MW00415694

BISON
BOOKS

Major League Baseball

VOLUME 1

Profiles, 1871–1900

THE BALLPLAYERS WHO BUILT THE GAME

Compiled and Edited by David Nemec

The Business of Baseball and Player Transactions by David Ball

UNIVERSITY OF NEBRASKA PRESS | LINCOLN AND LONDON

Photo editor: Erica Parise. All the visuals are from newspapers and books published prior to 1900 and have been in the public domain for years. These visuals are now part of David Nemec's collection.

The biographical entries of Bill Sweeney, Lew Brown, Em Gross, and Tommy Bond by David Nemec originally appeared in a different form in *Base Ball* 3, no. 1 (Spring 2009).

Library of Congress Cataloging-in-Publication Data

Major league baseball profiles, 1871–1900, volume 1 : the ballplayers who built the game / Compiled and Edited by David Nemec.
p. cm.
Includes bibliographical references and index.
ISBN 978-0-8032-3024-8 (pbk. : alk. paper)
1. Baseball players—United States—Biography.
2. Baseball players—United States—History.
3. Baseball—United States—History—19th century.
4. Baseball—United States—History—20th century.
I. Nemec, David.
GV865.A1M26 2011 796.357092—dc22
2010051805

Set in Minion Pro and Scala Sans Pro by Kim Essman.
Designed by A. Shahan.

To DICK THOMPSON, *a great friend, an invaluable colleague, and a Hall of Fame baseball historian*

CONTENTS

ILLUSTRATIONS

ACKNOWLEDGMENTS

Many baseball historians, researchers, editors, and publishers furnished us with information and guidance in our work. We are pleased to acknowledge their assistance and extend to them our deepest appreciation.

We thank Ken Samelson, former editor of *Macmillan Baseball Encyclopedia*, and Pete Palmer, coeditor of *The ESPN Baseball Encyclopedia*, for providing us with much of the nineteenth-century statistical data used by their respective publications, as well as for patiently responding to our many inquiries regarding disputed totals for individual and team pitching, batting, and fielding. We also thank Dave Smith, director of the SABR (Society for American Baseball Research) Retrosheet project, and the other members of the project for providing us with many requisite box scores of National Association games from 1871 to 1875.

A number of other SABR committee chairpersons and members rendered invaluable assistance during the preparation of this book, most notably Bill Carle, chairperson of the Biographical Committee; Peter Mancuso, chairperson of the Nineteenth Century Committee; Bill Hickman, chairperson of the Pictorial History Committee; and Carlos Bauer, former chairperson of the Minor League Committee. To the many members of their respective committees, who helped run to earth the information utilized in their invaluable committee newsletters, we extend a special note of gratitude.

Grateful acknowledgment is also made to the following researchers, writers, and historians for their help: Ray Nemec, Ev Cope, Bob Dolgan, Catherine Petroski, Cliff Blau, Wayne McElreavy, Mark Fimoff, Bob Richardson, Gary Gillette, Dixie Tourangeau, Frank Williams, Bob Tiemann, Walt Wilson, Bill Deane, Jules Tygiel, Angus McFarlane, Dennis Pajot, Leonard Koppett, Rich Topp, John Lewis, and Joe Wayman. Special thanks are owed to the leading authority on nineteenth-century minor leagues and their players, Reed Howard; SABR's most intrepid tracer of lost baseball players, Richard Malatzky; and baseball's leading necrologist, Bill Lee.

My personal thanks go to my wife, Marilyn, who kept my hands on the wheel throughout the long and bumpy ride; to my daughter-in-law, Erica

Parise Foster, for her help in assembling the photographs appearing in the book; to Scott Flatow, Al Blumkin, and Dave Zeman, for their steadfast interest and enthusiasm; and to Tony Salin, who was there with critically needed support and encouragement when the project was still in its embryonic stage.

Finally, I wish to thank the staff of the University of Nebraska Press, and especially Ann Baker and Rob Taylor, for believing in and publishing the work.

This book is dedicated to Dick Thompson, who had an abiding spirit and unquenchable thirst for knowledge about even the most obscure figures in the game's early history. Our greatest regret is that Dick is no longer with us now that we have touched the final base.

DAVID NEMEC
October 2010

INTRODUCTION

The original goal for this book was to create a unique history of major league baseball's tumultuous infant years by means of gathering the biographies of every man who played major league baseball, managed a major league team, owned a major league team, served as a regular major league umpire, or served as a major league president during the nineteenth century. Unlikely and even impossible as it might seem, we achieved our lifelong ambition only to discover that such a book would run in the neighborhood of twenty-five hundred pages. It then became a matter of economic necessity to hone our endeavor to a practical length and select from among the more than 2,400 biographies only those we judged to be the most interesting or significant. To facilitate the navigation of the final product we separated the selections into two volumes.

Volume 1 includes all of our nineteenth-century position player and pitcher selections. Volume 2 begins with nineteenth-century Hall of Fame members and twenty other figures that in our estimation also belong in the Hall of Fame; includes leading nineteenth-century managers, front office figures, and umpires; then concludes with thirteen special player sections.

The several objective standards for inclusion are:

For position players and pitchers: at least one season as a batting title or an ERA qualifier
For managers: at least one full season as a pilot
For umpires: at least half a season as a regular umpire
For executives: a significant length of time as either a league president or a principal team owner

This methodology assured inclusion of every key contributor to the major league game from May 4, 1871, through December 31, 1900, but also many other figures whose stories are either of special interest or else deepen the knowledge of what it was like in the roiling caldron of the last three decades of the nineteenth century and the arduous struggle many faced to succeed as a major league player, owner, umpire, manager, or league official.

Accordingly, volume 2 contains a wealth of figures who appeared in only one major league game; played a vital role in a rule change or court decision that altered the way the game was conducted either on or off the field; participated in a significant "first" or "last" in major league history; or were incomparable rogues, scamps, or hustlers who left their prints on the major league scene usually by dint of their nefarious behavior off the diamond rather than by their athletic achievements on it.

Each person appears in the section where he left his most indelible mark on the game, whether it was as a pitcher, a first baseman, a manager, or in one of the specialty categories such as Rogues Gallery, Clubhouse Lawyers, Hall of Famers, or Baseball's Most Wanted. The decision as to where to situate a figure was usually straightforward. Frank Killen, for example, is found among the pitchers, Cap Anson among the Hall of Famers, and Jim Mutrie among the managers. In the case of someone like the inimitable Charley Jones, the process required more thought. Jones was an outfielder, but he was also something of a rogue. In the end we decided that this peerless early day slugger's most notable feature is that his final disposition—to the frustration of scores of excellent and dedicated baseball researchers—remains unknown to this day. He is showcased among Baseball's Most Wanted.

In addition to providing both an overall and a detailed sense of the player's role in the nineteenth-century game, specific information is given on his major league debut game and finale, his most important achievements and life transitions (both on and off the field), an objective and, whenever possible, peer-driven analysis of his baseball-related skills (whether as a player, manager, executive, or umpire), his high and low points and personal tragedies, his relationship to any ground-breaking diamond occurrences, and the details of his demise (when known). Chronicled too are the reasons for his movement from team to team, whether it be via trade, free agency, contract jumping, or release; significant features of his minor league career; the reasons he changed or ought to have changed positions during his career; and, as in the case of someone like Jack Glasscock, judicious speculation on how his baseball experience and subsequent place in the game's history appear to have been dramatically altered by involvement or noninvolvement in certain key events.

With a player like Bill Everitt, whose .358 batting average in 1895 has remained the all-time record high by a National League or American League rookie for well over a century, a special citation is made of his achievement prior to the appearance of his biography. We also have highlighted outstanding home run performances, perfect games, unique no-hitters, landmark seasons, and career milestones. However, we have not highlighted every no-hitter, nor every batter who hit for the cycle, nor every .400 season or minuscule ERA; only those we judge to be the most significant appear within. The goal, above all, is to provide original, incisive, and thorough biographical information about the baseball-related ventures of each of our chosen subjects while keeping statistical information, most of which is readily available elsewhere, to a minimum. In conjunction with these efforts is the goal to provide readers with profuse samplings of the spirit and flavor of nineteenth-century baseball writing and the harsh and sometimes downright cruel eye with which the game's observers often viewed even its most revered figures. At the same time we have modernized to some extent team names, especially those of teams in the National Association and its forerunner, the National

Association of Base Ball Players. The Athletic Club of Philadelphia, for one, is called the Philadelphia Athletics or the Philadelphia A's. On the other hand, we use the nicknames by which teams were most commonly known at the time of discussion. The Philadelphia National League club is a prime example: as early as 1883 the club was sometimes referred to as the Phillies, even though writers and fans more frequently called the club the Quakers prior to 1890, when the Philadelphia Players League enterprise also adopted the Quakers nickname. The National League Brotherly Love entry then became universally known as the Phillies, to distinguish it from its rival.

The fifth and last edition of *The ESPN Baseball Encyclopedia* is the chosen authority for statistics except in the rare instances when that book has reference information that conflicts with the authors' own research findings. A more frequently occurring difference, however, exists with *The ESPN Baseball Encyclopedia* and other reference sources with respect to the names by which nineteenth-century players were most commonly known by their peers. The information also differs—and in each case the reason for differing is cited—with the debut and final appearance dates other sources list for certain players. One final note on the statistics used: for players and managers whose careers extended into the twentieth century, statistics are complete only through the 1900 season. Similarly, biographies of figures that either remained prominent or achieved most of their prominence in the twentieth century in most cases conclude with their activities through the 1900 season. The exceptions are players like Bill Bernhard, Klondike Douglass, Ollie Pickering, Bob Wood, Charlie Dexter, Harry Lochhead, Jock Menefee, Kit Kittridge, Jay Hughes, Emmet Heidrick, Dick Cooley, Charlie Irwin, and Tom McCreery, among numerous others, whose careers extended into the twentieth century but who have never before been the subject of a biography or, in rare instances, players such as Willie Keeler and Win Mercer, for whom we present an examination of their overall careers that is both fresh and significantly contrary to any previous biographical treatments. For biographies on many figures of considerable later significance like Ban Johnson, Danny Murphy, and Kid Elberfeld, who were lesser contributors to major league baseball in the nineteenth century and who are not included in this book, readers should consult the SABR biographical project at http://bioproj.sabr.org. Also available on the project's site are biographies of several nineteenth-century figures who went unexamined due to space limitations, as well as complete biographies for overlapping nineteenth- and twentieth-century figures like Nap Lajoie, Dan McGann, John McGraw, and Connie Mack, who in most cases are pursued only through the 1900 season. While readers are encouraged to explore the SABR site and others like it, we believe that our book offers a more unique, more incisive, and more objective portrait of the baseball aspects of all of our subjects' lives.

Significant points of demarcation for pitching and stolen base achievements are the 1893 season, when the current pitching distance was established, and the 1898 season, when the current rule for defining a stolen base was established. Consequently, achievements in these areas may be prefaced with post-1892 and post-1897. These dates are more precise than the term "modern" that arbitrarily, and senselessly, pertains to everything that happened after 1900. Other demarcations are the Deadball Era (1901–1919) and the creation of the National Association (1871–1875), which is recognized as the first major league.

For more about the lives of numerous nineteenth-century major league baseball figures and a general history of the game in its early years, please visit these extraordinary websites belonging to two of our writers, Peter Morris and Eric Miklich: www.petermorrisbooks.com and www.19CBASEBALL.com.

One final observation: If a book of this scope had been attempted fifty years ago, today it would seem pitiably incomplete and fraught with errors—not for a lack of diligence or devotion to the project by its architects but solely because of the rudimentary research tools and materials that formerly were available to even the most dedicated baseball historians. We certainly recognize that even though our book is as good as we can make it at the present time, the many technological advances that have sprung into existence just in the past few years may create a new state of the art in baseball research that will one day make some of our work seem similarly outmoded. Meanwhile, we want to hear from you about any blunders or omissions you find (we know there will be some) or about your research, which may be of tremendous importance to us in updated editions of *Major League Baseball Profiles*.

To simplify the reader's task in following a career line, teams mentioned in the players', pitchers', and managers' registers are designated N during the 1892 to 1899 period, when the National League was officially known as the National League and American Association. During the National Association's tenure as a major league (1871–1875), the abbreviation "Phi" represents the Philadelphia Pearls, as distinguished from "Ath" (the Philadelphia Athletics) and "Cen" (the Philadelphia Centennials).

ABBREVIATIONS AND SYMBOLS

Most abbreviations used will be familiar to the majority of baseball fans and students of the game, and all are spelled out in the text periodically so that the reader is reminded of what they signify. When a minor league, such as the International Association, the New England League, or the Southern League, is mentioned for the first time, the name is given in its complete form. Subsequent mentions will usually appear as abbreviations, e.g., IA, NEL, or SL. Postal abbreviations are used for state names. For the sake of brevity, numbers are presented in numeral form in player debut and final game profiles (1st, 2nd, 3rd, etc.). The names of newspapers, periodicals, and books—except *Sporting Life* and *The Sporting News*—are not abbreviated.

GENERAL

AA: American Association (as a major league)
ABs: at-bats
AL: American League
ALer: American Leaguer
AOPS: adjusted on-base percentage, for offensive level of the league and player's home park
BA: batting average
BR/9 IP: base runners allowed per every 9 innings pitched
CG: complete game(s)
DH: doubleheader
DL: disabled list
FA: fielding average
FL: Federal League
GM: General Manager
H/9 IP: hits allowed per every 9 innings pitched
HBP: hit by pitch(es)
HOF: Hall of Fame
HOFer: Hall of Famer
IPHR: inside-the-park-home run(s)

K/9: strikeouts per 9 innings
KC: Kansas City
LA: Los Angeles
ML: major league
MLB: Major League Baseball
MLer: major leaguer
NA: National Association (major league or minor league) or National Agreement, depending on the context
NL: National League
NLer: National Leaguer
OBA: opponents' batting average
OB: Organized Baseball (all major and minor leagues)
OBP: on-base percentage
OOBP: opponents' on-base percentage
OPS: on-base percentage plus slugging average
PAs: plate appearances
PCL: Pacific Coast League
PL: Players League
RBI: runs batted in
RC/G: runs created per game
SA: slugging average
SL: Sporting Life
SO/BB: pitchers' strikeouts to bases on balls ratio
TC/G: total chances per game
TSN: The Sporting News
UA: Union Association
WP: winning percentage

POSITIONS

All position names are abbreviated as follows (excludes catcher and pitcher when they appear as the name of the position):

1B: first base
2B: second base
3B: third base
SS: shortstop
LF: left field
CF: center field
RF: right field

CONTRIBUTORS

Each biography concludes with the initials of its primary author(s). When two or more authors contributed significantly to a biography, initials are listed in order of magnitude of contribution.

DB: David Ball
JK: Jeffrey Kittel
BM: Brian McKenna
EM: Eric Miklich
PM: Peter Morris
DN: David Nemec
LS: Lyle Spatz
DT: Dick Thompson
JT: John Thorn
FV: Frank Vaccaro
PVB: Philip Von Borries

TEAM LOCATIONS

Following the last two numerals of the year or years in which a man played or managed is an abbreviation of the city where his team resided.

Alt Altoona
Ath Philadelphia Athletics (NA)
Atl Brooklyn Atlantics (NA)
Bal Baltimore
Bos Boston
Bro Brooklyn
Buf Buffalo
Cen Philadelphia Centennials (NA)
Chi Chicago
Cin Cincinnati
Cle Cleveland
Col Columbus
Det Detroit
Eck Brooklyn Eckfords
Har Hartford
Ind Indianapolis
KC Kansas City
Kek Fort Wayne (NA)
Lou Louisville
Man Mansfield (NA)
Mar Maryland (NA)
Mil Milwaukee
Mut New York Mutuals (NA)
Nat Washington Nationals (NA)
NH New Haven (NA)
NWK Newark (FL)
NY New York
Oly Washington Olympics (NA)
Phi Philadelphia
Pit Pittsburgh
Pro Providence
Reds St. Louis Reds (NA)
Res Elizabeth Resolutes (NA)
Roc Rochester

Rok Rockford (NA)
StL St. Louis Brown Stockings (NA)
StP St. Paul
Syr Syracuse
Tol Toledo
Tro Troy
Vir Virginia
Was Washington
Wes Keokuk (NA)
Wil Wilmington
Wor Worcester

LEAGUE NAMES

Following the year and team information is the symbol for the league:

NA National Association (1871–75)
N National League (1876–present)
A American Association (1882–91)
U Union Association (1884)
P Players League (1890)
AL American League (1901–present)
F Federal League (1914–15)

OTHER SYMBOLS

[*] when it appears prior to player's name indicates that he had a brother or brothers who also played in the major leagues, although not always in the nineteenth century.

[#] when it appears prior to player's name indicates that he had a son or sons who also played in the major leagues, in every case in the twentieth century.

[* plus parenthetical team indication, e.g., (84NYA)] when it appears in a player's career profile indicates that the team was one with which he played that year only in a World's Series game or games; the example is taken from the profile of second baseman Tom Forster, but there are others. World Series eligibility rules in the nineteenth century were catch-as-catch-can.

[(P/M) prior to a team abbreviation] indicates the individual served as player-manager

[(M) prior to a team abbreviation] indicates the individual served as a manager only

[(*see* [name])] indicates that another biography, which appears in either volume 1 or volume 2, will provide more information about the game, incident, or imbroglio under discussion.

EXPLANATION OF PLAYER PROFILE STATISTICS

The twelve central pitching statistics are given for every player who pitched in a major league game between 1871 and 1900; twelve central batting statistics are given for every position player that took part in a major league game in that same thirty-year span. All players are listed alphabetically following standard alphabetizing conventions. Name(s) following a given name are the name or names by which that player was best known in the nineteenth century. Christy Mathewson, for instance, was called "Matty" as a rookie in 1900 but was not dubbed "The Big Six" until several years later. Hence his most famous nickname is not mentioned in Mathewson's profile in the Hall of Fame section. When a man played under a name other than his given name, his playing name is followed by the part of his given name that differed from it—in most cases a surname only. In the case of men who were known by more than one surname, the secondary surnames are given in parentheses and prefaced by "aka."

Following the name of each pitcher or position player is a chronological list of the team(s) for which he played. See the sample player, Charles Augustus Nichols (below), for an explanation of the year abbreviations.

Vital statistics—birth date, birthplace, death date, height, weight, batting, throwing—are furnished, when known. Gaps in information are indicated either by question marks or by the word "Unknown." Since knowledge of nineteenth-century baseball is expanding each and every day, it is hoped that many of the gaps will be filled in future editions.

Nichols, Charles Augustus / "Kid"

B	T	HGT	WGT	G	IP	H	GS
B	R	5'10½"	175	519	4227	4140	468

CG	BB	SO	SH	W	L	PCT	ERA
443	1073	1531	40	310	167	.650	2.98

B. 9/14/1869 Madison, WI **D.** 4/1/1953

TEAMS: 90–01BosN (P/M)04–05StLN 06PhiN

First is the player's surname (Nichols), followed by his given first and middle names, then the name (or, in other cases, names, in order of dominance) the player was usually called by his baseball peers ("Kid"). Next are statistics regarding how Nichols batted (B) and threw (T), followed by his playing height and weight, and his major league service in the nineteenth century as a pitcher: 519 games (G) in which he pitched 4,227 innings (IP), allowed 4,140 hits (H), started 468 games (GS), and pitched 443 complete games (CG). In his 519 games Nichols walked 1,073 (BB), struck out 1,531 (SO), threw 40 shutouts (SH), won 310 games (W), and lost 167 (L), for a .650 winning percentage (PCT) with a 2.98 earned run average (ERA). The next line includes his birth date, place of birth, and death date. Last is a chronological list of Nichols's major league seasons as a pitcher and the teams for which he pitched. Take note that although Nichols pitched for several years and all the teams during that period are listed, Nichols's statistics in this book reflect only his nineteenth-century major league achievements.

Albert Spalding is an example of a player who was primarily a pitcher but who also played other positions and served as a major league manager long enough to merit inclusion of both his batting statistics and his managing years prior to 1900.

Spalding, Albert Goodwill/ "Al"

B	T	HGT	WGT	G	IP	H	GS
R	R	6'1"	170	347	2886.1	3280	326
CG	**BB**	**SO**	**SH**	**W**	**L**	**PCT**	**ERA**
280	164	248	24	252	65	.795	2.13
G	**AB**	**H**	**R**	**2B**	**3B**	**HR**	
411	1959	613	417	86	19	2	
RBI	**BB**	**SO**	**SB**	**BA**	**SA**	**OBP**	
328	29	26	18	.313	.379	.323	
G	**W**	**L**	**PCT**	**PENNANTS**			
126	78	47	.624	1			

B. 9/2/1850 Byron, IL **D.** 9/9/1915
TEAMS: 71–75BosNA (P/M)76–77ChiN 78ChiN

Spalding's batting achievements reflect that in his eight-year career he played 411 games (G); compiled 1,959 at-bats (AB) and 613 hits (H); scored 417 runs ®; collected 86 doubles (2B), 19 triples (3B), and two home runs (HR); and totaled 328 RBI (RBI), 29 walks (BB), 26 strikeouts (SO), and 18 stolen bases (SB). He finished with a .313 career batting average (BA), a .379 slugging average (SA), and a .323 on-base percentage (OBP). Spalding's stolen base total is underscored, meaning that for some seasons his achievements in that department are unknown. As is the case for every man who played in both the National Association and another major league, Spalding's National Association statistics are incorporated into his total major league statistics. (Unlike some other reference works, we recognize the National Association as a major league and are not bound by Major League Baseball's decision to treat its statistics separately.) Finally, Spalding was a team manager for two seasons, during which his teams played 126 games (G), won 78 (W), and lost 47 (L), for a winning percentage of .624 that included one pennant-winning season.

1 | THE PITCHERS

From an original photo taken at the time.

Top Row—Billy Montjoy, P.; W. W. Carpenter, 3rd B.; John S. Corkhill, R. F.; Gus Shallix, P.; Will H. White, P.; Phil Powers, C.; Frank Fennelly, S. S. Bottom Row—C. G. Baldwin, C.; J. E. Peoples, C.; John A. McPhee, 2nd B.; Chas. N. Snyder, C.; C. W. Jones, L. F.; Jimmy Clinton, C. F.; John G. Reilly, 1st B.

THE CINCINNATI BASEBALL TEAM, 1885.

1. The 1885 Cincinnati Reds featured bespectacled Will White, one of the pitchers most responsible for the creation of the first hit-by-pitch rule the previous year, and Gus Shallix, who would probably have enjoyed a much longer ML career had the rule not been in force.

Abbey, Bert Wood / "Bert"

B	T	HGT	WGT	G	IP	H	GS
R	R	5'10½"	180	79	568	686	65

CG	BB	SO	SH	W	L	PCT	ERA
52	192	161	0	22	40	.355	4.52

B. 11/29/1869 Essex, VT **D.** 6/11/1962
TEAMS: 92WasN 93–95ChiN 95–96BroN
DEBUT: 6/14/1892 at Washington; caught by Jack Milligan and beat St. Louis's Charlie Getzein 13–7
FINALE: 9/19/1896 at Philadelphia; relieved Harley Payne in Payne's 17–16 loss to Philadelphia's Al Orth and Kid Carsey

The son of a minister, Bert Abbey was signed by Washington NL after Senators manager Arthur Irwin watched him hurl for the University of Vermont in the spring of 1892. It was his fifth year on the team since college eligibility rules then were negligible. After winning his ML debut, Abbey was just 4-18 the remainder of 1892 and was sold to Pittsburgh in the spring of 1893. The Pirates loaned him to Macon of the Southern League, where he hoped to stay long enough to regain his confidence and learn the intricacies of pitching at the new 60'6" distance. But in late June he was traded to Chicago for defiant holdout Ad Gumbert. Abbey at first refused to join the Colts, but when he was offered $1,000 to finish the season in the Windy City he reported in early August. He lost his first start in Chicago livery on August 5 to Cleveland and was just 4-12 before being released to Brooklyn early in the 1895 season.

Abbey went 13-10 with Brooklyn to lift his career record from 9-30 to a less appalling 22-40. During a second spell in the minors, he hurt his arm in 1899 while with Montreal of the Eastern League. Abbey retired to his farm in Vermont at the turn of the century and coached his alma mater. Discontented with farm life, he eventually began helping his son Fred run the Gardenside Nurseries in Shelburne, VT. At the time of his death in 1962, Abbey was the oldest living former major leaguer, since catcher Buster Burrell had died a month earlier. The pair had been batterymates with Brooklyn in 1895–96. (DN)

Amole, Morris George / "Doc"

B	T	HGT	WGT	G	IP	H	GS
R	L	5'9"	165	18	119.1	150	12

CG	BB	SO	SH	W	L	PCT	ERA
10	39	30	0	4	10	.286	4.75

B. 7/5/1878 Coatesville, PA **D.** 3/9/1912
TEAMS: 97BalN 98WasN
DEBUT: 8/19/1897 at Baltimore; caught by Wilbert Robinson and lost 3–0 to Cleveland's Cy Young
FINALE: 5/17/1898 at New York; relieved Bill Dinneen and led 10–6 in the 9th before losing 11–10 to New York's Cy Seymour
CAREER HIGHLIGHT: Caught by Al Shaw and pitched the first no-hitter in American League history, topping Detroit 8–0 on April 19, 1900, the loop's Opening Day under its new name.

Of Dutch ancestry, Doc Amole was discovered in 1895 by Ned Hanlon and recommended to Denny Long, the owner-manager of the Wilmington Atlantic League entry, after he pitched his hometown Coatesville team to the Chester County amateur championship. From Pennsylvania mining country, Amole was so ingenuous that he had never used a telephone or an electrical appliance of any kind until his emergence in pro ball. At Wilmington, Amole drew the team's Opening Day assignment in 1896 and went 22-24. While with Reading in 1897, he got Hanlon's full attention when he won both ends of a DH on June 27. Baltimore purchased Amole for $1,000 just as the 1897 pennant race was reaching a full head of steam. His first win, 5–3 over Cincinnati on August 27, put the Orioles temporarily in first place. Because he was a rookie, Amole was used sparingly in the final weeks of the season but was still voted a full Temple Cup series share by his teammates.

That winter Amole was part of a blockbuster trade between Baltimore and Washington that brought the Orioles' Doc McJames and Gene DeMont. On December 10 the *Washington Post* commented that Amole had "cyclonic speed and fine control, and in watching the bases he is the equal of old Mattie Kilroy." Still the deal was viewed as a poor one for Washington, and it looked even worse when Amole lost his first five starts and also dropped his Washington finale on May 17 in relief after giving up 5 runs in the bottom of the ninth. He had previously squandered what seemed a certain victory at Brooklyn just eleven days earlier, surrendering six runs in the ninth to blow a 9–4 lead. Some two weeks after his final ML appearance, Amole was released to Buffalo, where he spent the next four seasons.

Probably Amole arrived in the majors before he was ready. He had an excellent pickoff move and stepped toward 1B as he released his fastball, producing a crossfire delivery that was difficult to hit. But militating against his assets was what *TSN* called his "hayseed habit" of exposing his fingers to batters so that they could see when a curve was coming. Amole's personal habits were also not exemplary. In March 1899, while employed in Baltimore at a winter job as a steel worker, he was arrested for slugging a police sergeant during a drunken escapade. It did not help Amole, either, in his quest to return to the majors, that the Buffalo teams for which he pitched during his prime years were generally bad. In 1900 he won 22 games for the Bisons, just 1 behind the AL leader, but he also lost 22, leaving him only 1 short of topping the loop in losses.

Amole remained in the Eastern League until 1904 and drifted out of baseball soon thereafter. In 1912, still just 33 years old, he was found one morning dead in bed of lung congestion at his boarding house in Wilmington, DE, where he had been working as a carpenter. The source of his nickname is still unknown, but one theory is that his last name was pronounced Ah-MOH-lee, which, when combined with Doc, rhymes with guacamole. (DN)

Anderson, Warner Samuel / "Varn" "Varney"

B	T	HGT	WGT	G	IP	H	GS
R	R	5'10"	165	35	239.2	339	30

CG	BB	SO	SH	W	L	PCT	ERA
22	115	41	0	9	20	.310	6.16

B. 6/18/1866 Geneva, IL **D.** 11/5/1941
TEAMS: 89IndN 94–96WasN
DEBUT: 8/1/1889 at Pittsburgh; caught by George Myers in a 10–3 loss to Pittsburgh's Harry Staley
FINALE: 5/6/1896 at Cleveland; caught by Deacon McGuire in a 13–7 loss to Cleveland's Cy Young

Arm trouble early in his career prevented Varn Anderson, a fine all-around player, from fulfilling his potential. He first surfaced professionally in 1887 with Rockford, IL, but soon moved to Milwaukee, where he was regarded as the second best pitcher in the Western Association, following only Bill Hutchison. After spending 1888 with St. Paul, Anderson played that winter in California. During his stay there, he beat the All-American team 6–2 before it embarked on its famous world tour, but he also first experienced arm woes, possibly from trying to pitch year-around. In July 1889 Anderson was acquired by Indianapolis NL from Detroit of the International Association but was dropped after making two bad starts. He then went to Burlington of the Central Interstate League.

Anderson was named Burlington's player-manager prior to the 1890 season. By July, however, his arm was useless and he resigned his position when he felt that it was unfair to be paid just for managing and returned to his job as a watchmaker for a watch factory in Rockford, IL. That winter he eloped to Beloit, WI, with 17-year-old Florence Doughty of Rockford. Several comeback attempts failed before Anderson returned to pro ball three years later with Mobile of the Southern League, but he was released in May 1894 at his own request when he felt his arm was still not in proper shape. Later in the campaign, he tried again with Lynchburg of the Virginia League and looked sharp enough to be summoned in late September to Washington, where he made two starts and lost them both.

In 1895 Anderson did not make his first start for Washington until Decoration Day. Even though each of his first four starts resulted in Washington wins, he was used sparingly until June 26 when he made his first appearance in eighteen days and lost 1–0 to Brooklyn in thirteen innings. After his career-best performance, Anderson joined Washington's rotation. Also used as a pinch hitter, he beat New York 7–6 on September 25 with a 2-run pinch single in the bottom of the 10th. In addition to a solid .289 BA in 1895, Anderson scored 22 runs, tied for the most ever by a pitcher with less than 100 ABs. The puzzle is that he was not converted to another position after opponents ripped his slants that season for a .327 BA.

The following spring Washington released Anderson after he was shelled in his first two starts. When he fared no better with Minneapolis of the Western League, he returned home and became the player-manager of the Rockford Western Association club in 1897. No longer able to pitch, he switched to 1B. After agreeing to be Rockford's player-manager again in 1898, Anderson recanted when the league took control of the Rockford franchise in February 1898 following a dispute over the dispersal of its Decoration Day receipts the previous year. At that point team owner Arthur Vanderbeck, who also owned the Detroit club in the Western League, arranged to transfer all of Rockford's players to Anderson after he was installed as player-manager of Rock Island. But, after clashing with Rock Island's directors in May 1898 over which players to retain, Anderson quit pro ball to run a semipro team on weekends while working at the Rockford Watch Factory. When the factory closed he opened his own watch shop in Rockford and remained one of the city's leading citizens until his death in 1941. Among nineteenth-century pitchers with a minimum of 100 career ABs who played less than 50 games at other positions, Anderson ranks first in OPS (.737) and RC/G (6.10). (DN)

Atkinson, Albert Wright (aka Atkisson) **/ "Al"**

B	T	HGT	WGT	G	IP	H	GS
B	R	5'11"	165	106	915	943	106

CG	BB	SO	SH	W	L	PCT	ERA
99	209	435	3	51	51	.500	3.96

B. 3/9/1861 Clinton, IL **D.** 6/17/1952
TEAMS: 84PhiA 84Chi–PitU 84BalU 86–87PhiA
DEBUT: 5/1/1884 at Pittsburgh; caught by Jack Milligan and beat Pittsburgh's John Fox 9–2
FINALE: 8/13/1887 At New York; caught by Wilbert Robinson and lost 13–11 to New York's Al Mays

Al Atkinson's work with the amateur Chicago Prairie Queens in the early 1880s earned him a tryout with Dan O'Leary's independent Indianapolis team in 1883. When Atkinson bragged that no catcher on the Hoosiers could hold him, O'Leary assigned him to work with Jim Keenan, the club's top backstop. Atkinson proved as good as his word, striking out "sixteen of O'Leary's ball-pounders" in an eight-inning practice game, and then left in disgust when O'Leary offered him a mere $15 to stay overnight and pitch an exhibition game against Detroit NL the next day. The following spring the 1883 AA champion Philadelphia A's liked Atkinson's raw speed enough to give him the honor of being the lone rookie ever to start on Opening Day for a defending ML flag winner. Little more than two months later, Atkinson repaid the A's by jumping to the Union Association. More than money, he liked the idea of pitching closer to his Chicago home. To Atkinson's chagrin the team moved to Pittsburgh soon after he arrived and then disbanded entirely. Atkinson finished the season with Baltimore UA but found himself blacklisted in 1885 owing to his leap to the UA while under contract to the A's. He spent his year in exile working as a carpenter while pitching with the semipro Chicago Blues.

Returning to Philadelphia in 1886, Atkinson became the first hurler to pitch no-hitters in two different major leagues when he held the Mets hitless on May 1 in only his third start after rejoining the A's. That same month *TSN* declared that he and Ed Cushman were the "worst batters in the Association," an opinion that seemed justified when he hit just .122 that season. What pundits failed to notice was that it was an amazingly productive .122. Atkinson's 27 runs and 26 walks are both the most ever by a sub-.125 hitter.

In addition, Atkinson led the A's in both wins and losses in 1886. The following spring local papers predicted he would be one of the few pitchers who would be unfazed by the new pitching restrictions introduced in 1887 because he delivered the ball without first taking a running step or two, which was now forbidden. Instead he got off poorly, giving up 45 runs in his first four starts but somehow managing to win three of them. Three days after a 13–7 loss on July 5 at Louisville, Atkinson was warming up in Cleveland for his next start when he felt a cord behind his right elbow snap. He rested his arm for more than a month before returning on August 10 but to no avail. Beaten 13–10 by Brooklyn, he tried for a final time three days later against the Mets and was released when he again gave up 13 runs and lost.

Atkinson rebounded to a degree in 1888 with Toronto of the International Association, posting the loop's second-best ERA at 1.36 after he claimed that his arm had gone "out of place" in 1887 and that he accidentally threw it back into joint one day while hitting a heavy bag in the gym. Years later Atkinson told a different story. Then 90 years old and living in a cabin he had built for himself in the Ozarks, he revealed that his secret treatment had consisted of taking a sponge and soaking his sore flipper, then grabbing an electric battery with his wet hands. His arm instantly got better.

Atkinson's shock treatments failed in 1889. In July he requested his release from Toronto. Over the next few years Atkinson attempted a series of unsuccessful comebacks and then settled into a life in the Ozarks entirely of his own design with his wife, Mary Jane. A self-taught artist, he painted scenic oils and turned his carpentry skills to woodworking. An expert carver, at one point he spent two years building a combination radio-phonograph cabinet out of seventy three different kinds of wood. Atkinson died at his home in McNatt, MO, at 91 of Alzheimer's. (DN/DT/DB)

Bakely, Edward Enoch

(b. Bakeley) **/ "Enoch" "Jersey"**

B	T	HGT	WGT	G	IP	H	GS
R	R	5'8"	170	215	1782.2	1909	204

CG	BB	SO	SH	W	L	PCT	ERA
191	564	669	7	76	125	.378	3.66

B. 4/17/1864 Blackwood, NJ **D.** 2/17/1915
TEAMS: 83PhiA 84PhiU 84WilU 84KCU 88CleA 89CleN 90CleP 91WasA 91BalA
DEBUT: 5/11/1883 at Philadelphia; caught by Jack O'Brien and beat New York's Tim Keefe 4–3
FINALE: 8/20/1891 at Baltimore; caught by George Townsend and lost 8–4 to Washington's Buck Freeman in relief of Frank Foreman

Jersey Bakely was born in New Jersey, explaining his nickname, but his peers usually called him Enoch. After his winning debut in 1883, *SL* wrote, "Bakely, a West Philadelphia amateur, was put in the pitcher's box and his clever pitching delighted the crowd and demoralized the Metropolitans." He was nonetheless seldom used by the pennant-bound A's and spent much of the season on loan to teams in the Interstate Association. The A's apparently made minimal effort to retain him the following season, and their judgment seemed right when he led the UA in losses with 30 while pitching for three of the loop's poorer teams. Bakely returned to the A's in 1885 but did little more than pitch batting practice. Eventually he was sent to Portland, ME, of the Eastern New England League.

During the next two seasons Bakely toiled for Rochester of the International Association. Despite being arrested along with teammate Fred Lewis after a drunken spree in September 1887 and fined $50, a hefty amount in those days, Bakely was signed by Cleveland AA for 1888. After a basement finish in 1887, Cleveland named Bakely its ace, and it paid a rich dividend. By late July, Bakely was among the top flingers in the AA; after blanking the pennant-bound Browns 1–0 on July 30, he fashioned three more shutouts the following month, including two on consecutive days in Cincinnati. In early September, Bakely owned a 25-24 record. Even though he ended the season with nine straight losses to finish 25-33, he collected exactly half of Cleveland's wins.

The following year, after Cleveland moved to the NL, he led the team in ERA but fell to 12-22 when he received both poor fielding and run support. Jumping to the PL Cleveland entry in 1890, Bakely again found himself on a bad team, but this was one that he made no better. Expected to share top billing with Cinders O'Brien, Bakely instead joined O'Brien in posting a combined 20-41 record while the rest of the team's staff finished above .500 (35-34).

Slated to rejoin Cleveland NL after the PL folded, Bakely was jolted when the Spiders released him in February 1891 for his drinking. He joined the new Washington AA entry but was dumped after losing 10 of 12 starts. Unaccountably Baltimore hired him, and before he joined the Orioles it was written, "The man is too far gone for any hope of usefulness." But Bakely proved surprisingly effective, winning four of six starts, before his imbibing caused Baltimore to fire him on August 28.

Bakely drifted through the minors for several more years and boxed professionally on occasion. (In the fall of 1888, *TSN* related that he had once been scheduled to fight Jack Dempsey, the "Nonpareil," but Frank Bancroft had intervened and called off the bout.) Bakely's final opportunity to salvage his baseball career came in 1895 when Jack Milligan, his batterymate of ten years earlier, invited him to join the Allentown team Milligan was managing. Three months later Bakely's locker was empty when Milligan cleared all the lushers off the club. Upon his departure, *TSN* lamented, "His jaunty step as he walked to the pitcher's box was especially pleasing to the ladies, many of them attending games when they knew Bakely was going to pitch. He had such a bewitching smile also and it is to be regretted that his fondness for 'smiles' led to his release." Bakely was unemployed when he died at his Philadelphia home of a heart attack in 1915. (DN)

Baker, Kirtley / "Kirtley" "Whitey"

B	T	HGT	WGT	G	IP	H	GS
R	R	5'9"	160	58	371	483	44

CG	BB	SO	SH	W	L	PCT	ERA
34	186	115	2	9	38	.191	6.28

B. 6/24/1869 Aurora, IN **D.** 4/15/1927
TEAMS: 90PitN 93–94BalN 98–99WasN
DEBUT: 5/7/1890 at Cleveland; caught by Bill Wilson and lost 5–4 to Cleveland's Ed Beatin
FINALE: 6/14/1899 at Washington; relieved Bill Dinneen who took the 9–6 loss to Baltimore's Jerry Nops

In 1889 umpire Al Jennings observed Kirtley Baker pitching for the Cincinnati Blue Licks and recommended him to Reds owner Aaron Stern. But the boyish, sandy-haired Baker was too nervous to do well in a tryout. Returning to the Blue Licks, in July he struck out 77 batters over a 5-game stretch and produced "doubtless the best amateur pitching in the Ohio Valley." The accolade won him another failed tryout with Cincinnati in September, followed by a recommendation to Pittsburgh NL that winter from minor league manager Harry Smith, who had seen Baker pitch briefly for Quincy of the Central Interstate League.

Baker's first highlight with Pittsburgh came in a spring exhibition on April 1, 1890, when he beat McKeesport 31–1. However, once regular action was under way, he lost his first five starts before breaking into the win column on May 31 at Boston. Despite missing the last two months of the season with a bum arm, Baker led the NL's tail-ender in innings, losses, strikeouts and walks. Although he collected only three wins to go with his 19 defeats, two were shutouts and in each he allowed just two hits. Released by Pittsburgh in September when his arm faltered, Baker finished 1890 with an amateur team in his hometown of Aurora, IN, run by Harry Smith.

Baker played under Smith at Aurora again in 1891 until the Illinois-Iowa League disbanded and then began his trek back to the majors by toiling in the Southern League. In 1893 Baltimore acquired "the peroxide of hydrogen blonde" twirler. Manager Ned Hanlon kept him on the team all season but released him early in 1894 when he refused to give up pitching and become an outfielder. *TSN* deemed Baker a terrific hitter whose lone drawback was that he was "fast as a hay wagon" on the bases.

Stubbornly determined to make his mark as a moundsman, Baker labored in baseball's nether regions for the next five seasons before returning to the majors late in 1898 just in time to hurl an 11–4 loss to Boston on October 11 that clinched the NL pennant for the Beaneaters. A 1-7 start in 1899 convinced Washington pilot Arthur Irwin to cut Baker's release. Exiting the majors with a .191 winning percentage and a 6.28 ERA, he was out of the pro game entirely by the end of the century. Baker was a grocer when he died at 57 of a pulmonary embolism in Covington, KY. (DN)

Baker, Norman Leslie / "Norm" "Mikado"

B	T	HGT	WGT	G	IP	H	GS
?	L	?	?	30	253	250	29

CG	BB	SO	SH	W	L	PCT	ERA
28	86	94	1	14	15	.483	3.42

B. 10/14/1862 Philadelphia, PA **D.** 2/20/1949
TEAMS: 83PitA 85LouA 90BalA
DEBUT: 5/21/1883 at Philadelphia; caught by Amos Cross and lost 4–1 to Philadelphia's Bobby Mathews
FINALE: 8/30/1890 at Baltimore; caught by Eddie Tate and was relieved by Mike O'Rourke after his left arm was broken by an eighth inning line drive in a 7–4 loss to St. Louis's Joe Neale

Norm Baker was a "fine baritone singer and a good pianist," nicknamed "Mikado" for having sung in a production of it for the Ford Opera Company in the winter of 1885–86. *TSN* offered this appraisal of his pitching in 1893, when his career was near its end: "Baker, with a different temperament, might have made a big hit right in the center of fortune's bulls eye." Baker's temperament problems were not typical among ballplayers of his era. Unlike most, who were guilty of dissipation or laziness, he throve on simply being contrary. In 1894, after temporarily giving up active play to take a job as an umpire in the Western League, he was fired in July because he seemed to revel in "going against the opinion of the home crowd." Accordingly, he was loathed in almost every WL city, but rather than disappearing into the woodwork, Baker pitched batting practice for the Minneapolis club until it hired him and got a dazzling 14-6 performance for its money before he was laid up in September with pneumonia.

Baker pitched in the Philadelphia City League in the early 1880s before being hired by Pittsburgh AA while it was visiting the City of Brotherly Love. Released after going 0-2 in three starts, he joined Johnstown, PA, and then moved in 1884 to Springfield, OH, where he met catcher Amos Cross. Together, they left the Ohio State League for unaffiliated Nashville late that summer and then came to Louisville AA as a unit in the spring of 1885. In his initial start as a Colonel, with Cross as his receiver, Baker blanked Pittsburgh's Hank O'Day 11–0.

Baker continued to work with Cross all season and was bailed out of tight situations continually when Cross, the owner of one of the best catching arms of his time, either picked off napping runners or threw them out trying to steal. His reward, however, for finishing second on the Colonels in most pitching departments to Guy Hecker was his release back to Nashville (by then in the Southern League) when manager Jim Hart acquired Tom Ramsey near the close of the 1885 season and decided one capricious left-hander was all he could bear. Baker remained in the minors until August 1890, when his Baltimore Atlantic Association entry returned to the AA as a replacement team. In his first start with the Orioles on August 28, he beat the man who had usurped him five years earlier, Ramsey, 6–2. Baker's next appearance nearly resulted in a career-ending injury and revealed with which arm he threw. After a line drive broke "one of the smaller bones in his left arm near the shoulder," he was released by Baltimore that winter. As *TSN* reported, "His pitching arm is said to be almost entirely useless."

Baker left the game after a week's stint with Minneapolis in 1895 to work as a piano and organ salesman and for a time was affiliated with Foster & Waldo, a Minneapolis company owned by former ML outfielder Elmer Foster and his brother Robert. Baker and Foster, both unconventional sorts, not surprisingly hit it off and co-managed a company team for a time that also included former ML catcher Joe Crotty, another cut from a unique mold. Baker eventually returned to the East and died of a stroke in Hurffville, NJ, at 86. (DN)

Baldwin, Charles B. / "Lady"

B	T	HGT	WGT	G	IP	H	GS
R	L	5'11"	160	118	1017	921	116

CG	BB	SO	SH	W	L	PCT	ERA
112	233	582	9	73	41	.640	2.85

B. 4/8/1859 Oramel, NY **D.** 3/7/1937
TEAMS: 84MilU 85–88DetN 90BroN 90BufP
DEBUT: 9/3/1884 at Milwaukee; caught by Tony Falch and lost 5–3 to Washington's Charlie Geggus
FINALE: 6/26/1890 at Philadelphia; suffered the PL's most ignominious defeat when he was caught by Connie Mack and lost 30–12 to Philadelphia's Ben Sanders

Ned Hanlon called Charles Baldwin the greatest left-hander he had ever seen. Yet today he is remembered largely because his refusal to smoke, drink, or carouse led him to become known as "Lady." Baldwin was born in a New York farming community in 1859, and he moved with his family to Barry County, MI, after the Civil War. As a young man, he soon became known throughout western Michigan for his ability to "throw a fast one packed with dynamite" and "a puzzling curve which on account of its weaving in and out had been dubbed the 'snake ball.'" But, because no catcher in the area could handle his deliveries, he experienced limited success until word came of a stout-hearted receiver named Deacon McGuire, who lived fifty miles away in Albion. The two men were paired and became an instant success, even though their team could only play on weekends because McGuire was apprenticing as an iron molder in Albion and Baldwin was busy in Hastings. Eventually, both turned pro and went contrasting ways; McGuire took several years to establish himself but then had one of the longest ML careers ever, while Baldwin rocketed to stardom only to see his star quickly fade in a career that essentially lasted only four pro seasons.

Baldwin began his pro career with Milwaukee of the Northwestern Association in 1884. His rustic ways made him an easy target for his new teammates, and they were probably the ones who tagged him with the unflattering nickname. On one long train ride they talked two law enforcement officers into going through the pretense of arresting Baldwin and a teammate and then leaving them unattended. The teammate, who was in on the gag, promptly walked away, but the naïve young pitcher sat frozen in terror for the remainder of the trip.

Near the end of that year Milwaukee joined the UA and Baldwin made his first two ML starts. Milwaukee joined the Western League after the UA disbanded that winter, but when that loop followed suit in June of 1885, the southpaw was in demand. Chicago was among his pursuers, but Baldwin had given his word to Bob Leadley of Detroit that he would go with Leadley's club. He immediately proved to be a sensation. Although his record was a mediocre 11-9, he posted a sparkling 1.86 ERA. There had previously been numerous southpaws whose curves baffled left-handed batters, but most had short-lived success because they couldn't get right-handed batters out. Baldwin, however, featured a nasty in-shoot and drop ball that made him just as tough on right-handers. He built on that success in 1886. Detroit raced out of the gate, and in the first month of the season Baldwin won 11 games, culminating when he beat the Giants 4–1 on Decoration Day in front of a record Polo Grounds crowd estimated at over 26,000. His motion baffled NL hitters, prompting one writer to offer this description: "Usually he throws his arm in a circle about his head, then raises one leg, and a moment later comes down hard with both feet on the ground, when the ball leaves his left hand like a flash." Left-handed batters found Baldwin so difficult that many of them gladly sat out when he pitched.

Despite a phenomenal start, Detroit could not pull away from Chicago, and when injuries struck the Wolverines' pitching staff, the White Stockings passed them. Baldwin, however, remained brilliant, ending the season with 55 complete games, league-leading totals of 323 strikeouts and 7 shutouts, a 2.24 ERA, and 42 wins. The 1887 season was a different story. Most of the league's southpaws proved so ineffective that their struggles were generally blamed on a new rule that had eliminated the running start. In Baldwin's case, however, overwork in 1886 appears to have been his undoing. By the end of July, he had a disappointing 6-9 record and was sent home to Hastings without pay. He returned in September with Detroit clinging to a precarious lead in the pennant race and immediately showed his old form, beating archrival Chicago in his first start. Baldwin went on to win six more games in the final month to lead his team to its first pennant. He was just as stellar in the World's Series against St. Louis, pitching a shutout in his first start and following with three more wins, including the series clincher.

By the following spring, however, Baldwin's arm was ailing again, and this time there would be no comeback. He made only six starts in 1888 with little success. His Detroit finale came on July 28 when he lost to Chicago by the football score of 21–17. Except for a few humiliating appearances in the 1890 PL, that was essentially the end of his meteoric career. Rumors of his return to baseball surfaced annually, but his periodic failed comeback bids were compared by *TSN* to earlier embarrassments by Lee Richmond. Baldwin had married a Hastings girl after the 1886 season and eventually returned to Hastings for good. In 1910 he sold his farm and moved into town, where he ran an insurance business and managed a nine that was recognized as Michigan's best independent team for three straight years. After a full life, Baldwin died in 1937 of heart disease. (PM)

Baldwin, Marcus Elmore / "Mark" "Fido"

B	T	HGT	WGT	G	IP	H	GS
R	R	6'0"	190	347	2811.1	2695	328

CG	BB	SO	SH	W	L	PCT	ERA
295	1307	1354	14	155	165	.484	3.37

B. 10/29/1863 Pittsburgh, PA **D.** 11/10/1929
TEAMS: 87–88ChiN 89ColA 90ChiP 91–93PitN 93NYN
DEBUT: 5/2/1887 at Indianapolis; caught by Tom Daly and lost 9–1 to Indianapolis's Henry Boyle
FINALE: 9/30/1893; caught by Parke Wilson and lost 8–6 to Pittsburgh's Frank Killen
CAREER HIGHLIGHT: Led the 1890 Players League in almost every major pitching department

Mark Baldwin claimed an 1867 birth date when he joined Chicago in 1887, making him only 19 (as opposed to his real age of 23), which was in keeping with what others saw as his "childish ways" and extreme petulance. He, in contrast, envisioned himself as dapper, bright, articulate, outspoken, and an independent spirit. When Baldwin first met with

Pittsburgh owner J. Palmer O'Neill during negotiations with the Pirates prior to the 1891 season, he told O'Neill his name was too long and asked if he could call his future boss "Owny." Then, no sooner had Baldwin signed with his hometown team than he hired a personal valet, Reddy Mason, who later became the "rubber" (masseur) for all major sports teams that used the Pittsburgh grounds.

Baldwin pitched for a semipro team in Cumberland, MD, while attending Penn State. By 1886 he was ready for stiffer competition and joined Duluth of the Northwestern League. When he struck out 18 St. Paul hitters on June 18, including 12 in a row at one point, news of the feat spurred the World's Series–bound Chicago White Stockings to try to sneak him onto their postseason roster after rookie sensation Jocko Flynn hurt his arm. Unable to surmount the objections of AA champion St. Louis, Chicago had to wait until the following season to unveil Baldwin. Although he won 18 games as a rookie, he led the NL in wild pitches.

His control problems persisted in 1888, but he was invited to accompany the Chicago team that winter on its world tour. After staggering to a 13–8 win over the All-American team at London in the last "foreign" game on the junket, Baldwin was informed by Chicago on the eve of the 1889 season that Chicago no longer desired his services. That May he signed with Columbus AA as a free agent for $4,000 and fashioned one of the most extraordinary pitching seasons in ML history, giving up a then record 274 walks and leading the AA by a huge margin in almost every negative department but still managing to win 27 games with the sixth-place Senators. At the close of the season he blamed his wildly uneven performance on the vicious bench jockeying in the AA and then joined Charlie Comiskey, manager of the St. Louis Browns, the team guiltiest of the offenses he found so disturbing, in jumping to the Chicago PL entry.

In 1890 Baldwin led the strongest of the three big leagues that season in most major pitching departments, twice won both ends of a DH, and came within a hair of compiling 35 victories when rain ended his battle with New York on the closing day of the season in a 2–2 tie. When the PL folded he was required to return to Columbus AA and telegraphed a club official in February, "Depend on me; will not go back on my contract." Little more than two weeks later, however, Baldwin was in St. Louis after signing with Pittsburgh, attempting to bribe local players to break their AA contracts for 1891 and play in the NL. When Browns owner Chris Von der Ahe learned of Baldwin's perfidy, he had him jailed on a phony vagrancy charge, which was then changed to conspiracy, a criminal offense with possible prison time. (Baldwin countered by suing Von der Ahe for false arrest and winning, but he was unable to collect until 1898 when he finally had the St. Louis owner kidnapped and jailed. Von der Ahe ultimately had to buy his freedom for $2,625, the amount he still owed in damages.) Baldwin got out of the slammer in time to go to spring training with Pittsburgh but opened the season with a sore arm. He still led the last-place Pirates with 22 victories.

The following January, Baldwin developed a felon on his left hand and was facing possible amputation before it finally healed. On May 30, at Pittsburgh, he registered the last DH win ever by a Pittsburgh pitcher when he bagged two nine-inning CG victories over Baltimore. In August, however, he quarreled with the Pirates, testy new manager, Al Buckenberger, and was suspended. While absent from the team, he was arrested on September 1 in Homestead, PA, where he was then living, for complicity in instigating the famous Homestead strike and riots against Carnegie Steel. After posting $2,000 bail, Baldwin was allowed to rejoin the Pirates and the charges were eventually dropped when his father, an influential figure in the steel industry, intervened on his behalf. Baldwin again led Pittsburgh in wins with 26, giving him 108 victories in the past four seasons, more than any other pitcher during that span except Bill Hutchison, John Clarkson, and Gus Weyhing.

He appeared in just one more game in Pirates livery and was then given to New York NL for no compensation, suggesting that Pittsburgh owed the Giants a favor. When New York released him after the 1893 season, despite his having posted 16 wins, second on the staff only to Amos Rusie, he claimed it was because he was now a persona non grata along with Silver King and several other players who had jumped AA contracts in 1891 to join the NL, and he may have been right. In February 1900, the *Washington Post* revealed, "It's an open secret among the players, or rather, a suspicion, that Mark Baldwin and Charlie 'Silver' King were 'marooned,' left to seek employment in some other walk outside of baseball, with a sort of Mafia-like understanding among the magnates, that they were to be ignored and their services unsought as punishment for the part they played in the Association-League war of '91."

Baldwin pitched for Mike Kelly's Allentown club in 1894 and went to camp with the Phillies the following spring but was cut, and he later joined Rochester of the Eastern League for a time, before finishing his career with Pottsville or the Pennsylvania State League. He then enrolled in medical school at the University of Pennsylvania and played guard on the football team. Upon obtaining his medical license, he set up a dermatological practice in Pittsburgh, where he died in 1929 of a long-standing heart ailment. (DN/DB/BM)

Barr, Robert McClelland / "Bob"

B	T	HGT	WGT	G	IP	H	GS
R	R	6'1"	192	159	1328.1	1460	152

CG	BB	SO	SH	W	L	PCT	ERA
141	363	588	6	49	98	.333	3.85

B. 12/?/1856 Washington, D.C. **D.** 3/11/1930
TEAMS: 83PitA 84WasA 84IndA 86WasN 90RocA 91NYN
DEBUT: 6/23/1883 at Cincinnati; caught by Billy Taylor and lost 7–2 to Cincinnati's Will White
FINALE: 9/12/1891 at New York; caught by Artie Clarke and lost 8–7 to Cleveland's Henry Gruber when the Spiders scored 3 unearned runs in the ninth inning

Bob Barr's ML finale was typical of his career. Although far from a great pitcher, he hardly deserved to win only a third of his games in his five ML seasons. Barr worked for the Health Office in Washington and pitched for local teams until he was invited to join Pittsburgh AA in 1883. Given a temporary leave of absence from his job, he no doubt regretted it when he perceived the caliber of his new team. As a rookie he went 6-18 for an outfit that could not win even a third of its games. The following year he signed with Washington AA, another dreary group that was bringing up the rear of the loop when it disbanded. He then finished the year with Indianapolis, compiling a composite 12-34 mark. After his first two seasons Barr stood 18-52 for three teams that had an aggregate .259 winning percentage.

His luck was not about to change. After spending 1885 back in Washington with the Eastern League Nationals, he accompanied the team when it entered the NL the following year on the agreement that he would pitch only in home games. Released in July with a 3-18 record, he then watched his former team finish last without him. Even though his career figure had now slipped to 21-70, he nonetheless received an offer from Chicago NL for 1887 but could not get a leave of absence from his new job in the Patent Office and played in a Washington amateur league instead. The following year, Barr decided baseball held more intrigue than a government career, and he signed with Rochester of the International Association. Before the 1888 season was out his father had died and his "aged mother" took seriously ill, requiring him to return to Washington for several weeks. Barr still managed to notch a 1.58 ERA with Rochester. When he went 29-18 with a 1.68 ERA in 1889, he was among the cast of players Rochester retained upon joining the AA the following spring.

Barr celebrated his return to the majors in 1890 with a team that could win as often as it lost—Rochester finished exactly at .500—by notching 28 victories, but he pitched so often (493 innings) that he also led the loop in losses with 24. Still, he liked playing for manager Pat Powers enough that he accompanied him to Buffalo of the Eastern Association in 1891. Barr's arm soon had Buffalo in first place by so wide a margin in early August that Powers felt he could cash in his ace while his value was at a premium and sold him to the Giants for $1,000. In first place earlier in the 1891 season, the Giants were in complete disarray by the time Barr arrived. In his first appearance with his new club on August 13 at New York, a Cincinnati player fouled one of his pitches out of the park. Barr had just been given a new ball and was preparing to pitch when a policeman threw the old ball back into the park. It struck him in the head and knocked him unconscious. Barr was not fit to pitch again until twelve days later and was released after losing all four of his starts with the Giants, including his finale that he had been so close to winning before errors cost him the game.

He could not get back to Buffalo fast enough, but in April 1892 his honeymoon with that city ended when he was arrested in a raid on a bookie joint where he was working as a clerk. Less than a year later he escaped from a Harrisburg mental hospital by climbing over a fence, and although he suffered a broken leg, he managed to hop a boxcar before being captured. Barr may just have been bleeding the pent-up frustration out of his system after years of rotten luck pitching with rotten teams. By 1896 he had returned to Washington and been appointed the chief clerk of the engineering department, a position he held until his death at 73 from prostate cancer. (DN)

Bartson, Charles Franklin / "Charlie" "Old Reliable"

B	T	HGT	WGT	G	IP	H	GS
?	?	6'0"	170	25	188	226	20

CG	BB	SO	SH	W	L	PCT	ERA
17	66	47	0	8	10	.444	4.11

B. 3/13/1865 Peoria, IL **D.** 6/9/1936
TEAMS: 90ChiP
DEBUT: 5/14/90 at Buffalo; caught by Duke Farrell and beat Buffalo's Alex Ferson 4–1
FINALE: 9/16/1890 at Chicago; caught by Jack Boyle and was relieved by Frank Dwyer in his 3–1 loss to Buffalo's Larry Twitchell

In 1889 Charlie Bartson was in his second season with his hometown Peoria team in the Central Interstate League when he fanned 12 Chicago NL hitters in an exhibition game. Jimmy Ryan, a three-time victim of Bartson's, remembered him when the Chicago PL team was hunting for extra pitchers. The rookie did not make his debut until the 1890 PL season was well under way and subsequently got little work since Mark Baldwin and Silver King started 113 of Chicago's 138 games between them.

In July 1890 Bartson was offered to Buffalo to strengthen the last-place Bisons. But PL contracts stipulated that a player could not be transferred without his consent, so Bartson refused the deal, preferring to pitch one game a week for a good team than every third day for bad team that would grind him into the ground. He was let go before the season ended after he accompanied teammates on an off day to a NL game between Chicago and Boston at Boston's South End Grounds on September 18 and had a flask concealed under his jacket. Bartson proceeded to get drunk and then verbally abuse the Colts' Cap Anson so vilely that the police physically ejected him from of the park. A disgusted Charlie Comiskey, Bartson's manager, promptly recommended his release because "his work was not of such a kind as to warrant his retention" anyway.

Bartson pitched in Midwestern minor leagues until he was in his early thirties and then joined Ed Dugdale in establishing a Western Association team in Peoria. He later was president of the Peoria Three-I League club for some years. Bartson was employed by the Empire Cigar Store when he died of heart problems at his Peoria home at 71. (DN)

Beatin, Ebenezer Ambrose / "Ed"

B	T	HGT	WGT	G	IP	H	GS
R	L	5'9"	162	109	946	997	108

CG	BB	SO	SH	W	L	PCT	ERA
104	372	335	5	48	56	.462	3.68

B. 8/10/1866 Baltimore, MD **D.** 5/9/1925
TEAMS: 87–88DetN 89–91CleN
DEBUT: 8/2/1887 at Detroit; caught by Charlie Ganzel and beat Philadelphia's Charlie Buffinton 10–3
FINALE: 9/14/1891 at Philadelphia; caught by Chief Zimmer and lost 13–3 to Philadelphia's Bill Kling

Ed Beatin pitched for independent Fredericktown, MD, in 1886 after gaining acclaim while hurling for the unaffiliated Limekilns against a Hagerstown nine that included Tom Kinslow, who had recently been released by Washington. Remembering Beatin's dazzling assortment of curves when both he and Beatin joined Allentown of the Pennsylvania State Association the following spring, Kinslow convinced Allentown to keep Beatin after he had an attack of severe stage fright and pitched poorly. In July 1887 Beatin (known by now as the "Allentown Wonder") flirted with Cincinnati AA; meanwhile the Cleveland AA team also wanted both him and Kinslow. A controversy erupted when Detroit garnered Allentown's crack battery instead after Cincinnati insisted Allentown had agreed to its offer of $1,000 for them, but it was forgotten by the end of August after Detroit sent Beatin home with a sore wing that he acquired pitching an exhibition game in the rain.

Beatin began 1888 back in Allentown and did not make his first appearance with Detroit until July 10. Although he hurled only 12 games, he had the distinction of pitching Detroit's finale as a member of the NL when he beat Washington 7–4 on October 13. In the late fall of 1888, after shifting from the AA to the NL, Cleveland purchased Beatin from the disbanding Detroit club and happily watched him notch 20 wins in 1889 and lead the team in strikeouts despite having the least speed of any pitcher on the staff. He made up for it with a "teaser" that rivaled the best junkballers in the nineteenth century. Enoch Bakely and Cinders O'Brien, the Spiders' other two main pitchers, fled to the PL Cleveland entry in 1890, but Beatin remained loyal and further rewarded Cleveland NL by going 22-30 that season while the rest of the staff was 22-58. His star at its zenith, Beatin's name in Cleveland was so prominent that he was hired to work that winter as a sports reporter for a local paper.

Expected to be the team's ace again in 1891, Beatin left Cleveland's spring training site at Hot Springs, AR, in late March to attend his mother's funeral in Baltimore. Upon returning to the club, he hurt his arm and was unable to make his first start until May 14, when the season was already 20 games old. After absorbing a 12–6 loss to the Phillies, Beatin rested for a month and a half before testing his arm again against Pittsburgh. Trailing 4–0, he "was taken out of the box after the fifth when he had no speed" but escaped the loss when Cleveland rallied to win 9–4. Shortly afterward Beatin went to Mount Clemens, MI, to treat his arm with hot baths and massages. Returning to the Spiders in August, he was shelled 12–2 by Boston. Another rest period proved equally futile when he was removed in the second inning of a 13–3 loss to the Phils on September 14.

The following March, Beatin was assigned to Minneapolis when the eight Western League teams were drawn by lottery, but his arm was dead. In February 1900 the *Washington Post* reported he was working in a Baltimore restaurant, shelling oysters. Beatin died in Baltimore at 58. (DN/DB/PM)

Begley, Edward N. (b. Bagley) **/ "Ed"**

B	T	HGT	WGT	G	IP	H	GS
?	?	?	?	46	381	427	44

CG	BB	SO	SH	W	L	PCT	ERA
40	147	148	0	16	27	.372	4.39

B. 10/?/1863 New York, NY **D.** 7/24/1919
TEAMS: 84NYN 85NYA
DEBUT: 5/3/1884 at New York; caught by Buck Ewing and beat Detroit's Stump Wiedman 11–3
FINALE: 7/4/1885 at Louisville; caught by Bill Holbert and was relieved in the sixth inning by Dave Orr and charged with a 13–7 loss to Louisville's Guy Hecker

Ed Begley's arm hung by a thread by the time he made his final ML start, perhaps because he had employed an extremely unorthodox pitching delivery in 1884, which commenced with his back turned toward the plate, and injured himself trying to alter it the following season when a new rule disallowed such trickery. A member of the New York NL club's rotation in his rookie season, he was made part of a sham trade over the winter by the syndicate ownership of both the NL and AA New York entries when he went to the AA Mets along with third baseman Frank Hankinson for pitcher Tim Keefe and third baseman Tom Esterbrook. The Mets, as everyone expected, got the worst of the deal when Keefe matured into a 300-game winner and Begley had just four more ML wins left in his arm of choice, which remains unknown. He rebounded a bit in 1886 and in June was said by the *New York Times* to be "pitching strongly for the Bridgeports" of the Eastern League. But the following June he was released by Binghamton of the International Association. Begley died at his home in Waterbury, CT, in 1919. (DN)

Bentley, Clytus George / "Cy"

B	T	HGT	WGT	G	IP	H	GS
?	?	?	?	18	144	268	17

CG	BB	SO	SH	W	L	PCT	ERA
15	12	5	0	2	15	.118	6.19

B. 11/23/1850 East Haven, CT **D.** 2/26/1873
TEAMS: 72ManNA
DEBUT: 4/26/1872 at Troy; caught by John Clapp in a 10–0 loss to Troy's George Zettlein
FINALE: 8/9/1872 at Hartford; caught by John Clapp in an 11–8 loss to Jim Britt of the Brooklyn Atlantics

Cy Bentley's first ML win came on May 22 against Cleveland. Since the Mansfields won three of the seven decisions in which he did not figure and were only 2-15 in games he started, it will probably always be a puzzle that he was the club's ace pitcher. No less of a puzzle is that he batted in the middle of the order despite hitting only .219. Like several other members of the Mansfields, Bentley's ML career encompassed only the short period that the club was a member of the NA. He died in Middletown, CT, the following February of unknown causes. (DN)

Bernhard, William Henry / "Bill" "Strawberry Bill"

B	T	HGT	WGT	G	IP	H	GS
B	R	6'1"	205	53	351	404	39

CG	BB	SO	SH	W	L	PCT	ERA
30	110	72	1	21	16	.568	3.97

B. 3/16/1871 Clarence, NY **D.** 3/30/1949
TEAMS: 99–00PhiN 01–02PhiAL 02–07CleAL
DEBUT: 4/24/1899 at Philadelphia; relieved Wiley Piatt in Piatt's 10–8 loss to Brooklyn's Doc McJames and Jack Dunn
FINALE: 9/19/1907 at Cleveland; relieved Bob Rhoades in a 2–1 loss to St. Louis's Harry Howell and Bill Dinneen

Bill Bernhard was no starry-eyed teenager when the Phils sent him a contract after he had pitched well for Palmyra of the New York State League the previous year. He rejected it and spent the season pitching for independent teams after the Phils refused to up the ante. That winter Bernhard got what he wanted from the Phils and reported in the spring of 1899. Splitting his time between relief and starting roles, he went 6-6 and then joined the rotation in 1900. After a spectacular 12-1 start, Bernhard faded to 15-10 and, worse, was hammered for 11.69 hits per nine innings, the highest mark of any NL qualifier in 1900.

Obviously, when both Bernhard and second baseman Nap Lajoie jumped the Phils for the AL Philadelphia A's in 1901, Bernhard was the one less missed, especially when he repeated his negative feat and led all AL qualifiers with 11.49 hits allowed per nine innings. Still, the Phils took legal action against Bernhard as well as against Lajoie, and the pair was transferred to Cleveland to elude a court order to return to the NL. Lajoie hit .369 for Cleveland but missed over 50 games while Bernhard became the surprise acquisition in all of baseball in 1902, when he went from worst to first, allowing just 7.01 hits per nine innings, the most stingy figure in the majors. After being slowed by a broken finger in 1903, he rebounded to win 23 games in 1904 and remained a key member of the Naps staff through the 1906 season before his arm began to fail him.

Bernhard later managed in both the Southern Association and the PCL. In 1919 he relocated to Southern California and died in San Diego of leukemia in 1949. (DN)

Bond, Thomas Henry / "Tommy"

B	T	HGT	WGT	G	IP	H	GS
R	R	5'7½"	160	417	3628.2	3765	408

CG	BB	SO	SH	W	L	PCT	ERA
386	193	972	42	234	163	.589	2.14

G	AB	H	R	2B	3B	HR	RBI
488	1975	471	213	53	11	0	174

BB	SO	SB	BA	SA	OBP
22	63	5	.238	.276	.247

G	W	L	PCT	PENNANTS
6	2	4	.333	0

B. 4/2/1856 Granard, Ireland **D.** 1/24/1941
TEAMS: 74AtlNA 75HarNA 76HarN 77–81BosN (P/M)82WorN 84BosU 84IndA
DEBUT: 5/5/1874 at Brooklyn; caught by John Farrow in a 24–3 win over Baltimore's Asa Brainard
FINALE: 8/11/1884 at Columbus; caught by Charlie Robinson and lost 11–3 to Columbus's Dummy Dundon

Tommy Bond is the only pitcher since the inception of the NL in 1876 to win 40 or more games three years in a row. At age 23 he was the highest-paid player in the game, receiving $2,500. A year later, still short of his 25th birthday, he owned 221 career wins (although his salary had been cut to $1,500). From that point forward he never won another game in the NL. Were it not for the creation of the jerry-built UA in 1884, he probably never would have won another major league game.

Bond first tried out for the Brooklyn Atlantics in 1873 when he was only 17. However, he had not yet mastered control of his patented "rise ball," which he delivered with his right hand about six inches above the ground. Returning to the Atlantics the following spring, he helped achieve semi-respectability in the NA for the first time by winning 22 games. But he also led the loop in losses (32), runs (440), and home runs allowed (16). The latter total was astronomical for its time, representing a full 40 percent of the home runs surrendered in 1874. Bond's rookie high-point came on September 30 when he was the last pitcher on a visiting NA team to beat Boston in its home park. (The following year, the four-time NA champs set an all-time record when they went undefeated at home for the entire season.) Just a day later, however, the titleholders wreaked gleeful revenge, trouncing Bond and the Atlantics 29–0.

In 1875 Atlantics captain Bob Ferguson persuaded Bond to accompany him to Hartford, where he would share the pitching with Candy Cummings and play RF on days when he was not in the box. Bond's home runs allowed shrank from 16 to 3 after Cummings tutored him in how to add a curve to his rise balls. By the end of the season some observers believed that Bond's curve was even better than that of his mentor, the putative inventor of the pitch. Bond remained in Hartford when it joined the fledgling NL in 1876, and he replaced Cummings as the Dark Blue's ace. Nevertheless, at the close of the 1876 season, unhappy with Ferguson, who had suspended him in the late going after he accused Ferguson of throwing games, the 20-year-old righthander switched to Boston as soon as his Hartford contract expired. In his first three years with Harry Wright's Hub entry, Bond won 123 games and carried Boston to two pennants. A third was missed in 1879 largely because his arm woes near the end of the season forced Wright to use rookie Jim Tyng in key games against Providence, the eventual pennant winner.

After Bond slipped to just 26 wins on a dissension-ridden club in 1880, he opened 1881 by dropping his first three starts at the new fifty-foot pitching distance. Wright elevated rookie Jim Whitney to the team's ace and released his longtime stalwart, giving his roster spot to journeyman flinger John Fox. Still just 25, Bond returned to the Brooklyn Atlantics, now an independent team, and spent the summer trying to pamper his arm by playing the outfield. That winter the Worcester NL club signed him as a pitcher and captain solely on his reputation and against the wishes of manager Freeman Brown. When Bond's arm gave out on Opening Day in 1882 and then again in his second start, Brown released him as unfit to play. However, the pitcher surprised Brown by appearing in Cleveland before a game with a doctor's note clearing him to play. He even replaced Brown briefly as manager, although he knew better than to try to pitch again.

Two years later, when Boston was granted a franchise in the rebel UA, Bond was coaxed into trying out for the team and seemed at first to have undergone a miraculous renaissance. In April 1884 the *Boston Globe* reported, "Bond has changed his style of pitching, and now delivers the ball well up to the shoulder and with great speed." The former NL great won his Opening Day start against Philadelphia and five weeks later dealt the St. Louis Maroons their first loss after they had won a record 20 straight games to open the season. On June 20 Bond topped Washington to lift his mark to 13–7, but it would be his last ML win. After he lost his next two starts he was released, partly as a cost-cutting measure since his salary was the highest on a team that was losing money. But Boston's judgment proved correct when he signed with Indianapolis AA and was thrashed in his final five big league starts.

Still short of his 30th birthday, Bond umpired in a New England minor league in 1885 while trying (unsuccessfully) to learn the leather business. The following spring he made a brief comeback with Brockton of the New England League, winning his first three starts, but he was soon out of the game again. Beginning in 1891 he worked in the Boston City Assessor's office until his retirement thirty-five years later. Bond also umpired college games and coached the Harvard team on occasion, a role he had first undertaken on a volunteer basis in 1879. He died of myocardial insufficiency at his daughter's Boston home in 1941. (DN)

Borden, Joseph Emley (aka Josephs) **/ "Joe"**

B	T	HGT	WGT	G	IP	H	GS
R	R	5'9"	140	36	284.1	304	31

CG	BB	SO	SH	W	L	PCT	ERA
23	58	43	4	13	16	.448	2.56

B. 5/9/1854 Jacobstown, NJ **D.** 10/14/1929
TEAMS: 75PhiNA 76BosN
DEBUT: 7/24/1875 at Philadelphia Athletics; caught by Charlie Snyder and lost 11–4 to the Athletics' Dick McBride

FINALE: 7/15/1876 at Chicago; caught by Lew Brown and was relieved by Jack Manning in the 15–0 loss to Chicago's Al Spalding

CAREER HIGHLIGHT: 7/28/1875 at Philadelphia; caught by Charlie Snyder and hurled the first no-hit game in ML history, beating Chicago's Mike Golden 4–0

One of the classic early-day baseball tales is how Joe Borden joined the Philadelphia Pearls in 1875 under the name of Josephs to hide his pro ball aspirations from his father. Few know that on July 28 of the following year Borden tried to umpire an exhibition between the New York Mutuals and the Lynn Live Oaks under his former alias but was such a well known figure by then that New York threatened to walk off the field if he officiated.

Borden's groundbreaking no-hitter was his first ML win and came in his third start while he was still known as Josephs. The acclaim his achievement drew outed him and by September, when he signed a three-year contract with Boston for the following year, he was using his real name. Early in 1876 Borden shut out Cincinnati in a game that was considered by some at the time to be a second no-hitter but has since been ruled a two-hitter. Boston's ace from the outset of the season, he was given the ball by manager Harry Wright in 18 of the club's first 19 regular season games plus numerous exhibitions. It is unclear whether Wright wore out Borden's arm or his pitches simply no longer fooled batters. By late June teams were beginning to batter Borden and the Boston press was accusing him of "want of judgment" in the box. After an 8–6 loss at Louisville on June 29, Borden, who was making his fifth straight start at the time, went sixteen days before taking the box in Chicago for his final ML appearance. The long gap suggests that he may have been overused by then, but that can be only a surmise since Wright was never openly criticized for any facet of his managing during his days in the Hub. In any event, the Boston club had to buy out the exploded phenom's last two years of his contract after failing to get him to quit after he was assigned to maintain the team's home grounds.

By 1878 Borden was running a shoe factory near Philadelphia. Later an officer of the Guarantee Trust and Safe Deposit Company, he died at his daughter's home in Yeadon, PA, at 75. (DN/DB)

Boyle, Henry J. / "Henry" "Hank" "Handsome Henry"

B	T	HGT	WGT	G	IP	H	GS
R	R	6'1"	165	207	1756.1	1740	199

CG	BB	SO	SH	W	L	PCT	ERA
189	378	602	10	89	111	.445	3.06

G	AB	H	R	2B	3B	HR
291	1049	230	120	42	7	10

RBI	BB	SO	SB	BA	SA	OBP
70	51	129	7	.219	.301	.258

B. 9/20/1860 Philadelphia, PA **D.** 5/25/1932

TEAMS: 84StLU 85–86StLN 87–89IndN

DEBUT: 7/9/1884 at Baltimore; caught by George Baker and beat Baltimore's Jerry Dorsey and Yank Robinson 8–2

FINALE: 10/2/1889 at Indianapolis; caught by Con Daily and was relieved by Amos Rusie after six innings in his 12–2 loss to Philadelphia's Charlie Buffinton

After pitching for a pennant winner as a rookie, Henry Boyle was buried on a series of bad teams and lost 20 games or more four times in a relatively brief career. Nevertheless, with a good head for the game, as well as speed, control, and a sinker that tailed sharply away from right-handed batters, he was regarded as one of the NL's better pitchers during the late 1880s.

Boyle began as a versatile utility man who primarily played 1B for Reading, PA, and topped the Interstate Association with a .356 BA in 1883. With Reading collapsing in the summer of 1884 he signed with St. Louis, the runaway leader of the upstart UA. After a win over Baltimore in his debut, he was used heavily in the box for a few weeks until the Maroons corralled Charlie Sweeney, the pitching ace of Providence's NL club. After that, Boyle played more LF but remained the Maroons' backup pitcher. Against admittedly weak competition in the UA, he posted impressive results, with an ERA well over a run below the league average and a mere 118 hits allowed in 150 innings. Meanwhile, owner Henry Lucas so trusted him that he was named treasurer shortly after Boyle joined the club and handled all finances on its road trips. After the UA collapsed and the Maroons took a NL franchise, Sweeney hurt his elbow, leaving Boyle the ace on the staff. In 1886 Boyle was out with arm problems for more than two months but was back by the end of the season, and although he lost 15 of 24 decisions he logged the loop-leading ERA. When the St. Louis franchise was sold to Indianapolis the following spring, he was one of four Maroons stars who were allowed to play for the new team while remaining the property of the NL, lest the financially suspect Indianapolis management be tempted to sell off its best players.

In Indianapolis Boyle was trapped on a tail-ender with a miserly management. He remained the club's best pitcher but along with the rest of the staff was periodically accused of malingering, and when the team fared badly, as it usually did, the Indianapolis stars were suspected of deliberately playing poorly in hopes of forcing a trade. Outfielder Ed Andrews, an activist in the players' Brotherhood, later remembered that when the team traveled, three unnamed Indianapolis players would visit all the home team clubhouses to bewail their treatment at the hands of their club. Two of the players were Jack Glasscock and Jerry Denny; the third was almost certainly Boyle.

Yet when the Brotherhood established the PL after the 1889 season, Indianapolis club president John T. Brush opened his wallet and signed Boyle as well as most of his teammates. Shortly before play began the next spring, Indianapolis sold its team to New York, which had lost most of its own players to the PL. Boyle never played for the Giants, however. Over the winter his arm had gone bad, and by July he was begging in vain for a trial at 1B. Subsequently Boyle made attempts to come back as a position player in the minors but was described as "a back number of the first water, one of the great has-beens."

Once out of baseball, Boyle worked as a salesman. At one point he peddled picture books door to door in Indianapolis, and by the late 1890s he sold beer for a Philadelphia brewery. From time to time he dropped in on newspaper offices around the country and reported in the baseball weeklies reminiscences about his playing days. By the early twentieth century, however, he was largely forgotten. For many years it was not even known where and when he died, but it has lately been established that he passed away in 1932 in Philadelphia. (DB/DN)

Bradley, George H. / "Foghorn"

B	T	HGT	WGT	G	IP	H	GS
R	R	6'0"	175	22	173.1	201	21

CG	BB	SO	SH	W	L	PCT	ERA
16	16	16	1	9	10	.474	2.49

B. 7/1/1855 Milford, MA **D.** 3/31/1900
TEAMS: 76BosN
DEBUT: 8/23/1876 at Boston; caught by Lew Brown and beat Philadelphia's Lon Knight 7–6
FINALE: 10/21/1876 at Boston; caught by Lew Brown and lost 11–1 to Hartford's Candy Cummings

After "Foghorn" Bradley beat several NL teams in 1876 exhibitions while pitching for independent Lynn, MA, he was brought to Boston to replace Joe Borden. Bradley started 21 of Boston's final 22 games, missing only a September 5 contest against Cincinnati, when manager Harry Wright gave the ball to Jack Manning. Whether the task was too much for his arm or he simply couldn't agree to terms with Boston for 1877 is unclear, but in any case in mid-September 1876 the *Boston Herald* said the entire Boston team had signed for next year except for Bradley, who then played mostly 1B in 1877 for London, Ontario, in the International Association. Bradley later became an umpire and was a regular member of the NL staff off and on through the 1883 season.

He returned to umpiring in 1886 in the AA and was embroiled in an infamous incident in a Sunday game at Cincinnati on July 11. In the sixth inning Bradley was assailed by the crowd, which thought he favored the visiting Brooklyn club, and was hit by a beer mug hurled from the stands. He retreated to the directors' room under the grandstand but was coaxed after a long delay into returning to the field and finishing the game, won by Brooklyn 11–7. Bradley died in Philadelphia of chronic alcoholism at 44. (DN/DB)

Bradley, George Washington / "George" "Grin"

B	T	HGT	WGT	G	IP	H	GS
R	R	5'10½"	175	347	2940	3009	325

CG	BB	SO	SH	W	L	PCT	ERA
302	196	671	33	171	151	.531	2.44

G	AB	H	R	2B	3B	HR
567	2258	518	272	64	38	3

RBI	BB	SO	SB	BA	SA	OBP
172	40	150	5	.229	.296	.243

B. 7/13/1852 Reading, PA **D.** 10/2/1931
TEAMS: 75StLNA 76StLN 77ChiN 79TroN 80ProN 81DetN 81–82CleN 83PhiA 84CinU 86PhiA 88BalA
DEBUT: 5/4/1875 at St. Louis; caught by Tom Miller and beat Joe Blong of the St. Louis Reds 15–9
FINALE: 8/8/1888 at Cincinnati; played SS and went 0-for-3 in a 6–2 loss to Cincinnati's Elmer Smith
CAREER HIGHLIGHT: 7/15/1876; caught by John Clapp and pitched the first no-hitter in NL history, blanking Hartford's Tommy Bond 2–0 for one of his season-record (since tied) 16 shutouts

TSN explained George Bradley's nickname of "Grin" on April 23, 1892: "No one before ever had such a tantalizing smirk and none of the modern detachment has given evidence that they can successfully imitate it." Bradley's grin, which some called fiendish, symbolized his machinations in his early years in the game. Frank Bancroft described how Bradley would steam open a sealed box containing a new ball, put the ball in a vise and then seal up the box again and wait for an umpire to open it and toss him a sphere of mush. Bradley first learned the trick from Mike McGeary when McGeary joined him on the St. Louis Browns in 1876, and the two worked it to such perfection that he compiled a record 16 shutouts, 45 wins and a loop low 1.23 ERA.

Toward the end of the 1876 season Bradley signed with the Philadelphia Athletics for 1877 and then had to scramble to find a home with Chicago after the A's were ousted from the NL. Assuming the role of Chicago's ace after Al Spalding moved from the pitcher's box to 1B, Bradley was expected to carry the Second City club to a repeat NL pennant but instead sagged to 18-23 when opposing teams were warned of his trickery by McGeary and switched unsealed ball boxes prior to games he was due to pitch. In 1878, when Chicago made no effort to retain him, Bradley pitched for New Bedford of the International Association under Frank Bancroft. He returned to the NL the following spring with its new Troy entry and topped the loop in losses and earned runs allowed while fashioning a dismal 13-40 record. Bradley remained a capable second-line slinger and general utility player in the majors for another five years but was an ace on only one other occasion—in 1884, when he began the season in that role for the Cincinnati UA club and won 25 games before ceding his mantle to Jim McCormick late in the season.

Bradley first pitched for pay with independent Easton, PA, in 1874. That October he hurled a ten-inning exhibition game for the Philadelphia A's against the NA flag-winning Boston Red Stockings and distinguished himself to such a degree that both he and his catcher, Tom Miller, were hired as the battery for the new St. Louis Brown Stockings entry in the NA the following season. A month after winning his NA debut, Bradley repeated his earlier exhibition-game success against Boston by handing the Red Stockings their first defeat of the 1875 NA season. He finished his rookie year with 33 wins and won 45 more as a sophomore, but his total of 78 at that point represented nearly half of his final figure of 171.

Following his 25-win season in the 1884 UA, Bradley became primarily an infielder. Blacklisted by the majors in 1885 for being a UA jumper, he remained out of the pro ranks. The following year he returned to the majors with Philadelphia AA and opened the season at SS after impressing the team brass with his hard work in spring training. But after going 4-for-48, he was released. Bradley filled out the decade of the 1880s playing and managing in the minors, mostly in the Southern League. In 1890 he came full circle when he finished his pro career where it had begun fifteen years earlier—in Easton, but at 3B. Bradley worked as a night watchman for a while in a carriage store and was then hired on with the city of Philadelphia as a police officer. He died in Philadelphia of liver cancer in 1931, a year after retiring from the police department. (DN/DB)

Brainard, Asahel / "Asa" "Acey" "Count"

B	T	HGT	WGT	G	IP	H	GS
R	R	5'8½"	150	85	699.2	1109	82

CG	BB	SO	SH	W	L	PCT	ERA
77	78	25	0	24	53	.312	4.40

G	AB	H	R	2B	3B	HR
108	467	116	71	11	0	0

RBI	BB	SO	SB	BA	SA	OBP
43	10	7	4	.248	.272	.264

B. ?/?/1841 Albany, NY **D.** 12/29/1888
TEAMS: 71–72OlyNA 72ManNA 73–74BalNA
DEBUT: 5/5/1871 at Washington; caught by Doug Allison and lost 20–18 to Boston's Al Spalding
FINALE: 10/14/1874 at Baltimore; played 2B and went 2-for-5 in a 15–2 loss to Boston's Al Spalding

It is difficult to gauge whether Asa Brainard pitched for a string of bad teams in the NA because none of the good teams wanted him or whether he just had the poor judgment to consistently sign with bad teams. A mere five years before he appeared in his final NA game he had been the toast of baseball as the ace of the undefeated 1869 Cincinnati Red Stockings, so it would seem that the game could hardly have passed him by so quickly. Yet once the NA formed in 1871, very few pitchers from the pre-professional era successfully made the transition. Actually, in just the few short months between 1871 and 1872 the game changed dramatically as the pitching rules were liberalized to make way for the first curve ball pitchers to appear in ML livery. Brainard was not among them. His twin fortes were guile and his skill at watching base runners. By the early 1870s "scientific" pitchers dependent largely on changing speeds to retire batters were few, and those, like Harry Wright, who were successful usually pitched only a few innings and against certain types of teams.

Brainard first came to Cincinnati in 1868 after spending part of the previous season with the Washington Nationals. Upon arriving in the Queen City he boarded with a family named Truman and eventually married one of their two daughters, Mary, when a romance developed while she was helping to nurse him back to health from a bout with smallpox. In 1869 Brainard was financially ready for wedlock when Harry Wright offered him $1,100 to pitch for the Red Stockings, the first avowed all-professional team, a salary topped only by Wright's $1,200 and his brother George's $1,400. Even though Brainard pitched almost every one of the Red Stockings' 64 games in 1869 and was never beaten, all did not go smoothly between him and Wright, especially after rumors arose that a few Red Stockings were "enticed" on the morning of the infamous Haymaker tie game in which Haymakers then scored six runs in the first inning and hit Brainard hard. Something of a prima donna, he was also a raging hypochondriac, ready to beg off from a game at the first sign of a sniffle, let alone a hangover, of which there appear to have been a fair number during the Red Stockings' cross-country swing. On that score alone, it was not surprising that Wright would pursue a young Rockford, IL, slinger named Al Spalding rather than Brainard when he formed the Boston team prior to the inaugural NA campaign. Wright also could not have been pleased to learn that Brainard deserted his recent bride after the 1870 season, leaving her destitute and forced to rely on help from her family in raising their infant son.

Brainard received no further ML invitations upon finishing 1874 with a 4.40 career ERA, the poorest of any NA pitcher in 500 or more innings, and provided ample evidence that he could play no other position well enough to carry his .248 career BA. The following year he opened an archery range on Staten Island and in 1882 he was seriously injured when a customer accidentally shot an arrow through his hand. Later in the 1880s Brainard moved west to Denver and ran the Markham Hotel billiard room until he died of pneumonia in 1888, the first of the 1869 Red Stockings to pass away. (DN/BM)

Breitenstein, Theodore P. / "Ted" "Red Ted" "Theo"

B	T	HGT	WGT	G	IP	H	GS
L	L	5'9"	167	376	2949.1	3067	338

CG	BB	SO	SH	W	L	PCT	ERA
299	1203	886	12	160	167	.489	4.02

G	AB	H	R	2B	3B	HR
445	1344	289	173	27	15	4

RBI	BB	SO	SB	BA	SA	OBP
126	150	102	30	.215	.266	.296

B. 6/1/1869 St. Louis, MO **D.** 5/3/1935
TEAMS: 91StLA 92–96StLN 97–00CinN 01StLN

DEBUT: 4/28/1891 at St. Louis; relieved Jack Stivetts in the eighth inning of a 13–0 win over Louisville's Jack Doran and Ed Daily
FINALE: 5/9/1901 at Cincinnati; caught by Bill Schriver, lasted just one inning and gave up 6 runs before being relieved by Willie Sudhoff in a 9–3 loss to Cincinnati's Noodles Hahn
CAREER HIGHLIGHT ONE AND FAMOUS FIRST: 10/4/1891 at St. Louis; caught by Jack Munyan and became the first pitcher to throw a nine-inning no-hitter in his first ML start when he beat Louisville's Jouett Meekin 8–0
CAREER HIGHLIGHT TWO AND FAMOUS FIRST: 4/22/1898 at Cincinnati; caught by Heinie Peitz and pitched his second career no-no, beating Pittsburgh's Charlie Hastings 11–0 as Baltimore's Jay Hughes also threw a no-hitter on the same day, the first time in ML history that had happened

A product of a time when left-handers were still trained to write with their right hands, Ted Breitenstein had red hair and freckles and was challenged as a hitter until Roger Connor joined the Browns and changed his stance. (Breitenstein had always had a great eye—he walked 150 times in the decade of the 1890s, 19 times more than any other hurler.) But the jury will forever be out on whether he was a great pitcher whose prime years were wasted on a string of bad teams or simply a very durable pitcher capable of producing some terrific games along with some real clunkers. He led all nineteenth-century southpaws in starts and innings but ranked only third in wins behind Ed Morris and Killen and finished with just a .482 winning percentage even though he was never a member of a cellar dweller.

A stove maker by trade, Breitenstein first gained the spotlight as a pitcher-outfielder in 1889–90 with the Home Comforts, a St. Louis semipro outfit. Breitenstein joined the AA St. Louis Browns in the spring of 1891 and began the season as the Browns' mop-up flinger before being sent to Grand Rapids of the Northwestern League for further training. Shortly after being recalled to the majors, this time to stay, he celebrated by marrying Ida Uhlenschtick, who would remain his mate until her death in April 1935. Breitenstein continued to do only mop-up duty for the Browns until their final day as a member of the AA. Given his first ML start, he faced the minimum of 27 batters in no-hitting Louisville 8–0 and then went to work at his off-season job in a local wrought iron range works.

In 1892, after the Browns moved to the new loop formed by the NL-AA merger, Breitenstein was plagued by poor control in his official rookie year and finished just 9-19. But the following year, after the pitching distance was lengthened and most other hurlers struggled to adjust, he flowered out of the blue, leading the NL with a 3.18 ERA. His 1894 campaign was another gem, as he went 27-23 while the rest of the Browns' staff was a miserable 29-53. At that point Breitenstein grew disenchanted with owner Chris Von der Ahe and began to rouse himself only for games against top clubs. In 1895 he bested the pennant-winning Orioles five times in eight tries but was just 14-27 against the rest of the loop, and the Browns became known as "Chris's Counterfeits." Meanwhile Von der Ahe accused his ace of boozing during home games and ducking into the Sportsman's Park bar between innings. On September 14 Breitenstein was hit on the knee by a line drive in a game against Philadelphia, an injury that by rights should have shelved him for the rest of the season. But he feared Von der Ahe's notoriety for not paying players when they were injured. Eleven days later, with his knee still aching, he came back to beat Cincinnati, the last time the Browns would top the Reds until September 27, 1897.

In January 1896 *TSN* revealed that Breitenstein had made only $1,800 in 1895 in the course of stunning its readers with the news that he had jumped the Browns to become player-manager of the Chester Grays in the outlaw Southern Illinois League for $2,500 plus a half interest in a local billiard hall. Even though the move was largely a ploy to hold up Von der Ahe for more money, it succeeded marvelously. But once the owner overcame his panic at the prospect of losing his best player, he and Breitenstein immediately quarreled again as to when the pitcher should report and what his punishment would be if he was not in top condition. The left-hander then seemingly had only a mediocre year—18-26 with a 4.48 ERA—but his 18 wins represented almost half of the Browns' total of 40, and his ERA was nearly a full run below the team's 5.33 mark. That October, Von der Ahe, desperate for money to finance winter horseracing at Sportsman's Park, sold Breitenstein to Cincinnati for a reported $10,000 (which may actually have been as little as $4,000). In any case, the

27-year-old lefty subsequently became known as "The $10,000 Beauty" and gave the Reds three red-headed starters—he, Frank Dwyer, and Red Ehret.

Breitenstein proved worth the investment initially, leading Cincinnati in wins and almost every other major pitching department in 1897, but the following year he won 20 games for the last time. In 1899, after he slipped to just 13 victories, there was talk of making him an outfielder. Breitenstein meanwhile attributed his poor showing to manager Buck Ewing, whom he claimed had forced him to overtrain the previous spring and lose too much weight, but when his deterioration continued in 1900, he was allowed to return to St. Louis.

Released in 1901 by his hometown club after just three starts, Breitenstein blamed the poor spring weather for his rheumatism acting up and hampering his control. His career seemed over after a stint with St. Paul of the Western League ended in late August, but the following spring Charlie Frank, an old Browns teammate, induced him to give it one more try with Frank's Memphis Southern Association entry. Breitenstein found a second life in the game, collecting 151 victories over the next decade in the SA to lift his total pro-career win total to 328. He umpired awhile in the Texas League and then returned again to St. Louis to work as a watchman for the city park department. In 1935 he collapsed at his job in Forest Park when grief over his beloved wife's death just nine days earlier aggravated a preexisting condition and triggered a fatal heart attack. (DN)

Briggs, Herbert Theodore / "Bert" "Buttons"

B	T	HGT	WGT	G	IP	H	GS
R	R	6'1"	180	52	410.2	486	47

CG	BB	SO	SH	W	L	PCT	ERA
43	203	158	0	17	28	.378	4.84

B. 7/8/1875 Poughkeepsie, NY **D.** 2/18/1911
TEAMS: 96–98ChiN 04–05ChiN
DEBUT: 4/23/1886 at St. Louis; caught by Kit Kittridge and beat St. Louis's Ted Breitenstein 3–1
FINALE: 9/25/1905 at Chicago; caught by Johnny Kling and was relieved in the ninth inning by Jake Weimer who got the 3–2 win over Brooklyn's Harry McIntire

Known as "Bert" early in his career, Herbert Briggs grew up in the Glenville section of Cleveland and pitched for the Euclid Beach Parks, a local amateur team, before joining Little Rock of the Southern League in 1895. He was purchased by Chicago in September but could not join the NL club until the following spring because he had to attend to his ailing mother. Prior to his rookie season, Briggs married his Cleveland sweetheart. He then went 12-8 in twenty-one starts and was praised by manager Cap Anson for the way he "mixes 'em up." The following year Briggs lost his first start by one run after giving up just 6 hits and then dropped another one-run verdict in his second start despite firing a seven-hitter. After that he fell down a well and was 4-17 to finish with a .190 winning percentage, the lowest of any qualifier in 1897. Given a last reprieve when Tom Burns took over as Chicago manager in 1898, Briggs won his initial start of the season on April 25, beating Cincinnati 7–4, but he then dropped his next three decisions and was bounced.

By the close of the century Briggs was having to advertise for baseball jobs in *TSN*, but a good year with Utica of the New York State League in 1901 elevated him the following season to Toronto of the Eastern League, where he notched two successive 20-win campaigns. Briggs returned to Chicago NL in 1904 and narrowly missed a 20-win season when he lost his last start of the year to Boston 5–4 in ten innings. He remained in the Cubs' rotation early in 1905 but was able to complete only 13 of 20 starts. Briggs sat out 1906 and then spent two years in the American Association with Indianapolis before returning to Cleveland. He died of tuberculosis at his home there in 1911. (DN)

Britt, James Edward / "Jim"

B	T	HGT	WGT	G	IP	H	GS
?	?	?	?	91	816.2	1266	91

CG	BB	SO	SH	W	L	PCT	ERA
88	62	29	1	26	64	.289	4.26

B. 2/25/1856 Brooklyn, NY **D.** 2/28/1923
TEAMS: 72–73AtlNA
DEBUT: 5/2/1872 at Middletown; caught by Tom Barlow and lost 8–2 to Middletown's Frank Buttery
FINALE: 11/1/1873 at Brooklyn; caught by Tom Barlow and beat George Zettlein of the Philadelphia Whites 12–1

The son of Irish immigrants, Jim Britt was the youngest documented player in ML history after first pitching for the Brooklyn Atlantics as early as 1870, when he was just 14. He began his ML career two years later with nine straight losses before defeating New York 11–10 on July 2, 1872. Britt's career win-loss record is more a reflection of the quality of his team than of his pitching skills, although there were periodic mentions in the *Brooklyn Eagle* that he was under suspicion of game throwing. After leaving the Atlantics he toiled for the Flyaway club of Brooklyn in 1874, flirted with joining NA New Haven for a time the following spring, and instead remained in Brooklyn, pitching with clubs there for several more seasons.

In the late 1870s Britt headed west to the San Francisco Bay area, where he played ball for a few years, became a plumber, and also worked as a city fireman. He served for a time on the San Francisco Board of Supervisors and was a leader in the local plumbers' union. His son Jimmy was a boxer and won the world lightweight title. Britt died in San Francisco in 1923 after a long illness. (DN/DB)

Buffinton, Charles G. / "Charlie"

B	T	HGT	WGT	G	IP	H	GS
R	R	6'1"	180	414	3404	3344	396

CG	BB	SO	SH	W	L	PCT	ERA
351	856	1700	30	233	152	.605	2.96

G	AB	H	R	2B	3B	HR
586	2214	543	245	67	16	7

RBI	BB	SO	SB	BA	SA	OBP
255	91	114	14	.245	.299	.276

G	W	L	PCT	PENNANTS
116	61	54	.530	0

B. 6/14/1861 Fall River, MA **D.** 9/23/1907
TEAMS: 82–86BosN 87–89PhiN (P/M)90PhiP 91BosA 92BalN
DEBUT: 5/17/1882 at Boston; caught by Ed Rowen and blanked Worcester's Frank Mountain 6–0
FINALE: 6/28/1892 at Washington; caught by Wilbert Robinson and lost 12–8 to Washington's Phil Knell

Charlie Buffinton is one of seven pitchers that appeared in as many as 3,000 innings during his eleven-year career span (1882–92) and is the only member of the select group besides Tony Mullane that is not in the HOF. Mullane was a contract jumper and spent most of his career in the American Association. The only black mark against Buffinton is that during that eleven-year span he had the fewest career wins on the list (233 to Mickey Welch's 254), but he also had the best record as a manager and was second only to Mullane as a hitter. That is not to argue that Buffinton was a great pitcher, only that he was a very good one.

Blond, debonair, one of the few impact pitchers in the 1880s about whom nothing unduly derogatory was ever written, Buffinton was known for an overhand curve ball that on April 11, 1918, *TSN* said was really a "drop ball, which in later years they called it a spit ball." Originally a catcher in the early 1880s with semipro clubs, he turned to pitching after he was struck in the eye by a foul tip and was blasted by New Bedford, MA, in his first start but then beat New Bedford in each of his next two appearances to launch his new career path.

Buffinton joined the independent Philadelphias in the spring of 1882 but was released after just four games. Boston then signed him for its reserve squad and nursed him along all season, using him in exhibitions but only sparingly in official NL contests. Consequently, Buffinton appeared in just 15 games his rookie season—5 as a pitcher and the other 10 as a position player. The following year he alternated with Jim Whitney, both in the box and in RF, and was instrumental in Boston's surprise NL pennant triumph. Buffinton had a superb year in 1884 with 45 wins, 417 strikeouts and a .750 winning percentage but was second in all of these departments to Charley Radbourn, whose record 60 wins dwarfed every pitching season before or since.

That September, Buffinton married Alice Thornley of Providence, removing from circulation one of the game's most eligible bachelors. But marital bliss initially did not seem to agree with him. Over the next two seasons Buffinton went 29-37 and spent much of 1886 on the DL with arm trouble. The following April he was sold to Philadelphia NL along with catcher Tom Gunning. In his new surroundings he rebounded strongly, winning 73 games in 1887–89 before joining the majority of the NL's elite performers in jumping to the PL in 1890. Named playing captain of the Philadelphia entry shortly after the PL season started, he was effective as both a pitcher and a leader, lifting his club above .500 and going 10–6 against Boston, New York, and Chicago, the loop's top three teams.

After the PL collapsed, Buffinton was expected to return to Harry Wright's Philadelphia NL squad but instead signed with the renegade Boston Reds, which had retained the core of their 1890 PL flag winner, added a few new players like Buffinton, and joined the AA. In the spring of 1891 he developed a new delivery following several years of experimentation to revamp his technique after a rule change took away his two-step, jump-in-the-air and curve-the-ball style. The innovation produced such a striking result that in the tenth season of his career Buffinton suddenly emerged as the top pitcher in the game, sparking Boston to the final AA pennant and leading all ML qualifiers in base runners and hits per nine innings (10.47) as well as winning percentage (.763).

Buffinton's stay in the limelight was short. That December the NL and AA consolidated and much against his wishes he was assigned to Baltimore, destined to finish last in 1892, the first season the archrivals played in one twelve-team league. Not in the least hesitant to make his displeasure known, Buffinton pressured the Orioles to trade him but was rebuffed. When he refused to accept a pay cut from $100 to $75 a week as part of the NL's general belt-tightening, Baltimore released him on June 30. Informally blacklisted because of the circumstances of his release, Buffinton finished the season pitching for a semipro team in Massachusetts under an assumed name.

The following year he went into the lumber business in Fall River and turned so ferociously against baseball that he would not even go to the local team's New England League games. Later a successful salesman for the Bowenville Coal Company in Fall River, Buffinton was the city's most famous native son during his lifetime. He died in a Fall River hospital at 46 while preparing to undergo heart surgery. (DN)

Burdick, William Byron / "Bill"

B	T	HGT	WGT	G	IP	H	GS
R	R	?	?	30	221.2	226	24

CG	BB	SO	SH	W	L	PCT	ERA
22	56	71	0	12	14	.462	3.17

B. 10/11/1859 Austin, MN **D.** 10/23/1949
TEAMS: 88–89IndN
DEBUT: 7/23/1888 at Indianapolis; caught by Dick Buckley and beat Chicago's Mark Baldwin 2–1
FINALE: 7/2/1889 at Indianapolis; relieved Amos Rusie and took an 8–6 loss to New York.

Minnesota native Bill Burdick farmed for half a dozen years in South Dakota, a venture that delayed his start in pro ball until he was in his late twenties. He was considered a "jolly, fat little fellow" with a physical resemblance to Jim Galvin, and although he was not of Galvin's caliber, he was described as excellent as long as the bases were empty. With runners on, he had an incurable tendency to fall apart.

After a brief test with Nashville of the Southern League, Burdick returned to the upper Midwest to pitch for Eau Claire, Milwaukee, Oshkosh, and Omaha. In July 1888 he was acquired by Indianapolis. Burdick got off to a good start with the Hoosiers, beating Chicago 2–1 on July 23. For the rest of the season he pitched on a regular basis and finished 10-10, making him the first qualifier in ML history to post a .500 record while on a last-place team.

Notwithstanding his success in 1888 Burdick was caught in a numbers game in 1889, as Indianapolis added veteran pitchers Charlie Getzein and Jim Whitney to an already full pitching staff. He injured his arm in an April exhibition, and though he remained with the Hoosiers, he pitched seldom and then usually in relief as manager Frank Bancroft experimented with the newly liberalized substitution rule. After suffering a 10–6 loss to Boston in late June Burdick replaced Amos Rusie in the fourth inning against New York on July 2 and held down the Giants while Indianapolis came from behind to take a 6–4 lead. But Roger Connor belted a three-run homer in the seventh to give New York the win and Burdick a loss in his final ML appearance.

For Burdick it was back to the minors and the upper Midwest again, pitching for Omaha, Sioux City, and Minneapolis. With Sioux City, Burdick's work as a sub umpire against Milwaukee so enraged Brewers captain George Shoch that Shoch pulled his team off the field before the second inning, forcing Burdick to forfeit the game to Sioux City. Milwaukee was already more than happy to see the last of Burdick; during Sioux City's last game there, he got drunk at the bar under the grandstand and was forcibly ejected from the grounds as he yelled "like a wild Comanche." Burdick finished his pro career with Minneapolis of the Western Association in 1891 and was soon working as a grip man on electric cable cars in Minneapolis. He later operated Burdick's Resort on Newman Lake near Spokane, WA, for many years. Prior to his death in Spokane at 90, Burdick was the last surviving member of a nineteenth-century Indianapolis ML team. (DB/DN)

Calihan, William T. (aka Callahan) / "Will" "Billy"

B	T	HGT	WGT	G	IP	H	GS
?	R	5'8"	150	50	408.1	427	47

CG	BB	SO	SH	W	L	PCT	ERA
22	172	155	0	24	21	.533	4.14

B. 5/3/1868 Oswego, NY **D.** 12/20/1917
TEAMS: 90RocA 91PhiA
DEBUT: 4/17/1890 at Philadelphia; caught by Deacon McGuire and lost 11–8 to Philadelphia's Sadie McMahon
FINALE: 6/20/1891 at Philadelphia; replaced Tommy Corcoran at SS and was 0-for-1 in a 12–3 loss to Boston's George Haddock

Will Calihan began his pro career with Rochester of the International Association in 1888. His first batterymate was his brother Tom, but later that season he began to pair with Jim Toy after Tom left Rochester under a cloud. Calihan remained with Rochester in 1889 until trouble with the front office sent him to Buffalo; he finished a combined 20-19 with the two IA teams and owned a glittering 1.74 ERA.

Prior to the 1890 season Calihan was courted by the Buffalo PL entry but reluctantly signed with the new Rochester team in the American Association when the Bisons cooled on him. *TSN* predicted he would fare well with Rochester "in the absence of his incorrigible brother," but he was a management issue in his own right. In early August Calihan was suspended after club president Henry Brinker hired a detective hoping to catch him drinking, and Calihan flattened his tail when he spotted him and then thrashed a club official who tried to intervene. After a tough 3–1 loss to St. Louis at Rochester on September 8, he was shut down for the year. His salary probably became an issue after Rochester dropped out of the race. Some weeks after the 1890 season *TSN* reported that he had been Rochester's highest paid player at $312.50 per month.

Calihan signed for 1891 with Philadelphia AA but was released in June along with batterymate Dave McKeough. *TSN* at first said the reason was "they were tired of bench-warming," and later claimed there had been a clique on the A's working against them. Calihan finished the season with Buffalo of the Eastern Association and then returned to Rochester and remained in the Eastern League through 1894. Prior to the 1895 season he was expected to get a trial with Washington NL, but it never materialized and he signed with Atlanta of the Southern League. In June Calihan left the team for a month when his wife died. He began 1896 as Atlanta's second baseman and leadoff hitter but by July was back with Rochester. His arm dead, Calihan remained primarily a position player until giving up pro ball in 1898 after a short stint in the Southern League. He died in a Rochester hospital of pneumonia in 1917. (DN)

Callahan, James Joseph / "Jimmy" "Nixey"

B	T	HGT	WGT	G	IP	H	GS
R	R	5'10½"	180	130	1077.1	1226	121

CG	BB	SO	SH	W	L	PCT	ERA
117	293	288	8	67	49	.578	3.49

G	AB	H	R	2B	3B	HR
225	810	219	128	32	16	3

RBI	BB	SO	SB	BA	SA	OBP
96	28	7	29	.270	.365	.301

B. 3/18/1874 Fitchburg, MA **D.** 10/4/1934
TEAMS: 94PhiN 97–00ChiN 01–05ChiAL (P/M)11–13ChiAL (M)14ChiAL (M)16–17PitN
DEBUT: 5/12/1894 at Baltimore; caught by Jack Clements and was relieved by Jack Taylor in his 8–3 loss to Baltimore's Stub Brown
FINALE: 7/29/1913 at Boston; pinch hit unsuccessfully for pitcher Bill Lathrop in the eighth inning of a 5–3 loss to Boston's Dutch Leonard

Called "Nixey" as a boy, Callahan shunned the nickname in later life and insisted on being called "Jimmy" or "Jim." A sprinter before he became a pro ballplayer, he ran for prize money while working as a plumber's apprentice and pitching for semipro teams under the name of William Smith with the consent of his foreman, who was a baseball buff but could not voluntarily let him off work. Callahan would thus pretend to be sick on days he pitched and use the alias as a disguise. The ruse continued for some three years before he was found out and began pitching in 1893 for independent teams under his own name. Signed that winter as a combination pitcher-infielder by the Phillies, Callahan demonstrated that he needed further seasoning and finished 1894 in the Pennsylvania State League. Judging him no longer a prospect, the Phillies let him get away despite a 30-win season in the 1895 Eastern League but then retrieved him from the Kansas City Western League club in the fall draft after the 1896 season. At that point an embarrassed Jim Manning, the KC manager, revealed that Callahan had been sold to Chicago in July for 1897 delivery and he had been sworn to abide by Chicago GM Jim Hart's request to keep the transaction secret.

Philadelphia protested in vain that the draft should take precedence over the clandestine sale, and in 1897 Callahan became the last player in NL history to qualify for both the batting title and the ERA crown when he collected 189.2 innings and 360 ABs with Chicago. The following year he switched primarily to pitching and won 20 games in each of the next two seasons. Callahan later attributed his early hill success to Chicago teammate Clark Griffith, who had become the staff ace relying almost solely on excellent control and keeping batters off balance. Like Griffith, Callahan also appreciated the importance of pacing himself and usually grew stronger with each passing inning. Also aiding him in close battles were both his stickwork and his exceptional fielding. In his last three seasons with Chicago NL (1898–1900), Callahan averaged the most assists per inning (.31) among hurlers in a minimum of 750 innings during that span. At the close of 1900 Callahan became one of the first NL players to jump to the American League when he followed his mentor Griffith's lead and signed with the Chicago entry in the rebel loop. (DN)

*Campbell, Hugh F. / "Hugh"

B	T	HGT	WGT	G	IP	H	GS
?	?	?	?	19	165	250	18

CG	BB	SO	SH	W	L	PCT	ERA
18	7	5	0	2	16	.111	2.84

B. ?/?/1846 ?, Ireland **D.** 3/1/1881
TEAMS: 73ResNA
DEBUT: 5/6/1873 at Elizabeth; caught by John Farrow and lost 8–3 to Baltimore's Candy Cummings
FINALE: 7/17/1873 at Brooklyn; caught by Doug Allison and lost 23–1 to Brooklyn's Jim Britt

Hugh Campbell was the brother of first baseman Mike Campbell, his teammate on the 1873 Resolutes. After first appearing together in 1866 with Irvington, NJ, the pair moved to the Elizabeth team after the 1870 season and was on its 1872 New Jersey state championship squad. In several 1872 exhibition games against NA teams Campbell had fared reasonably well. These outings gave the Resolutes confidence that they could compete in the 1873 NA, but it was illusory. Campbell's only two wins came on June 5 at Brooklyn and, stunningly, in the first game of a July 4 DH at Boston when he beat Al Spalding 11–2. He died in Newark of tuberculosis in 1881. (DN/DB)

Carrick, William Martin / "Bill" "Poker Bill" "Doughnut Bill"

B	T	HGT	WGT	G	IP	H	GS
R	R	5'10"	150	167	1324.2	1650	155

CG	BB	SO	SH	W	L	PCT	ERA
138	400	239	4	63	89	.414	4.14

B. 9/5/1873 Erie, PA **D.** 3/7/1932
TEAMS: 98–00NYN 01–02WasAL
DEBUT: 7/30/1898 at Louisville; caught by Mike Grady and beat Louisville's Chick Fraser 7–3
FINALE: 9/23/1902 at Washington; caught by Boileryard Clarke and gave up four home runs in a 14–1 loss to Boston's Irv Young

Despite his slight frame, Bill Carrick was a workhorse, largely because his delivery put little strain on his arm. An avid poker player, explaining his primary nickname, he threw mostly "slow twisters." Able to keep hitters off balance early in his ML career, he was among the easiest pitchers in the majors to hit once batters realized they could sit on his slow curves since he had little else. In his final three ML seasons (1899–1902) Carrick led all ML pitchers that worked a minimum of 800 innings during that span in both the most hits allowed per nine innings (11.28) and the highest ERA (4.17).

The willowy right-hander learned the game in

Adrian, MI, and pitched for the local Michigan State League champions in 1895 as well as in the Interstate League. Late that season the NL Spiders invited him to hurl for the Cleveland Athletic Club, where they could inspect him more closely. Cleveland then put a string on him and sent him to Fort Wayne of the Interstate League in 1896 but no longer liked what it saw. Carrick spent 1897 with Newark, where he spearheaded the Atlantic League Colts by topping the loop in wins with 31. He returned to Newark in 1898 before being acquired by the NL Giants. Despite pitching well in his first taste of ML competition, he was used sparingly in the last ten weeks of the season and made only five starts.

The following year Carrick sprang forward as the Giant's ace, pacing the NL in starts and CGs. During the off-season he continued to live with his parents in Adrian and work as an electroplater. In 1900, when the Giants fell to the NL basement, Carrick again led the loop in starts but also ranked first in losses. At 19-22, however, he came within one win of joining the select circle of ML hurlers that have won 20 games for a cellar dweller. Sometime that year Carrick married and bought his own home in Adrian; mounting financial obligations no doubt helped persuade him to jump to the rebel AL in 1901 for more money. Unfortunately, he picked the wrong team, as Washington, in his two remaining ML seasons, spent both mired deep in the second division. At the close of his final campaign in 1902, the *Washington Post*, in its yearly assessment of the local club, reported, "Carrick was a dead one for over two months."

But while ML hitters were no longer gulled by his snail-speed curves, the rubber-armed righty would continue to fool minor league batsmen for the better part of another decade, although he first had to survive accusations of being a company plant during an electroplaters strike and was even forced for a time to play under an assumed name to escape reprisals. In 1903, after beginning the season with Toledo, Carrick fled to Seattle when union men accused him of acting as a spy for "The Manufacturers Association of Chicago" and threatened to boycott every game in which he appeared until they ran him out of the East. In September of that year, the *Washington Post* noted, "Poker Bill Carrick has been chased by the Seattle team. The unions are still on Bill's trail for spying during a strike."

Carrick spent 1904 in the New England League under the name of Page. Emboldened, he resumed his own name in 1905. Carrick later played in the Eastern and the Connecticut state leagues. In 1910 he took over as player-manager of New Haven, and in May the *New York Times* observed that he had sparked his team to 10 straight wins and the early lead. After the Prairie Hens finished fourth, Carrick was replaced at the helm. He died in Frankford, PA, of heart disease in 1932 and was returned for burial to Adrian, where he spent most of his life. (DN)

*Casey, Daniel Maurice / "Dan"

B	T	HGT	WGT	G	IP	H	GS
R	L	6'0"	180	201	1680.1	1664	198

CG	BB	SO	SH	W	L	PCT	ERA
182	543	743	14	96	90	.516	3.18

B. 11/20/1862 Binghamton, NY **D.** 2/8/1943
TEAMS: 84WilU 85DetN 86–89PhiN 90SyrA
DEBUT: 4/18/1884 at Washington; caught by Bill McCloskey and beat Washington's Charlie Geggus 4–3
FINALE: 10/4/1890 at Syracuse; caught by Herman Pitz and beat Philadelphia's Ed O'Neil 7–6

Dan Casey was the brother of outfielder Dennis Casey, who played CF behind him in his ML debut. The owner of a family farm in Binghamton, he had already established himself as the Quicksteps' ace and owned a 20-4 record in 1884 by the time the Delaware team was invited to replace disbanding Philadelphia in the UA. Casey featured a screwball—described as "a drop and out" to right-handed hitters—that may have been taught to him by McCloskey, his first catcher. After winning Wilmington's initial UA game, he was shelled by Washington 14–0 in his next start and then released. He began the following season with Indianapolis of the Western League. Reportedly 14-4 when the loop disbanded on June 15, he was sold to Detroit along with Deacon McGuire, his catcher at Indianapolis, and several other teammates. Casey's highlight in his official rookie season came on August 7 when he stopped Providence's NL record streak of 26 straight home wins over Detroit, but later that month he was fined $100 for poor work and had $50 added to the insult when he refused to take tickets before a game.

In November 1885 Casey and McGuire were donated by Detroit to the NL after the Wolverines acquired Buffalo's "Big Four" near the end of the season. The Phillies purchased Casey and McGuire from the senior loop in January and were rewarded with 24 victories after installing the southpaw in their 1886 rotation. The following year the lefty won a career high 28 games and topped the NL in shutouts and ERA. In 1888, however, Casey had little to cherish after he spoiled Boston's home opener with 15,000 on hand to inaugurate the unveiling of the new $70,000 Grand Pavilion section of stands by beating John Clarkson 4–1. He slumped to 14-18 and was dropped after winning just 6 games in 1889. Casey revived to go 19-22 with Syracuse in 1890 but was left high and dry when the PL folded after the season, cutting ML jobs by a third. He pitched in the minors until 1894 and then worked as a conductor on a streetcar line.

Upon his death in Washington in 1943, some of his obits mentioned that he had claimed for years to have inspired "Casey at the Bat." In a 1938 radio broadcast in Baltimore, Casey maintained that Mudville was the area around the Phillies' park at Broad Street and Huntington, which had been a vast mud hole before the park was built, and that Flynn and Blake were Charlie Bastian and Joe Mulvey. No historians have ever found his hypothetical correlations between himself and Ernest Thayer's fabled Casey more than mildly diverting. (DN/DB)

Chamberlin, Elton P. (b. Chamberlain) **/ "Elton" "Ice Box"**

B	T	HGT	WGT	G	IP	H	GS
R	B	5'9"	168	321	2521.2	2406	301

CG	BB	SO	SH	W	L	PCT	ERA
264	1065	1133	16	157	120	.567	3.57

B. 11/5/1867 Buffalo, NY **D.** 9/22/1929
TEAMS: 86–88LouA 88–90StLA 90ColA 91PhiA 92–94CinN 96CleN
DEBUT: 9/13/1886 at Baltimore; caught by Paul Cook and lost 6–2 to Baltimore's Matt Kilroy
FINALE: 5/13/1896 at Cleveland; caught by Chief Zimmer and was replaced by Nig Cuppy in the first inning of Cuppy's 14–4 win over Philadelphia's Bert Inks and Kid Carsey

The son of a Buffalo druggist, Elton Chamberlin delighted in tussling with professional wrestlers and pitched in more odd or famous games that any other hurler in the nineteenth century. Adept at changing speeds and angles of delivery, he was also able to pitch either underhand or overhand and with either arm. Since Chamberlin never wore a glove, "the ambidextrous wonder" would pitch with his right hand and use his left hand to catch runners napping or vice versa, and on at least two occasions—in 1888 and again in 1891—he pitched with both arms in the same game.

Among Chamberlin's many memorable outings was the most controversial contest in the AA's ten-year history on September 7, 1889, at Brooklyn when St. Louis manager Charlie Comiskey pulled his team off the field, claiming it was too dark to continue, and umpire Fred Goldsmith forfeited the "Candlelight Game" to Brooklyn. When AA president Wheeler Wikoff later overruled the forfeit, Chamberlin, who had been pitching at the time, was credited with a 4–2 win. Some five years later, in the afternoon game of a Memorial Day DH at Boston, he lost 20–11 to Kid Nichols when Link Lowe took him deep four times to render him the first ML pitcher to surrender four home runs in a game to the same batter. That same season, on July 20 at Cincinnati, Chamberlin won an eerie ten-inning game against Pittsburgh literally at gunpoint. Harry Vaughn hit a home run to tie the contest and Germany Smith followed by winning the game with a one-hop liner that bounced into the bleachers when Pittsburgh outfielder Elmer Smith was prevented from pursuing the ball into the stands (as the rules then allowed) by a spectator who held him off with drawn revolver.

According to historian Lee Allen, Chamberlin was nicknamed "Ice Box" for "his austere calm in the face of all hostility by the enemy." After pitching for various amateur clubs, he made his pro debut in 1884 with Quincy of the Northwestern League and Southern League by 1886 with Macon, where he went 13-20. Chamberlin came to Louisville once the SL season ended and by 1887 was sharing the bulk of the Louisville pitching load with Tom Ramsey. In the spring of 1888 he held out, refusing to join Louisville until early May. The Colonels quickly tumbled deep into the second division, to slash Chamberlin's payroll owner Mordecai Davidson peddled him to front-running St. Louis for a reported $4,000. Even though Chamberlin won 25 games that season and gave the Browns 32 victories in 1889, he was not among the pitchers the PL courted for 1890. The following June the Browns demonstrated why that was so when they sold him to Columbus AA, while he was under suspension, for perhaps as little as $1,000 and offered in explanation, "Chamberlin is of a sullen, sulky disposition and is very hard to manage." In addition, the pitcher was a skilled ventriloquist, who often disconcerted teammates, and was a "blue-ribbon gourmandizer," thinking ahead to his postgame meal the whole time he was in the box. Still, he was 12-6 with a 2.21 ERA in his limited use with Columbus and blanked Toledo 6–0 on the final day of the season after clashing with manager Gus Schmelz over what he felt was a childish set of rules that Schmelz had posted in the clubhouse.

That winter Columbus redoubled efforts to get rid of Chamberlin when he was involved in a boxing betting scam in his Buffalo hometown. In February 1891 he was sold to Philadelphia AA for more than Columbus had paid for him but still far less than what his work in the past four seasons should have merited. Although Chamberlin won 20 games for the last time in his career in 1891, his overall record was 22-23 while the rest of the A's staff went 51-42. Assigned to Cincinnati when the AA and NL merged the following year, he again underachieved, finishing 19-23 for a Reds team that was otherwise 63-45. An improvement to 16-12 in 1893 was marred when the *Cincinnati Enquirer* accused him of throwing a July 4 game to Philadelphia and of being in cahoots with a gambler named Brill, who was a club hanger-on.

Even though Chamberlin evaded the charge, he was never again entirely free of suspicion. By 1896 his arm had begun to fray from the heavy workload it had endured early in his career. After spending 1895 in the minors, he pitched his last ML game when he was still just 28 and then returned to Buffalo and played for semipro teams there until the late 1890s. At one point he tried to convince NL president Nick Young to hire him as an umpire. Thwarted in that ambition, he then tried his hand at professional boxing. Chamberlin died in Baltimore at 61. (DN/DB)

Clarke, William H. / "Dad"

B	T	HGT	WGT	G	IP	H	GS
B	R	5'7"	160	120	848.1	1061	92

CG	BB	SO	SH	W	L	PCT	ERA
77	191	174	2	44	51	.463	4.17

B. 1/7/1865 Oswego, NY **D.** 6/3/1911
TEAMS: 88ChiN 91ColA 94–97NYN 97–98LouN
DEBUT: 4/23/1888 at Indianapolis; caught by Duke Farrell and finished the game in CF in place of Jimmy Ryan, who relieved him and got the 11–10 win over Indianapolis's Lev Shreve
FINALE: 4/18/1898 at Louisville; caught by Charlie Dexter and lost 7–2 to Pittsburgh's Frank Killen

Originally a homely farm boy with frightful grammar and a perennial butt of crude practical jokes, Dad Clarke became an irreverent wag once he acquired some sophistication and learned to palaver so smoothly that he was constantly conning fellow players out of everything from meal money to their girlfriends. On the mound he kept up a steady stream of unsettling commentary to batters, and off the field newcomers to his teams were warned to stay away from him any time they saw a pair of dice in his hand. With a ball in his hand Clarke was seen as having only limited natural talent, but Hugh Fullerton regarded him as one of the most scientific and deceptive pitchers in the game, extraordinary at changing speeds and angles.

Clarke tried out with Oneida of the outlaw Central New York League in the spring of 1886 but was cut when the club's catcher couldn't hold him. He then went to Norwich, which had a better catcher, and in his first CNYL game pitched a no-hitter against Oneida in which he faced only twenty-seven men. Clarke began 1887 with Sandusky, OH, of the Tri-State League but was sold to Des Moines of the Northwestern League for $1,000 before being acquired by Chicago NL for 1888 delivery. In his Second City debut he failed to get a win but hit his only career home run. After staggering to an 11–7 victory in his second start eleven days later, he was cut and finished the season with Omaha of the Western Association, where he became known as "Oscar Wilde" Clarke because his control was so wretched.

The following year Clarke improved, walking only 110 batters in 462 innings, but despite going 35-15, he remained in Omaha while teammate Kid Nichols headed for Boston NL. He was still with the Omahogs when they disbanded in July 1891, freeing him to join Columbus AA. But 16 walks in 21 innings and remarks from the *Ohio State Journal* that he "fielded his position like an old woman with her shoes full of broken glass" consigned him to spend two more seasons in the minors before the New York Giants drafted him from Erie of the Eastern League in the fall of 1894. By then his control had sharpened, but he was slow in adapting to the new pitching rules.

Clarke turned 30 in January 1895 with a 5-6 career record and a 5.28 ERA but then suddenly put it all together. He led the Giants with a 3.39 ERA that season and won 18 games. Given the chance to assume Amos Rusie's crown as the club ace when Rusie held out all of 1896, Clarke lost to Washington on Opening Day and was 0-5 at the end of April. Although he led the Giants in innings and finished a semirespectable 17-24, his days in New York were numbered when Bill Joyce took over as manager. Clarke's floaters resulted in too many hard smashes hit to 3B, which Joyce could not tolerate since he played there. In August 1897 Clarke was sent to Louisville with cash for outfielder Tom McCreery. The following April, on the advice of "Orator" Jim O'Rourke, a staunch advocate of Cesare Lombroso's theories that certain physical stigmata indicated a born criminal, Clarke curiously let a phrenologist examine the odd bumps on his face and hands shortly after he made his last ML start. He then evidently received assurance that even though he had a face that would "turn cream into rich cottage cheese," according to *TSN*, he was not destined for a life of crime.

Clarke returned in 1899 to pitch for Worcester of the Eastern League and then joined Butte, MT, "while holding down a position in a mining company." In 1900 he appeared in three games with Buffalo of the newly renamed American League before heading west again. When he passed through the town where he had played the longest, someone from the *Omaha World-Herald* spotted him and wrote, "He still wears his face upside down, and is laughing when you think he is crying." After going 1-4 with Minneapolis of the independent American Association in 1902, Clarke left the game to be a bartender in Lorain, OH. He died in a hospital there in 1911 after having suffered a stroke several days earlier. (DN/DB)

---

*Clarkson, Arthur Hamilton / "Arthur" "Dad"

B	T	HGT	WGT	G	IP	H	GS
R	R	5'10"	165	96	704.2	873	81

CG	BB	SO	SH	W	L	PCT	ERA
63	325	133	2	39	39	.500	4.90

B. 8/31/1866 Cambridge, MA **D.** 2/5/1911
TEAMS: 91NYN 92BosN 93–95StLN 95–96BalN
DEBUT: 8/20/1891 at Philadelphia; relieved Amos Rusie in a 13–2 win over Philadelphia's Duke Esper and Bill Kling
FINALE: 8/8/1896 at Washington; relieved Sadie McMahon in McMahon's 21–16 win over Washington's Win Mercer and Effie Norton

The younger brother of HOF pitcher John Clarkson and the older brother of twentieth-century ML pitcher Walter Clarkson, Arthur Clarkson was "as blonde . . . as his brother is brunette" and also smaller in size and considerably less talented, although he had his days. After spending 1887 with Portland, ME, of the New England League, he joined Chicago of the Western Association in 1888 and showed "plenty of speed but a lack of control" and was soon dropped by the Windy City minor league club. In the spring of 1889 Louisville AA gave Clarkson a trail and was castigated, as he was regarded as a flop by then who had only his brother to thank for having had so many opportunities.

But Clarkson was tenacious. He pitched briefly for St. Paul of the Western Association in 1890 and then caught on with New Haven of the Eastern Association in 1891 before coming to New York NL for five games. Even though he did fairly well with the Giants, he began 1892 with Troy of the Eastern League. A 25-19 record warranted a start with Boston on October 8 several months after his brother had left the team for Cleveland. Clarkson showed potential, topping Amos Rusie 3–1, but was allowed to sign with St. Louis in 1893. At the finish of his 12-9 official rookie season, *TSN* observed that of all the new pitchers that year in the NL only he could be deemed a success.

But a year later it seemed an illusion that Clarkson had adjusted well to the new pitching distance, as he went 8-17 with a 6.37 ERA. A 1-6 start in 1895 made the Browns jump at an offer for him from Baltimore of utilityman Frank Bonner and pitcher Bill Kissinger. In his initial appearance with the first place Orioles, Clarkson beat Philadelphia 5–4 and at the close of his 12-3 half season in Baltimore was cited by *TSN* as a prime "illustration of what a good team can do for a pitcher."

Baltimore was still a very good team in 1896, but Clarkson reverted to his pre-Orioles form, giving up 72 hits in just 47 innings before pocketing his release in August. He complained that Orioles manager Ned Hanlon did him wrong since he had been with the team for so long that he deserved a cut of Temple Cup money, which his release denied him, but no one listened. Clarkson tried to come back the following year with Milwaukee of the Western League under Connie Mack but was soon pitching for semipro teams in the Boston area for a few dollars a game. Near the end of the century he briefly went into the cigar business with his brother in Michigan. Clarkson spent his final years as a tailor in Boston, with Harvard students his main clientele. He died in a Cambridge hospital in 1911 of peritonitis, the day after undergoing surgery for a gastric ulcer. (DN)

Clausen, Frederick William / "Fritz"

B	T	HGT	WGT	G	IP	H	GS
R	L	5'11"	190	42	324.1	315	41

CG	BB	SO	SH	W	L	PCT	ERA
36	159	134	2	16	22	.421	3.64

B. 4/26/1869 New York, NY **D.** 2/11/1960
TEAMS: 92–93LouN 93–94ChiN 96LouN
DEBUT: 7/23/1892 at Baltimore; caught by Jack Grim and lost 4–3 to Baltimore's Tom Vickery and George Cobb
FINALE: 5/4/1896 at Louisville; caught by Jack Warner and was relieved by Mike McDermott in his 12–7 loss to New York's Jouett Meekin

Fritz Clausen's first baseball paycheck came from independent Sheboygan, WI, in 1889. He spent the next two seasons in the Illinois-Iowa League and the Western Association and then joined Columbus, OH, in 1892. Clausen was the surprise sensation of the Western League, starting off 14-0 before suffering his first loss to Milwaukee on June 19, and finished the first half of the season 17-4. Sold to Louisville at that point for $500, he initially rebelled, refusing to play for a losing club. Eventually he relented but may have made a grave mistake in doing so. Clausen pitched excellent ball in the second half of the 1892 NL season but was just 9-11.

Released by Louisville in 1893 when he lost four of his first five starts, he moved to Chicago, a better team, and went 6-2, seemingly to prove that all he needed was decent support. But in 1894 he was cut after making just one bad start. By August Clausen was with Omaha of the Western Association when he was jailed for deserting his wife and children the previous winter. Released from custody after vowing to atone for his immaturity, Clausen joined Montgomery of the Southern League in 1895 and was pampered to the extent that team followers chipped in an extra $25 a month to increase his salary and provided other extra perks for his wife and family. The pitcher repaid their generosity by jumping to the Petersburg of the Virginia League, forcing Nick Young to intervene.

By the spring of 1896 Clausen's callow behavior had disgusted so many teams that he was probably relieved that anyone invited him to training camp, even if it was last-place Louisville. After he was thrashed 8–3 by Pittsburgh in his first start on April 22, manager John McCloskey sat him down for nearly two weeks before calling on him again. Even more abominable in his second appearance, Clausen was released to Milwaukee of the Western League, which also soon cut him. He returned to the Virginia League for a time but by August was in Louisville being treated for erysipelas. Clausen recovered to win 20 games in 1897 with Norfolk of the Virginia League and continued to pitch in the minors until 1902. He eventually settled in Memphis, TN, and worked as a carpenter until he retired in 1950 some ten years before his death at 90 from injuries he suffered in a fall. (DN)

Colcolough, Thomas Bernard / "Tom"

B	T	HGT	WGT	G	IP	H	GS
R	R	5'10"	160	49	319.1	397	31

CG	BB	SO	SH	W	L	PCT	ERA
22	166	66	0	14	11	.560	5.89

B. 10/8/1870 Charleston, SC **D.** 12/10/1919
TEAMS: 93–95PitN 99NYN
DEBUT: 8/1/1893 at St. Louis; relieved Frank Killen in a 25–2 win over St. Louis's Jimmy Bannon and Frank Pears
FINALE: 7/16/1899 at Weehawken, NJ; caught by Jack Warner and was relieved by Charlie Gettig in his 10–2 loss to St. Louis's Pete McBride

The pronunciation of Tom Colcolough's name befuddled everyone when he started his pro career until he finally said, "Call me Coakley," even though the correct pronunciation was Col-CO-lee. Consequently, he was listed in many box scores as Coakley when he returned to the majors in 1899 after a three-year absence, gulling some future researchers into thinking he was a hitherto undiscovered player.

Colcolough's father was a wealthy commissions agent in the Carolinas, precluding him from needing to play ball for a living, and he toyed for a time with the notion of leaving the game to study "for the ministry" instead. A product of the Charleston, SC, amateur scene, he tried pro ball initially with Atlanta of the Southern League in 1892 but was in over his head. Colcolough returned in 1893 with Charleston in the same loop and held Montgomery hitless on June 23, marking one of the first pro nonos at the new pitching distance. Toward the end of July he joined the Pirates. Used sparingly and mostly in relief, he did not log his first ML decision until September 29 when he beat New York's Amos Rusie 4–3. The following year Colcolough was bombed to the tune of a 7.08 ERA, but terrific run support enabled him to finish the year 8–5. He was released in June 1895 to Wilkes-Barre of the Eastern League and remained with that club for the better part of the next three and a half seasons before being dropped in June 1898 after an attack of Bell's palsy. His return to the majors in 1899 with the Giants is difficult to fathom. Colcolough nonetheless was actually pitching fairly well until late June, when Jennie Boyle, a woman he had wooed in Wilkes-Barre but then refused to marry, socked him with a breach of promise suit.

After leaving baseball in July 1899 Colcolough was in the produce business for a while, but his family money evaporated, forcing him to take a job as an acetylene torch welder at the Charleston Navy Yard. He died in Charleston of a heart attack in 1919, leaving a widow and four children. Colcolough's 7.08 ERA in 1894 when he went 8-5 is the highest in ML history by a qualifier with a winning percentage of .600 or better (.615). (DN)

Coleman, John Francis / "John"

B	T	HGT	WGT	G	AB	H	R	2B
L	R	5'9½"	170	629	2508	645	332	88

3B	HR	RBI	BB	SO	SB	BA	SA	OBP
56	7	279	152	154	71	.257	.345	.302

G	IP	H	GS	CG	BB
107	842.2	1182	93	84	102

SO	SH	W	L	PCT	ERA
224	4	23	72	.242	4.68

B. 3/6/1863 Saratoga Springs, NY **D.** 5/31/1922

TEAMS: 83–84PhiN 84–86PhiA 86PitA 87–88PitN 89PhiA 90PitN

DEBUT: 5/1/1883 at Philadelphia; caught by Frank Ringo and lost 4–3 to Providence's Charley Radbourn

FINALE: 7/18/1890 at Brooklyn; caught by Harry Decker, was relieved by Fred Osborne and finished the game in LF in his 17–7 loss to Brooklyn's Tom Lovett

The owner of an incredible arm early in his career—he reportedly once threw a ball 121 yards and 6 inches *underhanded*—John Coleman played amateur ball in Chicago before joining independent Peoria in 1882. In a biographical sketch of him on January 6, 1894, *TSN* said that he fanned 37 at one point with the Illinois club over a 2-game stretch.

Acquired by Philadelphia, an NL newcomer in 1883, Coleman and his team were competitive in an Opening Day 4–3 loss to Providence, but after that the roof collapsed. The 20-year-old rookie set all-time ML season records for losses (48), hits allowed (772), runs allowed (590), and earned runs allowed (291). Yet he hurled three shutouts, played a decent outfield on some days he didn't pitch, and posted a 12-48 record in contrast to the 6-43 mark the other Quakers pitchers logged. He was also never again the same. A chilling example of how Coleman and other young hurlers of his time were foolishly abused came on May 30, 1883, at Philadelphia. With the Quakers trailing Chicago 22–2 in the second game of a DH, the rookie was made to take Jack Neagle's place in the box while Neagle replaced him in the outfield. Coleman, who had worked the first game, then pitched to his max, hurling shutout ball the rest of the way in a meaningless effort, as the final score was 22-4.

By the close of his frosh season, Coleman was already suffering arm trouble. He finished the season in the outfield, leading team captain Blondie Purcell to take the box himself in some games and then end the season by using another rookie, Charlie Hilsey, in the last three contests, also probably ruining Hilsey's arm. Coleman opened 1884 in LF but hit poorly, and since he was of little more use in the box, he was let go to Philadelphia AA. After doing even worse against AA pitching (.206) he experienced a career revival in 1885, winning the A's RF job and finishing ninth in the loop among qualifiers in RC/G with 8.48. In addition, Coleman made history on May 10 at St. Louis and provoked a rules change when he finished the game as an injury substitute in RF, wearing street clothes after not suiting up that day. The following year, when his BA fell below .250, the A's cut him in late September and he finished the season in Pittsburgh, where he remained through 1888.

In October 1887, after leading the weak-hitting Smoke City entry in runs in its first season after transferring from the AA to the NL, Coleman had bladder surgery, confining him to his bed for a long spell while his father-in-law tried to talk him out of playing ball anymore, offering to set him up in business. Coleman demurred, but by the end of the 1888 campaign his arm was too weak even for the outfield, and Pittsburgh released him. In May 1889 he appeared to make a miraculous recovery. Catcher Jack Brennan swore Coleman was once again as fast as any pitcher in the game, inducing the A's to retrieve him and put him in the box. Coleman won his first start with Philadelphia, topping Cincinnati 6–1 on May 30, but he then came down with a case of malaria that shrank him to just 128 pounds. He returned to the A's late in the season and was effective, finishing with a 2.91 ERA in five starts. But evidently his arm either went back on him again or else he was still in ill health, for no ML team bid for his services that winter even though the majors expanded to twenty-four teams after the addition of the PL.

Coleman's ML coda came in July 1890 when last-place Pittsburgh NL paid him $100 to don its uniform again for two dreary pitching appearances. He essentially finished his career in the Pennsylvania State League in 1893 as a first baseman and died in Detroit twenty-nine years later after being struck by a car. At the time, he was working in a Motor City bowling alley. (DN)

Colliflower, James Harry / "Harry" "Collie"

B	T	HGT	WGT	G	IP	H	GS
L	L	5'11"	175	14	98	152	12

CG	BB	SO	SH	W	L	PCT	ERA
11	41	8	0	1	11	.083	8.17

B. 3/11/1869 Petersville, MD **D.** 8/12/1961
TEAMS: 99CleN
DEBUT: 7/21/1899 at Washington; caught by Ossee Schreck and beat Washington's Win Mercer 5–3
FINALE: 10/12/1899 at Cincinnati; caught by Joe Sugden in a 6–2 loss to Cincinnati's Emil Frisk

Harry Colliflower was a prominent figure on the Washington amateur sports scene that random chance thrust into an ML uniform for nearly three months. A carpenter by trade, he had passed his 30th birthday and was pitching for the Eastern Athletic Club in Washington when Cleveland tried him in the box one afternoon at D.C. on the recommendation of someone on the Washington club. His debut brought this tribute from the *Washington Post*: "Colliflower possesses every quality that is required in a major league twirler. He has fine control of the ball, good speed, and, the requisite amount of nerve." The game was a mirage. In his remaining eighty-nine innings with the last-place Spiders he allowed 146 hits, went 0-11, and compiled an ERA over 9.00. But on occasion, between Colliflower's box appearances, Cleveland manager Joe Quinn employed him either at 1B or in the outfield. Colliflower hit .303 in 73 ABs, but it was a hollow .303; he scored just five runs and finished with a .676 OPS.

Prior to 1899 Colliflower had pitched in several different minor leagues between 1894 and 1898, always with the same result: a quick release. He tried to parlay his Cleveland experience into a fresh stab at a pro career in the 1900 Connecticut State League but soon resumed playing amateur ball in Washington in the summer, football in the fall, and working as both a basketball referee and a baseball umpire. In 1909, while an assistant to the captain of the watch in the Washington Municipal Building, he was granted a fifty-day furlough without pay to take a job as a South Atlantic League umpire. The following August, Ban Johnson summoned him from the "Sally" League to finish the season as an AL arbiter, but he was replaced after working just 46 games. Colliflower later did some scouting for ML teams before taking a job as a clerk for his nephew's fuel oil and coal company in Washington. His death in D.C. at 92 left Sport McAllister the lone surviving member of the worst full-season team in ML history: the 1899 Spiders. (DN)

***Conway, James P. / "Jim" "Dark Days"**

B	T	HGT	WGT	G	IP	H	GS
?	R	?	?	56	452.2	485	52

CG	BB	SO	SH	W	L	PCT	ERA
44	107	140	0	22	29	.431	3.64

B. 10/8/1858 Clinton, PA **D.** 12/21/1912
TEAMS: 84BroA 85PhiA 89KCA
DEBUT: 5/5/1884 at Cincinnati; caught by John Farrow and beat Washington's John Hamill 11–3
FINALE: 10/5/1889 at St. Louis; caught by Joe Gunson in a 7–2 loss to St. Louis's Elton Chamberlin

Called "Dark Days" because of his somber bearing, Jim Conway flunked two early trials with the Brooklyn and Philadelphia AA teams, the second when he hurt his arm after just four innings on May 27, 1885, while leading Cincinnati 15–9, and John Coleman replaced him and got a 16–9 win that could as easily have been credited to him under the rules at that time. Returning to the minors, Conway enjoyed a successful 1887 season with Topeka in the Western League and signed for 1888 with Kansas City of the Western Association. After going 18-12, he became part of the 1888 KC Blues contingent that joined the AA KC Cowboys in 1889. Conway's final ML win on September 26 against Cincinnati was his nineteenth of the season. Plagued anew by arm trouble, he started only once more, on October 5. Failing in his bid for a twentieth win, he left the club before the end of the season and went to Mount Clemens, MI, for therapy along with his brother Pete, also a sore arm victim.

Conway remained with Kansas City after it deserted the AA in late 1889 and accompanied the club to the Western Association, where it won the 1890 pennant with minimal help from him. His arm still ailing, he began 1890 as an outfielder and was unable to take his turn in the box until mid-May. Conway returned to Kansas City in 1891 but was released in July, his arm so sore that he gloomily—and, alas, accurately—predicted to a *TSN* correspondent that he feared he would never pitch again. Conway was basically out of the game by 1892 and died in Clifton, PA, at 54. (DN)

*Conway, Peter J. / "Pete"

B	T	HGT	WGT	G	IP	H	GS
R	R	5'10½"	162	126	1040	1058	123

CG	BB	SO	SH	W	L	PCT	ERA
117	250	428	5	61	61	.500	3.59

B. 10/30/1866 Burmont, PA **D.** 1/13/1903
TEAMS: 85BufN 86KCN 86–88DetN 89PitN
DEBUT: 8/10/1885 at Philadelphia; caught by Jack Rowe and beat Philadelphia's Ed Daily 5–2
FINALE: 5/9/1889 at Chicago; caught by Fred Carroll, was relieved by Al Maul and finished the game in LF in his 7–6 loss to Chicago's John Tener

Pete Conway, the younger brother of ML pitcher Jim Conway, debuted at 18, was a surprise sensation at 21, and threw his final pitch in the bigs when he was just 22. So fast that Cap Anson loathed batting against him more than any other pitcher, Conway started his delivery facing 3B with his right foot slightly advanced, stepped quickly through the box with his left foot and brought his arm very high at the point of release so that his ball came at such a sharp downward angle to batters that he got an inordinate number of fly ball outs. However, the delivery put so much strain on his arm that he almost certainly injured his rotator cuff either toward the end of the 1888 season or else in the spring of 1889 and may have first torn it as early as 1887.

After pitching in the amateur Philadelphia Athletic Association in 1884, Conway joined the semipro Philadelphia Solar Tips the following year and was steered to Buffalo NL in August when it ran short of pitchers. On October 10, 1885, in what may have started him on the path to an early injury, he pitched a DH against Providence that represented the Bisons' last two games as a member of the NL, losing both to veteran Dupee Shaw. Although in the majors for just two months, he had already made 27 starts and fashioned 26 CGs.

Assigned the following year to Kansas City, an NL replacement club, Conway resumed his heavy workload, especially for a teenager, making twenty-seven starts before being sold on August 5 to Detroit for some $300, with KC manager Dave Rowe left holding the bag when he did not get either the price or the players he expected in return. In the spring of 1887 Conway was left behind in Hot Springs with arm trouble when Detroit broke camp. On May 18, in his first start of the season, he won 9–7 at Philadelphia, but he "trembled like a leaf at the close of the game" and a month later he was still so "broken down and useless" that he did not start again for the Wolverines until August 10. By the end of the year he was back in the rotation, indicating that his arm was on the mend.

In 1888 Conway may have been the best pitcher

in the NL. As of July 1 he was tied with John Clarkson for the loop lead in wins with 16, and he finished at 30-14 while the rest of the Detroit staff was a lame 38-49. Fought over by other NL teams once Detroit disbanded, Conway was awarded to Pittsburgh in 1889 along with teammates Deacon White and Jack Rowe. He won his first start on April 30, topping Cleveland 6–4 and hitting a ball over the CF fence that was said to be the longest home run ever to that point at a Pittsburgh park. But when he also won his second start on May 6 against Indianapolis, he was obviously laboring. Nevertheless, he was sent to the box again just three days later and lasted but four innings. The following week, the Pittsburgh papers stunned their readers with this announcement: "On Tuesday [May 14] the management decided that it was useless to carry Conway and [Ed] Morris with the team any longer, and they were suspended without pay and sent home to get in shape. It was a surprise, but as both were not in form, owing to illness from natural causes, the step was perfectly legal." A subsequent report confided, "Do you know where the trouble in Conway's arm lies? Well, it is just on the top of the right shoulder." He went to Hot Springs to recover but never did, although in December he came to Pittsburgh with his new bride to sign a contract and declare that Hot Springs had worked wonders.

Conway pitched a few games in 1890–91 for teams in places like McKeesport and Youngstown and then left the game to go to law school at the University of Michigan and coach the varsity team. In 1892 there were reports that he was also pitching for the Michigan nine under the name of Robinson, but the eligibility rules then were such that there would have been no reason to conceal his true identity unless he feared he might embarrass himself. Conway took up residence for a time in Detroit. In 1897 a court there awarded his wife Josephine a divorce on the charge of nonsupport, creating doubt that he ever finished law school, let alone went into practice. Some six years later, while working as a police officer in Clifton Heights, PA, Conway took ill in a local barbershop and was rushed to his home, where he died of neuralgia of the heart and fever (probably a rampant heart virus) and was buried at St. Charles Cemetery in Drexel Hill near his brother. Just 36, he was of an age where he might still have been in the majors if overwork and a lack of knowledge of pitching mechanics and the anatomy of the human arm—no one in 1888 had a clue how easily injured the rotator cuff muscle could be—had not destroyed his career when he was scarcely beginning to come into his own. (DN/DB)

---

*Conway, Richard Butler / "Dick"

B	T	HGT	WGT	G	IP	H	GS
L	R	5'7½"	140	41	352	404	41

CG	BB	SO	SH	W	L	PCT	ERA
39	137	121	0	15	24	.385	4.78

B. 4/25/1865 Lowell, MA **D.** 9/9/1926
TEAMS: 86BalA 87–88BosN
DEBUT: 7/22/1886 at Baltimore; caught by his brother Bill and lost 11–10 to Cincinnati's George Pechiney
FINALE: 10/8/1888 at Boston; caught by Eddie Tate and lost 10–6 to Indianapolis's John Healy

Dick Conway was the brother of ML catcher Bill Conway and was married to Katie Moolic, the sister of ML catcher Prunes Moolic. In 1884 he was patrolling the outfield for Salem in the Massachusetts State Association. When his brother signed to play with Philadelphia NL that July, Dick accompanied him and caught on as a pitcher with York, PA, of the Eastern League. The following year, with Conway as the team's ace and his brother the regular catcher, Lawrence, MA, captured the 1885 New England League pennant. One writer deemed Conway "the ball player who has probably gained more notoriety this season in the Eastern States than any other individual."

Not all of Conway's notoriety was of a positive nature. On July 23, in a game at Brockton, one of his pitches fractured the skull of Brockton player-manager Bill McGunnigle. The *Brockton Weekly Gazette* recounted that McGunnigle "dodged the first ball thrown at his head . . . with the second he needed to drop to all fours to save himself. . . . The unfortunate batsman could not avoid the [third] ball in time, and it struck him directly behind the left ear . . . Poor 'Mac' fell like an animal beneath the butcher's axe, and his quivering form was drawn up in agony as he lay upon the ground." The *Boston Globe* reported, "The only topic on the street tonight is the question of whether it was Conway's idea to frighten the batsman or if he was trying to get the balls as close to the batsman as possible."

In 1886 the Conways returned to Lawrence. By early July they had Lawrence in first place again in the New England League when friction on the team exploded. Despite the club's success, management persisted in handing out fines to players. On July 17 the entire Lawrence team, in protest, refused to play a game with Newburyport. William S. Knox, president of the club, then tried to blacklist all the truant players. The Conways were eventually reinstated after they paid a fine of $20 and admitted they had been wrong in striking against their club. Knox probably agreed to the modest punishment because he had already arranged to sell his crack battery. A few days after the Conways returned, they accompanied outfielder Pat O'Connell to Baltimore for $1,800 plus an agreement to transfer catcher Ned Bligh and pitcher Bill McCaffrey from Baltimore to Lawrence.

Conway's debut in Baltimore rated this appraisal from the *Lawrence Daily American:* "Judging by the way Dick Conway was batted at Baltimore yesterday, it will not be long before he will wish he had remained at Lawrence." He won his next 2 games but then lost 6 in a row, including a 22–5 drubbing by Louisville on August 15. By September, Conway was back in the New England League, this time with Portland, ME.

Conway helped Portland win the 1886 New England League pennant, pitching shutouts in his first four outings. On October 30 Boston NL signed him for 1887 delivery. Conway staggered to a 10–8 win over Washington in his NL debut on May 14, 1887, and won 5 of his first 6 decisions with Boston before enemy hitters caught up to him. He won just four of his remaining twenty starts to finish with a sore arm and a 9-15 record. The Beaneaters nonetheless reserved him for 1888 and paid him $2,000, but it proved to be largely to pitch batting practice after John Clarkson was acquired. Conway did not make his first box appearance of the season until August 7, when he stopped Pittsburgh 6–1. He then made only five more starts before Boston sold him to Worcester of the Atlantic Association for $1,000. In May 1889 Worcester manager Walter Burnham, his former manager with Lawrence in 1885, suspended him after it developed that perhaps the reason he had pitched so little in Boston the previous year was because he had a chronic sore arm. Conway tried to make several comebacks, the last with Lowell of the 1891 New England League, and then resigned himself to operating a clothing store he had opened with a partner in Lowell, MA. But the business failed and he spent the rest of his life as a clerk before dying in Lowell in 1926, leaving his wife and six children. (DN)

Corbett, Joseph Aloysius / "Joe" "Smiling Joe"

B	T	HGT	WGT	G	IP	H	GS
R	R	5'10"	175	48	373	387	43

CG	BB	SO	SH	W	L	PCT	ERA
40	141	180	1	27	10	.730	3.14

B. 12/4/1875 San Francisco, CA **D.** 5/2/1945
TEAMS: 95WasN 96–97BalN 04StLN
DEBUT: 8/23/1895 at Washington; caught by Deacon McGuire and lost 11–4 to Baltimore's Sadie McMahon
FINALE: 7/29/1904 at Pittsburgh; caught by Mike Grady and lost 10–1 to Pittsburgh's Patsy Flaherty

Joe Corbett was the younger brother of heavyweight champion Jim Corbett. The pair played together in a sporting writers-actors game on August 10, 1895, that was called "a lurid farce" by *SL*, and when the younger Corbett appeared in the majors two weeks later with Washington, Opie Caylor ranted that he was "purely a gate attraction" and there should be a rule against employing "sideshow" players like him. A San Francisco product, Corbett allegedly was discovered in California pitching for St. Mary's College by Cincinnati sportswriter Ren Mulford, who was there to cover one of his brother's fights. After Mulford donned a glove and caught the collegian, he recommended him to Washington. Washington also liked Corbett enough to try to sign him to a regular contract, but he refused when he learned that Baltimore manager Ned Hanlon had also been impressed by him.

Joining the Orioles in the spring of 1896, Corbett was farmed and pitched in two minor leagues before being recalled by Hanlon in September. A 3-0 mark earned him a crack at a spot in Baltimore's rotation in 1897, but the following March he nearly did not report after acting as a second in the ring when his brother lost the heavyweight title to Bob Fitzsimmons. Inconsolable for some time, Corbett eventually gathered himself to lead the Orioles in wins (24) with "a long swinging motion" and an underhand delivery similar to old-timer pitchers. In his official rookie season the only minor criticism of him in Baltimore was that he worked too slowly, taking as long as ten or twenty seconds between pitches, but censure mounted when he joined with several other Orioles in holding out in the spring of 1898. Unlike the others, who were upset when they were offered the same salary despite a schedule increase of 20 games from 134 to 154, with Corbett it seemingly was an affair of the heart and not money that restrained him from coming East to play. Meanwhile he took a job as a reporter on the *San Francisco Call* and pitched on occasion in the California League.

The following spring Corbett echoed his refusal to return to the Orioles, but now it was because he still bore the unpleasant memory of a romance in Baltimore that had been broken off by the girl's parents when they saw their daughter becoming serious about a ballplayer and, worse, the brother of a prizefighter. In June 1899 Corbett married Elizabeth Maloney, the daughter of a San Francisco contractor and managed a livery business that had been left him by his father, who had committed suicide."

Prior to the 1900 season the story changed again. Hanlon now said the reason Corbett refused to return East was because of a mix-up in his last game with the Orioles, when he had tossed Boston's Link Lowe a pitch different from the one catcher Wilbert Robinson signaled for and the team had then blamed him for the loss that decided the 1897 NL pennant race. Meanwhile Corbett contended that he couldn't play anymore even if he wanted to because he was sick, his muscles paralyzed from too much pitching. By the following season Corbett had miraculously recovered and was playing for Oakland of the California League. After appearing with Los Angeles in 1903, the Pacific Coast League's inaugural season, he at last consented to return to the majors. Tired of dealing with his "one-year wonder," Hanlon made no protest when Corbett signed with the St. Louis Cardinals and could not have been heartbroken when he fared poorly in fourteen starts before being released. Corbett returned to San Francisco and worked as a clerk with the Tidewater Associated Oil Company but continued to dabble in pro ball until age 40. He died from a heart attack at 69. (DN/DB)

*Corcoran, Lawrence J. / "Larry"

B	T	HGT	WGT	G	IP	H	GS
L	B	5'3"	127	277	2392.1	2147	268

CG	BB	SO	SH	W	L	PCT	ERA
256	496	1103	22	177	89	.665	2.36

B. 8/10/1859 Brooklyn, NY **D.** 10/14/1891
TEAMS: 80–85ChiN 85–86NYN 86WasN 87IndN
DEBUT AND FAMOUS FIRST: 5/1/1880 at Cincinnati; caught by Silver Flint and beat Cincinnati's Will White 4–3 when Chicago scored 2 runs in bottom of the ninth to win the first ML game in history ended via the new "sudden death" rule that halted a game as soon as a winning run scored; previously the bottom of the ninth inning had to be played to completion even if the team batting had already won the game
FINALE: 5/20/1887 at Boston; played CF and went 1-for-4 in an 8–7 loss to Boston's Bill Stemmeyer
CAREER HIGHLIGHT: 6/27/1884 at Chicago; in only his fourth ML season flipped his then record third career no-hitter (all caught by Silver Flint) in topping Providence's Charlie Sweeney 6–0

The brother of one-game ML pitcher Mike Corcoran, Larry Corcoran could pitch with both arms but not well enough with his left to continue his ML career after his right arm crumbled. In his tragically short career, the tiny Brooklyn native won an unbreakable rookie-record 43 games; became the first pitcher to toss two no-hitters, let alone three; won a fantastic 177 games before his 26th birthday; played on four pennant winners in his first five seasons; and demonstrated that he could play capably enough at both SS and in the outfield to have extended his career if he had been a better hitter.

After playing with amateur teams in Brooklyn, Corcoran joined independent Geneseo, NY, in 1877 and then finished the season with Buffalo of the International Association. In 1878 his 9-23 record in the box and .144 BA with Springfield of the IA gave no intimation that he was a star in the making. Corcoran remained in Springfield in 1879 until joining Worcester in September for a few games. By that time his skills in the box were so clearly superior that it was apparent his mediocre record to that point was the product of pitching for poor teams.

Aware that it needed only a pitching upgrade to overtake Providence at the head of the NL, Chicago hired Corcoran and comparative novice Fred Goldsmith for 1880 to replace its incumbent boxmen. Never before and never again have two newcomers to a team even come close to matching the pair's combined 64-17 record their first season in the Second City. In shepherding Chicago to its first of three straight pennants, Corcoran hurled his initial career no-hitter on August 19 when he topped Boston 4–0 for his third win over the Hub team in the space of just three days. It was an early sign of how little regard would be given to preserving his arm, as Chicago by then already had a prohibitive lead in the NL race.

By Opening Day in 1884 Corcoran had worked a total of 1,762 innings, an average of 440 a season in his first four ML campaigns, but the worst was yet to come. Prior to the season he flirted with the rebel Union Association, stirring up bad blood. When Chicago then struggled in the early going after Goldsmith began experiencing arm trouble and player-manager Cap Anson in desperation called on Corcoran for 60 games and 516 innings, he had the temerity to demand extra pay for his extra work. Chastised by Anson for being a baby and drawing little sympathy from the local press, the following spring Corcoran was able to start only 7 games in the first four weeks of the season, and although his record was 5-2, it was obvious that his deliveries no longer had the same zip. The club then revealed he had a strained shoulder (probably a torn rotator cuff). On July 11, with newcomer John Clarkson having established that he could handle the bulk of the pitching load and Jim McCormick recently arrived in a deal with Providence, Corcoran was first laid off without pay and then released after he pledged to return to Chicago if his shoulder mended. Instead, he went straight to New York NL and went 2-1 in three starts before his shoulder gave out completely.

Corcoran made one appearance with the Giants in 1886 as an outfielder and then was loaned to Washington on the agreement that New York could reclaim him if it wished. After he flunked an effort to make him a position player by hitting .185, the D.C. club released him and the Giants declined to take him back. Corcoran began 1887 with Nashville of the Southern League. In May the new Indianapolis NL entry, in search of a marquee player, paid Nashville $500 for Corcoran and immediately realized it was money lost when he was bombed in his first two pitching starts in Hoosiers garb and lacked even enough arm strength by then to play the outfield. Further comeback attempts in the minors were marred by weak play and suspensions for drunken benders. In 1891 Corcoran umpired in the Illinois-Iowa-Indiana League until illness forced him to return to his home in Newark. When he died that October, leaving a wife and four children, the cause of death was first reported as typhoid but was later changed to Bright's disease. (DN/DB)

Crosby, George W. / "George"

B	T	HGT	WGT	G	IP	H	GS
?	?	5'11"	178	3	28	27	3
CG	**BB**	**SO**	**SH**	**W**	**L**	**PCT**	**ERA**
3	12	11	0	1	2	.333	3.54

B. 9/?/1857 Lyons, IA **D.** 1/9/1913
TEAMS: 84ChiN
DEBUT: 5/22/1884 at Cleveland; caught by Mike Kelly and lost 3–0 to Cleveland's Jack Harkins
FINALE: 5/30/1884 at Chicago; caught by Silver Flint and beat Detroit's Dupee Shaw 11–10

Among the multitude of recruit players that came and went in the three major leagues in 1884 before anyone could even learn their names, George Crosby was one of the few that slipped away despite showing a spark of real talent. After beginning 1884 with the Chicago reserves, he was sent for by manager Cap Anson when the regulars reached Cleveland on the night of May 20 with both Fred Goldsmith and Larry Corcoran experiencing arm problems after pitching every game to that point. Two days later, in his ML debut, Crosby found himself locked in a scoreless tie with Cleveland at the end of regulation time that he eventually lost in the tenth inning when Cleveland scored three runs with the help of left fielder Billy Sunday's muff of Jack Glasscock's looping liner. Pitching on only one day's rest, Crosby lost 8–4 to Buffalo's Jim Galvin on May 24 and then was given five days off before making his third and final start on May 30. He entered the ninth inning leading Detroit 7–6, but aided by three walks the Wolverines tallied four runs to take a 10–6 lead. In the bottom of the ninth, Crosby then won his own game 11–10 by knocking home the winning run—he had earlier hit a two-run homer.

Crosby accompanied Goldsmith in a sale to

Baltimore AA in August. Though he pitched for the Orioles in exhibitions, he never saw action in an official AA game. After two seasons in the minors, Crosby signed with Andy Piercy's San Francisco California League team in March 1887. He later pitched semipro ball in the Los Angeles area for several years before returning to San Francisco, where he died in 1913 of cancer of the pylorus. He was working as a teamster at the time. (DN)

Crothers, Douglass / "Doug" "Dug"

B	T	HGT	WGT	G	IP	H	GS
R	R	5'9"	140	21	179	218	21

CG	BB	SO	SH	W	L	PCT	ERA
21	55	51	1	8	13	.381	4.63

B. 11/16/1859 Natchez, MS **D.** 3/29/1907
TEAMS: 84KCU 85NYA
DEBUT: 8/3/1884 at St. Louis; caught by Kid Baldwin and lost 4–3 to St. Louis's Charlie Sweeney
FINALE: 9/3/1885 at Brooklyn; caught by Charlie Reipschlager and beat Brooklyn's Henry Porter 14–5

Doug Crothers grew up in Texas and pitched for semipro teams there until moving to St. Louis. In his debut with Kansas City UA he was referred to as "Caruthers" and appeared in several box scores by that more famous baseball name before he was able to convey his real name to scorekeepers across the league.

After the 1884 season Crothers returned to the semipro ranks until the New York Mets visited St. Louis on May 19, 1885. Even though he lost his Mets debut 9–2 to the Browns' Dave Foutz, he showed enough promise to get another start two days later. On that occasion, with a wet ball, he lost 11–9 to Foutz in a sloppy game that consumed an unheard of one hour and thirty minutes just to play the first three innings. Strangely, one of Crothers's better games with the Mets was his last, after which he was released to Memphis of the Southern League. The SL at that time was an all white loop, so Crothers's Southern upbringing did not present a problem for him until 1887, when Syracuse of the International Association suspended both him and outfielder Hank Simon in June for refusing to sit for a team picture with African American pitcher Bob Higgins. Crothers's offense was the more serious of the two because it had been prefaced by a brawl with manager Joe Simmons, but it kept him out of uniform only a month and cost him just $50 when Simmons discovered he was making so much money pitching for local amateur teams that he scarcely felt punished by the suspension. Shortly after his return to the Stars, Crothers clashed with Simmons again and was released. He later played and managed in the Texas League and was among the circuit's early organizers. After leaving baseball Crothers was active in local politics in St. Louis and worked as a private secretary to the St. Louis postmaster. He died of tuberculosis in St. Louis at 47. (DN)

Crowell, William Theodore / "Billy"

B	T	HGT	WGT	G	IP	H	GS
R	R	5'8½"	160	64	549	765	64

CG	BB	SO	SH	W	L	PCT	ERA
62	205	138	1	19	45	.297	5.15

B. 11/6/1865 Cincinnati, OH **D.** 7/24/1935
TEAMS: 87–88CleA 88LouA
DEBUT: 4/20/1887 at Cincinnati; caught by Charlie Reipschlager and lost 14–6 to Cincinnati's Mike Shea
FINALE: 9/5/1888 at Cleveland; caught by Paul Cook and lost 14–3 to Cleveland's Cinders O'Brien

One of the top amateur pitchers in Cincinnati in 1884, Billy Crowell finished the season with Evansville of the Northwestern League and then toiled for Nashville of the Southern League in 1885. In 1886 he joined Altoona of the Pennsylvania State Association. After no-hitting Wilkes-Barre on June 15 he flipped two strong exhibitions against Pittsburgh NL and Philadelphia AA in August and was then courted by several ML teams. That same month he applied for a license to marry Adelaide Chichester.

Crowell eventually signed with the new Cleveland AA entry for 1887 and began an eighteen-month sojourn in which he frustrated the entire Forest City almost beyond endurance. It was one of the great puzzles in Frank Brunell's career as a baseball writer that Crowell did so poorly, because he had good speed, quick curves, a vast array of pitches, and was a crisp fielder and adept at holding runners. Yet he was hit hard in almost every game. Much of Crowell's problem was that he had a rank team behind him, but he also may have been affected by the pitching rules in 1887 that allowed a batter four strikes for the only time in history. However, when Crowell's troubles showed no sign of abating after the three-strike rule was restored in 1888, Cleveland cut him following a 10–0 thrashing at Cincinnati on July 14.

Crowell apparently remained in Cleveland after his release. He was given a gift start against his old team when Louisville came to town in September and then quickly dismissed by the Colonels. Crowell got a measure of revenge, however, on April 3, 1889, when he beat Cleveland and Cinders O'Brien 3–1 in an exhibition game after signing with St. Joseph of the Western Association. But after posting a 17-24 mark in that loop, he began to experience arm trouble and by the early 1890s was interspersing comeback bids with attempts to start a new career as a minor league umpire. Meanwhile, several of his business ventures failed. Crowell ran a fishery in New Orleans for a while and then bought into a Florida orange grove in 1896. By the following fall he was tending bar in Houston. His final comeback—in 1899 with Houston of the Texas League—resulted in an embarrassing 2-12 start before he quit. Eventually Crowell opened a successful army surplus store in Fort Worth and in 1935 died in a hospital in that city following surgery for prostate cancer. (DN)

Cunningham, Ellsworth Elmer / "Bert"

B	T	HGT	WGT	G	IP	H	GS
R	R	5'6½"	155	341	2725.2	3060	310

CG	BB	SO	SH	W	L	PCT	ERA
286	1061	716	4	142	166	.461	4.23

B. 11/25/1865 Wilmington, DE **D.** 5/14/1952
TEAMS: 87BroA 88–89BalA 90PhiP 90BufP 91BalA 95–99LouN 00–01ChiN
DEBUT: 9/15/1887 at Brooklyn; caught by Jim Peoples and lost 11–1 to Cincinnati's Elmer Smith
FINALE: 4/28/1901 at Chicago; caught by Frank Chance and lost 6–4 to Pittsburgh's Deacon Phillippe
CAREER HIGHLIGHT AND FAMOUS FIRST: 8/20/1890 at Buffalo; won both ends of a DH against Chicago, topping Mark Baldwin 6–2 in the first game and Charlie Bartson 7–0 in the nightcap to become the first and only pitcher from a last-place team ever to perform this feat

We will probably never know if the Bert Cunningham that returned to the majors from the minors in 1895 after a three-year exile was basically the same pitcher as the one that compiled the poorest ERA (4.39) and allowed the most base runners per nine innings (13.94) among all ML pitchers in 1,000 or more innings in his first five ML seasons (1887–91). Unhappily, all we have today are snippets describing Cunningham's pitching methods and clear statistical evidence that even in his early years he was the farthest from being a strikeout artist of any pitcher in the game. In 1891 he logged the poorest strikeouts-to-walks ratio (0.43) of any hurler that worked 200 or more innings in a season between the introduction of the four-ball rule in 1889 and the end of the fifty-foot pitching distance in 1892.

Cunningham grew up in Delaware a member of a family that owned horses, and he was an avid rider all of his life. It is not known how he came to pitch for an independent team in Peoria, IL, in 1887. He jumped the club along with his catcher to play for Champaign, IL, when Peoria fell behind in his salary. A few days later the Peoria manager found him in Champaign and told him the Brooklyn AA team had wired Peoria that it would pay him $200 a month. Cunningham thought it was a joke, but when he ran the story by umpire Jack Brennan, Brennan told him to check it out by wiring Brooklyn that he would come if he were sent $400 in advance plus a train ticket. He then headed east when Brooklyn owner Charlie Byrne did as he asked. When Brooklyn had no further use for him after just three games, he finished 1887 with independent Moline but remained Brooklyn's property and, as such, was sold to Baltimore the following March along with pitcher Jack Harkins for around $1,200.

Cunningham found himself at the head of Baltimore's rotation when Matt Kilroy showed the first signs of overwork in the spring of 1888. After beating Brooklyn on Opening Day, Cunningham proceeded to win 22 games and notch the best ERA on the team (3.39). The following year he seemed overworked himself, falling to 16-19 while the rest of the Orioles' staff went 54-46. In 1890 he led the PL in earned runs allowed and again pitched poorly when he returned to Baltimore in 1891. Banished to the minors, Cunningham struggled in 1892–93, pitching in six different leagues before he at long last found himself in 1894. His quantum leap to a 35-win season with Sioux City of the Western League suggests that he acquired a new pitch, but there is nothing to support that speculation. Upon returning to the majors in 1895, his first three seasons with Louisville offered no hint that in 1898 he would put together 28 wins and a .651 winning percentage, the highest of any 25-game winner on a sub-.500 team in the eight seasons when the NL was a twelve-team league. *TSN* afforded only this terse insight into his sudden success: "The slow ball is his strongest point," and he made no attempt to disguise it. Meanwhile, an incredulous J. Earle Wagner, Washington's owner, grumbled that Cunningham "hasn't enough speed to assassinate a mosquito."

After Cunningham's 28 wins in 1898 set a post-1892 season record for the most by a pitcher who failed to pitch a shutout, rival hurler Bill Hart predicted that he would be harshly affected by the new balk rule that was imposed that off-season. But when Cunningham fell to 17-17 in 1899, he blamed his slow start on the death of his beloved terrier and team mascot Monday, who had been mysteriously poisoned. Later in the season, after rolling up a six-game winning streak, he attributed his sudden turnaround to the release of catcher Kit Kittridge and claimed that Kittridge had unwittingly tipped off batters when his slow curves were coming.

Cunningham was among the trainload of Louisville players that were transferred to Pittsburgh that December when the NL laid plans to pare to eight teams in 1900. The following March the Pirates sold him to Chicago, but he refused to report until July and then pitched sparingly. Released after making only one appearance with Chicago in 1901, Cunningham agreed to serve as an NL replacement umpire for the rest of the season but quit in July under an unremitting attack by Giants owner Andrew Freedman after Chicago swept five games from Freedman's club in July. Cunningham umpired awhile longer in the minors and then worked as a typewriter salesman for the Remington-Rand Company. He died in Cragmere, DE, at 85 after a two-month illness. (DN)

Cuppy, George Joseph (b. Koppe) / **"Nig"**

B	T	HGT	WGT	G	IP	H	GS
R	R	5'7"	160	289	2189.2	2409	251

CG	BB	SO	SH	W	L	PCT	ERA
215	591	595	9	158	92	.632	3.45

B. 7/3/1869 Logansport, IN **D.** 7/27/1922
TEAMS: 92–98CleN 99StLN 00BosN 01BosAL
DEBUT: 4/16/1892 at Cincinnati; relieved Lee Viau in a 6–3 loss to Cincinnati's Elton Chamberlin
FINALE: 8/7/1901 at Baltimore; caught by Lou Criger and lost 10–4 to Baltimore's Joe McGinnity

Denton Young was 6'2" and threw so hard that he was nicknamed "Cyclone." His teammate from 1892–99, George Cuppy, was seven inches shorter, threw mostly junk, and received his nickname because of his "swarthy complexion and pearly teeth." Young won over 350 games more than Cuppy. Yet for the five-year period at the beginning of Cuppy's career (1892–96) he averaged 25 wins a season to Young's 32, and the Cleveland pair were the most successful pitching tandem in the 1890s despite the fact that the Spiders never won a pennant during their reign.

Cuppy pitched with Indiana independent teams until 1890, when he joined Dayton of the Tri-State League. He finished the season with Meadville, PA, and was spending his second season with the New York–Pennsylvania League team when Cleveland acquired him in July 1891 on the condition that he be allowed to finish the season with Meadville.

Cuppy impressed no one when he arrived in Cleveland's training camp in the spring of 1892. He had little speed, "an exasperatingly slow delivery," and only fair control. Expected to be no better than fourth in the Spiders' rotation behind Young, George Davies, and Lee Viau, he advanced to third when Viau lasted just one inning in his first start of the season and then climbed to second after Davies lost four of his first five decisions. By June 1892, Cuppy was starting nearly as often as Young and that continued even after the Spiders acquired John Clarkson from Boston. He finished the season with 28 wins, still a rookie record for a Cleveland ML franchise, and 103 strikeouts. Both figures proved to be career highs, and when Cuppy slipped to just 17 wins in 1893 and an awful 39–75 strikeouts-to-walks ratio, it was presumed that a combination of the dramatic changes in pitching rules and batters' growing familiarity with his off-speed deliveries would send him the way of Jesse Duryea, Frank Knauss, Gus Krock, and the flock of other pitchers in that era who flamed out almost immediately after brilliant rookie seasons.

Instead, Cuppy rebounded in 1894 to win 24 games, only 2 less than Young, and then followed with two more strong seasons, giving him 75 wins in 1894–96, tied for third with Jouett Meekin in that three-year span and trailing only Young (89) and Kid Nichols (88). In 1897, Cuppy lost his first two starts of the season but then won his next seven, seemingly dispelling a fear that he had hurt his arm that spring on a cold day in Toledo. But after May 29 he made only ten more starts before he was shut down for the year with elbow trouble. That winter Cuppy informed the Spiders that his elbow had been miraculously cured by "Reese, the bonesetter of Youngstown" who had done "some mysterious manipulations and made the pain disappear." In March, however, he had a relapse and his arm was put in a cast.

Eventually Cuppy went back to Reese "as a drowning man catches at a straw" and managed to appear in 128 innings before the 1898 season was out. Over the next three years he continued to pitch infrequently, and his slow pace, which had once been tolerated because he won so often, now began to exasperate teammates as well as opposing batters and umpires. The epitome of the frustration Cuppy wreaked came on August 15, 1900, at Chicago. The following day the *Chicago Tribune* wrote of a game that lasted three hours and two minutes, an unheard of length for that time, "Cuppy, who is slower than the relief of the Ministers at Pekin, pitched for Boston [NL]. It takes Cuppy 14 seconds to pitch a ball and from three to eight minutes to retire a batter." A year later in August the *Boston Globe* remarked, "In the second game Cuppy got away with his dinky pitching for five innings, which showed the nerve and luck of the man." But then in the sixth inning Baltimore tallied 7 runs to take the game away and soon afterward he was released.

Cuppy was player-manager of Elkhart in 1902 and then ran a billiard hall in that Indiana city in partnership with catcher Lou Criger. He married for the first time in 1910 and was in the retail tobacco business when he died of Bright's disease in Elkhart twelve years later. (DN)

Cushman, Edgar Leander / "Ed"

B	T	HGT	WGT	G	IP	H	GS
R	L	6'0"	177	147	1225.2	1264	145

CG	BB	SO	SH	W	L	PCT	ERA
137	359	607	4	62	81	.434	3.86

B. 3/27/1852 Eagleville, OH **D.** 9/26/1915
TEAMS: 83BufN 84MilU 85PhiA 85–87NYA 90TolA
DEBUT AND FAMOUS FIRST: 7/6/1883 at Detroit; caught by Deacon White and lost 3–2 to Detroit's Dupee Shaw
FINALE: 10/11/1890 at Columbus; caught by Harry Sage and was relieved by John Healy, who took the 7–4 loss to Columbus's Jack Easton in relief of Frank Knauss
CAREER HIGHLIGHT: 9/28/1884 at Milwaukee; caught by Cal Broughton and no-hit Washington's Abner Powell 5–0

Ed Cushman was the first southpaw to make his ML debut in a starting role against another southpaw, Detroit's Dupee Shaw. Released by Buffalo in September 1883, he finished the season with Toledo of the Northwestern League and then moved to Milwaukee of the same loop in 1884. After posting a 23-1 record, he accompanied Milwaukee to the UA as a late-season replacement team and went 4-0, racking up 47 strikeouts in 36 innings while allowing a mere 10 hits. In an October 4 win against Boston he fanned 16, and when Henry Porter struck out 18 Boston hitters the following day, it gave the pair 34 whiffs, still the most ever by two teammates on consecutive days.

Cushman's snazzy combined mark of 27-1 in 1884 made him the Philadelphia A's prize acquisition after the UA folded. He opened 1885 with a CG win over the defending AA champion Mets and at the end of April owned the lowest OBA (.174) of any pitcher in the circuit. But Cushman then began to struggle. Near the end of June he was released to the Mets and slowly regained his early form. When Cushman notched a win for the Mets in their season closer, it marked the first time in ML history that a pitcher had achieved an Opening Day CG win over the same team that he would post a CG win for in its season finale. But by 1886 the Mets were in such disrepair that Cushman is best remembered as part of the first ML pitching staff to have three 20-game losers. Nevertheless he had a strong year, going 17-21 while the other Mets boxmen were 36-61. A 5.97 ERA the following season triggered his release after a loss to Cleveland on September 14.

By 1889 Cushman was pitching for Toledo of the International Association. His season ended early on September 13 when a line drive broke his left wrist, but Toledo retained him on the strength of his 2.09 ERA when it joined the AA in 1890. Then 38, he was 17-21 with a first-division entry and returned to the minors when the majors pared from twenty-four teams to sixteen in 1891. Cushman joined Erie, PA, and settled in that town after the Blackbirds won the Eastern League pennant in 1893, his final season with the club. He was a conductor for several years with the New York Central Railroad before operating a restaurant in Erie on State Street. Cushman died at his Erie home in 1915 after an extended illness. If his birth year is correct, Cushman was 31 before he launched his pro career. His baseball experience prior to 1883 remains extremely sketchy. (DN)

Daley, William / "Bill"

B	T	HGT	WGT	G	IP	H	GS
?	L	5'7"	140	62	409.2	399	43

CG	BB	SO	SH	W	L	PCT	ERA
33	291	218	2	29	16	.644	3.49

B. 6/27/1868 Poughkeepsie, NY **D.** 5/4/1922
TEAMS: 89BosN 90BosP 91BosA
DEBUT: 7/17/1889 at Boston; caught by Charlie Ganzel and beat Indianapolis's Amos Rusie 7–5
FINALE: 6/30/1891 at Boston; caught by Duke Farrell and beat Philadelphia's Kid Carsey 16–4

In his inaugural ML appearance Bill Daley drew as his pitching opponent fellow rookie Amos Rusie, making for arguably the most frightening game for hitters on both sides ever played in the nineteenth century. Daley, without question, was the wildest good pitcher prior to 1901, and Rusie may have been the second wildest. Late in the 1890 season, a week after it had called the slender southpaw one of the three fastest pitchers in the PL, *TSN* wrote: "Daley . . . is probably the most erratic pitcher in the country." And in 1898, long after Daley was gone, Charlie Ganzel called him, "The craziest pitcher I ever faced. . . . He didn't have any command at all; not the least idea where the ball was going."

In 1889 Daley was in his third season with Jersey City of the Atlantic Association when Boston paid a steep $2,500 price for him. But bidding against Boston were the New York Giants, who had been interested in him since May after he beat Boston, the Giants and the Philadelphia Phillies in a rapid string of preseason exhibitions. In his first appearance with Boston, Daley ran the gamut of the extremes in performance that he would display all during his short but never dull ML career. He walked 10 Indianapolis batters, hit a man, made a throwing error, was fanned three times himself, and yet still won. For the remainder of the season, however, he was seldom used because Boston was fighting for the NL pennant. But when he pitched well for the Boston team that barnstormed over the winter, the Beantown PL entry pilfered him. Daley began 1890 fourth in the Boston PL rotation but soon slipped ahead of Matt Kilroy. Pitching every fifth game on the average, he led the team in walks by a wide margin but also led in strikeouts and shutouts. Moreover, he topped the PL with a .720 winning percentage, the highest ever by an ERA qualifier who allowed as many as 6 walks per every nine innings pitched.

Like most members of the Boston PL championship team, Daley remained with the club when it joined the AA the following year. To the surprise of many he was released by manager Arthur Irwin on July 17 for what Irwin called indifferent work and wildness. At the time, Daley was 8-6. He went home to Poughkeepsie and joined a local semipro team. After he fanned 21 batters in an August game, Giants scout Billy Primrose visited him near the end of the month with an eye toward signing him, but the two could not agree on terms. It was the closest Daley would ever come to returning to the majors. He signed with Buffalo of the Eastern League for 1892 but was released in August. By 1894, his control ever worsening, he was pitching out the string for Poughkeepsie of the New York State League. Daley later worked at a Poughkeepsie rolling mill and as a laborer in the local opera house. In 1922 he was found in bed at his Poughkeepsie home an undetermined number of days after he had died from an apparent heart attack. (DN)

Dammann, William Henry / "Bill" "Wee Willie"

B	T	HGT	WGT	G	IP	H	GS
L	L	5'7"	155	60	367.2	473	38

CG	BB	SO	SH	W	L	PCT	ERA
26	115	74	4	24	15	.615	4.06

B. 8/9/1872 Chicago, IL **D.** 12/6/1948
TEAMS: 97–99CinN
DEBUT: 4/24/1897 at Cincinnati; caught by Heinie Peitz and beat Chicago's Roger Denzer 4–3
FINALE: 6/22/1899 at Cincinnati; relieved Bill Phillips after one inning in Phillips's 9–5 loss to Philadelphia's Al Orth

Born in Chicago, Bill Dammann grew up in Spokane and started pitching for pay with minor league teams in Washington, Oregon, and Sacramento in the California League. In February 1894 he advertised in *TSN* for a playing job in the east. A week later, having already secured an offer from Atlanta, he sent *TSN* a letter of appreciation, but the Georgia club refused to send him travel money to come east, and Dammann wound up re-advertising.

The country had fallen into a severe depression, and in March 1894, Coxey's army, a group of unemployed men under the leadership of Jacob Coxey marched on Washington to demand that the government provide jobs. If a story told several years later is true, Dammann must have failed to find work of any kind, for he joined Randall's army, a Northwest-based offshoot group that reached northern Indiana around early May. In this peculiar way Dammann attained his goal of coming east. When Randall's army disbanded, Dammann signed with a team in Upper Sandusky, OH, to pitch for $10 a week, a decent wage for a skilled laborer even when work was not scarce. He moved to nearby Toledo in the stronger Western League in 1895.

In the fall of 1894 Dammann had received a chance to pitch against major leaguers when Cincinnati came through Upper Sandusky for an exhibition. The Reds rolled to a 14–5 win, but Frank Bancroft, Cincinnati's business manager, was impressed by the little left-hander with the big curve ball and sharp control who held the big leaguers down cold for several innings before his bush-league team came apart. Bancroft noted Dammann's name, and after the 1896 season Cincinnati acquired him for their Indianapolis farm club and then sent three players to Indianapolis for him the following off-season.

Bill Watkins, Indianapolis's manager, predicted a bright future for Dammann, comparing him to Lady Baldwin, and veteran infielder Jack Glasscock agreed he was the best southpaw prospect in the country. Dammann never lived up to these expectations, pitching with fair success but relatively infrequently for the Reds over three seasons, and then often in relief. An undersized control artist with a submarine delivery, he simply lacked the stuff to overpower ML hitters. However, a severe attack of typhoid soon after his arrival in Cincinnati may have permanently impaired his effectiveness to some degree.

Dammann began well, defeating Chicago 4–3 in his debut, and celebrated another big day three weeks later when he married Ida Lewis of Indianapolis. After starting seven times in the first month of the season with only one loss, though, he took sick and did not appear again for two months. He pitched rarely the rest of the season, working fewer than 100 innings. The following season he carried a heavier workload of 225 innings, but it was still a modest total by the standards of that day. Still, he could boast a 16-10 record and finished the season strongly. But in 1899 he missed time with a sprained ankle and then pitched poorly and was exiled to a relief role before being sent back to Indianapolis.

He then led the peripatetic existence of a successful career minor leaguer, pitching for a variety of teams, primarily in the Midwest. In 1903 Dammann returned home to play for a new club in Spokane, for which he won 26 games. In 1904, after winning 23 games with Spokane, he finished the season with Tacoma and eventually drifted back to the Midwest, where his pro career finished in 1908. Dammann died in Lynnhaven, VA, in 1948. (DB/DN)

Daub, Daniel William / "Dan" "Mickey"

B	T	HGT	WGT	G	IP	H	GS
R	R	5'10"	160	126	899.1	1065	103

CG	BB	SO	SH	W	L	PCT	ERA
74	327	185	0	45	52	.464	4.75

B. 1/12/1868 Middletown, OH **D.** 3/25/1951
TEAMS: 92CinN 93–97BroN

DEBUT: 8/31/1892 at Cincinnati; caught by Harry Vaughn and lost 5–1 to Boston's Jack Stivetts
FINALE: 7/1/1897 at Philadelphia; caught by Jack Grim and Aleck Smith in a 16–2 loss to Philadelphia's Jack Taylor

The cocky Dan Daub became insufferable after starring at Denison University in 1891 and fanning a reported 101 batters in a six-game stretch at one juncture. He continued to be a big frog in a small pond with Charleston, WV, in 1892, and his head swelled even more when he did so well against Cincinnati in an exhibition game that he was signed to a contract guaranteeing him $50 for every game he pitched with the Reds for the rest of the season. Stung when he worked only four contests after telling manager Charlie Comiskey that he expected to pitch at least three times a week, he was even more disconcerted when he was released to the Southern League in the spring of 1893.

Upon being summoned to Brooklyn in August of that season, Daub dropped his first Bridegrooms start to Boston but did well after that, logging a 3.84 ERA, 71 points below the team average. Hit hard the following year, he finished with a 6.11 ERA but pumped up his ego that fall when a 3-game series between two semipro Buffalo teams, Genesco and Mount Morris, boiled down to a rubber game. With Elton Chamberlin slated to pitch for Genesco, Mount Morris hired Daub and catcher Billy Earle as ringers and had them both play in street pants cut off at the knees. Daub could not refrain from gleefully revealing his true identity after he beat Chamberlin 10–2.

In 1895 Daub led Brooklyn in ERA once manager Dave Foutz began to spot him only against teams that were likely to have trouble with his off-speed pitches, but by 1897 he was no longer able to consistently beat even "fastball-hitting Cleveland" and was removed from the rotation in July and then sent home the following month with "serious stomach trouble." Daub pitched in the minors until 1901 when he was forced to quit the Marion Western Association team after suffering "a broken ligament in his right shoulder." He coached for a while at the University of Delaware and Amherst College and then worked for a cash register manufacturer in Dayton, OH. Daub died in Bradenton, FL, at 83. (DN)

Davies, George Washington / "George"

B	T	HGT	WGT	G	IP	H	GS
?	R	?	180	46	369	364	42

CG	BB	SO	SH	W	L	PCT	ERA
37	127	166	1	18	24	.429	3.32

B. 2/22/1868 Portage, WI **D.** 9/22/1906
TEAMS: 91MilA 92–93CleN 93NYN
DEBUT: 8/18/1891 at St. Louis; caught by Jack Grim and beat St. Louis's Jack Stivetts 7–2
FINALE: 7/20/1893 at Boston; relieved Amos Rusie after one inning in Rusie's 15–8 loss to Boston's Kid Nichols

TSN once referred to George Davies as "the tall sycamore of Wisconsin." A graduate of the University of Wisconsin, he subsequently attended medical school there and by the winter of 1891 was apprenticing under a doctor in Milwaukee. The 1891 season was Davies's third with Milwaukee and his best to date; he was wildly popular in the Wisconsin city until the fall of that year when the Brewers joined the minor Western League after the AA disbanded and he opted to sign instead with Cleveland NL for 1892. When Davies got off to a bad start the following spring, *TSN* predicted that he would be cut when Cleveland picked up John Clarkson from Boston in July. But he remained with the Spiders all year, finishing a poor 10-16 for a club that was 83-40 minus his negative contribution.

After being blistered in his first three starts with Cleveland in 1893, Davies was left behind in Brooklyn to care for teammate Jimmy McAleer in June while McAleer recovered from a leg injury. Once McAleer rejoined the Spiders, Davies was then loaned to New York and released in late July when the Giants had no more use for him and Cleveland did not want him back.

Davies at that point appears to have retired from the game to practice medicine in Waterloo, WI, although he flirted now and again with the notion of taking time away from his practice to "do a little twirling" for the local team in the Wisconsin State League. In 1906 he died in his office from what may or may not have been an accidental overdose of a medicine he was taking as a sedative, and he was survived by his wife, Grace. (DN)

Davis, John Henry Albert / "Daisy"

B	T	HGT	WGT	G	IP	H	GS
?	R	5'6½"	150	40	323.2	356	39

CG	BB	SO	SH	W	L	PCT	ERA
33	71	186	2	16	21	.432	3.78

B. 11/28/1858 Boston, MA **D.** 11/5/1902
TEAMS: 84StLA 84–85BosN
DEBUT: 5/6/1884 at St. Louis; caught by Pat Deasley and beat Toledo's Hank O'Day 6–3
FINALE: 7/29/1885 at Boston; caught by Tom Gunning and beat Buffalo's Billy Serad 1–0

Daisy Davis is among the select few hurlers to throw a shutout in his ML finale. When he joined St. Louis in 1884, he falsely claimed to be 24 and boasted of having pitched a game in Cairo, IL, in September of 1881 in which he fanned 24 batters. After scoring a victory in his first start with the Browns, he lost more often than he won until he was released in early September when St. Louis fell out of the race and began cutting costs. Davis then signed with Boston around September 19 for $400 a month, more than twice what the Browns were paying him.

In 1885 Davis did not pitch his first game for Boston until May 20 after spending most of the spring being loaned to local amateur nines. Unhappy with his limited role even despite pitching poorly in his first ten starts of the season, he was targeted for release in late July. On the final Wednesday of the month he reported to the Boston park expecting to pull gate duty. Instead, player-manager John Morrill surprised him by starting him in place of Jim Whitney, who had been announced to pitch but had to be excused "on account of indisposition." The change came after the lineups had already been posted, forcing Davis, a .157 career hitter, to bat in Whitney's cleanup spot in the order. Although the *Boston Globe* called his effort "a creditable game," it did not save his job.

Davis left baseball in 1888 after twirling for Portsmouth in the New England Interstate League, but the following fall the *Police Gazette* forecasted that he had "lost his swelled head" and was now ready to return to the game and "be paid and treated as any ordinary player." This did not occur, but the *Police Gazette's* description of Davis suggests that his nickname may have been self-coined. A daisy in 1880s parlance was an outstanding player, which he was not. (DN)

Deagle, Lorenzo Burroughs / "Ren"

B	T	HGT	WGT	G	IP	H	GS
R	R	5'9"	190	34	269.1	255	34

CG	BB	SO	SH	W	L	PCT	ERA
29	56	83	2	17	15	.531	2.74

B. 6/26/1858 New York, NY **D.** 12/24/1936
TEAMS: 83–84CinA 84LouA
DEBUT: 5/17/1883 at St. Louis; caught by Bill Traffley and beat St. Louis's Tony Mullane 6–3.
FINALE: 9/12/1884 at Louisville; caught by Len Stockwell and finished the game in RF after being relieved by John Reccius, who was credited with the 8–7 win over Virginia's Ed Dugan.

Ren Deagle's pro career is a puzzle in that he clearly had talent that was never utilized. He bears a tenuous connection to a colorful historical incident memorable because of its inclusion in Martin Scorsese's *Gangs of New York*. A few years before his birth his father, also named Lorenzo, had witnessed the murder of Bill "the Butcher" Poole in a saloon that Deagle himself partly owned. Around 1868 the family moved to Cincinnati, where the elder Deagle ran a saloon on Vine Street. By the middle 1870s young Lorenzo began to work as a clerk and then as a printer and mailer for local newspapers. In his free time he played baseball, a pastime for which he displayed considerable aptitude. A right fielder and change pitcher initially, he played for the local champion Mohawk Browns in the late 1870s along with future catching great Buck Ewing, then a second baseman, and Long John Reilly.

By 1882 Deagle was viewed as the best amateur player in Cincinnati, and yet, at the relatively advanced age of 24, he had never played a moment of pro ball until the Reds signed him that November. Will White, Cincinnati's ace pitcher, was quoted as praising him; catcher Phil Powers also spoke highly of him, telling a Chicago newspaper Deagle would do well provided he wasn't too fast for Powers himself to catch him. Early in the 1883 season Deagle sat on the bench, keeping in shape by pitching for the semipro Shamrocks. When both White and second-string pitcher Harry McCormick came down with physical ailments Deagle made his ML debut on May 17 with a victory at St. Louis. He won again at Louisville three days later and then followed with a four-hit shutout at Columbus.

In spite of his good start Deagle hurled only

18 games in 1883, largely because he was caught in the middle of a tug of war. The veteran White, with his underhanded delivery, could handle large workloads and was not only eager to do so but had considerable influence on club secretary and de facto manager Opie Caylor. For a second pitcher Caylor preferred McCormick, who lacked Deagle's stuff but had experience and poise and had helped the club win a pennant the previous year. Others felt White was being used too often while Deagle rusted away on the bench and then was criticized when he pitched badly in an occasional start. After an October exhibition loss to Toledo, Caylor complained that Deagle had stubbornly refused to profit from instruction and tried to strike out every hitter he faced.

With baseball salaries generally rising, Deagle was offered a raise from $600 to $1,000 for 1884, but he balked because rookie outfielder Podgie Weihe was getting $1,200. Threatening to quit if he did not get more than Weihe, he was given $1,300. Once the new season began, however, he pitched rarely and was forced to play on occasion with the club's reserves to keep in trim. Again, it required an injury to Will White to allow Deagle get into his first game, an 11–2 win at Toledo. Good days were otherwise few. On June 4 he lost at New York 19–2, and though 11 errors by infielders Chick Fulmer and Bid McPhee were an enormous handicap, his pitching was equally horrendous. Deagle was soon sent home to Cincinnati and on June 20 was released. He promptly signed with Louisville, where he reportedly offered to pay his new team's management to pitch every game against the Reds, promising he would never lose. When in his first appearance against Cincinnati he won 6–3, it prompted the *Cincinnati Commercial Gazette* to note, "Deagle's heart is filled with joy tonight." On August 23 he lost a 1–0 heartbreaker to Toledo's ace Tony Mullane. After that Deagle pitched only 2 games and failed to complete either; in a day when pitchers went the route in almost every start, his abbreviated efforts may have indicated arm problems.

In 1885, Deagle joined Cleveland of the Western League, but the loop soon went under. By the following year he was no longer pitching, a further indication that his arm was gone. Switched to 1B, Deagle showed considerable power for the era, at one point homering on consecutive days to earn his Topeka team a pair of 9-8 wins, but he batted only .209. He continued to play minor league and semipro ball in the Midwest for a few years and then took a clerical job with the American Railway Express Company in Kansas City, where he died of heart failure forty-six years later. (DB/DN)

Dean, Charles Wilson / "Dory"

B	T	HGT	WGT	G	IP	H	GS
R	R	5'9"	160	30	262.2	397	30

CG	BB	SO	SH	W	L	PCT	ERA
26	24	22	0	4	26	.133	3.73

B. 11/6/1852 Cincinnati, OH **D.** 5/4/1935
TEAMS: 76CinN
DEBUT: 6/22/1876 at Cincinnati; caught by Amos Booth and lost 8–5 to Boston's Joe Borden
FINALE: 10/9/1876 at Cincinnati; caught by Amos Booth and lost 11–0 to Hartford's Candy Cummings

Dory Dean joined the junior Cincinnati Red Stockings while their namesakes were thrilling the city by compiling an undefeated season in 1869. But pro ball left town a year later and it was six more years before Dean would get his chance to show his stuff in front of the hometown fans. When he finally did, it proved a mixed blessing.

Cincinnati gained a franchise in the NL's inaugural campaign of 1876, but the club it fielded often seemed to be major league in name only. After a 3-2 start, Cincinnati dropped 19 of its next 20 games and inexperienced club owner Josiah "Si" Keck overreacted, signing Dean and then releasing his primary pitcher, Cherokee Fisher. While no one could claim that Fisher had been effective, he at least was an experienced ML pitcher who could keep things respectable, whereas Dean was a novice. As Opie Caylor put it in the *Cincinnati Enquirer*, "We have no ill will toward Dean for yesterday's results. We believe he did as well as he could. But he is a boy."

Soon afterward Dean was replaced as Cincinnati's regular pitcher by Dale Williams and then restored when Williams hurt his arm to the delight of NL batters, who continued to pound his pitches. Despite his lack of success, Dean deserves credit for introducing a significant new tactic to the pitcher's repertoire. After Chicago hammered him in a 23–3 loss on July 25, he was sent out to face the same club again two days later. In desperation Dean "brought out a new delivery, which consisted in facing second base with the ball in hand, and then turning quickly, letting it come in the general direction of the stand, without any idea of where it really was going to land." After their initial surprise Chicago batters had little trouble with the new delivery and again feasted on Dean in a 17–3 win.

Dean compiled a dismal 4-26 record in 1876 and never again appeared in the majors. Nevertheless, his novel delivery found new practitioners. A Harvard pitcher named Harold Ernst began using a similar delivery and taught it to John M. Ward, whose "fore and aft style of delivery" made him one of the NL most "puzzling" pitchers in 1878. Ward's style indeed caused so much consternation that it was banned at season's end. Eventually, however, such deceptive deliveries made their way back to the majors, and, in a sense, Dean was the forefather of the likes of Luis Tiant and Fernando Valenzuela. While he never again played pro ball, he became an outstanding tennis player, competing in and winning tournaments into his eighties. Dean eventually moved to Nashville, where he and his son operated an electrotype business, and died there in 1935. His nickname remains a mystery. (PM/DN/DB)

Derby, George Henry / "George" "Jonah"

B	T	HGT	WGT	G	IP	H	GS
L	R	6'0"	175	110	964.1	1064	107

CG	BB	SO	SH	W	L	PCT	ERA
105	182	428	12	48	56	.462	3.01

B. 7/6/1857 Webster, MA **D.** 7/4/1925
TEAMS: 81–82DetN 83BufN
DEBUT: 5/2/1881 at Detroit; caught by Charlie Bennett and lost 6–5 to Buffalo's Jack Lynch
FINALE: 7/3/1883 at Chicago; caught by Dell Darling and lost 31–7 to Chicago's Larry Corcoran while giving up 32 hits, a record 16 for extra bases
CAREER HIGHLIGHT: 8/13/1881 at Chicago; caught by Charlie Bennett in front of a hostile Chicago crowd and beat the NL champion Chicagos and their ace Larry Corcoran 2–0, scattering just 6 hits in his rookie-record ninth shutout of the season

But for an arm injury late in his rookie year, George Derby might have become the premier pitcher of the 1880s. He was a good fielder, a hard hitter, and featured a variety of curves, but his best pitch was "a straight drop ball," the only one like it that his favorite catcher, Charlie Bennett, ever saw. In 1897 Bennett told *TSN* that even Chicago, the best-hitting club in the game, could not solve Derby. Bennett crowed that Chicago manager Cap Anson, knowing that none of his men could hit Derby's drop ball, would order everyone in the lineup to call for high balls (as permitted by the rules in 1881), but "upon seeing a low one coming, they would smash at it" and often the missed strike would come to Bennett on the bounce after hitting in front of the plate.

Prior to 1877 Derby played for amateur teams around Wellsboro, PA, his childhood home. His first pro experience came in 1877 with Hornellsville of the League Alliance. He returned to the Hornells in 1878 and finished the campaign with Syracuse, the International Association champion, but refused to accompany the club to the NL in 1879. Instead Derby joined Washington of the National Association and remained with the minor league club for two seasons, sharing the pitching with Jack Lynch and playing RF on the days when Lynch took the box.

In September 1880 Derby married Ella Robinson, spurring him to take an offer of more money from Detroit, the NL replacement for recently expelled Cincinnati. Bennett years later revealed that Detroit was regarded as an "experimental" team in 1881 and not expected to be a factor in the pennant race. Consequently, the Wolverines made little effort to acquire a first-rate pitcher to share the work with Derby. In Bennett's opinion, Detroit would have won the pennant if Stump Wiedman had been with the club all season. Instead Wiedman was not signed until there was only about a month left to go, by which time Derby had been for all intents used up. Bennett said that in 1883, shortly after Derby was released by Detroit, he "wrote me from Buffalo after he went there that a cord in his forearm was a quarter of an inch out of place, and he failed to ever distinguish himself after his work here."

There is also a possibility that Derby, sustained a torn rotator cuff, and we can point to the day it probably occurred. On September 15, 1881, Derby squared off against Providence ace John M. Ward and emerged with a 12–8 loss in which he gave up 12 hits with most of the damage inflicted in the last four innings. It was Derby's fifth loss in his last six starts and reduced his record to 29-26. Derby did not pitch again in 1881 after seeming a lock at the beginning of September to win between 35 and 40 games. Since the Wolverines were in a struggle for second place—they eventually finished fourth—it seems likely that Derby incurred an injury in what became his final start of the season. Though he rebounded to top Cleveland 5–4 on Opening Day in 1882, he had few good games after that and was less than a .500 pitcher for a Detroit team that broke .500.

When Detroit did not reserve him for 1883 Derby signed with Buffalo but won only twice in his thirteen starts. In early June Buffalo accused him of "playing for his release," but *SL* defended him, saying his right arm was now nearly useless. His final ML win came a few days later on June 18 against an abysmal Philadelphia team when he beat 48-game loser John Coleman 11–2. Derby was then thrashed in his next start by his old Detroit mates and ended his ML career with a thud on July 3, 1883, when he gave up 32 hits and 31 runs at Chicago, where he had pitched his finest game just two years earlier. Suspended by Buffalo after his 31–7 shellacking, Derby later turned down an offer from Cincinnati AA, claiming his arm was useless, and became a shoe salesman. He died in Philadelphia in 1925. (DN/DB)

Devlin, James H. / "Jim"

B	T	HGT	WGT	G	IP	H	GS
?	L	5'7"	135	23	170.1	161	21

CG	BB	SO	SH	W	L	PCT	ERA
17	58	90	0	11	10	.524	3.38

B. 4/16/1866 Troy, NY **D.** 12/14/1900
TEAMS: 86NYN 87PhiN 88–89StLA
DEBUT: 6/28/1886 at New York; relieved Tim Keefe in Keefe's 12–7 win over Kansas City's Pete Conway and Jim Whitney
FINALE: 6/17/1889 at Philadelphia; caught by Jack Milligan and lost 11–2 to Philadelphia's Ed Seward

The scandal-free Jim Devlin worked as a brush maker in the off-season. In the spring of 1886 the slightly built southpaw was in his second year with Troy when a dispute over his contract arose between the Hudson River League team and New York NL. Overriding Troy's protests that Devlin was being stolen, the Giants put him under the tutelage of sore-armed hurler Larry Corcoran. When Corcoran judged him to have "a good head, a twisting curve, and plenty of speed," Giants captain John M. Ward got permission from Kansas City to substitute him for Tim Keefe in the eighth inning of a 12–2 blowout. But Devlin, according to *SL*, "was badly rattled," and, Corcoran's plaudits notwithstanding, soon found himself back in the minors.

The following spring Devlin accompanied Philadelphia NL to training camp, where manager Harry Wright discovered that his revamped delivery, in accordance with the new pitching rule changes, was too deliberate, allowing base runners to run wild on him. But Wright worked patiently with his protégé until he was judged ready to take the box in his first official game with the Quakers on July 31. When Devlin was rocked 10–2 by Pittsburgh and then lost 9–6 at Detroit three days later, Wright's patience evaporated and the 21-year-old hurler went to Ashland of the Central Pennsylvania League.

Lacking a southpaw, St. Louis Browns manager Charlie Comiskey pilfered Devlin from the Western Association St. Louis Whites shortly after the 1888 season started and shoved him immediately into action against Cincinnati on April 24. Though Devlin showed well before losing 4–3 in ten innings, he did not take the box again for the Browns until early June. By late July, however, he and Silver King were Comiskey's entire pitching staff after family illness called Nat Hudson to Chicago. But shortly after beating Kansas City on July 20 to put the Browns permanently into first place that season, Devlin contracted malaria. He returned to beat Kansas City 8–1 on October 1 and then dropped his next two starts, including a 10–1 drubbing by Cincinnati in the final game of the regular season. Devlin pitched briefly in relief against the New York Giants in the World Series that fall and then returned to his Lansingburgh, NY, home.

He began 1889 as the Browns' fourth pitcher and seemingly should have moved up in Comiskey's estimation after he topped Louisville 3–2 in ten innings in the club's eleventh game of the season and then won again over the Colonels two days later. Instead Comiskey soured on Devlin after he was beaten handily in each of his next two outings and then ordered his dismissal the following month after an ugly loss to Philadelphia. Years later, Comiskey claimed Devlin's downfall was "a passion for mixed ale," but arm trouble also was a probable culprit.

Devlin kicked off the 1890 season by starting Sioux City's Western Association opener. He subsequently moved to Albany of the Eastern League and won 23 games for the Senators in 1892. Devlin remained active as a semipro after his pro career dimmed out before he was 30. As late as 1898 he was pitching for a club in Albany with Hugh Ahearn, later with Brooklyn NL, as his catcher. At the time of his death of pneumonia in 1900, Devlin was working for a cigar manufacturer in Troy. (DN)

Dinneen, William Henry / "Bill" "Big Bill"

B	T	HGT	WGT	G	IP	H	GS
R	R	6'1"	190	106	830	892	99

CG	BB	SO	SH	W	L	PCT	ERA
85	299	281	1	43	50	.462	3.63

B. 4/5/1876 Syracuse, NY **D.** 1/13/1955
TEAMS: 98–99WasN 00–01BosN 02–07BosAL 07–09StLAL
DEBUT: 4/22/1898 at Washington; caught by Deacon McGuire and was relieved by Doc Amole in his 12–7 loss to Brooklyn's Joe Yeager
FINALE: 8/26/1909 at St. Louis; caught by Jim Stephens and was pinch hit for in the seventh inning of his 5–1 loss to New York's Tom Hughes
CAREER HIGHLIGHT: Won 3 games for Boston AL in the first modern World Series in 1903

Bill Dinneen won 170 ML games, plus 3 more in the first modern World Series in 1903, and umpired twenty-eight years in the AL, appearing in eight World Series and working the plate in the first ML All-Star game in 1933. In 1911 he became the first man to both play and umpire in a World Series and is still the only hurler to both throw a shutout and officiate in a Fall Classic. In honor of his forty consecutive years of ML service (1898–1937), including both playing and umpiring, Dinneen was selected to throw out the symbolic first pitch to commemorate the fiftieth anniversary of the first modern World Series prior to Game 2 of the 1953 Series between the Yankees and Dodgers. For all that, he remains practically an unknown name to most current fans.

At 19, Dinneen was already so far along in his development that he jumped directly from the Syracuse sandlots to Toronto of the strong Eastern League and survived a horrendous introduction in which he went 0-4 and gave up 44 runs in 38 innings. After winning 21 games with the Maple Leafs in 1897, he was acquired by Washington NL and signed in 1898 for $130 a month, the same salary he got in the minors the previous year. Dinneen struggled at the start with the eleventh place Senators, waiting until May 11, 1898, to collect his initial ML win, but he remained in the rotation all year. The following season he led the Senators in ERA and also hit .303, a career high.

That winter, when Dinneen and teammate Buck Freeman were sold to Boston, it was correctly viewed as a sure sign that the NL would reduce to eight teams in 1900 and Washington would be among the four casualties. Expected to contend for the pennant with the addition of the two Washington mainstays, Boston instead finished below .500 but through no fault of Dinneen's, as he went 20-14 while the rest of the Beaneaters' staff was 46-58. Dinneen's first of what would be four career 20-win seasons was cemented when he beat a young novice named Christy Mathewson on August 26, 1900. After the season he committed to join teammate Jimmy Collins in jumping to the new Boston AL entry but then reneged when Beaneaters team official James Billings pressured him to remain in the NL. The Boston Americans then signed Cy Young in Dinneen's stead, but by the spring of 1902 he had reconsidered and joined Young in the Americans' livery. (DN)

Dolan, John / "John"

B	T	HGT	WGT	G	IP	H	GS
?	R	5'10"	170	39	286.2	314	33

CG	BB	SO	SH	W	L	PCT	ERA
26	122	87	0	15	16	.484	4.30

B. 9/12/1867 Newport, KY **D.** 5/8/1948
TEAMS: 90CinN 91ColA 92WasN 93StLN 95ChiN
DEBUT: 9/5/1890 at Chicago; caught by Jerry Harrington and lost 12–3 to Chicago's Jack Luby
FINALE: 9/4/1895 at Boston; caught by Tim Donahue and was relieved by Bill Terry in his 15–5 loss to Boston's Jim Sullivan

John Dolan pitched with his hometown Newport Ravens in 1887–88 but by the following September had ascended to Minneapolis of the Western Association. He started 1890 with Evansville and went to Chicago after the Indiana club disbanded. Released by the Colts that October, he signed in April 1891 with Columbus AA. Dolan was 12-11 with a second-division team when manager Gus Schmelz fined him $25 for failing to cover 1B in a game with Louisville on August 16. Dolan argued until Schmelz said, "That's $25 more, and now get out on the field and not another word from you." The *Ohio State Journal* reported that Dolan complied, but the next morning when players came down to breakfast he was missing. Said the *Journal*, "The wonder has been that Manager Schmelz didn't fine him to a stand-still long ago. He is lucky to be alive." Later that month *TSN* said that Dolan appeared at a game in Cincinnati and swore the reason he left was because Columbus was taking all of his money in fines for trivial offenses and for errors on the field that were part of baseball. Said Dolan, "The way I look at it is this: The club is not drawing well since it went down in the race and lost [Jack] O'Connor, and they are making their salaries by fining players." He then tried to play in Denver but upon being blacklisted was forced to return to Columbus and make amends. Eventually he was reinstated after he threatened to sue, enabling Ted Sullivan to sign him for Washington that November. The D.C. club cut Dolan in May 1892 although he was far from its worst pitcher. He finished the season in the Eastern League and then was the first player Bill Watkins signed when he was named St. Louis NL manager in 1893. He was also among the first players Watkins released the following spring.

Dolan was with Rockford of the Western Association in 1895 when Chicago sent Tom Parrott to Rockford on loan in return for an option on Dolan that was exercised in late August. Even though he did not appear with the Colts after September 5, he remained on the team until the end of the season and then was released the following April. Dolan hurled in the minors until leaving pro ball in 1900. For years afterward writers confused him with John Frank "Jack" Dolan, a minor league pitcher in the late 1890s and early 1900s. Dolan the major leaguer died in Springfield, OH, at 80. (DN)

Donahue, Francis Rostell / "Red"

B	T	HGT	WGT	G	IP	H	GS
R	R	6'0"	187	183	1431.1	1795	165

CG	BB	SO	SH	W	L	PCT	ERA
148	403	286	8	69	95	.421	4.61

B. 1/23/1873 Waterbury, CT **D.** 8/25/1913
TEAMS: 93NYN 95–97StLN 98–01PhiN 02StLAL 03–05CleAL 06DetAL
DEBUT: 5/6/1893 at New York; relieved Amos Rusie in Rusie's 18–8 win over Washington's Jesse Duryea and Duke Esper
FINALE: 9/28/1906 at Detroit; caught by Boss Schmidt and lost 7–4 to Philadelphia's Jack Coombs and Jimmy Dygert
CAREER HIGHLIGHT: 7/8/1898 at Philadelphia; caught by Ed McFarland and no-hit Boston's Vic Willis 5–0

Red Donahue was the son of a noted Connecticut criminal lawyer, a graduate of Villanova, an excellent pool player, and thrice a 20-game winner, but he is remembered today only for having lost a post-1892 record 35 games for the 1897 St. Louis Browns.

He joined the Giants in 1893 at age 20 after pitching for New Milford, CT, the previous year and was released to Lowell of the New England League after just two appearances. Two years later Donahue came to St. Louis late in the season from Grand Rapids of the Western League. In 1896, his official rookie year, Donahue went 7-24 with the Browns and experienced far too many games like the one on July 24 at St. Louis. With the Browns tied 8–8 with Baltimore going into the thirteenth inning, the Orioles scored 5 runs and umpire Bob Emslie then forfeited the game "because St. Louis would not field batted balls which they could not see." Spared a loss at first, Donahue later had it restored when Nick Young ruled the game official even though St. Louis, trailing 13–8, did not get to bat in the bottom of thirteenth frame.

But 1896 was a walk in the park for Donahue compared to 1897. Although he led the NL in every negative pitching department—most prominently losses with a whopping 35—he also topped the loop in CGs with 38 and the Browns in wins with 10. His lone season highlight came on September 27 when he broke a string of 23 consecutive losses to Cincinnati dating back to September 25, 1895, by edging Ted Breitenstein 5–4. Traded to the Phillies that November in a mammoth seven-player deal, he arrived in Philadelphia still shell-shocked and needed several weeks to acclimate to the fact that he was now with a team that could make plays behind him and score runs. By the following year Donahue was ready to emerge as one of the better pitchers in the NL, going 21-8 with a 3.39 ERA. In the six seasons that followed he reached the "Charmed Circle" twice more, won 19 on one occasion and bagged 15 wins in each of the other three campaigns. After slipping to just 6 wins with Cleveland in 1905, he rebounded to score 13 victories in his final ML season after joining the Tigers and Ty Cobb. Donahue then quit active play cold at age 33, ran a saloon in Philadelphia and coached baseball at both Yale and LaSalle University before dying of tuberculosis seven months after his 40th birthday. (DN)

Donovan, William Edward / "Bill" "Wild Bill"

B	T	HGT	WGT	G	IP	H	GS
R	R	5'11"	190	27	144	159	13

CG	BB	SO	SH	W	L	PCT	ERA
10	100	60	0	3	10	.231	4.81

B. 10/13/1876 Lawrence, MA **D.** 12/9/1923
TEAMS: 98WasN 99–02BroN 03–12DetAL (P\M) 15–16NYAL 17NYAL 18DetAL (M)21PhiN
DEBUT: 4/22/1898 at Washington; caught by Deacon McGuire and relieved Doc Amole, who had earlier replaced Bill Dinneen in Dinneen's 12–7 loss to Brooklyn's Joe Yeager
FINALE: 9/2/1918 at Detroit; caught by Oscar Stanage and Archie Yelle before being relieved by Ty Cobb and Bobby Veach in his 7–3 win over Chicago's Eddie Cicotte

Bill Donovan was acrobatic, a fast runner, and a fairly good hitter, but until 1901, his fourth ML season, he gave little sign that he would be one of the game's foremost pitchers in the first decade of the twentieth century. He was slated to pitch in the Connecticut State League for his second straight season in 1898 but was corralled by Washington manager Arthur Irwin instead. Arriving in D.C. with little pro experience, he displayed a live fastball and an equally live bat in spring training but lacked control and the necessary discipline as a hitter. But it was his volatile temper more than any skill shortcomings that led Washington to send him to Richmond of the Atlantic League with a string attached and then throw him into a deal with Brooklyn that was already tilted heavily in Brooklyn's favor. Late in the 1899 season, when several of the Superbas veteran pitchers were struggling, manager Ned Hanlon reclaimed him from Richmond for $500.

Again Donovan's erratic play and immature tantrums earned a quick return to the minors. He spent most of 1900 with Hartford of the Eastern League before being summoned by Hanlon in late September along with batterymate Farmer Steelman after Brooklyn had clinched its second straight NL pennant. Donovan saw no action in the postseason *Chronicle-Telegraph* club series against second-place Pittsburgh and in the spring of 1901 seemed a long shot at best to make the Brooklyn club. The situation changed abruptly, however, when Superbas ace Joe McGinnity jumped to the American League in 1901 and Roaring Bill Kennedy was of little use. (DN/DB)

Dowling, Henry Peter / "Pete"

B	T	HGT	WGT	G	IP	H	GS
L	L	5'11"	165	74	610	652	66

CG	BB	SO	SH	W	L	PCT	ERA
61	223	176	0	27	39	.409	3.69

B. 7/15/1876 St. Louis, MO **D.** 6/30/1905
TEAMS: 97–99LouN 01MilAL 01CleAL
DEBUT: 7/27/1897 at Louisville; caught by Bill Wilson and beat New York's Dad Clarke 12–6
FINALE: 9/28/1901 at Philadelphia; caught by Joe Connor and lost 3–1 to Philadelphia's Snake Wiltse

In 1898 *TSN* noted that Pete Dowling was "of a good parentage and has a college education." None of this information has ever been verified, leaving the left-hander nearly as enigmatic a figure as his Louisville hill teammate in the late 1890s, Bill Magee. Reportedly, Barney Dreyfuss signed Dowling in 1897 when he watched his Louisville club play Paducah, KY, in an exhibition game and the Colonels barely beat Dowling 2–1. Since St. Louisan Willie Sudhoff was also on the Central Kentucky League team, conceivably he and Dowling came to Paducah as a package.

Shortly after winning his first start with Louisville, Dowling was farmed to Milwaukee of the Western League and then recalled in September. The following season he went 13-20 as part of the Louisville rotation and then spent the winter superintending his zinc mine in southeast Missouri—or so he claimed. Dowling had a flair for tall tales, particularly when he had been drinking, which was not a rare occurrence. In 1899 he fashioned a 3.11 ERA, led the Colonels in pitching strikeouts, and yet was left out of the package of Louisville players that Dreyfuss ticketed for Pittsburgh when the two clubs came under syndicate ownership before the Kentucky faction formally disbanded. What cooked Dowling with Dreyfuss was a drinking spree following a game in Washington on September 2 that caused him to miss the team train to Cincinnati. The left-hander initially was suspended just for the season but later was released to Milwaukee of the newly renamed American League.

Viewed in the 1900 preseason as the Brewers' ace, Dowling beat Chicago in the season opener and topped the AL with five extra-inning wins but was only 16-19 for a team that finished 21 games above .500. When he got off to a 1-4 start with Milwaukee the following year after the AL went major, he was sold to Cleveland on June 1 and ended the campaign with 26 losses, still the loop season record for the most by a southpaw as well as the Cleveland season record of 22. Eventually Cleveland cut all ties to him but not without regret, for he had been the Blues' most effective pitcher at times in spite of his overall mark.

Dowling then went on a frenetic tour of teams in the West that took him from Montana to California and eventually to Hot Lake, OR. Sometime on the afternoon or early evening of June 30, 1905, he was decapitated while walking either on or along the railroad tracks from Hot Lake to LaGrande, OR. Whether he was drunk or sober at the time, or a suicide or accident victim, was never made public. (DN)

Driscoll, John F. / "Denny"

B	T	HGT	WGT	G	IP	H	GS
L	L	5'10½"	160	83	681	747	80

CG	BB	SO	SH	W	L	PCT	ERA
72	67	171	1	38	39	.494	3.08

B. 11/19/1855 Lowell, MA **D.** 7/11/1886
TEAMS: 80BufN 82–83PitA 84LouA
DEBUT: 7/1/1880 at Buffalo; played CF and went 1-for-4 in a 4–0 win over Troy's Mickey Welch
FINALE: 6/28/1884 at Louisville; caught by Ed Whiting and lost 7–6 to Bob Barr

Denny Driscoll was unimpressive as both a pitcher and an outfielder with Buffalo NL in 1880 but returned to the majors two years later to construct a partial season that today renders him a perennial first-round draft pick in historical simulation games. Despite not joining the Allegheny club in the fledgling AA until July 12, 1882, he set all-time season records for the fewest walks (0.54) and fewest base runners allowed per nine innings (7.79) by a left-handed qualifier. After being league adjusted, his numbers are not quite as awesome since the 1882 AA was a pitcher-dominated circuit, but they still convey that—statistically, at any rate—he was the best pitcher in the loop by a significant margin.

Driscoll's sudden ascension is difficult to comprehend. Nothing he had done previously offered any hint of what a bargain the Alleghenys might be getting when manager Al Pratt detoured en route from Philadelphia to Albany in early July 1882 to woo the left-hander away from Billy Barnie's minor league Brooklyn Atlantics. Nor was he ever again more than an average ML pitcher. Nicknamed "Denny" for an unknown reason, Driscoll grew up in Lowell in a family of textile workers but avoided the mills long enough to finish school. In 1875, at age 20, he was pitching for the Bartlett amateur team of Lowell. After beginning 1876 with independent Nashua, NH, he jumped to the semipro Our Boys club of Boston after facing them in a game and fancying their style. He remained with Our Boys through 1877 and then was with several New England independent nines before arriving in Buffalo in 1880 from Jersey City.

Unreserved for 1881, Driscoll started the season with the New York Mets of the Eastern Championship Association under Jim Mutrie but had trouble adjusting to the new fifty-foot pitching distance and drifted from team to team for most of that season. He almost certainly would have remained with Barnie's Atlantics in 1882 if the Alleghenys had not spent most of the first half of the inaugural AA season unsuccessfully auditioning pitchers that could alternate with Harry Salisbury. By the end of the summer Driscoll was the team's ace perforce after Salisbury was expelled for anticipated contract jumping and finished with a flourish, losing only to Louisville in his last seven starts of season when Guy Hecker no-hit the Alleghenys on September 19.

Upon learning he would be reserved for 1883 by the Pittsburgh-based club, Driscoll made plans to wed Mary Casey of Lowell in November and picked up extra money pitching exhibitions throughout the month of October. Installed as the Alleghenys' Opening Day starter in 1883, he lost 4–0 to Philadelphia and lost again the following day. One of his rare early-season wins came on May 11 when he beat Baltimore 7–6 by dint of what the Orioles deemed "a scurvy trick" that took advantage of a then extant rule quirk. In the first inning with one out Baltimore had already scored a run and had men on 2B and 3B when Bill Reid hit a foul ball. The ball was returned to Driscoll while he was purposely still outside the box, and he deliberately threw wild to third baseman Joe Battin. "The ruse worked charmingly." One runner went home and the other to 3B, but both were retired at their original bases after Battin returned the ball to Driscoll inside the box, ending the rally with just one run. The incident may help explain Driscoll's astonishing success in 1882. Pitching only a partial season in a novice league with an uneven cast of umpires and facing hitters to whom he was a new challenge on only one or two occasions before the season ended, Driscoll may have excelled largely on guile and trickery.

The Alleghenys did not invite Driscoll to return in 1884 even though he led a weak seventh-place team in most major pitching departments largely because he, Billy Taylor, and Buttercup Dickerson (who were also not asked back) "did more to demoralize the club than all else put together [with their] outrageous breaches of discipline." He signed with Louisville as support for Guy Hecker and won his first start but was soon replaced by Ren Deagle and faded to the minors until the spring of 1886, when he left the game after washing out with Binghamton of the International Association. That July Driscoll died at his home in Lowell of consumption, leaving his wife and two children. (DN)

Duggleby, William James / "Bill" "Farmer Bill" "The Oyster" "Frosty Bill"

B	T	HGT	WGT	G	IP	H	GS
?	R	?	?	9	54	70	5

CG	BB	SO	SH	W	L	PCT	ERA
4	18	12	0	3	3	.500	5.50

B. 3/16/1874 Utica, NY **D.** 8/30/1944
TEAMS: 98PhiN 01PhiN 01PhiAL 02–07PhiN 07PitN

DEBUT AND CAREER HIGHLIGHT: 4/21/1898 at Philadelphia; caught by Ed McFarland and became the first player to hit a grand slam homer in his first ML at-bat in the bottom of the second inning in a 14–4 win over the New York's Cy Seymour and Charlie Gettig
FINALE: 9/7/1907 at Pittsburgh; caught by George Gibson and was relieved by Deacon Phillippe in his 5–4 loss to Chicago's Ed Reulbach

Bill Duggleby learned the game in the Corn Hill section of Utica, where he acquired the nickname "Farmer Bill" while pitching for various amateur teams. After his 1897 season as a pitcher-outfielder with Auburn in which his .365 BA led all New York State League players with a minimum of 200 ABs, he moved up to the Phillies in 1898. Despite his heroics in his ML debut, Duggleby spent most of the season with Wilkes-Barre of the Eastern League joined by another Phils farmhand, first baseman Billy Goeckel. While there, with Goeckel's heady coaching, he mastered a timing pickoff player in which he would spin and throw to 1B without looking, as Goeckel, also counting silently to himself, sprinted for the bag.

After spending most of 1899 and 1900 in the Eastern League, Duggleby married Ethel Williams. He returned to the Phils a mature pitcher in 1901 and won a career-high 20 games. During the off-season Duggleby jumped to the AL Philadelphia Athletics, but when the Phillies dragged all their absconders into court, he rejoined the Phils rather than accompanying several of his ex-teammates who escaped to Cleveland.

Duggleby remained with the Phils until 1907 but never was able to match his 1901 success. Sold to the Pirates in July 1907, he was cut after a poor September start against the Cubs. Duggleby's obit claimed that his career ended in an exhibition-game plate collision with Ty Cobb in which his ankle was broken, but actually he pitched in the minors until he was in his late thirties and then worked at the Savage Arms plants in Ilion, NY, until shortly before his death in 1944. Researchers seeking oddities in baseball's rich history have found few more bizarre than the fact that it is still unknown which way the first player to hit a 4-run homer in his initial ML plate appearance batted. (DN)

Dundon, Edward Joseph / "Ed" "Dummy"

B	T	HGT	WGT	G	IP	H	GS
?	R	6'0"	170	31	247.2	298	28

CG	BB	SO	SH	W	L	PCT	ERA
23	53	68	0	9	20	.310	4.25

B. 7/10/1859 Columbus, OH **D.** 8/18/1893
TEAMS: 83–84ColA
DEBUT: 6/2/1883 at Philadelphia; caught by Rudy Kemmler and beat Philadelphia's Enoch Bakely 8–6
FINALE: 9/20/1884 at Columbus; played CF and switched positions with pitcher Frank Mountain in Mountain's 13–6 loss to Baltimore's Hardie Henderson

Dunny Dundon's brother was a prominent Ohio Democratic politician and lumber dealer. After losing his speech and hearing at age two following a bout with typhoid fever, he was educated at the Ohio School for the Deaf and was a classmate of Dummy Hoy. Dundon pitched for the Columbus mute team in 1879 and continued to play with the club off and on while also performing for various independent and semipro teams in the Ohio capital and working as a bookbinder. He joined the local AA club on an experimental basis as a pitcher-change outfielder in June 1883 and was not expected back after he "hinted . . . there was an element too prevalent in the sport, which was, to say the least, objectionable." Instead he returned for a second season despite hitting .161 and winning just 3 of 19 decisions. In 1884 Dundon improved marginally as a pitcher but was used more frequently in the outfield, a puzzle since he batted just .140.

Dundon then spent the next two seasons in the Southern League. In January 1887 he was stabbed outside a Columbus saloon during a fight with a gang of soldiers and was reported to be near death. Dundon recovered in Hot Springs, AR, however, and logged 20 wins the next season with Syracuse of the International Association. In March 1888 he married Emma Wooley of Columbus before rejoining Syracuse. Dundon had a 2.76 ERA in mid-August 1888 when he was fined and threatened with being blacklisted after jumping the team along with African American pitcher Bob Higgins when the Stars tried to reduce their salaries. Higgins went home to his barbershop in Tennessee and Dundon returned to his old job in a Columbus bindery but took time away from it late in the season to pitch a few games with the local team in the Tri-State League. He quit pro ball the following year after falling short of the Evansville Central Interstate League team's expectations.

In the early 1890s Dundon was still receiving periodic offers to return to baseball but refused them all. In 1893 *TSN* reported than he had "fallen a victim to quick consumption" and noted in its obit that about ten days before his death he grew annoyed by voices in his room at his home and witnesses confirmed that he had recovered his hearing before he died. It is probable that Dundon was related to twentieth-century ML infielder Gus Dundon, but to what degree is as yet unknown. (DN/DB)

Dunn, John Joseph / "Jack"

B	T	HGT	WGT	G	IP	H	GS
R	R	5'9"	?	127	981.2	1101	108

CG	BB	SO	SH	W	L	PCT	ERA
95	291	258	3	61	52	.540	4.07

G	AB	H	R	2B	3B	HR
150	479	116	66	7	2	0

RBI	BB	SO	SB	BA	SA	OBP
58	15	—	9	.242	.265	.268

B. 10/6/1872 Meadville, PA **D.** 10/22/1928
TEAMS: 97–00BroN 00–01PhiN 01BalAL 02–04NYN
DEBUT: 5/6/1897 at Brooklyn; relieved Sadie McMahon in the third inning of a 9–9 tie with New York's Dad Clarke and Cy Seymour
FINALE: 10/4/1904 at New York; played LF and got 1 hit in a 7–3 loss to St. Louis's Mike O'Neill

Jack Dunn is probably the most notable performer whose playing weight is still unknown. When he was a boy of nine, a handcar ran over his left shoulder and doctors debated for a time whether to amputate his arm. Dunn's left arm was never again as strong, and his right arm was also somewhat suspect by the time he was in his late twenties. From the outset of his career he relied on curves, guile, and his exceptional fielding ability to get by as a pitcher, but after the 1901 season he became almost exclusively a position player. By the end of his ML career he had played at least 5 games at every position except catcher.

A late starter, Dunn did not turn pro until 1895 with Binghamton of the New York State League. The following year Pittsburgh acquired him but then loaned him to Toronto of the Eastern League and lost faith in him, allowing Brooklyn to draft him for the standard $500 price in October 1896. The Bridegrooms used Dunn solely in relief until July 3, 1897, when he started at Philadelphia and won 5–2. He finished the season with the best record on the staff (14-9) but joined with Roaring Bill Kennedy and Joe Yeager the following year in giving Brooklyn three 20-game losers. In 1899, on a revamped team under manager Ned Hanlon, Dunn won 23 games and was a member of the first strict four-man rotation in ML history as each of the club's starters worked at least 275 innings and only Doc McJames (19-15) kept the club from being the first with four 20-game winners.

Early in the 1901 season Dunn injured his elbow. When he was still unable to throw his curve ball without pain in late July, Hanlon released him to Philadelphia. The Phillies gave up on Dunn the following April, but John McGraw, the player-manager of the new Baltimore AL entry, garnered him and made him the Orioles' leading utilityman. Dunn spent the rest of the ML portion of his playing career under McGraw, finishing with the 1904 Giants, McGraw's first pennant winner. In 1905 he led Providence to the Eastern League pennant as a player-manager, thereupon launching arguably the most successful minor league executive and managerial career in history.

After winning an Eastern League pennant with Baltimore in 1908, Dunn bought the club from Ned Hanlon and owned it until his death in 1928. Famed for his ability to find talented players in the rough and develop them into stars, he had a hand in discovering Babe Ruth, Lefty Grove, Jack Bentley, Joe Boley, Dick Porter, Ernie Shore, and numerous other prominent players, and then selling them to ML clubs for sums that enabled his Baltimore club to make a handsome profit each season. From 1919 through 1925 Dunn's International League Orioles won an OB record (tied by the 1919–25 Fort Worth Panthers of the Texas League) seven straight pennants. In 1928 he refused an offer from Braves owner Judge Fuchs to manage in the majors. That fall, while attending dog field trials in Towson, MD, Dunn became "overly excited" when his favorite dog, Belle the Devil, made a spectacular point and suddenly seized up in his stirrups and slipped out of his saddle. He was dead from a stroke "before he hit the ground." (DN)

Duryea, James Newton / "Jesse" "Cyclone Jim" "Farmer Boy"

B	T	HGT	WGT	G	IP	H	GS
R	R	5'10"	175	143	1088	1101	130

CG	BB	SO	SH	W	L	PCT	ERA
104	349	416	5	59	67	.468	3.45

B. 9/7/1859 Osage, IA **D.** 8/19/1942

TEAMS: 89CinA 90–91CinN 91StLA 92CinN 92–93WasN

DEBUT: 4/20/1889 at Cincinnati; caught by Kid Baldwin and lost 2–0 to St. Louis's Elton Chamberlin

FINALE: 7/15/1893 at Pittsburgh; caught by Duke Farrell in a 19–0 loss to Pittsburgh's Frank Killen in which he gave up 4 home runs and 4 triples.

Jesse Duryea was already 26 when he first played pro ball with St. Paul of the Northwestern League in 1886, but he gave a fictitious birth date that made him only 23. Previously he had been a farmer and was appropriately dubbed "Farmer Boy" by his teammates. Duryea was with St. Paul for three years until Cincinnati AA purchased him and his batterymate Billy Earle in the fall of 1888 for about $3,000.

After a somewhat slow start in 1889 Duryea won 32 games, a remarkable total for a rookie, and emerged as Cincinnati's best hurler. At the end of the season he beat St. Louis in an AA game that decided one of the nineteenth century's tightest pennant races in favor of Brooklyn. Doc Bushong, Brooklyn's reserve catcher, came to Cincinnati to offer Duryea and catcher Jim Keenan $100 if they won and during the game sat behind the backstop, close enough to keep reminding Keenan of the promise. Some observers objected, fearing this practice would blur the borderline between rewards for winning and bribery to lose.

The Brotherhood revolt in 1890 made Duryea's fine pitching in 1889 a coveted prize. He was reportedly offered a hefty $4,500 to jump to the Players League, but he demanded more. After much dithering he took advance money from Brooklyn PL but finally decided in March to return the money and stay with Cincinnati. According to his own story, he had been on his way to Brooklyn's spring training site, but as he passed through Cincinnati, Reds officials waylaid him and persuaded him to jump back. Many Cincinnatians greeted the vacillatory Duryea with disgust for his disloyalty, but he was nonetheless the Reds' Opening Day starter. Although he had decent numbers in 1890, he did not nearly approach his rookie success. The following season was much worse. After losing five straight Duryea seemed to be righting things in mid-May, when he pitched well in a 2–1 loss to Brooklyn and then beat Boston star Kid Nichols for his first win of the year, but after that he resumed his losing ways. Duryea did not pitch after June 13 and drew his release on July 1. A few weeks later he signed with St Louis. Pitching his first game in more than five weeks on July 22, he defeated Mike Kelly's Cincinnati AA team by a 10–2 count. After two less successful appearances, however, he was released for not being in condition to pitch and returned to his home in Goodell, IA. There, Duryea admitted alcohol had been his downfall and insisted that from now on he would "drink nothing stronger than ginger ale." *TSN* subsequently reported that late in the season Duryea had looked so emaciated that he appeared tubercular.

In 1892 he signed with Cincinnati again and reported healthy and "brown as a nut." He pitched poorly, though, and on June 17 was released. Hired by Washington when the Senators needed a pitcher for a Sunday game in Cincinnati and their extra man, Bert Abbey, was a Sabbatarian, Duryea pitched well in losing and spent two months as a Senator, but although most of his ancillary stats look strong, he lost 11 of 14 and by the end of August was released once more. The following season nonetheless found Washington giving Duryea another try, but he pitched dreadfully, 4-10 with a 7.54 ERA, almost 3 runs above league average. The final straw came on July 15 when Pittsburgh buried Duryea 19–0 in one of the most lopsided shutouts in history. After his latest release Duryea continued to pitch in the minors until 1896, exactly ten years after he had made his pro debut.

Nicknames such as "Farmer Boy" do not suggest a man of social graces, but Duryea was said to be a good violinist and accordionist. These talents may explain how he was able to woo and win a prominent St. Paul society woman in February 1891. He later operated small hotels in Britt and Algona, IA, and then worked for a number of years at a recreation center in Algona prior to his death at 82. (DB/DN)

Dwyer, John Francis / "Frank"

B	T	HGT	WGT	G	IP	H	GS
R	R	5'8"	145	365	2819	3312	318

CG	BB	SO	SH	W	L	PCT	ERA
271	764	565	12	177	151	.540	3.84

G	AB	H	R	2B	3B	HR
394	1252	287	178	28	21	5

RBI	BB	SO	SB	BA	SA	OBP
136	70	80	16	.229	.297	.273

B. 3/25/1868 Lee, MA **D.** 2/4/1943
TEAMS: 88–89ChiN 90ChiP 91CinA 91MilA 92StLN 92–99CinN
DEBUT: 9/20/1888 at Chicago; caught by Tom Daly and beat Washington's Hank O'Day 11–0
FINALE: 7/24/1899 at Cincinnati; caught by Heinie Peitz, was relieved by Jack Taylor in his 8–3 loss to Boston's Kid Nichols
CAREER LOWLIGHT: 9/30/1894 at Cincinnati; shooting for his twentieth win on the season's final day, Dwyer led Cleveland 16–1 in the bottom of the sixth but gave up 2 runs in the sixth and 11 in the seventh as Cleveland rallied to tie the game 16–16 against reliever Bill Whitrock before it was called due to darkness

A graduate of Hobart College, Frank Dwyer was a smart, boyish-looking control artist who led Cincinnati in wins for the decade of the 1890s. A mainstay on three straight contending Reds teams in the twelve-team NL, Dwyer legitimately could be considered an ace only in 1896, but no other pitcher in the team's long history appeared in nearly as many significant, interesting, or just plain wacky games.

Raised in Geneva, NY, Dwyer went west at the age of 19 and alternated with Ted Kennedy for La Crosse, WI, on the bumpy fields of the Northwestern League. Despite going just 13-18, he was purchased by Chicago NL for 1888 and placed with the club's new Chicago Western Association farm team, where he logged 312 innings. Dwyer threw a three-hit shutout in his ML debut after joining the NL Chicagos and was on track to be unbeaten in five September starts until he gave up nine runs in the seventh inning of a game in New York. In 1889 manager Cap Anson made Dwyer part of the first four-man rotation in ML history, but against Cleveland, in his tenth start of the season, he was embarrassed when Anson made him one of the first pitchers benched in the middle of an inning as per the new freer substitution rule.

League changes and franchise collapses accounted for most of Dwyer's early player movements. In 1891 he became one of only four players that Milwaukee kept from the Cincinnati AA club when it disbanded, but he was assigned the following February to the St. Louis Browns after Milwaukee was left out of the League and Association merger. Dwyer started slowly for the Browns and was summarily released after a 16–4 loss at Washington on June 11.

St. Louis soon regretted the move. With Cincinnati, Dwyer came into his own, winning 10 of 13 decisions down the stretch. Over the next six years Dwyer started a third of Cincinnati's games and made 30 relief appearances. In 1895 the Reds emerged as a contender after a long dry spell. That July 16, Dwyer beat Boston to lift his record to 12-5 and put Cincinnati a mere half game out of first place. But Dwyer won only twice more prior to Labor Day, and the Reds fell 20 games off the pace. The 27-year-old put it all together the following season with a 13-game winning streak beginning on June 15 that spearheaded Cincinnati to a 34-6 spurt. The team held first place as late as August 20 when an 11-game losing streak on an Eastern road trip scuttled their season. Dwyer lost three disheartening starts during that collapse, and while he finished with a career-best 24-11 record, it was still a disappointing season, for he had been a spectacular 20-3 on the morning of August 12.

Not physically strong enough to be a stopper or pitch on consecutive days, Dwyer was helpless to prevent similar team collapses the following two seasons. In the heat of the 1898 pennant race, hard-charging Boston rocketed past Cincinnati on September 7. Dwyer, sore-armed at an inopportune time, started against Philadelphia on ten days rest on September 17. Leading 8–1 in the fifth inning, he seemed a lock to end Cincinnati's 6-game losing streak. But then a line drive off the bat of opposing pitcher Al Orth caromed off his head. Dwyer was carried unconscious to the hospital, lost his hearing for two months, and suffered permanent dizzy spells that all but ended his career at the age of 30. Although he returned in 1899, he did poorly in five widely spaced starts and announced his retirement after the last of them to become an umpire.

Of upstanding character, in 1899 Dwyer worked as a regular NL umpire, and in 1900 he moved to the newly renamed minor American League. However, he quit his AL post one month into the season after a fan threw a chair at him from the stands during a near riot at Detroit. Following a period of reflection, he returned to umpiring in 1904 after the AL became a major circuit, and he was involved in a famous incident on May 29 when Cleveland second baseman Nap Lajoie spat a whole tobacco chaw in his face.

Dwyer then retired to quieter work in the game, taking a job as a scout for New York AL and later switching to Detroit in 1909. In 1916 he was named the New York state boxing commissioner and remained at the post until 1922. Dwyer died in Pittsfield, MA, at 74 of a heart attack. (FV/DN)

Easton, John S. / "Jack"

B	T	HGT	WGT	G	IP	H	GS
?	R	?	?	76	522.1	498	57

CG	BB	SO	SH	W	L	PCT	ERA
46	262	246	0	26	29	.473	4.12

B. 2/28/1865 Bridgeport, OH **D.** 11/28/1903
TEAMS: 89–91ColA 91StLA 92StLN 94PitN
DEBUT: 9/23/1889 at Brooklyn; relieved Mark Baldwin and earned a save in a 3–2 win over Brooklyn's Tom Lovett
FINALE: 7/7/1894 at Pittsburgh; relieved Red Ehret in a 12–0 loss to Philadelphia's Gus Weyhing

Jack Easton grew up just across the Ohio River from West Virginia and apprenticed with a Wheeling amateur team before turning pro with Sandusky in the 1887 Tri-State League. He began the following year with the same Ohio club before being acquired by Lima, OH, the eventual Tri-State champions that season. That winter Easton resumed his profession as a glass finisher in the expectation of moving up to a higher level of ball, but the spring of 1889 found him still in the Tri-State League, this time with Springfield, OH. His opportunity to advance finally came late that season when Columbus AA suspended Bill Widner for drunkenness and looked to nearby Springfield for a replacement. Used initially in relief, Easton got his first start on October 11, 1889, and beat Philadelphia 7–4.

When Columbus's ace, Mark Baldwin, absconded to the Players League in 1890, it opened a spot for Easton. He won his first start of the season, topping Toledo 4–3 in the second game of the campaign, but soon settled into mediocrity due to poor control. In 1890 Easton averaged a walk every other inning and finished with an OOBP over 100 points higher than his OBA, a clear mark of an erratic pitcher. When he continued to disappoint in 1891, Columbus released him in July. Browns manager Charlie Comiskey promptly signed Easton, having been gulled into believing the first-place Boston Reds were after his services. After learning otherwise Comiskey used his new pitcher only sparingly and then allowed him to return to Columbus for his final two starts in the AA when the Senators ran short of healthy arms toward the end of the season.

Easton began 1892 back in Browns livery but was released in May, the owner of a 6.39 ERA, although he staggered to wins in his only two starts. By the summer he was pitching for Green Bay in the Wisconsin-Michigan League. Easton spent most of the remainder of his playing career in eastern minor leagues except for a brief stint with Pittsburgh in 1894 that saw him lose 9–6 to George Hemming on June 19 in his final ML start, thereby ending a 20-game Louisville losing streak. Joining Guy Hecker's Oil City club of the Iron & Oil League in 1895, Easton both pitched and caught and worked winters for the Oil City Electric Railway. Later he worked at construction jobs and tried umpiring for a short while in the Interstate League after finishing his pitching days there in 1897.

In December 1897, Easton was dragged away in handcuffs from his job as a glass finisher at Aetna Standard Mill in Martins Ferry, OH, and charged with murdering a man in New York state in September 1897. A $250 reward for his capture was paid when it was seemingly established that Easton and his wife were living in Goshen, NY, at the time, and he was identified as the guilty man from a photograph. Within ten days, however, Easton was released when "it was proved he was not the man wanted" after his employer's books showed that he was on the job in Martins Ferry during the time the murder occurred. He later moved to Steubenville, OH, and was working at the Jefferson Glass Works when he died of stomach cancer in 1903. (DN)

Egan, James K. / "Jim" "The Troy Terrier"

B	T	HGT	WGT	G	IP	H	GS
B	L	?	?	12	100	133	10

CG	BB	SO	SH	W	L	PCT	ERA
10	24	20	0	4	6	.400	4.14

G	AB	H	R	2B	3B	HR
30	115	23	15	3	2	0

RBI	BB	SO	SB	BA	SA	OBP
10	1	21	—	.200	.261	.207

B. ?/?/1858 Derby, CT **D.** 9/26/1884
TEAMS: 82TroN
DEBUT: 5/15/1882 at Worcester; played LF and went 1-for-4 in a 5–1 loss to Worcester's Lee Richmond
PITCHING DEBUT: 5/17/1882 at Albany, NY; caught by Bill Holbert and beat Providence's John M. Ward 7–4
FINALE, FAMOUS LAST, AND CAREER HIGHLIGHT: 9/29/1882 at Troy; caught Mickey Welch, went 2-for-5 and scored 2 runs in a 10–7 win over Worcester's Jake Evans that marked Troy's last game as a major league team

Jim Egan could do just about everything necessary to succeed on the diamond except stay sober. He pitched with both arms on occasion, and there is a fair possibility that he was also a switch hitter. In his ML debut he replaced Pat Gillespie, a left-handed hitter, in the lineup on a day Troy faced left-hander Lee Richmond, suggesting that he could hit from the right side of the plate. Since Egan was a natural southpaw, it seems likely that he could also swing a bat from the port side.

A Connecticut native, Egan played for Waterbury in 1880 and returned there for most of 1881. He signed with Troy for 1882 as a tenth man. Egan made his first appearance in Troy's ninth game of the season and his first pitching start two days later. Expected to be only a change pitcher, Egan instead replaced Mickey Welch as the club's number two starter behind Tim Keefe when he won his first three decisions after Welch had been savaged in his first two appearances.

When Welch blanked Boston 1–0 in his third start, however, he regained his number two status. Egan, meanwhile, was rapidly drinking himself off the team. Released in June after an 11–8 loss to Detroit, he joined Billy Barnie's minor league Brooklyn Atlantics and by late July had redeemed himself under Barnie's supervision. Re-signed by Troy when both Keefe and Welch were in need of rest, he made his first appearance in the box for the Trojans in six weeks on July 26, losing a tough 5–3 verdict to Boston. Egan then proceeded to start Troy's next 3 games, all against Providence, winning 1 and losing 2, as both Keefe and Welch were still not in shape to pitch. After that, Keefe and Welch started every game for the rest of the season, and Egan played only sparingly, usually in CF, although his final appearance with Troy demonstrated that he was also a capable catcher. Unfortunately, that performance was not enough to prevail over his earlier history with the club.

When Troy went defunct after the 1882 season and many of its players were steered to New York, its replacement NL franchise, Egan was not among the chosen. He began 1883 with Brooklyn of the Interstate Association but soon returned to Waterbury to play for the independent Monitors. In September he was jailed for drunkenness. Ever restless, Egan barnstormed with comedic baseball teams for the rest of the fall and also worked in a circus. Late that winter he was jailed again, this time for robbery. Egan was subsequently sentenced to a year in the New Haven city jail for stealing a gold watch, despite testimony from several of his friends that the charge was fallacious. Some six months later he died of brain fever while incarcerated, still swearing his innocence. It is not clear whether Egan was actually nicknamed "The Troy Terrier" or whether the nickname was applied to him, perhaps posthumously, by a writer who mistook him in more ways than one for Dick Egan, a boxer of the same vintage, who was called "The Troy Terror" and was embarrassingly flattened in an exhibition match at Troy's Irving Hall on the opening night of Egan's lone ML season. (DN/DB)

Ehret, Philip Sydney / "Red"

B	T	HGT	WGT	G	IP	H	GS
R	R	6'0"	175	362	2754.1	3172	309

CG	BB	SO	SH	W	L	PCT	ERA
260	841	848	14	139	167	.454	4.02

B. 8/31/1868 Louisville, KY **D.** 7/28/1840
TEAMS: 88KCA 89–91LouA 92–94PitN 95StLN 96–97CinN 98LouN
DEBUT: 7/7/1888 at Kansas City; caught by Jim Donahue and beat Baltimore's Matt Kilroy 13–9
FINALE: 6/25/1898 at Louisville; relieved Bert Cunningham and was relieved by Bill Magee in a 7–3 loss to Philadelphia's Red Donahue that was charged to Cunningham
FAMOUS FIRST: 7/9/1892 at Pittsburgh; became the first pitcher since the introduction of the "modern" substitution rule in 1891 to serve as a pinch hitter for a pitcher and then not remain in the game to pitch when he singled in the fourth inning while batting for Will Thompson and Mark Baldwin then finished the 7–5 loss to Brooklyn's Bill Hart

Fun-loving and temperamental Red Ehret was named after a famous poet, brought alligators North from spring training, and ran his fingers through the hair of African American children "to put a kink in his pitches." The lanky redhead walked onto the Western League St. Joseph Reds at age 17 in 1886 and went 20-25 the next year in the same loop. Cut loose when the WL had financial troubles, he opened 1888 with Austin and was the Texas League sensation playing everywhere except catcher and batting cleanup. Ehret had an 8-4 record when Austin disbanded on June 30 and was sold to Kansas City AA three days later. Despite good work for the last-place Cowboys, he sat on the bench most of the year.

Ehret's hometown Louisville team purchased him in 1889. In his first full ML season he avoided 30 losses in his final start on October 12 when the last-place Colonels scored four runs in the ninth inning. In 1890, with Jack Chapman at the reins, Ehret's 16-5 mark in the second half of the season helped fellow Kentucky ace Scott Stratton bring Louisville its only ML pennant. In the final AA–NL World's Series, Ehret beat Brooklyn's 30-game winner Tom Lovett twice.

The redhead jumped Louisville for Lincoln, NE, of the Western Association just before the Fourth of July in 1891 and with three weeks remaining in the WA season was sold as a hired gun to first place Sioux City. Louisville spitefully noted that Ehret was still reserved "although not wanted," and the chance of a permanent blacklist loomed. However, when Sioux City manager Al Buckenberger secured the Pittsburgh VP role for 1892, he procured Ehret from the Colonels. He missed six weeks with a sore arm early in 1892 but logged over 250 innings after the Fourth of July. Ehret maintained the same workload in 1893 but was unable to win when the team slumped in June, a pattern that repeated in 1894. After he was traded that off-season to St. Louis for Pink Hawley, Pittsburgh writer Frank

McQuiston considered it a mistake and offered to bet that Ehret would win more games than Hawley in 1895. McQuiston was silenced when Ehret suffered through a miserable year with the eleventh-place Browns and at one point would have been winless in seventeen consecutive starts if he had not been credited with a specious win against Washington during that skein.

In late November 1895 Ehret went to Cincinnati in a multiplayer deal. With the Reds, he sported an 18-7 record to August 20 and helped Cincinnati hold first place for much of the summer. Then an 11-game losing streak hit the team. Before the Reds dropped from contention, however, Ehret created a scandal in August when he sold his potential share of Temple Cup proceeds to Frank Foreman for $100 and later tried to ameliorate the situation by claiming it was done only as a joke that neither Foreman nor he took seriously.

The following year Ehret slipped to just 8 wins. In February 1898 he was involved in another multiplayer trade that took him to Louisville in exchange for southpaw Bill Hill. When the Colonels released Ehret in 1898, a seven-year minor league career began with Cortland of the New York State League in 1899 followed by a 23-loss season with last-place Minneapolis of the upstart American League in 1900. Ehret umpired in the Southern Association in 1905 after going 10-11 for Memphis the previous year in his final full pro season. He officiated again in the Northwestern League in 1907 but quit that venue for good on August 4 after a surge of one-hundred angry fans threatening him from the RF bleachers in Seattle tumbled onto the field when a railing broke, leaving many injured. Hiding in the clubhouse, Ehret hastily wrote a resignation letter. When next heard from in 1908, he was running a saloon in Memphis. Ehret died at Cincinnati's General Hospital in 1940 of rectal cancer. (FV/DN)

Emslie, Robert Daniel / "Bob" "Wig"

B	T	HGT	WGT	G	IP	H	GS
R	R	5'11"	180	91	792.1	775	90

CG	BB	SO	SH	W	L	PCT	ERA
85	165	362	5	44	44	.500	3.19

B. 1/27/1859 Guelph, Ontario, Canada

D. 4/26/1943

TEAMS: 83–85BalA 85PhiA

DEBUT: 7/25/1883 at Baltimore; caught by Rooney Sweeney and beat Pittsburgh's Denny Driscoll and Billy Taylor 13–9

FINALE: 7/16/1885 at St. Louis; caught by Jack O'Brien, finished the game in RF and lost 13–11 to St. Louis's George McGinnis and Dave Foutz

Nicknamed "Wig" because he wore a hairpiece, Bob Emslie was said to be the "best wing shot" in Canada even before he began to make his way in baseball with the semipro Harrison Giants in the late 1870s. Also on the team for a time was outfielder Tip O'Neill. After spending 1880–81 with a club in his hometown of Guelph, Emslie joined the St. Thomas, Ontario, Atlantics in 1882 until he drew an offer from the Merritt club of Camden, NJ. He remained with the Merritts until they disbanded in 1883 while atop the Interstate Association. The highest paid team member at $150 a month, Emslie received little more than that when he left Camden to join the last-place AA Baltimore Orioles. In the remaining weeks of the 1883 season he compiled a 9-13 record, spectacular on a team that was otherwise a dreadful 19-55.

In 1884 Baltimore improved dramatically when several new players were added, and Emslie finished 32-17. Early the following season, probably in a game against Brooklyn on April 25, Emslie hurt his arm—*TSN*'s description of the injury in February 1896 made it appear to have been a torn rotator cuff—and was unable to pitch again until May 9 when he lost 9–1 to Louisville. Released by Baltimore soon thereafter, he suffered the same fate in Philadelphia after a four-game trial in which he went 0-4.

Emslie assayed a comeback with Toronto of the International Association the following year, winning 12 of his first 16 decisions, but then "wilted badly" and quit active play early in 1887 after an unsuccessful trial in the Southern League. Several weeks later he launched his second and more significant career in baseball on July 1, Dominion Day, when he was asked to umpire an International Association game between Toronto and Hamilton after the scheduled official failed to appear. He then served as a regular IA umpire until he joined the American Association staff in 1890. Poorly received in several AA bastions, and especially Columbus, he began the following year in the Western League. In August, Emslie was offered a job as a replacement umpire in the NL. He officiated his first NL game August 19, 1891, at Cincinnati and did not put his blue uniform in mothballs to stay until serving as the base umpire in both ends of a senior loop DH at St. Louis on September 28, 1924. Upon his departure, he held the record (since broken) for the most games as a ML umpire with 4,228.

Emslie is best remembered as the base umpire in the famous "Merkle Game" at New York's Polo Grounds on September 23, 1908. His reluctance to make a call at 2B on the play led Giants manager John McGraw to nickname him "Blind Bob." It was one of the milder examples of the cruel jibes umpires early in Emslie's career had to endure. In March 1897 *TSN* crowed how easy it would be for Indian outfielder Chief Sockalexis to scalp Emslie because he wore a wig.

After putting away his indicator Emslie served as NL Chief of Umpires for a time. Remaining physically active deep into old age, he coached youth baseball and was an excellent bowler and golfer as well as a top-notch curler with the St. Thomas Granites. He died at 84 in St. Thomas and was inducted into the Canadian Baseball HOF in 1986. (DN)

Esper, Charles H. (b. Esbacher) **/ "Duke"**

B	T	HGT	WGT	G	IP	H	GS
?	L	5'11½"	185	236	1727.2	2048	198

CG	BB	SO	SH	W	L	PCT	ERA
152	669	453	4	101	100	.502	4.39

B. 7/28/1867 Salem, NJ **D.** 8/31/1910
TEAMS: 90PhiA 90PitN 90–92PhiN 92PitN 93–94WasN 94–96BalN 97–98StLN
DEBUT: 4/18/1890 at Philadelphia; relieved Ed Seward in the fifth inning and bagged a 12–9 win over Rochester's John Fitzgerald
FINALE: 7/12/1898 at New York; caught by Jack Clements and lost 7–1 to New York's Jouett Meekin

A left-handed dipsy doodler that finished one game above .500 in 201 decisions, Duke Esper was one of three journeymen pitchers whose unforeseen success with Baltimore in the mid 1890s made Ned Hanlon look like a genius. His pitches had little speed; when he won he was a "puzzle" and when he lost he looked as hittable as a teenager at a Sunday school picnic. A slim Philadelphia ironworker, Esper was 21 and afflicted with heart palpitations when Billy Sharsig took him from Smyrna of the Delaware League to serve as an extra pitcher on Philadelphia AA in 1890.

Used mostly at home, Esper opened 7–4, and the A's held first place in the AA for fifty-six consecutive days. But the club then finished 14-57, arguably the worst late-season collapse in ML history, and Esper was among the team's first blunders when he was cut on August 2. Pittsburgh NL, headed for an even worse finish, gave Esper two late-August starts in the midst of a club-record 23-game losing streak. Harry Wright then corralled Esper as the Phillies embarked on their final road trip. The rookie won each of his five outings, securing a place on Wright's 1891 squad, where he won 20 games. Big victories included a May 13 outing, when Esper beat Cleveland in fourteen innings, prompting The *Philadelphia North American* to run this classified ad: "Wanted: Pitcher with heart disease." Esper's 3 wins in 1891 over Cleveland fireballer Cy Young were also impressive. Early in 1893 he upped his record against Young to 5-0 and became known as the "Cy Young beater." Esper would start more times against Young in his heyday than any other pitcher except Kid Nichols, although Young would eventually even their duel at 7-7.

In mid 1892 Wright acquired Phil Knell and released Esper despite the fact that his 6 straight wins nearly landed the Phillies the first half flag in that year's split-season schedule. Esper won both of his two starts with Pittsburgh to close out 1892 but was given another "unconditional release" in November. He worked that winter as a bartender in Philly amid talk that his heart problems would preclude his return to the diamond and then signed with lowly Washington, where he received execrable offensive and defensive support. Esper ended up logging 334 innings and a 12-28 record. Frustrated, he jumped the Senators on May 20, 1894, and was suspended for ten days for general misbehavior. The *Washington Post* announced, "He will never again wear the uniform of a National League club if Manager Schmelz can prevent it," but he returned to give up 116 runs in his next ten starts. Esper's nadir came in July 1894 when he lost an 11–4 lead in the ninth inning and then was forced to pitch the next day because Cy Young was announced for Cleveland. Drubbed 23–4, he was made to suffer through a complete-game 29-hitter.

At the time Baltimore surprisingly held first place after a string of sub-.500 years. But when the Orioles lost 7 straight games, manager Ned Hanlon bought Esper cheaply from Washington and put him in a rotation with his old Philadelphia pitching partners, Kid Gleason and Sadie McMahon. Working once a week, Esper reeled off a 10-2 record to help seal the Orioles' first pennant as the *Washington Post*, only weeks earlier his main denunciator, proclaimed:,"When everything is considered, Charley Esper is better entitled to the honor of being the League's star left-handed pitcher than any other southpaw in the League, Breitenstein not excepted." He then opened Game 1 of the Temple Cup series but lost to Amos Rusie, as New York went on to sweep four straight.

Esper gained weight and lost some stamina over his three years with Baltimore, but the Orioles put together a dynasty with him always doing well down the stretch. On October 7, 1895, he shut out Cleveland in the postseason for Baltimore's only win of that Temple Cup series. In 1896 he won 7 of his last 8 decisions. His drop ball was at its best and his change up "tantalizing." But the Orioles' stretch drive fatigued him, and he started only once after September 1.

Seemingly finished, Esper was sold to Milwaukee of the Western League on February 20, 1897, but the sale was canceled when St. Louis owner Chris Von der Ahe claimed he had not waived on the aging southpaw. Esper made his first start for St. Louis against his favorite foe, Cy Young, on April 29 and fashioned a 6-6 tie. After that he was winless until June and eventually was suspended for being "out of condition." Returning unwillingly to St. Louis in 1898, he started 3-0 but was released in July after losing his next five decisions. Esper appeared briefly in the Eastern League and then hired on as a policeman in his hometown of Philadelphia. Later he managed a restaurant there for ten years before declining health and liver failure claimed him at his home in Philadelphia at 45. He was buried under his birth name, Esbacher. We have yet to learn when he adopted the name of Esper and how he acquired the nickname of "Duke." (FV/DN/DB)

*Ewing, John / "John" "Long John" "Carmencita"

B	T	HGT	WGT	G	IP	H	GS
?	R	6'1"	168	129	1058.2	1113	121

CG	BB	SO	SH	W	L	PCT	ERA
113	390	525	9	53	63	.457	3.68

B. 6/1/1863 Cincinnati, OH **D.** 4/23/1895
TEAMS: 83StLA 84CinU 84WasU 88–89LouA 90NYP 91NYN
DEBUT: 6/18/1883 at St. Louis; played CF and went 0-for-5 in an 8–7 win over New York's Jack Lynch
FINALE: 10/1/1891 at New York; caught by Buster Burrell and lost 6–3 to Brooklyn's Dave Foutz

John Ewing was nicknamed Carmencita because his gyrations in the pitcher's box resembled those of Carmencita, a famous Spanish fan dancer in the South while he was pitching in the Southern League. For years, however, he was daunted by having to play in his older brother Buck's shadow. In early 1883, while Ewing was with the amateur Cincinnati Shamrocks, his brother convinced St. Louis Browns owner Chris Von der Ahe that his younger sibling was a hot prospect, but Ewing seemed anything but that when he appeared in St. Louis "as big around as a fishing pole" and was swiftly released after Mets outfielder Chief Roseman hit a ball over his head in CF and the crowd so rattled him that he was unable to pick it up in time to prevent Roseman from scoring a home run. Before leaving St. Louis, Ewing begged Al Spink not to write about his gaffe for fear it would appear in the Cincinnati papers and embarrass him. Word of the blunder got around, however, and for years Ewing had to live down a reputation for being brilliant in practice but so overcome by stage fright in games that his play "was decidedly yellow."

By 1884 Ewing's image as being too soft ever to succeed in baseball had reached such epic proportions that he no sooner appeared in uniform with the Washington UA club than manager Mike Scanlon complained, "That long stiff never saw Buck Ewing. Take him away before I kill him." The following two years Ewing turned entirely to pitching with an independent team in Richmond, IN, and then moved to the Southern League until June 1888 when Memphis sold him and catcher Harry Vaughn to Louisville. After his first eleven starts with the Colonels, Ewing had a dazzling 1.00 ERA but finished just 8-13 with the seventh-place club. In 1889 he started Louisville's season opener and also its finale and won both. In between, however, he was 4-30 and was in the box on July 22 at St. Louis when Louisville lost its all-time-record 26th straight game en route to a 27-111 finish. The owner of a 14-43 career record to that point, Ewing would hardly have been pursued by the Brotherhood had his brother not all but strong-armed the New York PL team to take him.

In 1890 the Ewing brothers were the most successful sibling battery in history prior to Wes and Rick Ferrell, as Buck logged a .951 OPS and the pitching half went 18-12. Nevertheless, Ewing was still suspect, and Buck first had to coax manager Jim Mutrie into hiring him for the NL Giants after the PL folded and then demand that he be put in the rotation after twin aces Mickey Welch and Tim Keefe both stumbled out of the starting gate. Ewing did not make his first start until May 8, when he blanked Boston 7–0. After that he cruised to a 21-6 record before losing his last two appearances of the season. Extolled by the local press, Ewing had only one critic in New York, catcher Dick Buckley, who accused him of lacking the necessary "sand" to pull himself together in games whenever he started to get hit.

That winter Ewing had a severe attack of the grippe and then suffered a relapse in February 1892. It soon emerged that he had something much more serious. Toward the end of the month, *TSN* proclaimed that he was lying in his home in Pendleton, OH, dying of consumption, but he then rallied miraculously and *TSN* happily reported that he was expected to be ready to pitch his first game in June.

Come June 1892, however, Ewing decided he would forgo trying to pitch that season. He ultimately quit the game and went to Colorado Springs for his health. In December 1893 *TSN* announced that he had been seen in Colorado and looked "as if he was good for many years to come." Two Aprils later Ewing's long battle with the one of the most dreaded diseases of his time ended when he was seized with violent hemorrhaging in Denver, where he had gone in an effort to acclimate himself to return east. Prior to his death he made out a will and stipulated that he wanted Long John Reilly and Harry Vaughn to act as pallbearers along with his brother. (DN)

Fagan, William A. / "Bill" "Clinkers"

B	T	HGT	WGT	G	IP	H	GS
?	L	5'11"	165	23	187.1	234	23

CG	BB	SO	SH	W	L	PCT	ERA
21	99	61	0	6	15	.286	5.28

B. 2/15/1869 Troy, NY **D.** 3/21/1930

TEAMS: 87NYA 88KCA

DEBUT: 9/15/1887 at Cincinnati; caught by Jim Donahue and lost 4–0 to Cincinnati's Tony Mullane

FINALE: 7/20/1888 at St. Louis; caught by Fatty Briody and lost 18–5 to St. Louis's Jim Devlin

The son of a Troy dump cart driver, Bill Fagan came to the Mets in 1887 from Lynn of the New England League with a reputation as a teenage phenom and a bit of a comedian. After his first look at his new pitcher, Mets skipper Opie Caylor compared him to 1887 rookie sensation Elmer Smith and declared, "I have seldom failed in my estimation of young pitchers, and I'll pit Fagan's professional future against the best of them." Although he won just one of six starts, Fagan truly did fare moderately well with a weak seventh-place finisher and on October 10 had the distinction of pitching the Mets' final game as a member of the AA, a 4–0 loss to Baltimore.

Sent to Kansas City when Brooklyn skimmed the cream off the disbanding Mets and sold the rest to the Mets' AA replacement entry, Fagan soon lived up to his nickname, although he originally earned it for his musical talents. He turned in a couple of well-pitched games early in the season, including his first win with his new team on May 4, when he edged Cincinnati 4–3. But after his final ML win on June 23 over St. Louis, he lost his next five starts, culminating with an 18–5 clinker that put the Browns in first place to stay for the rest of the season.

Upon his release Fagan went home to nurse his wounds. Still just turned 20, he joined Denver the following spring and started the 1889 Western Association season by reportedly winning his first 11 games, all of them on cloudy, cool days, only to wilt in his next start on a hot, sunny afternoon and be fined $100 by manager Dave Rowe for "indifferent" work. From that experience, Rowe, who had been Fagan's manager at Kansas City early in the 1888 AA season, learned to save his young pitcher for cooler weather, of which there was precious little once summer arrived in the Mile High City.

By the following year a limp arm compounded Fagan's troubles with heat. Released by Omaha of the Western Association, he returned to the East, his career in tatters at age 21. Two years later *TSN* reported that after his failed comeback in the Pennsylvania State League, he and a former Omaha teammate, Tom Flanagan, were working as a song and dance team in the Troy area. When Fagan's show business ambitions faded, he became a brush maker until he was confined to his Troy home with nephritis in 1912 and died there eighteen years later. (DN)

Ferson, Alexander / "Alex" "Colonel"

B	T	HGT	WGT	G	IP	H	GS
R	R	5'9"	165	48	368.1	424	45

CG	BB	SO	SH	W	L	PCT	ERA
36	151	106	1	18	25	.419	4.37

B. 7/14/1866 Philadelphia, PA **D.** 12/5/1957
TEAMS: 89WasN 90BufP 92BalN
DEBUT: 5/4/1889 at Washington; caught by Connie Mack and lost 3–2 to Boston's John Clarkson
FINALE: 7/25/1892 at Baltimore; relieved Sadie McMahon and was later relieved by George Cobb in McMahon's 10–1 loss to Chicago's Bill Hutchison

Alex Ferson's handicaps were being on the frail side and being so slow a worker that he maddened teammates who had to play the field behind him on a series of bad clubs. In each of his three ML seasons, he had the wretched luck to pitch for a cellar dweller. Ferson's pro unveiling came in the 1886 Pennsylvania State League. A good performance with Manchester of the New England League the following summer earned him an invitation to accompany the NL Quakers on a fall barnstorming tour with hopes of making the club in 1888. But when Ferson returned to Philadelphia before the trip was over with a sore arm, he was deemed a "dire failure." He thus started 1888 with Milwaukee of the Western Association but was released when his arm was still ailing. Given a second ML chance the following spring, he made a weak Washington entry, beginning the season as a regular member of the rotation and emerging as the staff ace with a 17-17 log for a team that was otherwise 24-66. His effort made him only the second qualifier in ML history to post a .500 record with a last-place club. But as effective as Ferson was his rookie season with a ball in his hands, he was equally dismal (.113) with a bat in them. The *Washington Star* unkindly noted in May 1889, "Ferson is another Gilmore at the bat. He strikes out with the greatest ease."

In 1890 Ferson went from the frying pan into the fire when he jumped from the NL's weakest team to Buffalo, fated to finished last in the PL, 20 games behind seventh-place Cleveland. With him also came a sore arm that he was warned to rest or risk ruining it. Instead Ferson foolishly tried to pitch through his pain. After winning his initial start with the Bisons on April 21, he lost all seven of his remaining decisions before belatedly taking his doctor's advice and shutting down for the season following an 18–4 pounding at New York on July 9.

Sent home without pay, Ferson sat idle until the spring of 1891 when he joined Syracuse of the Eastern Association. Except for a brief stint with last-place Baltimore in 1892, he labored for the rest of the century in the minors, primarily in northern New England. In retrospect, Ferson almost certainly had too fragile an arm to withstand the workload demanded of a frontline starter in his day, especially one with a weak team. On a unit that could have afforded to use him more sparingly, he might have developed into one of the better pitchers of the 1890s.

In later life Ferson operated restaurants in Worcester and Dorchester, MA. Upon his death in Boston at 91, he was buried in Manchester, NH. At the time Ferson was Connie Mack's last surviving Players League batterymate. (DN)

Fifield, John Proctor / "Jack"

B	T	HGT	WGT	G	IP	H	GS
R	R	5'11"	160	68	521.2	616	64

CG	BB	SO	SH	W	L	PCT	ERA
54	193	89	3	21	39	.350	4.59

B. 10/5/1871 Enfield, NH **D.** 11/27/1939
TEAMS: 97–99PhiN 99WasN
DEBUT: 4/28/1897 at Philadelphia; caught by Mike Grady and lost 6–5 to Boston's Fred Klobedanz
FINALE: 10/12/1899 at Washington; caught by Doc Powers and lost 5–4 to New York's Ed Doheny

Prior to turning pro, Jack Fifield played halfback for Dartmouth and also pitched for the school's baseball team; he later served as Dartmouth's head baseball coach. After spending 1894 with independent clubs in New Hampshire, he joined Little Rock of the Southern League in 1895. Late that summer he was nearly purchased by the Phillies but instead went to Detroit of the Western League. When he went 28-13 the following year, the Phillies no longer waffled over whether to acquire him.

Fifield's first ML appearance in 1897 resulted in the Phillies' first loss of the season after a 5-0 start as well as Boston's first win after a 0-5 start. The two clubs went opposite directions after that; Boston won the pennant while the Phillies sank deep into the second division under rookie pilot George Stallings, Fifield's skipper at Detroit. The fault, at least initially, was not Fifield's. After posting the Phils' 13th win of the season at Louisville on May 14, he then had to stop a 10-game club losing streak two weeks later at Chicago. When he followed with a prolonged losing skein of his own, rumors whirled that a clique of older team members viewed him as Stallings's pet and deliberately played badly behind him. Fifield finished his frosh year just 5-18 and lost a chance for a sixth win on July 24 when his teammates, perhaps in a calculated attempt to thwart him, erupted against umpire McGinty in the ninth inning while holding a 4–3 lead, forcing McGinty to forfeit the game to Cleveland. He was nonetheless reserved for the following year and celebrated by marrying Ethel Wolfroe in the spring of 1898 and then going 11-9 with a fine 3.31 ERA.

In 1899, Fifield began well, winning two of his first three starts, but then slumped, scoring just 1 more win in Phillies garb, an 8–4 verdict over St. Louis on June 9. After losing his next three starts Fifield was released to Minneapolis of the Western League. Less than a month later, however, Minneapolis returned him to the Phils for "indifferent work." In September 1899 Philadelphia unloaded Fifield on eleventh-place Washington, where he began poorly but fared better toward the end of the season. One of the many casualties of the NL's decrease in 1900 to just eight teams, Fifield returned to the minors with Detroit of the newly renamed American League but was held by injuries to just five appearances and a 0-2 record. He then spent eight more seasons in the New York State League before departing the pro arena in 1908. Fifield died in Syracuse at 68. (DN)

Fisher, Chauncey Burr / "Chauncey" "Peach" "Fish"

B	T	HGT	WGT	G	IP	H	GS
R	R	5'11"	175	65	435.2	583	44

CG	BB	SO	SH	W	L	PCT	ERA
36	140	80	3	21	26	.447	5.37

B. 1/8/1872 Anderson, IN **D.** 4/27/1939
TEAMS: 93–94CleN 94CinN 96CinN 97BroN 01NYN 01StLN
DEBUT: 9/20/1893 at Cleveland; caught by Chief Zimmer and lost 9–6 to Boston's Jack Stivetts
FINALE: 7/6/1901 at St. Louis; relieved Jack Harper and then was relieved by Farmer Burns in Harper's 14–9 loss to Philadelphia's Doc White
FAMOUS INCIDENT: *See* Alfred Manassau

The brother of twentieth-century ML pitcher Tom Fisher, Chauncey, the elder Fisher, may have been better at poker than baseball. During his scant time in the majors he often won as much as $100 at a sitting. Fisher first gained plaudits with the local Anderson independent team in 1890. He then pitched with several small minor league clubs before joining Buffalo of the Eastern League in 1893. After hurling three consecutive shutouts for the Bisons and faring well against Cleveland in an exhibition game, he was sold to the Spiders in September for $1,000. Unimpressive with Cleveland, he was released to Cincinnati in 1894 and did no better there, finishing the year with a composite 7.76 ERA.

In the spring of 1895 Fisher was farmed to Indianapolis along with several other players the Reds were not ready to quit on completely. That August, *TSN* proclaimed, "Fisher is the scrappiest pitcher in the Western," and Cincinnati owner John T. Brush swore he would be back with the Reds in 1896. Brush could not help but live up to his word when Fisher led the WL with 36 wins. In his second ML trial the Indiana righty showed improvement, particularly at holding base runners, and had 10 wins by August 1896 for the contending Reds when Brush suddenly farmed him again to Indianapolis, ostensibly to aid the Hoosiers in a late pennant bid of their own. That November, when Fisher was traded to Brooklyn along with Germany Smith and $1,000 for Tommy Corcoran, it emerged that Brush had farmed a useful pitcher in the heat of the 1896 NL pennant race to placate Buck Ewing, who disliked the young Hoosier. Although happy to escape Cincinnati and Ewing, Fisher evidently also had his problems in 1897 with Brooklyn manager Billy Barnie. Even though he was second on the team in ERA, he worked only 149 innings. Late in the season Fisher appeared to get it all together. On September 25 he blanked Philadelphia, and a week later he won Brooklyn's season finale against pennant-bound Boston. Yet he found himself farmed once again in 1898, this time to a weak Omaha Western League team, where he nonetheless won 23 games. Fisher acted as player-manager for part of the season before he was fired for dissipation but was still drafted by Baltimore NL for 1899.

Within days it developed that the Orioles had acquired Fisher solely to farm him to Buffalo. While *TSN* harrumphed that it was unfair to draft a man and then send him to a team in the same classification, thereby blocking his path to advance in his profession, Fisher spent the winter captaining the Indianapolis roller polo team and then, with Hoosier manager Bob Allen's complicity, wangled an assignment to Indianapolis of the Western League for the coming season. A member of Allen's WL pennant winner in 1899, Fisher had an even more rewarding championship thrill the following season when he went 19-9 for the 1900 Chicago White Stockings, the first flag winner in the newly renamed American League.

Rather than accompany Chicago when the AL went major in 1901, Fisher returned to the NL, signing with New York, where he was expected to be third in the rotation behind Dummy Taylor and Christy Mathewson. Instead he was released after one horrific start against Philadelphia and then had to wait until the Cardinals signed him. But a single relief appearance was all Patsy Donovan, Fisher's last ML manager, could abide. Fisher was released in late July for being overweight and spending too much time at racetracks.

Was Fisher potentially a good ML pitcher who played under the wrong managers and was an unfortunate victim of the NL's reprehensible farming practices in the late 1890s? Or did he get less than he deserved from his talents because he consistently alienated NL clubs he might otherwise have helped? The Fisher of 1895–1900, in any case, was unquestionably a pitcher of ML caliber. He later ran a wrecking business in his native Anderson for some thirty years before retiring to Los Angeles, where he died of prostate cancer. (DN)

Fitzgerald, Warren Bartholomew / "Warren"

B	T	HGT	WGT	G	IP	H	GS
?	L	5'9"	162	36	301	310	35

CG	BB	SO	SH	W	L	PCT	ERA
32	100	113	3	15	20	429	3.43

B. 4/?/1868 ?, Pennsylvania **D.** 11/7/1930
TEAMS: 91–92LouA
DEBUT: 6/4/1891 at Louisville; caught by Jack Ryan and beat Boston's Bill Daley 6–5
FINALE: 6/8/1892 at Washington; caught by Jack Grim and lost 12–1 to Washington's Frank Killen

Warren Fitzgerald was working as a sceneshifter at Taber's Opera House in Leadville, CO, when his coworkers formed a baseball team. The taciturn youth forgot his stage aspirations when he became the club's star pitcher. Shortly before his 19th birthday in the spring of 1891, Fitzgerald joined Seattle of the Pacific Northwest League, where he remained until Louisville acquired him. The southpaw was a surprise success with the Colonels, as was fellow rookie Hughie Jennings. In part because both were native Pennsylvanians, they became friends and road roommates.

After a solid rookie year Fitzgerald returned to Colorado and kept in shape over the winter ice skating. In 1892, however, he encountered arm trouble soon after reporting for spring training. He began the season still on the mend and apparently never fully recovered. Following four poor starts, he was released by the Colonels and joined the Deppens, a Louisville semipro team. Upon receiving an offer to return to the Pacific Northwest League with Spokane, Fitzgerald headed west. Soon after rejoining Spokane, he recognized that his arm would never again be sound and went back to Leadville and his old job as a sceneshifter. Fitzgerald remained in the West for the rest of his life, dying in Phoenix of asthma in 1930. (DN)

*Foreman, Francis Isiah / "Frank" "Monkey"

B	T	HGT	WGT	G	IP	H	GS
L	L	6'0"	160	202	1506	1606	180

CG	BB	SO	SH	W	L	PCT	ERA
148	599	542	6	84	84	.500	3.98

G	AB	H	R	2B	3B	HR
216	645	140	91	20	13	9

RBI	BB	SO	SB	BA	SA	OBP
62	59	109	17	.217	.330	.292

B. 5/1/1863 Baltimore, MD **D.** 11/19/1957
TEAMS: 84ChiU 84KCU 85BalA 89BalA 90–91CinN 91–92WasN 92BalN 93NYN 95–96CinN 01BosAL 01–02BalAL

DEBUT: 5/15/1884 at Chicago; caught by Tony Suck and beat Washington's Milo Lockwood 8–3
FINALE: 5/10/1902 at Philadelphia; caught by Wilbert Robinson and lost 13–4 to the A's Pete Husting

The brother of ML pitcher Brownie Foreman and his teammate for a time on the 1896 Reds, Frank Foreman is the only man to play in the UA, AA, NL, and AL, and also the last UA graduate to still be active in the majors in the twentieth century. Nicknamed "Monkey" for his facial antics, Foreman survived a myriad of changes in pitching styles and an increase in pitching distance, and he toiled under every major pitching rule change that occurred between 1884 and the present day except one; by spending his final two seasons in the AL he never reaped the benefit the NL handed pitchers when it introduced the foul-strike rule in 1901.

As a southpaw Foreman was seen as the perfect complement to staff ace Hugh Daily when he joined Chicago UA in 1884 but was released after he completed only one of his first three starts. He joined Kansas City UA just long enough to be belted in one start and then finished the season with Lancaster of the Keystone Association. Foreman was pitching for a semipro team in his Baltimore hometown in 1885 when Orioles manager Billy Barnie hired him for 3 games. Though he won 2 of them, he was hit hard and relegated again to the semipro ranks.

Foreman did not really begin to make his way in pro ball until 1888 when ex-Oriole Tom York hired him to pitch and play the outfield for Albany of the International Association. When he returned to the AA with Baltimore the following year, he won his first six starts and was particularly effective against the loop's two strongest teams, Brooklyn and St. Louis, owing to a live fastball that Cincinnati outfielder Bug Holliday said "has a jump to it which makes it mighty hard for a batsman to hit it safely." Foreman finished the season with 10.89 base runners allowed per nine innings, the best figure among AA pitchers in a minimum of 200 frames.

By the time Baltimore resigned from the AA late in 1889, Foreman had waffled repeatedly over whether to jump to the Philadelphia PL club or remain with the Orioles, until he was finally sold to Cincinnati, which had also resigned from the AA and moved to the NL. Regarded as a prize acquisition, he signed a three-year deal for $6,000 per annum but was just 13-10 for a contending team in 1890 and later tried unsuccessfully to sue the Reds for the remaining two years of his contract after the club was sold and its new owners gave him only one partial game the following spring (as an outfielder no less) to prove himself before dumping him. Foreman then signed with Washington AA, led the last-place club in wins with 18 and, more significantly, became the last player who was largely a pitcher to pace his team in home runs, albeit with just four.

The 1891 season would be Foreman's last as a staff leader. After two marginal seasons in 1892–93 that were spent partly in the minors, he was consigned to Toledo of the Western League in 1894. The following spring he returned to Cincinnati and was part of the Reds' four-man rotation but won just 11 games. In 1896 he improved to 14-7 and a career high .667 winning percentage. Even though he appeared in less than 200 innings, he bizarrely became a huge drawing card. After working in front of the two largest crowds to attend a Reds game the previous season, on Sunday July 19, 1896, with Cincinnati in first place, he started against Baltimore in front of over 24,000, the largest crowd in Queen City history to that point. Exactly a week later at Cincinnati, in front of 22,000, he beat Cy Young 10–1, but soon after that his arm went back on him, restricting him to the bench from August 23 until the last day of the season when he made his final NL start, again beating Young and the Temple Cup–bound Spiders, 7–3.

Foreman's trouble may have stemmed from a shoulder injury he suffered in a tussle with Pittsburgh first baseman Jake Beckley in May 1895. In any event, he was farmed to Indianapolis prior to the 1897 season and then released by the Hoosiers in April when manager Bill Watkins proclaimed: "He is done for." Foreman proved Watkins wrong, however, by winning 30 games after the Hoosiers rehired him and 24 more in 1898. After pitching for Buffalo of the Western League in 1899, he remained with the Bisons in 1900 when the WL became the newly renamed American League.

Buffalo was dropped from the AL after 1900 and Foreman signed for 1901 with the new Boston AL entry but was released after Washington pummeled him 9–4 on May 3. He then worked out at his Baltimore home until cajoling Orioles player-manager John McGraw to test him in a game and was signed for the balance of the season after he set down flag-winning Chicago 8–1 on June 12. Foreman's arm went back on him again in 1902, holding him to just 2 games before McGraw cut him. Credited by some sources with discovering HOFer Eddie Plank while coaching for Gettysburg College in the spring of 1901, Foreman was bedridden for the last eighteen months of his life before his death in Baltimore at 94 removed the last surviving UA participant. (DN)

Fox, John Joseph / "John"

B	T	HGT	WGT	G	IP	H	GS
?	?	?	?	45	356.2	440	43

CG	BB	SO	SH	W	L	PCT	ERA
38	98	104	0	13	28	.317	4.16

B. 2/7/1859 Roxbury, MA **D.** 4/16/1893
TEAMS: 81BosN 83BalA 84PitA 86WasN
DEBUT: 6/2/1881 at Boston; caught by Charlie Snyder and lost 6–1 to Cleveland's "The Only" Nolan
FINALE: 8/9/1886 at Washington; caught by Jackie Hayes and lost 13–3 to St. Louis's John Healy

John Fox was considered a "heavy ball tricky" pitcher and a good batter, but there is no surviving evidence of the latter and he appears to have been unable to keep pace with the rapid changes in pitching rules during the early 1880s. Invited to train with Boston in the spring of 1881, he was released but then rehired when Tommy Bond's arm failed and manager Harry Wright suddenly found himself with no one to spell rookie ace Jim Whitney. Like Whitney, Fox frequently played the outfield on days he didn't pitch, but when he hit just .178 and Bobby Mathews made a successful comeback in 1882, he was not reserved.

After a year in independent ball, Fox resurfaced with Baltimore AA in 1883 and was designated the team's ace in the preseason by manager Billy Barnie. On Opening Day Fox ruined the New York Mets' AA inaugural by beating Tim Keefe 4–3. He batted leadoff that day, as he did during most of his stay in Baltimore, and appears to have been the last ML pitcher to be used regularly as a leadoff hitter. Fox's usage in that critical spot in the order is an example of Barnie at his most bizarre, for the AA averages at the end of May ranked Fox the worst hitter in the loop. He finished his Baltimore sojourn with a .152 BA and was released to Trenton of the Interstate Association after winning just six of nineteen starts. By late August, Fox was with Wilmington in the same loop when Cleveland manager Frank Bancroft offered $300, catcher Cal Broughton, and rookie pitcher Will Sawyer for him, plus the promise to play an exhibition game in Wilmington, but the deal fell through when the Cleveland president refused to part with Broughton and Sawyer's parents would not let him play so far from home.

Notwithstanding Fox's numerous failures thus far, his arm was still promising enough to induce Pittsburgh AA to sign him for 1884 and pitch him on Opening Day. After losing 9–2 to Philadelphia Fox appeared the following afternoon at SS. It was his last ML game as a position player, but Pittsburgh's campaign to make him its frontline pitcher continued for another month. Released again to Trenton (now in the Eastern League) after winning just 1 game, Fox served out the remainder of his career in the minors save for his final ML appearance in 1886 at Washington. Soon after that he was out of baseball, but the December 1, 1889, *Boston Globe* noted, "John Fox, the old Boston league pitcher, talks of going back into the business. Few pitchers had a better arm than Fox." But it was only talk. Fox died in Boston at 34. (DN)

Fraser, Charles Carrolton / "Chick"

B	T	HGT	WGT	G	IP	H	GS
R	R	5'10½"	188	174	1382.2	1537	163

CG	BB	SO	SH	W	L	PCT	ERA
135	595	364	6	72	87	.453	4.21

B. 3/17/1871 Chicago, IL **D.** 5/8/1940
TEAMS: 96–98LouN 98CleN 99–00PhiN 01PhiAL 02–04PhiN 05BosN 06CinN 07–09ChiN
DEBUT AND FAMOUS FIRST: 4/16/1896 at Louisville; caught by Jack Warner and lost 4–2 to Chicago's Danny Friend as he became the first hurler at the 60'6" distance to make his ML debut by starting his team's Opening Day game
FINALE: 5/3/1909 at Chicago; relieved Andy Coakley in a 9–2 loss to Pittsburgh's Vic Willis
CAREER HIGHLIGHT: 9/18/1903 at Chicago; no-hit Chicago's Peaches Graham 10–0

Chick Fraser and Fred Clarke were married to sisters whom they met in Chicago in 1896, the first year they were teammates with Louisville after Fraser had won 23 games the previous season for Minneapolis of the Western League. Fraser set the tone for his career in his rookie season when he lost 27 games and led the NL in runs allowed, walks, and wild pitches. After a fourteen-year battle with erratic control that he never quite won, Fraser finished as one of only three pitchers in ML history to lose 200 games (212) and win less than 200 (175). Moreover, his .440 career winning percentage is the lowest among pitchers with 200 or more losses. On the positive side, he is on the select list of hurlers that have enjoyed 20-win seasons in both the AL and the NL.

Growing up in Chicago, Fraser was privileged to hone his craft in the fast Chicago City League in the early 1890s. He graduated to Minneapolis in 1894 and after two seasons with the Western League club had the ill fortune to be acquired by Louisville. In 1896 Fraser and fellow frosh Bill Hill combined to lose a post-1892 rookie tandem record 55 games. After marrying the following spring, he rebounded to go 15-19 for a bad team, only to lose complete command of his control the following year and amplify what had previously been only a minor drinking problem. Despairing of ever making his brother-in-law into a useful pitcher after he started 7-17, player-manager Clarke endorsed his sale to Cleveland in early September 1898. A 5.57 ERA in five starts induced the Spiders to peddle him to Philadelphia prior to the 1899 season for $1,000.

Fraser thrived in his new environment, winning 21 games for the Phillies in 1899 and then leading the team in both wins and ERA in 1900. Failing to get an appropriate salary increase for his good work, he jumped to the AL Philadelphia entry in 1901 and remained just long enough to win 22 games and become the new major loop's first leader in walks and wild pitches. Fraser returned to the Phils in 1902 under legal duress and was a capable starter for a string of NL teams for the next seven seasons. In 1904–06, he set a modern record when he lost 20 games for three consecutive years with three different teams. After finishing his playing career as a player-manager for Decatur of the Three I League in 1912, Fraser continued to manage in the minors and later coached and scouted for several ML teams, including his brother-in-law's Pirates. Fraser was scouting for the Yankees when he died in Wendell, ID, of an illness stemming from an infection that had resulted in the amputation of one leg and was about to force the other one also to be removed. (DN)

Friend, Daniel Sebastian / "Danny"

B	T	HGT	WGT	G	IP	H	GS
L	L	5'9"	175	67	551.2	612	64

CG	BB	SO	SH	W	L	PCT	ERA
58	249	158	1	32	29	.525	4.71

G	AB	H	R	2B	3B	HR
69	238	61	28	9	3	1

RBI	BB	SO	SB	BA	SA	OBP
20	9	6	3	.256	.332	.283

B. 4/18/1873 Cincinnati, OH **D.** 6/1/1942
TEAMS: 95–98ChiN
DEBUT: 9/10/1895 at New York; caught by Tim Donahue and beat New York's Amos Rusie and Les German 13–2
FINALE: 5/8/1898 at Chicago; caught by Tim Donahue and lost 8–2 to Cincinnati's Jack Taylor

Sulky and inconsistent, Danny Friend belied his surname and made few friends despite being a lefty with a good sharp-breaking curve and a live bat. He lacked an overpowering fastball, walked far too many batters, and constantly frustrated his teammates by trying to nibble at the strike zone. Nor was he a man with whom to sit down over a meal on days he pitched. Friend believed that if he dined with anyone who ate anything sour or pickled he was doomed to lose. Thus he refused to eat with Bill Dahlen, who always ordered that type of food, and usually found himself at a table alone once teammates learned of his hoodoo.

After pitching in the Illinois-Iowa League and Oconto of the Wisconsin State League at age 17, Friend became the ace on Fred Doe's 1895 New Bedford New England League team despite demonstrating repeatedly in his first four pro seasons that he was a chronic whiner. After his first loss under Doe, the young southpaw moaned, "Balls over the fence should be doubles." Doe countered by calling him a baby and said he would give him a rattle and "put him in the nursery with the quitters." Boston NL manager Frank Selee visited New Bedford on September 3, 1895, to personally scout the high-strung portsider. Although Friend beat Pawtucket 21–0, hitting a home run and a double, Selee did not sign him because he did not like his off-balance, all-arm pitching mechanics. A Chicago NL scout also happened to be at the game and convinced Colts player-manager Cap Anson that Selee had made one of his rare misjudgments. Anson named Friend his 1896 Opening Day starter, but the hurler, for all his splendid curves and body English, won only half his decisions. On July 1, Friend was having a particularly arduous day against Cleveland when pitcher Walter Thornton, occupying LF that day, misplayed a ball. "The idea of putting pitchers behind me," Friend raged. Then he stalked to the CF clubhouse, to the amazement of his teammates. As he shut the clubhouse door behind him Friend added in a rare moment of self-insight, "I do not seem to be liked by some members of the club." Walking three to five batters a game, Friend finished the year 18-14.

He opened 1897 farmed out to Kansas City of the Western League to work on his control. Chicago recalled him on June 22, and he showcased his new side-arm "Missouri River curves." But he was still as wild as ever. Friend beat Boston in his fifth start after opening the game by hitting the first two batters he faced and then walking the third. In his next start on July 12, at Brooklyn, he gave his arm a rest by lobbing every pitch to the plate in the fifth inning. Brooklyn promptly got five straight singles as his exasperated teammates swore at him. Against Baltimore five days later his teammates swore at Anson to remove him after catcher Kit Kittridge said the southpaw mixed up all the signals in a 20–2 loss. Prior to a later start in Philadelphia, teammates rode Friend so hard in the clubhouse that, in a pique, he went out and gave up seven runs in the first inning. Anxious not to further rattle the hothouse flower, the *Chicago Tribune* timidly commented in its evaluation of his 1897 season only that he was "not confident."

That August 30, in New York, in the top of the ninth inning with Chicago at bat and leading 7–5, home plate umpire Bob Emslie ejected Anson for arguing that it was too dark to continue. In the bottom of the frame Chicago was without a left fielder. Friend, who had the day off and was standing by the gate, threw a white robe over his street clothes and went to LF. New York captain Bill Joyce berated Emslie for permitting a player on the field without a uniform. Emslie countered that Friend *might* have a uniform on underneath the robe. When the Giants made two quick outs, Joyce ordered Tom McCreery, the next hitter due up, not to go to bat, whereupon Emslie called the game on account of darkness, reverting the score back to 7–5 Chicago at the end of the eighth inning and triggering a protest that was eventually disallowed, although it does seem that Joyce had a legitimate gripe in that Friend may have been the last to play illegally in an ML game in street clothes.

When Tom Burns became Chicago's manager in 1898, he gave Friend two early-season starts and then shipped him with pitcher Bert Briggs to Columbus of the Western League for outfielder Sam Mertes. Friend soon was sent from the Ohio capital to Milwaukee, where he was forced to sign a temperance clause just before getting into fight with hack driver Eddie McCloskey in Columbus and stabbing him in the back. He escaped felony charges when the cabbie refused to prosecute, but Milwaukee still suspended him. Sold to Minneapolis for $350, Friend survived a spider bite on his pitching arm while relaxing in a hammock at his home in Chillicothe, OH, to win 20 games in 1899 and help the Millers to first place in the Western League with a week to play but then suffered ugly losses in his last two starts, handing Indianapolis the pennant.

In 1900 Friend went 19-10 for Eastern League champions Providence after being 16-4 at the season's midpoint when his 9-game winning streak was snapped while hosting Hartford on the day the Connecticut club's manager, Billy Barnie, died. Friend later dated his subsequent arm trouble to that fateful day and finished the second half of the season just 3-6. He never again pitched with his old effectiveness but batted .330 as a part-time outfielder in 1901 and remained a pitcher-outfielder in the minors until 1908. The owner of a seventeen-year pro career but less than four of it spent in the majors despite a mountain of talent, Friend ran a manufacturing company that made rubber mats from old auto tires until he died of a heart attack in Chillicothe, OH, at 69. (DN/FV)

Gardner, James Anderson / "Jim"

B	T	HGT	WGT	G	IP	H	GS
?	R	5'10"	165	56	398.1	468	49

CG	BB	SO	SH	W	L	PCT	ERA
37	130	109	1	24	20	.545	3.75

B. 10/4/1874 Pittsburgh, PA **D.** 4/24/1905
TEAMS: 95PitN 97–99PitN 02ChiN

DEBUT: 6/20/1895 at Pittsburgh; caught by Joe Sugden and beat Louisville's Mike McDermott and Bert Cunningham 17–9
FINALE: 5/23/1902 at Chicago; caught by Frank Chance and lost 5–2 to Philadelphia's Chick Fraser

Jim Gardner was a "wealthy young law student" pitching for the Pittsburgh Athletic Club in 1895 and spurning pro offers until the Pirates agreed that he could pitch only home games while he continued his studies. A crafty junkballer, he enabled Pirates manager Connie Mack to gloat after a Gardner game against Brooklyn that all the Bridegrooms' hitters were "suffering from injured spines" going after his slow stuff. When he finished his rookie year at 8-2 with a 2.64 ERA, pressure was put on him to sign a regular contract with the club for 1896, but instead he devoted the year to his law classes.

Then, as happened in the nineteenth century to so many aspirants in other fields of endeavor, baseball won out, and Gardner went to spring training in 1897 "a full fledged member of the Pirates." His junk now more familiar, he was hit hard in the few games he pitched and spent nearly as much time playing other positions even though he was a poor hitter. Gardner may have acquired a new pitch in 1898, for he put together a career-high 10 wins and a 3.21 ERA. The following spring he came down with malaria and was released when he recuperated too slowly.

Deigning to go to the minors in an effort to resurrect his career, Gardner went 8-8 for Indianapolis of the newly renamed AL in 1900 and served as a pitcher-SS as well as player-manager for part of the season with Columbus of the Western Association in 1901. Signed that winter by Chicago NL, he was thrown from his buggy in March 1902 when his horse ran away, and he spent several weeks in a Pittsburgh hospital with a severe brain concussion before reporting to spring training. After arriving late, he showed so little effort while trying to round into shape that he nearly did not claim the sixteenth and final spot on Chicago's Opening Day roster. Gardner won his first start against Cincinnati on April 19 but got just two more starts before being released. After leaving pro ball in 1904 he worked in the sporting goods section of a Pittsburgh department store—he appears never to have practiced law—before dying in Pittsburgh in 1905 of surgical complications. *SL* attributed Gardner's death to the effects of a pitched ball that had fractured his skull six years earlier, but the only documented head injury he ever sustained was his 1902 brain concussion. Moreover, there is some evidence that he died after surgery for an abscessed ear. (DN)

Gastright, Henry Carl
(b. Gastreich) **/ "Hank"**

B	T	HGT	WGT	G	IP	H	GS
R	R	6'2"	190	171	1301.1	1337	143

CG	BB	SO	SH	W	L	PCT	ERA
121	584	514	6	72	63	.533	4.20

B. 3/29/1865 Covington, KY **D.** 10/9/1937
TEAMS: 89–91ColA 92WasN 93PitN 93BosN 94BroN 96CinN
DEBUT: 4/19/1889 at Baltimore; caught by Jim Peoples in an 11–0 loss to Baltimore's Frank Foreman
FINALE: 6/5/1896 at Brooklyn; relieved Frank Dwyer in a 10–1 loss to Brooklyn's Roaring Bill Kennedy

The most prolific winner in the brief ML history of Columbus, OH, ML teams, Hank Gastright was an avid hunter and outdoorsman but was often mistaken for a minister. Born Gastreich (which in German means "rich guest") the educated bilingual pitcher worked in his father's Newport rolling mill during the off-season, refrained from all the customary baseball vices and owned a remarkable tailing fast ball. Yet he struggled throughout his career with his control and a tendency to give up big hits in the late innings of close games.

Gastright debuted in 1888 with Toledo of the Tri-State League. Prior to 1889 Columbus manager Al Buckenberger obtained Gastright and helped steer Columbus into the AA as a replacement for NL-bound Cleveland. Gastright opened his rookie year poorly, missing most of June and July after catching "swamp fever" pitching on a wet day in Brooklyn's Washington Park. By Labor Day Gastright was 4-13 and easy to run on but then speeded up his delivery and finished strongly. Healthy all of 1890, the 25-year-old hurler responded with his career year, a 30-win season that sparked Columbus to a remarkable second-place finish. Gastright won 10 straight games before taking a loss on October 6 at Louisville the day Louisville clinched the AA pennant. To close the year, Gastright tossed a seven-inning no hitter against Toledo in front of 4,000 fans in Columbus.

In the strengthened AA of 1891 Gastright reverted to his losing ways, sat out two months with a sore arm, and then returned to win only one of ten starts. He would probably have lost 20 games had manager Gus Schmelz not laid him off without pay due to illness with three weeks left in the season. Gastright signed with the star-studded AA Boston Reds for 1892, but when the NL merged with the AA in December 1891, the Reds went defunct and Gastright was assigned to the weak Washington entry. He missed most of May with a stomach disorder and then pitched erratically. Knocked out after one inning in Boston on June 18, Gastright blamed his failure on forgetting to wear an undershirt on a chilly day. After coming down with typhoid, he was released in July and sat out the rest of the year.

On December 1, 1892, the NL assigned Gastright to Pittsburgh and his old manager Buckenberger. He helped the team hold first place in the early going, but his work gradually deteriorated until his removal in the third inning of a game he was winning in Brooklyn on June 1. At that point Buckenberger shopped Gastright around until Frank Selee, manager of first place Boston, gambled on him. Despite being "wild as a steer," Gastright won his first ten decisions behind Boston's powerful offense, making Selee seem a genius. He finally lost on September 18 at Cleveland when pitcher John Clarkson hit a tenth-inning home run.

Gastright sought a substantial pay raise for 1894. When he returned two contracts to Selee unsigned, he was seen as expendable and released the opening week of the season. Gastright signed with Brooklyn as a free agent and joined the team in midgame on April 30. He had time to shave and eat and was then sent to the mound, saving a win for Dan Daub. But after that he was an inconsistent spot starter. On June 1 he flipped the best game of his NL career: a one-hit win over Chicago to put Brooklyn above .500. Two starts later he got a no-decision after Brooklyn scored nine runs for him in the first inning. Released on August 6, Gastright went home to Kentucky and then sat out 1895, reportedly the "victim of an accident down South." In the spring of 1896 he latched on with Paris, KY, of the Blue Grass League and wrote to Cincinnati pilot Buck Ewing begging for a tryout. Ewing granted it to him on June 5 in Brooklyn, but Gastright had nothing left. A last moment of glory came in 1897 when Gastright went 13-7 to help the Hartford Atlantic League club to a third-place finish. He died at 72 in Cold Springs, KY. (FV/DN/DB)

German, Lester Stanley / "Les"

B	T	HGT	WGT	G	IP	H	GS
R	R	5'8"	165	130	858.2	1104	93

CG	BB	SO	SH	W	L	PCT	ERA
74	378	151	0	34	63	.351	5.45

B. 6/1/1869 Baltimore, MD **D.** 6/10/1934
TEAMS: 90BalA 93–96NYN 96–97WasN
DEBUT: 8/27/1890 at Baltimore; caught by George Townsend and lost 11–10 to St. Louis's Jack Stivetts
FINALE: 8/6/1897 at Brooklyn; replaced Doc McJames in the third inning of McJames's 15–5 loss to Brooklyn's Chauncey Fisher

With deep-set eyes and a thin handlebar mustache, the clever Les German could pitch a handful of innings as well as anyone—but seldom a full nine. A winner of 35 games in back-to-back minor league seasons, he offered a wide array of deliveries and speeds and until almost the very end of his career, managers and captains continually felt that between his cunning and knowledge of his craft he was on the verge of putting it all together. After playing semipro ball just north of his Baltimore hometown, German began in 1888 with the Allentown, PA, Central League club and then pitched for Lowell of the Atlantic Association in 1889. Joining Baltimore after it left the AA for the Atlantic Association in 1890, German put up a 35-9 record to August 27, when Baltimore returned to the AA, replacing the disbanded Brooklyn club. German made seventeenth starts in the Players League thinned loop but against sterner competition was winless in his first six and was released after the season.

Back in the minors with Buffalo of the Eastern Association in 1891, German went 35-11 but then surprised the baseball establishment by pitching for Oakland in the outlaw California League in 1892. Oakland finished last in both halves of the season, but German logged over 300 innings and paired with catcher Parke Wilson. The two signed as a unit in 1893 with Augusta of the Southern

League, where Opie Caylor called German the best pitcher in the loop. On June 19 he no-hit Mobile. Little more than three weeks later New York NL signed German and his batterymate, Wilson, and he finished the year in the Giants' three-man rotation, earning notice as a fly ball pitcher prone to giving up streaks of walks late in games.

The similarities between German and John M. Ward, his first manager with the Giants, ran deep. German, like Ward, who also started as a pitcher, was well spoken, well read, of small stature, could hit and run the bases well, and passed the ball between his hands right up to the start of his motion. In late May 1894 German wrote an incisive article on pitching for *TSN*. Earlier in the month he had missed several weeks with the flu and lost a few miles per hour off his fastball. When New York contended down to the wire, German's arm wilted. He started only twice after September first and missed New York's 4-game sweep over Baltimore in the first ever Temple Cup series. Still, when his August 18 loss to Chicago was thrown out, it gave him a 9-8 record in 1894 and the only winning season of his ML career.

German pitched well in 1895 until a July 17 victory over Ted Breitenstein. After that he had no arm strength left and resorted to tossing floaters and rainbow curves. A trial at 3B in September proved a failure. The following spring, after German was blasted in one final relief appearance with the Giants, Washington garnered the free agent pitcher. With the Senators, German was called "the best fielding and baserunning pitcher in baseball," but the same could not be said of his mound work. An atrocious 2-20 mark in 1896 (arguably the worst ever by a 20-game loser, as he finished with a 6.43 ERA and a .091 winning percentage) meant that German won only five of thirty total decisions in D.C. before being released in August 1897. He finished the year with Columbus of the Western League and played the infield for Rochester of the Eastern League in 1898 to essentially finish his career. German then opened a small hotel and saloon in his hometown of Aberdeen, MD, where he was a gun aficionado and loved to hunt. He died in Lanham, MD, at 65. (DN/FV)

Gettig, Charles Henry / "Charlie" "Sandow"

B	T	HGT	WGT	G	IP	H	GS
R	?	5'10"	172	42	276	345	26

CG	BB	SO	SH	W	L	PCT	ERA
22	110	51	0	15	12	.556	4.50

G	AB	H	R	2B	3B	HR
126	377	91	48	16	2	0

RBI	BB	SO	SB	BA	SA	OBP
47	28	—	12	.241	.294	.302

B. 12/?/1870 Baltimore, MD **D.** 4/11/1935
TEAMS: 96–99NYN
DEBUT: 8/5/1896 at Baltimore; relieved Dad Clarke in a 10–4 loss to Baltimore's Duke Esper
FINALE AND CAREER LOWLIGHT: 10/14/1899 at New York; led Washington's Dan McFarlan 9–0 after five innings but lost 12–9 after the Giants fell completely apart behind him and gave away the game

Nicknamed after strongman Gene Sandow, Charlie Gettig had a powerful body and a 48" chest. In four seasons with the Giants he appeared at every position without distinguishing himself at any of them. In the early 1890s Gettig pitched and played 2B for a string of teams around Baltimore before joining Hanover of the Cumberland Valley League in 1895. He moved to Newark of the Atlantic League early in the 1896 season and then joined the NL Giants in August. Gettig began 1897 with New York but was farmed to Newark for much of the season before being recalled in time to finish the year at 3B with the Giants. In 1898 he remained with the Giants all season as a scrub and spot pitcher, but it is hard to gauge where his value to the team lay.

The 1899 campaign was no better for Gettig, but by the season's end it was clear that he would not have been a Giant ever again even if he had hit .400 and won 30 games. The catalytic event came after a Sunday game at Weehawken, NJ, when team captain Kid Gleason ordered him to carry one end of the team bat bag to the ferry "as if he were common laborer." When Gettig refused, Gleason fined him $20 and was supported by owner Andrew Freedman to the disgust of rest of the Giants, many of whom had little respect for Gleason as a captain. After the incident, Gettig's loathing for Freedman, already substantial, ballooned until he could think only of escaping New York. Although he signed with Giants for 1900, it was with the understanding that he would be traded to another NL team as soon as a deal could be arranged. Instead he was sold prior to the season to Chicago of the still minor league AL and then suspended for the entire campaign when he took the ticket to Chicago given him by manager Buck Ewing and then went only as far as Newark before leaving the train and cabling Ewing that he would not be reduced to playing minor league ball. After serving his suspension Gettig resumed his pro career in 1901 and played in the minors until 1909. He died in Baltimore at 64. (DN)

Getzein, Charles H. (b. Goetzien) **/ "Charlie" "Pretzels"**

B	T	HGT	WGT	G	IP	H	GS
R	R	5'10"	172	296	2539.2	2670	292

CG	BB	SO	SH	W	L	PCT	ERA
277	602	1070	11	145	139	.511	3.46

B. 2/14/1864 ?, Germany **D.** 6/19/1932
TEAMS: 84–88DetN 89IndN 90–91BosN 91CleN 92StLN
DEBUT: 8/13/1884 at Detroit; caught by Ed Gastfield and lost 1–0 to Cleveland's John Henry
FINALE: 7/19/1892 at Brooklyn; caught by Dick Buckley and Bill Moran and lost 13–0 to Brooklyn's Ed Stein

During his playing career Charlie Getzein appears never to have persuaded scorekeepers to spell his surname "Getzien" as per his preference. The original German spelling was "Goetzien," which was changed when his family emigrated from Germany to Chicago in the 1870s. While Getzein and catcher Charlie Ganzel were both with Detroit they were known as "The Pretzel Battery," the same sobriquet later given St. Louis's Ted Breitenstein and Heinie Peitz.

The boyish-looking and, at the time, clean-shaven Getzein made his pro debut in 1883 with Grand Rapids and remained with the club the following year until the Northwestern League folded. Sporting a glittering 27-4 record at the time, he suffered a cruel initiation when he joined Detroit NL. Getzein lost his first eight starts with the last-place Wolverines before finally breaking into the win column on September 20 with a 7–1 triumph over Charley Radbourn of pennant-winning Providence. On a poor team again the following year, he lost 25 games, but when Detroit rose to second place in 1886 he contributed mightily with a 30-11 mark and was rewarded by being fined $300 by manager Bill Watkins when he slumped late in the season. In 1887, even though Detroit won its lone NL pennant, the occasion was still less than a joyous one for Getzein even though he ultimately won 29 games. In June he had another tiff with Watkins, who felt he wasn't watching base runners closely enough. Watkins then punished him by working him in 156 more innings than anyone else on the Detroit staff. Overtaxed again by Watkins in 1888, Getzein began experiencing arm trouble for the first time the following year after the Wolverines sold him to Indianapolis just prior to folding.

Getzein rebounded in 1890 to win 23 games as the third member of a three-man staff that accounted for all of Boston NL's 76 wins, giving him 135 career victories at age 26, but he had little left. Released on July 17, 1891, when Boston manager Frank Selee decided his lame arm would never repair, Getzein hurled one game with Cleveland and then shut down for the season. He returned in 1892 with St. Louis, sacrificing his speed, drop ball, and characteristic straight-armed backswing for an economical delivery that put less strain on his arm. But when his missiles were tattooed for 13.25 hits per nine innings, the worst ratio in 1892 of any pitcher in a minimum of 100 frames, he was released in July and soon was playing in the Chicago City League. Getzein was active in the City League until 1896 and then continued his duties as a typesetter with the *Chicago Tribune*. He died of a heart attack in Chicago at 68. (DN)

Gilmore, Frank T. / "Frank" "Bones" "Shadow"

B	T	HGT	WGT	G	IP	H	GS
R	?	5'11½"	164	49	405.1	435	47

CG	BB	SO	SH	W	L	PCT	ERA
46	143	212	2	12	33	.267	4.26

B. 4/27/1864 Webster, MA **D.** 7/21/1929
TEAMS: 86–88WasN
DEBUT AND CAREER HIGHLIGHT: 9/11/1886 at Washington; caught by Connie Mack in a 4–3 win over Philadelphia's Ed Daily in which he struck out 10, a then NL record by a hurler in his debut
FINALE: 7/4/1888 at Pittsburgh; caught by Connie Mack and lost 14–0 to Pittsburgh's Ed Morris

While with Hartford of the Eastern League in 1886, Frank Gilmore, then in his second pro season, and Connie Mack became lifelong friends and known as the "Bones Battery" because both were thin as rake handles. In late June Washington began negotiations to buy Gilmore from Hartford but had no interest in Mack. When Gilmore refused to sign without his catcher, Mack came in the bargain and the pair then lived together in Washington until Mack married in November 1887.

When Gilmore first came to the NL he had a distracting windup, generated by wildly gyrating his long arms and legs, and the widest curve ball in the game. In 1886 he fanned an astonishing total of 75 batters in his nine starts with Washington and averaged an ML-high 9 strikeouts per every nine innings pitched, but his career was ruined by pitching rule changes in 1887 that rendered his hop-and-skip delivery no longer legal. Gilmore was 7-20 in his sophomore season and gave up tons of walks. The skin-and-bones pitcher was also severely hampered in 1887 by another rule change that eliminated a batter's option to request either high or low pitches. Called by Mack the worst hitter he had ever seen, Gilmore swung at every pitch in the same place, around knee high, making him pie for balls above the waist. The *Washington Post* said of his stance at the plate: "He held his bat across his shoulder like an old lady with a broomstick awaiting the exit of a mouse from a trap." Under the new batting rule Gilmore hit .065 in 1887, the lowest BA in the majors among players with a minimum of 75 ABs. To compound his struggles he talked of marrying a Baltimore woman in early June but a few weeks later was panned by Washington papers for apparently jilting her. Even before the spring was out Washington wanted to trade him to Indianapolis, but the pitcher vacillated for weeks over whether to accept the move (as was still a player's right then), and on August 8 the *Indianapolis Sentinel* announced, "Pitcher Gilmore has refused to come to Indianapolis and the deal with the Washingtons is off."

By the following season Gilmore was one of the most unpopular players ever to wear a Washington uniform, so reviled that *TSN* reported that "as many as one hundred persons have turned away from the gates and gone home after hearing that he was billed to pitch in the game." His arm and confidence in shreds, he was released in July 1888 with a 1-9 record. His valise filled with snake oil and various liniments, Gilmore headed for Syracuse of the International Association but quit in September after he was beaned in a game at Rochester.

By the early 1890s Gilmore was collecting fares on a Washington Street car line and hoping that no passengers recognized him. He later relocated to Hartford and worked as a playground supervisor before dying in 1929 of complications following an attack of heat prostration. Mack, though by then unable to recall with which arm his first ML batterymate threw, sent the biggest wreath to his funeral. (DN/DB)

Golden, Michael Henry / "Mike"

B	T	HGT	WGT	G	IP	H	GS
R	R	5'7"	166	59	393	457	45

CG	BB	SO	SH	W	L	PCT	ERA
40	53	86	1	10	32	.238	2.79

G	AB	H	R	2B	3B	HR
107	415	90	38	9	3	0

RBI	BB	SO	SB	BA	SA	OBP
35	5	38	3	.217	.256	.223

B. 9/11/1851 Shirley, MA **D.** 1/11/1929
TEAMS: 75WasNA 75ChiNA 78MilN
DEBUT: 5/4/1875 at Keokuk; caught by Paddy Quinn and lost 15–1 to Chicago's George Zettlein
FINALE: 9/14/1878 at Milwaukee; played CF and went 1-for-5 in a 4–3 win over Providence's John M. Ward

Mike Golden grew up in Rockford, IL, and began playing on the local team in the late 1860s, although he was still "such a kid" that he seldom appeared in important games. Small and wiry with a strong arm, he was originally a catcher and occupied that position until 1874, by which time he had joined the independent Keokuk Westerns. When Al Pratt, who was supposed to pitch for the club, backed out, Golden was forced to take the box. Because he came late to pitching, he was still learning its intricacies the following year when Keokuk joined the NA.

In addition to arm strength Golden appears to have had speed but little control. After his ML debut the *Keokuk Daily Gate City* admitted that Golden "did some wild pitching," and after his lone appearance against his boyhood teammate Al Spalding, the *Boston Globe* complained,

"Several of the Bostons were hit by the swift pitcher of the Keokuks." Chicago nonetheless hired Golden after Keokuk disbanded to replace George Zettlein, who had moved to the Philadelphia Pearls. He won three of his first four outings with the Windy City entry but then dropped three of his next four and lost his job to Jim Devlin.

Golden began 1876 with the independent Covington Stars with Silver Flint as his catcher but joined unaffiliated Indianapolis later in the year. At the end of 1877 he accompanied the Milwaukee League Alliance team when it enlisted in the NL for 1878. Golden was retained largely because Milwaukee failed to secure George Bradley, its first choice to alternate with its putative ace, Sam Weaver. Having lost much of his speed since 1875, perhaps owing to arm trouble, Golden was used mainly on days when Milwaukee's regular catchers were recuperating from handling Weaver's speedballs. A poor season both in the box and at the plate left Golden unemployed, and he returned to Rockford, where he joined the police force and resumed playing for the local Northwestern League team. Golden continued to be active on the Rockford baseball scene as both a player and team organizer until the mid-1880s, meanwhile making police work his career. In the 1890s his son Charlie played quarterback for Northwestern and caught for the school's baseball team. Golden remained in Rockford until his death from heart disease at 78. (DN/PM)

Goldsmith, Fredrick Ernest / "Fred" "Goldie"

B	T	HGT	WGT	G	IP	H	GS
R	R	6'1"	195	189	1609.2	1685	185

CG	BB	SO	SH	W	L	PCT	ERA
174	171	433	16	112	68	.622	2.73

B. 5/15/1856 New Haven, CT **D.** 3/28/1939
TEAMS: 75NHNA 79TroN 80–84ChiN 84BalA
DEBUT: 10/23/1875 at New Haven; played 2B and went 2-for-4 in an 8–3 loss to Hartford's Candy Cummings
FINALE: 9/10/1884 at St. Louis; caught by Sam Trott, was relieved by Tommy Burns, and finished the game at 1B in his 8–3 loss to St. Louis's Dave Foutz
CAREER HIGHLIGHT: In 1880, his first full ML season, set a season record that lasted until 1931 for the highest winning percentage by a 20-game winner when he went 21-3 (.875)

Fred Goldsmith swore until his dying day that he was the true inventor of the curve ball and claimed he gave the first public demonstration of the pitch at Brooklyn's Capitoline Grounds on August 16, 1870, with Henry Chadwick in attendance. Chadwick denied the event had ever occurred and preferred Candy Cummings's claim that he first used the pitch in an 1867 game against Harvard to Goldsmith's that he developed the pitch as a teenager in New Haven and tried it on the Yale team.

If Goldsmith's contention were not baseless, then the wrong man would now be in the HOF, and certainly a less entertaining one. In his heyday Goldsmith was a skilled boxer after learning the sport while coaching at Yale one spring. According to Ned Williamson, "Goldie" cunningly enticed unwitting Chicago rookies to put on the gloves with him with no clue that they were about to face a skilled pugilist. To Cap Anson's consternation, Goldsmith also taught his teammates how to play football and introduced them to the wild side of life. Once, while Chicago was on the road, the club secretary fined Goldsmith three nights running for being out after curfew, left the amount of the fine in a sealed envelope at the hotel desk, and doubled it each day. When the team left town, the hotel manager returned all the envelopes unopened to the secretary because Goldsmith had never once come into the hotel during the team's stay.

But Goldsmith had lived on the edge almost from the first moment he picked up a baseball. In his youth he was in RF for a team in Bridgeport, CT, one day against the Milford Eurekas when he tried to throw a runner named Gilman out at 3B and the ball hit Gilman in the temple, sending him to a hospital, where he died a few hours later. It was perhaps this incident that led Goldsmith to take his game to Canada for several of what could have been his prime years. From 1876–78 he starred with the London Tecumsehs of the International Association and seemed reluctant to test himself against ML competition until late in the 1879 season after he had returned to the States a few months earlier with Springfield, MA, of the National Association.

A sensational 4-for-5 NL debut while serving in CF against Cincinnati on September 10, 1879, gave Troy manager Bob Ferguson a false picture of Goldsmith as a hitter, but even though his pitching was tops—a 1.57 ERA in 8 games—Ferguson was unable to retain him under the new reserve rule that came into effect after the season. Hence Goldsmith was free to sign with Chicago, and for the next four seasons he and Larry Corcoran formed the game's first pitching rotation, won 68 percent of their games, and spurred Chicago to three straight NL pennants and a second-place finish in 1883. Unlike Corcoran, who seldom complained about anything early in his stay with Chicago, Goldsmith was famous for moaning every spring that he had a sore arm but somehow would always manage to work out the kinks toward the end of the exhibition schedule. Soon after the 1884 season was under way, however, the soreness was genuine and involved his shoulder, suggesting rotator cuff damage. Never big on sentiment, Chicago president Al Spalding sold Goldsmith to Baltimore AA for $400 in August once it was apparent the injury was irreparable. When he beat Pittsburgh on August 25, an *SL* observer noted, "His shoulder still being lame, he was obliged to resort more to strategy than to speed or curves." Three days later Goldsmith likewise topped the pennant-bound New York Mets with his slow stuff, but it was his last win. Baltimore shut him down for the season after just one more start but continued to pay him, although the club refused to remunerate Spalding after Goldsmith frankly told Orioles manager Billy Barnie almost the moment he joined his new club that his arm was shot.

The following year Goldsmith umpired in the Canadian League awhile after pitching a few innings in that loop and then turned to tending bar and planning ways he might retrieve his former glory. In the spring of 1888 he dyed his gray hair black and went to Hot Springs, where he wheedled Anson into giving him a trial with Chicago, but bad weather early in spring training hampered his chances to be game tested and an ankle sprain later dashed his last hopes. In July Goldsmith was appointed a substitute umpire in the AA and almost immediately came under fire for his ball-strike work in a game between Louisville and St. Louis, an ominous sign that the Browns would have future trouble with him. Still, Goldsmith finished the season successfully and was hired as a regular AA umpire in 1889. As luck would have it, he was designated to officiate the critical September series in Brooklyn between the Bridegrooms and the Browns with first place on the line and a probable pennant hinging on the outcome. On September 7 he forfeited a game St. Louis had been leading 4–2 to Brooklyn when Browns manager Charlie Comiskey took his team off the field after contending that it was too dark to finish the ninth inning. When AA officials overturned Goldsmith's decision and awarded the game to St. Louis, he felt that his credibility had been tainted, and he resigned. By the end of the century Goldsmith was operating a little grocery store near Detroit's Recreation Park. He later was the postmaster in Clawson, MI, for a number of years before returning to storekeeping. Several of his obits said that at the time of his death of heart disease in Berkley, MI, at 82 he was holding a press clipping saying that he invented the curve ball. (DN/PM)

Gruber, Henry John / "Henry"

B	T	HGT	WGT	G	IP	H	GS
R	R	5'9"	155	151	1239.1	1328	139

CG	BB	SO	SH	W	L	PCT	ERA
129	479	346	5	61	78	.439	3.67

B. 12/14/1863 Hamden, CT **D.** 9/26/1932
TEAMS: 87–88DetN 89CleN 90CleP 91CleN
DEBUT: 7/28/1887 at Detroit; caught by Charlie Ganzel and lost 5–4 to New York's Tim Keefe
FINALE: 10/2/1891 at Cleveland; caught by Jack Doyle and beat New York's Silver King 9–1

Strong, with a fancy contortionist delivery, Henry Gruber never was able to command his fastball or reach his potential despite several outstanding minor league seasons. The 21-year-old Connecticut native entered the pro ranks to stay on September 4, 1885, when his Waterbury team replaced Norfolk in the Eastern League. He pitched in the New England League in 1886 and the next year was back in the Eastern League as Hartford's ace. On July 26, 1887, he signed with Detroit, which won a bidding war with the New York Giants for his services. Gruber went 4–3 filling in for Lady Baldwin, who was suspended a month. In his debut he walked 8 and lost in the ninth inning, harbingers of two pitfalls that would plague him throughout his career. From the outset Gruber was a deliberate worker, once said by *TSN* to be "as slow in the box as the seven ages of man." He would pose for what seemed like forever and then lift his left leg up to his chin before delivering with an audible grunt a live fastball that commonly sailed behind a batter or bounced in the dirt. Gruber had a slower drop ball, but he telegraphed that pitch to batters with a "peculiar squirm," as if he had just bitten something sour. "Green apple curves," his drops were called.

Gruber replaced Baldwin again early in 1888 but was winless in eight midseason starts as first-place Detroit lost 16 games in a row. When the Wolves disbanded after the season, Gruber became Cleveland property. Once again he lost seven starts in a row in midstream as Cleveland stumbled from first place. Boston president Jim Hart controversially offered the Spiders' hurler $500 if he beat New York in the final game of the season to enable Boston to cop the NL pennant, but the Giants clinched the flag after Mike Tiernan tapped Gruber for an inside-the-park homer.

He jumped to Cleveland PL in 1890 but held out until an attendance clause was removed from his contract. In his first PL start on April 19 against Buffalo, he walked 16, tying the single-game ML record for bases on balls. For the year, Gruber threw 47 wild pitches and, on August 23 in a 6–5 loss at New York, became one of the first pitchers to be charged with a game-ending balk—all in what turned out to be his best ML season. After the PL folded, Gruber went back to Cleveland NL, where he alternated with a young Cy Young. As if his control did not suffer enough on its own, on May 23, 1891, during a game against Boston, one of the Hub players coated the game ball with a veneer of grease. Umpire Phil Powers refused to issue a new ball and Gruber walked three in a row before teammate Jack Doyle threw the greasy ball to Cleveland substitute Ed Seward near the outfield bleachers and Seward heaved it out of the park. Powers promptly fined Doyle and Boston tried to claim a forfeit win, but Gruber prevailed 9–2.

Some four months later Gruber ended his ML career with a personal best two-hitter on October 2, 1891. Although his arm was still sound, he was unwanted the following spring when the NL-AA merger reduced the majors to twelve clubs. Respected baseball observers called Gruber a "head case" and said his value was less than "Panama Canal stock." Gruber coached Yale baseball in the spring of 1892 and then had a poor Eastern League season. Gruber rebounded to help Troy to a third-place finish in the EL in 1893 and then opened 1894 with a glittering 11-0 start but transferred to Tom Burns's Springfield team on August 1 after Troy went bankrupt and finished the year 26-11. He was a mainstay with Springfield in 50 games when they won the pennant in 1895, and he almost helped Buffalo to the same prize in 1896 until his arm finally gave out. Gruber umpired in the EL part of the 1897 season but quit when the Wilkes-Barre team refused to let him in the park on July 11 after he allegedly had shown partiality to Buffalo in the previous day's game. In 1932 he died of heart attack while crossing a downtown street in New Haven. (FV/DN)

Haddock, George Silas / "George"

B	T	HGT	WGT	G	IP	H	GS
R	R	5'11"	155	204	1580	1650	189

CG	BB	SO	SH	W	L	PCT	ERA
160	714	599	8	95	87	.522	4.07

B. 12/25/1866 Portsmouth, NH **D.** 4/18/1926
TEAMS: 88–89WasN 90BufP 91BosA 92–93BroN 94PhiN 94WasN
DEBUT: 9/27/1888 at New York; caught by Jim Banning until Banning was injured in a 3–0 loss to New York's Ed Crane
FINALE: 9/20/1894 at Washington; replaced Piggy Ward in RF and went 0-for-2 in a 14–8 loss to Cleveland's Bobby Wallace

George Haddock was the brother-in-law of pitcher Jim Whitney, who encouraged him to test the pro waters in 1886 with Topeka of the Western League. On Whitney's word, after Haddock had a good year in the same loop the following year, Washington invited him to spring training in 1888 and farmed him to Troy of the International Association when he proved unready. Although neither Haddock nor his batterymate, catcher Jim Banning, dazzled the IA in 1888, both were asked to finish the season with Washington. Banning was injured early in his first ML game and never did play a full contest in top company, but Haddock quickly showed he belonged, pitching well in each of his first two starts with Washington, although he lost both.

The following spring Haddock joined George Keefe and Alex Ferson in giving Washington an all-rookie rotation, but only Ferson had a decent record, and the Senators finished last. The trio then jumped as a unit to Buffalo of the Players League in 1890 and were an unequivocal disaster. Ferson ruined his arm, Keefe posted the worst ERA in the loop among qualifiers (6.52) and Haddock's 5.76 ERA was second only to his teammate.

At the close of his second full ML season Haddock's career record was a dismal 20-47, hardly the stuff to attract a manager looking to win a repeat pennant. Yet that is precisely what happened. When the PL folded Haddock joined its flag winning Boston Reds when they moved to the AA for 1891, minus only a few key members like pitchers Charley Radbourn and Ad Gumbert. In their stead, pilot Arthur Irwin garnered Charlie Buffinton, one of the game's top pitchers, and Haddock, seemingly one of its dregs. Then, even more astonishingly, he named Haddock his Opening Day starter. Irwin might have garnered Manager of the Year for that move alone, as Haddock paced the AA in wins and shutouts and clinched the pennant for Boston when he beat Baltimore 6–2 on September 5.

In the space of one season Haddock's career winning percentage had shot from .299 to .482, putting him among the game's most appetizing free agents when the AA and NL merged after the 1891 season and the disbanding Boston club's players were assigned to teams that comprised the new twelve-club loop. Awarded to Brooklyn, Haddock began 1892 as a holdout and threatened to tend to his flour and feed business in Dorchester, MA, rather than take a salary cut as mandated to reduce payrolls after the merger. He coached Williams College until finally signing with Brooklyn on May 20 for a reported $3,250. Despite his belated start, Haddock had another fine season, logging 29 victories and a .690 winning percentage that placed him among the game's elite pitchers.

Verging on greatness at 26, the slender righty abruptly had the rug pulled out from under him the following spring. After injuring his knee in an exhibition game, Haddock later hurt both his thumb and elbow and made his last start with Brooklyn on August 11 before being released. He signed for 1894 with his old manager, Irwin, who was now at the helm of the Philadelphia Phillies, the strongest-hitting team in the game, and needed only a modicum of pitching help to contend for the pennant. Though Irwin tried to nurse his former ace, it was obvious by July that Haddock's elbow was shot. His final ML win came at Pittsburgh on July 6, but when he was thrashed 17–8 by St. Louis in his next start four days later, Irwin acknowledged the inevitable and cut him. Fittingly, perhaps, Haddock finished his ML career where it had begun only six short years earlier, in Washington, with four quick losses in September, shaving his career winning percentage by 12 points. Just so, his final mark of .522 is tops among all nineteenth-century ML pitchers who were below .300 after their first sixty decisions. Sent home by the Senators after appearing in his ML coda as an outfielder, Haddock retired to his feed and grain business and later moved to Boston, where he died of a heart attack at 59. (DN)

Hagan, Arthur Charles / "Art"

B	T	HGT	WGT	G	IP	H	GS
?	R	?	?	22	178	277	21

CG	BB	SO	SH	W	L	PCT	ERA
19	43	50	0	2	18	.100	5.36

B. 3/17/1863 Providence, RI **D.** 3/25/1936
TEAMS: 83PhiN 83–84BufN
DEBUT: 6/30/1883 at New York; caught by Em Gross and lost 8–6 to New York's Tip O'Neill
FINALE: 5/13/1884 at New York; caught by George Myers and lost 20–5 to New York's John M. Ward
CAREER LOWLIGHT: 8/21/1883 at Providence; in a game witnessed by many of his friends and family from Lonsdale, RI, was caught by Em Gross and sustained the most lopsided shutout defeat in ML history when he lost 25–0 to Providence's Charley Radbourn

Strapped for pitching, Philadelphia NL tested Art Hagan, a member of the independent Webster, MA, club, in an exhibition against unaffiliated Newark on June 28, 1883. When the 20-year-old fared tolerably well against a lineup that featured Dave Orr, the Quakers turned him loose two days later against New York NL. By the time Philadelphia released Hagan in late August, he was well on his way to establishing himself as perhaps the worst ML pitcher in the dozen years (1881–92) when the pitching distance was fifty feet from home plate. Among hurlers during that twelve-year span in a minimum of 100 innings, Hagan was indisputably the most hittable, surrendering 14.01 safeties per nine innings, 1.08 more than second-ranked Frank Brill.

He left Philadelphia with a 1-14 log, his lone win coming on July 18 at Buffalo. Evidently the Bisons saw something that day that was invisible to every other team, for they gave him a two-game trial near the close of the 1883 season. A 5–3 loss to Charley Radbourn in his final appearance of the campaign encouraged Buffalo to invite him back for an encore. Hagan's second and last ML win occurred on May 10, 1884, when he took revenge on his old club, the Quakers, by staggering to a 9–7 verdict. Three days later, in allowing 26 hits in his wretched ML finale, "before the game terminated New York led him to believe he had no curves." The contest not only represented the departure of one of the game's worst pitchers but also one of its best. Hagan's 20–5 loss proved to be John M. Ward's final ML win. After leaving baseball Hagan was a grocer, a funeral director, and a partner with his brother in a brewery. He died at his home in Providence in 1936. (DN)

Hahn, Frank George / "Noodles"

B	T	HGT	WGT	G	IP	H	GS
L	L	5'9"	160	77	620.1	586	71

CG	BB	SO	SH	W	L	PCT	ERA
61	157	277	8	39	28	.582	2.97

B. 4/29/1879 Nashville, TN **D.** 2/6/1960
TEAMS: 99–05Cin 06NYAL
DEBUT: 4/18/1899 at Cincinnati; caught by Heinie Peitz and beat Pittsburgh's Billy Rhines 7–5
FINALE: 6/7/1906 at St. Louis; caught by Deacon McGuire and beat St. Louis's Jack Powell 6–4 in thirteen innings
CAREER HIGHLIGHT: 7/12/1900 at Cincinnati; caught by Heinie Peitz and no-hit the Phillies' Bill Bernhard, winning 4–0

Noodles Hahn had an older brother, Charles—nicknamed "Snooks"—who was also a promising pitcher in the mid 1890s before encountering arm trouble. The younger Hahn was reportedly an excellent piano player, talented enough that he might have become a concert pianist with more training. There are several versions of how he acquired his charming nickname. The one Hahn favored, as told to Harry Weldon of the *Cincinnati Enquirer* in 1899, was that when he was a boy in Nashville there was a poor old man in his neighborhood for whom his grandmother made food every day and then had her grandson deliver it. The man was especially fond of noodle soup, and Hahn's brothers, Snooks and Eddie, began ribbing him about being the noodle soup boy.

Hahn joined Snooks on Chattanooga at age 16 after flunking a tryout with his local Nashville entry in the Southern League when his insolence and immaturity grated on player-manager George Stallings. Lew Whistler, Chattanooga's thicker-skinned player-manager, sent him to the mound the day after signing him and then transported him to Mobile when the franchise moved there in July. Hahn returned to Mobile in 1896 but quit before the Southern League season ended when manager Paul Hines fined him $25 for refusing to pitch two days in a row, and he finished the campaign with Detroit of the Western League. Despite fashioning an uninspiring 17-17 record in the WL in 1897, he was drafted by Cincinnati and offered $1,500 for 1898. When Hahn brashly demanded $1,800, he was sent back to Detroit but reported fat and out of shape, pitched erratically, put on even more weight as the season progressed and finished with a composite 12-20 mark after he was released to St. Paul in the late going. Saints manager Charlie Comiskey nonetheless recommended that the Reds take a fresh look at him.

Hahn arrived at Cincinnati's training camp the following spring with a reputation for being too fond of beer and indifferent to learning his craft. Nothing was expected of him. Hahn then stunned Reds observers, including one who wrote glowingly that he featured "terrific speed, good curves and the best control ever displayed by a green southpaw." Manager Buck Ewing, notoriously reluctant to play rookies, was predictably against keeping him, but Reds veterans, who harbored little respect for their longtime pilot by 1899, persuaded owner John T. Brush to force Ewing to use the spring sensation. Hahn wobbled to a win in his ML debut but then caught fire and finished his frosh season as the NL strikeout king and the Reds' leader in almost every major pitching department.

Still, he was regarded with suspicion by pundits, who compared him to Frank Killen in that he did not have an effective curve ball and predicted he would not last more than a couple of seasons since southpaws traditionally had short careers. *TSN* went so far as to theorize that lefties were at an increased risk to develop heart trouble because the heart, which was on the left side, was under greater strain. Hahn amplified concern that he might be a one-year wonder when he held out in the spring of 1900. Brush, after being roasted for not giving his top pitcher the $2,100 he requested, relented in time for Hahn to pitch the Reds' third game of the season and edge Chicago 7–6. He then had a fine year with a dreary seventh-place team, topping the NL in shutouts and tying Rube Waddell for the strikeout lead. Already, though, Hahn inwardly feared that that he had to work too hard with such a poor team behind him. The following year he announced, "I am wise enough to know that I cannot last forever, and that I am greatly shortening my career by pitching as I did last season." (DN)

Handiboe, James Edward / "Nick" "Jim"

B	T	HGT	WGT	G	IP	H	GS
R	R	5'11"	160	14	114	82	14

CG	BB	SO	SH	W	L	PCT	ERA
12	33	83	1	7	7	.500	3.32

B. 7/17/1866 Columbus, OH **D.** 11/8/1942
TEAMS: 86PitA
DEBUT: 5/28/1886 at Baltimore; caught by Doggie Miller and lost 4–1 to Baltimore's Matt Kilroy
FINALE: 9/8/1886 at Pittsburgh; caught by Doggie Miller and finished the game in RF after he was relieved by Art Whitney in the second inning of his 6–2 loss to St. Louis's Dave Foutz

There appear to have been at least two and maybe even three pitching Handiboe brothers in the 1880s and the early 1890s, and it is not clear which of them wore a Pittsburgh uniform in 1886 and came down with a sore arm that sidelined him for a full month before he made his final ML start. Sold by Pittsburgh to Eau Claire of the Northwestern League in the spring of 1887, Handiboe was with his hometown Columbus team of the Tri-State League the following season along with his brother John.

Such is true anyway if "Nick" was indeed the nickname of James Edward Handiboe, who died of heart disease in 1942. But the August 19, 1893, *TSN* carried this obit: "Jim Handiboe, an old time ball player, boozed himself into eternity in Columbus. He was found dead in the parlor of his home." Hence Nick was perhaps the Pittsburgh pitcher's real first name and Jim was an altogether different Handiboe, and there is also of course the possibility that *none* of the Handiboe brothers were actually named Nick, at least as a first name, but *several* of them were called Nick. Whatever the case, the best pitcher among the brothers was probably John, who remained active in the minors until he hurt his arm in the early 1890s and then returned briefly to the game with Gallipolis, OH, in 1896. John's brother was likewise poised to make a comeback the following year. According to *TSN* in March 1897, "Nick Handiboe thinks there is still some pitch in him." Yet we cannot gainsay that the 1897 Handiboe was John once again on the comeback trail but now using the name Nick.

Handiboe is an unusual name, but there was yet another Handiboe who played in the same era and was probably a cousin of the pitching brothers. In September 1901 John Adam Handiboe, a third baseman with Memphis of the Southern Association, died when he sleepwalked out his hotel room window after his road roommate stayed out past curfew and left him unattended. (DN/DB)

Harkins, John Joseph / "Jack" "Pa"

B	T	HGT	WGT	G	IP	H	GS
R	R	6'1"	205	139	1183.1	1262	137

CG	BB	SO	SH	W	L	PCT	ERA
131	358	489	4	51	83	.381	4.09

B. 4/12/1859 New Brunswick, NJ **D.** 11/18/1940
TEAMS: 84CleN 85–87BroA 88BalA
DEBUT: 5/2/1884 at Providence; caught by Fatty Briody and lost 5–2 to Providence's Charley Radbourn
FINALE: 5/1/1888 at Baltimore; caught by Chris Fulmer and lost 12–7 to Cleveland's Billy Crowell

Jack Harkins was a chemistry student at Rutgers University, pitching summers for New Jersey semipro teams until 1881, when he joined an independent nine in Trenton. After flunking a trial with Baltimore AA in the spring of 1883, he remained with Trenton, now in the Interstate Association, until Cleveland NL acquired him for 1884 to replace Hugh Daily, who had jumped to the rebel UA. After Jim McCormick also bolted to the UA, Harkins became the Blues' workhorse and lost 32 games in his rookie year.

Among the crew of Cleveland players that Brooklyn AA bought after the season, Harkins started for his new club on Opening Day in 1885 and beat Baltimore 7–3. It was his peak moment in the majors. In three seasons with Brooklyn

Harkins never had a winning record and by 1887 was being hit so hard that he finished with a 6.02 ERA, the highest among AA qualifiers. That winter Brooklyn sold him to Baltimore for $600, and he lasted just one game with the Orioles before returning home to New Brunswick "completely worn out."

Harkins later was head coach of the Yale baseball team. One of his early players was Amos Alonzo Stagg, the legendary college football coach, who became a lifelong friend. After leaving coaching, Harkins was an alderman in New Brunswick and operated a café there for a time before taking a job as Sergeant-at-Arms of the local court. He died at his New Brunswick home of a heart attack at 81. (DN/DB)

Harper, George B. / "George" "Skirts"

B	T	HGT	WGT	G	IP	H	GS
R	R	5'10"	165	28	172.1	234	20

CG	BB	SO	SH	W	L	PCT	ERA
14	88	46	0	10	14	.417	5.43

B. 8/17/1866 Milwaukee, WI **D.** 12/11/1931
TEAMS: 94PhiN 96BroN
DEBUT: 7/11/1894 at St. Louis; relieved Gus Weyhing in the sixth inning and lost 13–12 to St. Louis's Pink Hawley
FINALE: 9/4/1896 at Philadelphia; caught by Jack Grim and lost 7–4 to Cleveland's Bobby Wallace and Cy Young

With the technique of a medium-arc softball pitcher and little more, George Harper wiggled in a sixteenth-year minor league career that brought him some 300 wins. Twice he bobbed up in ML company, only to be exposed each time as a curiosity when his dazzling assortment of junk deliveries that frustrated even the best hitters on occasion could not do so often enough for him to win in the show.

A change pitcher for both Oshkosh and Ted Sullivan's 1886 Milwaukee Northwestern League team, Harper also spent the following season in the Northwestern and Western leagues. Over the next six years the bulk of his career wins came in the California League. With a spotty fan base, terrible grounds keeping, and in an environment where most quality players fled east as soon as possible, Harper hurled for Oakland and Stockton before winning 41 games with a powerful Sacramento team in 1890. Perfect for that time and place, he spirited pennant-winning San Jose the following season, going 47-32 with a 0.96 ERA and then won 37 times in 1892, giving him a three-year victory total of 125.

Harper would never dominate again after taking his game east. In 1894 he tried his junk balls with Detroit of the Western League but was released after a 26–16 loss to Sioux City. George Stallings acquired him for Nashville of the Southern League on June 1, and after he beat Atlanta 1–0 on July 4, his mystical reputation on both coasts induced Phillies manager Arthur Irwin to pick him up for the last two months of the 1894 season. In his first ML start Harper beat overanxious Boston 9–2 with his slow curves and spins. Philadelphia, with arguably the greatest offense in ML history, supported Harper with 104 runs in his nine rookie starts, but he still could win only half of his decisions and pick up his release.

In 1895 Harper went 24-21 for last place Rochester of the Eastern League and was reportedly signed by Brooklyn sight unseen for 1896. But Bridegrooms manager Dave Foutz shuddered at his new pitcher's style, especially after pitcher Roaring Bill Kennedy hit 3 home runs off him in a scrimmage game. Foutz took Harper on the first road trip "because directors had put him on the roster," but the displeased skipper soon farmed his slowballer to Scranton of the Eastern League and then had to recall him in July when the team ran short of healthy arms. Harper finished the year 4-8, spent the next two seasons in the Eastern League, and then headed back to the West Coast with Watsonville of the Cal League in 1899. After serving as player-manager for Stockton in 1900 Harper finished his pitching career with Sacramento the following year. An excellent billiards player, he once beat nationally ranked Tom McCarthy. Harper made his living after leaving baseball operating a tailoring shop in Stockton, where he died at 65 of a severe upper respiratory infection. (FV/DN)

Hart, Robert Lee / "Bob"

B	T	HGT	WGT	G	IP	H	GS
?	?	5'8"	?	26	201.1	188	24

CG	BB	SO	SH	W	L	PCT	ERA
20	66	95	0	12	8	.600	3.67

B. 5/16/1866 Palmyra, MO **D.** 5/14/1944
TEAMS: 90StLA
DEBUT: 7/13/1890 at St. Louis; caught by Jake Wells and was relieved by Jack Stivetts who took the 8–7 loss to Philadelphia's Sadie McMahon
FINALE: 10/14/1890 at Louisville; caught by Jack Munyan and lost 13–7 to Louisville's Red Ehret

Bob Hart was a longtime minor leaguer whose career path was so intertwined with contemporary hurler Bill Hart that references still wrongly carry him as having been called Billy. After blanking the NL St. Louis Maroons in an 1886 exhibition game while pitching for Leavenworth of the Western League, Hart began 1887 with Milwaukee of the Northwestern League but finished with Kalamazoo in the Tri-State League. He remained in that loop for the next two seasons and then moved to Grand Rapids of the International Association in 1890 until the St. Louis AA acquired him in July. Despite being the Browns' most effective hurler in the last two months of the season, Hart was cut after he fared poorly in postseason exhibitions. Exiled to the minors, he refused an offer to return to the Browns the following August when his Duluth Western Association team disbanded, preferring to go to Green Bay of the Wisconsin State League. On Sunday September 20, 1891, Hart was allegedly offered a $300 bribe to throw that day's game in what was slated to be a best-of-five series with Marinette to decide the loop championship, but the affair was aborted when a gang of "three or four thousand toughs" from Marinette ringed the field that afternoon with foghorns and pea shooters and pelted the Green Bay team, cowing former ML second baseman Joe Quest, who was umpiring, into "practically giving the game" to the home nine and causing Green Bay to refuse to play the last 2 games of the series. Hart subsequently pitched in the California and Southern leagues before returning to Hannibal, MO, his adopted home, where he died at 77 after fracturing a hip. (DN)

Hart, William Franklin / "Bill" "Will" "Bond Hill Billy"

B	T	HGT	WGT	G	IP	H	GS
?	R	5'10"	163	186	1424.1	1599	171

CG	BB	SO	SH	W	L	PCT	ERA
146	647	383	5	59	109	.352	4.56

B. 7/19/1865 Louisville, KY **D.** 9/19/1936
TEAMS: 86–87PhiA 92BroN 95PitN 96–97StLN 98PitN 01CleAL
DEBUT: 7/26/1886 at Philadelphia; caught by Wilbert Robinson and lost 7–2 to Louisville's Guy Hecker
FINALE: 7/30/1901 at Cleveland; relieved Earl Moore in Moore's 11–5 loss to Philadelphia's Eddie Plank

Bill Hart won over 300 pro games, but only 59 of them were in the majors. In a career that encompassed some twenty-five seasons just eight of them were spent at the ML level and were punctuated by three significant interruptions, each lasting two years or longer. A product of the Bond Hill area of Cincinnati, a particularly fertile breeding ground for ballplayers, Hart was working as a printer's devil when he made his pro debut in 1884 with the Cincinnati UA reserves. The following year he moved to the fledgling Southern League, first with Memphis and then Chattanooga, and was still with the Tennessee club in July 1886 when he allegedly jumped his contract to join Philadelphia AA. In truth, Hart had been a victim of Philadelphia co-owner Lew Simmons's double dealing and escaped blacklisting when he apologized to Chattanooga via a letter that ended, "I have pitched four games this week [his first with Philadelphia], which you know are too many, and consequently have been pounded pretty hard." Hart predictably finished the 1886 season with a weary arm, started poorly in 1887, and then endured five successive seasons in the minors, debating after each whether to quit the game and work full-time at his winter job as a compositor for a Cincinnati newspaper. Finally, in 1892, he returned to the majors with Brooklyn but was only 9-12 with a first-division club. When he broke his arm sliding into 2B on September 8 against Chicago, he was released and had to sit out all of 1893 while the fracture mended.

After spending 1894 with Sioux City of the Western League Hart seemed about to get lucky when Cincinnati, his hometown team, took a shine to him, but before the Reds could act Pittsburgh drafted him for 1895. In his lone year with the Pirates he was second in wins only to Pink Hawley but was traded the following January to St. Louis along with Monte Cross and $750 for Bones Ely. Hart's two years with the Browns were his most abysmal in baseball, as he suffered 56 defeats, topped the NL in losses in 1896, and played on two successive cellar dwellers. In December 1897 he returned to Pittsburgh in a trade for Jim Hughey and $1,800 but was hit by a batting practice line drive in the spring of 1898 and sustained a broken jaw that left him temporarily gun-shy after it healed. Released to Milwaukee of the Western League in 1899, Hart shifted to Cleveland when the loop changed its name to the American League the following year and went 18-15 for the Lake Shores, earning a final return to top company when the AL went major in 1901. In July he was cut when Cleveland underwent a midseason overhaul, and he joined the AL umpiring staff as a temporary sub for injured Jack Haskell. In 1902, Hart launched a second career in the minors as a player, manager and umpire. He joined the NL umpiring staff in 1914 but left midway through the following season and returned to Cincinnati to work as an electrotyper. Hart died in the Queen City of a heart attack at 71. (DN)

Hawley, Emerson Pink / "Pink"

B	T	HGT	WGT	G	IP	H	GS
L	R	5'10"	185	367	2830.1	3106	321

CG	BB	SO	SH	W	L	PCT	ERA
280	933	818	11	160	165	.492	4.00

G	AB	H	R	2B	3B	HR
369	1157	278	128	47	20	11

RBI	BB	SO	SB	BA	SA	OBP
152	35	82	7	.240	.344	.268

B. 12/5/1872 Beaver Dam, WI **D.** 9/19/1938
TEAMS: 92–94StLN 95–97PitN 98–99CinN 00NYN 01MilAL
DEBUT: 8/19/1892 at Louisville; caught by Bill Moran and was relieved after six innings by Bill Hawke in a 4–2 loss to Louisville's Scott Stratton
FINALE: 8/20/1901 at Boston; caught by Tim Donahue and was relieved by Tully Sparks in the fourth inning in his 6–0 loss to Boston's Cy Young
CAREER HIGHLIGHT: In 1895 set the post-1892 season records for the highest SA (.497) and the most RBI (42) by a player appearing principally as a pitcher

Hot-tempered, ready to take a swing at any umpire who made a call against him, or bean any hitter he viewed as a threat, Pink Hawley pitched his first ML game when he was 19 and his last when he was just 28. Known by his middle name, he had a twin brother named Blue who was his batterymate until 1891, when Blue died of pneumonia. Also on their semipro Beaver Dam, WI, team that year was a third brother, T. W., who played 1B and remained Pink's traveling companion and adviser until the late 1890s. Shortly after Blue's death Hawley signed with Milwaukee in July 1891. A "big brawny fellow with lots of speed," he was so obviously a major talent that he went to spring training with Chicago in 1892 at Hot Springs, AR. Reportedly he failed to make the Colts' roster because player-manager Cap Anson, who seldom liked a new player unless he could take credit for his discovery, had not discovered him. Upon being cut Hawley signed with independent Fort Smith, AR, where he roomed with "Fish" Hall, a savvy minor league pitcher who advised him how to negotiate with Chris Von der Ahe when the St. Louis owner began courting him. Hawley had assumed Paul Bunyan proportions by the time he arrived in the Mound City accompanied by tales of how he had struck out 22 hitters in 1 game while with Fort Smith and hit for the cycle in another. Events would soon demonstrate that all of these stories may have been true. Pitching for an eleventh-place team in 1892, Hawley molded a 3.19 ERA but was just 6-14. On bad St. Louis teams again the next two seasons, he finished 1894 with a 30-58 record in Browns livery. Traded that winter to Pittsburgh for pitcher Red Ehret and $3,000, Hawley flowered into arguably the best pitcher in the NL in 1895, winning 31 games and setting several post-1892 season batting marks for pitchers, including the most RBI (42) and the highest SA (.497). Almost single-handedly he kept the Pirates in first place as late as August 3 before the team fell to seventh when manager Connie Mack could find only one other pitcher—Bill Hart (14)—that won more than 8 games.

The following May Hawley had the dubious good fortune of being the first MLer to appear on a team button when Red Mason, the Pirates' trainer, devised a button for fans to wear with Hawley's picture on it. Mason chose Hawley because he was regarded as not only Pittsburgh's best-looking player but also its best in general, an opinion that Pirates pitcher Frank Killen (who in 1896 was on his way to posting the last 30-win season by an NL southpaw) took violent exception to. Before Mack opened his eyes to what was happening, his team had divided into two camps, as Hawley and Killen each had his band of loyal followers and would openly pull for the other to lose. The situation grew so insufferable the following year that one of the two prima donnas had to go, and Hawley was chosen as the sacrificial lamb when Bill Watkins was appointed Pittsburgh's new manager for 1898. Watkins, after managing Hawley with St. Louis in 1893, made it clear he wanted no part of the querulous pitcher again. In November 1897 Hawley, outfielder Elmer Smith, and $1,500 went to Cincinnati in return for five players.

The discarded pitcher had a season in 1898 second only to his 1895 gem, winning 27 games for the third-place Reds. Just 25 when the campaign ended, he had already banked 138 career victories. But Hawley then crossed swords with Cincinnati owner John T. Brush and refused to sign a contract for a pay cut to $1,800 with a clause that he would get more only if he refrained from drinking all year. By rule then, because of the size of the pay cut, Hawley could have become a free agent if the National Board agreed with his case, but Brush happened to be on the board. Already deeply antagonistic toward Brush, Hawley was further unraveled by a new balk rule in 1899 that cost him several early-season games. Warned by Brush not to commit another balk, Hawley inevitably did, and Brush promptly suspended him. The 27-game winner in 1898 plummeted to just 14 victories.

Fed up with dealing with Hawley, Brush sold him to the New York Giants in March 1900 for an amount neither team ever disclosed. Stuck on a demoralized outfit that was headed for the first cellar finish ever by a New York big league team, Hawley started 0-7 but nonetheless finished with a .500 record and led the NL in CGs. He then jumped to the American League at his first opportunity and chose Milwaukee because of its proximity to his home. But his choice tied him to player-manager Hugh Duffy, another pilot who was less than an ardent admirer of his.

Hawley began 1901 with his team on the losing end of each of his first four starts, highlighted by an Opening Day fiasco that saw a near certain win snatched from him when Detroit rallied for a record 10 runs in the ninth inning against his relief help in a 14–13 win. In June, sensing the Brewers were going to be his second last-place team in a row, he embarked on a 7-game losing streak that turned Duffy irrevocably against him. At the end of August Duffy gave Hawley his ten days notice of release. He again pitched disappointingly the following year with both Milwaukee of the outlaw American Association and Buffalo of the Eastern League, finishing a combined 8-11, and then left pro ball to hurl for an independent team in La Crosse WI, until La Crosse joined the Wisconsin State League and he was named player-manager. Until 1909, his last year at the La Crosse helm, the team was called the Pinks in his honor. Hawley later returned to his hometown and was running a bowling alley until failing health confined him to his home just before his death at 66. (DN)

Healy, John J. / "John" "Long John" "Egyptian"

B	T	HGT	WGT	G	IP	H	GS
R	R	6'2"	158	227	1875	1920	222

CG	BB	SO	SH	W	L	PCT	ERA
208	599	822	9	78	136	.364	3.84

B. 10/27/1866 Cairo, IL **D.** 3/16/1899
TEAMS: 85–86StLN 87–88IndN 89WasN 89ChiN 90TolA 91BalA 92BalN 92LouN
DEBUT: 9/11/1885 at St. Louis; caught by George Baker and lost 2–0 to Chicago's Jim McCormick
FINALE: 7/6/1892 at Louisville; caught by Jack Grim and lost 6–5 to New York's Amos Rusie

John Healy was born in Cairo, IL, in an area known as "Little Egypt," and as a result was called "Egyptian." His career winning percentage is only .364 and the best season record he ever achieved was 22-21, yet, especially in his youth, he was counted as one of the most promising pitchers of the day, and he never lacked for a team that coveted his services.

Healy's family came to America from Ireland shortly before his birth, and of three siblings he was the youngest by more than ten years and the only one born in the United States. His mother, Bridget, was widowed when he was young, and his older brother Frank, a druggist, supported the family. In Cairo, catcher Tom Dolan discovered Healy, the prototypical wild but hard-throwing young pitcher, playing local ball, and Dolan recommended him to his St. Louis NL team. Still only 18 years old, Healy made an impressive debut, holding pennant-winning Chicago to 5 hits in a 2–0 loss. He later two-hit Boston for his first ML win but lost six other starts and walked batters at a rate almost 30 percent above NL average.

But he also fanned batters at a rate substantially above the league average and showed enough to be deemed ready to help the weak Maroons without minor league seasoning. In short time Dave Rowe, Kansas City's player-manager, described Healy as "the coming pitcher of the country" and reportedly offered two players and cash for him, only to be turned down by the Maroons.

Pitching for a succession of weak teams in St. Louis and Indianapolis over the next few years, however, Healy never fully lived up to his potential, averaging more than 25 losses a season. Like many of his Indianapolis compatriots, he frequently quarreled with team management, complained about low salaries and was accused of malingering. When he injured his wrist in a fight with teammate Con Daily late in the 1888 season, he was fined $300. Nevertheless, he was still well regarded by baseball men such as Cap Anson, and when Anson's Chicago team went on its famous world tour after the 1888 season, Healy was taken along as a pitcher for the All-America team that opposed Chicago. The always publicity-conscious Chicago club president Al Spalding naturally made sure that Egyptian Healy pitched the game the tourists played in the desert within sight of the pyramid of Cheops.

The Indianapolis management and Healy had by now wearied of one another, and while he was touring the globe the Hoosiers traded him for another malcontent pitcher, Jim Whitney of Washington. A good trade is supposedly one that helps both teams; the Healy-Whitney deal came about as close as possible to being an atrocity, for Healy and Whitney combined for a 3-18 record with their new teams and were both released long before the season was over. Chicago picked Healy up, but he pitched poorly and was released again. Even after Healy had accumulated a 2-15 record for two teams that had each released him, Boston reportedly was ready to sign him in September as insurance for its pennant drive, but he returned to Cairo to be with his dying mother and did not pitch again that year.

His serious collapse in 1889 suggests an arm problem; if so, the layoff late in the year may have helped him recover, for his next two seasons were much improved. But being out of action at the end of the 1889 season also took him out of the revolt by the players' Brotherhood that established the new PL. A Brotherhood sympathizer, he signed with Kansas City of the AA after the season because "he was against the [National] League," and he had not realized the NL players were organizing their own circuit. When KC descended to the Western Association, however, Healy objected to going to a minor league and claimed his KC contract was invalid because it had been signed sooner than the rules allowed and, moreover, on a Sunday. To avoid an appeal of the matter, KC sold him to the Toledo AA replacement team, for whom he recorded the only winning record of his career. After Toledo left the AA, he pitched for Baltimore and then 2 games for Louisville in July 1892 that finished his ML career.

Healy pitched well in his short stint with the Colonels, and the claim would later be made that new Louisville manager Fred Pfeffer had released him only because Pfeffer's predecessor, Jack Chapman, had signed him. However, for some while a trick knee had bothered Healy. Surgery during the 1891–92 off-season had supposedly been successful, but after his release by Louisville he stayed out of pro ball for nearly two seasons, suggesting that he was not physically sound. He does not seem to have fully recovered until 1895, when he returned to top-level minor league ball, going 17-13 for Minneapolis of the Western League before retiring for good the following season.

The sometimes headstrong and undisciplined fireballing youngster of the 1880s matured into a stable and substantial man, regarded in Minneapolis particularly as a smart pitcher and a steadying force on the team. In 1891 he had married Maggie Griffin in St. Louis and begun saving his money and thriving generally. During off-seasons he had worked in his brother Frank's drugstore and then taken a managerial position in a large St. Louis grocery. During his hiatus from pro ball, he had also organized his own cooperative team of unemployed pro players, with everyone paid a share of the gate. After playing his last pro game in 1896 Healy came back to St. Louis to join the police force. Very soon, however, he developed symptoms of tuberculosis. In 1898 Healy traveled to Nebraska, where the climate was thought to be better for his lungs and soon returned, reportedly much improved. But his condition continued to deteriorate. In March 1899 he died at his St. Louis home, survived by his wife and two young daughters. (DB/DN)

Hecker, Guy Jackson / "Guy"

B	T	HGT	WGT	G	IP	H	GS
R	R	6'0"	190	334	2924	2922	322

CG	BB	SO	SH	W	L	PCT	ERA
312	492	1110	15	175	146	.545	2.93

G	AB	H	R	2B	3B	HR
705	2876	812	504	117	47	19

RBI	BB	SO	SB	BA	SA	OBP
278	143	44	123	.282	.376	.324

G	W	L	PCT	PENNANTS
138	23	113	.169	0

B. 4/3/1856 Youngsville, PA **D.** 12/3/1938
TEAMS: 82–89LouA (P/M)90PitN
DEBUT: 5/2/1882 at St. Louis; played 1B and went 4-for-5 in a 9–7 loss to St. Louis's George McGinnis
FINALE: 9/30/1890 at Pittsburgh; played LF and went 1-for-4 in a 10–1 win over Philadelphia's Tom Vickery
CAREER HIGHLIGHT ONE: Won an American Association season record 52 games in 1884
CAREER HIGHLIGHT TWO: In 1886 became the only player in ML history to qualify for an ERA crown and win a batting title in the same season
CAREER HIGHLIGHT THREE AND FAMOUS FIRST: 8/15/1886 at Louisville; in the second game of a DH was caught by Amos Cross, went 6-for-7, became the first pitcher to hit 3 home runs in a game and scored a nine-inning single-game-record 7 runs in his 22–5 win over Baltimore's Dick Conway

Guy Hecker was the American Association's premier pitcher in its first four seasons as a major leaguer and led the loop in hitting in its fifth season. In his heyday he was so popular in Louisville that salesman would call their products Hecker this or Hecker that and claim the great pitcher used them all the time. It was said that if Hecker had professed to prefer moonshine to the best Kentucky sour mash, everyone in Louisville would have begun drinking moonshine.

Born in Youngsville, PA, Hecker moved down the Allegheny River with his family to Oil City, which remained his home until late in life. In 1877 he came to Ohio to play 1B for the independent Springfield Champion Citys behind pitchers Bobby Mitchell and Candy Cummings and then returned to Oil City to marry and play for the local exchange team. In the summer of 1879 Hecker joined semipro Warren, PA, in a tournament that also included Bradford, PA, which featured pitcher Tony Mullane. The two struck up a bond, and when Mullane signed with the Louisville entry in the fledgling American Association, he encouraged Hecker to accompany him. Resistant for years to numerous offers to turn pro, Hecker finally succumbed but, only after working out an arrangement with his wife whereby she would remain in Oil City while he went off to play.

Hecker occupied 1B exclusively with Louisville until August 18, 1882, when he switched places with Mullane and beat Pittsburgh 8–4, giving up just 6 hits in his nine frames of work. It was an average he would maintain in his twelve remaining box appearances in 1882, enabling him to hold opponents to a minuscule .188 BA and an even more remarkable .199 OBP in his rookie season. After Hecker added a no-hitter on September 19 at Pittsburgh, Louisville felt less bereft when Mullane grabbed an offer of more money to sign with St. Louis in 1883.

Installed as Louisville's bellwether in his sophomore season, Hecker won 28 games and followed with a year that brought him the AA season record for wins (52), complete games (72), and innings (670.2), as well as the ERA crown (1.80) and the strikeout lead (385). But for all that he could do no more than lift his club to a third-place finish. Hecker, not surprisingly, began 1885 with an ailing arm but pitched through it and won 30 games. The following spring he was said to be a "broken down pitcher" due to elbow trouble and was replaced as team captain in late May after a faction led by his chief rival for pitching plaudits, Tom Ramsey, alleged that Hecker was jealous of Ramsey's success and working to undermine him. Hecker's reaction was to win 11 straight games at one point and rank as the circuit's leading hitter at the end of July. By the end of August he had hiked his BA to .385, but his arm was now so painful after each game he pitched that he had to shock it with an electric battery before he could put his hat on. When Hecker slumped in September both in the box and at the plate, the team went down with him, spiraling from second place to 4 games below .500 at the season's end, although Hecker managed to win the batting title by the skin of his teeth with a .341 mark.

The 1887 season found Hecker at 1B more often than in the box after the new pitching rules eliminated his patented running start and his mounting arm woes curtailed the effectiveness of his overhand drop. Although he hit .319 and won 18 games, he missed substantial time after an errant pitch from New York's Ed Cushman dislocated his kneecap, and he later was sidelined with an abscessed ear. When Hecker slipped to .227 and 8-17 in 1888, Louisville merchants began looking for another name to put on their products. He was further embarrassed the following year, drawing his release in mid-September to cut the expense of his salary as the Colonels headed toward a 27-111 finish and .196 winning percentage, an ML record low to that point.

Hecker ended 1889 as an AA umpire and was contemplating retirement when the Pittsburgh NL club, which had been stripped by Players League raiders, offered to name him its player-manager. To his annoyance, Hecker found himself on a team even worse than his previous one, as his dismal, crudely patched-together Smoke City charges set a new ML nadir by winning just 23 games and logging a .169 winning percentage. In November 1890, Hecker announced his retirement but then became an agent for Pittsburgh NL, hired specifically to bribe AA players to jump their contracts and play in the NL, preferably with the Pirates. The following July restlessness drove him to agree to replace ex-ML pitcher Jake Aydelott as player-manager with Fort Wayne of the Northwestern League. Hecker took a similar post in 1892 with Jacksonville of the Illinois-Indiana League and then tried his luck in the oil business for a while. In 1893 he helped revive the independent Iron & Oil League with himself as Oil City's first baseman and manager. He remained active at the helm of his team—known as "Hecker's Hitters"—until 1898.

Eventually Hecker left the oil business and moved with his wife to Wooster, OH, where they opened a grocery store. Later he was a lease adjuster for the Ohio Fuel Gas Company. An auto accident in 1931 left Hecker with limited use of his right arm, and he died seven years later at his Wooster home from nephritis. (DN/PV)

Hemming, George Earl / "George" "Old Wax Figger"

B	T	HGT	WGT	G	IP	H	GS
R	R	5'11"	170	204	1587.2	1795	168

CG	BB	SO	SH	W	L	PCT	ERA
156	690	362	7	91	82	.526	4.53

B. 12/15/1868 Carrolton, OH **D.** 6/3/1930
TEAMS: 90CleP 90BroP 91BroN 92CinN 92–94LouN 94–96BalN 97LouN
DEBUT: 4/21/1890 at Buffalo; relieved Enoch Bakely in a 15–8 loss to Buffalo's Alex Ferson
FINALE: 6/12/1897 at Baltimore; relieved Bill Hill who took the 15–6 loss to Baltimore's Joe Corbett
FAMOUS FIRST: 9/7/1896 at Baltimore; became the first pitcher in ML history to win the third game of a tripleheader when he beat Louisville's Bert Cunningham 12–1

George Hemming was a cook at the Ohio state mental hospital and pitching for an amateur team in Columbus, OH, when Larry Twitchell introduced him to Cleveland PL club owner Al Johnson. He was released when Cleveland misguidedly thought it had enough pitching, and he joined independent Anderson, IN, until the Brooklyn PL entry acquired him in July. A strong 8-4 finish with Brooklyn ranked Hemming among the top rookies to make their ML debuts in the Brotherhood loop. After the PL collapsed, manager John M. Ward snatched the frosh for his Brooklyn NL club. Hemming had a great spring in 1891, raising Ward's expectations that he would be the one of club's best pitchers, but instead he was its worst. His low point came on August 25 at Chicago when he gave up 27 hits and 50 total bases in a 28–5 loss to the Colts' Jack Luby.

Threatened with a large salary cut, Hemming held out in 1892 along with two of Brooklyn's other pitchers, Tom Lovett and George Haddock, and Ward's response was to reconstruct almost his entire pitching staff, cutting not only Hemming but also Bob Caruthers and Bill Terry. Hemming pitched a trial game with Cincinnati, was not offered a contract, and finished the year with Louisville. The following year he went 18-17 with the weak Colonels, an achievement that did not escape Baltimore manager Ned Hanlon. On August 31, 1894, Hanlon sent pitcher Bert Inks and $2,000 to cash-poor Louisville for Hemming and received an immediate dividend when his new pitcher was a perfect 4-0 in the final weeks of the season. A member of a championship-caliber team for the first time in his career, Hemming followed with a 20-win season in 1895 and was 15-6 for the Orioles the next year before running aground. Correctly judging that Hemming's arm was gone, Hanlon sold him back to Louisville in April 1897. When the Colonels released him early that summer, he vowed that he would "rest his arm for a year at least" but returned the following spring with Newark of the Atlantic League.

Hemming remained active in the minors as an undistinguished pitcher-outfielder until 1904. The source of his most intriguing nickname, "Old Wax Figger," is unknown. A finesse pitcher who was the product of an era when strikeouts were infrequent, Hemming has the lowest strikeouts-to-walks ratio (0.52) among ML pitchers in a minimum of 1,500 career innings. He died in Springfield, MA, at 61. (DN)

Henderson, James Harding / "Hardie"

B	T	HGT	WGT	G	IP	H	GS
R	R	5'10"	200	210	1788.1	1800	206

CG	BB	SO	SH	W	L	PCT	ERA
197	522	930	4	81	121	.401	3.50

B. 10/31/1862 Philadelphia, PA **D.** 2/6/1903
TEAMS: 83PhiN 83–86BalA 86–87BroA 88PitN
DEBUT: 5/2/1883 at Philadelphia; played LF and made 2 hits in a 4–1 loss to Providence's Charley Radbourn
FINALE: 5/24/1888 at Pittsburgh; caught by Doggie Miller and lost 11–6 to Indianapolis's John Healy

Even though Hardie Henderson collected two hits in his ML debut, he was not a good hitter. He was also excruciatingly slow on the bases. In May 1886 he and behemoth first baseman Juice Latham as a joke were advertised to run a twenty-five-yard match race. But Henderson's biggest handicap was that all of his luck was bad. In 1882 he was a highly regarded 19-year-old slinger with the Philadelphia League Alliance team but lacked a catcher that could handle him. Moving with many of his teammates to Philadelphia NL the following year, he was paired with Bill Harbidge, a veteran NL catcher, in his first ML start on May 3, 1883. But Harbidge was felled by a foul tip, leaving Henderson at the mercy of rookie receiver Frank Ringo in what became a 24–6 loss. He then had the rare bad fortune to leave Philadelphia, the last-place NL finisher in 1883, for that season's AA doormat, Baltimore, where he suffered 32 losses in 42 decisions.

The 1884 campaign seemed to herald a change in Henderson's luck when he beat New York on Opening Day and rolled to 27 wins for an Orioles team that surprised by finishing in the first division. But 1885 was a complete reversion when Baltimore again sank to last place even though Henderson won 25 games and 61 percent of his club's victories. The following season he became a classic example of how much a pitcher's supporting cast could affect his record in the nineteenth century. Following a 3-15 start for yet another dreary Baltimore cellar dweller, he got his wish after months of begging for his release and signed with Brooklyn, where he went 10-4 despite injuring his arm in a late-September game against Cincinnati and having to resort to a lob ball for the rest of the year.

Henderson's arm woes pursued him into 1887 just when he was finally with a good team. Little used even after he healed, he worked only 111⅔ innings, and soon his arm was not the only part of his anatomy that was not in shape. Released after the season, he signed for 1888 with Pittsburgh but alienated manager Horace Phillips when he reported to spring training weighing 216. Ordered to get down to 190, Henderson made only a token effort to reduce when his arm went on the fritz again. After Pittsburgh released him, he pitched portions of the next two seasons in the minors and then took up umpiring.

Henderson officiated in the minors for several years before he was appointed a substitute NL umpire late in the 1895 season to work games at Philadelphia. That winter, when Nick Young hired him as a regular umpire, he joined three other ex-ML pitchers on the NL staff—Tim Keefe, Bob Emslie, and Stump Wiedman. Young's theory was that the quartet would excel at calling balls and strikes, but Henderson ran into another sort of problem. Although he was a staunch advocate of the double-umpire experiment that was tested on a regular basis for the first time in 1896, he had the misfortune to often be paired with callow rookie official Dan Campbell, resulting in frequent disorderly games, and left in disgust before the season was out.

By the end of the century Henderson was running Baker's Pool Room on Lancaster Avenue in downtown Philadelphia. He was often sighted by writers from *SL* and *TSN* who delighted in noting facetiously that he was "thin as ever." Luckless to his last day, on February 6, 1903, Henderson was run over by a trolley car when he tripped and fell in its path while he was on his way home from work. (DN)

Henry, John Michael / "John"

B	T	HGT	WGT	G	IP	H	GS
?	L	?	?	18	140.2	152	18

CG	BB	SO	SH	W	L	PCT	ERA
18	54	73	1	4	14	.222	4.09

G	AB	H	R	2B	3B	HR
60	218	53	28	9	0	0

RBI	BB	SO	SB	BA	SA	OBP
19	8	27	12	.243	.284	.273

B. 9/2/1863 Springfield, MA **D.** 6/11/1939
TEAMS: 84CleN 85BalA 86WasN 90NYN
DEBUT AND CAREER HIGHLIGHT: 8/13/1884 at Detroit; caught by Jerrie Moore and beat Detroit's Charlie Getzein 1–0
FINALE: 8/7/1890 at Philadelphia; replaced Jesse Burkett in LF when Burkett relieved pitcher Jack Sharrott and went 0-for-2 in a 5–4 loss to Philadelphia's Tom Vickery

John Henry spent part of 1883 with Wilmington of the Interstate Association and was with Grand Rapids in 1884 when the disbanding Northwestern League club sold one of its batteries to Detroit and the other to Cleveland. The quartet all made their ML debuts in the same game on August 13, 1884, with Henry's easily the most superlative. It was a one-time performance. Henry lost all four of his remaining starts with Cleveland and found himself with Norfolk of the Eastern League in the spring of 1885. To escape he complained that he could not pitch under the loop rule forbidding overhand deliveries, but Norfolk contended that he "was playing for his release, threw a game in Washington, and generally acted in a rebellious manner." The Virginia team then tried to blacklist him when it released him, but Henry fought it through and pitched in the Southern League awhile before being acquired by Baltimore AA. Despite a 2-7 mark with the Orioles, he was reserved for 1886 but then released the following spring. After summering with Hartford of the Eastern League, Henry hooked on with Washington NL late in the season and last appeared in a Senators uniform on October 19, 1886, when he lost 6–2 to Baltimore to give the Orioles the postseason series for supremacy between the last-place AA and NL finishers.

Probably wisely, Henry at that juncture began to fancy himself more an outfielder than a pitcher. In 1889 he hit .312 as player-manager for Hartford of the Atlantic Association and was rehired for the following season. Fired in June 1890, he seemed to hit the jackpot when the Giants grabbed him to fill an embarrassing hole in CF. Henry's luck was short-lived, however. On July 19 he gave his watch, diamond stud, and $56 to Samuel Goodman, a friend of his, to hold during a game that day at the Polo Grounds, and Goodman immediately went missing.

Henry played in the minors until 1895, finishing with Hartford in the Connecticut State League, and then opened a "fine saloon" in that city. Tired of being raided, he joined the other side and became a policeman. Henry rose to the rank of captain prior to his death at his Hartford home at 75. (DN)

*Hill, William Cicero / "Bill" "Still Bill"

B	T	HGT	WGT	G	IP	H	GS
L	L	6'1"	201	124	925	994	115

CG	BB	SO	SH	W	L	PCT	ERA
92	406	280	3	36	69	.343	4.16

B. 8/2/1874 Chattanooga, TN **D.** 1/28/1938
TEAMS: 96–97LouN 98CinN 99CleN 99BalN 99BroN
DEBUT: 4/18/1896 at Louisville; relieved Gus Weyhing in the ninth inning in Weyhing's 5–3 win over Chicago's Danny Friend
FINALE: 9/13/1899 at Brooklyn; caught by Deacon McGuire and beat Pittsburgh's Tully Sparks and Sam Leever 4–3

Bill Hill was dubbed "Still Bill" because he hailed from an area where moonshining stills flourished and he was a steady patron of them. "The sorrel-topped south-paw [*sic*]" pitched for a string of teams throughout the South without lasting long with any of them until he joined independent Knoxville, TN, in 1895 after pledging he would quit drinking. Upon fanning 102 batters and allowing just 24 hits over a 9-game stretch late in the season, he was acquired by Louisville in September 1895 but never got into a game.

The following spring Colonels manager John McCloskey nearly released Hill because he was atrocious at holding enemy runners on 1B despite being left-handed. He then pitched well in an intersquad game to keep his job and joined fellow rookie Chick Fraser at the head of the Louisville rotation. At the close of his first season Hill owned just 9 wins and a post-1892 rookie-record 28 losses.

But 10 were by just one run, and he topped the club in ERA and strikeouts and was second only to Fraser in wins. In his sophomore year Hill fell to just 7 wins, and veteran first baseman Perry Werden, who joined the team that season, drew the blame. Both Werden and Hill were arrested at 3 a.m. in a Louisville saloon in late September for trying to shake down another patron, and while the pitcher was only fined $300 for the indiscretion and suspended, Werden was told to look elsewhere in 1898 for a job.

Despite Hill's murky reputation, Louisville managed to swing perhaps its best trade ever the following February, sending the blond lefty with a career 16-45 record to that point to Cincinnati for pitcher Red Ehret, outfielder Dummy Hoy, and SS Claude Ritchey, three quality players. The trade was contingent on Hill signing a contract containing "an iron-clad temperance clause" and following through with his plan to marry his fiancé, Carrie Fletcher, but when ex-MLer Billy Klusman learned of the deal he warned the Cincinnati management of a night in the saloon he ran in the Queen City when Hill had punched out a partly crippled customer in an argument over the man's necktie. In August 1898 Reds manager Buck Ewing, against his better judgment, opted not to suspend Hill for assaulting the club masseur, but when the pitcher had mushroomed to 212 pounds by the end of the season, his vow to local writer Ren Mulford to turn over new leaf for 1899 after having again visited "The Altar of Thirst" was viewed so charily that he was sent to St. Louis accompanied by a hefty $4,000 check for pitcher "Brewery" Jack Taylor.

By the spring of 1899 Hill's stock had fallen so low that the syndicate owners of St. Louis and Cleveland earmarked him for the hapless Spiders. After swiftly failing in Cleveland, Hill did likewise in Baltimore but then won his only mound appearance with Brooklyn. Nevertheless Superbas manager Ned Hanlon left him home the following spring and then sent for him in desperation when Jerry Nops was a holdout and the team needed another lefty. Hill never pitched again for Brooklyn but that July joined Detroit of the newly renamed AL for a few games before returning to his adopted home in Cincinnati with an arm injury that would keep him from ever playing again. His friends took up a collection to tide him over until he found a job, and he talked of opening a saloon near the Cincinnati ballpark with catcher Heinie Peitz that the partnership would christen "The Battery." Instead, the brother of twentieth-century MLer Hugh Hill became a Queen City policeman and rose to the rank of detective before he was hit by a car while crossing a downtown street and died from a skull fracture. (DN)

Hodnett, Charles / "Charlie"

B	T	HGT	WGT	G	IP	H	GS
?	?	?	?	18	153	149	18

CG	BB	SO	SH	W	L	PCT	ERA
15	23	47	1	14	4	.778	1.88

B. ?/?/1861 Dubuque, IA **D.** 4/25/1890
TEAMS: 83StLA 84StLU
DEBUT: 5/3/1883 at Cincinnati; caught by Sleeper Sullivan and lost 3–2 to Cincinnati's Will White
FINALE: 7/4/1884 at Washington; caught by Jack Brennan and lost 12–1 to Washington's Aleck Voss

Charlie Hodnett came to the Browns in the spring of 1883 from the St. Louis sandlots. His brother Jack was also a prominent local amateur, and his father, John, helped found the *St. Louis Times*, a Democratic organ, in 1866. Both brothers worked as printers at their father's paper early in life.

After topping Columbus 5–1 on May 20, 1883, at St. Louis for his first ML win, Hodnett made only two more starts with the Browns, as the club's twin tandem of George McGinnis and Tony Mullane pitched every game that season but the four that fell to the rookie. The following year Hodnett started for the St. Louis Maroons on Opening Day and beat Chicago 7–2. More than a month later he sustained the UA club's first defeat after it had sprinted to a ML-record 20-0 start when he lost 8–1 to Boston's Tommy Bond. In his penultimate ML start Hodnett lifted his season log to 10-1 by topping Washington 12–7 on July 3. The following afternoon, back in the nation's capital after the Maroons had played a morning game in Baltimore, he endured a 12–1 blasting that dropped his final season mark to 10-2.

Though kept on the Maroons' payroll until September 1884, Hodnett never pitched in another official game. The likelihood is that he was already suffering from the rheumatoid condition that reduced him to a cripple within a few years. By 1886 Hodnett was able to walk only with the aid of a cane and relied on occasional benefit games as his main source of income. Though his exact birth date is unknown, as are all his vital statistics, he is believed to have been only around age 28 when he died a pauper in the St. Louis poor house, where he had been sent after his family could no longer care for him. (DN/DB)

Hoffer, William Leopold / "Bill" "Chick" "Wizard"

B	T	HGT	WGT	G	IP	H	GS
R	R	5'9"	163	145	1155.1	1220	132

CG	BB	SO	SH	W	L	PCT	ERA
115	428	295	10	89	38	.701	3.68

B. 11/8/1870 Cedar Rapids, IA **D.** 7/21/1959
TEAMS: 95–98BalN 98–99PitN 01CleAL
DEBUT: 4/26/1895 at Baltimore; caught by Wilbert Robinson and beat Brooklyn's Ed Stein 12–6
FINALE: 7/4/1901 at Cleveland; caught by Bob Wood and beat Chicago's Ervin Harvey 6–5
CAREER HIGHLIGHT: Won a post-1892 rookie-record 31 games in 1895
FAMOUS FIRST: 4/24/1901 at Chicago; caught by Bob Wood and lost the AL's inaugural game as a major league team 8–2 to Chicago's Roy Patterson

Bill Hoffer underwent a long apprenticeship in the minors before reaching Baltimore in 1895. After spending 1890–91 with his hometown Cedar Rapids club in the Illinois-Iowa League, he put in two more unremarkable minor league seasons before his 28 wins in 1894 with Buffalo of the Eastern League earned him a bid from the Orioles. Given little chance to crack the Baltimore rotation in 1895, Hoffer soon became manager Ned Hanlon's ace, winning 31 games. With ample reason to celebrate, he married his childhood sweetheart, Emma Vanous, that November.

Hoffer's fortes were that he owned a tailing fastball, hit decently, and was an outstanding fielder, particularly strong on bunts, even though as late as 1897 he was the only Baltimore pitcher that didn't wear a glove "when officiating in the box." Most important, Hoffer had the best team in the league behind him in his first two seasons and the second-best in 1897 when he assembled his third straight 20-plus-wins campaign. At that point he was 78-24; during his remaining time in the majors he went just 14-22. Hoffer's pitching was so rank at the beginning of the 1898 campaign that it is fair to assume he had arm trouble, but it could not have been serious, since he was healthy by the time he joined Pittsburgh in late July and won his first three starts before being kayoed for the rest of the season by typhoid fever. But Hanlon treated Hoffer's arm condition as if it were terminal, releasing him so callously after just four bad outings that for over a half century after the pitcher retired he refused to set foot in Baltimore.

In his first start for Pittsburgh in 1899 Hoffer was injured in a collision while covering 1B, and he did not appear again for twelve days. Other ailments brought him to September with a weak 4-10 record, but he then won his last four decisions with the Pirates. Despite his strong finish, Hoffer was dropped when Pittsburgh inherited the cream of disbanding Louisville's pitching staff over the winter. He spent 1900 with Cleveland of the newly renamed American League, going 16-12 with a seventh-place team. The following year he drew Cleveland's Opening Day assignment but lost 8–2 to Chicago and was just 2-8 before staggering to a win in his final ML appearance.

Hoffer played and managed in the minors until 1909 and then worked as a conductor and engineer on a transit line that ran between Cedar Rapids and Iowa City. In his spare time he explored an artistic bent by designing Christmas cards and sports cartoons. Hoffer died in 1959 just eight days prior to catcher Boileryard Clarke, who thus became the last surviving member of the Orioles' 1894–96 dynasty. (DN)

Hofford, John William / "John"

B	T	HGT	WGT	G	IP	H	GS
?	?	6'0"	168	12	106	116	12

CG	BB	SO	SH	W	L	PCT	ERA
12	49	46	0	3	9	.250	4.16

B. 5/25/1863 Philadelphia, PA **D.** 12/16/1915
TEAMS: 85–86PitA
DEBUT: 9/26/1885 at Baltimore; caught by Frank Ringo in a 5–4 loss to Baltimore's Hardie Henderson
FINALE: 7/24/1886 at Pittsburgh; caught by Fred Carroll and lost 7–6 to Philadelphia's Al Atkinson

John Hofford's favorite catcher was his brother, Chick, and the pair formed a sibling battery at various junctures during their amateur and minor league careers. The pitching half first made his mark in 1883 with independent Lancaster. Hofford hurled for Littleton of the Keystone Association the following season before joining Franklin and dominating the Iron & Oil League to such a degree that it disbanded, freeing him to sign with Cleveland for 1885. When the Blues dropped out of the NL, he went to Augusta of the newly formed Southern League instead.

Within weeks after his arrival in Georgia, he was proclaimed the top pitcher in the South, though he had competition from Matt Kilroy, a young teammate who was also from the Philadelphia area. Hofford was more highly regarded at the time, in part because he was the better hitter of the two. By August his reputation had lured both Pittsburgh manager Horace Phillips and an agent from the Baltimore AA team to Augusta in a feverish attempt to acquire him. Phillips arrived first and thus landed Hofford, which may have changed the course of baseball history. When Baltimore's agent found he had lost his chance at the brass ring, to save face he wired Orioles manager Billy Barnie that Kilroy was just as good. Had Pittsburgh landed the booby prize instead, Kilroy, a rookie sensation in 1886, as a lefty tandem with Ed Morris would have made the Alleghenys so strong that year in the box that they might have won the AA pennant and remained in the rebel loop rather than defecting to the NL and initiating a sequence of setbacks that would bring the AA to its knees some five years later. Too, Kilroy's career no doubt would have played out very differently.

Meanwhile, Hofford arrived in Pittsburgh in time to make three losing starts before the 1885 season expired. The following spring he was third on the pitching depth chart behind Morris and HOFer Jim Galvin. As such, he started the third game of the AA season and collected Pittsburgh's first win when he edged St. Louis 6–5. After that he was used only intermittently, as Morris and Galvin were each able to pitch almost every other game, and in late May Hofford claimed he had a sore wing. Phillips scoffed, contending the rookie was angling for his release so he could return to Augusta, which was prepared to pay him more than he was earning at the ML level. Hofford then changed his tune and said his real problem was that the veterans on the Pittsburgh team would not play their best when anyone except Galvin or Morris was pitching. After a bad performance against Philadelphia on June 5, he was suspended for a month, but Phillips lifted the ban early, allowing him to return on June 26 and beat Louisville in eleven innings. The win was Hofford's last in the majors. He received just two more starts, both 1-run losses, before being cut in early August.

Hofford returned to the Southern League in 1887 with Memphis but never again experienced the same success in that loop or any other, although he appears to have continued trying as late as 1896 in the outlaw Naugatuck Valley League. Following a fling with umpiring in the minors, he left the game and returned to Philadelphia where he became a police officer with the Chestnut Street squad. Details of Hofford's final years are sketchy and most of his vital statistics, including which arm he favored, are still unknown. He died in Philadelphia at 52. (DN)

Howell, Harry Taylor / "Harry" "Handsome Harry"

B	T	HGT	WGT	G	IP	H	GS
R	R	5'9"	170	51	337.2	394	37

CG	BB	SO	SH	W	L	PCT	ERA
30	116	86	2	21	13	.618	3.92

B. 11/14/1876 Brooklyn, NY **D.** 5/22/1956
TEAMS: 98BroN 99BalN 00BroN 01–02BalAL 03NYAL 04–10StLAL
DEBUT: 10/10/1898 at Brooklyn; caught by Jack Grim and beat Philadelphia's Red Donahue 7–3
FINALE: 5/14/1910 at New York; was the third Browns pitcher in Ed Kinsella's 14–0 loss to New York's Hippo Vaughn

Reference works list Harry Howell as having been born in New Jersey (exact location unknown), but *TSN* on several occasions said he was born in Brooklyn, the son of Edward Howell who had once played for the old Eckfords, and learned the game on the Brooklyn sandlots. After leaving school Howell worked as a plumber until he joined four other Brooklynites on Meriden in 1898 under manager Jack Chapman. An 18-13 record against Connecticut State League competition persuaded Brooklyn to buy him that fall. The following year Howell went to Baltimore when syndicate ownership brought most of Baltimore's top players to Brooklyn and shipped Brooklyn's lesser players to the Orioles.

A fine rookie season dispatched him back to Brooklyn for 1900. Used mostly in relief, Howell did not notch his first win of the year until June 14 and finished a mediocre 6-5 with the flag-winning Superbas. His future with Brooklyn seemingly dim, Howell might have wondered if he would join his younger brother, a southpaw pitcher in the New England League, in the minors the following season, but that winter he was presented with a far more attractive option when John McGraw, his manager with Baltimore in 1899, felt his rookie performance was a truer representation of his talent. (DN)

Hudson, Nathaniel P. / "Nat"

B	T	HGT	WGT	G	IP	H	GS
R	R	?	?	86	694.1	669	78

CG	BB	SO	SH	W	L	PCT	ERA
72	156	258	5	48	26	.649	3.08

G	AB	H	R	2B	3B	HR
125	446	110	56	14	3	3

RBI	BB	SO	SB	BA	SA	OBP
58	35	11	12	.247	.312	.304

B. 1/12/1859 Chicago, IL **D.** 3/14/1928
TEAMS: 86–89StLA
DEBUT: 4/19/1886 at Pittsburgh; caught by Doc Bushong and lost 6–3 to Pittsburgh's John Hofford
FINALE: 6/27/1889 at St. Louis; caught by Jack Boyle and was relieved by Jack Stivetts in his 8–6 loss to Cincinnati's Tony Mullane

Nat Hudson was among the many adolescents who graduated to the majors after apprenticing at Chicago's Lincoln Park. He started his pro career late, waiting until he was 24 before signing with independent Rock Island in 1883. After a good season in 1885, split between the Western League and the Colorado State League, he came to the Browns the following spring. A 16-win rookie season led Hudson to think he had Chris Von der Ahe over a barrel when the Browns' owner sold his twin aces Bob Caruthers and Dave Foutz to Brooklyn that winter. Hudson engaged in a protracted holdout in the spring of 1887, averring that he would pitch in the Chicago City League and stay home to attend to his recently deceased father's estate and his mother, who was ailing with stomach cancer. He finally signed around Memorial Day and did not pitch his first game of the season until June 3, when he beat Brooklyn 7–4. Thereafter he continued to feud with Von der Ahe and was used sparingly by manager Charlie Comiskey and not at all after he topped Cleveland on August 5.

Finishing the season with just four wins, Hudson boasted that he had "more money at his command than almost any ball player in the country" and understood the lumber business so thoroughly that he was ready to leave the game for it. Realizing Hudson's threat was no longer idle, Von der Ahe and Comiskey wooed him back into the Browns' fold and were rewarded in 1888 with 25 wins. That winter Hudson inherited around $70,000 from his late mother's estate and announced that from then on he would pitch only because he enjoyed it. But when he was blasted 17–7 by Louisville in his first start of 1889 on April 23, it sounded a warning note. By the time he made his final appearance with the Browns, his arm was so dead that he threw only "slow drops."

On July 17, 1889, the Browns traded him to Louisville for the Colonels' problem southpaw, Tom Ramsey, but he refused to report to the Kentucky team. Rather than rescind the deal, Louisville was so eager to get rid of Ramsey that it kept Hudson and sold him to Minneapolis for $1,000. Hudson's arm recovered enough that he was able to win 16 of his first 21 starts against Western Association competition in 1890 before Minneapolis had to release him in July because his salary was prohibitive. He returned to Chicago and played in the City League for several seasons, mostly as an outfielder.

Hudson seems either to have exaggerated the amount of his inheritance or else run through it rather quickly. By 1897 he was a clerk in the office of the election commissioners in Chicago. He later worked as the city treasurer and was active in city politics. By the turn of the century Hudson had made peace with Charlie Comiskey and was a frequent guest of the new owner of the Chicago White Sox at old-timers' events. He died in 1928 of a heart attack at his home in Chicago. (DN)

Hughes, James Jay / "Jay"

B	T	HGT	WGT	G	IP	H	GS
R	R	?	185	73	592.1	518	70

CG	BB	SO	SH	W	L	PCT	ERA
61	219	180	8	51	18	.739	2.95

B. 1/22/1874 Sacramento, CA **D.** 6/2/1924
TEAMS: 98BalN 99BroN 01–02BroN
DEBUT: 4/18/1898 at Washington; caught by Boileryard Clarke and beat Doc Amole 9–0
FINALE: 9/27/1902 at Brooklyn; caught by Lew Ritter and beat New York's Jack Cronin 12–4
CAREER HIGHLIGHT: 4/22/1898 at Baltimore; caught by Boileryard Clarke and no-hit Boston's Ted Lewis 8–0

Jay Hughes is listed as the brother of ML pitcher Mickey Hughes but on specious evidence (*see* Michael Hughes). He is one of a select group of pitchers to hurl shutouts in each of their first two ML starts. Furthermore, he followed his whitewash debut by no-hitting Boston in his next appearance on April 22, 1898. When Cincinnati's Ted Breitenstein also threw a no-no that afternoon, it marked the first time in ML history that two pitchers had hurled no-hitters on the same day.

A saddler by trade, the strawberry-blond Hughes was discovered by Hughie Jennings when a barnstorming Baltimore team playing postseason exhibitions on the West Coast against a ML all-star squad took a holiday to play Hughes's Sacramento Gilt Edge club and lost, 4–2. Awed by Hughes's array of curves, Jennings told Orioles manager Ned Hanlon his lone reservation was that the West Coast hurler lacked sufficient speed. Jennings's fears proved groundless. Although Hughes was far from a strikeout artist, he threw every pitch with the same easy overhand motion, making it impossible for batters to gauge what was coming.

After winning 23 games his frosh year, he went north to Brooklyn the following spring along with Hanlon when syndicate ownership dictated that the Orioles' best players be transferred to the City of Churches. Hughes gave Brooklyn the loop's win and winning-percentage leader in 1899 and helped assure Hanlon of his fourth ML pennant. That winter he married Mary Waters of Sacramento and complied with her wishes that he stay on the West Coast. Ignoring Hanlon's pleas that Brooklyn could not win again without him, he signed with Sacramento of the California League for $2,000, less than Hanlon offered him, and went 24-10. When Brooklyn ace Joe McGinnity jumped to the AL after the 1900 season, a desperate Hanlon upped the ante, and Hughes seized the improved offer since his wife had just borne twins. He won 32 games for Brooklyn in 1901–02 to bring his career total to 83 and then fled the majors again to play in the outlaw Pacific Coast League in 1903. Pitching for Seattle, a sub-.500 team, he went 34-15 and tied for the loop lead in wins. Following a 26-18 season for Seattle in 1904, Hughes turned his back on baseball, pitching only a few scattered innings after that.

In 1924 Hughes was working as a caretaker on a ranch near Walnut Grove, CA, when he slipped off a railway trestle overlooking the American River while returning on foot to the ranch and fell to his death. Although the Sacramento coroner ruled the incident an accident, there was some suspicion that it may have been suicide. At the time, Hughes's son, Pete, was playing with Evansville in the Three-I League. Some eleven years later, Pete drove to where his estranged wife was living, parked his car in front of her house and blew his brains out. (DN)

Hughes, Michael J. / "Mickey"

B	T	HGT	WGT	G	IP	H	GS
?	R	5'6"	165	75	623.2	594	70

CG	BB	SO	SH	W	L	PCT	ERA
63	235	250	2	39	28	.582	3.22

B. 10/25/1866 New York, NY **D.** 4/10/1931
TEAMS: 88–89BroA 90BroN 90PhiA
DEBUT: 4/22/1888 at Brooklyn; caught by Bob Clark and beat Cleveland's Billy Crowell 5–1
FINALE: 8/28/1890 at Philadelphia; relieved Ed Seward, was later relieved by Curt Welch, and finished the game in CF in a 21–8 loss to Columbus's Elton Chamberlin

Most reference works still claim Mickey Hughes was the older brother of ML pitcher Jay Hughes even though the two were born on opposite coasts and there is no evidence that the elder Hughes ever set foot on the West Coast, let alone even so much as met his supposed younger brother. While with Newark of the International Association in 1887 in his third pro season Hughes survived a near-fatal beanball dished up by Toronto's Ed Crane to reach the majors the following year with Brooklyn AA. The owner of a puzzling rising fastball and an excellent curve, Hughes promptly won his first eight starts before suffering his first ML loss on June 17 to Baltimore. After finishing his rookie season with 25 wins, he was expected to replace Bob Caruthers as the team's ace the following year but by

June was under suspension for being in poor condition. Rather than serving as the staff bulwark, Hughes lost his spot in the rotation to Tom Lovett and was usually left behind whenever the Bridegrooms went on the road. With Brooklyn bidding for its first AA pennant, manager Bill McGunnigle benched Hughes for the duration of the season after he lost 12–10 at Philadelphia on September 19.

Pledging to curb his drinking, Hughes began 1890 back in McGunnigle's good graces but was suspended without pay in early July "for dereliction of duty" and then released soon afterward. Signing with Philadelphia AA, he hurled one last good game, beating St. Louis 3–1 on August 17, but was gone by Labor Day after he quit a game against Columbus in disgust when a hungover Denny Lyons played third base like a sieve behind him.

In April 1891 Hughes was arrested for his role in a brawl and near-fatal stabbing at a saloon near Coney Island. The following May he was jailed in Brooklyn for grand larceny. Despite the repeated efforts of former teammates to reform him, Hughes continued on his downward path, appearing in Coney Island police court every few weeks with Milly Gorman, who owned a cheap hotel in the Coney Island area and with whom he had been living in a common-law relationship. Gorman also owned a saloon and frequently had the pitcher arrested for pilfering money out of the till, but each time she softened and took him back. At times the two would engage in drunken public spats and both be sentenced to the workhouse. Hughes meanwhile traced his incorrigibility to the beaning he had sustained in 1887.

After he had dropped out of sight for a time, on March 2, 1901, *TSN* said a short, stout fellow in Albany was claiming to be Mickey Hughes but must be an imposter, as the real Mickey was dead. *TSN* was wrong; Hughes was still very much alive. He worked as a shipping clerk in the New York area for a spell before dying of a cerebral hemorrhage in 1930. (DN/DB)

Hughey, James Ulysses / "Jim" "Coldwater Jim"

B	T	HGT	WGT	G	IP	H	GS
?	R	6'0"	?	145	1007.2	1271	113

CG	BB	SO	SH	W	L	PCT	ERA
100	317	250	0	29	80	.266	4.87

B. 3/8/1869 Wakashma, MI **D.** 3/29/1945
TEAMS: 91MilA 93ChiN 96–97PitN 98StLN 99CleN 00StLN
DEBUT: 9/29/1891 at Milwaukee; relieved Will Mains in Mains's 10–5 loss to Louisville's Warren Fitzgerald
FINALE: 9/30/1900 at Chicago; caught by Wilbert Robinson and lost 4–1 to Chicago's Tom Hughes

At a glance Jim Hughey must seem to have been just about the worst pitcher to appear in as many as 1,000 innings in the majors. Among the significant negative records he holds are: the most recent pitcher to lose 30 games in a season (1899), the most complete games in ML history without throwing a shutout (100), and the lowest career winning percentage among pitchers in a minimum of 100 decisions (.266). Furthermore, Hughey was weak on bunts and so awkward in general as a fielder that *TSN* once said that he was "lucky to get the man at second, when a double play would be a cinch under ordinary circumstances."

Yet when fully a third of the ML pitchers in 1899 either quit or went to the minors the following year after the NL pared from twelve to eight teams, St. Louis not only did not view Hughey's 4-30 record and 5.41 ERA as reason to dismiss him but kept him on its roster for the entire 1900 season.

After pitching for Joliet of the Illinois-Iowa League in 1890, Hughey first secured the spotlight on July 4, 1891, when he threw two-hit and no-hit shutouts for Fond du Lac against Appleton in a Wisconsin State League DH. Late that September he joined Milwaukee after the Brewers replaced the Cincinnati AA entry. Despite winning his only start with the club, he returned to the minors for the next four years save for a brief dalliance with Chicago in 1893.

In the fall of 1895 Pittsburgh NL drafted Hughey from Toledo after he logged 21 wins in the Western League. In his official rookie year he went 6-8 for the Pirates, followed with a 6-10 campaign in 1897, and then was traded to St. Louis that December for pitcher Bill Hart. Over the next two seasons Hughey was an aggregate 11-54 (.169) for teams that were an aggregate 59-245 (.194). He nonetheless experienced his ML career highlight on August 1, 1898, at St. Louis when he beat Charlie Hickman of the pennant-winning Boston club 3–1 on a three-hitter, with only a first-inning run preserving his record for never pitching a shutout.

Upon his departure from the majors, Hughey returned to Toledo, then in the Western Association, for 1901–02 and then spent two years in the Southern Association before retiring to open a general store in a rural area near Coldwater that he operated for many years. He died in a Coldwater hospital in 1945, leaving his wife, Alice, whom he had married in 1892. (DN)

Husted, William J. / "Bill"

B	T	HGT	WGT	G	IP	H	GS
?	?	?	?	18	129	148	17

CG	BB	SO	SH	W	L	PCT	ERA
12	67	33	0	5	10	.333	4.88

B. 10/11/1866 Gloucester, NJ **D.** 5/17/1941
TEAMS: 90PhiP
DEBUT: 4/29/1890 at Brooklyn; caught by Bill Hallman and beat Brooklyn's Con Murphy 14–7
FINALE: 10/4/1890 at Cleveland; caught by Jack Milligan and beat Cleveland's Henry Gruber 16–4

Under more propitious circumstances Bill Husted probably would have been a successful major leaguer. His first pro season of consequence came with Buffalo of the International Association in 1887. He remained in that loop in 1888, toiling for London, Ontario. Husted was regarded as the Philadelphia Brotherhood team's prize rookie in the spring of 1890. In his first exhibition-game appearance with the Quakers, he topped Brooklyn 9–4 on March 8 in Mobile, AL. After winning a spot in the rotation, Husted cruised to an easy win in his debut. Leading 12–1 after six innings, he then "eased up," allowing six runs in the final three frames. *SL* observers, who saw a lot of him since the paper was based in Philadelphia and was pro-Brotherhood, lamented early in the season, "Husted is a very clever pitcher and ought to get more work." But Charlie Buffinton, the team's top pitcher and also its field captain, preferred to use veteran arms until the Quakers were out of the PL race. It did not help Husted's case, either, that he went 3-10 between his first and last starts of the season.

After the PL folded, Husted signed for 1891 with Philadelphia AA. *SL* joyously predicted, "It will be a great and grievous disappointment to his [Husted's] many admirers if their expectations concerning him are not more than realized." Though Hu-sted made the A's roster in spring training, he was released on April 30 without having pitched in an official AA game. The struggling Washington AA club made overtures to him, but he chose to stay in Philadelphia and pitch for the Phillies. When the Phils tried to lowball him on salary, he refused to sign and was about to head for Kansas City of the Western Association instead. But he then decided minor league life and pay no longer appealed to him. Husted returned to the amateur ranks and by 1894 was the player-manager of the semipro Cape May team in the Landings Base Ball Association. He died in Gibbsboro, NJ, at 74. (DN)

Hutchison, William Forrest (aka Hutchinson) / "Bill" "Wild Bill"

B	T	HGT	WGT	G	IP	H	GS
R	R	5'9"	175	376	3079.1	3124	346

CG	BB	SO	SH	W	L	PCT	ERA
321	1132	1235	21	182	163	.528	3.59

B. 12/17/1859 New Haven, CT **D.** 3/19/1926
TEAMS: 84KCU 89–95ChiN 97StLN
DEBUT: 6/10/1884 at Kansas City; caught by Nin Alexander and lost 10–3 to Chicago's John Horan
FINALE: 5/20/1897 at St. Louis; caught by Ed McFarland and lost 11–4 to Boston's Ted Lewis
CAREER HIGHLIGHT: In 1891 became the last ML hurler to win 40 or more games two seasons in a row

Bill Hutchison's name was spelled Hutchinson during most of his career (and may actually have been Hutchinson, according to a Yale University census) and created havoc for researchers in 1941 when a James Hutchinson died in New York City at age 78 after claiming that he was the Hutchinson who pitched for Kansas City UA in 1884. That conundrum was soon resolved, but for years afterward a story continued to have life that Hutchison had never pitched a baseball until 1882 when Yale's regular pitcher's arm gave out and he offered to try his hand at it.

Later it emerged that Hutchison had pitched for the Yalies as early as 1878. In a life of 66 years that was riddled with paradoxes and contradictions, it is still difficult to determine what about Hutchison was true and what was not. Despite reputedly being the scion of a wealthy railroad official and never pressured to play ball for a living, he decided to take the plunge in 1887 and play for money;

and after leaving the game and devoting his full energy to railroading, he seems never to have risen much higher than a clerk's position in the Kansas City Southern Railroad hierarchy. But none of this should distract from the fact that in 1890 Hutchison suddenly sprang forth as the top pitcher in the game, led the majors in wins three years in a row, and was the last ML hurler to win 40 games in back-to-back seasons. Additionally, he was the only ML pitcher subsequent to Charley Radbourn and Jim Galvin in 1883–84 to log as many as 600 innings two years in a row and led all nineteenth-century hurlers in wins after age 30 with 167.

Despite all that, Hutchison is often regarded nowadays as a fluke, the last of the rubber-armed pitchers of the 1870s and 1880s who burned out quickly from overwork and at a tender age, when in actuality he pitched in the majors until he was nearly 38, was an ERA qualifier in seven consecutive seasons and never had serious arm trouble. The lone quirky feature of his ML career, apart from its late start, was that he appears to have had more difficulty adjusting to the dramatic changes in pitching rules in 1893 than any other ML hurler with the possible exception of Gus Weyhing. Previous to that, from 1890–92, Hutchison was the best pitcher in the game, collecting 28 more wins than any other ML hurler during that span; after 1892 he was among the loop's worst twirlers.

In 1877–78, Hutchison attended an academy in Norwich, CT, that was run by his father. Since no catcher on the school team could hold him, the academy hired a ringer named Mickey Miner to catch him even though Miner was a local hoodlum and was almost never sober on game days. Hutchison then spent the next four years at Yale playing SS beside second baseman Walter Camp on days when he did not pitch. In 1883 he agreed to play professionally for Springfield of the Northwestern League but only for two months and refused an offer from Cleveland manager Frank Bancroft to join the NL Blues. The following year, while working at his first railroad job in Kansas City, he was persuaded to pitch 2 games for the local UA team but then, again, resisted all pro offers until 1887, when he was given a leave of absence from his railroad job to play for Des Moines of the Northwestern League after refusing a similar arrangement with Chicago NL. Hutchison struck the same bargain with Des Moines and his railroad employers in 1888. Although the season was well under way when he joined the Iowa team, he still won 23 games.

At that point his success against minor league hitters made the temptation to test himself against ML competition too strong to resist any longer. Hutchison signed with Chicago in 1889 and was installed by manager Cap Anson in the ML's first four-man pitching rotation, going 16-17 in his official rookie season. When he remained loyal to the Colts rather than jump to the PL, Anson rewarded him by making him the staff ace in 1890 and continued to hold him in that regard as late as 1895, long after he had demonstrated that the new pitching rules were beyond his mastery. Still, both Anson and other team observers continued to blame Hutchison's decline on cigarette smoking, claiming it made him too nervous. Hutchison disagreed and solicited for a change in scenery. In 1896 he signed with Minneapolis of the Western League after Chicago released him, seemed to prove his point by leading the loop in wins with 38, and could only laugh at his critics when he was presented with a silver smoking set by admiring fans. Desiring to stay in Minneapolis, Hutchison asked Chicago GM Jim Hart to claim he was on loan to the WL club, but NL president Nick Young took the view that he had been legally drafted by the last-place St. Louis Browns and forced him to join the Mound City club after spring training was already under way in 1897. Disgusted, Hutchison won just one of five starts with the Browns before convincing them to trade him back to Minneapolis. Prior to leaving St. Louis, however, he first needed to get the $800 in cash he had stored in the office safe at the Lindell Hotel, where he had stayed until just a few days before his release. To his horror, he learned that a clerk had made off with the cash, and the hotel manager refused to make good on it, claiming the pitcher was no longer a guest of the hotel. Hutchison pitched in the Western League until 1899 and then played semipro ball until he was nearly 50 years old. He was a railroad clerk when he died in Kansas City at 66 of heart disease. (DN/DB)

Inks, Albert John / "Bert"

B	T	HGT	WGT	G	IP	H	GS
L	L	6'3"	175	89	603.2	780	77

CG	BB	SO	SH	W	L	PCT	ERA
59	266	167	2	27	46	.370	5.52

G	AB	H	R	2B	3B	HR
90	250	75	36	10	0	0

RBI	BB	SO	SB	BA	SA	OBP
18	17	22	2	.300	.340	.349

B. 1/27/1871 Ligonier, IN **D.** 10/3/1941
TEAMS: 91–92Bro 92WasN 94BalN 94–95LouN 96PhiN 96CinN
DEBUT: 9/2/1891 at Cleveland; caught by Tom Daly in an 8–1 loss to Cleveland's Cy Young
FINALE: 6/23/1896 at Chicago; caught by Harry Vaughn and was relieved by Chauncey Fisher in his 7–5 loss to Chicago's Bert Briggs

Bert Inks exemplified the lengths to which teams often go to give a left-handed pitcher every opportunity to develop into ML material. He also may have been a good B.S. artist, pitching for Notre Dame on occasion despite no evidence that he was a student and either claiming—or else allowing someone else to make the claim without refutation from him—that his real name was Inkstein, beguiling *TSN* to assert in April 1892 that he was one of the first "Hebrew" players in ML history.

After spending 1889 with an independent team in Goshen, IN, Inks signed with Indianapolis and then went to spring training with the Phillies when the defunct Hoosiers' roster was dispersed, but he was released on the eve of the 1890 season to Monmouth of the Illinois-Iowa League. He joined Brooklyn the following year after the Duluth Western Association team disbanded. Although just 3-10 with the Bridegrooms, he blanked the Giants 8–0 on October 2 and hit .286 for the year. Inks split 1892 between Brooklyn and Washington and then went back to the minors with Binghamton of the Eastern League. Baltimore manager Ned Hanlon liked his bat as well as his left arm and brought him to the Orioles' camp in the spring of 1894. Inks went 9-4 for the eventual NL flag winners, but an alarming 5.55 ERA provoked Hanlon to send him to Louisville along with $2,000 for pitcher George Hemming on the last day of August. Stuck on the NL's worst team in the mid-1890s, Inks went an aggregate 9-26 with the Colonels before being swapped to Philadelphia for Tom Smith in January 1896. Released to Cincinnati after just one start in a Phils uniform, Inks collared his last ML win on June 16, 1896, beating St. Louis 3–2, but by then was throwing mostly junk.

His arm trouble appears to have also affected his hitting—he batted just .083 (1-for-12) in 1896 to reduce his career BA from .311 to an even .300. It is surprising that his bat never earned him so much as a single inning as a position player. Inks returned to Ligonier, IN, after leaving the game in 1898 and operated a combination stage and movie theater there until his death in 1941. His 5.52 career ERA is the highest among nineteenth-century pitchers in a minimum of 500 innings. (DN/DB)

Jones, Albert Edward / "Cowboy" "Bronco"

B	T	HGT	WGT	G	IP	H	GS
L	L	5'11"	160	60	450	521	57

CG	BB	SO	SH	W	L	PCT	ERA
45	133	122	0	23	28	.451	3.46

B. 8/23/1874 Golden, CO **D.** 2/9/1958
TEAMS: 98CleN 99–01StLN
DEBUT: 6/24/1898 at Cleveland; caught by Lou Criger and was relieved by George Kelb in his 13–4 loss to New York's Cy Seymour
FINALE: 6/21/1901 at Philadelphia; relieved Jack Harper in the first inning in a 4–1 loss to Philadelphia's Al Orth

In June 1897 *TSN* predicted that Cowboy Jones "will be one of the greatest pitchers in the profession in 2 years, barring accident." Some four years later, former Milwaukee teammate Bill Reidy recalled that in a Western League game that year against Grand Rapids Jones had fanned the first 8 men who faced him without even a single foul ball being hit. At that juncture Jones was spending his second season with Milwaukee after coming to Wisconsin the previous July from the California League. That fall he was drafted by Cleveland, which had been trying to acquire him for several months, and seemed on his way to stardom. But over the winter Jones informed Cleveland that his arm "had gone back on him." When he failed to report in the spring of 1898, Cleveland suspected Milwaukee manager Connie Mack of a scam, telling Jones to feign arm trouble so the Spiders would be eager to relinquish him to the Brewers and recoup their draft money.

Ultimately, Jones did report—and for more money than Cleveland had offered him originally—after Nig Cuppy came to camp with the same elbow problem that had plagued him in 1897. But it soon emerged that Jones's arm truly was suspect. His Cleveland debut was delayed until June 1898, and by late September he had gone home to rest for the winter.

Jones was part of the Cleveland contingent that was assigned to St. Louis when syndicate ownership merged the two clubs prior to the 1899 season. His arm seemed hale again the following spring. In his first 1899 appearance on April 22 he beat Pittsburgh to extend his club's hot start to 5-0. But by the end of May, Jones had been removed from the rotation, and some two months later he exploded at manager Pat Tebeau for not pitching him more often. Soon after that Jones jumped the team, threatening to go back to his old job as a timekeeper in an Aspen, CO, mine, but a later report, perhaps emanating from Jones, said he had returned to Colorado for his health.

Whether Jones was a malingerer or truly had physical issues, the sorry fact is that after his first two seasons in the majors he had pitched in only 21 games and scarcely 150 innings. But in the spring of 1900, facing a threat of losing his job when the majors pared down to just eight teams, he seemed to regain his health, if not his former zip. In the St. Louis rotation all year, Jones performed erratically, finishing at 13-19 with a mediocre 3.57 ERA. That winter he ran his cigar store in Aspen and then in February announced that he was jumping to Baltimore of the rebel AL to join his St. Louis teammates from the previous year, John McGraw and Wilbert Robinson. Jones then reconsidered and remained in the NL.

In the spring of 1901 St. Louis's new manager, Patsy Donovan, replaced him in the rotation with rookie Ed Murphy after he got off to a 2-6 start and then authorized his release to Denver of the Western League in early July. Jones pitched in the minors until 1907, finishing with Topeka of the Western League, and may have later returned to the pro ranks in Canada. His failure to emerge as a frontline ML pitcher still lacks a satisfactory explanation. Jones died in Englewood, CA, in 1958. The Colorado School of Mines baseball field is named after him. (DN)

Jones, Alexander M. / "Alex"

B	T	HGT	WGT	G	IP	H	GS
L	L	5'9"	170	24	192.1	199	24

CG	BB	SO	SH	W	L	PCT	ERA
18	77	63	1	7	14	.333	3.32

B. 12/25/1869 Pittsburgh, PA **D.** 4/4/1941
TEAMS: 89PitN 92LouN 92WasN 94PhiN 03DetAL
DEBUT AND CAREER HIGHLIGHT: 9/25/1889 at Pittsburgh; caught by Fred Carroll and fanned 10 to tie the then NL record for the most strikeouts by a pitcher in his ML debut in beating Washington's George Keefe 8–5
FINALE: 5/16/1903 at Detroit; caught by Sport McAllister and was relieved by John Deering in his 9–6 loss to Boston's Cy Young

Alex Jones threw hard and had an excellent curve but seemingly was shortchanged because of his size. He came to Pittsburgh in 1889 from the amateur Homestead, PA, club and drew this accolade from *SL* after his debut: "Jones, a rising young pitcher . . . was put in the box by manager Hanlon, and he did remarkably well. He exhibited some very puzzling curves." At the time, Jones was working at the Edgar Thompson Steel Works in Pittsburgh and was given a three-week leave of absence to try his arm in the majors. When Pittsburgh attempted to reserve him for 1890, he fought against it, claiming he had never signed a contract and had only agreed to join the club on a trial basis.

Jones subsequently decided to cast his lot in pro ball in the 1891 New York–Pennsylvania League and resurfaced in the majors in 1892 with Louisville. Although he was effective with the Colonels, he was released to Washington when he failed to win much (5-11), and the same fate awaited him in Washington (0-3). Jones spent the next two seasons in the Pennsylvania State League before joining the Phils in 1894 for one last NL game, a neat 6–3 win over St. Louis on September 3. He then pitched in the minors for a number of years and appears to have left pro ball around 1898 after two seasons in the Atlantic League and not to have returned until 1902 with independent Homestead after reportedly refusing an offer to sign with the NL Cardinals for $250 a month. It is not clear how Jones came to Detroit in 1903, or even if he did. Conceivably, the "Aleck Jones" who was shellacked in two starts ten days apart with the Tigers and then pitched in the minors until 1907 was a different man. (DN)

Keefe, George Washington / "George"

B	T	HGT	WGT	G	IP	H	GS
L	L	5'9"	168	78	616.1	721	71

CG	BB	SO	SH	W	L	PCT	ERA
68	360	213	1	20	48	.294	5.05

B. 1/7/1867 Washington, D.C. **D.** 8/24/1935
TEAMS: 86–89WasN 90BufP 91WasA
DEBUT: 7/30/1886 at Washington; caught by Jackie Hayes in a 13–9 loss to Detroit's Charlie Getzein
FINALE: 4/28/1891 at Baltimore; caught by Joe Visner and Tom Hart, and lost 19–3 to Baltimore's Sadie McMahon
FAMOUS RECORD: 5/1/1889 at New York; caught by Buck Ebright and set a then ML record as well as a NL record he still shares when he walked 7 batters in the fifth inning in a 19–3 loss to New York's Ed Crane

The son of a Civil War veteran, George Keefe claimed to be a nephew of Tim Keefe's, but that remains unconfirmed. It did seem, however, that he could not have played in the majors as long as he did without having been somehow connected. Keefe's 5.13 ERA in 1889 is the highest of any qualifier that pitched in the Players League the following year. He also owns the highest career ERA (5.05) of any ML pitcher who hurled a minimum of 600 innings prior to the increased pitching distance in 1893.

Keefe came to Washington NL in 1886 from the D.C. Agricultural Department team. Talented but almost completely undisciplined, he was farmed to Binghamton of the International Association in 1887 but returned to Washington for one outing on August 24 and was blasted 20–1 by Detroit. After spending most of 1888 with Troy of the IA, he was reacquired by Washington when a restraining order prevented Bill Widner from pitching for the Senators. Keefe was such a pleasant surprise—6-7 with a 2.84 ERA—that he was not only handed a spot in the rotation the following spring but named to start the opening game. Despite losing on both Opening Day and closing day (the original Senators' last game as a member of the NL), Keefe joined batterymate Connie Mack on the Buffalo PL club the following spring. He posted a 6.52 ERA, the worst prior to 1893 by a pitcher in a minimum of 150 innings, and was fired by manager Jay Faatz when he went home in August with a sore flipper. Upon his departure *TSN* counseled, "Keefe must learn to bat or his usefulness as a baseball player will be seriously impaired."

Ironically, after struggling in the minors for a few more years as a pitcher, around 1894 Keefe became a pitcher-outfielder and matured into one of the better hitters in the lower minors toward the end of the century. In 1896 Keefe led the Texas League in batting at the halfway mark before fading. He continued to play in the South and Southwest while wintering in San Antonio and working in the Fort Sam Houston quartermaster's department until he finished his career in 1901 back on the mound with Birmingham of the Southern Association and went 7-15. Keefe then returned to Washington with his wife, Georgetta, after years of roaming the country and found both his parents dead and his fireman brother killed in the line of duty. He resettled in D.C. and played for amateur teams in the early part of the twentieth century while working at the Navy Yard. Eventually Keefe became a landscape gardener for the Washington school system. He died at Washington's Providence Hospital in 1935 of a staph infection he incurred when he scraped his leg on a car door. (DN/DB)

Kennedy, William Park / "Roaring Bill" "Bill" "Brickyard"

B	T	HGT	WGT	G	IP	H	GS
R	R	5'11"	160	368	2780.2	3018	325

CG	BB	SO	SH	W	L	PCT	ERA
274	1106	723	11	174	144	.547	4.01

G	AB	H	R	2B	3B	HR
361	1170	303	140	46	18	1

RBI	BB	SO	SB	BA	SA	OBP
135	39	38	13	.259	.331	.284

B. 10/7/1867 Bellaire, OH **D.** 9/23/1915
TEAMS: 92–01BroN 02NYN 03PitN
DEBUT: 4/26/1892 at Brooklyn; caught by Tom Daly and beat Baltimore's Sadie McMahon 12–10
FINALE: 9/26/1903 at Pittsburgh; caught by Ed Phelps and lost 4–1 to New York's Joe McGinnity
FAMOUS FIRST: 10/7/1903 at Pittsburgh; became the first pitcher to make his final ML appearance in a World Series Game when he started Game 5 against Boston AL and was relieved by Gus Thompson in an 11–2 loss to Boston's Cy Young

Bill Kennedy's greatest failing was an inability to cover 1B; he simply could never master the task and kept protesting in vain that it wasn't part of a pitcher's job description. Called "Roaring Bill" for his foghorn voice and the way he incessantly ragged on umpires, opposing batters, and even his own teammates, Kennedy frequently clashed with managers, most prominently Ned Hanlon (1899–1901), because of his wont to constantly blame teammates for errors behind him and umpires for the stunning number of batters he sometimes walked. On August 31, 1900, he gave a free ride to an NL-record 6 consecutive hitters in the course of a 9–4 loss to Philadelphia. His temper and erratic control were nonetheless tolerated because his lively fastball was nearly unhittable on days when he was right.

After growing up in Bellaire on the west side of the Ohio River as a protégé of ex-ML SS Bill Whites', Kennedy crossed the water to pitch for Wheeling of the Tri-State League in 1889 and then joined Denver of the Western Association for the next two years. He was headed for the Pacific Northwest League in 1892 when he received a last-minute offer in March from Brooklyn. Kennedy had never been east before and especially not in a city the size of New York or Brooklyn. After winning his ML debut he bought a loud $50 suit with his first paycheck and then took his change in dollar bills so he could flash a big wad. Swiftly taken to the cleaners by New York sharps, he fled home to Bellaire, was cleaned out of the rest of his cash by "sympathetic" locals and did not rejoin Brooklyn for several weeks. Even then player-manager John M. Ward did not risk starting him again until August 9 at Baltimore when he lost a 3–2 rematch with McMahon. By his second season, however, Kennedy was Brooklyn's ace and remained the club's strongest pitcher for six seasons. Even in 1899, when he lost his kingpin status to rookie 28-game-winner Jay Hughes, he bagged 22 victories and another 20 the following year after Joe McGinnity replaced Hughes as Hanlon's top gun.

In 1901, after winning two straight pennants in Brooklyn, Hanlon decided he could do without Kennedy's tantrums and released the churlish veteran that fall after he hurled less than 90 innings. Kennedy caught on the following spring with New York NL but was dropped after being crushed 15–1 by Cincinnati on May 18. He then went home to Bellaire to run his saloon and assemble a semipro team he dubbed the "Bill Kennedy All Stars." When his arm revived toward the end of the summer, he engineered a tryout with defending NL champion Pittsburgh in the spring of 1903 and made the club after stopping St. Louis 11–1 in a trial game on April 27. A spot starter during the regular season, Kennedy was called upon in the first modern World Series when two of the Pirates' primary starters, Sam Leever and Ed Doheny, were incapacitated on the eve of the affair. On his 35th birthday Kennedy started Game 5 at Pittsburgh in front of a throng of well-wishers who had made the trip from Bellaire. After battling Cy Young to a scoreless tie for five innings, he had his last opportunity to display his infamous temper to a big league audience when errors by Honus Wagner and Fred Clarke led to six Boston runs in the sixth frame.

Kennedy never again donned a ML uniform after the final game of the Series. He toiled a few more years in the minors amid stints with his semipro team and finished his active career in 1908 with Dayton of the Central League. Nearly seven years later he died of tuberculosis at his brother's home in Bellaire. (DN/DB)

Kennedy, Theodore A. / "Ted"

B	T	HGT	WGT	G	IP	H	GS
L	R	5'8"	178	33	283.1	340	32

CG	BB	SO	SH	W	L	PCT	ERA
31	109	118	0	12	21	.364	4.32

B. 2/7/1865 Henry, IL **D.** 10/30/1907
TEAMS: 85ChiN 86PhiA 86LouA
DEBUT: 6/12/1885 at Chicago; caught by Silver Flint and beat Detroit's Stump Wiedman 6–4
FINALE: 9/23/1886 at New York; caught by Paul Cook and lost 12–6 to New York's Al Mays
CAREER HIGHLIGHT: 7/16/1885 at Buffalo; on his final day with Chicago was caught by Mike Kelly and won both ends of a DH, beating Buffalo's Billy Serad 9–3 in the first game and then Pete Wood and Hardy Richardson 13–9 in the nightcap after being relieved in the eighth inning by Ned Williamson

Ted Kennedy was a finesse pitcher with an excellent change of pace. Much of his early box training came while he served as a batboy for Peoria in 1878 and was tutored by Charley Radbourn. Kennedy, who had moved to Peoria as a boy, played for various amateur teams in town until 1884, when he joined the independent Carson & Rand club of

Keokuk, IA, as a pitcher and third baseman. But it was soon apparent that he was not much of a hitter—his .060 ML career BA is the third worst among nineteenth-century players with at least 100 ABs—and it was once said of him that "his time in running the bases has been reckoned as about three hours." Consequently, and wisely, he became solely a pitcher. In seventeen starts with the Keokuk club, Kennedy was credited by *SL* in November 1884 with having struck out a phenomenal 277 batters.

That winter he remained in Keokuk and opened a saloon with his catcher, future MLer Ed Dugdale, called "Ted and Ned's." The partners paired again with Keokuk in 1885 until the club joined the Western League just as it was about to collapse. Kennedy was plucked from the sinking loop by Chicago NL as a backup for ace John Clarkson. When he won his debut, however, he found himself in the regular rotation and soon became practically a one-man staff after Clarkson temporarily drained his arm hurling 3 games in a row at Buffalo. The only able-bodied Chicago pitcher available on the morning of July 16, 1885, Kennedy worked both ends of a DH. Chicago then pitched him again the following day in an exhibition game at Syracuse. After losing 5–0 to the New York State League Stars, Kennedy came down with what he later deemed "a cold" in his shoulder and was unable to pitch anymore that season. In September, with Chicago about to play in the postseason against AA champion St. Louis, he was released and thus denied a World's Series share.

Over the winter Kennedy signed with Philadelphia AA and was effective early in the season but then suffered again from his shoulder ailment. He later remembered that by June 1886, "I was terribly lame—had to pitch underhand. Every game I pitched that season it was like a rusty knife was being thrust into my shoulder." As a result, Kennedy lost his last 10 decisions with the A's after starting the season 5-5. Released after his final A's appearance on July 8, he was given a reprieve by Louisville the following month but lost four starts in the space of eight days to finish the season with a 14-game losing streak and a final mark of 5-19 with a 4.66 ERA.

His ML career over, Kennedy rebounded to pitch awhile in the minors before quitting to become a sporting goods magnate, specializing in gloves and especially catcher's mitts. By 1890, purportedly his final minor league season, he had invented a new mitt (*see* Joseph Gunson) that former ML catcher Bill Traffley claimed would make him a millionaire because it made a catcher feel as if his hands were "made of iron." Wilbert Robinson also touted Kennedy's invention by using the glove to catch balls with one hand because the pocket in Kennedy's mitt was so deep. In the mid 1890s Kennedy sold the patent for "Ted Kennedy's Patent Protecting League Mitt" to the A. G. Spalding Company and returned to Peoria, where he continued to experiment with new ideas for improving gloves and ran a school for aspiring pitchers. He also invented an early form of a pitching machine, became a vegetarian, and went into the furrier business after relocating his family to St. Louis in the early 1900s. Early in the summer of 1907 Kennedy was rumored to be part of a group working to buy the moribund St. Louis Cardinals franchise, but nothing came of it. A few weeks after the season ended with the Cardinals buried deep in the NL cellar, Kennedy went to bed at his St. Louis home as usual on the last Sunday in October. During the night he began experiencing heart palpitations and died before a doctor could be summoned. (DN)

Killen, Frank Bissell / "Frank" "Lefty"

B	T	HGT	WGT	G	IP	H	GS
L	L	6'1"	200	321	2511.1	2730	300

CG	BB	SO	SH	W	L	PCT	ERA
253	822	725	13	164	131	.556	3.78

B. 11/30/1870 Pittsburgh, PA **D.** 12/3/1939
TEAMS: 91MilA 92WasN 93–98PitN 98–99WasN 99BosN 00ChiN
DEBUT: 8/27/1891 at Boston; caught by Jack Grim and lost 8–2 to Boston's George Haddock
FINALE: 6/27/1900 at Pittsburgh; caught by Art Nichols and lost 9–2 to Pittsburgh's Jesse Tannehill
CAREER HIGHLIGHT: In 1896 became the last NL southpaw to date to register a 30-win season

Frank Killen left the majors 7 wins short of Ed Morris's then career record for the most wins by a southpaw (171) but held the NL mark of 157 until it was broken by Ted Breitenstein with the last win of his ML career. One of the few 200-pound hurlers in his era, he lacked stamina in his teens but then put on weight and evolved into a workhorse by the time he was 21. Killen threw hard and had better-than-average control, especially for a southpaw, but his forte may have been that he perspired so heavily that he was always pitching with a wet hand, giving his deliveries weird twists and curves. While not a pioneering spitballer per se, he may be said to have been a sweatballer.

In 1889 Killen was a left-handed catcher in the Allegheny County League who sometimes pitched. He became largely a hurler the following year with Manistee in the Michigan State League and moved to Grand Rapids in the Interstate Association after Manistee folded. When the IA also disbanded, he joined Minneapolis in July and remained in Minnesota until the Western Association club went under. Killen added to his 30-win total in 1891 with Minneapolis by bagging 7 more victories with Milwaukee after it joined the AA late in the season.

Assigned to Washington in 1892 when the AA and NL merged, he went 29-26 for a D.C. team that was otherwise 29-67 and shared with Chicago's Bill Hutchison (51.4 percent) the distinction of becoming the last two pitchers in ML history to win as many as 50 percent of their team's games. The following spring, to Killen's joy, he was traded to Pittsburgh. He celebrated his escape by going 36-14 and leading the Pirates to a surprise second-place finish. Part of his success came from a sliding move at the new pitching distance that allowed him to vacate the pitcher's plate before he released the ball and steal a few inches on umpires. The gambit was seemingly removed from his arsenal the following year, but he simply refined it until a rule was finally adopted in 1897 requiring a pitcher to have his foot visibly on the rubber rather than just the back of his foot touching the rubber, which had led to Killen and others stealing ground. Killen nonetheless slumped to just 14 wins in 1894. In July he was hit in the pitching arm by a line drive. When ordered to report to the Pirates after a month on the DL, he claimed the team physician had made his condition worse. When the doctor denied having treated him at all during his supposed rehab, Pittsburgh seriously considered Chicago's offer of trading Willie McGill for him.

But if Killen's 1894 season was a disappointment, 1895 was almost a lost year entirely. In early June manager Connie Mack put him on notice that he would be released if his pitching didn't improve. Killen then won his next three starts but was spiked in the foot during a fight with New York catcher Parke Wilson on June 8 and finished the season recuperating at Mount Clemens, MI. In 1896 he returned to his former dominance with 30 wins, intimidating hitters with high inside fastballs and happy to fight any that took issue with his mode of pitching. Killen continued his renaissance in 1897, winning his first five starts, but then lost 23 of his remaining 35 decisions.

The following spring his days in Pittsburgh were numbered when Bill Watkins took over as manager of the team. The two clashed immediately over Watkins's edict that every player would be subject to the same club rules. Killen had been accustomed to special treatment, as had Pink Hawley. Under Mack and later Patsy Donovan, both had been permitted to sit in the grandstand with their wives or friends rather than on the bench in uniform on days they were not slated to pitch. In 1897 Killen had also been given permission to skip spring training when he insisted that his contract "did not begin until April 15" and that he preferred to train at home by taking lengthy daily horseback rides.

Even though Killen was having a decent year in 1898, Watkins released him to Washington on August as part of a salary purge. No happier in his second stint in D.C. than he had been in his first, the southpaw won just 6 games with the Senators before being released to Boston the following April and taking a $300 pay cut. Little more than a year later Killen's ML career was over at 29. He pitched in the minors until 1903, tried umpiring but was unsuited for it, and then returned to Pittsburgh, where he ran a saloon and dabbled in real estate. In 1939 he was found dead in his car of an apparent heart attack. (DN)

*Kilroy, Matthew Aloysius / "Matt" "Matches" "Bazazz"

B	T	HGT	WGT	G	IP	H	GS
L	L	5'9"	175	303	2435.2	2445	292

CG	BB	SO	SH	W	L	PCT	ERA
264	754	1170	19	141	133	.515	3.47

G	AB	H	R	2B	3B	HR
330	1062	236	163	24	17	1

RBI	BB	SO	SB	BA	SA	OBP
103	118	46	67	.222	304	.280

B. 6/21/1866 Philadelphia, PA **D.** 3/2/1940
TEAMS: 86–89BalA 90BosP 91CinA 92WasN 93–94LouN 98ChiN

DEBUT: 4/17/1886 at Baltimore; caught by Chris Fulmer in a 4–1 win over Brooklyn's Jack Harkins
FINALE: 8/17/1898 at Boston; caught by Tim Donahue and lost 6–2 to Kid Nichols
CAREER HIGHLIGHT ONE: Struck out an all-time ML season record 513 batters in 1886
CAREER HIGHLIGHT TWO: Won a left-hander's season record 46 games in 1887

Matt Kilroy was the brother of ML pitcher Mike Kilroy and had five ball-playing brothers altogether. The most famous of the six Kilroy brothers reputedly could pitch with either arm, though never effectively right-handed, and learned to throw with only a wrist snap after his upper left arm went dead in the early 1890s. Kilroy's strengths were speed, good control for a lefty, and a killer pickoff move that was later banned. He would stand facing the plate and then fire the ball to 1B without either looking or stepping in that direction, a move no longer permissible by the time he pitched his final ML innings in 1898.

Kilroy and his brothers grew up in the Fishtown section of Philadelphia. After pitching for the local Hartville amateur club in 1883, he joined the August Flower team of Atlantic City at the beginning of the 1884 season and moved to the Eastern League Newark Domestics in the late spring before finishing the summer with the independent Augusta, GA, Browns. Kilroy returned to Augusta the following spring when the team joined the fledgling Southern League and was regarded as the third-best pitcher in the loop by the end of the season. When the top two prizes, John Hofford and Tom Ramsey, went to other ML teams, Baltimore manager Billy Barnie settled for Kilroy and struck gold.

Although Ramsey in particular seemed superior initially, Kilroy threw harder, had better personal habits, and was a more accomplished all-around player. Unfortunately, he had the worst team in the majors behind him in his rookie year. After winning his first three career starts, Kilroy was 26-34 the rest of the way and topped the AA in losses and runs surrendered (350) along with an all-time record 513 strikeouts. The following year his strikeout total dropped to 217 when the four-strike rule was instituted for 1887 only, but he increased his wins to 46 with a first-division team supporting him and finished the campaign with back-to-back shutouts at St. George Grounds, the New York Mets' Staten Island home. The twin goose eggs also elevated his innings pitched to a ML high 589⅓ and a two-year total of 1,172⅓. Although Kilroy was rewarded for his colossal labors with a pay hike to $2,600 in 1888, not surprisingly he experienced his first serious bout of arm trouble and was idled for two lengthy stretches that season.

Kilroy rebounded strongly in 1889, topping the AA in CGs, as he and Frank Foreman started all but two of Baltimore's 139 contests. He then jumped to the PL in 1890, signing with Boston, and won the Reds' opening Brotherhood game on April 19 3–2 over Brooklyn. Years later Kilroy revealed that the game spelled his ruin in that Charley Radbourn had been slated to start but begged off at the last minute, saying he wasn't in shape yet. Neither was Kilroy, who was sent to the box before he was fully warmed up, and finished the campaign at 9-15, the poorest season to that point by a regular starter on a pennant winner. Worse, he completed only two-thirds of his starts and logged nearly twice as many walks as strikeouts. Seen as a back number even though he was just 24, Kilroy was signed almost out of sympathy by Mike Kelly, player-manager of the weak Cincinnati AA entry in 1891, and then released when he was just 1-4. His speed now gone, as well as "his old-time cunning," he tried to mount several comebacks, usually failed miserably, and finally quit the game after serving as a pitcher-outfielder with Syracuse of the Eastern League in 1895.

On January 8, 1898, *TSN* noted, "Matt Kilroy wants to break into baseball next year. His Philadelphia saloon is for sale and so is his service." Few readers paid any attention—such declarations coming from erstwhile stars were common and almost always meaningless—but then, a month later, *TSN* reported that Chicago manager Tom Burns believed Kilroy could have a future in the NL as a hitter. Astonishingly, a dozen years after setting the all-time pitcher's season strikeout record, Kilroy opened the 1898 campaign in RF for Chicago and batted leadoff. By early May, however, he had lost his post when he was hitting in the low .200s and returned to the box. Although he executed an occasional good game, his patented pickoff move to 1B was called a balk now, eliminating one of his main weapons. Kilroy finished the season 6-7, played RF for a time with Billy Barnie's Hartford Eastern League club in 1899, and then returned to his saloon, which was situated across the street from the Phillies' park. In 1909 he moved his business near to the AL Philadelphia A's new Shibe Park after serving as a pitching coach early in the twentieth century for A's manager Connie Mack. Until Kilroy gave up his business in 1935, he never missed an A's home game, leaving work every afternoon just prior to the first pitch. He died in a Philadelphia hospital at 73 after a long illness. (DN)

King, Charles Frederick
(b. Koenig) / **"Silver"**

B	T	HGT	WGT	G	IP	H	GS
R	R	6'0"	170	397	3180.2	3098	370

CG	BB	SO	SH	W	L	PCT	ERA
328	967	1222	19	203	152	.572	3.18

B. 1/11/1868 St. Louis, MO **D.** 5/21/1938
TEAMS: 86KCN 87–89StLA 90ChiP 91PitN 92–93NYN 93CinN 96–97WasN
DEBUT: 9/28/1886 at New York; caught by Mert Hackett and lost 3–2 to New York's Tim Keefe
FINALE: 8/19/1897 at Washington; caught by Duke Farrell and lost 10–4 to Chicago's Clark Griffith
FAMOUS GAME: 6/21/1890 at Chicago; caught by Duke Farrell and became the only pitcher in ML history not to receive credit for a CG no-hitter thrown in his home park when Chicago manager Charlie Comiskey opted to bat first, and King then worked eight hitless innings but lost 1–0 to Brooklyn's Gus Weyhing when Chicago failed to score in the top of the ninth after Brooklyn had tallied an unearned run in the seventh
CAREER HIGHLIGHT: Is the only the pitcher to lead two different nineteenth-century major leagues in ERA—the 1888 AA and the 1890 PL

Charles Koenig was nicknamed "Silver" by a St. Joseph sportswriter because his blond hair resembled burnished silver, and his last name was Anglicized early on in his baseball career so that for most of his life few knew him by any name other than "Silver King." An established ML pitcher before his 20th birthday, King won 32 games in 1887, his official rookie year, and his rapid emergence allowed Browns owner Chris Von der Ahe to sell both of his other two star pitchers, Bob Caruthers and Dave Foutz.

A hod carrier for his father in his youth, King grew into an imposing physical specimen by his midteens and was already starring in the vibrant St. Louis amateur baseball scene of the early 1880s as a member of an outstanding Peach Pies club that included the Tebeau brothers and Jack O'Connor. In 1885, at age 17, King, against his parent's wishes, joined an independent pro team in Jacksonville, IL, and the next season pitched for St. Joseph of the Western League. Late in the 1886 campaign King came to Kansas City NL and started 5 games before closing day. Over the winter the KC franchise folded, leaving King held on reserve by the National League but with no claimants for his services, in part because his asking price was too high. Since King was making $5 a day laying brick for his father (or so he claimed), he felt he was entitled to make much more than that for laying a baseball out of a batter's reach. Reportedly in late March or early April 1887 Browns official George Munson walked into The *Sporting News* offices one day and asked who was best pitcher available in St. Louis. When informed it was King, Munson journeyed to his house and left a note asking him to come into the *TSN* offices the next day. Signed almost as soon as he set foot inside the door (for around $1,800 according to *SL*), King became an immediate star with a veteran championship club.

TSN once wrote, "Possessing wide shoulders, a barrel chest, long, brawny arms, hands so big that they could completely surround and hide the ball, and iron nerves and muscles," King brought an ideal physical makeup to the game. While speed was his chief asset, he is credited with having been the first to use the crossfire, an extravagant sidearm delivery. He mixed curves and a change of pace with his speed, throwing them all with the same motion and with remarkable control without a windup. *TSN* added, "King's unique delivery of the ball is the subject of a great deal of speculation." It is generally agreed that he stood deep in the left corner of the pitcher's box, took a giant step to the right and fired the ball over his left shoulder. Although he often appeared to be out of the box when he released the ball, his movements were so quick that teams could not convince umpires to call balks on him. In addition, King's unorthodox mechanics made it difficult to steal against him. After leaving the game, the hurler himself acknowledged: "My pitching stock consisted mainly in speed. I threw some curves, but I never knew about such things as a spitball, a fadeaway, shine ball and all those tricks."

While his physical gifts and unique delivery made King a successful pitcher, he matured early in other ways as well. After signing for $1,800 in 1887 he demanded a raise to $3,600 the following year and finally agreed to sign one of the first bonus incentive contracts in ML history. King settled for $2,500 in base salary in 1888 but only on the condition that he receive an additional $500 if he won 40 games. He collected with room to spare when he led the AA with 45 victories, only to decide that Browns owner Chris Von der Ahe had cheated him out of his share of World's Series money. As a consequence he went on record as saying, "I will never pitch another ball for that fellow if I can help it. He has gouged every player in the club out of $300, for that is what is coming to us."

But his physical and financial maturation notwithstanding, King alienated not only owners with his temperament. Disagreeable, impatient, and sometimes downright intolerant, in October 1890, after his favored Chicago PL team finished out of the money, he disgustedly told *TSN* that he was tired of pitching for clubs that were expected to win but didn't and said he wanted to play next year for Cleveland PL, because if he were to pitch the near hopeless Infants into first place "there would be some glory in that." Later that fall, after the PL collapsed, he found himself at the center of what would become known as the Baldwin Affair (*see* Mark Baldwin), which swept him to Pittsburgh NL rather than his expected return to the AA. At the end of the following season, after Pittsburgh finished last, he began blaming his steady decline as a pitcher on the poor support he received from his teammates and actually quit during the 1893 campaign to join his father's contracting business rather than soldier on with a mediocre Cincinnati club.

King remained out of the game for more than two years until fellow St. Louisan Bill Joyce coaxed him into joining Washington in 1896. Still possessing his trademark crossfire delivery, King came to the Senators in late May and debuted with an 11–6 win over Pittsburgh. He seemed little affected by the long layoff from the game until July 21 at Cleveland when a line drive back through the box fractured his pitching forearm. King returned to action from the injury faster than his doctor recommended and was not the same. When he lost the season finale 9–1 to Boston, it cost Washington an undisputed ninth-place finish, its highest since joining the NL in 1892.

After finishing his renascent year 10-7, King began the following spring in the Washington rotation but left the team in August after winning just six of his first nineteen starts. He returned to St. Louis and ran such a successful contracting business that he was able to retire comfortably at 57. King died in a St. Louis hospital thirteen years later following surgery for gallstones and appendicitis. (DN/JK/DB)

Kirby, John F. / "Jack"

B	T	HGT	WGT	G	IP	H	GS
?	R	5'8"	172	75	611.1	640	75

CG	BB	SO	SH	W	L	PCT	ERA
68	258	200	1	18	50	.265	4.09

B. 1/13/1865 St. Louis, MO **D.** 10/6/1931
TEAMS: 84KCU 85–86StLN 87IndN 87CleA 88KCA
DEBUT: 8/1/1884 at St. Louis; caught by Kid Baldwin and lost 4–1 to St. Louis's Charlie Sweeney
FINALE: 6/29/1888 at Kansas City; caught by Jim Donahue and lost 7–0 to Philadelphia's Ed Seward

Among all ML pitchers who have worked 600-plus innings, Jack Kirby has the worst winning percentage, with the exception of John Coleman, who did most of his work for the woebegone 1883 Philadelphia NL club that won only 17 games all season. Kirby earned his mark pitching for a succession of wretched clubs over five years and losing 50 of 68 career decisions. He would not have lasted long enough to achieve this unenviable record, however, had he lacked talent. By some accounts Kirby was loaded with it actually, and the explanation for his failure to take advantage of it is not readily apparent. Some contended he was too stubborn ever to take coaching, yet there are also indications that his prospects were damaged when inept managers handled him poorly. His drastic 1887 falloff was due in large measure to arm trouble and also perhaps to difficulty adjusting to major revisions in the pitching rules.

After a brief trial the previous season with Kansas City UA, Kirby joined his hometown St. Louis Maroons in August 1885. The Maroons were a bad team, but Kirby was one of a trio of pitchers that gave them the nucleus of a promising young staff, although his stats generally lagged behind those of teammates John Healy and Henry Boyle. Nevertheless, he was considered "a comer" with a tantalizing drop ball, or slow curve.

In the spring of 1887 the Maroons franchise and players were taken over by Indianapolis. Unhappy with his new club's low salary offer, Kirby was the last former Maroon to sign. Beginning with his first game, a 10–8 loss to Detroit, he pitched poorly. After a string of bad performances he went home to St. Louis to rest a sore arm, but when he returned in June he fared no better. Along with shoulder problems, there were complaints about his attitude. Kirby was said to go to pieces with runners on base, and since he allowed 16.4 runners per nine innings, there were usually plenty on base. He was criticized for "lack of judgment or head work" and a *SL* correspondent labeled him "a bullhead, mulish ingrate, and apparently without sense of honor or a single manly instinct." Nor did Kirby pretend to be thrilled at being in Indianapolis, a baseball gulag with low pay and poor playing conditions. By late June he was telling reporters openly what others had been hinting for two months, that he was deliberately pitching badly in order to force a sale to another team. On July 2 he was at last waived out of the NL and went to Cleveland, moving from the basement team in the League to the tailender in the AA.

Kirby debuted with his new team at Cincinnati the next day, but the first ten batters he faced all scored. He excused his performance by claiming fatigue from a long train ride and was spared a loss in that game thanks to a rainout, but he went on to lose five starts in which the weather did not come to his rescue, pitching far worse than he had in Indianapolis. Kirby reportedly admitted that arm problems had caused his poor work with the Hoosiers and that he had hidden them because he wanted to escape to a new team. His attitude nonetheless caused as much disquiet as it had in Indianapolis, with Cleveland *SL* correspondent Frank Brunell calling him "always out of condition, lazy, and unambitious." By the time he was released Kirby was talking of suing Cleveland for $125 in unpaid salary, while Cleveland officials threatened a lawsuit against Indianapolis for selling damaged goods. Besides his arm problems, Kirby, whose control had never been the best, may have been disadvantaged more than most pitchers by 1887 rules changes that included an increase to four strikes for a strikeout.

In 1888 "three strikes and you're out" returned, and Kirby, who had finished 1887 pitching semipro ball in St. Louis, signed with Memphis of the Southern League. In May of that year he went back up to the AA with Kansas City. After being rocked by Brooklyn in his KC debut on May 20, he defeated the Athletics, 3–2—one of the only 2 games he won in ML competition after 1886. He did not pitch again for a month and then was cut after 3 more losses.

Like many pitchers of that day, Kirby's career was finished by the time he reached his midtwenties. He had married Jessie Hooper, a native of England, in 1885 when she was only about 17. They had three daughters. To support his family after his playing career was over, Kirby first walked a beat in St. Louis and later served as a prison guard and as police property custodian in St. Louis for fourty years. He died of diabetes in St. Louis in 1931. (DB/DN)

Kissinger, William Francis / "Bill" "Shang"

B	T	HGT	WGT	G	IP	H	GS
R	R	5'11"	185	53	319.1	500	32

CG	BB	SO	SH	W	L	PCT	ERA
23	123	61	0	7	25	.219	6.99

G	AB	H	R	2B	3B	HR
72	214	60	24	13	3	0

RBI	BB	SO	SB	BA	SA	OBP
26	3	16	1	.280	.369	.290

B. 8/15/1871 Dayton, KY **D.** 4/20/1929
TEAMS: 95BalN 95–97StLN
DEBUT: 5/30/1895 at Baltimore; caught by Boileryard Clarke and beat Louisville's Mike McDermott 8–4
FINALE: 6/10/1897 at Washington; caught by Klondike Douglass and was relieved by Bill Hart in his 12–3 loss to Washington's Silver King

A product of the University of Cincinnati, Bill Kissinger turned pro with Atlanta of the Southern League in 1894 but soon earned a reputation as "the big kid who had the speed of a cyclone in practice but who laid down as soon as he entered a game," and was released in May. He then went to the Virginia League and was signed that winter by Baltimore manager Ned Hanlon, who liked his size and speed but worried that he was too "boyish looking." After winning his Orioles debut in 1895 he was reamed in his next outing on June 7 and dealt the following day along with infielder Frank Bonner to St. Louis for pitcher Dad Clarkson.

He could not have gone to a worse team, not that his arrival was about to make it any better. By the time Kissinger finished his wretched ML tenure in 1897 he had compiled stats the likes of which have never been seen since. Among pitchers with a minimum of 250 career innings, he ranks first in the number of base runners allowed per nine innings with 17.78, as well as owning the worst ERA (6.99). Yet, if pitching wasn't his strong point, there was nothing terribly wrong with the rest of his game. In 1895, as a rookie, Kissinger led all NL pitchers in FA, and when he left the majors in 1897 he had seen action at every outfield position, as well as 3B and SS, in addition to his fifty-three appearances on the, mound. He also owned a .280 career BA, raising wonder that he was not made into a position player. Kissinger was out of baseball by August 1898 after failing to make the grade in the New York State League. He worked as a tailor in Cincinnati prior to his death from a heart attack, leaving behind his wife, Edith. (DN)

Kitson, Frank R. / "Frank" "Kitty"

B	T	HGT	WGT	G	IP	H	GS
L	R	5'11"	165	97	699.1	733	80

CG	BB	SO	SH	W	L	PCT	ERA
68	156	162	5	45	34	.570	3.37

G	AB	H	R	2B	3B	HR
119	329	86	46	8	4	0

RBI	BB	SO	SB	BA	SA	OBP
24	10	—	9	.261	.331	.287

B. 9/11/1869 Watson, MI **D.** 4/14/1930
TEAMS: 98–99BalN 00–02BroN 03–05DetAL 06–07WasAL 07NYAL
DEBUT: 5/19/1898 at Baltimore; caught by Mike Bowerman and beat Pittsburgh's Bill Hart 6–0
FINALE: 7/22/1907 at St. Louis; relieved Al Orth and was later relieved by Earl Moore in Orth's 6–4 win over St. Louis's Fred Glade

In 1892 Frank Kitson pitched for an amateur team in Benton Harbor, MI, but when he tried to turn pro in 1893 with Muskegon, MI, his father made him quit and go back to work on the family farm. By the time Kitson publicly went pro in the Virginia League three years later he was already 25. The following season he joined Burlington, IA, and was regarded as the best pitcher in the Western Association when F. S. Long, a Burlington sportswriter from Norwich, CT, Ned Hanlon's hometown, recommended him to the Baltimore manager. Hanlon had no use for Kitson but bought him to keep him away from Boston. When Kitson reported to Baltimore, Hanlon refused to pay Burlington, claiming the pitcher was not of ML caliber. Eventually Hanlon wired the money when Burlington got Nick Young to intervene. But he then clandestinely farmed Kitson to Reading of the Atlantic League while telling the press that the recruit pitcher was working out in Baltimore every day.

Kitson finally joined Baltimore in the spring of 1898. He split his rookie season between the mound and the outfield and did well at both but not so well that Hanlon chose to retain him when he moved to Brooklyn in 1899 with most of the Orioles' best players. Left behind in Baltimore, Kitson thrived under the club's new manager, John McGraw, winning 22 games. It convinced Hanlon that he belonged in Brooklyn. Kitson remained with Hanlon's Superbas through 1902 and then jumped to Detroit AL to be closer to his home. In December 1905 the Tigers sent him to Washington for Happy Townsend, but the trade of once-promising right-handers benefited neither team.

Kitson finished his pro career in 1908 with Kansas City of the American Association and returned to farming. He died of a heart attack at his home in Allegan, MI, after spending his entire life in that area. (DN)

Klobedanz, Frederick Augustus / "Fred" "Duke"

B	T	HGT	WGT	G	IP	H	GS
L	L	5'11"	190	88	694	733	84

CG	BB	SO	SH	W	L	PCT	ERA
68	264	177	2	52	25	.675	4.15

G	AB	H	R	2B	3B	HR
107	327	90	48	11	6	7

RBI	BB	SO	SB	BA	SA	OBP
46	9	11	1	.275	.413	.318

B. 6/13/1871 Waterbury, CT **D.** 4/12/1940
TEAMS: 96–99BosN 02BosN
DEBUT: 8/20/1896 at Cincinnati; caught by Marty Bergen and beat Cincinnati's Phil Ehret 8–6

FINALE: 9/5/1902 at Boston; caught by Pat Moran and beat Pittsburgh's Harvey Cushman and Honus Wagner 12–1

For a while Fred Klobedanz was said to be as hard to hit as his name was to pronounce, but after he logged by far the highest ERA on the Boston staff in 1898, his second full ML season, and won just one of five starts in 1899, he was released. Klobedanz resurfaced in Boston for a final appearance in 1902, on loan from Lawrence of the New England League, and seemed unperturbed when his fine showing yielded only a return to the Class B circuit. Earlier in the season the *Washington Post* had observed that he "seemed to be satisfied to pitch" in the NEL, where his salary couldn't be more than $150 a month. The same paper also noted after his ML finale, "The good natured Dutchman has a slow ball that is worth the speed of any pitcher in the league. What a prince of pitchers he would be except for his laziness."

Klobedanz won his first of over 240 games in the minors in 1892 with Portland, ME, and his last in 1907 with New Bedford, MA. His exceptional hitting ability also earned him frequent duty both at 1B and in the outfield. In 1894, Louisville, more interested in his bat than his arm, scouted him as a possible first baseman and then unwisely chose Lute Lutenberg. Klobedanz almost certainly would have outhit Lutenberg by 100 points but instead had to remain with Fall River of the New England League for nearly three full seasons before finally heading for the majors in August 1896. He supplemented his 26 wins in the NEL with 6 more in Boston livery. The following season he finished at 26-7 with a .788 winning percentage, a post-1892 ML record high by a southpaw 20-game winner that lasted until Eddie Plank's .813 in 1912. When Klobedanz slipped to 19 wins in 1898, it prevented the pennant-winning Beaneaters from being the first club in ML history with four 20-game winners when Kid Nichols, Vic Willis, and Ted Lewis all attained the charmed circle.

Although in later years Klobedanz was seemingly content to remain the minors, that was not true after Boston dropped him in 1899. Initially he went to Worcester of the Eastern League but ran into trouble with union workers there that had begun the previous winter when he worked as scab sceneshifter in Boston while regular stagehands were on strike. When all the unions in Worcester demanded that the club release Klobedanz, Chicago offered to take him off Worcester's hands, but he went home to Fall River instead upon learning that Chicago union men would likewise repulse him if he joined the Windy City team. In August 1899 *TSN* summarized the tawdry incident by remarking, "Klobedanz queered himself in labor circles by taking a 'scab' job in a Boston theater." Klobedanz's last job was as a hotel clerk in Waterbury. He died in that city of cancer at 68. (DN)

Knell, Philip Louis / "Phil"

B	T	HGT	WGT	G	IP	H	GS
R	L	5'7½"	154	192	1452.1	1478	163

CG	BB	SO	SH	W	L	PCT	ERA
141	705	575	8	79	90	.467	4.05

B. 3/12/1865 Mill Valley, CA **D.** 6/5/1944
TEAMS: 88PitN 90PhiP 91ColA 92WasN 92PhiN 94PitN 94–95LouN 95CleN
DEBUT: 7/6/1888 at Pittsburgh; caught by Fred Carroll and beat Washington's Jim Whitney 3–2
FINALE: 9/29/1895 at Louisville; relieved Nig Cuppy in Cuppy's 13–8 loss to Louisville's Tom McCreery
FAMOUS FIRST: 6/3/1892 at Washington; in the first ML game witnessed by a sitting U.S. President, Benjamin Harrison, was caught by Jack Milligan and lost 7–4 to Cincinnati's Tony Mullane
CAREER LOWLIGHT: In 1891 issued an all-time ML season southpaw-record 226 walks

Phil Knell was blond, wiry, a rabid bench jockey, and seldom a popular teammate, but he was so lethal against left-handed hitters that Dan Brouthers called him the toughest pitcher he ever faced. He starred with the Tufts-Lyon team of Los Angeles and Oakland's Greenhood & Morans club before Pittsburgh bought him from the latter team for $1,000 in June 1888. Although he was chastised by the California press for going east, after Pittsburgh released him in September 1888 for being too wild the California League happily welcomed him back but lost him again the following summer when Frank Selee acquired him in time to help Omaha win the Western Association pennant.

That winter, Philadelphia PL signed Knell as box insurance. Instead he emerged as the club's surprise ace, surviving 166 walks and 28 hit batsmen to go 22-11. Still legally bound to Omaha once the PL folded, Knell signed with Columbus AA in April 1891 after the AA withdrew from the National Agreement. He won a ML career-high 28 games despite surrendering a southpaw-season-record 226 walks, hitting 54 batters and heaving 24 wild pitches. Late that fall Knell married Fredericka Morsch of Los Angeles, just days before he learned that he had been assigned to Washington as part of the AA–NL merger in December 1891. Toiling for a weak team, he was a respectable 9-13 after a loss to Cleveland on July 4, when Washington pilot Arthur Irwin abruptly dumped him for insubordination. Knell signed with the Phils in late July 1892 and again fared reasonably well, going 5-5 for a composite 14-18 season, yet he was not rehired for 1893.

He spent the first year at the new 60'6" pitching distance back in the Cal League before Pittsburgh signed him for 1894. His Pirates contract was rescinded, however, after a sloppy relief appearance. About to return to the West Coast, Knell got an unexpected offer from Louisville and stayed to lead the Colonels in losses and strikeouts. His high-point in his last full ML season came on August 14 when he beat the Phillies 13–7 in a game that had to be played at the University of Pennsylvania field after Philadelphia's park was destroyed eight days earlier by a fire. During the contest he was the beneficiary of six Louisville home runs, including his own lone career four-bagger, courtesy of a RF fence that was markedly shorter than the prescribed ML distance at the time.

A 0-6 mark in his first six starts in 1895 bade Louisville to pull the plug on Knell after an 18–11 loss in the first game of a Memorial Day DH. Hired by Cleveland more for his base coaching and bench jockeying than pitching, he surprised manager Pat Tebeau by winning several key games in July but was cut when he logged a 5.40 ERA with the Spiders. Arm trouble appears to have accounted at least partially for his decline. In 1896 Tebeau farmed Knell to Fort Wayne of the Interstate League, where it was hoped that Tebeau's brother George, who managed the Farmers, could teach Knell to play the outfield. But Knell eventually took the mound again in addition to doing garden duty, and later, after finding himself back on the West Coast without an engagement in the spring of 1897, he returned to the Cal League and played in various incarnations of that circuit until 1908. He also served two separate stints as an umpire in the PCL, but each ended badly. In early September 1912 Knell dispensed with officiating when a livid crowd at Los Angeles's Washington Park mobbed him as he tried to fight his way through it backed by San Francisco players armed with bats. Knell was over 60 when he played in his last old-timers game preceding a PCL contest in 1926. He died eighteen years later in Santa Monica of a heart attack. Knell held the ML record for the most career walks issued (705) in less than 1,500 innings until Monte Pearson broke it in 1941. (DN)

Knepper, Charles / "Charlie"

B	T	HGT	WGT	G	IP	H	GS
R	R	6'4"	190	27	219.2	307	26

CG	BB	SO	SH	W	L	PCT	ERA
26	77	43	0	4	22	.154	5.78

B. 2/18/1871 Anderson, IN **D.** 2/6/1946
TEAMS: 99CleN
DEBUT: 5/26/1899 at Cleveland; relieved Willie Sudhoff in a 12–0 loss to Baltimore's Frank Kitson and Ralph Miller
FINALE: 9/26/1899 at St. Louis; caught by Joe Sugden and lost 15–3 to Cy Young

We will probably never know whether Charlie Knepper was a decent pitcher on an atrocious team or in perfect harmony with the rest of his abysmal teammates on the 1899 Spiders. In July 1899 *TSN* reported that Knepper "has nothing except a uniform to show that he is a National Leaguer," but at the end of the season Washington writer J. Edgar Grillo rated him the equal of Cy Young in Young's rookie year and expected good things from him in St. Louis in 1900. Previously, Grillo had noted, "Knepper bears a strong physical and facial resemblance to Jack Stivetts, and his breeze-warming shoot is as rapid as the sultry curve that proceeded from Stivetts' mitt early in the nineties." There is support for Grillo's view. On August 25 Knepper collected Cleveland's last home win of the season when he "pitched a gilt-edged game" and topped New York 4–2 on a three-hitter. Some two weeks later he led Chicago 6–4 in the bottom of the ninth with two out and the bases loaded when Bill Bradley hit a routine grounder to SS Harry Lochhead, whose throw to 1B was in time, but Tommy Tucker dropped the ball and then "stood motionless as a statue" while three runners scored to hand Chicago a 7–6 verdict that ought to have given Knepper his fifth win and the team lead for the season.

Old for a rookie at 28, the 6'4" right-hander came to Cleveland in 1899 with little experience even in top-minor league company after failing several trials with Indianapolis of the Western League in between stints in the Kentucky-Indiana League, an Indianapolis semipro team and, finally, the 1898 Interstate League, where *TSN* noted that he won 21 games for last-place Youngstown. In March 1900 the St. Louis–Cleveland syndicate ownership transferred Knepper to St. Louis as Grillo had predicted, but he was farmed to Minneapolis of the newly renamed AL in late May when he was still home in Indianapolis, confined to bed with inflammatory rheumatism. Knepper pitched a game for Minneapolis but remained St. Louis property. He tried to mount a comeback in 1901 with St. Paul but was released by manager Jimmy Ryan in June and eventually worked in the heat treatment department at the Warner Gear Company in Indiana. Knepper died in a Muncie hospital in 1946 after a long illness. (DN)

Knouff, Edward / "Ed" "Fred"

B	T	HGT	WGT	G	IP	H	GS
R	R	?	160	44	343	335	43

CG	BB	SO	SH	W	L	PCT	ERA
37	175	128	1	20	20	.500	4.17

B. 6/?/1868 Philadelphia, PA **D.** 9/14/1900
TEAMS: 85PhiA 86–87BalA 87–88StLA 88CleA 89PhiA
DEBUT: 7/1/1885 at Philadelphia; relieved Phenomenal Smith in the fifth inning of Smith's 12–11 loss to New York's Doug Crothers
FINALE: 6/7/1889 at Philadelphia; caught by Jack Brennan and was relieved by Mike Mattimore, who got the 9–7 win over Louisville's Tom Ramsey

Ed Knouff was just 17 when he made his ML debut. His deliveries came "from every conceivable angle" and were hard to hit when he could control them, which was too seldom to suit any of his five ML managers. In the spring of 1885, after failing a trial in the Eastern League, Knouff went to Macon, GA, of the Southern League but was released in late June and happened to be at the A's game on July 1, when he was summoned from the stands to relieve Phenomenal Smith. Knouff had some good days with the A's but was released after losing his final start in 1885 on September 23, to Louisville 11–5. He returned to the Southern League with Memphis the following year, came home after winning 24 games, and was again at the A's park on the last day of the season, when Baltimore manager Billy Barnie went on the prowl for a victim to pitch for his hapless Orioles.

Knouff's eight strikeouts that afternoon moved Barnie to invite him to Baltimore's spring camp in 1887. He survived a severe case of typhoid early in the season but continued to appear only sparingly because Barnie, surprisingly, had a decent team. When Barnie released Knouff in late August, St. Louis quickly snatched him. Baltimore followers were stunned by how well he did for the first-place Browns in the final month of the season. Knouff was doing even better in 1888 when his wing began ailing. Released on July 26 by St. Louis, he signed the next day with Cleveland but was able to make only one start, losing 2–1 to Kansas City on August 7, before being sent home in the hope that rest would mend him.

Knouff made the A's varsity in the spring of 1889 and won his first two starts. But they were spaced nearly a month apart, and when he was blasted in his third appearance after another lengthy rest, he was released. Knouff married the following April. Over the next several seasons he tried periodically to return to the game but by the mid 1890s was working in Philadelphia as a ball stuffer. A year or so later he hired on as a firefighter. While he was battling a blaze in 1897, a falling beam landed on his back, permanently disabling him. For the next three and a half years Knouff languished in Philadelphia's German Hospital, unable to walk, spending each day in a wheelchair by a window overlooking Girard College and the old ball grounds where he had debuted fifteen years earlier with the A's. He died at the hospital from uremia at 32. (DN)

Krock, August H. / "Gus"

B	T	HGT	WGT	G	IP	H	GS
R	R	6'0"	196	60	505.1	537	59

CG	BB	SO	SH	W	L	PCT	ERA
56	110	209	4	32	26	.552	3.49

B. 5/9/1866 Milwaukee, WI **D.** 3/22/1905
TEAMS: 88–89ChiN 89IndN 89WasN 90BufP

DEBUT: 4/24/1888 at Indianapolis; caught by Silver Flint and beat Indianapolis's Henry Boyle 5–2
FINALE: 7/26/1890 at Buffalo; caught by Connie Mack and lost 13–9 to Brooklyn's John Sowders and George Hemming

Gus Krock first came of age in 1886 with independent Decatur, IA. That August he joined Oshkosh and remained there in 1887, finishing with a .221 OBA, the second lowest in the Northwestern League. Grabbed by Chicago, Krock was about to be jettisoned in the spring of 1888 after Colts manager Cap Anson scoffed that NL players would steal on him at will because of his slow delivery. But helped by catcher Tom Daly, the rookie corrected his technique and soon was one of the hardest pitchers in the league to steal on. Featuring a slow drop ball and good control, he was also among the hardest to hit. After winning his ML debut Krock quickly assumed the lead role in Chicago's rotation and finished the campaign at 25-14.

As good as Krock's yearling season was, his sophomore year was as awful. In his first start of the season, on April 29 at Indianapolis, he was hit hard but escaped with no decision. When he continued to be pounded in each of his next six starts, Anson ordered his release in July. Krock hooked on with Indianapolis long enough to log four equally dreadful starts and then finished the season with Washington. His composite record with the three clubs added up to the second-highest number of enemy base runners per nine innings (16.12) among NL qualifiers, trailing only Washington teammate George Keefe (16.16).

Sympathetic observers contended that Krock had been damaged in 1889 by the new pitching rules enforced that year, but in actuality the only rule change of consequence was reducing the number of balls needed for a walk to four, a revision that should have impacted no more on Krock than any other hurler. The following spring, however, it grew apparent that his problem was physical. After signing with Buffalo PL, Krock spent most of the early season at Mount Clemens, MI, nursing his lame arm, but the treatment was unsuccessful. Returning to Buffalo in July, he did well for six innings in his final ML start and then was racked and released soon afterward. That December *TSN* reported that he was working in an Oshkosh foundry and moaning that "the work was too hard" and he wanted to play ball again.

Krock essayed a comeback in the 1891 Western Association, but by late spring he was playing independent ball in Bay View, WI. He later joined the Milwaukee police force after posting one of the top scores on the entrance exam but then decided to join the army and in June of 1898 was pitching for the First Wisconsin Regiment team stationed in Tampa, FL. Not long after that Krock began to manifest the first signs of consumption. He moved to Southern California, hoping for a miracle cure, but died at 38 in Pasadena. (DN/DB)

Lampe, Henry Joseph / "Henry"

B	T	HGT	WGT	G	IP	H	GS
R	L	5'11½"	175	9	49.1	85	4

CG	BB	SO	SH	W	L	PCT	ERA
2	40	19	0	0	3	.000	8.03

B. 9/19/1872 Boston, MA **D.** 9/16/1936
TEAMS: 94BosN 95PhiN
DEBUT: 5/14/1894 at Boston; relieved Kid Nichols with Boston trailing 12–5 in a 16–5 loss to Baltimore's Sadie McMahon
FINALE: 8/1/1895 at Philadelphia; caught by Mike Grady and was relieved by Jack Taylor, who took the 10–8 loss to Brooklyn's Ad Gumbert and Bert Abbey

Henry Lampe came to Boston in 1894 touted by *TSN* as "the best left-handed pitcher of New England." Nothing else even remotely complimentary was ever said about him. In Lampe's lone start for Boston on June 6, 1894, he was relieved in the third inning by Tom Smith in a 27–11 loss to Pittsburgh. Between them, Lampe and Smith gave up seven home runs, a one-game record at the time. When Lampe was released to the New England League two days after his pasting, *TSN* sighed, "He is of no earthly use."

Over the winter Lampe patched his shattered ego and was 17-3 in late June 1895 with Lawrence of the New England League when he was purchased by Philadelphia. In his first start with the Phillies he lost 11–10 at Washington to Al Maul in the only NL game a gentleman named Redheffer ever umpired. Bad as Lampe and Maul were, Redheffer was even worse, forcing Washington manager Gus Schmelz to haul former ML catcher Miah Murray out of the stands in the fourth inning to assist the beleaguered newcomer in keeping a lid on the chaos. Lampe pitched more credibly in his second start, losing 6–1 to St. Louis on July 12, but then, after being given nearly a three-week's vacation, again suffered a double-digit loss. Thereafter he exited the majors tied for the record for the most runs allowed of any hurler in a career of less than 50 innings (73). Lampe still is tied for the lead in that department, as well as for the mark of allowing the most enemy hits in less than 50 innings (85).

After finishing 1895 with Buffalo of the Eastern League, Lampe went to spring training the following year with New York NL and opened the campaign with the New York Mets, an Atlantic League farm club of the Giants. In July Giants owner Andrew Freedman agreed to loan Lampe to Portsmouth when the Mets disbanded. Scarcely a month later Lampe boarded a train to still another destination after Portsmouth dropped him because "his brilliancy had been dimmed by Virginia League batsmen." He spent the rest of his minor league career with teams in the Eastern League before retiring in 1899 to become a Boston police officer.

But Lampe found keeping the peace no easier than keeping ML runners off base. In June 1900 he was seriously injured while trying to stop a runaway horse. He had just returned to duty the following month in Division 6 in South Boston when he was hit over the head with a wood plank while quelling a domestic argument. Yet Lampe managed to survive another thirty-six years before dying at his home in Dorchester from surgical complications. (DN)

Lee, Thomas Frank / "Tom"

B	T	HGT	WGT	G	IP	H	GS
?	?	5'8"	155	20	167.1	176	19

CG	BB	SO	SH	W	L	PCT	ERA
17	44	95	0	6	12	.333	3.50

B. 6/8/1862 Philadelphia, PA **D.** 3/4/1886
TEAMS: 84ChiN 84BalU
DEBUT: 6/14/1884 at Detroit; played SS and went 1-for-4 in a 9–4 win over Detroit's Stump Wiedman
FINALE: 9/16/1884 at Baltimore; caught by John Cuff and lost 11–4 to Pittsburgh's Hugh Daily
CAREER LOWLIGHT: 6/28/1884 at Chicago; in his NL finale was caught by Mike Kelly in Chicago's undersized park and allowed a then record 6 home runs in a 13–4 loss to Providence's Charley Radbourn

After appearing at SS in his ML debut, Tom Lee made two losing starts before gaining his first victory on June 21 by topping Boston 11–7. He made two more losing starts with Chicago and was let go after the second, when Providence tattooed him for a new ML single-game-record six dingers. Dumped at the end of June, he was not picked up by Baltimore UA until late July.

Lee made just fourteen starts with Baltimore but was second on the team in both innings pitched with 122 and wins with 5. But it was a very distant second to the club's workhorse, 40-game winner Bill Sweeney. Baltimore cast Lee adrift when the Pittsburgh UA club disbanded, freeing the Maryland club to pick up Al Atkinson. At the time of Lee's departure he was unable to pitch, his "arm pounded black and sore" from having been hit by a line drive in his final ML appearance. The following year Lee played in the Southern League, where he contracted malaria that spiraled into "quick consumption," leading to his death at 24 in Milwaukee. (DN)

Leever, Samuel / "Sam" "Deacon" "The Goshen Schoolmaster"

B	T	HGT	WGT	G	IP	H	GS
R	R	5'10½"	175	86	644.2	615	71

CG	BB	SO	SH	W	L	PCT	ERA
62	175	220	7	37	36	.507	2.98

B. 12/23/1871 Goshen, OH **D.** 5/19/1953
TEAMS: 98–10PitN
DEBUT: 5/26/1898 at Pittsburgh; relieved Jesse Tannehill who had relieved Jim Gardner in Gardner's 11–7 loss to Washington's Win Mercer
FINALE: 9/26/1910 at Brooklyn; relieved Kirby White in White's 4–1 loss to Brooklyn's Nap Rucker

A small-town schoolmaster, Sam Leever appears to have given no thought to baseball as anything more than a summer job to supplement his teaching income until Richmond of the Atlantic League sold him to Pittsburgh in 1897. He made the Pirates' roster the following spring but was farmed to Richmond in May when the team had too many pitchers. Later recalled after a 21-18 season, he collected his first ML win on getaway day in 1898, beating Cleveland 9–1.

While with Richmond, Leever had grown accustomed to patrolling the outfield during batting practice on days when he wasn't pitching and wowing the crowd with long throws. He would also pitch batting practice on occasion, ignoring manager Jake Wells's monition to save his arm. In 1899 Leever tried to follow the same regimen in Pittsburgh, believing himself indestructible, but by July his arm was ailing for the first time in his life. Nevertheless, he led the NL in games, innings pitched, and saves in his official rookie year and finished with 21 wins. Expected to become the team's ace in 1900 and carry Pittsburgh to its first-ever pennant after the Pirates beefed up their roster by adding the core of Louisville's best players in the off-season, Leever had his hand severely cut in an Opening Day start at St. Louis and was idle for two weeks. Returning on May 2, he won his next three decisions, but after that he was only a .500 pitcher and a major disappointment as the Pirates fell 4½ games short in their bid to overtake defending NL-champion Brooklyn.

Leever thus finished the nineteenth-century portion of his career 37-36, just one game above .500, but would retire in 1910 with a winning percentage of .660, the ninth highest in history. (DN)

Lovett, Thomas Joseph / "Tom"

B	T	HGT	WGT	G	IP	H	GS
R	?	5'8"	162	162	1305.1	1341	149

CG	BB	SO	SH	W	L	PCT	ERA
132	444	439	9	88	59	.599	3.94

B. 12/7/1863 Providence, RI **D.** 3/19/1928
TEAMS: 85PhiA 89BroA 90–91BroN 93BroN 94BosN
DEBUT: 6/4/1885 at Philadelphia; caught by Jack Milligan and lost 8–3 to St. Louis's Bob Caruthers
FINALE: 9/9/1894 at Boston; caught by Charlie Ganzel and was relieved by Harry Staley, who took the 13–11 loss to Chicago's Scott Stratton
CAREER HIGHLIGHT: set a ML record, later tied by Scott Stratton, when he won 24 straight games in his home park from May 21, 1890, through September 3, 1890

Tom Lovett's arm of choice remains a mystery, but he was almost certainly right-handed since writers in the 1880s were wont to note pitchers that threw left. In any case, Lovett had an excellent change of pace, good control, and a talent for working out of jams. His alleged weaknesses were that he was an erratic fielder, particularly early in his career, and an impatient hitter who swung at everything, although his career .185 BA and .449 OPS were no worse than most pitchers in his time.

Lovett signed with the Providence reserves in the spring of 1885 after pitching for Waterbury, CT, the previous year. In May he was sold to Philadelphia AA. Even though he did moderately well in his rookie year (7-8 with a 3.70 ERA), the A's released him. Lovett then spent 1886 in the New England League and the first half of 1887 in the Eastern League before being sold to Oshkosh of the Northwestern League after his Bridgeport EL team folded. At the time he was 21-3 against EL competition. With Oshkosh he added another 20 wins in 22 decisions for a combined 41-5 mark, but when he refused several offers from ML teams, Cleveland writer Frank Brunell groused, "Lovett seems to be unapproachable by an Association or League club. He has, I suppose, fought off each of us in turn, and I am at a loss to see the reason, except he fears failure."

In truth, Lovett was probably well paid by Oshkosh and remained in the minors since the reserve power had been removed from them and he could pick where he played. The fact that he and others took this attitude was a key reason the majors restored reserve rights to the minors. But meanwhile, a 30-win season in 1888 with Omaha of the Western Association finally propelled Lovett to take an ML offer the following year from Brooklyn AA. He soon replaced 1888 rookie sensation Mickey Hughes in the Bridegrooms' rotation but was the least effective member. As a consequence, manager Bill McGunnigle used him strictly in relief in 1890 until the season was more than a month old. The date of Lovett's first start, May 21, marked the beginning of his record 24 straight wins at Brooklyn's home park before the Giants ended the skein on September 5. Not nearly as effective on the road, Lovett still finished 30-11 and then collected 2 more wins in the World's Series that fall against Louisville before dropping the final AA-NL postseason contest on October 28 to end the affair at 3 games apiece. He followed with 23 wins in 1891 but then sat out the entire 1892 season when Brooklyn would not meet his salary terms and spent the summer pitching for a Bridgeport semipro team and managing his Providence saloon before finally penning this note to Brooklyn owner Charlie Byrne: "Dear Byrne, I hear your loving call, / Though I must say I like your gall. / So send the contract, I will sign, / And be once more your Valentine."

During Lovett's absence, John M. Ward had taken over the Bridegrooms' reins. When the pitcher returned to the club in 1893, rather than the warm reception he might have expected from the anti-establishment Ward, he had a particularly chilly relationship with his manager. The fault admittedly might have Lovett's; he appears not to have kept in great shape in his year away from the majors. He may also have had trouble adjusting to the new pitching distance, for he appeared in only 14 games in the box. Released after the season, he signed with Boston for 1894, but local papers attest that he was not wanted there and that the Beaneaters deliberately played poorly behind him so he would lose. If so, Lovett foiled his teammates to an extent. He was 8-6 in July, but Boston nonetheless cut him. Lovett pitched effectively in the Eastern League through 1896 and then worked as a salesman for a while before becoming a night watchman at a warehouse in Providence. He died of a heart attack on a Providence street at 64 while taking a walk. (DN/DB)

Luby, John Perkins / "Jack" "Pat"

B	T	HGT	WGT	G	IP	H	GS
L	R	6'0"	185	106	797.1	810	88

CG	BB	SO	SH	W	L	PCT	ERA
73	311	215	1	40	41	.494	3.88

G	AB	H	R	2B	3B	HR
132	430	101	66	12	11	7

RBI	BB	SO	SB	BA	SA	OBP
70	37	52	11	.235	.363	.310

B. 6/?/1869 Charleston, SC **D.** 4/24/1899
TEAMS: 90–92ChiN 95LouN
DEBUT: 6/16/1890 at Chicago; caught by Jake Stenzel and lost 4–3 to Pittsburgh's Guy Hecker
FINALE: 6/11/1895 at Boston; caught by Fred Zahner and Tub Welch in an 11–0 loss to Boston's Harry Dolan

A tall, lean blond, Jack Luby pitched for his local independent Charleston team at the beginning of 1889 and finished the campaign with Grand Rapids of the Michigan State League. Still just 20 and socially immature, he remained in the South in 1890 with Galveston of the Texas League. When the TL folded in June, Luby came to Chicago NL, along with his catcher, Jake Stenzel.

After he lost five of his first six starts with Stenzel handling him in each, Chicago player-manager Cap Anson benched Stenzel in favor of another rookie backstop, Kit Kittridge, but the move failed to halt Luby's slide. On July 24, after a 10–4 blasting at the hands of Brooklyn, he was 3-9. Were it not for his bat (his .440 SA in 1890 led everyone on the Chicago team with as many as 125 PAs), he almost surely would have been released. Instead Anson gave Luby one final chance, against seventh-place Cleveland on August 6. Luby responded by reeling off a rookie-record 17 straight wins, the last at New York on October 3 when he nipped Amos Rusie 3–2. In so doing he became the only qualifier prior to John Tudor in 1985 to win more than two-thirds of his decisions after being as many as 6 games under .500 at one point in the season.

In the spring of 1891 Anson allowed Luby to train "at his Southern home" rather than with the team and regretted it when the sophomore reported in poor shape and was a major flop, finishing 8-11. Luby remained in Chicago that winter under Anson's close supervision, playing indoor baseball. After another poor start in 1892 he swore off cigarettes, with *TSN*'s support: "He lays all his stomach troubles to excessive smoking of the death's delight." Meanwhile Luby's bigger problem—drinking—went unaddressed, and he also had bouts of arm trouble. When he went 11-16 in 1892 and flunked a trial in the outfield, hitting just .190, he was released.

Luby spent 1893 in the Southern League with New Orleans, playing 1B and the outfield and pitching only when his arm allowed. The following January he signed to play RF and captain Milwaukee of the Western League, but he also pitched a fair amount and was recruited by Louisville for 1895. Luby recorded his final ML win on April 23, 1895, when he survived a ninth-inning salami by former teammate Jimmy Ryan to beat Chicago 16–14. Then on May 5 he reinjured his arm and did not reappear until June 1, when he lost 21–4 to Washington. Released after being thrashed by Boston in his final ML start, he joined Scranton of the Eastern League but was "fined $100 for impudence and mutiny" by manager Billy Barnie in August and later suspended for heaving a ball at a base coach who was riding him and allowing the winning runs to score. After that Luby's course was inexorably downward. He played with Carbondale of the Pennsylvania State League until he was jailed for a drunken escapade and then hooked on as a first baseman with Hornellsville of the New York State League for a while. Luby died at his Charleston home in 1899 after a long illness, perhaps consumption. (DN)

Lynch, John H. / "Jack"

B	T	HGT	WGT	G	IP	H	GS
R	R	5'8"	185	221	1924.1	2048	216

CG	BB	SO	SH	W	L	PCT	ERA
214	295	859	8	110	105	.512	3.69

B. 2/5/1857 New York, NY **D.** 4/20/1923
TEAMS: 81BufN 83–87NYA 90BroA
DEBUT: 5/2/1881 at Detroit; caught by Jack Rowe and beat Detroit's George Derby 6–5
FINALE: 4/19/1890 at Syracuse; caught by Jim Toy and lost 18–12 to Syracuse's Bill Sullivan and Frank Keffer

A "jolly humorist," chubby Jack Lynch pitched with a graceful waltz-skip and in 1884 worked in tandem with Tim Keefe to bring New York City its first ML pennant and the majors the first pair of 30-game winners on the same team. Lynch started with semipro Port Jervis, NY, in 1877 as an outfielder, joining Mike "King" Kelly on a veritable team of future stars. On May 14, 1878, he was signed by Billy Barnie to play for New Haven of the International Association. Two weeks later New Haven's ace Candy Cummings jumped the team, and Lynch volunteered to pitch. Soon after his box debut, a 5–2 loss to Utica on June 1, Barnie moved the team to Hartford in search of a better fan base. Lynch went 4-14 all told for Barnie, including three losses in a Fourth of July tripleheader with New Bedford. When Barnie was forced to disband Hartford on July 17, 1878, Lynch signed with Ormond Butler's Washington Nationals and produced a stunning 2–1 win against Providence's John M. Ward on August 20.

In 1879 Washington entered the National Association and Lynch arrived as a frontline player, going 27-13 in championship games plus 9-5 in tough exhibitions. Lynch's rubber arm kept Washington in the thick of the pennant race, and the humorist in him would turn somersaults for the crowd after an exciting win. Still, with 2 games remaining in the season, Albany clinched the flag on September 23 when Lynch was tagged for a Mike Muldoon home run that beat Washington 1–0. The following year Washington won the National Association pennant by virtue of the fact that every other team went belly-up while Lynch was 31-18. On September 29 he opposed Hugh Daily of the New York Mets in the first baseball game ever played at the Polo Grounds, with Daily winning 4–2.

As a Buffalo NL rookie in 1881, Lynch alternated with Jim Galvin until August, when Jim O'Rourke tried unsuccessfully to win the pennant using Galvin alone. Miffed, Lynch went to New York City and opened a sporting goods store on the current site of Madison Square Garden. In 1882, after refusing to return to Buffalo, he replaced Hugh Daily as ace of the League Alliance New York Mets and went 33-31, logging a staggering 586 innings. The ladies took a liking to his waltzlike delivery, and he became a fan favorite, beating visiting National League teams fourteen times. His Tammany Indian nickname was "Big Medicine."

The Mets squad was split in 1883 to seed New York teams in both major leagues, and Lynch was placed in the AA. In 1884 he alternated with Tim Keefe to bring New York its first ML flag, as both won 37 games. Having lost money despite copping the pennant, New York owners moved Keefe and Tom Esterbrook to the NL to profit from its 50¢ admission price. One of the few stars left on the Mets, Lynch became a rare pitcher-captain in July 1885 and gave the club a tinge of respectability by dint of his last winning season, at 23-21. The following year Lynch sank to 20-30 as part of the first ML staff with three 20-game losers. In 1887, his final full season, even at 7-14 he was accorded the honor of pitching the last game in Mets AA history, losing 10–0 to Baltimore. By then all those innings early in his career had taken their toll, and Lynch's embarrassing comeback attempt in 1890 with Brooklyn AA after struggling for two years to regain his form in the minors is best forgotten.

Lynch had opened a combination saloon and billiard room with veteran catcher John Clapp in 1884, just down the street from the Polo Grounds, which became a popular player hangout for a time. In future years he became a noted after-dinner speaker and in the off season entertained admirers around his hot stove in the back of his various saloon establishments. He had coached Princeton College in 1886 and continued to coach periodically, but it was not his forte. Lynch thought of himself as an innovator—in 1890 he invented a baseball puzzle that he claimed would be all the rage and would be played by benchwarmers during games. When the puzzle was a flop and his saloon ventures foundered, he became a New York City police officer late in 1891 and began pounding a beat around 60th Street and Lexington Avenue in Manhattan. Finding that law enforcement was not one of his gifts either, he changed occupations in the mid 1890s and became a boiler inspector, a job he held until retirement. Lynch died at his son John's home in the Bronx at 66. (FV/DN)

Madigan, William J. / "Tony" "Tice"

B	T	HGT	WGT	G	IP	H	GS
?	R	5'5½"	126	14	114.2	154	13

CG	BB	SO	SH	W	L	PCT	ERA
13	44	29	0	1	13	.071	4.87

B. 7/18/1868 Washington, D.C. **D.** 12/4/1954
TEAMS: 86WasN
DEBUT: 7/10/1886 at Washington; caught by Barney Gilligan and lost 6–1 to Boston's Bill Stemmeyer
FINALE: 9/4/1886 at Chicago; caught by Dave Oldfield and lost 13–6 to John Clarkson

Raised in the Swampoodle sector of Washington near the D.C. club's park in 1886, Tony Madigan remained a resident of that region all his life. After leaving baseball, he clerked for a law firm and then ran a liquor store. Eventually he worked for the Pabst Brewing Company, according to his obit, "until Prohibition's effects knocked him out of the job, in 1920."

Madigan first got the Washington NL club's eye in 1886 when he fanned 23 members of the Pension Office team while pitching for the amateur Merchants. Of his ML debut the *Washington Post* said, "Madigan, the young pitcher who made his first appearance yesterday, impressed . . . as a plucky one in the box and, as he expressed himself after the game, 'I expected to be hit, but they could not scare me.'" Though reference works list Madigan as having been 18 when he joined Washington and weighing 126 pounds, in August 1886 *TSN* reported that he was but 17 and weighed just 118. After a 0-3 start he won his only ML game on July 19 when he beat New York. Madigan then embarked on a 10-game losing streak that carried to the end of his short career. The following year he endeavored to learn his craft pitching in the minors but was released in August by Binghamton after going 6-12 against International Association competition. Madigan had no better success in 1888 in the Michigan State League and by the end of the summer was back in Washington pitching and playing RF for the Alerts, which also featured his brother Jack and future ML pitcher Harry Mace.

Whether Madigan was 17 or 18 in 1886, he holds the post-1876 record for the most innings pitched by a hurler whose ML career ended before his 19th birthday. He died at 86 in a Washington hospital after an illness of six weeks. (DN)

Martin, Alphonse Case / "Fahney" "Phonny"

B	T	HGT	WGT	G	IP	H	GS
?	R	5'7"	148	24	156.1	263	13

CG	BB	SO	SH	W	L	PCT	ERA
10	17	6	0	3	10	.231	4.03

G	AB	H	R	2B	3B	HR
74	337	82	52	4	2	0

RBI	BB	SO	SB	BA	SA	OBP
37	2	8	4	.243	.267	.248

G	W	L	PCT	PENNANTS
9	1	8	.111	0

B. 8/4/1845 New York, NY **D.** 5/24/1933
TEAMS: 72TroNA (P/M)72EckNA 73MutNA
DEBUT: 4/26/1872 at Troy; played RF and went 2-for-4 in a 10–0 win over Middletown's Cy Bentley
FINALE: 10/21/1873 at New York; played RF and went 1-for-6 in a 15–3 win over the Philadelphia Athletics' Cherokee Fisher

Surely Alphonse Martin was a right-hander, since he was a high profile pitcher in a time when there were almost no lefties and there was never any comment on which arm he favored. His nickname was a contraction of Alphonse and was pronounced "FAH-ney." Martin is among the crew of early-day pitchers for whom plausible credentials can be offered that they invented the curve ball. As early as April 1868 the *New York Clipper* wrote, "[Martin] is an extremely hard pitcher to hit, for the ball never comes in a straight line, but in a tantalizing curve." That same year *Wilkes' Spirit of the Times* said, "His great effectiveness is on account of his slow curve line of delivery." These quotes were cited in the early 1900s by writer June Rankin in building a case that the curve was in existence as early as Martin's tenure in the game, which began in 1860 with the Unions, a junior club, and perhaps existed even before that, for there are references to curve ball pitching as early as 1853.

Martin grew up in Manhattan and apprenticed at a ball ground on Third Avenue and 63rd Street. After serving in the Union Army and pitching for the Zouaves (Company A, 5th New York Volunteers), in 1864 he joined the Empire club of New York with Nat Jewett as his catcher and remained with them through 1865, playing 2B in addition to pitching. Martin then spent part of 1866 with the Unions of Morrisania before joining the New York Mutuals through 1867 and then served two seasons with the Brooklyn Eckfords before returning to the Mutes in 1870. The following year, rather than stay with the Mutes when they entered the all-professional National Association, he got a better offer from the Eckfords. In the NA's second season, Martin signed with Troy as a pitcher-outfielder but was more effective at the latter position, hitting .303 as opposed to logging a 5.79 ERA. After winning his pitching debut on May 7 by beating his former Eckfords team 17–11, he was winless for the rest of the season and collected only 2 victories the following year as a member of the Mutes. When his hitting lagged too, it grew apparent that the game had progressed too far for him to keep the pace any longer.

Martin was interviewed frequently when the controversy as to who invented the curve ball peaked in the early part of the twentieth century. In 1910 Sam Crane wrote that Martin said Bobby Mathews used a curve in 1869, a year before Candy Cummings developed his. According to Crane, Martin maintained that Tommy Bond and Terry Larkin were the first pitchers "who really developed and demonstrated the possibilities of the out-curve." Some eight years later the *New York Sun* said that Martin now claimed a New York Mutuals pitcher named McSweeney invented the curve in 1866. In 1931 Martin signed an affidavit that in 1868, while pitching for the Eckfords, he faced Mathews, who was then with Baltimore, and Mathews not only threw a curve but also a spitball. Subsequently, Ed Seward and Tony Mullane backed Martin by averring that Mathews threw a spitter for Philadelphia AA in the 1880s. Martin died in Hollis, NY, in 1933. (DN/PM/EM)

Mathews, Robert T. / "Bobby"

B	T	HGT	WGT	G	IP	H	GS
R	R	5'5½"	140	578	4956	5601	568

CG	BB	SO	SH	W	L	PCT	ERA
525	532	1528	20	297	248	.545	2.86

G	AB	H	R	2B	3B	HR
623	2486	504	318	48	9	1

RBI	BB	SO	SB	BA	SA	OBP
164	73	59	10	.203	.230	.225

B. 11/21/1851 Baltimore, MD **D.** 4/17/1898
TEAMS: 71KekNA 72BalNA 73–75MutNA 76NYN 77CinN 79ProN 81ProN 81–82BosN 83–87PhiA
DEBUT AND CAREER HIGHLIGHT: 5/4/1871 at Fort Wayne; in the first game in ML history was caught by Bill Lennon and beat Cleveland's Al Pratt 2–0, making him the only pitcher in National Association history to debut with a shutout
FINALE: 10/10/1887 at Philadelphia; caught by George Townsend and lost 7–5 to Brooklyn's Steve Toole

When Bobby Mathews fell 3 victories short of 300 wins, he spared MLB from being accused of holding the HOF door shut to the first 300-game winner in the eyes of the many that regard the National Association as a major league. Adding to his credentials for enshrinement are the distinction of being one of the first pitchers to throw a curve ball and of being among the early practitioners of the spitball (*see* Alphonse Martin). Mathews was also the lone pitcher from the first NA season to remain active long enough to hurl against a ML hitter that could no longer request either a high or a low pitch. But by then he had long been an ultimate survivor at the only occupation he knew.

At age 16 Mathews joined the Maryland Juniors. He then spent part of 1869 and most of 1870 with the professional Marylands before moving west to the Kekiongas club of Fort Wayne late in the latter campaign and remaining with them when they joined the first all-professional league the following year. Mathews returned to Baltimore after the Indiana club folded and then headed for New York in 1873. When the Gotham entry also folded after the 1876 season, he signed with Cincinnati, but between playing for a weak team and having to adjust to constant changes in pitching rules he seemed to be passé in 1877.

The following year, however, Mathews revamped his delivery while pitching in the minor league International Association. There, he strove to emulate the style of another pitcher he had faced on occasion over the years, a one-armed hurler named Hugh Daily, who had perfected a kind of double motion before delivering the ball. With his own exceptional headwork and refinements in the pitches he already owned, Mathews returned to the majors the following year and eventually to the front ranks after he joined Philadelphia AA in 1883. Mathews immediately led his new team to the pennant by bagging 30 wins and followed with two more 30-win seasons, swelling his career victory total to 281. Prior to the 1886 season it seemed only a question of whether he or Jim McCormick would reach 300 wins first. Mathews won his first two starts in 1886 and then began to stumble. He remained in the rotation until August 3 but made only one more start after that and finished the year still 6 wins short of 300. In 1887 Mathews began the season on the DL with an arm injury. When the A's tried to cut him in June, he threatened to sue the club for his full salary. Unnerved, the A's restored him to the payroll but used him only sparingly until the waning days of the season. On October 7 Mathews beat Brooklyn 10–3 for his last ML win. Three days later he threw his last ML pitch in Philadelphia's season finale.

Apparently the A's either re-signed him for 1888 or else he had a multiyear deal, for when the club cut him in the spring of 1888 he was prepared to sue it again until it made him a salaried "coach." Mathews's last active season as a player was in 1889 with independent Lebanon, PA. He then umpired in the Players League for part of 1890 and worked an indicator in the AA early in 1891 before writing race sheets at a New York track. Mathews last worked at Joe Start's roadhouse in Providence before paresis forced him to return to Maryland. After being hospitalized in Baltimore for a time, he was released to his boyhood home to live with his ailing and impoverished mother until he died in 1898. (DN/EM/BM)

Mattimore, Michael Joseph / "Mike"

B	T	HGT	WGT	G	IP	H	GS
L	L	5'8½"	160	58	490.2	514	51

CG	BB	SO	SH	W	L	PCT	ERA
50	184	132	5	26	27	.491	3.83

G	AB	H	R	2B	3B	HR
124	451	92	57	10	9	1

RBI	BB	SO	SB	BA	SA	OBP
36	40	29	34	.204	.273	.278

B. 8/?/1858 North Bend, PA **D.** 4/28/1931
TEAMS: 87NYN 88–89PhiA 89KCA 90BroA
DEBUT: 5/3/1887 at Washington; caught by Pat Deasley and lost 14–4 to Washington's Jim Whitney
FINALE: 7/21/1890 at Louisville; caught by Herman Pitz and lost 11–4 to Louisville's Herb Goodall

Mike Mattimore was in his midtwenties before he ventured into pro ball. After spending 1885–86 with four different minor league teams, Mattimore vied for the third spot in the New York NL rotation in the spring of 1887 but by early summer was pitching batting practice and reserve-squad games. Nevertheless, he received his salary for the full season and irked the Giants when he signed with the Philadelphia A's for 1888.

Serving as the A's third starter that year behind Ed Seward and Gus Weyhing, Mattimore fashioned four shutouts but was seldom used against the better teams. In March 1889 *TSN* predicted he would never make it as a pitcher but would soon be one of the hardest-hitting outfielders in the game. Despite this rosy forecast Mattimore hit just .233 as an outfielder–first baseman in 1889 and made only five pitching appearances with the A's before being released to Kansas City in early September when the Cowboys ran short of outfielders. Rather than accompany the Cowboys to the minors in 1890 after they left the AA, Mattimore joined the mishmash Brooklyn Gladiators and was the team's best pitcher before it folded, which is not a rich compliment. His 4.54 ERA in 1890 actually elevated his career ERA by a third of a run. Mattimore went to the Pacific Northwest League after leaving the majors and was among the many eastern MLers who fell in love with the Far West. He settled in Montana and worked as a boilermaker with the Anaconda Mining Company, moving back and forth between Butte and Helena prior to his death at 72. (DN)

Maul, Albert Joseph / "Al" "Smiling Al" "Berry"

B	T	HGT	WGT	G	IP	H	GS
R	R	6'0"	175	184	1412.2	1620	164

CG	BB	SO	SH	W	L	PCT	ERA
141	510	341	4	84	77	.522	4.34

G	AB	H	R	2B	3B	HR
408	1368	328	192	45	30	7

RBI	BB	SO	SB	BA	SA	OBP
178	182	170	44	.240	.332	.336

B. 10/9/1865 Philadelphia, PA **D.** 5/3/1958
TEAMS: 84PhiU 87PhiN 88–89PitN 90PitP 91PitN 93–97WasN 97–98BalN 99BroN 00PhiN 01NYN
DEBUT: 6/20/1884 at Baltimore; caught by Jack Clements and lost 7–2 to Baltimore's Bill Sweeney
FINALE: 9/9/1901 at New York; was relieved after one inning by Jake Livingstone in his 11–3 loss to St. Louis's Willie Sudhoff

Al Maul was the lone participant in the 1884 Union Association to play in a NL game in the twentieth century. How he did it is a story in itself. Maul was a master of the quick pitch and slow-breaking curve—his pitches were called "dinks"—of whom *TSN* said, "Only with the aid of a cannon could he have acquired more speed." Unlike most successful pitchers of his day, he got most of his outs via fly balls; hitters would lunge at his junk deliveries and pop them up. Yet even though his arm was scarcely taxed by his pitches and he also could play several positions, he never played more than 74 games in a season and on only four occasions pitched more than 62 innings. Near the end of his career *SL* mused, "No one else possessed his secret of enjoying sporting life without working very hard or successfully." Trenchant as it may be, the observation is not entirely accurate. At the close of the 1894 season Maul owned the highest ERA (5.15) among pitchers in 750 or more innings since the start of his ML career in 1884. He then stunned pundits by topping the NL in ERA in 1895 despite making just sixteen starts and appearing in only 135.2 innings, just barely enough to qualify. Almost three years later, after winning just 5 games in the two intervening seasons, Maul assembled one of the premier pitching performances in the 1893–1900 era, bagging 20 wins and a 2.10 ERA while allowing just 9.76 base runners per nine innings. His sudden (and brief) ascension to stardom was probably attributable as much as anything to the fact that his arm was sound enough for the first time since 1895 to fully utilize a fresh bit of artistry he had developed once rule changes allowed new balls to be introduced into play more frequently. When given a new sphere Maul would clandestinely rough it up with a piece of pumice stone concealed in a handkerchief, creating an early version of the "emery ball" that came to prominence some fifteen years later.

Maul was a 17-year-old pitcher-SS with the amateur Bridgeton team of Philadelphia in 1883. He played for a variety of other local teams before and after his one-game trial with the UA Keystones in 1884 and then began his pro career in earnest the following season with Binghamton of the New York state League. He remained in New York state in 1886 with Binghamton and Rochester before moving to Nashville of the Southern League in 1887. Midway through that campaign Philadelphia owner Al Reach purchased him for around $2,500. Finding little in his high-priced new acquisition to like, Reach peddled him for less than half that amount to Pittsburgh in January 1888. Maul opened 1888 as Pittsburgh's regular first baseman but lost his job when the club bought Jake Beckley. He then spent another six seasons as a pitcher-utilityman (including 1892 in the minors) before making the mound his permanent home. Following his breakthrough ERA crown in 1895, Maul developed his first serious bout of arm trouble, although Washington teammates who knew his history found it a bit too convenient to believe and accused him of being able "to lift his arm" only on the 1st and 15th each month to collect his pay. The 1897 season got Maul even more pay for less work since he spent part of the summer on Baltimore's Temple Cup qualifier while appearing in just nine innings. No one knows how he kept his arm healthy throughout 1898, but if he had a secret method he promptly lost it. In his final three ML seasons he appeared in just eighty-three innings.

After the Giants released Maul in 1901, he ran a grocery store in Philadelphia and scouted local college players for ML teams. Later he worked in the ticket departments of both Philadelphia ML clubs. Prior to his death he and Frank Foreman were the last two surviving UA participants. (DN)

Mays, Albert C. / "Al"

B	T	HGT	WGT	G	IP	H	GS
R	R	?	?	150	1251	1341	147

CG	BB	SO	SH	W	L	PCT	ERA
137	415	469	3	53	89	.373	3.91

B. 5/17/1865 Canal Dover, OH **D.** 5/7/1905
TEAMS: 85LouA 86–87NYA 88BroA 89–90ColA
DEBUT: 5/10/1885 at Louisville; caught by Dan Sullivan and lost 3–0 to Baltimore's Tommy Burns
FINALE: 5/2/1890 at Toledo; caught by Jack O'Connor and lost 13–3 to Toledo's Ed Cushman

Al Mays was discovered in 1884 by Louisville ace Guy Hecker pitching in Hecker's hometown of Oil City, PA. Ignoring Mays's already full-blown reputation for drinking and recklessly hitting batters, Hecker recommended him to Louisville. From his first game in the majors to his last, Mays pitched in extreme hard luck. In his initial appearance Louisville made just four hits on his behalf and was held scoreless. Mays also lost his next start and did not win his first game until June 30, 1885, when he beat first-place St. Louis 5–2.

The following year Mays was released by Louisville in March and landed on the weakling New York Mets, for which he lost 27 games and was a member of the first pitching staff in ML history with three 20-game losers. In 1887, after the Mets began the season by losing 10 straight games on the road, Mays broke the skid by beating Brooklyn in the team's home opener. Then on June 4 he hurled his best game of the season, giving up just four hits to the pennant-bound Browns, but nonetheless lost 1–0. Some ten weeks later Mays was the victim of one of the most notorious gaffes in nineteenth-century baseball. As he was about to deliver a pitch in the bottom of the tenth inning of a tie game with Baltimore runners on second and third and Orioles pitcher Matt Kilroy at bat, Mets manager Opie Caylor shouted from the bench for catcher Bill Holbert to order first baseman Jim Donahue to move in a few steps in case Kilroy tried a squeeze bunt. Distracted, Holbert turned his head toward Caylor, causing Mays to halt his delivery, at which point umpire Jack McQuaid properly called a balk, enabling the winning run to score.

In 1888 Mays received the lone good break of his career by landing on Brooklyn, which skimmed off the cream of the disbanded Mets. Prior to the 1889 season, however, with Brooklyn on the threshold of breaking St. Louis's four-year monopoly on the AA pennant, Mays was sent to the neophyte Columbus entry in the AA. Soon after he won Columbus's opening game as a member of the AA, his arm failed, sending him to Mount Clemens, MI, in June in the vain hope the waters there would work magic. The following March, even though there were now three major leagues with the addition of the PL, Mays was still without a team. Claiming his arm was as good as new, he finally convinced Columbus to hire him on a per diem basis, only to be released when he was rocked by Toledo in his first appearance of the season.

In the spring of 1891 the best Mays could land was a job with Erie of the New York–Pennsylvania League. Meanwhile his wife, whom he claimed he had married in 1889 while intoxicated, sued him for divorce on the grounds of chronic drunkenness and abandonment. Mays remained in Erie for the next several years, working as a laborer and pitching when his ailing arm and general rheumatic condition permitted. In 1893, for the only time in his career, he was on a pennant winner when Erie copped the Eastern League flag, but Mays took little joy in the triumph since he was able to play in only 16 games before leaving the club in early September totally disabled by rheumatism. Approximately twelve years later he accidentally drowned in the Ohio River near Parkersburg, WV, and Blennerhasset Island, once a hideout for Aaron Burr. (DN)

McBride, John Dickson / "Dick"

B	T	HGT	WGT	G	IP	H	GS
?	R	5'9"	150	237	2082	2420	237

CG	BB	SO	SH	W	L	PCT	ERA
227	174	150	10	149	78	.656	2.71

G	W	L	PCT	PENNANTS
252	161	85	.654	1

B. 6/14/1847 Philadelphia, PA **D.** 10/10/1916
TEAMS: (P/M)71–75AthNA 76BosN
DEBUT: 5/20/1871 at Boston; caught by Ned Cuthbert and lost 11–8 to Boston's Al Spalding
FINALE: 7/13/1876 at Chicago; caught by Lew Brown and lost 11–3 to Chicago's Al Spalding

It is only fitting that Dick McBride began and ended his ML career losing to Al Spalding, for the two vied for recognition as the game's top pitcher throughout the NA's five-year history, with Spalding performing a cut better in almost every respect.

A skilled cricket player in his youth, in 1861 the acerbic and temperamental McBride joined an embryonic version of the Athletics Base Ball club that won the first NA pennant. Mainly a SS in his early years, he gravitated to the box in the mid-1860s and by 1866 was the Athletics' main pitcher. Restricted to an underhand delivery without even a wrist snap, he specialized in spotting his pitches and trying hitters' patience until eventually they swung at his serving rather than one to their liking. When the Athletics entered the fledgling National Association in 1871, McBride was their captain and was expected to pitch every game. In September, when he was forced to miss 2 games against Cleveland, the Athletics lost 1 of them behind change pitcher George Bechtel, and it nearly cost them the pennant.

After Boston emerged as the NA's dominant team and swept the next four pennants, by 1875 the A's were losing money and opted to pare McBride's team-high salary from the payroll. Even though he had already won 44 games and was having his best season, he was cut after a 17–13 loss to Boston on October 9, and the A's finished the year with rookie Lon Knight in the box. When Spalding and three other Boston players skipped to Chicago for 1876, leading to the dissolution of the NA and the rise of the NL in its stead, the Hub team signed McBride to replace Spalding, but he was unable to pitch until June. In late May 1876 the *New York Clipper* contended, "When the Bostons have McBride in the pitcher's position things will be different. Then the rest of the nine will play with more confidence." McBride did indeed do well in his first two starts once he rounded into shape. On June 8 he lost 3–1 to Louisville's Jim Devlin, and two days later he lost another narrow decision to Devlin 4–3. But in his final two ML starts he was hammered for a total of 31 runs and 43 hits.

A possible explanation for his sudden decline is that he tried to change his delivery to keep up with the times, encountered arm trouble in 1876, recovered briefly, and then began ailing again. McBride played for the Athletics' minor league and independent team until the late 1870s and then became a successful merchant and also was the superintendent of a sub–post office in Philadelphia for a while. In 1888 *TSN* reported him to "have the appearance of a man of fifty-eight years," his beard completely gray. McBride's birth date is suspect. It is doubtful that he was only 14 when he first joined the Athletics in 1861. He died in Philadelphia at 69 or thereabouts. (DN/EM)

McCormick, Patrick Henry / "Harry"

B	T	HGT	WGT	G	IP	H	GS
R	R	5'9"	155	103	884	922	103

CG	BB	SO	SH	W	L	PCT	ERA
96	115	157	10	41	58	.414	2.66

B. 10/25/1855 Syracuse, NY **D.** 8/8/1889
TEAMS: 79SyrN 81WorN 82–83CinA
DEBUT: 5/1/1879 at Chicago; caught by Kick Kelly and lost to Chicago's Terry Larkin 4–3
FINALE: 9/20/1883 at Cincinnati; beat Baltimore's Bob Emslie and Hardie Henderson 3–2

Harry McCormick joined the Stars in his native Syracuse in 1875 after beating that team while pitching for the amateur Geddes Plaid Stockings. Having developed a curve ball, still a novelty in the baseball world, he became a sensation in 1876. McCormick first earned fame by pitching a 0–0 tie against the NL St. Louis Browns and quickly became the Stars' mainstay, hurling almost all their games for three seasons. With pinpoint control that enabled him to motion his fielders into position and induce the hitters to hit the ball right to them, he was known as heady and cool under pressure and probably benefited even more than most pitchers would from the support provided by a strong fielding team featuring Jimmy Macullar, Jack Farrell, and Hick Carpenter.

The Stars nearly nosed out Buffalo for the 1878 International Association championship, as McCormick won 26 of 36 decisions and garnered a badge from the *New York Clipper* as the best fielding pitcher in the IA. However, when Syracuse, unable to make IA baseball a paying venture, somewhat reluctantly chose to enter the NL in 1879, the move turned out badly, as the team lost 48 of 70 games and disbanded before the season ended. Perhaps the Stars were simply in over their heads in the tougher NL, but they also had the bad luck to step into deeper competitive waters just as the strong right arm of McCormick, on which they had depended so heavily, began to falter.

Certainly the magic faded for McCormick in 1879, leaving him never again a dominant pitcher. Aside from any wear on his arm from the heavy workload of the previous three seasons, hitters had probably begun to catch up with his curve ball. McCormick also failed to stretch the rules requiring underhanded pitching, as others were doing, leaving him behind as pitching techniques developed. In the wake of his unfortunate 1879 season McCormick had a hard time reestablishing his career. On May 21, 1880, he hurled for Albany of the National Association, his first game since Syracuse had disbanded early the previous September, and beat Worcester but did not play again and was released a few weeks later. In 1881 he was signed by Worcester in June but lost 8 of 9 games as the backup to Lee Richmond, the newest hot, young pitcher, and then remained without a job until just after the beginning of the 1882 season when Cincinnati signed him to replace Dave Rowe, who had bombed as the team's change pitcher during the preseason. With another sharp fielding team behind him, including Carpenter and Macullar as well as the great Bid McPhee, McCormick pitched strong ball, helping Cincinnati win the first AA championship.

The next season was another disappointment. McCormick pitched well at times but was arrested in June for shooting off fireworks and carrying a concealed "pop" (slang in the 1880s for gun) and briefly suspended by the Reds. He vied for playing time with rookie Ren Deagle behind staff ace Will White until he begged for his release, complaining that he was handicapped by "the dislike of certain parties." In 1884 McCormick pitched for Minneapolis of the Northwestern League and then Trenton of the Eastern League before being blacklisted for jumping the latter team. The following spring he paid $100 to procure reinstatement and tried out for a new Syracuse International League team but no longer had his control. McCormick then worked as a barge tender on the Erie Canal. When he died in 1889 of cholera, he was still popular enough in his hometown that in 1904 the street where he had lived was renamed McCormick Avenue. (DB)

McCullough, Charles F. / "Charlie" "The Tammany Tiger"

B	T	HGT	WGT	G	IP	H	GS
?	R	6'1"	185	29	241.2	276	28

CG	BB	SO	SH	W	L	PCT	ERA
27	116	69	0	5	23	.179	4.88

B. ?/?/1866 Dublin, Ireland **D.** 4/13/1898
TEAMS: 90BroA 90SyrA
DEBUT: 4/23/1890 at Brooklyn; caught by Jim Toy and lost 7–2 in ten innings to Rochester's John Fitzgerald
FINALE: 8/29/1890 at Syracuse; caught by Grant Briggs and lost 10–9 to Louisville's Red Ehret

The team comedian everywhere he went, Charlie McCullough toiled in two small Pennsylvania circuits in 1888, his frosh pro season. After spending 1889 in the Southern League, the Ireland native returned to his adopted Brooklyn home the following season to pitch for the local AA Gladiators. McCullough appears to have been completely out of his depth even in the weakest of the three major leagues in 1890. His .179 winning percentage was by far the worst of any qualifier that season—and his pitching was of All-Star caliber compared to his hitting! Among all players in the nineteenth century with a minimum of 100 PAs, McCullough posted the lowest career BA (.032), SA (.032), and OPS (.121).

Yet he was not so dreadful as his stats make it appear. In his ML debut McCullough had a shutout through the first six innings and would have won with just a smidge more offensive support. Following a 0-7 start he garnered his first ML win in neat fashion on May 23, topping Louisville, the eventual AA pennant winner, 4–2. Later in the season, before the Gladiators disbanded, he also beat second-place Columbus, and in his ML finale he lost largely because second baseman Cupid Childs played an abnormally poor game and committed several crucial errors.

McCullough signed for 1891 with Rochester of the Eastern Association and was pitching in the minors as late as 1896 when he hurled three straight shutouts in June for independent Allentown. Disappearing from view soon after that, not until the twenty-first century was McCullough learned to have died in Brooklyn less than two years after pitching his last pro game. (DN)

McDermott, Michael Joseph / "Mike"

B	T	HGT	WGT	G	IP	H	GS
?	R	5'7"	180	58	355.2	443	47

CG	BB	SO	SH	W	L	PCT	ERA
27	191	69	1	11	33	.250	6.17

B. 9/7/1872 St. Louis, MO **D.** 6/30/1943
TEAMS: 95–96LouN 97CleN 97StLN
DEBUT: 4/20/1895 at Louisville; caught by Tub Welch and was relieved after only one inning by Jack Wadsworth in Wadsworth's 16–9 loss to Pittsburgh's Frank Killen
FINALE: 7/31/1897 at St. Louis; caught by Morg Murphy and was relieved by John Grimes, who got the 11–6 loss to Louisville's Bill Magee

Current reference works list Mike McDermott as being born in 1862, which would make him nearly 33 when he debuted and the oldest rookie pitching qualifier in the nineteenth century. But the April 18, 1896, *TSN* said he was 23 years old. Since he does not appear to have begun his pro career until the mid 1890s, an 1872 birth year seems more reasonable.

McDermott hurled for a series of Illinois semipro teams in 1894 and earned a bid from Louisville when he threw a no-hitter for the Hillsboro club against Vandalia. In the spring of 1895 his behavior was more like that of a 22-year-old than a 32-year-old when he and another rookie, Sandy McDougal, were accused of ruining their chances by "letting themselves out" in exhibitions in an effort to bedazzle manager John McCloskey. Yet McDermott's strategy seemed to work since McCloskey was smitten enough to keep him in the Louisville rotation all year despite a wretched overall performance. In addition to logging a 4-19 record and a 5.99 ERA, the rookie led the NL in both wild pitches and pitcher errors. By August, after continual sulking and drinking sprees, McDermott was heavily fined by McCloskey, removed from the rotation and made to carry the team's bat bag. But no sooner was he benched than Louisville began receiving trade offers for him, causing McCloskey to reevaluate his feckless pitcher. Outfielder Tom Brown once explained why McDermott was so highly coveted by other teams early in his career. During the warmup period he looked unhittable, but once the game started, "under fire he is in danger of having his heart take an upshot and collide with his Adam's apple."

After disappointing observers who had predicted he would be the most brilliant rookie pitcher in the NL in 1895, McDermott returned to St. Louis after the season and found that his brothers had abandoned the family, leaving his younger sisters and father destitute and homeless, scattered all over the city. McDermott had to round them up, find new lodgings for them, and then go to work supporting them. He reported for duty the following spring with a new strategy: to round into shape more slowly. It appeared to work when he produced his career game on May 21, 1896, at Louisville, blanking Baltimore, that season's NL pennant winner, 1–0 and allowing just two hits. But McDermott then lapsed into his old ways. Toward the end of June he was farmed to Rochester of the Eastern League and then cut free altogether in late July. Said to have "cried when told of his release," McDermott regained equilibrium when Cleveland signed him later that summer and put him on its reserve squad.

Elevated to the Spiders' roster in the spring of 1897, McDermott again had intermittent flashes of brilliance. On May 2 he topped St. Louis 3–1, allowing just four hits. Then on the 27th he replaced shell-shocked Cy Young in the second inning and held hard-hitting Baltimore to a mere four hits the rest of the way in gaining an 8–7 win. Nevertheless, he was released after a couple of bad games the following month. Upon returning home to St. Louis, McDermott begged Browns owner Chris Von der Ahe for one last chance, but after topping Washington 4–3 on July 25, he was removed early on in his next start six days later. The official explanation for his short-lived stint was "heat prostration," but it seems likely that he arrived at the park hungover, for he was released shortly thereafter.

That winter McDermott married Bridget Gillon and vowed to reform, but after spending parts of the next two seasons in the minors without living up to his pledge, he was out of pro ball by 1900. McDermott then worked as a laborer for the Laclede Gas Company and died in St. Louis at 68 of stomach cancer. (DN)

*McFarlan, Anderson Daniel / "Dan" "Silver"

B	T	HGT	WGT	G	IP	H	GS
R	R	6'0"	178	40	263.2	354	35

CG	BB	SO	SH	W	L	PCT	ERA
28	82	51	1	8	25	.242	5.02

B. 11/6/1874 Gainesville, TX **D.** 9/23/1924
TEAMS: 95LouN 99BroN 99WasN
DEBUT: 9/2/1895 at Washington; caught by Jack Warner in a 9–7 loss to Washington's Jack Gilroy

FINALE: 10/14/1899 at New York; caught by Doc Powers and beat Charlie Gettig 12–9

Dan McFarlan hurled Washington's last game as a member of the twelve-team NL and seemed certain to finish his career with a .212 winning percentage when the Nationals trailed New York 8–0 after five innings, but instead he elevated his final mark to .242 by dint of the Giants' wretched late-inning support of Charlie Gettig. Both Gettig and McFarlan were history the following year when the NL lopped off four teams, cutting jobs by a third.

The brother of ML outfielder Alex McFarlan, ML umpire Horace McFarlan, and at least two other ball playing brothers, McFarlan was a graduate of Washington & Lee and said by *TSN* to be "the wealthiest player" in the majors in the fall of 1899 thanks to a "$165,000 trust" left by his father twenty years earlier that could not be touched until his youngest sister came of age. McFarlan and his brother Alex, upon finally coming into their inheritance, debated using the money to buy the Louisville club until a wiser head said, "There are better and safer ways of investing money."

Much about the McFarlan clan is still fair game for researchers. The family appears to have been in Texas in the 1870s, but *TSN* at one point claimed McFarlan grew up in New Jersey and learned the game from Al Nichols, the banned ex-ML infielder. By the time McFarlan joined Louisville in 1895, he had pitched with several Kentucky teams and in the Texas, Southern, and Western leagues and was renting a home in Louisville after marrying the previous December. In his ML debut he lost 9–7 when a bases-loaded overthrow by SS Frank Shugart rolled into a hole in the grandstand and down into the park cellar, allowing all four runners to score. Six starts later McFarlan was still looking for his first win. After finishing the season 0-7, he was farmed to Rochester of the Eastern League in 1896 but would have been recalled that June by Louisvilles new manager, Bill McGunnigle, along with "his beautiful young wife" if Rochester manager Dan Shannon had not put up a fuss at the notion of losing his best pitcher.

McFarlan remained in the Eastern League for three full years before Baltimore drafted him in the fall of 1898 after a 27-win season with Montreal. Transferred to Brooklyn in April 1899 in a Baltimore-Brooklyn syndicate deal, he made one relief appearance there and then was part of a trade with Washington that brought Duke Farrell and Doc Casey to Brooklyn. McFarlan lost his first four starts with Washington to approach the then record of 13 straight losses to begin a ML career. He finally broke his 0-11 skein by topping Pittsburgh 10–2 on May 19. After leaving Washington McFarlan spent five seasons in the minors before returning to Kentucky, presumably to enjoy what was left of his inheritance, although he appears to have been a near invalid in his later years, perhaps a result of a beaning at some point in his career. McFarlan died in Louisville at 59 of acute indigestion. (DN)

McGill, William Vaness / "Willie" "Kid" "The Boy Boozer"

B	T	HGT	WGT	G	IP	H	GS
?	L	5'6½"	170	166	1235	1363	148

CG	BB	SO	SH	W	L	PCT	ERA
114	696	502	2	71	73	.493	4.57

G	AB	H	R	2B	3B	HR
167	476	96	66	19	2	0

RBI	BB	SO	SB	BA	SA	OBP
40	98	77	9	.202	.250	.340

B. 11/10/1873 Atlanta, GA **D.** 8/29/1944
TEAMS: 90CleP 91CinA 91StLA 92CinN 93–94ChiN 95–96PhiN
DEBUT: 5/8/1890 at Cleveland; caught by Charlie Snyder and beat Buffalo's George Haddock 14–5
FINALE: 6/12/1896 at Philadelphia; caught by Mike Grady and was relieved in the second inning by Al Orth, who got the 9–8 win over Louisville's Bill Hill and Tom Smith
CAREER HIGHLIGHT: Won 21 games in 1891 at age 17 to become the youngest 20-game winner in ML history

Willie McGill apparently came to Chicago at an early age after being born in Atlanta and began to be groomed by his father, Thomas, for a career in baseball even before he was out of elementary school. By the time he was in his early teens he already possessed "some of the most tortuous, sinuous, and puzzling curves ever seen." After beginning 1889 in the Chicago Commercial League, McGill was given his father's permission to sign with Evansville of the Central Interstate League in June once his school year ended. At the time he reportedly was 5'3" and 133 pounds, but he still had some growing to do. McGill gained only three inches in height but nearly forty pounds in weight, most of it in his lower body, giving him tremendous leg strength.

The teenager was so pumped when he joined Evansville that he lasted only a few weeks before he ran dry of adrenaline and had to be sent home to rest. Shortly after he returned, he hurled a 6–0 no-hitter against Davenport on July 26 but after twelve starts was just 5-7 and was released to Burlington "owing to his almost total failure of late to fill his position." But some of McGill's teammates contended the real reason was that Frank Nicholas, Evansville's first-string catcher, could not handle the little southpaw's low curves and drops and kept signaling for high pitches, which either were hit or went wild.

Someone connected with the Cleveland PL club, probably catcher Charlie Snyder, invited the 16-year-old to try out the following spring. McGill's father accepted the offer on his behalf, but on the condition that he could travel with the team to monitor his son. In his initial ML appearance on May 8, 1890, McGill fanned 10, became the youngest hurler since 1876 to pitch a CG, and faced Deacon White, who was playing ML ball before McGill was even born. Used sparingly but to great effect, he went 11-9 for a seventh-place team.

Once the PL disbanded, McGill, who had played without a contract in 1890, signed with the new Cincinnati AA entry and started on Opening Day against St. Louis. Less than a month later, after he and Ed Crane were arrested in Louisville for knocking over garbage cans, Browns owner Chris Von der Ahe bought the problematic left-hander. Within days of the sale McGill's father died of head injuries sustained in a railway accident while en route to join his son, leaving the 17-year-old without a chaperone. Bereft, McGill struggled on alone against evil influences until early August, when his mother came to St. Louis to comfort him. He then accompanied her back to Chicago, vowing as he boarded the train that he was through with baseball forever. But scarcely a week later he was back in St. Louis to beat Washington for his fifteenth victory. McGill finished with 21 wins but just a .150 BA. In October 1891 Al Flournoy told *TSN*, "He is the poorest batter, I think I ever saw stand up to the plate." No one at the time appeared to notice that while McGill notched just 15 hits, he bagged 34 walks, uniquely paradoxical stats that he would repeat almost every season throughout his career.

Assigned to the Cincinnati Reds when the AA and NL consolidated in December 1891, McGill held out in the spring of 1892. While dickering for a salary increase he pitched for the University of Notre Dame in its first varsity baseball game on April 24, beating Michigan 6–4. Exactly a week later he made his initial appearance with the Reds in the first ever NL Sunday game at Cleveland and stumbled to a 12–7 win. He then embarked on a flurry of benders and was released after just two more starts. Given the money to pay his outstanding bills in Cincinnati and train fare home to Chicago, McGill instead loitered in Cincinnati and squandered it on "German tea." His mother, who had been advised of his release, cabled Reds manager Charlie Comiskey as to his whereabouts when he did not appear at her door. At that point the club learned he had never left town. McGill remained in Cincinnati for several more weeks, "haunting the park" every day in search of another chance before finally reconciling himself to serve his penance for the rest of the season with Menominee in the Wisconsin-Michigan League. Shortly before his departure the *Cincinnati Enquirer* wrote he was "a miserable little tough, who should be taken by the police and given about sixty days on the rock pile at the work-house."

That winter Chicago president Jim Hart gambled on McGill after hearing that the wife of stockholder in the Menominee club had reformed McGill and he hadn't touched a drop since she began supervising him. The 19-year-old lefty showed his gratitude by leading the Chicago staff in wins and strikeouts and adapting far better than most hurlers to the new pitching distance. But McGill's reformation ended almost as soon as the 1894 season began. Released after logging a 7-19 mark and a 5.84 ERA, he signed with the Phillies. McGill seemed to be making a genuine effort to stay on the wagon until June 22, 1895, when he was spiked while sliding into a base in a game at Brooklyn. During his stint on the DL he was "indiscreet enough to break discipline" and won only 1 more game all season. When his indiscretions continued to mount in the spring of 1896, he was traded to St. Paul of the Western League for outfielder Sam Mertes. McGill hurled just 4 games with the Minnesota club before breaking his pitching hand. Around that time he seems to have finally matured and begun to take better care of himself, but it was too late. His hand never fully healed. Although McGill continued pitching for another dozen years or so, most of it was spent in the low minors and the Chicago City League.

McGill might have allowed his father's death and his own immaturity to spoil a highly promising baseball career, but he learned a hard lesson from it and later became the athletic trainer at the Northwestern University as well as its head baseball coach. He then was associated with the Butler University Athletic Department for a time before working for Indianapolis Power and Light. McGill died in Indianapolis at 70. (DN/DB)

McGinnis, George Washington / "George" "Jumbo"

B	T	HGT	WGT	G	IP	H	GS
?	R	5'10"	197	187	1603.2	1572	186

CG	BB	SO	SH	W	L	PCT	ERA
177	294	562	18	102	79	.564	2.95

B. 2/22/1854 St. Louis, MO **D.** 5/18/1934
TEAMS: 82–86StLA 86BalA 87CinA
DEBUT: 5/2/1882 at St. Louis; caught by Sleeper Sullivan and beat Louisville's Tony Mullane 9–7
FINALE: 6/10/1887 at Brooklyn; caught by Kid Baldwin and lost 17–5 to Brooklyn's Henry Porter

George McGinnis's vital statistics have long been a source of conflict. His birth year is now listed as 1854 even though in 1897 *TSN* gave it as 1857, and his death certificate lists an 1864 birthdate, making him only 18 when he won 25 games as a rookie in 1882. What makes his tender age so implausible is that he was first discovered on the sandlots in 1879 by Charlie Hautz while working as a glass blower in East St. Louis and, at 15, would have almost certainly been too young for Hautz to make the ace of his crack St. Louis Browns semipro club. Moreover, Hautz claimed that McGinnis had been particularly appealing because he was so hard on left-handed batters, which suggests that he was a southpaw. However, in the October 12, 1887, *SL* McGinnis, in accounting for why he had been so ineffective that season, said, "I caught a severe cold and it settled in my right shoulder. I tried to pitch underhanded—my old style of delivery—but I could not get command of the ball," which would seemingly make him a righty, and that is how we are listing him here. For the moment.

Then there is the matter of McGinnis's nickname. Though there are references to him as "Jumbo," his teammates called him George. By any name, he was the present-day St. Louis Cardinals franchise's first great pitcher and among the AA's finest arms in its first three seasons as a major loop with 78 wins, ranking him behind only Will White, Guy Hecker, and Tony Mullane. Yet in 1885 when the Browns first emerged as an AA powerhouse, McGinnis could win only 6 games and was reduced largely to gate duty.

That winter he lost weight and came to spring training in 1886 "thin as a race-horse" in an effort to reclaim his status as the team's ace, but once the season started his teammates always seemed to play badly behind him (some thought on purpose). In McGinnis's first start he lost 6–5 to Louisville. Several more demoralizing losses followed, culminating with a 13–12 setback in a Sunday game in Brooklyn on May 23, in which Browns shortstop Bill Gleason made six errors. McGinnis made just two more starts with the Browns. The last, on July 8 at St. Louis, may have been a showcasing, for when he blanked Baltimore 10–0, Orioles manager Billy Barnie swiftly bought him. McGinnis could only have felt vindicated when he was matched against his old team in his first start with the Orioles on July 11 and edged the Browns 3–2, leading an Orioles writer to exclaim, "McGinnis is the handsomest man on the Baltimore club including Muldoon." But after that he was less than a .500 pitcher, winning 10 and losing 13, still not a bad performance for a team that won just 48 games, and he was second on the staff only to rookie wonder Matt Kilroy.

Nevertheless, Barnie dropped him when he wanted more than a pittance in salary, leaving him jobless until Cincinnati signed him in early April 1887. McGinnis won his first exhibition appearance with the Reds, beating Toronto on April 10, and was in the rotation at the beginning of the year. In the second game of the season he topped Cleveland 13–6, and four days later, at St. Louis, he won his own game 6–5 when he led off the ninth inning with a hit, "actually stole second" and then scored on Frank Fennelly's single. But he won only one of his next six starts, growing progressively worse in each.

His arm obviously ailing, McGinnis tried to regroup with Milwaukee of the Northwestern League after Cincinnati cut him but could do nothing in

1887 even against minor league batters and returned to St. Louis, where he was playing RF for the Prickly Ash club by the end of the summer. For the rest of the 1880s McGinnis worked winters at his trade as a glass blower and then each spring broadcast that his arm was sound again, only to embarrass himself when he tried to prove it. Advertised to pitch a benefit game now and then, he would always wind up umpiring it instead and eventually officiated 3 AA games in between stints as an arbiter in the Interstate League. His quest to be hired as a regular AA umpire also became an annual occurrence that each year came to naught, perhaps because his eyes had begun to weaken.

By 1891 McGinnis and Tom Dolan were the St. Louis battery in a series of "Fat Men's" games with a team from Chicago. Also on the St. Louis squad was Dick Mappes, an ex-Brown with whom McGinnis had opened a local saloon several years earlier on Warren Street called The Battery, and John Peters, "now plump as a partridge." In all, *TSN* said, everyone on the team was "weighty enough to sink a large-sized life preserver." It was probably at this juncture, that McGinnis became known as "Jumbo." An ardent fisherman, McGinnis made that his new pastime after his vision grew too cloudy even for heavyweight games. At one juncture, he took a job in a glass blowing factory in Alton, IL, where he was once believed to have been born—another vital statistic about which historians still differ. His eyesight continued to deteriorate until eventually he went blind. The problem would appear to have been cataracts, because corrective surgery was eventually able to restore some of his vision. McGinnis died at his St. Louis home in 1934. (DN/DB)

McKeon, Lawrence G. / "Larry"

B	T	HGT	WGT	G	IP	H	GS
?	?	5'10"	168	116	979	979	115

CG	BB	SO	SH	W	L	PCT	ERA
110	206	474	4	46	64	.418	3.71

B. 3/25/1866 New York, NY **D.** 7/18/1915
TEAMS: 84IndA 85–86CinA 86KCN
DEBUT: 5/1/1884 at St. Louis, caught by Jim Keenan and lost 4–2 to St. Louis's Tip O'Neill
FINALE: 9/15/1886 at Kansas City; caught by Fatty Briody and lost 14–2 to Pete Conway of Detroit

At age 18 Larry McKeon lost 41 games to set an American Association rookie record. Then, two years later and still just 20 years old, he threw his last big league pitch, and long before he turned 25 his pro career was over. McKeon made his pro debut in 1883 with New Haven, but the independent club disbanded in May and the 17-year-old went to unaffiliated Indianapolis along with his veteran batterymate, Jim Keenan. Reputedly "exceedingly swift," he first gained national attention on July twelve when he lost 1–0 to Hugh Daily of Cleveland NL. The following year McKeon accompanied Keenan and many of his other Indianapolis teammates to the American Association when it expanded to 12 teams. He got off the mark poorly by losing his first eight decisions and causing the Hoosier management headaches with his drinking and unruliness, but as the season progressed his work improved and by October he was regarded as one of the better young pitchers in the loop. Starting well over half of his team's games in 1884, McKeon collected 18 of the Hoosiers 29 wins, but due to the poor quality of the team behind him he also led pitchers in all three major leagues in losses with 41.

When the rebel UA ceased operations after the 1884 season and the AA trimmed to eight teams, McKeon's Indianapolis club was among the casualties and descended to the minor Western League in 1885. That June Detroit NL bought out the Indianapolis club for $5,000, $1,000 being stock in the Detroit club, with the proviso that $2,000 would be paid immediately and the rest would come only if all the key Indianapolis players signed with Detroit as agreed. But when the two most coveted members of the Hoosiers, McKeon and Keenan, made a deal on their own with Cincinnati AA, Detroit reduced its buy-out price to $2,000 and the transaction became the subject of a lawsuit. Despite not joining the Reds until June 26, McKeon led the team in wins with 20. The following spring he reported to Cincinnati sporting a new "brick colored, tan barked mustache." By May his Reds teammates were urging him to shave it off, claiming it was a "Jonah," but it was too late. Earlier that month a fire had destroyed McKeon's family home and all its contents, and meanwhile an arm injury he had incurred during a spring workout in the gym worsened, reducing him to throwing only slow balls.

McKeon was already "considered the most tiresome pitcher in the profession" because he took so long between pitches, wiping his pitching hand (though which hand that was is still unknown) endlessly on the bottom of his trousers and all the while staring the batter in the eye, striving to make him nervous and impatient. His ailing arm only increased his penchant for stalling. Yet he was still capable of an occasional good effort. At one point in 1886 McKeon won 3 games in a row before his arm betrayed him again in early August and Cincinnati released him. He returned home to Indianapolis and soon arranged for it to be announced in the local press that he had been released only because the Cincinnati club was losing money and needed to save the cost of his salary. Obviously eager to dispel the impression that his arm was gone, McKeon had hopes of signing with Detroit, now an NL pennant contender with spectacular hitting but holes in its pitching staff. Rather than joining a team in the pennant hunt, however, the best he could do was to coax Dave Rowe, manager of the NL's weak Kansas City entry, into giving him a trial. He was dropped after 3 starts resulted in 2 bad losses and a 4–4 tie.

In the spring of 1887 McKeon was given a brief look by Indianapolis's new NL entrant but was not signed when he pitched indifferently in an exhibition appearance. Although he was probably invited to try out only because the new club was having a difficult time signing some of the players awarded to it, McKeon and his local admirers were indignant when he was cut, claiming that he had been jettisoned by club directors who had been investors in the old Indianapolis club and still held a grudge against him for the loss of money in the Detroit deal.

McKeon eventually hooked on with a new Kansas City entry in the Western League and was bombed 20–3 by St. Joseph in his first start on April 28, 1887. Rather than quit when the humiliating defeat proved conclusively that his arm was gone, McKeon moved to 1B and ended the season hitting .335. The mark was deceptively high, however, because walks were counted as hits in 1887. That winter McKeon worked in the city assessor's office in Indianapolis while he tried unsuccessfully to convince Harry Spence, the new manager of the local NL franchise, to make him the team's first baseman. After also failing in a bid to get a tryout with Cleveland AA, McKeon joined a semipro team in Lafayette, IN. When he was released in July 1888, the *Lafayette Journal* remarked, "He may be a ball player, but he did not overturn the grand stand here."

The remaining years of McKeon's life were dark and downhill. Early in his time in Indianapolis a local paper had described him as a clean-living young man who did not drink. If this was ever true, the Indianapolis team, a notoriously hard-living and riotous bunch, soon proved an unfortunate influence on the impressionable teenager. Late in the 1883 season he got into a drunken fight with a bootblack and was fined by the club management. That August he missed a ball game to go on what the press described as a picnic out of town with a young lady and then the next day failed to show up at the train station when the team left for a road trip. Twenty-four hours later a club director saw him off on another train. According to *SL*, "But before he reached the outskirts he jumped off and about the time to directors were felicitating themselves on a happy deliverance he turned up in the Oriental Hotel saloon and continued to have a time with the boys."

McKeon's behavior improved after that, and while he was with Cincinnati he appears to have stayed on the straight and narrow. However, his problems became more serious again as his career declined. In his remaining years McKeon gained attention from the press only for matters that were unsavory or simply sad. In 1888 he was arrested and accused of stealing $40 from a companion with whom he had been painting Indianapolis red. Almost six years later he appeared on the front page of several Midwestern newspapers when a drinking cohort of his was the victim of a particularly brutal and gruesome murder in an Indianapolis roadhouse, although McKeon was only involved as a witness. In February 1896, already long forgotten by most of the baseball public, he was discovered tending bar at Andy Wetzel's saloon on Vine Street in Cincinnati. McKeon was not yet 30 years old. Some thirty months later he was arrested in Indianapolis for robbing a traveling salesman and his female companion. Told that the charges would be dropped provided he left town for good, McKeon instead remained in Indianapolis, and in March 1899, just fifteen years after he had been the toast of the Hoosier metropolis, he was sentenced to the local workhouse as a "virtual vagrant." McKeon died in Indianapolis at 49 from tuberculosis and chronic alcoholism. (DN/DB)

McMahon, John Joseph / "Sadie"

B	T	HGT	WGT	G	IP	H	GS
R	R	5'9½"	165	321	2634	2726	305

CG	BB	SO	SH	W	L	PCT	ERA
279	945	967	14	173	127	.577	3.51

B. 9/19/1867 Wilmington, DE **D.** 2/20/1954
TEAMS: 89–90PhiA 90–91BalA 92–96BalN 97BroN
DEBUT: 7/5/1889 at Louisville; caught by Wilbert Robinson and beat Louisville's Tom Ramsey 9–1
FINALE: 7/12/1897 at Chicago; relieved Harley Payne and took the 13–9 loss to Chicago's Danny Friend

There are several stories to account for Sadie McMahon's nickname, but none are particularly plausible. Just before his death McMahon himself said it had originated in 1891 when teammate Perry Werden had called out to a woman of his acquaintance, named Sadie, and bystanders thought he meant the pitcher. All considered, astonishingly little is known about McMahon despite his longevity and high profile during his ML career. In October 1888, following his second season with an independent team in Westchester, PA, McMahon was tried in a Wilmington court for killing a peanut vendor the previous May on the Forepaugh circus grounds. Because the evidence against him was flimsy, he was exonerated, but rather than becoming a morsel for opposing-team bench jockeys to use on him, the tawdry incident appears mysteriously to have disappeared from memory even before he made the majors the following year.

McMahon began 1889 sharing the box with Jack Stivetts for Norristown, PA, and joined Philadelphia AA when his independent club was about to disband. The following season, with most of the AA's top pitchers in the PL, he burst forth as the loop leader is almost every major pitching department. In 1891 McMahon joined Bill Hutchison and Amos Rusie as the last ML hurlers to work as many as 500 innings two years in a row. The heavy load continued in 1892 when the NL and AL merged and McMahon's Baltimore club sank to last place, saddling him with a career-high 25 losses. In September he clashed with the Orioles' new manager, Ned Hanlon, over his nocturnal doings and was suspended. Aware of McMahon's precarious status on the Baltimore club, Cincinnati approached Hanlon at the NL winter meeting with an offer of Tony Mullane for him. Hanlon replied, "Not on your life," and added, "McMahon is the greatest pitcher I ever saw."

The increased pitching distance in 1893 forced McMahon to add more pitches to his repertoire, and he adapted so well that he went 23-17 while the rest of the Baltimore staff was 37-52. He continued to be Hanlon's ace the following year when the Orioles launched their three-year pennant run but tore a ligament in his shoulder in late August and was shut down for the season. McMahon's injury not only prevented him from pitching in the Temple Cup but also was still plaguing him the following spring. In April 1895 owner Harry Vonderhorst accused him of not working hard enough to get in shape. The *New York Herald* added gasoline to the ruckus by reporting that McMahon's injury was not incurred in a game but came when he was hit on the elbow by a bottle in a barroom brawl. Inclined to sulk anyway, the pitcher grew even more lax in his workout regimen. With the Orioles struggling in late August and no one but rookie Bill Hoffer winning consistently, the local press clamored for Hanlon to start using McMahon regardless of his condition. Finally, on August 9, McMahon made his initial appearance of the season and topped New York 8–2. It launched perhaps the most spectacular six-week pitching stretch seen in the 1893–1900 era. Using his recently developed change of pace almost exclusively, McMahon completed 15 of 15 starts, went 10-4 and collected 4 shutouts, enough to lead the NL even though he was technically not a qualifier.

It was all but his last gasp. In 1896 McMahon received the Orioles' Opening Day starting assignment, lost to Brooklyn, and finished with the poorest record of Hanlon's five starters. The following April Hanlon released him, but only after McMahon had reimbursed the Orioles for his "training expenses" as a way of escaping Louisville's offer to buy him from Baltimore. McMahon struggled on for a while in Brooklyn and then returned to his original trade as a house carpenter. He died in New Castle, DE, at 86 from complications following foot surgery. (DN)

Meakim, George Clinton / "George"

B	T	HGT	WGT	G	IP	H	GS
R	R	5'7½"	154	39	256.2	268	32

CG	BB	SO	SH	W	L	PCT	ERA
23	100	142	3	15	13	.536	4.03

B. 7/11/1865 Brooklyn, NY **D.** 2/17/1923
TEAMS: 90LouA 91PhiA 92CinN 92ChiN 95LouN
DEBUT: 5/2/1890 at St. Louis; relieved Red Ehret in Ehret's 11–3 loss to St. Louis's Jack Stivetts
FINALE: 9/3/1895 at Washington; caught by Jack Warner and beat Washington's Andy Boswell 5–2

Because he was a good base runner and hitter, George Meakim served as a utilityman in the minors in addition to pitching. The book on his pitching was less kind. He was said to be "speedy but erratic," with a habit of coming apart in crucial situations. Meakim first gained attention in 1885–86 with the Long Island Athletic Club and joined Scranton, PA, the following year. After struggling in his first two pro seasons, he enjoyed a good year with Grand Rapids of the Michigan State League in 1889 and was signed by Indianapolis NL for 1890 before the formation of Players League launched the tumultuous sequence of events that ultimately stripped the Indiana club of its senior loop franchise.

Meakim joined Louisville AA instead for his maiden ML experience and was used solely in relief until May 18, 1890, in a Sunday game at Gloucester, NJ, when he beat Philadelphia 5–2, but his off-the-field behavior undermined his chances of becoming a regular member of front-running Louisville's rotation. In August 1890, after ignoring several warnings from manager Jack Chapman, Meakim was suspended for drunkenness. Upon being reinstated he threatened to sue the *Louisville Courier-Journal* for $70,000 over what he said was a false report the paper had printed of his capers. No sooner had that furor died down than Meakim got into a fight with Harry Taylor over a card game, causing Taylor to vow never to play 1B again when Meakim pitched. To cover 1B in the event Taylor meant business, Chapman was forced to hire ancient Chief Roseman.

That winter, to the joy of most of his Louisville teammates, Meakim was released despite a fine 12-7 record. Signed by the Philadelphia A's, he pitched poorly in each of his six starts and was cut in June. After returning to form in the Western Association in the second half of the 1891 season, Meakim signed with Chicago for 1892. But when he was thrashed 14–10 by his old Louisville mates in his first start with the Colts on April 16, he was released to Rochester of the Eastern League. By September, however, Meakim was back in the majors after going 15-2 with Rochester. His initial appearance with Cincinnati on September 20, 1892, may have marked a ML first. When he entered the contest as a pinch runner for pitcher Elton Chamberlin and at the close of the inning Frank Dwyer, rather than Meakim, replaced Chamberlin in the box, the maneuver may have been the first time in ML history a pitcher appeared as a pinch runner (as opposed to a courtesy runner) and then did not remain in the game; some historians believe it marked the first use of a pinch runner, period.

Meakim perhaps should have remained no more than a pinch runner with Cincinnati, for he was hammered in three of his four subsequent pitching starts with the club, doing well only on September 25, when he beat St. Louis 5-2. For nearly three years that victory seemed as if it would be his last in the majors, as he was again relegated to the minors. In the interim the pitching distance had lengthened and the craft had changed so radically that many star pitchers, let alone their marginal brethren, could not make the necessary adaptations, but Meakim demonstrated that he was the exception when he returned to Louisville late in 1895 after spending most of the campaign with Wilkes-Barre of the Eastern League. In his first ML appearance since 1892 he allowed just 2 runs. But almost immediately after his dazzling return, he took ill in Philadelphia—probably with a flare up of a rheumatoid condition that had been plaguing him for several years—and was left behind when Louisville finished its series with the Phillies. Meakim returned to Wilkes-Barre the following year, but his rheumatism by then relentlessly hampered his effectiveness. He gave up the game soon thereafter and opened a corner dairy store in Brooklyn. Meakim died in Queens, NY, at 57. (DN)

Meekin, George Jouett / "Jouett" "Jo"

B	T	HGT	WGT	G	IP	H	GS
R	R	6'1"	189	324	2605.1	2837	308

CG	BB	SO	SH	W	L	PCT	ERA
270	1056	901	9	152	133	.533	4.07

G	AB	H	R	2B	3B	HR
338	1099	267	163	30	24	15

RBI	BB	SO	SB	BA	SA	OBP
131	69	87	16	.243	.355	.289

B. 2/21/1867 New Albany, IN **D.** 12/14/1944
TEAMS: 91LouA 92LouN 92–93WasN 94–99NYN 99BosN 00PitN
DEBUT: 6/13/1891 at Louisville; caught by Jack Ryan and lost 8–2 to Cincinnati's Willie McGill
FINALE: 7/8/1900 at St. Louis; caught by Bill Schriver and was relieved by Tom McCreery in his 17–3 loss to St. Louis's Cy Young

Jouett Meekin began as a catcher with his hometown New Albany Browns and changed to the opposite end of the points when New Albany's regular pitcher was unavailable for a game against the Louisville Deppens. By 1891 he was in his third season with St. Paul of the Western Association when the Louisville AA club induced him to jump his contract. NL president Nick Young ordered Meekin to return to St.Paul even though the AA was no longer a member of National Agreement, but he refused, maintaining that he hadn't left St. Paul to better himself but to escape its tyrannical manager, Bill Watkins. It did not take Meekin long to realize his mistake. Little more than a year after he arrived in Louisville, Colonels manager Fred Pfeffer weighed his 4.19 ERA to that point and released him. When Meekin wanted to sign with Cincinnati, Young again intervened and gave him to Washington, deep in the NL second division at the time, and he finished the season a composite 10-20. In 1893 his 10-15 record, mediocre as it seemed, was the best on the Washington club. Taking notice, New York sent pitcher Charlie Petty, catcher Jack McMahon, and $7,500 to the Senators for him and catcher Duke Farrell.

Meekin swiftly demonstrated Washington's foolishness by winning 33 games and helping to carry the Giants to the 1894 Temple Cup over the pennant-winning Orioles. That fall a novel was published with him as its hero. Not only was Meekin's biography used in the book but its title was *The Mighty Meekin.* In 1895 Meekin dropped to 16 wins and a 5.30 ERA after tearing a muscle in his forearm early in the season while trying to strike out Phillies slugger Ed Delahanty in a key situation. Soon afterward he took a brutal beating on June 1 to St. Louis, giving up 30 hits in a 23–2 loss. When Meekin was still unable to throw his curve ball without terrible pain by the end of 1895, *TSN* predicted he would be moved to 1B to utilize his bat since his "arm was gone." But over the winter he healed sufficiently to replace holdout Amos Rusie as the Giants' ace the following year, going 26-14 while the rest of the staff was 38-53.

Meekin fashioned his third and final 20-win season in 1897 and then slipped below .500 (16-18). When he had just 5 wins after his first 18 starts in 1899, he was sold to Boston for a reported $5,000. However, many sources believed the second-division Giants gave Meekin to Boston gratis in order to shed a high-priced player and help Boston in its pennant bid against Brooklyn (testy New York owner Andrew Freedman was on particularly bad terms with the Brooklyn club). There was also speculation that Boston owner Arthur Soden owned $50,000 worth of stock in the Giants and that Meekin's dispersal was yet another evil of syndicate ball. When New York writer Joe Vila said that "it was common talk" and Meekin had merely been loaned to beat Brooklyn out of the pennant, most agreed with Vila. Only Henry Chadwick felt that Soden would never engage in anything so rank.

It is impossible at this late juncture to sort out which side was closer to the truth. Boston failed to overtake Brooklyn for the 1899 pennant, and even though Meekin remained with the Beaneaters, it may only have been because New York no longer wanted him back. In March 1900 Boston released him. That June Pittsburgh owner Barney Dreyfuss signed Meekin to a conditional contract and predicted that he was "far from being a has-been and will be heard from before the snow flies," but he was released a few weeks later after being hammered for 21 runs in just sixteen innings. The following year Meekin quit the pro game after a brief sojourn with the Louisville Western Association club but later returned to pitch a few games in the lower minors and to umpire in the Three-I League. He then worked as a pipe man for the New Albany fire department until his retirement in 1939. Meekin died five years later in New Albany of a heart attack while hospitalized with injuries he had sustained in a fall at his home a week earlier. (DN)

Menefee, John / "Jock"

B	T	HGT	WGT	G	IP	H	GS
R	R	6'0"	165	76	584.2	730	67

CG	BB	SO	SH	W	L	PCT	ERA
59	175	149	2	30	38	.441	4.17

G	AB	H	R	2B	3B	HR
86	253	50	28	4	3	0

RBI	BB	SO	SB	BA	SA	OBP
27	26	15	6	.198	.237	.283

B. 1/15/1868 Rowlesburg, WV **D.** 3/11/1953
TEAMS: 92PitN 93–94LouN 94–95PitN 98NYN 00–03ChiN
DEBUT: 8/17/1892 at Pittsburgh; replaced Doggie Miller in RF and had no at bats in a 3–1 win over Washington's Frank Killen
FINALE: 9/7/1903 at Pittsburgh; started both ends of a DH, "but he lasted less than two innings in the forenoon and retired before the close of the first frame in the afternoon" as Clarence Currie got the 11–8 win over Pittsburgh's Ed Doheny in the a.m. game and Menefee lost 7–4 to Sam Leever in the p.m. game

Jock Menefee was a capable hitter but "awfully slow in his delivery, with a long arm swing which lets a base runner steal bases right along" and relied on guile, slow curves, and drops. By the time he made his ML debut in 1892 he had accumulated some six years of experience in independent leagues, a year in the New York–Pennsylvania League, and enough cheap real estate near Pittsburgh that he became moderately wealthy when it was chosen as the construction site for several new factories.

Menefee joined the Pirates around the same time as Jake Stenzel and was one of the many victims of manager Al Buckenberger's reluctance to try new players unless injuries made it absolutely imperative. Dropped after just 2 games, Menefee went to Chattanooga in the Southern League in 1893 but jumped the team when manager Gus Schmelz fined him $10 for disobedience, forcing Billy Barnie to pay Schmelz $200 for Menefee's contract to get him off Chattanooga's blacklist when he wanted the pitcher-outfielder for Louisville.

Barnie was handsomely rewarded when Menefee was by far his most effective pitcher in the second half of the 1893 season, at 8-7 with a 4.24 ERA. The Pirates, realizing their mistake, traded George Nicol for him in August 1894 and added five-hundred dollars to sweeten the pot. By the end of the year Menefee had a composite 13-25 mark and was released by Pittsburgh after just 2 games in 1895 when his arm went bad. For the next four seasons he worked largely as an outfielder in the minors but reverted to pitching upon joining Minneapolis of the Western League in 1899.

The following year Menefee returned to the majors with Chicago and won the season opener in relief but was used sparingly after that even though he was quite effective, finishing 9-4 in 16 appearances. He was then a periodic member of the Chicago rotation in 1901–03 and is the only ML hurler to finish his career by starting both ends of a DH. Menefee remained in the game for the love of it after leaving the majors. In 1905 he was hospitalized in Monongahela, PA, after suffering a fractured skull when he was beaned in a semipro contest against Donora on April 7. By that time Menefee was serving as the director of numerous banks in Monongahela Valley in addition to owning brickyards and business lots in Monessen and McKeesport. He was reportedly worth $75,000.

Five years later Menefee suffered a terrible personal tragedy when his 17-year-old son, Fred, was buried alive in a bin of loose dirt at a factory site Menefee owned in Monessen after the boy "apparently slipped feet first into the dirt and sank out of sight." When Menefee died in 1953 at the Restful Acres Nursing Home in Belle Vernon, PA, it removed one of the last remaining pitchers who had hurled in the majors at the fifty-foot distance. (DN)

Miller, Joseph H. / "Cyclone"

B	T	HGT	WGT	G	IP	H	GS
?	L	5'9½"	165	27	222.1	215	26

CG	BB	SO	SH	W	L	PCT	ERA
23	76	125	1	13	11	.542	3.04

B. 9/24/1859 Springfield, MA **D.** 10/13/1916
TEAMS: 84Chi-PitU 84ProN 84PhiN 86PhiA
DEBUT AND CAREER HIGHLIGHT: 7/11/1884 at Boston; caught by Em Gross, beat Boston's Fred Tenney 10–2, and fanned 13 to set a new ML record for the most strikeouts by a player in his pitching debut that was broken later that season by Charlie Geggus
FINALE: 10/14/1886 at Philadelphia; caught by Wilbert Robinson and beat Baltimore 5–1

The *Atlanta Constitution* in 1907 recalled Cyclone Miller as a "short, closely built, apple-butter Dutchman" during his brief stay in the Southern League more than twenty years earlier. It would be a mystery why a pitcher of Miller's obvious talent never seemed to stay anywhere for long were it not for frequent veiled allusions to his being ornery in addition to being very hard to catch. Called "Cyclone" for the obvious reason—he fanned 13 in his ML debut, a southpaw record prior to 1954—Miller had a great move to 1B that snared numerous pickoffs but probably was illegal. Moreover, he was the second most prominent rookie southpaw in 1884, bowing only to Ed Morris, as well as the most notorious.

On July 22, 1884, Miller started the game in RF but was summoned to the box by Providence manager Frank Bancroft in the eighth inning to replace Charlie Sweeney with the Grays comfortably leading Philadelphia 6–2. Sweeney, rather than take RF as per the rule at that time, stormed out of the park, forcing Providence to finish the game with eight men and ultimately saddling Miller with a 10–6 loss. Nine days later Providence arrived at the Polo Grounds to find the grounds wet for its game that afternoon against New York, but Bancroft insisted on playing and got New York to agree to let Miller umpire in the absence of the regular umpire, who called in sick. Miller's decisions were so one-sided that it appeared he was trying to throw the game to Providence. When action was finally stopped by darkness with the score 3–3, the *Providence Journal* reported, "The police had to escort Miller off the field, the crowd had become so threatening in its demonstration."

Miller's mere presence on the Providence team in 1884 was viewed askance. He was supposedly under contract to Worcester, MA, at the time he joined the Grays even though he had pitched for the Chicago UA club just four days earlier. By the time the fog around him had lifted he had been a member of at least five different pro teams in 1884 without clearly belonging to any of them and then finished the campaign with an army team from Fortress Monroe, VA, on loan from Providence, who might never have had possession of him in the first place. The following season, after escaping censure for his contract jumping in 1884, Miller showed the danger in allowing him to go unreprimanded by signing with Indianapolis of the Western League and then skipping to unaffiliated Springfield, MA, after receiving a $50 advance from the Hoosiers, only to jilt Springfield too and head for Macon of the Southern League. Despite demands that he be blacklisted, the spring of 1886 still found Miller with Macon—his longest tenure by far with any one team—until he was sold on June 7 to Augusta for five-hundred-dollars.

The Georgia team recouped its money and more in August when it peddled Miller to Philadelphia AA for five-hundred dollars, plus an A's reserve battery. In the final two months of the 1886 AA season he was the A's best pitcher, bagging 10 wins with a 2.95 ERA that ranked third in the loop. When he was reserved for 1887, the A's no doubt had a few trepidations that Miller might not return when he headed for Cuba that winter with a touring team.

After practicing during the off-season under the new pitching rules now in force, Miller foresaw no problem and eagerly awaited the A's training camp the following spring. In mid-April, however, he was waived out of the AA and sold to Lincoln of the Western League for $500. Some eight weeks later Miller injured his arm in a game against Topeka, and when it failed to respond he was sent home to Philadelphia after the Nebraska club took up a collection for $188 to help pay his way and give him a purse upon which to live until he found another means of support. Our surmise is that, contrary to his initial bolt of confidence, Miller had trouble adapting to the 1887 pitching rules and ruined his arm trying, perhaps while in Cuba, since he passed through waivers even before the AA season started. In any case, he quit the following year after being cut by Jackson of the Tri-State Leagues. Miller died at Lawrence Hospital in New London, CT, at 57. (DN/DB)

Miller, Ralph Darwin / "Ralph"

B	T	HGT	WGT	G	IP	H	GS
R	R	5'11"	170	29	188.2	205	25

CG	BB	SO	SH	W	L	PCT	ERA
19	100	46	0	5	17	.227	5.15

B. 3/15/1873 Cincinnati, OH **D.** 5/7/1973
TEAMS: 98BroN 99BalN
DEBUT: 5/6/1898 at Brooklyn; relieved Jack Dunn and got the win when Brooklyn scored 6 runs in the bottom of the ninth to beat Washington's Doc Amole 10–9

FINALE: 5/26/1899 at Cleveland; was credited with pitching a combined shutout when he relieved Frank Kitson late in a 12–0 win over Cleveland's Charlie Knepper

Ralph Miller was a member of Interstate League–champion Kenton, OH, in 1895 before joining Jackson, MI, the following year. In 1897 he was acquired by Portland, ME, and later went to Fall River, where his 1.06 ERA ranked him the best pitcher in the New England League by the time Brooklyn purchased him for 1898 delivery. Miller began well in 1898, winning his debut in relief and then stopping Reds outfielder Elmer Smith's 30-game hitting streak on the last day of May, although he lost the game when his Brooklyn teammates made 5 errors behind him. But he finished his rookie campaign with a dismal 4–14 mark and a 5.34 ERA.

Shipped to Baltimore when Brooklyn and the Orioles consolidated in 1899, leaving Baltimore with most of Brooklyn's rejects, Miller posted his lone win as an Oriole on May 6 when he drubbed the Phillies 11–3. Several weeks later, when he refused to be farmed, he was released outright. Miller finished his pro career in 1902 with Indianapolis of the outlaw American Association when he was just 29 after a line drive broke a bone in his pitching arm. He returned to Cincinnati and worked as the shipping department manager for Ault and Wilborg for 25 years. Miller lived to be 100. When he died at a rest home in Cincinnati in 1973, he was believed to have been the last surviving nineteenth-century ML player, but that honor was later found to belong to Charlie Emig. (DN)

Morris, Edward / "Ed" "Cannonball"

B	T	HGT	WGT	G	IP	H	GS
B	L	5'7"	165	311	2678	2468	307

CG	BB	SO	SH	W	L	PCT	ERA
297	498	1217	29	171	122	.584	2.82

B. 9/29/1862 Brooklyn, NY **D.** 4/12/1937
TEAMS: 84ColA 85–86PitA 87–89PitN 90PitP
DEBUT: 5/1/1884 at Cincinnati; caught by Fred Carroll and beat Cincinnati's Will White 10–9
FINALE: 10/1/1890 at Pittsburgh; caught by Jocko Fields and beat Philadelphia's Bill Husted 9–7
CAREER HIGHLIGHT ONE: In 1886 hurled a southpaw season record 12 shutouts and won a then southpaw season record 41 games
CAREER HIGHLIGHT TWO: from 9/10/1888 through 9/15/1888 threw 4 consecutive shutouts to set a NL record that lasted until 1968

Ed Morris was irremediably temperamental, apt to go to pieces if a critical error was made behind him, and often accused of sulking and not giving his best. When things went right for him, however, he was probably the premier southpaw in the game prior to Lefty Grove. Prior to pitching rules changes in 1887 Morris was the best quick pitcher in baseball, especially when he was teamed with his favorite batterymate, Fred Carroll. As soon as the ball was delivered, Carroll would wing it back to Morris and then the lefty would instantly fire it in again. In the days before advance scouting, teams seeing Morris for the first time were cowed by this maneuver. The pair of batterymates were also among the best of their time at holding runners—Morris had an excellent pickoff move and Carroll had an extremely quick release on steal attempts.

Born in Brooklyn, Morris moved to San Francisco with his family at an early age and by 1879 was catching for the local Eagles. The following year he caught for the San Francisco Nationals, the amateur champions of the Pacific Coast, and then joined the Mystics in 1881. That winter he caught John M. Ward when Ward barnstormed on the West Coast and was persuaded by the future HOFer to take his game east in 1882. After the Mystics staged a final benefit game for him on April 23, 1882, Morris signed with the independent Philadelphias and arrived in time to catch Jack Neagle on May 8. Later that season he moved to independent Reading and pitched for the first time in his career after swapping places with a pitcher that had been knocked out of the box. By 1883 Morris was largely a pitcher and played CF rather than caught on days when he was not on the points, because Reading, now part of the Interstate Association, had a better backstop in Carroll. The pair went to Columbus AA as a unit in 1884 and sparked the Ohio club to a surprising second-place finish. They were then among the players that Pittsburgh purchased from Columbus when it left the AA and, after unsuccessfully trying to avoid the transfer, were teammates on Smoke City clubs in three different major leagues until Morris left the game in 1890.

Morris's first two seasons with Pittsburgh produced 80 wins, giving him 114 career victories as of October 11, 1886, just twelve days after his 24th birthday. But once the Smoke City club absconded to the NL that winter, he fell victim to changes in the pitching rules that put a severe crimp in his delivery. The 1887 season was scarcely underway when Morris refused to pitch in Detroit on May 9, claiming his arm hurt. Pittsburgh manager Horace Phillips accused him of being too "faint hearted" to face the hard-hitting Wolverines and suspended him for three weeks without pay. The incident set the tone for the remainder of his tenure with Pittsburgh NL. In July the Allegheny club weighed a $2,000 offer for Morris from the Giants but ultimately rejected it, fearing a hostile fan reaction. Morris then got in trouble with Phillips again when he and outfielder Tom Brown were heavily fined after a detective tailed them when they went on a toot the night before a game in Philadelphia. His all-but-lost 14-22 season ended in an October exhibition game when he was hit in the left temple by a beanball and seriously hurt.

In 1888, after working out at a YMCA all winter, Morris seemed to make a remarkable adaptation to the new pitching rules when he rebounded to win 29 games and at one point surrendered just 2 runs in 56 innings sandwiched around 4 consecutive shutouts. But he reverted to his 1887 form after he and teammate Willie Kuehne were charged in March 1889 with running a gambling house in the guise of a billiard hall. Although they successfully fought the charge, the time Morris had to spend in court away from spring training forced him to try to get into shape too quickly and he began the season with a sore arm. Able to make only 21 starts and log just 40 strikeouts in 170 innings, he was saved from a probable release when the PL formed over the winter and Carroll, Kuehne, and Jake Beckley, after jumping to the Pittsburgh PL entry, persuaded manager Ned Hanlon to add their struggling teammate. Midway through his final ML season Morris was released but refused to accept it, claiming his contract was ironclad. He continued to report to the Pittsburgh park twice a day and work out until the club finally relented. Although he made only fifteen starts and was heavily battered, he reeled to an 8-7 record and went out a winner when he topped Philadelphia in his final ML appearance.

Morris remained in Pittsburgh after leaving the game and opened a saloon. In 1895 he was called on to umpire a Pirates game against Washington and was so pleased by his performance that he applied for a job as a regular NL umpire in 1896. He was rejected, however, because of his condition—or lack of it—he weighed over 210 by then. Morris later served as a deputy warden at the Western Pennsylvania Penitentiary and as an Allegheny county employee. He died in a Pittsburgh hospital at 74 from an infection that originated in his big toe. (DN/DB)

Morrison, Michael / "Mike"

B	T	HGT	WGT	G	IP	H	GS
R	R	5'8½"	156	65	504.2	571	62

CG	BB	SO	SH	W	L	PCT	ERA
55	325	254	1	20	39	.339	5.14

B. 2/6/1867 Erie, PA **D.** 6/16/1955
TEAMS: 87–88CleA 90SyrA 90BalA
DEBUT: 4/19/1887 at Cincinnati; caught by Charlie Snyder and lost 13–6 to Cincinnati's George McGinnis
FINALE: 9/21/1890 at Columbus; caught by Eddie Tate and lost 7–4 to Columbus's Hank Gastright

After two seasons with Hamilton, Ontario, of the International Association, Mike Morrison came to the majors scarcely two months after his 20th birthday with an arm that reportedly could throw a ball on a line from deep CF to home plate, but he was very raw in all other aspects of his pitching as well as his level of socialization. Originally the property of the AA New York Mets, Morrison was sold to Cleveland for $500 in January of 1887 before he ever wore a Mets uniform. On May 26, 1887, he brought a halt to Cleveland's 0-6 start in the AA when he beat Louisville to garner both his and the Forest City franchise's first victory. But in his next start, four days later in St. Louis, he went from the sublime to the ridiculous by giving up 10 walks and 26 hits in a 28–11 loss to the Browns. Morrison finished the season with a 4.92 ERA and a record for the most enemy base runners allowed per nine innings by a qualifier (17.39) in any season prior to 1889 when the four-ball rule first went into effect. Teammate and fellow rookie Billy Crowell was not far behind him with 16.16.

Crowell would only get worse in 1888, but at least he survived the season in the majors, whereas Morrison, after an unsettling winter—in which his brother John, a minor league catcher, was beaten nearly to death with a beer stein in a barroom fracas—wound up in the Tri-State League following his released by Cleveland in late June for being lazy and refusing to work on correcting "bad pitching habits." Another rocky minor league season awaited Morrison in 1889. In his first start with Minneapolis of the Western Association he surrendered 20 hits and 3 home runs and then was tagged for 18 hits in his second outing en route to a 10-15 record.

Notwithstanding Morrison's dreary 1889 performance, Syracuse hired him when it joined the AA in 1890, only to release him in April for not being in condition and then take him back again for the lack of anyone better. In his Syracuse debut on April 22 at Philadelphia, Morrison lost 17–6 to the A's. After posting a 5.88 ERA in seventeen appearances, he was released permanently by Syracuse in early August and immediately engaged an attorney and referred the matter to the board of directors. Morrison contended that the Stars' owner-manager, George Frazier, had withheld much of his salary, claiming that Morrison had been fined and suspended for poor play. According to Morrison he had never been informed of his punishment at the time it occurred and had actually pitched an exhibition game for Syracuse in late July at the very time Frazier testified he had been suspended. To support his case he got an affidavit from Syracuse's interim manager, Wally Fessenden. Amid the row with his old team, Morrison joined Baltimore when it reenlisted in the AA, replacing the disbanded Brooklyn Gladiators. His lone win with Baltimore and the last of his brief, tumultuous ML career came on September 8, 1890, when he beat Louisville's ace, Scott Stratton, 3–1 on a two-hitter.

After eventually settling up with the Syracuse club, Morrison returned to the Stars in 1891 when they switched from the AA to the Eastern Association. By 1893, though still just 26 years old, the once gifted but unruly righty was back in his hometown of Erie, PA, pitching for the Eastern League Blackbirds for $50 a month. Among all nineteenth-century ML pitchers in a minimum of 500 career innings, none allowed more enemy base runners per nine innings than Morrison, with 16.57. A lifelong resident of Erie, he operated a grocery store there until 1935 and died twenty years later in a local nursing home. (DN)

Mountain, Frank Henry / "Frank"

B	T	HGT	WGT	G	IP	H	GS
R	R	5'11"	185	143	1215.2	1273	142

CG	BB	SO	SH	W	L	PCT	ERA
137	309	383	9	58	83	.411	3.47

G	AB	H	R	2B	3B	HR
194	717	158	84	28	13	9

RBI	BB	SO	SB	BA	SA	OBP
13	39	35	3	.220	.333	.265

B. 5/17/1860 Ft. Edward, NY **D.** 11/19/1939
TEAMS: 80TroN 81DetN 82WorN 82PhiA 82WorN 83–84ColA 85–86PitA
DEBUT: 7/19/1880 at Troy; caught by Joe Straub and beat Chicago's Larry Corcoran 12–9
FINALE: 8/17/1886 at Pittsburgh; caught by Doggie Miller and lost 7–5 to New York's Jack Lynch
CAREER HIGHLIGHT AND FAMOUS FIRST: 6/5/1884 at Washington; caught by Rudy Kemmler, went 2-for-5 and was the first ML pitcher to hit a home run in the course of pitching a no-hitter when he went deep against Washington's Bob Barr in his 12–0 win

Frank Mountain and his 1880 Union College batterymate, catcher Bill Ahearn, both appeared with Troy NL later that season, but whereas Ahearn was a one-gamer, Mountain had a seven-year career awaiting him that included moments of brilliance. There were few in his first two ML seasons. Troy dropped him after he lost his second start, 8–4 to Cleveland, and Detroit, which signed him in 1881 after he beat the minor league New York Mets 9–0 in an exhibition on June 21, 1881, released him two months later, reducing him to finishing the season with Joe Mack's semipro Haverly's Mastodon Minstrels and then singing with them that winter.

The following year Mountain was the centerpiece of a curious sequence of transactions. After starting the season 0-5 with Worcester NL, he was loaned in late May to Philadelphia of the rival AA, made eight starts in a twenty-one-day period with the A's, and then was summoned back to Worcester. A player loan of this nature was rare in the majors at that time; such a loan between teams in two separate leagues that were supposedly engaged in bitter warfare was unprecedented, but it seems to have sent no shock waves through the baseball community, suggesting that the hostility between the two rival major leagues may not have been as intense as it was made out to be.

After Worcester disbanded Mountain signed for 1883 with the AA expansion team in Columbus and added 33 more losses to his career total, giving him 55 over the course of his first two full ML seasons, the most of any hurler in the majors during that span. But he also attained 22 wins. The following year, with a strengthened team that contended for the AA pennant, Mountain shot to near stardom when he bagged 23 wins and a 2.45 ERA. On July 22 he put Columbus briefly in first place when he beat Toledo 5–1, but in his next start two days later, his carelessness cost his team dearly. In a ten-inning battle with Indianapolis, he suffered an embarrassing 3–2 defeat by serving weak-hitting outfielder Podgie Weihe a changeup that allowed Weihe to rap a game-winning triple.

Both Mountain and Ed Morris joined Pittsburgh in 1885 when it absorbed the cream of the disbanded Ohio club, but while Morris emerged as the top lefty in the game, arm woes (which had begun the previous year) held Mountain to just five starts before he was shut down for the season after an 11–6 loss to Philadelphia on July 4. No longer able to throw overhand by the following spring, he was blasted by St. Louis 14–7 in his first start of the season on May 4 and then given a whirl at 1B that ended after he hit just .145. In August Mountain begged Pittsburgh manager Horace Phillips for one last trial in the box but was so wild he would have been dangerous if his deliveries had still had any speed.

Mountain went into business in Schenectady in 1887, failed a comeback attempt with Columbus of the Tri-State League in the spring of 1888, and then went to Toledo of the TSL later that season as a non-playing manager. Soon the ex-pitcher was embroiled in internal team strife when several players went on a strike led by the preternaturally rebellious Ed Reeder. After Mountain refused to reinstate popular Ed Sales on the team along with Reeder and four other players, he was fired on July 20.

Returning to Schenectady after a bid to become a minor league umpire also ended badly, he then was turned down in his effort to become the local police chief. By the end of the century, however, Mountain was chief engineer of the General Electric fire department in Schenectady and remained with GE until his retirement. He died in Schenectady at 79. (DN/DB)

Mountjoy, William Henry / "Billy" "Bill"

B	T	HGT	WGT	G	IP	H	GS
L	R	5'6"	150	57	503.2	504	57

CG	BB	SO	SH	W	L	PCT	ERA
56	110	164	5	31	24	.564	3.25

B. 12/11/1858 London, Ontario **D.** 5/19/1894
TEAMS: 83–85CinA 85BalA
DEBUT: 9/29/1883 at Cincinnati; caught by Charlie Snyder and lost 4–1 to New York's Tim Keefe
FINALE: 8/18/1885 at Brooklyn; caught by Phil Powers and lost 8–3 to Brooklyn's Henry Porter

Billy Mountjoy probably would have been one of the better pitchers in his era were it not for his lack of size and the yearly pitching rule changes that appeared to take a particularly heavy toll on his stamina and arm. He grew up in London, Ontario, home to two famous teams in his youth: the Mutuals, limited to boys sixteen and under, and the professional Tecumsehs. He played with both and remained with the Tecumsehs until 1882, when he left his native Canada to play with independent Port Huron, MI. Mountjoy returned to Port Huron in 1883, joining Bill Watkins and several other future ML players. In September 1883 he was acquired by Cincinnati and stunned Queen City observers in his first game with the club on September 23, when he beat Baltimore 2–0 in an exhibition game that was stopped by rain after five innings with Baltimore still looking for its first hit according to the *New York Clipper*, although other sources credited the Orioles with 1 hit. After losing his official ML debut, Mountjoy ended the season 0-1 but remained in Cincinnati through the month of October to play in a string of postseason exhibition games. In the first, on October 2, he blanked Chicago's ace, Larry Corcoran, 5–0 to pull Cincinnati even in a best-of-three series that the Reds won the following day behind Will White and later, on October 23, he no-hit the Toledo Northwestern League champions.

Having pitched shutout wins in two of his first three appearances with Cincinnati, Mountjoy, according to the *Clipper*, had "placed himself on record as one of the coming pitchers of the country." So highly vaunted that he came to spring training in Cincinnati in 1884 behind only White in the club's rotation, he accordingly started the second game of the Reds' season, beating Columbus 4–3 for his first official ML win. Mountjoy's zenith came on July 27 when he bested Louisville's Guy Hecker, the AA's top pitcher in 1884, 6–2 in eleven innings after engineering the tying run in the ninth inning by convincing umpire Robert Ross that a pitch nicked his uniform blouse with the bases loaded, only to jubilantly admit later that the ball had never touched him. Soon thereafter, however, Mountjoy lost his number two spot in the rotation to Gus Shallix when his arm began to tire. It revived enough over the winter for him to begin 1885 sharing the pitching load with Will White, but by June he began to lose zip again. Released to Baltimore after a 7–6 loss to Brooklyn on July 5, 1885, Mountjoy did not make his first appearance with the Orioles until July 28. The twenty-three-day layoff appeared to rejuvenate him, as he blanked Philadelphia 6–0 on a four-hitter, but his wing again began to falter, quickly bringing his release.

After another short layoff, Mountjoy signed with Binghamton of the New York State League largely owing to his connection with fellow Canadian Jon Morrison, an outfielder on the club. Some three weeks later *SL* observed, "The State League clubs all seem to take kindly to Mountjoy's delivery." For several more years the once promising Canadian rode the rails from one minor league team to another, ranging as far west as Denver and as far south as Nashville, until the close of the 1888 season, when he briefly became an umpire in the International Association. The following spring Mountjoy unsuccessfully tried his hand at managing the Toledo club and then abandoned the game to go into the hotel business in Michigan. He died of consumption five years later in his native London. (DB/DN)

Murphy, Joseph Akin / "Joe"

B	T	HGT	WGT	G	IP	H	GS
?	?	5'11"	160	11	95	113	11

CG	BB	SO	SH	W	L	PCT	ERA
10	44	30	0	4	7	.364	5.97

B. 9/7/1866 St. Louis, MO **D.** 3/28/1851
TEAMS: 86CinA 86StLN 86–87StLA
DEBUT: 4/28/1886 at St. Louis; caught by Kid Baldwin and lost 7–3 to St. Louis's Dave Foutz in ten innings
FINALE: 8/19/1887 at St. Louis; caught by Jack Boyle and beat Philadelphia's Bobby Mathews 7–4

A prominent amateur athlete in St. Louis in the mid-1880s who would go on to become the sports editor of the *St. Louis Globe-Democrat* and the *Chicago Tribune*, Joe Murphy pitched a handful of major league games while he continued to play amateur baseball in St. Louis and run in track and field events for the Missouri Amateur Athletic Association. Endeavoring to maintain his status as an amateur sprinter, Murphy repeatedly attested that he was not a pro baseball player and that he received no compensation from the clubs he played for except for transportation and hotel expenses. When asked why he declined a $2,000 contract from Cincinnati in April 1886, Murphy said that he would never turn pro and that, "I only pitched for [Cincinnati] to satisfy my own curiosity and to see what I could do against a professional team."

A month later Murphy and Opie Caylor, Cincinnati's manager, exchanged telegrams arranging for Murphy to pitch in another Reds game against St. Louis. On May 16, in his second ML appearance, the 19-year-old nipped the defending AA champions 7–6 at Sportsman's Park. The performance made young Murphy the toast of St. Louis; according to *TSN*, "With him in the box, the Cincinnatis could probably win every day in the week from any club in the American Association excepting, of course, the Browns."

Murphy then returned to the amateur ranks with the local Prickly Ash Club, until June 1886 when he pitched 3 more games with Cincinnati, 2 of them against the Browns, which beat him in both. His amateur standing by then in serious peril (and even more so after he was suspected of playing a game with Louisville on June 17 as "Clarence Murphy"), Murphy nonetheless agreed to join the NL St. Louis Maroons in July without a contract when the club ran short of healthy pitchers, and he was beaten soundly in all four of his NL starts. Then, on October 5, 1886, with the AA pennant clinched, the Browns put him in uniform for one day to face Philadelphia. After Murphy won 9–4 he steadfastly refused numerous offers to turn pro on a full-time basis in 1887, agreeing only to hurl a token last ML game for the Browns on August 19, again against Philadelphia.

By 1888 Murphy was the sports editor of the *St. Louis Globe Democrat* and still the "champion sprint runner of St. Louis," described as "one of those athletes who never complain, no matter how heavily he is handicapped." Murphy held the same position two years later on the *Chicago Tribune* but had put on too much weight to still run competitively, although he continued to pitch on weekends with a Chicago press team. In the February 28, 1891, *TSN*, he accurately predicted that the AA had only one more year to live as major league and contended that it was stupid and had made an ass of itself time and again in being outsmarted by NL because its owners were all schoolboys in comparison to NL moguls. By the mid-1890s Murphy had taken a post as secretary of the Harlem Race Track in Chicago. He remained active in sports for the rest of his life but never again approached the heights he had reached before his 21st birthday. Murphy died in Coral Gables, FL, at 84. (DN/JK)

Neale, Joseph Hunt / "Joe"

B	T	HGT	WGT	G	IP	H	GS
R	R	5'8"	153	31	227.2	233	25

CG	BB	SO	SH	W	L	PCT	ERA
21	73	58	1	12	12	.500	4.59

B. 5/7/1866 Wadsworth, OH **D.** 12/30/1913
TEAMS: 86–87LouA 90–91StLA
DEBUT: 6/21/1886 at Louisville; played RF as an injury replacement and went 0-for-1 in an 8–2 loss to Pittsburgh's Nick Handiboe
FINALE: 6/29/1891 at St. Louis; caught by Jack Munyan, was relieved by Jack Stivetts, and took the 11–10 loss to Columbus's Jack Dolan

Savannah of the Southern League sold Joe Neale to Louisville for $600 shortly after he beat Pittsburgh AA 1–0 in a sixteen-inning exhibition game that *SL* later said "almost destroyed the use of the boy's arm." In truth, Neale's arm was never again wholly sound. Sent home in August 1886 when he was still unable to pitch, Neale worked in an Akron rolling mill that winter and then tried again with Louisville the following season but was terrible in five starts. He did his career no service in 1888 when he pulled a leg muscle in a Tri-State League game and was told by Columbus to stay in his hotel room at full pay while the team went on the road but then was caught flagrantly disobeying orders and was suspended. Neale went on the wagon in 1889, however, and started the season 8-0 with Springfield of the Illinois-Iowa League after recovering his "Savannah drop." He moved to Quincy, IL, the following year and signed with St. Louis after the Central Interstate League folded in mid-August.

The Browns' most effective pitcher in the closing weeks of the 1890 season, Neale began 1891 in the rotation but encountered arm trouble again in hurling a one-hitter against Cincinnati on April 30 and was out for three weeks. After that he pitched only sporadically before being released in early July. Neale dropped down to the Southern League in 1892 and appeared in the loop's best pitching duel that season, a 0–0 tie in fourteen innings against Chattanooga's Jack Keenan. The game may have been more than his arm could bear, for he was working in construction in Akron soon afterward. Neale subsequently became a machinist and died at his Akron home in 1913 of a perforated ulcer that developed into peritonitis. (DN)

Newton, Eustace James / "Doc"

B	T	HGT	WGT	G	IP	H	GS
L	L	6'0"	185	35	234.2	255	27

CG	BB	SO	SH	W	L	PCT	ERA
22	100	88	1	9	15	.375	4.14

B. 10/26/1877 Indianapolis, IN **D.** 5/14/1931
TEAMS: 00–01CinN 01–02BroN 05–09NYAL
DEBUT: 4/27/1900 at Pittsburgh; caught by Heinie Peitz and was relieved by Ed Scott, who earned a 19–5 win over Pittsburgh's Jesse Tannehill
FINALE: 5/7/1909 at New York; relieved by Joe Lake in Lake's 4–3 win over Boston's Charlie Chech

Doc Newton was a fast worker and owned one of the best change-ups of any lefty in the game. A streak of rebelliousness, a bent toward wildness and an inclination to dissipate denied him what might otherwise have been a substantial ML career. The son of an Indianapolis doctor, Newton attended Moores Hill College (now Evansville University) in the off-season while pitching in the minors, beginning in 1896 with Maysville of the Bluegrass League. After a 15-21 year with Norfolk of the Virginia League in 1897, Newton was purchased by Baltimore in August and later sold to Louisville without ever being tested by Orioles manager Ned Hanlon in a game. In 1898 Newton reported to spring training with Louisville but was jettisoned when he wanted too much money and was labeled a "swellhead" for his ingratitude, though he claimed he only asked for $900 in salary. Returning to Norfolk, he pitched and played CF in 1898 and then in 1899 moved to his city of birth, Indianapolis, where he clinched the Western League pennant for the manager Bob Allen by beating Milwaukee on September 9.

On the strength of his 1899 season, Newton made the Cincinnati club under Allen in 1900, joining fellow Hoosiers hurler Ed Scott as the only two impact rookie pitchers in the senior loop that season. That fall his father died, and the following spring he finished medical school. The two events may have turned Newton's mind away from baseball, for he started poorly with Cincinnati in 1901 and was released on July 13 to Brooklyn, where he rejoined Hanlon, the pilot who had refused to pitch him in 1898. Though Hanlon treated Newton more kindly this time, his reputation for being effective for six or seven innings and then coming unglued exasperated Hanlon despite the lefty's well-above-average overall showing with Brooklyn in both 1901 and 1902. Rather than endure another year of Hanlon, Newton jumped Brooklyn the following spring and signed with Los Angeles in the new outlaw Pacific Coast League. Over the course of the next two seasons, the southpaw won 74 games in the PCL, inducing the AL New York Highlanders to make him a Rule 5 draft selection in the fall of 1904 (after the PCL became part of OB).

Newton remained with New York until early in the 1909 season even though he never retrieved the promise he had shown early in his career. A typical year for him in that stretch was 1906, when manager Clark Griffith was forced to suspend him for chronic dissipation and then later blamed him for the loss of the AL pennant to the White Sox. Following the cessation of his baseball career in 1915, Newton worked as a warehouse superintendent, perhaps realizing that his temperament was not fit to practice medicine. He died from food poisoning at his home in Memphis, TN, while under treatment for a severe nervous disorder. (DN)

Nichols, Frederick C. / "Tricky"

B	T	HGT	WGT	G	IP	H	GS
R	R	5'7½"	150	106	881	1045	98

CG	BB	SO	SH	W	L	PCT	ERA
90	91	174	1	28	73	.277	3.04

B. 7/26/1850 Bridgeport, CT **D.** 8/22/1897
TEAMS: 75NHNA 76BosN 77StLN 78ProN 80WorN 82BalA
DEBUT: 4/19/1875 at Boston; caught by Studs Bancker and lost 6–0 to Boston's Al Spalding
FINALE: 7/11/1882 at Baltimore; caught by Ed Whiting and beat Cincinnati's Will White and Harry Wheeler 9–6

Tricky Nichols was considered one of the game's fastest underhand pitchers in the mid-1870s, but he had difficulty making the transition in 1881 to the increased fifty-foot pitching distance and the more liberal rules regarding deliveries. A victim of bad teams during most of his career, he first made a name for himself in 1874 playing for his hometown independent Bridgeport nine along with his brother Ferry and Jim O'Rourke's brother John.

The following year the righthander with the "tricky delivery joined the woeful New Haven NA entry and suffered a broken finger and 13 straight losses, a nineteenth-century ML record for a pitcher beginning his career, before notching his first ML win on July 3, when he beat pennant-bound Boston 10–5. Nichols returned to New Haven in 1876 after it became an independent team, leaving the club for only one game, on August 22, when he hurled for Boston against Hartford while the Hub team awaited the arrival of Foghorn Bradley. Nichols then headed west to St. Louis the following spring but in his first full NL season was hampered by wildness and finished with a sub-.500 record at 18-23.

When St. Louis folded after the 1877 season, Nichols signed with a new NL entry in Providence. Expected to be no more than a change pitcher, he received this glowing tribute from the *New York Clipper* after beating Boston's Tommy Bond in his first start with the Grays on May 4: "Nichols is a first-class strategist. . . . Strategy combined with speed and the curve is now the only testing battery in the field." Though he beat Bond again four days later, he won only two of his other nine decisions and spent 1879 with the Worcester minor league entry. Hitching a ride when the Massachusetts club joined the NL the following spring, he lasted only two starts, losing both.

Nichols returned to the majors for one last time in 1882, the year after the pitching distance lengthened five feet. He opened the season as the Baltimore AA club's ace but lost his first two starts and soon ceded his status to Doc Landis. By late June he was reduced to relieving Landis in blowouts on days when he played CF. On the morning of July 11, 1882, Nichols's record stood at 0-12. He topped Cincinnati, the eventual AA pennant winner, that afternoon to break his losing skid, but it was not enough to prevent his release.

Unlike most of the hurlers who struggled at the new fifty-foot pitching distance, Nichols eventually achieved a fair amount of mastery at it, albeit in the minors. In 1888, at age 38, he was still active in the Texas League, where he was known as Fred "Tricky" Nichols, "an old hand." Nichols died at his sister's home in 1897 in the town where he was born. His .277 winning percentage is the third worst in ML history among pitchers with a minimum of one-hundred decisions. (DN)

Nolan, Edward Sylvester / "The Only Nolan"

B	T	HGT	WGT	G	IP	H	GS
L	R	5'8"	171	79	676	720	78

CG	BB	SO	SH	W	L	PCT	ERA
74	135	274	1	23	52	.307	2.98

B. 11/7/1857 Paterson, NJ **D.** 5/18/1913
TEAMS: 78IndN 81CleN 83PitA 84WilU 85PhiN
DEBUT: 5/1/1878 at Indianapolis; caught by Silver Flint and lost 5–4 to Chicago's Terry Larkin
FINALE: 10/9/1885 at Chicago; caught by Andy Cusick and beat Chicago's Jim McCormick 12–11

There is a fair possibility Edward Nolan' was the first MLer born in Canada. His nickname came to him in 1878 when Indianapolis team president William Pettit adorned the entire town with pictures of him and his catcher Frank Flint billing him as "The Only Nolan." In 1900 Nolan conceded that Candy Cummings may have invented the curve ball but contended he originated the "inshoot," a form of the modern-day screwball. He first gained notoriety in 1877 with Indianapolis when he lost 2–1 to Pittsburgh's Jim Galvin on Memorial Day and then hurled a 2–2 tie against Galvin the following afternoon that was halted after thirteen innings when Indianapolis had to catch a train. After Nolan and his Hoosier League Alliance club were accepted into the NL in 1878, Nolan presumed he would pitch almost every game. He also expected to bring with him a stratagem that had worked brilliantly in the past, but the May 28, 1878, *Rochester Evening Express* warned that he would have to find a new one: "Nolan, the famous Indianapolis pitcher, when he has a hard hitter to face, whom he is afraid of, pitches the ball at him two or three times, and hits him if he can. The result is that he flurries the batter and spoils his effectiveness. In a recent game with the Chicagoes he hit Cassidy with the ball and disabled him. Thereupon two of the Chicagoes made little speeches to Nolan as to what would happen if he hit them. They were not hit." Nolan's expectations that he would pitch at will were likewise thwarted when he lied to the team, telling them he had been called home by his brother's funeral, in order to go on a bender and was blacklisted. The following month the *Chicago Tribune* chortled: "'The Only' Nolan owes his downfall to the fascinations of a beautiful habitué of an avenue assignation house, who has ruined more men in this city than she can count on the jeweled fingers of both her hands." Meanwhile the *Indianapolis Journal* told its readers: "'The Only' is now showing his inamorata the sights of New York City. He will be carrying the hod in a few months."

At a loop meeting in December 1878 Nolan's appeal for reinstatement was denied and he spent most of 1879–80 in California before being allowed to return to the NL in 1881 with Cleveland. On July 23 Nolan not only pitched Cleveland to a 7–3 win over Buffalo but also went 4-for-4. Two months later, however, he and teammates John Clapp and Jim McCormick missed Cleveland's September 20 game in Worcester when a train wreck interrupted their return from a junket to New York. The three were each fined $100, and Nolan, seen as the ringleader, was also put on the NL's blacklist later that month for "confirmed dissipation and general insubordination." He remained out of the majors on this occasion until 1883, when the AA began employing blacklisted NL players. Joining Pittsburgh, he lasted only seven starts, losing them all. In 1884 Nolan had slightly better luck, winning one of five starts after his Wilmington club abandoned the Eastern League to join the UA. The following year he came back from the dead one final time, walking the straight and narrow all season under Philadelphia NL manager Harry Wright, but managed to win only one of seven decisions (most record books incorrectly list him as 1-5 rather than 1-6), which came in his final ML appearance.

Nolan finished his pro career in 1886 with Jersey

City and then got involved in horse training before taking a job as a truant officer on the Paterson, NJ, police force. In October 1900 he proudly informed *TSN* that he had won a sergeant's job when he heard a shot and a moment later observed a well-dressed young man emerge from former New Jersey senator Robert Williams's house in Paterson and announce that his uncle had just shot himself. The man then asked Nolan to attend to the victim while he went for a doctor. Suspicious, Nolan moved to detain the man and was confronted by a pistol. Thinking quickly, he cajoled the man into not being afraid of him since he was stranger there, at which point man went off down the street with Nolan following him at a distance and seeing him board a New York train. Nolan, who had a pistol of his own, boarded behind his quarry and arrested him. When it transpired that the transgressor was a burglar named "Red Jim" McGrath, who had stolen jewels and shot at a servant who came upon him during the robbery, McGrath got ten years and Nolan got his promotion. He remained on the Paterson force until 1913, when he died of nephritis. (DN/DB/PM)

Nops, Jeremiah H. / "Jerry"

B	T	HGT	WGT	G	IP	H	GS
L	L	5'8½"	168	109	811.2	891	99

CG	BB	SO	SH	W	L	PCT	ERA
82	222	251	6	60	31	.659	3.61

B. 6/23/1875 Toledo, OH **D.** 3/26/1937
TEAMS: 96PhiN 96–99BalN 00BroN 01BalAL
DEBUT: 9/7/1896 at Philadelphia; caught by Jack Boyle and beat Chicago's Bill Terry 10–5
FINALE: 9/23/1901 at Baltimore; in the second game of a DH was caught by Roger Bresnahan and was relieved by Frank Foreman in his 5–4 win over Milwaukee's Bill Reidy

From the outset of his first pro season with Lima, OH, in 1894, Jerry Nops was compared to Duke Esper, also a southpaw who featured a variety of slow curves, and the time he took between pitches was said to make him nearly as infuriating as Nig Cuppy. Like Cuppy, his career winning percentage is also somewhat deceptive inasmuch as he was always on strong teams.

Nops came to the Phillies in 1896 from the Wilmington Atlantic League team, where he had shared the pitching for a time with his brother Billy. Even though he won his debut, beating Chicago when the Phillies rallied late in the game, he was not particularly impressive. The explanation for Orioles pilot Ned Hanlon's interest in him may lie in his stylistic resemblance to Esper, who had produced good results with Baltimore.

The explanation for how he got to the Orioles from the Phillies is considerably murkier. Apparently the Phils put him in uniform before they had title to him. Although Phils owner John I. Rogers claimed Nops had been pledged to his team, Wilmington owner Denny Long denied it and also denied he had promised to sell the pitcher to Cincinnati for $1,000. Possibly Hanlon outbid Cincinnati at the last minute, but, as in any transaction in that period that involved Long or Hanlon, let alone the two of them together, nothing can be assumed for certain. In any event, Hanlon made an agreement with Nops that he would not get an 1896 Temple Cup share but rather $50 for each game he pitched and won and $25 for any he lost. Prior to the Cup series, Nops, who was living in Norwalk, OH, was taken to Cleveland and given $25 and expenses, much appreciated because otherwise he would have had to pay his own way home from Baltimore. In addition, he was given a full share of gate receipts from an exhibition game following the Cup series, which came to about $18, and, most important of all, an invitation to the Orioles' spring camp in 1897.

Hanlon's recompense for his machinations was a 20-6 season from Nops in his official rookie year and a team-leading 2.81 ERA. In 1898 the slow-working southpaw slipped to 16-9 but was still so valued that John McGraw successfully fought to prevent him from joining the cream of the Orioles Hanlon took to Brooklyn in 1899 when the two clubs combined. In late July 1899, after Nops was suspended for "convivial behavior," *TSN* wrote that he was "like the little girl of Mother Goose fame—when good he is very, very good but when bad he is horrid." He was subsequently traded to Brooklyn and then made to return to Baltimore when John McGraw, Hanlon's replacement at the Orioles' helm, forced a reversal in accordance with an agreement not to meddle with his roster after the season started. Despite it all, Nops won 17 games and celebrated by opening a saloon in Baltimore opposite the B & O Railroad station.

Assigned to Brooklyn in 1900, when Baltimore

was among the franchises dropped to shave the NL to eight teams, Nops held out until late April and then was "no longer the ruddy picture of health he had been in 1896" when he finally reported. Slow to round into shape, he seemed to regain his stride in early July when he joined Frank Kitson in pitching back-to-back one-hit wins at Cincinnati, but by the end of the month he was headed back to the minors with Norwich of the Connecticut State League. In September 1900 *TSN* reported that he had sold his saloon in Baltimore and inherited $100,000, but while the former was true, the money must never have reached his hands, for he was quick to sign for 1901 with McGraw's new Baltimore entry in the rebel American League. A 12-10 record induced McGraw to invite him to spring training in 1902, but Nops remained out of the game for the next two seasons before returning in 1904 with Providence of the Eastern League. He lingered in the minors until 1908 and then worked as a bartender and at times had an interest in a taproom of his own before suffering a cerebral hemorrhage in 1937 and dying at West Jersey Hospital in Camden, NJ. (DN/DB)

O'Day, Henry Francis / "Hank"

B	T	HGT	WGT	G	IP	H	GS
?	R	6'0"	180	201	1651.1	1655	192

CG	BB	SO	SH	W	L	PCT	ERA
177	578	663	5	73	110	.399	3.74

B. 7/8/1862 Chicago, IL **D.** 7/2/1935
TEAMS: 84TolA 85PitA 86–89Wasn 89NYN 90NYP
DEBUT: 5/2/1884 at Louisville; caught by Sim Bullas and lost 7–4 to Louisville's Denny Driscoll.
FINALE: 10/3/1890 at Chicago; caught by Harry Vaughn in a 10–0 loss to Chicago's Silver King
CAREER LOWLIGHT: In 1888 started the season 0-9 with 1 tie when his Washington teammates scored a total of 9 runs on his behalf in his first ten starts of the season
FAMOUS FIRST: On September 6, 1895, at New York, became the only umpire ever to eject Connie Mack while Mack was a ML manager when he fined Mack $100 in addition to tossing him for using abusive language in arguing a call in Pittsburgh's 6–3 loss to the Giants
FAMOUS EVENT: Was the home plate umpire who ruled Fred Merkle out on a disputed force play at 2B in the famous Giants-Cubs tie game at the Polo Grounds on September 23, 1908

Hank O'Day came from a family of brothers who all played with Charlie Comiskey in the 1870s on the prairies west of Chicago; his oldest brother, James, died in 1892 when he jumped from a moving train in a state of delirium after suffering severe head injuries as a Pinkerton man in the coal mining battle at Homestead, PA. After playing in the Chicago City League in the early 1880s, O'Day joined Al Spalding's Amateurs in 1882 and turned pro the following year with Bay City, MI, of the Northwestern League. He led the team in hitting in June but was released when captain Dave Foutz had to get rid of a player and reportedly drew his name out of a hat. Fortunately for O'Day, he landed on an even better team: Toledo, the 1883 Northwestern League champion. In 1884 he accompanied the Blue Stockings to the AA and split the pitching chores with Tony Mullane. Although O'Day was not a strikeout pitcher, catcher Deacon McGuire, who worked with him often in 1884, said the Chicagoan "threw the hardest and heaviest ball I ever saw. It was like lead and it came to me like a shell out of a cannon." Late that summer O'Day also got his first taste of his future vocation when he substituted for missing umpire Will Holland on September 11 at Toledo and executed his duties "very acceptably," according to *SL*.

After Toledo dropped out of the AA, O'Day split 1885 between Pittsburgh AA and the Eastern League Washington Nationals. A 26-win season with Savannah of the Southern League in 1886 earned his permanent return to the majors after the SL season ended. At first O'Day thought he was going to Detroit, a hot contender in the NL race, but instead, after purchasing him from Savannah, the Wolverines sold him to last-place Washington NL for a $400 profit. He suffered for nearly three years in D.C. and compiled a dreary 28-61 record with the perennial tailenders before being sold to the first-place New York Giants in July 1889. O'Day swiftly confirmed what it could mean to a pitcher to go from worst to best when he went 9-1 with New York to lift his overall record to 11-11 after arriving from D.C. with a 2-10 mark. That fall he was one of the Giants' World's Series heroes when he went 2-0 in two starts against AA champion Brooklyn.

Along with many other Giants stars, O'Day jumped to the New York Brotherhood club in 1890. Even though he fashioned his career year, leading his PL team in wins, for an unknown reason he opted not to return to the majors in 1891. It may have been that O'Day knew his arm was flagging, for after three bland seasons in the minors he began umpiring in 1894 in the Northwestern League. The following year he finished the season as a regular member of the NL staff but did not become a senior loop fixture until 1897. By the turn of the century his effusive safe and out calls and unswerving intolerance for rowdy players had branded him one of the NL's best officials. Christy Mathewson once said the arguing a call with O'Day was like "using a lit match to see how much gasoline was in a fuel tank." (DN)

Orth, Albert Lewis / "Al" "The Curveless Wonder"

B	T	HGT	WGT	G	IP	H	GS
L	R	6'0"	200	158	1223	1437	130

CG	BB	SO	SH	W	L	PCT	ERA
119	282	267	8	80	60	.571	3.78

G	AB	H	R	2B	3B	HR
199	583	176	74	27	13	6

RBI	BB	SO	SB	BA	SA	OBP
83	13	17	12	.297	.417	.313

B. 9/5/1872 Sedalia, MO **D.** 10/8/1948
TEAMS: 95–01PhiN 02–04WasAL 04–09NYAL
DEBUT: 8/15/1895 at Philadelphia; relieved Kid Carsey in Carsey's 23–9 win over New York's Jouett Meekin
FINALE: 9/20/1909 at New York; started and was relieved by Rube Manning, who got the 9–4 win over Cleveland's Walt Doan

Batters who faced Al Orth swiftly realized that his nickname was a misnomer. From a distance his deliveries seemed straight as a string, but he had a wide assortment of short curves and jump balls that either moved or hopped just enough to keep hitters off balance and may have been an early form of the slider. Prior to 1904 he also had a decent fastball, and after that he relied on junk and pinpoint control. Ossee Schreck reportedly once caught a pitch of Orth's barehanded while batting and fired it back at him, saying, "Can't you throw any harder than that?"

Orth grew up in Danville, IN, and knew outfielder Sam Thompson as a teenager. In 1894 he quit DePauw University to pitch for independent teams in Indiana after failing a trial with Indianapolis of the Western League. Later that season Orth joined Lynchburg, where he met Jennie Allen, his future wife, and was so effective against Virginia League hitters (24-7 in 1895) that Thompson recommended the Phillies purchase him. In the final two months of the 1895 season Orth hit .356 and was 8-1 on the hill, but his .889 winning percentage was delusive, as he was supported by an average of 11.30 runs per game.

Orth's first career start, on August 17, was typical; aided by a 21-hit Phillies barrage, he topped Boston 17–7. On the morning of September 24, 1895, he was a perfect 8-0. That afternoon Orth led Baltimore 7–6 in the bottom of the ninth when first baseman Jack Boyle muffed a low throw from SS Joe Sullivan, allowing Willie Keeler to tally the tying run. When darkness halted the game moments later with the score 7–7, there was speculation that Sullivan deliberately threw low and that Boyle deliberately dropped it so that Baltimore would not lose a critical game, and the Phillies finally had to offer $1,500 to anyone with proof "to convict any of its players before the National Board of any intentional misplay . . . during the season of 1895." The offer went unclaimed, but Orth nonetheless lost his final start of the season four days later to finish 8-1.

The following year, despite logging just 23 strikeouts in 196 innings, he was the only member of the Phils staff to compile a winning record (15-10). In 1897 Orth had his career year at the plate, hitting .329, and frequently was used either in the outfield or as a pinch hitter, but his hill work slumped to 14-19. Although effective the next two seasons, he was hampered by a string of minor injuries and a bout with malaria that held him to just 144 innings in 1899.

The Phillies began the final year of the nineteenth century with soaring hopes owing to a solid everyday lineup built around Nap Lajoie and Ed Delahanty accompanied by the five-man rotation led by Orth and southpaw Wiley Piatt. But while the three subsidiary starters all had good years, Piatt was just 9-10 and Orth little better at 14-14. The six-year veteran, if not a disappointment, had yet to deliver on his early promise. (DN)

Parsons, Charles James / "Charlie"

B	T	HGT	WGT	G	IP	H	GS
L	L	5'10"	160	8	59	83	7

CG	BB	SO	SH	W	L	PCT	ERA
6	16	12	0	1	4	.200	4.58

B. 7/18/1863 Cherry Flats, PA **D.** 3/24/1936
TEAMS: 86BosN 87NYA 90CleN
DEBUT: 5/29/1886 at Boston; caught by Eddie Tate and lost 9–4 to Detroit's Charlie Getzein
FINALE: 4/23/1890 at Pittsburgh; relieved Vint Dailey in a 20–12 loss to Pittsburgh's Pete Daniels and Chummy Gray

Charlie Parsons came of age in the yearling Southern League in 1885 and hurled the first no-hitter in SL history on May 29 of that season against Matt Kilroy of Augusta. Acquired by Boston prior to the 1886 campaign, Parsons was highly regarded during spring training but received just two chances once the bell rang and was betrayed by his Hub teammates in both. In his debut the entire Boston team played a ragged game, especially Sam Wise who "was utterly unable to play shortstop owing to the condition of his arm." His second outing two days later ended in a 4–1 loss to Cleveland when Boston left ten men on base.

Oddly, in both games Boston, the home team opted to bat first, resulting in Parson logging an eight-inning CG on each occasion. In late June he was sold to Rochester of the International Association for less than $600 against the wishes of Rochester manager Frank Bancroft. Years later Bancroft, in discussing his dissatisfaction with his new pitcher, told of a game against Syracuse in which Parsons was getting hammered. Since the rules in 1886 prevented Bancroft from replacing him, the manager snuck out of the park between innings and bought some purgative in a nearby drugstore that he gave Parsons to drink telling him it was a tonic. When the pitcher vomited on the grass between the box and the platter, Syracuse quickly consented to his removal. The story has a ring of truth, particularly since Parsons was fined $50 the following year and released after an altercation with Bancroft. But before departing the upstate New York club, he had already caught the interest of New York Mets manager Opie Caylor.

Caylor brought Parson to Staten Island, the Mets' home ground, in early September 1887 on speculation, and he continued his curious streak by pitching his third consecutive eight-inning CG in his first three ML starts, an 11–11 tie with Cincinnati. On September 13, just three days later, Parsons made it 4-for-4 in 8-inning complete games when he garnered his lone ML win, beating Cleveland 9–6. The streak was broken in his next start on September when he was hooked up in a 4–4 ten-inning tie with Philadelphia. Parsons then began a new streak in his final start of the season when he lost 15–7 to his old Augusta opponent, Matt Kilroy, in a game that darkness held to eight innings.

The Mets folded after 1887, and in 1888 Parsons started the season with Minneapolis, where he and catcher Frank Graves, in the words of Peekie Veach, were "the skinniest battery I or anyone else ever saw." Parsons received one final ML opportunity two years later when the Players League triggered expansion to twenty-four teams. He went to spring camp with Cleveland NL but later claimed that he injured his arm in a preseason exhibition game with Omaha and lost his fastball. The results reflect it. He was hammered in successive appearances two days apart at Pittsburgh NL, the weakest team in the majors in 1890. His finale, in which "the men played as though they cared nothing about the game," ironically lasted only eight innings, though he was gone by the finish. His arm shot, Parsons turned to umpiring in the minors before going home. He died in Mansfield, PA, in 1936. (DN/DB)

Payne, Harley Fenwick / "Harley" "Lady"

B	T	HGT	WGT	G	IP	H	GS
B	L	6'0"	160	80	557	678	72

CG	BB	SO	SH	W	L	PCT	ERA
57	136	148	3	30	36	.455	4.04

B. 1/9/1864 Windsor, OH **D.** 12/29/1935
TEAMS: 96–98BroN 99PitN
DEBUT: 4/18/1896 at Baltimore; caught by Jack Grim and was relieved by Ad Gumbert in his 6–2 loss to Baltimore's Arlie Pond
FINALE: 6/8/1899 at Baltimore; caught by Bill Schriver and was relieved in the first inning by Jim Gardner in his 11–5 loss to Baltimore's Harry Howell

Nicknamed "Lady" because of his resemblance to former-Detroit star Lady Baldwin in style and physical appearance, Harley Payne was heralded as early as 1890 while with Youngstown of the Tri-State League but nonetheless took a long time to climb the minor league ladder. He finally reached the top rung with Brooklyn in 1896 after going 10-11 with a .347 BA the previous season as a pitcher-outfielder with Toronto of the Eastern League. A staff-leading 3.39 ERA and 14 wins as a rookie with a bad team earned him Brooklyn's Opening Day assignment in 1897. Payne again won 14 games, but his ERA climbed to 4.69. The following year the death of his mother and sister kept him home during spring training. Health problems of his own—probably a heart arrhythmia—followed the long delay before he could start his conditioning regimen. Payne made just one appearance with Brooklyn, a start on April 23 at Washington in which he stumbled to a 9–8 win with help from his own bat, as he went 3-for-4 and drove in 3 runs. It would be his last game in a Brooklyn uniform. His health still poor, Payne was released to Pittsburgh but was unable to report in 1899 until May 1. When his physical condition continued to be precarious, the Pirates cut him in June.

Payne remained out of the game in 1900 and failed in a comeback bid with Omaha of the Western League in 1901. The following year the *Washington Post* reported that he owned a library in Geneva, OH, and had become a "veritable bookworm." Payne died from chronic heart disease at his farm in Orwell, OH, in 1935. (DN)

Pechiney, George Adolphe / "George" "Pisch"

B	T	HGT	WGT	G	IP	H	GS
R	R	5'9"	184	61	514.1	568	61

CG	BB	SO	SH	W	L	PCT	ERA
56	207	183	3	23	34	.404	4.23

B. 9/2/1861 Cincinnati, OH **D.** 7/14/1943
TEAMS: 85–86CinA 87CleA
DEBUT: 8/4/1885 at Cincinnati; caught by Kid Baldwin and beat Pittsburgh's Jim Galvin 4–1
FINALE: 6/24/1887 at Cleveland; caught by Charlie Reipschlager and lost 17–7 to St. Louis's Dave Foutz

George Pechiney's name was pronounced PEESH-en-ney but was often mistakenly pronounced Petchiney, and the joke in 1887 when his arm had clearly begun to sour was that he would not "petch iney more." After failing to light up the Southern League, he was working as a carriage blacksmith and hurling for the semipro Cincinnati Clippers in the summer of 1885 when the Reds signed him. Because Pechiney was still a work in progress, he was tutored by Tony Mullane, who had been suspended for the year but remained in Cincinnati drawing his salary and serving as a kind of pitching coach.

After a brilliant start that saw him post the best ERA of any AA rookie with at least 10 complete games, Pechiney went home early with arm trouble and then was awful in 1886, finishing with the worst SO to BB ratio and the second worst BR per 9 IP ratio among AA qualifiers. His weak performance suggests that his arm woes were now chronic. In any case, Pechiney came in for his share of the blame for the team's second-division finish, and on December 15, 1886, he and catcher Charlie Snyder were sold as a package to the Cleveland AA replacement team.

On May 10, 1887, Pechiney staggered to an 8–7 verdict over Baltimore to notch both Cleveland's first home victory as a member of the AA and his final ML win. By the time Cleveland released him, he so obviously had nothing left that the only invitation he received came from tiny Crawfordsville, IN, of the Central Interstate League. Pechiney tried to return in 1888 with Canton of the Tri-State League but was released in June and later tried unsuccessfully to convert to being a position player. Before his 27th birthday arrived, he was back in Cincinnati playing for a local amateur team. *TSN* joined Cincinnati papers in blaming Pechiney's rapid descent largely on his drinking and remarked, "There never was a more promising boy in the ranks than George, but his friends provided his greatest enemies." A toolmaker later in life, Pechiney died in Cincinnati at 81 of a cerebral hemorrhage. (DN/DB)

Phillippe, Charles Louis / "Deacon" "Phil"

B	T	HGT	WGT	G	IP	H	GS
R	R	6'½"	180	80	600	605	71

CG	BB	SO	SH	W	L	PCT	ERA
62	106	143	3	41	30	.577	3.02

B. 5/23/1872 Rural Retreat, VA **D.** 3/30/1952
TEAMS: 99LouN 00–11PitN
DEBUT: 4/21/1899 at Louisville; relieved Bill Magee in the fourth inning and earned an 11–4 win over Cleveland's Harry Maupin
FINALE: 8/13/1911 at Cincinnati; relieved Howie Camnitz in a 4–0 loss to Cincinnati's Harry Gaspar

Nicknamed "Deacon" for his straitlaced demeanor and his off-season management of a church choir, Charles Phillippe (pronounced Phil-AH-pee) was a descendant of the royal Phillippe family of France, according to Harry Pulliam. At age 3, Phillippe moved with his family from the small Virginia town where he was born to the Dakota Territory. He appears never to have discussed his early baseball experiences or the reasons he delayed starting his pro career until he was in his midtwenties. By 1896 Phillippe was residing in Minnesota and pitching for an independent team in Mankato. The following year he graduated from Fargo of the Red River Valley League to Minneapolis of the Western League. After going 21-19 in his second season with the Millers he was drafted by Louisville for 1899 delivery. Expected to vie for a spot in the rotation, he emerged instead as the Colonels' ace when Bert Cunningham, a 28-game winner in 1898, fell to 17-17. Even though Phillippe did not make his first start until the 1899 season was nearly three weeks old, he led the club in games, starts, and wins, and, most significantly, displayed extraordinary control for a rookie, walking just 64 batters in 321 innings. Among pitchers that year in 300 or more innings, only Cy Young issued fewer free passes, and over the next dozen years the pair would compete for the honor of being arguably the best control pitcher ever.

When syndicate ownership moved Louisville's best players to Pittsburgh after the Colonels were dropped from the NL prior to the 1900 season, Phillippe had a much better supporting cast in his sophomore year and showed his appreciation by supplanting the Pirates' twin stalwarts in 1899—Jesse Tannehill and Sam Leever—as the staff leader in innings, starts, and complete games while tying Tannehill for the club lead in wins with 20. With Phillippe at the head of a rotation that included Jack Chesbro in addition to Tannehill and Leever, the Pirates seemed poised to leap to the top of the NL once the new century began. (DN)

Phillips, William Corcoran / "Bill" "Cyclone" "Whoa Bill"

B	T	HGT	WGT	G	IP	H	GS
R	R	5'11"	180	90	627	712	70

CG	BB	SO	SH	W	L	PCT	ERA
50	211	134	4	33	36	.478	4.67

B. 1/9/1868 Allenport, PA **D.** 10/25/1941
TEAMS: 90PitN 95CinN 99–03CinN (M)14IndFL (M)15NWKFL
DEBUT: 8/11/1890 at Pittsburgh; caught by Harry Decker and beat Chicago's Ed Stein 6–4
FINALE: 9/22/1903 at Cincinnati; caught by Lee Fohl and lost 12–7 to Philadelphia's Bill Duggleby

The half brother of Barney Wolfe, an AL pitcher in the early 1900s, Bill Phillips left school in the mid-1880s to work in the Pennsylvania coal mines and continued to be a miner even after he made the majors to stay in the late 1890s. After the long winters in the mines he usually reported to spring training in peak shape and weighing less than he had the previous fall.

Phillips made his pro debut with Troy of the International Association in 1888 and was invited to finish the season with Washington NL but never did more than pitch batting practice. Washington appears to have attached a string to him, however, for it rehired him after he spent 1889 with independent McKeesport, PA. He remained with the D.C. club when it left the NL prior to the 1890 season and enlisted in the Atlantic Association. Working under manager Ted Sullivan, he soon emerged as the team's top pitcher and acquired the nickname of "Cyclone" at about the same time that it was bestowed on one Denton True Young. Phillips came to Pittsburgh NL after Washington disbanded on August 2, 1890. He won his ML debut but was reamed 18–5 by Chicago in his next start as he became the first big league pitcher to surrender two grand-slam homers in the same game (to Tom Burns and Kit Kittridge) and then lost his next eight starts as well to finish 1-9 with a 7.07 ERA and 8 dingers allowed in just 82 innings.

Over the next three years Phillips must have often been tempted to quit the game while pitching in such humble stations as Meadville, PA, and Owensboro, KY. Following a strong season with Indianapolis of the Western League in 1894, he returned to the majors with Cincinnati but soon found himself back in Indianapolis after being given only a handful of starts by Reds manager Buck Ewing. Phillips later admitted to loathing Ewing, whom he felt had not given him a fair chance, but claimed he held no grudge against the Cincinnati club even though it froze him in Indianapolis from August 1895 through the close of the 1898 season.

Drafted by Chicago after he went 28-9 and, according to catcher Mike Kahoe, beat Detroit on one occasion while pitching the whole nine innings smoking a pipe (there was no rule at that time against smoking on the field), he returned to Cincinnati in 1899 when it was forced to keep him after Chicago refused to waive its claim on him. In his first full ML season Phillips went 17-9, was second on the Reds in several major pitching departments only to rookie sensation Noodles Hahn and raised eyebrows as to why he had been buried in the minors so long. He remained a Cincinnati mainstay until 1903, all the while continuing to work in the mines and play the trombone in a band comprised of fellow miners.

In 1901 Phillips recommended his half brother to the Reds, and Ted Sullivan, his old manager with Washington, concurred, claiming that Wolfe's style of delivery made him think he was watching Phillips. The Reds passed on Wolfe, however, allowing him to sign elsewhere. Meanwhile, Phillips began his career as a pilot with Indianapolis of the American Association in 1904. He continued to serve as a player-manager until he was past 40 and then remained in the game, hoping for an opportunity to manage in the majors. It finally came in 1914 when he was hired to pilot Indianapolis of the rebel Federal League. Despite leading the Hoosiers to the initial FL pennant, he lasted only two months in the dugout after the franchise moved to Newark, NJ, in 1915 and never managed in the majors again. Among the FL players Phillips mentored were future HOFer Edd Roush, two-time FL batting champ Benny Kauff, and future HOF pilot Bill McKecknie. He died at his home in Charleroi, PA, in 1941. (DN)

Phyle, William Joseph / "Bill"

B	T	HGT	WGT	G	IP	H	GS
?	R	?	?	13	106.2	116	12

CG	BB	SO	SH	W	L	PCT	ERA
12	35	14	2	3	9	.250	3.46

B. 6/25/1875 Duluth, MN **D.** 8/6/1953
TEAMS: 98–99ChiN 01NYN 06StLN
DEBUT: 9/17/1898 at Washington; caught by Art Nichols and blanked Washington's Bill Donovan 9–0
FINALE: 9/15/1906 at St. Louis; played 3B and made 1 hit in a 4–0 loss to Chicago's Orval Overall

It is surprising that so few of Bill Phyle's vital statistics are known—he was hardly a low profile player, and he remained active in the game into the 1930s. In 1897 *TSN* suggested he had a serious weight problem but then, three years later, described him as "Little Phyle." He was reputedly part Indian "of Sioux descent" and first began to carve a name for himself with unaffiliated St. Cloud, MN, in 1893–94. Phyle joined Dubuque of the Eastern Iowa League in 1895 and was regarded so highly that St. Paul of the Western League traded pitcher Alex Jones plus cash for him in September. He remained with St. Paul through 1898 and finally captured the interest of Chicago NL on August 20 of that year when he no-hit Milwaukee.

Traded for Frank Isbell, Phyle joined Chicago in time to make three late-season starts and won two of them via shutouts. He then began 1899 in Chicago's rotation but alienated manager Tom Burns when he contracted malaria and was mistakenly identified as being part of a group that was out carousing while he was supposed to be in bed recuperating. Given a second chance in 1900 by Burns's replacement, Tom Loftus, while at Chicago's spring camp in West Baden, IN, in a fit of pique Phyle broke a slew of glass objects in the team headquarters. Loftus settled the matter before the Chicago team moved south to Selma, AR, for spring training by making the pitcher pay for the damages. Phyle then refused to go to Kansas City when he was traded for first baseman John Ganzel and played semipro ball in northern Minnesota instead. That winter Phyle ran a saloon in Minneapolis with lightweight boxer Ed Santry, for whom he sometimes acted as a second, and somehow finagled it so that he could join New York NL in 1901. Phyle earned a spot at the rear of a rotation led by Christy Mathewson and Dummy Taylor and made nineteen starts. His last ML appearance as a pitcher came on September 28, 1901, at Chicago, when he lost 5–2.

The following season Phyle signed with Minneapolis of the American Association as a third baseman and hit .281 before jumping to San Francisco. He then returned to Minneapolis, and was traded in the spring of 1903 to St. Paul, which promptly swapped him to Milwaukee. By the end of that summer Phyle was wearing yet another uniform when he was named captain of Memphis. After Memphis captured the Southern Association pennant by a one-game margin over Little Rock with Phyle contributing a .300 BA, he openly blared that Atlanta had purposely lost the pennant-clinching game to Memphis because Crackers manager Abner Powell loathed Little Rock pilot Mike Finn. It was a belief many held, but "Billy Phyle was the only man who was foolish enough to open his face, and he got soaked proper" when the loop voted to blacklist him after he failed to go before a board and substantiate his charges.

Made to look foolish when Phyle presented evidence that he was sick in bed at the time of the board hearing, the Southern Association attempted to save face by offering to reinstate him if he apologized for his actions. Phyle refused and instead played outlaw ball for the next two years, creating constant trouble by adopting assumed names and then merrily airing his true identity after games against OB teams. In September 1905 Cincinnati president Garry Herrmann fined him $75 when he discovered his Reds had played an exhibition against a Youngstown team that employed Phyle.

Finally, in February 1906, the Southern Association voted to reinstate the unrepentant third baseman. Phyle then immediately began a fresh roller-coaster ride from one team to another when Memphis traded him to Nashville, which in turn dealt him to Kansas City of the American Association, where he lasted only until August, when he was sold to St. Louis NL. He finished the season with the Cardinals, was released in January 1907, and spent three seasons with Toronto of the Eastern League, including 1908, when he led the loop with 16 homers, before retiring as a player. A vastly reformed Phyle later umpired in the PCL from 1913–31 and then worked twelve years in Los Angeles as a movie studio technician. He died in Los Angeles General Hospital in 1953 of heart disease and was survived by his widow, Anna, and a daughter. (DN)

Piatt, Wiley Harold / "Wiley"

B	T	HGT	WGT	G	IP	H	GS
L	L	5'10"	175	100	771.2	802	95

CG	BB	SO	SH	W	L	PCT	ERA
80	254	257	9	56	39	.589	3.61

B. 7/13/1874 Blue Creek, OH **D.** 9/20/1946
TEAMS: 98–00PhiN 01PhiAL 01–02ChiAL 03BosN
DEBUT: 4/22/1898 at Philadelphia; caught by Ed McFarland and beat New York's Amos Rusie 13–7
FINALE: 8/1/1903 at Boston; started and was relieved by John Malarkey in his 5–2 loss to New York's Joe McGinnity, who won both games of a DH that day

The first prominent Ohio State graduate to reach the majors, Wiley Piatt arrived in Philadelphia unheralded from Dayton, the 1897 Interstate League champs. Signed for $150 a month, he was promised a raise by manager George Stallings if he pitched well, and presumably he got it. Piatt was the surprise 1898 rookie sensation, leading the Phils with 24 wins. His sophomore year was only slightly less superb, as he again topped the club in wins with 23. In 1900 Piatt slipped badly after encountering arm trouble and was shut down for the season after an 8–2 loss at New York on August 22. The following year he joined the mass exodus of NL players to the higher paying AL, signing with Connie Mack's first Philadelphia A's entry.

Accused of being cocky, not in shape, and "carelessly indifferent," he was jettisoned on July 3, 1901, with a 5-12 record, as Mack earned *TSN's* praise for doing "right in ridding himself of the worse than useless drag of a pitcher." Piatt then spent six weeks in Atlantic City and apparently was reinvigorated by the summer air on the Jersey shore, for he went 4-2 with a 2.79 ERA after linking up with the AL-pennant-winning White Sox for the last month of the 1901 season. That winter he was caught in the smallpox epidemic that forced the closing of all the area schools near his home in West Union, OH. But by the time the season started he was well enough to win a spot in the White Sox' five-man rotation, joining Ned Garvin, Jimmy Callahan, Roy Patterson, and Clark Griffith. Even though the only serious mark against him was the league lead in pitching errors (13), Chicago made little effort to retain him. Piatt returned to the NL in 1903, signing with Boston for $3,000 plus a $500 signing bonus. He pitched well in the early going but was often betrayed by his supporting cast. On June 25 he joined a select list of luckless hurlers when he pitched two CGs in a DH against the Cardinals and lost both, 1–0 and 5–3. Some five weeks later he was released and finished the season pitching for whatever independent team would pay him the most money on a given day.

Piatt signed with Nashville of the Southern Association in 1904 and was the club's Opening Day starter but tried the patience of catcher-manager Newt Fisher with his bouts of indifference. The following year Piatt pitched very well at times with Toledo of the American Association but too infrequently, logging only fourteen decisions, his typical pattern toward the end of his career. He continued to play in the minors until 1908 and taught part-time in the winters. Around 1910 he became a full-time teacher in southeastern Ohio but quit to become a common laborer. Piatt later did defense work during World War II just prior to his death in Cincinnati at from colon cancer. (DN)

Porter, Walter Henry / "Henry"

B	T	HGT	WGT	G	IP	H	GS
R	R	?	142	207	1793.1	1893	206

CG	BB	SO	SH	W	L	PCT	ERA
201	466	659	9	96	107	.473	3.70

B. 6/?/1858 Vergennes, VT **D.** 12/30/1906
TEAMS: 84MilU 85–87BroA 88–89KCA
DEBUT: 9/27/1884 at Milwaukee; caught by George Bignell and beat Washington's Charlie Geggus 3–0
FINALE: 5/23/1889 at Kansas City; caught by Jim Donahue and lost 17–3 to Brooklyn's Tom Lovett
CAREER HIGHLIGHT: 6/6/1888 at Baltimore; caught by Law Daniels and no-hit Baltimore's Matt Kilroy 4–0

Henry Porter was an outfielder–first baseman converted into a pitcher. His one asset, a fastball, could never offset his many shortcomings in the box. Even as a 30-game winner for Brooklyn in 1885 he failed to earn the respect of teammates, management, and fans. Despite having played for strong Natick and Westboro, MA, independent teams in the late 1870s, Porter was a small, weak-hitting first baseman for his hometown Webster, MA, team in 1880–81 who occasionally pitched while his brother Albert caught. The following season, at 23, he was pressed into service more often as a pitcher for the independent Rhode Island Woonsockets. That winter he signed with Bay City, MI, of the Northwestern League for 1883, leaving his wife and newborn son in Webster. In 1884 Porter went 18-10 in a two-man rotation with Dave Foutz, keeping Bay City in first place until mid June. Six weeks later Bay City folded and auctioned off its team. Porter at first pledged to join Foutz in St. Louis but then agreed to be sold to Milwaukee along with his catcher George Bignell for $2,800 and went 9-2. On September 19 Milwaukee joined the UA, and eight days later Porter pitched the team's ML inaugural, a one-hit win over Washington.

When the UA disbanded Porter signed with Brooklyn AA on February 7, 1885. He closed the year 33-21 and became known as "Byrne's Pet," a reference to his chummy relationship with team owner Charlie Byrne. Teammates felt differently about him, however. Porter was given to temper tantrums in the box after suffering errors behind him, and his outbursts were usually followed by ugly streaks of walks and wild pitches. He was also chided for relying on superstition, to the extent of pitching even on the hottest days with the same red jersey under his uniform. When a St. Louis laundry lost the jersey in 1885, Porter was beside himself with rage.

Drinking was blamed for the 142-pounder's early 1886 inconsistency. Even though he was leading the team in wins on July 23, the *Brooklyn Eagle* wrote, "When Porter is in the box . . . the home team does not go into the field with that feeling of confidence." At the time he ranked among the league leaders in hit batsmen, walks, and wild pitches. Porter finished the year 27-19, but his 1887 contract included a clause against imbibing. He injured his hand on August 5, finished the season winning only two of his final eleven starts, and was among the Brooklyn discards to the new Kansas City franchise prior to 1888 after the Bridegrooms signed superstar Bob Caruthers. KC was a cellar club and Porter had to overexert himself for wins. While he hit his career high for shutouts with 4, in 12 of his starts he allowed 10 runs or more. A June 6 no-hitter at Baltimore came between 2 starts in which he allowed 30 hits, and by the end of the season his arm was stretched to the breaking point.

Porter was released by four minor league clubs over the next eighteen months to end his pro career. He then worked at the Douglas Shoe Factory in Brockton, MA, and died at his home there of tubercular meningitis in 1906. (FV/DN/DB)

Powell, John Joseph / "Jack" "Red"

B	T	HGT	WGT	G	IP	H	GS
R	R	5'11"	175	155	1227.2	1331	147

CG	BB	SO	SH	W	L	PCT	ERA
128	336	318	13	78	60	.565	3.53

B. 7/9/1874 Bloomington, IN **D.** 10/17/1944
TEAMS: 97–98CleN 99–01StLN 02–03StLAL 04–05NYAL 05–12StLAL
DEBUT: 6/23/1897 at Louisville; caught by Lou Criger and beat Louisville's Bill Magee 18–1
FINALE: 9/24/1912 at St. Louis; was relieved by Mack Allison and lost 6–2 to Chicago's Ed Walsh

After Jack Powell married catcher Jack O'Connor's sister Nora in 1902, the pair was known thereafter as "the Brother-in-law Battery." They also ran a saloon together in St. Louis for a number of years before Powell and his wife divorced in 1907. Powell is remembered today mostly for his stunning array of negative achievements. In his sixteen-year ML career he surrendered 110 home runs, 31 more than any other pitcher did during that span (1897–1912), and also was a league leader at various times in losses and earned runs allowed. He is known best, however, for notching the most losses (256) of any ML pitcher with a sub-.500 career winning percentage (.489).

Not surprisingly, Powell was actually one of the better pitchers of his time and was victimized largely by the quality of his teams. He never played on a pennant winner, only once (in 1904) pitched on a club that finished as high as second, and was on three cellar dwellers. Powell's main attributes were his extraordinary endurance, a quick no-windup delivery that often caught batters off guard, and a talent for being able to take the hill with little warmup, enabling him to appear often in relief.

An apprentice boilermaker prior to starting his pro career, Powell was recommended to Chicago manager Cap Anson in 1896 while pitching for the Maroons, a Windy City amateur team. When Anson passed on Powell, he joined George Tebeau's Fort Wayne Farmers. The Interstate League club operated as a kind of farm team for the Cleveland Spiders (hence its nickname), and at the end of the season both Powell and his main batterymate, Lou Criger, headed for the Forest City. Although Powell's official ML debut did not occur until June 23, 1897, he started at 1B in a Sunday game at Cleveland on May 13 that was halted by the police after only one inning. All records of the game were expunged, but Powell, the most expendable Cleveland participant in the game, was the one thrown to the wolves when prosecutors decided to charge one player to test the validity of the local Sunday Blue Law. He was fined $5 plus court costs, but the Cleveland club picked up the tab.

Despite not joining the Spiders' rotation until the season was nearly two months old, Powell won 15 games in his rookie season and established himself as a perfect complement to the club's ace, Cy Young, for the remainder of the decade. In 1898 he and Young were 48-28 while the rest of the staff was 33-40. The following year, after syndicate ownership transferred him to St. Louis along with Young, he led the NL in starts and tied for the top spot in complete games while going 23-19. After both Powell and Young slipped below 20 wins in 1900 as St. Louis tumbled into the second division, they parted ways, with Young jumping to Boston of the fledging American League. The next year Powell followed suit, joining the St. Louis AL entry, where he would remain for most of the rest of his career. (DN)

Pratt, Albert George / "Al" "Uncle Al" "The Five-Inning Wonder"

B	T	HGT	WGT	G	IP	H	GS
?	R	5'7"	140	43	330.1	446	40

CG	BB	SO	SH	W	L	PCT	ERA
30	61	41	0	12	26	.316	4.41

G	W	L	PCT	PENNANTS
111	51	59	.464	0

B. 11/19/1847 Allegheny, PA **D.** 11/21/1937
TEAMS: 71–72CleNA (M)82–83PitA
DEBUT: 5/4/1871 at Fort Wayne; in the first ML game in history was caught by Deacon White and lost 2–0 to Fort Wayne's Bobby Mathews
FINALE: 8/19/1872 at Cleveland; caught by Scott Hastings and finished the game in RF after switching places with Rynie Wolters, who took the 12–7 loss to Boston's Al Spalding

Al Pratt claimed to have learned to play ball while serving in the Union Army in the Civil War and that the first catcher's glove he ever saw was a "yellow buckskin gauntlet in which the fingers had been cut out and the palm padded by a tailor" worn by Cleveland receiver Deacon White at Brooklyn's Capitoline Grounds in 1872 when his hands began to hurt. Both claims may be true and, in any case, are hardly controversial, but another of Pratt's assertions—that Bobby Mathews and Candy Cummings invented the curve ball simultaneously—if true, could stir up a hornets' nest. Pratt's memory may have been skewed in that he faced Mathews in the first ML game and lost, for Mathews himself once professed that he learned the pitch from Cummings.

Upon being mustered out of the army, the tiny, baby-faced Pratt pitched for the amateur Atlantics of Allegheny, PA, in 1866 and then joined the

Allegheny Enterprise the following year before coming to Ohio with the Portsmouth River Rats. Already known as an elfin speedballer who wore down in the late innings, by 1869 he was with the Cleveland Forest Citys. A year later Platt's Forest City crew was the first pro team beaten by an amateur nine, when the Chicago Aetnas snuck a mushy ball into a game at Lakeside Grounds in the Windy City. He remained with Cleveland until it left the NA in 1872 and then played for a string of Midwestern teams before returning to the Pittsburgh area in 1877 and pitching for the Xanthes club.

By the early 1880s Pratt was no longer an active player and had become a sporting goods dealer for the Spalding Company but was still very involved with the game. Instrumental in the formation of the American Association, he was named manager of its Pittsburgh (Allegheny) entry but held the job only one year when he realized his players were making a fool of him whenever he attempted to curb their profligacy. Through the remainder of the 1880s Pratt continued to serve as an adviser to the Pittsburgh team, an occasional umpire, and a scout while deriving his major income from his sporting goods store. In July 1890 the *Chicago Tribune* announced that Pratt had denied rumors that he would accept the management of Pittsburgh NL, but a few weeks later *TSN* reported he had bought a share of the club and would help resurrect it since he was much better at the business end of baseball than any of its present owners. Apparently *TSN* jumped the gun. A month later the St. Louis paper informed its readers that rather than serving in Pittsburgh's front office Pratt was suing the club for $740 owed him for uniforms and equipment he had supplied to the team. Over the next few years Pratt expanded his local sporting goods empire. He died at his Pittsburgh home in 1937 at 90 and was buried in his Grand Army of the Republic uniform. (DN/DB)

Ramsey, Thomas H. / "Tom" "Toad"

B	T	HGT	WGT	G	IP	H	GS
R	L	5'9½"	180	248	2100.2	1941	241

CG	BB	SO	SH	W	L	PCT	ERA
225	671	1515	5	113	124	.477	3.29

B. 8/8/1864 Indianapolis, IN **D.** 3/27/1906
TEAMS: 85–89LouA 89–90StLA
DEBUT: 9/5/1885 at St. Louis; caught by Jack Kerins and lost 4–3 to St. Louis's Dave Foutz
FINALE: 9/17/1890 at Columbus; caught by Jack Munyan and was relieved by Jack Stivetts in a 6–1 loss to Columbus's Jack Easton

A bricklayer in his youth, despite losing a finger on the job, the redheaded Tom Ramsey developed such a strong left hand that he was able to twist the cover partially off a ball to give it weird spins and breaks; in addition, the skin on his pitching fingers was "as horny and rough as a nutmeg grater [or a toad]" according to Hugh Fullerton. At issue is whether he threw an early form of a knuckleball, a kind of screwball, or even a spitball. Here is a Louisville writer on the Colonels' problematic southpaw after the 1887 rule change eliminated a batter's choice to designate whether he wanted high or low balls: "[Ramsey's best pitch is] a combination down and in ball. He brings a ball higher than any pitcher in the profession. When it starts out it seems above the batter's head, but, taking a quick shoot, it passes over the plate waist high, having taken a wonderful drop." In 1886, Ramsey's first full ML season, his pitching style was different. His curve would start in the strike zone and drop out of it before crossing the plate to the consternation of lowball hitters. Highball selectors fared better against him in that his pitch would start at their belt line and drop to knee level by the time they swung.

Withal, it would seem that Ramsey must have been nearly unhittable when he was on his game, and indeed he was. But he was far from unbeatable. For one, Ramsey was a miserable fielder and hitter, one of the worst ever at both phases of the game. Among all pitchers in roughly 150 or more ML games there is no one even close to being as error prone; Ramsey's 107 bobbles in his 248 box appearances translate to a .761 FA, 76 points worse than the next hurler on the list, Elmer Smith. What's more, *TSN* observed, "There never was a pitcher who let personal feeling enter his work so much as Tom Ramsey." It was said that if he bore a batter or a team animosity he was nearly invincible, but otherwise he often pitched indifferently or worse. In the late 1880s with abominably bad Louisville teams, Ramsey seldom paid attention to the score and just tried to hurry and get the game over so he could hit the saloons.

Ramsey first appeared on the scene as a catcher with semipro Shelbyville, IN, in 1883, but by 1885 it was clear that he belonged at the other end of the points. He was already so devastatingly effective a ground ball and strikeout pitcher by then that in two of his 1885 games with Chattanooga of the Southern League his catcher and first baseman made all the put-outs. In August of that season Louisville sent pitcher John Connor and $750 to Chattanooga for Ramsey in what was probably the first genuine player trade in history between two professional teams. Ramsey had been personally scouted by Louisville manager Jim Hart, who was so ecstatic to steal him from under the nose of Baltimore manager Billy Barnie that he helped steer Matt Kilroy to Barnie as a way of atoning. In nine late-season starts with the Colonels in 1885, Ramsey logged a 1.94 ERA and a .150 OBA but was given so little support that he won just three of them.

The following spring Ramsey shouldered past Guy Hecker as Louisville's ace and roared to 38 wins and 499 strikeouts, the second highest season total in ML history. Yet by June he was viewed by his teammates as no more than "a young tough" and was thoroughly disliked by most of them, although a few took his part in what would become a vicious feud between him and Hecker until both left the club in 1889. Hart had also begun to regret his choice of Ramsey over Kilroy when the team's new ace began to make even Pete Browning seem like a temperance crusader.

Still, in 1887 Ramsey amassed an even more phenomenal array of stats, winning 37 games for a fourth-place team and bagging 355 strikeouts, 118 more than any other ML pitcher in the lone year batters were given four strikes. On June 21 he struck out a single-game record 17 Cleveland Blues under the four-strike rule and nine days later fanned 16 members of the first-place St. Louis Browns. But by the following June, under Louisville's refractory new owner, Mordecai Davidson, Ramsey's career had begun to unravel. First, Davidson suspended him without pay for excessive drinking; then a month later Ramsey purposely missed the team train to Cleveland in order to avoid a warrant for his arrest at the railroad station for the stack of bar tabs he owed in Louisville; and finally he was jailed in Louisville anyway and released only after he "took the insolvent debtor's oath" that all he owned were the clothes on his back. After winning 75 games in his previous two seasons, Ramsey sank to 8-30. In 1889, pitching for a Louisville team that finished 66½ games out of first place, he dipped even lower to 1-16. Yet his lone win of the season in a Colonels uniform broke a ML-record 26-game losing streak when he topped St. Louis 7–3 on June 23. The previous month Davidson had put Ramsey on the market with a $10,000 price tag, and there were enough nibbles to suggest that if he lowered the damages a little he would find a taker. Instead Louisville held on to its plummeting pitcher until July, by which time the Colonels were able to obtain in a trade with St. Louis only a pitcher (Nat Hudson) who refused to play for them and had to be sold to a minor league team.

Even though he was finally on a winner, Ramsey was not about to do himself any favors. Browns manager Charlie Comiskey abhorred his new pitcher's attitude to the extent that he used him in only 5 games down the stretch in 1889, preferring to go with a three-man rotation of Silver King, Elton Chamberlin, and rookie Jack Stivetts. In 1890, with Comiskey gone to the PL, Ramsey vied with Stivetts all season for the honor of being the Browns' new ace. On the morning of September 17 each had 24 wins. When Stivetts won the first game of a DH with Columbus that day, Ramsey had a chance to match his rival in the second contest, but he was released when he lost and never pitched in the majors again.

Some historians are of the opinion that Ramsey was unofficially blacklisted once the Players League folded and 33 percent fewer pitchers were needed in the majors in 1891, but it is doubtful that anything short of a written mandate could have persuaded every ML team to pass on a 24-game winner unless there was also a physical problem. Ramsey had no history of serious arm trouble prior to 1890, but the following year he was unable to get anybody out, even during Denver's Western Association exhibition season. In October 1892, after he flunked out of the Illinois-Iowa League, *TSN* reported that Ramsey was "living quietly in Indianapolis, working out, had given up drinking," and had written to Browns owner Chris Von der Ahe pleading for a minimal contract with a clause that it would end instantly if he drank.

Von der Ahe seemingly never replied, for the following year Ramsey served as player-manager of independent Shelbyville, IN, and swore he had been on the wagon for three years. Still no bids came from NL teams, so he signed for 1894 with Savannah of the Southern League under John

McCloskey. In April Ramsey seemed unbeatable, winning 4 straight games at one point, but writers soon were noting in their columns that he looked old and lacked spark, and his pitches had no speed. McCloskey released Ramsey sometime in early July. The following spring, after washing out with St. Joseph of the Western Association, Ramsey began dreaming of umpiring in the minors. As late as 1899 *TSN* was still positing that he might get a trial with Indianapolis, then in the Western League. Ramsey did indeed relocate to the Hoosier capital around that time but never played there again. He died in Indianapolis of pneumonia at 41. (DN/DB)

Reis, Laurence P. / "Laurie"

B	T	HGT	WGT	G	IP	H	GS
R	R	5'9"	160	8	72	84	8

CG	BB	SO	SH	W	L	PCT	ERA
8	10	19	1	4	4	.500	2.00

B. 11/20/1858 Chicago, IL **D.** 1/24/1921
TEAMS: 77–78ChiN
DEBUT: 10/1/1877 at Chicago; caught by Cal McVey and beat Cincinnati's Bobby Mitchell 10–3
FINALE: 9/3/1878 at Chicago; caught by Phil Powers and lost 8–0 to Providence's John M. Ward

Laurie Reis began 1877 with the semipro Fairbanks club of Chicago and finished in September with independent Valley City, IA, before returning home to start the Chicago NL club's last 4 games of the season, losing only to Louisville's Jim Devlin on October 5. His stunning 0.75 ERA (or, anyway, what composed it) did not go unnoticed—ERA stats as such were not as yet kept officially. Reis made the White Stockings' varsity the following spring but was sent off to regroup after two wretched starts in May. He returned in early August to play LF in a game and then beat Providence's John M. Ward 17–3 on August 15. A losing rematch with Ward nineteen days later marked his ML finale.

Reis spent the next two seasons with Dubuque, IA, and ran a poolroom there between pitching dates. By the early 1880s he had returned to Chicago, where he played in the Chicago City League for a time and later worked for the Pullman Palace Car Company. Reis died in Chicago at 62. (DN)

Rettger, George Edward / "George"

B	T	HGT	WGT	G	IP	H	GS
R	R	5'11"	175	21	139.2	125	18

CG	BB	SO	SH	W	L	PCT	ERA
14	92	62	1	9	6	.600	3.67

B. 7/29/1868 Cleveland, OH **D.** 6/5/1921
TEAMS: 91StLA 92CleN 92CinN
DEBUT: 8/13/1891 at St. Louis; caught by Dell Darling and beat Washington's Ed Eiteljorge 11–9
FINALE: 7/16/1892 at Baltimore; caught by Jerry Harrington and beat Baltimore's George Cobb 16–5

In 1890 Meadville of the Pennsylvania State League signed George Rettger off the Cleveland sandlots. He also pitched some for independent Moundsville, NY, and then split 1891 between the Northwestern League and the Western Association before joining the Browns late in the AA season. Rettger was arguably St. Louis's most effective pitcher during its last two months as a member of the rebel AA. In a key game on September 12 at St. Louis that kept the Browns' faint pennant hopes alive, he beat Boston's ace, Charlie Buffinton, 4–2.

When the AA and NL combined over the winter, Rettger was assigned to Cleveland, where his girlfriend lived, and went into training to box T. M. Ryan, the Forest City light-heavyweight champion. By the time spring training began, he had given up his fight plans and was regarded as the best pitching prospect at Cleveland's Hot Springs, AR, camp. But he may have incurred an injury, for he did not make his first start of the season until June 3 at Washington, when he lost 9–4. Soon afterward Cleveland acquired John Clarkson from Boston, removing Rettger from the pitching mix. After his release he pitched a winning game for Cincinnati, only to be cut again.

If Rettger did indeed have an injury or arm trouble in 1892, there was no evidence of it during the remainder of his lengthy career, all of it spent in the high minors. He finished in 1901 with Kansas City of the Western League after logging a 7–11 mark with Milwaukee of the newly named American League the previous season. The 1900 campaign was his sixth with Milwaukee. It would seem that surely, at some point during all that time, an ML team would have drafted or purchased Rettger, a consistent 20-game winner in the 1895–98 Western League, but it never happened. Instead he became an auto mechanic in his native Cleveland. He died of tuberculosis in Lakewood, OH, in 1921, leaving behind his wife, Catherine. (DN)

Rhines, William Pearl / "Billy" "Bunker"

B	T	HGT	WGT	G	IP	H	GS
R	R	5'11"	168	248	1891	1961	222

CG	BB	SO	SH	W	L	PCT	ERA
187	576	553	13	113	103	.523	3.48

B. 3/14/1869 Ridgway, PA **D.** 1/30/1922
TEAMS: 90–92CinN 93LouN 95–97CinN 98–99PitN
DEBUT: 4/22/1890 at Cincinnati; relieved Lee Viau in a 13–3 loss to Chicago's Bill Coughlin
FINALE: 6/22/1899 at Pittsburgh; caught by Mike Bowerman, was relieved by Tully Sparks, and took the 11–6 loss to New York's Cy Seymour
CAREER HIGHLIGHT: Is the only ML pitcher to win an ERA crown at both the 50-foot and the 60'6" distances.

The fifth child of lumberman George Rhines and his wife, Nancy, Billy Rhines grew up in Ridgway, a prosperous small town in northwestern Pennsylvania. Raised in middle class circumstances, he attended Bucknell University, later the alma mater of Christy Mathewson. But unlike Mathewson he did not play much ball until he casually tried pitching to a friend at Bucknell and found he had a natural aptitude for it.

Rhines broke into pro ball with Binghamton of the International Association in 1887 and by 1889 was with Davenport of the Central Interstate League, where he formed a battery with Jerry Harrington. After Davenport folded in September 1889, peripatetic freelance scout Ted Sullivan signed both Rhines and Harrington for Cincinnati. Rhines made his ML debut on April 22, 1890, mopping up in a 13–3 loss to Chicago, and did not get his first start until the eighth game of the season. Once he was given a chance to pitch regularly, he won his first six starts, lost to Brooklyn, and then won seven more. By then it was the middle of June and the Reds were leading the NL. They cooled off to finish fourth, and Rhines ended the season with a 28-17 record, completing all forty-five of his starts. In 1891 he fell to 17-24, but pitched effectively for a troubled seventh-place team.

Rhines not only threw hard but had a reputation as a smart pitcher who delivered the ball from a variety of angles. He often threw sidearm and could drop down to deliver the ball from below his knee, firing it with a rising trajectory. Jim McCormick, an earlier-day star, threw a "rise ball" that may have been similar, but McCormick had started when underhanded pitching had still been required by the rules. By the time Rhines came of age, his pitching style seemed so unusual that he was considered something of a pioneer in reintroducing the underhand delivery, and for years afterward every submariner was compared to him, most notably Joe McGinnity. After 1891, however, Rhines ran into difficulty. NL hitters may have caught up with his peculiar style, but since he had worked successfully for two full years, it seems likely his problems had more to do with a serious drinking problem once he and his batterymate, Harrington, began imbibing with Eddie Burke and the notoriously bibulous Pete Browning. Rhines reported late in 1892 due to an injury suffered falling off a horizontal bar at a gym in March, hurt himself probably in an alcohol-stimulated wrestling match after he came to Cincinnati, and then was suspended and sent home in May after a fracas in a downtown saloon with Burke over the respective merits of their Pennsylvania home towns. Rhines appears to have had a physiological problem coping with alcohol. According to the *Cincinnati Enquirer*, he had never been a drinker before 1892, and a teammate said even a couple of beers would render him helplessly intoxicated.

Rhines returned to the Reds in July 1892 but could not regain his stride. He was released and pitched ineffectively for Louisville in 1893 before being demoted to Grand Rapids of the Western League the following season. There he made a comeback, and in December he and his catcher, Harry Spies, were selected in the minor league draft by Cincinnati after Grand Rapids reportedly made the Reds an unsuccessful offer of twice the draft price to retain the pair. Rhines made the most of his second lease on life in Cincinnati, putting in three good years for the Reds, and then was traded to Pittsburgh in November 1897. He disappointed the Pirates, however, and late in the season was suspended again for drinking. His performance dropped off more drastically in 1899, and he was released in June after running up a 6.00 ERA in nine starts.

After a feeble comeback attempt in the 1901 Western Association, Rhines retired to his home in Ridgway, where he managed the local team and enjoyed hunting in the hills surrounding the town; a crack shot, he had set a record at a Cincinnati shooting gallery and won several trap shooting contests. His father died in 1899, and Rhines seems to have inherited control of the family lumber business. But things apparently went poorly, for by 1920 he was driving a taxi. He did not marry until he was in his forties and then had four children in quick succession. Sadly, however, he would not see them grow up. Rhines died at his home in Ridgway of heart disease when he was only 52 years old, after a long illness that reportedly left the family impoverished. (DB/DN)

Rhodes, William Clarence (b. Rotes) **/ "Bill" "Dusty" "Poodles"**

B	T	HGT	WGT	G	IP	H	GS
?	?	?	?	20	151.2	244	19

CG	BB	SO	SH	W	L	PCT	ERA
17	66	22	0	5	12	.294	7.60

B. 6/27/1871 Pottstown, PA **D.** 3/7/1934
TEAMS: 93LouN
DEBUT: 6/14/1893 at Washington; caught by Jack Grim and beat Washington's Jesse Duryea 9–5
FINALE: 8/15/1893 at Chicago; caught by Jack Grim and lost 11–6 to Chicago's Frank Donnelly
CAREER LOWLIGHT: 6/18/1893 at Cincinnati; caught by Henry Cote, allowed 14 runs in the first inning, and became the last pitcher in ML history to give up 30 runs in a game in a 30–12 loss to Cincinnati's Elton Chamberlin

The first MLer with his last name to be nicknamed "Dusty," Bill Rhodes lived in Pottstown all of his life. His first momentous baseball achievement came in October 1891, when he hurled the independent Pottstown team to a 1–0 postseason exhibition win in ten innings over Philadelphia AA after going 11-21 for Danville of the Pennsylvania State League. That winter Rhodes appears to have been contacted by Fort Worth of the Texas League and signed for 1892, but he finished the season back with Danville and by the following spring had joined Johnstown of the Pennsylvania State League.

Johnstown accused Rhodes of jumping his contract when he joined Louisville in June 1893 but soon probably was happy to disassociate itself from him. The marvel is not how awful Rhodes was with Louisville but that he managed to win 5 games. Rhodes's 14.48 hits allowed per nine innings are still the ML-record high by a rookie qualifier. If he can be said to have had a career highlight, it came on July 9, 1893, when he drew the honor of pitching Louisville's first Sunday game at Parkland Field after the team annexed the land on which the facility was located so that Parkland suburban residents could no longer protest Sunday ball and alcohol sales. Rhodes lasted only until the third inning before giving way to George Hemming, who earned a 19–9 win over the Giants' Ed Crane.

There is some evidence that in 1893 Rhodes had more trouble than most pitchers adjusting to the increased distance and in particular to having to anchor one foot to a tiny rubber plate as he started his delivery. We would all like to know which foot that was. After his unhappy ML experience with Louisville, Rhodes returned to the Pennsylvania State League and remained in the pro game until 1898, presumably faring better once the pitchers' plate (or rubber) was expanded in size. Rhodes later worked as a riveter until his death in 1934 and left two daughters and his wife, the former Laura Levengood. (DN/PM)

Richmond, J. Lee / "Lee"

B	T	HGT	WGT	G	IP	H	GS
?	L	5'10"	155	191	1583	1763	179

CG	BB	SO	SH	W	L	PCT	ERA
171	269	552	8	75	100	.429	3.06

G	AB	H	R	2B	3B	HR
251	1018	262	169	29	20	3

RBI	BB	SO	SB	BA	SA	OBP
113	46	73	0	.257	.334	.289

B. 5/5/1857 Sheffield, OH **D.** 10/1/1929
TEAMS: 79BosN 80–82WorN 83ProN 86CinA
DEBUT: 9/27/1879 at Boston; caught by Charlie Snyder and beat Providence's John M. Ward 12–6
FINALE: 10/4/1886 at Cincinnati; caught by Kid Baldwin and lost 6–4 to New York's Jack Lynch
CAREER HIGHLIGHT: 6/12/1880 at Worcester; caught by Charlie Bennett and pitched the first perfect game in ML history, beating Cleveland's Jim McCormick 1–0

Like many of his baseball contemporaries, Lee Richmond played under his middle name (partly perhaps because his first name was only an initial) and is largely remembered for a single isolated event from an interesting and important career, but his authorship of the first ML perfect game is only the highlight of his brief tenure as the most sensational pitcher in baseball. Even more important, as the first significant left-handed hurler in baseball history he played a key role in the development of the modern batter-pitcher relationship.

Born in northern Ohio, Richmond went east to Brown University, where he played baseball first as an outfielder then as a pitcher for Brown's championship team. Before the rise of college football, star players for Ivy League colleges were celebrities of some note and the recipient of fancy offers to play pro baseball. Only in rare cases did the collegians do more than dabble their toes in the waters of professional sports, but Richmond is an exception. In 1879 he accepted an offer from Frank Bancroft to pitch an exhibition game for Bancroft's National Association Worcester team against Chicago NL. Richmond traveled to Worcester on June 2 and electrified the baseball public by no-hitting the White Stockings in a seven-inning game.

Bancroft was quick to sign Richmond to finish the season with Worcester, although he continued to take classes and play for the Brown team until school ended. Richmond dominated minor league and independent teams, pitching a second no-hitter, and in late September was loaned by Worcester to Boston, where he made his first NL appearance, allowing 4 hits and beating Providence's John M. Ward, another fine young pitcher whom he would anticipate by just a few days in throwing the initial ML perfect game. During the 1879–80 off-season Worcester was admitted to the NL, with Richmond signing to return to the team at a healthy salary hike. Although he was not the first left-handed pitcher in the game, he may reasonably be viewed as the first to achieve stardom. Until the early 1870s pitchers were limited to a straight-armed, underhanded delivery. Under these limitations favoring one hand over the other was little more than an accidental characteristic of a pitcher, like hair color. Over the course of the 1870s, however, pitchers began to learn to throw breaking balls. They also started bending the rules, raising the angle of delivery, and since umpires found it too difficult to monitor them, rules makers were led in gradual stages to legalize what could not be prevented, until eventually the modern overhand delivery was born. That point was not achieved until the mid-1880s, however. In the late 1870s the curve ball had become a key ingredient in most pitchers' repertoires, and a submarine delivery was standard. Handedness naturally became a crucial element of the pitcher-batter relationship.

The result was not a spate of left-handed pitchers, however. Because a left-handed batter has a shorter run to 1B, larger numbers of left-handed hitters began to appear in lineups, and the best left-handers, with the advantage in hitting against the almost exclusively right-handed pitchers, became dominant offensive forces. As early as 1877 the NL saw a left-handed pitcher in Bobby Mitchell, and Curry Foley debuted two years later with Boston, but neither achieved lasting prominence. When Richmond appeared with a devastatingly effective curve ball, he redressed the balance of power in the pitcher-batter relationship. Indeed, lefty hitters had even more trouble with the best early southpaws, such as Richmond, than right-handed hitters did against righty pitchers, presumably because the left-handers rarely saw a left-handed pitcher and had scant opportunities to adjust to them.

Historian Peter Morris thus writes of "an awed reaction when the first great post-curve southpaw, J. Lee Richmond, burst on the scene in 1880," while the contemporary *Cincinnati Enquirer* complained in less elegant terms of "Richmond, Worcester's wonderful left-handed pitcher, about whom the newspapers in the East have been slobbering." Not especially fast, he was a smart pitcher, the first one known to literally keep a book on opposing hitters, and he had a variety of breaking pitches that left-handers in particular found devastating. The *Enquirer's* slighting remarks appeared early in April, during the preseason; when league play began Worcester started playing midwestern teams as well as eastern ones, and Richmond made an impression in that region as well. On June 26—two weeks after Richmond had pitched his perfect game against Cleveland—three of Chicago's left-handed hitters batted right-handed against him.

Richmond became the focal point for the development of other tactics that are standard now but were new at the time. Teams juggled lineups to drop left-handed hitters to the bottom end of the order, and in late May Boston sat down left-handed John O'Rourke against Richmond, and Providence's veteran lefty first baseman Joe Start was benched in favor of George Bradley. Meanwhile

Worcester used Richmond as the first situational lefty. The rules of the day allowed substitutions only in the event of injury, but Richmond played the outfield when he did not start in the pitcher's box, for he was a good fielder and hitter and, in Harry Wright's words, "a remarkably clever man on the bases."

Largely through Richmond's efforts, Worcester, despite bringing a patchwork roster into the NL and being handicapped by a small market from which to draw revenue, finished a respectable 40-43. The following years were progressively worse for the team. By 1882 Richmond's record was 14-33, but the rest of the Worcester pitchers were a wretched 4-33. Meanwhile, almost 1,500 innings pitched in three years had put considerable stress on Richmond's arm, even with the submarine motion then prevalent. By the time he signed with Providence for 1883 after Worcester was dropped from the NL, he was afflicted with a sore arm. For a time early in the 1883 season he alternated in the pitcher's box with Charley Radbourn, but then he gave way to Charlie Sweeney and played primarily as an outfield sub, getting only two pitching starts after June 22.

Like many pitchers of his day, Richmond had become an "exploded phenomenon," a briefly brilliant hurler who had lost his effectiveness due to the killing workload expected of pitchers or to an inability to adjust to rules changes and rapid advances in pitching techniques. Exploded phenoms were often poor boys whose ability to throw a baseball hard had lifted them out of humble circumstances, and to be dumped suddenly back into obscurity was a harsh experience, psychologically devastating for many. Richmond was fortunate enough to have resources most of his peers lacked. His baseball earnings had financed a master's degree from Brown and then a medical degree from the New York College of Physicians and Surgeons, which he attained just as his baseball career was winding down. After practicing medicine in several northern Ohio cities, he settled around 1890 in Toledo, where he married and turned from medicine to a long career as a high school math teacher. Richmond also coached baseball, numbering among his charges a young Fred Merkle. Upon retirement he became a faculty member and dean of men at the University of Toledo. Richmond died in Toledo at 72 of a stroke after being in ill health for several weeks before leaving behind his wife, Mary.

Before all that happened, however, Richmond made one final attempt to recapture baseball glory. Early in the 1886 season Cincinnati's Hick Carpenter was chatting with St. Louis's Doc Bushong, and Bushong mentioned he had seen their mutual former Worcester teammate Richmond recently and that after several years of rest the stiffness had left his arm. Cincinnati needed pitching, and eventually manager Opie Caylor was able to get in touch with Richmond. On August 11 a story headlined "AN IMPORTANT ENGAGEMENT" appeared in the *Cincinnati Commercial Gazette* announcing that Cincinnati had signed Richmond, the onetime "king bee in the profession."

Caylor expected Richmond to pitch the following day, but it transpired he would need more practice. Not until August 27 did he debut for the Reds, but he was hit hard, could not control the ball, and was removed from the box to CF in the middle of a game lost by Cincinnati 11–8. After that he was used occasionally as an outfielder, and once he relieved, but he did not get another pitching start until October 4, near the season's end, when he pitched marginally better than in his debut but allowed 4 earned runs and lost again. At that point Richmond went back to his medical practice.

With his arm perhaps still not healthy and coming off a layoff of nearly three years, Richmond probably had too many handicaps to have made a successful comeback. Nevertheless, there are indications that his effort gave witnesses an invaluable view of the remarkably rapid pace at which the craft of pitching was advancing. In the space of half a dozen years Richmond had gone from defining the state of the art in pitching to being a sort of living fossil. Louisville star Guy Hecker was quoted as saying Richmond's success had never been due to exceptional talent but simply to the fact that no one had ever seen a left-handed curveballer when he arrived on the scene. Hecker, it should be said, had never played in the same league as Richmond prior to 1886 and can rarely if ever have seen him play in his glory days, but observers in Cincinnati found Richmond's submarine motion oddly quaint once overhand pitching had been legalized. He lacked "the drops and shoots that the present pitchers rely upon for success," noted the *Cincinnati Enquirer*: "It was old-time pitching against modern batsmen." A mere six years earlier the "old-time pitcher" had terrorized the NL's best left-handed hitters, but even Caylor observed in the *Commercial* after Richmond's final ML appearance that the southpaw had been practicing overhand pitching with "his hand away up on a level with his head, but in the game yesterday he seemed afraid to try it, and at no time did he get above the shoulder." (DB/DN/PM)

Salisbury, Henry H. / "Harry"

B	T	HGT	WGT	G	IP	H	GS
L	?	5'8½"	162	48	424	418	48

CG	BB	SO	SH	W	L	PCT	ERA
47	48	166	1	24	24	.500	2.55

B. 5/15/1855 Providence, RI **D.** 3/29/1933
TEAMS: 79TroN 82PitA
DEBUT: 8/28/1879 at Boston; caught by Charlie Reilley and lost 15–1 to Boston's Tommy Bond
FINALE: 9/22/1882 at Pittsburgh; caught by Billy Taylor and lost 20–6 to Louisville's Tony Mullane

At age 18 Harry Salisbury was playing 2B for the Webster Clippers in the Massachusetts Junior Association. He remained in the East until he graduated from Brown University and then was drawn westward and began pitching. Salisbury occupied the box for two months with St. Paul of the League Alliance in 1877, with the Cleveland Forest Citys the following year until he was "bounced out in the cold," and then with Detroit in 1879 before the Troy NL club brought him to Boston to face Hub ace Tommy Bond three times in three days. On the first occasion the *New York Clipper* said he was "batted in every direction, while his delivery was very wild." But by the third try Salisbury was able to defeat Bond 4–1 and end an eleven-game Boston winning streak against Troy.

Although Salisbury pitched decently for the Trojans (4-6 in ten starts) he returned to the minors until the AA was born as a rival major league in 1882. Joining Pittsburgh, he quickly emerged as the staff ace and took a 20-17 record into his final ML start on September 22. Reputedly Salisbury was fired immediately after absorbing a 20–6 drubbing, partly for his poor effort but more because Pittsburgh learned that he had already signed with another team for 1883. But actually Salisbury pitched for Pittsburgh in several postseason exhibition games, including a 6–6 tie with St. Louis on October 11.

Salisbury then surprised by taking a job with the Union Pacific Railroad. For the next four seasons he pitched on occasion in the Colorado State League and for Omaha of the Western League but mainly for the local Union Pacifics, a strong independent team that included catcher Stub Bandle. Salisbury then retired to his Nebraska farm in 1887, though Bandle, by then the Union Pacifics' manager, claimed the ex-MLer would pitch occasionally for his team "but would not leave town with them." Soon farm and family life were no longer enough challenge for the pitcher, and he came out of retirement to work for some years as an accountant for the Pacific Express Company in Omaha. Salisbury later relocated in Chicago and served as the vice president for a rubber goods firm until his death in 1933. Although his throwing arm is still unknown, the probability is strong that he was a righty. (DN/DB)

Sanders, Alexander Bennett / "Ben"

B	T	HGT	WGT	G	IP	H	GS
R	R	6'0"	210	168	1385	1496	157

CG	BB	SO	SH	W	L	PCT	ERA
144	297	468	14	80	70	.533	3.24

G	AB	H	R	2B	3B	HR
247	948	257	132	43	16	5

RBI	BB	SO	SB	BA	SA	OBP
113	47	62	27	.271	.366	.310

B. 2/26/1865 Catharpin, VA **D.** 8/29/1930
TEAMS: 88–89PhiN 90PhiP 91PhiA 92LouN
DEBUT: 6/6/1888 at Philadelphia; caught by Deacon McGuire and lost 6–3 to Chicago's Gus Krock
FINALE: 10/14/1892 at Cleveland; played RF and went 2-for-4 in a 16–10 loss to Cleveland's John Clarkson

Ben Sanders had good speed and was a skilled enough hitter to bat leadoff on occasion, but some sources contend he was an outstanding fielder while others maintain that he had an unorthodox delivery that finished with him off-balance, his back to the plate, making it hard for him to react quickly on batted balls. His so-so .916 career FA does little to settle the debate.

Sanders attended Roanoke College in 1885–86 and later graduated from Vanderbilt with a degree in civil engineering. He always carried a Bible with him along with his school texts and was a faithful churchgoer and a staunch YMCA member. After a brief trial as a pitcher-outfielder with Nashville in the Southern League in 1886, the following year Sanders turned mainly to pitching upon joining Canton of the Ohio State League and was coveted by both Cleveland AA and the NL Quakers. The Philadelphia club won his services for 1888, although he did not report for duty until after he finished the school year. Sanders proceeded to win 19 games as a rookie and lead the NL in shutouts with eight despite his late start. When he won 19 again the following year and also hit .278, 12 points above the team BA, the Philadelphia PL club made his acquisition for 1890 a top priority. Again Sanders did not make his first start until the season was well under way, but by June he had already become the staff workhorse and for the third successive year logged 19 wins plus a .312 BA.

When the PL folded, Philadelphia NL pilot Harry Wright was prepared to welcome Sanders back, only to be stunned by a letter from the pitcher on the eve of the 1891 season averring that "all the money in Philadelphia" could not induce him to play ball again. Wright then received a second jolt when he learned that George Wagner, the treasurer of Philadelphia AA, had visited Sanders in his Nashville home as the college term was about to end and induced him to join the A's for the rest of the campaign in return for $5,000. If that figure is genuine, Sanders was probably the highest-paid partial-season player in the nineteenth century, for the AA season was already more than two months old by the time he made his first appearance with the A's on June 17. With time to make just nineteen pitching starts, he finished 12-5 but gave the A's a bit more bang for their buck by also playing 22 games in the outfield.

Remarkably, since there were no eligibility rules then for college sports, Sanders, despite being a four-year ML veteran, was permitted to pitch yet another season for Vanderbilt in the spring of 1892 after making the same arrangement with Louisville as he had with the A's the year before, when the off-season AA-NL merger assigned him to the Kentucky team. Making his first appearance with the Colonels on June 21, he beat Pittsburgh 5–1. Determined to get full value for their dollar, the Colonels cast Sanders as their staff workhorse and put him either at 1B or in the outfield on days his arm needed rest. In return the ex-Vandy student gave them 12 wins, second on the staff only to Scott Stratton, and a .729 OPS, the highest of any Colonel with a minimum of 200 PAs. Now 27, Sanders decided it was time to put his degree to use. Although he experienced twinges of longing for the game every now and then, he worked as a civil engineer until retiring a few years before succumbing to gall bladder problems at 65 in a Memphis hospital. (DN)

Schappert, John (aka Sheppert and Shappard) **/ "John"**

B	T	HGT	WGT	G	IP	H	GS
R	R	5'10"	170	15	128	131	14

CG	BB	SO	SH	W	L	PCT	ERA
13	32	38	0	8	7	.533	3.52

B. ?/?/? Brooklyn, NY **D.** 7/27/1917
TEAMS: 82StLA
DEBUT: 5/3/1882 at St. Louis; caught by Ed Fusselbach and beat Louisville's Tony Mullane 6–4
FINALE: 7/6/1882 at St. Louis; caught by Sleeper Sullivan and was relieved by Ed Fusselbach in his 21–17 win over Louisville's John Reccius

John Schappert's birth date is unknown, but he was playing with New York–area semipro teams as early as the mid 1870s. In 1882 he came to the upstart AA Browns from Billy Barnie's Eastern Championship Association Brooklyn Atlantics. His release in early July proved to be a mistake since the Browns never found a capable backup pitcher to George McGinnis for the rest of the season. But Schappert's erratic performances perhaps played only a minor part in his early dismissal. The Browns may have dismissed him for their own self-protection.

In a time when a batter was not yet given his base after being hit by a pitch, Schappert was fond of throwing at opponents indiscriminately, making it probable that St. Louis hitters found themselves ducking swarms of retaliatory beanballs on the days he pitched. While he was toiling for Harrisburg of the Interstate Association the following May, a Wilmington paper cited "the cowardly habit of Schappert . . . in maliciously crippling men at the bat," and pointed out that nearly all the players are afraid to stand in front of the fellow's balls." The previous week Columbus AA manager Horace Phillips had attributed his team's unexpected exhibition loss to Harrisburg to "men being afraid to stand up at the plate."

Schappert also faced frequent accusations that he was throwing overhand. Yet he appears to have adjusted his modus operandi well enough to chisel out a living in the minors as late as 1886. By the end of that summer he had eight children to feed, at which point Syracuse of the International Association callously released him and he had to look elsewhere for a means to support his growing family after Bradford of the Pennsylvania State Association did likewise the following June. Schappert died in Brooklyn in 1917. (DN)

Serad, William I. / "Billy" "The Little Frenchman"

B	T	HGT	WGT	G	IP	H	GS
R	R	5'7"	156	95	787.1	935	92

CG	BB	SO	SH	W	L	PCT	ERA
86	290	278	4	35	55	.389	4.13

B. ?/?/1863 Philadelphia, PA **D.** 11/1/1925
TEAMS: 84–85BufN 87–88CinA
DEBUT: 5/5/1884 at Providence; caught by George Myers and after giving up 3 walks in the first inning was relieved by Jim O'Rourke in his 5–2 loss to Providence's Charley Radbourn
FINALE: 7/7/1888 at Cincinnati; caught by Jim Keenan and was relieved by John Weyhing in his 7–0 loss to Philadelphia's Ed Seward

After playing with the August Flower club of Woodbury, NJ, and the amateur Houstons of Chester, PA, Billy Serad was signed by Buffalo in 1884 as the second pitcher on a two-man staff featuring Jim Galvin. Serad lost his first four starts, twice having to be replaced by outfielder Jim O'Rourke, and then improved, winning half his decisions the rest of the way. However, while pitching fewer than half as many innings as Galvin he allowed more earned runs and many more walks. He returned in 1885 but pitched poorly again, and although a disintegrating Buffalo club sold Galvin to Pittsburgh in mid-July, Serad pitched less than he had in 1884.

Buffalo disposed of its franchise after Detroit acquired four of the Bisons' top players. The best of the leftover Bisons stocked two new NL teams, with the remnants held for sale to outside teams at prices set by the league. Serad drew little interest even with a price tag reported at a modest $300 but was finally acquired in late March 1886 by Utica for $250. After he led the International Association in wins with 30, Cincinnati AA brought him back to the majors. Competing in 1887 for a job with several other newcomers, Serad fared badly in the preseason, won his first championship game, and then did so poorly that by May 15 the *Cincinnati Commercial Gazette* was predicting his release. He pulled out of the doldrums with wins over Baltimore and Philadelphia, and by the end of the month, with Tony Mullane, the team's lone established pitcher, having jumped the club in a money dispute, Serad and Elmer Smith emerged as the staff's leaders. Serad's workload declined when Mullane returned to the team, but the season was still the best of his ML career.

In the 1888 preseason Serad beat St. Paul 10–0, in a game one Cincinnati paper called a no-hitter, although another scored a wind-blown fly a triple. Once the season began, however, he rarely pitched when rookie Lee Viau got off to a hot start. Serad did not get a chance until June and showed the rust, walking 6 and losing to the Athletics, 14–7. Cincinnati found another strong pitching prospect, John Weyhing, and Serad was released on August 18. For several years he continued pitching in the minors, mainly with Toronto, where he won 19 games in 1889. Soon after breaking his arm in a game at Detroit in 1890, Serad turned to umpiring. He briefly worked an indicator in the Western and Southern leagues and then settled down at his home in Chester, PA, umpiring local games. Returning home from a game in 1907, Serad was struck down by an electric trolley and seriously injured. Fortunately, he recovered and lived another eighteen years. Serad was working for the South Chester Tube Company at the time of his death in Chester at 62. (DB/DN)

Seward, Edward William (b. Sourhardt) / "Ed"

B	T	HGT	WGT	G	IP	H	GS
?	R	5'7"	175	176	1485.2	1369	169

CG	BB	SO	SH	W	L	PCT	ERA
159	451	589	13	89	72	.553	3.40

B. 6/19/1867 Cleveland, OH **D.** 7/30/1947
TEAMS: 85ProN 87–90PhiA 91CleN
DEBUT: 9/30/1885 at Detroit; caught by Barney Gilligan and relieved Dupee Shaw in Shaw's 9–5 loss to Detroit's Stump Wiedman

FINALE: 6/8/1891 at Brooklyn; replaced Jimmy McAleer in LF and went 0-for-1 in a 7–6 loss to Brooklyn's Tom Lovett

Short but with powerful legs, Ed Seward threw hard and had a knee-buckling curve. In 1883, although just 16, he was already making his living pitching for independent Terre Haute, IN. Two years later he traveled from London, Ontario, where he had played that summer in a Canadian league, to make his ML debut for the about-to-disband Providence Grays against Detroit. Seward then spent 1886 with at least three different eastern minor league teams before being acquired by Philadelphia AA. In 1887, his official rookie season, he combined with Gus Weyhing to give the A's the most remarkable rookie tandem in ML history when the pair collected 51 of the team's 64 victories.

Envisioning an AA pennant, A's manager Billy Sharsig rode his star duo hard in 1888 and was rewarded with 63 of his club's 81 wins, 35 by Seward alone. The Cleveland-born righty had his feet put mercilessly to the fire by Sharsig in mid-September when the A's pennant chances were about to extinguish. Following a rainout on September 11, Seward pitched 4 complete games in the next 4 days and 7 in the next 9. The results were predictably tragic. In 1889 he slipped from 35 wins to 21 and also hurled nearly two-hundred fewer innings. As if sniffing a badly overworked arm, PL raiders left Seward alone that winter while making Weyhing a top priority. When the 22-year-old Clevelander came to the A's training camp the following spring barely able to brush his teeth, Sharsig threw him in the A's second game of the season and then laid him off without pay while he "got into shape" after staggering to a 12–9 win over Rochester. It was exactly a month before Seward was healthy enough to make his next start on May 18 and then exactly another month before he could take the box again. After that he pitched more often but even less effectively. When Seward left the team in September after the A's announced that he had been laid off without pay because his arm had gone bad, he ranked among the ten worst qualifiers in the 1890 AA in hits and base runners allowed per nine innings.

By June 1891 the little pitcher had played his last ML innings—as an outfielder no less—after coming to the Cleveland NL training camp that spring in the hope of finding a new niche in the game. Hard pressed to believe a career-.170 hitter could suddenly blossom into a competent batter, Spiders manager Bob Leadley persisted in pitching Seward until his arm went completely dead after a 7–0 loss at New York on June 2. By July 1891 the 24-year-old who had once won 81 games over a three-year span was playing the outfield for Meadville, an unofficial Cleveland farm team in the New York–Pennsylvania League. Still unable to hit enough, Seward tried to master "the double hand delivery" (learning to pitch with his other arm). When that experiment failed he signed for 1892 as a 5'7" first baseman for Menominee in the Wisconsin-Michigan League, found the position beyond him, and tried the pasture again only to learn that now his "arm was too weak for an outfielder."

That winter Seward applied for a job as an umpire in the NL, having worked 2 games as a sub the previous year. He gave up the post in mid-July 1893 and resumed treatment for his arm at a Baltimore hospital. Over the next few years he tried every conceivable type of ointment, patent medicine, and quack remedy, all with predictably dreary results. Rumored to be ready to go into the provision business in Louisville, Seward instead changed his mind just as he was about leaving his hometown and chose to stay at his job with the Cleveland fire department. In early November 1898, while fighting a blaze, he fell three stories down an elevator shaft "head foremost" and was saved from certain death only by his helmet. Complimented on his good luck, Seward probably replied . . . well, perhaps we shouldn't speculate. By the time he died at his Cleveland home of kidney cancer at 80, none of the local papers remembered him as having been the city's only native son to post a 35-win season in the majors. (DN/DB)

Seymour, James Bentley / "Cy"

B	T	HGT	WGT	G	IP	H	GS
L	L	6'0"	200	140	1035	950	124

CG	BB	SO	SH	W	L	PCT	ERA
105	656	589	13	61	56	.521	3.71

G	AB	H	R	2B	3B	HR
248	669	187	95	13	5	8

RBI	BB	SO	SB	BA	SA	OBP
66	20	<u>7</u>	13	.280	.350	.302

B. 12/9/1872 Albany, NY **D.** 9/20/1919

TEAMS: 96–00NYN 01–02BalAL 02–06CinN 06–10NYN 13BosN
DEBUT: 4/22/1896 at New York; relieved Jouett Meekin in the third inning in Meekin's 14–3 loss to Philadelphia's Jack Taylor
FINALE: 7/7/1913 at Philadelphia; pinch hit unsuccessfully for catcher Bert Whaling in the twentieth inning of a 3–2 loss to Philadelphia's Pete Alexander and Tom Seaton

Cy Seymour and Babe Ruth are the only two ML players to pitch more than 100 games and collect as many as 1,500 hits since 1893, when the pitcher's plate was planted 60'6" from the platter. They are also the only two since 1893 to lead a ML in both a positive major season batting and pitching department. In Ruth's case, it was readily apparent that the talent was there for him eventually to achieve both. With Seymour the only thing apparent early in his career was that while he had the capability to lead in strikeouts and win games, he was also a likely candidate to lead in almost every negative pitching department. In 1898 Seymour became the only hurler at the 60'6" distance to post as many as 25 wins despite leading his league in walks, wild pitches, and hit batsman.

Called "Cy," short for cyclone, Seymour loathed the nickname and preferred to be called either James or "Bent," an abridgement of his middle name. Because he was making a reported $1,000 a month pitching semipro ball in Plattsburgh, NY, more than he would have made in even a top minor league in the mid 1890s, he delayed starting his pro career until 1896 when he reported directly to the New York Giants. Seymour's very first ML appearance suggested that his control needed tweaking, and he was soon farmed to Springfield of the Eastern League, recalled in August, still seemed skittish, and was shipped to the Atlantic League New York Mets and then recalled again in September. The following season player-manager Bill Joyce, in his only full season at the Giants' helm, decided he could live with Seymour's wildness in return for his strikeouts and got an 18-14 performance that actually should have been 20-14. On May 3, Seymour lost a near certain win when the game was forfeited to New York in the fourth inning after Washington, down 9–0, began to stall, hoping the game would be called by rain. Exactly a month later Seymour beat Louisville in both ends of a DH, only to have the first game expunged because it had been transferred to New York from Louisville without the NL's consent.

In 1898 Seymour seemed ready to emerge as one of the NL's premier hurlers when his devastating "indrop" (an early version of a screwball) enabled him to top the loop in strikeouts and share with Pittsburgh's Jesse Tannehill the distinction of being the last southpaw in the nineteenth century to win as many as 25 games. His new status as the team's ace brought him the honor of pitching the Giants' first Sunday home game, when the club played Washington in Weehawken, NJ, on September 11 at the grounds of the West New York Field Club. Batting second in the order, Seymour beat the Senators' Frank Killen 8–2 and scattered just three hits. But the following year he tumbled to 14 wins when his walks outnumbered his strikeouts. For the first time serious thought was given to making him an outfielder after he hit .327 and his indrop began taking a heavy toll on his arm.

Meanwhile one of Seymour's still-infrequent games in the outfield fanned the argument that, in fairness to spectators, all last-minute substitutions should be posted on the team blackboard prior to a game when he played RF in place of Mike Tiernan at St. Louis on July 25 and "not more than one in fifty of the 12,000 spectators recognized the pitcher" since both he and Tiernan were left-handers and built alike. The 1900 season was even more frustrating for Seymour. In the spring his experiment in learning to switch hit fizzled and he developed a sore arm. Clashes with manager Buck Ewing were followed by even worse run-ins with SS George Davis after Davis took over the club's helm. In addition to being farmed as punishment to Worcester, MA (which refused to take him), Seymour was suspended at least twice during the season without pay, and a local paper chortled that "each time he has returned as meek as Moses." When the curtain dropped on the last season in the nineteenth century he had pitched just 53 innings with a 6.96 ERA and collected a mere 40 ABs and no extra base hits. His future in the game seemed in serious peril. (DN)

Shaffer, John W. / "John" "Grocer Boy" "Cannon Ball"

B	T	HGT	WGT	G	IP	H	GS
?	R	5'10"	?	21	181	188	21

CG	BB	SO	SH	W	L	PCT	ERA
21	82	58	1	7	14	.333	4.57

B. 2/18/1864 Lock Haven, PA **D.** 11/21/1926
TEAMS: 86–87NYA
DEBUT: 9/13/1886 at New York; caught by Jim Donahue and beat St. Louis's Nat Hudson 6–3
FINALE: 6/30/1887 at New York; caught by Andy Sommers in a 15–4 loss to Baltimore's Matt Kilroy

A product of his local Lock Haven semipro team, John Shaffer arrived in Atlanta, GA, late in the 1885 season. He remained with the pennant-winning Southern League city in 1886, going 24-11, and then headed home after its season ended. En route to Lock Haven his train was either intercepted or else he was cabled to go to New York instead, where the AA Mets eagerly awaited him. Shaffer was an immediate sensation, topping the 1886 AA champion St. Louis Browns in his first two starts and finishing 5-3 for the seventh-place Mets with a 1.96 ERA and a stunning .164 OBA.

That winter the Mets offered Shaffer $2,000 for 1887, but he threatened to keep his $8-a-day job in a Lock Haven grocery store unless he got $3,000. When it later emerged that he was really working for only $8 a week "mixing sand and sugar," he was nicknamed "Grocer Boy." By that time he was being called other things too, but no longer "Cannon Ball." It will probably never be determined whether Shaffer hurt his arm in the spring of 1887, was undone by the harsh pitching rule changes that were imposed that season, or simply did not work hard enough to get into playing shape during the training period. In any event, he began 1887 by losing his first eight starts, all by a margin of 4 runs or more. He then won his next two appearances before losing twice to Louisville. On the final day of June, Shaffer returned after a "long rest," was blasted by Baltimore, and was sent home with a 2-11 log and 6.19 ERA.

After his frantic pleas over the winter that his arm was sound again, Shaffer played in the Southern League in 1888 and was 11-6 with a .328 BA before the loop folded. He then signed with Omaha of the Western Association, but the local press drummed for his immediate release: "Pitcher Shaffer . . . is no good and should not lay claim to being good." A few weeks later some of the same writers were claiming he was one of the top pitchers in the league. Shaffer pitched steadily in the minors until 1889 and then worked at the Demorest Sewing Machine Company in Williamsport, PA. He later moved to Endicott, NY, where he died in 1926 after being in poor health for some years. (DN)

Shallix, August (b. Shallick) **/ "Gus"**

B	T	HGT	WGT	G	IP	H	GS
R	R	5'11"	165	36	291	258	35

CG	BB	SO	SH	W	L	PCT	ERA
30	86	93	0	17	14	.548	3.56

B. 3/29/1858 Paderborn, Westphalia, Germany
D. 10/28/1937
TEAMS: 84–85CinA
DEBUT: 6/22/1884 at Cincinnati; caught by George Miller and beat Pittsburgh's Jack Neagle 4–3
FINALE: 6/2/1885 at Philadelphia; relieved by Pop Corkhill in the second inning after being struck on his pitching elbow by a Bobby Mathews pitch and was credited with the 12–8 loss that by today's rules would be attributed to Corkhill

Gus Shallix was one of the most dangerous pitchers in baseball, a man who put nearly half as many batters on base by hitting them as he did through walks, averaging more than one HBP per nine innings in 1884 and still more the following season. Yet he was no cold-eyed beanballer; blessed with tremendous speed and a wicked inshoot, he simply lacked even the rudimentary ability to control his pitches. In later years Shallix was sometimes identified as the pitcher who inspired the HBP rule—mistakenly, for he was still playing semipro ball when the rule went into effect prior to the 1884 AA season—but the faulty ascription suggests the vivid impression made on contemporaries by a pitcher whose career profile otherwise looks unremarkable.

The German-born Shallix grew up in Cincinnati and by the early 1880s was a well-known local amateur, making forays to New Orleans and Wilmington but in each case quickly returning home with his reputation for chronic wildness ever growing. When Cincinnati AA organized a reserve team in 1884, Shallix was its regular pitcher. The reserves proved a costly luxury and were disbanded early in

June, but Shallix was retained to play for the Reds. He became the third pitcher on the staff, used largely against weak teams. Shallix beat Pittsburgh in his June 22 debut but then, on July 2, showed his full capabilities, both positively and negatively. In a one-hit win over Washington he allowed no base runners after the third inning but also beaned Ed Yewell in the first frame, putting him out of the game and leaving him still afflicted with "flighty spells" months later. Even more frightening was a game on August 26 in which Shallix knocked Indianapolis's Bill Watkins unconscious with an in-shoot in the first inning and then hit Watkins's 3B replacement, Jim Donnelly, in the ribs later in the game. Watkins regained consciousness to find his hair turned gray (perhaps a slight exaggeration but only that) and subsequently spent two weeks in bed and lost sixteen pounds. While he recovered to play again, he was gun-shy at the plate and soon quit to manage.

Shallix went a respectable 11-10, and 1885 brought hope that a year's experience would make him an improved pitcher. From the start of pre-season exhibitions his arm bothered him, however. Switching intermittently between his usual "cannonball style" and a repertoire of off-speed pitches, he was fairly effective but could not consistently complete his starts. In early May he seemed to have righted himself. Reverting to speed, he beat Brooklyn 8–3 on May 8 and then came back the next day to relieve the injured Will White in the fifth inning, limiting Brooklyn to 1 hit. When he returned on May 12, however, he walked 2 batters after a lead-off double and then wild-pitched the run home and wound up being touched up for 13 hits and 7 walks. The following day, with Billy Mountjoy's arm sore and White still incapacitated, captain Charlie Snyder put Shallix in to pitch again. He did well for six innings throwing junk and then faltered but struggled to a 14-10 win. On May 17 Shallix was back in the box, but his arm soon tired and he changed places with right fielder Pop Corkhill.

Even by the rugged standards of the day Snyder had worked a sore-armed pitcher very hard, yet he had his reasons. In the 1880s arm trouble could act as a sort of communicable disease on a roster, since the incapacity of one pitcher threw a heavy load on the rest of his team's small staff. His hand injury aside, erstwhile iron man White was aging and could not carry the workload he once had, while Mountjoy was afflicted with arm problems as bad as Shallix's. With a staff consisting of two sore-armed pitchers and an aging one, Snyder occasionally used catchers Kid Baldwin and Jimmy Peoples in the box, but this was a tactic he could not employ often if he was to have a contending team. As a result, he was constantly tempted to overwork all his pitchers or push one of them hard in order to rest the others. How much the careers of Mountjoy, Shallix, and many contemporaries suffered in this way we cannot know with certainty, but undoubtedly the damage was substantial.

Shallix pitched rarely and ineffectively over the next few weeks. After a final injury-plagued appearance on June 2, he remained on the payroll for a month before receiving his release. His 1885 statistics are generally acceptable, but he completed only seven of twelve starts, making him and his .194 career OPS practically useless at a time when substitutions were allowed only in the event of injury and a pitcher in need of relief normally had to exchange places with an outfielder.

He signed with Nashville of the Southern League but was soon back home. A few years later Shallix tried a comeback with Leadville, CO, but realized he could no longer compete in pro ball and returned to Cincinnati, where he worked as a molder in a foundry and then as a policeman, continuing to play for a time on local teams.

Genial and something of a storyteller, during his years in baseball retirement Shallix was an occasional source of copy for newspaper reporters. He prided himself on his ability to spot talent and liked to tell how he had discovered stars such as Matt Kilroy and future HOFer Sam Thompson. Shallix died of a heart attack in 1937 in Cincinnati. (DB/DN)

Sharrott, John Henry / "Jack"

B	T	HGT	WGT	G	IP	H	GS
R	R	5'9"	165	48	311.1	264	32

CG	BB	SO	SH	W	L	PCT	ERA
26	157	137	0	20	17	.541	3.12

G	AB	H	R	2B	3B	HR
96	299	71	47	9	5	2

RBI	BB	SO	SB	BA	SA	OBP
43	9	31	15	.237	.321	.260

B. 8/13/1869 Staten Island, NY **D.** 12/31/1927
TEAMS: 90–92NYN 93PhiN

DEBUT: 4/22/1890 at New York; relieved Jesse Burkett in Burkett's 7–3 loss to Philadelphia's Kid Gleason

FINALE: 9/30/1893 at Cleveland; played LF and went 1-for-4 in a 10–2 win over Cleveland's Cy Young

A cousin of ML pitcher George Sharrott, in 1890 Jack Sharrott came to the Giants with no previous experience and was their most pleasant rookie surprise, going 11-10 with a 2.89 ERA. The following spring, when Buck Ewing returned to the team from the Players League, he singled out Sharrott as the best young pitcher in the NL, praising him for being very heady and especially good at holding runners. *TSN* echoed, "Little Sharrott . . . watches the bases like a lynx," and umpire Jack McQuaid lauded his "drop curve."

At the beginning of the 1891 season Sharrott joined HOFers Amos Rusie, Tim Keefe, and Mickey Welch in the Giants' rotation. On June 11 he beat Pittsburgh 10–2 to vault the Giants into first place but dislocated his shoulder in the fifth inning sliding into a base, and Rusie had to finish the game. The injury shelved Sharrott for the season and still bothered him that fall to the extent that he tried to learn to throw left-handed. In 1892 Sharrott was able to pitch only two innings and was released at the end of June and then reacquired by the Giants when it seemed he might be on the mend. The following March, New York traded Sharrott and Jack Boyle to the Phillies for Roger Connor. Harry Wright tried to make Sharrott into an outfielder when it became apparent that his arm would never be sound again. Though he led the loop in pinch hits, he hit just .250 in 1893. The following April the Phillies released him near the end of spring training and he then embarked on a long tenure as an outfielder in Eastern minor leagues, finishing his active playing career in the 1906 New York State League. Sharrott later worked as an elevator operator and died of a stroke in Los Angeles at 58. (DN)

Shaw, Frederick Lander / "Dupee" "The Wizard"

B	T	HGT	WGT	G	IP	H	GS
L	L	5'8"	165	211	1762	1710	207

CG	BB	SO	SH	W	L	PCT	ERA
196	396	950	13	83	121	.407	3.10

B. 5/31/1859 Charlestown, MA **D.** 6/11/1938

TEAMS: 83–84DetN 84BosU 85ProN 86–88WasN

DEBUT: 6/18/1883 at Providence; played RF and went 0-for-4 in a 7–3 loss to Charley Radbourn in relief of Charlie Sweeney

FINALE: 7/17/1888 at Indianapolis; caught by Tug Arundel and lost 11–5 to Indianapolis's John Healy

Dupee Shaw pitched for four ML clubs between 1883–88 and achieved a winning record only in the weak UA. Those numbers suggest a pitcher unable to retire ML batters on a regular basis, but nothing could be farther from the truth. Instead, Shaw's career resembled those of many pitchers whose careers overlapped with the advent of legal overhand pitching: He could be all but unhittable when paired with a catcher who could handle his offerings but at the batter's mercy when he lacked one.

Shaw was discovered by catcher Lew Brown while playing for a Boston amateur club. On Brown's recommendation, independent Lynn, MA, signed him for 1883 but had no catchers who could stand up to his deliveries, rendering him so ineffective that he was moved to the outfield. Despite the setback, Shaw's work came to the attention of Detroit, which acquired him in June and gave him another chance to pitch. Paired with standout catcher Charley Bennett, Shaw proved very effective, posting a 2.50 ERA although he won only 10 of 25 decisions.

At a time when pitchers delivered the ball with little preliminary motion, Shaw used an elaborate windup that "caused much merriment and good-natured joshing wherever he appeared." According to one writer, "Shaw's preliminary motions are enough to give a timid batsman the delirium tremens." Jack Gleason, who faced him in 1884, complained, "He . . . watches first so closely that you can't get a yard away. Then when he pitches the ball, it comes in like a blue streak. . . . I've faced all of them and Shaw, I think, is the swiftest and trickiest of the lot."

All this frantic activity allowed Shaw to unleash an overpowering fastball and a devastating array of curves, earning him the nickname of "The Wizard." But his offerings were as difficult to catch as they were to hit, and that became a huge issue in 1884 when Detroit manager Jack Chapman tried to pair the young southpaw with rookie one-gamer Walter Walker. The acid test proved a disaster for both men. Meanwhile Bennett had an injury-plagued season, and Detroit brought in a string of would-be catchers who proved no better at handling Shaw. Forced to ease up, he began to be hit hard and became increasingly frustrated. Matters came to a head when he committed a throwing error that cost Detroit yet another game, and Chapman fined him $30 out of his yearly salary of $1,500. Shaw caught a train back to Massachusetts that evening and refused to return unless the fine was remitted.

When Detroit stonewalled him, Shaw jumped to Boston UA when he was offered $350 a month for the rest of the season and was reunited with Lew Brown. The erratic Brown had in fact been under suspension, but the club lifted it to allow him to handle his onetime protégé. Over the remainder of the season, when given the chance to work with Brown, Shaw was brilliant. He struck out 309 batters in little more than two months and, despite the lively ball used by the UA, often was all but unhittable. In one game he struck out 18 and allowed only a single hit, but still lost 1–0. When he struck out 16 in his next outing two days later, it gave him a ML record 48 whiffs in 3 consecutive games. On the final day of action in UA history, October 19, he dealt pennant-winning St. Louis its lone shutout that year, 5–0 in front of 12,000 St. Louis faithful.

Brown remained unreliable, however, which again demonstrated how dependent Shaw was on a competent receiver. When Brown did not show up for a game on August 16, rookie Ed Crane was forced to fill in. In the second inning one of Shaw's offerings "nearly tore Crane's forefinger out by the roots." A man named Murphy (first name unknown) replaced Crane, but it was taken for granted that Murphy would not be able to handle Shaw's deliveries, so Shaw switched places with the team's right fielder that day, James Burke.

The UA folded after one year and Shaw returned to the NL, but the "Wizard" had lost some of his magic. His problems began when stricter delivery restrictions were enacted for the 1885 campaign. In June the revised rules were abruptly discontinued, but new obstacles presented themselves. According to John M. Ward, Shaw often tipped his pitches during his elaborate windup. Finding a catcher who could handle his deliveries continued to be a problem, and, perhaps most important, he developed a sore wing. An even bigger crisis for Shaw emerged after the 1885 season when Providence folded and he was stuck on the newly formed Washington NL team. In 1886 he went 13-31 while the rest of the staff, minus late-season rookie sensation Frank Gilmore, was an appalling 8-57. On October 9, in a season-ending series that amounted to a battle for last place in the NL, Shaw was scheduled to pitch with Barney Gilligan catching, but when big money began to be bet on the Missouri club despite its being a decided underdog, bookmakers grew suspicious and phoned Washington manager John Gaffney not to use his scheduled battery, and he chose Gilmore and Connie Mack instead. When Washington won 3–0, it further aroused suspicion about a game some weeks earlier in Kansas City when Shaw had been beaten by the weak Cowboys and seemed surprisingly ineffective.

Despite this litany of issues, Shaw soldiered on and sometimes showed flashes of his old brilliance. But then in 1887 the NL instituted a new barrage of delivery restrictions that marked the end of him as a formidable pitcher. He was released at midseason and returned to the minor leagues, where he briefly regained his old effectiveness. Shaw got one more chance with Washington the following year but had little left and was cut after 3 games. He pitched sporadically in the minors for several more years and then returned to Charlestown, where he operated a billiard hall and hotel and participated frequently in Boston AL old timers events after the turn of the century despite carrying in the neighborhood of 200 pounds now on his 5'8" frame. Shaw died in 1938 in Everett, MA. The source of his primary nickname—"Dupee"—is unknown. (PM/DN)

Shreve, Leven Lawrence / "Lev"

B	T	HGT	WGT	G	IP	H	GS
R	R	5'11"	150	57	473.1	551	57

CG	BB	SO	SH	W	L	PCT	ERA
53	189	141	3	19	37	.339	4.89

B. 1/14/1867 Louisville, KY **D.** 10/18/1942
TEAMS: 87BalA 87–89IndN
DEBUT: 5/2/1887 at Baltimore; caught by Law Daniels and beat New York's Ed Cushman 15–9
FINALE: 9/27/1889 at Indianapolis; caught by Andy Sommers and was relieved by Jack Fee in his 15–8 loss to Boston's John Clarkson

A member of one of one of Louisville's leading families, Lev Shreve could be devastatingly effective—witness his one-hit 9–0 shutout of Louisville in an exhibition game on April 8, 1889. Dick Buckley, a catcher known for his skill in working with young pitchers, later recalled that Shreve had an unsettling slow drop ball that "went part way and then stopped," tying the hitters in knots when he was on his game. Tall by the standards of the day but slender, he suffered from a lack of stamina. Whether physical development and experience might have turned him into an effective major league pitcher can never be known, for like so many hurlers of his day, about half a dozen years of heavy work were all he could withstand before his arm gave out.

Shreve began his pro career in the tough Southern and Northwestern leagues at age 19. In his first pro season he lived the typical nomadic life of a minor leaguer, playing for five different teams, until Baltimore signed him in the fall of 1886. Shreve pitched a few good games for the Orioles the next season, winning three of four starts, but was pushed aside by the comparatively experienced Phenomenal Smith and Matt Kilroy. In early August manager Billy Barnie began trying to find a buyer for Shreve, and in short order the young Louisvillian was waived out of the AA and acquired by last-place Indianapolis NL. The Hoosiers were also stockpiling young arms, but unlike the Orioles, they had few talented ones. Shreve was able to crack the regular rotation, going 5-9 down the stretch for a weak team. In 1888 he continued to pitch regularly, leading the Hoosiers in innings but was the least effective of the club's four main starters and lost 24 of 35 decisions.

Shreve was stigmatized as "a vain young man and what you would call a matinee favorite," although these sentiments may reflect prejudice due to his wealthy family background. Moreover, he was considered an effective pitcher for only six or seven innings, a serious drawback in a day when players could not leave a game unless they were injured. He saw the handwriting on the wall in 1888, although he may not have recognized it, when he watched an amateur game featuring Amos Rusie, an Indianapolis neophyte gifted with blinding speed. Shreve could hardly have overlooked Rusie's talent, but he may not have expected that by the spring of 1889 Rusie would be wearing an Indianapolis uniform. The club had also acquired two well-known NL veteran pitchers, and after new manager Frank Bancroft complained that Shreve lasted about seven innings and then "he goes all to pieces and breathes as though his lungs are all gone," Shreve was released in May to Detroit, by then a minor league team, and went 18-9 with a 2.07 ERA for the International Association champion. "From the moment of his engagement dates the team's upward march to the pennant," a Detroit writer crowed. However, Shreve suffered a hand injury late in the season, and with first place assured he was released. The arrangement seems to have been mutually satisfactory. Shreve returned to Indianapolis, where he got one more start but lasted only two innings.

The hand injury may actually have been the beginning of arm problems. Early in Shreve's career, according to a later account, he liked to show off his arm in preseason exhibition games. Later on, "it took a derrick to hoist him out of the dressing-room for practice." In the spring of 1890 he took a late winter trip to Hot Springs, AR, returned saying his arm was healthy, and then signed with Minneapolis after much coquetting, only to be released in late July. He played for Rochester of the Eastern Association for two months in 1891 but no more after that. As late as 1897 he was said to be claiming his arm was as healthy as it had been seven or eight years before and wanted to get back into the game. Shreve may have moved to Detroit by then, because he wanted to sign with that club. He worked as an executive for the Ford Motor Company until his retirement in the late 1920s and died at his Detroit home in 1942. (DB/DN)

Smith, John Francis (b. Gammon) **/ "Phenomenal"**

B	T	HGT	WGT	G	IP	H	GS
L	L	5'6½"	161	140	1169.1	1177	129

CG	BB	SO	SH	W	L	PCT	ERA
123	479	519	2	54	74	.422	3.89

G	AB	H	R	2B	3B	HR
148	472	118	80	16	10	2

RBI	BB	SO	SB	BA	SA	OBP
47	54	13	17	.250	.339	.332

B. 12/12/1864 Philadelphia, PA **D.** 4/3/1952
TEAMS: 84PhiA 84PitA 85BroA 85PhiA 86DetN 87–88BalA 88–89PhiA 90PhiN 90PitN 91PhiN
DEBUT: 8/14/1884 at Philadelphia; caught by Jack O'Brien and lost 6–5 to New York's Jack Lynch

FINALE: 6/15/1891 at Philadelphia; caught by Jack Clements, was relieved by Kid Gleason and lost 10–8 to Cleveland's Henry Gruber

Known in 1884 as The Manayunk Wonder, John Smith pitched briefly that year in the AA and then had meteoric success again with independent Allentown early in 1885. Beckoned to Brooklyn for a trial, he arrived so full of himself that his Brooklyn teammates decided to teach him a lesson and committed 14 errors behind him, most of them intentional, in his 18–5 loss to St. Louis on June 17, 1885. Afterward Brooklyn owner Charlie Byrne said, "It's an outrage the way my men treat this new player, and I will take steps to punish them for it." He then fined several Grays but released Smith to restore team harmony.

Two weeks later another trial with the Philadelphia Athletics ended even more abortively. On July 1 in New York, Smith pitched effectively until the fifth inning when umpire Nat Hicks gave two batters their bases on balls. Smith then stalked off the field, complaining that Hicks was squeezing him on pitches and that catcher Jack O'Brien was not supporting him properly. Ed Knouff finished the game, and the Athletics released Smith.

Was he so headstrong and immature that he simply could not be handled? Was he an insecure young man rendered excessively sensitive by harsh treatment at the hands of intolerant veteran players and umpires? All we can say with certainty is that any problems with Smith's head did not affect his strong left arm. Upon leaving Philadelphia he went to Newark of the Eastern League, where he was an immediate phenom, explaining his more familiar nickname. On August 29, 1885, he beat his last previous team, Philadelphia AA, 6–0 and allowed just 1 hit. Twelve days later he blanked Pittsburgh AA 4–0 on just 3 hits. By 1886 Smith was arguably the hottest property in minor league baseball, touted by some as the best left-handed pitcher in the game. Late that summer he stirred up another hornet's nest, however, when he signed to play for New York NL in 1887 and then changed his mind and decided to go to Detroit instead, claiming the Giants had gotten him drunk to get his name on a contract. On September 30 at the Polo Grounds, Smith was warming up for his Detroit debut when he was served an injunction forbidding him from pitching. Afterward the two clubs came to an agreement whereby the Giants, by now out of the NL race, would allow Smith to remain in Detroit for its stretch run, while Detroit would refrain from reserving him after the season. He did well for the Wolverines in three starts but could only break even in two decisions as Detroit fell 2½ games behind Chicago for the NL title.

After the season more fireworks in baseball or juridical law seemed on the horizon, but Smith cut the Gordian knot by signing with Baltimore AA instead. He was hardly a flop with the Orioles, yet as often happened with hotly disputed players he proved not to have been worth the immense trouble he had caused. Not only was he not the best left-hander in baseball, he was not even the best on the Orioles' staff, an honor that fell to Matt Kilroy, who won 46 games. Nevertheless, Smith had his career year, winning 25 games and sharing almost the entire Orioles pitching load with Kilroy; between them the pair started 127 of the club's 141 games.

Smith never again was nearly as effective. He won just 33 games over the next three seasons. His final win came with the Philadelphia Phillies in 1891 when he beat Chicago 4–3 in the morning game of a Memorial Day DH. Still just 27, Smith worked in a Philadelphia cotton mill that winter, ran an independent league in the Bristol, PA, area for a while, and then returned to the pro scene as a player, manager, and sometimes owner in the minors, finishing in 1904 with Manchester of the New England League. During his lengthy minor league second career he became primarily an outfielder, won several batting titles, managed Nap Lajoie at Pawtucket in 1896 while hitting .405 to Lajoie's loop-leading .429, and is also credited with having a part in discovering Christy Mathewson. Smith's last minor league batting crown came with Manchester in 1901 at age 37. During the off-season he played semipro basketball and later, when he coached the St. Anselm's college basketball team, some might have seen it as ironic that the once seemingly uncoachable pitcher had become a coach at a sport that had not even existed when he was in his baseball prime. In 1932 Smith retired from the Manchester police department after twenty-eight years of service. He died in Manchester in 1952, leaving five sons and seven daughters. We are still awaiting an explanation for when and why Smith dropped his original surname of Gammon. (DN/DB)

*Sowders, John / "John"

B	T	HGT	WGT	G	IP	H	GS
R	L	6'0"	150	65	497	573	60

CG	BB	SO	SH	W	L	PCT	ERA
48	271	195	1	25	32	.439	4.29

B. 12/10/1866 Louisville, KY **D.** 7/29/1939
TEAMS: 87IndN 89KCA 90BroP
DEBUT: 6/28/1887 at Indianapolis; relieved Hank Morrison and later switched places again in RF with Morrison, who took the 24–0 loss to Philadelphia's Charlie Ferguson
FINALE AND CAREER HIGHLIGHT: 10/4/1890 at Buffalo; caught by Con Daily and blanked Buffalo's Larry Twitchell 5–0

John Sowders's ML career went from the ridiculous to the sublime, as his debut was one of the most wretched introductory pitching exhibitions in ML history and his finale was among the very best of its kind. One of four ball-playing brothers, despite being a left-hander he specialized in catching unwary base runners with a right-handed pickoff move—an accepted strategy at a time when rules required the pitcher to face the batter and the modern stretch position was unknown.

Sowders and his brother, fellow MLer Bill, both started with an Indianapolis club sponsored by the When Department Store, owned by John T. Brush. John went pro with Sandusky of the Ohio State League early in 1887 but was released in May. In dire need of pitching, his hometown Indianapolis club signed him on June 23. Five days later Sowders made his ML debut under singular circumstances. Four Indianapolis players had engaged in a nightlong spree and others were injured, leaving the team shorthanded with players out of position. The result, a humiliating 24–0 loss to the Phillies in which the *Indianapolis Sentinel* said Sowders was "as nervous as a cricket," was the sum total of his ML experience in 1887. He returned to the majors early in 1889 when Kansas City AA purchased him and infielder Jack Pickett from St. Paul in a well-publicized, big money deal. Much was expected of the pair in KC, but Pickett suffered injuries and Sowders did not pitch well, losing 16 of 22 decisions.

In 1890 Sowders landed with Brooklyn of the outlaw Players League, a seemingly bizarre transition in that the PL had its pick of the top pitchers in the game, of which the 23-year-old lefty was hardly one. Yet Brooklyn pilot John M. Ward appeared to have an affinity for ex-Hoosiers and also to know his man, for Sowders was surprisingly effective in the toughest of the three major circuits in 1890, winning 19 games. In spite of his strong showing he never played again in the majors, in part because KC reclaimed him after the PL folded, and no ML team cared to war over his services. Consequently, in 1891 Sowders returned to the minors until finishing his pro career in the 1896 Interstate League. After leaving baseball he operated a fish and game market in Indianapolis and died at his home there in 1939. (DB/DN)

*Sowders, William Jefferson / "Bill" "Little Bill"

B	T	HGT	WGT	G	IP	H	GS
R	R	6'0"	155	71	517.2	542	61

CG	BB	SO	SH	W	L	PCT	ERA
55	149	205	2	29	30	.492	3.34

B. 11/29/1864 Louisville, KY **D.** 2/2/1951
TEAMS: 88–89NBosN 89–90PitN
DEBUT: 4/24/1888 at Boston; caught by Tom O'Rourke and beat Philadelphia's Charlie Buffinton
FINALE: 6/19/1890 at Pittsburgh; relieved George Ziegler in the sixth inning in a 7–1 loss to Cleveland's Ezra Lincoln

For a brief time Bill Sowders looked like a coming star. One of four ball-playing brothers who were born in Louisville and grew up in Indianapolis, he first began to find his way in pro ball in the 1886 Northwestern League after being released by Nashville of the Southern League. Just before Christmas in 1887 the free-spending Boston team acquired Sowders after a stormy negotiation with St. Paul. The Saints had originally agreed to terms and then refused to honor the deal and demanded more money. An angry Boston management paid the higher price but then publicly denounced St. Paul's tactics, and the whole affair blew up into a loud newspaper controversy, with St. Paul retaliating by claiming they had suckered Boston into paying the extravagant price of $7,500 for a pitcher who had a bad arm. In fact, the cost was probably about $3,800, still a considerable wad of cash for a minor league pitcher.

In his rookie season Sowders held his own with a strong pitching staff, but he pitched rarely and ineffectively the following season. His best pitch was a slow sinker, called a "drop," which one observer said "broke near the batter and passed over the plate at an elevation of about 6 inches." In 1889 he lost the ability to control his pet pitch—or perhaps NL hitters simply laid off it—and in mid-July was sold to Pittsburgh for a reported $1,000. Newspaper reports of sales prices are always questionable, but there can be no doubt that Boston lost heavily on its investment in Sowders. Reluctant to accept the deal to a weak club, Sowders eventually was persuaded to go where he could pitch regularly, but he fared poorly again. In 1890 he was one of very few Pittsburgh players not to jump to the new Players League and was traded to Milwaukee of the Western Association in late June for pitcher Charlie Heard. An obit claimed that "illness and an operation terminated his career" in 1890, which is not the case, but he may have had physical problems, for he could not compete successfully even back in the minors, quitting, for all intents and purposes, in 1892.

Everyone seems to have liked Sowders. Longtime minor league umpire Abner Moreland remembered many years later that his first assignment had been a 2–1 loss Sowders pitched for St. Paul. Probably as a joke, both managers had warned Moreland beforehand that Sowders was likely to be confrontational, so when he responded to a knock and found Sowders and two teammates at his door, Moreland braced for an argument or even a beating. But Sowders simply congratulated him on a fine game, telling him he had not missed a single ball or strike call all afternoon. In 1887 Sowders married Lulu Alexander of Indianapolis, and the Hoosier capitol remained his home after he retired from baseball. He operated a seafood business there in addition to coaching baseball at Wabash College, some 50 miles northwest of Indianapolis, and lived to be 86 years old. (DB/DN)

Sparks, Thomas Frank / "Tully"

B	T	HGT	WGT	G	IP	H	GS
R	R	5'10"	160	29	178	192	18

CG	BB	SO	SH	W	L	PCT	ERA
9	86	53	0	8	7	.533	4.15

B. 12/12/1874 Etna, GA **D.** 7/15/1937
TEAMS: 97PhiN 99PitN 01MilaAL 02NYN 02BosAL 03–10Phi
DEBUT: 6/15/1897 at Boston; caught by Jack Boyle and lost 9–1 to Boston's Jack Stivetts
FINALE: 6/8/1910 at Philadelphia; caught by Red Dooin and was relieved by Jim Moroney in his 7–3 loss to Chicago's King Cole.

A graduate of Beloit College in Georgia, Tully Sparks pitched in the Southern and Texas leagues before joining the Phillies toward the end of the 1897 season. Ineffective in his initial appearance, he was cut but returned to the majors with Pittsburgh in 1899 after going 23-10 with Richmond of the Atlantic League. Used as a combination starter-reliever, Sparks left the Pirates in mid-September as per his special contract, which stipulated that he could go home on September 15 to "attend to cotton interests" on his Southern plantation.

After the majors contracted to eight teams prior to the 1900 season, Sparks signed with Milwaukee of the newly renamed AL and went 16–12, guaranteeing him a spot in the Brewers' rotation when the AL went major in 1901. A lackluster 7–16 mark in his first full ML season sent him in search of a new home. Sparks had pitched for five teams in his first four ML seasons before returning to the Phillies, his original club, in 1903. He then improved with each passing year, peaking with 19 wins in 1906 and a 22–8 log in 1907. Sparks finished his ML career in 1910 with 107 wins and returned to his cotton interests. Restless, he added selling real estate to his portfolio and eventually dabbled in mining bauxite ore before finding a permanent niche in the insurance business. He died in Anniston, AL, of heart trouble at 72. The source of Sparks's nickname is unknown. (DN)

Sprague, Charles Wellington / "Charlie"

B	T	HGT	WGT	G	IP	H	GS
L	L	5'11"	150	24	161.2	162	17

CG	BB	SO	SH	W	L	PCT	ERA
13	101	76	0	10	7	.588	4.51

G	AB	H	R	2B	3B	HR
60	219	50	27	5	6	1

RBI	BB	SO	SB	BA	SA	OBP
20	17	2	11	.228	.320	.293

B. 10/10/1864 Cleveland, OH **D.** 12/31/1912
TEAMS: 87ChiN 89CleN 90TolA
DEBUT: 9/17/1887 at Chicago; caught by Tom Daly and hurled a 5–5 tie against New York's Mickey Welch

FINALE: 10/10/1890 at Louisville; caught by Harry Sage and lost 7–6 to Louisville's Red Ehret

An electrician by trade, Charlie Sprague was deemed "a Green Mountain boy" when he joined the Chicago NL club in 1887, but that was a media error, as he was from Cleveland and had been in Vermont only to play for a team in Rutland before joining Lynn of the New England League. After working a tie game in his ML debut, Sprague beat Washington 12–2 in his next start and showed enough promise that Chicago reserved him for 1888. But the following spring Chicago manager Cap Anson thought he needed "a little more meat on his bones." Sprague went to the Western Association Chicago Maroons and then trained with Cleveland NL in the spring of 1889. Manager Tom Loftus hoped for a hometown gate attraction but entrusted his young pitcher to make only two widely spaced starts—on April 26 and June 21—before releasing him to Toledo when he was unable to do as well as anticipated against teams top heavy with left-handed hitters. Sprague accompanied Toledo in 1890 when it moved up from the International Association to the AA as an interim replacement club. Before long he was appearing more often in the outfield than in the box after he began experiencing arm trouble. Despite his sporadic use, Sprague carried a 9-4 season log into his October 10 start against Louisville that turned out to be his last ML appearance, and he would have finished 10-4 if he had not worn down and lost a 6–2 lead. The following year, his arm shredded, Sprague converted to the outfield upon joining Denver of the Western Association but could not hit well enough to make his way back to the majors and was out of the pro game by the end of that season. He died in Des Moines on New Year's Eve in 1912 of a head injury. (DN)

Staley, Henry Eli / "Harry"

B	T	HGT	WGT	G	IP	H	GS
L	R	5'10"	175	283	2269	2468	257

CG	BB	SO	SH	W	L	PCT	ERA
231	601	746	10	136	119	.533	3.80

G	AB	H	R	2B	3B	HR
288	955	174	91	20	7	7

RBI	BB	SO	SB	BA	SA	OBP
109	65	160	7	.182	.240	.237

B. 11/3/1866 Jacksonville, IN **D.** 1/12/1910
TEAMS: 88–89PitN 90PitP 91PitN 91–94BosN 95StLN
DEBUT: 6/23/1888 at Chicago; caught by Fred Carroll and relieved Ed Morris in Morris's 12–1 loss to George Borchers
FINALE: 7/30/1895 at Louisville; caught by Doggie Miller and was relieved by Bill Kissinger in an 18–2 loss to Bert Inks and Tom McCreery
CAREER HIGHLIGHT: 6/1/1893 at Boston; caught by Bill Merritt, beat Cincinnati's Billy Rhines 15–4, and went 3-for-4 with 2 home runs and 7 RBI, tying the ML single-game record for the most RBI by a pitcher that lasted until Tony Cloninger broke it in 1966

Harry Staley was a fly-ball pitcher with excellent control and kept his games moving along at a brisk clip. A decent hitter for a pitcher, at his peak he approached stardom, and in 1890 he had arguably the finest season of any pitcher in the nineteenth century when he held opposing batsmen to a nineteenth-century record 3.55 BR/9 IP below the league average. Staley's achievement has remained buried until recently because it occurred in the Players League, a hitters' heaven in 1890.

A graduate of the Decatur, IL, semipro ranks, Staley pitched for the independent Springfield Reds in 1886 before returning to Decatur's new Illinois-Iowa League team in 1887. The following year he joined the Western Association St. Louis Whites, which were under the control of the AA St. Louis Browns. Although the Whites were a poor team and Staley's record with them was below .500, Browns owner Chris Von der Ahe sought $3,000 for him alone before selling him to Pittsburgh as a package with first baseman Jake Beckley for $4,500. Staley's rookie highlight came on July 28 when he beat Indianapolis 8–0 and allowed only 1 hit. But the following month he went into a losing skid when he kept getting rattled with men on base because catcher Doggie Miller was unable to prevent them from stealing. Staley's work improved when Jocko Fields was made his batterymate, and he finished 12-12.

In 1889, his first full ML season, despite leading the NL in losses Staley was Pittsburgh's most coveted pitcher by Players League raiders. He signed with the Smoke City PL entry and, though he again found himself on a second-division team and finished with just a 21-25 record, he produced some of the PL's best pitching performances of the year. After the PL collapsed, Staley returned for a time to Pittsburgh and then was allowed to sign with the Boston NL club for a reported $3,500 plus a bonus that Boston paid to the Pirates for releasing the rights to him after the Phillies, who had first claim on his services, declined because manager Harry Wright did not like his "habits." Wright's puritanical streak was Boston's gain when its new acquisition went 20-8 in Hub livery and curbed his drinking enough that pilot Frank Selee could look the other way. Staley repeated his success in 1892 with a 22-10 mark but then fell off somewhat in 1893 when the pitching distance increased. By 1894, even though he was still just 27, dissipation had taken its toll, as he plummeted to just 12 wins and a 6.81 ERA. At the close of the season Staley reportedly weighed well over two hundred pounds and was released, although he claimed he had signed with Boston for 1894 at salary lower than he wanted only after the reserve clause was removed from his contract, thus enabling him to sign for 1895 with St. Louis as a free agent.

The following spring ex-Boston teammate Jack Stivetts was overheard saying: "Western dispatches say that Harry Staley reported in St. Louis [at about forty pounds less than last year's weight]. . . . If the figures are correct Staley has either lost a leg or is in the clinch of consumption." Whatever Staley weighed, he had a bad year for a very bad team, hitting just .134 and winning only 6 of 19 decisions. Staley later umpired in the minors after pitching in them until 1899 and then failing abysmally to impress Baltimore AL manager John McGraw in his final comeback bid in the spring of 1901. He lived near Pittsburgh for a while in the early part of the twentieth century before moving to Battle Creek, MI, to work in a box factory. He was buried there after dying in the cereal capital in 1910 following stomach surgery. (DN)

Stearns, William E. / "Bill"

B	T	HGT	WGT	G	IP	H	GS
?	R	?	?	84	699.2	1167	79

CG	BB	SO	SH	W	L	PCT	ERA
73	45	23	0	13	64	.169	4.26

B. 3/20/1853 Washington, D.C. **D.** 12/30/1898
TEAMS: 71OlyNA 72NatNA 73WasNA 74HarNA 75WasNA

DEBUT: 6/26/1871 at Washington; caught by Doug Allison and beat Cleveland's Al Pratt 16–3
FINALE: 6/12/1875 at Philadelphia; played CF and went 1-for-3 in a 10–2 loss to the A's Dick McBride

Bill Stearns won his only two starts in 1871 but then went 11-64 for the rest of his career. In 1872 he lost all eleven of his box appearances to set a season futility mark for the most losses without a win that lasted until 1928 when the Phils' Russ Miller went 0-12. In 1873 Stearns broke his 11-game losing skein by winning his first two outings against a pitifully weak Maryland club but then embarked on a new streak, dropping 16 straight before winning again on August 8 over the Philadelphia Pearls.

The following year he abandoned the Hartford team a few days before the end of the season while owing money to his landlord and local merchants. When the judiciary committee expelled him from the NA for his delinquent behavior, the contract that he had previously signed with Chicago for 1875 was rescinded. Stearns was eventually reinstated, but in the interim Chicago had filled its roster, forcing him to sign with Washington's newest NA entry. His final win in seemingly the most undistinguished pitching career in ML history came on May 15, 1875, when he beat New Haven 8–4. But as ghastly as Stearns's career stats appear to be, we wonder what he might have done with a decent team behind him at some point in his career. For most of his five-year sojourn in NA, the restrictions on pitchers were such that the number of hits and runs a hurler allowed were far more indicative of the kind of fielding support he had than of his own pitching prowess.

A Civil War veteran and a member of the Grand Army of the Republic, Stearns at one point served in Company H of the Army Corps of Engineers in Puerto Rico and upon his death in 1898 was buried at Arlington National Cemetery. (DN)

Stecher, William Theodore / "Bill"

B	T	HGT	WGT	G	IP	H	GS
?	?	?	?	10	68	111	10

CG	BB	SO	SH	W	L	PCT	ERA
9	60	18	0	0	10	.000	10.32

B. 10/29/1869 Riverside, NJ **D.** 12/26/1926
TEAMS: 90PhiA

DEBUT: 9/6/1890 at Philadelphia; caught by John Riddle and lost 7–0 to Louisville's George Meakim
FINALE: 10/12/1890 at Gloucester, NJ; caught by Joe Daly and lost the A's season finale 12–2 to Syracuse's Ed Mars

Not only does Bill Stecher hold the nineteenth-century record for the most career losses without a win, but he leads all pitchers who made a minimum of ten career starts in almost every conceivable negative department, including BR/9 IP (22.63), ERA (10.32), and H/9 IP (14.69). Still, it must be noted that he had a wretched unit behind him in every start, not just your garden-variety bad team but one stocked with semipros and marginal minor leaguers (*see* Billy Sharsig).

Stecher came to the A's from the Harrisburg, PA, Eastern Interstate League team and was the sinking club's main starter in the last weeks of the 1890 season. The closest he came to earning an ML win was on September 26, when he lost 7–3 to St. Louis. Stecher later pitched in small unaffiliated Pennsylvania leagues and died in Riverside, NJ, in 1932. (DN/DB)

Stein, Edward F. / "Ed"

B	T	HGT	WGT	G	IP	H	GS
R	R	5'11"	170	215	1656	1689	183

CG	BB	SO	SH	W	L	PCT	ERA
158	732	535	12	109	78	.583	3.97

B. 9/5/1869 Detroit, MI **D.** 5/10/1928
TEAMS: 90–91ChiN 92–96BroN 98BroN
DEBUT: 7/24/1890 at Chicago; caught by Kit Kittridge and lost 8–4 to Brooklyn's Bob Caruthers
FINALE: 6/27/1898 at Chicago; caught by Jack Ryan and lost 9–4 to Walt Woods

Ed Stein had an unorthodox delivery that was "very wearing" on his arm and made him require more rest between starts than the average pitcher in the 1890s. Indicative of the toll his poor technique took on him, only 2 of his 109 career wins came after he celebrated his 26th birthday in 1895. After pitching for several minor league teams in his home state of Michigan, Stein joined Chicago in July 1890 and collected his first ML win on the 29th when he topped Philadelphia 8–6. He was off to a fine 12-6 start when his arm miseries started in September. Still plagued by an ailing arm the following spring, Stein did not make his first start in 1891 until the season was two weeks old and then had to wait two more weeks before he was able to pitch again. Convinced that his young pitcher's unsound mechanics were uncorrectable, Cap Anson engineered Stein's release in July 1891 to Omaha of the Western League.

Anson soon came to regret his haste when Stein signed with Brooklyn for 1892, won 27 games, and led the Bridegrooms in strikeouts and ERA. Predictions that he would have trouble at the new pitching distance the following season were quashed when he was second on the staff only to Roaring Bill Kennedy in every major pitching department. In 1894 Stein produced his career year with a 26-14 mark, but his arm was never entirely right again. Although he remained Brooklyn property for all or part of the next four seasons, he spent more time in recovery at Mount Clemens, MI, and in court battling with Brooklyn owner Charlie Byrne over how much of his salary he was entitled to receive while on the disabled list than he did in uniform.

Stein returned to Detroit after leaving the majors. He worked for a cigar maker and then held a variety of city jobs until he was elected sheriff of Wayne County, MI. His term in office was marred by a financial scandal. Stein died of pneumonia in a Detroit hospital at 58. (DN)

Stemmeyer, William / "Bill" "Cannon Ball"

B	T	HGT	WGT	G	IP	H	GS
R	R	6'2"	190	60	495	482	59

CG	BB	SO	SH	W	L	PCT	ERA
59	205	295	1	29	29	.500	3.67

B. 5/6/1865 Cleveland, OH **D.** 5/3/1945
TEAMS: 85–87BosN 88CleA
DEBUT: 10/3/1885 at Buffalo; caught by Eddie Tate and blanked Buffalo's Pete Conway 16–0
FINALE: 6/15/1888 at Cleveland; played 1B and went 1-for-4 in an 11–8 win over Philadelphia's Mike Mattimore

Called "Cannon Ball" and "the Cleveland Cyclone," Bill Stemmeyer was an earlier, more successful version of Steve Dalkowski. As a rookie in 1886 he led the NL with a record 63 wild pitches as well as strikeouts per nine innings and finished his ML career two years later having given up 205 walks in just 495 innings (when walks were still relatively infrequent). Stemmeyer made his pro debut in 1884 with Hamilton of the Ohio State League and the following spring joined Toledo. He lost Toledo's Western League opener at Cleveland 11–5, and then played in Canada with Toronto after the WL folded. When he pitched a superb exhibition game against Boston in September 1885, he was invited to cross the border to make a start for the Hub team against Buffalo. Boston third baseman Billy Nash later would say that with almost the first pitch Stemmeyer threw he established himself as the fastest pitcher Nash ever saw. The following spring it soon became clear that while Stemmeyer had a "terrific delivery," Boston had no catcher that could handle him on days when he was even slightly off target. In his first start of the 1886 season, on May 3 at Washington, he threw 5 wild pitches to go with his 11 strikeouts, and his battered catcher, Pat Dealy, allowed 10 passed balls, enabling Washington to stage a 5-run rally in the bottom of the ninth inning to win 12–11. But then, eight days later at Chicago, the rookie was so completely on target that he won 5–1 and allowed just 1 hit. By the end of May, Stemmeyer was paired mainly with Tom Gunning, the only catcher he ever found who could work compatibly with him. Praised constantly for his pluck, Gunning allowed only one passed ball on June 1 at Boston as Stemmeyer blanked St. Louis 4–0 and threw no wild pitches. Stemmeyer eventually logged 22 wins with Gunning's help.

The following April, however, Gunning, in disfavor with Boston owner Arthur Soden for his involvement with the players' Brotherhood movement, was sold to Philadelphia. Gunning's departure and the drastic new pitching restrictions spelled almost an immediate end to Stemmeyer's effectiveness. In his first 1887 start on April 30 he beat Washington 6–4, but five days later he was creamed 13–0 by the weak-hitting Philadelphia Quakers and after that the wheels began to come off. Stemmeyer's last good day in the box came on August 20 at Washington when he lost a DH to Jim Whitney, 3–1 and 4–3. Tom O'Rourke, who, like Gunning, seldom played unless Stemmeyer pitched and was jettisoned after the 1887 campaign, caught him in both games.

Stemmeyer may have encountered arm trouble toward the end of that season, or perhaps Boston player-manager John Morrill simply sensed that without O'Rourke he would have no catchers able to work with his cannonballer. But arm concerns seem the more likely explanation. Released in 1888 to his hometown team in the AA, "The Cleveland Cyclone" was no longer even a stiff breeze. In his two starts with Cleveland in the spring of 1888 he was blasted 14–3 and 28–7. Prior to his release team captain Jay Faatz pushed to have Stemmeyer used "on the O'Neill system," referring to Tip O'Neill, who became an outfielder after he could no longer pitch, claiming that he would make a fine hitter. But Cleveland skipper Jimmy Williams dismissed the suggestion after trying Stemmeyer in just one game at 1B.

Stemmeyer played with amateur teams in Cleveland for a time and tried unsuccessfully to make himself into a catcher. In the spring of 1888 *TSN* observed, "Pitcher Stemmeyer now acknowledges he is a back number." But baseball's loss was Cleveland gourmet diners' gain. By 1897 Stemmeyer owned a very prosperous buffet and restaurant on Lorain Avenue in the Forest City and was said by Cleveland team observer Charles Mears to be well on his way to becoming a very rich man. Stemmeyer died in Cleveland just three days shy of his 80th birthday. (DN/DB)

Stocksdale, Otis Hinkley / "Otis" "Old Gray Fox"

B	T	HGT	WGT	G	IP	H	GS
L	R	5'10½"	180	54	347	521	46

CG	BB	SO	SH	W	L	PCT	ERA
30	136	48	0	15	31	.326	6.20

G	AB	H	R	2B	3B	HR
68	203	63	33	5	5	0

RBI	BB	SO	SB	BA	SA	OBP
28	8	18	4	.310	.384	.340

B. 8/7/1871 Arcadia, MD **D.** 3/15/1933
TEAMS: 93–95WasN 95BosN 96BalN
DEBUT: 7/24/1893 at Washington; caught by Duke Farrell and beat Boston's Kid Nichols 17–15
FINALE: 5/2/1896 at Boston; relieved Bill Hoffer in the bottom of the ninth with Baltimore ahead 8–6, gave up the tying runs, and then took a 10–9 loss when Boston scored 2 unearned runs in the bottom of the tenth

Raised in Maryland, Otis Stocksdale attended Johns Hopkins in Baltimore before trying pro ball. He was successful in every facet of the game but least so as a pitcher (in the majors at least), the position where he served most of his career. It was a puzzle why he was not made an outfielder even as far back as 1893 when he made his pro debut with Wilkes-Barre of the Eastern League. Probably part of the reason why managers were patient with Stocksdale's early pitching endeavors was that almost every pitcher struggled in 1893, the first year the mound was set at its present distance, and the assumption was that the stocky Marylander simply needed time to relearn his craft. In any event, Stocksdale's ragged win over Boston in his ML debut was but a prelude to one of the worst seasons ever by a pitcher who made as many as ten starts. In 69 innings he was rapped for 111 hits and 82 runs, enough of them earned that he finished 1893 with a wretched 8.22 ERA.

Despite being blasted in every ML park, Stocksdale was retained and again seemingly pitched poorly in 1894, going 5-9 and collecting only 10 strikeouts against 42 walks in 117 innings. But his overall stats are only a part of the story. After starting the campaign 0-6, Stocksdale returned to the box on August 15 after a brief illness and reeled off 5 straight wins for the last-place Washingtons before reverting to form and dropping his last three starts. He then took a turn in the outfield and as the club's lead-off hitter, finishing the season there on September 30 in both ends of a DH. After he talked that winter of quitting the game, Stocksdale returned to Washington the following spring. Named the Opening Day starter, he responded with an 11–6 loss at Boston on April 19, and four months later, almost to the day, found himself back in Boston but in a Beaneaters uniform facing Louisville. In his Hub debut Stocksdale took the cellar dwellers' measure 15–2 but won only 1 more game in Boston garb. Picked up that winter by defending champion Baltimore, Stocksdale again made an Opening Day appearance in 1896 but this time only as an unsuccessful pinch hitter. Little more than two weeks later his ML coda came after a single unfortunate hill appearance with the Orioles. Poised to get a save after pinch-hitting for starter Bill Hoffer during a 3-run rally that put the Orioles ahead of Boston 8–6 in the top of the ninth, Stocksdale was tapped for the tying runs in the bottom half. In the tenth Baltimore scored a single run, but Stocksdale again could not hold the lead, although through no fault of his own. With the bases loaded and two out, he seemingly worked out of the jam when he induced Hugh Duffy to slap a potential game-ending grounder to SS Hughie Jennings. But instead it proved to be Stocksdale's last pitch in the majors when Jennings booted the ball and then threw wildly to 1B, allowing the tying and winning runs to score.

After leaving Baltimore, Stocksdale went 32-16 in the 1896 Virginia League and then pitched and managed in the minors until he was past 40, winning well over 150 games, and also coached the Trinity College team in Durham, NC. When he was approaching 50 he tried umpiring, joining the International League staff. But he lost the confidence of IL officials when he was forced to forfeit a game at Baltimore on August 12, 1921, after he was unable to persuade two ejected Toronto players to leave the field and the police ultimately had to remove them. Stocksdale finished his life working as a security guard in Arcadia, MD, where he was buried after succumbing to heart disease. (DN)

Stratton, Chilton Scott / "Scott"

B	T	HGT	WGT	G	IP	H	GS
L	R	6'0"	180	231	1892.1	2177	214

CG	BB	SO	SH	W	L	PCT	ERA
199	434	570	10	97	114	.460	3.86

G	AB	H	R	2B	3B	HR
391	1390	381	202	37	32	8

RBI	BB	SO	SB	BA	SA	OBP
163	109	93	56	.274	.364	.335

B. 10/2/1869 Campbellsburg, KY **D.** 3/8/1939
TEAMS: 88–90LouA 91PitN 91–94LouN 94ChiN 95ChiN
DEBUT AND RECORD ACHIEVEMENT: 4/21/1888 at St. Louis; on Opening Day was caught by Paul Cook and lost 11–7 to St. Louis's Silver King but at age 18 and 6 months became the youngest player ever to hit a home run in his first ML game
FINALE: 7/2/1896 at Chicago; caught by Bill Moran and was relieved by Bill Hutchison in his 15–9 loss to St. Louis's Red Ehret and Bill Kissinger
CAREER HIGHLIGHT: Tied the ML record for the most consecutive wins by a pitcher in his home park when he won 24 straight home victories for Louisville AA from 4/28/1890 through 8/3/1891
FAMOUS LAST: 5/22/1893 at Louisville; caught by Jack Grim in the first game played in Louisville's Eclipse Park II (aka Parkland Field) and beat Cincinnati's Elton Chamberlin 3–1 in what may

have been the last contest in ML history at the fifty-foot distance when the game was "played by mutual agreement with the pitcher under the old rules"

Playing for amateur Taylorville in 1887, Scott Stratton was dubbed the "Taylorville Wonder" and was Louisville's prize catch that off-season. The following spring he started the Colonels' opening game of the campaign. Three days later Stratton collected both his first career win and Louisville's first win of the season when he topped Kansas City. By July, Bob Ferguson was so impressed by the rookie that he averred, "If . . . Stratton had a good instructor and was not worried by the older players, I believe he would soon be the best twirler in the Association." After that monition from "The King of Umpires," teammate Jack Kerins took Stratton in tow and helped him learn the finer points of his craft, but the Colonels were so poor in 1888 that he had to wait until the last day of the season to reach double digits in wins. The following year Louisville assembled the worst team in AA history and Stratton had a 3-13 record that would likely have been worse if he had not torn a muscle in his arm in July and been relegated to playing either 1B or the outfield the rest of the season. Heightening his misery was an unceasing battle with team officials after he refused to play on Sundays when he taught a Sunday-school class in his hometown church.

In January 1890 Stratton ran off with Bessie Anderson, the underage daughter of a wealthy Taylorville farmer, and set out on a sixty-five-mile buggy ride on a bitter winter night to be married in Jeffersonville, KY. Although Bessie's parents did not embrace him until the following summer when she gave birth to a son, the entire city of Louisville went gaga over him in the summer of 1890 when he came out of nowhere to emerge as the top pitcher in a loop riddled by PL defections and spark Louisville from worst to first. His 34-win season may have gone to his 21-year-old head. The following February he allowed Guy Hecker to induce him to jump his Louisville contract and sign with Pittsburgh NL for $4,000. Already nicknamed "the Pirates" for pilfering second baseman Lou Bierbauer, the Smoke City management never received its added due for netting Stratton, especially after he came down with typhoid before reporting to Pittsburgh, pitched 2 losing games with the Pirates, and then suffered a typhoid relapse compounded by a severe case of homesickness and a sore pitching shoulder. By late June, Pittsburgh was only too glad to let Stratton squirm out of his contract.

Stratton never again even remotely approached his 1890 form, but he did have one good year left in him. In 1892 he went 21-19 for a Louisville team that finished 26 games under .500. After that he was not even an average ML pitcher—in his three remaining seasons he rolled up a 6.07 ERA—but he was a terror at times as a hitter. In 1894, split between the mound and other positions, he batted .361 with a .974 OPS. Early the next season he drew his release from Chicago and signed with St. Paul of the Western League as an outfielder. Stratton spent two years with St. Paul before manager Charlie Comiskey cut him because his arm was now so dead that he couldn't even lob the ball back to the infield. At that point he may have learned to throw left-handed—it was not uncommon then for dead-armed pitchers to return as opposite-armed position players. Stratton played four more seasons in the minors, in any case. To the end of his career he was a formidable hitter and remained one of the few pro players who refused to play on Sunday. Stratton ran a farm outside of Bloomfield, KY, until his death in 1939 from a heart attack. (DN)

Sudhoff, John William / "Willie" "Wee Willie"

B	T	HGT	WGT	G	IP	H	GS
R	R	5'7"	165	104	799.1	933	94

CG	BB	SO	SH	W	L	PCT	ERA
81	247	152	2	34	60	.362	4.32

B. 9/17/1874 St. Louis, MO **D.** 5/25/1917
TEAMS: 97–98StLN 99CleN 99–01StLN 02–05StLAL 06WasAL
DEBUT: 8/20/1897 at Brooklyn; relieved Red Donahue in the second inning of Donahue's 12–7 loss to Brooklyn's Jack Dunn
FINALE: 6/16/1906 Detroit; caught by Howard Wakefield and was relieved in the third inning by Charlie Smith, who got the 5–3 win over St. Louis's Ed Smith and Fred Glade

Willie Sudhoff was pitching for Paducah in 1897 when the Central Kentucky League collapsed. He went home to play for the St. Louis A.B.C. semi-pro nine until he was invited to accompany the NL Browns on an eastern road trip in August. Sudhoff ended his first ML season just 2-7 but seemed promising enough that manager Tim Hurst put him in the rotation in 1898. That year Jack Taylor and he won two-thirds of the Browns' games between them but were just 26-56 combined, as the rest of the staff went 13-55. In 1899 Sudhoff's experience typified syndicate ball at its worst. Initially he refused to play for St. Louis again and took less money to go to Cleveland, where he felt he would have more chance. Sudhoff started for Cleveland on Opening Day, but when Nig Cuppy failed to round into form, the syndicate owners yanked him back to St. Louis.

Sudhoff had another unpleasant season in 1900. Despite the best overall stats on the St. Louis staff, he appeared in just 126 innings and was farmed for part of the summer to an East St. Louis semipro team. Nevertheless Sudhoff wanted to stay in St. Louis the following year when he and his wife had a baby. Meanwhile the team played poorly behind him, and there was speculation that it was deliberate because he had carried tales about teammates to the front office, although he denied having done so. Offered a token $100 raise for 1902 by owner Frank Robison, he instead jumped to the new AL entry in St. Louis. Sudhoff won just 12 games his first season in the junior loop but collected a career-best 23 victories in 1903. When he fell to 10-20 two years later, he was dealt to Washington for Beany Jacobson, a trade that worked out poorly for both teams. Released by Washington in June 1906, Sudhoff pitched in the American Association until 1908 and then returned to St. Louis. He died of paralysis at a city sanitarium in 1917, purportedly from factors stemming from a train wreck he had been in while traveling with the Browns, but more likely it was syphilis. (DN)

Sullivan, Daniel James / "Jim"

B	T	HGT	WGT	G	IP	H	GS
R	R	5'10"	155	70	514	621	57

CG	BB	SO	SH	W	L	PCT	ERA
46	171	97	2	26	28	.481	4.50

B. 4/25/1869 Charlestown, MA **D.** 11/30/1901
TEAMS: 91BosN 91ColA 95–98BosN
DEBUT: 4/28/1891 at Philadelphia; relieved John Clarkson in the ninth inning and was later relieved by Kid Nichols who finished Clarkson's 11–6 win over Philadelphia's Kid Gleason
FINALE: 5/6/1898 at Boston; caught by Marty Bergen and was relieved by Vic Willis in his 7–5 loss to New York's Ed Doheny

Other reference works list the wrong debut date for Jim Sullivan, and until recently both his debut and final appearance dates were wrong. For years his games in 1898 were attributed to pitcher Mike Sullivan, even though the *Boston Globe* made it clear that the Sullivan who pitched for Boston on May 6, 1898, was Jim. The *Globe* once described Sullivan as "not a man that requires much training, being of slight built and with no superfluous flesh to reduce." His slender frame was not always a plus, though; the *Washington Post* noted that he lacked stamina throughout his career, relied almost wholly on guile, and could only pitch once a week, unheard of in the 1890s.

Sullivan was with the semipro Chammont Athletics of the New Brunswick League in 1891 until arriving in Boston after making "such a favorable showing against the [NL] Brooklyns on Fast Day" and remaining just long enough to make one catastrophic relief appearance in which he allowed seven enemy runners in just a third of an inning. Later that season Sullivan made a losing start for Columbus AA in a game at Boston and then apprenticed with Providence of the Eastern League for some two and a half seasons before returning to Boston to stay in 1895.

After going 11-9 in his official rookie season, Sullivan married Minnie McMahon of Charlestown, MA, in January 1896. Used more often that year, he fell to 11-12. Sullivan spent most of the following season sidelined with lung trouble. He returned to Boston in 1898 to make three poor appearances and then finished the season with Lanconia, NH, in a semipro league. Sullivan signed with Manchester of the New England League in 1899 but was too weak by then to keep the pace and spent less than a week in New Hampshire. He died of consumption at his home in Roxbury, MA, in 1901. (DN)

Sullivan, Michael Joseph / "Mike" "Big Mike"

B	T	HGT	WGT	G	IP	H	GS
L	R	6'1"	210	160	1111.1	1292	119

CG	BB	SO	SH	W	L	PCT	ERA
99	568	285	1	54	65	.454	5.04

B. 10/23/1866 Boston, MA **D.** 6/14/1906
TEAMS: 89WasN 90ChiN 91PhiA 91ColA 91NYN 92–93CinN 94WasN 94–95CleN 96–97NYN 99BosN
DEBUT: 6/17/1889 at Boston; relieved Alex Ferson, who was charged with the 11–5 loss to Boston's John Clarkson
FINALE: 8/18/1899 at Boston; caught by Boileryard Clarke and beat Louisville's Harry Wilhelm and Walt Woods 7–6

Mike Sullivan was fast for a big man, a fairly good hitter and probably would have done better as an outfielder. Tom Brown identified his problem as a lack of heart when he pitched. Sullivan lived in fear of hitting batters and conceded the plate to any like Bill Joyce who crowded it. But Sullivan had plenty of heart when it came to a brawl or a political battle. A devout Catholic who was appalled by the foul language and rowdyism (but not the drinking) that permeated the game, he was pitching for Worcester in the Atlantic Association in 1889 when Washington NL found him. After five relief appearances with the Senators, he made his first start on August 7, 1889, and gave up 14 runs to Cleveland in the third inning, a record high for that frame. Released a few months later with a 0-3 record and a 7.24 ERA, he was as shocked as anyone when Chicago signed him for 1890. But Sullivan lasted less than four months with the Colts and finished the year with John Morrill's semipro team in Boston. The following spring he went to camp with the AA Boston Reds but failed to make the club and pitched for three more ML teams before the season was out. It was a pattern Sullivan would follow for the rest of his career. In 1892, after starting the season in the minors, he joined Cincinnati in August and had his finest season in the majors, going 12-4 with a 3.08 ERA. Never again would he have an ML season in which he produced both a winning record and an ERA under 5.00.

In the spring of 1895 Sullivan announced that he would quit the game after that season to enter the bar since he was due to graduate from law school the following spring. He then gave a retirement speech: "It being my last season on the diamond, I will at least try and make the Omega a creditable one." But when Cleveland released him in May with an 8.42 ERA, he opted to exit on a more positive note. Sullivan then pitched two more seasons with the New York Giants before quitting. After devoting 1898 to his budding law practice, he agreed to make one last ML appearance with Boston in 1899 when scheduled starter Ted Lewis was unable to work the second game of a DH. The club had to round up a uniform that would fit Sullivan, but once he wriggled into it he staggered to a 7–6 win and then retired for good.

Two years later Sullivan was elected to the Massachusetts state senate. By 1906 he had been a member of the governor's council for three years and was regarded as a rising political star in the Democratic Party when he died suddenly of a brain hemorrhage five days after suffering a heart attack. Among pitchers in a minimum of 1,000 career innings, Sullivan holds the record for allowing the most enemy BR/9 IP (15.28) by a slight margin over Chief Hogsett. Both Sullivan (1890s) and Hogsett (1930s) were active in times that were the least friendly in history to pitchers. (DN)

Sullivan, Thomas / "Tom"

B	T	HGT	WGT	G	IP	H	GS
?	?	5'10"	165	47	408	474	47

CG	BB	SO	SH	W	L	PCT	ERA
46	152	147	0	14	33	.298	4.04

B. 3/1/1860 New York, NY **D.** 4/12/1947
TEAMS: 84ColA 86LouA 88–89KCA
DEBUT: 9/27/1884 at Brooklyn; caught by Rudy Kemmler and beat Brooklyn's Bill Terry 10–4
FINALE: 6/23/1889 at Cincinnati; caught by Joe Gunson and lost 15–7 to Cincinnati's Jesse Duryea

Tom Sullivan came to Columbus in September 1884 from Springfield of the Ohio State League. With the Senators all but out of the AA race, manager Gus Schmelz started the rookie four times in the final nineteen days of the season. Sullivan's finale with the club came on October 13 at Philadelphia when he won 3–2 to finish the season 2-2. When Columbus ceded its AA franchise, Sullivan, Al Bauer, and Dummy Dundon all signed with Atlanta of the novice Southern League under Schmelz in 1885. Years later the *Atlanta Constitution*, reminiscing about the city's first pro team, remembered him as "a slender, agile ever-smiling worker" who featured a change of pace and was a good fielder, but contemporary observers described a pitcher who had a "jump in the box" delivery and constantly was outside the box at time of release but got away with it because of his hard-to-follow style of pitching. Unfortunately none of Sullivan's appraisers were kind enough to recall with which arm he threw. Louisville, in any case, bought what fellow SL pitchers like Tom Ramsey had to say about Sullivan and hired him for the 1886 campaign. But after losing seven of his first nine starts with the Kentucky entry, he found himself on a train back to Atlanta, where he finished 14-8.

The following year Sullivan blossomed unexpectedly into arguably the best pitcher in the minors, winning a loop-leading 36 games for Western League champion Topeka. Still, all it earned him was a return to the Southern League in 1888 with Birmingham. Sullivan remained in the Alabama city until June, when he was released as part of a cost-cutting measure. Now a free agent, he signed with the Kansas City AA expansion club and was the team's best pitcher over the rest of the season despite leading the Association in both wild pitches and HBPs. But his final start of the year on October 14 typified his luck with the last-place Cowboys, as he lost 2–1 in thirteen innings. Expected to be Kansas City's ace in 1889, Sullivan was plagued by control problems and a sore arm, probably stemming from his unorthodox delivery. His attitude was also a problem. After a 14–2 loss at Philadelphia on June 8, he was threatened with release when he announced that he would not pitch winning ball until his salary was raised from the meager $1,800 he was receiving. Kansas City continued to keep him on the payroll, however, even after his bad arm permanently sidelined him in late June.

Released finally in August 1888, Sullivan returned to his home in Cincinnati, opened a saloon and made periodic comeback attempts before reconciling himself to the fact that his career was at an end. Using his popularity with the baseball public in Cincinnati to advantage, Sullivan started a successful local advertising agency. Some years after retiring he was struck by a car while crossing a street and died in Cincinnati's General Hospital at 87 of a fractured skull and internal injuries. (DN/DB)

Swaim, John Hillary / "Cy" "Hillary"

B	T	HGT	WGT	G	IP	H	GS
?	R	6'6"	180	42	285.1	338	32

CG	BB	SO	SH	W	L	PCT	ERA
23	87	82	0	12	22	.353	4.48

B. 3/11/1874 Cadwallader, OH **D.** 12/27/1945
TEAMS: 97–98WasN
DEBUT: 5/3/1897 at Washington; relieved Win Mercer in a rain-soaked game that was forfeited in the fourth inning when Washington, behind 9–0, began stalling in the hope umpire Tom Lynch would call the contest before it became official
FINALE: 7/21/1898 at Washington; caught by Deacon McGuire and lost 7–4 to Cincinnati's Ted Breitenstein

The gangly Hillary Swaim came from a baseball family and had twin brothers who formed a battery with Geneva College in 1897. He was almost certainly a right-hander, as per a note in the *Washington Post* prior to the 1897 season that the Senators would probably carry no southpaws that year. Called "Cy" because he was seen as a big, naïve, hard-throwing country boy on the order of Cy Young, Swaim went by his middle name of Hillary in the mid-1890s while working as a small-town Ohio schoolmaster.

Swaim first played for pay for Twin Cities, OH, of the Interstate League in 1895. After attending Scio College that winter, he signed with Cleveland but was farmed to Fort Wayne of the Interstate League. Wild, and so fast that no Fort Wayne catchers could hold him, he finished 1896 with New Castle of the same circuit. That fall Washington drafted him, but when the NL club sent a check to Nick Young to forward to New Castle, it was returned because New Castle inexplicably had released Swaim even though Washington had announced it would draft him. The gaffe cost the minor league club $200.

Swaim's ML debut was delayed by a severe case of grippe in the spring of 1897. Once under way, however, he joined the Senators' rotation and was reasonably effective even though runners stole him blind because of his long swing before releasing his pitches and a penchant for giving away his curves by exposing his fingers to batters. Swaim was also a poor fielder, exceptionally vulnerable to bunts because of his height. After beginning 1898 in the Washington rotation, he was released in July with a 3-11 mark. Swaim returned to Fort Wayne in 1899. Near the close of the season *TSN* said that he was the class of the Interstate League pitchers, but the problem was his looping delivery tied "his rangy shape into pretzels while in the act of fielding his position." In 1900 Swaim jumped Fort Wayne in

July when he was fined for poor play. Soon thereafter he threw his last pro pitch for Terre Haute of the Central League and then returned to the classroom. Swaim died in 1945 in Eustis, FL, where he had first gone in the fall of 1897 to take an off-season teaching job in a "cracker hamlet" on the banks of the Indian River. (DN)

Sweeney, Charles J. / "Charlie"

B	T	HGT	WGT	G	IP	H	GS
R	R	5'10½"	181	129	1030.2	928	123

CG	BB	SO	SH	W	L	PCT	ERA
113	172	505	8	64	52	.552	2.87

G	AB	H	R	2B	3B	HR
233	894	224	117	39	7	2

RBI	BB	SO	SB	BA	SA	OBP
84	59	71	11	.251	.317	.297

B. 4/13/1863 San Francisco, CA **D.** 4/4/1902
TEAMS: 82–84ProN 84StlU 85–86StLN 87CleA
DEBUT: 5/11/1882 at Boston; played RF and went 0-for-4 in a 5–1 loss to Boston's Bobby Mathews
FINALE: 7/9/1887 at Cleveland; played SS and went 1-for-4 in a 9–7 loss to Philadelphia's Gus Weyhing
CAREER HIGHLIGHT: 6/7/1884 at Boston; caught by Sandy Nava and fanned a then record 19 batters in a 2–1 win over Boston's Jim Whitney

Charlie Sweeney was married to the sister of ML player and umpire Jim McDonald. Perhaps the progenitor of the "fadeaway" (screwball), he was also its greatest casualty. In a letter to *TSN* in 1897 from his prison cell at San Quentin, Sweeney described how he began 1884 as Providence's workhorse, pitching 19 of 23 games until he "snapped a cord" in his arm at Chicago on June 27 and hurled in pain ever after that. On the day in July (the 22nd) that he jumped the Grays and eventually signed with St. Louis of the UA, his letter maintained that manager Frank Bancroft ordered him from the box to RF in a "surly tone," and when he protested that he wanted to finish his own game, Bancroft threatened to fine him $50, at which point he walked off the field. When Bancroft pursued him to the dressing room, Sweeney "told him what he thought of him," peeled off his uniform, and never put it on again. Sweeney is no doubt too kind to himself in his version of a famous game (Providence was forced to finish with eight men and lost what had seemed a sure victory), but his description of his injury is accurate. By the following spring his elbow was in ruins, and after struggling to win four of his first six starts in 1885 to lift his career record at that point to 52-24, he was a weak 12-28 for the remainder of his short, sad stay in the majors.

Sweeney first gained repute in 1881 with the San Francisco Athletics of the California League. His purported ML debut on May 11, 1882, begs further study. It seems unlikely that he would have come all the way east to play a single game in May at Boston as an outfielder with Providence since he spent the better part of the season nearly 2,500 miles away with a team in Eureka County, NV. However, he was definitely the Sweeney who reported to Providence from California in July 1883 and was deprived of a probable win on Independence Day in his initial ML pitching appearance when the Grays were forced to quit to catch a train to New York while leading 11–9 after seven innings and had to forfeit the game. He was just 7-7 for the rest of the season, seemingly no threat to steal Charley Radbourn's mantle as the Grays' ace, but when Radbourn's drinking led to his suspension the following spring, the 21-year-old Californian was suddenly Providence's kingpin hurler and responded by holding enemy hitters to just a .185 BA in 221 innings before his own proclivities for "German tea" put Bancroft on his case as well.

Sweeney finished the season with a composite 41 wins after going 24-7 against tepid UA hitters. Over the winter debate raged whether the NL would reinstate him once the UA dissolved, but no sooner was that matter resolved in his favor than his arm and temper became even bigger issues. A mean drunk, Sweeney turned most of his St. Louis teammates permanently against him in 1886 after he flattened outfielder Em Seery and was referred to afterward in *SL* as a "whiskey-guzzling cowardly nincompoop." Then in July he and catcher Tom Dolan were both released after a clubhouse brawl. Sweeney tried to catch on with Syracuse of the International Association but was dropped after just 3 games. He then fled to California trailed by taunts of "Dead Army Charlie."

Sweeney's faint hope of returning to the majors as a position player met with unexpected success when the Cleveland AA replacement team installed him as its Opening Day first baseman in 1887, but he was gone by July after hitting just .226

in 36 games. Vowing to return home to San Francisco and give his arm a long rest, Sweeney lost his resolve that fall and played in an exhibition game against a touring team of New York Giants. That evening he got into a fistfight with Giants star Roger Connor. When he came away badly battered, he went hunting for Connor with a pistol, and Connor quickly scooted out of town (although he later claimed he had left because he got homesick).

Sweeney's life then became a monotony of running his San Francisco saloon, playing benefit and exhibition games that he declared on each occasion would be his farewell but never were, and getting into headline-grabbing scrapes. In July 1891 he was "jailed in San Francisco for whipping a street car conductor so severely that Grim Death is likely to punch his ticket." Somehow he escaped conviction on that one, and he escaped again in January 1894 when he beat up a patron who tried to defend an old beggar woman he threw out of his saloon. But his string ran out in July of that year when he shot and killed one Con McManus amid a knock-down, drag-out quarrel. On November 1 Sweeney was convicted of manslaughter and sentenced to eight years at San Quentin. After some forty months of incarceration, however, he was pardoned by California governor James Budd when his legal counsel established that he was convicted on the perjured testimony of King McManus, Con's brother, who had furthermore intimidated other witnesses to the shooting from testifying on Sweeney's behalf.

Shortly after his release from prison Sweeney umpired a California League game on June 13, 1898, but any thoughts of returning to the sport in that role were truncated when it developed that he had contracted tuberculosis while at San Quentin. Sweeney died in San Francisco at 38. (DN)

Sweeney, William J. / "Bill"

B	T	HGT	WGT	G	IP	H	GS
?	R	5'11"	160	82	708	700	80

CG	BB	SO	SH	W	L	PCT	ERA
76	116	422	4	49	31	.613	2.67

B. ?/?/1858 Philadelphia, PA **D.** 8/2/1903
TEAMS: 82PhiA 84BalU
DEBUT: 6/27/1882 at Pittsburgh; played CF, batted cleanup, and went 1-for-4 in a 6–4 win over Pittsburgh's Harry Salisbury
FINALE: 10/14/1884 at Cincinnati; caught by Yank Robinson and lost 8–0 to Cincinnati's Jim McCormick

Blond, clean-cut, worldly at an early age, Bill Sweeney was both the Union Association's leading pitcher and its greatest casualty, falling prey to a team captain who abused him mercilessly. As a result he is the lone pitcher never to resurface in the majors after enjoying a 40-win season. Capable of playing every position on the diamond, Sweeney might have remained in the bigs even after his arm all but fell off had he been a better hitter, but his .221 career average and .497 OPS—mostly compiled against suspect UA competition—hardly tempted post-1884 major league teams.

Born in Philadelphia, Sweeney began his career as a catcher in 1877 for the amateur Fairmonts and moved to the box the following year. After hurling a twenty-one-inning win and driving home the winning runs with a triple, he was invited to join the independent Philadelphia Athletics for the remainder of the 1878 season. Lured to faraway California that winter, Sweeney launched his pro career in San Francisco as a teammate of Bob Blakiston on the 1879 Californias by winning 13 of 17 decisions and hitting .349. His season highlight came on July 20 when he fanned 18 in an 8–2 win over Oakland. The following year Sweeney switched to the San Francisco Athletics, where he shared the pitching in the early spring with ML star Jim Galvin, who was toying with the notion of jumping the Buffalo NL team, and Jim Devlin, the banned ex-Louisville hurler. His catcher generally was future big leaguer Tom Dolan. In such company Sweeney could only hope to serve as a utility player and change pitcher, although he did begin to get more work in the box after Galvin ended his holdout in May and headed east to Buffalo. When he slipped to 8-8 and a .241 BA, California swiftly lost its appeal and he returned to Philadelphia.

Slow to mature as a pitcher, Sweeney was not ready to test his mettle against big league competition until 1882 when he was 25 and the AA's inaugural season was already well under way. Inexplicably, Philadelphia A's captain Juice Latham installed him in CF and batted him cleanup in his ML debut, and then put him at cleanup again three days later when he made his maiden pitching appearance. Sweeney performed passably as a pitcher in his rookie season, logging a 9-10 record and a 2.90 ERA, but he hit just .159, offering the A's no inspiration to reserve him. Consequently, he spent 1883 with Peoria of the Northwestern League under captain–first baseman Charlie Levis. His principal catcher, Ed Fusselbach, was also born in Philadelphia and likewise had flopped in the AA the previous year. The redoubtable Dick Phelan, a longtime minor league veteran, played behind him at 2B. Levis, Fusselbach, and Phelan all accompanied Sweeney to the rebel Union Association the following season as members of the Baltimore entry, with Levis again named captain.

Levis designated Sweeney, a known quantity, as his ace from the outset, but initially alternated him with rookie Ed Smith. Unhappy with Smith's work, Levis dumped him scarcely a month into the season but never found an adequate replacement. By late May, Sweeney had graduated from being Baltimore's ace to its only reliable pitcher. As a result, he started 60 of the club's 105 games and pitched 416 more innings than its second most active hurler, Tom Lee. The torturous workload Levis imposed on his former Peoria teammate appears to have been an attempt to make a respectable showing and keep his job. Ultimately the captain failed; he was replaced at the team's helm in the final weeks of the season and released to Indianapolis AA. Sweeney, meanwhile, finished the year with the loop lead in wins, innings, starts, CGs—and a dead arm.

The wonder is that Sweeney never seems to have protested his dreadful abuse in a public forum, as did other overtaxed pitchers in his time. There is no indication that he even expressed his displeasure to Levis. Perhaps, after laboring for years in near oblivion, he was simply too enamored of the acclaim suddenly lavished on him as he piled up win after win. Against every UA team but one, Sweeney was a composite 39-11 with a .780 winning percentage. He was just 1-10 against the team that counted most, however: the champion St. Louis Maroons.

When Sweeney lost five of his last six starts in 1884, most by a lopsided margin, his arm was so obviously in shreds that no other ML team made a bid for him after the UA folded, forcing him to return to the minors in 1885 with Cleveland of the Western League. Posting just a 2-5 record before the WL folded on June 15, Sweeney dropped down another rung, joining his old batterymate Fusselbach on the Oswego, NY, club. By September the Starchboxes had shut Sweeney down for the season to save his arm for 1886, but the following July the International League club realized there was nothing left to save. Reduced to playing for a semipro team in tiny Little Falls, NY, Sweeney opened his copy of *Sporting Life* one evening in the summer of 1886 and must have given a sour laugh when he read that "lack of speed" was keeping him "out of the top rungs of his profession." Now and again over the remainder of the decade he tried to sell himself to a team in either the semipro ranks or the low minors, never to last more than a few games. Unmarried, Sweeney died of consumption in Philadelphia in 1903. (DN)

---

*Tannehill, Jesse Niles / "Jesse" "Powder"

B	T	HGT	WGT	G	IP	H	GS
B	L	5'8"	150	135	1053.2	1155	119

CG	BB	SO	SH	W	L	PCT	ERA
102	198	255	11	79	42	.653	3.19

G	AB	H	R	2B	3B	HR
203	593	164	84	29	8	1

RBI	BB	SO	SB	BA	SA	OBP
68	39	2	12	.277	.359	.327

B. 7/14/1874 Dayton, KY **D.** 9/22/1956
TEAMS: 94CinN 97–02PitN 03NYAL 04–08BosAL 08–09WasAL 11CinN
DEBUT: 6/17/1894 at Cincinnati; caught by Morg Murphy and was relieved by Tom Parrott and later Frank Dwyer, who took the 9–8 loss to St. Louis's Dad Clarkson
FINALE: 4/12/1911 at Cincinnati; relieved Art Fromme in a 14–0 loss to Pittsburgh's Babe Adams

Not one baseball fan in a million knows that Jesse Tannehill began and ended his ML career with Cincinnati, and precious few know that he is the only man to be a mainstay on three twentieth-century pennant winners and yet never receive a World's Series share. Tannehill was a member of the 1901–02 Pirates and 1904 Boston AL, flag winners in the only three seasons since 1900 (save for 1994) without postseason play. More significant, among lefties eligible for or already enshrined in the HOF, none had better control than Tannehill, and few hurlers during his career span (1894–1911) could rival him as a hitter.

Born in a small Kentucky town across the river from Cincinnati, Tannehill learned the game on the Queen City sandlots. In the spring of 1894 the NL Reds spotted him pitching for the semipro Shamrocks and put him in uniform. In a *TSN* interview years later Tannehill recalled his early tribulations with Cincinnati and how he learned from them to succeed with Pittsburgh when he returned to the majors three years later. Tannehill admitted that veteran Cincinnati players had broken his heart with their cold treatment and observed: "The first two or three months in a big league are the hardest in a player's experience. If he is game enough to stand up and play winning ball in the chilly atmosphere he is sure to encounter, he is pretty apt to hold on to this job in fast company." Released by Cincinnati after walking 16 batters in just 29 innings and logging a 7.14 ERA, Tannehill then apprenticed for two seasons with Richmond of the Virginia League under manager Jake Wells, perhaps the most unsung developer of young pitchers in the nineteenth century. By 1896 local writers were already noting his remarkable control built around a "tantalizing slow curve ball" and many variations on it. Arriving in Pittsburgh the following spring, Tannehill failed to impress manager Patsy Donovan with his off-speed pitches. Donovan preferred hard throwers like Pink Hawley and Frank Killen and for a time even considered converting the rookie southpaw into an outfielder. In early August the 23-year-old lefty played CF and batted leadoff on consecutive days against Cincinnati, but a few weeks later a shoulder injury sent him home for the year.

Tannehill returned in 1898 under a new manager, Bill Watkins, who disdained both Killen and Hawley for their spoiled brat attitudes and had already traded Hawley. Given Hawley's spot in the rotation, Tannehill promptly won his first three starts and by midseason was not only the Pirates' ace but also one of their top pinch hitters. It was a role he would retain for the rest of the century. In 1900 Tannehill was at his peak, going 20-6 and also hitting .336. Yet even though the Pirates were on the brink of emerging as the NL's next dynasty, all was not serene for the loop's leading southpaw. In December 1900 Pirates owner Barney Dreyfuss tried to trade Tannehill to Cincinnati for Noodles Hahn even as his pitcher denied a story that he had refused to pitch in the postseason *Pittsburgh Chronicle-Telegraph* cup series against pennant-winning Brooklyn. Tannehill averred that Pirates manager Fred Clarke had never asked him to pitch in any of the cup games, which the local press found incomprehensible. It was clear, in any case, that a major rift was developing between the pitcher and his team. (DN)

Taylor, John Besson / "Jack" "Brewery Jack" "Bowery Jack"

B	T	HGT	WGT	G	IP	H	GS
R	R	6'1"	190	271	2091	2476	235

CG	BB	SO	SH	W	L	PCT	ERA
209	583	529	7	120	117	.506	4.22

G	AB	H	R	2B	3B	HR
287	930	234	100	46	8	5

RBI	BB	SO	SB	BA	SA	OBP
135	44	58	9	.252	.335	.289

B. 5/23/1873 Staten Island, NY **D.** 2/7/1900
TEAMS: 91NYN 92–97PhiN 98StLN 99CinN
DEBUT: 9/16/1891 at New York; caught by Dick Buckley and lost 2–0 to Pittsburgh's Mark Baldwin
FINALE: 9/12/1899 at Washington; caught by Heinie Peitz and was later relieved by Peitz in a 7–2 loss to Washington's Roy Evans
FAMOUS LAST: In 1899 Taylor became perhaps the last ML pitcher to play his entire career without using a glove. As *TSN* noted, "He believes that he can do more effective work in the box with both hands bare."

TSN said of Jack Taylor after his death in 1900 from Bright's disease: "Nature gave him ability, but unfortunately the balance wheel was omitted from his make up. Had he ever realized how much harm he was doing himself he might have been one of the greatest pitchers the game ever knew." It then added, "Nature always sounds a warning before exacting a penalty, but Jack never took a tip of any kind in his life." In commenting on the fact that Bright's disease takes a while to develop and Taylor must have been under its effects for some time, the paper pointed to the drop-off in his play late in 1898, which continued in 1899. But in actuality Taylor had led the NL in appearances, starts, CGs and innings in 1898. Then, the following spring, after being traded to Cincinnati, he got off on a bad foot with manager Buck Ewing by skipping afternoon practices at the Reds' training site in Columbus, GA, claiming he was too sore, and then disappearing for several days on a bender. Taylor further antagonized Ewing in June when he missed a team train from New York to Boston and, upon arriving late, told Ewing he had gone sailing with an old Staten Island friend and they had gotten stuck when an unexpected and almost unearthly calm prevented them from returning to shore. Unbeknownst to him, however, reports came to Ewing that gale force winds were in effect that day. At that point another manager might have invoked the temperance clause in Taylor's contract and booted him off the team, but Ewing was frantically trying to save his own job. Taylor escaped with a $700 fine and a five-week suspension. He returned to the rotation on July 11 and pitched several good games, including a 1–0 gem on August 15 at Boston.

Then, less than a month later, a sharp pain struck Taylor in his right side in the fifth inning of his final ML appearance. He was removed from the game and a doctor was called. By then the pain had subsided, but he was sent back to Cincinnati and remained out of action as a precaution until he returned to his home at the end of the season. That December, Taylor mingled with the crowd at the NL's winter meeting in New York City, actively lobbying for a trade, ideally to Brooklyn. He seemed in good health, but in January 1900 his mother died of pneumonia. In the days immediately following her passing, Taylor admitted to "feeling unwell." Less than three weeks after losing his mother, he died following an operation. Although his official cause of death was acute nephritis, commonly referred to as Bright's disease, there is a strong possibility, given Taylor's history, that his trouble might have either been brought on or else aggravated by a drinking binge pursuant to his mother's death. Taylor's sudden demise, in any case, removed one of the game's best pitchers in the 1890s. His 120 wins are the most by any pitcher in the final decade of the nineteenth century who won his last game at age 26 or younger.

After serving most of the 1891 season in the Eastern Association, Taylor was pulled from the Corinthian Athletic Club to pitch one brilliant game for the New York Giants and then, bafflingly, allowed to escape. He returned to the majors with Philadelphia late in 1892 from Albany of the Eastern League and was the Phillies' most consistent winner for the next five seasons. Despite recurrent drunken altercations with teammates, Taylor remained highly regarded throughout the league. After he was traded to St. Louis in a seven-player deal in December 1897 along with Jack Clements and several other players whom Phils manager George Stallings felt were sabotaging his authority, Boston offered $5,000 plus Jack Stivetts and Charlie Ganzel for him and Clements. The deal fell through when Browns owner Chris Von der Ahe demanded $7,500 in cash rather than the players in order to clear debts, and Von der Ahe later also rejected an offer from Washington of nine players for Taylor. Stuck on one of the worst teams in the nineteenth century, Taylor nonetheless went 15-19 while the rest of the Browns' hill staff finished 24-82. Desperate to leave St. Louis and play on a contender, Taylor only partially got his wish. Cincinnati in 1898 had been a third-place team but dropped to sixth in his final ML season thanks in part to his own spotty contributions. (DN)

Taylor, John W. / "Jack"

B	T	HGT	WGT	G	IP	H	GS
R	R	5'10"	170	74	618	638	70

CG	BB	SO	SH	W	L	PCT	ERA
69	142	135	3	33	38	.465	3.22

B. 1/14/1874 New Straitsville, OH **D.** 3/4/1938
TEAMS: 98–03ChiN 04–06StLN 06–07ChiN
DEBUT: 9/25/1898 at Chicago; caught by Art Nichols and beat Pittsburgh's Bill Hart 7–4
FINALE: 9/2/1907 at St. Louis; relieved Chick Fraser in Fraser's 6–0 loss to St. Louis's Art Fromme
CAREER HIGHLIGHT: hurled a record 187 consecutive CGs from 6/20/1901 to 8/9/1906

Scouted by Connie Mack while pitching for semipro teams in Marietta, OH, and Parkersburg, WV, Jack Taylor signed with Milwaukee of the Western League in January 1897 after Mack became manager of the Brewers. Taylor's first season under Mack was marred when he dislocated his shoulder in a midseason collision at home plate. While spending the winter as a brakeman on a passenger train, Taylor agreed to sign with Milwaukee in 1898 for only $750 since his shoulder was suspect but got Mack to promise him another $600 if he did well. Although he won 28 games that year for the Brewers, Mack never gave him an extra cent. When Louisville NL, which had a string on Taylor, agreed to relinquish him in return for Chicago pitcher Walt Woods, he finished 1898 in the Windy City. Still bitter over his treatment at Mack's hands, Taylor threatened to quit baseball and go back to work for the railroad unless Chicago paid him what he felt he was worth the following year. He acquired considerable leverage with the Second City management after debuting with 5 late-season wins in 5 starts.

Taylor extended his consecutive wins streak at the start of his career to seven before suffering his first loss on April 23, 1899, to Cincinnati but nonetheless finished with a sub-.500 record (18-21) in his official rookie year. Despite posting the third-best ERA in the NL (2.55), he was even unluckier in 1900, going just 10-17 and missing several starts after contracting blood poisoning in his pitching arm. In addition, the opportunity to begin his career with 70 straight CGs was denied him when he was relieved for the first time in a September 10 loss to Philadelphia. Then, in his last appearance of the season, Taylor was nearly killed after throwing the final pitch of the nineteenth century in Chicago's park. On October 8, in the ninth inning of the second game of a DH, the right-hander was struck over the heart by a line drive off the bat of Cincinnati's Tommy Corcoran. When he was unable to rise and Chicago had no other pitchers on the bench, umpire Hank O'Day immediately stopped the game so that he could get medical attention. When the team left for Pittsburgh the following morning to play its final series of the season, Taylor stayed behind in a Chicago hospital, his baseball future in doubt. (DN)

Terry, William H. / "Bill" "Adonis"

B	T	HGT	WGT	G	IP	H	GS
R	R	5'11½"	168	440	3514.1	3525	406

CG	BB	SO	SH	W	L	PCT	ERA
367	1298	1553	17	197	196	.501	3.74

G	AB	H	R	2B	3B	HR
667	2389	594	314	76	54	15

RBI	BB	SO	SB	BA	SA	OBP
287	146	139	106	.249	.344	.295

B. 8/7/1864 Westfield, MA **D.** 2/24/1915
TEAMS: 84–89BroA 90–91BroN 92BalN 92–94PitN 94–97ChiN
DEBUT AND FAMOUS FIRST: 5/2/1884 at Brooklyn; caught by John Farrow and collected the Brooklyn–Los Angeles franchise's first win when he beat Washington's Bob Barr 7–5 and went 2-for-3
FINALE: 4/27/1897 at St. Louis; caught by Kit Kittridge and lost 10–4 to St. Louis's Red Donahue
CAREER HIGHLIGHT: 7/24/1886 at Brooklyn; caught by Jimmy Peoples in his 1–0 no-hit win over Dave Foutz of pennant-bound St. Louis

Because Bill Terry's very appearance on the field could evoke a hysterical reaction from the women in the crowd, the press liked to refer to him as "Adonis," but his teammates knew him as Bill. A fastball pitcher with a decent curve, he was the only pitcher prior to the AA–NL merger in 1892 to spend his first eight ML seasons in the same city with the same franchise. Actually, Terry had been with Brooklyn for nine years by then and was a member of City of Churches pennant winners in three different leagues—the Interstate Association, the AA, and the NL. At the close of the 1896 season he suddenly found himself the recipient of considerable attention for having survived for so long as a ML pitcher under so many different rule changes. *TSN* ran a ghostwritten column under his name on how the art of pitching had evolved since his rookie season in 1884. That year he won 19 games in a loop that still forbade overhand pitching, later he had 20-win seasons at the 50-foot distance in two different leagues after the four-ball rule was introduced and in 1895 he won 21 games at the 60'6" distance.

Terry spent 1879–80 pitching for the amateur Racket Club of Ludlow, MA, before joining the semipro Bridgeport Rosedales in 1881. After a second season in Bridgeport, he came to Brooklyn in 1883 and pitched the Interstate Association pennant clincher on September 29, beating Harrisburg 11–6. Only 19 when he moved with Brooklyn to the AA the following year, he quickly established himself as the Grays' ace and played an additional 13 games in the outfield. Terry lost his top dog status the following year to Henry Porter but remained an effective pitcher-utilityman for the next four seasons. In 1889 he blossomed into a 20-game winner for the first time, joining Bob Caruthers and Mickey Hughes in leading Brooklyn to its initial AA pennant. He repeated his success in 1890, bagging 26 wins for the first team in ML history to win a repeat pennant after changing leagues. Terry then slipped to 6-16 in 1891 and began experiencing the arm problems that would haunt him for the rest of his career.

Released by Brooklyn in June 1892 after he staged a nine-week holdout, he pitched 1 game for Baltimore and then was traded to Pittsburgh for

Cub Stricker. Terry underwent a temporary resurgence with the Pirates when a Brooklyn physical education instructor gave him a regimen of exercises that were surprisingly modern to strengthen his arm, but by 1894 he again seemed near the end and was released to Chicago. A second renaissance resulted in his last 20-win season in 1895 and another 15 wins the following season, including a one-of-a-kind game. On July 13, 1896, Terry became the only pitcher in ML history to collect a CG win despite giving up 4 home runs to the same batter when Ed Delahanty's quartet of dingers was not enough to counter the 9 runs Chicago compiled off Philadelphia pitching.

Just 32 when he hurled his last ML pitch, Terry joined Milwaukee of the Western League for two seasons after the Brewers agreed to let him pitch only in home games and was an aggregate 33-13. He then opened a billiard hall in Milwaukee and later also operated the Second Street Alleys, one of the leading bowling emporiums in the country. A ranked bowler himself, Terry frequently entered tournaments in the Midwest. He died in 1915 of pneumonia at his Milwaukee home. (DN)

Thornton, John / "Jack"

B	T	HGT	WGT	G	IP	H	GS
R	R	5'10½"	175	41	290	292	35

CG	BB	SO	SH	W	L	PCT	ERA
25	139	57	1	15	19	.441	4.10

B. 5/22/1869 Washington, D.C. **D.** 4/26/1935
TEAMS: 89WasN 91–92PhiN 92StLN
DEBUT: 8/14/1889 at Indianapolis; caught by Connie Mack and lost 11–9 to Indianapolis's Charlie Getzein
FINALE: 9/15/1892 at Washington; played RF and went 0-for-3 in a 2–0 loss to Washington's Jouett Meekin

During Jack Thornton's lengthy pro career, his death or near-death was reported on several occasions. Yet what happened to him after his playing days remained a mystery until recently. Thornton grew up in Washington, D.C., and was pitching for Mount Pleasant, an area amateur nine, in 1889 when he made his ML debut under bizarre circumstances. Given a tryout with the local NL club, he was warming up with pitcher George Keefe when one of his pitches struck Keefe in the head and kayoed him. When Keefe was unable to join Washington on its next road trip, Thornton took his place and started against Indianapolis on August 14. The novice walked 8 batters and surrendered 11 runs in the game, yet it was not entirely his fault, as he was undone by 8 errors behind him. Thornton did not pitch for Washington again but had showed enough potential to be offered an 1890 contract by Milwaukee of the Western Association. There he fashioned a WA-best 29 wins and twirled a no-hitter on June 12. The stellar year earned him a ticket back to the bigs with the Phillies, for whom he was a creditable 15-16 in 1891.

Thornton's official rookie year would prove to be his only full season in the show and practically the end of his pitching career. After a few weak outings at the start of 1892, he went back to the minors with Syracuse of the Eastern League and began making the transition to 1B. Thornton made his final ML appearance with St. Louis when the Browns visited Washington after the EL season ended. Over the next decade and a half he made the rounds of minor league circuits. These years saw several references to Thornton's mortality. After the 1893 season the death of a Pensacola, FL, pitcher named William Thornton led the 1894 baseball guides to report that Jack Thornton had died. As a result, he aroused quite a stir when he turned up at the Phillies' park in May 1894 during a game the Phils lost, leading one of his exteammates to quip, "That's what we get for having a dead man on our bench." Then, during an eventful 1903 season with Milwaukee of the Western League, a train carrying Thornton and his teammates was caught in a flood. A few weeks later, several Milwaukee players had to flee their hotel in the middle of the night to escape a fire.

Yet Thornton was still alive and well when his association with pro ball ended in 1906 after he was fired as manager of Dayton in the Central League. It appears that he and his wife, Nina, moved from Colorado Springs to Chicago at that point, as he pitched and played 1B for the Artesians in the Chicago City League in 1907. A full decade later, there were references to a "Big Jack" Thornton pitching for a Second City indoor baseball team called the Marquettes. But it remains far from certain that this was the former major leaguer who would have then been in his mid forties. Thornton is believed to have died in his native Washington on April 26, 1935. (PM/DN)

Titcomb, Ledell / "Cannonball" "Little Tit"

B	T	HGT	WGT	G	IP	H	GS
L	L	5'6"	157	63	528.2	492	62

CG	BB	SO	SH	W	L	PCT	ERA
61	239	283	5	30	29	.508	3.47

B. 8/21/1866 West Baldwin, ME **D.** 6/8/1950
TEAMS: 86PhiN 87PhiA 87–89NYN 90RocA
DEBUT: 5/5/1886 at Philadelphia; caught by Deacon McGuire and lost 4–2 to New York's Tim Keefe
FINALE: 10/15/1890 at Baltimore; began the game at 2B and finished at 3B, thus playing two infield positions left-handed as he went 0-for-2 in a 9–5 loss to Baltimore's Sadie McMahon
CAREER HIGHLIGHT: 9/15/1890 at Rochester; caught by Deacon McGuire and pitched a 7–0 no-hitter against Syracuse's Ed Mars

Early in his career Ledell Titcomb was mortified when teammates nicknamed him "Little Tit." Sources list his playing height and weight as having been 5'6" and 157, yet his obit in the *New York Times* described him as having been "a rugged 200-pounder." But there is no dispute about Titcomb's main pitching weapon: he threw hard, accounting for his other nickname—Cannonball. Titcomb first pitched for pay with independent Haverhill, MA, in 1883, when he was just 17. The following year he remained with Haverhill when it joined the East New England League. On June 12, 1885, Titcomb beat Philadelphia NL 2–1 in an exhibition game, spurring Quakers manager Harry Wright to acquire him.

Titcomb's rookie season in 1886 was marred by wildness and injury. After losing his first four starts and spending most of his time on the bench, he broke his right (non-pitching) arm in August while engaging in horseplay. Highly regarded by Wright prior to then, in his first game back from the injured list Titcomb made his final appearance with the Quakers, losing 11–0 to Detroit's Lady Baldwin on October 8 in what became Baldwin's NL southpaw-season-record forty-second win.

Released by the Quakers after the season, Titcomb joined Philadelphia AA. After winning his first start in 1887, 10–9 over Brooklyn on April 30, Titcomb then gave up 21 runs in his next two starts, saddling him with an average of 10 runs per game, too high for the A's taste. Discarded in May, Titcomb went to Jersey City, where he hooked up with catcher Pat Murphy. The two became known as the "water-wheel" battery and were sold as a unit to the New York Giants for a reported $3,000 in late August after Titcomb went 13-10 against International Association competition. Titcomb and Murphy made their Giants debut on September 2, 1887, beating Detroit 2-1.

Based on their late-season showing the Titcomb-Murphy battery was accorded the honor of starting together on Opening Day in 1888 at Washington, as Titcomb blanked the Senators 8–0 to gain the first victory for what would be the Giants' initial pennant-winning team. In his final start of the season Titcomb was equally effective, topping Pittsburgh's Ed Morris 1–0 on October 10 on a one-hitter, with Morris making the lone enemy hit. It is conceivable that Titcomb hurt his arm in that game, however, for he made only one appearance for the Giants in their World's Series triumph over AA champion St. Louis, and that did not come until seventeen days after his final regular season outing. In a game that no longer mattered since the Giants had already clinched the Series, Titcomb was lifted after surrendering 6 runs in 4 innings of an eventual 18–7 St. Louis win.

Buoyed by his World Series share, Titcomb took the winter off, hunting bear in the Maine wilds when he was not at his home in Haverhill with his wife and children. He began 1889 with a rocky 11–10 win in his first Giants start on April 25 but then lost his next two outings and was dispatched to Toronto, where he fashioned a 1.29 ERA to top the International Association. Despite the addition in 1890 of the PL, a third major league, Titcomb remained with Toronto until the IA collapsed. He then joined Rochester AA and pitched brilliantly before contracting a sore arm near the end of August. He continued to take his regular turn in the box, however, and even logged a no-hitter against Syracuse on September 15 and pitched Rochester's last victory to date as a member of a major league, when he topped Baltimore 4–3 in a six-inning game on October 11. Over the winter Titcomb tried in vain to pamper his arm and finally, on the prayer that it might yet recover, he signed in March 1891 with Rochester, which had moved to the Eastern Association. But the pipe dream ended quickly. On May 2, 1891, Buffalo blasted Titcomb 18–1. He left pro ball after hurling one last game with Providence of the same circuit and worked for some years for the United Shoe Machinery Corp. Titcomb died at 80 in Kingston, NH. (DN)

Toole, Stephen John / "Steve"

B	T	HGT	WGT	G	IP	H	GS
R	L	6'0"	170	55	443	457	52

CG	BB	SO	SH	W	L	PCT	ERA
49	259	141	1	27	26	.509	4.79

G	AB	H	R	2B	3B	HR
59	228	60	34	15	2	1

RBI	BB	SO	SB	BA	SA	OBP
31	5	—	9	.263	.360	.282

B. 4/9/1859 New Orleans, LA **D.** 3/28/1919
TEAMS: 86–87BroA 88KCA 90BroA
DEBUT: 4/20/1886 at Philadelphia; caught by Jim McCauley in a 7–3 loss to Philadelphia's Al Atkinson
FINALE: 5/9/1890 at Brooklyn; caught by Herman Pitz in a 4–2 loss to Philadelphia's Eddie Green

Steve Toole was among the least heralded of the many rookie southpaws who debuted in 1886 but soon established that he was the best hitter among them. He batted .351 as a frosh with Brooklyn and .263 for his career. His .351 season mark ranks first among all AA players with a minimum of 50 ABs who served primarily as pitchers. Though born in New Orleans, Toole grew up in Pittsburgh and first turned heads in 1883 while pitching for the amateur R. D. Woods club. Nevertheless, the spring of 1885 found him no higher than the Iron & Oil League with Youngstown at age 26—too old to be so far down the pro ladder and have any reasonable hope of making the majors. But when Toole went to Rochester after Youngstown folded and fared well against International League hitters, Brooklyn took him for 1886.

Toole served his entire rookie campaign fourth in the Brooklyn rotation and as a result made only twelve starts. His first victory came on April 25 when he beat Baltimore 11–1. Toole's sixth and final win in 1886 brought his season to an unpleasant halt. On October 2 at Pittsburgh he sprained his ankle running to 1B. Brooklyn requested a substitute runner, but Pittsburgh captain Tom Brown would allow only first baseman Bill Phillips to replace Toole. Since Phillips had a sore knee, Toole gamely stuck it out and was finished for the year after hanging on to beat Ed Morris 4–2. As always, he wintered in Pittsburgh, where he was already developing "something of a reputation as a politician." Despite improving to 14-10 the following year, Toole became expendable after Brooklyn purchased St. Louis's twin aces, Bob Caruthers and Dave Foutz, and was ticketed for the expansion Kansas City Cowboys in 1888. Barely two months into the 1888 season, KC manager Sam Barkley released him following a 7–6 loss to Louisville. Bark-ley might have noticed the southpaw's 6.61 ERA, but Toole claimed Barkley cut him because he refused Barkley's request to let another player wear his uniform in a game. Upon returning east the budding politician rejoined Rochester, which was now a member of the International Association. Toole returned to Rochester in 1889 and went just 9-16 despite posting a glittering 1.60 ERA. When both Rochester and a new club in Brooklyn, known as the Gladiators, were late additions to the AA the following spring, Rochester supplied Toole, Billy O'Brien, Jack Peltz, and Jim Toy to bolster weak sister Brooklyn. Toole hurled the Gladiators' opening game, losing 3–2 to Syracuse on April 17. Despite pitching nearly as well in each of his next five starts, he was let go in May. Since he was easily Brooklyn's best pitcher at the time, his release probably came at his own request so that he could be appointed a regular AA umpire in place of recently resigned Frank O'Brien.

But officiating proved hazardous to Toole. In addition to dealing with kicking players that had once been his teammates, on June 9 he was arrested along with members of the Rochester and Philadelphia teams for participating in a baseball game the previous Sunday at Windsor Beach Park, Rochester's Sabbath facility. A few weeks later he officiated his last game in the AA.

That winter Toole was appointed wharf master of Pittsburgh, spurring locals wags to venture that he would now be responsible for brushing mud off wharves rather than off home plate with his cap. His political rise was swift once he got his foot on the ladder. By the spring of 1892 Toole was a justice of the peace in Pittsburgh's first Ward. He was alderman of the first Ward only six years later. Toole remained active in Pittsburgh politics until his death from a stroke at 60. (DN)

Valentine, John Gill / "John"

B	T	HGT	WGT	G	IP	H	GS
?	?	?	?	13	102	130	12

CG	BB	SO	SH	W	L	PCT	ERA
11	17	13	0	2	10	.200	3.53

B. 11/21/1855 Brooklyn, NY **D.** 10/10/1903
TEAMS: 83ColA
DEBUT AND FAMOUS FIRST: 5/3/1883 at Columbus; caught by Pop Schwartz and beat Louisville's Guy Hecker 6–3 for Columbus's first win as a major league entry
FINALE: 8/3/1883 at Columbus; beat Louisville's Sam Weaver 3–2 (some sources credit this win to Frank Mountain, in which case Valentine's last game was a 3–1 loss at Cincinnati on 7/31/1883)

John Valentine has yet to be credited by some reference works with being both a ML player and umpire. After quitting pitching he officiated in both the AA and the NL from 1884 through 1888. In all, for someone who was relatively prominent on the baseball landscape for over a decade, Valentine seems scarcely to have cast a shadow. His year of birth also is in question. In 1891 a New York sportswriter ran into him on a Manhattan street and described him as very stout. At the time Valentine would have been 36, according to his baseball birth date, but the writer thought he looked considerably older. Furthermore, Valentine confided that he had a daughter who was about to get married, a somewhat unlikely intimacy from a man only in his midthirties.

Valentine first gained eminence with Winona of the League Alliance in 1877 and pitched all over the country for the next five years before signing with Columbus after it joined the AA in the winter of 1882–83. His most recent stop had been with the 1882 minor league New York Mets under Jim Mutrie, who recommended him to Columbus AA expansion franchise pilot Horace Phillips when Mutrie's own new AA entry Mets had no need for Valentine after signing Tim Keefe and Jack Lynch. In his younger days Valentine had owned a fair fastball, but by 1883 he was relying almost entirely on guile and had a sore arm for most of his Columbus stay. Phillips released him in early August, and Valentine joined Trenton of the Interstate Association some five days later. By the following year he had turned to officiating. Valentine died at 47 in Central Islip, NY. (DN/DB)

Viau, Leon A. / "Leon" "Lee"

B	T	HGT	WGT	G	IP	H	GS
R	R	5'4"	160	178	1442	1441	162

CG	BB	SO	SH	W	L	PCT	ERA
146	526	554	5	83	77	.519	3.33

B. 7/5/1866 Corinth, VT **D.** 12/17/1947
TEAMS: 88–89CinA 90CinN 90–92CleN 92LouN 92BosN
DEBUT: 4/22/1888 at Kansas City; caught by Jack O'Connor and beat Kansas City's Steve Toole 10–8
FINALE: 8/27/1892 at Louisville; caught by Mike Kelly and beat Louisville's Scott Stratton 8–1

Many examples of labored Victorian newspaper wordplay testify to the fact that the stocky little right-hander's name was pronounced "view," and in fact the 1870 census report spells the family name that way. During his career Lee Viau was said to be the son of a Dartmouth professor and a graduate of that university, but his father was actually a French Canadian carpenter who worked for Dartmouth. Viau himself genuinely was a student in the science department, however, although his athletic skill may have helped him obtain an opportunity that few carpenters' sons could enjoy,

When Viau broke in with Cincinnati in 1888 after moving up from St. Paul of the Northwestern League, he won his first eight starts and had the Queen City in a furor, but he soon showed that he was not only unable to keep up the fast pace but could be notably erratic, prone to tire in the late innings. Viau was also thought to have let his early popularity turn his head. Considered narcissistic, a lady's man, and a clotheshorse, he was stigmatized as lazy and stubborn, more interested in being seen in public by a theater crowd than a baseball crowd. After a late season loss to Brooklyn on a long drive by light-hitting Jack Burdock, exasperated manager Gus Schmelz told the *Cincinnati Commercial Gazette,* "I hardly know what to say about Viau," who had been told Burdock could not hit a high fast ball and then "nodded, went in and gave him a slow incurve."

Viau had shocked respectable opinion even before his rookie season by passing off a prostitute as his wife while playing winter ball in San Francisco. His most serious problem, however, was an alcohol habit that began to manifest itself in 1889. In obedience to his parent's wishes, Viau was exempted from having to play on Sundays, and it left a particularly bad taste when he spent his Sabbaths drinking. Promises to reform were made in vain and heavy fines proved ineffective. By September 1889 a Cincinnati newspaper wrote, "No player connected with the Cincinnati team was ever so generally unpopular as Lee Viau. The Dartmouth man would do better in some other city. Give him a chance." It is unclear whether the reporter meant Viau should be given an opportunity to reestablish himself in the Cincinnati public's good graces, or he hoped Viau would to given a chance to go to another city. Viau, hit heavily by fines for his drinking, was more than ready to move on.

He got that chance when he was released in mid-summer of 1890. Viau went to Cleveland, where he had a modest comeback in 1891 with an 18-17 record but then bounced among three NL teams in 1892 before ending his ML career with the lowest BA (.139) and fewest RC/G (1.85) of any nineteenth-century player with a minimum of 500 ABs.

Viau went on to a long minor league career before finishing at age 41 in the New York State League, but alcoholism continued to darken his achievements. When he played at Paterson, NJ, with Honus Wagner, the usually mild-mannered Wagner is said to have almost strangled his teammate after the pitcher drenched him with a bucket of water during an argument over Viau's drinking. After 1908 Viau settled down in Paterson, where he managed the game room at the local Elks Club. Drink and womanizing brought many contemporary players with habits like Viau's to early graves, but even though he never married or quit the bottle, he lived to see his 80th birthday before dying in Hopewell, NJ, in 1947. (DB/DN)

Vinton, William Miller / "Bill" "Cully"

B	T	HGT	WGT	G	IP	H	GS
R	R	6'1"	160	37	314	302	37

CG	BB	SO	SH	W	L	PCT	ERA
34	73	160	2	17	19	.472	2.46

B. 4/27/1865 Winthrop, MA **D.** 9/3/1893
TEAMS: 84–85PhiN 85PhiA
DEBUT: 7/3/1884 at Chicago; caught by John Crowley and was relieved by John Coleman, who got the 15–13 win over Chicago's Larry Corcoran
FINALE: 9/16/1885 at Philadelphia; caught by Frank Siffel and was relieved by John Coleman in his 15–6 loss to St. Louis's Bob Caruthers

In 1882 Bill Vinton played for the school team at Phillips Andover, where he was nicknamed "Cully." He then attended Yale the following year but pitched professionally that summer for independent Springfield, MA. On September 22 Vinton hooked up with Holyoke's Henry Porter but lost 2–1 despite allowing just 1 hit when Porter threw a no-no. Vinton then returned to Yale and did not pitch professionally again until the summer of 1884 when he joined Philadelphia NL. After being rocked in his first effort, he garnered his initial ML win five days later, beating Detroit 11–4. For the remainder of the season Vinton pitched effectively for a mediocre team and as a result was allowed to delay his return to the Quakers in 1885 until the college year ended. Vinton left the Quakers that season with a 3-6 record after losing 6–0 to Chicago on August 5. Two weeks later he joined the rival AA Philadelphia A's and seemed to hit his stride again before losing his last two starts. He then left the team to return to college and pitched for Yale in the spring of 1886, but the A's did not invite him back. Instead Vinton signed in May with Meriden of the Eastern League.

In the spring of 1887 Vinton finally, after 3 years as a pro, was deemed ineligible to pitch for Yale. After graduating from Yale in 1888 he joined Lowell of the New England League for a time but then quit pro ball. The September 8, 1893, *Boston Globe* accurately reported that he had died in the house of his father, Rev. P. H. Vinton, in Pawtucket, RI, but said his death was due to "heart disease induced by excessive athletic work" rather than dysentery, the true cause. (DN)

Voss, Alexander / "Aleck"

B	T	HGT	WGT	G	IP	H	GS
R	R	6'1"	180	34	239.1	280	26

CG	BB	SO	SH	W	L	PCT	ERA
24	39	129	0	5	20	.200	3.72

G	AB	H	R	2B	3B	HR
77	290	51	34	9	0	0

RBI	BB	SO	SB	BA	SA	OBP
—	5	—	—	.176	.207	.190

B. 5/16/1858 Roswell, GA **D.** 8/31/1906
TEAMS: 84WasU 84KCU
DEBUT: 4/17/1884 at Baltimore; played 1B and was 1-for-4 in a 7–3 loss to Baltimore's Bill Sweeney

FINALE: 9/12/1884 at Boston; played LF and went 0-for-3 in a 6–2 loss to Boston's James Burke

Aleck Voss developed his game on the Cincinnati sandlots and joined the independent Cumminsville, OH, Blue Sox in 1875. The following season he was a member of the Cincinnati NL reserves but then made baseball only a sideline for some years while he worked in the decorating trade. After playing with the Cincinnati Shamrocks in 1882, he joined the Dayton, OH, independent club the following year and showed enough to be among the first men Washington added to its roster when it enlisted in the upstart UA in 1884. A combination pitcher, first baseman, and outfielder, Voss opened the season at 1B and did not make his first appearance in the box for Washington until May 10 at St. Louis, when he lost 8–4. His final game with Washington came some four months later when he lost 8–3 to Baltimore on August 5.

Eight days afterward Voss made his first appearance with the Kansas City UA team, losing 6–4 to Cincinnati. He lasted scarcely a month under manager Ted Sullivan. In 1885 and part of 1886 Voss played in the Southern League before joining Leadville of the Western League, where *TSN* reported in August that his "arm has given out." He recovered sufficiently over the winter to pitch for Denver of the Western League in 1887 and beat Omaha in a DH, throwing a no-hitter in the opener. In October 1887 two of his children died, however, and his wife reportedly "lay at the point of death." The personal setback, coupled with another bout of arm trouble, kept Voss "at his old home, Cumminsville, without an engagement" as late as July 4, 1888, according to *SL*. Voss eventually took a job with the Pullman Palace Car Company, where he remained until the spring of 1890 when he signed to manage and play 1B for McKeesport of the Tri-State League. Fired as manager soon after the season started for being "careless and negligent in his duties," Voss tried to remain on the team solely as a player but was released after hitting just .196 in 11 games. Soon after that his life also came undone. In March 1900 *TSN* reported that he had been sentenced to thirty days in the Cincinnati workhouse and fined $50 for chronic drinking and nonsupport of his wife and family. Voss died in Cincinnati six years later. (DN)

Wadsworth, John L. / "Jack" "Waddy"

B	T	HGT	WGT	G	IP	H	GS
L	R	?	180	47	367.2	524	44

CG	BB	SO	SH	W	L	PCT	ERA
39	199	87	0	6	38	.136	6.85

B. 12/17/1867 Wellington, OH **D.** 7/8/1941
TEAMS: 90CleN 93BalN 94–95LouN
DEBUT: 5/1/1890 at Cleveland; caught by Chief Zimmer and lost 12–11 to Cincinnati's Lee Viau in relief of Jesse Duryea
FINALE: 4/29/1895 at Louisville; was the third Louisville pitcher in a 19–8 blowout loss to Cleveland's Nig Cuppy
CAREER LOWLIGHT: 8/17/1894 at Philadelphia; allowed a record 36 hits to Philadelphia in a 29–4 loss to Kid Carsey

Jack Wadsworth claimed during his playing days that he was born in 1872, shaving a nifty five years off his real age. He also reportedly had been a college pitcher in the Cleveland area, but there is no record that he was ever a matriculated student anywhere. Said by *TSN*, when Cleveland signed him in the closing days of 1889, to have "the speed of Bakely and the cunning of Beatin," he showed only rare flashes of either attribute during his stay with the Spiders. In 1890 Wadsworth registered the poorest strikeouts-to-walks ratio of any ML qualifier prior to the increase in pitching distance in 1893 (0.32) as well as the lowest winning percentage of any pitcher between 1876 and 1892 in as many as 160 innings (.111).

Following a decent season with St. Paul of the Western League in 1892, Wadsworth was given a trial by Baltimore in the spring of 1893 and then released after he was hammered in three straight starts. He began 1894 with Memphis and was acquired in July by Louisville after the Southern League folded. Bad as his 4-18 record with the Colonels might seem, it was actually better than it should have been. Wadsworth sandwiched a 2-18 mark between winning his first start with Louisville on July 9 and his final start on the last day of the season, when he outlasted Brooklyn 10–6. In a year when almost all pitchers were tattooed, Wadsworth fared the worst of all; his 7.60 ERA was more than half a run higher than any other qualifier in 1894.

Two abysmal relief outings at the start of the 1895 season, in which Wadsworth surrendered 24 hits in nine innings of work, spelled the end of one of the least illustrious pitching careers in ML history. He labored onward in the minors with a series of teams and did his best work for New Castle of the Interstate League in 1899 when he complemented his pitching duties by hitting .343 in 140 ABs. Wadsworth then hit only .244 the following year and was out of the pro game by 1902. He later operated a restaurant in his town of birth. An inveterate hunter, he trained bird dogs as a side venture. Wadsworth died a widower of the long-term effects of syphilis in Elyria, OH. (DN)

Weaver, Samuel H. / "Buck" "Sam"

B	T	HGT	WGT	G	IP	H	GS
R	R	5'10"	175	153	1307.2	1438	150

CG	BB	SO	SH	W	L	PCT	ERA
141	106	348	7	68	80	.459	3.21

B. 7/20/1855 Philadelphia, PA **D.** 2/1/1914
TEAMS: 75PhiNA 78MilN 82PhiA 83LouA 84PhiU 86PhiA
DEBUT: 10/25/1875 at Philadelphia; caught by Charlie Snyder and beat the St. Louis Browns' George Bradley 17–2
FINALE: 5/29/1886 at Philadelphia; caught by Jack O'Brien and lost 20–1 to St. Louis's Bob Caruthers
CAREER HIGHLIGHT: 5/9/1878 at Indianapolis; caught by Bill Holbert in a 2–1 win over Indianapolis's "The Only" Nolan and either threw a no-hitter or else gave up 1 hit to Indianapolis catcher John Clapp—historians will probably always be at odds as to whether Clapp reached base on a single or an error

Sam Weaver was the original "Buck" Weaver. Teammates called him Buck throughout his career (we wish we knew why) and afterward Frank Bancroft, his manager while he was with Worcester, MA, in 1879, remembered him as Buck. After debuting with a win in his hometown on one of the NA's last days as a major league, Weaver pitched for the League Alliance Philadelphia Athletics before jumping to Milwaukee after the 1877 season was under way. Accompanying the independent Wisconsin club when it joined the NL, he set about disproving the popular theory that pitching is anywhere from 60 to 90 percent of the game. In 1878 Weaver had one of the most remarkable rookie years of any pitcher in ML history, with a 1.95 ERA and an NL-low .247 OOBP, but all he showed for it was the all-time season record for the fewest BR/9 IP (9.21) among qualifiers with a winning percentage below .300 (.279)—and a return ticket to the minors once Milwaukee disbanded.

Weaver joined independent Worcester in 1879 under Bancroft and was a member of the first team—in a time still without scorecards, let alone numbered uniforms—whose players sported a form of individual identification. According to the *Chicago Tribune*, each Worcester worthy wore a colored band around his cap an inch wide, "the color to be printed against the player's name in the scorecard, as follows": Charlie Bennett, blue; Weaver, red; Frank Heifer, yellow; Steve Brady, green; Art Whitney, brown; Jim Mutrie, orange; Ike Benners, black; Tricky Nichols, white; Lon Knight, crimson; and Doc Bushong, purple.

By July 1879, however, Bancroft had "gotten down" on Weaver, preferring Lee Richmond, and the original Buck began pitching for hire on a temp basis with such unheralded independent teams as Campello, MA. The following year he returned to his hometown to hurl for the Globe team and by 1881 had joined the Eastern Championship Association Athletics. When the A's advanced to the rebel AA in 1882, Weaver was expected to be their ace but began the season with a lame arm, causing his teammates to curse when management did not hire a quality pitcher to replace him but instead tried to get by with marginal types, like Harry Arundel, until he healed. Despite eventually winning 26 games, he was allowed to sign with Louisville the following year and then jumped to the Philadelphia UA Keystones in 1884 after another big season in 1883 with 24 wins as second fiddle to Guy Hecker.

Back to first fiddle, Weaver was creamed 14–1 by Boston on Opening Day in 1884 and was released by the Keystones even before the club disbanded on August 7. The excuse given was that his salary was too high, but the truth was he was the least effective pitcher in the UA. In his seventeen starts with the Keystones, Weaver allowed 14.36 BR/9 IP and logged a 5.76 ERA, the poorest among UA qualifiers. Arm or shoulder trouble was almost certainly the culprit for the Philadelphian's rapid decline. Weaver tried to come back with the A's in 1886 but was hurriedly scrapped after his first two starts in Philly yielded a 14.73 ERA. By the end of the decade he was a policeman in Philadelphia, and his arm eventually was useful enough again to play SS on a team of Philadelphia "bobbies" that challenged police teams in surrounding cities. In 1908 Weaver retired from the force with twenty-one years of service when an operation failed to remedy a serious heart condition. He died of a heart attack at his Philadelphia home in 1914 as he sat down to breakfast. Local obits referred to him as "Buck Weaver" and extolled his terrific speed. (DN)

White, William Henry / "Will" "Medicine Bill" "Whoop-La"

B	T	HGT	WGT	G	IP	H	GS
B	R	5'9"	175	403	3542.2	3440	401

CG	BB	SO	SH	W	L	PCT	ERA
394	496	1041	36	229	166	.580	2.28

G	W	L	PCT	PENNANTS
72	44	27	.620	0

B. 10/11/1854 Caton, NY **D.** 8/31/1911
TEAMS: 77BosN 78–80CinN 81DetN 82–86CinA (P/M)84CinA
DEBUT AND FAMOUS FIRST: 7/20/1877 at Cincinnati; was the first pitcher to be caught by his brother (Deacon White) in his ML debut and lost 13–11 to Cincinnati's Candy Cummings
FINALE: 7/5/1886 at Philadelphia; caught by Charlie Snyder and beat Philadelphia's Ted Kennedy 14–7
CAREER HIGHLIGHT: In 1879 compiled the following ML season records: most starts (75), most CGs (75), most innings pitched (680), and most batters faced (2,906)

Will White grew up on a farm in western New York playing ball with his older brother Jim, nicknamed "Deacon." By the early 1870s, while the elder White was developing into one of the top players in the country, Will remained on his father's farm, honing his pitching talents. After the younger White had spent 1876 with independent Binghamton, Boston signed the two siblings that winter, and in late February manager Harry Wright wrote Deacon, mentioning that if Will wanted to take on the job of caring for the team's grounds and clubhouse, the club would pay him an extra $60 a month.

He saw more action in that job than he did pitching. With Tommy Bond, the best hurler in the game, taking care of nearly all the work for Boston, White hurled only three contests, all against weak Cincinnati. Still, he showed enough that both White brothers were signed by Cincinnati for the ensuing year. It was thought that White might back up Bobby Mitchell, another young pitcher who had made a splash the previous fall with the Reds, but he won the regular job and became a Cincinnati mainstay for most of the next decade. In 1878 he pitched Cincinnati to a strong second-place finish. The following year Cincinnati went much of the season without a backup pitcher except right fielder Blondie Purcell, leaving White to start 75 of the team's 81 games. Even by the standards of that time, when pitchers threw underhanded, his iron man work that season, which featured four all-time records, was remarkable.

In 1881 Cincinnati was dropped from the NL. White could undoubtedly have signed elsewhere, but he preferred to remain in Cincinnati to watch his business interests there. Just before the season started Detroit was desperate for a replacement pitcher. Not anxious to leave his business, White set his terms high, but manager Frank Bancroft made him a generous enough offer that he agreed to go to Detroit on a one-month contract. White was expected to alternate with an overworked George Derby, but the *Cincinnati Enquirer* predicted that with no spring training he would "get little glory out of it," and so it proved. White was ineffective and returned to tending his store and pitching occasional games with local semipro teams. When a reorganized Cincinnati club entered the upstart AA in the fall of 1881, White became one of the first players signed. With Charlie Snyder, a fine thinking man's catcher, White formed a battery that was the heart of the AA's inaugural pennant winner and remained a mainstay for Cincinnati until 1885.

In 1884 White replaced Snyder as team captain, in effect acting as a modern manager, but with the added responsibility he did not pitch up to his usual standard. In August, Snyder was returned to command, White having reportedly stepped down because managing was affecting his pitching. The fact was that his skills were in decline. In January 1885 Snyder set off a furor in Cincinnati when he told a reporter that the Reds played without confidence when White was in the box "because they are always expecting to see [his] delivery pounded all over the field." Late in the 1885 campaign White went to the bench, and after that season he announced his retirement.

In June 1886 White was persuaded to give it another try and was welcomed roundly by a huge Cincinnati crowd when he first took the box on June 10 against Pittsburgh. It was soon apparent, however, that manager Opie Caylor, who had predicted White would be the answer to his club's pitching woes, was in for a disappointment. White was only 31 at the time, not old for a smart, well-conditioned pitcher with good control, but while he had been considered a hard thrower in his youth, by the mid-1880s he was almost antediluvian in retaining an underhanded pitching style while other hurlers were transitioning to overhand pitching. It is likely that his career may have been shortened by stubbornness about adjusting to new techniques.

The first bespectacled player in ML history and the only documented one for many years, White looks out from the middle of team photos from the early 1880s with rimless eyeglasses, a walrus mustache, and prematurely white hair, appearing like the kindly grandfather of the young men around him. His mild appearance is to some degree deceiving, although White certainly shared many of the virtues of his brother Deacon. He was intelligent, sober, and almost sedate in comparison to many ballplayers, a churchgoer who refused to play on Sunday. While teammates drank their salaries away, White saved his money and ran a succession of retail establishments in Cincinnati, including a teashop, groceries, and a drug store. The nickname "Medicine Bill" was given to White for the apothecary he owned.

Yet for all his air of middle-class rectitude, White had an edge to him. To keep hitters loose, he purposely threw at them, and although his underhanded slants probably did not frighten them as much as the deliveries of faster pitchers, he was intimidating enough that he was singled out as the pitcher most responsible for the AA's adoption of the first hit-by-pitch rule in 1884. He was a man of pronounced opinions, and the comments of club secretary and journalist Opie Caylor when White took over the captaincy in 1884 demonstrate he was not as gentle and indulgent as he appeared in team pictures. Caylor promised that White would impose "a better discipline . . . more system and less dependence on the ability of the team to manage itself. . . . All the players will be asked to obey orders. . . . If a batter [has] six balls and strike at the seventh [then required for a base on balls], he will be knocking a slice off his next salary installment."

In his AA years White was so close to the Cincinnati management, especially Caylor, that some players regarded him as a stool pigeon and nicknamed him "The Telephone" because they found that everything they said in his vicinity ended up in the ear of club president Aaron Stern. White was also outspoken, though unsuccessful, in advocating the retention of slick-fielding, light-hitting Jimmy Macullar in the regular lineup in 1883, and he used his influence to put himself in the lineup as often as possible. The unfriendly *Cincinnati Enquirer* remarked that Billy Mountjoy would never have pitched at all had White not had religious scruples about Sunday ball. The most striking example of White's influence, however, was the brief benching of SS Chick Fulmer during a series at St. Louis in 1883. There was no love lost between Fulmer and White, and although the full story was not revealed at the time, it appears that White convinced the sometimes impulsive and excitable Caylor that Fulmer was being paid by St. Louis president Chris Von der Ahe to throw games. The rest of the Cincinnati club quickly united in forcing Caylor to restore Fulmer to the lineup.

After the 1886 season White retired to his grocery in Fairmount, a Cincinnati suburb. He left Cincinnati for Buffalo, near his boyhood home, where his brother Deacon and Jack Rowe took over a minor league team in 1889. After Deacon White and Rowe left Buffalo in midseason to play for Pittsburgh, Will filled in as team manager. He subsequently left baseball, partnering with his brother as an optician in Buffalo. White drowned in 1911 when he suffered a heart attack while teaching a niece to swim at his summer home in Port Carling, Ontario. (DB/DN)

Whitney, James Evans / "Jim" "Grasshopper"

B	T	HGT	WGT	G	IP	H	GS
L	R	6'2"	172	413	3496.1	3598	396

CG	BB	SO	SH	W	L	PCT	ERA
377	411	1571	26	191	204	.484	2.97

G	AB	H	R	2B	3B	HR
550	2144	559	316	139	39	18

RBI	BB	SO	SB	BA	SA	OBP
280	161	211	20	.261	.375	.313

B. 11/10/1857 Conklin, NY **D.** 5/21/1891
TEAMS: 81–85BosN 86KCN 87–88WasN 89IndN 90PhiA
DEBUT: 5/2/1881 at Providence; caught by Charlie Snyder and went 3-for-4 in a 4–2 win over Providence's John M. Ward
FINALE: 7/16/1890 at St. Louis; caught by Wilbert Robinson and lost 9–8 to St. Louis's Tom Ramsey after giving up 5 hits to Ramsey, a notoriously weak hitter
CAREER HIGHLIGHT: In 1882 became the only player ever to lead a ML team in wins (24), home runs (5), batting (.323). OBP (.382), and slugging (.510)
FAMOUS FIRST: In 1881, his rookie year, became the first pitcher to lead a major league in both wins (31) and losses (33) in the same season
FAMOUS FIRST: Was the first pitcher in ML history to retire with 200 losses (204) and less than 200 wins (191)

During the final years of the 1870s and the early 1880s, pitching deliveries were liberalized, allowing pitchers to throw from shoulder-height or above. No one exemplified the dramatic consequences better than Jim Whitney. Born on a farm near Binghamton, NY, Whitney began playing baseball with area nines and joined the local International Association club in 1878. At some point he acquired the unflattering nickname of "Grasshopper" for his elongated body and relatively small and narrow head. In 1879 Whitney signed to pitch for an Omaha club that made a trip to California but ran out of funds while there. He remained in San Francisco, where his 23-6 log with the local Knickerbockers led the California League. Whitney was a giant by the standard of the times at 6'2", and the elimination of the pitching restrictions together with his development of a running start enabled him to throw with fearsome speed.

Signed to pitch for Boston NL in 1881, Whitney was an immediate sensation. A Buffalo sportswriter gave this description: "With the batsman in position, Whitney revolves the ball in his hands several times, then suddenly he curls himself up like a boy attacked with the gripes or a dog retiring for the night, whirls his leg, his right arm shoots straight from the shoulder, and the first thing the sorely perplexed striker knows the sphere has . . . started on its errand. For a few minutes the batter is uncertain whether or not the man has a fit, and two or three balls pass by before he fully realizes the situation."

As that account suggests, it was not just that Whitney threw hard—he also had a mean streak and no compunction about trying to intimidate batters. "After a player has faced him once and had several ribs staved in by one of his chain lightning shots," noted another writer, "he comes to the bat the second time and strikes at balls he couldn't reach with a ten-foot pole, in order to get out of the way of another shot." Still another was even more blunt, observing that Whitney was "so notorious for 'accidentally' hitting the batsman with a hard-pitched ball that he has been dubbed the 'man-hitter' throughout the league." Whitney's overpowering fastball made him extremely successful early on. Many terrified batters seem to have all but given up trying to hit his offerings after one or two at-bats, as he struck out 16 in a game with Chicago and 13 against Detroit. He followed with 24 wins in 1882 despite missing a week in June when he was subpoenaed to testify in a murder trial in Omaha and then had his best season in 1883, helping Boston to claim the NL pennant while alternating with Charlie Buffinton to keep hitters off stride as they faced a pure power pitcher one day and a fine drop curve the next.

Gradually, however, batters grew more accustomed to Whitney and to other pitchers who relied solely on tremendous speed. While he remained an effective pitcher—averaging nearly 27 wins per season and compiling a 2.49 ERA in his five years with Boston—it gradually became clear that he was not as valuable to the team as his gaudy statistics suggested. In particular, Whitney's lightning-fast deliveries took a dreadful toll on catchers. Worse, he showed no compassion for his receivers, never modulating his pace and becoming angry with any whose hands became too sore to handle his fastballs. Although good-natured when off the field, such actions, coupled with his constant arguing with umpires, earned Whitney a reputation as a prima donna. Finally, he was hoisted on his own petard, as the legalization of overhand pitching reduced him from the best-hitting pitcher in the game in the early 1880s to no more than an average batsman by the middle of the decade.

After Whitney went 18-32 in 1885, Boston signed Charley Radbourn to replace him. Henry Chadwick aptly commented that the acquisition of Radbourn "throws the pacer Whitney out of the Boston market. He was too costly in wearing out catchers last season. His great pace is his only point. He knows nothing of strategic play." Whitney made a triumphant return to Boston the following June. Wearing a Kansas City uniform, he allowed his old teammates only 2 hits and beat Radbourn. But over the next five seasons, he experienced only sporadic success as he pitched for KC, Washington, Indianapolis in the NL, and Philadelphia of the AA. He was released by Philadelphia in July 1890. Whitney had married a sister of Washington teammate George Haddock, and he began making plans for life after baseball by entering the hay and grain business. But his health failed and, only ten months after his final ML appearance, he died of tuberculosis in Binghamton. (PM/DN/DB)

Whitrock, William Franklin / "Bill"

B	T	HGT	WGT	G	IP	H	GS
?	R	5'7½"	170	37	235	296	29

CG	BB	SO	SH	W	L	PCT	ERA
24	102	57	0	9	19	.321	5.44

B. 3/4/1870 Cincinnati, OH **D.** 7/36/1935
TEAMS: 90StLA 93–94LouN 94CinN 96PhiN
DEBUT: 5/3/1890 at St. Louis; relieved Elton Chamberlin in Chamberlin's 10–6 loss to Louisville's Scott Stratton
FINALE: 7/11/1896 at Louisville; relieved Jack Taylor in Taylor's 9–1 loss to Louisville's Chick Fraser

Bill Whitrock's first pro experience came with Springfield, OH, of the Tri-State League in 1889. He went to camp with Cincinnati NL the following spring, but his hopes of making his ML debut in his home city were squelched when holdout Jesse Duryea joined the Reds in March. After signing with St. Louis AA, Whitrock was used exclusively in relief until May 17, 1890, when he lost to Syracuse 5–0 as the Stars' John Keefe held the Browns to just 1 hit, a bloop double. Previously, Whitrock had broken up a no-hitter himself with his first ML hit when he doubled in the seventh inning against Columbus's Hank Gastright on May 8. After St. Louis released him in July, he finished the season with Portland of the Pacific Northwest League.

Although Whitrock later returned to the majors on two separate occasions, his rookie year proved to be his best: 5-6 with a 3.51 ERA. Haunted throughout his career by streaks of wildness, he was nonetheless a popular presence on all of his teams for his fine tenor voice and his quirky inventions. In 1897, while with Canandaigua, the New York State League champs, Whitrock developed what he called a "dead arm cure" by using a hot iron to press out ailing muscles and tendons in his arm. The treatment formed a bad blister on his arm that "reeked of foul smelling pus," but after avowing that his arm was better once the blister healed, he persuaded teammates to try his new cure. His credibility was undermined when his arm miseries returned and he was unable to return to pro ball until 1900 for one last unmemorable season. Whitrock later settled in Derby, CT, and worked at a restaurant and then at the Robert N. Bassett Company in Shelton. He died in Derby of a heart attack at 65. (DN)

Widner, William Waterfield / "Bill" "Wild Bill"

B	T	HGT	WGT	G	IP	H	GS
R	R	6'0"	180	69	522	606	59

CG	BB	SO	SH	W	L	PCT	ERA
48	137	110	3	22	36	.379	4.36

B. 6/3/1867 Cincinnati, OH **D.** 12/10/1908
TEAMS: 87CinA 88WasN 89–90ColA 91CinA
DEBUT: 6/8/1887 at Philadelphia; caught by Kid Baldwin and beat Philadelphia's Ed Seward 9–8
FINALE: 7/23/1891 at Cincinnati; caught by Mike Kelly and lost 7–4 to St. Louis's Jack Stivetts

The son of a school janitor in Cumminsville, a northern suburb of Cincinnati, Bill Widner first drew kudos pitching for the local Cumminsville Blues and signed with Cincinnati AA in late May 1887. Widner won his only game against an AA opponent, beating Philadelphia, but did not play again in an official game prior to his release on August 13. He signed with New Orleans of the Southern League for a reported $175 a month, which if accurate was nearly double what the Reds had been paying him.

The clock started ticking on Widner's fifteen minutes of fame when the SL folded on July 4, 1888, and representatives of ML clubs descended on the Crescent City to bid for the Pelicans' best players. Widner signed with Washington, but New Orleans reorganized, entered the Texas League, and wanted him back. The resulting legal maneuvering sidelined Widner for much of September, but when not out of action he pitched 12 games for the Senators and ultimately remained Washington property after New Orleans disbanded for good. As frequently happened, the intensity of the pursuit for a disputed free agent was out of proportion to his value. Widner was a good minor league pitcher and did respectable work in Washington, but he was inconsistent, and by the following winter the D.C. club had him up for sale. His brief tenure in Washington ended when he and outfielder Ed Daily were waived out of the NL and purchased for a modest price by Columbus AA in January 1889. Widner proved he could live up to his "Wild Bill" nickname and be part of a hard-drinking team when he and catcher Ned Bligh stayed out all night on the eve of the season and were fined. By midsummer the club was embroiled in a player revolt over fines withheld from salaries, with Widner reportedly short $175 from his bimonthly pay. If he could not stay sober, Widner at least remained healthy, unlike many of Columbus's pitchers. He worked more than anyone except team ace Mark Baldwin, but the *Columbus Dispatch* called him "a woeful disappointment" and the *Ohio State Journal* said he had been periodically "less than useless to the club."

Nevertheless, Widner returned for another season, having signed "an iron-clad agreement" prohibiting drinking, but he had physical problems in 1890 and pitched sparingly. In late June the *Journal* observed that, while it disapproved of fighting, it sympathized with Widner's actions in knocking down a man who had accused him of drinking, for he had stayed sober all season and said he was glad of it: "If I was released tomorrow"—a real possibility by that point—"the bad luck would not drive me to drink." In spite of everything, Widner was exceptionally popular with Columbus denizens, and in deference to public sentiment the management reluctantly gave him a last chance on July 10. He was knocked out of the box in the seventh inning of an 11–9 loss to Rochester and drew his release that evening.

News reports refer to a thumb injury, but it is likely that Widner had arm problems as well, for his pitching days were numbered. He went to Sioux City of the Western Association, where he had a close call when he and his roommate were nearly asphyxiated after neglecting to turn off the gas in their hotel room. By season's end he was playing 1B. He subsequently went back to pitching for local teams around Cincinnati and obtained one final ML box appearance with Cincinnati AA in 1891. After unsuccessful ventures in the Southern and Western leagues in 1892, Widner left baseball. He enlisted in the army during the Spanish-American War but otherwise worked at a variety of blue-collar jobs. In the early 1900s his health began to decline. Widner died at his Cincinnati home of diabetes at 41. (DB/DN)

Wiedman, George E.
(aka Weidman) **/ "Stump"**

B	T	HGT	WGT	G	IP	H	GS
R	R	5'7½"	165	279	2318.1	2594	269

CG	BB	SO	SH	W	L	PCT	ERA
249	459	910	13	101	156	.393	3.61

G	AB	H	R	2B	3B	HR
379	1401	248	132	28	4	2

RBI	BB	SO	SB	BA	SA	OBP
112	45	193	11	.177	.209	.203

B. 2/17/1861 Rochester, NY **D.** 3/2/1905
TEAMS: 80BufN 81–85DetN 86KCN 87DetN 87NYA 87–88NYN
DEBUT: 8/26/1880 at Buffalo; caught by Tom Kearns in a 3–3 tie with Boston's Tommy Bond
FINALE: 7/5/1888 at Detroit; caught by Buck Ewing and lost 18–13 to Detroit's Pete Conway
CAREER HIGHLIGHT: Led the NL in ERA in 1881 despite not throwing his first pitch of the NL season until September

Originally a hard thrower with no frills, the stumpy George Wiedman was a poor hitter but saw considerable outfield duty because managers in that era still felt that his able fielding was more essential than having a stronger bat in the lineup. At age 22 Wiedman already had two 20-win seasons to his credit, but a lethal combination of overwork at an early age and laboring for a string of bad teams caught up to him by the time he was 25, and he finished his ML career just two years later.

Born in Rochester, Wiedman played locally and worked out with the Rochester University baseball squad in the spring of 1880. He signed on June ninth with Rochester the same day that player-manager Horace Phillips landed the resurrected Hop Bitters in the minor league National Association. The 19-year-old found himself on a team with Dan Brouthers and Buck Ewing, alternating in the box with Hugh Daily. When Wiedman beat the slugging Buffalo club of the NL twice in early July exhibitions, six weeks later Buffalo signed him to spell its ace, Jim Galvin.

Too green as yet for NL competition, Wiedman was 0-9 in thirteen appearances and slid to Washington of the Eastern Championship Association in 1881. He went to Albany after Washington disbanded and had a 13-17 overall record in 1881 when he signed with Detroit. Despite not returning to the NL until early September, Wiedman fashioned a 1.80 ERA in thirteen starts and won the retrospective loop ERA crown. The youngest regular pitcher in the majors, he was so dominant that manager Frank Bancroft dropped another promising young arm, Tony Mullane.

Bancroft alternated Wiedman with George Derby in 1882, and Wiedman responded with 25 wins and made Detroit the surprise first-place club until July 13. On August 17 he lost the famous eighteen-inning 1–0 game to Providence that was resolved by Charley Radbourn's solo home run. But Bancroft's wife died after the season, and Jack Chapman took over the Detroit reins in 1883. Even though the Wolverines were never in serious contention, Chapman used Wiedman in 52 games and over 400 innings. Wiedman lost the 1883 season opener and then won 9 straight until a 6-run third inning facing Boston on May 28 signified that he needed rest. Instead Chapman started him in 7 of the club's next 10 games. The following year Detroit suffered the most losses of any team in the majors (84) under Chapman while a sprained wrist saved Wiedman from further abuse and held him to just 212 innings. Chapman's departure in 1885 saw Detroit move out of the cellar and Wiedman regain a semblance of form after a 3-15 start. His fastball was gone, however, and when he told the Detroit press that Bill Watkins "is no good as a manager, and I would not play under him," he was among the players Detroit gave the NL to stock the new Kansas City and Washington franchises, and KC claimed him. Forming a two-man staff with Jim Whitney, in 1886 he led the NL in both hits and runs allowed.

When KC left the NL after just one season, Detroit reclaimed Wiedman for 1887. Returning to the city where he once starred, he opened the season 9-0 with excellent run support. He continued to be effective, but meanwhile Detroit loaded up on promising young pitchers, rendering him nearly superfluous. When Wiedman lost 12–2 on July 18 at Philadelphia, Watkins labeled him as "indifferent" and took the opportunity to make some quick money on him by selling him on August 9 to the AA New York Mets for $600. Wiedman finished the AA season 4-8 and went to the NL New York Giants after the Mets disbanded. Arm trouble delayed his Giants debut until June 4, 1888, when he beat Indianapolis 3–2. But it was a month before he could pitch again, and his second outing made it depressingly clear that his arm could no longer take the strain. He finished the year with Toronto of the International Association, sat out most of 1889, and then went 16-11 for a Dunkirk, PA, semi-pro team in 1890 and later suffered through two dismal comeback attempts in the Eastern League.

In 1896 Wiedman worked as a regular NL umpire for three months but quit after a game at Louisville on June 26 that *TSN* described as "almost a riot from start to finish." After Cleveland's Jesse Burkett homered in ninth to tie the game 4–4, Louisville made three outs deliberately, claiming it was too dark to continue. But Cleveland manager Pat Tebeau prevailed upon Wiedman to start the tenth, and the Spiders scored 5 runs on homers by Jimmy McAleer and Chippy McGarr. Louisville had loaded the bases in the bottom half of the frame when Wiedman abruptly called the game, with the score reverting to a 4–4 tie, so enraging Cleveland that McAleer slugged him as he tried to leave field. Wiedman later managed the Rochester Eastern League club in 1897 until the team moved to Montreal in July. He then married the daughter of AL umpire Silk O'Loughlin and was part owner of a summer resort in suburban Rochester until his death in New York City at 44 from throat cancer. (DN/FV/DB)

Wilson, Frank Ealton / "Zeke"

B	T	HGT	WGT	G	IP	H	GS
R	R	5'10"	165	120	882	1054	106

CG	BB	SO	SH	W	L	PCT	ERA
84	270	198	3	52	44	.542	4.03

B. 12/24/1869 Benton, AL **D.** 4/26/1928
TEAMS: 95BosN 95–98CleN 99StLN
DEBUT: 4/23/1895 at Washington; caught by Jack Warner and lost 4–1 to Washington's Al Maul

FINALE: 6/28/1899 at St. Louis; relieved Willie Sudhoff in a 5–0 loss to Baltimore's Joe McGinnity

Zeke Wilson was an outfielder in 1890 when he first surfaced with a semipro team in Troy, AL. He then pitched for parts of three seasons in the Southern League before journeying north in 1894 to play for the Pottsville Pennsylvania State League champions. Scouted by Cleveland outfielder Jimmy McAleer, who was also interested in pitcher Bobby Wallace, Wilson was McAleer's choice, but by then Boston had also joined the chase. The pitcher was awarded to Boston after a dispute and trained with the Hub team in the spring of 1895. But late that June, Boston opted to let Wilson join Cleveland after all. He pitched sporadically with the Spiders until September, when he contracted malaria. Wilson rebounded strongly in 1896, winning 17 games as he, Cy Young, Bobby Wallace, and Nig Cuppy accounted for all of Cleveland's 80 victories and spurred the Spiders to their second straight Temple Cup appearance. His performance fell off in 1897 and was even more disappointing the following year, when he went 13-18.

That winter Wilson was shot in the hip in a roadhouse melee near Montgomery, AL, after stabbing his assailant in an altercation over a woman both men had been buying drinks. He recovered in time to report to spring training with St. Louis after syndicate ownership shifted most of Cleveland's better players to the Mound City club. Unwanted by the Perfectos, he was cut on July 6, 1899, after he refused to go back to Cleveland "except as a last resort." Wilson later pitched in the Southern Association in the early 1900s but was only a marginal contributor after enjoying a 16-win season for Atlanta in 1903. He died in a Montgomery, AL, hospital in 1928 after an extended illness. (DN)

Wise, William E. / "Bill"

B	T	HGT	WGT	G	IP	H	GS
?	?	5'7"	142	54	393.1	419	45

CG	BB	SO	SH	W	L	PCT	ERA
37	66	277	4	24	21	.533	3.07

B. 3/15/1861 Washington, D.C. **D.** 5/5/1940
TEAMS: 82BalA 84WasU 86WasN
DEBUT: 5/2/1882 at Philadelphia; played CF and went 1-for-5 in a 10–7 loss to Philadelphia's Sam Weaver
FINALE: 7/17/1886 at Washington; caught by Phil Baker and finished in RF after being relieved by Ed Fuller in his 8–1 loss to Philadelphia's Charlie Ferguson

Bill Wise was capable of playing both SS and CF between box appearances. In 1880 he joined the National Association Washington entry and remained with the Nationals through 1881. The following year proved him unready for faster company, and he appeared in just 5 games with Baltimore AA, spending most of the season on the club's reserve squad. Wise did, however, gain the distinction of earning Baltimore's first win as a member of the AA, topping Philadelphia's Sam Weaver 6–4 on May 4, 1882, in his first ML pitching stint.

He returned to the Nationals late in 1883 from Harrisburg of the Interstate Association and was among the club members that moved to the rebel UA in 1884. Expected by manager Mike Scanlon to serve as the club's ace, Wise lost the job to Milo Lockwood but quickly reclaimed it after Lockwood was battered in the season opener while he played RF and batted second. Wise continued to bat high in the order all season, sometimes even leading off on days he pitched. Though he hit just .233, he led the team in every major pitching department while collecting exactly half of Washington's 46 wins. Wise later claimed he also sometimes ran the club while Scanlon was on scouting trips for new players, but there is no evidence of that.

Wise remained with the Nationals when they left the UA and dropped down to the minor Eastern League in 1885. He returned to the majors for one game with the fledgling Washington NL entry the following year and later pitched in the minors with Hartford of the Atlantic Association, where Prunes Moolic caught him. Wise remained a resident of the nation's capitol for his entire life and died there at 79. (DN)

*Wood, Peter Burke / "Pete"

B	T	HGT	WGT	G	IP	H	GS
?	R	5'7"	185	27	217.2	263	24

CG	BB	SO	SH	W	L	PCT	ERA
23	69	46	0	9	16	.360	4.51

B. 2/1/1857 Hamilton, Ontario, Canada
D. 3/15/1923
TEAMS: 85BufN 89PhiN

DEBUT: 7/15/1885 at Buffalo; caught by George Myers in a 4–2 loss to Chicago's John Clarkson
FINALE: 6/29/1889 at Pittsburgh; caught by Harry Decker in an 8–0 loss to Pittsburgh's Harry Staley
CAREER HIGHLIGHT: 9/30/1885 at Boston; Wood and his brother Fred became the third sibling battery in ML history in his 5–3 loss to Boston's Jim Whitney

Pete Wood's birth date is questionable. Against his having been born as early as 1857 are the facts that he does not appear to have started his pro career until 1883 and the August 22, 1885, *SL* said that he was 20 years old and Buffalo manager Jack Chapman had difficulty securing the necessary consent for him to leave Canada and pitch in the United States because his parents were against the move. In 1883 Wood pitched for independent Hamilton, Ontario, with his brother Fred as his catcher, and *SL* called them "the finest battery in Canada." He was still with Hamilton in 1885 when Chapman finally persuaded his parents to let him pitch for Buffalo. In his very first game Wood committed a gaffe that pointed up a still-existing flaw in the rulebook when his towering fly ball down the LF line fell safely among three Chicago fielders. Wood only got as far as 2B on the hit because he had presumed the ball would go foul and did not run until the ball landed fair. Cap Anson played the game under protest because umpire John Gaffney refused to declare Wood out for not running as soon as the ball was hit as per a rule that had been introduced after a Boston batter (*see* Joseph Hornung) had helped his team win a game against Chicago two years earlier by refusing to run after hitting a potential double play ball.

Wood remained with Buffalo in 1886 after the city left the NL and put a team in the International Association before returning to Hamilton after Buffalo released him in August. That fall he enrolled in the University of Toronto and attended it in the off-season while continuing to pitch for Hamilton. In 1888 Wood hit .322 for Hamilton in 96 games as a combination pitcher-outfielder and posted a 1.80 ERA in the 50 International Association contests in which he occupied the box. St. Louis, embroiled in a tight AA pennant race, tried to buy him in August but blanched when Hamilton wanted a reported $8,000 for him. Hamilton eventually received considerably less that that but still, reportedly, received a healthy $3,500 from Philadelphia NL in November 1888, some of which may have gone to Wood in addition to the $3,000 salary he reportedly was given by Philadelphia. Wood appears either to have arrived at the Quakers' spring training site in 1889 with a sore arm or else to have injured his arm during the exhibition season. There is also a possibility that Wood pampered his arm that spring to a degree that convinced Quakers manager Harry Wright he was a malingerer. In any event, the expensive off-season purchase did not make his first appearance with the Quakers until May 31, when he beat Indianapolis 11–4. Wood may have reinjured his arm in the game since he did not appear again for nearly a month, or he may simply have aggravated Wright again. About a week after what would be his final ML appearance, the *Chicago Tribune* commented, "Manager Wright admits that Pete Wood is not strong enough for the league." Meanwhile, Wood blew the whistle to *TSN* that Wright had the Quakers playing a seven-inning practice game every afternoon, either before or after the regularly scheduled game that day, and that pitchers were not excused from the game even on days they were slated to pitch. Wood then grumbled that Wright was way "too much of a disciplinarian to be a successful manager." Two weeks after Wood's comments appeared in *TSN*, Wright bit the bullet and released his $3,500 acquisition, and by late August, Wood was back in the International Association and admitting that his career in Philadelphia had been "short and sweet."

In October 1889 Wood married a woman from Watertown, NY, and may have decided at that juncture that he needed something more stable than pro baseball. After one last season in the minors he enrolled in medical school at Western University in Toronto and pitched for the school team. By 1892 he was practicing medicine in Hamilton but subsequently returned to the States and moved his practice to Anaconda, MT, where he also found time to be a choir leader. Wood died in Chicago of anemia and cirrhosis of the liver, leaving behind his wife, Bertha. (DN/DB)

Woods, Walter Sydney / "Walt"

B	T	HGT	WGT	G	IP	H	GS
R	R	5'9½"	165	54	404.1	449	43

CG	BB	SO	SH	W	L	PCT	ERA
35	97	48	3	18	26	.409	3.34

G	AB	H	R	2B	3B	HR
91	281	46	31	2	1	1

RBI	BB	SO	SB	BA	SA	OBP
22	14	—	8	.164	.189	.206

B. 4/28/1875 Rye, NH **D.** 10/30/1951
TEAMS: 98ChiN 99LouN 00PitN
DEBUT: 4/20/1898 at Louisville; played 2B and went 0-for-4 in a 7–6 loss to Louisville's Bill Magee
FINALE: 4/27/1900 at Pittsburgh; relieved Jesse Tannehill, who took the 19–5 loss to Cincinnati's Ed Scott
CAREER ODDITY: 6/22/1898 at Chicago; caught by Tom Donahue and lost 6–5 to Ted Lewis of Boston in fourteen innings when Lewis singled home the winning run; in his last start, five days earlier, Woods had also lost by 1 run in fourteen innings when his pitching opponent, Louisville's Bill Hill, singled home the winning run

In 1894 Walt Woods attended Phillips Exeter Academy and played summers for the Portsmouth, NH, Athletic Club. Upon turning pro he climbed the ladder in the New England minor leagues as a combination pitcher-outfielder. By 1897 Woods was with Springfield, MA, of the Eastern League under Tom Burns. Woods then accompanied Burns when Burns replaced Cap Anson as the Chicago NL manager in 1898 but nearly didn't make the team when he spent his every waking hour in the spring that he was not on the ball field carrying on a torrid correspondence with his girlfriend in New Hampshire. Woods eventually debuted at 2B and, despite hitting just .175, played everywhere except catcher and 1B for Chicago in his rookie season. For religious reasons, he refused to play on Sunday, and Burns respected the wishes of the hurler (who became known as "the Sunday School Pitcher") even though Chicago had Sunday ball by 1898.

In January 1899 Woods went to Louisville as compensation for the Colonels having waived their option on Milwaukee pitcher Jack Taylor the previous August. He remained in the Louisville rotation all year and also showed enough as a position player, even though he continued to hit poorly, that he was among the crew Colonels owner Barney Dreyfuss, who also owned a slice of the Pittsburgh franchise, targeted to take to Pittsburgh after Louisville folded following the 1899 season. To Woods fell the honor of pitching the final home game in the Louisville franchise's history on September 2, 1899, against Washington. Supported by 6 Louisville home runs, just 1 short of the single-game team record at that time, he triumphed 25–4.

Over that winter, Woods saved the life of a boy who had fallen through the ice in Portsmouth, NH, where Woods was then residing, but he could not save his big-league career when the NL shrank to eight teams, reducing ML pitching jobs by some 50 percent. Following his coda relief appearance with Pittsburgh in 1900, he finished the season with Springfield, where he led all Eastern League hurlers in fielding after handling over one-hundred chances without making an error. Some years after Woods quit the game to run a grocery store in Portsmouth, Hugh Fullerton compared him to Cubs hurler Carl Lundgren, in that both survived primarily on trickery and guile. In addition, Woods had an eerie knack for picking off base runners even though he never seemed to watch the bases. Opposing players said it was as if he had eyes in the back of his head. But even with the extra edge Woods's fielding and base-watching skills gave him, he was barely adequate against ML hitters. Since the advent of the 60'6" pitching distance in 1893, no pitcher who worked as many as 250 innings at the big-league level ever notched fewer strikeouts per nine innings than Woods (1.07). After coaching baseball for a number of years at the University of New Hampshire and Dartmouth College, Woods adapted to a less exciting life as a mail carrier in his hometown of Portsmouth, NH. He died in that city at 76. (DN)

Yeager, Joseph F. / "Joe" "Little Joe"

B	T	HGT	WGT	G	IP	H	GS
R	R	5'10"	160	48	356	410	39

CG	BB	SO	SH	W	L	PCT	ERA
36	101	78	1	15	25	.375	3.94

G	AB	H	R	2B	3B	HR
69	190	35	24	5	2	0

RBI	BB	SO	SB	BA	SA	OBP
19	13	—	1	.184	.232	.255

B. 8/28/1875 Philadelphia, PA **D.** 7/2/1937

TEAMS: 98–00BroN 01–03DetAL 05–06NYAL 07–08StLAL
DEBUT: 4/22/1898 at Washington; caught by Jack Ryan and beat Bill Dinneen, Doc Amole, and Bill Donovan 12–7
FINALE: 9/29/1908 at St. Louis; played 2B and went 1-for-3 in a 2–1 win over New York's Rube Manning

Joe Yeager eventually quit pitching and became a position player despite showing scant promise as a hitter early in his career. In his fourth pro season he was purchased by Brooklyn from Lancaster of the Atlantic Association in late September 1897 for considerably less than the $3,000 Lancaster had demanded the previous year when the Phillies sought his services. Lacking a change of pace and chided for failing to follow through on his pitches, Yeager joined Jack Dunn and Roaring Bill Kennedy in giving Brooklyn three 20-game losers in 1898, but he had two highlights. On May 17 at Boston he spoiled a potential Ted Lewis no-hitter by singling with two out in the ninth, although he lost the game 12–0. Then in early October, while out rowing in Jamaica Bay, he and teammate Jack Grim combined to rescue a man who had fallen out of his rowboat.

When Ned Hanlon took charge of Brooklyn in 1899, Yeager was very diffident at first around the famous manager but gradually began to thaw after Hanlon praised him for his fielding and worked with him on not letting go of his pitches too soon. Still, he was used infrequently, appearing in more games as a SS than as a pitcher, and was farmed to Detroit of the newly renamed AL in 1900. Recalled in October after the AL season ended, he split two decisions with Brooklyn and then jumped to Detroit over the winter when it became apparent he did not fit into Hanlon's plans for 1901. By 1903 Yeager had become largely a position player, usually appearing at 3B, but never hit enough to claim a regular post for more than a one-year stretch.

He finished the ML portion of his career with the 1908 Browns and then played in the minors for a time before settling in Detroit and working as a city employee. Upon Yeager's death at his Detroit home in 1937 after a long illness, an obit credited him with inventing the squeeze play, but the device was part of the game long before he appeared on the scene. (DN)

Zettlein, George / "Charmer" "George" "The Lively Tortoise"

B	T	HGT	WGT	G	IP	H	GS
R	R	5'9"	162	250	2176.2	2678	244

CG	BB	SO	SH	W	L	PCT	ERA
228	145	143	13	129	112	.535	2.49

B. 7/12/1844 Williamsburg, NY **D.** 5/22/1905
TEAMS: 71ChiNA 72TroNA 72EckNA 73PhiNA 74–75ChiNA 75PhiNA 76PhiN
DEBUT: 5/8/1871 at Chicago; caught by Charlie Hodes and beat Cleveland's Al Pratt 14–12
FINALE: 9/16/1876 at Philadelphia; caught by Bill Coon and lost 7–6 to Louisville's Jim Devlin

George Zettlein claimed (probably falsely) that he served in both the army and the navy in the Civil War and was on Admiral Farragut's flagship in the Battle of New Orleans. According to James Terry, the pitcher was "a big-footed, buffoonish character," and William Ryczek depicted him as famous for getting hit in the head with a line drive, taking a drink of water, and going back to work. Yet outfielder Ned Cuthbert claimed that the "Charmer" was the speediest pitcher of his day, and he was also said to be the first pitcher to give pickoff signs to his infielders and then to throw to a base without looking, expecting them to have gotten the sign and be on the bag. But while reports as to his skill and acumen may be contradictory, Zettlein was undeniably the first pitcher in ML history to give up a home run (on May 8, 1871, to Cleveland's Ezra Sutton) and also the first to surrender a grand slam (on September 5, 1871, to Boston's Charlie Gould).

A Brooklyn native, Zettlein tossed for the Brooklyn Atlantics in 1870 and beat the Cincinnati Red Stockings 8–7 in eleven innings on June 14 to end their record 97-game winning streak. Probably he would have remained with the Atlantics if they had joined the NA in 1871, but instead he went to Chicago and won his first seven starts of the fledgling ML season before losing 8–5 at New York on June 5. After that he went just 11-8 but led the loop with a 2.73 ERA. Zettlein moved to Troy in 1872 when the Great Fire forced Chicago to disband but returned to the Windy City in 1874 when it rejoined the NA. The following year he severed connections with Chicago on August 3 for what he considered "arbitrary and unjust treatment by the managers" and joined the Philadelphia Pearls, only to run into trouble again almost immediately. On August 30, in the clubhouse after a loss to Hartford, Mike McGeary accused both Zettlein and outfielder Fred Treacey of selling out the game. Both were initially suspended, but at a team meeting that night Treacey accused McGeary of offering Jack Burdock of Hartford $1,000 prior to the game to throw the decision to Philadelphia and suggested McGeary was angry was because he had lost money on the game and not because he believed Zettlein and Treacey had thrown it.

Even though the pitcher finished the season back in the team's good graces, he considered quitting the game to run a restaurant in Far Rockaway, NY. He then decided belatedly to return, but since the Pearls were not part of the newly formed NL, he signed in May with the Philadelphia Athletics and was a bleak 4-16, leading the loop in every negative pitching department except losses and BR/9 IP. After leaving the game, Zettlein worked in the Brooklyn district attorney's office for some years. He died of Bright's disease in Patchogue, NY, while visiting his brother-in-law. Zettlein acquired his most popular nickname from a dancer with Hooley's Minstrels, called "George the Charmer." (DN/DB/EM)

2 | THE CATCHERS

2. Tom Deasley, considered by some observers to have been the best defensive catcher in the majors during his prime years, displays the tools of his trade while he was a member of the 1887 New York Giants.

☆Allison, Douglas L. / "Doug"

B	T	HGT	WGT	G	AB	H	R	2B
R	R	5'10½"	160	318	1407	381	236	44

3B	HR	RBI	BB	SO	SB	BA	SA	OBP
10	2	140	24	40	5	.271	.321	.284

G	IP	H	GS	CG	BB
1	5	11	0	0	1

SO	SH	W	L	PCT	ERA
0	0	0	0	—	1.80

G	W	L	PCT	PENNANTS
23	2	21	.087	0

B. 7/12/1846 Philadelphia, PA **D.** 12/19/1916
TEAMS: 71OlyNA 72TroNA 72EckNA (P/M)73ResNA 73–74MuTNA 75HarNA 76–77HarN 78–79ProN 83BalA
DEBUT: 5/5/1871 at Washington; caught Asa Brainard and made 3 hits in a 20–18 loss to Boston's Al Spalding
FINALE: 7/13/1883 at Baltimore; caught Hardie Henderson, moved to CF and went 2-for-3 in a 9–4 loss to New York's Jack Lynch

A gunner with the Pennsylvania 192nd Infantry in the Civil War, Doug Allison suffered a significant hearing loss during his service. After mustering out of the Union Army, he worked as a marble cutter and played ball on weekends with the Manayunk club of Philadelphia. Allison joined the Geary club, a stronger team, in 1868 until July when the Cincinnati Red Stockings, soon to become baseball's first all-professional nine, courted him. Freckled and fair-complexioned, Allison belied his boyish appearance by proving that he could handle the hard tosses of pitcher Asa Brainard with no more protection than a small circular piece of rubber held between his teeth to prevent a foul tip from shattering them (although on at least one occasion, in 1870, he reportedly wore a pair of buckskin gloves to save his sore hands). Poorly educated in addition to being partially deaf, he had to convince Red Stockings captain Harry Wright that his guarded and sometimes surly demeanor was no more than an attempt to conceal his social unease.

By 1869, with the Red Stockings poised to launch their record winning streak, Wright shared the view of a San Francisco newspaper that Allison was "the best and most sure ball-catcher in the land." The following year, however, Allison began to manifest lackadaisical play behind the plate. Whether out of laziness or to teach the frequently hungover Brainard a lesson, he often made the pitcher chase his own wild tosses when the bases were empty. Yet the pair was still a compatible battery when it signed as a unit with the Washington Olympics for the first organized professional season in 1871. The two separated when financial problems beset the Olympics, with Allison joining Troy in 1872. He had to move yet again after the Haymakers were forced to exit the NA. Allison began 1873 as captain of the Elizabeth Resolutes, playing professionally with his brother Art for the first time, but when the New Jersey club defaulted after just 23 games, he found himself on his fifth NA team in just his third ML season.

In all, Allison played with eight different ML franchises and participated in his final ML game the day after his 37th birthday when Baltimore called in a favor while he was working in the dead letter branch of the Governmental Postal Service. The final member of the fabled Red Stockings to be active in the majors, during the first decade of ML play Allison caught more of the top pitchers than any other backstop. In 1886, after temporarily losing his government post, he moved back to Cincinnati and resumed his old trade as a marble cutter. By the end of the decade, Allison had returned to Washington and was working in a museum for $720 a year. He later reentered the Postal Service and was still on the government payroll in 1916 when he dropped dead of a heart attack at his home one morning while preparing to go to work. (DN/EM)

Baker, George F. (b. Boecke) / "George"

B	T	HGT	WGT	G	AB	H	R	2B
?	?	5'11"	162	126	474	74	45	6

3B	HR	RBI	BB	SO	SB	BA	SA	OBP
0	0	5	14	29	0	.156	.169	.180

B. 8/20/1857 St. Louis, MO **D.** 1/29/1915
TEAMS: 83BalA 84StLU 85StLN 86KCN
DEBUT: 5/24/1883 at Baltimore; played SS and went 2-for-4 in a 16–4 loss to Pittsburgh's Norm Baker
FINALE: 5/1/1886 at Kansas City; caught Pete Conway and went 1-for-4 in a 17–8 loss to Chicago's Jocko Flynn

A member of the 1877 Winona Clippers, George Baker was slated to try out for the St. Louis NL team in 1878 before it disbanded. He then spent 1878 with Springfield, MA, in the International Association and remained with Springfield in 1879 but was ill most of the season and returned to St. Louis, where he played for the semipro Standards in 1881–82. Of German-born parents, the bilingual Baker reentered the pro arena in 1883 with Peoria of the Northwestern League but jumped his contract in June to sign with Baltimore AA. He played just 7 games with the Orioles and spent most of his time trying to keep scorekeepers from confusing him with teammate Phil Baker.

In 1884 Baker shared St. Louis Maroons catching duties with Jack Brennan and compiled the lowest BA in the UA (.164) among players with at least 250 ABs. However, he was the receiver of choice for most of the Maroons' pitchers. Invited to return to the Maroons in 1885 after they switched to the NL, Baker caught Charlie Sweeney in the club's Opening Day win over Chicago but did little after that. His BA dropped to .122, and he found it difficult to catch faster overhand pitching once it was legalized. Released at the end of the season, he caught on with the Kansas City NL replacement team in the spring of 1886 but lasted only 1 game after Pete Conway, the owner of a high-angled fastball, "had to slack off on his delivery" because Baker was unable to handle him and committed 7 passed balls.

Baker played a while longer in the minors but was so often in poor health that reports appeared that he was either near death or may even have already died. But then in February 1889 *TSN* crowed, "George Baker has so many offers he does not know which one to take." He is believed to have finally signed with Leadville of the Colorado State League, but three years later the same paper carped, "George Baker . . . is making sad lies in St. Louis. George says that he will play ball again next year." By 1895 Baker was working in the mailing department of the Republic Company in St. Louis. He subsequently disappeared until the twentieth century when he was found to have died of kidney disease in St. Louis in 1915 while working as a stereotyper for the *Westliche Post*. Baker's .349 OPS is the lowest among position players with a minimum of 400 career ABs. (DN/DB)

Baldwin, Clarence Geoghan / "Kid"

B	T	HGT	WGT	G	AB	H	R	2B
R	R	5'6"	147	441	1677	371	186	56

3B	HR	RBI	BB	SO	SB	BA	SA	OBP
27	7	178	36	38	40	.221	.299	.243

G	IP	H	GS	CG	BB
2	4	5	0	0	6

SO	SH	W	L	PCT	ERA
1	0	0	0	—	9.00

B. 11/1/1864 Newport, KY **D.** 7/10/1897

TEAMS: 84KCU 84PitU 84KCU 85–89CinA 90CinN 90PhiA

DEBUT: 7/27/1884 at Kansas City; caught Ernie Hickman and went 1-for-4 in a 9–4 loss to St. Louis's Henry Boyle

FINALE: 9/16/1890 at Philadelphia; played 3B and went 0-for-4 in a 5–1 loss to Baltimore's Les German

CAREER HIGHLIGHT: Caught the most games (396) of any player who never appeared in an ML game after the age of 25

FAMOUS FEAT: Played in an official ML game with a team while under contract to another ML team (Kansas City UA) when he caught for Pittsburgh UA on 9/18/1884 at Baltimore after Orioles manager Billy Barnie agreed to let him come out of the stands, where he had been watching the game, and replace injured catcher Tony Suck because Pittsburgh had no other catchers available

Kid Baldwin moved in childhood to St. Louis, probably in connection with his father's work as a riverboat pilot. He entered pro ball in 1883 and was with Quincy of the Northwestern League in 1884 when he left the financially troubled team in late July to join Kansas City UA. Baldwin signed that winter with Milwaukee, another UA team, only to be left high and dry when the UA disbanded and Milwaukee entered the Western League, accepting the requirement that it drop blacklisted players. But Cincinnati outfielder Charley Jones had been impressed with Baldwin's play and recommended him to Reds club secretary Opie Caylor. Caylor had Jones take Baldwin hunting in Virginia, out of the way of rival clubs, until he engineered his removal from the blacklist. Baldwin's play in the next two seasons lived up to Jones's glowing reports, but friction due to his penchant for drinking and the high life frayed his relations with Caylor, who also wrote for the *Cincinnati Commercial Gazette* and subjected Baldwin to humiliating public lectures in his baseball columns.

Caylor's departure from the Reds in the fall of 1886 benefited Baldwin by breaking the cycle of recrimination and resentment into which his relations with the club had sunk. In 1887 Baldwin still had a taste for the high life but had "simmered down to an alarming extent and is not half as 'fresh' as he used to be," and his play improved correspondingly. The highlight of his season was a streak of consecutive games caught, which reached 50 just before the campaign ended. Over the entire season he caught 96 games, more than any other ML catcher, and topped AA receivers in assists. While his conduct was not irreproachable, he could hardly have played so well without staying generally clean.

In subsequent seasons, unfortunately, Baldwin reverted to his old ways, until the Reds finally released him on July 28, 1890. He signed with Philadelphia AA, but after a good start his play deteriorated. Baldwin had other problems as well. The Athletics were not meeting their salary payments and eventually released all their players at the beginning of September. Baldwin was one of the few who agreed to finish the season, but when it was learned he had been telling people he would revenge himself for the missed paydays by jumping the team in St. Louis, he was fired unceremoniously and left to scrounge contributions from other players in order to get home to Quincy.

Early in 1891 Baldwin signed with St. Paul of the Western Association. When the WA disbanded in midseason, he went to Spokane and remained on the west coast with Portland and Los Angeles in 1892, catching over 150 games. Still the old Kid Baldwin, he was sued for jumping an $80 board bill in Los Angeles, but a heavy workload again indicated he was keeping reasonably sober. In 1893 Baldwin signed with New Orleans, where he again shouldered a heavy workload. In July, however, his play slipped after he injured himself in a foolish wrestling match with the club groundskeeper, and he probably began drinking again. When the Southern League collapsed he hired on with Harrisburg of the Pennsylvania State League in April 1894. After catching well during the preseason he was benched due to eye problems and drew his release in late May. Baldwin had now been bounced from the weakest professional league he had ever played in, and something inside him broke. He remained in Harrisburg, no doubt drinking heavily and so isolated that his family had to advertise in the newspapers to contact him after his father died. He was probably already estranged from his wife, Mary (Mamie) Killiger Baldwin, whom he had married in Quincy in 1889. The loss of a newborn child in 1891 must have tested their marriage early on, and a statement Mamie Baldwin made later suggests that a brief sojourn in New Orleans in 1893 may have been the last time they were together. Continuing eye problems eventually threatened Baldwin with blindness, but members of the Philadelphia NL club raised money for a necessary operation, and in July 1895 he was reported on his way home to St. Louis. The operation had saved his sight, but drink and his private demons now took a firm hold of him. He went on the road, gravitating periodically to Cincinnati, usually homeless. When he was found living in a 10¢ lodging house, Tom Loftus hired him as a groundskeeper for his Columbus Western League team, but the job either fell through or Baldwin drank his way out of it.

In the summer of 1897, around the time Mamie Baldwin was requesting a divorce in Quincy, Baldwin was taken to Cincinnati's City Hospital a physical wreck. On July 3 he appeared in Probate Court to be examined for commitment to a mental hospital. *TSN* illustrated his decline with a grim pair of drawings, one showing Baldwin confident and handsome in a Reds uniform, the other showing him as he was now, a battered and bedraggled little man with a full beard and chalky complexion. When told he would be sent where he would have no choice but to stay sober he said he would "go any place where he could be cured." That place was Longview Insane Asylum, but a cure was no longer possible. Scarcely a week after his commitment, Baldwin breathed his last. Word was passed to one of his few remaining friends, who notified Marmie Baldwin in Quincy. (DB/DN)

Bligh, Edwin Forrest / "Ned" "Nelly Bly"

B	T	HGT	WGT	G	AB	H	R	2B
R	R	5'11"	172	66	209	34	17	3

3B	HR	RBI	BB	SO	SB	BA	SA	OBP
1	1	19	16	14	3	.163	.201	.232

B. 6/30/1864 Brooklyn, NY **D.** 4/18/1892
TEAMS: 86BalA 88CinA 89–90ColA 90LouA

DEBUT: 6/26/1886 at Brooklyn; caught Hardie Henderson and was 0-for-3 in a 1–0 loss to Brooklyn's Bill Terry

FINALE: 10/14/1890 at Louisville; caught Phil Ehret and went 2-for-5 in a 13–1 win over St. Louis's Bob Hart

Ned Bligh was an amateur third baseman that was made to catch in an emergency and proved a natural at the position. When the Baltimore AA club arrived in Brooklyn short of catchers in June 1886, Bligh was recommended to manager Billy Barnie by someone who had spotted him catching on occasion for the local amateur Nassau Athletic Club. He proved a capable receiver but could not hit a curve ball and after going hitless in 3 games was traded to Lawrence, MA, of the New England League (*see* Dick Conway). A similar situation arose in 1888 when Cincinnati signed him as a hedge against Kid Baldwin, who had been "getting into paths other than sobriety and peace." Although strong defensively, Bligh was not the player Baldwin was and appeared in only 3 games, again going hitless in all of them. He was then sold to the new Columbus AA entry in December 1888.

Bligh collected his first ML hit in his initial game with Columbus on April 19 at Baltimore. He played quite a bit early in the season but by July was a backup. In August a Columbus woman, Zella Coleman, sued Bligh on the charge that he had fathered her illegitimate child, and he and Columbus club president Conrad Born had to post a $400 bond so the catcher would remain at liberty. The issue was resolved in a way that allowed Bligh to continue his baseball career unfettered. After beginning the 1890 season as a backup again with Columbus, he went to Louisville. His final appearance in ML garb came against Brooklyn NL in the last game of the 1890 World's Series.

Bligh's ML career illustrates the value placed in his era on a catcher with reasonable defensive skills. Although he played two full seasons and parts of two others in the majors, he got into only 66 games and logged a .201 career SA. Bligh was clearly not a star in anyone's eyes, yet neither was he a mere replacement level player. No marginal player would last almost twelve more months with a team after costing its president the trouble and expense of bailing him out of jail. By 1891, with the Players League gone and the number of ML teams cut by a third, Bligh was with Troy of the Eastern Association but soon was out of baseball and tending bar in south Brooklyn. The following spring he died of inflammation of the bowel following a bout with typhoid of only twenty-four hours duration. His nickname "Nelly Bly" establishes that his last name was pronounced the same as the infamous captain's. (DN/DB)

Booth, Amos Smith / "Amos" "The Little Darling"

B	T	HGT	WGT	G	AB	H	R	2B
R	R	5'9"	159	110	438	98	47	5

3B	HR	RBI	BB	SO	SB	BA	SA	OBP
1	0	27	21	21	—	.224	.240	.259

G	IP	H	GS	CG	BB
15	95.2	136	9	6	13

SO	SH	W	L	PCT	ERA
18	0	1	8	.111	4.14

B. 9/4/1852 Cincinnati, OH **D.** 7/1/1921

TEAMS: 76–77CinN 80CinN 82BalA 82LouA

DEBUT: 4/25/1876 at St. Louis; played 3B and got Cincinnati's first hit as a member of the NL when he singled in the first inning and later scored the team's first run in a 2–1 win over St. Louis's George Bradley

FINALE: 9/28/1882 at Cincinnati; played 2B and went 0-for-4 in a 1–0 loss to Cincinnati's Harry McCormick

During Amos Booth's 110-game ML career, he played every position except 1B and CF, and in 1877 he became the first player in NL history to both catch and pitch as many as 10 games in the same season. Booth's hitting declined precipitously after his rookie year, no doubt owing to sharper pitching. In 1878, playing for Lowell, MA, in the International Association, he batted just .204 but nonetheless was invited to join the strong National Association Washington club the following year. Booth then spent two seasons with the semipro Cincinnati Buckeyes, with time out to play one game for the local NL club on August 18, 1880. His participation in the AA's fledgling season as a major league is strange in that it consisted of two games with two different teams spaced more than fourteen weeks apart. But knowing that both took place in Cincinnati suggests that he was called on in separate emergencies. Booth later became a Cincinnati police officer until he was fired for riding his horse into a canal. He then ran a saloon and died of a stroke in Miamisburg, OH, in 1921. The source of his nickname—"The Little Darling"—is unknown. (DN/DB)

Bowerman, Frank Eugene / "Mike" "Frank"

B	T	HGT	WGT	G	AB	H	R	2B
R	R	6'2"	190	307	1101	292	114	33

3B	HR	RBI	BB	SO	SB	BA	SA	OBP
16	5	150	29	—	28	.265	.338	.292

B. 12/5/1868 Romeo, MI **D.** 11/30/1948
TEAMS: 95–98BalN 98–99PitN 00–07NYN 08BosN (P/M)09BosN
DEBUT: 8/24/1895 at Baltimore; replaced catcher Boileryard Clarke and went 0-for-1 in a 22–5 win over Cincinnati's Tom Parrott
FINALE: 7/13/1909 at Chicago; caught Al Mattern and went 0-for-3 in an 8–0 loss to Chicago's Floyd Kroh

Mike Bowerman grew up on a farm near Romeo, MI, and was an excellent defensive catcher, particularly deft at bunts, but too cantankerous ever to be a popular batterymate. He claimed that his great-grandfather came over with Hessians during the Revolutionary War and also that in his early twenties he became the first in his family to go to college, studying chemistry at the University of Michigan, but the school has no record of him. What has been validated is that he caught for the Detroit Athletic Club and also for the Detroit Western League reserve squad before joining Twin Cities of the Tri-State League in 1895. Later that year he moved to the Norfolk, VA, club before Baltimore acquired him. Bowerman caught only 1 game with the Orioles before being farmed and was farmed again for most of the following season to Scranton of the Eastern League. Twenty-eight when he returned to Baltimore to stay, he caught a fair amount in 1897 and played a game in the Temple Cup series against Boston. The following season he was hitting .438, but in only 16 ABs, before he was sold to Pittsburgh in June along with outfielder Tom O'Brien for $2,500.

After sharing the Pirates' catching with Bill Schriver in 1898, Bowerman played a career-high 109 games in 1899, but when Pittsburgh acquired Chief Zimmer and Jack O'Connor that winter, he was handed to New York along with several other players in an effort to bolster the NL's signature franchise. At the close of the gift-giving from other NL teams, the *Cincinnati Enquirer* wrote, "It would not be stretching matters to say that the New York Club has been given players worth at least $15,000."

Although never among the Giants' leading lights, Bowerman was the first man to catch Christy Mathewson in the majors and became a favorite in New York, especially after John McGraw took over as manager. In the winter of 1905–06 he bought a peach farm in the Romeo area with his World Series winnings and then played two more seasons under McGraw before being part of a massive seven-player trade with the Boston Doves in December 1907. Bowerman spent his last two ML seasons with the Doves and managed the club in the latter part of 1909. After two years in the minor American Association, Bowerman operated his farm until his death and was survived by his widow Rose and seven children. When he was interviewed late in life, he claimed to have brought out Mathewson. There is some truth to the story, but others have stronger claims than Bowerman's to Matty's discovery. Bowerman was one of several players in the 1890s that were nicknamed "Mike" for reasons we do not know. (DN/PM/DB)

Briggs, Grant / "Grant"

B	T	HGT	WGT	G	AB	H	R	2B
?	?	5'11"	170	110	378	62	46	7

3B	HR	RBI	BB	SO	SB	BA	SA	OBP
5	0	22	21	17	9	.164	.209	.212

B. 3/16/1865 Pittsburgh, PA **D.** 5/31/1928
TEAMS: 90SyrA 91LouA 92StLN 95LouN
DEBUT: 4/17/1890 at Brooklyn; caught Dan Casey and went 0-for-3 in a 3–2 loss to Brooklyn's Steve Toole
FINALE: 6/22/95 at Pittsburgh; caught Gus Weyhing and went 0-for-2 in a 5–2 loss to Pittsburgh's Bill Hart

Grant Briggs broke in with Worcester of the New England League in 1888 before landing in Syracuse in 1889 and hitting .252 in 53 International Association games as a backup catcher to Moses Walker. Since Walker was African American, barring him by a gentlemen's agreement from accompanying the Stars when they joined the AA the following season, the door was ajar for second-stringer Briggs. Midway through his rookie ML season Briggs received this bit of flattery from *TSN*: "He is deaf as a post and too easily rattled, and is no good in any other position." The catcher did indeed have a severe hearing problem and the rest of it was also depressingly accurate. Before Briggs's first week in the AA was out, the Philadelphia A's stole a record 19 bases on him and pitchers Dan Casey and Mike Morrison on April 22, 1890. Tested at other positions as well that season, Briggs was found wanting at all of them if only because his .180 BA could not be tolerated unless he caught.

In 1891 Briggs returned to the minors except for one game with Louisville but tried again in the majors the following year, first signing with his hometown team in Pittsburgh. That winter, while driving a hack in Pittsburgh, he was indignant when the Columbus, OH, minor league team approached him in early February as if unaware that he was already under contract, until he discovered it was ploy by the Pirates to get rid of him. The end result was that Briggs ended up in the lowly Illinois-Iowa League until August, when a sincere ML offer beckoned from St. Louis. In 22 games with the Browns he hit .073. Axed by St. Louis prior to the 1893 season, Briggs went to Binghamton of the Eastern League and two years later caught for Guy Hecker's Oil City team in the Iron & Oil League. He liked his new town so well that he opened a bowling alley there, but he was back in Pittsburgh when Louisville, for the second time, needed him as a one-day fill in. Briggs subsequently returned to the Iron & Oil League in 1895 and played for a time in the Interstate League before settling permanently in Pittsburgh. He died there in 1928. Briggs's .421 career OPS is the third lowest in ML history among positions players with a minimum of 400 PAs. (DN)

Briody, Charles F. / "Fatty" "Alderman" "Falstaff"

B	T	HGT	WGT	G	AB	H	R	2B
?	R	5'8½"	190	323	1186	271	134	52

3B	HR	RBI	BB	SO	SB	BA	SA	OBP
7	3	115	44	113	6	.228	.292	.257

B. 8/13/1858 Lansingburgh, NY **D.** 6/22/1903

TEAMS: 80TroN 82–84CleN 84CinU 85StLN 86KCN 87DetN 88KCA

DEBUT: 6/16/1880 at Troy; caught Mickey Welch and went 0-for-4 in a 9–5 loss to Cleveland's Jim McCormick

FINALE: 7/24/1888 at Cincinnati; caught Red Ehret and went 0-for-4 in a 6–4 loss to Cincinnati's Lee Viau

Fatty Briody grew up in Wisconsin but spent most of his life in Lansingburgh, NY, where he conducted a trucking business for a time and then ran a hotel while serving as a committeeman from the seventh Ward and a church-going Episcopalian. In his final ML season *TSN* referred to him as "that parcel of German obesity," but the unflattering portrait was probably not one he could have escaped. Briody's weight appears to have been either a genetic or physiological problem rather than a disinterest in taking care of himself.

At age 20 he was playing 2B for the semipro Lansingburgh Haymakers after being dismissed by Troy of the League Alliance. By 1879 Briody had moved up to independent New Bedford, MA, of the National Association and was still primarily a second baseman but fancied himself a catcher by the time he came to Troy in June 1880. After 8 passed balls in his ML debut demonstrated that he had not yet mastered his new trade, Briody returned to 2B the following year with Albany of the Eastern Championship Association. But by then his weight was already such a severe handicap that his lack of range left him no alternative but to resume catching.

Briody's second ML game was nearly as disheartening as his first; on May 25, 1882, he replaced Kick Kelly in a 20–1 blowout loss to Buffalo. Briody then shared the catching duties in Cleveland until August 1884 when he and teammates Jack Glasscock and Jim McCormick jumped the Blues to join Cincinnati of the outlaw Union Association. The enormous disparity between Briody's performance that season in the NL and the UA would later provide considerable ammunition to historians eager to denigrate the UA's quality. In 47 NL games he hit .169, whereas he batted .337 in 22 games after jumping to the rebel loop.

The following year Briody accompanied Glasscock to the St. Louis Maroons once the team was accepted into the NL after the UA folded. Sharing the catching with George Baker, he slipped back into his customary sub-.200 mode against ML pitching. In 1886, however, after joining the new Kansas City NL entry, he batted .237 and exceeded the team BA, a rarity for him. Said to weigh upward of 250 by then, he was dubbed "the Falstaff of his profession" by the KC press. The 1887 season was Briody's career high point after Detroit purchased him in March from the disbanding KC entry. Though he played only 33 games, he was a member of the best team in the majors. To his disappointment, Briody saw no action that fall in Detroit's World Series win over the AA champion St. Louis Browns and was released soon afterward. He finished his ML career with the new Kansas City AA franchise in 1888.

Briody had been so obese when last seen by ML audiences that in 1893–94 no one doubted reports that he was dead until ex-ML outfielder Em Seery ran into him in October 1894 and pronounced him in good health. Two years later he was again said to have died and ex-ML pitcher Henry Boyle even claimed to have gone to his funeral. Then in the spring of 1897, Briody was found still very much alive running a hotel in his native city. Soon after that Briody moved to Kansas City and worked at the Armour Meat Packing Company for two years before relocating to Chicago. He died in Chicago of heart disease in 1903. (DN)

Brown, Lewis J. / "Lew" "Blower"

B	T	HGT	WGT	G	AB	H	R	2B
R	R	5'10½"	185	378	1531	379	205	83

3B	HR	RBI	BB	SO	SB	BA	SA	OBP
31	10	169	45	155	—	.248	.362	.269

G	IP	H	GS	CG	BB
2	2	6	0	0	5

SO	SH	W	L	PCT	ERA
0	0	0	0	—	27.00

B. 2/1/1858 Leominster, MA **D.** 1/15/1889
TEAMS: 76–77BosN 78–79ProN 79ChiN 81DetN 81ProN 83BosN 83LouA 84BosU
DEBUT: 6/17/1876 at Boston; caught Jack Manning and also played CF and RF and went 1-for-4 in a 12–8 loss to St. Louis's George Bradley
FINALE: 10/19/1884 at Boston; caught Dupee Shaw and went 1-for-4 as Shaw blanked St. Louis's Charlie Sweeney 5–0, handing the Maroons their only whitewash all year.

Lew Brown was nicknamed "Blower" in honor of the famous British race-walker Blower Brown, who died ironically in the same year that his namesake played his last ML game. Even though Brown was only 26 at the time and died two weeks short of his 31st birthday, his athletic feats and firsts dwarf those of most Hall of Famers. Brown was one of the last catchers to disdain both a mitt and mask, let alone a chest protector, and was reportedly the first catcher to bluff a throw to 2B on a steal attempt and snap the ball instead to his third baseman to nail a runner there who had broken toward the plate anticipating the throw to second. The March 8, 1902, *TSN* also credited him with being the only man to whip John L. Sullivan in his prime, "the affair being a rough-and-tumble fight in a New Hampshire saloon." Some twenty years earlier, however, the *Chicago Tribune* said that Brown had fought Sullivan in Boston under the name of "Robbins" and suffered a severe beating. To further complicate the task of separating truth from fiction for anyone wishing to tackle a biography on Brown, after his death, Tim Murnane, Brown's manager in 1884 when both were with the Boston UA team, described him as being, contrary to his size and demeanor, of very timid disposition. Murnane told of a Sunday game in 1884 at Kansas City when several cowboys in the stands fired their six-shooters during the action until Brown stopped play and approached Murnane, trembling and pale, to plead, "Say, for goodness sake, give them anything they want." In any event, Brown is unquestionably the only man since the inception of the NL in 1876 to catch as many as 100 games in the majors before his 20th birthday.

Brown came from an affluent family and scorned their wishes when he quit school to pursue baseball as a career. His introduction to the pro game came with Lowell, MA, in 1875 at age 17. Among his teammates were two other future Boston stars, John Morrill and Curry Foley. Brown began 1876 with Lowell, catching Foley for the second year in a row. After facing the St. Louis Browns in an exhibition game at Lowell on June 16, Brown was summoned to Boston and signed by Harry Wright in time to face the Browns again the following afternoon in a Boston uniform. Immediately upon his arrival, Brown took over the bulk of Boston's catching duties and within weeks had established himself as not only an outstanding receiver but also one of the most popular men on the club. The following year he became the youngest man ever to serve as a regular catcher on a pennant winner when Boston romped to the NL flag. Nevertheless, Wright opted to sign Charlie Snyder from the disbanded Louisville franchise for 1878 and let Brown drift to replacement Providence. Wright's reasons for abandoning arguably the best catcher in the League in 1877 were never made public, but future events suggest that, even though Brown was just 19, he was already an irredeemable alcoholic.

In 1878 Brown customarily batted third with Providence and was second on the Grays in RBI and third in runs. At some point the following year he injured his arm and subsequently lost his job in August, just about the time the Grays were gearing up to make a serious pennant bid. The *New York Clipper* gave as the reason for his release that he was "shoulder bound and his wild throwing has been extremely disadvantageous." Apparently that observation was accurate, because when Brown joined Chicago in early September, he was put at 1B, where his lame arm could cause the least damage. After appearing in just 6 games, however, he jumped the team, perhaps because he foresaw no future with the White Stockings once Cap Anson returned from the disabled list to reclaim the gateway post.

Brown signed to play for Boston in 1880 but showed up drunk for a preseason exhibition game and was suspended for the year under the NL's new "Get Tough" policy. He served his penance that season in Canada with the Woodstock Actives, where he caught a young pitcher named Tip O'Neill, and then returned to the NL in 1881 with the newly formed Detroit club. His arm problems recurred, consigning him to 1B. On June 13, when Detroit made its first appearance of the season in Boston, umpire Herm Doscher presented Brown with a gold watch from "his Boston friends" prior to the game. But if Brown was still a fan favorite in Boston, he was rapidly losing respect with the Detroit management. By the time the Wolverines reached Providence, the next stop on their eastern trip, he was gone, replaced at 1B by rookie Mart Powell. Brown played in the Eastern Championship Association for a time, but by late August he was back with Providence as an outfield fill-in while Charley Radbourn was pressed into emergency duty at SS. After the 1881 season Brown was placed on the NL blacklist, presumably for his chronic alcoholism. In 1882 he put in a third stint in Canada, this time with a Toronto team, but he returned to Boston in time for a benefit game held for him by his many friends at the Boston park on June 26. That autumn a Hub stage producer took advantage of Brown's name and reputation to cast him in the part of Charles the Wrestler in *As You Like It* at the Globe Theater.

Even though his arm was still ailing, Brown's popularity with fans and fellow players alike was so enormous that he was invited to rejoin the Boston club in 1883 now that Harry Wright was no longer running the team. Still shoulder bound, he occupied 1B early in the season when Boston suffered a rash of injuries and his versatile former Lowell teammate, John Morrill, was needed elsewhere. By the end of May, with all of the regulars once again healthy, Brown's usefulness ended. In late August he got a call from Louisville, and on the basis of his first few games with the club, the *Police Gazette* said, "The Louisvilles have caught on to Lew Brown, and if they can keep the little brown jug away from him they have a good ball player." But his chance of returning to the Kentucky team in 1884 evaporated after he made 4 errors in a game at New York on September 6 and finished the season with an .891 FA at 1B.

Luckily for Brown, the UA formed in 1884 as a third major league, and Tim Murnane, who had always been fond of him, was hired to manage the Boston entry. Over the winter Brown, who had been battling a weight problem for the past several years along with his arm troubles, fought to get into his best shape since 1878. After winning the honor in spring practice of catching on Opening Day, Brown teamed with his old 1877 batterymate, Tommy Bond, in the UA lidlifter on April 17, 1884, and beat the Philadelphia Keystones, 14–2. Although his arm was still not right, he finished second among UA catchers in assists. But his .231 BA, coupled with his imbibing, attracted no pursuers when the rebel loop folded, reducing ML jobs by a third.

Brown's baseball career essentially ended in 1884 at age 26, although he continued to play on occasion in sandlot games. In 1885 the *Boston Globe* reported that Brown, now "one of the leaders of Boston society," gave a picnic on his own behalf at which his friend John L. Sullivan put on a sparring exhibition. But it was no doubt an exaggeration on the *Globe's* part, for while Brown may have hobnobbed in the best Boston social circles, he was hardly a community pillar. By 1887 he was working at Joe Goss's saloon, the Saracen's Head, on Lagrange Street. Late that summer he appeared on the field at South End Grounds for the final time when he caught for the 1876 team that included Dave Birdsall and Jack Manning against a picked nine in a benefit game for Manning. Now extremely corpulent, Brown's performance was judged by the *Globe* to have been "very rusty."

In late December of the following year Brown got into a wrestling match at the Saracen's Head one evening with a patron named Chris O'Brien. When Goss's widow could not separate them, she came at them with a length of gas pipe and hit Brown across the shins, destroying his kneecap. He was taken to city hospital after never having been seriously ill before in his life. When he was told his leg would have to be amputated, he came apart over the next three days, grew delirious, and soon died. Reports on the cause of his death varied from pneumonia to a complete mental breakdown. Brown's funeral was held at 22 Lagrange Street, not far from the Saracen's Head. After the service his pallbearers, former teammates Harry Schafer, Murnane, Manning, Tommy Bond, Lon Knight, Joe Hornung, and Mike Slattery helped bury his body at Boston's Forest Hills Cemetery in the same grave with Goss, a former pugilist. Many eulogies were delivered by his former teammates and sportswriters, not all of them flattering, but the *Chicago Tribune* wrote that the consensus was that the big catcher had "one virtue that must not be lost sight of, and that was that, in his long baseball career, he was never suspected of a piece of crooked ball-playing, and yet he was with sporting people all the time." (DN/DB)

Buckley, Richard D. / "Dick"

B	T	HGT	WGT	G	AB	H	R	2B
R	R	5'10"	195	524	1833	449	213	72

3B	HR	RBI	BB	SO	SB	BA	SA	OBP
14	26	216	98	188	25	.245	.342	.291

B. 9/21/1859 New York, NY **D.** 12/12/1929
TEAMS: 88–89IndN 90–91NYN 92–94StLN 94–95PhiN
DEBUT: 4/20/1888 at Indianapolis; caught Henry Boyle and went 0-for-4 in a 5–4 loss to Chicago's George Van Haltren
FINALE: 9/28/1895 at Philadelphia; caught Al Orth after replacing Mike Grady and went 0-for-2 in a 6–3 loss to Brooklyn's Bert Abbey

Dick Buckley was born in New York and moved to Troy at an early age before his family finally settled in Pittsburgh. He worked as a laborer in Pittsburgh until returning to Troy to play with the semipro Haymakers in the early 1880s. He then spent two seasons with independent and minor league teams in Pennsylvania and Ohio before joining Binghamton, NY, in 1885. By the end of that season Buckley was with Syracuse and remained with the Stars until the fall of 1887 when the Indianapolis NL team acquired him. He debuted on Opening Day the following spring, hit well, and also played some 3B but was too slow afoot ever to be used anywhere besides catcher except in an emergency. Buckley again caught the season opener in 1889 and hammered 8 homers that year in just 260 ABs while sharing the receiving with Con Daily. Over the winter he was among the select Indianapolis players that New York obtained from the NL after the Hoosiers were erased from the loop.

After coming to New York, Buckley never again approached his early power numbers but grew in value because of his skill in helping young pitchers to develop. Buckley's special project was Amos Rusie, who was too fast and too wild for almost every other catcher to handle. In the flurry of player raids and transfers that grew out of the NL-AA merger in December 1891, he moved to St. Louis in 1892 while Browns catcher Jack Boyle headed east to New York, but there is no indication that the two were traded for one another. Buckley caught 119 games in his first year in the Mound City, a record high for a 32-year-old receiver that lasted until 1908, before breaking his right wrist on October 12 in a collision at home plate. The injury not only was slow to heal, keeping him out of action until August 1893, but caused his weight to balloon. No longer did he look "as though he could stop a locomotive full of railroad curves"—a description that had accompanied him when he first came to the Giants—and he also temporarily lost his status as the game's top handball player. He was once so skillful according to Bill Joyce that he could beat most men with his hands tied behind him just by using his feet to kick the ball. By the fall of 1893 Buckley reportedly weighed 270 pounds but managed to shrink to 190 prior to spring training in 1894 with a strict regimen at Mount Clemens that he claimed also improved his wrist. Yet in April the *Washington Post* noted that his "arm does not seem to be much better than last year," and when he twisted his ankle while chasing a pop foul Browns owner Chris Von der Ahe immediately put him up for release. The Phillies claimed Buckley as a stopgap replacement for Jack Clements, who was also ailing, and then rehired him for 1895 after he hit .294.

Nearing 36 by the time the 1895 season began, Buckley lost his backup role to Mike Grady and was sent to Louisville in December along with $500 for Dan Brouthers. When he refused to go to the Colonels, the deal was restructured so he could stay in Philadelphia, but the following spring the Phils released him anyway. Buckley worked winters as a foreman at a sand pit in Wisconsin and had an interest in a pool hall in Chicago, where he was living with his wife Katie, and could have retired from baseball. Instead he returned to Indianapolis, which was now in the Western League, and promptly duped pitcher Willie McGill, a former teammate on the Phils, by telling the left-hander just prior to a series with McGill's St. Paul club that he had been released because his arm was shot. In the first game of the series Buckley then threw out the first six St. Paul runners trying to steal on McGill's tip. He caught 84 games before a hand injury idled him and was back the following year with Grand Rapids. In June 1897 Buckley was traded to Columbus and was seen by player-manager George Tebeau as a major catalyst in the Senators' rise to second place in the WL by the season's end. He remained in the WL long enough to play in its first season after it renamed itself the American League. Slated to be the first-string catcher for Chicago, the eventual first AL champion, he broke a finger on Opening Day and lost his job to Joe Sugden while he mended.

The first year of the new century found Buckley with Omaha of the newly reorganized Western League. In October *TSN* noted, "Forty-four [*sic*] is his figure, and it is very probable that he has played his last season." The paper was wrong about his age—he was only 41—but right in a way. Although Buckley went to spring training with Omaha in 1902, he failed to make the team.

Three years later Buckley told the *Washington Post* that the big catchers mitts nowadays cut down stealing because mitts used in the late 1880s when he first caught Rusie were thin and small and catchers had to draw back their hands when catching a fastball whereas now they could stop it head-on and throw a runner out. He apparently was still living in Chicago at the time, but he eventually returned to Pittsburgh, where his last known job was as an elevator operator. Buckley died at his Pittsburgh home in 1929. (DN/DB)

Burrell, Frank Andrew / "Buster"

B	T	HGT	WGT	G	AB	H	R	2B
R	R	5'10"	165	122	390	96	42	13

3B	HR	RBI	BB	SO	SB	BA	SA	OBP
3	3	47	32	28	4	.246	.318	.305

B. 12/22/1866 Weymouth, MA **D.** 5/8/1862
TEAMS: 91NYN 95–97BroN
DEBUT: 8/1/1891 at New York; caught John Ewing and was 1-for-4 in a 9–8 loss to Brooklyn's Tom Lovett
FINALE: 10/2/1897 at Brooklyn; caught Chauncey Fisher and was 1-for-5 in a 15–6 win over Boston's Ted Lewis

Buster Burrell had a good arm, was durable and hit well in the minors but could never hit enough to win a regular ML job. His rookie season in 1891 saddled him with an image that was all but impossible to erase. In 15 games with the Giants, Burrell batted .094, exiling him to the minors for the next three years before a Western League season at Minneapolis in 1894 in which he caught a reported 111 straight games led Brooklyn to test him briefly in 1895. Again Burrell failed to hit (.143), but when catcher Con Daily was disabled in a heroic swimming rescue, the Weymouth native at last had his big chance. Yet even though Burrell batted .301 in 62 games in 1896, he scored just 19 runs. The following year he dropped to third on Billy Barnie's depth chart behind Jack Grim and rookie Aleck Smith. Over 30 by then (although he claimed he was born in 1868), he was too old to be a prospect any longer and too expensive to keep on the bench.

Returning to the minors in 1898, Burrell experienced a rejuvenation that enabled him to play pro ball for another 11 seasons. Finally, he finished in Woonsocket, RI, a career that had begun with the East Weymouth, MA, club in 1885. But Burrell's baseball longevity was no match for his overall longevity. Prior to his death at 95 at a South Weymouth nursing home, he was the oldest living former MLer at the time. (DN)

Bushong, Albert John / "Doc"

B	T	HGT	WGT	G	AB	H	R	2B
R	R	5'11"	165	672	2397	514	287	58

3B	HR	RBI	BB	SO	SB	BA	SA	OBP
13	2	184	124	97	39	.214	.252	.255

B. 9/15/1856 Philadelphia, PA **D.** 8/19/1908
TEAMS: 75AtlNA 76PhiN 80–82WorN 83–84CleN 85–87StLA 88–90BroN
DEBUT: 7/19/1875 at Philadelphia; caught Harry Arundel and went 3-for-5 in a 23–3 loss to the Athletics' Dick McBride
FINALE: 9/9/1890 at Philadelphia; caught Bill Terry and Bob Caruthers and went 0-for-2 in a 13–6 loss to Philadelphia's Kid Gleason.
FAMOUS FIRST: In 1886 became the first man in ML history to catch as many as 100 games in a season

Doc Bushong was an 18-year-old student at Philadelphia High School when he appeared in his first ML game for the Brooklyn Atlantics. The following spring he joined the West Chester Brandywines. Some historians have theorized that Bushong played pro ball to pay his way through dental school at the University of Pennsylvania, but it is hard to imagine that in his early years in the game he could have made enough money to have any left over for tuition at the end of a season. By 1879 it was apparent that Bushong played for one reason: he loved it.

After a 5-game NL stint in 1876 before the Philadelphia club disbanded, he journeyed to Janesville, WI, of the League Alliance the following year and caught young John M. Ward for a time before returning to the East with Buffalo. At his request Bushong was allowed to go to Utica of the International Association so that he could play more often, but his plan backfired when Utica released him in 1879 and he was left without a team because the supply of catchers in the East exceeded the demand. An aspirant dentist in the game solely for the money would have quit at that juncture, but Bushong sought a new bastion. On August 23, 1879, he was hired by the Beacon semipro club to catch Brown student Lee Richmond, on loan from Worcester, in an exhibition game against Richmond's team. Impressed by the ease with which Bushong handled Richmond's southpaw slants, Worcester signed him after the game. The next spring, when Worcester joined the NL, Bushong caught Richmond in an Opening Day 13–1 win over Troy and from then on was an entrenched major leaguer until his last game with Brooklyn more than a decade later.

Bushong remained Richmond's favorite catcher until Worcester left the NL following the 1882 season. He then joined Cleveland, pairing with righthander Jim McCormick. Even though his managers were still obeying the prevailing custom that a catcher should be used no more than two or three times a week, Bushong's effortless receiving style made it apparent that he could work more often. To protect his right hand for future dental surgery, he pioneered the technique of catching one-handed. Remarkably, in his eleven full ML seasons, his method stood him in such good stead that he appears never to have suffered a serious hand or finger injury. Moreover, Bushong, Charlie Bennett, and Silver Flint were the only NLers to catch 60 or more games in every season between 1881–84, the years when the lean, strong-armed Philadelphian was just coming into his prime, and during that span Bushong was second in the majors in catching assists only to Flint.

Yet when Cleveland abandoned its NL franchise at the close of the 1884 season and sold its best players to Brooklyn of the AA, Brooklyn chose Bill Krieg over Bushong, allowing him to sign with the St. Louis Browns. The catcher quickly showed Brooklyn its mistake, working a then AA record 85 games behind the plate in 1885, hitting a career-best .266 and earning this accolade from a St. Louis observer: "While he is hardly as capable a man as [Pat] Deasley, he more than makes up for any small inferiority in his excellent habits and strict reliability," in addition to being good at curbing would be base thieves and bolstering hurlers' confidence that he could handle their swiftest pitches.

If Bushong's work was instrumental in St. Louis's pennant march in 1885, his role was even larger in his second season with the club. In 1886 he became the first to catch as many as 100 ML games in a season (107) and also served notice that he could act as an enforcer. In a game with Baltimore in early June, Bushong flattened teammate Arlie Latham after Latham backed off from making a tag to avoid Baltimore catcher Chris Fulmer's hard slide into

3B. The incident presented Wheeler Wikoff with his first major challenge, and the new AA president initially suspended both players for thirty days but then weakened and merely fined them for fear of being accused of unfairly crippling the front-running Browns. In 1887, however, Bushong's six consecutive seasons in which he had caught well over half of his team's games began to take its toll. After working the Browns' Opening Day contest, he suffered an injury and soon ceded his top-dog status to a much younger Jack Boyle. In November 1887 Brooklyn tried to rectify its earlier error by purchasing the 31-year-old receiver along with Dave Foutz for $5,500. Bushong revived to catch in over half the Bridegrooms' games in 1888 but hit just .209.

When he was reduced to a backup role the next two seasons, it seemed time to launch his dental practice. Instead Bushong joined Syracuse of the minor league Eastern Association. In August 1891 *TSN* predicted, "He will never turn his attention to decayed molars as long as he can hang on to the profession in any capacity." Bushong may have taken umbrage, for that fall he opened a dental facility in Hoboken with two of his brothers. Eventually three of his sons also became dentists but not until after he died of renal cancer in 1908. (DN/DB)

Carroll, Frederick Herbert / "Fred" "Big Head"

B	T	HGT	WGT	G	AB	H	R	2B
R	R	5'11"	185	754	2892	820	546	146

3B	HR	RBI	BB	SO	SB	BA	SA	OBP
66	27	366	348	136	137	.284	.408	.370

B. 7/2/1864 Sacramento, CA **D.** 11/7/1904
TEAMS: 84ColA 85–86PitA 87–89PitN 90PitP 91PitN
DEBUT: 5/1/1884 at Cincinnati; caught Ed Morris and went 1-for-4 in a 10–9 win over Cincinnati's Will White
FINALE: 8/18/1891 at Pittsburgh; played RF and went 2-for-4 in a 4–3 loss to Chicago's Ad Gumbert

Most historians rate either Buck Ewing or Charlie Bennett the best defensive catcher in the nineteenth century, but there is room for debate as to the best offensive backstop. Was it Ewing? Mike Kelly? Jack Clements? Deacon White? Jack Milligan? All are strong candidates, but the best one may be a man who is seldom even listed among the top ten catchers in the nineteenth century. Counting only stats achieved while catching, Fred Carroll ranks second in OPS (.799) to Ewing (.805) among all backstops with as many as 2,000 PAs between 1871 and 1892, the last year before changes in pitching rules brought about a hitting explosion. What's more, Carroll's stats, unlike Ewing's, came with teams that afforded him little protection in the batting order.

Nicknamed "Big Head" because of the size of his head rather than his ego, Carroll was also an excellent defensive receiver early his career before hand injuries exacted their fee and had a quick release that held steals to a minimum. To keep his bat in the lineup on days when his hands were too sore to catch, Pittsburgh stationed him at 3B or in the outfield, and it was as an outfielder that he finished his ML career after his arm went.

Carroll began as a 16-year-old first baseman in 1880 with the San Francisco Athletics of the California League. By the spring of 1883 he had turned to catching and gone east to join fellow Californians Ed Morris and Hen Moore on the Reading Actives. It was with the Interstate Association team that Carroll first connected with Morris, the left-handed pitcher who would remain his favorite batterymate until 1890. The pair moved as a unit to Columbus AA in 1884. Carroll immediately established himself as an offensive force as well as an excellent receiver, hammering 6 home runs to go with a .440 SA. When Columbus disbanded after the season, Pittsburgh bought its top players for $8,000, with Morris and Carroll the jewels in the bargain. In 1886, Carroll's second season in Pittsburgh, he was leading the AA in batting in mid-July but slipped to .288 when hand injuries shaved his catching time and contributed heavily to his league-leading total of 92 passed balls. The following year he logged his first .300 season while playing the outfield, 1B, and catcher, and unfortunately—since he could only play one spot at a time—was the best Pittsburgh had at all three positions. After an off year in 1888 Carroll led the NL in OBP in 1889, hit .330, and collected 85 walks in 91 games. Jumping to Pittsburgh PL the following season, he began to spend more time in the outfield when his arm weakened.

Carroll returned to the NL Smoke City entry in 1891 after marrying Nellie Claire of San Jose on New Year's Day. He brought his new bride east with him to spring training, and it may have been a mistake. Already prone to reporting overweight, Carroll had more trouble than usual getting into shape while doing battle to resist his wife's cooking. It was apparent as soon as the season began that he no longer could throw and now lacked the range even to play the outfield. Released in August when his hitting sagged as well, Carroll underwent a spell of soul-searching after returning to the West Coast and decided that at 27 he was too young to lose out on a profession he loved. That fall he fought to regain his form while playing in the California League. After terrorizing pitchers in the CL for the next two seasons, he ventured back east to play in the Southern League and in 1895 hit a rousing .415 while captaining Grand Rapids of the Western League. He then returned to California and came east one final time in 1898 when he finished his pro career in the Interstate League. For several more years Carroll continued to play intermittently, but his passion now lay elsewhere. Almost a true Renaissance man, he had always saved his money while playing and used it to go into the express business. Meanwhile he had more time to devote to his avocation as a landscape artist. Carroll kept an art studio in Marin County and had several local one-man shows before dying suddenly of a heart attack at his San Rafael home in 1904 at 40. (DN)

*Clapp, John Edgar / "John" "Honest John"

B	T	HGT	WGT	G	AB	H	R	2B
R	R	5'7"	194	588	2523	714	457	91

3B	HR	RBI	BB	SO	SB	BA	SA	OBP
35	7	274	112	51	17	.283	.355	.313

G	W	L	PCT	PENNANTS
420	174	237	.423	0

B. 7/17/1851 Ithaca, NY **D.** 12/18/1904
TEAMS: (P/M)72ManNA 73–75AthNA 76–77StLN (P/M)78IndN (P/M)79BufN (P/M)80CinN (P/M)81CleN (P/M)83NYN
DEBUT: 4/26/1872 at Troy; caught Cy Bentley and went 2-for-4 in a 10–0 loss to Troy's George Zettlein
FINALE: 9/28/1883 at New York; played CF and made 1 hit in an 8–7 win over Detroit's Dupee Shaw

The brother of MLer Aaron Clapp, John Clapp was one of baseball's best catchers at a time when a catcher was a top commodity. Without ever compromising his reputation for honesty and loyalty, he was very aware of his value and took full advantage. While still a teenager Clapp spent 1868–69 playing for a club in Mansfield, OH, where he had the opportunity to face Harry Wright's mighty Red Stockings of Cincinnati. He then returned home and played the next two years for Ithaca area teams while hankering for another chance to prove himself against the nation's best players. Finally, Clapp wrote to Wright, who now managed Boston, after the 1871 season and inquired about a position. Wright replied with a long list of questions, and while Clapp's answer is not known, he signed with a new NA club in Middletown instead. The Connecticut club was short-lived, but Clapp's talents drew attention and he signed to catch for the Philadelphia Athletics, where he spent the next three seasons handling the offerings of Dick McBride and emerging as a star. A ponderous runner, Clapp was known for hitting every ball to RF, yet he somehow managed to post solid BAs. It was his play behind the plate, however, that made him one of the game's most valuable players. He also earned a reputation for honesty. Before one game, Chicago bookmakers offered him the phenomenal sum of $5,000 "to allow one or two 'pass-balls' when one or two men happened to be on base." But Clapp turned down the bribe and, as a result, became known as "Honest John."

Clapp's integrity did not mean that he was unaware of his value. In July 1875, Clapp had gone home to represent his hometown club in a game against its archrivals from Binghamton. The Athletics fined him for his absence and Clapp angrily refused to play. When the fine was still not remitted, he took an unprecedented step and met with representatives of the Boston, Hartford, and St. Louis clubs at Earle's Hotel in New York, where he "stated to them that he was on the auction block; that he had a surety offered him of $2,500, and that the club paying the largest amount over that sum would secure his services. He then left them to make their 'sealed proposals,' and the result was that Clapp opened the envelopes in their presence, and said, in a moment: 'Gentlemen, I will play in St. Louis.' The offer accepted was in the neighborhood of $3,000, but what the others were it is difficult to state."

The next two seasons provided dramatic proof of just how valuable Clapp was. Philadelphia suffered through a disastrous season without him and had its franchise revoked by the NL. Meanwhile, having Clapp behind the plate enabled St. Louis's George Bradley to emerge as one of the game's best pitchers. In previous seasons the lack of a capable enough catcher had forced Bradley to let up. But as Tim Murnane explained, after Clapp's arrival, "Bradley became the talk of the country." Bradley's breakout season caused Chicago to sign him for 1877, but the team management made the mistake of not signing Clapp. Bradley struggled, and as one sportswriter put it, "In 1876 [Bradley] was given by Clapp's efforts a great leeway in his work, and no man used strategy more; but in 1877 he claims that he felt himself confined to a narrower circle by the necessity of always thinking about his catcher, and pitching to him."

St. Louis also fell off in 1877 without its star pitcher, but Clapp played a role in an historic event. That March, Harvard catcher James Tyng had unveiled the first catcher's mask, but most pro catchers refused to wear the new contraption. In August, however, Clapp was struck in the face by a foul ball and had to wear a mask for protection. He continued to wear the mask even after his injury healed and is now credited with helping to introduce the new piece of protective equipment.

Clapp spent 1878 with Indianapolis, mostly playing the outfield and serving as player-manager, and then caught for Buffalo and Pud Galvin in 1879. After that campaign, the first version of the reserve clause was introduced, and Buffalo complained because it claimed to have reserved Clapp, only to have him sign with Cincinnati when that club's management produced cash. Clapp had another fine season as Cincinnati's player-manager in 1880, but the club lost its franchise over a dispute about selling liquor in the stands. He joined Cleveland in 1881, but it would prove a long season. Clapp was installed as manager early in the year, but even so, he struggled to work with pitcher Jim McCormick. The two men had previously been teammates in Indianapolis, but they now found that they could not "work together as a team. Both are capable of running the battery, and both want to boss the job, and as neither will yield to the other in occupying a subordinate position in directing the battery, they necessarily clash, and the result is divided opinions and ideas and a failure in team work together."

Clapp caught for the League Alliance New York Mets in 1882, his last full season of catching. He was only 31 at the time, but he had been catching the game's best pitchers for fifteen years and his body had taken its full quota of abuse. When asked by a naïve reporter in 1879 if he had suffered any injuries while catching, Clapp smiled wryly and, "pointing to a scarcely noticeable hollow in his left cheek bone, he said that one side of his face had once been knocked in by a hot ball. His left eye had been closed once, his right eye three times, and his nose broken. 'From 1873 to 1877,' continued he, 'I was very fortunate, and not the slightest accident occurred to me. I have been lucky this season also, and the only accident has been the knocking off of a finger nail.'"

In 1883 Clapp became manager of New York's National League team, while also catching occasionally. He was let go after the season, ending an outstanding career. His playing days over, Clapp and pitcher Jack Lynch operated a saloon in New York, called The Old Club. But he suffered a run of bad luck that included a lengthy illness, the loss of the business, and the death of his wife. Eventually he returned to his native Ithaca and became a policeman. On December 18, 1904, after carrying a drunk several blocks to jail, Clapp collapsed and died of a stroke. (PM/DN)

Clark, Robert H. / "Bob"

B	T	HGT	WGT	G	AB	H	R	2B
R	R	5'10"	175	288	1011	233	145	25

3B	HR	RBI	BB	SO	SB	BA	SA	OBP
11	1	107	85	29	71	.230	.280	.296

B. 3/18/1863 Covington, KY **D.** 8/21/1919
TEAMS: 86–89BroA 90BroN 91CinN 93LouN
DEBUT: 4/17/1886 at Brooklyn; caught Jack Harkins and went 0-for-3 in a 4–1 loss to Baltimore's Matt Kilroy.
FINALE: 8/3/1893 at Louisville; replaced Jack Grim, caught Bill Rhodes and went 0-for-2 in a 7–4 loss to St. Louis's Pink Hawley

In 1885, while catching for Atlanta in the Southern League, Bob Clark missed significant time due to illness, setting the tone for his entire career. The following season, in his very first ML appearance, he was hurt seriously enough that he was out for several weeks, but he still participated in 71 games, the most he would play in any of his seven ML seasons. Clark's usual pattern was to win the Brooklyn backstopping job in the spring, catch on Opening Day and then spend half the year or more on the DL. If it was not arm trouble, it was a broken finger or a serious illness. The shame of it for Brooklyn manager Bill McGunnigle was that Clark was the club's best catcher. In 1888 his absence behind the plate in all but 36 games may have cost Brooklyn the AA pennant, and an injury to him late the following season forced McGunnigle to use weaker receivers in the World's Series against the NL Giants. Active in just 43 games in 1890, Clark managed to be healthy enough to catch Brooklyn's final regular season game and then a World's Series game against Louisville, his lone postseason appearance.

The following spring, Brooklyn, deep in catchers, let him go to Cincinnati, but he seldom played. That winter Clark married second baseman Reddy Mack's sister and worked for a liquor emporium in Covington, KY. His arm all but gone and his hands battered, Clark caught a few games with Louisville in 1893 and then umpired in the minors off and on for a few years but was unable to coax Nick Young to hire him for an NL position. By the summer of 1897 Clark was working in the Covington revenue office as a tax collector, a job in keeping with his reputation as an umpire whose buttons should not be pushed. The previous year, while Clark was officiating a Western League game, Minneapolis catcher Bill Wilson had grabbed his mask during an argument and Clark had proceeded to beat Wilson nearly senseless with it. Eventually Clark turned to the occupation that served so many ballplayers in a time of need. He became a saloonkeeper in Newport, KY. When his business failed he worked in a Cincinnati chemical factory until he died at home in Covington of chemical burns he had received at his job some months earlier. (DN)

Clarke, Arthur Franklin / "Artie"

B	T	HGT	WGT	G	AB	H	R	2B
R	R	5'8"	155	149	569	122	72	14

3B	HR	RBI	BB	SO	SB	BA	SA	OBP
10	0	70	47	54	49	.214	.274	.279

B. 5/6/1865 Providence, RI **D.** 11/14/1949
TEAMS: 90–91NYN
DEBUT: 4/19/1890 at New York; played RF and was 0-for-3 in a 4–0 loss to Philadelphia's Kid Gleason
FINALE: 9/30/1891 at Boston; caught Bill Coughlin and went 0-for-3 in a 16–5 loss to Boston's Kid Nichols

Artie Clarke played for Williams College in 1889 and appears to have joined New York NL in 1890 without any previous pro experience. Judged too light to catch Giants ace Amos Rusie, he opened the season in RF but soon lost his job to fellow rookie Jesse Burkett. Clarke remained on the team because of his adaptability. He played every position as a rookie except 1B and pitcher and managed to collect almost 400 ABs despite never having a regular post. In his sophomore year Clarke began as a backup catcher to Dick Buckley but played little when his hitting fell off after he broke his thumb in May. That fall he set up a law practice in Charlestown, MA, and talked of quitting the diamond but was lured back to the game in 1892 for one final season when he was named captain of the Troy Eastern League team and hit .256. Clarke later became a Boston attorney and died in Brookline, MA, at 84. (DN)

Clarke, William Jones / "Boileryard"

B	T	HGT	WGT	G	AB	H	R	2B
R	R	5'11½"	170	511	1843	484	245	58

3B	HR	RBI	BB	SO	SB	BA	SA	OBP
20	8	276	84	58	28	.263	.331	.315

B. 10/18/1868 New York, NY **D.** 7/29/1859
TEAMS: 93–98BalN 99–00BosN 01–04WasAL 05NYN
DEBUT: 5/1/1893 at New York; caught Kirtley Baker and went 1-for-3 in a 7–5 loss to New York's Silver King
FINALE: 10/7/1905 at New York; played 1B and was hitless in a 6–1 loss to Philadelphia's King Brady

Boileryard Clarke's family moved to New Mexico when he was a boy, and he was reared in Indian Territory. Later in life he studied engineering at Brotherhood College in Santa Fe and coached baseball at Princeton for thirty-four seasons over forty-seven-year span after settling in the East. His nickname came from his raucous voice that "could be heard all over the diamond." In 1888 Clarke first caught for pay in the New Mexico League. After spending 1889 in the Colorado State League, he caught several exhibition games that fall for Chicago but was not invited to train with the ML club the following spring. Instead Clarke spent three more seasons in the minors, the last in the 1892 California League, before Baltimore hired him as a backup to Wilbert Robinson. Appearing in 49 games as a rookie in 1893, he batted just .175. Although Clarke's hitting improved over the next few years, he remained in Robinson's shadow until he was sold to Boston in March 1899. Once there, he again found himself second fiddle, ranking behind Marty Bergen in 1899 and then rookie Billy Sullivan the following year.

Having reached the age of 32 without as yet doing regular duty for any length of time, Clarke was ripe for a career change. After flirting with a group trying to reorganize the American Association as a major league, he welcomed an offer from the Washington entry in Ban Johnson's upstart American League. Clarke appeared in more than half of Washington's games in each of his four seasons in D.C. and twice played over 100 contests, including his career high of 126 in 1903. By that point, however, advancing age and the coming of the Deadball Era and its corresponding lack of offense had severely impaired his bat work. In Clarke's final three ML seasons his career BA fell 10 points from .266 to .256, but he had the satisfaction of finishing with his old Baltimore teammate John McGraw's pennant-winning 1905 Giants, although he saw World Series action that fall only as a coach before descending to the minors for four seasons. Clarke died in 1959 at Princeton Hospital of complications from a hip fracture. His passing at 91 just eight days after the death of pitcher Bill Hoffer removed the last surviving member of the 1894–96 Orioles dynasty. (DN)

Clements, John J. / "Jack"

B	T	HGT	WGT	G	AB	H	R	2B
B	L	5'8½"	204	1163	4295	1231	619	226

3B	HR	RBI	BB	SO	SB	BA	SA	OBP
60	77	687	341	301	55	.287	.421	.348

G	W	L	PCT	PENNANTS
19	13	6	.684	0

B. 7/24/1864 Philadelphia, PA **D.** 5/23/1941
TEAMS: 84PhiU 84–97PhiN (P/M)90PhiN 98StLN 99CleN 00BosN

DEBUT: 4/22/1884 at Philadelphia; played RF and went 2-for-6 in a 15–5 win over Baltimore's Ed Smith

FINALE: 10/2/1900 at Boston; pinch hit unsuccessfully for Bill Dinneen in the eighth inning of a 7–7 tie with Brooklyn's Bill Donovan and Frank Kitson

CAREER HIGHLIGHT ONE: Was the first to catch 1,000 ML games and remains the only left-hander to catch 1,000 ML games

CAREER HIGHLIGHT TWO: Hit .394 in 1895, still the record high for a catcher in enough games to be a batting-title qualifier

Jack Clements was the lone position player to debut in the tumultuous 1884 season and still be active in the final year of the nineteenth century. Like many nineteenth-century batsmen, he experimented with switch-hitting before finally settling on swinging mostly from the left side in the late 1880s. Clements also experimented with catchers' gloves before adopting one that teammate Jack Boyle said was "as straight as a shingle" and designed that way so the ball would ricochet off it into the wearer's hand and enable him to be ready almost instantly to throw. He likewise developed a unique chest protector, one that required him to blow it up before every game, and was also known for his trademark "indispensable sweater" that he wore even on the bench during hot summer games, ostensibly to shield his throwing arm, although by the late 1890s fellow players whispered it was really donned to help him sweat off poundage after he developed a serious weight problem.

As early as his first ML season in 1884 Clements wore a form of chest protection that was termed a "sheepskin," suggesting that it was considerably thinner than the balloon-style protector he later employed. After playing the outfield initially with the Philadelphia Keystones, he went behind the plate for the first time in Chicago on May 8 and ten days later reportedly was the first catcher in Cincinnati ever seen garbed in a chest protector when he handled Enoch Bakely in a game against the UA Outlaw Reds. Philadelphia NL acquired Clements in August 1884 as the Keystones were about to fold in return for settlement of a $500 claim against the Keystones for the lumber used in building their park. He remained with the Quakers until long after they became more popularly known as the Phillies. An erratic hitter with little power initially, he did not really begin to flower at the plate until 1890, his seventh ML campaign, when he posted a .864 OPS. Clements led the NL in home run percentage three years later when he went deep 17 times in just 376 ABs and set a season record for catchers that lasted until 1925 when Gabby Hartnett swatted 24 jacks.

In 1894 Clements was off to his best start ever until a broken ankle held him to just 46 games. He then hit a record .394 the following year despite suffering all season from hemorrhoids. In 1896 Clements was batting .359 and fighting off a string of nagging injuries when he was stricken with typhoid on a hot August day in Baltimore and missed the rest of the season. His 1897 campaign was equally marred when he grew to loathe Philadelphia after becoming one of the first victims of the City of Brotherly Love's soon-to-be-famed "Boo Birds." Although he played much better on the road than at home, he hit poorly overall and seldom appeared after catching on Opening Day.

That November, Clements was part of a huge six-player swap between the Phillies and lowly St. Louis. The 1898 Browns were no improvement on the 1897 bottom-feeders, but Clements had a personal highlight. On June 3 at Baltimore he became the first to catch 1,000 games in the majors. A .257 BA and a mushrooming weight problem consigned Clements to the even more dreadful Cleveland Spiders in 1899 when syndicate ownership swapped Cleveland's best players from 1898 for St. Louis's worst. Released early in the season when he refused a pay cut to $1,500, he sat idle until the following spring when Boston hired him as a backup and occasional pinch hitter. Clements finished his playing career later that season with Providence of the Eastern League and then worked at the A. J. Reach Sporting Goods manufactory in Philadelphia. When it closed he took a similar job in Perkasie, PA. Clements died in Norristown, PA, of a heart ailment at 75.

Casual students of the nineteenth-century game are naturally puzzled that Clements's groundbreaking achievements and overall career performance have never merited even token consideration for the HOF, especially since his defense seems to have been at least adequate. The reason may simply be that he was not particularly well-liked by many of his teammates and was despised by almost every young pitcher that debuted with the Phils during his later years with the team. By the early 1890s Clements had developed an utter disdain for rookie hurlers and would mock their deliveries by catching them barehanded and deliberately returning the ball at their feet whenever they missed his target or threw a pitch he did not like. His attitude got worse as he aged, and it probably is as good a reason as any that the Phillies' teams in the mid-1890s had so little luck with young arms and such poor pitching in general. (DN)

Cook, Paul / "Paul"

B	T	HGT	WGT	G	AB	H	R	2B
R	R	5'10"	185	378	1364	304	172	27

3B	HR	RBI	BB	SO	SB	BA	SA	OBP
9	0	114	67	87	52	.223	.256	.270

B. 5/5/1863 Caledonia, NY **D.** 5/25/1905
TEAMS: 84PhiN 86–89LouA 90BroN 91LouA 91StLA
DEBUT: 9/13/1884 at Philadelphia; caught Bill Vinton and went 0-for-4 in a 5–2 loss to Chicago's Larry Corcoran
FINALE: 7/16/1891 at Baltimore; caught Jack Stivetts and went 1-for-3 in a 3–1 loss to Baltimore's Sadie McMahon

Described as "a big, stout man" who ought to be able to hit well, Paul Cook was actually a weak hitter who just poked at the ball and hit lazy flies to LF. Defensively, he was no more than adequate, although in 1889 he led all AA catchers in assists as well as passed balls. The former triumph was courtesy of his pitching staff, which allowed the most hits and runs of any club in the majors that year, assuring him of the most opportunities to throw out would-be base stealers. Yet, when the Brotherhood raided the two existing major leagues that autumn, Cook was among the few AA catchers that were tapped for the PL. Part of the explanation that he was so richly rewarded for what was an otherwise mediocre career was his extraordinary popularity with both fans and fellow players.

Cook was spending his second year with Muskegon, MI, of the Northwestern League club in 1884 when he was summoned to Philadelphia NL in September. Following a 3-game trial with the Quakers, he returned to the minors and finished the 1885 season with the Eastern League Washington Nationals. Acquired by Louisville for 1886, Cook seized the Colonels' first-string catching assignment and retained it all season despite hitting just .206. He held out the following spring, hoping to play for Rochester, where he was then living, but was too well-liked by the new Colonels' manager, John Kelly, to obtain his release. Again he caught the most games on the club, if only because Kelly's other catchers were injured so often. The 1888 campaign once more found Cook behind the plate on Opening Day, though Louisville's busiest backstop collected just 36 total bases and 20 runs in 57 games. His most active season came the following year when he played in 81 games, and seemingly his most productive was in the 1890 PL when he hit .252, but the loop was built on offense and his BA was actually 22 points below the league average.

In Cook's year away from Louisville, the club had won a surprise AA pennant, but he had still been missed. When he caught the Colonels' second game of the 1891 season, a local paper noted, "Paul Cook was treated to an ovation on his return to the Association." But less than three months later manager Jack Chapman cut his walking papers. Cook played a handful of games with St. Louis and then joined Lincoln, NE. He went home to Rochester after the Western Association team disbanded and later ran a hotel in that city and opened the Oasis Café, one of the town's most popular watering holes at the turn of the century. In addition, he worked as a trainer for a local semipro football team prior to his death in 1905. (DN)

Criger, Louis / "Lou"

B	T	HGT	WGT	G	AB	H	R	2B
R	R	5'10"	165	282	976	255	118	29

3B	HR	RBI	BB	SO	SB	BA	SA	OBP
16	5	136	96	—	27	.261	.339	.334

B. 2/3/1872 Elkhart, IN **D.** 5/14/1934
TEAMS: 96–98CleN 99–00StLN 01–08BosAL 09StLAL 10NYAL 12StLAL
DEBUT: 9/21/1896 at Cleveland; pinch hit for pitcher Nig Cuppy in the seventh inning and walked in a 4–1 win over Cincinnati's Frank Dwyer
FINALE: 6/3/1912 at St. Louis; caught George Baumgardner and Curly Brown and went 1-for-2 before being replaced by Fred Walden in a 13–4 loss to Joe Engel and Tom Hughes

Born on a farm, Lou Criger pitched and caught for Elkhart, IN, amateur teams in the early 1890s. After gaining notice in 1894 in a game at Dowagiac, MI, against a Dowagiac team stacked with ringers like ML pitcher Danny Friend, he signed the following season with Kalamazoo of the Michigan State League but finished the summer with a semipro team in Goebelville, where he was caught that fall in an exhibition game by Charlie Ganzel, who touted him to Cleveland as a pitcher. The Spiders essentially farmed him to Fort Wayne of the Interstate League, where Cleveland pilot Pat Tebeau's brother George could keep watch on him. Upon arriving in Cleveland in September 1896, Criger immediately cemented what his position in the majors would be when he dazzled Tebeau and the rest of the Spiders in his first infield practice with the club. The following year, in his first full ML season, only weak hitting prevented him from claiming the regular catching post.

That winter, rather than return to the family farm, Criger worked at the C. G. Conn band instrument factory in Elkhart as a horn maker. Expected to be only third on the catching depth chart when spring training began in 1898, he wrested the first-string job from Jack O'Connor when incumbent regular Chief Zimmer was held by injuries to just 20 games. By producing career highs in runs (43) and BA (.279), he convinced Tebeau that his bat could support his exemplary defensive skills. After syndicate ownership decreed that Criger move to St. Louis in 1899 with most of the Spiders' regulars, only a rash of carbuncles followed by a torn muscle in his side stopped him from catching over 100 games. In 1900 he again lost significant time to an injury when he suffered a midseason broken rib but hit .271 and was then regarded as one of the best catchers in the NL. That fall Criger used his growing name recognition to open a saloon in Elkhart with former teammate Nig Cuppy as his partner. He was probably either at his saloon or on the family farm with his wife, the former Belle Wolhaupter, when a recruiter from the new Boston American League entry called on him soon after the holidays. (DN)

*Cross, Amos C. (b. Emile Kriz) / "Amos"

B	T	HGT	WGT	G	AB	H	R	2B
?	?	?	?	117	441	118	62	16

3B	HR	RBI	BB	SO	SB	BA	SA	OBP
7	1	56	45	—	13	.268	.342	.338

B. 2/?/1860 Milwaukee, WI **D.** 7/16/1888

TEAMS: 85–87LouA

DEBUT: 4/22/1885 at Louisville; caught Norm Baker and was 0-for-4 in an 11–0 win over Pittsburgh's Hank O'Day.

FINALE: 6/23/1887 at Cleveland; caught Guy Hecker and went 0-for-5 in an 11–10 win over Cleveland's Hugh Daily

FAMOUS LAST: 7/12/1886 at Louisville; in a 14–3 win over Baltimore's Abner Powell hit his only career home run in what was perhaps the last game in ML history that batterymates ranked one and two in a team's batting order when Cross batted second and pitcher Guy Hecker batted leadoff.

Amos Cross was the older brother of MLers Lave and Frank Cross, the former of which successfully concealed for well over a century that the true family surname was Kriz. An outstanding catcher, the eldest Cross was besieged by health problems from the outset of his ML career. In the spring of 1884 Pittsburgh of the AA released him owing to his "continued illness." Cross then joined Oil City of the Iron & Oil Association and paired with one of his spring Pittsburgh batterymates, Norm Baker. The following year he and Baker came to Louisville as a duo and debuted brilliantly with the Colonels, beating their former Pittsburgh club 11–0. From his first day in ML garb Cross was superlative defensively but struggled initially at the plate with impatience. In his rookie season he failed to collect a walk in 130 ABs, but he learned discipline quickly and the following year topped the team in the highest percentage of walks per at-bat (44 in just 283 ABs).

Like many young players of his time, Cross was not beyond falling prey to the wiles of women. In November 1886 he was arrested in Cleveland on a "serious charge" by one Dora Benns, and a week later *TSN* reported that another woman, a stranger to Cleveland, was also on the lookout for him. But the charges may have been trumped up, for he spent the winter without further incident, working out with his brother Lave in the Cleveland Armory. Still, when Cross reported to Louisville in the spring of 1887, he was ailing again. Since he was obviously not himself, the Colonels put him up for sale, but when there were no bidders he was released in September. The December 10, 1887, *TSN* sadly recounted, "Amos Cross of Louisville is dying with consumption of the lungs." But the following week the same paper brought hope when it retracted its gloomy forecast and said he was "not dying with consumption." As late as January 1888 Cross was reported to be recovering, but six months later he expired at his Cleveland home. (DN)

Crotty, Joseph P. / "Joe"

B	T	HGT	WGT	G	AB	H	R	2B
R	R	?	?	87	308	56	34	7

3B	HR	RBI	BB	SO	SB	BA	SA	OBP
3	1	9	11	—	3	.182	.234	.220

B. 12/24/1859 Cincinnati, OH **D.** 6/22/1926

TEAMS: 82LouA 82StLA 84CinU 85LouA 86NYA

DEBUT: 5/4/1882 at St. Louis; caught John Reccius and went 0-for-4 in a 14–5 loss to St. Louis's George McGinnis

FINALE: 7/5/1886 at Louisville; caught Al Mays and went hitless in a 5–4 loss to Tom Ramsey

Joe Crotty was a marginal talent but got his fair share of ML playing time because he was a willing worker and a good schmoozer. In 1878, at age 17, he played for the semipro Eclipse team of Louisville in return for his board only, although the owner gave him a new suit of clothes as a bonus after the season. Crotty remained with the Eclipse until it joined the AA in 1882. Dropped by the Kentucky club after just 5 games, he traveled to St. Louis, where he caught Ed Fusselbach, himself a catcher by trade, in a 14–3 loss to Pittsburgh. After the game the Browns released Fusselbach but kept Crotty, if only for a few more weeks.

In 1884 Crotty was with Bay City, MI, of the Northwestern League when Cincinnati UA acquired him to back up Fatty Briody. Given a second chance with Louisville in 1885, Crotty began the season third on the catching depth chart behind Dan Sullivan and Amos Cross but lost his bid to claim the job after both players faltered when Crotty hit just .155 in 39 games. His final ML opportunity came in 1886 under New York Mets manager Jim Gifford, who strove for team chemistry, but when crusty Bob Ferguson took over the club after it started 5-12, Crotty was soon released. He finished the season with Syracuse of the International Association and then played several more years in the minors. By 1893 he was out of the game and back in Louisville. Crotty remained in Louisville for a while, working for the local gas company. He then moved to Minneapolis and started a house furnishing business. By the close of the century Crotty had taken on a partner, expanded his business to include clothing and was among Minneapolis's most prosperous citizens. He died of a heart attack in the Minnesota city in 1926. (DN)

Cusick, Andrew J. / "Andy"

B	T	HGT	WGT	G	AB	H	R	2B
R	R	5'9½"	190	95	332	64	27	7

3B	HR	RBI	BB	SO	SB	BA	SA	OBP
1	0	15	8	42	1	.193	.220	.214

B. 12/?/1857 Limerick, Ireland **D.** 8/6/1929
TEAMS: 84WilU 84–87PhiA
DEBUT: 8/21/1894 at Wilmington; caught Jim McElroy, switched positions with left fielder Tom Lynch when John Murphy replaced McElroy in the sixth inning and went 0-for-3 in a 12–1 loss to Washington's Charlie Geggus
FINALE: 6/15/1887 at New York; caught Dan Casey and Ed Daily and went 0-for-3 in a 29–1 loss to New York's Tim Keefe

Andy Cusick was a sure-handed receiver, excellent on pop fouls, and, the Wilmington press wrote, "his throwing to the bases is perfection at least on home grounds." The same Wilmington reporter extolled, "Once on first he is sure to steal second. Your correspondent has not seen him fail at it." Cusick was also capable of playing anywhere, but no matter where he was put he failed to hit.

After playing with teams in Massachusetts and Connecticut, Cusick joined Interstate Association Wilmington in 1883 and was among the few players from the 1883 Quicksteps still with the club when it joined the UA in August 1884. He caught in a number of brutally ragged games, including both his debut and finale. Among the other debacles were the September 4, 1884, contest at Wilmington, which had to be stopped when a foul tip nearly made umpire Pat Dutton the first on-field fatality in ML history. The tipped ball apparently skipped off Cusick's shoulder and struck Dutton, who was officiating behind the plate, in the throat, instantly cutting off his breath.

Cusick joined Philadelphia NL in 1885, and then was followed a year later by his former Quicksteps batterymate, southpaw Dan Casey. But while Casey became a staff bulwark, Cusick seldom played once he began battling a growing waistline. After appearing even less often in 1886 he rebelled at his sub status early in the 1887 season, especially when he got off to a 10-for-24 start and was leading the team in hitting even after drawing the collar in what proved to be his final ML game on June 15. Near the end of June, Cusick was suspended without pay after not reporting to the club in over a week. He then was sold to Washington along with pitcher Ed Daily but was released instead when he could not come to terms with the Senators. Later that season Cusick claimed the real reason for his dismissal was that his arm was now permanently lame, and that may have been true, for when he attempted a comeback in the 1888 Western Association he could only play 1B. Cusick then tried umpiring in the WA but was fired two years in a row for excessive drinking. Late in 1892 he was jailed in Edwardsville, IL, unable to post bail or pay his fine after conspiring to rig a boxing match. Upon getting out of prison, he found a safer niche in the fight game and became a boxing trainer. At some point Cusick settled in Chicago. When he died in 1929, he left behind his widow, Mary, five children and his brother, Dennis, a former minor leaguer. (DN)

Darling, Conrad / "Dell" "Wiener"

B	T	HGT	WGT	G	AB	H	R	2B
R	R	5'8"	170	175	628	151	109	24

3B	HR	RBI	BB	SO	SB	BA	SA	OBP
13	7	83	91	96	29	.240	.354	.340

B. 12/21/1861 Erie, PA **D.** 11/20/1904
TEAMS: 83BufN 87–89ChiN 90ChiP 91StLA
DEBUT: 7/3/1883 at Buffalo; caught George Derby and made 1 hit in a 31–7 loss to Chicago's Larry Corcoran
FINALE: 9/10/1891 at St. Louis; caught George Rettger and went 0-for-3 in an 11–3 loss to Boston's George Haddock

We do not know why Conrad Darling was called "Dell," but his secondary nickname of "Wiener" was given him in 1887 because of his fondness for wienerwurst. Never the luckiest player, he came to Buffalo in 1883 from the Erie Gas & Oil League just in time to take part in a monstrous embarrassment at the hands of Chicago and by August was quarantined at his house in Erie with small pox. Darling then played in four different minor leagues over the next three years before returning to the majors with Chicago in 1887. After going 2-for-4 in his Windy City debut against Indianapolis's John Healy on May 4, he had one of the most outstanding seasons in the nineteenth century by a backup catcher (.900 OPS) but was never able to crack the regular lineup. Darling remained a sub for the next two years but became such a local favorite that he was taken aboard the Chicago PL team in 1890. Serving as a backup, Darling had a fine season and probably would have helped Charlie Comiskey's Pirates to a better finish if Comiskey had played him at 1B all year and benched himself.

But in jumping to the PL, Darling infuriated Cap Anson and, since he was no more than a scrub, was no longer welcome on the Colts. He spent 1891 with the Minneapolis Western Association club until it was about to disband and then headed for St. Louis AA. Darling reported to the Browns with a check in his purse for $90, his final salary payment from Minneapolis. St. Louis owner Chris Von der Ahe cashed the check for him, but when it was sent to Minneapolis for payment, officials of the disbanded team refused to reimburse Von der Ahe, and Darling thus was "the direct loser" when Von der Ahe held him responsible for the money. Adding to his misery was a .132 BA with the Browns after 17 games, earning him a quick release.

That $90 meant a great deal to Darling, who had a wife and six children to support. The following December, after spending the early summer with Toledo before the Western League disbanded, he and Lou Bierbauer's brother Charlie were implicated in a ring that robbed railroad cars on the Lake Shore, Nickel Plate, and other lines. The ring would break into sealed cars and then ride the train and throw off goods that could be easily fenced at stops along the way where confederates waited in hiding for the loot. The police in Erie, PA, obtained search warrants and raided the homes of "sometimes upstanding citizens" whose sons or "giddy daughters" had made themselves an unwitting part of the ring by harboring stolen goods. Bierbauer was soon captured, but Darling remained on the loose until the flap took a new turn after it was discovered that the shippers had grossly exaggerated the value of the goods the thieves had stolen.

A blacksmith during the off-season, Darling began to devote more time to his trade once it grew apparent that he would never again be able to support his family on baseball earnings. He also acquired part ownership in an Erie restaurant and worked for the Scott Coal Company until shortly before his death in 1904. Reportedly, Darling died of complications from an old baseball groin injury, but the true cause may have been testicular cancer. His widow later married his former crime cohort, Charlie Bierbauer. (DN/BM)

Dealy, Patrick E. (aka Dealey) **/ "Pat"**

B	T	HGT	WGT	G	AB	H	R	2B
R	R	5'8"	145	131	469	113	71	14

3B	HR	RBI	BB	SO	SB	BA	SA	OBP
4	2	34	19	26	45	.241	.301	.275

B. 11/12/1861 Underhill, VT **D.** 12/16/1924
TEAMS: 84StPU 85–86BosN 87WasN 90SyrA
DEBUT: 10/1/1884 at Cincinnati; caught Lou Galvin and went 0-for-3 in a 7–0 loss to Cincinnati's George Bradley
FINALE: 6/5/1890 at Syracuse; played 3B and went 0-for-3 in a 3–2 loss to Philadelphia's Sadie McMahon

Easterner Pat Dealy played with St. Paul UA in 1884 and then returned east with westerner Gurdon Whiteley to play for Boston NL in 1885. With the Hub team from the outset of the season, he irked most of his teammates early on when he convinced the Boston brass that Whiteley was a better player than Jim Manning, and the popular Manning was then benched while Whiteley proved to be a horrible bust. Meanwhile, evidence of Dealy's own playing skills was contradictory. On May 3, 1886, early in his second ML season, he committed 10 passed balls while catching Bill Stemmeyer in a 12–11 loss at Washington. Yet the previous year *SL* had written, "He is a little fellow, but solid, and holds [Jim] Whitney with ease and grace. The way he gathers in the foul tips and flies is something astonishing, while his throwing to the bases is not second to that of Charlie Bennett and Buck Ewing." Regardless, Dealy appeared in just 15 games with Boston in 1886 and then was released to Washington. In August 1887 Washington sent him home with a sore arm and suspended him on top of it for drinking and indifferent play. Dealy then spent the next two seasons in the minors scarcely distinguishing himself—in 1889 he hit just .170 for Buffalo in 70 International Association games—but nonetheless was signed by Syracuse for 1890 after the Stars joined the AA. In his Syracuse debut on April 18, 1890, Dealy again carved a negative niche in the record book when the Brooklyn Gladiators ran wild against him and pitcher Toby Lyons, stealing 16 bases. Dealy returned to the minors in 1891 and the following September was arrested in Buffalo for assaulting a man with a slingshot so severely that his victim nearly died. He remained in Buffalo after his baseball days ended in 1894 to work as a bricklayer and died there at 63. (DN)

*Deasley, Thomas H. / "Pat" "Tom"

B	T	HGT	WGT	G	AB	H	R	2B
R	R	5'8½"	154	402	1466	358	161	37

3B	HR	RBI	BB	SO	SB	BA	SA	OBP
9	0	120	49	89	7	.244	.282	.271

B. 11/17/1857 Philadelphia, PA **D.** 4/1/1943
TEAMS: 81–82BosN 83–84StLA 85–87NYN 88WasN
DEBUT: 5/18/1881 at Cleveland; played 1B and went 0-for-2 in a 3–2 win over Cleveland's Jim McCormick
FINALE: 9/12/1888 at Pittsburgh; caught Jim Whitney and went 0-for-2 in a 2–0 loss to Pittsburgh's Ed Morris

Pat Deasley's reputation had tarnished irrevocably long before the end of the nineteenth century, but in his prime he was considered the premier defensive catcher of his day. In the February 12, 1899, *Washington Post*, Tom Brown rated Deasley the best receiver he ever saw, a master at purposely dropping a pitch to delude a runner into breaking for the next base and then snapping up the ball and throwing him out. Catchers' fielding stats during the decade of the 1880s bear out Brown's assessment. Among receivers in 300 or more games between 1881 and 1890, Deasley ranks fourth in FA (.927) even though the bulk of his career came in the early part of the decade before fielding averages began to climb dramatically as catching gear grew increasingly sophisticated.

The brother of MLer John Deasley, the Philadelphia-born catcher was a near illiterate everywhere but on the playing field when he began making his name with local amateur and semipro clubs in the mid 1870s. By 1879 he and Harry Stovey, then still a pitcher, formed the battery for the semipro Defiance club. After spending most of 1880 in the minor National Association, Deasley signed with Boston NL in 1881 but was soon subjected to manager Harry Wright's bile for his off-the-field deportment. Addicted at a young age to alcohol, the catcher was so raucous and flamboyant when he was under the influence that Wright refused to play him unless he was cold sober. When Boston withheld money from his salary in 1882 after he led NL catchers in fielding, he told the *Boston Globe* he would "not play in the league again if the Boston Club had the power to retain [him] . . . and not keep their contract."

Deasley then jumped from the NL to its new rival and signed with St. Louis AA for a reported $257 a month in 1883 that advanced to $350 a month when he began the season temperate. Among the AA's highest-paid players even though, as a catcher, he appeared in little more than half his team's games, he repeated as his loop's fielding champion. But there were early warning signs—in late July owner Chris Von der Ahe suspended Deasley ten days for drinking—and by 1884 manager Charlie Comiskey had him on a short leash. Angry over Deasley's alcohol intake and repeated disciplinary infractions, Von der Ahe reneged on a promise not to reserve him for 1885 and sold him to New York NL in December 1884 for just $400 even though he had led all AA catchers in games played. According to some reports, the catcher paid for his own release when the Giants dangled a contract in front of him for even more money than the club's premier catcher, Buck Ewing, was receiving.

Deasley spent the next three seasons as a backup to Ewing, his playing time diminishing each year as his behavior grew increasingly "erratic and boyish." In 1887 he fancied himself a temperance orator for a time but soon backslid. That fall the Giants quit on him even though he hit .314 in spot appearances. Deasley signed with Washington and caught Hank O'Day in the Senators' 1888 Opening Day loss to New York. After that he was seldom used, missing time with a broken thumb and more time when he hit just .157 until Washington tired in mid-September of having to watch him "very closely to keep him on the beaten path" and dismissed him.

The following year, after flunking out of the lowly Central Interstate League, Deasley was reported to have come so unraveled that he was in an insane asylum. In April 1891 the *Boston Globe* sadly recounted that he was reporting to the Philadelphia Players League park every day under an illusion he was the groundskeeper. The *Washington Post* revealed five years later that ex-Senators player Harry O'Hagan had once said that on his way to the Phils' park he saw a decrepit man sitting on curbstone, stuffing a cigar butt into a pipe bowl so he could smoke it, and learned it was Deasley. Yet Deasley lived to be 85 before dying at his home in Philadelphia. (DN/DB)

Dolan, Thomas J. / "Tom"

B	T	HGT	WGT	G	AB	H	R	2B
R	R	5'11"	185	225	808	165	95	25

3B	HR	RBI	BB	SO	SB	BA	SA	OBP
7	1	40	9	23	11	.204	.256	.242

G	IP	H	GS	CG	BB
1	4	4	0	0	0

SO	SH	W	L	PCT	ERA
0	0	0	0	—	4.50

B. 1/10/1855 New York, NY **D.** 1/16/1913
TEAMS: 79ChiN 82BufN 83–84StLA 84StLU 85–86StLN 86BalA 88StLA
DEBUT: 9/30/1879 at Buffalo; caught Frank Hankinson and went 0-for-4 in a 10–2 loss to Buffalo's Bill McGunnigle
FINALE: 10/14/1888 at St. Louis; caught Jim Devlin and had 1 hit in a 10–1 loss to Cincinnati's Lee Viau

A master of deception his entire career, Tom Dolan claimed to be 17 when he caught for the independent St. Louis Reds in 1876, but he was really 21. He then spent the next dozen years deceiving ML teams into believing he was a good player even though most of the evidence was to the contrary. His grandest deception of all was actually not of his making—seemingly not, anyway. For a number of years *The Sporting News Official Baseball Record Book* recognized him as the record holder for the most outfield assists in a season with 63 in 1883 even though most of his assists that year came as a catcher.

Nevertheless, Dolan truly does own some significant distinctions. Beginning in 1877, he was Jim Galvin's most frequent catcher until Galvin became an established ML pitcher in 1879. Later in his career he became the only man ever to catch for three different St. Louis teams in three different major leagues in three consecutive seasons (1883–85). But perhaps his chief claim to sports fame is that in the mid-1880s he was the best handball player in baseball, so good that even Fred Dunlap, who fancied himself the kingpin, assiduously avoided playing Dolan. Finally, Dolan perpetrated one of the bloodiest on-field fights in baseball history on May 11, 1887, while playing for Lincoln of the Western League, when he and Denver's Pat Tebeau went at it so savagely that each was fined the munificent sum of $5. It was his customary way of taking care of business on and off the field. Soon after joining the Browns in 1883, Dolan, according to the *St. Louis Republican*, hired a teammate to beat up first-string catcher Pat Deasley so that he could obtain the job.

The son of John Dolan, a saloonkeeper whose business catered to a rough, working-class crowd that disregarded the racial boundaries then in sway in St. Louis, Dolan and his father openly bankrolled a local "colored" team in St. Louis called the Black Stockings in the early 1880s after he had already begun to play professionally. Dolan remained an active player until 1890, when his 3-year-old son died while he was playing in the Western Association. The following year he joined the St. Louis fire department, having earlier been a fireman during the off-season. Seriously injured in an electrical accident in 1894, he recovered to captain the fire department team for several more years. Never one for taking great care of himself, Dolan died in St. Louis in 1913 of cirrhosis of the liver. (DN/DB)

Donahue, James Augustus / "Jim" "Biddy" "Bridget"

B	T	HGT	WGT	G	AB	H	R	2B
R	R	6'0"	175	341	1275	298	133	24

3B	HR	RBI	BB	SO	SB	BA	SA	OBP
11	2	133	104	38	33	.234	.275	.295

B. 1/8/1862 Lockport, IL **D.** 4/19/1935
TEAMS: 86–87NYA 88–89KCA 91ColA
DEBUT: 4/19/1886 at Philadelphia; caught Ed Cushman and went 0-for-3 in a 4–1 win over the A's Ted Kennedy
FINALE: 10/2/1891 at Milwaukee; played RF and went 0-for-4 in a 5–0 loss to Milwaukee's Frank Killen

Jim Donahue was the first Donahue in ML baseball to be nicknamed "Bridget," albeit for an unknown reason, but he was more commonly called "Jim" or "Biddy." He received his initiation to the ML milieu when he began 1884 with the Philadelphia Quakers' reserves. Donahue joined the Muskegon, MI, Northwestern League team later in 1884 and then received his second ML opportunity after catching Matt Kilroy with Augusta of the Southern League in 1885. Ironically, he made his first ML hit off Kilroy on May 4, 1886. One of four catchers the Mets carried early in the 1886 campaign, Donahue remained with the club all year, and by the end of the following season he was viewed as one of the Mets' better players. He went to the new Kansas City AA entry in 1888 along with several teammates after the Mets disbanded and caught both the club's first game in the AA on April 21, 1888, and its final AA game on October 14, 1889. The following season Donahue remained loyal to Kansas City after the club deserted the AA for the minor Western Association, but in the spring of 1891, after a bitter holdout, he "jumped to Columbus" in April when he and KC could not come to terms. Idled for some time by typhoid, Donahue finally went home to recover. Upon returning to Columbus, he became the team's main catcher in the latter months of the season but hit just .218.

After Columbus disbanded when the NL and AA merged, Donahue put his name in the hat to play in the Western League in 1892 but balked when he was assigned to Milwaukee. Before the issue could be resolved, the WL collapsed and he headed to Marinette, WI, to finish his pro career in the Wisconsin-Michigan League. Donahue died in 1935 after a lengthy illness in Lockport, IL, where he had operated a liquor store for a number of years. (DN)

Douglass, William Bingham / "Klondike"

B	T	HGT	WGT	G	AB	H	R	2B
L	R	6'0"	200	480	1832	516	273	62

3B	HR	RBI	BB	SO	SB	BA	SA	OBP
21	9	178	165	15	62	.282	.354	.353

B. 5/10/1872 Boston, PA **D.** 12/13/1953
TEAMS: 96–97StLN 98–04PhiN
DEBUT: 4/23/1896 at St. Louis; caught Ted Breitenstein and went 3-for-4 in a 3–1 loss to Chicago's Bert Briggs
FINALE: 4/16/1904 at Philadelphia; played 1B and was 1-for-4 in an 8–7 loss to Boston's Kaiser Wilhelm

Klondike Douglass grew up in Wellsville, MO, and played with an independent team in nearby Moberly and later with Sherman of the Texas-Southern League before joining the Browns in the spring of 1896. The following year Douglass led a miserable St. Louis team in runs, BA, and SA despite slugging just .405. On November 10, a month after the season ended, Douglass was part of a seven-player trade that sent him to Philadelphia. The December 11, 1897, *TSN* said that he had "started for the Klondike" and then stopped when he learned of the trade because "he looks upon the deal whereby he comes to the Quaker City as good as a gold mine." Forever afterward Douglass was known as "Klondike."

In his first season with the Phils, Douglass moved from catcher to 1B and generally batted second in the order, an odd place for someone who seldom walked, had almost no power, and was not a particularly good base runner. In 1899 Douglass lost his job at 1B and became a backup catcher. He alternated between catcher and 1B for the remainder of his stay with the Phils without ever satisfying the club at either position. Douglass finished his pro career in the 1912 Virginia League and eventually did go west, dying in Bend, OR, at 81. (DN)

Dowse, Thomas Joseph / "Tom"

B	T	HGT	WGT	G	AB	H	R	2B
R	R	5'11"	175	160	590	116	62	12

3B	HR	RBI	BB	SO	SB	BA	SA	OBP
1	0	46	29	66	7	.197	.220	.243

G	IP	H	GS	CG	BB
1	5	6	0	0	1

SO	SH	W	L	PCT	ERA
0	0	0	0	—	5.40

B. 8/12/1866 Mohill, Ireland **D.** 12/14/1946
TEAMS: 90CleN 91ColA 92LouN 92CinN 92PhiN 92WasN
DEBUT: 4/21/1890 at Pittsburgh; played CF and went 0-for-4 in a 11–9 loss to Pittsburgh's Crazy Schmit and Bill Sowders
FINALE: 10/12/1892 at Philadelphia; played LF and went 2-for-4 in an 8–5 loss to Philadelphia's Kid Carsey

After spending 1888 with Wilkes-Barre of the Central League, Tom Dowse traveled to Atlanta of the Southern League the following spring but was forced to return north when the SL folded. It was a blessing for him, as he finished the season with Albany's independent pro team under manager Tom York, who recommended him to Cleveland. At the end of the 1890 season Dowse signed with Columbus AA where there would be "no [Chief Zimmer] to overshadow him completely." He participated in only 55 games for the Solons in 1891 but his final appearance came on October 4 at Milwaukee when he caught Columbus's last game as a major league entry, an 8–4 loss to the Brewers' Jim Hughey. After Columbus folded, Dowse embarked on an odyssey that put him in a record four different ML uniforms in 1892, none of them enamored of him enough to keep him for more than a few weeks. His .165 composite BA was largely to blame, but in at least one case Dowse found a unique way to grease the skids for himself. Released by Louisville, he was picked up by Cincinnati in mid-August and caught a good game at Pittsburgh. To celebrate, Dowse boarded the train to Cincinnati in the company of a pair of "two flashily dressed, paint-bedaubed females," who joined him in his sleeping compartment. When Dowse disobeyed manager Charlie Comiskey's orders to send the women on their way, Comiskey asked the conductor to have the women thrown off the train, only to learn that Dowse had paid their fares and they could not be ejected. Dowse could be released, however, and Comiskey took care of that as soon as possible.

Less puritanical managements in Philadelphia and Washington found him wanting for other reasons, and after spending the winter in Philadelphia stuffing mattresses Dowse played several more years in the minors, finishing in the 1897 Eastern League. Even in the minors Dowse was the same weak hitter who compiled just 130 total bases in 160 ML games, and he was also an inordinately slow runner. His main assets were a strong arm and "his boisterous coaching and rough style of play" that made him extremely unpopular in rival cities. In 1893, while Dowse was playing for Buffalo of the Eastern League, the Wilkes-Barre press vilified him as the dirtiest player in the loop and "suffering with an abnormally large cranium" to boot. But when Buffalo cut him in late July for poor hitting, none other than Wilkes-Barre manager Dan Shannon promptly signed him. Dowse remained in the Eastern League until 1897 and died from bronchopneumonia in Riverdale, CA, in 1946. (DN/DB)

Farrell, Charles Andrew / "Duke"

B	T	HGT	WGT	G	AB	H	R	2B
B	R	6'1"	208	1319	4863	1348	759	181

3B	HR	RBI	BB	SO	SB	BA	SA	OBP
112	51	836	440	246	135	.277	.382	.342

B. 8/31/1866 Oakdale, MA **D.** 2/15/1925
TEAMS: 88–89ChiN 90ChiP 91BosA 92PitN 93WasN 94–96NYN 96–99WasN 99–02BroN 03–05BosAL
DEBUT: 4/21/1888 at Indianapolis; played RF and went 0-for-4 in an 8–5 win over Indianapolis's John Healy
FINALE: 6/13/1905 at Boston; caught Bill Dinneen and made 2 hits in an 11–2 loss to Cleveland's Earl Moore
CAREER HIGHLIGHT: Retired in 1905 with the then career record for pinch hits with 23

Duke Farrell caught for an amateur team in Marlborough, the Massachusetts town where he grew up, in 1885–86 before joining the New England League the following season. Acquired by Chicago in 1888, he shared the club's catching with Tom Daly. Tall and agile, Farrell was capable of playing other positions as well. After jumping to Chicago PL in 1890, he joined the AA Boston Reds once the PL folded and topped the loop in both homers and RBI while serving most of the season at 3B as a stand in for the injured Bill Joyce. When Farrell was assigned to last-place Pittsburgh after the NL and AL merged in December 1891, he threatened to go back to his original trade as a shoemaker. Even though he eventually relented, he reported to the Pirates fat and out of shape and hit just .215, an ML season-record low for a hitter with a minimum of 600 ABs. One pleasant development in an otherwise dreary year for Farrell was that concessionaire Harry Stevens gave him his nickname, "The Duke o' Marlborough."

In December 1892 Farrell went from a poor team to an abysmal one when he was sent to Washington along with $1,500 for pitcher Frank Killen. He still did his best to win a game now and then for the Senators. On August 20, 1893, while batting in a game at Chicago he "innocuously" asked Colts catcher Kit Kittridge to sweep the plate, and when Kittridge reached behind him for the whisk broom, Cub Stricker, who had been on 3B, stole home as part of a planned play, but Washington still lost. Also that year Farrell led NL catchers in assists and was rewarded when the New York Giants acquired him in a four-player deal the following February. His 1894 season in New York marked his sixth different team in six years. Although he hit .284 and helped New York win the inaugural Temple Cup series, he scored just 47 runs in 114 games, an amazingly low total for a player with a good team, and followed by tallying just 38 times in 90 contests in 1895. In the spring of 1896, Farrell, previously a right-handed batter, learned to hit lefty as well, but manager Arthur Irwin still preferred Parke Wilson behind the plate, and in August Farrell was returned to Washington along with pitcher Carney Flynn and $2,500 for third sacker Bill Joyce.

The Senators were no better than they had been during Farrell's earlier visit, but he again gave it his best during the months he languished in Washington. Meanwhile he developed into one of the most unique switch hitters in the game's history. Not only did Farrell wait until fairly late in his career to begin batting from both sides of the plate, but he seems to have paid little regard to the arm a pitcher favored in deciding which way to bat. In the summer of 1896 he began swinging strictly left-handed when he fell into a hot streak from that side. The following season he hit only from the right side after a power surge in August. Farrell appears to have followed a similar policy throughout the rest of his career.

In 1898 he surmounted the loss of his wife to consumption to enjoy his last season as a semi-regular and was even leading the NL in batting for a time before finishing at .314. The following April he and Deacon McGuire, with whom he had shared the catching load since arriving in Washington, were both traded to Brooklyn for three lesser players and $2,500. The one-sided deal practically assured the City of Churches of the 1899 NL pennant. Brooklyn repeated the following year with Farrell sharing the catching with McGuire, but in 1901 he was spiked and missed a sizeable portion of the season with blood poisoning. During the layoff he put on weight and was released at the end of the 1902 season when he continued to balloon. Farrell caught on with Boston AL in 1903 and appeared to be returning to form until he broke an ankle sliding and was held to just 17 games. He returned to collect a pinch-hit AB in the first modern World Series that fall but ignored *SL's* monition to lose about sixty pounds prior to the 1904 season. After leaving the majors in June 1905, Farrell ran a hotel in Marlborough and then coached and scouted for a number of seasons with the Yankees. During World War I he served as a deputy U.S. marshal in Boston. Farrell was a coach for the Boston Braves when he died in Boston in 1925 following surgery for stomach cancer. (DN/DB)

Flint, Frank Sylvester / "Silver"

B	T	HGT	WGT	G	AB	H	R	2B
R	R	6'0"	180	760	2913	687	380	129

3B	HR	RBI	BB	SO	SB	BA	SA	OBP
34	21	295	54	471	10	.236	.325	.250

G	W	L	PCT	PENNANTS
19	5	12	.294	0

B. 8/3/1855 Philadelphia, PA **D.** 1/14/1892
TEAMS: 75RedsNA 78IndN (P/M)79ChiN 80–89ChiN
DEBUT: 5/4/1875 at St. Louis; played 3B and made 2 hits in a 15–9 loss to the St. Louis Brown Stockings' George Bradley
FINALE: 7/18/1889 at Boston; caught John Healy and went 1-for-4 in an 8–1 loss to Boston's John Clarkson

In an era when catchers were renowned for their mangled hands, Frank Flint had the most famous fingers of all. In 1888 he regaled an awed reporter with a guided description of the specific events that had disfigured nine of his ten digits. Yet remarkable as his hands were, people couldn't resist the urge to exaggerate. One tale had Flint visiting the White House and shaking the hand of President Cleveland, causing the president to reach his own hand into his pocket under the mistaken impression that he had been given a handful of walnuts.

Called "Silver" because of his whitish-blond hair, Flint was born in Philadelphia but grew up in St. Louis and first drew attention while catching for a local club called the Elephants. He was a large, powerfully built man at a time when most catchers were small and agile, but he soon showed he could handle the demanding position. By 1878 he was paired for the second year in a row with the hard-throwing "The Only" Nolan in Indianapolis, where team president William Pettit plastered the town with photos of the duo that bore the inscriptions "The Only Nolan" and "The Champion Catcher of America."

The following season Flint joined Chicago, where his ability to get the most out of pitchers like Larry Corcoran, Fred Goldsmith, John Clarkson, and Jim McCormick had much to do with the White Stockings' five pennants during his eleven seasons with the club. There were many theories as to why Chicago kept coming up with new pitching stars throughout the 1880s, but those who knew baseball understood that Flint's steadying hand in their support was a prime reason.

When Flint began his career, catchers wore no visible protective equipment at all, though many used mouth guards and some wore light kid gloves. By its end, however, catchers were wearing masks, chest protectors, and mitts, and each new addition to the catcher's garb lessened the skill needed to play the position. Flint had always been a weak hitter, so in 1889 he "went behind the bat but fifteen times. This was too much for his proud nature, and he decided to step down and out." When Flint finally retired, in addition to his many defensive kudos he took with him the lowest career OBP in history to that point (.250) by a position player with a minimum of 2,500 PAs.

What made Flint so invaluable despite his paltry offensive contributions? Perhaps his strongest asset was his ability to catch any pitch, regardless of how fast or from what angle in came, which allowed his pitchers to use their entire repertoires. Flint was also known for his firm handling of young pitchers. Whenever player-manager Cap Anson had him try out an aspirant arm, Flint would take off his catching glove, even though "in nine cases out of ten the pitchers that Anson assigned to Flint were lusty young fellows with more strength than accuracy." Flint would take the pitcher "down to the corner of the park, and with bare hands stop balls as fast as they were thrown. It was his policy to make the 'young blood' think they were pitching very slow balls until they became tired. Then he would don gloves and begin to do coaching. However, he would never give any advice to a 'colt' until he was sure he was tired out and convinced that he was not a 'cyclone.'"

Less than three years after playing his final game for Chicago, Flint was dead in that city, the victim of tuberculosis. He had been a heavy drinker and was broke when he died as a result of "the wide-open policy he pursued in helping his friends." But Flint had "not an enemy," which was symbolized when his ex-wife, who divorced him two years before his death because of his drinking, took him back and nursed him through his fatal illness. She explained, "Frank is a good fellow and I'm not going to say one word against him." (PM/DN)

Fulmer, Christopher / "Chris"

B	T	HGT	WGT	G	AB	H	R	2B
R	R	5'8"	165	252	876	216	176	37

3B	HR	RBI	BB	SO	SB	BA	SA	OBP
9	1	85	122	12	76	.247	.313	.343

G	IP	H	GS	CG	BB
1	2	2	0	0	11

SO	SH	W	L	PCT	ERA
0	0	0	0	—	4.50

B. 7/4/1858 Tamaqua, PA **D.** 11/9/1931
TEAMS: 84WasU 86–89BalA
DEBUT: 8/4/1884 at Washington; caught Abner Powell and went 2-for-4 in a 7–2 loss to Baltimore's Bill Sweeney
FINALE: 6/27/1889 at Baltimore; played CF and went 0-for-4 in a 10–0 win over Louisville's Red Ehret

Chris Fulmer's career took off in 1883 when he and Abner Powell formed a crack battery with the independent Woonsocket Comets. Both requested their releases in July so they could play for the newly formed Chicago Unions but ended up with Peoria of the Northwestern League instead when the Unions were slow to materialize. Fulmer broke his finger in the last game of the season against Toledo but healed over the winter, and he and Powell were again Peoria's leading battery at the beginning of the 1884 Northwestern League season. They traveled as a unit to the Washington Unions in August and remained with Washington in 1885 when it moved to the Eastern League after the UA collapsed.

Upon learning that Baltimore AA had signed Fulmer for the 1886 season, Washington manager Mike Scanlon tried to enjoin him from leaving, claiming that he really preferred to stay with Washington, which was about to become part of the NL. In truth, Scanlon may have been right, for Baltimore was the worst team in the majors in 1886. Apart from rookie sensation Matt Kilroy, Fulmer was probably the team MVP, as he led all Baltimore players that played in more than half the team's games in every major batting department despite hitting just .244. The club was so ghastly that Fulmer's mediocre .674 OPS topped runner-up Jack Manning (.577) by nearly 100 points.

Fulmer did well again the following year until he was shelved by a broken finger that was set badly. The finger continued to plague him in 1888, holding him to just 52 games and causing his BA to shrivel to .187. In 1889 Fulmer caught Baltimore's Opening Day game but then went behind the plate only once more when his finger still could not withstand the rigors of catching. After a short trial in CF to utilize his strong arm, he was released when he was unable to cover enough ground.

Upon leaving the Orioles, Fulmer joined Shenandoah of the Middle States League and then played in the International Association for part of 1890 before moving to Washington of the Atlantic Association by August. He appears to have left the game quietly at that point, but years later he circulated a story that his career ended when he injured his arm on a hard slide into the plate. Fulmer died in Tamaqua, PA, in 1931. (DN)

Fusselbach, Edward L. (aka Fusselback) **/ "Ed" "Ned" "Eddie"**

B	T	HGT	WGT	G	AB	H	R	2B
R	?	5'6"	156	109	462	124	75	19

3B	HR	RBI	BB	SO	SB	BA	SA	OBP
3	1	3	8	—	0	.268	.329	.281

G	IP	H	GS	CG	BB
4	23	34	2	2	2

SO	SH	W	L	PCT	ERA
3	0	1	2	.333	4.70

B. 7/4/1858 Philadelphia, PA **D.** 4/14/1926
TEAMS: 82StLA 84BalU 85PhiA 88LouA
DEBUT: 5/3/1882 at St. Louis; caught John Schappert and went 1-for-4 in a 6–4 win over Louisville's Tony Mullane
FINALE: 8/28/1888 at Philadelphia; played RF and went 1-for-4 in a 5–3 loss to Philadelphia's Ed Seward

Ed Fusselbach broke in with the Wright club of Philadelphia in 1875 and remained an amateur until joining the independent Philadelphia Athletics in 1878. Subsequently, he became a baseball vagabond. In 1880 he caught Bobby Mathews while both were with the San Francisco Stars and then returned to the Athletics for the 1881 Eastern Championship Association season. That winter he caught for the Lone Star team of New Orleans before reporting to the St. Louis Browns for his inaugural ML season in the fledgling AA. From the outset he was gauged to have one of the best arms in the game, strong enough to be used in the box on August 23 when injuries depleted the Browns' pitching staff. But while the talent was there, Fusselbach's resolve for staying in shape was capricious. In late August 1883 St. Louis sent him to Hot Springs, AR, "for his health" and then released him.

Fusselbach spent 1883 with Peoria of the Northwestern League, where he first teamed with pitcher Bill Sweeney, a fellow Philadelphian, and then accompanied Sweeney in 1884 to Baltimore UA, where he shared the catching with Rooney Sweeney. On Opening Day his "sharp throwing" produced 6 assists in Bill Sweeney's 7–3 win over Washington. Even though Fusselbach easily led the UA in catching assists with 137, he subsequently caught in only 5 more ML games, all with Philadelphia AA in 1885. His last big league appearance came in 1888 when he was back in Philadelphia after having been released by Portland of the New England League and convinced Louisville's Jack Kerins to give him a trial when the Colonels were short an outfielder, only to be left behind when Louisville went to its next stop.

Although Fusselbach was not a model player, his failure ever to play substantially again in the majors after 1884 is difficult to explain. As his career wore on, he learned to play SS, 3B, 1B, and the outfield, as well as catch, and seems usually to have hit reasonably well. Always welcomed in his home city, he was a member of Billy Sharsig's popular Philadelphia A's semipro team in 1891 and afterward resumed playing with pro teams in the Midwest. His last known port of call was Green Bay of the Wisconsin-Michigan League in 1892. Fusselbach was a plumber when he died in Philadelphia in 1926. (DN)

---

*#Ganzel, Charles William / "Charlie"

B	T	HGT	WGT	G	AB	H	R	2B
R	R	6'0"	161	787	2987	774	421	91

3B	HR	RBI	BB	SO	SB	BA	SA	OBP
45	10	412	162	121	60	.259	.330	.301

B. 6/18/1862 Waterford, WI **D.** 4/7/1914
TEAMS: 84StPU 85–86PhiN 86–88DetN 89–97BosN
DEBUT: 9/27/1884 at Cincinnati; caught Jim Brown and went 2-for-4 in a 6–1 loss to Cincinnati's Dick Burns
FINALE: 9/21/1897 at Boston; caught Kid Nichols and Charlie Hickman and went 1-for-4 in a 22–5 loss to Brooklyn's Jack Dunn

Charlie Ganzel was the brother of ML first baseman John Ganzel and the father of ML outfielder Babe Ganzel. He also had two other brothers, George and Joe, who played minor league ball. In his fourteen ML seasons Ganzel caught more than half his team's games just once—in 1895 with Boston—and played enough to qualify for a batting title only in 1888, when he not only caught but filled in capably for injured second baseman Hardy Richardson for some two months. Yet he was always regarded as one of the most valuable members of his team, a steady, consistent, and versatile hand who arrived at the park every day expecting to play and never was heard to complain when his name was not on the lineup card.

After growing up in Racine, WI, Ganzel moved with his family to Minneapolis, where he was living when he joined the St. Paul Northwestern League team in 1884. He accompanied the Apostles to the UA late that season and wore an ML uniform ever afterward until he served as the player-manager of several New England semipro teams for a time upon leaving the Boston club in 1897 and then later coached at Williams College. In the course of his career, Ganzel played on six pennant winners in two different NL cities and participated both in nineteenth-century World's Series and Temple Cup games. He married Alice Carter of Dubuque, IA, on February 8, 1885, in Minneapolis just prior to joining the Philadelphia Quakers for his first NL season. Upon his death in 1914 after a long battle with jaw cancer, he was survived by a daughter, with whom he was living at the time, and five sons, four of whom were ballplayers.

Ganzel's two defining moments in his career were refusing to desert the NL for the Brotherhood PL in 1890, although he was lavishly courted, and joining Dan Brouthers, Charlie Bennett, and Hardy Richardson in the quartet of Detroit players in November 1888 that was sold to Boston for a then record sum of $30,000. A few months prior to his death, when his old baseball friends learned of his dire circumstances, they started a fund for him and raised over $1,000 to ease his final days. (DN)

Gastfield, Edward / "Ed"

B	T	HGT	WGT	G	AB	H	R	2B
R	?	5'9½"	155	25	88	6	6	1

3B	HR	RBI	BB	SO	SB	BA	SA	OBP
0	0	2	2	37	—	.068	.080	.089

B. 8/1/1865 Chicago, IL **D.** 12/1/1899
TEAMS: 84–85DetN 85ChiN
DEBUT: 8/13/1884 at Detroit; caught Charlie Getzein and was 0-for-3 in a 1–0 loss to Cleveland's John Henry
FINALE: 7/11/1885 at Chicago; caught Ted Kennedy and was 0-for-3 in a 6–1 loss to Providence's Charley Radbourn

Ed Gastfield had an exceptional arm and was said to be able to throw a runner out at 2B on a short passed ball while still on his knees, but his throws who often too hot to hold, especially by infielders that were still playing barehanded. He began his pro career at 17 in 1883 with Grand Rapids of the Northwestern League, where he joined with fellow Chicagoan Charlie Getzein to form the "G" battery that was sold to Detroit as a unit in late July of 1884. Gastfield continued to serve as Getzein's personal catcher with the Wolverines until he left the club in 1885 and was behind the plate when Getzein, after a 0-7 start, recorded his first ML win on September 20, 1884, beating Charley Radbourn and pennant-bound Providence 7–1. Not surprisingly, Gastfield went 0-for-4 against the Grays' ace.

Fifteen days earlier at Philadelphia, Gastfield had celebrated his first ML hit off Bill Vinton of the Quakers. There would only be 5 other hits in his 88 ML ABs, marking him arguably the worst-hitting position player ever. Indeed, among those with at least 90 career PAs he ranks dead last with a .068 BA. Gastfield hit little better in the minors. In 1887, with walks counting as hits, he was batting just .191 (22-for-115) for Oshkosh of the Northwestern League in mid July. Gastfield spent two seasons with Oshkosh, where he caught several future ML hurlers, including Gus Krock and Bill Burdick. He moved to Omaha in 1888 but was released early in the year and returned to Chicago to play in the local City League, where he won praise for his superb work at 3B, making "stop after stop." Gastfield remained a fixture in the CCL for the next decade, playing every position except SS and pitcher but seldom hitting above .200. Near the end of his CCL career he teamed up with his old batterymate Getzein again on the Franklins in 1892. Gastfield died in Chicago seven years later. (DN)

Gilligan, Andrew Bernard / "Barney"

B	T	HGT	WGT	G	AB	H	R	2B
R	R	5'6½"	130	523	1873	388	217	68

3B	HR	RBI	BB	SO	SB	BA	SA	OBP
23	3	167	147	235	8	.207	.273	.265

B. 1/3/1858 Cambridge, MA **D.** 4/1/1934
TEAMS: 75AtlNA 79–80CleN 81–85ProN 86–87WasN 88DetN
DEBUT: 9/25/1875 at Brooklyn; caught Frank Fleet and went hitless in a 10–7 loss to New York's Bobby Mathews
FINALE: 4/27/1888 at Indianapolis; caught Lady Baldwin and went 1-for-5 in a 16–7 loss to Indianapolis's John Healy

Barney Gilligan was the lightest man to catch as many as 400 games in the majors. He was also among the lightest hitters to do so. Versatile enough to play SS and CF in addition to catching, Gilligan survived for some ten years in the majors almost solely on his defense. By the time he was 30, however, his small body had taken a terrific pounding, and his arm was in such bad shape that in his ML finale with Detroit he could only allow Indianapolis players to "run pretty much as they pleased."

Late in the 1874 season Gilligan joined a newly formed New York amateur team called the Fly-aways and remained with them except for two games in September 1875 when he was "loaned" to the NA Brooklyn Atlantics. He then underwent a lengthy apprenticeship with various Massachusetts semipro teams before joining Cleveland NL in 1879. Blues pitcher and captain Jim McCormick liked working with the rookie so much that his .171 BA was forgiven, but even though Gilligan hiked it by one point the following year, McCormick decided he preferred Doc Kennedy. Signing with Providence for 1881 when Cleveland did not reserve him, Gilligan soon became the pet receiver of rising pitching star Charley Radbourn. In the five seasons the pair worked together, Radbourn assembled a .687 winning percentage as opposed to a .529 percentage for the rest of his career. Gilligan's apex came on September 2, 1884, when, with Providence en route to the NL pennant, both he and Radbourn received gold-framed crayon portraits of themselves as the circuit's "king battery." In addition, he hit a career-high .245 and caught all 3 of Radbourn's victories in the first ever World's Series against the AA champion New York Mets.

After slipping to .214 the following year, Gilligan was assigned to the new Washington NL entry once Providence disbanded. He caught 81 games for the Senators in 1886 and led all NL catchers in assists but hit just .190 and lost his job to Connie Mack when he incurred arm trouble. Adding to his discouraging season in 1887 were intimations in September that he and pitcher Dupee Shaw were throwing games. Although the charges were never substantiated, Washington released him the following March.

After his embarrassing one-game trial with Detroit in April 1888, Gilligan finished the season in the New England League and then left the pro arena. Two years later *TSN* reported that he was now catching for a semipro team "in some jay town in New Hampshire." Gilligan's only job of substance after leaving baseball was the twenty years he spent as a garbage collector in Lynn, MA. He died there in 1934 of erysipelas after squeezing a pimple on his face. (DN/BM)

Grady, Michael William / "Mike"

B	T	HGT	WGT	G	AB	H	R	2B
R	R	5'9"	170	530	1747	525	314	92

3B	HR	RBI	BB	SO	SB	BA	SA	OBP
36	15	294	173	40	74	.301	.420	.383

B. 12/23/1869 Kennett Square, PA **D.** 12/3/1943
TEAMS: 94–97PhiN 97StLN 98–00NYN 01WasAL 04–06StLN
DEBUT: 4/24/1894 at Brooklyn; replaced injured Jack Clements, caught Kid Carsey, and went hitless

in a 22–5 win over Brooklyn's Roaring Bill Kennedy and Jim Korwan
FINALE: 9/19/1906 at Philadelphia; caught Ed Karger and got 1 hit in a 4–0 loss to Philadelphia's John Lush

Mike Grady was the original "Duke of Kennett Square" and was actually a neighbor of Hall of Famer Herb Pennock, the much more famous "Duke," and helped him develop as a pitcher. Grady played with the amateur Kennett Square Mohicans and the semipro Brandywines of West Chester, PA, before making his pro debut with Allentown of the Pennsylvania State League in 1893. That July he was courted by New Orleans but wanted too much money and was fair game for the Phillies to sign come fall.

An all-around athlete—he played tackle on the Westchester semipro football team in the off-season—he was equally resourceful on the ball field and could play everywhere except pitcher. Grady's downfall was that he never found a position that he could play well. Because he was rugged and had a good arm, he caught all through his youth and arrived in the majors in 1894 as a backup to Jack Clements. When he hit .363 in 60 games as a rookie but fielded just .848 behind the dish, it should have been obvious that he belonged in the lineup every day—but not as a catcher. Rather than move Grady to 1B, where he could do the least harm defensively, the Phillies went with Jack Boyle in 1895 and were rewarded with a .253 BA and .600 OPS while Grady hit .325 with a .797 OPS but got into just 46 games.

The situation improved in 1896, as he played in 71 games. But early the following season Grady was traded to last-place St. Louis. In his debut with his new club on June 3, 1897, he immediately "put lots of like into the Browns' playing," as they won 1–0 behind Red Donahue. That November he escaped St. Louis when he was traded to the Giants, but New York was on the skids and slid all the way to the basement in 1900 when he had his poorest season, hitting just .219. Grady had an excuse inasmuch as he had badly damaged his knee the previous September 9 in a game with Baltimore, and the injury had robbed him temporarily of his ability to squat behind the plate for long periods of time. As a result he played every position but pitcher in 1900. The Giants unsurprisingly put up little opposition when Grady jumped to Washington of the upstart AL in 1901. Even though he led the fledgling Senators in both home runs and OPS, he was allowed to drift to Kansas City of the independent American Association the following year. On the heels of a .355 season with KC, in 1904 Grady returned to the majors with the Cardinals and led the club in OPS, but because 1B was the province of Jake Beckley he was forced to do most of the catching and fielded just .946. Now in his midthirties, he played two more seasons with the Cards and then finished his career in 1910 with Chattanooga of the Southern Association. Grady worked with his brother Tom as a contractor in Kennett Square until retiring. A widower, he died at the home of his sister, Mrs. Albert Keating, in 1943.

Among men appearing in 500 or more games as catchers with a minimum of 2,000 PAs during his thirteen-year career span (1894–1906) Grady ranked as both the worst fielder (.946 FA) and the best hitter (.799 OPS). Had he been at 1B the whole time instead, his OPS would have ranked third at that position, behind only Frank Chance and Beckley—HOFers both. (DN)

Gross, Emil Michael / "Em"

B	T	HGT	WGT	G	AB	H	R	2B
R	R	6'0"	190	248	987	291	141	67

3B	HR	RBI	BB	SO	SB	BA	SA	OBP
21	7	107	51	52	—	.295	.427	.329

B. 3/4/1858 Chicago, IL **D.** 8/24/1921
TEAMS: 79–81ProN 83PhiN 84Chi-PitU
DEBUT: 8/13/1879 at Troy; caught John M. Ward and went 0-for-5 in an 11–3 win over Troy's Pat McManus
FINALE: 7/14/1884 at Washington; played RF and went 1-for-3 in a 4–2 loss to Washington's Aleck Voss
CAREER HIGHLIGHT: In 1880 caught every inning of every one of Providence's 87 official NL games

Throughout his career Em Gross stood accused of playing for his own selfish interests rather than for his team, but he may simply have been too self-reliant to care what his peers, let alone management, thought of him. He played his last ML game at age 26 and never looked back. At the time his .756 career OPS ranked first among all post-1875 catchers with a minimum of 1,000 PAs and the only enduring negative remark about his actual play was that he was said to be dreadful on pop fouls, often not coming within ten feet of them.

At age 18 Gross joined his brother Charlie, a first baseman, on the Chicago Acme Amateurs and served as both his team's lead-off hitter and catcher before moving north in August to sign with the St. Paul Red Caps. He remained with St. Paul in 1877, working with pitchers Harry Salisbury and Charlie Witherow, and then accompanied Salisbury to the Cleveland Forest Citys the following year. When Cleveland enlisted in the NL in 1879, it brought in an almost entirely new cast, and Gross was left to sign with the independent Detroit club. In August 1879 he became available after Detroit disbanded and was grabbed by the Providence Grays, who were in hot contention for the NL pennant. Gross's acquisition was something of a desperation move in that Lew Brown, the Grays' frontline catcher, had injured his arm, leaving the club with only one experienced backstop, Jim O'Rourke, who was needed in the outfield.

After drawing the collar in his initial NL game, Gross caught fire when he went 4-for-6 two days later in a 16–7 win over Troy's George Bradley. He finished with a .348 BA in 30 games and was a key asset in the Grays' down-to-the-wire pennant triumph over Boston. The following season Gross became the first performer in NL history to catch every inning of every one of his team's regular season games, leaving change catcher Mike Dorgan to work only an occasional exhibition contest. In 1881, however, he seemed to lose interest, appearing in only 51 contests and scoring a mere 15 runs, the second fewest in the NL among players in a minimum of 50 games. That winter Gross fell victim to an accelerated crackdown on players who were ill behaved in the judgment of their teams and was blacklisted by Providence. Whether the action was taken at the behest of the somewhat puritanical Harry Wright, who was about to take over the Grays' reins, is unclear, but it appears to have been arbitrary in any event. Gross sat out the 1882 season, probably making nearly as much money playing semipro ball in the Chicago area, and then was permitted to return in 1883 with fledgling Philadelphia NL, a replacement for the disbanded Worcester franchise. Playing for the worst team in NL history to that point, he perhaps could not be blamed for seeming to care about only his personal numbers. As if reconciled to the reality that the Quakers' pitchers were so awful nothing could help them, Gross led NL catchers with 74 errors and fielded .789, the lowest mark ever by a catcher in a minimum of 50 games. But at the plate, when he had only himself to consider, he led the Quakers by a wide margin in every major offensive department.

We will never know what would have happened if the UA had not formed that winter to give Gross an escape hatch when he learned that Wright was about to abandon Providence to take the controls in Philadelphia. In any case, he at first appeared to have no interest in playing ML ball anymore. Gross had inherited some $50,000 the previous year and was content to let the Chicago UA team court him to no purpose all through the spring of 1884. Finally, in late May, he agreed to sign and in his first game with Chicago on June 3 went 2-for-4 against St. Louis's Billy Taylor, the top pitcher in the UA at that juncture. Gross continued to hit at a torrid pace in the next 22 games but had trouble handling Hugh Daily's nasty fastballs and was casual beyond tolerance when he was tried in the outfield, fielding .545 in his 9 games there. Whether he lost vigor, refused to catch Daily ever again, or just grew bored with the level of play in the UA will probably never be known, but he left the team after the first game of its 4-game series in Washington in July and returned to Chicago. Gross departed with a .986 season OPS—the pre-1893 high by a catcher with a minimum of 100 PAs—and *SL's* assessment that as an outfielder he had the same problem he did as a catcher on pop fouls, in that "he couldn't judge a flour barrel twenty feet in the air."

The following season Gross appeared on occasion with the Franklins in the Chicago City League. When ML representatives came to the Windy City to woo him, he played cute, making it seem that he could be had but then lowering the boom and demanding a minimum salary of $5,000 to return. The cat-and-mouse game continued for several more years. Gross meanwhile enjoyed the good life and by 1891 was playing for the Chicago heavyweights along with Ned Williamson. Reports of his movements after that are contradictory. In the winter of 1907–08 the *Chicago Tribune* informed its readers that he was the uncle of mayor-elect Fred Busse and would be organizing a team in the Chicago City League the following season with ex-ML first baseman Mort Scanlan. But that August the *Detroit News* gloomily reported that ex-ML second baseman Joe Quest was dying of consumption on Em Gross's Georgia plantation. In May 1912 Hugh Fullerton received a letter from Quest, who was then in Citronelle, AL, confirming that he had been in bad shape after first being stricken five years earlier on Em Gross's farm. Gross died in Eagle River, WI, in 1921. (DN)

Gunning, Thomas Francis / "Tom"

B	T	HGT	WGT	G	AB	H	R	2B
R	R	5'10"	160	146	537	110	79	12

3B	HR	RBI	BB	SO	SB	BA	SA	OBP
4	2	46	16	70	38	.205	.253	.235

B. 3/4/1862 Newmarket, NH **D.** 3/17/1931
TEAMS: 84–86BosN 87PhiN 88–89PhiA
DEBUT: 7/26/1884 at New York; caught John Connor, went 0-for-4 and committed 6 passed balls in a 12–3 loss to New York's Mickey Welch
FINALE: 6/18/1889 at Philadelphia; replaced injured catcher Lave Cross and went 0-for-2 in a 22–6 win over Columbus's Mark Baldwin

Tom Gunning attended Holy Cross and Boston University before enrolling in the University of Pennsylvania medical school in the fall of 1887. After playing for the Eastern Championship Association Brooklyn Atlantics in 1882, he spent 1883 with Springfield, IL, of the Northwestern League and agreed that fall to play for the Chicago Union Association team in 1884. Two months later Gunning became the first player to be expelled from the UA when he reneged on his Chicago contract to sign for 1884 with Boston NL but was consigned to the reserve squad. Never more than a backup in the Hub, Gunning was nonetheless so respected by his teammates that he was selected to be the Boston chapter's Brotherhood representative. He resigned his post at the close of the 1886 season when he was sold to Philadelphia, where he filled the same role for the Quakers. Prior to the 1886 campaign, in part because of his Brotherhood activities, Gunning was sent home from spring training and told he was being laid off and would get no pay while he was idle. When Gunning demanded his release, Boston owner Arthur Soden, reluctant to surrender him for nothing, told captain John Morrill to keep him on the team, although he was seldom used.

In 1888, now with Philadelphia AA, Gunning spent his fifth straight year in the majors as a backup catcher. After starting the season by going 6-for-12 in the first 2 games, he hurt his arm, appeared in only 21 more games and hit just .150 in his 80 remaining ABs. Following his release by the A's, Gunning announced he was leaving baseball to study medicine. He caught later that summer, however, for Hartford of the Atlantic Association and in 1890 accepted a position as a Players League umpire. Gunning lasted as a PL official only until June, when he resigned after he fined the loop's organizer John M. Ward in a game at Brooklyn and thereafter was greeted with boos from fans each time he stepped on the field. In 1891 Gunning graduated from medical school and by the following year had his own practice in Fall River, MA. It was a successful one, he married well, and in time he became the Fall River medical examiner, a job he still held when he died of a heart attack in 1931. (DN)

Gunson, Joseph Brook / "Joe" "Gunnie"

B	T	HGT	WGT	G	AB	H	R	2B
R	R	5'6"	160	229	826	174	96	21

3B	HR	RBI	BB	SO	SB	BA	SA	OBP
6	0	68	34	40	4	.211	.251	.254

B. 3/23/1863 Philadelphia, PA **D.** 11/5/1942
TEAMS: 84WasU 89KCA 92BalN 93StLN 93CleN
DEBUT: 6/17/1884 at Boston; played CF and went 0-for-3 in an 11–1 loss to Boston's James Burke
FINALE: 9/18/1893 at Cleveland; caught John Clarkson and went 1-for-4 in a 7–6 win over Boston's Hank Gastright

Joe Gunson was a journeyman catcher for some seventeen pro seasons, finishing in 1900 with Harrisburg of the Atlantic League. He was typical of many catchers in his era in that he was a capable receiver and a poor hitter, but he had one memorable achievement—or so he claimed. In 1888, while catching for Kansas City of the Western Association, he decided on Decoration Day that the leather work glove he was wearing was insufficient protection for his hand and, in his own words, "I took a piece of strong wire and got the castoff belts from our Norfolk jackets and wrapped them around the wire, making a roll about an inch and a half thick. Then I sewed the roll around the finger ends of the glove." In a letter he wrote to *TSN* in 1939 Gunson went on to explain, "I began to leave other catchers to try it . . . the first one to try it was Thomas E. Nagle, catcher for the Omaha Club in the Western League, and while he was using it I sat on the bench with his pitcher, Ted Kennedy, and foolishly explained to him in full the exact making of it. . . . And behold early in the winter of 1889 I received a letter at home in Philadelphia from Mr. Kennedy containing a blue print of my own catchers mitt. A poor imitation of the real thing. He was supposed to have patented the wire protective mitt and not the mitt proper. Then catcher [Harry] Decker of Chicago [*sic*] club sensed his mistake and began to make them without the wire. Then everybody began to make them and I am satisfied that no one made much out of it. I never cared much about losing the patent on it. But of course I felt as though I deserve full credit for the invention. . . . I have the names, addresses and affidavits of 6 living witnesses who pitched to, or caught with the mitt during the season of 1888. Among them Kid Charles Nichols one of the greatest pitchers. . . . Yours Respectfully, Joseph B. Gunson."

There is probably a good deal of truth in much of what Gunson claimed for himself in 1939, but his contention that Ted Kennedy didn't improve on his invention is debatable. Others seem to have viewed Kennedy's mitt as less primitive than Gunson's, including Joe Cantillon (later the discoverer of Walter Johnson). Meanwhile, John McCloskey also staked his claim, maintaining that it was he who introduced Kennedy to a simpler form of the glove that subsequently became Kennedy's paradigm. In addition, in 1915 the *New York Times* credited Doc Bushong with using the first padded device, and supporters of almost every leading catcher in the 1880s have either before or since come forward with tales of how their man was the originator of the embryonic type of mitt that is still used today.

After leaving baseball Gunson was a private detective for a number of years and then worked as a house sergeant for the Philadelphia Bureau of Police prior to his death from natural causes in 1942 at his Philadelphia home. (DN/PM)

*Hackett, Mortimer Martin / "Mert" "Myrtle"

B	T	HGT	WGT	G	AB	H	R	2B
R	R	5'10½"	175	256	939	203	87	42

3B	HR	RBI	BB	SO	SB	BA	SA	OBP
15	8	83	16	225	5	.216	.318	.231

B. 11/11/1859 Cambridge, MA **D.** 2/22/1938
TEAMS: 83–85BosN 86KCN 87IndN
DEBUT: 5/2/1883 at NY; played CF and went 0-for-4 in a 3–2 loss to New York's John M. Ward
FINALE: 10/6/1887 at Indianapolis; caught Sam Moffet and went 0-for-4 in a 7–6 loss to Detroit's Charlie Getzein

Mert Hackett and his older brother Walt were first cousins of pitcher John Clarkson and similar players—versatile, decent fielders who lacked plate discipline and hit a combined .221, with Mert contributing a mere .216. The younger Hackett began his pro career with Fall River of the loosely run 1877 New England League at age 17 and gradually worked his way up to the Boston NL club. In 1883 he and fellow rookie Mike Hines split the Boston catching duties, making the Red Stockings the first of only two ML pennant winners to feature an all-freshman catching corps; the 1890 Louisville AA club is the other.

After debuting in CF, Hackett caught his first ML game on May 4, 1883, when he handled Charlie Buffinton in an 11–10 win over Philadelphia. Some four weeks later he was presented with a gold watch by team followers from his Cambridge hometown after a game with Buffalo. Hackett caught only 44 games as a rookie, but the following year he worked the plate in over half of Boston's games, earning him the Opening Day assignment in 1885. Following a 2–1 loss to New York, however, he dropped to third on the Boston depth chart behind Tom Gunning and Pat Dealy. By the end of May, Hackett was so seldom in the lineup that *SL* observed, "Much of the time Myrtle Hackett has been playing in the grand stand ticket office."

When he tucked only 34 games under his belt during the 1885 season, he was allowed to drift to Kansas City, a replacement for the failed Buffalo NL franchise. Far from his native Cambridge now, Hackett no longer had a personal fan club at his home games. One KC writer was even unkind enough to remark that he was "a rather giddy young man, parts his hair in the middle, wears patent leathers and dotes on the ladies." Yet Hackett revived his career somewhat, playing in 62 games, including Kansas City's finale in the NL, when he guided fledgling pitcher Silver King to a 7–5 win at Washington.

On March 9, 1887, Kansas City threw in the towel and sold its franchise and players to the National League for $6,000. The NL subsequently peddled Hackett and his KC teammate, Charlie Bassett, to KC's replacement, Indianapolis, for $1,000. In his final ML season, Hackett hit a personal high .238 but appeared in only 42 games with the Hoosiers. When he was suspended in July for drawing the color line and refusing to catch in an exhibition game against the Cuban Giants, a local scribe wrote, "He has always been a lazy, unmanageable fellow, and the players claim that he is the only troublesome, disorganizing man in the team." Another mark against Hackett was that he scored just 12 runs, bringing his career total to 87, the fewest by a nineteenth-century position player who took part in as many as 250 games.

After Indianapolis released him, Hackett began 1888 in the New England League but moved to Troy in the International Association when NEL teams began to run on him at will. In one game 19 stolen bases were procured with him behind the plate, as *SL* wrote: "Truly Myrtle Hackett is becoming a back number." Hackett briefly managed Troy after that and subsequent to 1888 remained active for a time in semipro circles. In 1891 he acted as catcher-manager for a team in Hyannis, with his brother at 2B. The following year he played for a nine in Northampton, MA, and then appears to have left the game and returned to his Cambridge home, where he become a policeman. A lifelong resident of Cambridge, Hackett died there in 1938. (DN/DB)

Hastings, Winfield Scott / "Scott"

B	T	HGT	WGT	G	AB	H	R	2B
R	R	5'8"	161	294	1328	371	264	44

3B	HR	RBI	BB	SO	SB	BA	SA	OBP
8	0	139	31	43	40	.279	.325	.296

G	W	L	PCT	PENNANTS
45	10	35	.222	0

B. 8/10/1847 Hillsboro, OH **D.** 8/14/1907
TEAMS: 71RokNA (P/M)71RokNA (P/M)72CleNA 72CleNA 72–73BalNA 74HarNA 75ChiNA 76LouN 77CinN
DEBUT: 5/6/1871 at Rockford; caught Cherokee Fisher and went 0-for-3 in a 13–4 loss to Cleveland's Al Pratt
FINALE: 9/1/1877 at Boston; played catcher, later switched to CF, and went 0-for-3 in an 8–3 loss to Boston's Tommy Bond.

A Civil War veteran, Scott Hastings was just 16 when he enlisted in the Union Army in April 1864 as a private from Illinois. Even though he mustered out after less than five months of service, he was eligible later in life to reside in a soldiers' home if he fell on hard times, and he died of stomach cancer in one such abode in Los Angeles at age 60.

Rockford's first 4 wins of the season in 1871 were declared forfeit losses when it was decreed that Hastings, the team captain and a member of the club in 1869–70, had appeared in the Rockford lineup before he was eligible as per the signing rules at that time (although most sources have since restored the wins, lifting Rockford's record from 4-21 to 8-17). When the Rockfords disbanded, Hastings joined Cleveland as team captain in 1872 but was replaced by Deacon White at the end of May after the Forest Citys concluded a disastrous Eastern trip and was never asked to captain a team again. He finished the year with Baltimore and then signed with Baltimore again for 1873, the lone time in his seven-year ML career that he played with the same club for more than one season.

Primarily a catcher early in his NA years, Hastings was installed in CF when he joined Louisville in 1876 for the NL's maiden season. That fall the *Chicago Tribune*, which had covered Hastings firsthand in 1875, explained why the Grays did not ask him to return: he played for himself rather than the team. In all likelihood other teams had previously experienced this side of Hastings, perhaps explaining why he changed nines annually. When no other NL clubs made him an offer, Hastings began 1877 with the International Association Maple Leaf club of Guelph. He joined Cincinnati on July 3 after the Reds had disbanded and then reorganized and caught Candy Cummings in a 6–3 loss to Louisville in Cincinnati's initial game back in the NL's good graces. Toward the end of his stay in the Queen City, the August 22 *Boston Globe* noted, "Hastings, when playing close behind the bat, wore the wire mask invented by Thayer of the Harvards, he being the only League catcher who has adopted it."

After leaving baseball Hastings purportedly worked for a time in Chicago as a clerk with A. T. Stewart and Company. In November 1888 *TSN* reprinted a letter from college student who said that in 1887 he had been playing in Santa Cruz and on his team at 1B was Hastings, who by then was fat, had a big black mustache, and worked in a local electric company. He was later a box maker in Santa Cruz until failing health forced him to enter the local soldiers' home. Although Hastings is listed as having been right-handed, the April 7, 1894, *TSN* said he was a "left-handed artist," and the April 1, 1894, *Chicago Tribune* and December 18, 1897 *TSN* also remarked on his left-handedness. If those observations are correct, he should be added to the short list of left-handers who caught 100 or more ML games. (DN/EM)

Hayes, John J. / "Jackie"

B	T	HGT	WGT	G	AB	H	R	2B
?	R	5'8"	175	300	1148	267	106	63

3B	HR	RBI	BB	SO	SB	BA	SA	OBP
10	10	81	39	53	0	.233	.331	.260

B. 6/27/1861 Brooklyn, NY **D.** 4/25/1905
TEAMS: 82WorN 83–84PitA 84–85BroA 86WasN 87BalA 90BroP
DEBUT: 5/2/1882 at Worcester; caught John Clarkson and went 3-for-5 in an 11–10 over Boston's Bobby Mathews and Jim Whitney
FINALE: 8/23/1890 at Brooklyn; played SS and went 1-for-4 in a 9–8 win over Pittsburgh's John Tener

Jackie Hayes's first team was the New York Astors, a thuggish semipro bunch that thrived on intimidating their opposition, and the newcomer blended in perfectly. Throughout his career Hayes had trouble with teammates, opponents, managers, owners, umpires, and even fans everywhere he went. Yet he somehow stayed under the radar on everyone's list of disorderly players if only because there was never a signature incident that punctuated his reputation for brutish behavior

Hayes graduated to Worcester of the NL in 1882 from the minor league New York Mets and had a fine rookie season, serving most of it in CF. After Worcester lost its NL franchise, he moved to Pittsburgh AA in 1883. Switched to catcher, he again had a solid year at the plate but led the loop in passed balls and clubhouse brawls with teammates. When Pittsburgh realized it was going nowhere in 1884, he was cut after 33 games to play in his hometown with the new Brooklyn AA entry. Hayes began 1885 as Brooklyn's frontline receiver but was axed after batting just .131 in 42 games. He then split the next two seasons between the minors and the majors and seemingly brought the ML portion of his career to a halt on August 24, 1887, when he caught Gid Gardner and Tommy Burns in a dismal 23–6 loss at St. Louis.

The following season Hayes was released by Scranton of the Central League in August when he could no longer throw anyone out. He fared little better with Newark in 1889, but in January 1890 John M. Ward stunned the baseball community when he signed trouble with a capital T to a Brooklyn PL contract after Charley Jones assured him Hayes was back in shape and had been dry for two years. Though Hayes played only 8 games with Ward's Wonders, he remained on the club all year and led the team in fiendish pranks. At a dinner feting Ward after the season, Paul Cook drunkenly displayed his new double-action revolver, and Hayes led the rest of the club in embarrassing their backup catcher. First, Ward removed the bullets from the revolver and threw them away, claiming that he feared having a loaded gun on the premises. After the festivities ended, Hayes and Con Daily lay in the weeds along the route they knew Cook would take back to his boarding house in Brooklyn. As Cook passed them, Hayes let out a blood curdling yell, and when Cook turned to run, Daily tripped him and the pair then acted like highwaymen and "robbed" him of all his valuables, including the gun. When Cook went to the nearest precinct the following morning to report the crime, a detective, who was in on the joke, accompanied Cook back to the saloon where the party had been night before. The landlord thereupon produced all of Cook's valuables and claimed that Cook had left them with him previous night for safekeeping.

Hayes subsequently played in the Pacific Northwestern League, but his movements after that remained a mystery for over a century. In 2005 researcher Richard Malatzky learned that Hayes had left the game in 1893 after the death of his first wife. He then remarried and worked as a shipping clerk in Brooklyn with the Valentine and Company Paint Manufacturers until his demise from a bleeding ulcer. (DN/DB)

Hicks, Nathan Woodhull / "Nat"

B	T	HGT	WGT	G	AB	H	R	2B
R	R	6'1"	186	257	1142	301	173	35

3B	HR	RBI	BB	SO	SB	BA	SA	OBP
6	1	116	25	23	9	.264	.307	.279

G	W	L	PCT	PENNANTS
129	59	67	.468	0

B. 4/19/1845 Hempstead, NY **D.** 4/21/1907
TEAMS: 72–73MutNA (P/M)74PhiNA (P/M)75MutNA 76NYN 77CinN
DEBUT: 4/22/1872 at Baltimore; caught Candy Cummings after starting the game in RF and switching positions with Charlie Mills and went 1-for-4 in a 14–8 loss to Baltimore's Cherokee Fisher
FINALE: 6/5/1877 at Chicago; caught Bobby Mathews and went 0-for-3 in a 12–5 loss to Chicago's George Bradley

To those who saw him in action, Nat Hicks made every other player look like a sissy by comparison. When he died in 1907, a lengthy *New York Times* obit described how he "created a sensation by catching behind the bat with his naked hands and body unprotected. His endurance was phenomenal in the face of the awful punishment he sustained. . . . He caught behind the bat close under the batsman and forced the other old line catchers to follow his example." In a legendary performance on July 4, 1873, Hicks "went into the game with his right eye almost knocked out of his head, and his nose and the whole right side of his face swollen to three times their normal size; and yet, notwithstanding this, nothing seemed too difficult for him to take. Player after player sank before his unfaltering nerve; and although struck four times during the game—once squarely on the mouth with the ball, once on the chest, and twice with the bat—he could not be driven away from his post."

Hicks was born in 1845 and served briefly in the New York Infantry's 15th Regiment at the tail end of the Civil War. He took up baseball after the war with the amateur Eagles of Brooklyn and rose to prominence in 1869 when he joined the semipro Harmonics of Brooklyn. Over the next eight years he acquired a reputation so outsized that he was still held in awe decades after his 1877 retirement. One of Hicks's legacies was that his skill at receiving the curve ball helped that pitch to revolutionize baseball. When he joined the Stars in 1869 Hicks was paired with Candy Cummings, reputedly the man most responsible for introducing the curve. The pitch achieved its full value, however, only if a catcher was able to handle it, and Cummings stressed the importance of Hicks's role in two accounts of the pitch's origins. Throughout his career Hicks was almost always paired with either Cummings or Bobby Mathews, the only other pro pitcher in Hicks's time who mastered the underhand curve. Hicks became even more celebrated for the courage with which he stood directly behind home plate while wearing no protective equipment except for light kid gloves. Several earlier catchers had tried playing close to the plate, but by the end of the 1860s pitchers' release points were on the rise, and the increased speed they generated caused most catchers to retreat to safety. Not Hicks. Over the course of his career, "the punishment the stout-hearted and thick-skinned Hicks absorbed was amazing. He lasted only eleven years in the big time, but during that period he had every finger in his hand broken at least once, his wrist broken, his eyebrow shattered, his nose smashed, and, in a career-ending climax, his kneecap broken while trying to block off famed Pop Anson at the plate." Aside from the knee injury, which helped to end his career, the only injury that idled Hicks for a prolonged period came on July 24, 1873, during a game with Baltimore when he became embroiled in a protracted argument with umpire Bob Ferguson, who responded by hitting Hicks with a bat. Although Hicks ended up with a broken arm and would not play for two months, he refused to press charges after Ferguson paid his "$80 medical bill for surgical services."

The Ferguson incident was but the worst of several like it, as Hicks was known for his bad temper and umpire baiting, and at various points in his career, other rumors swirled that he was involved in game fixing. No actual evidence was ever presented, however, and the rumors may only have been a reflection of how important Hicks really was to his team. Any time he had a bad game, a few disappointed spectators were sure to wonder what was wrong with him and the whispers would begin again. But Henry Chadwick, a passionate crusader against gambling, always maintained that Hicks was an honest player.

Hicks abruptly quit baseball in May of 1877. His bad knee seems to have been the biggest factor in his decision. With his playing days over, Hicks moved to Hoboken and operated the billiard room at the Naegelis Hotel. He also joined a choir and became known for his bass voice. In 1907 he died in his room at the Naegelis Hotel, the victim of accidental asphyxiation. His passing occurred only a few weeks after Roger Bresnahan had reputedly become the first catcher to wear visible shin guards, and the coincidence struck many of the writers who paid tribute to Hicks. "If poor old Nat," one sarcastically wrote, "had lived to trim his lamps on Roger Bresnahan behind the bat fortified behind his shin guards, bird cage, wind pad and pillow mitt, he probably would have died laughing, anyway." (PM/DN/DB/EM)

Hines, Michael P. / "Mike"

B	T	HGT	WGT	G	AB	H	R	2B
R	L	5'10"	176	120	451	91	69	20

3B	HR	RBI	BB	SO	SB	BA	SA	OBP
3	0	26	16	67	0	.202	.259	.229

B. 9/?/1862 ?, Ireland **D.** 3/14/1910
TEAMS: 83–85BosN 85BroA 85ProN 88BosN
DEBUT: 5/1/1883 at New York; in the first NL game played at the Polo Grounds caught Jim Whitney and went 2-for-4 in a 7–5 loss to New York's Mickey Welch
FINALE: 8/18/1888 at Boston; played LF and went 1-for-4 in a 15–5 win over Chicago's Mark Baldwin

Mike Hines was a weak hitter with poor plate discipline and no power. Yet he scored a rather phenomenal 69 runs in just 451 ABs despite a .229 OBP.

Hines also ranks sixth in games caught by a left-handed thrower.

After dividing 1882 between independent teams in Atlantic City and Harrisburg, PA, Hines joined with Mert Hackett, almost his exact opposite in the ability to score runs, to give Boston an all-rookie backstopping corps in 1883. When he and Hackett caught every inning for Boston, they enabled the club to become the first to win an ML pennant using only frosh receivers. By 1885, however, Hines and Hackett began the season third and fourth, respectively, on Boston's catching depth chart behind Pat Dealy and Tom Gunning. Hines was released in June after getting into just 14 games with Boston and signed with Brooklyn AA. He made his first appearance with Brooklyn on July 1 but was cut as soon as the club's other catchers were healthy.

Hines spent the next three years in the minors before rejoining Boston for his final 4 ML games. He then put in another three seasons in the minors, and by 1893 he was in the liquor business. Eventually Hines transferred a New Bedford liquor license to one Pat O'Leary for twice what he had paid for it and then arranged to work as a wine clerk for the gullible O'Leary, who was required by law to do business in Hines's name. Hines soon stopped coming to work altogether but insisted that O'Leary continue to pay him. His partner eventually gave him the slip. Not long afterward, Hines died in Taunton, MA, of progressive paralysis. (DN)

Holbert, William Henry / "Bill"

B	T	HGT	WGT	G	AB	H	R	2B
R	R	?	197	623	2335	486	182	41

3B	HR	RBI	BB	SO	SB	BA	SA	OBP
7	0	144	58	91	16	.208	.232	.228

G	W	L	PCT	PENNANTS
1	0	1	.000	0

B. 3/14/1855 Baltimore, MD **D.** 3/20/1935
TEAMS: 76LouN 78MilN (P/M)79SyrN 79–82TroN 83–87NYA 88BroA
DEBUT: 9/5/1876 at Hartford; caught Jim Devlin and went hitless in a 6–1 loss to Hartford's Candy Cummings
FINALE: 7/12/1888 at Kansas City; caught Al Mays and went 0-for-3 in a 3–1 loss to Kansas City's Henry Porter

Bill Holbert was an outstanding catcher—some say the best of his time—but arguably the worst hitter in the nineteenth century who had a substantial ML career. His .460 OPS is the lowest among all pre-1901 players with a minimum of 2,000 PAs, pitchers included. Moreover, he holds the record for the most career ABs (2,335) without hitting a home run.

Holbert was good with his hands and not only behind the plate. He perfected a trick of lighting a cigar and then snapping his fingers to knock off the end of it and make it sound as if it were an exploding cigar. When he left baseball he worked as a stereotyper at several New York papers, his longest stint coming with "the old *New York World*," according to one obit. A popular tale has Holbert coming to Louisville NL in 1876 with no previous pro experience after volunteering to replace injured Charlie Snyder while umpiring an exhibition game between the Alleghenys of the Pittsburgh area and the Kentucky club, but he had caught earlier in the season for the Wilmington Quicksteps, a top semipro team at the time. Although he did reasonably well with Louisville, hitting .256 in 12 games, he was not retained and played with the Alleghenys in the International Association the following year before returning to the majors with Milwaukee in 1878.

By the beginning of the 1884 season Holbert had established himself as the best in the game at handling hot pitchers (hard throwers), and the *New York Clipper* characterized his career to that point as "a remarkably brilliant one" even though his career BA was just .213. That year he played on his only pennant winner when he handled one of the AA New York Mets' twin aces, Tim Keefe, while his understudy, Charlie Reipschlager, worked with Jack Lynch. For the next two seasons it was Holbert who was the backup to Reipschlager after his BA dropped to .173 in 1885, but he regained his regular status with the Mets in 1887, his last full ML season.

In 1879 Holbert acted as interim manager of the NL Syracuse club for just one game, a 13–4 loss to Boston, and then ceded the reins to Jimmy Macullar. He frequently served as a field captain in later years, however, before his ML career came to a sad end in 1888. Brooklyn, by whom he had been purchased when the Mets folded, really had no use for him, and owner Charlie Byrne even took his uniform away in July, forcing him to borrow uniforms from other players just to continue to work out with the team. Holbert nonetheless kept in good shape and could probably have been useful to another ML team that season with thinner catching. After leaving the majors, Holbert continued to be active in the players Brotherhood. In 1890 he was rewarded when he was named a regular umpire in the Players League, but it was not a profession he cared to pursue after the PL disbanded. Instead he worked at a wide variety of jobs, ranging from running a laundry business to reportedly being affiliated with the U.S. Secret Service (which may have been utter fiction—Holbert was an incurable gagster) before turning to newspaper work. Although he returned to Maryland, his native state, before he died, he lived for many years prior to that on a large farm in New Jersey. (DN)

Keenan, James W. / "Jim"

B	T	HGT	WGT	G	AB	H	R	2B
R	R	5'10"	186	527	1886	453	255	61

3B	HR	RBI	BB	SO	SB	BA	SA	OBP
36	22	208	177	111	41	.240	.346	.312

G	IP	H	GS	CG	BB
4	19	17	0	0	4

SO	SH	W	L	PCT	ERA
2	0	0	1	.000	2.37

B. 2/10/1858 New Haven, CT **D.** 9/21/1926
TEAMS: 75NHNA 80BufN 82PitA 84IndA 85–89CinA 90–91CinN
DEBUT: 5/17/1875 at New Haven; replaced injured Studs Bancker at catcher and went hitless in a 10–7 loss to Washington's Bill Parks
FINALE: 10/3/1891 at Cincinnati; played 1B and went 1-for-5 in a 15–9 win over Chicago's Tom Vickery and Jack Luby

Always a good hitter and receiver, although his arm was a doubtful commodity and he was slow on the bases, Jim Keenan's real distinction may lie in the fact that he was perhaps the only severe baseball alcoholic of his generation to climb successfully on the wagon in midcareer and remain there, probably for the rest of his life.

Shortly after his 17th birthday, Keenan played 4 games for New Haven NA. During the ensuing six years he appeared with minor teams in the East plus 2 games for Buffalo NL. In 1882, Keenan joined Pittsburgh in the newly formed AA, but he fit in all too well with a particularly hard-drinking team and was suspended for insubordination in July and dumped soon afterward. Keenan began 1883 with his native New Haven, where he teamed with talented 17-year-old pitcher Larry McKeon. When the New Havens disbanded early in the season, the McKeon-Keenan battery signed with a successful independent team in Indianapolis. Keenan was made captain, and when Indianapolis entered the AA in 1884, he finally established himself as of ML caliber. One of the few quality players on a very bad club, he was the Hoosiers' best catcher and their leader in most offensive categories.

After the season the AA contracted, dropping Indianapolis, which entered the minor Western League, but by mid-June, the WL was tottering toward disbandment and Indianapolis sold its entire league-leading team to Detroit. While the other players went willingly to the Wolverines, Keenan and McKeon signed lucrative contracts with Cincinnati instead, a move that was legal because a team then could not transfer contract rights directly without a player's consent. Keenan was actually an afterthought in the Cincinnati signing. The Reds needed another good pitcher and McKeon was Indianapolis's most prized player. Well equipped with catchers, they brought Keenan aboard simply because batteries in the 1880s often went together as a pair.

As matters turned out, however, McKeon threw his arm out the next spring, effectively ending his career, while Keenan took a sobriety pledge in the fall of 1885 and made a new man of himself. At Indianapolis and later Cincinnati he had continued his wayward ways. In the last inning of a game against a Cincinnati semipro team in 1883, an inebriated Keenan had ordered McKeon into the outfield and gone into the pitcher's box himself, suffering humiliating punishment until manager Dan O'Leary took charge. Late the following season, the catcher had been suspended after going on yet another spree. Cincinnati owner Aaron Stern might have been forgiven for doubting Keenan's sincerity when he took the pledge, but he stayed sober and hit a solid .270 while sharing the Reds' catching with Kid Baldwin in 1886. Although he showed up lighter, quicker, and even more active the following spring, he played relatively little after he was sidelined for several weeks with a leg injury and came back to find Baldwin in the middle of a record streak of consecutive games caught. As a result, Keenan served mostly as a sub at 1B until Baldwin's streak had stretched to 50 games near the end of the 1887 season.

Baldwin's own drinking problems began to haunt him after that. Keenan replaced him as the Reds' frontline receiver and put up one last big offensive season with a .287 BA in 1889. In 1890 Keenan again reported in excellent shape but hit an anemic .138, consigning him to a sub role as the season progressed. After another poor year at the plate in 1891, he retired to run a saloon in Cincinnati's West End, near the Reds' ballpark.

In 1893 two stories in *TSN* claimed that Keenan was drinking secretly, his wife was divorcing him, and he had been institutionalized. Both tales must have been a considerable exaggeration if not an outright hoax, for he continued to operate his saloon, sometimes described in more elegant terms as a café, for many years and became something of a power in Cincinnati politics as a ward leader for George Cox's Republican machine and a two-term member of the city council. Around 1914 Keenan fell into difficulties, however. He lost his council seat and some time later had his saloon sold out from under him. Keenan then took a patronage position as a clerk at the city yard. Exactly what his duties consisted of are unknown, but one surviving letter in the Reds' archive suggests that, while certainly literate, Keenan lacked the education necessary to fill a clerical position—an impression strengthened by a story that, while testifying in court during his café days, he replied to a routine question about his occupation with the reply, "I keep a calf at Freeman and Liberty." Whatever his qualifications for the City Yard position, when a reform group turned out the remnants of the Cox machine, the nearly 70-year-old Keenan lost his job. One afternoon the following fall he suffered a stroke and was found unconscious on the floor of his room on Freeman Street, near his old saloon. Taken to a hospital, he passed away an hour later. His wife had died some years before, and only a daughter living in Connecticut survived him. (DB/DN)

Kelly, John Francis / "Kick" "Father"

B	T	HGT	WGT	G	AB	H	R	2B
R	R	6'0"	185	121	465	105	48	17

3B	HR	RBI	BB	SO	SB	BA	SA	OBP
3	1	5	10	26	—	.226	.282	.242

B. 3/3/1859 Paterson, NJ **D.** 4/13/1908
TEAMS: 79CleN 82CleN 83BalA 83PhiN 84CinU 84WasU
DEBUT: 6/7/1879 at Troy; caught Bobby Mitchell but switched places with first baseman Bill Phillips after he hurt his finger and went 1-for-4 in a 19–4 loss to Troy's George Bradley
FINALE: 10/19/1884 at Kansas City; played RF and went 1-for-3 in a 12–1 loss to Kansas City's Bill Hutchison

Historians often confuse John Francis Kelly with John O. Kelly, whose primary nickname was "Honest John" and not "Kick," as is commonly listed. The Paterson-born Kelly was "Kick," partially confirmed by the November 26, 1892, *TSN*, which noted, "Kelly will kick for Mobile" again in 1893. After leaving the majors, Kelly played for some six seasons with the Auld Iron Earth team of Mobile. He also ran the team part of the time and signed to manage Mobile of the Southern Association in 1892. Kelly remained connected with the Mobile team throughout the 1890s but by 1899 was only an "interested party" after taking a job as a sewer inspector. He later returned to Paterson before dying of diabetes in 1908. In 1883 Kelly became yet another subject of one of Baltimore manager Billy Barnie's bizarre experiments when Barnie batted him leadoff for a good part of the season despite his .239 OBP. (DN)

Kemmler, Rudolph (b. Kemler) **/ "Rudy"**

B	T	HGT	WGT	G	AB	H	R	2B
R	R	5'11"	208	236	862	168	79	18

3B	HR	RBI	BB	SO	SB	BA	SA	OBP
6	0	11	42	5	0	.195	.230	.234

B. 1/?/1860 Chicago, IL **D.** 6/20/1909
TEAMS: 79ProN 81CleN 82CinA 82PitA 83–84ColA 85PitA 86StLA 89ColA
DEBUT: 7/26/1879 at Buffalo; caught John M. Ward and went 0-for-3 in a 6–2 loss to Buffalo's Jim Galvin
FINALE: 8/11/1889 at Kansas City; caught Mark Baldwin and went 1-for-3 in a 6–4 loss to Kansas City's Jim Conway

At 15, Rudy Kemmler was already catching for the amateur Chicago Oaklands and the South Side Aetnas; two years later he and a young pitcher named Charlie Comiskey were the battery for the semipro Elgin Bluff Citys, and by 1879, still short of his 20th birthday, he was briefly a member of the NL-pennant-winning Providence club. Yet even though Kemmler appeared in ML box scores for over a decade, he seemed to regress rather than improve with each passing year. The likely explanation for his downward spiral is the rapid change in pitching styles over the course of his career, saddling him with batterymates who were increasingly harder to handle and opposing pitchers who were progressively harder to hit. Among all nineteenth-century position players with a minimum of 800 ABs, he has the second-lowest OPS, his .464 mark trailed only by Bill Holbert's .460. In addition, Kemmler was not only a slow runner but also an inept one; *TSN* once described a game in 1885 in which he "made his famous slide of two inches to within three feet of the home plate."

Kemmler's first pro experience came in 1878 with independent Davenport, IA, where he worked with pitcher W. E. Rockwell, later the president of the Pacific Northwest League (*see* Pete McNabb), who was said to have major league potential until he injured his arm the following year. In the spring of 1879 Kemmler trained with Chicago NL before returning to Davenport until it disbanded. Providence acquired him in the hope he could replace a faltering Lew Brown, but he was quickly jettisoned when he committed 7 errors in his second game with the club. In 1880 catcher, now 20, played for Kansas City and then joined independent Akron, OH, after the Missouri entry disbanded. He remained with Akron until 1882—with time out to catch one game for Cleveland in an emergency—when Charley Jones signed him over the winter for Cincinnati. As a backup to Charlie Snyder, he got little use and was released, signing with Pittsburgh after Cincinnati acquired Phil Powers. The following year he was among leftover players handpicked by the Columbus AA expansion team and earned his first chance at regular duty. But a .478 OPS in 84 games consigned him to share the job with Fred Carroll in 1884 and then back up Carroll in 1885 after Pittsburgh absorbed the Columbus franchise.

Kemmler then had the good fortune to catch on with the St. Louis Browns in 1886 and earned a World's Series share. On the team all year, he hit just .138, collected only 19 total bases in 123 ABs, and was on bad terms with owner Chris Von der Ahe. Although he went to spring training with the Browns in 1887, by late March he had joined Duluth of the Northwestern League. Kemmler moved to the Western Association in 1888, and the following August, after Columbus had rejoined the AA, he became the only player to perform on both of the Ohio capital's ML incarnations. Dismal hitting again doomed him to a short stay but not before he and Von der Ahe made amends. While Columbus was visiting St. Louis just before his release, Kemmler was nonplussed to see Von der Ahe approaching him prior to a game, axe in hand. When Von der Ahe explained that people had advised him to bury the hatchet with Kemmler, the two took turns with a shovel and did just that beside home plate. The incident characterizes Kemmler, a hardworking but somewhat undisciplined player with an occasional drinking problem who was too amiable to dislike for long—all in all, someone easy to become annoyed with but in the long run hard not to forgive—not unlike Von der Ahe himself, really.

By 1894 Kemmler was long since out of the game and working as a police officer in Minneapolis. He died of heart disease at 49 in Chicago, his place of birth. (DN/DB)

Kennedy, Michael Joseph / "Doc"

B	T	HGT	WGT	G	AB	H	R	2B
R	R	5'9½"	185	160	615	160	67	25

3B	HR	RBI	BB	SO	SB	BA	SA	OBP
4	1	53	15	37	—	.260	.319	.278

B. 8/11/1853 Brooklyn, NY **D.** 5/23/1920
TEAMS: 79–82CleN 83BufN
DEBUT: 5/1/1879 at Cleveland; caught Jim McCormick in Cleveland's inaugural game in the NL and went 0-for-4 in a 15–4 loss to Providence's John M. Ward
FINALE: 7/6/1883 at Detroit; played 1B and collected 1 hit in a 3–2 loss to Detroit's Dupee Shaw

Doc Kennedy's final ML game was an illustration of early-day platooning in that Deacon White, a left-handed hitter, was benched in favor of righty Kennedy because Dupee Shaw, a particularly troublesome southpaw, was hurling for the opposition. After spending 1876 and part of 1877 with the League Alliance Memphis Reds, Kennedy played for Rochester in the International Association in 1878 before joining the independent Cleveland Forest Citys late that summer. He then accompanied most of Cleveland's better players when it joined the NL in 1879.

Kennedy soon acquired a reputation as a strong-hitting catcher whose value was diluted because he spent too much time on the DL. Some of Kennedy's problems were caused by his stubbornness; he was among the last catchers to play in the majors without a mask, glove, or chest protector. But the injury that finally sank him came on Opening Day in 1882 when he hurt his knee stealing 2B in a 5–4 loss to Detroit. He was released soon thereafter, as was common then among most ML teams rather than continue to pay a disabled player.

The following year Kennedy's lame knee was compounded by a lame arm, producing a pink slip from Buffalo. At that point he was nearly 30 years old, could no longer crouch behind the plate owing to his bum knee, and continued to refuse to play with any equipment beyond his spikes. Kennedy could still swing a bat, however, leading independent Elmira to sign him after he left Buffalo and put him on 1B despite his unwillingness to use a glove. He then embarked on a long minor league career that rendered him almost certainly the last first baseman in pro ball to play the position barehanded. In 1896, when he was nearing age 43, *TSN* wrote, "His hands are a study." At the time he was with Fall River of the New England League under manager Charlie Marston and hit .325. Also on the pennant-winning Indians that season was a young centerfielder named Nap Lajoie, whom Kennedy called "Slashaway," and *TSN* commented that the misnomer was not far wrong. Kennedy was released in August, however. He returned to his off-season job as a New York City policeman, but in the spring of 1898 *TSN* reported that he was emerging from retirement to become the manager–first baseman of Palmyra in the New York State League. But by then his age—he was nearly 46—abbreviated his comeback attempt.

In addition to police work, Kennedy moonlighted as an umpire after his playing days ended. For years he worked semipro games in the New York City area and also an occasional New York AL exhibition game. In 1910, Kennedy was umpiring in the New York Department Store League when he was borrowed on August 20 for the day to work a DH with regular AL umpire Bull Perrine in Highlander Park between New York and the St. Louis Browns. He later moved to a farm near Swains, NY, where he died of an abscessed liver. (DN)

Kinslow, Thomas F. / "Tom"

B	T	HGT	WGT	G	AB	H	R	2B
R	R	5'10"	160	380	1414	376	186	40

3B	HR	RBI	BB	SO	SB	BA	SA	OBP
29	12	222	67	93	18	.266	.361	.301

B. 1/12/1866 Washington, D.C. **D.** 2/22/1901
TEAMS: 86WasN 87NYA 90BroP 91–94BroN 95PitN 96LouN 98WasN 98StLN
DEBUT: 6/4/1886 at Washington; caught Bob Barr and went 0-for-2 before hurting his thumb and being replaced by Barney Gilligan in a 1–1 tie with Detroit's Charlie Getzein
FINALE: 9/3/1898 at Louisville; caught John

Callahan and went 1-for-3 in a 13–1 loss to Louisville's Pete Dowling

Tom Kinslow was a respectable hitter for a catcher and above average defensively but was all but blacklisted from the majors just as he seemed to be making his mark. The cause: being perpetually on the edge of falling off the wagon. In the July 13, 1895, *TSN*, Kinslow revealed that after Pittsburgh fined him $25 a day and then released him when he went home to Washington and did not return promptly to the team as promised, "When I start drinking, which is about once a year, I cannot stop it."

He was also injury prone. After hurting his thumb in his pro debut with his hometown Washington NL club in 1886, he was removed from his last game with the team eleven days later when he broke a finger and was then released even as he was in the process of having it treated. The following spring Kinslow signed with Allentown of the Pennsylvania State Association along with pitcher Ed Beatin. After the Allentown team folded, both came to Detroit in midseason as the "Allentown battery," but whereas Beatin stuck with the Wolverines, Kinslow never played and in September went to New York AA. When Brooklyn owner Charlie Byrne bought the Mets' player stock once the club disbanded, he was startled to learn that four of the players, Kinslow included, had signed only thirty-day contracts with the Mets' and thus were not reserved for 1888. A free agent, Kinslow signed with London of the International Association and had a rare injury-free year but hit just .200. When he hiked that mark to .343 with the Canadian club the following year, John M. Ward grabbed the catcher for his Brooklyn Players League entry.

Kinslow followed Ward to the Brooklyn NL club after the PL collapsed. Reunited with owner Charlie Byrne, he remained in good standing with the Bridegrooms until he and fellow catcher Con Daily staged a mock prizefight in a St. Louis hotel lobby during the 1894 season and broke a glass door. When Kinslow was fined triple the amount deducted from Daily's paycheck, he developed an instant antipathy toward Byrne and in January 1895 was exhilarated to learn he had been traded to Pittsburgh for pitcher Ad Gumbert, until he discovered his new manager would be teetotaler Connie Mack. Upon drawing his release from Mack after his July 1895 binge, Kinslow considered retiring to work in a "lucrative business" he and his father ran in D.C., which was no more than a fancy term for a saloon.

After falling off the wagon again in Louisville in 1896, Kinslow quit to run the family establishment but was derailed on September 16, 1897, when he was arrested on charges of "fast driving, profanity and cruelty to animals" for driving his buggy too fast and whipping his horse. Threatened with losing his liquor license, he renewed his pledge to reform and decided to return to baseball while he was about it. But a year away from the game had rusted him. Kinslow worked out with Washington for several weeks before manager Arthur Irwin had little choice but to use him after both Deacon McGuire and Duke Farrell were injured. Released once both returned to action, he was summoned to St. Louis in late August to replace the injured Jack Clements and then dumped when Browns manager Tim Hurst held him responsible for a rank outing by rookie hurler John Callahan.

Kinslow became a fight manager in 1899. He was handling bantamweight Casper Leon in August when *TSN* reported that Brooklyn manager Ned Hanlon had signed him to have a warm body to foist on Baltimore in return for catcher Wilbert Robinson. If the story was true, it exemplified syndicate baseball at its worst. The following September local papers noted that Kinslow was suffering from consumption at his Washington home. When he died in 1901, he left behind his wife, Pauline, and a son, Paul. (DN)

Kittridge, Malachi Jeddidah / "Kit" "Mal" "Jed"

B	T	HGT	WGT	G	AB	H	R	2B
R	R	5'7"	170	745	2521	547	283	66

3B	HR	RBI	BB	SO	SB	BA	SA	OBP
30	13	258	213	166	53	.217	.283	.279

G	IP	H	GS	CG	BB
1	1.2	2	0	0	1

SO	SH	W	L	PCT	ERA
0	0	0	0	—	5.40

B. 10/12/1869 Clinton, MA **D.** 6/23/1928
TEAMS: 90–97ChiN 98–99LouN 99WasN 01–03BosN 03–06WasAL (P/M)04WasAL 06CleAL
DEBUT: 4/19/1890 at Cincinnati; caught Bill Hutchison and went 0-for-4 in a 5–4 win over Cincinnati's Jesse Duryea

FINALE: 8/8/1906 at Cleveland; replaced Fritz Buelow behind the plate in the ninth inning, caught Bob Rhoads and had no ABs in a 1–0 loss to Boston's Joe Harris

CAREER HIGHLIGHT: 8/16/1890 at Chicago; in an 18–5 win over Pittsburgh's Bill Phillips followed Tom Burns's first inning grand slam homer by hitting a grand slam in the fifth frame to mark the first time in ML history that a team hit 2 jackpot blows in the same game

Kit Kittridge was an agile receiver that stood 25 feet behind home plate with no one on base and dazzled fans with diving catches of foul tips. A converted second baseman, he was also one of the few catchers who called every pitch and became the fifth player to catch 1,000 ML games. Initially at least, he was a sanguine clubhouse presence, a free-thinker, comedian, and entertainer. In later years, however, his humor grew progressively sardonic and sometimes crossed lines with managers who would then punish him as an agitator.

Kittridge began on the independent Fitchburg Rollstones while still in high school. He spent three years with Fitchburg, was moved to catcher, and by 1888 had advanced to Portsmouth, NH, of the New England Interstate League. Now called "Kit" by teammates, he went west the next year and made a national reputation for himself by catching 111 games for the Quincy, IL, Central Interstate League champions. Chicago NL scooped Kittridge up for 1890 when the rebel PL forced the majors to expand to twenty-four teams. The stocky catcher blended well with staff ace Bill Hutchison, serving as his batterymate for back-to-back 40-win seasons. Unfortunately, Kittridge hit worse than most pitchers. He often batted at the bottom of the order and was sometimes embarrassed by having a pitcher pinch hit for him. In September 1891, after being suspended by manager Cap Anson for oversleeping, Kittridge had his job as Hutchison's batterymate given to Bill Schriver. He angrily complained, especially when the team lost a 6½-game lead with 17 to play.

On November 1, 1890, Kittridge and Walt Wilmot jumped to the prospective new Chicago AA team but were retrieved by Anson in the NL-AA merger shortly before Christmas that eliminated a potential second Windy City entry. Kittridge seemed to bond with Anson after that, to the point where the rest of the Colts viewed him as Anson's pet until mid-1895 when Anson did away with pitcher-catcher pairings and, barring injury, slated each catcher to appear in a strict rotation.

When Anson was let go after the 1897 season, Kittridge hoped to replace him. Once Tom Burns got the job instead, to guard his interests he tried to demote Kittridge to Omaha of the Western League, but other NL teams refused to waive on the catcher. He remained on the Chicago roster for two months, collecting full pay for sitting idle, until his transfer to Louisville on June 20. Chicago received $750, seemingly slight compensation for the nine-year veteran but later also appears to have received minor league pitcher Jack Taylor in partial payment when Louisville waived its option on him.

With Kittridge playing full-time, the Colonels had the best second-half season of their short NL history, and manager Fred Clarke made his new catcher his first lieutenant. But when Kittridge grew critical of Clarke the following year, he was benched after a 0-for-24 stretch, and Clarke labeled his clubhouse chatter backstabbing dissent. On June 30, 1899, Kittridge was released to Washington, temporarily without a frontline catcher while Deacon McGuire was out with a groin injury. When he batted .150 in 44 games, he departed from the NL in 1900. That season Kittridge invested in the Worcester Eastern League franchise, installed himself as his own manager, and caught 127 games while batting .300. The performance earned him a contract from Frank Selee of Boston NL in 1901.

When Selee moved to Chicago in 1902, Kittridge badmouthed his replacement, Al Buckenberger, and was sold to Washington AL on July 2, 1903. He finished the season in D.C. and invested in Worcester again the next spring. But when Patsy Donovan, who was expected to be Washington's 1904 manager, had trouble negotiating his release from St. Louis, Washington refused to let Kittridge go to Worcester and even made him interim pilot. The team opened the year 0-13, the worst AL start until the 1988 Orioles. Washington GM Bill Dwyer rewarded Kittridge by giving him his first paycheck in nickels and dimes. Tongue in cheek, Kittridge informed the local press that he had sprained his ankle carrying the bag of coins, causing him to miss a train out of New York on May 5. Dwyer then suspended him for being AWOL in Philadelphia, but the catcher, in his role as manager, rescinded the suspension with a telegram to Ban

Johnson and then traded himself to New York AL along with star outfielder Kip Selbach for two prospects. The ridiculous one-sided deal was quickly nullified, and Kittridge remained with Washington until he was loaned in 1906 to Cleveland, where he coached and caught in emergencies. Returned to Washington on August 13, he went to Montreal instead as player-manager. Between squabbles with front-office personnel, Kittridge was a successful player-manager in the minors for several years, finishing in 1911 with the Southern Michigan League Saginaw Krazy Kats, before taking a sales job with the National Cash Register Company. He later sold peanut and popcorn vending machines before dying at 58 in Gary, IN, of a cerebral hemorrhage while on a sales trip. (FV/DN)

Krieg, William Frederick / "Bill" "Stonewall"

B	T	HGT	WGT	G	AB	H	R	2B
R	R	5'8"	180	141	535	127	62	29

3B	HR	RBI	BB	SO	SB	BA	SA	OBP
8	4	37	23	19	4	.237	.344	.270

B. 1/29/1859 Petersburg, IL **D.** 3/25/1930
TEAMS: 84Chi-PitU 85BroA 85ChiN 85ChiN 86–87WasN
DEBUT: 4/20/1884 at St. Louis; caught Hugh Daily and went 2-for-2 in a 7–2 loss to St. Louis's Charlie Hodnett
FINALE: 6/15/1887 at Boston; replaced Cliff Carroll in LF and went 1-for-2 in a 13–4 win over Boston's Charley Radbourn

Bill Krieg was tough, durable, and oozing with raw catching talent but at times "showed clearly that in a crisis he seems to lack ability to grasp the situation." He might have made a successful ML first baseman if he had been taller than 5'8"—and perhaps he was. In October 1884 *SL* listed him as 6' and weighing 190. If true, his size was not a factor in his failure to capitalize on his ML opportunities.

After playing with the amateur South Bend Notre Dames in 1882, Krieg was cut by the Peoria Northwestern League club the following year despite hitting .286 at the time, and he then captained unaffiliated Dayton, OH, for a while before finishing the season back in the Northwestern League with Springfield, IL. He was regarded as one of the key components of the Chicago club when the UA organized in 1884, but he hit a disappointing .247 and had trouble handling staff ace Hugh Daily.

After Krieg's UA franchise disbanded, he signed with Cleveland NL for 1885, but when the Blues went defunct that winter he was part of the Forest City package that was sold to Brooklyn AA. Krieg was still so highly regarded at that point that Brooklyn manager Charlie Hackett let Doc Bushong go to St. Louis, a decision that menaced his job security when Krieg again was a disappointment. Released by Brooklyn after being injured in an exhibition game against Trenton, he caught Chicago's final game of the 1885 NL season after spending most of the summer with independent Hartford and then captained Hartford's Eastern League entry the following year until summoned to Washington in September. Krieg ended 1886 as the Nationals' regular first baseman and held the job in the spring of 1887 before losing it to Billy O'Brien, the surprise rookie NL home-run king. Released in late June, he refused an offer from Philadelphia AA when it did not include a signing bonus and went to Minneapolis of the Northwestern League instead.

The following season Krieg alternated between the outfield and catching, working the plate whenever Ed Klopf pitched; the two earned renown in the Western Association as Minneapolis's "Ku Klux" battery. He then spent thirteen more seasons in the minors, mostly in the Western Association where he won back-to-back batting titles in 1895–96. Krieg's last pro engagement was in the 1901 Central League as player-manager of Terre Haute. Finishing with a .335 career BA in the bushes, he continued to manage in the minors for another fifteen years or so and then worked for the Santa Fe Railroad in Chillicothe, OH, where he died in 1930. (DN/DB)

Leahy, Thomas Joseph / "Tom" "The Stoker"

B	T	HGT	WGT	G	AB	H	R	2B
R	R	5'8"	175	131	410	105	54	15

3B	HR	RBI	BB	SO	SB	BA	SA	OBP
9	0	42	44	—	18	.256	.337	.348

B. 6/2/1869 New Haven, CT **D.** 6/11/1951
TEAMS: 97PitN 97–98WasN 01MilAL 01PhiAL 05StLN
DEBUT: 5/18/97 at Pittsburgh; replaced Bill Merritt

at catcher, caught Jim Gardner and went 0-for-1 in an 11–5 loss to New York's Ed Doheny
FINALE: 10/7/05 at Cincinnati; caught Rip Vowinkel and had 3 hits in an 8–6 loss to Chicago's Three Finger Brown

Tom Leahy played summers with the amateur Brattleboro, VT, team while catching pitcher John Stafford during the college season for Holy Cross. Described as a "short, blocky, plucky," he was nonetheless an excellent sprinter, swift enough at times to beat Bernie Wefers, the sprint champion in the 1890s. Leahy spent four seasons with Springfield, MA, of the Eastern League before being acquired by Pittsburgh in the fall of 1896. Used in the infield and outfield nearly as much as at his regular position in his sporadic ML career, he did not serve exclusively as a backstop until 1905, his last taste of the bigs. Leahy's life fell apart for a time in the fall of 1898 when both his wife and infant daughter died in childbirth, but after working that winter as a roller polo referee, he pulled himself together and rejoined Providence of the Eastern League, where he had finished the previous season. Leahy may have been misplaced at catcher despite his build and pluck. Susceptible to passed balls and lacking a strong arm, he would seem to have done better at 2B. After retiring from baseball in 1910, Leahy served as an athletic trainer at Yale for thirty-two years. He died in New Haven in 1951. (DN/PM)

Malone, Fergus G. / "Fergy"

B	T	HGT	WGT	G	AB	H	R	2B
R	L	5'8"	156	220	1052	288	200	32

3B	HR	RBI	BB	SO	SB	BA	SA	OBP
7	1	159	32	19	17	.274	.320	.295

G	W	L	PCT	PENNANTS
156	75	91	.452	0

B. 8/?/1844 County Tyrone, Ireland **D.** 1/1/1905
TEAMS: 71–72AthNA (P/M)73PhiNA (P/M)74ChiNA 75PhiNA 76PhiN (P/M)84PhiU
DEBUT: 6/3/1871 at Philadelphia; caught Dick McBride in a 15–5 win over Troy's John McMullin
FINALE: 4/17/1884 at Philadelphia; caught Sam Weaver, went 1-for-4 and had 5 passed balls and dropped 2 pop fouls in a 14–2 loss to Boston's Tommy Bond

The first left-handed catcher of note, Fergy Malone was born in Ireland and raised in Philadelphia, where he came to enjoy baseball more than cricket. He began as a southpaw SS with an early version of the Philadelphia Athletics in 1862. Malone then played with several other teams over the next seven seasons, including the Olympics of Washington in 1868–69, before returning to the reorganized Athletics in 1870 as a catcher. After three more years in Philadelphia with the NA Athletics, Malone signed with Chicago in 1874 for $2,200, making him the highest paid club member. Recurring arm problems led him to return to Philadelphia in 1875 and abort his ML career after just 22 games the following year.

Malone continued to serve as player-manager for minor league and semipro outfits ranging as far as San Francisco until 1884 when the UA formed and ex-ML first baseman Tom Pratt helped install a team in Philadelphia and named his old Athletics teammate its manager. Malone was once believed to have been the first 40-year-old catcher in ML history when he went beyond the plate with disastrous results in the Keystones' opener but now appears to have been only 39 at the time. He consigned himself to running the team from the bench the following day. When the Keystones folded, Malone was offered dismissed NL umpire John Burns's job in August 1884. He was out of his element. After Malone officiated a game in Boston, a local writer deemed him "a gentleman of preternatural stupidity." After receiving a similar review of his work in every NL city, he had so much trouble keeping his games moving at an acceptable pace that he opted to remain in Philadelphia after umpiring a game there on September 6.

Malone then returned to managing in the minors for a time while acting as a scout for Philadelphia NL. In 1890 he brought suit for $3,000 against team owner John I. Rogers for nonpayment of his services in aiding the club to sign Jack Clements, Bill Hallman, Cupid Childs, Kid Gleason, and Bill Schriver over the years. Having alienated himself from the Phillies, Malone took a job as a special inspector for the Philadelphia branch of the U.S. Treasury. Some ten years later he was transferred to the customs office in Seattle, where he died in 1905 from alcohol poisoning after a prolonged drinking spree. (DN/PM/EM)

McFarland, Edward William / "Ed"

B	T	HGT	WGT	G	AB	H	R	2B
R	R	5'10"	180	471	1646	477	259	80

3B	HR	RBI	BB	SO	SB	BA	SA	OBP
34	10	241	147	19	33	.290	.398	.352

B. 8/3/1874 Cleveland, OH **D.** 11/28/1959
TEAMS: 93CleN 96–97StLN 97–01PhilN 02–07ChiAL 08BosAL
DEBUT: 7/7/1893 at Cleveland; played 3B and went 0-for-4 in a 10–5 loss to Baltimore's Sadie McMahon
FINALE: 6/26/1908 at Boston; caught Tex Pruitt and Fred Burchell and went 1-for-4 in an 8–0 loss to Washington's Cy Falkenberg

Ed McFarland was among the few players that appear to have made a mistake in jumping from the NL to the AL in the early part of the twentieth century. A regular from 1897–1901 with the Phillies, he was never able to do more than split the catching duties with Billy Sullivan in his six years with Chicago White Sox and collected just 1 pinch-hit AB against the Cubs in the 1906 World Series.

A Cleveland native, McFarland played for the Forest City Paint & Varnish Company team in 1891, with Will Sawyer of the 1883 Cleveland Blues as one of his batterymates and Frank Mears, the brother of Cleveland team historian Charles Mears, in RF. The following year he and Mears both joined the semipro Old Cuyahogas, and he then launched his pro career in 1893 with the Akron Summits of the Ohio-Michigan League. McFarland spent the next two seasons in the Western League and twice became a source of controversy in 1895 while with Indianapolis. In the spring he drew sneers when *TSN* called attention to the fact that he had "taken advantage of the rule that allows the catcher to wear a mitt of unlimited size. He has brought along a mitt that would easily do for a cushion for a good sized chair." Then in November, McFarland found himself caught between Browns owner Chris Von der Ahe, who claimed he had been given his pick of Indianapolis's players in return for outfielder Marty Hogan, and Cincinnati owner John T. Brush, who screamed that McFarland had been "loaned" to Indianapolis and could not be moved elsewhere.

The issue was resolved when McFarland was traded to St. Louis on November 23 in a six-player deal that was the largest in ML history to that time. Upon learning his son had gone to the lowly Browns, McFarland's father redoubled his efforts to get him to enter the family shoe business and might have succeeded if McFarland had not won St. Louis's Opening Day catching assignment. But when he hit just .241 in his official rookie year, the Browns viewed his hot start in 1897 (.327 in 31 games) as a fluke and sent him to the Phillies on June 1, 1897, for Mike Grady and Kid Carsey. McFarland came back down to earth that year, finishing at a composite .270, but over the next four seasons (1898–1901) led all ML catchers with a minimum of 1,000 PAs in every major batting department.

	OPS	AB	AVG	SLG	OBA
1. Ed McFarland	.760	1392	.300	.399	.362
2. Duke Farrell	.743	1161	.297	.387	.356
3. Heinie Peitz	.707	1183	.276	.357	.351
4. Chief Zimmer	.705	905	.276	.359	.346
5. Deacon McGuire	.690	1387	.283	.354	.336

Moreover, he topped NL receivers in assists and FA in 1900 and led again the following year in most assists per game before joining the mass exodus of Phillies stars to the AL. McFarland returned to Cleveland after retiring in 1908 and died there at 85 from injuries he sustained in a fall. (DN)

McGuire, James Thomas / "Deacon"

B	T	HGT	WGT	G	AB	H	R	2B
R	R	6'1"	185	1317	4808	1382	661	233

3B	HR	RBI	BB	SO	SB	BA	SA	OBP
69	42	686	397	215	103	.287	.391	.349

G	IP	H	GS	CG	BB
1	4	10	0	0	1

SO	SH	W	L	PCT	ERA
1	0	0	0	—	6.75

G	W	L	PCT	PENNANTS
70	21	47	.309	0

B. 11/18/1863 Youngstown, OH **D.** 10/31/1936
TEAMS: 84TolA 85DetN 86–88PhiN 88DetN 88CleA 90RocA 91WasA 92–99WasN (P/M)98WasN 99–01BroN 02–03DetAL 04–07NYAL (P/M)07-08BosAL 08CleAL (M)09CleAL (P/M)10CleAL (M)11CleAL 12DetAL
DEBUT: 6/21/1884 at Toledo; caught Tony Mullane and went 0-for-3 in a 7–1 loss to Baltimore's Hardie Henderson

FINALE: 5/18/1912 at Philadelphia; caught Al Travers in the famous Ty Cobb Strike Game and went 1-for-2 in a 24–2 loss to Philadelphia's Jack Coombs, Boardwalk Brown, and Herb Pennock

Of temperate habits, Deacon McGuire was sturdy, the first to catch 1,200 ML games in a long twenty-six-year career before retiring with the (since broken) career games caught mark. Not an innovator and not a superstar, McGuire cared for his hands, doted on his fielding mitts, and adopted new equipment as it appeared. An Ohioan who grew up in Albion, MI, he was large and plodding at a time when many believed the optimum catcher should be small and spry. In the top fifth of his era's catchers in both batting and slugging, for most of his career McGuire nonetheless choked up on his bat and stabbed at pitches rather than take a full swing.

After catching with numerous semipro teams near his Albion home, in 1883 McGuire played with independent Terre Haute, IN, and was good enough to sign a contract with Cleveland NL on December 5. But he never appeared with Cleveland, serving on its reserve team until June 1884 when Toledo AA signed him to back up its star African American catcher Moses Walker. After Walker broke his collarbone in July, McGuire got regular work.

Toledo was discarded when the AA contracted in 1885, and McGuire signed with Bill Watkins, manager of Indianapolis in the Western League. When Watkins's team disbanded six weeks into the season, he left to manage Detroit NL, hauling McGuire and left-hander Dan Casey with him accompanied by numerous other Hoosiers. The "Indianapolis battery" debuted on June 25, and McGuire in particular did well, but both were assigned along with outfielder George Wood to Philadelphia NL in 1886 as part of the NL's price for agreeing to Detroit's dubious "Big Four" purchase. McGuire's new manager, Harry Wright, frequently asked him to catch "up close" to the batter even without runners on base, and he took a beating. On August 28, 1886, his hands were so sore he reportedly dropped 7 third strikes by the third inning of a game with Chicago. McGuire cried injury, but Chicago manager Cap Anson refused to allow a replacement for him. Chicago president Al Spalding had to walk on the field to order Anson to agree to a substitution. Wright eventually released McGuire after two and a half seasons for iffy throwing. He then returned to Detroit but was cut in July 1888 and finished the year with Cleveland AA under Tom Loftus.

Loftus sold McGuire to Toronto of the International Association for 1889, perhaps influenced by an off-season misadventure. In February 1889, to the mortification of his widowed mother with whom he was living in Cleveland, the catcher eloped with one Julia Beebe. Friends were skeptical of the union because even though Beebe was pretty and petite, her reputation was that of a sporting woman, and a teammate said, "Mack is known among his friends as the biggest sucker a woman ever had on the string." Still, the newlywed caught 93 games for Toronto and hit .282. McGuire was a different catcher when he returned to the bigs in 1890 with Rochester AA; his stats across the board improved and stayed solid until the end of the 1890s.

In 1891, the final year of the AA, he joined Washington and remained in D.C. for eight more seasons after the club was included in the AA-NL merger, catching close to 100 games a year and running up more assists than games played. McGuire was now "one of the best throwers in the business," a prized team member and the lieutenant of Washington managers. In 1895 he became the first MLer to catch in every one of his team's games at the 60'6" distance. During that period Washington rarely escaped the second division, and in 1898 McGuire tried managing but was replaced because "he was too easy going and conscientious." The following year Brooklyn skipper Ned Hanlon traded for McGuire, enabling him to play for back-to-back pennant winners.

On June 14, 1900, McGuire caught in his 1,124th game to surpass Wilbert Robinson and set a new catcher's mark for games, a figure he extended to 1,611, a record that held until surpassed by Ray Schalk on September 12, 1925. Jumping to the AL in 1902, McGuire caught for Detroit for two forgettable seasons. But he was in still such great shape that at age 40 he signed with New York AL for $6,000 per annum. In 1904, his first season in New York, the Highlanders vied for the pennant as McGuire helped Jack Chesbro to win 41 games. But it was Red Kleinow who was catching Chesbro on the final day of the campaign when Chesbro was charged with a pennant-losing wild pitch.

McGuire became a full-time manager for Boston AL in mid-1907 but quit the following August after owner John Taylor traded Frank LaPorte against his wishes and signed on as a coach for Cleveland under Nap Lajoie. Early in 1909 Lajoie sent McGuire to California on a scouting trip, but McGuire's recommendation—outfielder Duffy Lewis—went unsigned. There was no animosity later that year when McGuire replaced Lajoie as manager. But early in 1911 McGuire lost the respect of his men when he tried to make them play instead of attending teammate Addie Joss's funeral, and on May 1 team captain George Stovall replaced him. McGuire coached in his fourth stint with hometown Detroit from 1912–14 and appeared in one last game as a player on May 18, 1912, when Tigers players went on strike to show support for the suspended Ty Cobb. That day, McGuire caught Al Travers, a divinity student plucked from the crowd, ordering him not to throw a fastball "if you value your life." Philadelphia beat Detroit 24–2. McGuire was 48 years and 6 months old. He scouted briefly for Detroit after that and managed Lonaconing in the Potomac League for half a season in 1916. McGuire then bought a flour mill near Albion, MI. He later ran a chicken farm until his death from pneumonia at his home on Duck Lake near Springport, MI. In 2006, Mike Piazza bumped McGuire out of the top twenty list for career games played as a catcher, but McGuire almost certainly will remain the all-time assist leader at the position with 937. (FV/DN/PM)

Merritt, William Henry / "Bill"

B	T	HGT	WGT	G	AB	H	R	2B
R	R	5'7"	160	401	1414	384	182	40

3B	HR	RBI	BB	SO	SB	BA	SA	OBP
12	8	196	110	71	21	.272	.334	.327

B. 7/30/1870 Lowell, MA **D.** 11/17/1937
TEAMS: 91ChiN 92LouN 93–94BosN 94PitN 94–95CinN 95–97PitN 99BosN
DEBUT: 8/8/1891 at Boston; caught Ad Gumbert and went 0-for-4 in a 4–3 loss to Boston's Harry Staley
FINALE: 10/14/1899 at Boston; caught Jouett Meekin and went 0-for-2 in a 6–1 loss to Philadelphia's Bill Bernhard

Bill Merritt hit well for a catcher, but his size was against him. Considered too frail to catch regularly or handle hard throwers, he worked only 353 games behind the dish in eight seasons, averaging a mere 44 a year. In 1898 *TSN* claimed that in 1891 he turned up at the Chicago team's hotel in Boston barefoot and ill clad to beg Cap Anson for a chance and then caught Bill Hutchison and Ad Gumbert "without a passed ball and hit the ball on the nose" in a DH that afternoon. Merritt later wrote an angry denial of the entire story.

In truth, he came to Chicago in 1891 from the Woonsocket New England League club after catching collegiate pitchers at Holy Cross, and *SL* at once said of him, "He is hardly heavy enough to catch Hutchison." The following season, however, Merritt reportedly caught 43 consecutive games for Louisville after coming to the Colonels in the late summer from the Southern League. Foolishly, the Kentucky club released him to Boston. Merritt got off to a torrid start in 1893 and was leading the NL in batting in early July before he was idled by a broken thumb. Even though he was not the same hitter when he returned, he still topped the Beaneaters with a .496 SA. Merritt did not get another chance at regular duty behind the plate until late in the 1895 season. He was hitting .285 for the Pirates when third baseman Billy Clingman threw a ball to him when he wasn't looking during infield practice prior to a late-September game at Louisville and shattered his jaw.

Merritt was reduced to a backup role when he returned to action the following year and did well but was mysteriously sold to Kansas City of the Western League in 1898. When he complained, it emerged that he had alienated his Pittsburgh teammates during an 1897 exhibition game at Atlantic City when they angered him by rooting for their underdog "college-boy" opponents, and he then chewed them out publicly after they razzed him. The razzing continued the rest of season and intensified whenever Pink Hawley pitched, and his "posing in the box" allowed teams to steal almost at will with Merritt getting the blame.

Unable to persuade Kansas City manager Jim Manning to release him, Merritt stubbornly remained at home in 1898 and most of 1899, playing in the outlaw Blackstone Valley league. After Pirates manager Patsy Donovan finally prevailed on Manning to waive all claims on Merritt, he joined Boston and made a token appearance in the last game of the 1899 season. Gone was the wiry catcher of the early 1890s. One reporter said of the new version: "Behind the plate stood William Merritt, who has been out of the game for a year. Billy was fat as butter and displayed a porcelain wing. One time he chased a foul fly near the fence and puffed like a flat boat steaming the Ohio River."

Merritt returned to semipro ball in 1900 but then got back into shape and served as a player-manager in the New England League for the next five seasons. He later managed Calgary in the Northwest League and scouted for both Boston ML clubs. Merritt died in a Lowell hospital in 1937 after a lengthy illness. (DN)

Miller, George Frederick / "Doggie" "Foghorn" "Calliope"

B	T	HGT	WGT	G	AB	H	R	2B
R	R	5'6"	145	1318	5171	1381	839	192

3B	HR	RBI	BB	SO	SB	BA	SA	OBP
57	33	567	467	129	260	.267	.345	.333

G	W	L	PCT	PENNANTS
133	56	76	.424	0

B. 8/15/1864 Brooklyn, NY **D.** 4/6/1909
TEAMS: 84–86PitA 87–93PitN (P/M)94StLN 95StLN 96LouN
DEBUT: 5/1/1884 at Pittsburgh; played RF and went 2-for-4 in a 9–2 loss to Philadelphia's Al Atkinson
FINALE: 9/25/1896 at Cleveland; caught Bert Cunningham and went 2-for-2 in a 10–7 win over Cleveland's Zeke Wilson

During his thirteen-year career, Doggie Miller became the only player in ML history to play at least 20 games at each of the eight nonpitching positions. In his own day, however, he may have been best known for the idiosyncrasies that earned him several enduring nicknames. Miller reached the majors with Pittsburgh AA in 1884 after a trainee season with Harrisburg of the Interstate Association. His primary position was catcher, but the recent arrival of overhand pitching had made it all but impossible for any man to catch on a daily basis, and the versatile Miller was often used at other positions when not stationed behind the plate. He soon became known less for his play on the field than for his performances in the coaching box. The American Association was noted for the energy and volume of its coaches, but even by the standards of the league, Miller was a revelation. He possessed a voice that could be heard all over the ballpark and lost no opportunity to use it. One sportswriter marveled that Miller kept up a continual chorus of "Get away," "Go along," "Go way up, "Go on," "What are you doing?" and "Whoa!" throughout his team's at-bats.

In 1887 Pittsburgh deserted the AA for the NL and brought the upstart AA's coaching style with it. Most fans in NL cities had never seen anything like Miller, and he was greeted with amazement. On Pittsburgh's first trip to Detroit, he was said to be "a pronounced type of the American Association coacher, and nothing like his bray has ever before been heard at Recreation Park. It is startling to spectators seeing his squatty, Quilp-like form to suddenly hear his foghorn tones exhorting a Pittsburger [*sic*] to 'Getwaygetwaygetway.'" As a result, he earned the nicknames "Foghorn" and "Calliope." He became just as well known by the nickname of Doggie, which may have been a tribute to his peculiar batting style. According to sportswriter Hugh Fullerton, "the oddest of all batters was Doggy [*sic*] Miller. He was short and stout with plump little legs. He stood perfectly still at bat until just as the pitcher was winding up to deliver the ball, then he suddenly stuck his left leg out straight in front of it, gave a funny little ballet girl kick, and threw himself forward to meet the ball. His performance caused so much laughter that Doggy tried earnestly to stop kicking—but he couldn't hit unless he did."

Miller continued to catch and play the outfield for his first five ML seasons, but things changed in 1890. He had stayed with Pittsburgh while many established players jumped to the Players League and the club had several holes to fill. Meanwhile, the introduction of catcher's equipment had revolutionized Miller's original position. When Miller continued to refuse to wear a chest protector, he was the only ML catcher to do so, and the new piece of protective equipment and the brand-new mitt wrought a dramatic change to the requirements of the position. Catchers began to use their bodies to stop pitches, and small, agile men like Miller were moved to positions that made better use of their dexterity. He spent most of his time at 3B in 1890 and thereafter was used wherever needed. By the time his career ended in 1896, Miller had caught 636 games, played 22 at 1B, 51 at 2B, 83 at SS, 243 at 3B, 146 in LF, 68 in CF, and 96 in RF.

After a decade in Pittsburgh, Miller joined St. Louis in 1894. In a tribute to the respect in which he was held, he was immediately named as the team's captain and de facto manager. The Browns, however, were in such disarray that no amount of leadership could turn the team around. Miller was replaced as manager after a ninth-place finish in 1894, and the club ran through four different managers in 1895. After that campaign Miller moved on to Louisville and then to the minors, where he ended his career in 1903 as player-manager of Dayton in the Central League. He passed away just six years later of Bright's disease at the too-young age of 44. (PM/DN)

Milligan, John / "Jack" "Jocko"

B	T	HGT	WGT	G	AB	H	R	2B
R	R	6'0"	192	772	2964	848	440	189

3B	HR	RBI	BB	SO	SB	BA	SA	OBP
50	49	497	210	134	41	.286	.433	.341

B. 8/8/1861 Philadelphia, PA **D.** 8/29/1923
TEAMS: 84–87PhiA 88–89StLA 90PhiP 91PhiA 92WasN 93BalN 93NYN
DEBUT: 5/1/1884 at Baltimore; caught Al Atkinson and went 2-for-4 in a 9–2 win over Baltimore's John Fox
FINALE: 9/29/1884 at Pittsburgh; caught Amos Rusie and went 0-for-3 in a 4–3 loss to Pittsburgh's Tom Colcolough

Strong if somewhat mechanical on defense, Jack Milligan led his league in fielding as a rookie, frequently led in double plays and was among the best catchers in his time at cutting down would-be base thieves. A poor base runner himself, he scored only 440 runs in a career that spanned ten seasons and was so often a victim of being picked off 1B by left-handed pitchers, particularly Matt Kilroy, that he finally began to stand on the bag until the ball was hit and then was so slow that he would sometimes be forced at 2B on a clean single. Largely for this reason Milligan often was not in the lineup when southpaws like Kilroy or Tom Ramsey pitched even though he was a right-handed hitter. Still, his vulnerability on the bases is insufficient reason for why he only appeared in an average of 77 games a year despite owning one of the most productive bats of any catcher in the nineteenth century. In 1889, Milligan belted 12 home runs in just 273 ABs, a season record for the most dingers in fewer than 300 ABs that survived until 1925. In the only year he played as many as 100 games (two years later), he topped the AA in doubles and ranked second in both SA and OPS. His .903 OPS remained the season standard until 1927 among catchers with a minimum of 400 ABs.

Orphaned at age 8, in January 1870 Milligan was sent by the courts to Girard College, the famous (many would say infamous) nineteenth-century Philadelphia school for boys without parents or legal guardians. After graduating in 1879, he became a blacksmith's apprentice. In between shoeing horses, he played baseball for various amateur and semipro teams in the Philadelphia area until 1883, when he joined the Pottsville Anthracite of the Interstate Association. Sharing the catching with John Grady, he faced pitchers like Bob Emslie, Sam Kimber, and Jack Harkins whom he would later meet in the majors.

That winter Philadelphia A's owner-manager Billy Sharsig signed Milligan on the recommendation of A's outfielder Lon Knight, himself a graduate of Girard. The rookie receiver won the A's Opening Day starting assignment in 1884 and shared the catching with Jack O'Brien for his first two seasons but then was relegated to a backup when Wilbert Robinson joined the club in 1886. The A's thinking eludes historians. Milligan had much better stats than Robinson, both offensively and defensively, yet by 1887 was appearing more often at 1B than behind the plate. Even so, he paced AA catchers in double plays that season despite catching just 47 games. In November 1887 Milligan was part of one of the first large player trades when he and two other A's went to St. Louis for Bill Gleason and Curt Welch. As though he knew in advance that he was not going to like playing under Browns manager Charlie Comiskey, he immediately tried to buy his release from St. Louis for $600, claiming that he wanted to play closer to his home in the east because his wife, Isabella, was sick. When Browns owner Chris Von der Ahe discovered his true motive was to play under Baltimore manager Billy Barnie, a former catcher who might be more appreciative of his work, his offer was refused.

Milligan then found himself serving as a backup for the next two seasons to Jack Boyle, a catcher whose stats were only marginally better than Robinson's. In 1888 he at least had the satisfaction of playing on a pennant winner and appearing in his only World's Series when the Browns claimed their fourth straight AA flag and faced the New York Giants, but the following year he watched impotently from the bench fully half the time despite his team-leading 1.030 OPS. Even before the season was over Milligan announced that he loathed playing in St. Louis and would quit rather than play there another year. He was spared from having to challenge the reserve clause when the PL formed. Among the first to jump to the Brotherhood loop, Milligan played with his hometown Philadelphia team and then returned in 1891 to a revamped A's franchise. After the AA and NL merged in December 1891, Milligan spent an unhappy year with Washington, where he was assigned in the merger, and began to put on weight. In July 1893 *TSN* judged him "the fattest catcher in the League," and a knee injury in August that abscessed made him all the more ponderous. Even though Giants ace Amos Rusie announced that he would pitch again for New York in 1894 only if Milligan was his catcher, player-manager John M. Ward jettisoned both Milligan and Mike Kelly after the 1893 season, in part because they ran practically a perpetual floating craps game in the New York clubhouse.

The two resumed their dice diversions the following season and also added drinking in the clubhouse prior to games after Milligan agreed to share the catching with Kelly on Kelly's Pennsylvania State League entry, Allentown Kelly's Killers. After Kelly's death, Milligan took over the club and helped move it to Reading for a time in 1895 before poor attendance forced the franchise to play all its games on the road. Through it all, he guided the club to a spot in the league championship series and led the loop in batting with an astronomical .452 BA.

Milligan played one more year in the minors, hitting a combined .372 in two different leagues, and then returned to his Philadelphia home. He worked as a tipstaff (sheriff's deputy) and made some money in real estate by buying vacant lots in South Philadelphia. In 1923 Milligan died of a heart attack at his home and was survived by his wife, whom he had married eleven days after making his ML debut. (DN)

Mills, Charles / "Charlie"

B	T	HGT	WGT	G	AB	H	R	2B
?	?	6'0"	165	38	177	40	33	4

3B	HR	RBI	BB	SO	SB	BA	SA	OBP
3	0	24	1	0	2	.226	.282	.230

B. 9/?/1844 Brooklyn, NY **D.** 4/10/1874
TEAMS: 71–72MutNA
DEBUT: 5/18/1871 at Troy; caught Rynie Wolters in a 14–3 win over Troy's John McMullin
FINALE: 9/28/1872 at Brooklyn; played RF and went 1-for-4 in a 9–5 loss to the Brooklyn Atlantics' Jim Britt

Charlie Mills's brother Andy was a first baseman with the Brooklyn Eckfords for a time. Mills also was with the Eckfords in 1865 and in the late 1860s played for the New York area's other leading clubs, the Atlantics and Mutuals, holding down the key position of catcher and establishing himself as one of the better players in the country. Tall by the standards of the day, his long reach was a significant advantage at a time when catchers, lacking protective equipment, usually stood far behind the plate and tried to corral the ball on the bounce. Mills was also well known as an able umpire whose high-profile assignments included the famous 1870 game in which the Atlantics ended the Cincinnati Red Stockings' long winning streak.

When the NA formed in 1871, Mills was the Mutuals' regular catcher, but by the following year he had begun to develop signs of the consumption that would take his life and could make only six appearances. He returned to the Atlantics in 1873, but his condition had deteriorated to the point that he could not play at all, although he continued to umpire to the end of the season. When he died the next April, sportswriter Henry Chadwick was shocked to find only two other baseball men at his funeral. However, in August the Mutuals and the Atlantics each played a benefit game to raise money for Mills's survivors. (DN/EM)

Munyan, John Baird (aka O'Rourke) / "Jack"

B	T	HGT	WGT	G	AB	H	R	2B
?	?	?	?	174	583	147	112	20

3B	HR	RBI	BB	SO	SB	BA	SA	OBP
11	4	67	76	39	28	.252	.345	.350

B. 11/14/1860 Chester, PA **D.** 2/18/1945
TEAMS: 87CleA 90ColA 90–91StLA
DEBUT: 7/12/1887 at Cleveland; played RF and went 0-for-4 in a 5–1 loss to Baltimore's Phenomenal Smith
FINALE: 10/4/1891 at St. Louis; caught Willie McGill and went 2-for-3 in a 4–3 loss to Louisville's Warren Fitzgerald

CAREER HIGHLIGHT: 10/4/1891 at St. Louis; caught Ted Breitenstein and went 1-for-2 in an 8–0 win over Louisville's Jouett Meekin 8–0 as Breitenstein became the first pitcher in ML history to throw a full-length no-hitter in his initial ML start

Jack Munyan was a gritty, hard-edged type with substantial boxing skills. Although his height and weight are unknown, he was evidently quite small. In 1891 he admitted to *TSN* that he had trouble handling tall pitchers because of his "diminutive" size and preferred working with men like Wee Willie McGill as opposed to someone like 6'2" Will Mains. Munyan began with semipro teams in Philadelphia. In 1882 he was briefly a member of the Philadelphia Athletics' reserves but never got into an official AA game. The following year he caught for at least three semipro teams and capped his season in July by hitting the first home run ever over the right-field fence in Philadelphia's Jumbo Park against the Foley club's Bert Dorr, who would finish the year pitching for the St. Louis Browns. In 1884 Munyan began with Harrisburg, PA, of the Eastern League and then went to Williamsport, PA, where he elicited this comment from *SL* after he was released in early October: "He has been playing with the utmost carelessness for the past three weeks. . . . He evidently wanted what he got."

Perhaps because of the stigma attached to him after the Williamsport incident, Munyan played the first part of the 1885 International League season with Binghamton under the name of "O'Rourke" but had resumed his real name by his second year with the Crickets. Munyan was with Bridgeport in the Eastern League in 1887 until the club disbanded in July, at which point he joined AA cellar-dweller Cleveland. After drawing the collar in his ML debut, he collected his initial hit the following day in an 8–1 loss to Matt Kilroy. But after that he seldom played, and signed with Columbus of the Tri-State League in 1888 when he was not invited to return to Cleveland.

Munyan's career seemed to be going nowhere when he spent 1889 with Springfield in the lowly Central Interstate League. In July he got into a highly publicized "nose-chewing, ear-biting and finger-swallowing" fight with teammate Ed Stapleton after accusing Stapleton of flirting with his wife, "a very handsome little brunette." His scrappy attitude earned offers that fall from both Columbus AA and Pittsburgh NL. Munyan chose Columbus because he had played there in 1888 but failed to impress manager Gus Schmelz and was let go after just 2 games. He quickly hooked on with St. Louis, however, and in short time became the club's front-line catcher. By the end of the 1890 season Munyan was hitting cleanup for the Browns, but he began 1891 on the bench after the PL collapse brought catcher Jack Boyle back to St Louis. When he was released at the close of the season, *TSN* said it was because he "could not catch a string of sausages nor hit a dead elephant with a club" and then responded to Munyan's claim that he might retire, with: "Well he never will be missed." But Munyan had no intention of retiring even though he was no doubt stung by the largely unfair appraisal of his skills. He began 1892 with Minneapolis and then joined Butte of the outlaw Montana State League after the Western League folded. His career seemed over two years later when he broke his right ankle sliding in a Western Association game at Lincoln, NE, in August, but he again rebounded from adversity and by 1896, although approaching his 36th birthday, was still a nimble backstop while acting as the Norwich, CT, club's player-manager. Munyan died in Endicott, NY, in 1945. (DN)

Murphy, Morgan Edward / "Morg"

B	T	HGT	WGT	G	AB	H	R	2B
R	R	5'8"	160	559	1949	438	242	55

3B	HR	RBI	BB	SO	SB	BA	SA	OBP
12	10	221	157	239	52	.225	.282	.284

B. 2/14/1867 E. Providence, RI **D.** 10/3/1938
TEAMS: 90BosP 91BosA 92–95Cin 96–97StLN 98PitN 98PhiN 00PhiN 01PhiAL
DEBUT: 4/22/1890 at Brooklyn; caught Charley Radbourn and went 1-for-4 in a 10–8 loss to Brooklyn's John Sowders.
FINALE: 5/31/1901 at Cleveland; replaced Doc Powers behind the plate and went 1-for-2 in a 15–14 win over Earl Moore, Dick Braggins, and Bill Hoffer

Cheeky, innovative, redheaded Morg Murphy had one of the finest throwing arms of any nineteenth-century catcher before being struck with typhoid at age 25. A Rhode Island native, Murphy played for teenage teams in East Providence before joining the independent Southern New England League in 1885. When Tim Murnane was named manager of the Boston Blues New England League entry for

1886, he signed Murphy as his catcher. Murphy remained with the Blues until they moved to Haverhill in 1887. He then spent two and a half seasons with Lowell, MA, and became one of only a handful of significant rookie contributors in the Players League after batting an uninspiring .249 for Lowell in 1889 against Atlantic Association competition. Also joining Murphy on the PL Boston Reds in 1890 was fellow frosh receiver Pop Swett. The two shared the catching initially with manager Mike Kelly, but Murphy gradually assumed the club's regular backstopping burden owing to his superior defensive skills. In 1891 Murphy remained with the Reds when they moved to the AA with most of their core players and thus began his career playing on two successive pennant winners in two different leagues. In the remaining nine years of his ML career he never again played on a championship team, nor did he ever again catch 100 games in a season.

In 1892, when the NL and AA consolidated and the Reds were dispersed, Murphy was awarded to Cincinnati despite wanting to play for the Boston NL entry. His disappointment probably contributed to his failure to approach the 1892 season with the same zeal he had brought to the game while playing in Boston. Also, he fell in with Arlie Latham; the two roomed together on Findlay Street, about half a block from the Reds' park, and alienated themselves from teammates when they disdained the team clubhouse and snobbishly dressed in their room and then walked to the park wearing their street clothes over their uniforms. Manager Charlie Comiskey soon accused Murphy of having "the big head" since coming to Cincinnati. When Murphy contracted a severe case of typhoid in July, he lost his job as the Reds' regular catcher to Harry Vaughn and never regained it in his remaining three years with Cincinnati.

In the fall of 1895 Murphy was traded to St. Louis along with Latham and two other players for Red Ehret and Heinie Peitz. He spent two dreary seasons with the Browns, capped by 1897 when he produced a dismal .377 OPS in 211 ABs, and then was traded to Pittsburgh for Joe Sugden. Murphy lasted only 5 games with the Pirates before being let go to the Phillies. He was seldom used by Philadelphia in 1898 and appeared in no games at all in 1899 even though he remained on the team all year as the head of the Quaker Signal Bureau. Until he was outed, Murphy's job, according to *TSN*, was to sit in a clubhouse window in CF with a pair of field glasses and signal to Phillies batters what kind of pitch was coming by raising a section of the window awning. The scheme was exposed when Dave Fultz, who had begun the season with Philadelphia, revealed the trick after he was sent to Baltimore, and Orioles catcher Wilbert Robinson then began changing his signs to confound Murphy.

Early in the 1900 campaign Murphy was farmed to Syracuse in the Eastern League but was retrieved in time to appear in 11 games and develop a new twist to the Quaker Signal Bureau. That year, with his "extracurricular" help, the Phillies' home winning percentage was 233 points higher than their road percentage. On a rainy September 17 Cincinnati captain Tommy Corcoran noticed that Phils third base coach Bull Chiles kept his foot in the same spot in the coaches' box despite a deepening puddle. In the bottom of the third inning the game was delayed when Corcoran began digging frantically at the spot with his cleats. He reached into the mud and pulled up a wooden box with a buzzer in it. Corcoran then followed the wire to deep center field and up into the stands, straight to Murphy. When Corcoran inquired what the catcher was doing, Murphy, who was concealing a buzzer, had no choice but to say, "I guess you've got the goods." The Phillies nonetheless won both ends of a DH that day, but two weeks later, in their final series at front-running Brooklyn, Superbas manager Ned Hanlon spotted Murphy across the street from the park with a pair of field glasses. In the course of a 2–1 loss to the Phils, pitcher Harry Howell was sent to investigate and discovered that Murphy was signaling the type of pitch coming to Chiles with a newspaper. Chiles was then relaying the information to the batter with a prechosen word. *TSN* noted that the following day, after Brooklyn's signals changed, Frank Kitson blanked the Phils 12–0.

Unlike other Phils, Murphy was not the subject of a legal suit when he joined Philadelphia AL in 1901 largely because the Phils released him beforehand. After 9 games under rookie ML manager Connie Mack, he was cut and went into the hotel business. Murphy died in Providence in 1938. Of the many lame-hitting catchers with a minimum of 1,000 ABs in the 1893–1900 era, he was the weakest in RC/G with just 3.35. (DN/FV)

Murphy, Patrick J. / "Pat"

B	T	HGT	WGT	G	AB	H	R	2B
R	R	5'10"	160	86	309	68	34	9

3B	HR	RBI	BB	SO	SB	BA	SA	OBP
2	1	21	24	28	7	.220	.272	.278

B. 1/2/1857 Auburn, MA **D.** 5/16/1927
TEAMS: 87–90NYN
DEBUT: 9/2/1887 at New York; caught Cannonball Titcomb and went 0-for-2 in a 2–1 win over Detroit's Pete Conway
FINALE: 10/3/1890 at Chicago; played LF and went 1-for-4 in a 3–2 loss to Chicago's Jack Luby

Until 1887, Pat Murphy, who had delayed his pro entry until age 28, seemed destined to be a shoemaker in Worcester and play minor league ball in the summers as long as his body could hold out. But that season, his second with Jersey City, then in the International Association, he was paired with a young southpaw named Ledell Titcomb, soon to be known as "Cannonball." The pair came to the Giants as a unit in September 1887 when Murphy was already past 30. The following year the early day prototype for Duane Decker's novel *The Catcher from Double-A* earned recognition as the least known member of New York's first ML pennant winner but appeared in all the team pictures and even played three games in the World's Series that fall against the St. Louis Browns. Murphy's role grew still more limited in 1889. He appeared in just nine games but hit a torrid .357, collected eight assists and no passed balls and was team pilot Jim Mutrie's favorite at leading the Giants famous "We are the people" chant. Murphy thought all that deserved a 3-year contract to assure his loyalty to the Giants when the PL began stripping the NL team of players, but Mutrie jolted him back to reality. Although used more often in 1890, he was released when Buck Ewing returned from the PL to share the catching with Dick Buckley but might not have been jettisoned if Mutrie had been prescient enough to know that Ewing would hurt his arm in the spring of 1891.

By that time Murphy owned a sizable chunk of property in Worcester and could have gone there to live in the large home he shared with his mother, but he returned to the minors for several more seasons. In 1894 he began the year as a player-manager with his hometown Worcester club in the New England League but was fired in June owing to the public's apathy toward the team. Murphy later worked as a Worcester policeman for some 10 years and then hired on as a special police officer with the local Plaza Theater. He died at his daughter's Worcester home in 1927. (DN)

Murray, Jeremiah J. / "Miah"

B	T	HGT	WGT	G	AB	H	R	2B
R	R	5'11½"	170	34	120	17	6	1

3B	HR	RBI	BB	SO	SB	BA	SA	OBP
0	0	7	4	16	0	.142	.150	.176

B. 1/1/1865 Boston, MA **D.** 1/11/1922
TEAMS: 84ProN 85LouA 88WasN 91WasA
DEBUT: 5/17/1884 at Providence; caught Charley Radbourn and went 1-for-3 in a 5–2 win over Detroit's Stump Wiedman
FINALE: 10/3/1891 at Boston; caught Kid Carsey and went 0-for-4 in a 6–2 loss to Boston's George Haddock

At age 19 and in his second pro season, Miah Murray played a cameo role as a catcher on Providence's famous 1884 champions, spending the entire season on the Grays' roster even though he appeared in only 8 games, the majority of them after Providence clinched the pennant and second-string catcher Sandy Nava had been released. In his debut on May 17 Murray had the privilege of working with Charley Radbourn, but in his future games he was primarily teamed with another prospect, a young all-around athlete named Jack Cattanach, whom the Grays were attempting to turn into a pitcher. The *Providence Journal* thought so highly of Murray that it noted, "He is a better thrower than either [Barney] Gilligan or Nava, is a free batsman and needs practice simply to accustom himself to quicker work in handling the ball." But while Murray may have been a free swinger, he so seldom made solid contact that his subsequent ML career was extremely modest. He signed with Indianapolis, a very strong minor league team, in 1885 but was again a backup to more experienced catchers Deacon McGuire and Jim Keenan, and was soon released so the club could save money. He latched on with Louisville for a few games later that season, and after bouncing around the minor leagues awhile again, he resurfaced briefly with Washington in 1888.

By 1890, still only in his midtwenties, Murray

was though with pro ball. When Washington AA showed up for a series in Boston at the tail end of the 1891 season with a roster shaved by injuries and financial need to ten healthy men, Murray played for one of the two local semipro teams that battled for a trophy awarded by the Boston club in a contest preceding the official Boston-Washington game. The following two days, Murray marked the end of his ML career when he spelled catcher Deacon McGuire for Washington's final 2 games of its Boston visit.

Murray subsequently became a more prominent figure in a variety of roles around the Boston and New England sporting scene than he ever had been as a player. In 1895 he worked as a regular NL umpire with less-than-stellar notices; a contemporary writer observed, "Jeremiah Murray needed more postgame escorts than a president," but it was common for umpires to get such harsh treatment in the 1890s. Murray then operated a succession of billiard rooms and bowling alleys in Boston, meanwhile umpiring for the Harvard University baseball team and serving as vice president of the semipro Cambridge Reds. Whenever the police refrained from intervening in a sport that was illegal but sporadically tolerated, he operated as a boxing promoter with the Criterion Athletic Club in 1902–1903 and later the Armory Athletic Club. In 1908 Murray joined many other local baseball veterans for an old-timers' day hosted by the Boston club, and he can be seen in a large group photo in *Baseball Magazine*, the once fresh-faced Providence catcher now balding and distinguished, or at least natty in appearance, like a maitre d' at a fine restaurant. He died in 1922 at his home in North Dorchester, MA. (DN)

Myers, George D. / "George"

B	T	HGT	WGT	G	AB	H	R	2B
R	R	5'8"	170	424	1578	321	183	43

3B	HR	RBI	BB	SO	SB	BA	SA	OBP
8	5	126	109	149	72	.203	.250	.260

B. 11/13/1860 Buffalo, NY **D.** 12/14/1926
TEAMS: 84–85BufN 86StLN 87–89IndN
DEBUT: 5/2/1884 at Boston; caught Art Hagan and went 2-for-5 in an 11–10 loss to Boston's Charlie Buffinton and John Morrill
FINALE: 8/3/1889 at Pittsburgh; played CF and went 0-for-4 in an 8–6 win over Pittsburgh's Harry Staley

An amateur sprinter and distance runner, the compactly built George Myers had the tools that would have made him a star in the 1870s, and even though catchers' equipment by the late 1880s made the speed necessary to chase after passed balls and wild pitches a less important skill, he remained one of the better catchers of his era until his arm betrayed him.

Plucky to an extreme, Myers used every part of his body to block pitches in the dirt and yet still avoided serious injury. He hands suffered, however, which may help explain his awful batting stats. On Opening Day, Myers always hit well. In the 1888 season lidlifter he slammed 3 doubles and a home run for Indianapolis. Then on May 23 a Dick Johnston foul ball dislocated one of Myers's fingers. After hitting .429 that April, Myers would bat just .123 over the season's last twelve weeks. As his short career progressed, he improved only at getting hit by pitches and drawing walks. On June 29, 1889, Myers had a 0-for-0 game with 4 walks.

After catching Billy Mountjoy for the Port Huron, MI, independent team in 1883, Myers earned a backup catcher's spot with Buffalo NL in 1884. Manager Jim O'Rourke used essentially a one-man pitching staff—Jim Galvin. Myers had trouble catching him and usually paired with change pitcher Billy Serad. Finally, on August 12, with Galvin going for his thirtieth win, Myers was forced to work with him. Galvin had to reduce his speed in winning 11–9 despite being "hit freely and loosely supported."

Jim McCauley was signed in 1885 to catch Galvin but was a disappointment, and Myers became Galvin's regular catcher. When Buffalo sank to last place on July 13, new manager Jack Chapman sold Galvin to Pittsburgh, which tried to buy Myers as well but balked at the Bisons' stiff asking price. Myers then finished 1885 with more regular work than in any other season and ended with 27 errors and 18 passed balls in his last 13 games. After the famous September 16 sale of four Buffalo stars to Detroit, the team was understaffed and Myers caught as many as 10 consecutive games for the only time in his career.

Once Buffalo disbanded, Myers was awarded to St. Louis and became Henry Boyle's pet receiver. He would remain Boyle's catcher, following him to Indianapolis in 1887 with mixed results, until he was released in August 1889 due to arm problems, just days after Jack Glasscock took over the management of the team from Frank Bancroft. That season most of Myers's appearances were as an outfielder while Con Daily and Dick Buckley did the bulk of the catching. He was saved only for emergencies and for dangerously wild rookies like Amos Rusie. Myers caught Rusie's first three major league starts and barely survived.

A skilled carpenter, Myers built houses in the winter months to substantial financial gain and by the early 1890s owned considerable property in the Buffalo area. Prior to the 1890 season Deacon White and Jack Rowe, former Buffalo teammates, tapped their old catcher for startup money for the new Buffalo Players League franchise. Myers had hoped to play as his reward but was not invited. He appeared with Syracuse of the Eastern Association in 1891 and then with Syracuse and Rochester the following year, batting .262 in 84 games. His arm shot, Myers then devoted himself to his real-estate investments until his death in Buffalo in 1926. (FV/DN/DB)

O'Brien, John K. (b. Byrne) / **"Jack" "Philadelphia Jack"**

B	T	HGT	WGT	G	AB	H	R	2B
R	R	5'10"	184	555	2169	577	366	106

3B	HR	RBI	BB	SO	SB	BA	SA	OBP
42	11	308	180	—	76	.266	.369	.331

B. 6/12/1860 Philadelphia, PA **D.** 11/20/1910
TEAMS: 82–86PhiA 87BroA 88BalA 90PhiA
DEBUT: 5/2/1882 at Philadelphia; caught Sam Weaver and went 1-for-5 in a 10–7 win over Baltimore's Tricky Nichols
FINALE: 9/16/1891 at Philadelphia; played 1B and was 2-for-4 in a 5–4 loss to Baltimore's Les German

Jack O'Brien was an outstanding defensive catcher and also played an excellent CF before finishing his career as a first baseman. In addition to being multitalented defensively, he hit with power and also ran well, at least early in his career. In 1886 *TSN* cited the reason he failed ever to achieve stardom: "O'Brien has but one fault and that is getting hurt in almost every game in which he takes part . . . long ago he was put down as the unluckiest man in the profession."

At age 18 in 1878 while catching for the Yeager Amateur Club of Philadelphia on June 20, O'Brien took part in one of the early-day classics when the Yeagers battled Girard College and its star catcher, Jack Milligan, in a contest played on a hard gravel field that lasted twenty-one innings before the Yeagers prevailed 10–7. The following year O'Brien played with the San Francisco–based California Club before returning to Philadelphia in 1880–81 to perform for the minor league Athletics. He made his ML debut in 1882 with the A's in the fledgling AA.

On June 2, 1882, in a 7–1 loss to Cincinnati, O'Brien sustained his first serious ML injury when he collided with Bid McPhee in a baserunning mishap. McPhee's spikes severely lacerated O'Brien's face, and the impact knocked him senseless. He was carried to the Philadelphia dressing room, where he remained unconscious "fully an hour." Fortunately, *SL* said, there was a doctor at the game, "but for whose timely services O'Brien might have been past all suffering." The following day O'Brien was back behind the plate, and he finished the season leading the second-place A's in BA, OBP, and SA. In 1883, O'Brien began July as the top hitter on the pennant-bound A's at .337, but a succession of injuries eventually reduced his mark to .290. The following year a lengthy bout with pneumonia held him to just 36 games, and he lost not only his salary during his illness but also the regular catching job to his 1878 Girard College rival, rookie Jack Milligan. O'Brien did not become a full-time player again until 1886 when his versatility enabled him to play everywhere except pitcher. Nevertheless the A's released him that fall owing to "strained relations for several years with one of the proprietors," probably the petulant Charlie Mason. O'Brien was quickly signed by Brooklyn and installed as the club's regular catcher on Opening Day in 1887. Injuries again caught up to him when backup receiver Jimmy Peoples was idled by a sprained ankle, forcing him to catch almost every game until his hands were so badly battered by June that Peoples then had to catch most of the time for the rest of the season. In 1888 O'Brien was again the Opening Day catcher, this time for Baltimore and injuries again hampered him, pushing him eventually to 1B.

O'Brien apparently sat out the 1889 season, limiting himself to sandlot games. When the Players League siphoned numerous players from both major leagues in the winter of 1889–90, in January 1890 O'Brien was coaxed into trying a comeback with the A's now that the team had a new front office. He caught only part of 1 game in 1890 but was the A's everyday first baseman and also their most productive hitter with the sole exception of Denny Lyons. O'Brien led the A's in RBI and triples and was second only to Lyons in walks, home runs, and SA. In mid-September he joined most of the other A's veterans in a mass exodus when the club's owners fell far behind in salaries.

Having ended the 1890 season injury-free, O'Brien opted to play in the minors in 1891 with St. Paul and Duluth, perhaps hoping to earn his way back to the majors. But since he was a widower by then, he had to leave his young daughter back home in the care of relatives. In 1892 O'Brien stayed in Philadelphia, caring for his daughter while working as "a boss teamster" and serving on weekends as Bobby Mathews's batterymate with the Mountain Leaguers in a local semipro league. He later became a pressman before dying in 1910 of Bright's disease. He was buried near the local Elks Home, where he was a resident toward the end of his life. (DN/DB)

O'Connor, John Joseph / "Jack" "Peach Pie"

B	T	HGT	WGT	G	AB	H	R	2B
R	R	5'10"	170	1183	4489	1229	658	186

3B	HR	RBI	BB	SO	SB	BA	SA	OBP
60	18	659	277	152	207	.274	.354	.320

B. 6/2/1866 St. Louis, MO **D.** 11/14/1937
TEAMS: 87–88CinA 89–91ColA 92–98CleN 99–00StLN 00–02PitN 03NYAL 04–07StLAL (P/M)10StLAL
DEBUT: 4/20/1887 at Cincinnati; caught Mike Shea and went 0-for-5 in a 14–6 win over Cleveland's Billy Crowell
FINALE: 10/9/1910 at St. Louis; replaced Bill Killefer late in the game and caught Alex Malloy in a 3–0 loss to Cleveland's Cy Falkenberg.

Jack O'Connor was a center of controversy from almost the first day to the last of his wildly uneven twenty-five-year career. A boyhood associate of Pat Tebeau and Bill Joyce in the Goose Hill Section of St. Louis, he played for the semipro Peach Pies (explaining his nickname) along with Tebeau and Silver King before accompanying King to the unaffiliated Jacksonville, IL, club in 1885. The following year he teamed with King on St. Joseph of the Western League and played under the name of Connors. In the spring of 1887, using his own name and claiming he was only 17, O'Connor seemingly became the youngest man ever to catch an AA game but spent most of that season and the next on the Reds' bench. Used primarily in the outfield in 1888 because he was still too raw as a catcher, that June he began clamoring for his release, complaining that he wasn't getting a fair chance and wasn't an outfielder, where manager Gus Schmelz insisted on playing him.

O'Connor got his wish and then some after the season when he was first ticketed to go to Columbus, an AA replacement team for Cleveland, and then traded by Columbus to his hometown St. Louis Browns for SS Bill White. Informed of the deal by Browns owner Chris Von der Ahe while he was in the midst of a poker game, O'Connor retorted that he would agree to catch only 1 game a week and then nearly caused Von der Ahe to faint when he mentioned the salary he wanted. The trade was quickly rescinded.

Perhaps realizing he was about to burn one too many bridges, O'Connor then claimed Columbus's first-string catching assignment in 1889 and led all AA receivers in games and FA. After he flirted with the rebel PL over the winter but could not strike a satisfactory deal, he stayed with Columbus and had his career year, catching 106 games and hitting .324. Toward the end of the 1890 season, however, Schmelz took over as manager of the club and the pair renewed their mutual dislike. That winter O'Connor clandestinely signed with Pittsburgh NL for a reported $700 advance. When Schmelz learned he was about to lose his catcher, he gulled O'Connor into remaining with Columbus by telling him to pocket the advance and think of it as "bribe money." Schmelz then decided to teach his brash catcher a hard lesson by suspending him on July 3 for "perpetual drunkenness" and "conduct unbecoming a gentleman." Eight days later O'Connor was expelled from the AA despite the intervention of a priest from his local parish vouching for "his future good conduct." He was allowed to sign with Denver of the Western Association because the AA in 1891 was considered an outlaw loop and the National Agreement thus did not recognize its blacklist, but before he could don a Denver uniform he was made to return the $700 he had bilked Pittsburgh out of in the spring.

After the AA and NL merged in December 1891,

Tebeau, by then piloting Cleveland NL, restored O'Connor to the majors. Upon being reunited with his old Peach Pies crony, the catcher became a changed man. He agreed to play wherever Tebeau put him, spending most of 1892 in RF, and in July married Cora Hunt of Columbus. That fall he played in the NL split-season championship series against Boston and later appeared with Cleveland in the 1896 Temple Cup series, but missed the lone postseason affair that Cleveland won, in 1895, with injuries. A player much like Tebeau—scrappy, versatile, a proponent of rowdy ball—O'Connor personified the Spiders throughout the 1890s and often ran the club unofficially on days when Tebeau was away on a scouting trip. In the winters he managed a grocery store in St. Louis and kept in shape playing handball; for a time he and Bill Joyce were the reigning doubles champions in the Mound City.

When syndicate ownership transferred most of the Spiders' top players to St. Louis in 1899, O'Connor became the club's field captain after Tebeau quit playing temporarily to manage from the bench. The following spring, however, the two had a falling out that would result in their not speaking for several years when Tebeau would not reappoint him captain. On May 22 O'Connor was sold to Pittsburgh for $2,000, half of which may have come to him as a bonus for agreeing to the transaction. He reunited with Chief Zimmer, his old road roommate on the Spiders, and vied with Zimmer and Bill Schriver for catching time. The following season O'Connor was a member of Pittsburgh's first NL flag winner but blew his chance for a repeat performance when Pittsburgh owner Barney Dreyfuss suspended him late in the 1902 campaign for allegedly acting as a liaison for AL president Ban Johnson to lure Pirates teammates to the proposed new AL franchise in New York. Dreyfuss's suspicions proved warranted when O'Connor and two of Pittsburgh's top pitchers, Jesse Tannehill and Jack Chesbro, skipped to Gotham in 1903. Once there, he quarreled with Highlanders manager Clark Griffith over the way Griffith ran his pitching staff, was suspended for a time, and then traded after the season to the St. Louis Browns for John Anderson.

O'Connor played sparingly with the AL Mound City club for the next four years and spent most of his time on the coaching lines. In 1909 he served as manager Mike Finn's chief assistant on Little Rock of the Southern Association before returning late in the season as a coach with the Browns in the expectation that he would be named manager the following year. The appointment came as he had hoped, but he soon regretted taking it. Not only did the Browns finish dead last in 1910, but O'Connor was accused of ordering rookie third baseman Red Corriden to play inordinately deep every time Cleveland's Nap Lajoie came to bat in a season-ending DH. Lajoie as a result bunted Corriden's way six times for hits en route to an 8-for-8 day that appeared to have been engineered by O'Connor to bring him the AL batting title over much loathed Detroit outfielder Ty Cobb. But when the final averages were calculated, O'Connor's skullduggery appeared to have gone for naught, as Cobb emerged the winner anyway (although it has since been established that Lajoie really won). While O'Connor was never formally banned for his role in the episode, neither he nor his chief assistant Harry Howell ever worked in the majors again (although Howell umpired in the rebel Federal League). He later managed the St. Louis FL entry in 1913 before the loop declared itself a major circuit and then promoted boxing matches in the Mound City Area. O'Connor died at his St. Louis home in 1937 of a multitude of life-threatening conditions. (DN/DB)

Oldfield, David / "Dave"

B	T	HGT	WGT	G	AB	H	R	2B
B	L	5'7"	175	46	155	31	11	4

3B	HR	RBI	BB	SO	SB	BA	SA	OBP
0	0	9	10	15	1	.200	.226	.253

B. 12/18/1864 Philadelphia, PA **D.** 8/28/1939
TEAMS: 83BalA 85–86BroA 86WasN
DEBUT: 6/28/1883 at Columbus; caught Hardie Henderson and committed 5 passed balls in a 4–2 loss to Columbus's Frank Mountain
FINALE: 10/11/1886 at Washington; caught John Henry and was 0-for-3 in a 7–5 loss to Kansas City's Silver King

In 1898 *TSN* conjectured that the only successful left-handed catchers were Jack Clements, Sam Trott, and Dave Oldfield. The switch-hitting lefty began his career with semipro Hartville, PA, in 1883. Among his teammates were two other future MLers, Walter Prince and Jim McTamany. Later in

1883 Oldfield played with the independent Lancaster Ironsides, where he formed a battery with Jim Hyndman. The circumstances under which Oldfield was called upon to catch for Baltimore in Columbus, OH, on June 28, 1883, are unclear, but he probably cost the Orioles the game by missing two third strikes on batters who later scored. In 1884 Oldfield shared the Ironsides catching duties with Gene Derby; also on the team again was McTamany. Oldfield made his debut with Brooklyn AA, as did Ironsides teammate McTamany, in an exhibition game against Philadelphia AA in Atlantic City on August 14, 1886, and went 3-for-4 against Tom Lovett. He proceeded to hit .320 in the 10 league games he played, including a one-pitch appearance on August 31 at Baltimore when he entered the game for injured Jim Peoples with two out and swiftly ended the contest by catching a pop foul.

Brooklyn carried four catchers at the outset of 1886, and all caught at least 1 game in the first week of the season. Oldfield was the last of the four to make his initial appearance but after that became the club's regular receiver for a spell before being cut, probably because of an injury. He joined Washington NL for the last two months of the season and was not asked to return when he hit just .141. By June 1887 Oldfield had joined Toronto of the International Association, which also had speedballer Ed Crane and the inimitable Harry Decker. Nearly a quarter of a century later Kid Bernstein, a Washington, D.C., ticket broker, recalled how as a boy he had witnessed Oldfield catch Crane with a huge handmade glove nearly the size of a pillow that Decker had fashioned out of mattress stuffings. Oldfield played several seasons with Toronto and was rated one of the top receivers in the International Association, but weak hitting prevented him from returning to the majors; in 1888 he led the IA with a .965 FA but batted just .194 and was out of pro ball two years later. Oldfield died in Philadelphia at 74. (DN)

O'Rourke, Thomas Joseph / "Tom" "Red"

B	T	HGT	WGT	G	AB	H	R	2B
?	R	5'9"	158	85	312	58	32	11

3B	HR	RBI	BB	SO	SB	BA	SA	OBP
0	0	26	21	15	8	.186	.221	.242

B. 10/?/1865 New York, NY **D.** 7/19/1929
TEAMS: 87–88BosN 90NYN 90SyrA
DEBUT: 5/11/1887 at Boston; caught Bill Stemmeyer and went 0-for-4 in a 9–4 loss to Philadelphia's Charlie Ferguson
FINALE: 8/1/1890 at Louisville; caught Dan Casey and went 0-for-4 in a 6–5 loss to Louisville's Mike Jones

Tom O'Rourke was a wiry redhead "liable to get rattled at critical points" and a poor hitter. He played with the semipro New York Senators under Charlie Murphy, later a Tammany Hall boss, and had a year of pro ball with Portland of the New England League before joining Boston as a backup receiver in 1887. After filling a similar role the following year, he returned to the minors until Players League raiders stripped many ML teams of their frontline catchers prior to the 1890 season. O'Rourke caught two games with New York NL early in that campaign and then was released to Syracuse AA. A regular for a time, he was fined $50 by Stars manager George Frazier for a misplay and refused to accompany the team on a road trip the night of August 9 unless the fine was remitted. He was then released and went home to New York. O'Rourke last played with Denver in 1891 and was later secretary for the Board of Water Supply in New York City. He died of heart trouble in 1929, leaving behind five children. (DN)

*Peitz, Henry Clement / "Heinie"

B	T	HGT	WGT	G	AB	H	R	2B
R	R	5'11"	165	721	2431	661	345	111

3B	HR	RBI	BB	SO	SB	BA	SA	OBP
50	13	357	275	76	70	.272	.375	.313

G	IP	H	GS	CG	BB
4	16	22	1	1	7

SO	SH	W	L	PCT	ERA
3	0	0	1	.000	7.31

B. 11/28/1870 St. Louis, MO **D.** 10/23/1943
TEAMS: 92–95StLN 97–04CinN 05–06PitN 13StLN
DEBUT: 10/15/92 at Kansas City; caught Pink Hawley and went 0-for-3 in a 1–0 loss to Chicago's Bill Hutchison
FINALE: 6/1/1913 at St. Louis; caught Bob Harmon and went 1-for-3 in a 4–2 loss to Chicago's Larry Cheney

Heinie Peitz was the younger brother of MLer Joe Peitz and the last nineteenth-century big leaguer to make his debut in Kansas City, where the Browns moved their final game in 1892. At age 15 he joined the St. Louis L. X. L. team, playing SS initially with his brother Joe at 3B. Peitz began catching for the L. X. L. club in 1888 and remained with it until 1890 when he made his pro debut with Jacksonville, IL, and then moved to Hillsboro, IL, later in the season. After spending most of 1891 with Hillsboro, he finished with Montgomery of the Southern League. At the close of the 1892 SL season the Browns purchased him for $500 after he had returned home to St. Louis and played several exhibitions with the club, filling in for injured Dick Buckley.

In 1893, his official rookie year, Peitz won the St. Louis catching job but was not the steady hand with pitchers that Buckley had been. When he contracted typhoid in September, leaving the team without a catcher, Art Twineham was acquired from the minors. The following year Peitz was moved to 1B and played there until Roger Connor joined the Browns; he then caught for a time before finishing the season at 3B. In 1895 Peitz played the same three positions but by now was among the top defensive catchers in the league, compiling 80 assists in just 71 games behind the plate. That November he was involved in the largest player trade to date when he accompanied Red Ehret to Cincinnati while four players headed for St. Louis along with an unknown amount of cash. Peitz then missed most of the next two seasons with injuries before finally giving the Reds a full return on their investment when he caught a career-high 101 games in 1898 and also often pitched batting practice, especially on days when the club was scheduled to face a dipsy doodler. According to teammate Elmer Smith, Peitz had a "flutter" pitch, probably a sort of knuckleball, that was nearly as good as Tom Ramsey's.

Peitz remained with Cincinnati until 1904, never quite achieving the potential that he had seemed to possess early in his career. In February 1905 he was traded to Pittsburgh for catcher Ed Phelps. Peitz was able to fend off rookie George Gibson's challenge for the Pirates' catching job that season but took on a backup role in 1906. After that he played and managed in the minors until 1913, when he returned to the majors as a player-coach with St. Louis NL. He then briefly umpired in the minors and did some scouting before leaving the game to work at Bruckman's Brewery in Cincinnati. Peitz retired in 1941 just two years before he died in Cincinnati of an intestinal blood clot. (DN)

Peoples, James Elsworth / "Jimmy"

B	T	HGT	WGT	G	AB	H	R	2B
?	R	5'8"	200	344	1251	264	157	38

3B	HR	RBI	BB	SO	SB	BA	SA	OBP
13	7	141	62	8	55	.211	.279	.252

G	IP	H	GS	CG	BB
2	15	30	2	1	2

SO	SH	W	L	PCT	ERA
4	0	0	2	.000	12.00

B. 10/8/1863 Big Beaver, MI **D.** 8/29/1920
TEAMS: 84–85CinA 85–88BroA 89ColA
DEBUT: 5/29/1884 at Baltimore; caught Will White and went 0-for-3 in a 2–0 loss to Baltimore's Bob Emslie
FINALE: 7/23/1889 at Columbus; caught Mark Baldwin and made 1 hit in a 9–3 loss to St. Louis's Silver King

Jimmy Peoples was remarkably fast for his size. His surprising speed, coupled with a strong arm, enabled him to play every position, including SS, where he served briefly as a regular for Cincinnati in his rookie season. He had two faults, however, that finished him as an MLer before age 26. Peoples was a chain smoker and frequently lit up on the bench during games. But what finally shortened his career was his fondness for abusing his great arm by making needlessly long or hard throws. He paid the price when it went permanently lame on him in 1889.

Peoples made his pro debut with independent Indianapolis in 1883. After observing his arm, Cincinnati AA garnered him in September and farmed him to the Shamrocks, a Queen City semipro nine, with the intention of grooming him to replace a fading Chick Fulmer at SS. But that plan was put on hold when Peoples made 4 errors in an exhibition game against his old Indianapolis teammates on September 18, 1883, and he began 1884 on the Cincinnati reserves. In late May, Peoples was summoned east to join the varsity in Baltimore when second-string catcher Phil Powers was injured. After working behind the plate in his ML debut, Peoples began to demonstrate his versatility four days later in Washington when he stood in at 3B for Hick Carpenter, who was out for the day with boils. At Pittsburgh, the Reds' last stop on their first eastern swing of the year, Peoples supplanted Fulmer at SS and kept the job until early August, when Cincinnati acquired Frank Fennelly from Washington AA. But through it all he failed to hit, posting the lowest OPS (.389) of any AA performer in 1884 with a minimum of 250 ABs.

When Peoples's stickwork continued to lag in the spring of 1885, Cincinnati let him go to Brooklyn. Even though he hit just .199 for the remainder of 1885, he led all Brooklyn catchers by a healthy margin, as the club's other six backstoppers that year weighed in with an aggregate .140 BA (42-for-300). The following season, Peoples took over the bulk of Brooklyn's catching and remained the Bridegrooms' primary receiver in 1887 despite spraining his ankle in March in a bowling alley fracas and being unable to play until late May. But he lost his job in the spring of 1888 to Doc Bushong, newly acquired from the St. Louis Browns, and became a seldom-used utilityman until receiving his release after the season.

Peoples gained a reprieve in the spring of 1889 when he tried out with the new Columbus AA franchise and proved to be the only receiver on the club that could handle Mark Baldwin's heavy fastballs. He was released in late July when his bad arm failed to heal and his throws on steal attempts consistently landed short of 2B. Peoples finished the season umpiring in the Tri-State League and was appointed to that loop's regular officiating staff the following spring. He remained an arbiter until late May when he resigned to become a player-manager for the Canton, OH, club. Ineffective in both roles, he then left baseball to return to Columbus and work as the membership chairman of the local athletic club. Soon, however, he was forced to resign after he was accused of absconding with some $260 in membership dues. Since he had also incurred many outstanding debts along Columbus's High Street, he fled east and convinced Eastern League president Pat Powers to make him a loop umpire in 1893. But officiating still was not Peoples's forte, and he again attempted a comeback the following spring, signing to manage and play 1B for Waterbury, CT. That job also was short-lived, lasting only until June when he lost the club's franchise after piling up too many unpaid bills. Peoples briefly resumed umpiring in the Western League and then went east again. In August of 1896 New York mayor William Strong appointed him a city marshal. It was to be his highest station outside of baseball, and like everything else in his itinerant and profligate life, he did not hold it for long. Peoples eventually drifted into real estate in Detroit and died there in 1920 of heart failure. (DN)

*Pierson, David P. / "Dave"

B	T	HGT	WGT	G	AB	H	R	2B
R	R	5'7"	142	57	233	55	33	4

3B	HR	RBI	BB	SO	SB	BA	SA	OBP
1	0	13	1	9	—	.236	.262	.239

G	IP	H	GS	CG	BB
1	0	2	1	0	0

SO	SH	W	L	PCT	ERA
0	0	0	1	.000	—

B. 8/20/1855 Wilkes-Barre, PA **D.** 11/11/1922
TEAMS: 76CinN
DEBUT: 4/25/1876 at Cincinnati; caught Cherokee Fisher in Cincinnati's inaugural NL game and went 0-for-4 and played errorless ball in a 2–1 win over St. Louis's George Bradley
FINALE: 9/28/1876 at Cincinnati; played RF and made 3 hits in a 10–7 loss to Boston's Foghorn Bradley

Dave Pierson would have been a capable catcher and outfielder if not for a scatter arm. He nonetheless started one game in the box, on May 13 at St. Louis, but was removed after facing just three batters and charged with the loss. After 1876 he played with numerous unaffiliated teams in the East until finding a home in the early 1880s with the Newark Domestics. Pierson became very popular in Newark, nearly too popular actually. On April 8, 1886, the Newark team chose him to umpire an exhibition game against the AA New York Mets. Pierson soon incensed the Mets by giving Newark pitcher Phenomenal Smith too many good strike calls in their estimation. Hoping to assuage the angry Mets, he then called a dubious balk on Smith that enraged the Newark team and started a near riot. Alarmed, Mets manager Jim Gifford pulled his team off the field and cancelled all future exhibition dates with Newark.

Pierson continued to be active on the New Jersey baseball scene for several more years as both a player and a promoter. In appreciation of his long service, in July of 1897 a testimonial game was held on his behalf in Newark. Pierson later worked for the Domestic Sewing Machine Company and also as a prison guard before dying in Newark of gall bladder cancer. (DN)

Powers, Philip J. / "Phil" "Grandma"

B	T	HGT	WGT	G	AB	H	R	2B
R	R	5'7"	166	155	573	103	56	12

3B	HR	RBI	BB	SO	SB	BA	SA	OBP
6	0	42	19	22	—	.180	.222	.206

B. 7/26/1854 New York, NY **D.** 12/22/1914
TEAMS: 78ChiN 80BosN 81CleN 82–85CinA 85BalA
DEBUT: 8/31/1878 at Chicago; caught Terry Larkin and went 0-for-4 in a 5–2 loss to Boston's Tommy Bond
FINALE: 8/26/1885 at New York; caught Shorty Wetzel and went 0-for-3 before being replaced by Ed Greer in an 8–2 loss to New York's Jack Lynch

Phil Powers spent some of his best seasons from 1876–78 with the strong Tecumsehs of London, Ontario, where he was the batterymate of future Chicago star Fred Goldsmith, played for the International Association's first champions in 1877, and met his wife, Mary. Over the next few years he bounced around among minor teams in the intervals between trials with several NL clubs, most notably spending much of 1880 as one of several catchers Boston tested after Charlie Snyder jumped to Washington and Lew Brown was blacklisted for drunkenness.

By 1882 Powers was back in London as player-manager, but the Tecumsehs lost money and were ripe to disband when they accepted an offer for Powers from Cincinnati. Little more than a month after coming to Cincinnati, he injured his right wrist in a collision at home plate and missed most of the rest of the season. Nevertheless, he was part of a championship campaign when Cincinnati rolled to the initial AA pennant.

A weak hitter whose .428 OPS is lower than that of any catcher in ML history with a minimum of 500 ABs, save the inimitably light hitter Bill Bergen, Powers's obits describe him as exceptionally durable, and the *New York Times* noted that in his day catchers wore no mitts, "and Powers won the title of 'Leather Fist' Powers," implying that his hands could take considerable punishment. Conversely, contemporaries thought Powers lacked the durability to work as a regular ML catcher, but his defensive skills were good enough that he provided a solid backup. When Cincinnati signed pitcher Larry McKeon from the disbanding Indianapolis club in June 1885 and took Jim Keenan simply because he had been McKeon's battery mate, an oversupply of catchers resulted in Powers's release. Club secretary Opie Caylor gave him an unusually warm sendoff and hoped that he would soon sign with an AA club so his friends in Cincinnati might see him again.

And so it happened. Powers and his batterymate Billy Mountjoy, also released, signed as a unit with Baltimore, but both were cut after just a month. The following season Powers spent some time with St. Louis AA but was released without having played a game. After a few more months in the minors, his pro career was over. During his playing years Powers had occasionally worked as an umpire, and now he made that his primary employment. Powers finished the 1886 season as a regular NL arbiter, was rehired for 1887, and continued to officiate off and on in the senior loop until August 1891. The umpire's lot was never easy in the 1880s and 1890s, but Powers seems to have had far more than his share of trouble with players, managers, and fans. Even in Cincinnati, where he had been a very popular player, he was vigorously roasted whenever he officiated.

Powers's last baseball job was as London's player-manager in 1888. By 1892 he had found humble but more peaceful employment in his native New York City, working as a messenger for the Manhattan Bureau of Buildings. Powers was still employed in that capacity when he died of pneumonia just before Christmas in 1914, survived by his wife and four daughters. (DB/DN)

Quinn, Thomas Oscar / "Tom"

B	T	HGT	WGT	G	AB	H	R	2B
R	R	5'8"	180	113	412	78	42	6

3B	HR	RBI	BB	SO	SB	BA	SA	OBP
4	2	30	36	30	8	.189	.238	.261

B. 4/25/1864 Annapolis, MD **D.** 7/24/1932
TEAMS: 86PitA 89BalA 90PitP
DEBUT: 9/2/1886 at Pittsburgh; caught Ed Morris and went 0-for-4 in a 6–2 with over Louisville's Guy Hecker

FINALE: 10/4/1890 at Pittsburgh; caught Al Maul and went 2-for-4 in a 10–6 win over Boston's Bill Daley

Tom Quinn was another rugged physical specimen who was solid behind the plate but helpless as spaghetti when he stood beside it. In 1889 he began the season 0-for-25 with Baltimore (and 0-for-29 in his career) before getting his first ML hit on May 2 at Columbus off Mark Baldwin. It is difficult to fathom why Quinn was invited to play in the elite Players League in 1890, let alone why he was allowed to transfer to Pittsburgh (his team of choice) from Brooklyn, where he was originally assigned. In honor of Quinn's hitting prowess, Pittsburgh manager Ned Hanlon generally batted him last. When the PL collapsed Quinn expected to sign with Pittsburgh NL and came to the club offices in January of 1891 to learn where matters stood. He was told not to give up his day job at the Edgar Thompson Street Works. Quinn eventually hired on with the Syracuse Eastern Association club but not before the *Pittsburgh Dispatch* printed a story that he was in the slammer for committing a murder at a picnic. In June of 1891 he sued the paper for libel after it sheepishly acknowledged that the accused was a different Quinn. Quinn later caught in the Eastern and Western leagues, finishing his pro career in 1892. By the turn of the century he owned a prosperous café in Braddock, PA. Quinn died in 1932 at his home in Pittsburgh. (DN)

Reilley, Charles Augustine (b. Charlse Augustine O'Reilley) / **"Charlie"**

B	T	HGT	WGT	G	AB	H	R	2B
R	R	5'10"	165	119	439	92	36	8

3B	HR	RBI	BB	SO	SB	BA	SA	OBP
1	0	34	3	38	—	.210	.232	.215

B. ?/?/1856 Providence, RI **D.** 11/4/1904
TEAMS: 79TroN 80CinBN 81DetN 81WorN 82ProN 84BosU
DEBUT: 5/1/1879 at Cincinnati; caught George Bradley and went 1-for-4 in a 7–5 loss to Cincinnati's Will White
FINALE: 4/26/1884 at Washington; played 3B and went 0-for-5 in a 10–6 win over Washington's Bill Wise

Charlie Reilley was born in Providence but grew up in Hartford. At age 18 he was catching for the Hartford Juniors and also the amateur Lone Stars. In the spring of 1877 he graduated from the independent Hartford Charter Oaks to Lynn of the International Association and then spent 1878 with three different IA teams. The following spring he caught Troy's first game as a member of the NL and remained on the club all season, sharing plate duty with Ed Caskin. He then played with four other NL teams over the next three seasons, failing to please any of them. Reilley finished 1882 with the independent Philadelphias and continued to play in that city until 1884, when the NL Quakers released him after he trained with them in the spring. At that point he joined the Boston Unions with hopes of making the team as a utilityman but was cut when he went hitless in each of his first 3 games. Leaving baseball in 1885 after being released by New Britain, CT, Reilley worked as a laborer and steam fitter in Providence before dying in 1904 of chronic interstitial nephritis. (DN)

Reipschlager, Charles W. / **"Charlie"**

B	T	HGT	WGT	G	AB	H	R	2B
R	R	5'6½"	160	296	1109	246	99	40

3B	HR	RBI	BB	SO	SB	BA	SA	OBP
14	0	63	34	—	9	.222	.283	.248

B. 2/7/1856 New York, NY **D.** 3/16/1910
TEAMS: 83–86NYA 87CleA
DEBUT: 5/2/1883 at Baltimore; caught Jack Lynch and was hitless in a 2–1 win over Baltimore's Bill Gallagher
FINALE: 9/6/1887 at Philadelphia; played 1B and was 2-for-4 in a 9–6 win over Philadelphia's Ed Seward

On September 28, 1960, *TSN* reported the death of Fred Strothkamp at age 96. For years Strothkamp had claimed that he had played in baseball's infant years as Ripschlager and someone had mistakenly added an *e* to his name. Strothkamp's story was that he had adopted the pseudonym because baseball was not a respectable profession in his youth and he had been called Rip as a sandlotter. Since Strothkamp was German, he had simply added *rip* to *schlager*, which is the German word for hitter. At the time of his death Strothkamp was a member of the St. Petersburg, FL, "Three Quarters of a Century Softball Club," all of whom were age 75 or older. The story was accepted as true for years because until the 1990s no one knew enough about the real Reipschlager's life to dispute it.

Reipschlager has now been documented as having died in Atlantic City in 1910. At 16 he was a member of the New York Silver Stars, the amateur champions of Manhattan Island. He played with a host of other New York amateur teams until 1876, when he joined the semipro Union club of Newark. The following year he moved to the Brooklyn Enterprise, where careless scorekeepers sometimes listed him as "Ripsticker," and also played with the Staten Island Alaskas, the Brooklyn Chelseas, and an Orange, NJ, cooperative team. Reipschlager continued his itinerant path through the minors and semipro ranks until 1882 when he accepted manager Jim Mutrie's invitation to join the League Alliance New York Mets. He accompanied the Mets when they joined the AA in 1883 and for the next four seasons shared the catching duties on the club with Bill Holbert and also had occasion to play every other position except pitcher. The better hitter of the pair, Reipschlager eventually began to see more action than Holbert, but when his BA sagged to .211 in 1886 he was sold that December to Cleveland and was the first player signed by the AA's newest replacement entry. In his final ML season he hiked his BA a point to .212 but scored just 20 runs in 63 games.

When Reipschlager fell into a substantial inheritance in July 1887 upon his mother's death and announced he might quit the game, Cleveland manager Jimmy Williams somehow restrained himself from weeping. Instead Reipschlager returned to the minors after the Blues released him, spending part of 1888 with Jersey City of the Central League. He resurfaced for a last time in the spring of 1890 when the Brooklyn Gladiators, a last-minute AA replacement team, took him to spring training along with Herman Pitz and Frank Bowes and manager Jim Kennedy let the trio battle it out for the catching job. Pitz won, Bowes was named the backup, and Kennedy released Reipschlager in May along with pitcher Jack Lynch, one of his ex-Mets batterymates. (DN)

Ryan, John Bernard / "Jack"

B	T	HGT	WGT	G	AB	H	R	2B
R	R	5'10½"	165	388	1396	315	177	54

3B	HR	RBI	BB	SO	SB	BA	SA	OBP
19	3	144	64	80	23	.226	.298	.262

B. 11/12/1868 Haverhill, MA **D.** 8/21/1952

TEAMS: 89–91LouA 94–96BosN 98BroN 99BalN 01–03StLN 12–13WasAL

DEBUT: 9/2/1889 at Baltimore; caught Mike McDermott and went 1-for-4 in a 10–2 loss to Baltimore's Matt Kilroy

FINALE AND RECORD ACHIEVEMENT: 10/4/1913 at Washington; when Ryan entered the game in the eighth inning to catch Clark Griffith and went 0-for-1 in a 10–9 win over Boston's Fred Anderson, he and Griffith formed the oldest battery in ML history, as the two were a combined 88 years and 276 days old at the time

As late as the 1980s, Jack Ryan was believed to have played every position in his ML career by dint of having been wrongly credited with pitching 1–0 shutout against Boston NL on August 4, 1902, that properly belonged to his Cardinals teammate Clarence Currie, whom he caught that day. Some eleven years later, in his final ML game, he was rightly credited with being one half of the oldest battery in ML history. In that game he also briefly caught Walter Johnson, marking him the only receiver to have worked with Johnson, the record holder in his time for the most career strikeouts, and Tom Ramsey, who will always remain the record holder for the most strikeouts in the lone season (1887) when four strikes were needed for a whiff.

Ryan played with semipro teams before joining Haverhill of the New England League in 1887. He was hitting .297 two years later with Auburn of the New York State League when he was summoned to last-place Louisville. In his official rookie year he served as the Kentucky club's regular backstop the following season when it won the first ever "Worst-to-First" pennant in ML history. Ryan again was Louisville's Opening Day catcher in 1891 but lost his job when he landed in manager Jack Chapman's doghouse after being stabbed in the leg by teammate Tim Shinnick during a scuffle with a knife. The club initially claimed the injury came under game conditions but grudgingly revealed the truth in January 1892 and released Ryan soon afterward. He went to spring training with Boston in 1893 but failed to make the club and spent the season with Springfield, MA, of the Eastern League. A second opportunity with the Hub outfit landed in his lap when Charlie Bennett lost both legs to the wheels of a train prior to the 1894 season. Ryan profited from Bennett's tragedy to play two full seasons with Boston and part of a third before rookie Marty Bergen claimed his roster spot in 1896.

After another two-year hitch in the minors, Ryan opened 1898 as Brooklyn's main receiver but hit just .189 in 87 games. Another lengthy minor league sojourn followed before he received a final opportunity to win a full-time ML job with the Cardinals in 1901. Even at age 33 his defensive skills were sharp enough that he was still on the club in 1903 despite hitting well below the Mendoza line in the previous two seasons.

Ryan finished his ML career with a .217 BA, down 9 points from his nineteenth-century mark. He later coached the baseball teams at the University of Washington and the University of Virginia and managed in the minors before serving as a coach for both the Red Sox and Senators. Ryan died in Boston at 83. (DN)

Sage, Harry / "Harry" "Doc"

B	T	HGT	WGT	G	AB	H	R	2B
R	R	5'10"	185	81	275	41	40	8

3B	HR	RBI	BB	SO	SB	BA	SA	OBP
4	2	25	29	—	10	.149	.229	.235

B. 3/1/1864 Rock Island, IL **D.** 5/27/1947
TEAMS: 90TolA
DEBUT: 4/17/1890 at Columbus; caught John Healy and was 2-for-4 in a 14–9 loss to Columbus's Hank Gastright
FINALE: 10/12/1890 at Columbus; caught Fred Smith and was 0-for-2 in an 8–0 loss to Columbus's Hank Gastright

In his lone big-league season Harry Sage generally batted last—and for good reason. He posted the worst career BA of any nineteenth-century catcher with a minimum of 300 PAs. Yet because he had a fair amount of power and plate discipline he also notched the highest RC/G ratio among all ML players with at least 300 PAs and career BAs below .160 (3.00).

Sage began his pro career in his hometown of Rock Island, IL, in 1883 and was a favorite batterymate of Nat Hudson for the better part of three seasons. After beginning a fourth season with independent Rock Island in 1886, he moved up to St. Paul, where he hit just .146 (30-for-206) against Northwestern League pitching. Sage showed little improvement with Des Moines in 1887, but in this case there were mitigating circumstances as his three-month-old daughter died in late June. After splitting 1888 between Des Moines and Kansas City of the Western Association, Sage joined Toledo of the International Association in 1889 and hit .196 in 71 games behind the plate. Doubtlessly his .149 BA came as little surprise when Toledo moved up to the AA in 1890 and met with stiffer competition.

Despite his monumental offensive shortcomings, Sage's defense skills were so good that he continued to catch in the minors until 1899, finishing where he began, with Rock Island. He then turned to both managing and umpiring in the minors before retiring from the game to work at the Rock Island Arsenal until 1921. After that he worked at various silent movie theaters in the Rock Island area until he was named stage manager of the Fort Theater, where he remained until he retired in 1941. When Sage died in 1947 after a three-month illness, he left five children and twelve great-grandchildren. (DN)

Schreck, Ossee Freeman (b. Freeman Osee Schrecongost) / "Ossee"

B	T	HGT	WGT	G	AB	H	R	2B
R	R	5'10"	180	126	465	135	62	22

3B	HR	RBI	BB	SO	SB	BA	SA	OBP
8	2	57	14	—	15	.290	.385	.315

B. 4/11/1875 New Bethlehem, PA **D.** 7/19/1914
TEAMS: 97LouN 98–99CleN 99StLN 01BosAL 02CleAL 03–08PhiAL 08ChiAL
DEBUT: 9/8/1897 at Baltimore; caught Rube Waddell and went 0-for-3 in a 5–1 loss to Baltimore's Jerry Nops
FINALE: 10/2/1908 at Cleveland; caught Ed Walsh and went 0-for-2 before he broke a finger and was replaced by Al Shaw in Addie Joss's 1–0 perfect-game victory for Cleveland

Ossee Shreck's first and last names were both mangled by the press throughout his career despite his diligent efforts to have each spelled as it appeared on his birth certificate. He made his play-for-pay debut with the independent Demorest Bicycle Boys of Williamsport, PA, in 1895 while working at the Demorest Sewing Machine Works in town. By 1897 he had made stops in four minor league towns before joining Louisville NL in September. In his initial NL game he served as the batterymate of Rube Waddell, the pitcher with whom he would eventually be linked forever in both fact and legend. Even though Shreck acquitted himself well in the contest, he was released soon afterward and finished the season with Brockton, MA, of the NEL, where teammates who found his name amusing as well as unpronounceable called him "Shrieking Ghost."

Shreck spent the latter part of 1898 in the Interstate League. At some point that season he met June Reed on a road trip to New Castle, PA. The two were married on December 5, 1899, by which time he had completed his official ML rookie season and begun playing as Schreck. In a normal year his .290 BA in 115 games split between Cleveland and St. Louis would have been worthy of notice, especially for a catcher, but 1899 was the most atypical season in history for rookies. Schreck's performance was not only greatly overshadowed; it was almost completely overlooked. When the NL dropped four teams prior to 1900, reducing jobs by a third, he was among the many quality players who were casualties, and he was forced to spend 1900 back in the minors with Buffalo of the newly renamed American League. His .282 BA in 125 games earned a contract with Boston, which was granted an AL franchise in place of Buffalo in 1901 when loop president Ban Johnson declared his enterprise was now a rival major league. (DN)

Schriver, William Frederick / "Bill" "Germany" "Pop"

B	T	HGT	WGT	G	AB	H	R	2B
R	R	5'9½"	172	750	2567	676	351	110

3B	HR	RBI	BB	SO	SB	BA	SA	OBP
37	15	354	215	118	44	.263	.352	330

B. 7/11/1865 Brooklyn, NY **D.** 12/27/1932
TEAMS: 86BroA 88–90PhiN 91–94ChiN 95NYN 97CinN 98–00PitN 01StLN
DEBUT: 4/29/1886 at Baltimore; caught Steve Toole, went 0-for-4 and committed 5 passed balls in an 11–9 loss to Baltimore's Matt Kilroy
FINALE: 10/6/1901 at Cincinnati; caught Stan Yerkes and went 1-for-3 in a 9–2 win over Cincinnati's Archie Stimmel and Crese Heisman

In 1899 *TSN* said that Bill Schriver's real name was "Schreiber," which means writer in German, and ten years earlier *SL* maintained that his Philadelphia teammates called him "Germany." If Schrieber was indeed his real surname, the evidence of it has yet to surface. Schriver grew up in the Williamsburg section of Brooklyn. When he signed with the Brooklyn AA team in 1886, he reputedly had never been west of Manhattan until he accompanied the team via train to Baltimore for its opening game of the season. After the train stopped in Newark, he reportedly jumped off, thinking they had arrived, and said, "I never knew Baltimore was so far." The problem with this story is that Schriver had played with Jersey City in the 1885 Eastern League, which also had clubs in Richmond and Washington. In any case, he botched so many balls in his Brooklyn debut that he was soon ticketed for the minors. After spending 1887 with Scranton of the International Association, he returned to the majors with Philadelphia NL in 1888 a more polished player with an excellent arm but still took too long to get rid of the ball and was victimized too often by base thieves as a result.

Schriver's defense remained a problem throughout his career. In his fifteen ML campaigns he appeared at every position except pitcher but never played in as many as 100 games in a season. The four years he spent with Chicago in the early 1890s epitomized his plight. Even though he outhit Kit Kittridge by 40 points during that span and his OPS was 111 points higher, he could never convince manager Cap Anson to do more than let him share the job with Kittridge. In 1895 Schriver's career hit bottom when the Giants, who had acquired him for free when Chicago dumped him after drafting Tim Donahue, released him in August even though he was hitting .315. But he revived in 1896 with Minneapolis when he led all Western League catchers in batting. After a year as a backup in Cincinnati to Heinie Peitz, Schriver had one final chance to win a regular job in the majors. Acquired from the Reds in a gigantic seven-player off-season trade, he opened 1898 as the Pirates' primary receiver with light-hitting Mike Bowerman his only competition but hit just .229, his career low, and by the end of the summer had lost the job to Bowerman.

Schriver remained with the Pirates until the spring of 1901. Now incredibly slow, he was released even though he could still hit because a new rule forcing a catcher to play up close to the batter even when there were no runners on base made it nearly impossible for him to chase down pop fouls hit behind him. Slated to go to Columbus of the Western Association as player-manager, he ended up with the Cardinals instead when the Columbus management made such a botch of his name that it could not get a telegram to him in time to sign him. Schriver played in the American Association with Louisville until 1905 and remained a minor leaguer as late as 1907, when he was 42 years old. He then returned to Brooklyn, where he died 25 years later. (DN)

Sellman, Charles Francis (aka Frank C. Williams) / "Frank"

B	T	HGT	WGT	G	AB	H	R	2B
?	?	5'9"	145	37	167	43	27	8

3B	HR	RBI	BB	SO	SB	BA	SA	OBP
2	1	16	4	3	3	.257	.347	.275

G	IP	H	GS	CG	BB
1	9	21	1	1	0

SO	SH	W	L	PCT	ERA
0	0	0	1	.000	8.00

B. ?/?/1852 Baltimore, MD **D.** 5/6/1907
TEAMS: 71KekNA 72OlyNA 73MarNA 74BalNA 75WasNA
DEBUT: 5/4/1871 at Fort Wayne; played RF in the first game in ML history, batted leadoff, and went 0-for-4 in a 2–0 win over Cleveland's Al Pratt
FINALE: 5/3/1875 at Washington; played 1B and went 1-for-3 in a 21–0 loss to the Athletics' Dick McBride

A Baltimore native, Frank Sellman met Bobby Mathews in 1869 while playing SS for the Marylands and later followed Mathews and numerous other Baltimoreans to Fort Wayne in the spring of 1871. Despite having played in the first ML game, for years he was a near cipher and made himself even less memorable by often playing under the name Frank Williams. Probably the most obscure player who participated in all five NA seasons, Sellman later became an umpire and in May 1882 officiated Baltimore's first series hosting Cincinnati after the AA was formed. Sellman died in Baltimore in 1907. Although he played in just 37 ML games, he appeared at every position except LF at least once and excelled at none of them. In his 18 games as a catcher, he fielded .657 and compiled the same FA in 1 less game at 3B. (DN/PM/EM)

Smith, Alexander Benjamin / "Aleck" "Broadway Aleck"

B	T	HGT	WGT	G	AB	H	R	2B
?	R	?	?	183	642	186	86	25

3B	HR	RBI	BB	SO	SB	BA	SA	OBP
11	1	96	14	—	28	.290	.368	.311

B. ?/?/1871 New York, NY **D.** 7/9/1919
TEAMS: 97–99BroN 99BalN 00BroN 01NYN 02BalAL 03BosAL 04ChiN 06NYN
DEBUT: 4/23/1897 at Washington; caught Dan Daub and Roaring Bill Kennedy and went 0-for-4 in an 8–7 win over Washington's Doc McJames and Silver King
FINALE: 10/5/1906 at New York; played 1B and made 2 hits in a 7–1 loss to Boston's "Big" Jeff Pfeffer

Surprisingly few of Aleck Smith's vital statistics are known considering that he was a high profile player for nearly a decade, most of it spent with New York–area teams. What sparse descriptions there are of him put him on the small side with a strong but erratic arm and powerful legs that he developed by spending his winters ice-skating. Despite being a teetotaler, Smith had almost every other baseball vice imaginable. A compulsive bettor on both horses and boxers, he spent most of his free days at New York racetracks wearing "razzle dazzle cravats and heavyweight diamonds" and his nights in escapades that alternately frightened and frustrated his wife, Adelaide. While playing with Brooklyn in 1900 Smith had one May Miller arrested after she robbed him of $200 at the Bath Beach Hotel in Coney Island. Miller, who specialized in snatching the wallets of her "johns" and fleeing while they were removing their trousers, had been caught in the act of lifting Smith's roll of $1,400, and it was short $200 when he wrestled it away from her.

After playing for a semipro team in Paterson, NJ, in 1893, Smith spent most of 1894 with New Bedford of the New England League. The following season he went to spring training with the Giants and was signed in late April but never played in an official NL game. Smith's ML debut had to wait until 1897 when he accompanied Billy Barnie, his manager at Hartford in 1896, to Brooklyn. He appeared in 66 games in his rookie year with the Bridegrooms, hit an even .300, and then never played as much again in any of his eight remaining ML seasons.

Smith began 1899 as Brooklyn's regular catcher but lost his job when the team acquired Duke Farrell. In July he was traded to Washington but refused to report and was subsequently sold to Baltimore, where he backed up Wilbert Robinson. In the waning weeks of the 1899 season, when Robinson was injured, Smith played regularly, was named team captain, and went on a tear, hitting .383 in 41 games with the Orioles. Rather than earn him increased duty in 1900, his hot streak resulted in a return to Brooklyn, where he rode the bench until he was farmed to Hartford of the Eastern League in late July. Smith again refused to report and also rejected an offer from Cincinnati, claiming the money was too little to induce him to leave the New York area and its many racetracks.

In his five remaining ML seasons, he played with five different teams, none for a full season, and left little mark on any of them. The 1903 Boston Americans—the first modern World Series champion—had seventeen players who played in 10 or more games. Even in Boston, precious few know Smith belongs on that select list. He died in New York of chronic endocarditis at 48. (DN)

Snyder, Charles N. / "Charlie" "Pop"

B	T	HGT	WGT	G	AB	H	R	2B
R	R	5'11½"	184	930	3643	855	433	124

3B	HR	RBI	BB	SO	SB	BA	SA	OBP
41	9	385	83	127	33	.235	.299	.254

G	W	L	PCT	PENNANTS
288	163	122	.572	1

B. 10/6/1854 Washington, D.C. **D.** 10/29/1924
TEAMS: 73WasNA 74BalNA 75PhiNA 76–77LouN 78–79BosN 81BosN (P/M)82–84CinA 87–88CleA 89CleN 90CleP (P/M)91WasA
DEBUT: 6/16/1873 at Washington; caught Bill Stearns and went 1-for-5 in a 7–6 loss to Baltimore's Candy Cummings
FINALE: 7/4/1891 at Washington; caught Buck Freeman, went 0-for-2 and committed 3 passed balls before being replaced by Deacon McGuire in an 8–7 win over Louisville's John Fitzgerald

Although listed in reference works as "Pop," Charles Snyder was known to teammates as Charlie and not dubbed Pop until his career was nearly over. He caught the underhand lobs of Bill Stearns at age 18 in his first ML game with Washington in 1873 and, in his final appearance eighteen years later, the wild lefty slants of Buck Freeman, who went on to become one of the premier hitters in the majors at the turn of the twentieth century. In addition to spanning several eras in the rapidly changing game, he both managed and umpired with distinction and was 47 when he officiated his last ML contests, a DH at the Polo Grounds on September 13, 1901.

Never much of an offensive player except against the weak competition prevailing during the earliest days of the AA, Snyder was the finest defensive catcher of the late 1870s and early 1880s. He was a master at faking a throw to catch a runner stealing 2B and then snapping the ball to nail a napping runner on 3B instead. He was also adept at making a clicking sound to fool the umpire into thinking a batter had tipped a pitch, when a caught foul tip would put out a hitter regardless of the count. Snyder was also reputedly the first man to wear a mask in a NL game after Harvard pitcher Jim Tyng had developed it. His ML record for the most career passed balls (647) reflects the length of his career and the primitive equipment used by catchers in his day rather than any lack of skill, but it speaks even more of his willingness to catch the most difficult pitchers in his time, such as Jim Devlin, Jim Whitney, Will White, and Gus Shallix.

Snyder grew up in Washington, D.C., where he broke in with the Creightons as a teammate of Joe Gerhardt. He was spotted by Nick Young and added to Young's Washington NA club in June 1873. The inexperienced Washingtons lost 31 of 39 games but featured some excellent young talent in Snyder, Gerhardt, and Paul Hines. Snyder's mature skills even at his tender age assured that he would soon move up to stronger clubs, and by 1877 he was with Louisville NL. Along with pitcher Jim Devlin and outfielder George Hall, he signed to play for St. Louis the following year, but at season's end Devlin and Hall confessed to having fixed games, a deathblow not only for their careers but for the already financially pressed Louisville and St. Louis teams. Snyder lost his lucrative contract with St. Louis and probably never recovered the $250 in back salary that Louisville owed him for his final weeks with the team. Instead he spent the next two years in Boston and then signed in 1880 with the National Association club in his native Washington. The D.C. nine that year may have been the strongest of the era outside the NL, featuring Snyder and Gerhardt as well as such fine players as Jack Lynch, Sam Trott, Mart Powell, and George Derby.

Snyder had gone to Washington in spite of being reserved by Boston at the end of the 1879 season, and one of the conditions the Bostons set for supporting a renewal of the reserve agreement in 1880 was that they be allowed to reserve Snyder again even though he was not on their roster. Accordingly, he returned grudgingly to Boston in 1881 but jumped again the following year to Cincinnati in the fledgling AA, a coup the *Cincinnati Commercial* greeted as "the best news yet given the baseball lovers in Cincinnati." Boston had lost money for five consecutive years and was slashing player salaries and cutting other expenses to the bone. Snyder reportedly did not receive his last month's pay in 1881 and no doubt was disgruntled, accounting for his deserting Boston a second time.

Snyder spent half a dozen seasons in Cincinnati, serving as team captain most of that time with the exception of a few months at the start of the 1884 season when Will White held the job. Lists of the Reds' managers during those years differ from source to source, but Snyder unquestionably ran the team on the field and carried most of the responsibilities associated with the modern manager's position. By 1886 he was beginning to show his age, and in December he and pitcher George Pechiney were sold to Cleveland's new AA team for a modest sum. In the Forest City, Snyder became team captain and the right-hand man to manager Jimmy Williams, and he enjoyed a revival as a player in 1887 as well, appearing in more games than he had since 1879 and batting a respectable .255. After he turned 33 that winter, his playing time and performance diminished sharply.

In 1891 Snyder had an unhappy experience as manager of a new AA team in Washington. When Sam Trott was fired only 12 games into the campaign, Snyder resigned as an AA umpire to take the job but found himself with the dual burden of a very weak team and an officious board of directors. His post was soon in jeopardy, as he was accused of lacking "assertiveness and force," a charge that would have surprised the many umpires he had bullied over the years. The Washington *Star* and *Post*, on the other hand, both used the same phrase to describe the team's real problem: "too many bosses." In mid-July Snyder was fired, leaving with a 23-46 record.

Snyder played in a few games for Washington in 1891, but he was merely filling in for injured regulars, and his playing career was essentially finished. Subsequently, he worked from time to time as an umpire in the NL and the minors. By 1905 he was acting as doorkeeper at the Columbia Theater in Washington but also did some scouting for the Washington Senators. He died in his hometown in 1924.

In all, Snyder was a man of large virtues and pronounced character flaws. He contributed as much as anyone to the umpire baiting that infected baseball in the last two decades of the nineteenth century. A handsome man with a dashing mustache and penetrating eyes who never married, he was a dedicated womanizer, but the vice that dominated his life was gambling. Snyder loved to bet on his own formidable pool-playing skills or on "faro, poker, the races, a craps game, in fact any sport where there is a chance to wager money," never stopping until he had no money to put up, so that he was constantly broke. A more negative account of his managerial tenure in Washington says he was axed because, not content just to gamble on his own, he promoted it among his players. As early as 1877 Nick Young wrote Boston manager Harry Wright, advising Wright not to offer Snyder a high salary because he was the kind of player "not loaded down with brains" who wanted high pay merely for the prestige, and, like other injudicious players "at the end of the season they are hard up as usual, and have little or no idea what has become of it, unless, perchance, some one has induced him to invest in a large gold watch." The letter survives and, with reason, has been taken as evidence of early club executives' condescension and contempt for their players; what is not usually recognized is that Young, Snyder's former manager, was speaking about a particular man he knew well, and accurately put a finger on his gravest weakness.

On the positive side, Snyder was a natural leader who seems to have been the glue keeping together a clique-ridden Cincinnati team in the early 1880s. The physical toughness required to catch so many years was matched by a considerable moral strength as well. When Jim Devlin was accused of game throwing, Snyder, not realizing his batterymate had already confessed, stood up for Devlin so manfully that in the tense atmosphere prevailing he himself fell under suspicion of having sold games. Years later, Snyder recalled that he had no awareness of the Louisville fixers in 1877, although in retrospect he remembered that Devlin had complained of a sore arm in key games and also that a base-path stumble by Hall had prevented the winning run from scoring in a game against Chicago. Hall moaned that he had sprained his ankle, but that night Snyder noticed Hall had no limp as he played pool with Devlin. Consequent to the Louisville scandal, Snyder later anointed himself a veritable saint in the eyes of Cincinnati club secretary Opie Caylor and baseball executives everywhere when he told Caylor a proffered raise was more money than he was worth and volunteered to give up half the extra money, telling Caylor to use it to sign a better first baseman, advice that led to Cincinnati's acquisition of John Reilly. (DB/DN)

Sommers, Joseph Andrews / "Andy" "Pete"

B	T	HGT	WGT	G	AB	H	R	2B
R	R	5'11½"	181	98	339	67	35	13

3B	HR	RBI	BB	SO	SB	BA	SA	OBP
4	3	36	16	43	8	.198	.286	.242

B. 10/26/1866 Cleveland, OH **D.** 7/22/1908
TEAMS: 87NYA 88BosN 89ChiN 89IndN 90NYN 90CleN
DEBUT: 4/27/1887 at Baltimore; caught Al Mays and went 0-for-3 in an 8–0 loss to Baltimore's Matt Kilroy
FINALE: 10/4/90 at Cleveland; caught Cy Young and went 0-for-2 in a 5–1 win over Philadelphia's Tom Vickery

We would love to know if Andy Sommers was named for the title character of Henry Fielding's 1742 novel. Born in Cleveland, he played for the Blues' reserves in 1884 before joining the Forest City's Western League entry in 1885 until the loop collapsed. Sommers then played with teams in Sandusky and Geneva, OH, before traveling to Hamilton, Ontario, of the International Association in 1886. Signed by the New York Mets that fall, he played with the AA club until his release in July 1887 and then finished the year in the Tri-State league. He spent 1888 in that same loop, hitting .342 for Lima, before being sold to Boston in September for $1,000. In March 1889 Chicago purchased Sommers from Boston for $500 to replace Tom Daly who had returned from the 1888–89 world tour badly banged up. Before the season was out, Sommers was with his fourth ML team in three seasons when he signed with Indianapolis after Chicago cut him.

After Indianapolis folded as an offshoot of the Players League threat, Sommers began 1890 with the Giants but lost his chance at a regular job when he was unable to handle fireballer Amos Rusie. By the following month Sommers was playing for unaffiliated Evansville, but he returned to the NL with Cleveland before the end of the season, putting him in a final total of six different ML uniforms even though he played just 98 games. In 1891 Sommers returned to Evansville as player-manager of its new Northwestern League entry. Later that season he joined Minneapolis of the upper-echelon Western League for a brief time, but after that he played and managed in the lower minors until 1896. Sometime around 1897 Sommers built a billiard hall on Pearl Road in suburban Cleveland and then added the first bowling emporium in that city. By the end of the century he was known as "The Father of Bowling in Cleveland." Sommers died at his Cleveland home of syphilis-related causes in 1908. (DN)

Suck, Charles Anthony / "Tony"

B	T	HGT	WGT	G	AB	H	R	2B
?	?	5'9"	164	58	205	31	21	2

3B	HR	RBI	BB	SO	SB	BA	SA	OBP
0	0	0	14	4	—	.151	.161	.205

B. 6/11/1858 Chicago, IL **D.** 1/29/1895
TEAMS: 83BufN 84Chi-PitU 84BalU
DEBUT: 8/9/1883 at Cleveland; caught Jim Galvin and went hitless in a 14–5 loss to Cleveland's Will Sawyer
FINALE: 10/15/1884 at Cincinnati; caught Al Atkinson and went 0-for-4 in a 3–2 loss to Cincinnati's George Bradley

Tony Suck caught for a string of amateur and semipro teams beginning in the late 1870s. In 1882 he batted leadoff for the semipro Chicago Green Stockings in the team's memorable 3–2 loss in fourteen innings to the independent Janesville, WI, Mutuals on July 22 at Janesville. The following year Suck was playing for pay with Fort Wayne of the Northwestern League when he was summoned to join Buffalo in Cleveland but was cut after just two games and moved to Brooklyn of the Interstate Association. Suck initially signed for 1884 with Brooklyn but was released in December when it grew evident the team would be invited to join the AA. He then went with the rebel UA's Chicago entry, where he shared catching duties with Bill Krieg until the team disbanded when it was transferred to Pittsburgh. At that point he moved to Baltimore UA for his final 3 ML games.

In 1885 Suck joined the semipro Chicago Blues, which featured Al Atkinson, the last pitcher he had caught in the majors. He remained with the Blues until the spring of 1886, when he signed with Augusta of the Southern League. No sooner had he joined Augusts than he was called home to Chicago by his wife's illness. While still in Chicago, Suck signed on with the NL White Stockings in July, specifically to catch Jim McCormick, but never appeared in an official game. That fall there was speculation that both he and the mercurial Hen Moore would play for the Kansas City Cowboys in 1887, but when the Cowboys ceded their NL franchise Suck signed to umpire in the Southern League in 1887 and then quit in August to give it another try as a player with the Memphis SL team. That winter he worked as a gravedigger in Chicago; the job convinced him that he was better off in life even as an umpire. Planning to officiate in the Southern League again, he traveled south but lost his enthusiasm for umpiring professionally when Kid Baldwin slugged him in an exhibition game in New Orleans in March 1888.

Suck again returned to Chicago, this time to stay. For the next several years he umpired summers in Chicago semipro circles and worked winters as a bartender. On January 30, 1895, the *Chicago Tribune* reported he had died at his home of pneumonia the previous day, leaving behind a wife and children. Later *TSN* related that some years prior to his death, while working as a bartender at Frank Flint's saloon on 35th Street, Suck had grown jealous of all the attention being paid to Flint's gnarled hands from his years of catching. To remind patrons that he too had once been quite a catcher, Suck hacked up his hands with a hatchet and feigned an illness so as to get time off to heal. But when he returned to the saloon and began flaunting his mangled hands, he was greeted by hoots of laughter and derision rather than the awe and sympathy he had anticipated. (DN)

Sugden, Joseph / "Joe"

B	T	HGT	WGT	G	AB	H	R	2B
B	R	5'10"	180	445	1517	413	213	44

3B	HR	RBI	BB	SO	SB	BA	SA	OBP
19	3	174	199	34	29	.272	.332	.329

B. 7/31/1870 Philadelphia, PA **D.** 6/28/1959
TEAMS: 93–97PitN 98StLN 99CleN 01ChiAL 02–05StLAL 12DetAL
DEBUT: 7/20/1893 at Chicago; caught Red Ehret and went 1-for-4 in a 9–7 win over Chicago's Willie McGill
FINALE: 5/18/1912 at Philadelphia; played 1B in the Ty Cobb Strike Game and went 1-for-3 in a 24–2 loss to Jack Coombs, Boardwalk Brown and Herb Pennock

Joe Sugden was fast for a catcher, hit fairly well, and was adequate defensively but spent most of his career as a backup or platoon player because he lacked durability. After Connie Mack took over as player-manager of the Pirates, while catching he frequently used Sugden as a runner for himself, a courtesy that teams as late as the mid-1890s routinely extended to each other when a catcher with a minor injury got on base and did not want to leave the game. Hence the likelihood is that Sugden participated in a number of games for which he did not receive credit because he never appeared either at bat or in the field.

The switch-hitting backstop came to Pittsburgh in July 1893 after his Charleston club folded along with the rest of the Southern League. He caught only 107 games in his first two and a half seasons with the Pirates before bidding for regular duty in 1896 when he hit .296 in 301 ABs. Sugden would have to wait until 1904 to get as many as 300 ABs in a season again. Nevertheless, prior to Wally Schang he held the record for the most career games caught (708) by a player who switch-hit for his entire career. Duke Farrell, still considered the earlier record holder by many, was a switch hitter only periodically.

Sugden was a coach with Detroit when he was thrust into duty in the famous 1912 "Strike Game" after having been active in the minors until 1911. He later was a longtime scout for the Cardinals but had been out of the game for a number of years when he died in Philadelphia in 1959. (DN)

Sullivan, Daniel C. / "Dan" "Link"

B	T	HGT	WGT	G	AB	H	R	2B
?	R	5'11"	198	197	786	183	86	24

3B	HR	RBI	BB	SO	SB	BA	SA	OBP
10	0	33	29	—	0	.233	.289	.262

B. 5/9/1857 Providence, RI **D.** 10/26/1893
TEAMS: 82–85LouA 85StLA 86PitA
DEBUT: 5/2/1882 at St. Louis; caught Tony Mullane and went 2-for-5 in a 9–7 loss to St. Louis's George McGinnis
FINALE: 4/18/1886 at Pittsburgh; caught Jim Galvin and went 0-for-4 in a 10–3 loss to St. Louis's Nat Hudson

Poor conditioning habits and a hair-trigger temper truncated Dan Sullivan's otherwise promising ML career. After catching for a variety of teams in the East, he joined the Albany National Association club in 1879 and received his first ML opportunity that August when Providence invited him to replace Lew Brown. Sullivan never played for the Grays, as the job instead went to Em Gross, but he made the most of his second ML opportunity in 1882 when he took command of the Louisville catching job and posted a respectable .610 OPS to go with a fielding average of .878 that was second among regular AA catchers only to Charlie Snyder. A broken finger and a severe leg injury curtailed Sullivan's duty in 1883 to just 35 games. In 1884 he caught Louisville's Opening Day win over Cincinnati and resumed service as the club's regular catcher, but his carousing and vitriolic verbal jousts with Cincinnati scribe and Reds official Opie Caylor made him a constant target in Caylor's baseball columns.

Caylor's savage attacks on Sullivan—he once wrote, "A keg of beer will catch for Louisville today"—were redoubled in 1885 by Ben Ridgley, a writer for the *Louisville Commercial.* When the local team went on a prolonged losing streak after beginning well, Ridgley laid the blame on Sullivan. Upon reading Ridgley's latest diatribe against him, Sullivan punched out the reporter the next day at the Louisville park while drunk and was released summarily by manager Jim Hart. Sullivan was a marked man in Louisville until that November when he patched up his troubles with the reporter.

After a poor performance in his initial game with Pittsburgh in April 1886, Sullivan played no more but lingered in town until his official release in early June. He then joined Savannah of the Southern League and later moved to Memphis of the same loop but was blacklisted by the Tennessee club after jumping his contract in August and returned to Pittsburgh, where he had a saloon. By 1890 Sullivan was living in Chicago and working as a scene setter at the Chicago Opera House. Two winters later he attended an NL meeting in Chicago in a last-ditch bid to land a job somewhere in baseball, but he failed to connect. Perhaps Sullivan already knew his days were numbered. On October 28, 1893, *TSN* reported that he had "taken sick at the World's Fair" and died 10 days later of consumption at his home in Providence. (DN)

Sullivan, Thomas Jefferson / "Sleeper" "Old Iron Hands"

B	T	HGT	WGT	G	AB	H	R	2B
R	R	5'7"	175	97	351	64	39	7

3B	HR	RBI	BB	SO	SB	BA	SA	OBP
4	0	15	4	21	—	.184	.228	.194

G	IP	H	GS	CG	BB
1	6	10	1	0	0

SO	SH	W	L	PCT	ERA
3	0	1	0	1.000	4.50

B. ?/?/1859 ?, Ireland **D.** 10/13/1909
TEAMS: 81BufN 82–83StLA 83LouA 84StLU
DEBUT: 5/3/1881 at Detroit; caught Jim Galvin and went 0-for-4 in a 4–2 loss to George Derby
FINALE: 5/29/84 at St. Louis; caught by Jack Brennan and pitched the first 6 innings before being relieved by Billy Taylor in his 13–8 win over Philadelphia's Sam Weaver

One of Thomas Sullivan's nicknames, "Old Iron Hands," proved to be highly ironic. He was also known as "Sleeper," stemming from an incident with his first organized team, the 1876 St. Louis Reds, one of the top independent clubs in the game. The team was run by Tom McNeary, who gave Sullivan his nickname when the Reds headed east on what was his first train trip and the 17-year-old catcher mistakenly thought the coach car was a sleeper because it was so luxurious. He told McNeary the team needn't have bought him a special sleeper berth because he was happy to sleep right where he was.

By 1879 Sullivan had moved up to the Northwestern League Dubuque team, where he made

$85 a month, the most on the club, and caught both Charley Radbourn and Billy Taylor barehanded, sparking his second colorful nickname. Sullivan remained with Dubuque in 1880 and moved to the independent Topeka Westerns after the Iowa outfit disbanded. The following year the now experienced train traveler made his ML debut with Buffalo and served all season as the Bisons' backup catcher to Jack Rowe.

Determined to live up to one of his nicknames and see more action behind the plate, Sullivan jumped to the rebel AA in 1882 and was favored to win St. Louis's first-string job. But a .181 BA in 51 games forced him to split time with rookie Ed Fusselbach. The following year Sullivan was unable to dislodge two newcomers, Tom Dolan and Pat Deasley, and was loaned to Louisville in August for ten days when the Kentucky club suffered a rash of catching injuries. Sullivan started behind the plate for the Colonels on August 10 at Cincinnati but was hurt in the third inning and played no more that season. Now regarded as overmatched at the plate and spotty behind it—in 1882 with the Browns he committed 97 passed balls in 51 games—Sullivan caught on briefly with the St. Louis Unions in the spring of 1884. His last ML appearance was an experiment to test if he could help the Maroons as a pitcher, and he failed to impress, though he staggered to a victory that Billy Taylor saved for him.

Sullivan harbored hopes of playing again in the majors until early January 1886, when he "met with an accident" while out on a bitter cold night and froze both hands. Initially, he had the fingers of his right hand amputated, and John Magner later held a benefit game for him in St. Louis on May 2, 1886. Sullivan subsequently needed further surgery. In November 1891 *TSN* wrote that he had had his once iron hands amputated, leaving him "to show nothing for them now but a pair of stumps." In later life Sullivan worked as a night watchman at St. Louis's South Side Park. He died at 50 in St. Louis. (DN)

#Sullivan, William Joseph / "Billy"

B	T	HGT	WGT	G	AB	H	R	2B
R	R	5'9"	155	94	312	85	46	8

3B	HR	RBI	BB	SO	SB	BA	SA	OBP
0	10	53	10	—	6	.272	.394	.304

B. 2/1/1875 Oakland, WI **D.** 1/28/1865
TEAMS: 99–00BosN 01–12ChiAL 14ChiAL 16DetAL
DEBUT: 9/13/1899 at Boston; caught Ted Lewis and went 0-for-3 in a 6–3 win over St. Louis's Cy Young
FINALE: 4/15/1916 at Chicago; replaced Oscar Stanage at catcher and was later replaced by Del Baker after George Burns pinch hit for him in the eighth inning of a 9–4 loss to Chicago's Eddie Cicotte and Reb Russell
FAMOUS FIRST: 4/24/1901 at Chicago; caught the first game in American League history, Roy Patterson's 8–2 win over Cleveland.

Billy Sullivan played SS at Fort Atkinson High School in Oakland, WI, until a leg injury forced him to move behind the plate. He remained there the rest of his career. After playing with an independent team in Edgewater, WI, in 1895, he appeared briefly in the Wisconsin State League the following year before moving to Cedar Rapids of the Western Association. Sullivan remained in that loop in 1897 when he joined Dubuque, IA, where he fell in with an venturesome group of teammates led by Peck Sharp, Bill Baer, Joe Cantillon, Joe Nonnemaker, and Gus Dundon that bought a houseboat for $100, dubbed it "Tom Loftus" after the longtime manager, and used the vessel for extended hunting and fishing expeditions in the Midwest. As luck would have it, Sullivan was purchased that fall by Loftus and in 1898 played for Loftus's Columbus club in the Western League. The following season he left Loftus's command when Columbus was transferred to Grand Rapids and George Tebeau took over as player-manager.

In September 1899 Boston bought Sullivan from Tebeau for $1,000 and the loan of outfielder Charlie Frisbee for 1900. Expected to be no more than a backup to Marty Bergen, Sullivan caught 22 games in the closing weeks of the season after Bergen was injured. That winter Bergen's tragic suicide provided Sullivan with an opportunity to become Boston's regular catcher, but he was not yet the defensive equal of Boileryard Clarke, and the pair shared the job. However, Sullivan led all NL catchers in home runs with 8 and hit a solid .273. After his first season and a fraction in the majors he gave every appearance of materializing into one of the best-hitting catchers in the game.

Boston, meanwhile, was powerless to stop its promising young receiver from jumping to the rebel American League. When Sullivan had joined the

Beaneaters in 1899, he had signed an agreement only to finish the season with Boston. That fall he had refused to sign a contract for 1900 and had played the entire 1900 season without one, entitling him to go wherever he pleased as the new century began. (DN)

Tate, Edward Christopher / "Eddie" "Pop" "Dimples" "Jumbo"

B	T	HGT	WGT	G	AB	H	R	2B
R	L	5'10"	200	227	822	179	101	22

3B	HR	RBI	BB	SO	SB	BA	SA	OBP
9	2	71	41	73	17	.218	.274	.269

B. 12/22/1860 Richmond, VA **D.** 6/25/1932
TEAMS: 85–88BosN 89–90BalA
DEBUT: 9/26/1885 at St. Louis; caught Charlie Buffinton and went 0-for-2 in a 5–2 win over St. Louis's John Healy.
FINALE: 10/15/1890 at Baltimore; caught Sadie McMahon and went 1-for-3 in a 9–5 win over Rochester's Bob Miller and Jack Grim

Eddie Tate was called "Pop" toward the end of his career but was known throughout the greater part of it as "Eddie," "Dimples," and "Jumbo" depending on his size at the time. In 1885 the left-handed catcher was still lean and wiry, fast enough to bat leadoff on occasion for the Virginias of the Eastern League, and was referred to as Eddie Tate when he joined Boston near the close of the NL season. In his debut he failed to distinguish himself but stuck with the Hub team the following spring because captain John Morrill, a former catcher turned first baseman, had a unique philosophy for his time. In addition to his putative regular, Con Daily, Morrill kept three backup receivers and used them all in a rotation depending on the pitcher on a given day with the result that, unlike most teams in 1886, Boston got a full nine innings out of its catchers because each worked only after his hands were well rested. Too, Morrill, who had won a pennant at the Boston helm in 1883 with two left-handed receivers, was among the few captains left in the game that bore no prejudice as yet against southpaw backstops.

In his official rookie season Tate was second only to Daily in catching time, and the two retained the same status in 1887. That winter Tate was handed a raise from $1,750 to $2,000 but had his playing time cut by almost 50 percent and ended his NL career on a sour note when he was injured by a foul tip in his final appearance with Boston on October 13 and had to be replaced by Mike Kelly. The following year Baltimore AA manager Billy Barnie borrowed a page from Morrill's playbook and hired four catchers, with Tate at the bottom of the list. Though he batted just .182, he eventually moved to the head of the rotation, primarily because none of Barnie's other three receivers could hit either. In 1890 when Baltimore abandoned the AA, Tate accompanied the Orioles to the Atlantic Association and remained on the team when it returned to the AA after the Brooklyn franchise folded. By then arm trouble and a disturbing weight gain had made him primarily a first baseman.

In 1891, Tate, now called Dimples, signed with Lebanon, PA, of the Eastern Association for lack of a better offer and then refused to report to the small market minor league club until threatened with being blacklisted. He finished the season in New Haven and then gravitated back to his hometown in 1892. Called the "adipose catcher" in the Richmond press, he now weighed well over two-hundred pounds and was stationed at 1B with the locals. Dropped at the end of the year by the Virginia League club, he ran his cigar business in Richmond the following season and captained an independent team in town called the Giants, perhaps in his honor, for he was reportedly "as big now as a prize pig at a country fair."

Evidently, at that point Tate began to exploit his ample weight. He resumed playing in the Virginia League, where everyone now called him "Jumbo," got married, and in 1895 reached his career apex when he topped the VL in batting with a .412 mark. Tate repeated as loop bat titlist in 1896 and then began to run out of steam. In 1897 he drew his release first from Norfolk and later from Sunbury of the lowly Central Pennsylvania League, but it was still not quite the end of the road. Two springs later the *Washington Post* announced that "Old Pop Tate" had signed with Allentown. In his sixteen-year pro career to that point, it was just about the first time he was called Pop. At the time of his death in Richmond from a heart attack in 1932, Tate's weight was unknown. His last reported job was as a bailiff at the Richmond City Police Court. (DN)

Townsend, George Hodgson / "George" "Sleepy"

B	T	HGT	WGT	G	AB	H	R	2B
R	R	5'7½"	180	152	541	101	60	18

3B	HR	RBI	BB	SO	SB	BA	SA	OBP
5	0	53	31	21	16	.187	.238	.239

B. 6/4/1867 Hartsdale, NY **D.** 3/15/1930
TEAMS: 87–88PhiA 90–91BalA
DEBUT: 6/25/1887 at Baltimore; caught Al Atkinson and went 1-for-4 in an 8–5 loss to Baltimore's Phenomenal Smith
FINALE AND FAMOUS LAST: 10/6/1891 at Washington; in the final game in AA history caught Kid Madden in a 15–11 win over Washington's Frank Foreman

On the final day of his ML career, George Townsend not only caught in the last official AA game before the loop disbanded, but he also caught Sadie McMahon's league-leading thirty-sixth win in the first game of a DH. Only 24 at the time, he seemingly was squeezed out of a job when the AA and NL merged due to an utter inability to hit—he ranks eighth on the nineteenth-century list of lowest OPS figures by position players with a minimum of 500 career ABs (.477). But there were other factors as well. Although Townsend had a great arm—*SL* once observed that "his throwing is like lubricated lightning"—but unfortunately he was also notorious for being able to sleep anywhere at any time. Some pitchers loved working with Townsend because he could handle with ease even the swiftest deliveries, but his detractors scoffed that he missed few swifties only because he was too slow and lazy to get out of their way.

In 1888, his second ML season, Townsend received much of the blame for the Philadelphia A's failure to make a stronger run at the AA pennant. His .155 BA as the chief backup to regular receiver Wilbur Robinson was the least of his problems. Team observers faulted manager Billy Sharsig for pairing Townsend with Gus Weyhing while Robinson caught the A's co-ace, Ed Seward. It was felt that Weyhing had a relatively poor year in 1888 because he feared runners would steal at will on Townsend ("Townsend's sleepy movements and indifferent throwing is enough to make even a more flighty man than Weyhing erratic") and became too preoccupied with base runners to focus on hitters.

Townsend came to the A's midway through 1887 after beginning the season with Reading of the Pennsylvania League before being acquired by the Orioles, for whom he never played that year. His rise had been swift—in 1886 he had played with Newburg, NY, in the lowly Hudson River League—and his descent was nearly as swift. After spending 1889 playing semipro ball, he returned to Baltimore in 1890 after it left the AA and enlisted in the minor league Atlantic Association. When the Orioles rejoined the AA, replacing disbanded Brooklyn, Townsend shared the receiving and also was pressed into service as an umpire on occasion. Billy Barnie reportedly respected not only the catcher's loyalty but also his intelligence. If Townsend appeared lazy at times on the field, he was industrious in all other respects. Upon leaving the majors, he spent the 1892 season in the Eastern League while studying dentistry in Philadelphia and later switched to medicine at Hillsdale College. Townsend died in New Haven in 1930 after practicing medicine for some years in nearby Brandford, CT. (DN)

*Traffley, William Franklin / "Bill"

B	T	HGT	WGT	G	AB	H	R	2B
R	R	5'7"	170	179	663	116	85	13

3B	HR	RBI	BB	SO	SB	BA	SA	OBP
12	1	36	34	1	8	.175	.235	.220

B. 12/21/1859 Staten Island, NY **D.** 6/23/1908
TEAMS: 78ChiN 83CinA 84–86BalA
DEBUT: 7/27/1878 at Chicago; caught Terry Larkin and went 1-for-4 in a 4–3 loss to Indianapolis's "The Only" Nolan
FINALE: 7/29/1886 at Baltimore; caught Hardie Henderson and went 0-for-2 in a 6–0 loss to Louisville's Tom Ramsey

The brother of John Traffley, a one-game MLer, Bill Traffley was noted for being a consummate team player. A skilled bunter, he sacrificed selflessly when a sacrifice was still counted as a time at-bat, and he was an excellent base runner, especially for a catcher, at least early in his career. In his later years his inability to push himself away from the table caught up to him; Traffley was reputedly pitcher Ed Crane's closest rival for the title of the most prodigious eater in the game and could routinely down three steaks at a sitting. But from the first day he played to the last, the same weakness prevailed. Traffley simply could not get on base often enough to take full advantage of his exceptional ability to advance himself on the rare occasions when he did.

Traffley played on Chicago amateur clubs before catching 2 games for the NL White Stockings in 1878 while Bill Harbidge was injured. He then played five seasons with the unaffiliated Omaha Union Pacifics while working as a railroader for the Union Pacific company. In 1883 Traffley joined Cincinnati as Ren Deagle's personal catcher and appeared in only 30 games. Skipping to Baltimore after Cincinnati was guilty of a contract-signing faux pas, he caught 108 games for the Orioles over the next two seasons but hit just .164.

After leaving Baltimore in 1886, Traffley played and managed in the minors until the late 1890s. For a time he ran a poultry farm during the winter, and he later worked as a sewer inspector. Traffley was especially popular in Des Moines, where he operated successful minor league clubs at two separate junctures, first in the late 1880s and then in the mid-1890s upon returning from an 1892 stint as the player-manager of the Deadwood, SD, team in the Black Hills League. His last post was as player-manager of the 1898 Hartford Atlantic League club. Traffley died in Des Moines in 1908 of tuberculosis after working for several years as a brakeman on a gravel train. (DN/DB)

Trott, Samuel W. / "Sam" "Babe"

B	T	HGT	WGT	G	AB	H	R	2B
L	L	5'9"	190	360	1354	338	166	73

3B	HR	RBI	BB	SO	SB	BA	SA	OBP
22	3	123	54	44	9	.250	.343	.280

G	W	L	PCT	PENNANTS
12	4	7	.364	0

B. 3/?/1859 Washington, D.C. **D.** 6/5/1925
TEAMS: 80BosN 81–83DetN 84–85BalA 87–88BalA (M)91WasA
DEBUT: 5/29/1880 at Boston; caught Tommy Bond and went 0-for-2 before being injured and replaced by Phil Powers in an 11–10 win over Chicago's Larry Corcoran
FINALE: 7/28/1888 at Cleveland; caught Bert Cunningham and went 1-for-2 before being injured and replaced by Chris Fulmer in an 11–7 loss to Cleveland's Cinders O'Brien

Sam Trott was probably the finest left-handed catcher in ML history except for Jack Clements and was Clements's superior defensively. He was also a good base runner and hit with moderate power. His gravest flaw was being injury prone—witness both his first and his last ML games. At age 15 Trott was already catching for the independent Washington Nationals. With time out in 1876 to play for unaffiliated Mansfield, OH, and in 1877 to catch for the independent Philadelphia Athletics, Minneapolis, and the Fairbanks club of Chicago, where he handled Laurie Reis, he remained with the Nationals until May 1880, when Boston purchased him for an undisclosed sum. After Trott stumbled with the Hub team, hitting just .206 and allowing 25 passed balls in 39 appearances, he was not reserved for 1881 and returned to the Nationals, by then a member of the Eastern Championship Association. Injuries and lax play led to his release, after which he joined Albany and then came to Detroit in September in time to catch 6 games.

Trott remained with the Wolverines in 1883, playing a fair amount at 2B in addition to backing up regular receiver Charlie Bennett. After some confusion as to whether Detroit would retain him, he was allowed to move to Baltimore in 1884, served as the Orioles' Opening Day receiver, and led all AA catchers in both put-outs and double plays. In the spring of 1885 he injured his throwing arm, leading to his release. Later that season, after his arm healed, he rejoined the Eastern League Washington Nationals for his fourth stint with the team. In 1886 he played for Newark of the Eastern League, but the following year found him back with the Orioles, where he replaced Chris Fulmer as the club's top receiver. Fulmer complained that manager Billy Barnie favored Trott solely because the two were partners in a local roller-skating rink, but the reality was that the southpaw receiver was the better all-around player. Nevertheless, Barnie released one of the game's best roller skaters on July 31, 1888, ostensibly because the Orioles had too many catchers and were losing money, but later it emerged that Trott's arm was shot.

A Baltimore writer bid the left-handed receiver this fond farewell: "He is way above average in education and native intelligence, and requires absolutely no looking after whatsoever in the way of discipline." Trott spent most of 1890 managing Newark (by then in the Atlantic Association) and playing occasionally and then signed to pilot Washington AA in 1891 after his brother Charles was made a director of the club. He lasted scarcely two weeks, leaving after only 12 games. The club's owners reported that Trott had quit, but he claimed otherwise and in January 1892 accepted $125 in lieu of bringing suit for the salary he said was still owed him from 1891. Trott then went into the cigar business in Baltimore and maintained interests in local roller rinks. By the turn of the century he was back in Washington, working as a contracting carpenter. Though no longer actively involved in the game, he kept up a close friendship with evangelist and former player Billy Sunday and was also an avid supporter of Jack Dunn's Baltimore International League dynasty in the early 1920s. A longtime asthma sufferer, he died in 1925 of a heart attack in Baltimore. (DN/DB)

Vaughn, Henry Francis / "Harry" "Farmer" "Zeke"

B	T	HGT	WGT	G	AB	H	R	2B
R	R	6'3"	177	915	3454	946	474	147

3B	HR	RBI	BB	SO	SB	BA	SA	OBP
53	21	525	151	128	92	.274	.365	.307

G	IP	H	GS	CG	BB
1	7	12	0	0	1

SO	SH	W	L	PCT	ERA
0	0	0	0	—	3.86

B. 3/1/1864 Ruraldale, OH **D.** 2/21/1914
TEAMS: 86CinA 88–89LouA 90NYP 91CinA 91MilA 92–99CinN
DEBUT: 10/7/1886 at Cincinnati; caught Bill Irwin and went 0-for-3 in a 9–4 loss to New York's John Shaffer
FINALE: 7/15/1899 at Philadelphia; caught Jack Taylor and Ted Breitenstein and went 0-for-4 in a 4–2 loss to Philadelphia's Bill Magee

Harry Vaughn was said to bear a strong resemblance to the fighter Jake Kilrain and to own one of the champion throwing arms of his time. He often boasted that he had beaten Ed Crane, another great thrower, in every contest the two had undertaken. If his bragging were not enough to make him somewhat overbearing, Vaughn also fancied himself a comic and exasperated teammates by conducting his lame version of snappy patter with spectators during games. Yet he spent thirteen years in the majors, primarily with Cincinnati, as a catcher and utility player known not only for his arm but his defensive versatility. Primarily called Harry, he was also known pejoratively as "Zeke" and "Farmer".

Born near Columbus, Vaughn grew up in southwestern Ohio and entered pro ball in the mid-1880s. In the fall of 1886 he received a trial with Cincinnati along with Bill Irwin, his batterymate at Lebanon, OH, in the Blue Grass League. Vaughn failed to stick with the Reds and wound up in the Southern League, where he caught John Ewing, the brother of catcher Buck Ewing. On June 25, 1888, Louisville purchased the pair from Memphis as a package. At Louisville, Vaughn found himself with a cash-starved team in free fall toward the bottom of the AA standings. In 1889 he suffered through a 26-game losing streak and experienced the Colonels' revolt against slow salary payment and fines imposed by hard-pressed owner Mordecai Davidson. After the season Vaughn jumped along with John Ewing to New York PL, where he played sparingly as a backup to Buck Ewing. After the PL folded, Vaughn was assigned to a new team hurriedly organized by the AA in Cincinnati, where he again backed up a future Hall of Famer, Mike Kelly. When the Cincinnati team disbanded, Vaughn went to Milwaukee, which replaced Cincinnati in the AA and then disbanded in its turn.

The NL and AA merger into one twelve-club league significantly tightened the job market, and Vaughn was one of a number of veteran players left homeless in 1892 until May when he caught on with the Cincinnati Reds, which had just suspended catcher Jerry Harrington. He wound up splitting the catching job with Morg Murphy and then remained with the Reds for nearly eight years. In 1897 he began the season as the regular first baseman but was replaced by Jake Beckley in late May. At the last, with his BA having fallen off from .305 in 1898 to .176, he was released in July 1899. He continued during the next several years as a minor leaguer and in 1904 became a player-manager at Birmingham, where he won a Southern Association pennant before being discharged during the 1908 season. Following an unsuccessful appeal to baseball's National Board for his full year's salary, he retired from baseball.

Vaughn could be a rough customer. In 1887 he was arrested in New Orleans after a drunken altercation with a prostitute named Emma Conrad, who jumped out a second-story window to escape his antics, and in 1898 he punched umpire Ed Swartwood following a game but remarkably was not punished because the NL's disciplinary provisions as yet did not allow for the punishment of players for actions away from the playing field. Vaughn's wife sued him for divorce two years later, claiming he had been abusive and threatened to kill her, and in 1902 he shot the proprietor of a Peoria hotel in the hand during an argument over attentions Vaughn had been paying the man's stepdaughter. Yet he also seems to have been a man of some substance, business, and executive ability, as his successful tenure as Birmingham's manager demonstrates. While with the Reds, Vaughn began dealing in tobacco, and after his departure from Birmingham he opened the W and V café and hotel in downtown Cincinnati with his nephew, Reds outfielder Sam Woodruff. Prior to his death in Cincinnati from pneumonia, he accumulated an estate of $5,000, a fairly substantial sum for the time.

Modern sources list Vaughn as 197 pounds, but that is probably his weight at a relatively early age, for he was a champion eater, even by baseball standards, and his weight began to rise dramatically as he reached early middle age, probably affecting his health. He died of pneumonia at his home in 1914 after what was said to have been an illness of a few days, but Cincinnati sportswriter Ren Mulford wrote that his health had actually been so tenuous for some time that his death came as no surprise. Along with Jim Keenan, another former Cincinnati catcher turned saloonkeeper, Vaughn had lost his liquor license after a recent change in the method of licensing, a particularly heavy blow, as he had no other occupational prospects. (DB/DN)

Warner, John Joseph / "Jack"

B	T	HGT	WGT	G	AB	H	R	2B
L	R	5'11"	165	445	1577	412	183	44

3B	HR	RBI	BB	SO	SB	BA	SA	OBP
15	4	193	121	33	61	.261	.306	.324

B. 8/15/1872 New York, NY **D.** 12/21/1943
TEAMS: 95BosN 95–96LouN 96–01NYN 02BosAL 03–04NYN 05StLN 05–06DetAL 06–08WasAL
DEBUT: 4/23/1895 at Washington; caught Zeke Wilson and went 0-for-3 in a 4–1 loss to Washington's Al Maul
FINALE: 9/30/1908 at Detroit; pinch hit unsuccessfully in the 9th inning for Gabby Street in a 7–5 loss to Detroit's Bill Donovan and George Mullin

Jack Warner was the only receiver to catch both Amos Rusie and Walter Johnson in ML action. He had an excellent arm, worked well with even the most difficult pitching types, and was a good enough batsman to be used as a pinch hitter on occasion. In 1897 he appeared to be on the brink of emerging as one of the NL's premier catchers. Yet he never again played in as many as 100 games after 1898 or had as many as 300 ABs in a season. Some of the explanation probably lies in his disposition. Crabby, surly, and sullen, Warner was the victim in Louisville of a clique called "the Galt House trio" that declared war on him and was also labeled a "knocker" by manager Bill McGunnigle. It is almost certainly not a coincidence that the only team he ever lasted with for any length of time was the Giants, which always had more than their share of prickly and ill-tempered players.

Warner was discovered on the Brooklyn sandlots by pitcher George Meakim, who brought the catcher with him in 1894 to Wilkes-Barre of the Eastern League. Under manager Dan Shannon's grooming, Warner soon replaced Fred Lake as the club's top receiver and was drafted by Boston for $500 after he worked 107 regular-season games and another 3 postseason exhibitions against the Hub team. Early in the 1895 season Beaneaters manager Frank Selee released Warner to Louisville when he decided Jack Ryan was the better catcher. Warner played well enough as a rookie to claim the regular Louisville backstopping job in 1896 but only until McGunnigle found him a discordant force. The Giants then became Warner's third ML stop in less than two seasons and, except for 1902 when he misguidedly jumped to the AL, he remained with the Gotham club long enough to share in its first pennant under John McGraw.

Warner appears to have gotten on well with McGraw, no easy feat, but even more impressively, he was also one of the few team members whom Giants owner Andrew Freedman seemed to fancy. On July 31, 1900, he fractured his left elbow chasing a pop foul into the railing of the stands behind home plate, putting him out for the season. The flint-hearted Freedman assured Warner he would be paid his regular salary for the rest of 1900 and also for the 1901 campaign as well if he still could not return.

Warner finished his pro career in 1912 with independent Poughkeepsie. He then coached at Fordham University for a while and umpired in the International League. His last job prior to his death in Queens, NY, was as a New York City cab driver. (DN)

Wilson, Parke Asel / "Parke"

B	T	HGT	WGT	G	AB	H	R	2B
R	R	5'11"	166	370	1280	339	194	37

3B	HR	RBI	BB	SO	SB	BA	SA	OBP
15	3	173	107	45	56	.265	.324	.326

B. 10/26/1867 Keithsburg, IL **D.** 12/20/1934
TEAMS: 93–99NYN
DEBUT: 7/19/1893 at New York; caught Les German and went 2-for-4 in a 12–6 loss to Boston's Hank Gastright
FINALE: 10/14/1899 at New York; caught Charlie Gettig and went 2-for-4 in a 12–9 loss to Washington's Dan McFarlan

In his seven ML seasons, all spent with the Giants, Parke Wilson was a regular only for short stretches but was an excellent backup catcher and a valuable utilityman. He made his pro debut in the Colorado State League in 1889 with Colorado Springs after previously playing amateur ball in Denver. The following year he graduated to the Denver Western Association club and by 1893 had moved to Augusta of the Southern League along with pitcher Les German, whom he caught in his ML debut. Praised immediately by the local press ("Wilson, New York's catcher, is showing up strongly"), he continued to do well and caught Mark Baldwin in Baldwin's ML finale and the Giants' final game in 1893.

In 1894 Wilson hit well in a backup role and scored 35 runs in 49 games while Duke Farrell, the Giants' first-string receiver, tallied only 47 times in 114 contests. That winter, Giants ace Amos Rusie publicly stated that he preferred having Wilson behind the plate when he pitched, resulting in Wilson getting more work in 1895. The following season he seemed on the verge of wresting the regular job away from Farrell but hit poorly and logged just a .245 SA when his 60 hits earned only 62 total bases. Despite lifting his BA to .299 in 1897, 1898 was a lost year for Wilson. After his brother Claude was killed in a bar fight in Kansas City that January, Wilson and pitcher Mike Sullivan were sold as a package to KC in April. When Wilson was recalled late in the season by the simple expedient of refunding the Western League club's $500 purchase money, it strongly suggested that he had actually been loaned to KC.

The 1899 season, Wilson's last in the majors, was the closest he came to regular duty. He appeared in 97 games at six different positions and played all of them competently. After spending that winter working in the grocery store he co-owned with Bill Everitt in the Five Points section of Denver, he went to camp with the Giants expecting to vie with Mike Bowerman and Jack Warner for full-time plate duty. Instead he ended up with Kansas City in the newly renamed American League after failing to mesh with the team's new manager, Buck Ewing. Wilson finished his active pro career in 1906 Pacific Coast League. He was living in Hermosa Beach, CA, in 1934 when he died after a short illness, leaving a wife and five children. (DN)

Yeager, George J. / "George" "Doc"

B	T	HGT	WGT	G	AB	H	R	2B
R	R	5'10"	190	103	329	84	59	25

3B	HR	RBI	BB	SO	SB	BA	SA	OBP
6	5	73	45	1	7	.255	.371	.290

B. 6/4/1873 Cincinnati, OH **D.** 7/5/1940
TEAMS: 96–99BosN 01CleAL 01PitN 02NYN 02BalAL
DEBUT: 9/25/1896 at Washington; played 1B and went 1-for-3 in a 6–3 win over Washington's Doc McJames
FINALE: 8/5/1902 at St. Louis; replaced Aleck Smith behind the bat and was 0-for-1 in an 8–7 loss to St. Louis's Jack Harper

An extreme extrovert who yammered unremittingly about himself, George Yeager at times was far from an idle boaster. In 1893, while playing with an independent club in Celina, OH, he earned the nickname "Home Run" for his long-ball exploits. Though his natural position was catcher owing to his durability, he fancied himself a better infielder and especially liked to play both keystone positions barehanded. After splitting 1894 between Celina and the New England League, Yeager let his inflated sense of his worth cost him a job with Ted Sullivan's Atlanta team in the Southern League the following spring. Returning to the NEL, he became strictly a catcher and a first baseman.

Yeager received a late-season trial in Boston in 1896 after clubbing 24 homers with Pawtucket to pace the NEL. Frank Selee saw enough promise in him to install him as the chief backup to both catcher Marty Bergen and first baseman Fred Tenney. A hand injury curtailed Yeager's season in 1897, but he rebounded to play in more than half of Boston's games the following year. Boileryard Clarke's acquisition prior to the 1899 season made Yeager expendable, and he spent most of that year with Worcester of the Eastern League. He remained in the minors in 1900 with Milwaukee of the newly renamed American League and considered leaving baseball when he helped patent a new water filter that *TSN* contended "will be the means of putting George on easy street." His interest in the game was replenished, however, when the AL went major in 1901 and Cleveland offered him a contract.

Toward the end of the 1901 season Yeager was let go to Pittsburgh, the NL front-runner, in time to help the Pirates celebrate their first pennant. He remained in the senior loop in 1902 as a backup with the Giants until a series of machinations instigated by John McGraw and John T. Brush resulted in a swarm of quasi-legal player transactions between the Giants and McGraw's former Baltimore club that brought the utilityman to the Orioles for his final ML innings. Yeager spent most of the rest of his pro playing career in the American Association, remaining a valuable backup receiver until he was in his late thirties. His misfortune seems to have been spending his prime years with talent-rich Boston, with whom his skills, particularly as a hitter, grew rusty rather than flourish. Yeager later worked as a railroad-switch tender and died of a stroke in Cincinnati, leaving behind his wife, Tillie. (DN)

Zearfoss, David William Tilden / "Dave"

B	T	HGT	WGT	G	AB	H	R	2B
?	R	5'9"	174	25	71	17	6	3

3B	HR	RBI	BB	SO	SB	BA	SA	OBP
3	0	17	9	5	2	.239	.310	.279

B. 1/1/1868 Schenectady, NY **D.** 9/12/1945
TEAMS: 96–98NYN 04–05StLN
DEBUT: 4/16/1896 at Washington; caught Dad Clarke and went 1-for-4 in a 6–3 loss to Washington's Win Mercer
FINALE: 7/8/1905 at Cincinnati; caught Jake Thielman and went hitless in a 6–3 win over Cincinnati's Jack Harper

Dave Zearfoss graduated from Washington College in Chesterton, MD, and was discovered playing for an independent team in Dover, DE, at age 27. Only someone like Arthur Irwin, the Giants' new manager in 1896, would make a player in his late twenties without any minor league experience his Opening Day catcher. Zearfoss immediately staked a claim to being the first receiver to wear overt shin guards—one anyway—in a ML game when he appeared on the field in Washington with a cricket shield on his left leg to avert being spiked in plays at home plate. He eventually was farmed to the Atlantic League when he failed to hit but remained Giants property until he was released in July 1898. Zearfoss then played for Minneapolis and Toronto before trying his luck out West.

After finishing the 1900 season in the Montana State league, Zearfoss served as Tacoma's leadoff hitter in the spring of 1901 until he broke his thumb prior to the start of the Pacific Northwest League season, leaving manager John McCloskey temporarily without a catcher. Zearfoss returned east to Kansas City for a while before McCloskey, who by then was managing the San Francisco Pirates in the Pacific National League, lured him back to the West Coast. Near the close of the 1903 season Zearfoss refused to join Brooklyn even though he was living in Newark, NJ, at the time because he felt the travel expenses would be too steep. That fall he dickered with Pittsburgh before signing with St. Louis NL as a backup to Mike Grady. Thirty-seven when he left the Cardinals, he remained active until 1907, when he quit Franklin, PA, of the Interstate League, after hitting .217 in 82 games and then managed in the minors for a spell before taking a job with the Delaware Power and Light Company. Zearfoss retired in 1939 and died in a Wilmington hospital six years later after a lengthy illness. (DN)

Zimmer, Charles Louis / "Chief"

B	T	HGT	WGT	G	AB	H	R	2B
R	R	6'0"	190	1132	4050	1109	578	208

3B	HR	RBI	BB	SO	SB	BA	SA	OBP
70	25	578	350	323	138	.274	.378	.343

B. 11/23/1860 Marietta, OH **D.** 8/22/1949
TEAMS: 84DetN 86NYA 87–88CleA 89–99CleN 99LouN 00–02PitN (P/M)03PhiN
DEBUT: 7/18/1884 at Cleveland; caught Frank Brill, batted cleanup and went 0-for-3 in an 11–2 loss to Cleveland's Jack Harkins
FINALE: 9/27/1903 at Pittsburgh; caught Chick Fraser and was hitless in a 6–3 win over St. Louis's Pat Hynes
CAREER HIGHLIGHT ONE: In 1890 set a new NL record when he caught 125 games, including a then season record 107 games in a row from 4/19/1890 through 9/2/1890 before family illness intervened
CAREER HIGHLIGHT TWO: In 1902 became the first man to catch 100 ML games after age 40

Chief Zimmer may have had the most durable and deft hands of any catcher in ML history. He boasted that in twenty years of pro play he had never suffered a finger injury and in 1893 was dexterous enough to assemble an intricate parlor baseball game with a ball pitched from 2B and an iron stick two inches long for a bat that was a forerunner of penny arcade games popular as late as the 1950s. While other catchers of his day were unable to pursue off-season trades that required the efficient use of their hands, Zimmer also made most of his family's furniture. Arguably the best defensive catcher in the 1890s, he was likewise among the better hitters at the position once he overcame a tendency to go into a defensive crouch at the plate against speedballers like Amos Rusie, preventing himself from taking a full swing.

In 1882 Zimmer was working in an Ironton, OH, tin shop for $15 a week when he took a $5 a week pay cut to play for the local semipro team. The gamble paid off although it took a long while. Zimmer played for independent Portsmouth, OH, in 1883 and then returned to Ironton before being summoned to Cleveland in July to replace injured Detroit receiver Charlie Bennett. Initially he appeared in ML box scores as "Ziller," and before manager Jack Chapman got his name straight he was back in the low minors. As of 1886 Zimmer had still climbed no higher than Poughkeepsie of the Hudson Valley League. The team was so fleet that it was nicknamed the Indians, and he was appointed the titular leader and nicknamed "Chief" after catching 27 straight games. Still, Zimmer did not reach the majors to stay until midway through the 1887 season, when he was approaching his 27th birthday. He then more than atoned for his late entry by embarking on a seventeen-year ML sojourn before exiting in 1903.

After splitting the catching with veteran Charlie Snyder in his first two seasons with Cleveland, Zimmer took on full-time duty in 1889. Near the end of the season, however, he was hit in the neck in a game against Philadelphia, and the injury was at first feared to be fatal. Zimmer was still less than 100 percent when the 1890 campaign began and made just 4 hits in the first 14 games of the season. But as team captain, he obstinately kept himself in the lineup, and even though he hit only .214, he first began to gain recognition for his durability and defensive acumen. Ever since 1887 Zimmer had been positioning himself closer to the plate than other catchers so that he could both provide a better target for his pitchers and throw out more would-be stealers. Owing largely to his contributions and the arrival of rookie hurler Cy Young in 1890, Cleveland's hill staff was the envy of the rest of the NL throughout the 1890s.

When injuries held Zimmer to just 20 games in 1898, he lost his job to Lou Criger and was assumed to be finished. The following year, at his request, he remained with Cleveland after syndicate ownership moved most of the Spiders' players to St. Louis. Zimmer finished the season with Louisville and played 1B on closing day in what many expected to be his ML finale. But to everyone's surprise, including probably his own, he won the Pirates' regular catching job in 1900 after coming to Pittsburgh in the mass transfer of Louisville players when the Kentucky club was about to dissolve. That spring he was also appointed president of the new Players Protective Association, the players' most successful attempt yet to unionize their demands.

Seemingly sympathetic at first to fellow NL players who were jumping to the rival AL, in the spring of 1901 Zimmer stood accused by John McGraw of betraying the association and secretly signing a NL contract. A few weeks later AL president Ban Johnson severed all ties with the PPA after Zimmer induced Emmet Heidrick and Bobby Wallace to renege on their AL contracts and return to the St. Louis Cardinals and then unsuccessfully pushed Cy Young to do likewise. Zimmer tried to save face by claiming that he was quitting the game to go into business in Cleveland, only to return for a second season with Pittsburgh and experience playing on his first ML pennant winner.

Zimmer remained with the Pirates when they repeated as NL champs in 1902 and then finished his ML career as player-manager of the Phillies the following year. After umpiring in the NL in 1904, he returned to the minors for several seasons as a player, umpire, manager, and part-owner. He then left the game to work as a cabinet-maker and building inspector before opening a cigar store and making his own cigars. Zimmer was a widower when he died of Alzheimer's in his daughter Leona's home in Cleveland. (DN)

3 | THE FIRST BASEMEN

3. In his first three seasons switch-hitting, Jake Virtue looked as though he would be one of the top first basemen in the game throughout the 1890s. But he was gone from the majors by the middle of his 5th campaign.

Baker, Philip / "Phil"

B	T	HGT	WGT	G	AB	H	R	2B
L	L	5'8"	152	195	817	212	134	20

3B	HR	RBI	BB	SO	SB	BA	SA	OBP
11	3	34	39	32	16	.259	.322	.293

B. 9/19/1856 Philadelphia, PA **D.** 6/4/1940
TEAMS: 83BalA 84WasU 86WasN
DEBUT: 5/1/1883 at Baltimore; played RF and made 2 hits in a 4–3 win over New York's Tim Keefe
FINALE: 9/2/1886 at Chicago; played 1B and went 0-for-3 in a 5–4 loss to Chicago's Jocko Flynn

Phil Baker caught for amateur teams in Philadelphia before joining Altoona in 1876. By the late 1870s and seeing little future in the game as a principal occupation, he had relocated to Washington as captain of the local Nationals and taken a job as a messenger in the Department of the Treasury. In 1881 Baker signed to play RF for the Providence NL club but backed out before the season started. He then resumed playing with the Nationals only in home games or when the team traveled to nearby Baltimore so that he would not have to take time away from his job.

In the spring of 1883 Baker got a thirty-day leave from the Treasury Department and signed a six-month contract with Baltimore AA for $80 a month. When he was successful beyond his expectations, his thirst for the game drove him to try to arrange to have his Treasury work covered while he traveled with the Orioles, but he managed to get into only 23 games and was absent from the club for several long periods of time. That winter Baker apparently affirmed that he preferred the vagaries of a baseball career to the security of his Treasury Department job and agreed to captain the new Washington UA entry. He opened 1884 in CF and soon demonstrated that he was also the best the club had at both 1B and catcher.

Baker remained with Washington when it joined the Eastern League in 1885 after the UA folded and then accompanied the core of the team when it was elevated to the National League in 1886. In his final ML season he led Washington in games played at 1B but otherwise seemed overmatched, collecting just 91 total bases in 81 games. Still, Louisville AA showed an interest in buying him toward the end of the season, but he refused to leave Washington and *SL* said: "He also objects to being bartered against his will." Baker returned to amateur ball the following season and opened a cigar and stationery store in Washington. He subsequently got back into the pro game in eastern minor leagues but severely injured his shoulder in 1889 while with Rochester of the International Association. After umpiring in the minors for a time, he resumed government work and played on occasion for "picked nine" and "married men's" teams. Baker's last known job was as a collator in the night proof section of Government Printing Office. He died in 1940 at his daughter's home in Washington after a long illness. (DN)

Brown, William M. / "Will" "Reddy" "Big Will" "Sailor" "California"

B	T	HGT	WGT	G	AB	H	R	2B
R	R	6'2"	190	418	1589	415	236	70

3B	HR	RBI	BB	SO	SB	BA	SA	OBP
17	6	252	123	124	39	.261	.338	.319

B. ?/?/1866 San Francisco, CA **D.** 12/20/1897
TEAMS: 87–89NYN 90NYP 91PhiN 93BalN 93–94LouN 94StLN
DEBUT: 5/10/1887 at New York, played RF and was 0-for-1 in an 8–3 loss to Washington's Jim Whitney
FINALE: 5/20/1894 at St. Louis, played 1B and was 1-for-3 in a 7–1 loss to Cincinnati's Frank Dwyer

When not working as a teamster in San Francisco, Will Brown caught in 1887 for Greenhood & Morans in the California League as George Van Haltren's batterymate. After joining New York NL the following year, once Brown proved himself defensively he ended up catching the most games for the team (albeit just 46) when Buck Ewing was used primarily in the infield. A thumb injury hampered Brown in 1888, holding him to just 20 games for the Giants' first pennant winner. He also played sparingly for the repeat NL champs in 1889 but was such a popular and valued team member despite his limited use that he was among the Giants who were invited to join the New York PL entry in 1890. Brown's particular forte was rattling batters with a constant stream of mind-boggling chatter. He reveled in giving false tips as to what pitch was coming and then, at the last second, shouting at the batter what the real pitch would be. A great prankster, the big redheaded backstop would also play on a batter's nerves by pretending sotto voce to side with him in protesting an umpire's questionable strike call.

The Giants reclaimed Brown after the PL folded, but he reported late the following spring and on the eve of the season was released to the Phillies. The New York press bemoaned his departure, claiming he was the Giants best catcher outside of Ewing and had been for years, but Phils manager Harry Wright deployed him primarily at 1B. Brown flubbed his first chance to be a full-time player, hitting just .243. That winter, while playing in the Cal League, he injured his leg, causing him to miss the entire 1892 season.

Released by the Phils, Brown opened 1893 at 1B for Baltimore but was jettisoned after 7 games when he was hitting just .125. Picked up by Louisville to replace Lew Whistler, he suddenly exploded at the plate and led the Colonels in SA, BA, total bases, and RBI. By the spring of 1894, however, Brown had "grown to be enormous," weighing around 240 pounds. Dropped by Louisville after he started poorly, he signed with St. Louis but was cut after just 3 games. Brown played on the Pacific Coast for the next two years. His last engagement came in 1896, when he signed in April with Seattle of the New Pacific League. Already in the early stages of consumption, Brown was forced to quit after just 17 games and travel first to Hawaii and then Arizona, hoping in vain for a cure. He died at his home in San Francisco on Christmas Day in 1897. Local ballists flocked to the funeral of the popular redhead. (DN/PM)

Carey, George C. / "Scoops"

B	T	HGT	WGT	G	AB	H	R	2B
R	R	5'11"	175	131	522	134	60	22

3B	HR	RBI	BB	SO	SB	BA	SA	OBP
7	1	76	28	32	2	.257	.331	.311

B. 12/4/1870 Pittsburgh, PA **D.** 12/17/1916
TEAMS: 95BalN 98LouN 02–03WasAL
DEBUT: 4/26/1895 at Baltimore; played 1B and was 1-for-4 in a 12–6 win over Brooklyn's Ed Stein
FINALE: 7/6/1903 at Washington; pinch hit in the ninth inning for pitcher Abe Wilson and skied out to Elmer Flick in a 3–1 loss to Cleveland's Addie Joss

The uncle of George McAvoy, a 1-game MLer in the twentieth century, Scoops Carey holds a distinction that is unlikely ever to be matched: he is the lone position player to lead two different major leagues in fielding in the only two seasons he played in enough games to qualify as a fielding leader. Carey also owns a second distinction that helps explain why he was a regular in only two ML seasons. His 59 runs for Baltimore in 1895 are the fewest ever by a regular on a team that scored 1,000 runs.

Carey's fielding crowns were richly deserved. His rep as a defensive wizard was already in full bloom by the time he signed with Baltimore after finishing 1894 with Milwaukee of the Western League. Carey was particularly adept on throws in the dirt, accounting for his nickname. Dan Brouthers, Baltimore's incumbent first sacker, was understandably nonplused by Carey's acquisition, especially when *TSN* touted the rookie as being a dead ringer for Charlie Comiskey in size, build and, above all, in the deft way he played 1B. Brouthers's still potent bat enabled him to open 1895 as the Orioles' gateway guardian, but complaints from the other Baltimore infielders that he was missing too many of their throws led manager Ned Hanlon to turn to Carey after the campaign was scarcely a week old.

Although Carey initially took Brouthers's cleanup spot in the batting order, he was swiftly dropped to seventh when it grew clear that he would hit well below the team average. In addition to a long, looping swing that produced a plethora of lazy fly balls, Carey was agonizingly slow, swiping just two bases for a team built on speed. Despite winning the pennant with the slick-fielding rookie, as soon as the season ended Hanlon began angling to replace him. He settled on Giants first sacker Jack Doyle, trading the New York club Kid Gleason and $1,500 for Doyle on November 14, 1895. Henry Chadwick viewed the move as foolish and wrote, "Carey at first base was one of the strongest points of the Baltimores' citadel in 1895."

Baltimore nonetheless formally released the NL's top-fielding first baseman in 1895 to the Syracuse Eastern League team as per a bulletin of April 17, 1896, from NL president Nick Young. David Ball has written that the transaction was "the earliest example I have seen of a reference to the direct transfer of players other than draftees from the minor leagues in a bulletin. Although no actual change had taken place, this was a tacit acceptance of the fact that clubs now in practice transferred their rights in player contracts to each other, rather than purchasing a player's release from his old team and then signing him to a separate contract."

After spending 1896 with Syracuse, Philadelphia plucked Carey from the Stars' roster as per an agreement the two clubs had struck in which the Phils would get their choice of Stars players when Philadelphia allowed Charlie Reilly to go to Syracuse earlier in 1896 to serve as the Stars' player-manager. But rather than retain Carey, the Phils farmed him in 1897 to the Atlantic League, where he finished the season with Reading and led the loop, as usual, in FA and assists and hit .354.

In the fall of 1897 Louisville drafted Carey but released him just 8 games into the 1898 season when (alas, also as usual) he failed to hit ML pitching. Carey spent the next three years in the Western and Eastern leagues before joining Buffalo of the fledgling AL in 1900. To no one's surprise, he topped the AL in fielding but posted only the sixth, highest BA among the loop's eight regular first basemen. The following year, when Buffalo was dropped from the AL and moved to the Eastern League, Carey was named the Bisons' manager, captain, and highest-paid player at $300 a month and responded unexpectedly by losing the loop fielding crown but leading all Buffalo hitters with a .316 mark.

That winter, Carey was acquired by Washington, which had struggled through its maiden AL season in 1901 without a reliable first baseman, but his career in the nation's capitol seemed as if it would be short-lived when Senators manager Tom Loftus announced that he was about to trade for Baltimore's hard-hitting Dan McGann. The McGann deal fell through, however, giving Carey the Senators' 1B post by default. By the morning of April 28, 1902, his job was already in jeopardy as he was hitting just .188. But he survived if for no other reason than Loftus feared to break up a team that was unexpectedly leading the league in the early going. The Senators then immediately went into a tailspin while Carey's average oddly began to climb. Despite missing a number of games in midsummer with a broken bone in his hand, his hot hitting continued and he finished third on the team in batting at .314, trailing only Jimmy Ryan (.320) and loop-bat-crown winner Ed Delahanty (.376).

A slow start in 1903 doomed Carey to the bench. Though he lingered on Washington until early August, he seldom played after dropping a throw from Rabbit Robinson on June 5 that opened the gates for the St. Louis Browns to tally 3 unearned runs and beat luckless Happy Townsend 4–3. Carey finished 1903 back in the Eastern League with Buffalo. To the end of his career in the minors he continued to pile up fielding crowns, although his batting by the time he reached his late thirties slid into the low .200s. Carey died in 1916 in East Liverpool, OH, his adopted home, of mitral stenosis when he was only 46 years old.

Carleton, James Jr. / "Jim"

B	T	HGT	WGT	G	AB	H	R	2B
?	?	5'8"	155	36	165	44	39	9

3B	HR	RBI	BB	SO	SB	BA	SA	OBP
1	0	22	9	3	3	.267	.333	.305

B. 8/20/1848 Clinton, CT **D.** 4/25/1910
TEAMS: 71–72CleNA
DEBUT: 5/4/1871 at Cleveland, played 1B in the first ML game in history and went 0-for-3 in a 2–0 loss to Fort Wayne's Bobby Mathews
FINALE: 5/22/1872 at Middletown; played 1B and went 1-for-5 in a 10–5 loss to the Mansfields' Cy Bentley

Jim Carleton began with the New York Mutuals in 1869, playing mostly SS. He moved to the Forest City Club for the 1870 season as its regular first baseman. Carleton joined the embryonic Bell Telephone Company after leaving baseball. He moved rapidly up the corporate ladder and was a wealthy man by the time he moved to Detroit, where he became a prominent stockbroker prior to his death there from pneumonia in 1910. (DN/EM)

Carney, John Joseph / "Jack" "Handsome Jack"

B	T	HGT	WGT	G	AB	H	R	2B
R	R	5'10½"	175	252	946	258	120	30

3B	HR	RBI	BB	SO	SB	BA	SA	OBP
13	7	129	83	59	40	.273	.354	.338

B. 11/10/1866 Salem, MA **D.** 10/19/1925
TEAMS: 89WasN 90BufP 90CleP 91CinA 91MilA
DEBUT: 4/24/1889 at Washington; played 1B and went 1-for-4 in an 8–4 loss to Philadelphia's Charlie Buffinton

FINALE: 10/4/1891 at Milwaukee; played 1B and went 1-for-4 in an 8–4 win over Columbus's Phil Knell and Jack Leiper

A fastidious dresser who changed his necktie three times a day, Jack Carney was also a "Fancy Dan" fielder. In July 1892 *TSN* rued, "If Carney could hit a little better he would be the peer of anybody in the business," which creates something of a puzzle. With the sole exception of his freshman year with Washington, Carney hit ML pitching quite well—.290 in 673 ABs—and was clearly superior to several first basemen in the early 1890s that had substantial ML careers.

Carney turned pro in 1886 with unaffiliated Concord, NH, and then spent two years with Manchester in the New England League before winning the Washington 1B job in the spring of 1889. Hampered by a torn ligament in his left shoulder, he hit just .231 as a rookie but was nonetheless corralled by Deacon White and Jack Rowe for their Buffalo PL club in 1890. Released when White decided to played 1B himself, Carney finished the season in RF with the Cleveland PL team and stroked .348 in 25 games. In 1891 he was the Opening Day first baseman for his third different ML team in yet a third different league in his third and final ML season when he took the field with the new Cincinnati AA entry. Following 1891 Carney served as a player, captain, and manager in the minors until he was past 40. In 1894, while with Toledo of the Western League, he severely sprained both ankles, sidelining him for several weeks, and one ankle never entirely healed. Although he continued to hit in the .300s, his fielding suffered markedly.

Early in his career Carney was part owner of the Carney Brothers wholesale shoe company in Salem, MA, but in 1899 he married Grace Baker of Manchester and began studying pharmacy at the Boston College of Pharmacy. Soon afterward he opened his own drugstore in Manchester but continued to be active in pro ball and later coached at Phillips Exeter Academy, New Hampshire State, and Boston College before becoming the longtime coach at Cornell. In his spare time Carney raised a rare species of rabbit. He died of a heart attack in Litchfield, MA. (DN)

Cartwright, Edward Charles / "Ed" "Jumbo"

B	T	HGT	WGT	G	AB	H	R	2B
R	R	5'10"	220	495	1902	562	348	100

3B	HR	RBI	BB	SO	SB	BA	SA	OBP
44	24	333	202	128	144	.295	.432	.368

B. 10/6/1859 Johnstown, PA **D.** 9/3/1933
TEAMS: 90StLA 94–97WasN
DEBUT: 7/10/1891 at St. Louis; played 1B and was 2-for-5 in a 15–13 loss to Syracuse's Mike Morrison
FINALE: 6/4/1897 at Washington; played 1B and was 2-for-4 in an 8–5 loss to Chicago's Jimmy Callahan
CAREER HIGHLIGHT: on 9/23/1890 at St. Louis; played 1B and hit a grand slam and 3-run homer in the same inning as he drove in a then record 7 runs in the third inning in a 21–2 win over Philadelphia's Eddie Green; Cartwright's single-inning RBI record stood for 109 years until it was broken by Fernando Tatis

Ed Cartwright possessed "warning track power." In summing up his career in 1899, the *Washington Post* wrote that he "could hoist a fly higher than a sky-rocket." Unhappily Cartwright's towering fly balls that sailed out of small minor league parks were no more than loud outs in most ML facilities.

The burly Cartwright began as a catcher for small minor league teams in northern Ohio in the early 1880s. Due to an injury, at the late age of 25 he first launched his pro career in 1885 as an umpire in the Southern League before turning to playing with Nashville. After spending the winter of 1886–87 with the Acid Iron Earth team in New Orleans, he joined the New Orleans Southern League entry in 1887 and began the year as the team's leadoff hitter despite being its top slugger. After just 16 games he carried a .430 BA (with bases on balls being counted as hits as per the 1887 rule) and had tallied 30 runs.

The following year Cartwright moved up to Kansas City of the Western Association. Then in 1889 he joined St. Joseph of the WA and hit .278 with 13 home runs. That winter, Cleveland NL, riddled by PL defections, pondered acquiring Cartwright despite his age—as early as 1888 he was already being referred to by Kansas City writers as "the old man"—but were dissuaded by a St. Joseph scribe who claimed that Cartwright was too afraid of being hit by the ball to stand in against tough pitchers and also smote too many routine fly balls. Cartwright was labeled as having these same flaws for the remainder of his career.

Rejected by Cleveland, he began 1890 with Hamilton, Ontario, of the International Association. When the IA disbanded with Cartwright hitting only .243, he signed with St. Louis AA. Despite an outstanding half season with the Browns that included a .300 BA and 60 RBI in just 75 games, Cartwright was released when the PL folded and first baseman–manager Charlie Comiskey rejoined St. Louis. He spent 1891 working at the Union Iron Works in San Francisco and playing for the local Friscos in the California League. At the close of the campaign he stood first in batting in the pitching-dominated circuit despite hitting just .285. That winter he served as foreman for the gang of ironworkers that was building the U.S. warship *Monterey* in San Francisco Bay.

In the spring of 1892 Cartwright journeyed north with pitcher George Borchers to play for the Tacoma in the newly formed Pacific Northwest League. Since both were married, they rented a house together in Tacoma large enough to accommodate the two couples, and Cartwright took over as team captain in June. When the PNL collapsed, Cartwright finished the year in the Montana State League and then retraced his steps across the country to play for Memphis of the Southern League. Now nearing his 34th birthday, the big first baseman enjoyed a banner year, leading the SL in batting (.373) before the loop folded in August. Cartwright's showing at Memphis induced J. Earle Wagner, owner of last-place Washington NL, to ignore his age, and in 1894 the jumbo first baseman immediately repaid Wagner's faith in him by topping the D.C. club in home runs and RBI while playing every inning at 1B.

Making his home now in the nation's capital, Cartwright spent the winter hunting and hiking and trying unsuccessfully to take off weight. Owing to the trifling results of his dietary efforts, distaff fans of the Washington team took to calling him "Piano Legs" in 1895. Despite his bulk, Cartwright gained a growing reputation as a fielder especially adept at handling errant throws from third baseman Bill Joyce and second sacker Jack Crooks, both of whom had accuracy problems. He was even named team captain in the process of leading the club in doubles and finishing second in both BA and SA.

Cartwright was replaced as captain the following year, however, when Gus Schmelz decided that he was too quiet and turned instead to Joyce, who had more "sand." Furthermore, Cartwright's age was catching up to him in 1896, as he lost 54 points off his batting average and saw his SA shrink by a whopping 132 points. When Cartwright's offensive deterioration increased in 1897—no home runs or triples and only 4 doubles in 124 ABs—he was released on June 5, two days after Washington purchased Tommy Tucker from Boston. After a short stay in the Western League with Minneapolis, where he was still a passable fielder but hopeless at the plate, Cartwright resumed his trade as an iron molder. He died at his home in St. Petersburg, FL, of pneumonia in 1933. More than a century after Cartwright tallied 106 RBI to lead Washington in 1894, he and Luke Easter remain the only two men to compile 100-RBI seasons in the majors despite not playing their first ML games until they were past 30 years old. (DN)

Clark, William Otis / "Bill" "Big Bill" "Willie" "Wee Willie"

B	T	HGT	WGT	G	AB	H	R	2B
L	L	6'1"	195	349	1275	366	188	54

3B	HR	RBI	BB	SO	SB	BA	SA	OBP
35	2	199	114	18	38	.287	.389	.359

B. 8/16/1872 Pittsburgh, PA **D.** 11/13/1932
TEAMS: 95–97NYN 98–99PitN
DEBUT: 6/20/1895 at New York; played 1B and was 1-for-4 in a 15–6 win over Washington's Otis Stocksdale
FINALE: 8/3/1899 at Pittsburgh; played 1B and went 1-for-4 in a 5–4 loss to Baltimore's Harry Howell.

"Wee Willie," the nickname listed for Bill Clark in many reference works, was meant facetiously and not commonly used by his fellow players. Clark was more often called either "Bill" or "Big Bill." The August 5, 1899, *TSN* not only confirmed that he was a southpaw but also offered his views on why a left-hander had an advantage over a righty at playing 1B. Clark grew up in Pittsburgh. After spending his first pro seasons in the Pennsylvania State League, he moved in 1895 to Scranton of the Eastern League, where he beat out veteran Dan Stearns for the 1B job. That June, while hitting .391, he was traded to New York NL for Andy Boswell, Tom Bannon, and Tot Murphy after first baseman Jack Doyle was injured. Clark failed to hit enough to keep the job once Doyle was healed and further jeopardized his chances with the New Yorkers when he told Scranton sportswriter J. S. Kay in August 1895 that he disliked playing for the Giants because the team was riddled with factions. Clark furthermore opined that Doyle, also the Giants' manager at the time, should be a player only.

Clark was nonetheless retained in 1896 when Doyle was traded to Baltimore but lost the battle for the 1B post, first to Harry Davis and then to Jake Beckley after Beckley arrived from Pittsburgh in a trade for Davis. Since his services were seldom needed, he spent part of the season with the New York Mets, a Giants farm team, and earned a fresh look when he smoked Atlantic League pitchers, hitting .420 in 24 games. After a serious offseason illness, Clark began 1897 on the bench but assumed 1B when Beckley was let go to Cincinnati. By that point Clark was using one of the biggest bats in the majors, and the choice appears to have been to his detriment as he hit with little power and scored just 63 runs in 116 games. Clark's uninspiring year led Giants owner Andrew Freedman to cut his salary, and Clark responded by engaging in a protracted holdout that finally convinced Freedman to sell him to Pittsburgh on August 4, 1898. In a somewhat ironic turn of events, Clark replaced Harry Davis as the Pirates' first baseman. Though he hit well in the remaining two months of the season and was happy to be playing in his hometown, he continued to display little power and scored just 29 runs in 57 games.

Clark spent the winter of 1898–99 working in a Pittsburgh rolling mill, perhaps in an attempt to add muscle. He then began the 1899 season batting cleanup but soon dropped down in the order when his stroke still lacked punch. By the end of July *TSN* was already predicting that he would soon be released for dull play. Clark was also accused of having taken a rookie—probably Jimmy Williams—out on the town in July to show off his old haunts while the team was in New York.

Finally released after the finish of a home series with Baltimore on August 3, 1899, Clark joined Milwaukee of the newly christened American League prior to 1900 but after just 19 games broke his ankle sliding on June 2. The injury not only ended his season but his career. Clark died at his Pittsburgh home in 1932 of cancer. (DN)

Cogswell, Edward / "Ed"

B	T	HGT	WGT	G	AB	H	R	2B
R	R	5'8"	150	109	496	146	102	16

3B	HR	RBI	BB	SO	SB	BA	SA	OBP
4	1	32	25	21	—	.294	.349	.328

B. 2/25/1854 ?, England **D.** 7/27/1888
TEAMS: 79BosN 80TroN 82WorN
DEBUT: 7/11/1879 at Cincinnati; played 1B and went 1-for-5 in an 11–2 win over Cincinnati's Will White
FINALE: 5/30/1882 at Troy; played 1B and went 0-for-4 in a 10–2 loss to Cleveland's Jim McCormick

Ed Cogswell was an excellent contact hitter, a skillful bunter and fine first baseman despite his small size. In 1874 he was a member of the semipro Rollstone club of Fitchburg, MA, along with his brother, who caught for the team. By 1877 Cogswell was with Manchester of the International Association. He remained with the Connecticut team until it disbanded in 1879, allowing him to join Boston NL. Cogswell immediately established himself as the team's lead-off hitter and a reliable fielder and base runner but could not be accommodated on Boston's elite five-man reserve list after his rookie season. He signed with Troy but appears to have been unhappy with the Trojans. In late July he announced he was "permanently retired from baseball" after his finale on July 30, a 7–6 win over Worcester's Denny Driscoll.

The following year Cogswell remained away from the ML arena but was lured back to it in 1882 when Worcester appointed him both its captain and lead-off hitter. Near the end of May he was dropped in the order when his BA shrank to barely over .100. Soon after that Harry Stovey was moved to 1B when Worcester reorganized and released Cogswell. Our surmise is that Cogswell was injured early in the season—one report spoke of a "lame arm" in commenting on his release—and it permanently impaired both his fielding and his batting. But it is also conceivable that even a year off from ML competition failed to rekindle his enthusiasm for the game. Cogswell worked during his few remaining years as an overseer at the Fitchburg, MA, Worsted Mill and died at his mother's home in Fitchburg at 34. (DN)

Davis, Harry H. / "Harry" "Jasper"

B	T	HGT	WGT	G	AB	H	R	2B
R	R	5'10"	180	340	1281	341	190	40

3B	HR	RBI	BB	SO	SB	BA	SA	OBP
63	6	190	99	41	62	.266	.411	.328

B. 7/19/1873 Philadelphia, PA
D. 8/11/1947 Philadelphia, PA
TEAMS: 95–96NYN 96–98PitN 98LouN 98–99WasN 01–11PhiAL (P/M)12CleAL 13–17PhiAL
DEBUT: 9/21/1895 at Boston; played 1B and went 3-for-4 in a 13–12 loss to Boston's Jim Sullivan
FINALE: 5/30/1917 at Philadelphia; pinch hit unsuccessfully for Bill Johnson in the thirteenth inning of a 2–0 loss to New York's Slim Love and Urban Shocker
CAREER HIGHLIGHT: Set an all-time ML record by a qualifier in 1897 when his loop-leading 28 triples represented 70 percent of his total of extra-base hits

The only ML slugger to win four consecutive loop home run crowns and not reside in the HOF, Harry Davis lost his father at age 5 and was sent by his mother two years later to Girard, a Philadelphia school for orphaned and disadvantaged boys. A fertile breeding ground for young baseball talent, Girard had already spawned Lon Knight and Jack Milligan and eventually would produce thirteen MLers, including Davis. While at Girard he was nicknamed Jasper for an unknown reason and learned accounting.

At age 18 Davis left Girard to take a banking job and catch for the Bank Clerks Athletic Association team in a Philadelphia amateur league. He spent the next two years with the Pennsylvania Railroad team until he nabbed the eye of scout and minor league manager Billy Murray and was signed by the Providence Eastern League entry. In the spring of 1894 Davis was traded to Pawtucket of the New England League and became player-manager of the Rhode Island club the following season shortly before he departed for New York in September. An outfielder by now, Davis tripled in his first ML game with the Giants, a sign of events to come, but had trouble with the LF sun in the Polo Grounds and was relocated to 1B. When he continued to flash extra base power in 1896, the Giants seduced Pittsburgh into parting with longtime Pirates stalwart Jake Beckley for him by adding $1,000 to the kitty. Davis then tanked, hitting just .190 for the rest of the season, but rebounded in 1897 to top the NL with 28 triples.

The following March, before heading off to spring training with the Pirates, he married Emma Hicks, the daughter of the woman he had boarded with after leaving Girard. Davis opened 1898 at 1B with Pittsburgh and hit well but was then sold under mysterious circumstances to Louisville in July. *TSN* darkly hinted that "a tale is behind his release from Smoketown that will do no one good to unfold," and evidently no one ever did. At the time of his departure, Davis led the NL in triples with 13 but again tanked after joining a new team and hit just 2 more triples and .217 all told with Louisville before being released in early September to Washington. By the time Washington dismissed him in May 1899, Davis had hit just .205 in the 56 games he had played since leaving Pittsburgh and gave every appearance of a hitter with a serious flaw that pitchers had recently detected. He went to Providence after leaving Washington and remained with the Clamdiggers through the 1900 under Billy Murray, his original savior. If Davis indeed had a batting fault, Murray seemingly was of no help in correcting it. His protégé had two decent but hardly sensational seasons in the Eastern League. Then, in the winter of 1900–1901, Davis headed home to Philadelphia and returned to his old job with the Pennsylvania Railroad when none of the many jobs that had suddenly opened on eight new ML teams after the American League declared itself a major circuit were offered to him. (DN)

Dehlman, Herman J. / "Herman" "Dutch"

B	T	HGT	WGT	G	AB	H	R	2B
?	?	?	?	307	1219	262	226	34

3B	HR	RBI	BB	SO	SB	BA	SA	OBP
5	0	83	46	65	34	.215	.251	.245

B. ?/?/1852 Brooklyn, NY **D.** 3/13/1885
TEAMS: 72–74AtlNA 75StLNA 76–77StLN
DEBUT: 5/2/1872 at Mansfield; played 1B and went 0-for-4 in an 8–2 loss to Mansfield's Frank Buttery
FINALE: 9/8/1877 at Brooklyn; played 1B and went 2-for-2 in a 15–6 loss to Hartford's Terry Larkin

Called "Dutch" because he wore a peculiar peaked cap of a type that the Dutch often wore in the 1870s, Herman Dehlman revolutionized the 1B position by dropping to one knee on throws and stretching to the limit in whatever direction was necessary. His infielders thus could throw lower to him than to other first basemen of his time. He also revolutionized his position insofar as hitting was concerned. Even in Dehlman's day first basemen were expected to hit a bit, but he succeeded in playing six ML seasons despite posting the lowest OPS (.496) of any first sacker in history with a minimum of 1,000 career ABs.

Ironically, Dehlman began his ML career batting cleanup. That foolishness did not last long. By 1876 in his fledgling NL season he was often batting last, owing to his stellar .202 BA. Even though Dehlman never learned to hit, not even in the minors, he was a respected figure in the game until his sudden death in 1885. That March, after a .220 season in the Eastern League, Dehlman brought his family with him to Wilkes-Barre while he discussed terms to manage the minor league team there for the coming season. He died after a two-day illness. There are conflicting reports as to whether the cause was typhoid or peritonitis, perhaps the result of a ruptured appendix. (DN)

Doyle, John Joseph / "Jack" "Dirty Jack"

B	T	HGT	WGT	G	AB	H	R	2B
R	R	5'9"	155	1151	4480	1389	776	241

3B	HR	RBI	BB	SO	SB	BA	SA	OBP
51	23	788	314	132	453	.310	.402	.360

G	W	L	PCT	PENNANTS
81	40	40	.500	0

B. 10/25/1869 Killorgin, Ireland **D.** 12/31/1958
TEAMS: 89–90ColA 91–92CleN 92–95NYN (P/M)95NYN 96–97BalN (P/M)98WasN 98–00NYN 01ChiN 02NYN 02WasAL 03–04BroN 04PhiN 05NYAL
DEBUT: 8/27/1889 at Columbus; caught Hank Gastright and went 0-for-3 in a 10–5 loss to Philadelphia's Sadie McMahon
FINALE: 7/13/1905 at Detroit; played 1B and went 0-for-3 in a 6–3 loss to Detroit's George Mullin

Dubbed "Dirty Jack" in his playing days for his aggressive and despised approach that featured slashing slides, deliberate spikings of opponents and brawls with anyone who riled him, including teammates and umpires, Jack Doyle paradoxically was one of the most revered figures in the game by the time of his death. In his seventy some years in baseball he was everything at one time or another except an owner or league official, and he awakened on his last morning the oldest living ex-member of both the Brooklyn Dodgers and the New York Yankees franchises. Doyle's leading assets were versatility—he played at least 13 games at every position except pitcher—steady play and baserunning. Among the first to perfect the hook slide, he was so masterful at it that in 1900 Cincinnati pitcher Ed Scott moaned to *TSN*: "I'll venture to say that on one-third of the stolen bases Doyle gets credit for he was really out," implying that his rival's deft sliding earned him every close decision on steal attempts.

A native of County Kerry, Ireland, Doyle came with his parents to Holyoke while still a boy and made that Massachusetts city his residence for the rest of his life. After leaving school in the ninth grade, Doyle played semipro ball in neighboring towns until 1887, when he enlisted in the New England League as a 17-year-old catcher. Moving to Canton of the Tri-State League in 1889, Doyle boarded around the corner from the house belonging to an Ohio congressman named William McKinley, who became one of his most ardent fans. An immediate sensation in the TSL, that August he was courted vigorously by the Louisville AA club but made his ML debut at age 19 with Columbus AA instead when Columbus manager Al Buckenberger snuck in ahead of Louisville and paid Canton $300.

In 1890, his first full ML season, Doyle was unhappy with his role as a utilityman. Prior to the 1891 campaign he joined two other Solons, Ralph Johnson and Frank Knauss, in jumping to Cleveland NL after the AA withdrew from the National Agreement. Of the trio, only Doyle was a helpful addition to the Spiders, although arm trouble prevented him from serving as an adequate backup to catcher Chief Zimmer. The following June he asked for his release when he was still only a part-timer and was granted it so the Spiders could get down to the roster limit. Doyle joined the Giants on June 23, 1892, for the first of his three separate stints with the club and got into as many as 100 games for the initial time in his career even though he still was without a regular position. The following spring he was behind the plate on Opening Day for the Giants but caught only 47 more games and again was reduced to part-time duty.

When Roger Connor was traded prior to the 1894 season, Doyle finally won his first regular job in the majors, playing 99 games at 1B and hitting a career high .367. By finishing second the Giants qualified to play pennant-winning Baltimore that fall in the first ever Temple Cup series. Prior to the affair players on both teams made a secret pact to split the take regardless of which side won, but some apparently did not honor their commitment. Several years later, when Doyle, who had since moved on to Baltimore, was traded to Washington, an unnamed Orioles player leaked, "[Doyle] did McGraw dirt over the Temple Cup money when New York beat us [in 1894] and he had hardly a friend in the team." The revelation helped to explain the savage feud that erupted between Doyle and McGraw almost from the moment the Giants sent Doyle to Baltimore in November 1895 for Kid Gleason and cash. The pair came to blows on at least one memorable occasion while Doyle was with the Orioles and only accelerated their antipathy toward one another as the years passed. On June 9, 1900, matters between them reached a new hot point when Doyle, back with the Giants, deliberately spiked McGraw, by then with St. Louis, in a play at 3B. Further bloodshed was averted when the Giants released Doyle two years later, once it grew apparent that McGraw was going to bolt the AL and take over the reins in New York.

Oddly enough, however, Doyle's career peaked during the two seasons he teamed with McGraw on the Orioles, resulting in a personal-best 116 runs in 1896 and a third and final Temple Cup appearance the following year when he hit a healthy .354. Similarly, his release by the Giants in 1902, which seemed to signal that his career was winding down, did him a favor. The following year, reunited in Brooklyn with his old Orioles manager, Ned Hanlon, Doyle played a career-high 139 games and enjoyed his last .300 campaign. But less than two years after that he left the majors after an embarrassing finale on the only day he saw action in a New York Yankees uniform.

Doyle's departure was little mourned at first. In March 1902 *TSN* had said in effect that the sport should welcome the day it came: "[Doyle] belongs to that type of performers, who affect a contempt for patrons and boast that they are in base ball for the money . . . his disappearance from the profession would remove one of the worst examples that young players have ever had." In 1906 Doyle managed Des Moines to the Western League pennant but had less luck with Milwaukee of the American Association the following season and left the game in 1908–09 to become the police commissioner of Holyoke. Ill-suited to deskwork, he next tried umpiring and in 1911 was appointed to the regular NL officiating staff but left after working a game at Pittsburgh on June 1. Doyle then umpired in the minors awhile before finding his most enduring niche in the game. For the last thirty-eight years of his life he worked for the Cubs as a scout and later in an advisory capacity, helping to uncover such future Bruins stars as Gabby Hartnett, Charlie Root, Stan Hack, and Phil Cavarretta. A lifelong bachelor, Doyle died in a Holyoke hospital in 1958 following a heart attack at 89. (DN/LS)

Everitt, William Lee (aka Everett) **/ "Bill" "Wild Bill"**

B	T	HGT	WGT	G	AB	H	R	2B
L	R	6'½"	185	665	2727	880	521	82

3B	HR	RBI	BB	SO	SB	BA	SA	OBP
41	11	333	197	85	179	.323	.395	.371

B. 12/13/1868 Fort Wayne, IN **D.** 1/19/1938
TEAMS: 95–00ChiN 01WasAL
DEBUT: 4/18/1895 at St. Louis; played 3B and was 1-for-3 in a 10–7 loss to St. Louis's Ted Breitenstein
FINALE: 6/24/1901 at Washington; played 1B and was 0-for-3 in a 9–8 loss to Milwaukee's Pete Husting, Pink Hawley, and Ned Garvin

Bill Everitt holds two significant records. In 1895 he compiled the highest BA ever by an NL or AL rookie with at least 400 ABs when he debuted with a .358 mark for Chicago. Three years later, in his first season as Cap Anson's replacement at 1B with Chicago, Everitt collected 596 ABs, the most ever by a gateway guardian who went homerless for an entire season. These two records symbolize Everitt's paradoxical career.

In his early days in the game, Everitt allowed himself to be carried in box scores as "Everett" but fought for the correct spelling once he made the majors. (Nevertheless, the *Macmillan Baseball Encyclopedia* continued to carry him as "Everett" throughout its twenty-eight-year history.) Born in Indiana, he gravitated slowly westward and learned the game on the Denver sandlots. Everitt had already passed his 24th birthday before first drawing national notice in 1893 as an SS with San Francisco in his fourth year in the California League. The following year he came east permanently to play for

Detroit of the Western League. During the winter of 1894–95 a dispute arose when Detroit tried to retain Everitt after the NL Chicago Colts claimed the rights to him. Colts president Jim Hart contended that Chicago had loaned second baseman Bob Glenalvin to Detroit in 1894 in exchange for the pick of any player on Detroit's roster at the end of the season. Hart had at first claimed outfielder Sam Dungan but argued that Chicago was entitled to replace Dungan after he broke his thumb and choose Everitt instead. When Nick Young sided with Chicago, Colts manager Cap Anson owned a 26-year-old rookie who had to find a new position because the club already had Bill Dahlen at shortstop. Anson made Everitt compete for the 3B job with incumbent Charlie Irwin in spring training, and Everitt won out when Irwin developed arm trouble.

After a stellar rookie year in which he led the club in runs and hits in addition to setting his frosh BA mark, Everitt slipped to .320 in 1896 and was moved to the outfield when his fielding also declined. The following spring he regained his 3B job but injured his shoulder in May in a basepath collision and played in just 92 games after not missing a contest in his first two ML seasons. Anson's retirement from active play that fall proved to be Everitt's salvation in that it allowed him to move to 1B and pamper his still-ailing shoulder, which considerably hindered his throwing. In mid-July 1898, he led the NL in hits and was among the batting leaders, but his average plummeted after a fistfight with teammate Barry McCormick during a game at Baltimore on July 15. The melee was set off when McCormick jeered Everitt for making yet another rotten throw.

Following the first game of the 1899 season, Everitt was named team captain by Chicago manager Tom Burns as a compromise to appease both the Jimmy Ryan and Bill Lange factions on the club that each wanted their man as captain. The new responsibility did little to perk Everitt's play. Although he batted .310 and again led the club with 166 hits, he collected only 196 total bases. Considered by some observers to be the best bunter in the NL during his peak years, Everitt had always been able to hit for average, but now that he was a first baseman more production was expected from his bat. He was traded to Kansas City of the then minor AL for first sacker John Ganzel in May 1900 after compiling just 28 total bases in the first 23 games of the season. Rather than join KC, Everitt stayed in Chicago that summer playing the horses.

Still the property of KC, Everitt reported in the spring of 1901 after the team and its manager, Jim Manning, were transferred to Washington for the AL's first season as a major circuit. When he was hitting just .191 two months into the season, he was released by Manning the morning after a 2-error finale on June 24. Everitt returned to Denver, where he now had a commission business, and was a player-manager with Colorado Western League entries until 1905 before retiring to run his ranch and act as president of the Colorado Wrecking Company. He died of complications arising from diabetes at 69. (DN)

Faatz, Jayson S. / "Jay"

B	T	HGT	WGT	G	AB	H	R	2B
R	R	6'4"	196	298	1135	274	159	24

3B	HR	RBI	BB	SO	SB	BA	SA	OBP
12	3	105	39	33	93	.241	.292	.293

G	W	L	PCT	PENNANTS
33	9	24	.273	0

B. 10/24/1860 Weedsport, NY **D.** 4/10/1923
TEAMS: 84PitA 88CleA 89CleN (P/M)90BufP
DEBUT: 8/22/1884 at Baltimore; played 1B and went 0-for-5 in an 8–6 loss to Baltimore's Bob Emslie
FINALE: 9/10/1890 at Buffalo; went 1-for-4 in an 11–3 win over Chicago's Charlie Bartson

Said to be "as slender as a knitting needle and long as a fence rail," Jay Faatz is the type of player who befuddles modern historians who see only a first baseman with a .584 OPS in more than 1,200 PAs and marvel at the connections he must have had to remain in the majors so long. In actuality, Faatz was among the more intriguing and innovative players of his time. An expert poker player with a fondness for diamonds and all forms of jewelry, he was a fine field leader but not always a popular one due to a quick temper and an inability to hold his tongue. After the close of the 1889 season, Faatz was among John M. Ward's chief assistants in organizing the Players League, but while Ward and most of his subordinates were later welcomed back into the NL, in the end Faatz's imprudence and lack of tact damned his chances of ever working again in the majors.

Among the least-talented players to participate in the PL, at least on the surface, Faatz had two fortes, neither of which can readily be detected from his career stat profile. He was an exceptional base runner, especially for a first baseman, and skilled at getting hit by pitches, sticking his arm out as if by accident while pretending to dodge them, and so subtly that he almost always got his base. Faatz and Curt Welch were the two most instrumental players in forcing rulesmakers to take hard look at the HBP rule after the 1888 season and think seriously of abolishing it, since a HBP was not automatically awarded at that time but left to an umpire's judgment as to whether the batter made a genuine effort to avoid being hit.

Faatz first turned heads in 1882 with the independent St. Thomas Atlantics, where he played 1B with his brother Charlie (a longtime minor league player and manager) at SS. In 1883 he moved to Saginaw, MI, of the Northwestern League and then joined the feeble Pittsburgh AA team late the following season, hitting just .241. Faatz returned to the minors for the next three years before being acquired by Cleveland AA. In the spring of 1888, manager Jimmy Williams installed his new first baseman as team captain and was richly rewarded when Faatz got off to a torrid 32-for-77 start (.416) and in mid-May was second in hitting in the AA only to Tip O'Neill's .420. By June, however, Williams had replaced him as captain after accusing him of not pulling pitcher Doc Oberlander out of a game when Oberlander was being bombarded. Also said to be lax in enforcing club rules, Faatz was replaced by catcher Charlie Snyder, but after Tom Loftus took over the club's reins from Williams, one of his first moves was to reinstate Faatz as captain. The promotion failed to revive the first sacker's bat, as he hit just .234 in his final 393 ABs of the season.

Faatz continued as captain in 1889 when Cleveland switched to the NL but fell off even more dramatically in almost every offensive department due to a lingering wrist injury and personal tragedy. On March 8, just before the Blues were to go to Hot Springs, AR, for spring training, his wife Nellie died of typhoid scarcely three weeks after the couple was married. One of Faatz's few bright spots in an otherwise saddening year came on July 26 at Pittsburgh when his shot down the 3B line hit Deacon White on the foot and ricocheted under a row of seats, giving him time to circle the bases for a historic three-run homer that never reached the outfield.

That winter Faatz's poor year and his stubborn wrist ailment led him to assume strictly an advisory role with Cleveland PL. But in July, when both he and outfielder-pitcher Larry Twitchell were transferred to the Buffalo PL club as per a covenant to bolster the weaker teams, Faatz reactivated himself and became the last-place Bisons' player-manager for 34 games before being either fired or "laid off" with pay—reports conflict—on September 14 and replaced by Connie Mack.

The following season Faatz joined Syracuse after it dropped down to the Eastern Association from the AA, and he served as captain and first baseman. He remained a force in Syracuse's fortunes until moving to Toronto in 1895 and then taking the reins of New Castle of the Interstate League in 1896. After leaving the game, Faatz returned to Syracuse and sold insurance until shortly before his death of sinus cancer in 1923. (DN)

Farrar, Sydney Douglas / "Sid"

B	T	HGT	WGT	G	AB	H	R	2B
?	R	5'10"	185	943	3573	905	497	157

3B	HR	RBI	BB	SO	SB	BA	SA	OBP
53	18	412	233	269	92	.253	.342	.305

G	W	L	PCT	PENNANTS
33	9	24	.273	0

B. 8/10/1859 Paris Hill, ME **D.** 5/7/1935
TEAMS: 83–89PhiN 90PhiP
DEBUT: 5/1/1883 at Philadelphia; played 1B and went hitless in a 4–3 loss to Providence's Charley Radbourn
FINALE: 10/4/1890 at Cleveland; played 1B and went 1-for-4 in a 16–4 win over Cleveland's Henry Gruber

Sid Farrar was living in Melrose, MA, in 1882, working winters in a box factory and singing in the church choir when his wife, Henrietta, gave birth to a daughter, Geraldine. At age 3 Geraldine was singing with her father in the Melrose choir; eighteen years later she created a sensation in Berlin with her debut as Marguerite in Charles Gounod's *Faust*, and afterward she was renowned as the "It" girl of the opera until her retirement in 1922 at age 40. At the height of her career, her striking beauty, enchantingly lyrical voice, and faultless stage presence earned her such a fanatical following, particularly among young women, that her worshippers were nicknamed "Gerry-flappers." Meanwhile, her torrid love affair with Arturo Toscanini and her subsequent marriage to the nefarious film actor Lou Tellegen were the sources of considerable scandal.

In the spring of 1883, when Geraldine was less than a year old, her less famous father won the 1B job on the Philadelphia Quakers, an NL replacement team, at the last minute when Alex McKinnon took ill. Farrar had been active in the game since 1876 when he played with the semipro General Worth team of Stoneham, MA, in the Eastern Massachusetts Association but had never been among the more prominent minor league or independent team first basemen before getting his unexpected opportunity. He hit just .233 as a rookie and scored only 41 runs in 99 games but nonetheless held the Quakers' gateway post until 1890 when he jumped to the Players League, where he finished his career the owner of the lowest OPS (.647) among all first basemen in the decade of the 1880s (1881–90) with a minimum of 2,000 PAs.

Farrar's only offensive season of merit came in 1887 when he hit .282 and scored 83 runs. He was a mediocre base runner, his fielding, although sound, was hardly electrifying—he led NL first basemen once each in FA, assists, and double plays—and it is probably only fitting that after he left the scene no one could ever remember which way he had batted. Farrar's strengths were that he kept his head in the game at all times and was regarded as a clean player, attributes that often were enough to keep a job for quite a while under Harry Wright, his manager in every season but his first and last. His career appears to have been saved by the PL—at least for one more year. Reportedly, Wright had booked him for release after the 1889 season.

When Farrar tried without success after the PL collapsed to convince Columbus AA that he would be an improvement on the Senators' present first baseman, Mike Lehane, the *Philadelphia Press* had this to say: "Farewell, Sidney, we will probably never see a man on the Philadelphias at first base that can field the position better or run slower." Farrar quit play after a .282 season with Providence in the 1892 Eastern League. He then went into the furniture business in Melrose with Frank Selee and later bought a turkey farm near Ridgefield, CT. After his wife died in 1923, he regularly traveled with his famous daughter, even abroad to places like Berlin to watch her give emeritus performances. When Farrar died in 1935 following surgery he left Geraldine an estate worth $80,900. In her later years she lived in total seclusion on the family farm in Ridgefield. Geraldine Farrar died in 1967 died from a heart attack at 85. (DN/FV)

*Field, James C. / "Jim"

B	T	HGT	WGT	G	AB	H	R	2B
L	?	6'1"	170	332	1270	292	180	38

3B	HR	RBI	BB	SO	SB	BA	SA	OBP
21	10	50	77	—	9	.230	.317	.289

G	IP	H	GS	CG	BB
2	9.2	7	1	1	4

SO	SH	W	L	PCT	ERA
2	0	1	0	1.000	2.79

B. 4/24/1863 Philadelphia, PA **D.** 5/13/1953
TEAMS: 83–84ColA 85PitA 85BalA 90RocA 98WasN
DEBUT: 6/2/1883 at Philadelphia; played 1B and went 0-for-4 in an 8–6 win over Philadelphia's Enoch Bakely
FINALE: 7/21/1898 at Washington; played 1B and went 0-for-4 in a 7–4 loss to Cincinnati's Ted Breitenstein

Jim Field's ML career spanned sixteen seasons, and he was a regular in several of them but played only 332 games. Until a few years ago his ML debut date was believed to be May 30, 1883, but Columbus's game in New York that day has since been credited to Yale first baseman Sam Childs. Field actually first appeared with Columbus in an exhibition game win at Brooklyn on June 1. He filled a huge hole—the Ohio team had begun 1883 without a genuine first baseman and had already run through four candidates—but was no all-star either. Field's biggest offensive contribution in his first three ML seasons came on May 7, 1885, at Pittsburgh, when he was hit a record 3 times in 3 plate appearances in a 3–1 loss to New York's Ed Begley.

After spending 1886 in the Southern League, Field expected to play 1B in his hometown in 1887, but the AA Philadelphia Athletics decided Ed Flanagan's bat had more pop. Field then spent the better part of the next four seasons with Newark minor league clubs before being purchased by

Rochester AA in late July 1890 for $600. Although he hit just .202 in 52 games, he displayed surprising power (.356 SA). Field finished 1890 at 1B for Rochester and then played in the Eastern League, mostly with Buffalo, until 1898, when Washington, which used eleven different first basemen that year, tried him in desperation. Released after just 5 games, Field was feared to be dying of consumption, but writer Harry Merrill said the rumor came from "his always cadaverous appearance," coupled with the fact he was ill early in the season, coughing and spitting up blood. In any case, Field went to Hot Springs in late August after leaving Washington, recovered to serve as a player-manager for a time with Newark of the Atlantic League in 1899 and operate a tavern for a number of years near Shibe Park in Philadelphia. The brother of marginal MLer Sam Field lived to the ripe age of 90 before dying after falling down a flight of stairs at his home. (DN)

Fisler, Weston Dickson / "West" "Icicle" "The Dandy of the Diamond"

B	T	HGT	WGT	G	AB	H	R	2B
R	R	5'6"	137	273	1335	414	258	72

3B	HR	RBI	BB	SO	SB	BA	SA	OBP
14	2	189	15	17	14	.310	.390	.318

B. 7/5/1841 Camden, NJ **D.** 12/25/1922
TEAMS: 71–75AthNA 76PhiN
DEBUT: 5/20/1871 at Boston; played 1B and went 1-for-5 in an 11–8 loss to Boston's Al Spalding
FINALE: 9/16/1876 at Philadelphia; played RF and went 0-for-5 in a 7–6 loss to Louisville's Jim Devlin

The son of physician Lorenzo Fisler, an early mayor of Camden, NJ, West Fisler was small, quiet, proficient at almost every position, and known as "The Dandy of the Diamond" because of the way he always wore his uniform in pristine condition, complete with tie and collar. He broke in with the Equity club of Philadelphia at age 18 in 1860 and played with several other nines in Philadelphia and New Jersey prior to joining the Philadelphia Athletics on June 8, 1866, as a center fielder and third baseman. Fisler took over as the A's first baseman in 1867 despite his lack of size and played either 1B or 2B for the next ten seasons with occasional games in the outfield and at SS. He topped NA first sackers in fielding in 1871 and two years later led all second baseman in FA. Excellent at every phase of the game, Fisler probably could have played in the NL for a few more years if he had chosen to leave Philadelphia. Instead he remained with the A's after they reorganized as part of the loosely run League Alliance, and he also returned to cricket, his original sport.

In 1883 Fisler was managing the Camden Merritts when they disbanded on July 20 while leading the Interstate Association. Sometime in the mid-1870s he opened a men's clothing store with former teammate Count Sensenderfer, also a noted dandy. The pair went separate ways after their partnership dissolved, with Fisler taking a sales post with Wanamaker's. He later was a clerk for one of Philadelphia's leading attorneys and was still working when he died in a Philadelphia hospital at 81. (DN/EM)

Flynn, William / "Clipper"

B	T	HGT	WGT	G	AB	H	R	2B
?	R	5'7"	140	38	182	57	47	7

3B	HR	RBI	BB	SO	SB	BA	SA	OBP
1	0	29	4	2	3	.313	.363	.328

B. 4/29/1849 Lansingburgh, NY **D.** 11/11/1881
TEAMS: 71TroNA 72OlyNA
DEBUT: 5/9/1871 at Troy; played RF and went 0-for-4 in a 9–5 loss to Boston's Al Spalding
FINALE: 5/24/1872 at Washington; played 1B and went 3-for-5 in an 11–7 win over the Washington Nationals Bill Stearns

Clipper Flynn played with the Haymakers in 1869 in the controversial August 26 match against the undefeated Cincinnati Red Stockings in which the Haymakers withdrew from the field with the score 17–17 due to perpetual disagreements with umpire J. R. Brockway. He then moved to Chicago the following year before returning home to Troy for the inaugural NA season. Flynn is probably best remembered for picking a fight with New York's Dick Higham before a game on June 11, 1871. Higham bloodied Flynn, and when Flynn jumped into the press box to hide, a general melee ensued highlighted by a fistfight between the respective presidents of the Troy and New York teams. Flynn hit .338 in hitter-friendly Troy in 1871 but was batting only .225 despite his gala day in the Olympics' finale before they disbanded. The source of his nickname is unknown, as is the reason why he chose not to sign with Troy again in 1872. In 1877 Flynn returned to baseball for two years with the Troy area Lansingburghs. He then helped run the family business, Flynn Brothers Manufacturing, in Troy until he died in 1881. (DN/FV/EM)

*Foutz, David Luther / "Dave" "Scissors"

B	T	HGT	WGT	G	AB	H	R	2B
R	R	6'2"	161	1136	4537	1253	784	186

3B	HR	RBI	BB	SO	SB	BA	SA	OBP
91	31	750	300	136	260	.276	.378	.323

G	IP	H	GS	CG	BB
251	1997.1	1843	216	202	510

SO	SH	W	L	PCT	ERA
790	16	147	66	.690	2.84

G	W	L	PCT	PENNANTS
532	264	257	.507	0

B. 9/7/1856 Carroll County, MD **D.** 3/5/1897
TEAMS: 84–87StLA 88–89BroA 90–92BroN (P/M)93–96BroN
DEBUT: 7/29/1884 at Cincinnati; caught by Pat Deasley and beat Cincinnati's Will White 6–5
FINALE: 5/14/1896 at Cincinnati; played RF and went 1-for-4 in a 13–2 loss to Cincinnati's Frank Dwyer
CAREER HIGHLIGHT: 9/12/1886 at St. Louis; according to *TSN*, "Foutz played the sharpest trick ever seen on the ball field" when he snuck over from the pitcher's box and recorded an unassisted pick-off of base runner Pete Browning at 1B.

Dave Foutz was a multifaceted player who was a member of five pennant winners in two different cities and two different major leagues between 1885–90. Despite a frail, elongated, scissorslike appearance that lead many to think he suffered from consumption and others to believe (correctly) that he was asthmatic, Foutz, according to Al Spink, "was the possessor of considerable strength and while he was one of the speediest of pitchers he could also hit the ball an awful hard crack."

Born in the Baltimore area, Foutz began his baseball career in that city with the amateur Waverlys in 1878 at 1B. The following year he journeyed to Colorado to seek his fortune as a gold miner in the Leadville area and instead found fame as a pitcher. In 1882, while hurling for the semipro Leadville Blues, Foutz claimed to have gone 40-1 with ex-MLer Jake Knowdell as his catcher, earning his first pro contract with Bay City, MI, of the Northwestern League the following season. In his second season with Bay City, Foutz caught the eye of several ML teams. Upon the collapse of the Northwestern League, there was a bidding war for the pitcher–first baseman with a .333 BA and 18-4 record in the box, and the Browns paid a then astronomical $2,000 in July 1884 to secure Foutz's services. St. Louis owner Chris Von der Ahe proudly described his new acquisition as "a bewilderer," an assessment of Foutz's pitching style rather than his character that proved wholly accurate when the rookie went 15-6 in the remaining ten weeks of the season despite missing nearly a month with malaria.

A side-armer with an easy motion, Foutz was unaffected by the blizzard of pitching rule changes in the mid-1880s and won 99 games between 1885–87 while serving in RF between box assignments, since he was also one of the club's better hitters. In 1886 he was arguably the best pitcher in the AA, leading the circuit in wins and ERA. The following year his pitching season was truncated on August 14 when a line drive broke his right thumb, but he nonetheless had his best year at the plate, hitting .357 in 102 games. His effectiveness as a pitcher was essentially ended, however, as the thumb injury reduced his ability to throw a curve ball. After winning 114 games in his first four ML seasons, Foutz would only win 33 more.

During the 1887 World's Series against NL champion Detroit, Foutz was singled out by Von der Ahe as one of the causes of the Browns' ignominious defeat. Still suffering the lingering effects of his injury, he pitched poorly, losing 3 decisions, including a 9–0 rout in Game 6. To make matters worse, he only hit .169. Foutz also committed a baserunning blunder in Game 2 when he stopped at 2B after hitting the ball into the overflow crowd in RF although the rules of the time would have allowed him to keep running. After the Series he and catcher Doc Bushong were sold to Brooklyn for $5,500 as part of Von der Ahe's massive housecleaning, which the owner maintained was a financial necessity but in Foutz's case was probably designed to eliminate manager Charlie Comiskey's chief competition for his 1B roost, as 1B was Foutz's best position in the event his pitching days proved to have been numbered by his injury. In Brooklyn, Foutz did indeed become the club's first baseman and contributed heavily to championships in 1889 and 1890 with both his bat and his sharp defensive work. While he only occasionally took the box, Foutz led Brooklyn in RBI in 1888 and 1889 and in total bases in 1888 and 1890.

In 1892, with Dan Brouthers available to play 1B, Foutz again returned to splitting time between the outfield and the box. Although unable to regain his old form, he went 13-8 in twenty starts. His 1892 effort made him the first hurler in ML history to pitch two-hundred innings after a four-year gap since his previous two-hundred-inning season. It was all but his last gasp as a hurler, however. When the pitching distance increased the following season and Foutz took over as manager of the Brooklyn club, he played less often with each passing season.

While not a great success during the four years he ran the Bridegrooms, he was able to keep the team over .500 in his first three years. By 1896, his final season at the helm, Foutz allowed outfielder Mike Griffin to run the club on the field while he made the personnel decisions and spent most of his time at the racetrack. In October he resigned his Brooklyn post and was reported to be considering an offer to manage the Browns in 1897, but negotiations appear to have ground to a halt when Foutz said he would only serve as a bench pilot after claiming heart trouble would prevent him from ever playing again.

In truth, Foutz's health had begun to deteriorate badly in the mid-1890s. In 1894 he suffered bouts of rheumatism and pneumonia, and in 1896 he was forced to retire as a player after just two early-season games. In the winter of 1896–97, Foutz was living at his mother's house in Waverly, MD, while seeking medical treatment in Baltimore when, on March 5, he died suddenly of what appears to have been an asthma attack. In addition to his mother, Foutz was survived by his wife, who had suffered a series of mental breakdowns in recent years that contributed to his own decline in health, and a brother, Frank, a Baltimore amateur who would eventually play in the American League in its inaugural season as a major loop. (DN/JK)

Gould, Charles Harvey / "Charlie" "Bushel Basket"

B	T	HGT	WGT	G	AB	H	R	2B
R	R	6'0"	172	221	964	248	138	37

3B	HR	RBI	BB	SO	SB	BA	SA	OBP
12	2	111	19	24	7	.257	.327	.272

G	IP	H	GS	CG	BB
2	4.1	10	0	0	0

SO	SH	W	L	PCT	ERA
0	0	0	0	—	0.00

G	W	L	PCT	PENNANTS
88	11	77	.125	0

B. 8/21/1847 Cincinnati, OH **D.** 4/10/1917
TEAMS: 71–72BosNA 74BalNA (P/M)75NHNA (P/M)76CinN 77CinN
DEBUT: 5/5/1871 at Washington; played 1B and made 1 hit in a 20–18 win over Washington's Asa Brainard.
FINALE: 7/12/1877 at Cincinnati; played 1B and went 1-for-4 in a 15–9 loss to Chicago's Terry Larkin
FAMOUS FIRST: 9/5/1871 at Boston; hit the first grand slam homer in ML history in the ninth inning to top Chicago's George Zettlein 6–3

The first baseman for the legendary 1869 Cincinnati Red Stockings was a Queen City native and the scion of an old and cultured Ohio family. Charlie Gould was not a fast runner and only a fair hitter (he had the lowest BA of all the starters on the 1869 club, hitting .457). In the field he was weak on pop-ups and scoops but excellent at snagging even the hardest thrown balls. As for his managerial record, it is more a reflection on the quality of the teams he ran than on his leadership.

After hitting just .255 for the pennant-winning Bostons in 1872, Gould intended to quit the game but could not stay away and returned with Baltimore in 1874. The following year he again tried to retire after he was canned as field captain of New Haven but then agreed to return to Cincinnati as player-manager when it joined the NL in 1876. Gould and second baseman Charlie Sweasy were the only two members of the 1869 Red Stockings on the Queen City's first major league entry. He finally made good on his pledge to quit for good the following year when Cincinnati temporarily dropped out of the NL.

Gould later worked for the Cincinnati police department and then served as a streetcar conductor and a storeroom manager for the Pullman Palace Car Company before becoming a Cincinnati insurance agent. He was living with his son in Flushing, NY, in 1917 when he suffered a fatal stroke. (DN/DB/EM)

Kerins, John Nelson / "Jack"

B	T	HGT	WGT	G	AB	H	R	2B
R	R	5'10"	177	557	2227	561	392	72

3B	HR	RBI	BB	SO	SB	BA	SA	OBP
51	20	217	165	5	95	.252	.357	.308

G	W	L	PCT	PENNANTS
24	12	12	.500	0

B. 7/15/1858 Indianapolis, IN **D.** 9/8/1919
TEAMS: 84IndA 85–89LouA (P/M)88LouA 89BalA (P/M)90StLA
DEBUT: 5/1/1884 at St. Louis; played 1B and was 0-for-5 in a 4–2 loss to Tip O'Neill of the Browns
FINALE: 6/15/1890 at St. Louis; replaced injured catcher Jack Munyan and went 0-for-2 in a 9–1 loss to Columbus's Hank Gastright

In 1897 Tom Brown told *TSN* that Kerins was once the toughest man in baseball. Brown recounted that when he had been running his saloon in Louisville in the mid-1890s Joe Goddard's manager had stopped by one day looking for someone to box four rounds with the Australian slugger, and Jack Kerins, after volunteering, had held Goddard to a draw and nearly knocked him out in the first round. Yet by 1896 a reporter who saw Kerins tending bar at Brown's place sadly noted that he sported "a figure as ample as Old King Cole."

Kerins was a welter of contradictions both on and off the field. A boilermaker by trade, he was allegedly temperate, but there is at least one report that he was fined (by Jim Hart in 1886) for drunkenness. Too, Kerins was viewed as an excellent-fielding first baseman but a weak hitter, yet his .357 SA is good for a .252 career hitter and especially for a catcher, his position about a third of the time. Kerins began his career catching with the semipro Indianapolis Capital Cities in 1878 and remained in the Midwest, mostly with independent teams, until he joined Fort Wayne of the Northwestern League in 1883 and was acquired later that season by independent Indianapolis. The following year he made his ML entrance when Indianapolis moved up to the AA. Kerins served as team captain until Bill Watkins took over on August 1. Despite a .214 BA and a low OBP, he led the team in runs with 58. Under suspension for an unknown offense at the time the Hoosier club folded, Kerins transferred to Louisville in 1885 and again was named captain but this time served only until SS Tom McLaughlin replaced him on June 5. In 1886 Kerins led the Colonels in runs with 113 despite hitting only .269, in part because he was such a good base runner that he often batted leadoff. Current reference works rate Kerins one of the top players in the AA in 1886, but many of his rating points stem from credit he received as a catcher for fielding runs, which can be derived speciously. Because he was the only catcher on the Louisville team who could handle Tom Ramsey's knuckle-ball deliveries, Kerins caught most of Ramsey's starts and compiled mammoth put-out and assist totals from either catching the third strike on Ramsey's 499 strikeouts (for a put-out) or else muffing it and then needing to throw the batter out at 1B (for an assist).

In 1887 Louisville's new manager, "Honest John" Kelly, to spare Kerins injury began to use him as a catcher only when necessary. As it was, a broken thumb suffered in a plate collision held him to just 112 games. Kerins appears to have never been the same after the injury. By 1888 he was seen mostly in the outfield, and the following year he was released in late May for being in poor condition. Kerins then turned to umpiring and was more or less a regular AA ump until its demise after the 1891 season, although he took leave from officiating in 1890 to mount a comeback with St. Louis as a player. When he was hitting just .127 after 18 games, the Browns released him.

Kerins applied to umpire in the NL after the AA folded but was rejected. He later officiated for a time in the Western League and then managed Tom Brown's saloon. Kerins died a pauper in Louisville's City Hospital in 1919, and members of the Louisville baseball community had to organize a fund drive to get the money to give him a "Christian burial." (DN/DB)

LaChance, George Joseph / "Candy"

B	T	HGT	WGT	G	AB	H	R	2B
B	R	6'1"	183	684	2703	793	424	121

3B	HR	RBI	BB	SO	SB	BA	SA	OBP
62	30	467	137	124	192	.293	.417	.338

B. 2/15/1870 Putnam, CT **D.** 8/18/1932
TEAMS: 93–98BroN 99BalN 01CleAL 02–05BosAL
DEBUT: 8/15/1893 at Brooklyn; played LF and went 1-for-4 in a 5–0 win over Washington's Les German
FINALE: 4/28/1905 at Boston; played 1B and went 1-for-3 in a 1–0 loss to Washington's Casey Patten

Someone may have given George LaChance his nickname jokingly, for his disposition was anything but sweet. He was the first baseman on the 1904 Boston Americans' "iron man" infield that featured four men who all played 155 or more games. Although the club won the AL pennant, he hit .227 and was gone after just 12 games in 1905 when he got off to a .146 start. LaChance had previously been a member of the 1903 Boston Americans, the first modern World Series winner, after coming to the Hub in a November 1901 trade with Cleveland AL for catcher Ossee Schreck. The deal was made when the surly LaChance threatened to quit Cleveland over the harsh roasting he was given by local fans and several times had to be restrained from going into the stands in Cleveland's park in pursuit of a tormentor.

A switch hitter who could play both the infield and outfield as well as catch, LaChance seemed on the verge of stardom when he first arrived in the majors. He was sold to Brooklyn in August 1893 at Wilkes-Barre manager Dan Shannon's behest when his club was anchored in last place in the Eastern League. A center fielder prior to arriving in Brooklyn, LaChance was not about to replace Mike Griffin and was forced to seek other employment. He did not find his permanent niche at 1B until 1895, when he led Brooklyn in RBI as well as stolen bases. The following year LaChance missed the last two months of the season when a line drive off Jake Beckley's bat broke his hand. He returned in 1897 to post decent numbers but collected just 15 walks and then slumped to .247 the following year. When Brooklyn and Baltimore came under syndicate ownership in 1899 and most of the combine's stronger players were assigned to Brooklyn, LaChance headed for Baltimore. But even a .307 season could not save him from being dropped once the NL pared from twelve teams to eight in the spring of 1900. LaChance connected with Cleveland of the newly renamed AL and remained with the Forest City club when the loop went major in 1901.

LaChance finished his pro playing career in 1908 where it had begun in 1891, with Waterbury, CT. He umpired in the Connecticut League for a while and then settled on a small farm in Waterville, CT, and later worked as a watchman at a Waterville factory. LaChance left a wife and three children when he died at his Waterville home after a long illness. (DN)

Lane, George M. / "Chappy"

B	T	HGT	WGT	G	AB	H	R	2B
R	?	?	165	114	429	87	52	17

3B	HR	RBI	BB	SO	SB	BA	SA	OBP
7	4	—	7	—	—	.203	.303	.219

B. ?/?/1856 Pittsburgh, PA **D.** 10/9/1901
TEAMS: 82PitA 84TolA
DEBUT: 5/16/82 at Cincinnati; played CF and went 1-for-4 in a 9–4 loss to Cincinnati's Harry McCormick
FINALE: 9/9/84 at Toledo; played 1B and RF and went 1-for-4 in a 4–0 win over Brooklyn's Jim Conway

Born in the Pittsburgh area around 1856, Chappy Lane first played for pay as an outfielder with the independent 1876 Alleghenys. He later was with the Wheeling Standards before returning to the Alleghenys and remained with independent teams in the Pittsburgh area until the city seized one of the AA's six original franchises in 1882. Lane soon proved that he could hit the ball with power—when he hit it. Though batters' strikeout totals were not kept in the AA's early years, he almost certainly was a leading K victim in 1882. Among nineteenth-century first baseman with a minimum of 200 ABs after the pitching distance was set at 50 feet in 1881, his 1882 .178 BA is second only to Juice Latham's mark of .169 in 1884.

Lane opened 1884 as Toledo's first baseman but again failed to hit and rode the bench much of the season. Little is known of his movements after he left the Ohio club. He died in Philadelphia in 1901 after a barrel of brass fell on his head. The source of his nickname is unknown.

Larkin, Henry E. / "Ted"

B	T	HGT	WGT	G	AB	H	R	2B
R	R	5'10"	175	1184	4718	1429	925	259

3B	HR	RBI	BB	SO	SB	BA	SA	OBP
114	53	836	464	141	129	.303	.440	.380

G	W	L	PCT	PENNANTS
79	34	45	.430	0

B. 1/12/1860 Reading, PA **D.** 1/31/1942
TEAMS: 84–89PhiA (P/M)90CleP 91PhiA 92–93WasN
DEBUT: 5/1/1884 at Pittsburgh; played CF and went 0-for-4 in a 9–2 win over Pittsburgh's John Fox
FINALE: 8/3/1893 at Philadelphia; played 1B and made 1 hit in a 22–7 loss to Philadelphia's Jack Taylor

Ted Larkin was in his second season with the Interstate Association Reading Actives in 1883 and prior to his death in 1942 was reportedly the last surviving member of this famous minor league team that furnished the majors with so many players in 1883–84. The following spring, when he opened the season in CF for the Philadelphia A's, he was one of three rookies on the defending AA champs, joining catcher Jack Milligan and pitcher Al Atkinson. The club also had a new SS, Sadie Houck, and was never able to play cohesively enough to defend its title. Unfortunately, a similar situation prevailed in all of Larkin's seven seasons with the A's. The team began each spring with high hopes, usually remained in contention until August, and then faded and finished somewhere between third and sixth. Larkin in some ways personified the A's. A good player throughout his career, he was a cut below stardom. His AA career OPS ranks sixth among players with a minimum of 2,000 ABs in that loop, but the gap between him and Harry Stovey's fifth best mark (37 points) is wider than between his .815 and the tenth-best figure of .788.

Ironically, Larkin was never even the main cog on his own team, thanks to Stovey, who not only paced the A's each season in most major batting departments but also was their recognized field leader. In 1888, when Larkin assumed the captaincy at the beginning of season after Stovey refused the job, he was accused by both teammates and manager Billy Sharsig of being too hard on the club's twin pitching aces, Gus Weyhing and Ed Seward, and not "kicking" enough at umpires' decisions. Larkin's defense was that Philadelphia was a town where fans got down on their players who kicked (certainly not true today), but he could offer no explanation for his own .269 BA, his career season nadir. He recovered to hit .318 in 1889 and then joined the exodus of discontented players who jumped to the PL in 1890. Serving for most of the season as Cleveland's playing captain, he combined with Pete Browning and Ed Delahanty to give the Infants a potent middle of the batting order, but their pitching was no match for the rest of the loop.

Larkin returned to the A's when the PL folded, but then both he and catcher Jack Milligan had the ill luck to be assigned to lowly Washington when the NL and AA merged in December 1891. When he hit just .280 and was marked by Washington for release, he fully welcomed it until Jim O'Rourke took over the club's reins after the 1892 season ended and intervened.

Forced to return to D.C. in 1893 against his wishes, Larkin was leading the team with a .317 BA when he sensed the club was headed for a cellar finish and decided enough was enough. He jumped to Reading of the Pennsylvania State League along with teammate Joe Mulvey, knowing that he could play for his hometown team without fear of reprisals because it was not part of the National Agreement. But when Reading chose to play as a National Agreement team in 1894, he moved to Mike Kelly's freewheeling Allentown club that had become a haven for disgruntled ex-ML stars. Larkin had a final big year in 1895, his last pro season, when he hit .358 while splitting his time among three Pennsylvania State League teams. After leaving the game, he was a boilermaker in Reading for many years before taking a job with the city park system. He died of a sudden illness at a Reading hospital in 1942. Most reference works contend that Larkin was known by his first name of Henry, but his teammates and the media called him "Ted" throughout his career for a reason we do not know. (DN)

Latham, George Warren / "Juice" "Jumbo"

B	T	HGT	WGT	G	AB	H	R	2B
R	R	5'8"	210	334	1431	353	209	35

3B	HR	RBI	BB	SO	SB	BA	SA	OBP
17	0	101	35	6	6	.247	.295	.266

G	W	L	PCT	PENNANTS
93	45	48	484	0

B. 9/6/1852 Utica, NY **D.** 5/26/1914
TEAMS: 75BosNA (P/M)75NHNA 77LouN (P/M)82PhiA 83–84LouA
DEBUT: 4/19/1875 at Boston; played 1B and made 1 hit in a 6–0 win over New Haven's Tricky Nichols
FINALE: 10/11/1884 at Richmond; played 1B and went 0-for-3 in an 11–6 loss to Virginia's Pete Meegan

Juice Latham is the only first baseman in ML history to compile as many as 1,400 ABs and never hit a home run. To those who saw him play early in his career, that might come as no surprise, for he was small for a first baseman and quite slim, weighing only around 160. By the time he finished playing, however, he probably weighed over 230 pounds. Notwithstanding his massive girth, he loathed being called either "Juice" or "Jumbo," feeling that both nicknames were beneath his dignity.

After playing for an independent team in Toronto early in 1874, Latham was observed playing somewhere in New York state later that summer by Harry Wright and signed for a three-month trial in 1875. Unable to dislodge Cal McVey at 1B, Latham played for Wright's Boston club only on days that McVey caught until his three months expired and then served for a time as New Haven's playing captain before finishing the season in Canada. After spending 1876 with independent London, Ont., and Binghamton, NY, he signed with Louisville in 1877. Though he played regularly for the Grays and had his best season, hitting .291, he is perhaps the most forgotten regular on the only club ever thought to have deliberately lost a pennant. Though he was not implicated in the ensuing scandal and was one of the few Grays not even suspected, he was relegated to the minors again when Louisville disbanded.

Latham did not return to the majors until five years later when the rebel AA formed and he was named the Philadelphia entry's playing captain. Relieved of his command after the season ended, he went back to familiar ground, signing with Louisville. In 1883, despite his ample midsection, Latham was tried briefly as a SS, but the experiment ended when he fielded .688 in 9 games and was fined $50 for falling "into evil ways." His reputation for the "hard stuff" growing by the day, he nonetheless was named Louisville's captain and cleanup hitter at the beginning of the 1884 season. Latham was swiftly relieved of the latter assignment after he went 0-for-5 on Opening Day and swam well below the .200 watermark all season, resulting in a .395 OPS, by far the lowest of any 1B batting-title qualifier in history. But the captaincy appears to have remained his until his final day in a Louisville uniform. And the AA pennant, which might have been Louisville's, went to the New York Mets when the Colonels decided that a jolly drinking companion was worth more than a first baseman who could still deliver an occasional hit.

If Latham went on a rigorous training regimen after the 1884 season in an attempt to turn his career around, it was an abject failure. In 1885 he joined Virginia and was hitting .201 for the Eastern League team as the season headed into August. Yet he continued to land one minor league assignment after another, meanwhile driving a horse car in the winter months. In 1888 Latham suffered his ultimate indignity when *SL* reported, "An earthquake took place on the Elmira grounds recently in the vicinity of second base. It was only Juice Latham sliding to the second bag." The following March he was rumored to have committed suicide, but it turned out that he had just disappeared for a while to escape paying a string of bar tabs in Oneida, NY, his last pro stop.

By 1900 Latham had returned permanently to Utica, using the city as his perch to regale gullible writers with stories of how he had originated base coaching and intimate fallaciously that teams all over the area were constantly soliciting him to stage a benefit game on his behalf. He died in 1914 at a Utica hospital after an illness of several months. (DN/DB)

McAtee, Michael James / "Bub"

B	T	HGT	WGT	G	AB	H	R	2B
?	R	6'1"	160	51	264	65	64	11

3B	HR	RBI	BB	SO	SB	BA	SA	OBP
3	0	25	6	4	5	.249	.314	.271

B. 3/?/1845 Troy, NY **D.** 10/18/1876

TEAMS: 71ChiNA 72TroNA
DEBUT: 5/8/1871 at Chicago; played 1B and went 1-for-4 in a 14–12 win over Cleveland's Al Pratt
FINALE: 7/23/1872 at Middletown; played 1B and went 2-for-4 in a 7–0 win over Middletown's Cy Bentley

Bub McAtee wore a makeshift knee brace after dislocating his knee on a play at 1B. He was also a prizefighter and was regarded as one to approach gingerly on the ball field. McAtee grew up in Lansingburgh, where his father was a saloonkeeper, and played for the Haymakers club from 1866–69. In 1870 he seceded to Chicago along with Mart King and Clipper Flynn. When the Great Fire ruined Chicago's NA franchise, McAtee returned to Troy for the 1872 season. It is not known why he did not connect with another NA team after Troy folded following its game on July 23, 1872. McAtee died of consumption at his home in Troy in 1876. His nickname was often given to rugged customers in his day. (DN)

McCauley, Allen A. / "Al"

B	T	HGT	WGT	G	AB	H	R	2B
L	L	6'0"	180	192	677	170	106	30

3B	HR	RBI	BB	SO	SB	BA	SA	OBP
16	2	78	99	51	17	.251	.352	.357

G	IP	H	GS	CG	BB
10	76	87	9	9	25

SO	SH	W	L	PCT	ERA
34	0	2	7	.222	5.09

B. 3/4/1863 Indianapolis, IN **D.** 8/24/1917
TEAMS: 84IndA 90PhiN 91WasA
DEBUT: 6/21/1884 at Indianapolis; played 1B, relieved Jake Aydelott in the box, and went 2-for-5 in Aydelott's 17–6 loss to Philadelphia's Bobby Mathews
FINALE: 10/6/1891 at Washington; played 1B and got 1 hit in a 15–11 loss to Baltimore's Kid Madden

Al McCauley was playing for a local Indianapolis team in 1884 before he joined the city's AA entry in June. Released to Portsmouth of the Ohio State League before the season ended, he went to Birmingham of the Southern League in 1885 and continued to split his days between pitching and 1B. By the time McCauley returned to the majors with the Phillies in 1890 he was strictly a first baseman. Dropped after he hit just .244 against PL-diluted NL pitching staffs, he signed with Omaha of the Western Association for 1891 and was among the Nebraska team's players who accompanied player-manager Dan Shannon to Washington in July. Acquired to replace slumping Mox McQuery at 1B, McCauley hit well in his second stint in the AA but was released after the season. He played in the California League for the next two years and then returned to Indianapolis in 1893 when the Cal loop folded and played on a local semipro team with the Sowders brothers.

The following year McCauley resumed his pro career with Sioux City of the Western League and remained a journeyman minor leaguer until 1897. McCauley's .251 ML-career BA seems reason enough that he never established himself as a ML first baseman. However, his .709 career OPS is the highest of any first baseman prior to World War II with so low a BA and a minimum of 600 career PAs. McCauley died at an Indianapolis nursing home in 1917. (DN/DB)

McSorley, John Bernard / "Trick"

B	T	HGT	WGT	G	AB	H	R	2B
R	R	5'4"	142	43	146	34	19	5

3B	HR	RBI	BB	SO	SB	BA	SA	OBP
0	0	11	5	4	3	.233	.267	.258

G	IP	H	GS	CG	BB
1	2	5	0	0	0

SO	SH	W	L	PCT	ERA
1	0	0	0	—	4.50

B. 12/16/1852 St. Louis, MO **D.** 2/9/1936
TEAMS: 75RedsNA 84TolA 85StLN 86StLA
DEBUT: 5/6/1875 at Keokuk; played LF and went hitless in a 15–2 loss to Keokuk's Mike Golden
FINALE: 5/6/1886 at Pittsburgh; played SS and went 0-for-3 in a 6–0 loss to Pittsburgh's Ed Morris

Trick McSorley was a notorious "kicker," regularly fined or ejected by umpires and called "the true sportsman of the gang" because he was involved year-round in either horse racing, cockfighting, dogfighting, or hunting. He was a member of the St. Louis Reds from 1873 through 1875 when they were briefly part of the NA. Late in the 1875 season he jumped to Covington, KY, and remained there in 1876. McSorley spent 1877 with Indianapolis of the League Alliance and then played with Buffalo,

Detroit, the semipro Cincinnati Buckeyes, the independent St. Louis Browns, Kansas City, and Peoria. He was with Peoria in 1884 when the Northwestern League folded, enabling Toledo AA to hire him at no cost and put him into the record book when it installed him as its regular first baseman for a time. McSorley purportedly is the only man in ML history to play as many as 10 games (16) at 1B despite being listed as under 5'6" (though in team pictures he looks taller than that).

The following year he was with Milwaukee until the Western League folded and then joined Memphis of the newly formed Southern League before coming to the St. Louis Maroons for his only 2 games in the NL. McSorley remained in St. Louis with the AA Browns in the early part of 1886 as an injury replacement for SS Bill Gleason. He then returned to Memphis and was leading the team in hitting when the Southern League folded, sending him to Hot Springs, AR, with teammate Ed Fusselbach. Now 35, instead of declining he seemed actually to be peaking when he batted leadoff for Denver in 1887 and ranked among the top hitters in the Western League. McSorley then captained Davenport of the Central Interstate League for part of 1888, also spent more time with Denver, and then in early March of the following spring joined Lou Sylvester and Charlie Krehmeyer as part of a group of ex-Browns players whom St. Louis sportswriter Joe Pritchard recruited for the Sacramento team of the California League. Nearly 37 by then, McSorley left active play shortly thereafter and umpired briefly in the minors before returning to St. Louis to work as a bartender. Around 1901 he joined the St. Louis Police Department and remained on the force for some thirty years before dying of a stroke in St. Louis at 83.

McSorley will always be the lone man who performed with St. Louis teams in the NA, the NL, and the AA. His longevity and versatility for a player his size (if indeed his listed height is correct) are also almost unparalleled. (DN/DB)

McVey, Calvin Alexander / "Cal"

B	T	HGT	WGT	G	AB	H	R	2B
R	R	5'9"	170	530	2513	869	555	133

3B	HR	RBI	BB	SO	SB	BA	SA	OBP
44	11	448	30	51	25	.346	.447	.354

G	IP	H	GS	CG	BB
34	176.1	235	19	12	16

SO	SH	W	L	PCT	ERA
37	0	10	12	.455	3.83

G	W	L	PCT	PENNANTS
157	91	64	.587	0

B. 8/30/1849 Montrose, IA **D.** 8/20/1926
TEAMS: 71–72BosNA (P/M)73BalNA 74–75BosNA 76–77ChiN (P/M)78–79CinN
DEBUT: 5/5/1871 at Washington; caught Al Spalding and made 2 hits in a 20–18 win over the Olympics' Asa Brainard
FINALE: 9/30/1879 at Cleveland; played RF and went 1-for-5 in a 9–6 loss to Cleveland's Jim McCormick

Cal McVey may have been the most multitalented athlete on the 1869 Cincinnati Red Stockings—he was also an excellent boxer—and was almost certainly the team's best all-around player over the long haul. Still a teenager when he left the Indianapolis Actives in 1868 to join the Queen City club, he nonetheless had been playing in fast company ever since 1866. McVey was initially regarded by some on the team as an experiment because of his tender age, but he quickly established himself as a dominant hitter on the game's most dominant team. He also owned arguably the best arm on the club, allowing him to serve as both a change pitcher and catcher despite some defensive shortcomings when he was not stationed at his customary post in RF. In the 1870 eleven-inning loss to the Brooklyn Atlantics at Capitoline Grounds that snapped the Red Stockings' record winning streak, McVey nearly extended the game when he dug Joe Start's drive out of the hostile Brooklyn crowd in deep RF and fired a strike to catcher Doug Allison, who muffed the throw as Start stumbled across the plate with the winning run. Writing about the game in 1894, Tim Murnane called McVey's heave the greatest throw he ever saw.

In 1871 McVey and first baseman Charlie Gould were the lone Red Stockings regulars who accompanied the Wright brothers to the Boston NA club, as the rest of the team helped form the Washington Olympics. McVey remained with Boston long enough to be part of its first pennant winner in 1872 and then switched to Baltimore in 1873 when the Maryland entry offered him more money plus its captaincy. Primarily a catcher in his first two NA seasons, he played every position but pitcher with Baltimore. In 1874 McVey returned to Boston and shared the catching with Deacon White, who had joined the club in the interim. When not behind the plate, McVey was usually found at his old post in RF. In 1875, for the first time in his career, he played 1B on a full-time basis. At the close of 1875, the NA's final season, he owned a .362 career BA, third only to Ross Barnes's .391 and Levi Meyerle's .365.

The following year two of the NA's top three hitters joined White and pitcher Al Spalding, the NA's best battery, on the Chicago White Stockings. The quartet's covert signing with the Second City entry during the 1875 season was instrumental in causing the unbalanced and poorly organized NA to disband in favor of the upstart National League. Led by the Boston "Big Four," Chicago made the initial NL race nearly as much of a mockery as most of its NA counterparts had been, and McVey, in addition to hitting .347, logged a 1.52 ERA and 5-2 record, the best showing of any change pitcher in the loop. But when White returned to Boston in 1877 and Spalding quit pitching to play 1B, McVey replaced White at catcher and was inadequate to the task, as Chicago tumbled into the second division.

Invited to return to Cincinnati in 1878 and manage the club that had brought up the rear in each of the NL's first two seasons, McVey rose to the challenge and also moved to 3B, his fourth different position as a regular. Despite a rocky year in the field, he again topped .300 and spurred Cincinnati to a surprise second-place finish, but Cincinnati dropped to fifth in 1879 and he fell below .300 (.297) for the only time in his career. When the Reds released all their players toward the end of the season to help cut their losses, it rescinded the final year of McVey's three-year contract with the club, and he decided to relocate to the San Francisco Bay Area after visiting it during a fall barnstorming tour.

In 1880 McVey played in the California League, undertook a few mining ventures, and began to acclimate to western life. He remained active in the Pacific Coast game for several more years and experimented with a number of different lifestyles but never found one completely to his satisfaction. In the 1890s he worked in wine country and kept in shape wrestling and sparring despite now weighing close to 200. By the turn of the century he was back in the San Francisco Bay Area, running a cigar store. In 1906 McVey wrote a long letter to the *Boston Globe* after he was involved in the San Francisco Earthquake, saying that he had saved his wife and his 82-year-old father and was now reduced to living in a ten-by-twelve shack on almost no money, but at least he was not among the nearly 100,000 in the city who were homeless because "everything sent here in the shape of food and clothing has been ransacked and plundered by the so-called relief committees. It is simply awful." McVey later worked as a night watchman for a San Francisco lumber company. He died in San Francisco at 76 and was cremated. (DN/DB/PM)

Mills, Everett / "Everett" "Ev"

B	T	HGT	WGT	G	AB	H	R	2B
L	?	6'1"	174	337	1525	433	283	62

3B	HR	RBI	BB	SO	SB	BA	SA	OBP
21	2	205	13	12	10	.284	.356	.290

G	W	L	PCT	PENNANTS
14	8	6	.571	0

B. 1/20/1845 Newark, NJ **D.** 6/22/1908
TEAMS: 71OlyNA (P/M)72BalNA 73BalNA 74–75HarNA 76HarN
DEBUT: 5/5/1871 at Washington; played 1B and went hitless in a 20–18 loss to Boston's Al Spalding
FINALE: 10/17/1876 at New York; played 1B and went 1-for-3 in a 3–0 win over New York's Bobby Mathews

In 1886 Ned Cuthbert told *TSN* of a game he recalled in 1871 in which Everett Mills had lined a shot back through the box that had nearly decapitated Chicago's Ed Pinkham. Cuthbert also recollected that Mills liked low pitches and Pinkham, a southpaw, threw him a steady diet of outcurves, suggesting that Mills was a left-handed hitter. Mills began with the Eureka club of Newark, NJ, in 1864 and by 1869 had joined the New York Mutuals, remaining with them through 1870.

A steady performer throughout the NA's five-year history, Mills tumbled in 1876 when he scored just 28 runs for Hartford in 63 games. He played with Milwaukee of the League Alliance in 1877, briefly in the 1878 International Association, and then served as sergeant-at-arms in Quarter Sessions Court in Newark, NJ, before dying a heart disease in 1908. (DN/EM)

Morrill, John Francis / "John" "Honest John"

B	T	HGT	WGT	G	AB	H	R	2B
R	R	5'10½"	155	1265	4912	1275	821	239

3B	HR	RBI	BB	SO	SB	BA	SA	OBP
80	43	643	358	656	61	.260	.367	.310

G	IP	H	GS	CG	BB
18	58.2	75	2	2	12

SO	SH	W	L	PCT	ERA
22	0	1	2	.333	4.30

G	W	L	PCT	PENNANTS
696	348	334	.510	1

B. 2/19/1855 Boston, MA **D.** 4/2/1932
TEAMS: 76–88BosN (P/M)82–88BosN (P/M)89WasN 90BosP
DEBUT: 4/24/1876 at Philadelphia; played CF and made 1 hit in a 20–3 loss to Philadelphia's Lon Knight
FINALE: 7/8/1890 at Boston; played SS and went 1-for-3 in a 9–7 loss to Cleveland's Henry Gruber
FAMOUS FIRST: In 1883 became the first manager to win a ML pennant after taking the reins after the season started

John Morrill's main distinction was his rare ability to play every position well. He had a sensational arm and could throw from all angles even while falling to the ground. Believed by many historians to have been the best fielding first baseman in the nineteenth century, he was not far behind as a third baseman and had the unique experience of playing his first ML game in CF and his finale, fourteen years later, at SS. More important in some ways, he played all but 44 of his 1,265 games in a Boston ML uniform and was the city's first homegrown star of the first magnitude.

Morrill performed for amateur clubs in Boston before joining independent Lowell, MA, in 1875 as a combination second and third baseman. The following season he was claimed by both Syracuse and Boston but agreed to terms with his hometown club when manager Harry Wright offered him a three-year contract after he demonstrated that he was a capable catcher in addition to being a crack infielder. In his first season with the Hub NL entry, Morrill played six positions and then served at four the following year. The 1878 campaign was unique for him in that he was stationed at 1B in 59 of Boston's 60 games.

Morrill had yet to show much prowess as a hitter, however. He was in his fifth ML season before he hit his first career home run, victimizing Providence's John M. Ward on May 19, 1880. Subsequently his hitting began to improve, peaking in 1883 when he stroked .319 and compiled 212 total bases, second in the NL only to Dan Brouthers. That year he also hurled his only CG pitching win on May 5, beating Philadelphia 5–3, and became the first pilot in history to win a pennant after taking over a club in midstream. Morrill had served as Boston's field leader the previous year before relinquishing control to Jack Burdock at the start of the 1883 campaign and then assuming it again when Burdock felt the extra burden affected his play. He remained the club's pilot for the better part of the next five seasons but failed to repeat his magic as either a hitter or a leader. Morrill's nadir came in 1888 when he quarreled with teammate Mike Kelly, who was named the club's captain and then constantly criticized both his play and his field generalship to other players. The incessant bickering between the two helped sink Morrill's BA to .198, a record low by a 1B qualifier in either the NL or the AL. He reached his boiling point the following spring when Kelly, and not he, was named captain of the regular Boston nine in the annual Fast Day game. The next day Morrill was shipped to Washington along with Sam Wise for a reported $6,000.

Restored to his customary player-manager role once he joined the Senators, Morrill hit just .185 in 44 games and had his new team headed for a cellar finish when he was released in July. The following spring Morrill formed an independent team that he called the John F. Morrills and kept it extant for several years. He also wrote about sports for the *Boston Journal* until 1892 when he joined George Wright in the Wright & Ditson sporting goods enterprise after the death of Wright's partner and remained with the firm for over thirty-five years. In 1894 Morrill survived a near-fatal bout with appendicitis but did not fare as well that November when he came under vicious attack by members of the local press for refusing to attend Mike Kelly's funeral "right in his own backyard."

Morrill became an excellent golfer in his later years and was chairman of the New England Senior Golf Association for a time. He died at his Brookline home of double pneumonia in 1932, leaving behind a widow and four daughters. (DN/DB)

Murnane, Timothy Hayes
(b. Murnan) / **"Tim"**

B	T	HGT	WGT	G	AB	H	R	2B
L	R	5'9½"	172	383	1632	426	336	32

3B	HR	RBI	BB	SO	SB	BA	SA	OBP
9	5	130	60	54	39	.261	.301	.287

G	W	L	PCT	PENNANTS
111	58	51	.532	0

B. 6/4/1852 Naugatuck, CT **D.** 2/7/1917
TEAMS: 72ManNA 73–74AthNA 75PhiNA 76–77BosN 78ProN (P/M)84BosU
DEBUT: 4/26/1872 at Troy; played 1B and went 1-for-4 in 10–0 loss to Troy's George Zettlein
FINALE: 10/19/1884 at St. Louis; played 1B and went 0-for-4 in a 5–0 win over St. Louis's Charlie Sweeney

Although born in Connecticut, almost from the day Tim Murnane uttered his first word he spoke with an Irish brogue that some thought affected once they learned he was not really from "The Old Sod." While attending Holy Cross Prep, he began his career as a catcher with the amateur Stratford, CT, nine in 1869 and left the club the following year to play for the amateur Savannahs. In 1871 Murnane moved to the independent Middletown Mansfields and abandoned his catching aspirations to play 1B and the outfield. The following year he accompanied the Mansfields when they joined the NA and led the club in runs and BA while playing every inning of every game at 1B.

Murnane would never again approach his rookie heights and actually had to struggle for several years after that before he achieved even mediocrity again as a hitter. His fortes were his daring baserunning and his field leadership. On June 14, 1873, Murnane stunned onlookers in Philadelphia when he leaped over the head of Boston second baseman Andy Leonard to escape a rundown play. He reportedly collected the first stolen base in NL history three years later.

Murnane's spirited brand of ball impressed Boston manager Harry Wright sufficiently that he installed the first baseman as the Red Stockings' cleanup hitter in the club's yearling season as a member of the NL. Even though Murnane served as no more than a sub with Boston the following year, his reputation was such that the Providence Grays made him the first player they signed upon joining the NL in 1878. But when he hit just .239 in 49 games, he took his final bow in front of an NL audience on September 30, 1878, in a 2–1 win over his former Boston mates. After spending the next two seasons with Albany minor league teams, Murnane left the game to open a combination saloon and billiard hall in Boston.

Four years later he agreed to return to the diamond as a player-manager when his old Boston teammate, George Wright, helped install a Hub entry in the rebel Union Association and offered him a piece of the action. Murnane assembled one of the better clubs in the loop but undermined his work when he served as his own first baseman and logged a dismal .549 OPS. After the UA collapsed, he played awhile with Jersey City of the Eastern League in 1885 and then retired to start the New England League Boston Blues in 1886 and found a new sporting paper, the *Boston Referee*, that covered baseball and roller polo.

Murnane's first publishing venture failed, but it led to a position on the *Boston Globe*. His way with words and knowledge of the game were such that within a few years he was the *Globe's* sports editor and also writing regular columns on baseball for both *SL* and *TSN*. In addition to being a keen observer, if a somewhat conservative one who preferred the playing style of old-time stars like Wright and Ross Barnes, Murnane kept an active role in the game by scouting young talent and serving as longtime president of the New England League. Meanwhile his columns grew in popularity despite their sometimes partisan nature. Along with being a champion of the players of his day, Murnane usually took the side of the Boston NL club in disputes. Yet he had an analytical and foresighted mind that conceived as early as 1900 the notion of a designated hitter for the pitcher. In the late summer of 1895 Murnane's first wife died at their summer home in Nantucket after a "long battle with the enemy," leaving him with two young daughters. He was wed for the second time in February 1898 to Agnes Dowling, who bore him four more children. On February 17, 1917, a few hours after writing his daily column for the *Globe*, Murnane escorted his wife to an opera at Boston's Shubert Theatre. He remained in the lobby while she went to check her coat. When she returned she found him dead on the floor of a heart attack. Murnane is the only ML player to receive the J. G. Taylor Spink Award (in 1978) "for meritorious contributions to baseball writing." (DN)

O'Brien, William Smith / "Billy"

B	T	HGT	WGT	G	AB	H	R	2B
R	R	6'0"	185	356	1424	364	164	59

3B	HR	RBI	BB	SO	SB	BA	SA	OBP
22	32	206	59	88	26	.256	.395	.289

G	IP	H	GS	CG	BB
2	10	8	0	0	3

SO	SH	W	L	PCT	ERA
7	0	1	0	1.000	1.80

B. 3/14/1860 Albany, NY **D.** 5/26/1911
TEAMS: 84StPU 84KCU 87–89WasN 90BroA
DEBUT: 9/27/1884 at Cincinnati; played 3B and went 1-for-4 in a 6–1 loss to Cincinnati's Dick Burns
FINALE: 7/24/1890 at New York; played 1B and went 2-for-4 in a 9–3 loss to St. Louis's Bill Hart

Billy O'Brien is the only future ML home run king to debut in the UA. As a teenager he pitched for an Albany team with Mike Lanahan as his catcher. Lanahan was mysteriously murdered in August 1896, by which time O'Brien was wrapping up his career after Toledo of the Interstate League axed him for being "too slow in fielding his position." An absence of speed was O'Brien's perennial bane. In 1889 the *Washington Post* lamented when the D.C. club dismissed him that "his greatest drawback is his inability to run."

Still a pitcher-infielder in the early 1880s, O'Brien was in his second year with St. Paul of the Northwestern League when the Apostles joined the UA late in the 1884 season. After 8 games with St. Paul, he was permitted to go to Kansas City, where he made his home at the time. O'Brien remained with KC the following year until the Western League folded and then moved to Memphis of the Southern League. An encore season in the SL with Nashville earned a contract from the NL St. Louis Maroons in the fall of 1886. When St. Louis sold its franchise to Indianapolis that winter, O'Brien was the only Maroon that went to Washington rather than the Hoosier city. Still without a set position, he opened 1887 at 3B for the D.C. club and on May 3 homered in his first NL game. After also being tried at 2B and in the outfield, O'Brien was permanently planted on 1B.

More than any other hitter in 1887, O'Brien benefited from the experimental four-strike rule in effect for only that one season. A free swinger with tremendous power, he used the cushion of an extra strike in each at-bat to compile 97 of his 223 total bases on extra-base hits and lead the NL in seat rattlers with 19. It was a rule-created feat, as fluky in its way as Ned Williamson's record 27 homers in 1884. The following season was barely underway when a local Washington writer observed, "O'Brien, known and dreaded by pitchers as a long, hard hitter, has weakened lamentably under the [restoration of the] three-strike rule and has lost his old average." Though he still showed occasional flashes of power, he totaled only 9 walks, 42 runs, and a .225 BA in 528 ABs. O'Brien also fanned 70 times as opposed to just 17 the previous year.

In 1889 Washington released him just 2 games into the season, but when he hit .317 for Rochester of the International Association, Jim Kennedy, manager of the Brooklyn Gladiators, the AA's least auspicious replacement team in 1890, offered him a contract. O'Brien was leading the Gladiators in just about every major batting department when Kennedy folded the team. Upon arriving home in Kansas City, he learned that Dave Rowe's Denver Western Association club needed a first baseman. Already past 30, O'Brien was further slowed the following year when he suffered a severe knee injury and was released by Denver. A Kansas City fireman in the off-season, he nonetheless had trouble staying active enough to avoid putting on weight. After suffering through several more releases and increasing ridicule for his poor fielding—he was now an atrocity even on routine pop flies—O'Brien quit the game and left firefighting for police work. He had risen to the rank of sergeant when he died from heart disease in Kansas City at 51. (DN)

Orr, David L. / "Dave" "Sadie"

B	T	HGT	WGT	G	AB	H	R	2B
R	R	5'11"	250	791	3289	1126	536	198

3B	HR	RBI	BB	SO	SB	BA	SA	OBP
108	37	627	98	50	66	.342	.502	.366

G	IP	H	GS	CG	BB
3	10	11	0	0	5

SO	SH	W	L	PCT	ERA
1	0	0	0	—	7.20

G	W	L	PCT	PENNANTS
8	3	5	.375	0

B. 9/29/1859 New York, NY **D.** 6/3/1915
TEAMS: 83NYA 83NYN 83–87NYA (P/M)87NYA 88BroA 89ColA 90BroP
DEBUT: 5/17/1883 at New York; played 1B and went 1-for-4 in a 7–5 loss to Pittsburgh's "The Only" Nolan
FINALE: 10/4/1890 at Buffalo; played 1B and went 2-for-4 in a 5–0 win over Buffalo's Larry Twitchell
CAREER HIGHLIGHT: Set a then ML record for triples in 1886 with 31

In 1887 many of Dave Orr's teammates began calling him "Sadie." The nickname originated when New York Mets manager Opie Caylor received a telegram that summmer signed Sadie, informing him that Orr was incapacitated with a sprained ankle. Upon inquiry, Caylor discovered the injury had occurred when a man threw Orr down the stairs outside the apartment of a woman named Sadie whom Orr had stopped to "visit" on the way to the ballpark, only to find his rival swain already there.

Had he been born fifty years later, Orr might also have been nicknamed "Ducky" in honor of being perhaps the best bad-ball hitter ever outside of Joe Medwick. Tony Mullane called Orr the most dangerous batsman he ever saw, bar none. The big first baseman feasted on outside pitches, pivoting on his right foot as he swept his bat across the plate to propel balls with vicious topspin, but allegedly could hit any delivery, whether an inch from the ground or a foot over his head. A free swinger to a ridiculous extreme, Orr went to the plate with only one goal in mind: to get his hacks. After walking just 7 times in 1888, the last year the five-ball rule was in effect, Orr collected only 9 bases on balls in 560 ABs in 1889, the first year of the four-ball rule, and from April 24 through July 13 did not draw a single walk in a span of 268 ABs. As a consequence of his complete disdain for the concept of plate discipline, Orr owns the lowest career OBP (.366) among all players with a minimum of 3,000 ABs who averaged at least 1 hit per every 3 ABs.

The son of Irish immigrants, Orr left school at age 13 to work as an apprentice butcher and later became a granite cutter, pursuing his father's profession. Some ten years later, when he was nearing 23, he played for the semipro Alaska club of Staten Island. The following year Orr joined independent Newark after failing a trial with Brooklyn of the Interstate Association as an outfielder when manager George Taylor would not let him play 1B because the team already had Oscar Walker at that position. By the close of the season Orr had played with both the AA and NL New York entries on loan from Newark and cemented his claim on the AA club's 1B job for the following year when he hit his first 2 ML home runs and also tripled in a 7–1 win over Columbus on September 22, 1883.

The following year Orr went 0-for-5 for the Mets on Opening Day but then smote .357 for the rest of the season to cop the AA bat crown as a rookie. Hitting out of the fifth spot in the order, he also topped the loop in hits and RBI. Orr followed with equally brilliant seasons in 1885 and 1886 but with a weak supporting cast, as syndicate ownership had downsized the Mets in favor of the NL New York Giants. In 1887, his final season with the Mets, he was held to just 84 games after he collided with teammate Andy Sommers on April 27 while chasing a pop fly and suffered multiple injuries. When the Mets disbanded that October, Orr was among the club's elite players that were sold as a package to Brooklyn AA for somewhere around $20,000.

Injuries again hampered him in 1888, reducing his BA to a career low .305. With Dave Foutz on hand to take Orr's place, Brooklyn pilot Bill McGunnigle contrived to sell the big first baseman and pitcher Al Mays to the Columbus AA replacement team for $3,000. Orr seemed a bargain when he rebounded to play 134 games, led the Ohio club in hitting, and finished the 1889 season as captain. When he jumped to the PL in January 1890, however, his departure was greeted with whoops of joy from his former Columbus teammates, who regarded him as "big, flabby," one of the worst "back-cappers" in the game, and so devious that they would have refused to accept him as captain again.

In what proved to be his final ML season, Orr

led his Brooklyn Brotherhood club in most offensive departments and lost the PL batting crown to Pete Browning by a fraction of a percentage point. At the close of the campaign John M. Ward took his Brooklyn team west to play a string of exhibition games. According to *TSN*, when the club stopped on October 13 in Bellefonte, PA, Orr came down with a flare-up of his chronic rheumatoid condition. The following day, just before a game in Renovo, PA, he suffered a stroke during pregame practice that paralyzed his left side. His frightened teammates strove to rouse him out of his "depression" until his wife, Emily, arrived.

The couple returned to their home in Brooklyn, where Orr was confined to bed for some weeks. They then undertook a tortuous trip to Hot Springs AR. Once there, Orr gradually regained the use of his left arm and was able to walk by the following September, although he was still "very lame." At that point he remained convinced he would one day return to the playing field, especially after he was able to umpire an NL game in late September 1891. In the interim he took a job at a Brooklyn hotel, but by 1894 he had accepted the inevitable and was hired by the Giants to "have charge of the gate through which New York's sun gods pass this year." Orr continued to work at the Polo Grounds for a time and later served as a caretaker for Ebbets Field after it opened in 1913. His last connection with baseball came in 1914 when he worked as a press attendant at Washington Park for the Brooklyn Federal League club. The following year Orr died of heart disease at his niece's home in Richmond Hill, NY. (DN)

Phillips, William B. / "Bill" "Willie" "Silver Bill"

B	T	HGT	WGT	G	AB	H	R	2B
R	R	6'0"	202	1038	4255	1130	562	214

3B	HR	RBI	BB	SO	SB	BA	SA	OBP
98	17	534	178	215	39	.266	.374	.299

B. 4/?/1857 St. John, New Brunswick, Canada
D. 10/7/1900
TEAMS: 79–84CleN 85–87BroA 88KCA
DEBUT: 5/1/1879 at Cleveland, played 1B and went 0-for-4 in a 15–4 loss to Providence's John M. Ward
FINALE: 10/14/1888 at Louisville; played 1B and went 1-for-4 in a 9–1 loss to Louisville's Tom Ramsey
HISTORIC EVENT: 6/12/1880 at Worcester; Phillips lined an apparent single to RF to break up Lee Richmond's perfect game in the offing, but Worcester's Lon Knight charged the ball and threw Phillips out at 1B to preserve the first perfect game in ML history

Bill Phillips was the first documented Canadian-born major leaguer. One of ten children, he moved to Chicago with his family in early childhood and launched his career in 1875 as a catcher with the local amateur Enterprise club. The following year he headed north to catch for independent Winona, MN, and then spent most of 1877 with Minneapolis of the League Alliance.

Phillips joined the independent Cleveland Forest Citys prior to the 1878 campaign as a catcher–second baseman but was playing 1B by summer and led the team with a .296 BA, making him a lock to accompany it when it enrolled in the National League for 1879. Although hired to play 1B, he also caught 11 games as a ML frosh and led his weak-hitting team in runs by a wide margin despite logging just 58 scores. The next year Phillips played every inning of every game at 1B as part of the Blues' new "Stonewall Infield" that also featured Jack Glasscock at SS and rookie second baseman Fred Dunlap. Durability would be Phillips's long suit in his six-year tenure with Cleveland, for his .264 BA and .655 OPS marked him as the weakest-hitting first baseman with a minimum of 1,500 PAs during that span (1879–84).

When the Cleveland franchise disbanded following the 1884 season, Phillips was among the Blues players who were sold to Brooklyn AA. His first season in a new uniform brought a career-high .302 BA and 63 RBI despite spending several weeks on the DL. Phillips also topped the AA in fielding, strengthening his reputation for providing solid defense, especially on low throws. He repeated as fielding leader in 1887 and also led the club in RBI but was then part of a six-player, $7,000 fire sale to the new Kansas City AA entry in January 1888 after Brooklyn snared first sacker Dave Orr from the disbanding New York Mets.

Whether Phillips was simply unhappy in Kansas City or already suffering the early effects of the disease that would claim his life little more than a decade later, his bat grew so lethargic that pitchers were told simply to groove pitches to him rather than waste energy nibbling at the corners of the plate. He finished the season at .236 and stole only 10 bases. The following March he was released by

KC for "being too slow on the bases" and joined the Hamilton, Ontario, International Association team for a time but hit just .245. By that fall he was working as a policeman in Chicago. The following year, when Phillips played in the Chicago City League, he was reported to "weigh a ton." He died in Chicago ten years later of locomotor ataxia, a disease often associated with syphilis. (DN)

Powell, Martin J. / "Mart"

B	T	HGT	WGT	G	AB	H	R	2B
L	L	6'0"	170	229	1163	329	213	43

3B	HR	RBI	BB	SO	SB	BA	SA	OBP
11	3	115	75	59	—	.283	.347	.326

B. 3/25/1856 Fitchburg, MA **D.** 2/5/1888
TEAMS: 81–83DetN 84CinU
DEBUT: 6/18/1881 at Providence; played 1B and went 2-for-5 in a 10–3 win over Providence's Bobby Mathews and John M. Ward
FINALE: 8/10/1884 at Cincinnati; played 1B and went 1-for-4 in a 7–4 win over St. Louis's Charlie Sweeney

Mart Powell played for several years with Lowell, MA, while it was both an independent and a minor league club before joining Holyoke of the National Association in 1879. The following spring found him at 1B with the Washington NA entry. He remained with the D.C. club until June 1881, when he was acquired by Detroit. Powell's outstanding rookie performance—his .810 OPS led all NL yearlings—catapulted the expansion Wolverines to a surprise first-division finish. He continued to hit well in his next two seasons with Detroit and then jumped to the UA in 1884. His ML career ended little more than three years after it began when Cincinnati dropped him after he battled with illness most of the early summer.

For years Powell was credited with having played a game with Philadelphia of the AA in 1885, but it has now been established that the game belongs to a contemporary first baseman, Jim Powell. Mart Powell's pro career appears to have come to an abrupt end after his final game with Cincinnati UA. He may have already been in the early stages of consumption, the illness that claimed his life less than four years later and also caused his sister's premature death in 1882. (DN)

Reilly, John Good / "John" "Long John"

B	T	HGT	WGT	G	AB	H	R	2B
R	R	6'3"	178	1142	4684	1352	898	215

3B	HR	RBI	BB	SO	SB	BA	SA	OBP
139	69	740	157	156	245	.289	.438	.325

B. 10/5/1858 Cincinnati, OH **D.** 5/31/1937
TEAMS: 80CinN 83–89CinA 90–91CinN
DEBUT: 5/18/1880 at Cincinnati; played 1B and went 1-for-4 in a 6–5 loss to Buffalo's Tom Poorman
FINALE: 10/3/1891 at Chicago; played LF and went 4-for-5 and in a 17–9 win over Chicago's Tom Vickery and Jack Luby
CAREER HIGHLIGHT: In 1888 hit a nineteenth-century season-record 8 inside-the-park home runs

Born in Cincinnati, John Reilly passed his earliest years at his family home within walking distance of the Ohio River. The family's circumstances were comfortable, as Reilly's father worked as a riverboat pilot and captain. When the Civil War broke out he was assigned to serve as pilot of the *St. Louis*, the flagship of Adm. Andrew Foote, who commanded the gunboat flotillas that cooperated so effectively with Ulysses Grant's armies early in the war. During the Federal Navy's assault on Fort Donelson in Tennessee on February 14, 1862, a Confederate shell burst in the cabin of the supposedly invulnerable ironclad. Foote suffered a minor ankle wound, but Frank Reilly's injuries were mortal. Reilly's widowed mother endured several lean years, and he was sent to live on his grandfather's farm in Illinois. But then, in the early 1870s, his mother remarried and was able to bring her son back home to live with her. After his return Reilly quickly became active at the two pursuits in which he would spend the rest of his life. On May 5, 1873, his mother signed a contract on his behalf to become an apprentice at the Strobridge Lithographing Company, a thriving commercial art firm. Soon afterward he began to play baseball for a team of 14-year-olds across the Ohio River in Latonia, KY.

Reilly's work at Strobridge affected his baseball career significantly. He started with Latonia as a catcher, but the rigors of playing in a day of minimal protective equipment made that position hazardous to a player's hands and more so to the career of the budding commercial artist. As a result, he switched to 1B, a spot that proved ideal for a lanky beanpole, standing 6'3" in a day when few men reached six feet.

By the late 1870s Reilly was advancing in both his professions. After completing his apprenticeship, he was taken on by Strobridge as a professional artist and was soon playing for the best semipro baseball clubs in the city. Cincinnati had been a charter member of the NL in 1876, but a succession of financial failures caused its current owners to fold the team late in the 1879 season, releasing all players. A new group emerged from the seeds of the amateur Cincinnati Stars, one of Reilly's clubs in 1879, and built its own ballpark on Bank Street in the West End, near downtown Cincinnati. As a result of the reorganization the new club lost the rights to reserve the old team's players and fell behind in the race to sign free-agent talent. Though unfortunate for local fans, it would turn out to be a boon for several of the city's young players. One was Reilly when the new 1880 Reds gave him a contract as the eleventh man on an eleven-player squad.

As a 21-year-old rookie, however, he was outmatched by most NL pitchers and batted a meager .206. An unselective free swinger throughout his career, Reilly walked a mere 3 times and recorded 36 whiffs in 272 ABs, more than 50 percent above the NL's average strikeout frequency, but the most memorable event of his rookie season occurred far from any ball field. A few weeks after he was put in the lineup the Reds went on an extended road trip. June 10 found them at Providence. With the prospect of a couple of off days, Reilly made a quick visit to New York. On the evening of June 11 he boarded the steamer *Narragansett*, sailing up the Long Island Sound to begin the return voyage to Providence. Reilly was asleep around midnight when he was thrown from his berth. The *Narragansett* had collided with another ship, the *Stonington*. Reilly hastened to the already water-covered deck, where a fire had started and passengers were beginning to panic. He climbed a mast and went to work with a knife supplied by another passenger to help free the ship's lifeboats. At one point he fell into the water and nearly drowned. Fortunately, he was able to grab a ladder and climb back on board. Reilly would recall seeing a man, maddened by fear and preferring a quick death to one by fire or drowning, raise a revolver to his head and shoot himself. He encountered an agitated woman who had stepped out of her stateroom at the time of the collision, accidentally locking her small children inside. Unable to find an axe, Reilly tried to break down the door with his shoulder, but the ship was listing so violently that he had to push upward and could not gain the traction he needed. With the vessel in danger of sinking, he had to give up his efforts and abandon the children to their fate. Returning to the deck, he threw a plank into the water and then jumped in himself and grabbed it. Reilly found the tide carrying him away from the rescue ships that were now coming into the area. He floated alone in the dark for what he later estimated might have been about an hour. Reilly was so tired that he had given up paddling and was drifting aimlessly when a boat from the City of New York found him and took him aboard. In midmorning he arrived back in New York, where he sat on a dock for about five hours in his soaked underwear until a friend finally brought him some clothes.

That same day, June 12, the Reds resumed their series with Providence. The survivors had been taken to different cities, and no one knew whether Reilly was alive or dead, but the Reds were expecting the worst. The *Cincinnati Gazette* the next day observed: "The sad news of the loss of John Reilly on the ill-fated Narragansett seemed to have a depressing effect on the Cincinnatis," who lost 11–4. The *Cincinnati Commercial* had also received an unconfirmed report of Reilly's death but wisely withheld it for fear of alarming Reilly's family prematurely. Two days later, the *Commercial* happily reported that Reilly had telegraphed to say he was safe. On June 15 he was back in the lineup. When he took the field, spectators who had read accounts of his harrowing experience gave him a warm welcome.

Nothing remotely as exciting happened during the rest of the 1880 baseball season. Among the young players the Reds tried in a vain attempt to escape the NL cellar were Joe Sommer and Hick Carpenter, who would be Reilly's teammates on future Queen City teams. That fall, Cincinnati encountered yet another management crisis, and this time no reorganization took place. The city spent 1881 without a professional team. Reilly likewise took the year off from pro ball, working for Strobridge and from time to time appearing as a member of various amateur and pickup teams. In the fall, a new pro club was organized, but Reilly disappointed local fans by signing instead with the New York Mets. A strong independent team, the Mets played 162 games, more than any team had yet played in a season. Reilly appeared in 159 of them, all the while carrying on a separate career. Since the Mets rarely played on the road, he was able to spend most mornings at the New York office of the Strobridge firm before commuting to the Polo Grounds for ball games in the afternoon.

Meanwhile, the reorganized Cincinnati team had entered the American Association, an upstart rival to the NL. As the summer of 1882 waned its six charter franchises put their substantial profits to work signing stars from the NL and other clubs to contracts for the next season. Reilly, in fact, committed himself to not one but two lucrative deals for 1882, first signing a contract with Cincinnati and then pledging to sign with a new NL team in New York. In the process he embroiled himself in an embarrassing situation. Cincinnati's club secretary had signed Reilly in New York during August, but by the fall there were reports that he was claiming he had not actually signed with Cincinnati but only made a promise to do so, conditional on Strobridge's agreeing to transfer him back to the team's home office in Cincinnati. Since Strobridge refused to do this, Reilly claimed the Cincinnati agreement was invalid. Cincinnati newspapers told a different story. They said that Reilly had come home expecting the local team to grant him an honorable release from his contract with them. Angered by Buck Ewing's similar repudiation of a Cincinnati contract to play for New York, the Reds' management surprised Reilly by refusing his request and then placated him by raising their salary offer. Reilly finally promised owner Aaron Stern he would ask for a release from his oral promise to sign with the New York team. The whole matter was not solved until a peace treaty between the two leagues the following spring awarded him to Cincinnati.

Reilly returned home having matured as an offensive player. Perhaps his finest performance occurred on September 12, when Cincinnati rolled over the Alleghenys, and he went 6-for-7 with 2 stolen bases and 6 runs scored. In the bottom of the eighth, he drove an opposite field drive to right field to tally Cincinnati's fourth home run of the game. The hit completed a cycle for Reilly, who had already hit a double and triple to go with his 3 singles. Between September 10 and September 22, Reilly notched 19 hits in 41 ABs for a BA of .463 and an SA of .639. The surge assured him of the ownership of a bat inscribed in silver that was presented to the team BA leader. Reilly's next season was still better. In 1884 he belted .339 and led the Association in home runs and SA. Modern readjustments of nineteenth-century statistics leave him second to Dave Orr in the batting race and among the leaders in most other significant categories.

Two years later Reilly's season was marred after a broken leg in mid-May put him out of action for a month. He rebounded to hit .309 in 1887, and his ten home runs made him the only man in the AA besides batting champ Tip O'Neill to reach double figures in that category. Reilly followed in 1888 with his best season since 1884. After beginning the year by homering in 5 consecutive games, he led the league again in homers and slugging, as well as RBI, and finished near the top in BA. In a day when up-to-the-moment statistics were not available to everyone with a computer, hopes persisted into November that Reilly had won the AA batting crown. After a long delay, the official stats finally showed Reilly finishing fourth. Today, stat readjustments have moved him up two places, but O'Neill is still given credit for his second consecutive batting title.

At the peak of his career Reilly was a cornerstone of a strong and very stable Cincinnati team. Although the Reds were unable to repeat their 1882 championship, the club remained a consistently high finisher. The team's core was its infield, especially Reilly together with future HOFer Bid McPhee at 2B and Reilly's 1880 teammate Hick Carpenter at third. This trio was a regular unit from Reilly's debut with the team in 1883 until Carpenter was released on the eve of the 1890 season. "The seasons come and go," the *Pittsburgh Dispatch* remarked, "but Biddy McPhee, Long John Reilly and Hick Carpenter always come winner in the shuffle, and look as natural around the bases as sign-boards at the forks of country cross-roads."

Despite difficulty in adjusting his stroke to the bunting and place hitting that came into fashion during the late 1880s, Reilly nonetheless continued to record consistently high BAs. He had a strong throwing arm, and while a man of his size would hardly be a speed demon, with his long legs he was among the Reds' most effective base runners. In a day when most home runs were hit inside the park, his high totals for homers as well as triples testify to his speed as well as his power. Throughout his career Reilly maintained the superior defensive skills that had kept him in the majors before his hitting had matured and contributed to his team in other ways as well. He was an intelligent and sensitive man, of whom a rather florid obit writer for the Cincinnati *Enquirer* would say: "An omniverous [*sic*] reader and student of human nature, 'Long John' found the characters of Dickens on every field and Thackeray's folk on the highways and byways leading thereto. Had he cared to devote his pen to biography instead of the sketching pad, the ball-player artist might have been his own Boswell."

Reilly's self-disciplined habits extended even to his care for his playing equipment, particularly his bats. According to the *Cincinnati Enquirer*, he scraped them with glass to get them just the right size and texture. Reilly was equally renowned for his devotion to his team. He once explained, "I like to see your crazy-mad players. The smiling fellows care only for their salaries and are no good to a team. . . . I've been in tight games when the paternity of every member of the team has been questioned, and after that it was over—the harsh words had all been forgotten." Reilly's intense nature combined with a lively sense of humor and pungent manner of expressing his opinions made him a favorite of sportswriters, and as the newspaper space devoted to baseball increased during the later years of his career, reporters found him a prolific source of quotes and quips. When Reilly was not having fun, however, he was sometimes at odds with less team-oriented players. He stayed sober and in shape, expected his teammates to do the same and could be outspoken in criticizing those who failed to live up to his standards. According to a report in the *Cincinnati Enquirer*, Fred Lewis, a brilliant outfielder who was drowning in an ocean of alcohol, ended his big-league career in late August of the Reds' nightmare 1886 season by punching Reilly and chasing him half naked out of the dressing room when Reilly castigated him for not being in shape to play a game.

Nor was Reilly pleased after the 1888 season when catcher Kid Baldwin was given a contract containing a bonus provision for staying sober for the coming year. Club president Stern was trying to find an imaginative approach that might produce better results with Baldwin. Some of the Reds' veterans did not like Stern's idea, however, and Reilly bluntly told the *Cincinnati Commercial Gazette* on October 3, 1888, that the Baldwin contract showed it paid for a ballplayer to drink, for "then the management will pay him a big bonus to keep sober," a prime example of the candor that made Reilly a reporter's favorite.

In spite of his fine play, the season of 1888 left Reilly with a bitter taste in his mouth. A clubhouse scrap with diminutive teammate Hugh Nicol and a season-long feud with umpire Herman Doscher blighted his year, and for the sixth consecutive season his team had failed to grab the pennant. By that time Reilly's off-season conversations had begun to include talk about retiring—perhaps a salary ploy, perhaps a genuine sign of waning enthusiasm in a man of whom the *Cincinnati Enquirer* had once said, "When that player quits baseball, boys will refuse to eat mince pies."

Still, after 1888, Reilly's hitting began a slow decline that turned into a precipitous drop in 1891, when he batted .242 for a seventh-place Cincinnati team racked by dissension. Following that season, the Reds brought in Reilly's longtime rival Charlie Comiskey to play 1B and manage. There had been talk of moving Reilly to the outfield, but Comiskey seems to have vetoed that move, ending Reilly's tenure as a Red. Although he was now 33 and coming off his worst performance since his rookie season eleven years before, Reilly still had options that would have allowed him to continue his ML career. But as much as he loved playing ball, he could do so only at a financial sacrifice, since his current work for the Strobridge lithography firm was now earning him at least $50 every week, and sometimes as much as $80 (presumably due to overtime). These were substantial sums in a day when an ordinary skilled or semiskilled laborer thought he had had a good year if he earned $500.

Reilly had an additional reason for staying in Cincinnati—his comfortable and inexpensive living arrangements in his hometown. He never married and continued to live with his mother's family. Her second husband seemingly died about 1880, and the family soon moved east to Columbus Tusculum, now a neighborhood in the middle of Cincinnati's east side but then a rather distant suburb along the river. Reilly would remain in this home until he died on May 31, 1937, after an illness of several years. In his last years, a niece, who shared the house with Reilly and her husband, maintained his home.

Reilly continued to work for Strobridge until the early 1930s, specializing in circus posters. This was a particular staple of the firm's business, especially after the Ringling Brothers and Barnum and Bailey circuses merged to become the country's dominant circus and gave Strobridge all their poster business. Although Reilly made his living as a commercial artist, on his own time he liked to paint nature scenes copied from his wanderings in local woods or on the shores of the Ohio River. In a short reminiscence, Elizabeth Kellogg, who worked at the Cincinnati Art Museum, recalled that "just once—for he was a modest soul," Reilly put his paintings on exhibition. Kellogg and a friend who worked at the Cincinnati Art Museum were surprised to see such delicate workmanship from the hands of a man who was large even for a professional athlete.

Although Reilly was not by any means a superstar, his local connections and his strong character and vivid personality made him the most popular player of his generation in Cincinnati. During his playing days, a local tobacconist had named a brand of cigars the "Long John Reilly," and long after his retirement his name continued to appear in newspapers as a former baseball luminary. More than ten years after his death he still remained a name of note in his hometown, for in 1948 the *Times-Star* announced news "of special interest to baseball fans" when it was reported that the home at Columbia Parkway and Stanley Avenue in which John Reilly had spent most of his life had been sold to make way for a gas station, and the house itself would be moved to an empty lot farther up Stanley Avenue. (DB/DN)

Rogers, James F. / "Jim"

B	T	HGT	WGT	G	AB	H	R	2B
?	?	5'8"	180	151	597	140	82	17

3B	HR	RBI	BB	SO	SB	BA	SA	OBP
12	3	90	48	23	20	.235	.318	.294

G	W	L	PCT	PENNANTS
44	17	24	.415	0

B. 4/9/1872 Hartford, CT **D.** 1/21/1900
TEAMS: 96WasN 96–97LouN (P/M)97LouN
DEBUT: 4/16/1896 at Washington; played 2B and went 1-for-3 in a 6–3 win over New York's Dad Clarke
FINALE: 6/15/1897 at Baltimore; played 1B and went 2-for-4 in a 7–5 loss to Baltimore's Arlie Pond

At age 20 Jim Rogers was already in his fourth season of pro ball and led the 1892 New England League in hitting with a .323 BA while playing 1B for Portland, ME. It was a position he handled well despite his size, *TSN* claimed, because like Jake Beckley, "he extends himself instead of standing like a sphinx on the base" when taking throws. Rogers moved up to Providence of the Eastern League the following year and continued to flash surprising power for a relatively small man. He remained with Providence through 1895, when he was sold to Washington for $1,000 after a .327 season. In early May 1896 Orioles manager Ned Hanlon stopped a game at Baltimore to make the umpire measure Rogers's glove, which he contended was more than the legal size. It proved not to be, but the incident suggests that Rogers may have been playing 2B with a first baseman's mitt, which was still permissible in 1896 as long as the mitt did not exceed the fourteen-inch size limit. Some two months later, he and Jack Crooks were sent to Louisville along with $2,000 for Jack O'Brien. Rogers finished the season as the Colonels' regular first baseman and then married Nora Begley that November at his home in Bridgeport, CT.

In January 1897, after Louisville's board of directors had assured Bill McGunnigle that he would be rehired as manager for the coming season, the Board reconvened and, after a heated debate, named Rogers as its controversial choice to run the club. Rogers had no previous managerial experience. He was handed the only team in the league that at the beginning of the 1897 campaign not only had no ten-year ML veterans but lacked even a five-year veteran. Working under the dual responsibility of managing and playing 1B, Rogers started the year hitting .121 (7-for-58). He succeeded in lifting his BA to .147 (22-for-150) by the time he was fired as both a player and a manager on June 15. Fred Clarke took over the club while Rogers went to Springfield, MA, after negotiations with Pittsburgh fell through. Later that season he was nearly slain after an Eastern League game at Wilkes-Barre on August 8 when he broke the leg of an African American fan who had been razzing him and barely escaped an angry mob of his combatant's friends.

Rogers played with Lyons in the New York State League in 1898 and in the Connecticut State and Eastern leagues for parts of the following year. In January 1900 he died at his mother-in-law's home in Bridgeport, reportedly from the effects of a beaning he had sustained in 1898 when he was struck in the "right temple and knocked insensible" in an exhibition game against the Giants. Other sources contend that Rogers died of kidney trouble, but if the description of the beaning is true, then it is likely he batted left-handed since the pitch hit him in the right side of his head. The same year he was purportedly beaned, the *Cincinnati Enquirer* lamented, "If ever a player had the earmarks of a first-rater Rogers had when he first came to Washington. He simply fooled everybody." (DN/DB)

Schoeneck, Louis W. / "Jumbo"

B	T	HGT	WGT	G	AB	H	R	2B
R	R	6'3"	256	170	657	186	79	30

3B	HR	RBI	BB	SO	SB	BA	SA	OBP
4	2	28	20	27	12	.283	.350	.308

G	IP	H	GS	CG	BB
2	4.1	5	0	0	1

SO	SH	W	L	PCT	ERA
1	0	0	0	—	0.00

B. 3/3/1862 Chicago, IL **D.** 1/20/1930
TEAMS: 84Chi-PitU 84BalU 88–89IndA
DEBUT: 4/20/1884 at St. Louis; played 1B and went 1-for-3 in a 7–2 loss to St. Louis's Charlie Hodnett
FINALE: 5/11/1889 at Cleveland; played 1B went 0-for-4 in a 4–2 loss to Cleveland's Ed Beatin

Jumbo Schoeneck is listed in most reference works as having weighed 223, but that figure probably came from the late 1870s when he was still a Chicago amateur. By ten years later he tipped the scales at upward of 270 and may have been the heaviest nineteenth-century MLer. Schoeneck came to Chicago UA in 1884 from the Springfield, IL, Northwestern League club and quickly established himself as the team's best hitter. He then went to Baltimore, replacing weak-hitting Charlie Levis, and played independent ball for a year after the UA folded before returning to the pro arena in 1886 with Portland, ME, of the New England League.

In 1888 Schoeneck began the season with the Chicago Maroons of the Western Association and was acquired by Indianapolis NL in August despite carrying just a .247 BA at the time. When he was measured for a uniform while with the Maroons, Schoeneck was found to have a 46" waist, 51" hips and a size 18½" collar. Disregarding his .237 BA in the closing weeks of the season, Indianapolis opened 1889 with Schoeneck at 1B, but he held the job less than three weeks. Schoeneck finished the year with New Haven and then captained the Connecticut club in 1890 before beginning a gradual descent through the minors that ended in 1892, when he played his last pro innings with Green Bay of the Wisconsin-Michigan League. He died in Chicago at 67. (DN)

Schomberg, Otto H. (b. Schoemberg) (aka Shomberg) **/ "Otto"**

B	T	HGT	WGT	G	AB	H	R	2B
L	L	5'11"	175	214	777	220	155	29

3B	HR	RBI	BB	SO	SB	BA	SA	OBP
23	7	122	123	44	34	.283	.407	.389

B. 11/14/1864 Milwaukee, WI **D.** 5/3/1927
TEAMS: 86PitA 87–88IndN
DEBUT: 7/7/1886 at Pittsburgh; played 1B and went 1-for-4 in a 6–2 win over Brooklyn's Jack Harkins
FINALE: 7/14/1888 at Indianapolis; played 1B and went 0-for-4 in a 5–2 win over Washington's Hank O'Day

Had Otto Schomberg played a century later he would have been a DH and his ML career would likely have been much longer. He began pro play in 1884 at 1B for Milwaukee's reserve team and finished the season with Stillwater, MN, of the Northwestern League. By late June 1886 he was with Utica and leading the International Association in batting when he was purchased by Pittsburgh, which had been making do with a variety of out-of-position players at 1B. Schomberg's arrival instantly added significant punch to Pittsburgh's attack, making pundits wonder if the Alleghenys might have challenged St. Louis for the AA pennant if he had arrived as little as a month earlier.

Schomberg's family was upper middle class, with money made in his father Henry's Michigan planing mill. Schomberg himself had a good head for business and no firm commitment to baseball, drank nothing strong than seltzer water, and seems to have been regarded by many teammates as priggish, aloof, and superior. A few weeks after he joined Pittsburgh, a fight with Fred Carroll led to punishment for the veteran Carroll that seemed grossly unjust to an anti-rookie faction on the club. It is likely that Schomberg's difficult relations with teammates led the Pittsburgh management to send its promising young first baseman to the St. Louis Maroons in return for Alex McKinnon, a much older first sacker, in December 1886. However, the *St. Louis Post-Dispatch* claimed that Pittsburgh would never have disposed of Schomberg had it not been for manager Horace Phillips's "infatuation" with McKinnon.

Schomberg never played for the Maroons because Indianapolis took over their franchise prior to the 1887 season. He provided much-needed clout to a light-hitting Hoosiers lineup, finishing among NL leaders in OBP and OPS. However, he was last among the Hoosiers regulars in stolen bases and played badly in the field, developing serious trouble making throws and committing 55 errors. Schomberg's arm eventually grew so erratic that manager Horace Fogel, casting about for other options at 1B, gave amateur Henry Jackson a trial late in the season.

Jackson flopped, but the next spring Indianapolis brought in several more candidates for Schomberg's position. A move to the outfield had previously been considered, and he was given a chance to play RF when Jack McGeachy held out well into the season. A slow runner whose arm was a liability at 1B seems a poor choice for the outfield, but Schomberg had played the position at Utica, and it was felt he might be able to handle it again because his 1887 errors had come primarily on short throws to 2B and home. The experiment failed. Schomberg made few plays in RF and recorded a FA of .857, nearly 50 points below the league average. Any chance of remaining in the lineup was scotched when he broke an ankle just as McGeachy finally reported to the club. When he was able to play again he got occasional spells at 1B but played too little to get untracked and batted only .214. Nevertheless, his offensive production was still superior to Tom Esterbrook's. At last the Indianapolis management cut the Gordian knot, acquiring minor leaguer Jumbo Schoeneck and releasing both Esterbrook and Schomberg.

Schomberg's services were still in demand, but at the early age of 23 he had already begun to experience the first symptoms of a serious heart ailment and retired from baseball. Always a lover of horseflesh, he said he would settle in Indianapolis and run a livery stable. When those plans went awry, he went on to a successful business career elsewhere. Maintaining a residence in Milwaukee, where he continued to play amateur ball, he joined his brothers, Henry and Richard, in establishing the Schomberg Lumber Company as well as a store in Good Hope, MI. At one point Schomberg's concern employed as many as one-hundred teams hauling logs. In the late 1890s he came to be on sufficiently good terms with Milwaukee manager Connie Mack that he continued to scout for Mack's Philadelphia Athletics years later. Schomberg died in 1927 in Ottawa, KS, of a heart attack on a train bound from his winter home in California to Milwaukee. (DB/DN)

Scott, Milton Parker / "Milt" "Mikado Milt"

B	T	HGT	WGT	G	AB	H	R	2B
R	?	5'9"	160	341	1285	293	107	42

3B	HR	RBI	BB	SO	SB	BA	SA	OBP
10	5	132	40	78	11	.228	.288	.257

G	IP	H	GS	CG	BB
1	3	2	0	0	2

SO	SH	W	L	PCT	ERA
0	0	0	0	—	3.00

B. 1/17/1861 Chicago, IL **D.** 11/3/1938
TEAMS: 82ChiN 84–85DetN 85PitA 86BalA
DEBUT: 9/30/1882; played 1B and went 2-for-5 in a 6–5 win over Buffalo's Jim Galvin
FINALE: 10/14/1886 at Philadelphia; played 1B and went 0-for-3 in a 5–1 loss to Philadelphia's Cyclone Miller

A relatively small man for a first baseman, Milt Scott may have hindered himself with his eating habits. He was compared to outfielder Jack Remsen as another of the prodigious overeaters who "never seem to know when they have enough" and was said to be "an amiable elephant" on the bases. Yet he drew praise from *SL* as late as his final ML season as "a very graceful fielder," one that was never "flashy" and made even the hardest plays "modestly."

Before spelling Cap Anson in the closing game of the 1882 campaign, Scott had been playing for Al Spalding's Amateurs. The following season he was among the Amateurs that Jack Remsen recruited to help form the Fort Wayne Northwestern League team and by August, with the club in disarray, had replaced Remsen as captain. That November, *SL* reported the Fort Wayne players were demanding to be released because of misconduct by club officials, and two months later the *Detroit Free Press* said Scott's father had declared that if his son couldn't be set free by Fort Wayne he would put him to work in his store. The matter was resolved when Detroit NL signed Scott and installed him as its regular first baseman. In 1884 the rookie tallied just 29 runs, a season-record low by a first baseman with a minimum of 400 ABs. Nevertheless, Scott held his job and actually seemed to be improving as a hitter when he was sold to Pittsburgh AA in June 1885 after Detroit acquired Mox McQuery. By the end of the season Scott had hiked his composite BA to .254 but again scored only 29 runs, this time in 358 ABs. Released to Baltimore in April 1886, the Chicagoan produced unequivocally the worst offensive season ever by a first baseman with 400 or more ABs, ranking last in OPS (.481), BA (.190), SA (.242), and OBP (.239).

Recognizing that if he was to have a future in the game it must lie at another position, Scott returned to the minors with Kansas City of the Western League in 1887, intending to convert to pitching. But KC soon released him and he moved to La Crosse, WI. In September he was among the leading hitters in the Northwestern League when he broke an ankle sliding. Back on his feet by November, Scott wintered in Chicago and worked out daily in gym. When he was still without an engagement in the early spring, he joined the Picketts of the Chicago City League until he was signed by the local Western Association Maroons and hit .200. Failing again in his ambition to become a pitcher, he joined Utica of the New York State League in 1889 but batted just .224. The following season Scott came full circle in his career when he hired on as Fort Wayne's player-manager. But by the spring of 1891 he was ostracized around town after reportedly running up several debts the previous fall and then leaving without paying them off. A local paper grumbled, "There are many people in this city who would like to see Scott. They are his creditors." But in April 1891 *TSN* licensed Scott to tell his side of the story and it was very different. According to Scott, he had led the Indiana League in batting and fielding and the team had made money all season with him not only its manager but also a partner of the owner, but the owner then closed the books to Scott at the end of the season and claimed the club had lost money. Finally, the owner gave him "the razzle" by falsely asking him to return in 1891 and then hiring Guy Hecker to replace him. Scott finished his letter to *TSN* with, "Does this case not cap the climax in base ball history?"

Rather amazingly, notwithstanding his embarrassingly awful season in Baltimore in 1886, Scott returned to that city later in life and died there at 72. (DN/DB/PM)

Smith, John Joseph / "Jack" "Big Jack"

B	T	HGT	WGT	G	AB	H	R	2B
?	?	5'11"	210	54	219	53	37	7

3B	HR	RBI	BB	SO	SB	BA	SA	OBP
5	0	19	8	34	—	.242	.320	.269

B. ?/?/1858 San Francisco, CA **D.** 1/6/1899
TEAMS: 82TroN 82WorN
DEBUT: 5/1/1882 at Providence; played 1B and went 1-for-4 in 9–3 loss to Providence's John M. Ward
FINALE: 9/27/1882 at Worcester; played 1B and went 1-for-3 in an 11–8 loss to Troy's Tim Keefe

Born in New York, Jack Smith moved to Chicago with his family around 1870 and then relocated to San Francisco in 1878. The following year he joined the local Knickerbockers and soon became the most renowned hitter in the San Francisco Bay Area. In 1880 Smith topped the California League with a .358 BA and also paced the loop in hits, SA (.582), and home runs. He finally consented to come east to play for Troy NL in the spring of 1882.

Smith had been acquired to enable Roger Connor to play elsewhere besides 1B, where his fielding skills seemed wasted, but when he failed to hit Connor was forced to return to the bag. Released by Troy in August, Smith was picked up by Worcester and hit better with the Massachusetts club but not enough to induce any NL clubs to fight for his services in 1883. The following year, however, Columbus AA thought it had signed him to fill a gigantic hole at 1B, but he failed to report.

Smith continued to play cat and mouse with ML teams for several more seasons until they all despaired of enticing him to come east again. He and his brother Hughie, a second baseman, by that time were teammates on the San Francisco Pioneers. Smith remained an active player in the Bay Area until a few years before his death from stomach cancer in 1899. At the time he was working for a local wholesale firm in San Francisco. His brother meanwhile had been appointed supervisor of Recreation Park—the hub of San Francisco amateur baseball from the late 1890s to the present day—and had a son, Hugh Jr., who played in the Pacific Coast League. (DN)

Start, Joseph / "Joe" "Old Reliable" "Rocks"

B	T	HGT	WGT	G	AB	H	R	2B
L	L	5'9"	165	1070	4743	1417	852	147

3B	HR	RBI	BB	SO	SB	BA	SA	OBP
67	15	545	164	109	18	.299	.368	.322

G	W	L	PCT	PENNANTS
25	18	7	.720	0

B. 10/14/1842 New York, NY **D.** 3/27/1927
TEAMS: 71–75MutNA (P/M)73MutNA 76NYN 77HarN 78ChiN 79–85ProN 86WasN
DEBUT: 5/18/1871 at Troy; played 1B and went 2-for-5 in a 14–3 win over Troy's John McMullin
FINALE: 7/9/1886 at Washington; played 1B and went 0-for-3 in a 19–1 loss to Boston's Charley Radbourn

Considered the best defensive first baseman in history prior to the advent of Charlie Comiskey, Joe Start joined the Enterprise club of Brooklyn in 1860 when he was only 17 and remained in the game until he was nearly 44. Prior to the formation of the NA he had been a member of the Brooklyn Atlantics for nine seasons and played a key role in the Atlantics' famous streak-stopping defeat of the Cincinnati Red Stockings in 1871 by scoring the winning run when the throw home from Cal McVey escaped catcher Doug Allison. Start then spent the next six seasons with the New York Mutuals but seemed to be on the decline when the Mutes were ousted from the National League following the 1876 season. Instead, many of his best years were still ahead of him.

In 1877, as he approached 35, Start hit .332 with Hartford and followed with a .351 campaign in his lone year with a team west of the East Coast when he was the last man prior to 1898—other than Cap Anson—to serve as Chicago's regular first baseman. Returning to the East in 1879, Start immediately played for his first of two pennant winners in Providence and in 1884 was the first 40-year-old MLer to participate in a World Series, when he was party to the Grays' 3-game sweep of the AA champion New York Mets. The following season was Start's last as a regular. He notched another 40-year-old achievement—the first at that ripe age to play in as many as 100 games (101) in a season—and then finished his career in 1886 with Washington, where he was sent against his will after Providence lost its NL franchise.

Start achieved still another significant distinction in 1885 when he became the first to play as many as 1,000 ML games at 1B. In addition, even though the credit has mostly gone to Charlie Comiskey, many historians believe that Start was actually the first gateway guardian to play a substantial distance from the bag, commencing as far back as the 1860s, some twenty years before Comiskey adopted the strategy.

After leaving baseball Start and his wife, Angeline, whom he married in 1885, ran the Lakewood Inn in Warwick, RI, just south of Providence, until they sold it in 1919 and eventually retired to Providence, where he died eight years later. (DN/DB)

Stearns, Daniel Eckford / "Dan" "Ecky"

B	T	HGT	WGT	G	AB	H	R	2B
B	R	6'1"	185	509	2025	491	295	72

3B	HR	RBI	BB	SO	SB	BA	SA	OBP
36	8	173	173	117	67	.242	.325	.306

B. 10/17/1861 Buffalo, NY **D.** 6/28/1944
TEAMS: 80BufN 81DetN 82CinA 83–85BalA 85BufN 89KCA
DEBUT: 8/17/1880 at Buffalo; played SS and went 3-for-4 in a 6–1 win over Worcester's Lee Richmond and Fred Corey
FINALE: 10/14/1889 at Louisville; played 1B and went 1-for-4 in an 8–7 loss to Louisville's John Ewing

An inveterate banjo player who aggravated more than one road roommate with his incessant strumming, Dan Stearns played pro ball for over twenty years and was the consummate "mascot" in the minors, perennially on winning teams. In 1879, at age 17, he caught an exhibition game for Buffalo NL on July 14 at Rochester. Twenty years later he finished the Eastern League season with Buffalo. There is evidence that Stearns wore "the lightest glove of any first baseman in the business," barely larger than a kid glove, along with several references to his having been a switch hitter even though he is still not credited as such in most reference works. In addition, Stearns, more than any other first baseman, caused a rule change owing to his proficiency at leveling runners when they rounded 1B en route to an extra-base hit, secure in the knowledge that they would be given only 2B. Stearns's ploy resulted in granting umpires the discretion to award runners more than one base when they witnessed obvious interference. Yet Stearns never really was able to distinguish himself in the majors and played his final game in top company while still just 27 despite hitting a solid .286 with Kansas City in 1889. Part of the reason was that Stearns refused an offer to join Boston NL in 1890, volunteering to remain with KC even though it was abandoning the AA to join the minor Western Association. Regardless, he was unquestionably a rugged piece of work, even for the rough-and-tumble times in which he played. In late August 1891, while the Kansas City club was visiting Lincoln, NE, for an exhibition game, Stearns and several teammates stopped after the contest at Lindsley's Saloon before returning to their road abode at Lincoln's Capital Hotel. There, Stearns became embroiled in an argument with a drunken off-duty police officer named Malone. Later, while Stearns and teammates Bill Wilson, Jim Manning and Jack Pickett were gathered in front of the Capital Hotel, Malone spotted Stearns and resumed the argument, larding it with a stream of verbal abuse. When Stearns replied in kind, Malone drew his service revolver and pressed it to Stearns's heart. Stearns continued to taunt his adversary, daring him to shoot. When Malone let his guard down for an instant, Stearns decked him and was joined in giving him a thrashing by Wilson and Pickett. Thinking Malone was unconscious, Stearns and his teammates left him on the street and turned to enter the hotel, whereupon Malone opened fire, forcing them to flee to the hotel roof. Malone later tried to press charges against Stearns but was dissuaded when it was obvious to his fellow officers that he was intoxicated.

Compounding Stearns's bellicose nature was a deadly gambling addiction. By the end of the 1891 season he had dropped most of his KC salary in local poolrooms and bookie joints. That November he signed with a group that had been awarded a Chicago AA franchise for the following season, but his contract was voided when the AA disbanded, dissolving the Chicago entry. The following spring Stearns was still "hangtailing" in KC poolrooms, awaiting an offer after refusing to enter the Western League lottery pool because he felt the loop's $1,000 salary limit was beneath him. His judgment was rewarded when he was named captain of the Buffalo Eastern League team. Stearns later played in the Southern League and umpired for a time in the Eastern League before joining Buffalo in 1899 for his final pro fling. He later relocated to the Los Angeles area and worked as a U.S. court bailiff. In his early eighties he was moved to a sanitarium in Glendale, CA, and died there in 1944, leaving his wife Julia and several siblings. (DN/DB)

Sullivan, John Franklin / "Chub"

B	T	HGT	WGT	G	AB	H	R	2B
R	R	6'0"	164	112	442	114	55	10

3B	HR	RBI	BB	SO	SB	BA	SA	OBP
5	0	24	7	15	—	.258	.303	.269

B. 1/12/1856 Boston, MA **D.** 9/12/1881
TEAMS: 77–78CinN 80WorN
DEBUT: 9/24/1877 at Cincinnati; played 1B and went 0-for-4 in a 5–1 win over St. Louis's Tricky Nichols
FINALE: 7/17/1880 at Worcester; played 1B and went 0-for-4 in a 7–1 win over Cleveland's Jim McCormick

In 1903 Tim Murnane said of Chub Sullivan: "This player was the most finished first baseman the game ever saw." Sullivan appears to have played his entire career barehanded. He first came to prominence in 1874 with the amateur Boston Stars after learning the game on the Boston Commons. In 1875, playing with Taunton, he led the New England Association in batting and fielding and graduated to independent Ithaca the following year. Sullivan went west to join the unaffiliated Columbus Buckeyes in 1877. After leading the Buckeyes in batting, he was summoned to Cincinnati in late September and recommended that the NL club also hire one of his Columbus teammates, Mike "King" Kelly.

Cincinnati made Sullivan its first baseman in 1878. Although he played every inning and led the NL in fielding, he was dropped when he scored just 29 runs in 61 games and had only 6 extra-base hits. Sullivan spent 1879 with Worcester of the National Association and then accompanied the team when it enlisted in the NL the following year. He left the club in July when he took ill, but in October, when

Worcester held a benefit game for him, he played 1B in the contest in addition to receiving a $200 purse, and there was some talk that he was on the road to recovery. But the following spring Worcester officially released him because, as reported in the *New York Clipper*, "his lungs are affected, and it is thought his ball-playing days are over." Sullivan died that fall of consumption at his home in South Boston, and the entire Worcester team wore crepe armbands for a week after his death, the first time an ML club had ever done so for a fallen comrade.

Sullivan holds a spurious record. He is currently credited with the most ABs in a season without collecting any RBI (166 in 1880) despite unquestionably logging at least one ribby. On May 14 at Boston, Sullivan singled home Art Whitney from 3B in the ninth inning after Whitney hit an apparent home run over the LF fence but missed 3B and was allowed to return there when umpire Billy McLean contended that Boston pitcher Tommy Bond failed to do "what should be done" to have Whitney ruled out. (DN)

Tenney, Frederick / "Fred"
"The Soiled Collegian"

B	T	HGT	WGT	G	AB	H	R	2B
L	L	5'9"	155	673	2701	869	545	105

3B	HR	RBI	BB	SO	SB	BA	SA	OBP
35	8	361	256	26	115	.322	.398	.383

B. 11/26/1871 Georgetown, MA

D. 7/3/1852 Boston, MA

TEAMS: 94–04BosN (P/M)05–07BosN 08–09NYN (P/M)11BosN

DEBUT: 6/16/1894 at Boston; caught Tom Lovett in a 16–10 win over Chicago's Scott Stratton and went 1-for-3 before breaking a finger on his left hand and being replaced by Jack Ryan

FINALE: 10/7/1911 at New York; finished the game at 1B and went hitless in a 5–2 win over New York's Rube Marquard, Louis Drucke, and Charlie Faust

Fred Tenney's obits claimed that he originated the 3-6-3 double play in an 1897 game against Cincinnati and was the first lefty catcher in the majors. Both assertions are false, although it is certainly true that he made his ML debut as a catcher and was one of the most artful first basemen in his day. Eight times during his seventeen-year career he led his loop in assists, once in FA, and twice in double plays. When he retired in 1911, he ranked first in career assists at 1B with 1,363, third in DPs, and sixth in FA. He also had only 597 RBI while serving at 1B, the fewest in history among gateway guardians with 2,000 or more hits and 125 less than runner-up Jake Daubert.

The son of a Civil War veteran, Tenney graduated from Brown University after playing on a college nine that was stocked with future MLers. He was just sitting down to his "senior dinner" on the evening of June 15, 1894, when he received an urgent telegram from the Boston NL club requesting his services for the following afternoon as an injury replacement behind the bat. Tenney lasted less than five innings before being injured himself but was offered a contract and hit a breathtaking .395 in 27 games. His catching was too raw, however, for manager Frank Selee's taste, and he spent parts of the next two seasons in the New England League while learning to also play the outfield and 1B. After he appeared in 88 games as an outfielder-catcher in 1896 and slapped .316, Selee named him Boston's Opening Day right fielder the following year and then moved him to 1B after 4 games, replacing slumping veteran Tommy Tucker. Tenney proceeded to lead the NL in ABs in 1897 and post career highs in both runs (125) and RBI (85) but weighed just 155 pounds at the end of the season and was encouraged to add weight over the winter after producing a mere 28 extra-base hits. Apparently he demurred, for he remained about the same weight for the rest of his career.

After missing significant time with injuries in 1898, Tenney was given grudging permission by Selee not to go south to Durham, NC, with Boston the following spring but rather to train in the North and coach the Dartmouth team. Selee actually had little choice but to assent since Tenney's contract didn't officially commence until April 15, 1899, and numerous other players were taking similar advantage to make extra money after the schedule was increased to 154 games in 1898 without a corresponding increase in salary. Tenney then belied the theory that participation in organized spring-training sessions was essential by notching 209 hits, 17 triples, and a .347 BA in 1899, all of them personal full-season career highs by a wide margin. That winter *TSN* added to his growing reputation by rating him the best first baseman in the game at stretching for errant tosses and also at coming off bag, ready to throw elsewhere as soon as he had tagged it.

Tenney was also excellent at charging bunts and getting the lead runner at 2B, making him one of first gateway guardians to demonstrate the value of a left-hander playing the position. In 1900 he logged Boston's first RBI of the season when he tripled in the eleventh inning to plate the winning run and hand Kid Nichols a 1–0 victory over Brooklyn, but he finished with just 56 ribbies, the fewest among the seven first basemen in the NL with a minimum of 300 ABs. Tenney would play ten more ML campaigns without ever achieving as many as 50 RBI in a season again. (DN)

Tucker, Thomas Joseph / "Tommy" "Foghorn" "Tommy Talker"

B	T	HGT	WGT	G	AB	H	R	2B
B	R	5'11"	165	1688	6482	1882	1084	240

3B	HR	RBI	BB	SO	SB	BA	SA	OBP
85	42	932	481	223	352	.290	.373	.364

G	IP	H	GS	CG	BB
2	3.1	7	0	0	0

SO	SH	W	L	PCT	ERA
2	0	0	0	—	5.40

B. 10/28/1863 Holyoke, MA **D.** 10/22/1935
TEAMS: 87–89BalA 90–97BosN 97WasN 98BroN 98StLN 99CleN
DEBUT: 4/16/1887 at Baltimore; played 1B and went 1-for-3 in an 8–3 win over Philadelphia's Ed Seward
FINALE: 9/13/1899 at Philadelphia; played 1B went 0-for-2 in an 8–2 loss to Philadelphia's Red Donahue

In 1889 Tommy Tucker experienced his career highlight when he hit .372 in becoming the first switch hitter to win a ML batting title. Through the 1892 season he owned a .297 BA at approximately the halfway mark in his career. The increased pitching distance the following year fattened batting averages across the board for the remainder of the decade of the 1890s. In every case but one, position players at the midpoint of fairly lengthy ML careers lifted their BAs after 1892. The lone exception was Tucker, who actually hit 15 points *less* in the second half of his ML sojourn to finish at .290. If his hitting decay were not burden enough, he also grew increasingly unpopular among fellow players with each passing year, so that by the time he took his last throw at 1B in a ML game, no one was sorry to see him go.

Tucker played for a semipro team representing his hometown of Holyoke in 1882–83 before turning pro in 1884 with Holyoke of the Massachusetts State Association. He began the following season with Springfield, MA, before moving to Newark of the Eastern League. Returning to Newark in 1886, he was acclaimed the best all-around first baseman in the loop, inducing Baltimore AA manager Billy Barnie to fire weak-hitting Milt Scott and replace him with the fancy-fielding switch hitter. Tucker followed an outstanding rookie season in 1887 by leading the Orioles in homers and RBI in 1888 and then topping the AA in batting in 1889. When Baltimore abdicated its AA franchise that fall and moved to the minor league Atlantic Association, Tucker tied himself in knots over whether to jump to the PL before finally signing a personal services contract allowing Baltimore to assign him to any team he wanted and then being sold to Boston NL for $3,000.

Whether it was a change to the NL brand of ball or playing for a better caliber of team, he evolved into a different sort of player than he had been with Baltimore. Always an aggressive, in-your-face type—he led his league five times in being hit by pitches—he became downright fractious, perfecting a trick on wild pickoff throws of falling heavily on top of the runner to prevent him from advancing. His language, particularly when he was acting as a base coach, grew increasingly vulgar, and his off-field activities began engaging him in frequent skirmishes with manager Frank Selee. On September 21, 1892, Tucker showed up drunk for a game at Cincinnati. When Selee refused to put him in the lineup, Tucker cursed out the manager to the extent that he finally had to be dragged out of the park by the police. The following year, on May 15 at Boston, Tucker and John McGraw got into a savage fight on the field, which triggered an unruly section of the crowd to set a bonfire in the RF stands that stopped the game and ultimately burned down not only the ballpark but over 150 nearby buildings. Then in 1894 Tucker's jaw was broken by an angry mob in Philadelphia when he went back to retrieve a sweater he had forgotten on the visitors' bench after a particularly contentious game.

Following years of trying unsuccessfully to trade his querulous first baseman whose defense had begun to decline as much as his hitting, Selee gave up hoping for a decent player in return and sold him to Washington for $800 in June 1897. Tucker seemingly thrived on the change of scene, hitting .338 for the D.C. club to post a composite .333 mark, his highest since winning the AA batting title eight years earlier. But Washington officials must have sensed that the revival was illusory, for they sold him to Brooklyn in March 1898 and recouped their $800 when they could not get waivers on him so they could send him to minor league Omaha. The 34-year-old first sacker lasted less than four months in Brooklyn before being peddled to last-place St. Louis. The next spring, when St. Louis and Cleveland consolidated under syndicate ownership, Tucker went to the Forest City along with the rest of St. Louis's dregs. He played in 1899 as if he were sleepwalking, compiling an abominable .593 OPS and scoring just 40 runs in 127 games for the equally abominable Spiders, and was axed for "indifferent play" a full month before the season ended.

After spending three undistinguished seasons in the minors, Tucker left the game to work in Holyoke paper mills. At the time of his death in Montague, MA, in 1935 his son Raymond was a political journalist in Washington. Tucker's .372 mark in 1889 still stands as the season record for a switch hitter. (DN)

Virtue, Jacob Kitchline / "Jake" "Guesses"

B	T	HGT	WGT	G	AB	H	R	2B
B	L	5'9½"	165	474	1764	483	321	60

3B	HR	RBI	BB	SO	SB	BA	SA	OBP
50	7	256	275	140	50	.274	.376	.376

G	IP	H	GS	CG	BB
2	5	3	0	0	4

SO	SH	W	L	PCT	ERA
2	0	0	0	—	1.80

B. 3/2/1865 Philadelphia, PA **D.** 2/3/1943
TEAMS: 90–94CleN
DEBUT: 7/21/1890 at Boston; played 1B and went 2-for-2 in a 12–5 loss to Boston's Charlie Getzein
FINALE: 7/20/1894 at Louisville; played 1B and went 1-for-3 in a 7–4 loss to Louisville's Jock Menefee

Jake Virtue had an exceptional arm. He could take a relay throw deep in the outfield and routinely gun down a runner at the plate. Virtue was also outstanding on pop flies and would chase down even balls that his right fielder properly should have taken. Said to actually be less than his listed height, he was nonetheless so agile and reached so many off-the-mark throws that he belied the age-old notion that a first baseman had to be tall. On offense he was always hustling, frequently slid into 1B in an attempt to beat out a hit, and was equally effective from both sides of the plate. Yet Virtue was one of few hitters whose BA declined in 1893 at the increased pitching distance. A highly regarded player prior to then, he had only one major weakness: reportedly, he was totally lacking in confidence—1 error or strikeout early in a game would ruin him for the rest of the day.

Virtue first made his name known with the amateur 1885 Philadelphia Somersets, which also numbered catcher Billy Earle. A second baseman at the time, he turned pro the following year with Lancaster of the Pennsylvania State Association and by 1890 had converted to 1B and was spending his second season with Detroit under manager Bob Leadley when the International Association disbanded. The NL Cleveland Spiders at that point hired Leadley, who brought Virtue with him. The switch-hitting first sacker posted a .836 OPS in the second half of the 1890 season to lead all NL rookies with a minimum of 200 ABs. Two solid seasons followed, but Virtue's 1892 campaign was marred when he collided with catcher Chief Zimmer in a late-season game against Boston after Mike Kelly hollered from the Boston bench for first one of them and then the other to take a high foul pop. He never again was able to play 1B with the same abandon, and his hitting likewise deteriorated. The following year Virtue lost his job to Pat Tebeau, filled in for injured players at other positions, and finally was instructed to use his great arm to learn how to pitch and to expect his release if he failed at it. Virtue opened 1894 at 2B in place of ailing Cupid Childs, played CF for a time, and pitched twice in relief but was wild. After that he rode the bench until he was cut in late July. Virtue refused offers from other NL teams, preferring to play SS for Guy Hecker's Oil City club, but then signed with Louisville in December to replace feeble-hitting Lute Lutenberg for 1895.

Several weeks later Virtue suffered "some sort of paralytic stroke" that affected his right side and rendered him unable to walk until the fall of 1895. Then in July 1896 *TSN* put out a plea to send contributions to Chief Zimmer, who would distribute the money to Virtue's family, which needed aid after he was hit with a second stroke at his home in Philadelphia. Virtue's former Cleveland teammate Jack O'Connor told a story three years later that, one day in 1894 shortly before his release, Virtue had been unable to find his sweater and said, "May the devil paralyze the man who stole my sweater." Later he found it where he had forgotten he himself put it and soon afterward had his first stroke. The story may have been apocryphal, but, in any case, by that time Virtue had also been involved in a near-fatal train wreck in which twenty-five people were killed. His life now a complete shambles, he spent time in and out of hospitals with further strokes but eventually regained his health sufficiently enough to be in charge of the Philadelphia A's press box in the early part of the twentieth century. He remained a partial invalid until 1943 when he died at his son's home in Camden, NJ.

Although listed as a left-handed thrower, there is a possibility that Virtue was a righty. The January 20, 1900, *TSN* reported that after he had his first major stroke his right arm hung limp at his side and he could only throw with a wrist snap without raising the arm. The source of his nickname "Guesses" is still anyone's guess. (DN)

Werden, Percival Wheritt / "Perry"

B	T	HGT	WGT	G	AB	H	R	2B
R	R	6'2"	220	695	2746	774	444	109

3B	HR	RBI	BB	SO	SB	BA	SA	OBP
87	26	439	282	140	151	.282	.413	.358

G	IP	H	GS	CG	BB
16	141.1	113	16	12	22

SO	SH	W	L	PCT	ERA
51	1	12	1	.923	1.97

B. 7/21/1861 St. Louis, MO **D.** 1/9/1934
TEAMS: 84StLU 88WasN 90TolA 91BalA 92–93StLN 97LouN
DEBUT: 4/24/1884 at St. Louis; caught by Jack Brennan and beat Altoona's John Brown 11–2
FINALE: 10/3/1897 at Louisville; played 1B and went 3-for-4 in a 9–7 loss to Cincinnati's Billy Rhines
CAREER HIGHLIGHT: Set the pre-1920 professional record for the most home runs in a season with 45 for Minneapolis of the Western League in 1895

Perry Werden successfully shaved four years off his birth date and until recently was believed to have been only 18 when he made his ML debut. Knowing this only deepens the mystery of why his ML career was not more extensive. Considered by many authorities to have been the best minor league player in the nineteenth century, Werden won five minor league home run crowns, two batting titles, led in triples twice in the majors and once in the minors, led in doubles twice in the minors, and once paced his league in steals. Then, to that, one must add his ML season record for the highest winning percentage by a qualifier with a sub-2.00 ERA, which he set as a rookie and then never again threw a single pitch in the majors after going 12-1 (.923).

Werden began as a pitcher in the early 1880s with the amateur St. Louis Libertys and had for his batterymate his boyhood friend, neighbor, and future ML umpire, Jack Brennan. According to Brennan, it was common for the strong-armed Werden to pitch 2 or 3 games in one day. He also often tossed batting practice against the St. Louis Browns in 1883 and beat them on one occasion in an exhibition game. One of the first players the UA St. Louis Maroons signed for 1884, Werden was used only sparingly despite his dazzling stats and did not appear in a single inning at 1B, the position where he would later make his lasting mark. It is possible that he suffered an arm injury at some point in 1884, for he seldom pitched during his next few seasons in the minors and stopped appearing in the box altogether around 1888. An injury would also explain why he last appeared in the box with the Maroons on September 5, 1884, and traded places during the game with left fielder Henry Boyle.

In 1885 Werden joined Memphis of the Southern League, where he began to play 1B but appeared in only 28 games. The following season, while captain of the Lincoln Western League club, he won his first minor league home run crown. Werden did not really start to peak as a hitter, however, until 1889, when he moved to Toledo and topped the International Association in batting. He accompanied the Ohio club to the majors the following year, led the AA in triples, and was then sold to Baltimore AA prior to the 1891 season after the Black Pirates returned to the minors. In the AA's last hurrah as a major league entity, Werden paced it in batting the first month of the season and finished as the Orioles' team leader in RBI. When the AA and NL merged in December 1891, the big first baseman was assigned to St. Louis. Even though he led the Browns in homers and RBI, many observers soured on him, and Charles Mears wrote, "There are times when [Werden] seems to be afraid of his own capabilities as a ballplayer. Championships never are won by men who are the least bit afraid."

The 1893 campaign was the first at the 60'6" pitching distance and brought a proliferation of glittering hitting stats. High among them was Werden's 29 triples, but when they were accompanied by a .276 BA, four points below the NL average, the Browns rejected his salary demands for 1894 and sold him to Minneapolis of the Western League under cruel circumstances, handing him his release on April 18, 1894, just two days after his father's death. Werden spent the next three seasons feasting on WL pitching in Minneapolis's tiny Nicollet Park and collected an aggregate total of 676 hits and 106 home runs in addition to a composite .408 BA. Meanwhile, quality first basemen in the NL were in short supply, especially in Louisville, where the Colonels had made do in 1896 with a trio of journeymen who were better suited to other positions. Upon arriving in the Falls City in 1897, Werden led the team in RBI. Still, it was clear by the end of the season that the rough-cut first sacker was history, for player-manager Fred Clarke viewed him as a bad influence, particularly on immature and impressionable pitcher Bill Hill. When Werden and Hill were arrested in late September at 3:00 a.m. in a local saloon for allegedly trying to shake down another patron, Hill was fined $300 for his part and Werden was told to look for another job.

Werden returned to Minneapolis in 1898 but broke his right kneecap during spring training when he turned his ankle and fell on a sidewalk. Out the entire season, he was still hobbled in 1899 but nonetheless hit .346 in 111 games. When the WL changed its name to the American League prior to the 1900 season, Werden carved his niche in AL history when he became its first leader in SA, total bases, and doubles and tied Socks Seybold for the loop home-run crown. Probably because of his age (he admitted to being 35 in 1900 but was really 39), he was dropped from the AL rolls when it claimed ML status the following year. Werden remained a significant offensive force in the minors for three more seasons and then became a part-time player for several more. Fittingly, when his playing days finally ended, he became the first known full-time minor-league hitting coach, hired in that capacity by Indianapolis in 1908 while also serving as the team's trainer. He also umpired in several minor loops and headed Werden's All-Stars, a barnstorming team, before settling in Minneapolis with his wife, the former Mamie Hardy, whom he had married in 1888. Werden died in Minneapolis of a heart attack in 1934. (DN/PM)

Whistler, Lewis W. (b. Wissler) **/ "Lew"**

B	T	HGT	WGT	G	AB	H	R	2B
?	R	5'10½"	178	272	1014	247	150	29

3B	HR	RBI	BB	SO	SB	BA	SA	OBP
28	12	133	100	156	39	.244	.363	.318

B. 3/10/1868 St. Louis, MO **D.** 12/30/1959
TEAMS: 90–91NYN 92BalN 92–93LouN 93StLN
DEBUT: 8/7/1890 at Philadelphia; played 1B and went 1-for-2 in a 5–4 loss to Philadelphia's Tom Vickery
FINALE: 6/15/1893 at Boston; played 1B and went 0-for-4 in a 5–1 loss to Boston's Harry Staley

Lew Whistler was an excellent defensive first baseman, said to be the best in the NL at making pickoff plays on throws from his catcher, and had good power. Since he was weak on high pitches and thrived on low ones, he probably hit left-handed. Whistler began his pro career with Wichita of the Western League in 1887 as a middle infielder. He moved to San Antonio of the Texas League in 1888 and came to maturity as a hitter the following year, when he led the Central Interstate League with 22 home runs while playing 1B for Evansville. In 1890 Whistler was pacing Washington of the Atlantic Association in all slugging departments when the team folded in early August, allowing the Giants to acquire him. After an excellent rookie year at 1B, he was reduced to a utility role in 1891 when Roger Connor rejoined the Giants. On June 19, on a muddy field at Philadelphia, Whistler made a single-inning record 4 errors at 3B shortly after he rejoined the team following his father's death. As soon as the season ended, he signed with Baltimore after making it known that he felt he had been shabbily treated in New York.

Whistler opened 1892 with the Orioles at 1B and batting cleanup. He went 3-for-4 on Opening Day but hovered around the .200 mark after that and was released in late June. Signed by Louisville after Harry Taylor broke a rib, he led the Colonels in home runs but otherwise hit poorly. When he continued to exhibit little punch the following spring after the pitching distance increased and other hitters were prospering, he was released in June to Albany of the Eastern League. Whistler immediately regained his home-run stroke against lesser pitching and remained a force in the minors for another dozen years. He finished his active playing career in 1905 as player-manager with Memphis of the Southern Association, hitting .234 in 105 games. Whistler was the oldest surviving member of the New York Giants at the time of his death in St. Louis at 91. (DN)

4 | THE SECOND BASEMEN

4. Bill Greenwood, the all-time ML leader in the most games played at second base by a left-hander.

Ardner, Joseph A. / "Joe" "Old Hoss"

B	T	HGT	WGT	G	AB	H	R	2B
R	R	?	160	110	415	88	34	14

3B	HR	RBI	BB	SO	SB	BA	SA	OBP
2	0	39	18	64	9	.212	.255	.248

B. 2/2/1858 Mount Vernon, OH **D.** 9/15/1935
TEAMS: 84CleN 90CleN
DEBUT: 5/1/1884 at Providence; played 2B and went 0-for-4 in a 2–1 win over Providence's Charlie Sweeney
FINALE: 8/18/1890 at Cincinnati, played 2B and went 0-for-3 in a 14–3 loss to Cincinnati's Tony Mullane

The May 25, 1898, *Chicago Tribune* suggested that Joe Ardner may have coined the classic baseball expression, "The season is young yet." He began his career as a pitcher-infielder with his hometown Mount Vernon, OH, amateur team in 1876. By 1882 he was catching for an independent Philadelphia club. Ardner remained in Pennsylvania in 1883 with Reading of the Interstate Association until he was released in July. He then signed with Altoona but left the Mountain Citys before they affiliated with the UA in 1884 to join Cleveland NL as a replacement for arguably the best second baseman in baseball at that time, UA jumper Fred Dunlap.

Ardner lost his job to Germany Smith after Altoona left the UA, freeing Smith to sign with Cleveland. By the end of his stay with the Blues, Ardner owned a .183 OBP. He continued to exhibit a weak bat as he moved through the minors for the remainder of the 1880s. After hitting .239 with Oswego in 1886, in 1887 he was batting .247 for Topeka in midseason, the lowest BA of any Western League regular even with walks counting as hits.

As the UA encroachment gave Ardner his first ML opportunity in 1884, his second big-league job coincided with the Brotherhood war in 1890. Again it came with a Cleveland franchise after the NL Spiders lost second baseman Cub Stricker to Boston PL. Ardner opened 1890 in Stricker's stead and lost his job on August 21 to Bill Delaney. After spending that winter working at as a sceneshifter at the Cleveland Opera House, Ardner traveled west to play for Tacoma but left the Pacific Northwest League club late in 1891 to join Jamestown, the New York State League pennant winner. He moved south the following May to play 2B for Atlanta and by July formed a keystone combination with Pop Smith that was among the best in the Southern League even though both men were well past 35. Ardner left Atlanta when the SL folded and resumed his globetrotting. By 1896 he was back where he had started his career some twenty years earlier, in Ohio, latching on with the Youngstown Interstate League team. A widower, he died of pneumonia in Cleveland, his adopted home, at 77. (DN)

Barkley, Samuel W. / "Sam"

B	T	HGT	WGT	G	AB	H	R	2B
R	R	5'11½"	180	582	2329	602	362	125

3B	HR	RBI	BB	SO	SB	BA	SA	OBP
39	10	231	176	44	51	.258	.359	.314

G	W	L	PCT	PENNANTS
58	21	36	.368	0

B. 5/24/1858 Wheeling, WV **D.** 4/20/1912
TEAMS: 84TolA 85StLA 86PitA 87PitN (P/M)88KCA 88–89KCA
DEBUT: 5/1/1884 at Louisville; played 2B and went 3-for-4, getting all 3 of Toledo's hits in a 5–1 loss to Louisville's Guy Hecker
FINALE: 7/12/1889 at Kansas City; played 1B and went 1-for-3 in a 4–0 loss to Baltimore's Matt Kilroy

After getting three hits on Opening Day in 1884, Sam Barkley was off to a brilliant rookie campaign and ratings that, in the judgment of some reference works, made him the best overall player in the AA that year. He seemed to emerge out of nowhere, for he was then in his eighth pro season, having begun playing for pay with his hometown Wheeling Standards in 1877, and had previously played for minor league and independent entries in Detroit, Akron and, finally, the Toledo Northwestern League champions in 1883. Still, after his rookie performance, only his age (26) seemed to bar a lengthy and illustrious ML career. Well before he was 30, however, Barkley had already long since begun his downward descent when "hotel life and fan homage bred a spirit of indifference to training [in one who was] naturally a man inclined to avoirdupois accumulation."

One of the most highly coveted free agents in the game following the 1884 season when Toledo left the majors, the West Virginian's services went to St. Louis. Although he was instrumental in helping St. Louis win its first of four straight AA pennants, Barkley was put up for sale that winter, a puzzling development that only time would explain. For the moment, St. Louis alone knew what remained for other teams to discover: Barkley was an egomaniac and not a team player. A complicated dispute for his services between Baltimore and Pittsburgh culminated in the ousting of Pittsburgh owner Denny McKnight as AA president even though the Smoke City team ultimately garnered the ex-Browns second baseman (*see* Harmar McKnight).

Pittsburgh officials soon perceived why St. Louis had been so eager to shed Barkley. He was both a chronic malcontent and one to "play for the crowd" by trying for circus catches and dazzling one-handed stops rather than making plays as expediently as possible. Still, much was forgiven him until the following year when his BA dropped to .224, his arm went bad, and he was moved to 1B after Alex McKinnon died. His high salary, a source of friction on the Pittsburgh team ever since his arrival in 1886, was slashed, leading him to hold out the following spring. The 1888 season had already begun when the Alleghenys broke the logjam by selling Barkley to the new Kansas City AA entry for a reported $2,000. It was tantamount to robbery inasmuch as Barkley hit just .216 for the Cowboys, continued to have a lame arm, and was an abject failure after he replaced Dave Rowe as the club's player-manager. Criticized initially for "changing the men too much to get any real good work out of them," by September, just before he was fired, he stood accused of being "violently overbearing," along with the more serious charge of having deliberately tried to give away 2 games earlier in the month to the Philadelphia A's in an attempt to thwart the Browns (which he loathed after they sold him) in their bid for a fourth straight AA pennant.

Yet Barkley remained with KC in 1889 as a player only and opened the season at 2B. Even though he was hitting better than he had at any juncture since his rookie season, he was traded in July to Toledo, now a minor league club, for third baseman Billy Alvord. Barkley hit .248 for Toledo in some 50 games, moved on to Wheeling of the Tri-State League, and left baseball soon thereafter to become a cigar maker and salesman.

After several narrow brushes with the law, Barkley landed in Chicago in the mid-1890s, where he opened a saloon with ex-ML pitcher Al Atkinson. Having "grown large and fleshy" by now, he flirted with the Second City underbelly and was married for a time to Dora Feldman. After their divorce Feldman wed Chicago crime boss Mike McDonald. Soon afterward she blatantly shot and killed her lover, the artist Webster Guerin, but was found not guilty in a 1908 trial, owing perhaps to McDonald's persuasive presence in the courtroom. Long before then Barkley's saloon had failed and he had returned to Wheeling and opened another cigar store. In the winter of 1912 evangelist Billy Sunday converted him when Sunday visited Wheeling on one of his national tours. Once cleansed of sin, Barkley died at his home shortly thereafter of a surfeit of ailments, with the official cause listed as chronic parenchymal disease. (DN/DB)

Bassett, Charles Edwin / "Charlie"

B	T	HGT	WGT	G	AB	H	R	2B
R	R	5'10"	150	917	3493	806	392	114

3B	HR	RBI	BB	SO	SB	BA	SA	OBP
49	15	402	239	312	116	.231	.304	.285

B. 2/9/1863 Central Falls, RI **D.** 5/28/1942
TEAMS: 84–85ProN 86KCN 87–89IndN 90–92NYN 92LouN
DEBUT: 7/22/1884 at Providence; played 2B and went 0-for-5 in a 10–6 loss to Philadelphia's Jim McElroy
FINALE: 10/15/1892 at Cleveland; played 3B and was 1-for-2 in an 11–2 loss to Tom Williams

After playing with the independent Pawtucket Aetnas, in the fall of 1882 Charlie Bassett entered Brown University and starred on the school's baseball team for the next two springs. In July 1884, after Brown's collegiate season ended, he signed with Providence. Bassett's debut came in the famous game when Charlie Sweeney stalked off the field and forced Providence to finish the contest with just eight men. After filling in for second baseman Jack Farrell in his debut, later that season Bassett subbed occasionally for both SS Arthur Irwin and third baseman Jerry Denny. There were numerous favorable accounts of Bassett's fielding, but all conveniently ignored that he hit just .139. Regardless, he celebrated being a member of the game's first World's Series winner by marrying Ethel Esten of Lincoln, RI, a few weeks after the Grays beat the AA titlist New York Mets.

Rather than return to Brown and continue his studies, Bassett and his new bride decided that he should continue in pro baseball when the Grays invited him back in 1885. Injuries at various junctures in the season to Farrell, Irwin, and Denny increased the utility infielder's playing time to 82 games, but his execrable BA froze at .144. After the Grays folded at the close of the 1885 season, despite his atrocious stickwork Bassett's versatile glove was so coveted that he was grabbed by Kansas City, an NL replacement team in 1886. He rewarded the Cowboys with his career year, hiking his BA to .260 and posting a .380 SA, a personal high. After that, however, Bassett's hitting declined again. His fielding, in contrast, only improved, producing three FA crowns, two at 2B and one at 3B.

Let go by Louisville following the 1892 season, Bassett finished his pro career in 1897 where he had begun it fourteen years earlier, by playing five seasons with Providence, then in the Eastern League. Early in life he had harbored aspirations of making his living as a writer when he left baseball, but in 1898 he returned to the town where he had first played for an organized team and joined the Pawtucket police force. Over the next thirty years Bassett boasted to his fellow officers of his friendships with Babe Ruth, Wilbert Robinson, and Judge Landis. While these tales may have been somewhat fabricated, Bassett did maintain a close association with at least one of his famous playing contemporaries, Billy Sunday. On one occasion, after holding a revival meeting at a theater in Pawtucket, Sunday accompanied Bassett to the police station to join him in regaling the audience there with their mutual memories of Cap Anson, Mike "King" Kelly, and other stars of their time.

After retiring from the Pawtucket police force, Bassett worked for a time as a security guard and then lived the remainder of his life with his second wife, Florence Sprague, on his pension. He died at Pawtucket Memorial Hospital at 79. (DN)

Bierbauer, Louis W. (aka Bauer) **/ "Lou"**

B	T	HGT	WGT	G	AB	H	R	2B
L	R	5'8"	140	1385	5713	1524	821	209

3B	HR	RBI	BB	SO	SB	BA	SA	OBP
95	34	839	268	130	206	.267	.354	.301

G	IP	H	GS	CG	BB
4	14.2	13	0	0	5

SO	SH	W	L	PCT	ERA
5	0	0	0	—	3.07

B. 9/28/1865 Erie, PA **D.** 1/31/1926
TEAMS: 86–89PhiA 90BroP 91–96PitN 97–98StLN
DEBUT: 4/17/1886 at Philadelphia; played 2B and collected 1 hit in a 10–3 win over New York's Jack Lynch
FINALE: 4/30/1898 at Cleveland; played SS and went 0-for-5 in a 4–1 win over Cleveland's Jack Powell

In 1883, at age 18 and weighing only around 130, Lou Bierbauer was a semipro catcher in his native Erie. After producing 7-hit and 6-hit games with the Erie Olympics early in the 1885 season, Bierbauer went to Canada to play for the Hamilton Primroses and Guelph. Philadelphia AA invited him to training camp in 1886, expecting him to vie for the catching job, but when he also proved to be the club's best second baseman, the extra backstop berth went instead to rookie Wilbert Robinson. Even though he was almost instantly compared to Bid McPhee, the AA's premier second sacker, Bierbauer was loath to play there because the incumbent, Joe Quest, had been influential in his joining the A's, never expecting his protégé would usurp his position. Bierbauer at first was no improvement over Quest as a hitter, tallying a dismal .545 OPS in 137 games. His marks were better in his sophomore season, but a career-long weakness surfaced when he walked just 13 times in 530 ABs.

By 1889 Bierbauer had established himself as arguably the best second baseman in the AA, hitting .304 and knocking home 105 runs despite losing his wife in July. Yet his stats had an ominous tinge, as he scored just 80 runs and manager Billy Sharsig generally batted him near the bottom of the order. But if there was a flaw in Bierbauer's game, at that point only Sharsig appeared to sense it. When the PL formed after the 1889 season, Brooklyn SS-manager John M. Ward seized the AA's new 2B kingpin to serve as his keystone partner with the Brooklyn entry. Bierbauer did not disappoint Ward, hitting .306 and pacing all PL second basemen in assists and double plays.

Expected to return to Philadelphia AA after the PL collapsed, Bierbauer instead became an off-season tempest when it developed that the A's had carelessly neglected to reserve him. When he was awarded to Pittsburgh of the NL after a stormy battle between the two loops, the Smoke City entry was dubbed the "Pirates" for having snatched him. By the close of the 1891 season the delight in Pittsburgh over Bierbauer's bold acquisition had tarnished somewhat when his BA dropped exactly 100 points from the previous year. Some observers recalled a warning that had appeared two years earlier in *TSN* soon after his wife's death to the effect that she had "exerted a salutary restraining influence over her husband," but since he had played well the previous year, others were more inclined to attribute his drop at the plate to being spiked in a base-path collision with Boston's Tommy Tucker on May 27 that put him out of action for several games. Given the future direction Bierbauer's career took, the latter assessment would appear to have been on the mark. In any event, on August 21 he stunned Pittsburgh by asking for his release, saying that "he was sick of playing" for a losing team, but a local reporter wrote, "He is probably the last man, however, that would be released by the officials."

The Pirates continued to stand by him in 1892 even though he hit just .236 and were gratified when he lifted his BA to .284 in 1893. Even though Bierbauer openly admitted that he had become gun shy about covering 2B on steals and double plays because of the spiking he had sustained in 1891, in November 1893 Pittsburgh refused Philadelphia's offer of Bill Hallman for him. Hallman had scarcely been in Bierbauer's class a few years earlier, but within another year or so Pittsburgh would have welcomed Hallman in return for him. For some while Bierbauer had fooled team observers into thinking he was a decent hitter because he seldom struck out, but by 1895 the deception was over when he scored just 53 runs in 117 games and logged a .290 OBP. In addition, *TSN*, while careful not to identify Bierbauer by name, clearly was referring to him when it labeled a certain Pittsburgh infielder a "shirker," especially when the club went on the road where home fans were unaware of how zealously he dodged hard-hit balls and sliding runners. Still, he retained his regular post the following spring and was off to his best start in several seasons when he injured his ankle sliding in a game against Cincinnati on July 3 and had to be removed from the field by ambulance. Initially thought to be just a bad sprain, the ankle turned out to be broken, shelving him for the season. The irony was that Bierbauer was hurt as a base runner rather than as a fielder in the very sort of play that he had lived in fear of ever since his first serious injury in 1891.

The following March, satisfied that Dick Padden could do the job as well as Bierbauer and for less money, Pittsburgh sold the veteran second baseman to St. Louis. Loath at first to report to the dreary "Done" Browns, Bierbauer finally relented, but he then jumped the team in early May while it was in Louisville and claimed he preferred to play in an outlaw league near his home in Erie. Repentant the following spring, he opened 1898 at 2B for St. Louis but parted company with the Browns after going hitless in his first 4 games. Bierbauer then played out the string in the minors, finishing with the Newark Eastern League entry in 1902. Returning to Erie, he worked as a molder for several years and then managed in the low minors for a time. Upon leaving the game permanently, he took a job as a night watchman at the Oden Stove factory in Erie.

Bierbauer died at his home in 1923 of pneumonia. Many years later sportscaster Bill Stern announced that Bierbauer was the father of Elsie Janis, a vaudeville star in the early 1900s. Even some officials of the Pirates club bought the story until it emerged that her father was a different Bierbauer. (DN)

Bonner, Frank J. / "Frank" "Flea"

B	T	HGT	WGT	G	AB	H	R	2B
R	R	5'7½"	169	153	600	161	88	33

3B	HR	RBI	BB	SO	SB	BA	SA	OBP
8	3	88	43	22	25	.268	.370	.324

B. 8/20/1869 Lowell, MA **D.** 12/31/1905

TEAMS: 94–95BalN 95StLN 96BroN 99WasN 02CleAL 02PhiAL 03BosN

DEBUT: 4/26/1894 at Baltimore; played 2B and went 1-for-4 in a 13–7 loss to Boston's Jack Stivetts

FINALE: 6/26/1903 at Boston; played 2B and went 0-for-2 in a 5–4 win over Chicago's Jack Taylor

With the right ML team and sharper coaching Frank Bonner might have emerged as one of the better NL second basemen in the 1890s. A molder by trade, he first played semipro with a Worcester team in 1887. Later that summer he joined Providence, a member of the Rhode Island State League. A catcher at the time, he remained with Rhode Island teams for several seasons, gradually converting to the infield. Bonner's progress through the minors was arduous until 1893 when he arrived in Wilkes-Barre. Early in the Eastern League season he met a local woman whom he married the following year and suddenly became a different ballplayer. Always a gritty competitor—some unkind souls said dirty—but a suspect hitter, Bonner instantly thrived at the new pitching distance. After collecting 16 total bases in one game, he entered September with a .368 BA and an EL-leading 16 home runs. His season abruptly ended on Labor Day when he broke his shoulder while chasing a pop fly, but Baltimore manager Ned Hanlon nonetheless drafted him with the expectation that he would replace John McGraw at SS in 1894 while McGraw moved to the outfield. Late that winter the *New York Times* remarked, "The [Baltimore] organization is about the youngest and liveliest of all. If Bonner comes anywhere near realizing the many good things said of him he will be a great acquisition."

But by the following spring the Orioles' team composition had altered dramatically, as Hughie Jennings claimed SS, allowing McGraw to move to 3B, and Willie Keeler and Dan Brouthers arrived in a trade, relegating Bonner to the bench. The lone rookie on the NL's new powerhouse, he got into only 33 games but did well, hitting .322. Bonner began 1895 still as the Orioles' tenth man and again was hitting well—.333 in 11 games—when he was traded to St. Louis on June 8 for pitcher Bill Kissinger. Immediately, he announced that he would refuse to report to the Browns and wanted to return to Wilkes-Barre, his wife's home. Not only did Bonner hate to lose the Temple Cup playoff money he was almost certain to earn that season if he remained in Baltimore, but two Orioles teammates who had previously played with the Browns, Kid Gleason and Steve Brodie, told him he had best "jump into the river" because "most of the league players would as soon don convicts' stripes as put on a St. Louis uniform."

Eventually Bonner went to the Browns, if only because he had little choice, but his career never recovered. He did so miserably in St. Louis that in August he was finally granted his wish to play in Wilkes-Barre. In 1896 he was acquired by Brooklyn, which he liked no better than St. Louis, and again played for his release so that he could return to Wilkes-Barre. After that, Bonner seemed to find his niche in the Eastern League and was one of the loop's top players for the next three seasons. His peak came in 1897 when he was runner-up to Dan Brouthers for the EL batting title. In 1899 Bonner was with Hartford and about to turn 30 when he was sold to Washington, yet another lowly NL club, for a reported $1,000. Handed the Senators' 2B post, Bonner had his top ML season, batting .274 in 85 games. He probably would have been caught in the numbers crunch anyway when the NL lopped off four teams prior to 1900, including Washington, but the Senators let him go even before disbanding after the *Washington Post* termed him a hitter unable to pull the ball and a fielder that didn't know how to play the hitters.

Bonner returned to the EL in 1900 with Rochester, convinced that this time he was there to stay. The following season he joined Toronto, where manager Ed Barrow appointed him captain, and was thinking of relocating to the Canadian Eastern League city when a final ML opportunity came his way. Longstanding acrimony between Cleveland second baseman Erve Beck and the Blues' new manager, Bill Armour, drove Armour to acquire Bonner in November 1901. But as had happened with Baltimore in 1894, the little infielder had the rug pulled out from under him. Soon after the 1902 AL season began, legal issues forced the Philadelphia A's to let star second baseman Nap Lajoie go to Cleveland, which then sold Bonner to the A's, where Connie Mack kept him on the bench.

Bonner worked his way back to the NL in 1903, spending the first two months of the season with Boston, and then finished his career in the minors. He played with Louisville in 1904 before rejoining his old Washington manager, Arthur Irwin, at Kansas City in 1905 and hitting a solid .278. Bonner remained in KC that fall and was hospitalized around Christmastime with blood poisoning. He died on the last day of the year. Bonner's pesky style of play, rather than his size, led to him being called "Flea." (DN)

Burdock, John Joseph / "Jack" "Black Jack" "Birdie"

B	T	HGT	WGT	G	AB	H	R	2B
R	R	5'9½"	158	1187	4915	1230	777	164

3B	HR	RBI	BB	SO	SB	BA	SA	OBP
50	18	502	140	328	59	.250	.315	.273

G	W	L	PCT	PENNANTS
54	30	24	.556	0

B. 4/?/1852 Brooklyn, NY **D.** 11/27/1931
TEAMS: 72–73AtlNA 74MutNA 75HarNA 76–77HarN 78–88BosN (P/M)83BosN 88BroA 91BroN
DEBUT: 5/2/1872 at Mansfield; played SS and went 0-for-4 in an 8–2 loss to Mansfield's Frank Buttery
FINALE: 7/23/1891 at Boston; played 2B and went 0-for-5 in an 8–6 loss to Boston's John Clarkson

A formidable fielder who won seven FA crowns during his eighteen years in the majors, from the outset of his career Jack Burdock harbored a reputation as one of the dirtiest players in the game's history. In his NA days, when many of the fields he played on were in unkempt condition, he would fill his pockets between innings with gravel and then spread it in front of 2B whenever a dangerous base thief reached 1B so that he would be cut like glass if he tried to slide. Even after Burdock came to Boston in 1878, where his iniquitous tactics were little appreciated by manager Harry Wright, he continued to sharpen his spikes in full view of opponents so as to intimidate them when he got on base. That practice was met in kind one afternoon in a game against Providence when he encountered Jack Farrell, who wore barbed wire wrapped around his shins. Farrell cut Burdock to ribbons by landing on his legs after jumping to avoid his hostile spikes when he slid into 2B on a steal attempt. Later in his career Burdock was beaned so seriously by New York ace Tim Keefe that Keefe was almost too terrified to visit him in the hospital.

But it was the introduction of overhand pitching rather than injuries or his reprehensible style of play that reduced Burdock in the short space of two seasons from a star to a scrub. In 1883 the second baseman was at his apex. Selected to run Boston on the field at the beginning of the year, he ceded control in July to John Morrill, who proceeded to win the NL pennant, but the loss in status seemed only to sharpen Burdock's play. That season he batted a career high .330 to lead all NL middle infielders. Two years later, however—with overhand pitching now a permanent fixture—he hit just .142 while playing in only 45 games. Injuries were initially blamed for the sudden drop, but when his deterioration as a hitter accelerated in 1886, he was suspended in late September for "irregular habits" that were "leaving him without means with a large family to support." Exactly how many mouths Burdock had to feed was never certain. In 1888 *TSN* reported that Mickey Welch had five children and Jim Galvin had six and then asked, "How about Jack Burdock who is afraid to count his?" The implication was that Burdock, a reckless womanizer, probably had several illegitimate offspring in addition to the many he acknowledged.

Reinstated by Boston in 1887, Burdock strained an Achilles tendon in June and was sent home again in September, this time while "suffering from a tumor in his side." He then spent the off-season carousing and in January was being hunted by the New York Police Department for impersonating an officer. Yet Boston still retained him in 1888. In desperation, Burdock had taken to batting left-handed in 1887 but abandoned the experiment when his hitting failed to revive. Boston finally released him in late June 1888 while he was batting just .203. Hoping Burdock still retained at least a modicum of his earlier skills, Brooklyn hired him and put him at 2B in place of Bill McClellan. After his first 12 games with the Bridegrooms, Burdock was at .087 (4-for-46), but manager Bill McGunnigle was still not convinced. When his efforts in both Boston and Brooklyn in 1888 were combined, Burdock posted the lowest season BA in ML history by a position player other than a catcher with a minimum of 300 ABs (.142), and history views McGunnigle's obstinate experiment with him as likely to have cost Brooklyn the 1888 AA pennant.

Burdock then served for several seasons as a player-manager in the minors except for 3 games in 1891 when he returned to Brooklyn as a fill in for critically injured second baseman Hub Collins. Some thirty months later he reached his nadir when he was found dead drunk in a Brooklyn gutter by a police officer and taken into custody. In court the following day his wife testified that he seldom contributed to the support of her and their nine children, and the ensuing public opprobrium appears to have helped him pull his life together. Burdock worked at a variety of factory jobs in Brooklyn, reaching the position of foreman in at least one, and lived until 79. (DN)

Childs, Clarence Lemuel / "Cupid" "Fatty"

B	T	HGT	WGT	G	AB	H	R	2B
L	R	5'8"	185	1394	5386	1660	1190	196

3B	HR	RBI	BB	SO	SB	BA	SA	OBP
101	20	722	961	117	266	.308	.393	.415

B. 8/14/1867 Calvert County, MD **D.** 11/18/1912
TEAMS: 88PhiN 90SyrA 91–98CleN 99StLN 00–01ChiN
DEBUT: 4/23/1888 at Philadelphia, played 2B and went 0-for-4 in a 3–1 loss to Boston's John Clarkson
FINALE: 7/8/1901 at Chicago; played 2B and made 1 hit in an 8–5 loss to Brooklyn's Frank Kitson

Built like a catcher, Cupid Childs nonetheless possessed exceptional speed and agility early in his career and laid immediate claim to being the best second baseman in the game in 1890, when he had arguably the best frosh season of any middle infielder in ML history. As early as July 1890, *TSN* noted, "Fatty Childs is a fine second baseman for so bulky a lad." In 1892, his second year with Cleveland, the same paper wrote, "At a distance he looks like a big Easter egg done in blue and white." That season Childs was credited by some sources with winning the NL batting title, and he is still deemed the leader in hits and runs in the first year that the NL and AA merged.

A member of a farming family with eleven children who moved to Baltimore after his father died, Childs first wore a pro uniform in 1886 with Scranton of the Pennsylvania State Association and less than two years later exhibited the crusty disposition that led to him being facetiously nicknamed "Cupid" when he refused to let the Philadelphia NL team trade him to lowly Washington and compelled them to release him instead so that he could join Kalamazoo of the Tri-State League. He was a natural to return to the majors in 1890 with the Syracuse AA replacement team after hitting .341 for the Stars International Association entry the previous season. Syracuse left the AA after just one year, but not before selling its crack second baseman to Boston AA prior to the 1891 season for $2,000. Boston then traded Childs to Cleveland NL for Paul Radford and Cub Stricker, overriding the protests of Baltimore AA, with whom Childs had signed before the AA withdrew from the National Agreement, allowing Childs to argue successfully that his Orioles contract was invalidated. Childs's acquisition gave SS Ed McKean a four-star keystone partner and helped make the Spiders one of the NL's premier teams for the next eight seasons. Batting leadoff, the 5'8" second sacker yearly ranked among the NL leaders in runs and walks as well as several fielding departments. With the sole exception of 1895, when his poor season may have cost Cleveland the NL flag, he remained one of the loop's principal luminaries through 1897. In 1898, at age 31, Childs slipped to .288 as his nonconforming body design began to betray him. After a bout with malaria two years later, he struggled to break .240 with Chicago, although he led NL second basemen in total chances. By the spring of 1901 Childs's legs were nearly gone, and the crowning moment, according to a later report in the *Washington Post*, came in a game at Boston when he refused to handle a throw from catcher Johnny Kling in an attempt to nail a runner stealing at 2B, allowing it to go through to CF. When Childs's excuse was that it was "too hard" a throw, that night Chicago manager Tom Loftus decided to get rid of him.

Childs finished the following year with Syracuse of the New York State League and hit .358 but without enough ABs to qualify for the batting title. He then played a season in the Southern Association and part of 1904 back in the New York State League before returning with his wife to Baltimore. The couple was successful for a while in the coal business and bore a daughter, Ruth, but fell into debt when Childs took ill with Bright's disease, compounded by cirrhosis of the liver. After Childs died in a Baltimore hospital at 45, his former Spiders teammates helped to collect enough money to pay his medical expenses and establish a small fund for his wife and daughter. During his eight peak years (1890–97), Childs easily outranked every other ML second baseman with a minimum of 2,000 PAs in BA (.325), walks (761), runs (960), and OPS (.858). (DN)

Connor, James Matthew
(b. O'Connor) / **"Jim"**

B	T	HGT	WGT	G	AB	H	R	2B
R	R	5'10½"	179	293	1058	247	117	26

3B	HR	RBI	BB	SO	SB	BA	SA	OBP
15	3	129	85	7	27	.233	.295	.296

B. 5/11/1863 Port Jervis, NY **D.** 5/3/1950
TEAMS: 92ChiN 97–99ChiN

DEBUT: 7/11/1892 at Boston; played 2B and went 1-for-3 in a 3–2 loss to Boston's Kid Nichols
FINALE: 9/9/1899 at Chicago; played 2B and went 0-for-5 in an 11–0 win over Cleveland's Creed Bates

Jim Connor shortened his surname, perhaps to prevent people from automatically assuming he was Irish. The most complimentary thing ever said about him was that he was liked by all and avoided cliques on the Chicago team, not easy to do in the 1890s. A weak hitter and not a particularly daring base runner, he was regarded as even less of an offensive threat in the Colts' lineup than Barry McCormick, who sometimes played beside him. The pair rank first and second in the race for the lowest OPS among all position players except catchers who compiled as many as 1,000 ML at bats in the 1893–1900 era, which goes a long way toward explaining why Chicago was never much of a factor during the years the two of them and catcher Kit Kittridge, an equally severe offensive liability, staffed the same batting order.

Connor played intermittently for teams in the New England area before joining Joliet of the Indiana-Illinois League in 1892 at the rather ripe age of 29. In early July, Chicago purchased both George Decker and Connor from manager Billy Murray's first-place club for $500. Connor's initial stay in the Windy City lineup was short-lived; after going 1-for-3 in his debut, he went just 1-for-31 in his next 8 games and was released. He then played four seasons in the high minors before Chicago overrode Cap Anson's objections and drafted him from Minneapolis of the Western League after the 1896 season as a backup at 2B for veteran Fred Pfeffer. By the summer of 1897 Connor had the job when age caught up to Pfeffer and hit surprisingly well (.291). But after he was beaned and knocked unconscious in a late-season game, his next two years were so dismal that only his popularity in the clubhouse kept him at his post.

Connor remained a good-field, no-hit infielder in the minors until he was 45, finishing in the 1908 New England League, and then both managed and umpired in the minors for a time. After leaving the game, he worked as a janitor at a public school in Providence until his retirement. Connor died at St. Joseph's Hospital in Providence in 1950. (DN/PM)

Crane, Samuel Newhall / "Sam"

B	T	HGT	WGT	G	AB	H	R	2B
R	R	6'0"	190	373	1359	276	183	30

3B	HR	RBI	BB	SO	SB	BA	SA	OBP
18	3	45	60	127	25	.203	.258	.237

G	W	L	PCT	PENNANTS
155	73	79	.480	0

B. 1/2/1854 Springfield, MA **D.** 6/26/1925
TEAMS: (P/M)80BufN 83NYA (P/M)84CinU 85–86DetN 86StLN 87WasN 90NYN 90PitN
DEBUT: 5/1/1880 at Cleveland; played 2B and went 0-for-4 in a 7–4 win over Cleveland's Jim McCormick
FINALE: 6/28/1890 at Pittsburgh; played 2B and was 0-for-3 in a 9–1 loss to Boston's Kid Nichols

When Tim Murnane died in 1918, Sam Crane inherited his mantle as the dean of American sportswriters. By then he was in his twentieth year with the *New York Evening Journal* after previously working with the *New York Press* from 1890–98. Crane maintained a close friendship with John McGraw even though the two often clashed, and he lived and died with the Giants. He made all road trips with the team and in 1925 developed pneumonia during a Giants western swing. Upon arriving at his Bronx home, he went straight to bed, but by then it was too late. Liked by everyone (with the exception of Giants owner Andrew Freedman, whom he roasted almost daily in his *New York Press* columns in the mid-1890s until Freedman banned him from the Polo Grounds), Crane was best described in his later years by F. C. Lane, who wrote in a 1918 piece on him for *Baseball Magazine*, "His kindly face, with its drooping white mustache is known to thousands. His tall, dignified presence, his freedom from all snobbishness, his accommodating ways, the unconsciousness friendliness for all which shown forth, from his eyes are familiar features of the Polo Grounds press box. And may they continue to be such for many years to come." But revered as Crane may have been while alive, he quickly fell into neglect after his death. His writing was seldom quoted in future years, let alone anthologized.

Crane attended MIT for two years in the late 1870s, studying electrical engineering and playing ball summers in Eastern minor leagues. After spending most of 1879 with Springfield of the National Association, he left school when the Buffalo

NL club hired him not only to play 2B in 1880 but also to run the team on the field despite his complete lack of previous ML experience. Even after benching his own lame .129 BA, the best Crane could do, according to most reference works, was bring the Bisons home seventh at 24-58. In actuality, there is evidence that Crane quit the job in disgust, giving it over to pitcher Jim Galvin, who in turn passed it on to the club official John Page before the Bisons began their final western road trip.

Seemingly through with baseball, Crane spent two years as a traveling salesman for a Holyoke envelope company. In 1883 he gave the game another whirl when the New York Mets, a fledgling AA entry, offered him their 2B post. Crane hit just .235 in 96 games but would never have another ML season as good. He began 1884 on the sidelines again. After the UA campaign was already well under way, the Cincinnati Outlaw Reds, frantic for an experienced hand at 2B, put him back in uniform. Crane made his UA debut on May 22 and by August was also managing the club; most sources say he took over the reins in June, but, again, the best evidence indicates otherwise. By October he had elevated Cincinnati to the equal of the first-place St. Louis Maroons.

When the UA folded that winter, Crane joined Indianapolis of the Western League and was among the swarm of Hoosiers players that found their way to Detroit NL during the 1885 season. He finished the campaign at 2B with the Wolverines but hit .192. When he was batting .141 after 47 games in 1886, the Wolverines acquired Fred Dunlap from St. Louis NL, and Crane, with no other good option available, was eventually persuaded to play 2B for St. Louis in Dunlap's stead. A .158 composite BA in 86 games effectively spelled the end of his ML career, although he subsequently played a handful of NL games with Washington, New York, and Pittsburgh.

In March 1889 Crane caused a stir in the New York press when he attempted to reorganize the old New York Mets as a cooperative team, but it was mild compared to the lurid stories he sparked that August after he ran off with Hattie Frankenfeller, the wife of a Scranton hoodlum. The pair was jailed on her husband's word that they were illegally living together as man and wife. Crane swore he would sue Frankenfeller for perjury but meanwhile was detained when he could not post a $750 bond. Eventually Crane and Hattie, "by direction of the court," were found not guilty when Frankenfeller, who was about to be indicted for receiving stolen goods, failed to appear in court to testify against them. The fate of their relationship is unknown. However, Crane was married to a woman named Gertrude at the time of his death and was survived by both her and his son Elmer. (DN/DB)

Creamer, George W. (b. Triebel) **/ "George"**

B	T	HGT	WGT	G	AB	H	R	2B
R	R	6'2"	?	500	1862	400	234	55

3B	HR	RBI	BB	SO	SB	BA	SA	OBP
28	1	99	71	89	—	.215	.276	.244

G	W	L	PCT	PENNANTS
8	0	8	.000	0

B. ?/?/1855 Philadelphia, PA **D.** 6/27/1886
TEAMS: 78MilN 79SyrN 80–82WorN 83–84PitN (P/M)84PitA
DEBUT: 5/1/1878 at Cincinnati; played CF and went 2-for-5 in a 6–4 loss to Cincinnati's Will White
FINALE: 10/2/1884 at Pittsburgh; played 2B and went 1-for-4 in a 10–5 loss to St. Louis's Dave Foutz

Beginning in his late teens, George Creamer played for the amateur Shibe club of Philadelphia until 1876 when he joined the semipro Neshannocks of New Castle, PA, and then moved to the unaffiliated Detroit Aetnas in August. He spent 1877 in the International Association with the Allegheny club. A poor year as an ML rookie with Milwaukee in 1878 sent him back to the minors the following year with Rockford of the Northwestern League until Syracuse summoned him in July to fill in for injured second baseman Jack Farrell. Creamer then signed with Worcester, the NL's newest entry, in 1880 and played every inning at 2B despite posting a wretched .448 OPS. He improved little as a hitter during his next two seasons with Worcester but then rapped a career-high .255 in 1883 upon joining Pittsburgh AA after the Massachusetts club folded. A card-carrying member of the Allegheny club's infamous "Brewery 9," he was involved in a drunken street brawl at 3:00 a.m. in Cincinnati that season but avoided a possible suspension when he went out that afternoon and played one of his best games of the year while still under the influence.

In 1884 Creamer led all Pittsburgh players in

games played with 98 but may have already been suffering from the illness that caused his death less than two years later. In any case, he did not play during the final ten days of the season. Over the winter Creamer was released to Baltimore but was unfit to play by the spring of 1885. Soon he was confined to his bed with consumption. In April 1886 some $50 was raised in his behalf by the Waterbury, CT, Eastern League team, where he had friends. On May 21, 1886, as he lay destitute and dying, the Syracuse International Association team played a benefit game for him in Syracuse, where he had once played. Less than two months later he expired at his home in Philadelphia. (DN/DB)

Crooks, Charles John / "Jack"

B	T	HGT	WGT	G	AB	H	R	2B
R	R	5'10"	170	795	2783	671	537	74

3B	HR	RBI	BB	SO	SB	BA	SA	OBP
44	21	314	612	195	220	.241	.322	.386

G	W	L	PCT	PENNANTS
62	27	33	.450	0

B. 11/9/1865 St. Paul, MN **D.** 2/2/1918
TEAMS: 89–91ColA (P/M)92StLN 93StLN 95–96WasN 96LouN 98StLN
DEBUT: 9/26/1889 at Brooklyn; played 2B and went 1-for-4 in a 7–7 tie against Brooklyn's Bill Terry
FINALE: 8/3/1898 at St. Louis; played LF and went 0-for-3 in a 4–3 win over Brooklyn's Joe Yeager
CAREER HIGHLIGHT ONE: 6/8/1889 at St. Paul; went 5-for-5, hit 4 home runs, and had 13 RBI in a 19–15 win over St. Paul's Will Mains
CAREER HIGHLIGHT TWO: 5/11/1892 at St. Louis; became the first MLer to lead off 2 consecutive games with a home run in a 5–3 loss to Baltimore's John Healy after hitting a lead-off home run the previous day against Philadelphia's Jack Thornton
CAREER HIGHLIGHT THREE: In 1892 set an NL record that lasted until 1911, when he collected 136 walks

Jack Crooks claimed to be the son of Gen. George Crook of Civil War and Indian Wars fame, but it appears to have been only one of his many efforts to puff up his resume. At the outset of his career his gigantic ego continually put him at odds with fellow players and made him the frequent butt of practical jokes that took advantage of his inflated opinion of his abilities. Yet his view of himself was not entirely wrong. Crooks was a good fielder, had an exceptional eye, and knew how to make his way around the bases. Off the field, he was "a walking fashion plate . . . one of the nobbiest dressers in the profession."

Crooks followed in his alleged father's footsteps and joined the army in his early teens. In 1885 he captained the Company E 1st Regiment N.G. State of Minnesota team before mustering out of the service. He then appears to have played for Racine College for a time before beginning his pro career the following year with Minneapolis of the Northwestern League. A catcher in his youth, he switched to the infield with the Millers. After spending 1887 with St. Paul, he joined the St. Louis Whites of the Western Association until he was sold to Omaha of the same loop. In September 1889, following a .326 season under Omahahogs pilot Frank Selee, Columbus AA purchased him.

Named Columbus' captain in the spring of 1890, Crooks was replaced on May 18 by Jim McTamany after he alienated most of his teammates and hit just .130 in the first 21 games of the year. He finished with a mere 123 total bases but garnered a phenomenal 96 walks and scored 86 runs. These were the sorts of numbers that his remarkable expertise at fouling off pitches would enable him to replicate in almost every season for the remainder of his ML career. Yet in 1893 he became the only player in ML history to be banished to the minors after leading his loop in walks when he hit just .237 in the first year the 60'6" pitching distance triggered a massive offensive explosion.

Crooks spent 1894 with Minneapolis of the Western League and then returned to the NL with Washington. But he continued to winter in St. Louis, where he had played in 1892–93, and work as a ticket seller at Browns owner Chris Von der Ahe's racetrack. In the winter of 1895–96 Von der Ahe accused him of shortchanging customers and pilfering track proceeds but still allowed him to spend his final ML season in a St. Louis uniform after another Western League stint in 1897. Crooks then quit the game to work as a traveling salesman for the Rosenthal Brothers Cigar Company but returned to play briefly with Buffalo of the newly renamed AL in 1900. After a stint with St. Paul of the Western League in 1901, Crooks resumed his sales career. In his late forties he contracted elephantiasis and reportedly weighed over 300 pounds when he died after spending seventeen months in a St. Louis insane asylum. (DN/DB)

*Daly, Thomas Peter / "Tom" "Tido"

B	T	HGT	WGT	G	AB	H	R	2B
B	R	5'7"	170	1175	4235	1188	818	177

3B	HR	RBI	BB	SO	SB	BA	SA	OBP
81	44	610	554	402	324	.281	.393	.371

B. 2/7/1866 Philadelphia, PA **D.** 10/29/1938
TEAMS: 84PhiU 87–88ChiN 89WasN 90–96BroN 98–01BroN 02–03ChiAL 03CinN
DEBUT: 6/9/1884 at Philadelphia; caught Bill Gallagher and went 0-for-4 in a 6–4 win over Washington's Bill Wise
FINALE: 9/27/1903 at Cincinnati; played 2B and made 1 hit in a 7–6 win over Brooklyn's Grant Thatcher
CAREER HIGHLIGHT: 5/14/1892 at Boston; batted in the ninth inning for Hub Collins and hit the first documented pinch home run in ML history off Boston's John Clarkson to tie the game 6–6
HISTORIC INCIDENT: 5/2/1896 at Louisville; was hit on the right wrist by a Chick Fraser pitch and had to persuade Louisville hurler Bert Cunningham, who was umpiring that day, that he was hit on the shoulder in order to get his base; after the game it emerged that Daly's wrist had been broken by Fraser's pitch, a ludicrous development that led to rescinding the unwritten Welch Amendment to the rule book (*see* Curtis Welch)

Tom Daly was the older brother of MLer Joe Daly. In the spring of 1884 he was playing for independent Millsville, NJ, where he was discovered by Philadelphia UA manager Fergy Malone and given a 2-game tryout. Two winters later he caught the attention of Chicago NL while playing in San Francisco and catching young southpaw prospect Phenomenal Smith. Expected to replace heavily battered Silver Flint as Chicago's regular backstop in 1887, Daly failed to hit in his two seasons with Chicago and was released to Washington in April 1889. He came to Brooklyn NL the following year after Washington disbanded and never played in another ML uniform until 1902. Daly had a hiatus, however, in 1897–98, when he was more or less sentenced to Milwaukee of the Western League on loan before being recalled in September 1898. He then remained with Brooklyn until he jumped to Chicago AL in 1902 after topping the NL in doubles. Daly played poorly in his eighteen-month AL sojourn but revived after returning to the NL with Cincinnati in July 1903 to hit .293 and lift his career BA to .278. At his retirement his 1,582 career hits ranked third among players MLB recognizes as having been switch hitters.

Daly's career year came in 1894, when he hit .341. The following February he married divorce Priscilla McCormick just before the Brooklyn team headed south but then almost lost his job in spring training to ancient Joe Mulvey. In 1896 Daly's twin foibles—drinking and a reputation for being gun-shy at standing tall against a base runner to turn a double play—caught up to him, and he was fined and suspended for the rest of the year after trying to play a game against Washington while drunk. He apparently improved both weaknesses during his two-year exile in the Western League, for he hit .313 in 1899, his first full season after returning to Brooklyn, and led all NL second basemen in double plays. Daly finished his active career as a player-manager in the Tri-State League in 1907 and later coached and scouted for the Indians and the Yankees. He died at his Brooklyn home in 1939 of colon cancer. Daly was the lone performer to play on three Brooklyn pennant winners in the nineteenth century. The source of his nickname, "Tido," is still unknown. (DN)

*Demont, Eugene Napoleon (b. Demontreville) / "Gene"

B	T	HGT	WGT	G	AB	H	R	2B
R	R	5'8"	165	642	2504	785	403	98

3B	HR	RBI	BB	SO	SB	BA	SA	OBP
26	12	369	143	35	180	.313	.388	.356

B. 3/26/1874 St. Paul, MN **D.** 2/18/1935
TEAMS: 94PitN 95–97WasN 98BalN 99ChiN 99BalN 00BroN 01–02BosN 03WasAL 04StLAL
DEBUT: 8/20/1894 at Baltimore; played SS and went 1-for-4 in a 7–5 win over Baltimore's Duke Esper and Bill Hawke
FINALE: 4/26/1904 at Detroit; played 2B and went 1-for-4 in a 6–5 along with win over Detroit's Jesse Stovall

Gene Demontreville played as "Demont" for most of his career and was the brother of MLer Lee Demontreville. He became a cause celebre in 1899 when Washington owner J. Earle Wagner joyfully confided to Cincinnati writer Harry Weldon that in 1897 Washington scorekeepers had inflated Demont's average from .285 to .345 (since reduced to .341) to make him salable to Baltimore and admitted the club had done similar padding with Bill Joyce, which was why Joyce's BA had dropped so precipitously after he was traded to New York. When Ned Hanlon later queried Wagner about Demont's hitting decline, the Washington owner admitted the deception (or so he said), and Hanlon then pulled the same stunt with Demont in 1898 so that Chicago would be willing to deal Bill Dahlen for him. Wagner later recanted his story, claiming he had made it up because Weldon needed a scoop, and *TSN* concurred, saying it would be impossible to hike a BA such a large amount by crediting errors as hits, and any other method would be such an obvious fraud that it would be detected immediately. The supposition was that Wagner had manufactured the tale to make it seem he had not been as badly outfoxed in the Demont deal with Baltimore in December 1897 as the press believed. Whatever the truth, if Demont's three seasons in question (1896–98) are deducted from his career totals, his BA plummets from.303 to .274.

Demont played with the Allentown, PA, Eastern League club before joining Pittsburgh in 1894 to replace injured SS Jack Glasscock. The Pirates released him when his arm was inadequate for short, and manager Connie Mack laughed in his face when he vowed that he would soon be back in the majors, by which time Mack would be in the minors. Such nearly came to pass when Washington drafted Demont and his .316 BA after the 1895 Eastern League season ended and Pittsburgh fired Mack the following year.

The son of a recently deceased dentist, Demont took up residence in D.C. with his widowed mother, who didn't want him to play ball for fear of injury but ultimately decided to let her son do as he wished and came to all of Washington's home games when she was given a box seat by Wagner. In 1896, his official rookie year, he led Washington in BA and total bases. Moved to 2B the following year, Demont continued to lead his team in most batting departments but by midseason had begun to be scolded for arrogance and selfish play. He grew increasingly unpopular with teammates and fans when the press began accusing him of playing for his release. Traded to Baltimore, Demont continued to hit for average, but his power numbers dropped and he was criticized by Hanlon for persistently "advancing a step or two" after fielding a ball before throwing it to 1B. Baltimore still was able to unload him when Chicago manager Tom Burns desperately wanted to dispose of "disorganizer" Bill Dahlen. Demont lasted only four months in Chicago when he "mixed with the worst set in the team" and showed up for a game with a head injury from being beaned by a popcorn bowl another bar patron threw at him. On August 2, 1899, he was returned to Baltimore for lightly regarded infielder George Magoon.

That winter, syndicate ownership moved Demont to Brooklyn, where he was expected to hold down 3B, but he lost the job to Lave Cross. In August 1900, Demont married Anna Kelly of Toronto and seemed ready to take himself less seriously and his profession more so. He let it be known that he intended to claim Tom Daly's 2B job in 1901, but instead he was sold to Boston NL. In the first year of the new century he hit an even .300. When he dipped to .260 in 1902, Boston was happy to let him jump to the AL. By age 30 Demont was no longer a ML regular. After St. Louis AL released him in 1904, he played and managed in the Southern Association until 1910 (when he hit a paltry .189 for New Orleans in 107 games) before becoming involved in the Tri-State Fair project in Tennessee. In 1935 he died of a heart attack while running to investigate a minor fire at Mid-South Fairgrounds in Memphis, where he was the concessions manager. (DN)

Dunlap, Frederick C. / "Fred" "Sure Shot" "Dunny"

B	T	HGT	WGT	G	AB	H	R	2B
R	R	5'8"	165	965	3974	1159	759	224

3B	HR	RBI	BB	SO	SB	BA	SA	OBP
53	41	366	283	263	85	.292	.406	.340

G	IP	H	GS	CG	BB
2	2.2	6	0	0	0

SO	SH	W	L	PCT	ERA
2	0	0	0	—	6.75

G	W	L	PCT	PENNANTS
252	145	102	.587	1

B. 5/21/1859 Philadelphia, PA **D.** 12/1/1902
TEAMS: 80–83CleN (P/M)82CleN (P/M)84StLU

(P/M)85StLN 86StLN 86–87DetN 88–90PitN 89PitN 90NYP 91WasA

DEBUT: 5/1/1880 at Cleveland; played 2B and went 1-for-5 in a 7–4 loss to Buffalo's Bill McGunnigle

FINALE: 4/20/1891 at Washington; after making a hit in the first inning, he broke his left leg sliding and was replaced at 2B by Will Smalley in an 8–4 loss to Baltimore's Sadie McMahon

CAREER HIGHLIGHT: 7/10/1880 at Cleveland; in the bottom of the ninth inning, with Jack Glasscock on 1B, hit a 2-run homer to give Cleveland's Jim McCormick a 2–0 win over Fred Goldsmith and end Chicago's then NL-record 21-game winning streak (although technically Dunlap's hit should have been a triple as per a rule installed just that year, which decreed that the game ended as soon as Glasscock touched the plate)

Fred Dunlap and his first ML keystone partner Jack Glasscock are inextricably linked. Dunlap's arrival in Cleveland forced Glasscock to move from 2B to SS, and the two were teammates for the next six years except for 1884 when both jumped to the rebel Union Association and effectively destroyed the Cleveland franchise when pitcher Jim McCormick also deserted. The pair parted ways in 1886 when Dunlap was traded to Detroit, which won the NL flag in 1887 whereas Glasscock's teams continued to languish near the bottom, and again in 1890 when Dunlap jumped briefly to the PL after Glasscock, one of the leading Brotherhood fomenters, reneged on his pledge to join the PL, but they still will always remain linked in the eyes of most baseball historians.

Orphaned before he was 10, Dunlap was raised by a foster family of little means and by 15 was playing for pocket money with a team in Gloucester, NJ. A catcher at the time, he began the conversion to SS the following year with the semipro Camden Cregars. By 1878 he had risen to Hornellsville of the International Association. When the IA club disbanded he joined Albany, champions of the Minor League National Association. Long before Dunlap arrived in Cleveland in 1880, and despite being illiterate he had already become such a skilled negotiator that *SL* would write eleven years later, "He will be remembered as the artist who blazed the road to high salaries, and who never got the short end of a deal, even when dickering with men skilled in financiering. When he made a contract he always had a lawyer draw it up in proper airtight shape, and we never heard of any of them being set aside as 'vague and indefinite.'" Some years afterward MLer Gene Demont also told of how, while in the minors, veteran players had told him to pattern himself after Dunlap, who "squeezed every nickel" and retired a rich man.

Dunlap first served notice of his financial acumen in the winter of 1883–84 when Henry Lucas courted him for Lucas's St. Louis entry in the Union Association. The second baseman whose throws with either hand were "as accurate as the best rifle shot" had already earned him the nickname "Sure Shot" reputedly received $5,000 to enlist with Lucas, although some sources put the figure as low as $3,400. With Lucas as his new employer he then compiled the finest all-around season ever by a second baseman, leading the UA in almost every major batting and fielding department and piloting the Maroons to a post-1875-record .832 winning percentage. Even though the overall caliber of Lucas's loop was dubious, Dunlap's performance during his prime years was such that *TSN* editor Al Spink would contend as late as 1910 that he "was far and away the greatest second baseman that ever lived." Meanwhile, the *Cleveland Herald* was of the opinion that "Dunlap is of good habits, a fine player, and with no book learning, knows what is good for Fred Dunlap," making it one of the first contemporary sources that confirmed, if in somewhat delicate terms, that Dunlap was illiterate.

Dunlap remained loyal to Lucas when the UA folded and the young entrepreneur was permitted to transfer his Maroons to the NL (to replace Cleveland, the club Dunlap had helped ruin), but relations between them gradually eroded until the owner sold his second baseman to Detroit for $4,700 of August 6, 1886. "Dunny" agreed to the deal, however, only after he negotiated a $2,500 salary from Detroit for the remainder of the 1886 season and a guarantee of $4,500 in each of the next two seasons. He began 1887 as not only the top second baseman in baseball but also arguably the best handball player. In February of that year he challenged catcher Tom Dolan for the "championship of all balldom," but the rivals could never agree on a court. A few months later Dunlap's handball reign ended abruptly. On July 5, 1887, in a game with Boston, Dunlap and Wolverines right fielder Sam Thompson collided while chasing a pop fly off the bat of Billy Nash into short RF. Dunlap made the catch but limped off field. He was still limping around his hotel in Detroit that evening when he suddenly vomited. A doctor was summoned and pronounced that a small bone in his leg was broken. The doctor could only marvel at Dunlap's tolerance for pain in remaining ambulatory for several hours with so severe an injury. The second baseman went to Mount Clemens, MI, to speed his recovery and returned to the lineup on September 20, much sooner than expected. That fall he came to hate Wolverines manager Bill Watkins when Watkins rode him all during the World's Series against the AA Browns, claiming he had lost the speed to get to grounders that Dunlap contended no second baseman could have reached even with "a scoop net." Less than two weeks after the Series ended, Watkins engineered Dunlap's sale to Pittsburgh NL for around $5,000, but not until Dunny had negotiated to get part of the sales price, lifting his already stupendous salary of $4,500 for 1888 to somewhere in the neighborhood of $7,000.

Now the highest-paid player in the majors, Dunlap was physically no longer able to perform up to his previous standard. A bad-hop grounder in July 1888 broke his jaw, limiting him to just 82 games. The following year he took over as Pittsburgh captain when Ned Hanlon replaced Horace Phillips as manager but hit just .235 and no longer had even average range as a fielder. He initially remained with Pittsburgh in 1890, but after Guy Hecker replaced him as field leader, he accepted an offer to jump to the Pittsburgh PL entry, only to be told the club no longer needed him. Dunlap played 1 game with the New York PL club and then sat out the year, hoping to heal his many injuries. His comeback attempt with Washington AA was aborted when he suffered yet another broken leg sliding. Released in June, he argued that since he had been injured in play he should have been retained until he was healed, as had happened in Detroit in 1887. He then wrote a letter to *TSN* warning all players not to play for Washington because of the ill treatment he had been given, and the paper editorialized, "Such is one of the dark sides of a player's life, who is condemned by all."

At the time, Dunlap was believed to own around $25,000 worth of real estate in Philadelphia, enough to live comfortably off the income from his holdings. He invested some of his money in racehorses and as late as 1895 *TSN* could still say his hardest job was collecting the rents from his many properties. But soon thereafter Dunlap began to lose heavily at the track and his health failed. In August 1899 *TSN* said that he was "now a cripple, but he can still play a brilliant game of pool." Three years later Dunlap died of rectal cancer in abject poverty in his native Philadelphia. (DN/DB)

Evers, Thomas Francis / "Tom"

B	T	HGT	WGT	G	AB	H	R	2B
?	L	5'9"	135	110	431	99	54	6

3B	HR	RBI	BB	SO	SB	BA	SA	OBP
1	0	—	7	—	—	.230	.248	.242

B. 3/31/1852 Troy, NY **D.** 3/23/1925
TEAMS: 82BalA 84WasU
DEBUT: 5/25/1882 at Baltimore; played 2B and went 0-for-4 in a 6–5 win over Cincinnati's Harry McCormick
FINALE: 10/16/1884 at Kansas City; played 2B and went 0-for-3 in a 10–4 loss to KC's Bob Black
FAMOUS FIRST: In 1884 became the first player in ML history to play as many as 100 games in his official rookie season when he was past the age of 30

Tom Evers's famous first in his official rookie season is newly noted here; his two previous claims to fame were being the uncle of HOFer Johnny Evers and the lone left-hander besides Bill Greenwood to play as many as 100 games in a season at 2B. Though Evers had a lengthy pro and semipro career, curiously there was no mention of his baseball exploits in his *Washington Post* obit. Built like his famous nephew, small-boned and slat-thin, Evers began play in his hometown of Troy in 1876 as the first baseman on the local independent team. The following summer he joined the independent Albany Nolans. By 1880 Evers was back in Troy, playing for the semipro Tibbitts, and two years later, after playing one game for Baltimore AA, he joined the Washington Nationals, where he would remain for the rest of his pro career.

Evers's only full ML season came in the 1884 UA. During the preseason Washington manager Mike Scanlan viewed him with skepticism, always batting him last. But after going 0-for-3 in Washington's Opening Day game at Baltimore, Evers caught fire, collecting 3 hits the following day. At the end of the first week of the season Evers was batting .400 (10-for-25), but it was a mirage. After that he hit just .221. Nevertheless, Evers was Washington's only Opening Day starter to still be at his same post in the final game of the season.

Evers remained in Washington after the UA collapsed and resided there for the rest of his life. He continued to play with local teams until he was past 40. Meanwhile, he worked as a clerk in the War Department. Evers died at his Washington home in 1925 after a lengthy illness. (DN)

Farrell, John A. / "Jack" "Modoc Jack"

B	T	HGT	WGT	G	AB	H	R	2B
R	R	5'9"	165	884	3613	877	584	148

3B	HR	RBI	BB	SO	SB	BA	SA	OBP
55	23	370	197	205	87	.243	.333	.283

G	W	L	PCT	PENNANTS
51	24	27	.471	0

B. 7/5/1857 Newark, NJ **D.** 2/10/1914
TEAMS: 79SyrN 79–85ProN (P/M)81ProN 86PhiN 86–87WasN 88–89BalA
DEBUT: 5/1/1879 at Chicago; played 2B and went 0-for-5 in a 4–3 loss to Chicago's Terry Larkin
FINALE: 6/11/1889 at Baltimore; played SS and went 0-for-3 in a 7–5 win over St. Louis's Silver King

Born in New Jersey, Jack Farrell began his career in 1874 with the amateur Newark Modocs, providing the source of his nickname, and spent 1875 with the amateur Newark Unions. He then served three pro seasons with Syracuse and accompanied the Stars when they left the International Association for the NL in 1879. After Syracuse became the last NL team to fold without playing its full schedule of games, Farrell joined Providence on September 12. His arrival instantly shored up a weak spot at 2B and practically assured the Grays of their first pennant.

Although Farrell's career batting stats seem unimposing now, in his early years he was one of the best-hitting second basemen in the game. Entering the 1884 season, he occupied fifth place on the NL's all-time home run list with 14. Farrell was also a strong defensive player; in 1883 he led the NL in FA and assists. His hitting evaporated in 1884, however, although he was only 26 and should have been in his prime. Facing a steady diet of overhand pitching for the first time, he batted only .217 during Providence's second championship year, but his FA remained just a fraction below the league leader.

Writer Bill James put Farrell on his list of "drinking men" of the 1880s, and there were strong intimations as early as 1884 that alcohol would be his downfall. According to the *Providence Journal*, on May 31, when the Grays were riddled with injuries and needed every man on the field, Farrell showed up for the game claiming to be ill and asked to be excused. His request was denied, and he then looked "listless" in the field. When this pattern persisted, future reporters were not so gentle, and by the late 1880s there were frequent remarks such as, "Farrell is sick again, and this time it really is malaria."

On September 13, 1884, at the last Providence home game of the season, "Farrell was made the recipient of a handsomely framed crayon portrait of himself, and an excellent gold watch, chain and charm in the form of a $20 gold piece prettily monogrammed." But the highlight of his year (and one of the last positive moments in his career) perhaps came when he scored the winning run in the championship-clinching 3–1 victory against the New York Mets in the 1884 World's Series. Farrell remained in the majors for five more years, but his batting grew progressively weaker. He never hit over .225 again and left the game soon after the 1889 season to work as a hospital attendant in New Jersey. In the years ahead he would frequently appear in local papers, but it was seldom for his former connection to the game. Party to a mutually abusive marriage ever since 1887, Farrell was featured on page 3 of the August 16, 1892, *New York Times* after being arrested two nights earlier at his wife's home in Newark and fined by a judge when his wife swore that she had separated from him because of his uncontrollable drinking. Farrell countered by saying that if he had married the woman at all, it must have been at a time when he was so intoxicated as not to know what he was about, but he admitted living with her until she had persuaded him to deed to her what little property he owned. She had no use for him after that, he sheepishly acknowledged, and "turned him out of doors." Farrell said he had only gone to the house to get a baseball contract he had left behind, and when she saw him at the door, she started shooting at him from an upper window. Both were taken to the police station, but only Farrell, because he was completely drunk, was locked up. The *Times* story concluded, "The woman said that only the failure of her supply of cartridges prevented her from continuing the shooting till she had killed her husband."

Farrell died in a hospital in Overlook, NJ, in 1914 after suffering a heart attack. His obit asserted that "in his prime, he was regarded as the best second basemen in the country," and it was no more than the truth, especially in the years prior to Fred Dunlap's emergence. (DN/FV/DB)

Fleet, Frank H. / "Frank"

B	T	HGT	WGT	G	AB	H	R	2B
?	?	?	?	88	372	85	53	6

3B	HR	RBI	BB	SO	SB	BA	SA	OBP
0	0	36	3	5	2	.228	.245	.235

G	IP	H	GS	CG	BB
9	75.1	136	8	7	6

SO	SH	W	L	PCT	ERA
4	0	2	6	.250	5.02

B. ?/?/1848 New York, NY **D.** 6/13/1900
TEAMS: 71MutNA 72EckNA 73ResNA 74AtlNA 75StLNA 75AtlNA
DEBUT: 10/18/1871 at Philadelphia; caught by Charlie Mills and lost 21–7 to the Athletics' Dick McBride
FINALE: 10/9/1875 at Brooklyn; played SS and made 2 hits in a 20–7 loss to Hartford's Tommy Bond

Frank Fleet was given a free train ride to Philadelphia so he could pitch the Mutuals' final game of the 1871 NA season against the soon-to-be champion Athletics. Chicago and Boston, the other two teams in contention for the flag, could not have been thrilled with New York's pitching selection. Fleet demonstrated that he could play a bit, however, even if the box wasn't his forte. He participated in all five NA seasons, notwithstanding the fact that he was never good enough at any one position to win a regular job with any of his five different teams. Fleet's highpoint came in 1875 with the St. Louis Brown Stockings when he beat Keokuk on consecutive days, but after losing his next start six days later he apparently was released.

What was a player from New York who had never previously played for a team west of New Jersey doing in St. Louis in the spring of 1875? For one, Fleet had a propensity for playing everywhere and never in any one place for long, constantly jumping from team to team. We also think the Brown Stockings had a contact in the East who recommended him—perhaps Al Wright of Philadelphia, who may also have recommended several of the other eastern players on the Brown Stockings' roster. But perhaps the most important reason Fleet had never ventured west before was that prior to 1875 pro ball opportunities beyond the Ohio River were comparatively few. Last seen by pro fans in 1877 with clubs in Columbus and Springfield, OH, Fleet died at his home on the Lower East Side of Manhattan of heart disease in 1900. (DN/DB)

Forster, Thomas W. / "Tom"

B	T	HGT	WGT	G	AB	H	R	2B
R	R	5'9"	153	180	666	131	76	15

3B	HR	RBI	BB	SO	SB	BA	SA	OBP
4	1	40	49	12	9	.197	.236	.256

B. 5/1/1859 New York, NY **D.** 7/17/1846
TEAMS: 82DetN 84PitA *(84NYA) 85–86NYA
DEBUT: 8/4/1882 at Worcester; played 2B and went 1-for-4 in an 8–2 win over Worcester's Fred Corey
FINALE: 8/23/1886 at Brooklyn; played 2B and went 0-for-4 in a 16–6 loss to Brooklyn's Henry Porter

Tom Forster was a reliable fielder whose ML career was curtailed by his minuscule offensive production. He played with three teams in the 1881 Eastern Championship Association before signing with the independent Philadelphias in 1882 just prior to receiving an invitation to join the Detroit NL club in Worcester. After an outstanding ML debut afield on August 4, he made 3 errors the following day to help give Worcester its first win of the season over Detroit. When his fielding continued to be erratic and he collected just 7 hits in 76 ABs, Forster played himself out of any further ML opportunities until the Pittsburgh AA club, after running through a string of weak shortstops, handed him the job near the end of the 1884 season.

After playing in Pittsburgh's finale on October 15, Forster returned to his home in New York. On the morning of October 25, he received a wire from New York Mets manager Jim Mutrie inviting him to fill in that afternoon for second baseman Dasher Troy in the third and final game of the first-ever World's Series between the Mets and the NL-champion Providence Grays. Forster thereupon became the sole player ever to participate in a nineteenth-

or twentieth-century World Series while still technically the property of another ML team.

The following spring, Forster was with Milwaukee of the Western League, but the Mets still remembered him. When the WL disbanded he became an official member of the New York AA team and finished the season at 2B. In 1886 Forster performed in his lone Opening Day game in his four partial ML seasons. He was released after hitting just .195 in 67 contests. Two years later he hit a feeble .205 in the Western Association. Forster finished his career in 1890 with Hartford of the Atlantic Association. A lifetime resident of New York, he worked for Consolidated Edison for a number of years before dying at a Bronx hospital in 1946. (DN)

---

*Geiss, William J. / "Bill"

B	T	HGT	WGT	G	AB	H	R	2B
?	?	5'10"	164	75	283	50	22	11

3B	HR	RBI	BB	SO	SB	BA	SA	OBP
4	2	16	6	60	—	.177	.265	.194

G	IP	H	GS	CG	BB
14	100.2	98	13	10	24

SO	SH	W	L	PCT	ERA
11	1	4	9	.308	5.27

B. 7/15/1858 Chicago, IL **D.** 9/18/1924
TEAMS: 82BalA 84DetN
DEBUT: 7/19/1882 at Baltimore; caught by Ed Whiting and lost 7–1 to Louisville's Tony Mullane
FINALE: 8/13/1884 at Detroit; played 1B and went 0-for-2 in a 1–0 loss to Cleveland's John Henry

The brother of ML pitcher Emil Geiss, Bill Geiss's 1882 stats were at one time credited to an Emil Geis, who was probably E. M. Geiss, a minor league pitcher. In July 1883 a Fort Wayne paper reported that Geiss, then a pitcher-outfielder with the local Northwestern League club, had been suspended for sixty days for throwing a game he pitched against Toledo at the request of gamblers, but the president of the Indiana club denied the story and compromised the suspension with a $50 fine for "indifferent and careless playing."

Despite Geiss's unappealing record and his near illiteracy—he signed contracts by making his mark—Detroit hired him to man 2B in 1884 and inanely stuck with him until August despite his atrocious hitting stats. Geiss later developed into a fairly good minor league player, lasting in the Southern League until 1894, and subsequently played in the Chicago City League until he was past 40. He may have been held back as a hitter by fantasizing for too long that he was a pitcher. Geiss's obit in 1924 said that he had a brother Frank but made no mention of Emil, who died in 1911. Since both ML Geisses are buried at St. Boniface Cemetery in Chicago, chances are this baseball family tree needs no further research. (DN/DB)

Gerhardt, John Joseph / "Joe" "Move Up Joe"

B	T	HGT	WGT	G	AB	H	R	2B
R	R	6'0"	160	1071	440	939	493	122

3B	HR	RBI	BB	SO	SB	BA	SA	OBP
55	7	382	162	195	37	.22	.288	.258

G	W	L	PCT	PENNANTS
191	111	79	.584	0

B. 2/14/1855 Washington D. C. **D.** 3/11/1922
TEAMS: 73WasNA 74BalNA 75MutNA 76–77LouN 78–79CinN 81DetN (P/M)83–84LouA 85–87NYN 87NYA 90BroA (P/M)90StLA 91LouA
DEBUT: 9/1/1873 at Philadelphia; played SS and went 0-for-4 in a 14–7 loss to the Philadelphia Pearls' George Zettlein
FINALE: 4/29/1891 at St. Louis; played 2B and went 0-for-3 in a 12–8 win over St. Louis's Clark Griffith and Ted Breitenstein
CAREER HIGHLIGHT: Holds the ML record for the most chances per game (7.11) among second basemen in a minimum of 880 games

Joe Gerhardt was the eldest son of Union general Joseph Gerhardt and had a brother, Abraham Lincoln Gerhardt, who was a prominent amateur first baseman in the Washington area during the 1880s. An epileptic, he was often idled for a day or two by an attack but nonetheless played fifteen seasons in the majors and logged the best career fielding marks of any second baseman in history. Among players in less than 900 games at the keystone sack subsequent to 1876, when fielding stats were first accurately recorded, Gerhardt ranks first in assists by a wide margin and also stands first in range among all at the position in a minimum of 500 games. Indeed, his fielding prowess was of such towering repute that comments like "Gerhardt's second-base play was again the fielding feature" time and again highlighted accounts of games in which he participated, and he was able to keep his job deep into his thirties despite scoring the lowest offensive marks of any position player (.495 OPS and .194 BA with just 3.39 runs created per game) with a minimum of 1,500 PAs between 1885 and his ML finale in 1891.

Gerhardt made his pro debut at 18 in 1873 when he came to his hometown Washington club from the junior Creightons along with another teenager, catcher Charlie Snyder. The pair separated when Washington folded, Gerhardt heading to nearby Baltimore in 1874 but, for just 14 games and then playing his first full ML season the following year with the New York Mutuals. He left New York for Louisville when the NL formed in 1876 and spent most of the season at 1B, leading the loop in assists. In 1877 Gerhardt was one of only five members of the Grays were retained. Although he had what was arguably his career year, hitting .304 and topping the loop's second basemen in assists and double plays, it went for naught when four Grays conspired to throw the NL pennant to Boston. Untarnished by the scandal, he signed with Cincinnati but was dropped in the fall of 1879 when he suffered the first of his record three sub-.200 seasons as a qualifier and scored just 22 runs in 79 games.

Gerhardt went home to D.C. in 1880 to play for the National Association Washington club. Hired by the new Detroit NL entry that off-season, he captained the Wolverines in 1881 and was reserved for 1882 but refused to return, hoping to play for Louisville in the fledgling AA. When Detroit declined to release him and the money he wanted was too steep for Louisville's minuscule salary budget (the team's star, Pete Browning, reportedly only earned $60 a month), he opted to sit out 1882 rather than honor his Detroit contract and was blacklisted by the NL. The following season Gerhardt agreed to serve as player-manager of the Kentucky club on the condition that he not be reserved for 1884. He installed himself in the cleanup spot but finished the campaign batting last, the spot in the order he would occupy for most of the rest of his career.

In 1884 Gerhardt signed with Louisville under the same terms as the previous year but hit .220, was replaced as Colonels manager in midstream by Mike Walsh, and then exercised his free-agent rights by joining the NL New York Giants for a tidy pay increase. On Opening Day in 1885 he experienced his career offensive highlight when he singled in the eighth inning and later scored the winning run in a 2–1 victory over Boston's Jim Whitney. But even though he played every inning of every game at 2B, he scored just 42 more times that season. Gerhardt hit below .200 again the following year and was saved from extinction only by his superb defense and gift of gab that made him enormously popular with New York fans and the envy of every other Giants player, especially captain Buck Ewing. In May 1887 Ewing used a minor arm ailment as an excuse to quit catching and claim Gerhardt's 2B post on the assumption that everyone would agree the team needed an upgrade there, but he was stung when Gerhardt, prior to the game on the day he was released, emerged from the Giants' clubhouse wearing his trademark red jacket with his gear under his arm and was given a standing ovation after the crowd sensed what was occurring. He then joined the AA Mets but was weakened part of the season by malaria and sent home in September.

Gerhardt spent the next season and a half with minor league Jersey City under manager Pat Powers and then joined Hartford of the Atlantic Association after the New Jersey club folded in July 1889. He was added to the roster of the hastily assembled Brooklyn Gladiators, an AA replacement team in 1890, and had his usual dismal season at the plate but still retained his fielding artistry. When Brooklyn collapsed, he was hired as player-manager of the St. Louis Browns. Released despite pacing AA second basemen in every major fielding department, he played 2 games with Louisville in 1891 and then finished his active career in 1893 as player-manager of Albany in Eastern League.

Gerhardt died of a heart attack in Middletown, NY, in 1922 while on his way to work, leaving behind a wife and daughter. He was nicknamed "Move Up Joe" for constantly exhorting teammates to "move up, move up" when they were on base. (DN/DB)

*Gleason, William J. / "Kid"

B	T	HGT	WGT	G	AB	H	R	2B
B	R	5'7"	158	1127	4241	1128	657	110

3B	HR	RBI	BB	SO	SB	BA	SA	OBP
54	9	530	287	131	215	.266	.324	.316

G	IP	H	GS	CG	BB
299	2389.1	2552	266	240	906

SO	SH	W	L	PCT	ERA
744	10	138	131	.513	3.79

B. 10/26/1866 Camden, NJ **D.** 1/2/1933
TEAMS: 88–91PhiN 92–94StLN 94–95BalN 96–00NYN 01–02DetAL 03–08PhiN 12ChiAL (M)19–23ChiAL
DEBUT: 4/20/1888 at Philadelphia; caught by Jack Clements and lost 4–3 to Boston's John Clarkson
FINALE: 8/27/1912 at Boston; entered the game as a sub at 2B and went 1-for-2 in an 8–8 tie against Boston's Hugh Bedient

Kid Gleason was the brother of twentieth-century MLer Harry Gleason. He is best remembered as the manager of the 1919 Chicago White Sox—the most infamous team in ML history—but was known prior to then for having been a scrappy, versatile player and one of the game's top early-day mentors. Called "Kid" because of his small size and boyish appearance, Gleason was born in Camden, a sizeable city in 1866, but soon moved with his family to the Pennsylvania coal-mining country. He made his pro debut in 1887 with Williamsport of the Pennsylvania State Association as a pitcher-second baseman and moved to Scranton of the International Association midway through the season. Despite Gleason's composite 10-24 record in 1887, Philadelphia NL manager Harry Wright invited him to train with the Quakers in the spring of 1888. He made the club largely on the basis of an exhibition win against the University of Pennsylvania in which he fanned 12 but hardly demonstrated enough promise to merit Wright's strange decision to name him the Quakers' Opening Day starter. After losing 4–3 to Boston, Gleason pitched sporadically for the rest of the season and finished 7-16. Following another poor year in 1889, he unexpectedly found himself Wright's ace after PL raiders decimated Wright's staff.

Gleason won 38 games in 1890 against watered-down NL lineups and 24 the following year but then, unaccountably, was allowed by Wright to leave Philadelphia and join St. Louis after the NL and AA merged. Perhaps Wright thought the little pitcher was on the verge of wearing down after his early workload, but Gleason remained an effective ML hurler through 1894 and finished that campaign with 15 wins in his last 20 starts after he was traded to Baltimore. In June 1895 Orioles manager Ned Hanlon moved Gleason to 2B to replace the injured Harry Reitz and then traded him to New York that November for Jack Doyle in the expectation that Reitz would resume his station in 1896.

Gleason hit a composite .270 in his five seasons in New York (1896–1900), below the league average, but seemingly made up for it with crisp defensive work and aggressive field leadership. Subsequently, however, he hit only .254 over the remainder of his career (1901–12). After leaving the Phillies following the 1908 season, Gleason spent several years in the minors and then returned to the show as a White Sox coach. In 1919 Gleason was promoted to manager and piloted the Sox to the AL pennant in his rookie season as a helmsman. Chicago led the AL in almost every offensive department and reflected the same aggressive style of play that had been Gleason's trademark in his active days. He later said, "I think they're the greatest ball club I've ever seen. Period." But when the Sox came apart during the World Series, suspicions sprouted immediately. The discovery that the Series had been rigged for Cincinnati to win affected Gleason for the rest of his life even though he personally had no part in the scandal. He remained at the Sox' helm through the 1923 season and then left the game a badly disillusioned figure. But after two years in retirement in Philadelphia, he agreed to return as a coach under Connie Mack and played a vital role in the A's 1929–31 dynasty before a heart condition sidelined him permanently. Gleason died at his daughter's Philadelphia home in 1933. (DN)

Greenwood, William F. / "Bill"

B	T	HGT	WGT	G	AB	H	R	2B
B	L	5'7½"	180	574	2170	490	381	56

3B	HR	RBI	BB	SO	SB	BA	SA	OBP
26	8	185	201	71	194	.226	.287	.298

B. ?/?/1857 Philadelphia, PA **D.** 5/2/1902
TEAMS: 82PhiA 84BroA 87–88BalA 89ColA 90RocA
DEBUT: 9/16/1882 at Philadelphia; played RF and went 3-for-4 in a 6–3 loss to Pittsburgh's Denny Driscoll

FINALE: 10/15/1890 at Baltimore; played 2B and went 1-for-4 in an 11–10 win over Baltimore's Les German before spraining his ankle
FAMOUS GAME: 6/16/1887 at Baltimore; with the score tied 8–8 in the ninth inning was involved in a violent collision at 2B with St. Louis outfielder Curt Welch, triggering a riot that forced the game to be stopped and St. Louis players to run for the exits when angry fans stormed onto the field

Bill Greenwood holds three unique ML records, only one of which even his most ardent admirers are aware of. Historians recognized long ago that his 567 games at 2B are the most in ML history by a left-handed thrower. We have the pleasure, however, of announcing here that Greenwood also holds the season record for the most stolen bases (46) by a player with a sub-.200 BA (.191 in 1888) and the lowest career OPS (.584) among switch hitters with a minimum of 2,000 ABs prior to expansion in 1961.

During his day Greenwood was known as perhaps the most reckless base runner in the game, notorious for being suckered into taking longer and longer leads at 1B as the first baseman played deeper and deeper on every pitch, until finally the right fielder would sneak in to pick him off. Greenwood was also famed for his gigantic slides that incurred frequent hand injuries when he scraped a fielder's spikes on a dive into a base. His fielding and hitting did not earn him high praise either. Greenwood maintained that his handicap in playing 2B left-handed was not throwing to 1B but picking up ground balls, and that did indeed appear to be a problem. Among all who played a minimum of 500 games at 2B during the 1880s his 5.52 range factor was the second worst only to Yank Robinson's 5.29. But Greenwood was fooling only himself if he truly believed his throwing also was not an issue. In May of his final ML season a Columbus writer wrote, after watching him in action for Rochester, "Columbus ball patrons know how much time Greenwood loses in turning around to make a double. He missed many a one here last season when a right handed man would have had no trouble at all." As for Greenwood's hitting, Tom Brown recalled in 1897 that he had a bad habit of pulling away on pitches and "an awkward way of tweaking the ball . . . as he stepped back" so that "the sphere was met by the end of the bat."

What excuse could there have been then for five different ML teams to employ Greenwood for five full seasons and a part of a sixth? The answer is probably none that would make sense to the average fan today. Among his peers, though, Greenwood was respected as a scrappy, hustling player who got on base much more often than most players with a .298 career OBP. Along with being a slapdash runner, he was fast, bunted a lot, and forced fielders to hurry and throw errantly.

Greenwood played with amateur and semipro teams in the Philadelphia area until 1882, when he joined Atlantic City as a second baseman. He played a handful of games with the AA Athletics that September and looked good but was back in the minors the following year with the Merritt club of Camden. When the Merritts disbanded on July 20, 1883, while leading the Interstate Association, Brooklyn owner Charlie Byrne signed him along with five of his teammates. He finished the season with Brooklyn and transitioned with Byrne and all of his Camden compadres to the AA in 1884. Greenwood batted leadoff all season for Brooklyn despite hitting .216 and collecting just 10 walks. He then spent 1885–86 in the minors before returning to the AA in 1887 with Baltimore. Greenwood fell out of favor with Baltimore manager Billy Barnie in 1888 because of his drinking and letting public acclaim go to his head, and that winter the *Ohio State Journal* speculated "his wonderful ability as a tank artist is likely to leave him high and dry when the base-ball tide goes out." Nevertheless the Columbus AA expansion club signed him a few weeks later, but he lost his job when Jack Crooks joined the team late in the season, and, finished his ML career the following year with Rochester AA. Greenwood dropped dead of a heart attack at Kensington and Lehigh Avenue in Philadelphia on the evening of May 2, 1902, while discussing the Athletics—Washington AL game that afternoon. (DN/DB)

Hallman, William Wilson / "Bill"

B	T	HGT	WGT	G	AB	H	R	2B
R	R	5'8"	160	1243	5114	1450	890	203

3B	HR	RBI	BB	SO	SB	BA	SA	OBP
72	21	679	368	283	177	.284	.364	.338

G	IP	H	GS	CG	BB	SO	SH	W
1	2	4	0	0	2	0	0	0

L	PCT	ERA
0	—	18.00

G	W	L	PCT	PENNANTS
50	13	36	.265	0

B. 3/31/1867 Pittsburgh, PA **D.** 9/11/1920
TEAMS: 88–89PhiN 90PhiP 91PhiA 92–97PhiN (P/M)97StLN 98BroN 01CleAL 01–03PhiN
DEBUT: 4/23/1888 at Philadelphia; played SS and went 0-for-4 in a 3–1 loss to Boston's John Clarkson
FINALE: 9/27/1903 at St. Louis; played 2B and went 2-for-4 in a 5–3 loss to St. Louis's Three Finger Brown

Bill Hallman was an actor and vaudeville song-and-dance man in the off-season during his playing days. It kept his legs in shape and seems to have earned him more recognition than he ever received for what appears on the surface to have been a solid fourteen-year ML career. But that appearance is deceiving. Hallman's peak years came in 1893–96, when anything less than a .300 BA was a mark of failure. Consequently, his .272 career BA (built around four consecutive .300 seasons during his peak) was about average for his position and some 10 points below the league mark of .282. Hallman was also about dead average as a fielder and achieved black ink in a positive department only twice in his fourteen seasons. In 1891 he tied for the AA lead in games played, and ten years later he topped the NL in sacrifice hits.

Hallman turned pro in 1886 with Wilkes-Barre of the Pennsylvania State Association as a pitcher but moved behind the plate when the regular catcher took sick one day prior to an exhibition game and hit a grand slam home run in his first at-bat. He opened the following season with Hamilton, Ontario, of the International Association but returned to Wilkes-Barre when the Canadian club signed Chub Collins. Philadelphia NL acquired him in the spring of 1888 for insurance behind incumbent second baseman Charlie Ferguson. Although Hallman failed to win the job after Ferguson unexpectedly died, he claimed the spot in 1889. He then joined George Wood and Joe Mulvey in playing with Philadelphia teams in three different major leagues in three consecutive seasons before returning to the Phillies in 1892.

Hallman remained a Philadelphia fixture until June 1897 when he and Dick Harley were traded to St. Louis for outfielder Tommy Dowd. Initially a favorite of Browns owner Chris Von der Ahe's, he swiftly lost the fickle mogul's support once he was named manager of the club. Hallman was fined $200 by Von der Ahe after he broke his thumb in Cleveland and then contracted malaria that he claimed was brought on because "the dressing rooms which Von der Ahe furnishes his players are never clean." Hallman also contended that while the Browns were on the road for six weeks in 1897 the team wasn't paid, and he threatened, after he was traded to Brooklyn in November 1897, to "tie up" the St. Louis gate receipts when the Browns came to Brooklyn the following year in order to recover the $200 fine that had been deducted from his pay unfairly. Meanwhile he hit just .244 for the Bridegrooms and spent the next two seasons in the minors.

A good year in 1900 with Buffalo in the newly renamed American League earned Hallman a contract with Cleveland when the AL went major in 1901. He lasted only 5 games in the Forest City before returning to the Phillies to fill the hole vacated by Nap Lajoie when he jumped to the Philadelphia AL club. While Lajoie was hitting .426 to lead the AL in 1901, Hallman batted .184, a mere 242 points less, to bring up the rear among NL qualifiers. He was retained as a utilityman for two more seasons and then drifted back to the minors, where he finished his career in 1909 with Denver of the Western League. Hallman died in a Philadelphia hospital of a heart attack in 1950. (DN)

Keister, William Hoffman / "Bill" "Wagon Tongue"

B	T	HGT	WGT	G	AB	H	R	2B
L	R	5'5½"	168	287	1108	340	187	53

3B	HR	RBI	BB	SO	SB	BA	SA	OBP
26	4	154	44	5	69	.307	.412	.350

B. 8/17/1874 Baltimore, MD **D.** 8/19/1924
TEAMS: 96BalN 98BosN 99BalN 00StLN 01BalAL 02WasAL 03PhiN

DEBUT: 5/20/1896 at Cleveland; played 3B and went 2-for-4 in a 12–7 loss to Cleveland's Nig Cuppy
FINALE: 8/25/1903 at Philadelphia; played RF and went 0-for-3 in a 6–0 loss to Pittsburgh's Lave Winham

Bill Keister was the nephew of Washington owner J. Earle Wagner. Reportedly he had "trepanning" surgery early in life and had a silver plate put in his head, which caused him to suffer occasional memory lapses. Nicknamed "Wagon Tongue" because he used one of the longest bats in the game, the pint-sized Keister thrived on pitches up around his eyes, usually a guarantee of failure as a ML hitter. Yet he finished with a .312 career BA and topped the .300 mark in each of his five seasons as a qualifier. His defensive work was something less. In 1901 Keister made 97 errors and finished with a .851 FA, a post-1900 season low for a SS qualifier. At the time of his release in 1903, though, he ranked 2nd that season to Jimmy Sheckard in NL outfield assists, and only Sheckard and Sam Mertes surpassed his final mark of 22 that was compiled in just 100 games.

Baltimore acquired Keister from New Haven of the Atlantic League in May 1896 to replace third baseman Jim Donnelly, whose weak hitting frustrated manager Ned Hanlon. When Keister's fielding was too raw, Donnelly kept the job as an interim replacement for ailing John McGraw. After finishing the season with Scranton of the Eastern League, in November Keister married Blanche Carnes, the daughter of a conductor on the Baltimore and Ohio Rail Road. The couple resided in Baltimore with Keister's parents while he played for Paterson of the Atlantic League. Keister then spent most of 1897 in the Eastern League after failing a second ML trial with Boston. Back with Baltimore in 1898, he began the campaign on the bench but finished as the Orioles' regular SS after banging 41 hits in his first 22 games. A .329 BA in his official rookie year assured he would remain in the NL after the Orioles folded.

On March 23, 1900, St. Louis shelled out $19,000 for McGraw and Wilbert Robinson and demanded Keister in addition. Moved to 2B, he hit .300 and then followed McGraw and Robinson to the fledgling Baltimore AL entry in 1901. It is unclear why McGraw was uninterested in retaining the hometown infielder after he hit .328, led the AL in triples, and was leading the loop with 19 steals in early June. Keister drifted from Washington back to the NL with Philadelphia prior to the 1903 season. Although he played his final ML game more than a month before the campaign ended, he remained the Phils' property until early 1904, when he was sold to Jersey City of the Eastern League.

For the next seven seasons Keister continued to hit well in the minors and finished his career by rapping .282 in the 1910 Tri-State League. He died in Baltimore fourteen years later, leaving behind many unanswered questions regarding his abrupt departure from the majors and the reasons he never played for the same team two years in a row. Among the fifty-eight ML players who collected a minimum of 2,000 PAs during Keister's five seasons as a qualifier (1899–1903), he ranks thirteenth in BA (.315) and twelfth in SA (.446). Keister died in Baltimore two days after his 53rd birthday. (DN)

Kimball, Eugene Boynton / "Gene"

B	T	HGT	WGT	G	AB	H	R	2B
?	?	5'10"	160	29	131	25	18	1

3B	HR	RBI	BB	SO	SB	BA	SA	OBP
0	0	9	3	2	5	.191	.198	.209

B. 8/31/1850 Rochester, NY **D.** 8/2/1882
TEAMS: 71CleN
DEBUT: 5/4/1871 at Fort Wayne; in the inaugural ML game played 2B and went 0-for-4 in a 2–0 loss to Fort Wayne's Bobby Mathews
FINALE: 9/27/1871 at Cleveland; in a 9–7 loss to Boston's Al Spalding.

Gene Kimball appeared in all 29 of Cleveland's games and played six different positions, most of them adequately, but was dead weight at the plate. He nonetheless batted high in the order most of the season. A top-notch billiards player, Kimball died at his Rochester home in 1882. (DN/PM)

Lowe, Robert Lincoln / "Link" "Bobby"

B	T	HGT	WGT	G	AB	H	R	2B
R	R	5'10"	150	1284	5140	1486	956	175

3B	HR	RBI	BB	SO	SB	BA	SA	OBP
70	67	839	394	215	239	.289	.390	.346

G	IP	H	GS	CG	BB
1	1	3	0	0	1

SO	SH	W	L	PCT	ERA
0	0	0	0	—	9.00

B. 7/10/1868 Pittsburgh, PA **D.** 12/8/1951
TEAMS: 90–01BosN 02–03ChiN 04PitN (P/M)04DetAL 05–07DetAL
DEBUT: 4/19/1890 at Boston; played 3B and went 3-for-5 in a 13–9 win over Brooklyn's Bob Caruthers and Bill Terry
FINALE: 10/6/1907 at St. Louis; played 2B and made 2 hits in a 10–3 loss to St. Louis's Harry Howell
CAREER HIGHLIGHT: 5/30/1894 at Boston's Congress Street park; became the first player in ML history to hit 4 home runs in a game in a 20–11 win over Cincinnati's Elton Chamberlin, as a pre-1947 record 9 homers were hit in the game

Playing in Boston NL home parks that had short LF porches for most of his career, Link Lowe hit 70 career dingers, an exceptionally high number for a middle infielder in that time, but only 1 four-bagger after he left Boston following the 1901 season. In his last four ML campaigns he hit so little, period, that it is hard to fathom what kept him in the majors long past the time when he was no longer a particularly useful player.

Called "Link"—a derivative of his middle name—by teammates throughout his career, Lowe was discovered in 1885 by Charlie Powers, a compositor in the office of the New Castle, PA, Courant Company, where the 17-year-old was working as a printer's devil. When Lowe begged his way onto Powers's company team, he shone so brightly that he was playing with the New Castle minor league club by the end of the season. Powers also graduated to the pro ranks as a pitcher, and the pair went as a unit to Eau Claire of the Northwestern League in 1887. When Abe Devine, the Wisconsin club's manager, released Lowe as "too light," Powers again came to his rescue, advising Devine to rescind the release when another player was injured. After Lowe did so well at 3B upon returning to the club, the Eau Claire owners realized Devine was a fool not to have used him earlier and fired him.

Lowe spent 1888 and 1889 with Milwaukee of the Western Association before being acquired by Frank Selee when Selee took over as Boston NL pilot. He began 1890 at 3B but moved to the outfield to make way for Chippy McGarr. Lowe remained in LF the next two seasons, working winters in a New Castle machine shop, before replacing Joe Quinn at 2B in 1893. By the end of 1897, Lowe had been a member of five Boston pennant winners and was completing a 106-RBI and .309 season even though a case of pneumonia forced him to miss significant playing time for the third year in a row. Although only 29, he never again hit .300 or drove in 100 runs.

In December 1901 Lowe was sold to Chicago NL and rejoined Selee, who had left Boston to take the Windy City pilot's job. His career seemed at an end when Chicago sold him to Pittsburgh in April 1904 and the Pirates let him play only part of 1 game before passing him on to Detroit manager Ed Barrow, who was short a second baseman. Even though Lowe hit all of .208 with the Tigers in 1904, he not only kept his job but by midseason had also taken Barrow's. The following year Bill Armour replaced Lowe as pilot, and Germany Schaefer took over at 2B, but Lowe remained with the club as a player-coach under Hughie Jennings long enough to collect a World Series share as a member of Detroit's initial AL pennant winner.

Lowe had married Hattie Hughes of New Castle on April 2, 1894, and remained a winter resident of the Pennsylvania city until coming to Detroit. After a season as player-manager of Grand Rapids in the Central League at age 40, he scouted for the Tigers and then worked for the Detroit Department of Public Works. Lowe died at a Detroit retirement home in 1951. (DN)

Mack, Joseph (b. McNamara) / "Reddy"

B	T	HGT	WGT	G	AB	H	R	2B
R	R	5'8"	182	550	2062	524	381	87

3B	HR	RBI	BB	SO	SB	BA	SA	OBP
36	6	262	275	79	83	.254	.340	.352

B. 5/2/1866 ?, Ireland **D.** 12/30/1916
TEAMS: 85–88LouA 89–90BalA
DEBUT: 9/16/1885 at Brooklyn; played 2B and went 0-for-5 in an 8–5 loss to Brooklyn's Jack Harkins
FINALE: 9/30/1890 at Louisville; played 2B and went 1-for-3 against Louisville's Jouett Meekin in a 1–1 tie

Reddy Mack was born in Ireland as Joseph McNamara but grew up in northern Kentucky as Mack and was dubbed "Reddy" because of his flaming red hair. He was a coarse, scrappy player and patient hitter whom managers liked but only if they could abide his profligacy. Fellow players likewise either shunned or embraced him. In 1884, his first year of pro ball, Mack was accused of selling out a game for $200 while playing for Springfield of the Ohio State League. The charge was never proved, allowing him to travel to Macon, GA, in the spring of 1885 as a member of the fledgling Southern League. Mack led the circuit in runs and also topped it in batting for much of the season before departing for Louisville. Even though he struggled initially against AA pitching, he swiftly became a fixture at 2B and was respected around the loop for his hustle and hard play. He was also Louisville's best base coach, known for his chant, "Come on now, let's get in those scores."

In 1887, when walks counted as hits, Mack had his career year, batting .410 (.308 by current rules), thanks largely to his team-leading 83 walks. The following year, after a new owner, Mordecai Davidson, took command of the club, Mack became Davidson's pet target for his nocturnal revelry and general disinterest in conditioning. After hitting just .217 he was released and went home to Newport, KY, to cool his heels until an offer came from Baltimore. Though Mack hiked his BA only to .241 in 1889 and collected just 32 extra-base hits, he finished second on the Orioles in RBI with 87 owing to manager Billy Barnie's typical unorthodox batting order, which installed Mack as the cleanup hitter. The second baseman repaid Barnie's faith in him by remaining with Baltimore after it dropped off the ML map in 1890 and joined the minor Atlantic Association. Barnie in turn tolerated more carousing than he otherwise might have from his fier second baseman while Baltimore remained a minor league entity. But once Baltimore rejoined the AA, Mack was suspended twice for insubordination. The second occasion, following a game at Louisville, marked the last time he donned a ML uniform on the field of play.

After languishing in the Eastern Association in 1891, Mack seemed to gain a reprieve when Giants captain Buck Ewing, a close friend of his, convinced manager Pat Powers to take the turbulent second baseman to the club's training camp in Richmond, VA, in the spring of 1892. Ewing made it clear to Powers that he favored Mack over Charlie Bassett, who had been slated to take over the Giants 2B post after Danny Richardson went to Washington. But when Mack failed to "set the world on fire," Powers gave Bassett the job. As a sop to Ewing, however, Powers reluctantly agreed to keep Mack on the team as a substitute, which brought this from Opie Caylor's pen: "The second day after Reddy's arrival [in New York], the entire Tenderloin District closed up as tight as a tin can of tomatoes." Caylor also correctly predicted that Mack would never be more than a supernumerary for which "the duties are to sit near the water keg, keep the lid on, stir up the oat meal occasionally with a bat, hold the arnica bottle, dispense from the team's plug, blow up the chest protector and perform such other menial duties as are beneath the dignity of the manager." Near the end of April 1892 Mack was released to Providence of the Eastern League. He then drifted through the minors and outlaw leagues until 1900 when he turned up in New Orleans drunk and destitute. Given train fare at Tom Sullivan's behest, Mack was accompanied north by one "Giblets" McCafferty. Subsequently, Mack pulled himself together and reverted to using his birth name. As Red McNamara, he managed periodically in the low minors until a few years before he died from a cerebral hemorrhage after falling down a flight of stairs at his home in Newport, KY. (DN)

Manning, Timothy Edward / "Tim"

B	T	HGT	WGT	G	AB	H	R	2B
R	R	5'10"	170	200	730	138	99	28

3B	HR	RBI	BB	SO	SB	BA	SA	OBP
6	2	24	56	24	—	.189	.252	.256

B. 12/3/1853 Henley-on-Thames, England
D. 6/11/1934
TEAMS: 82ProN 83–85BalA 85ProN
DEBUT: 5/1/1882 at Providence; played SS and went 1-for-5 in a 9–3 win over Troy's Tim Keefe
FINALE: 7/20/1885 at Buffalo, played SS and went 0-for-3 in a 5–3 loss to Buffalo's Pete Wood

Tim Manning won the Providence SS post in the spring of 1882 as a 28-year-old pro rookie. He also served as the club's third-string catcher and was pressed into action behind the bat on four occasions, including a 6–3 loss to Buffalo on June 3 when his 4 passed balls helped lead to 4 unearned runs. Twelve days later he played his last game for Providence, a 4–2 loss to Cleveland, and was released shortly afterward, the owner of a glorious .105 BA in 76 ABs. Manning finished 1882 with the League Alliance Philadelphias before joining Brooklyn of the Interstate Association. Considered "the heavy batter on the team" in the early part of 1883, he was allowed to go to Baltimore AA when

Brooklyn corralled Bill Greenwood of the defunct Camden franchise. Replacing Tom O'Brien at 2B for the last six weeks of the 1883 season, he hit just .205 but was rehired when the Orioles could find no one better.

Manning began 1884 by scoring 5 runs in the first 3 games of the campaign against the New York Mets. He then reverted to form and hit just .202 for the balance of the season. Retained nonetheless for 1885, Manning lost his job after going 0-for-4 on June 24 in a 10–5 loss to Philadelphia. Following Baltimore's series with the A's, he was released along with pitcher Bob Emslie, as the Baltimore press celebrated by deeming both "useless and high-priced drones."

A versatile player with rare plate discipline for one with so wretched a career BA (his 56 walks rank first among all players with less than 740 career ABs between 1882 and 1885 and strengthen his case for being the most productive sub-.200 hitter in ML history), Manning finished 1885 with Toronto of the International Association and then spent 1886 with Augusta of the Southern League. He moved again the following season to Kansas City of the Western League but was let go in late June. His release became a blessing when he was hired almost immediately to serve as player-manager for Birmingham of the Southern League. Manning's natural intransigence reappeared some six weeks later when he mysteriously disappeared. Foul play was initially feared, but it developed that he had merely taken "French leave" after a disagreement with Birmingham officials.

Manning played four more seasons in the lower minors, peaking in 1890 when he won the Illinois-Iowa League batting championship by hitting .381 for Aurora and was also managing the club late in the season. After wintering in Chicago, he was again hired as player-manager when Aurora reorganized the following spring and tried without success to sign Windy City denizen pitcher Nat Hudson. Shortly after Hudson refused his offer, Manning quit, claiming the team was much weaker than he had been given to believe when he was rehired, and jumped to Joliet, IL. Nearing 40, he retired soon thereafter and became a park policeman in Chicago. Manning died at his home in Oak Park, a Chicago suburb, in 1934, surviving his wife by nearly forty-one years. Several decades later his 99-year-old daughter, a retired nun, remembered him as a "devil of a man" with blond hair and blue eyes. Among all sub-.200 hitters with a minimum of 500 career ABs, Manning rather remarkably ranks first in runs created per game with 4.00. (DN/DB)

McClellan, William Henry / "Bill"

B	T	HGT	WGT	G	AB	H	R	2B
B	L	5'5½"	156	792	3197	773	533	129

3B	HR	RBI	BB	SO	SB	BA	SA	OBP
33	6	304	274	95	132	.242	.308	.305

B. 3/22/1856 Chicago, IL **D.** 7/3/1929
TEAMS: 78ChiN 81ProN 83–84PhiN 85–88BroA 88CleA
DEBUT: 5/20/1878 at Chicago; played 2B and went 2-for-4 in a 3–1 win over Indianapolis's "The Only" Nolan
FINALE: 10/17/1888 at Philadelphia; played SS and went 0-for-4 in a 14–4 loss to Philadelphia's Gus Weyhing

Bill McClellan is the only southpaw to accumulate 1,000 ABs as both a SS and a second baseman and also ranks second in games played by a southpaw at both positions to Jimmy Macullar and Bill Greenwood, respectively. Throughout his career he was regarded as a model player, who seldom kicked, never drank, and was always a pleasure to have on a team, if never its greatest asset. McClellan's forte was speed and stealing, but he diminished that strength somewhat with his reputation for being notoriously easy to pick off base. In other respects, he seemingly was an offensive handicap to most of his teams. Among left-handed or switch-hitters in the nineteenth century with a minimum of 3,000 ABs, he posted the second-lowest OPS and also the second-worst SA, trailing only Arthur Irwin in both departments.

And yet, as a further illustration of how deceptive statistics can sometimes be, among all players in ML history with a minimum of 3,000 ABs and a sub-.250 career BA, McClellan ranks an astonishing ninth in runs created per game (5.28) despite having the next to lowest OPS of anyone on the list.

Prior to joining the NL White Stockings in 1878, McClellan had played in the Chicago City League and had also spent time with the League Alliance Memphis and St. Paul teams. In his rookie season he was solid defensively but weak at the plate, and though he held the Chicago 2B job until the end of the season, he could foresee a pink slip in the mail when Joe Quest, who had been with Indianapolis all season, played with Chicago in postseason exhibitions. Signing with the Washington Nationals for 1879, McClellan played with the D.C. club for two full seasons before receiving his second ML invitation in 1881 from Providence. Overwhelmed in his initial season facing pitchers at the new fifty-foot distance, McClellan hit just .166, lost his SS post in late August, and played RF for the remainder of the 1881 campaign—when he played at all.

In 1882 he performed with the League Alliance Philadelphias that provided the fabric for the NL's new franchise in the City of Brotherly Love the following year. Despite leading all NL shortstops in 1884 in games, chances, assists, and errors, he fell out of favor for holding out and was sold the following January to Brooklyn AA for an undisclosed amount and split 1885 between 3B and 2B. In 1886 McClellan had his finest all-around season to date, leading the AA in games played and his team in runs and stolen bases. The following year he again led the loop in games played but also topped it in errors with 105, diminishing his offensive contributions, which featured the team lead in steals and a career-high .263 BA.

Just 31 at the time, McClellan seemingly was at his peak, but the following spring he was suddenly no longer the same player. After opening the season for Brooklyn at 2B, he lost his job on July 3 to a washed-up Jack Burdock (who would hit .122 in 70 games after coming to the Bridegrooms) and played RF for a time before being sold on September 15 to seventh-place Cleveland, which did not reserve him for 1889. While it is true that McClellan hit just .209 overall in 1888, the suspicion is that even if he had matched his career mark of .242 his fate might have been sealed. By the late 1880s a bias had developed against left-handed infielders, especially among the better teams, and Brooklyn in 1888 was not only a good team but, in retrospect, might have won the AA pennant that year if it had stayed with McClellan rather than burdening itself with Burdock.

Whatever the case, McClellan's hitting, while adequate for a middle infielder, was not nearly strong enough to carry him as an outfielder. He went to Denver in 1889 and hit .283 against Western Association competition, remained with Denver until 1891, and then played three more years in the minors before returning to Chicago, where he died in 1929. (DN/DB)

Myers, James Albert / "Al" "Cod"

B	T	HGT	WGT	G	AB	H	R	2B
R	R	5'8½"	165	834	3222	788	429	135

3B	HR	RBI	BB	SO	SB	BA	SA	OBP
34	13	359	294	263	111	.245	.320	.314

B. 10/22/1863 Danville, IL **D.** 12/24/1927
TEAMS: 84MilU 85PhiN 86KCN 87–89WasN 89–91PhiN
DEBUT: 9/27/1884 at Milwaukee; played 2B and went 1-for-4 in an 8–4 win over Washington's Charlie Geggus
FINALE: 10/3/1891 at Philadelphia; played 2B and went 1-for-3 in a 5–2 win over Boston's John Clarkson

Al Myers joined independent Terre Haute in 1881 when he was only 17 and remained with the Indiana club for three years before making his minor league debut in the 1884 Northwestern League with Muskegon, MI. Later that season he joined Milwaukee in time to accompany the Wisconsin entry when it left the Northwestern League to join the UA as a replacement team. Myers led the late-year entry in both BA and SA.

The following year Myers demonstrated why he would emerge as one of the top graduates of the UA when he won the Philadelphia NL 2B post and led all rookie qualifiers in both major leagues in batting. Still, he became expendable when Philadelphia garnered veteran second sacker Jack Farrell from the disbanding Providence club. Sold to the new Kansas City NL entry, Myers placed the Cowboys in BA and SA while Farrell flopped in Philadelphia. That fall a cacophony of team observers noted to Quakers manager Harry Wright that if he had kept Myers and passed on Farrell his team would have been a strong flag contender. Wright took the message, and in July 1889 when Washington, which had acquired Myers after the Kansas City club folded, was strapped for cash, Philadelphia purchased him for $4,000, one of the highest sums paid to that time for a middle infielder. Bitter at the cavalier way Philadelphia had disposed of him four years earlier, now that he held the whip hand Myers demanded part of the purchase price before he would consent to the sale. By the time he extorted a reported $600 out of Washington owner Walter Hewett, more than two weeks had elapsed since his purchase was announced, and during the long wait for his arrival the Quakers fell too far off the pace to mount a pennant bid.

That winter, while many of Wright's other stars were jumping to the PL, Myers remained loyal to the venerable skipper and further rewarded him in 1890 with his best all-around season in the majors. Despite missing a number of games with minor injuries, the second baseman finished second or third on the team in most major offensive departments, trailing only future HOFers Sam Thompson and Billy Hamilton. Still just 26 years old when the season ended, Myers seemed to have his prime years still ahead of him. Instead he slumped to .230 in 1891 and was released in October for "indifferent play." The following month Myers announced his retirement from baseball to run a saloon and rather astonishingly submitted to a candid interview with a *TSN* correspondent in which he revealed why he had lost his appetite for the game: his parents were getting older, his wife was increasingly unhappy with the time he spent away from home during the season, and he had had enough of baseball in general. Myers later became a boxing promoter and managed a stable of fighters in addition to operating a saloon in Terre Haute with Sam Thompson. He died of nephritis in Terre Haute in 1927. (DN)

Nicholson, Thomas Clark / "Parson"

B	T	HGT	WGT	G	AB	H	R	2B
?	?	5'9"	148	168	646	169	96	20

3B	HR	RBI	BB	SO	SB	BA	SA	OBP
15	5	86	51	11	58	.262	.362	.325

B. 4/14/1863 Blaine, OH **D.** 2/28/1917
TEAMS: 88DetN 90TolA 95WasN
DEBUT: 9/14/1888 at Detroit; played 2B and went 1-for-4 in a 7–5 win over Philadelphia's Dan Casey
FINALE: 5/6/1895 at Chicago; plated 2B and went 1-for-2 in a 4–0 loss to Chicago's Bill Hutchison

Parson Nicholson entered the baseball world in 1885 as a 120-pound second baseman with semipro Bellaire, OH, playing alongside SS Bill White. In 1886 he joined semipro Barnesville, OH, and finished the season as a catcher with the D'Nice club of Wooster. When he made his pro debut in 1887 at age 24 with Steubenville, OH, and Wheeling, WV, two lower-echelon minor league teams, he hardly seemed a ML prospect. Yet the St. Louis Browns thought so highly of him that he was expected to occupy 2B in the Mound City in 1888, with Yank Robinson moving to SS in place of the recently traded Bill Gleason. Although Nicholson flunked the test in spring training, he began the season playing 2B in the Mound City—only it was with the Western Association St. Louis Whites. On February 25, 1888, *TSN* featured a likeness of him and said he was 6'6", a mistake that led future reference works to mark him the tallest second baseman in the nineteenth century for well over one-hundred years.

When the Whites folded in 1888, Nicholson returned to Wheeling in the Tri-State League until he was sold to Detroit for $400 in September. He did well enough with the Wolverines but was cut loose when the club folded and its established players were either sold or distributed to other NL teams. A .302 BA with Toledo in 1889 insured that manager Charlie Morton would retain Nicholson when the Black Pirates moved up from the International Association to the AA the following year. In his official rookie ML season, Nicholson missed only 2 games, tied for the Toledo team lead in RBI with Perry Werden, and rated among the best second basemen in the AA defensively. Still, 1891 found him back in the minors, seemingly to stay. In November 1894, after finishing his second consecutive season with Erie of the Eastern League at age 31, Nicholson, probably to his surprise, was hired by Washington's new manager, Gus Schmelz, to replace incumbent second baseman Piggy Ward. He opened 1895 at SS instead when Washington reacquired second sacker Jack Crooks over the winter but was jettisoned when, in Schmelz's judgment, he let Chicago second baseman Ace Stewart get away with interfering with him on a double play.

Sold to Detroit, Nicholson remained with the Western League club awhile and then finished his playing career in 1899 back in Wheeling. After his third stint with the West Virginia club, he returned to Bellaire, where he had grown up and begun his career. Nicholson bought a shoe store in town and served a term as mayor before contracting tuberculosis and dying in 1917 from bronchopneumonia. (DN)

O'Brien, John Joseph / "Jack"
"Chewing Gum Johnnie"

B	T	HGT	WGT	G	AB	H	R	2B
L	R	5'9"	175	501	1910	486	246	47

3B	HR	RBI	BB	SO	SB	BA	SA	OBP
17	12	229	154	58	24	.254	.316	.322

B. 7/14/1870 St. John, New Brunswick, Canada
D. 5/12/1913
TEAMS: 91BroN 93ChiN 95–96LouN 96–97WasN 99BalN 99PitN
DEBUT: 7/25/1891 at Brooklyn; played 2B and went 3-for-5 in a 15–2 win over Philadelphia's Duke Esper and Jack Thornton
FINALE: 10/7/1899 at Pittsburgh; replaced Heinie Smith at 2B and had no ABs in a 16–8 win over Cleveland's Jack Harper

Jack O'Brien was highly educated, a linguist, and had studied briefly for the priesthood. Paradoxically, he was also a skilled boxer and helped train his brother Dick, a welterweight out of Lewiston, ME, where the pair grew up. Unaware of O'Brien's pugilistic skill, former ML pitcher Tom Vickery, one of the game's great bullies, accused him of trying to throw a game by making errors while the two were teammates in the Southern League. After the contest (which O'Brien actually won for Vickery with a late-inning home run), the two put on the gloves and O'Brien massacred the pitcher, thereby ending Vickery's taunting him for being a "mick" and "the little priest."

A good fielder, O'Brien's failure to make a more indelible mark in the majors was a mystery until Tom Brown, one of his longtime ex-teammates, put his finger on the problem: O'Brien's habit of leaning in on pitches made him a ready target. According to Brown, the second baseman "walked into Rusie's in-benders and Joe Corbett's drops as though he was going to shake hands with them" and as a result launched too many weak grounders and pop-ups off the handle of his bat.

Brooklyn acquired O'Brien from Portland, ME, of the New England League in 1891 after second sacker Hub Collins was critically injured in a fly-ball collision. A sensational debut labeled him a phenom, but in his next game he made 3 errors, contributing to 9 unearned Philadelphia runs. When O'Brien's hitting also sagged, he lost all chance of claiming the Brooklyn 2B job after Collins was moved to the outfield. A second opportunity came his way in 1893 with Chicago, but even though he did well in a 4-game trial Chicago kept former Colts second sacker Bob Glenalvin instead.

The following year Louisville signed O'Brien for 1895 as a replacement for the aging Fred Pfeffer. Batting second and playing 2B, he stamped his first full ML season a partial success by leading the Colonels in walks and finishing second on the club in runs but produced only 15 extra-base hits for a meager .295 SA. Named captain of the club in 1896, he cajoled his manager, John McCloskey, into batting him cleanup but quarreled with teammates after McCloskey was axed and the new pilot, Bill McGunnigle, replaced him as captain. Despite hitting .339 and slugging .430 after 49 games, he was shipped to Washington for Jack Crooks and Jim Rogers plus $1,000. The steep price proved embarrassing to Washington's front office when O'Brien came resoundingly back to earth soon after he reported to the D.C. club and hit a bland .267. Although he opened 1897 at 2B for Washington, he finished the season with Providence of the Eastern League and spent 1898 in the bushes as well before being acquired by Baltimore. O'Brien played some 15 games with the Orioles in 1899 before learning he had a broken finger. Sold the next month to Pittsburgh, he finished his final ML season with a composite .215 BA, the lowest of any NL player with as many as 400 ABs in the last year the loop had twelve teams.

In 1900 O'Brien signed as player-manager with Oswego of the New York State League but became the subject of considerable intrigue when it emerged that Anaconda of the Montana State League had also wanted the second baseman. For some perverse reason, O'Brien sent Jim McHale, a novice player, to Montana in his stead with instructions to impersonate him. McHale was recognized as a fraud by catcher Dave Zearfoss, who was sworn to secrecy, but when Anaconda played Great Falls under John McCloskey and McCloskey asked McHale what teams he had played for and he mentioned Louisville, McCloskey's suspicions were aroused since he had managed O'Brien at Louisville. McCloskey was then distracted by something else, however, and the ruse was not exposed until "O'Brien" was hired by Helena to play against Great Falls in the league championship series in October.

As in all impersonation cases in pro baseball in that era, the crime exceeded the punishment.

O'Brien was never so much as reprimanded, nor apparently was his stand-in, McHale, who played several more seasons in the minors. O'Brien meanwhile retired from the game after 1900 to become a boxing and wrestling trainer and referee. He died of kidney trouble in 1913 in Lewiston, ME. (DN)

O'Brien, Thomas H. / "Tom"

B	T	HGT	WGT	G	AB	H	R	2B
R	R	6'1"	185	270	1111	257	158	50

3B	HR	RBI	BB	SO	SB	BA	SA	OBP
20	4	61	52	10	16	.231	.323	.267

B. 6/22/1860 Salem, MA **D.** 4/21/1921
TEAMS: 82WorN 83BalA 84BosU 85BalA 87NYA 90RocA
DEBUT: 6/14/1882 at Worcester; played 3B, later moved to CF and went 1-for-3 in an 11–2 loss to Buffalo's Jim Galvin
FINALE: 7/28/1890 at Rochester; played 2B and went 0-for-3 in a 12–2 loss to Louisville's Scott Stratton

In his ML debut Tom O'Brien muffed his first two chances at 3B and was moved to the outfield, where he did no better. Tried at 2B, he dropped an easy pop on June 22, 1882, at Chicago that cost Lee Richmond the game. A product of the Worcester amateur ranks, he seemed slated for a short pro career the following year when his arrival in Baltimore spurred the local *Herald* to recommend that the AA Orioles swap places with Camden in the Interstate Association since the Baltimore management was "determined not to pay enough to get good players." The following year, despite there now being three major leagues, O'Brien was without a team until the eve of the season, when the Boston UA club dropped two novices at the last moment. He made the most of his reprieve, going 5-for-5 on Opening Day, but after he drew the collar in the next game the bloom came off the rose completely when he made 4 errors in his third appearance of the season with Boston.

O'Brien began 1885 with Kansas City of the Western League and moved to Memphis of the Southern League when the WL folded. After the SL season ended, Billy Barnie gave him a second chance with the Orioles but then released him to Jersey City the following spring. O'Brien played with Jersey City through 1889, with time out to participate in 31 games with the about-to-disband 1887 New York Mets and half a season in 1889 with Rochester. A first baseman now, he remained with the upstate New York club in 1890 when it enrolled in the AA but was released after hitting just .190 in 73 games.

At age 30, O'Brien would seemingly have been nearing the end of a not particularly noteworthy career, but he was actually less than midway through it. O'Brien remained in pro ball until he was well past 40 as a first baseman and sometimes player-manager. A wobbly fielder early in his career, he became an excellent first sacker as he aged and a frequent loop FA leader. In December 1900, when two teams fought over his services for 1901, *TSN* remarked, "Tom has been connected with the game for many years and knows base ball so thoroughly." O'Brien later scouted for the Indians and Athletics before dying at a Worcester hospital in 1921 of complications from a ruptured appendix. (DN)

Padden, Richard Joseph / "Dick" "Brains"

B	T	HGT	WGT	G	AB	H	R	2B
R	R	5'10"	165	457	1650	443	254	47

3B	HR	RBI	BB	SO	SB	BA	SA	OBP
31	8	186	111	9	64	.268	.349	.335

B. 9/17/1870 Martins Ferry, OH **D.** 10/31/1922
TEAMS: 96–98PitN 99WasN 01StLN 02–05StLAL
DEBUT: 7/15/1896 at Pittsburgh; played 2B and went 0-for-3 in a 2–1 loss to Boston's Kid Nichols
FINALE: 5/2/1905 at Detroit; played 2B and was hitless in a 4–0 loss to Detroit's Frank Kitson

Dick Padden pitched for amateur teams along the Ohio River until he was in his midtwenties. Upon stating his wish to turn pro, he was in hot demand when Columbus, Wheeling, and Roanoke all competed for his services in the winter of 1894–95. Roanoke won out, and by the end of the 1895 Virginia League season he had moved to the infield, hit .316, and been elevated to the role of player-manager.

In July 1896 Padden made the majors after little more than one season in the minors, replacing Harry Truby at 2B for the Pirates. The following year, in his first full ML campaign, he missed only one game. But that winter, while working as a fireman in his Martins Ferry hometown, he read in *TSN* that he would have to battle for Pittsburgh's

2B post in 1898 with Bill Eagan because his manager, Patsy Donovan, felt that he was too slow getting to the bag on double-play attempts. Padden outshone Eagan in the spring when Bill Watkins took over the Pirates' reins and began the year hitting leadoff. In May, however, he jumped the team after Watkins fined him $25 when he was ejected from a game on April 30 for excessive arguing. His departure gave Eagan a second opportunity to claim his job, but even after Eagan blew his chance, Padden remained on Watkins's private blacklist.

That December he was traded with minor league outfielders Jimmy Slagle and Jack O'Brien to Washington for second baseman Harry Reitz. Under manager Arthur Irwin, Padden took a new lease on his ML career. He opened the season at 2B, moved to SS when Billy Hulen failed there, and in late June was handed the dual role of captain and unofficial manager while Irwin was on a scouting trip. Despite a solid season with a weak team, Padden found himself back in the minors in 1900 when Washington was among the clubs the NL jettisoned when it shrank to eight teams.

After captaining flag-winning Chicago in the newly renamed AL, Padden returned to the NL with St. Louis in 1901. That fall he joined the mass exodus of Cards players that fled to the new junior loop entry in St. Louis and remained with the Browns until the spring of 1905. Padden then played with St. Paul of the American Association until 1907. A diabetic, he died of a stroke in Martins Ferry, leaving behind his wife, Mary. (DN)

Phelan, James Dickson / "Dick" "Daddy"

B	T	HGT	WGT	G	AB	H	R	2B
R	R	?	?	107	422	102	66	14

3B	HR	RBI	BB	SO	SB	BA	SA	OBP
3	4	4	12	5	—	.242	.318	.263

B. 12/10/1854 Towanda, PA **D.** 2/13/1931
TEAMS: 84BalU 85BufN 85StLN
DEBUT: 4/17/1884 at Baltimore; played 2B and went 0-for-4 in a 7–3 win over Washington's Milo Lockwood
FINALE: 10/3/1885 at St. Louis; played 3B and made 1 hit in a 10–3 loss to Philadelphia's Ed Daily

Near the close of the nineteenth century, *TSN* opened its eyes to the fact that Dick Phelan had been playing professionally since 1872 and reported that "a list of the players who have been members of teams which have claimed 'Old Dad' . . . would look like a good-sized section of the city directory. Many of his contemporaries of the early days have tallied their last runs." On January 11, 1902, the baseball publication featured his biography, only part of which was true. Phelan was not the last to play barehanded, as *TSN* contended, but he was certainly among the last. His age was also a matter of dispute. In 1899 *TSN* said he was nearing 50, but records indicate that he was still only 44 years old.

No contemporary publication ever adequately explained how Phelan survived in the game for so long, but his durability helped. He also had rare courage at turning double plays even when it meant taking a ferocious hit from a base runner. Phelan nonetheless incurred his share of serious injuries on the field—and not only as a player. After spending part of 1901 umpiring in the Southern League, he laid plans to captain a team in Natchez, MS, in 1902, only to have his thirty-year playing career halted in early April after suffering a broken hand umpiring behind the plate in a New Orleans–Cleveland preseason exhibition when rookie Cleveland catcher Harry Bemis failed to handle a pitch. In 1931 the *Washington Post,* in reporting Phelan's death at his home in San Antonio of uremia after being confined there for about a year with chronic nephritis, feted him for never having worn a glove and never being ejected from a game. (DN)

Pierce, Grayson S. (aka Pearce) / "Grayce" "Gracie"

B	T	HGT	WGT	G	AB	H	R	2B
L	R	5'11"	176	84	307	57	21	4

3B	HR	RBI	BB	SO	SB	BA	SA	OBP
2	0	2	5	9	—	.186	.212	.199

B. ?/?/? New York, NY **D.** 8/28/1894
TEAMS: 82LouA 82BalA 83ColA 83NYN 84NYA
DEBUT: 5/2/1882 at St. Louis; played 2B and went 1-for-4 in a 9–7 loss to St. Louis's George McGinnis
FINALE: 8/1/1884 at Washington; played CF and went 2-for-4 in a 5–4 loss to Washington's Bob Barr

Grayce Pierce's personal life remains an enigma despite a professional life that put him frequently on public display, usually in a negative light. Never much of a player and too much of a talker ever to be an appealing teammate, Pierce was even less of a success as an umpire. Yet he was called on to officiate a NL game as late as July 28, 1893, just a year before his death.

Pierce played 2B for Louisville in the club's opening game in the AA but mysteriously lost his job barely two weeks into the season although he was hitting .303 at the time and fielding tolerably. Moving to Baltimore in June, he dropped to just .199, was cut after 41 games, and finished the year with a string of Columbus, OH, semipro teams. In 1883 Pierce crashed, both with the yearling Columbus AA entry and the yearling New York NL entry. Having shown nothing since leaving Louisville, he was nonetheless handed the Mets' 2B job in the spring of 1884 but lost it by the fourth game of the season. How he spent the rest of the spring and the early summer is a mystery, but he apparently was still tangentially attached to the Mets, for he turned up in Baltimore on August 1 to play for the pennant-bound New Yorkers in the last game of his ML career. By late September he was in New Orleans, intending to play there that winter. The following summer the Binghamton International Association team expelled him, allowing him to sign on for the rest of 1886 as a regular NL umpire.

Rehired as an NL official for 1887, Pierce lasted only 33 games before Detroit manager Bill Watkins forced his ouster for allegedly crooked umpiring. Upon hearing the news, a Chicago *SL* correspondent chirped, "Chicagoans are glad of Grace Pearce's retirement. His connection with the game did it no good." Switching his indicator to the minor league International Association, Pierce swiftly encountered the same charges. Yet the IA rehired him in 1888, and two years later, when the PL organized with the purpose of implementing a swarm of reforms, its prime mover, John M. Ward, endorsed Pierce as one of the loop's regular umpires when a replacement was needed in July.

While there is no signature incident to cite, Pierce appears to have used up all his baseball lives during his PL tenure. Over the next three seasons he officiated just 3 games in the NL on a substitute basis, and on July 22, 1894, shortly before his death, the *Washington Post* reported that he had been arrested when he was caught trying to pilfer $30 from a cash register in a 3rd Avenue saloon in Manhattan when he thought he saw the barkeep napping in his chair behind the bar. Pierce died in New York little more than a month later. (DN/DB)

Quest, Joseph L. / "Joe"

B	T	HGT	WGT	G	AB	H	R	2B
R	R	5'6"	150	596	2295	499	300	78

3B	HR	RBI	BB	SO	SB	BA	SA	OBP
17	1	161	104	161	5	.217	.268	.252

B. 11/16/1852 New Castle, PA **D.** 11/14/1924
TEAMS: 71CleNA 78IndN 79–82ChiN 83DetN 83–84StLA 84PitA 85DetN 86PhiA
DEBUT: 8/30/1871 at Cleveland; played SS and went 1-for-4 in a 17–12 loss to Troy's John McMullin
FINALE: 7/13/1886 at St. Louis; played 2B and went 0-for-3 in a 7–1 loss to St. Louis's Bob Caruthers

Joe Quest was a sharp fielder and light hitter who played continuously for numerous pro teams between 1871 and 1889 and is best remembered for his reputed role in coining the term "Charley Horse." The son of a blacksmith, he made his ML debut with Cleveland at age 18. Quest then played for Pennsylvania semipro and independent teams until signing with Indianapolis in 1877 and accompanying the Hoosiers to the NL in 1878. He joined Chicago the following year and became a fixture there as the White Stockings won three straight pennants between 1880 and 1882 with the Pennsylvanian anchoring the team's infield defense. When he was briefly benched in 1882, the club missed his sharp fielding and surged to the pennant only after he returned to the lineup.

It was while Quest was with Chicago that the term "Charley Horse" became the name of the muscle injury that ballplayers often suffer. Numerous versions of the term's origins have surfaced over the years, but in most of them the events took place while Quest and several teammates were spending an off day at a racetrack. The running style of one of the horses reminded the players of an injured teammate, and some joshing took place. It appears that Quest then offered another comparison—to the gait of a workhorse, or "charley horse," in his father's blacksmith shop—and the term stuck. It soon became an enduring part of the baseball lexicon.

Quest came under fire from the Chicago press over an "affair of the heart" and begged manager Cap Anson to send him elsewhere before he was shot. Sold to Detroit after the 1882 season, he put in brief stints with the Wolverines, St. Louis, Pittsburgh, and Philadelphia before dropping down to the minors until the early 1890s after he had tried umpiring in the NL for a while and officiated in the 1886 World's Series. Eventually, Anson got him a job at Chicago City Hall, but his tenure ended when he was accused of embezzlement. Quest then moved to Citronelle, AL, where he lived on a farm owned by another former Chicago teammate, Em Gross. In 1912 Quest was reported to be dying there of a lung ailment, but instead he relocated to San Diego, where he died in 1924. Although he was then nearly 72 years old, his death certificate listed his occupation as "ballplayer." (PM/DN)

Quinn, Joseph J. / "Joe" "Old Reliable"

B	T	HGT	WGT	G	AB	H	R	2B
R	R	5'7"	158	1703	6617	1733	860	217

3B	HR	RBI	BB	SO	SB	BA	SA	OBP
68	28	762	354	215	261	.262	.328	.302

G	W	L	PCT	PENNANTS
155	23	132	.148	0

B. 12/25/1864 Sydney, Australia **D.** 11/12/1940
TEAMS: 84StLU 85–86StLN 88–89BosN 90BosP 91–92BosN 93–96StLN (P/M)95StLN 96–98BalN 98StLN 99CleN (P/M)99CleN 00StLN 00CinN 01WasAL
DEBUT: 4/26/1884 at St. Louis; played 1B and went 2-for-5 in a 9–3 win over Altoona's Jack Leary
FINALE: 7/23/1901 at Cleveland; played 2B and went 2-for-4 in a 4–4 tie against Cleveland's Ed Scott

The first MLer born in Australia, Joe Quinn graduated from cricket to baseball when he came to America as a young boy. Ted Sullivan signed him for the UA St. Louis Maroons after a friend of Sullivan spotted him playing for an amateur team in Dubuque the previous year. His first night in St. Louis, Quinn stayed at the home of Al Spink, then the secretary of the Maroons. When he arrived at Union Park the following day, his appearance was a disappointment to Sullivan, but when Billy Taylor was unable to play 1B on April 26, 1884, Quinn was substituted and did so well that he won the job for the rest of the season and hit a respectable .270

After the UA disbanded that winter, Quinn accompanied the Maroons to the NL in 1885 but found the pitching there beyond him. Two consecutive poor seasons (.213 and .232) left him unwanted when the Maroons ceded their NL franchise to Indianapolis, and he was eventually sold to Duluth of the Northwestern League. Quinn returned to the majors in August 1888 with Boston NL and remained in top company until July 1901, when the Washington AL team sent him home with an injury to his arm that he had sustained a week earlier on a snap throw to 1B. His arm recovered enough with rest to allow him to play in the minors until 1904, by which time he was just a few months short of his 40th birthday.

Unlike most players of his day who lingered in the game until they were approaching middle age for the lack of anything better to do, Quinn played solely for the love of the sport. By 1895 he owned a thriving undertaking business in St. Louis with his father-in-law and was not only a skilled embalmer but also a capable veterinarian who possessed sufficient medical knowledge to be of service in on-field injury situations. Never idle for a moment, he dabbled in real estate, ran a livery stable for a while, played several musical instruments, sang in the choir of St. Bridget's Catholic Church in St. Louis, and by 1898 had six children, including a 10-year-old daughter who was thought to be a musical genius.

But for all of Quinn's many talents, he never learned to hit a baseball with any degree of consistency. In 1892, at 27, when he should have been at his peak, he hit .218 for the pennant-winning Boston Beaneaters. Traded to St. Louis in January 1893, he celebrated the first year the pitching distance was set at 60'6" by batting .230 and compiling a .564 OPS, the lowest by a qualifier that season. Notwithstanding his offensive inadequacies, Quinn was the lone player to perform as a regular on pennant winners in three different major leagues in the nineteenth century despite never playing in the American Association. His championship clubs were the 1884 UA St. Louis Maroons, the 1890 PL Boston Reds, the 1891–92 NL Boston Beaneaters, and lastly, the 1896 NL Baltimore Orioles. Ironically, however, his best seasons, all considered, came with miserable teams. In 1895 he hit .300 for the last time (.329) with the eleventh-place St. Louis Browns, and four years later he led the hapless 1899 Cleveland Spiders in BA and hits. As a further irony, Quinn's lone ML managerial experiences came with these two doormats and resulted in him posting a .148 career winning percentage, the lowest of anyone who acted as a pilot in a minimum of 150 ML games. But for him even to be given the opportunities he had, savvy baseball people needed to recognize his corresponding assets.

Quinn's fielding earned him the nickname "Ol'

Reliable," and he was universally respected for his honesty, integrity, and, above all, his concentration. He is one of only a handful of players from his era of whom it was never said that he gave less than his best or that his head was elsewhere than in the game. Quinn was suffering from Alzheimer's when he died in St. Louis of arteriosclerosis at 75. (DN)

*Reach, Alfred James / "Al"

B	T	HGT	WGT	G	AB	H	R	2B
L	L	5'6"	155	80	393	97	89	15

3B	HR	RBI	BB	SO	SB	BA	SA	OBP
7	0	57	9	10	7	.247	.321	.264

G	W	L	PCT	PENNANTS
11	4	7	.364	0

B. 5/25/1840 London, England **D.** 1/14/1928
TEAMS: 71–75AthNA (M)90PhiN
DEBUT: 5/20/1871 at Boston; played 2B and went 2-for-4 in an 11–8 loss to Boston's Al Spalding
FINALE: 5/21/1875 at New Haven; played RF in a 15–2 win over New Haven's Tricky Nichols

The son of a cricketer and trading agent and the older brother of MLer Bob Reach, Al Reach peddled newspapers on the streets of Brooklyn and later worked as an iron molder while playing baseball for recreation only. His first organized team was the Brooklyn Jacksons in 1858. Three years later he moved to the Brooklyn Eckfords and remained with them until he was given a princely offer of $25 in "expense money" to switch to the Philadelphia Athletics. The move, which was made primarily for money—and a meaningful amount then to someone who had grown up in near poverty—branded Reach a "revolver" as well as one of the first "professional" players. He debuted with the Athletics on June 9, 1865, and became the club's second baseman the following year, a position he would hold through the fledgling NA season. Reach played only a handful of games with the Athletics in their final year in the NA but continued to play with an offshoot of the club through 1877. Then in his late thirties, the onetime newsboy opened a sporting goods emporium in Philadelphia and later expanded his business into the A. J. Reach Company, one of the first manufacturers of sporting goods and the producer of both the ball (beginning in 1883) and the baseball guide that carried the AA's imprimatur during its ten seasons as a major league. The guide continued after the AA dissolved and in 1901 became the official guide of the American League while Reach's ball and the Spalding ball were the two balls adopted when the NL and AA merged in 1892.

In 1892, Reach, who had surrendered a substantial portion of his sporting goods empire to Al Spalding some ten years earlier, combined what interests he had left with Spalding's company and others to form A. G. Spalding and Brothers. Meanwhile, he had been actively involved in the business of the Philadelphia NL Quakers ever since 1883 when he and John I. Rogers took control of the franchise after it replaced Worcester. Reach retained his interest in the Quakers until 1903, long after they became more popularly known as the Phillies, and then sold his shares to devote his time to other business pursuits. He maintained a close association with the game, however, and in 1907 was a member of the misbegotten committee that determined that West Point cadet Abner Doubleday had invented baseball.

In his later years Reach took up golf and developed into a polished player, but unfortunately there is no record of whether he stroked from the same side as he once had swung a bat. He died in Atlantic City in 1928 at 87. (DN/EM)

Reitz, Henry Peter / "Harry" "Heinie" "Pepper"

B	T	HGT	WGT	G	AB	H	R	2B
L	R	5'7"	158	724	2744	801	447	108

3B	HR	RBI	BB	SO	SB	BA	SA	OBP
65	11	463	266	99	122	.292	.391	.363

B. 6/29/1867 Chicago, IL **D.** 11/10/1914
TEAMS: 93–97BalN 98WasN 99PitN
DEBUT: 4/27/1893 at Washington; played 2B and went 0-for-4 in a 7–5 loss to Washington's Jouett Meekin
FINALE: 6/3/1899 at Philadelphia; played 2B and went 0-for-3 before being replaced by Art Madison in a 15–3 win over Al Orth
CAREER HIGHLIGHT: In 1894 set the all-time ML season record for the most triples by a second baseman with 31

Often called Harry Reetz during his career, Reitz finally put everyone straight in 1899 when he informed *TSN* that his name was pronounced Rights.

Also called "Heinie" at times, he preferred "Harry" or "Pepper," the nickname given him when he played for Washington. Reitz had five brothers who ventured into pro ball, all of them second basemen, and all, like himself, graduates of the Chicago City League. In 1890, already almost 23, Reitz made a belated foray into the play-for-pay ranks when he joined Sacramento of the California League. Taking a liking to the West Coast, he married Maggie Lynch of Yolo City, WA, that October and planned to return to Sacramento the following year. When the club refused to meet his salary demands, he signed instead with Rochester for 1891. By July, however, Reitz had tired of the New York town and jumped his contract to return to the Cal League. His move triggered a threat by that loop to abandon the National Agreement if there were repercussions, as its teams had already had many players pirated that year by eastern circuits.

Allowed to stay in the Cal League, Reitz put in his third straight season there in 1892, joining San Francisco. That winter he played under John McCloskey, an ex–Cal Leaguer who had a pipeline to its players. McCloskey at first signed Reitz for his Montgomery club of the Southern League and then, when several big league teams showed interest in him, pitted Louisville against Baltimore to see which would pay the most for him. Baltimore won, enabling Reitz to become part of baseball's most famous dynasty of the 1890s: the 1894–96 Orioles.

In his rookie season of 1893 Reitz played every inning of every game at 2B for Baltimore and tied for the club lead in RBI. The following year injuries held him to just 108 games, but he still took a large hand in Baltimore's first pennant win as he set the all-time record for the most triples in a season by a second baseman with 31 and led the NL in FA. By 1895 Reitz was regarded as the best second baseman in the league at turning a double play but suffered a serious setback when he broke his shoulder in a game at New York on June 28 in a fall while chasing a pop fly. Reitz reclaimed his 2B post the following season after his interim replacement, Kid Gleason, was traded and produced a career-high 106 RBI. When he scored just 76 runs in 1897, the fewest of any Orioles regular, he was sent to Washington that winter in a six-player deal that brought second baseman Gene Demont to Baltimore. Before joining the second-division Senators, Reitz demanded a pay hike and held out until the 1898 season was under way. Upon donning his new duds, he hit .303, led the loop in FA for the third time, and beamed when his manager, Arthur Irwin, told the *Washington Post*, "Henry Reitz, to my mind, is the best second baseman in the League, and one of the greatest artists that ever played the sack."

That December, Washington made one of its few good trades in the 1890s, sending Reitz to Pittsburgh for second baseman Dick Padden and outfielders Jimmy Slagle and Jack O'Brien. Washington observers moaned initially, but Reitz injured his ankle against Philadelphia on June 3, 1899, was removed from the game, and never played in the majors again. The following year he played a few games with Milwaukee of the newly renamed AL and then returned to the California League but started drinking heavily after his wife died. He put on so much weight that when John McGraw signed him for Baltimore in 1901 after the AL went major, *TSN* noted, "The once great second baseman is all in, hopelessly fat and slow." After McGraw released him, Reitz finished his career in the minors, relying on his name alone to keep him in the game until 1908. He was working as a laborer in 1914 when he died after being struck by a car while crossing a Sacramento street. (DN)

Richardson, Daniel / "Danny"

B	T	HGT	WGT	G	AB	H	R	2B
R	R	5'8"	165	1131	4451	1129	676	149

3B	HR	RBI	BB	SO	SB	BA	SA	OBP
52	32	558	283	289	225	.254	.332	.301

G	IP	H	GS	CG	BB
15	100	91	9	8	30

SO	SH	W	L	PCT	ERA
38	1	7	3	.700	3.24

G	W	L	PCT	PENNANTS
43	12	31	.279	0

B. 1/25/1863 Elmira, NY **D.** 9/12/1926
TEAMS: 84–89NYN 90NYP 91NYN (P/M)92WasN 93BroN 94LouN
DEBUT: 5/22/1884 at New York; played SS and went 1-for-3 in a 7–1 win over Boston's Jim Whitney
FINALE: 9/24/1894 at Louisville; played 2B and went 0-for-2 in an 8–7 loss to New York's Jouett Meekin
CAREER HIGHLIGHT: 6/22/1892 at Washington; in a 16–14 win over New York handled a 2B-record 19 chances in a nine-inning game

Prolific at putting up gloveless .950 FAs when few others could field .900, Danny Richardson was spotted at the age of 21 by New York NL outfielder Mike Dorgan and then signed by Giants manager Jim Mutrie right off his hometown Elmira, NY, semipro team despite having no established position, no minor league credentials, and a weak bat. Immediately realizing the gem he had in the sure-handed Richardson, Mutrie used him at all positions except catcher until planting him at 2B in 1887. When Tim Keefe had the flu early in 1885, Richardson filled in as a pitcher and won 7 of 8 decisions, helping New York to a 17-3 start. Later Richardson's solid infield play made him an integral part of New York's back-to-back world championship teams in 1888–89. In the former year he led NL second baseman with a then near-record .942 FA, and in the latter year he logged 100 RBI.

Later compared to Rabbit Maranville in both size and value, Richardson could make one-handed grabs with either hand. During the winter months he bolstered his strength by digging cellars so that he could play through injuries and rarely missed a game. His only major injury was a broken jaw suffered in an 1887 postseason exhibition against the Cuban Giants. Following his two straight championship seasons, in 1890 Richardson joined in the exodus of NL players and signed to play for the New York PL entry but had a difficult adjustment when team captain and former Giants teammate Buck Ewing moved him to SS. Returning to the Giants after the PL collapsed, Richardson and teammate Roger Connor surprised the baseball world on October 28, 1891, by jumping to Billy Barnie's new Philadelphia AA franchise. Richardson signed for $4,000, an especially heady figure for a fielding specialist, but the team was dissolved over the winter when the NL and AA merged and, much against his wishes, he was "assigned" to play for Washington.

With the Senators, Richardson rose to assistant captain on April 19 and became manager of the team on August 24. On June 20, 1892, he set a still-extant nine-inning fielding record at second base, handling 19 of 20 chances. But Richardson hated the hot weather in Washington. Traded to Brooklyn the following season for Bill Joyce, he saw limited duty after being struck in the face by a ground ball on July 14. Claiming a weak stomach and an unspecified lung problem, he began taking days off for what were viewed to be specious reasons, and was finally suspended without pay on July 30 after missing a train connection in Jersey City. There followed several weeks of trading insults with Brooklyn owner Charlie Byrne. After Richardson finally announced that he would never play for Brooklyn again, the local press roasted him for thinking he was "bigger than baseball," and he finished the year managing a department store in tiny Blossburg, PA. Richardson returned to physical form in 1894 for Barnie's misguided Louisville team but failed to hit. The growing popularity of the fielder's glove in the early 1890s allowed many stronger batters to match Richardson's fielding numbers—on the surface at least—and made his special skills seem obsolete.

At age 31 Richardson moved back to Elmira and opened a dry goods firm. By the 1920s he was connected with Sheehan, Bean & Company, the largest department store in Elmira. Richardson died of a heart attack as he lunched in a New York restaurant with his brother-in-law, George Horgan. (FV/DN)

Ritchey, Claude Cassius / "Claude" "Little All Right"

B	T	HGT	WGT	G	AB	H	R	2B
B	R	5'6½"	167	523	1904	536	251	55

3B	HR	RBI	BB	SO	SB	BA	SA	OBP
23	10	232	166	—	69	.282	.350	.348

B. 10/5/1873 Emlenton, PA **D.** 11/8/1951
TEAMS: 97CinN 98–99LouN 00–06PitN 07–09BosN
DEBUT: 4/22/1897 at Chicago; played SS and went 3-for-4 in an 8–7 win over Chicago's Clark Griffith
FINALE: 6/24/1909 at Boston; pinch hit unsuccessfully for pitcher Jake Boultes in the ninth inning of a 12–5 loss to New York's Red Ames

Claude Ritchey was raised by his mother and stepfather and may have been illegitimate. Reportedly, his nickname stemmed from his talent for hitting in the clutch, but a suspicion lingers that it may have been related to his contrary and sometimes downright annoying disposition. A vegetarian when he arrived in the majors, he alienated steak-eating teammates with his discourses on why no sane man would fill his gullet with anything but fish and may have been traded at the request of manager Buck Ewing as a consequence.

Ritchey played in the Interstate League and the Iron & Oil League before moving up to Buffalo in the Eastern League in 1896. He opened the season in LF but was shifted to 3B by manager Jack Rowe when he was a flop in the outfield, and then to SS when he was physically inadequate at 3B. Drafted by Brooklyn that fall, he was sold to Cincinnati for $500 in March 1897 before he ever wore a Brooklyn uniform. Brooklyn manager Billy Barnie later claimed he had sold Ritchey as a favor to Cincinnati, which needed a SS when Tommy Corcoran held out, and was angry when Cincinnati did not return him after Corcoran rejoined the Reds. In any event, Ritchey did well as a Reds rookie and fans were unsettled when Cincinnati traded him to Louisville along with center fielder Dummy Hoy and pitcher Red Ehret for nothing more than Bill Hill, a terminally erratic left-hander.

After opening 1898 at SS with Louisville, he was eventually replaced by Bill Clingman, who had a stronger arm, and relocated to 2B. It would remain his province for the rest of his 13-year career. In 1899 Ritchey dispensed with vegetarianism and finished second on the Louisville team in RBI only to Honus Wagner but scored just 65 runs while batting fifth behind Wagner. Moved to Pittsburgh the following year when Louisville abandoned its NL franchise and shipped its best players to the Pirates, he resumed his anti-meat stance and hit well again but scored only 62 runs even though he was elevated to second in the order.

Ritchey's low run totals even while playing with good teams and hitting decently would remain a career long enigma. Not until 1901, however, would his exceptional fielding prowess first manifest itself. That year, Ritchey led all NL second baseman for the first time in a positive fielding department—put-outs—but before he finished he would claim a then record five NL fielding average crowns and rank second only to Nap Lajoie in career FA (.962 to .957). After leaving baseball Ritchey was a partner in an Emlenton clothing store for a while and then worked for the Emlenton Refining Company, which changed to Quaker State Oil a few years before his retirement in 1941. A vegetarian in his twenties, he later succumbed to the chronic ballplayer's affliction and died from cirrhosis of the liver in the small Pennsylvania town where he was born. (DN)

Robinson, William H. / "Yank"

B	T	HGT	WGT	G	AB	H	R	2B
R	R	5'6½"	170	978	3428	825	697	148

3B	HR	RBI	BB	SO	SB	BA	SA	OBP
44	16	399	664	181	272	.241	.324	.375

G	IP	H	GS	CG	BB
14	89	109	4	4	29

SO	SH	W	L	PCT	ERA
62	0	3	4	.429	3.34

B. 9/19/1859 Philadelphia, PA **D.** 8/25/1894
TEAMS: 82DetN 84BalU 85–89StLA 90PitP 91CinA 91StLA 92WasN
DEBUT: 8/24/1882 at Boston; played SS and went 0-for-3 in a 4–0 loss to Boston's Jim Whitney
FINALE: 8/10/1892 at Baltimore; played 3B and went 0-for-4 in a 7–2 loss to Baltimore's George Cobb

Yank Robinson played at least 14 ML games at every position except 1B. Considered the top second baseman of his day at standing his ground on double plays or steal attempts, in 1888 he was named the best player in the entire game by Bob Ferguson, who lauded him for being a consummate rug rat: hyperactive, shrewd, constantly thinking and devising plays, and, above all, willing to sacrifice himself for the team.

Ironically, Robinson was an even better SS than second baseman but was kept at 2B because of St. Louis manager Charlie Comiskey's stubborn loyalty to veteran Bill Gleason, and his best position of all may have been catcher. Like Bid McPhee and several other crack middle infielders in the 1880s who still played without gloves, Robinson was ambidextrous and never found a taker for his longstanding challenge to an ambidextrous throwing match. Robinson was also capable of hitting from both sides of the plate—or neither, according to his detractors, who cited his .241 career BA, lack of power, and affinity for slapping short opposite-field flare hits. Moreover, he reportedly was so raw at the start of his career that he held the bat crosshanded.

Yet Robinson's supporters among historians—and there are many—produce a persuasive case that he was the most productive sub-.250 hitter in history. In 1888 Robinson created 7.43 runs per game, the season record by a qualifier with a sub-.240 BA, and he also holds the career record (7.03) for the most RC/G by a player with a sub-

.250 career average and a minimum of 3,000 PAs. His secret for getting on base inordinately often for someone who posed almost no threat when he swung a bat was actually no secret. He was peerless at seemingly accidentally slicing, slapping, and bunting pitches foul—the rules in his day permitted a batter an unlimited number of foul balls, including bunts, without being assessed a strike—until eventually he either frustrated a pitcher into walking him or caught a fielder napping and dumped a ball out of his reach.

Born into poverty, Robinson left Philadelphia at a young age to make his way in the Boston area. He was playing for a semipro team in Natick, MA, when Detroit arrived in Boston needing a SS to replace the injured Arthur Irwin. A .179 BA and .800 FA failed to electrify the Wolverines, and Robinson spent 1883 with Saginaw, MI. Disregarding his .220 BA against middling Northwestern League pitching, Baltimore UA hired him and moved him all around the infield before planting him at 3B, where he led the loop in FA as well as walks. Robinson's flexibility induced St. Louis AA to hire him for 1885 at a salary of $2,100 in the expectation he would become its new catcher. He refused to play that position on a regular basis but proved worth his keep when he filled in for injured left fielder Tip O'Neill for nearly three months and appeared in 78 games altogether.

When the Browns won their first of four consecutive AA flags in 1885, Robinson took part in all 7 World's Series games against Chicago. The following season he replaced Sam Barkley at 2B and held the job without any serious black marks against him until May 2, 1889, when he was fined $25 and suspended after a shouting match with Browns owner Chris Von der Ahe. Both the fine and suspension were rescinded, however, when the entire team threatened to go on strike in his support. Near the end of the 1889 season he was fined again, this time without recourse, when he failed to show up for a game with Kansas City.

Irked, Robinson jumped to the PL in 1890 but ended up with the Pittsburgh entry rather than Brooklyn, where he had hoped to play. When he hit .229 and scored just 59 runs despite the livelier ball the PL employed, he attributed his collapse to losing too much "flesh" and being forced to play ball his manager Ned Hanlon's way, which was not at all his style. Unwelcome back in St. Louis after the PL folded, he caught on with the Cincinnati AA replacement team but again found a poor fit when he could not get along with many of his teammates, especially catcher Harry Vaughn, and led AA second basemen in errors even though he played less than 100 games at the bag. In fairness to Robinson, the club's home field at Pendleton was hastily constructed and had very poor drainage, and its infielders generally played better on the road, suggesting that his problems may have been partly due to poor playing conditions. Robinson appeared in a token game with St. Louis after Cincinnati disbanded and then, his career in jeopardy, signed with Washington after the AA and NL merged. He tried to get himself back into shape and give it his all but reported weighing only 146 pounds, and shortly before he was released in August 1892, the D.C. press sadly remarked that the game was now too swift for him.

The following spring Robinson was ready to sign with Louisville when it looked as though Fred Pfeffer would quit the game, but then rumors surfaced that he was dying of consumption. Although the April 8 issue of *TSN* reported they were false, claiming that Robinson remained idle because he had injured his knee in a workout and gone to Hot Springs to recover, it soon grew apparent that his health truly was declining. By the fall of 1893 Robinson seldom left his home in St. Louis, and most of the money he had made a few years earlier in real estate was gone. On December 29, 1893, his friends staged a benefit for him at the Standard Theatre in St. Louis with the expectation that the money they collected would send him to Las Vegas in a last effort to regain his health. Instead Robinson went to San Antonio. Interviewed in the Texas city by a *TSN* correspondent the following June, he could barely speak above a whisper. Robinson returned to St. Louis in August 1893 and died at the home of Pat and George Tebeau, where he was cared for in his last days by their mother. In gratitude, he willed the Tebeaus half of his estate, amounting to about $750, which they used to buy a "handsome" headstone for what otherwise would have been an unmarked grave in St. Louis's Calvary Cemetery. (DN/DB)

*Shaffer, Zachary Taylor
(b. Shafer) **/ "Taylor"**

B	T	HGT	WGT	G	AB	H	R	2B
L	?	5'7"	155	116	438	74	47	6

3B	HR	RBI	BB	SO	SB	BA	SA	OBP
6	0	21	43	—	19	.169	.210	.246

B. 7/13/1866 Philadelphia, PA **D.** 10/27/1945
TEAMS: 84KCU 84BalU 90PhiA
DEBUT: 6/7/1884 at Kansas City; played RF and went 2-for-5 in a 6–5 loss to Chicago's John Horan
FINALE: 7/16/1890 at St. Louis; played 2B and went 1-for-4 in a 9–8 loss to St. Louis's Tom Ramsey

Taylor Shaffer was the younger brother of Orator Shaffer and was reputedly nearly as loquacious as his sibling, putting up a constant stream of chatter both on and off the field. His career has some specious aspects. The 1884 portion of it until recently was attributed to one Frank Shaffer, who actually was responsible only for the games with Altoona. What is more, reference works incorrectly list the date of Shaffer's final game as September 20, 1890, which was actually the date of his brother's finale.

What do we know for certain about the younger Shaffer brother? We know he was with Minneapolis of the Northwestern League in 1886. Soon after his 20th birthday he and teammate George Rhue, later a minor league umpire, went to St. Paul one afternoon when Minneapolis had the day off to watch St. Paul play league-leading Duluth. Shaffer was chosen to umpire when the regular umpire failed to appear. According to Rhue, St. Paul manager Jack Barnes offered Shaffer $25 to assure a St. Paul victory and, even though Shaffer disdained the bribe, he took $25 from Barnes after the game when St. Paul won. But again, that's only according to Rhue.

In any event, by 1888 Shaffer had joined St. Paul and was working under Barnes when he was injured in July. Even as a St. Paul scribe was penning that "spectators will miss Shafer's easy graceful work and brilliant manner of touching runners," Barnes was cutting his second baseman's release form rather than continuing to pay him while he was disabled. So rewarded, Shaffer signed with Toledo in 1889 but hit just .237 and was released in January 1890 when Toledo joined the AA because he was deemed "not strong enough for the American Association." He was then rumored to be headed for Louisville, which lacked a second baseman after Dan Shannon jumped to the PL, but again the assessment was that he was "hardly heavy enough to play in the Association." Finally, Shaffer and his brother Orator signed with the Philadelphia A's as a package in mid-April. The assessments of his chances in the AA proved to be accurate. After hitting .172 in 69 games, Shaffer was released in late July. By age 25 he was out of baseball and running a hotel in Coatesville, PA, a town known today as "the Pittsburgh of the East." Shaffer died in 1945 in Glendale, CA. (DN)

Shannon, Daniel Webster / "Dan"

B	T	HGT	WGT	G	AB	H	R	2B
?	?	5'9"	175	242	964	225	171	36

3B	HR	RBI	BB	SO	SB	BA	SA	OBP
21	8	111	77	107	54	.233	.339	.291

G	W	L	PCT	PENNANTS
109	25	80	.238	0

B. 3/23/1865 Bridgeport, CT **D.** 10/24/1913
TEAMS: (P/M)89LouA 90PhiP 90NYP (P/M)91WasA
DEBUT: 4/17/1889 at Louisville; played 2B and went 1-for-4 in a 7–4 loss to Kansas City's Parke Swartzel
FINALE: 9/16/1891 at Louisville; played SS and went 0-for-4 in a 7–0 loss to Louisville's Jouett Meekin

The brother of Henry Shannon, sports editor of the *Bridgeport Daily Standard* in the 1890s, Dan Shannon enjoyed an eighteen-year career in the game as a player and a manager but was much better at the latter. Unhappily, his only two opportunities as a ML pilot came with deplorable teams. From the very outset of his career Shannon was recognized as a natural field leader. A lifelong resident of Bridgeport, CT, in 1882 he piloted and played 2B for his hometown semipro Nationals and then entered the pro ranks in the 1884 Connecticut State League. He remained with New England teams until July 1887 when Bridgeport sold him to Oshkosh with two other players for $3,000. Shannon immediately was named field captain of Frank Selee's eventual 1887 Northwestern League flag winner. The following year he returned east to play for Newark and that winter was hired by Louisville for 1889 to replace longtime incumbent Reddy Mack at 2B.

Shannon put together a solid rookie season, leading the dreadful last-place Colonels in runs, doubles and steals but was nonetheless released the following January. The PL immediately called Louisville's wisdom into question by putting him in a Brotherhood uniform, first with Philadelphia, where he was made captain, and then with New York, which needed a second baseman and lead-off hitter. Shannon brought Louisville's brain trust a measure of revenge when he hit .221 in 102 games and was left dispossessed when the PL folded. He signed in January 1891 to serve as player-manager of Omaha. In July he jumped his contract when the Western Association team fell into financial trouble, and he pirated five of his players to accompany him to the Washington AA entry.

On July 30, 1891, Shannon took over the Senators' managerial reins from Charlie Snyder and was given to understand that he would be absolved of blame for the club's last-place showing and rehired in 1892. Instead he was fired in late September. Team moguls complained that his health kept him out of the lineup too often and that he had failed to "develop any particular strength on the team," but Shannon said the real reason was that, being a teetotaler, he did not hang out at Mike Scanlon's pool-room and therefore was not popular with Scanlon and his cronies, who in essence ran the club. Meanwhile, the *Washington Star* wrote, "Perhaps he has not done any more than keep his head above the water, but when one thinks of the terrible handicap under which he labored when he arrived . . . it is no wonder that Shannon's showing has not been brilliant. He did not come here to win the pennant, but to keep the team going profitably and has done well enough."

Shannon survived a severe beaning in 1892, a near-fatal bout with pneumonia in 1894, and his daughter's death from diphtheria in 1898 to play and manage in the high minors until 1899, when he was fired by Buffalo of the Western League for drunkenness. Prior to his dismissal he had been responsible for helping to develop many future ML players and bringing at least one former MLer back from oblivion (*see* William Halligan). Shannon umpired briefly in the minors in the early part of the twentieth century and ran a café in Bridgeport. Around 1909 he took a job as a messenger for the Yost Typewriter Company and was still in their employ when he died in 1913 after a short illness. (DN)

Shinnick, Timothy James / "Tim" "Dandy" "Good Eye"

B	T	HGT	WGT	G	AB	H	R	2B
B	R	5'9"	150	259	929	222	164	25

3B	HR	RBI	BB	SO	SB	BA	SA	OBP
22	2	134	116	46	98	.239	.320	.332

B. 11/6/1867 Exeter, NH **D.** 5/18/1944

TEAMS: 90–91LouA

DEBUT: 4/19/1890 at Louisville; played 2B and went 3-for-3 in a 4–3 win over St. Louis's Jack Stivetts

FINALE: 10/4/1891 at St. Louis; played 2B and went 0-for-2 in a 4–3 loss to St. Louis's Willie McGill

Tim Shinnick played for two scholastic championship teams at Phillips Exeter Academy in 1885–86 and followed by playing for Lowell, the New England League pennant winner, in 1887 before being loaned to Farmington, NH, in August to help it win the Stratford County championship. He returned to Lowell in late September in time to join the pennant-clinching celebration and then remained with Lowell in 1888 when the club repeated as the NEL kingpin. After leading the New York State League in steals in 1889 while playing 3B for Auburn, the loop flag winner, Shinnick was able to boast with utter sincerity that he had never in his life played on anything but championship teams when he reported for spring training with Louisville in 1890.

Since the Kentucky city had finished a sorry last in 1889, Shinnick's teammates mocked his gloating until the 1890 AA season entered its final weeks with Louisville solidly in first place. Much of the credit belonged to Shinnick, who got off to one of the hottest starts of any rookie in history, going 7-for-7 in the first 2 games of his ML career before settling into his role as a solid run producer and the best all-around second baseman in the league apart from fellow rookie Cupid Childs. Shinnick's streak of being on only winners got a push when Louisville tied the favored Brooklyn Bridegrooms in the 1890 World Series, but then came to a sad halt in 1891 when the Colonels dropped to seventh place and he was nailed by the sophomore jinx, losing 36 points off his batting average and accounting for 40 fewer runs. He then fell prey to the AA and NL merger that winter, which cut ML jobs by 25 percent and forced him back into the minors in 1892 with Minneapolis of the Western League.

Shinnick subsequently spent the last ten years of his playing career in the minors, ending in 1901 with Ilion of the New York State League, where he served as player-manager until he was released in late May. Shortly afterward Shinnick tried his hand at umpiring in the NSL before returning to his Exeter home. He died in an Exeter hospital in 1944. (DN)

Smith, Charles Marvin / "Pop"

B	T	HGT	WGT	G	AB	H	R	2B
R	R	5'11"	170	1112	4238	941	643	141

3B	HR	RBI	BB	SO	SB	BA	SA	OBP
87	24	358	325	345	160	.222	.313	.287

G	IP	H	GS	CG	BB
3	5.2	10	0	0	0

SO	SH	W	L	PCT	ERA
0	0	0	0	—	6.35

B. 10/12/1856 Digby, Nova Scotia, Canada
D. 4/18/1927
TEAMS: 80CinN 81CleN 81BufN 81WorN 82PhiA 82LouA 83–84ColA 85–86PitA 87–89PitN 89–90BosN 91WasA
DEBUT: 5/1/1880 at Cincinnati; played 2B and went 0-for-4 in a 4–3 loss to Chicago's Larry Corcoran
FINALE: 6/9/1891 at Cincinnati; played 2B and went hitless in a 5–1 loss to Cincinnati's Ed Crane

Although Pop Smith was born in Canada, he moved to Boston at such an early age that it seems a stretch to rank him as the best Canadian-born second baseman in ML history even though technically he qualifies. But there is at least one significant distinction that he does unequivocally own: the most career runs by a player with a sub-.225 BA (643). Since Smith's departure from the majors in 1891, only two players have ever even remotely threatened his record, and the closest, Rob Deer, fell 65 runs short with 578.

More than anything else, Smith's mark is a testimony to his longevity despite his severe offensive shortcomings. Even though Bid McPhee and half a dozen other second basemen overshadowed him during his career, his defensive work, consistent effort, and durability did not go unappreciated. In 1890, after rookie manager Frank Selee named Smith captain of his Boston NL club, *TSN* observed of Selee's choice, "He knows every point of the game, is thoroughly familiar with the tricks of the business [and] quick to take advantage of every play that will help his side win." Yet while his teams usually finished above .500 and sometimes as high as second, Smith never had the good fortune to play on a pennant winner. His high-water mark may have occurred in 1882 when he began the season with a Philadelphia club that was expected to snare the initial pennant in the rebel AA, but instead a .092 BA earned his release after just 20 games and he finished the season as an AA umpire working in a string of late-season games between Cincinnati and Louisville that helped bring the flag to the Queen City. The following year Smith returned to the playing ranks full-time and achieved his only positive season batting feat when he led the AA in triples while manning 2B for the AA expansion Columbus team.

Smith began his pro career in 1876 with independent Binghamton and remained active in the game until 1899, when he was nearing his 43rd birthday. Upon leaving baseball he returned to his home in Boston and worked as a motorman for a Hub streetcar firm. Married with one son, Arthur, Smith died in 1927 in Allston, MA. (DN)

Somerville, Edward G. / "Ed" "Eddie"

B	T	HGT	WGT	G	AB	H	R	2B
R	R	5'7"	158	111	449	90	49	13

3B	HR	RBI	BB	SO	SB	BA	SA	OBP
1	0	27	3	12	2	.200	.234	.206

B. 3/1/1853 Philadelphia, PA **D.** 10/1/1877
TEAMS: 75CenNA 75NHNA 76LouN
DEBUT: 4/30/1875 at Brooklyn; played 2B and went 1-for-4 in a 4–3 loss to New York's Bobby Mathews
FINALE: 10/5/1876 at Louisville; played 2B and went hitless in an 11–2 loss to Hartford's Candy Cummings

Ed Somerville was the first participant in the NL's inaugural 1876 season to die. After breaking in with the Centennials, one of the three NA teams representing his hometown in 1875, he moved to New Haven when his initial club folded. In 1876 he started off well with Louisville and in midseason was offered $1,600 to sign for 1877. The offer was then rescinded when his play slipped in the second half of the season. Known as a chronic complainer, he was overheard by Boston manager Harry Wright bemoaning to a teammate after Louisville had traveled by streetcar to a game in the Hub, "It's strange these fools can't make cars that don't rattle and shake folks a-pieces!"

Somerville joined the London Tecumsehs in 1877 and served as the International Association club's SS until late in the season. He died of consumption in Ontario in the fall of 1877 and his body was taken to New Haven for burial, suggesting that he may have married a woman from there while playing with the Elm Cities in 1875. (DN)

Stricker, John A. (b. Streaker) **/ "Cub"**

B	T	HGT	WGT	G	AB	H	R	2B
R	R	5'3"	158	1196	4635	1107	790	128

3B	HR	RBI	BB	SO	SB	BA	SA	OBP
47	12	411	414	105	278	.239	.294	.306

G	IP	H	GS	CG	BB
8	27.2	30	0	0	11

SO	SH	W	L	PCT	ERA
10	0	2	0	1.000	3.58

G	W	L	PCT	PENNANTS
23	6	17	.261	0

B. 6/8/1859 Philadelphia, PA **D.** 11/19/1937
TEAMS: 82–85PhiA 87–88CleA 89CleN 90CleP 91BosA (P/M)92StLN 92BalN 93WasN
DEBUT: 5/2/1882 at Philadelphia; played 2B and went 0-for-4 in a 10–7 win over Baltimore's Tricky Nichols
FINALE: 9/29/1893 at Cincinnati; played RF and went 0-for-3 in a 10–4 loss to Cincinnati's Tom Parrott

Scrappy, hotheaded, and a perennial fan favorite, Cub Stricker played 2B on AA championship teams in Philadelphia and Boston. Philadelphia born, he changed his name to Stricker prior to joining the amateur Schusters in 1878 and remained on local amateur teams until coming to Harry Diddlebock's independent Philadelphias in 1879 as a SS at age 19. In 1881 he moved to Chick Fulmer's Philadelphia Athletics of the Eastern Championship Association and began playing 2B against NL teams in exhibitions. When the Athletics joined the AA in 1882, Stricker was in the Opening Day lineup and had a strong enough arm to pitch exhibitions and occasionally relieve in official games.

Stricker broke a finger in the pre-1883 season city series against the new Philadelphia NL team and missed the start of the year. The Athletics won the pennant that season under new captain Harry Stovey, but back-to-back errors by Stricker on July 26 cost them dearly. When he bobbled a grounder with a man on 3B in a 1–1 game, Stovey, playing 1B, yelled for a play at the plate. Instead Stricker fired the ball into Stovey's chest. The next batter hit a soft pop-up to Stricker and he muffed it. When the A's lost 8–1, Stovey was so disgusted that he suspended Stricker "indefinitely." Without a capable tenth man, pitcher Bobby Mathews tried to play RF and sprained his ankle. Stricker's suspension was rescinded in time for some of his biggest career hits. The most critical was a 2-out, game-winning double off St. Louis's Tony Mullane on September 6 before 12,000 home fans, giving the Athletics a 2-game lead with 14 to play. That week he made the cover of *Sporting Life.*

Despite his newly won local fame, Stricker delivered milk that winter and sold Christmas trees. Philadelphia sank lower in each of the next two seasons, and Stricker was released after a poor year in 1885. He signed with Scranton of the Pennsylvania State Association for 1886 but left early in the year for Atlanta of the Southern League. Stricker hit .243, as Atlanta won the pennant. He then spent four years with Cleveland, the first two as team captain. Stricker moved with Cleveland from the AA to the NL in 1889 and then jumped to the city's PL entry in 1890, but none of his Forest City clubs finished better than sixth.

During that period Stricker gained notoriety for baiting umpires and was named Cleveland's Brotherhood representative. After the PL disbanded, Arthur Irwin invited him to play with the new star-studded Boston AA franchise. Stricker batted eighth in the order, played every game, and Boston won the AA championship. When Boston was dissolved in the NL-AA merger, Stricker signed with St. Louis and replaced Jack Glasscock as player-manager in the team's eighth game of the season. After Stricker served 23 games in the dual role, Jack Crooks replaced him. On June 14 Stricker was traded to Pittsburgh for over-the-hill pitcher Pud Galvin but then was swapped again to Baltimore for pitcher Bill Terry before he could appear with Pittsburgh. Bad blood soon developed between Stricker and teammate Jocko Halligan, culminating the night of August 3, when Halligan broke Stricker's jaw during a poker game. An arrest warrant for Halligan was issued, but before it could be served manager Ned Hanlon suspended him and he never played in the majors again.

In 1893 Stricker signed to captain Washington NL but lost that title when the team was one game under .500 on June 15. Under manager Jim O'Rourke the Senators eventually sank to last place. On August 5, while losing a blowout in Philadelphia, Stricker tried to scare taunting Philly fans by firing a ball off the fence in front of their seats. The throw slipped and Stricker broke the jaw of 18-year-old spectator William Wright, who promptly sued. Unruffled, Stricker stole home scarcely two weeks later while fans howled as Chicago catcher Kit Kittridge was sweeping dirt off the plate with the umpire's broom. It was his last memorable moment in an always-eventful if seldom-feted career that produced the lowest OPS (.600) of any ML player that scored as many as 750 runs (790).

Stricker captained Providence of the Eastern League for the next two seasons, winning a pennant in 1895. He appeared with Pottsville of the Pennsylvania State League and Springfield, MA, of the Eastern League in 1896. A few appearances with the Philadelphia Athletics in the 1897 Atlantic League marked the end of his pro playing career. By the end of the century Stricker sporadically coached high school and college teams, usually on a volunteer basis, while continuing to play semipro ball with the Philadelphia Crescents. For much of his adult life he delivered milk with a horse and cart. Stricker died in Philadelphia at 78. (FV/DN)

Strief, George Andrew / "George" "Daisy"

B	T	HGT	WGT	G	AB	H	R	2B
R	R	5'7"	172	362	1360	281	145	50

3B	HR	RBI	BB	SO	SB	BA	SA	OBP
14	5	64	64	28	—	.207	.275	.242

B. 10/16/1856 Cincinnati, OH **D.** 4/1/1946
TEAMS: 79CleN 82PitA 83–84StLA 84KCU 84ChiPitU 84CleN 85PhiA
DEBUT: 5/1/1879 at Cleveland; played 2B and went 0-for-4 in a 15–4 loss to Providence's John M. Ward
FINALE: 9/8/1885 at Philadelphia; played 3B and went 1-for-4 in an 8–7 win over Cincinnati's George Pechiney
CAREER HIGHLIGHT: 6/25/1885 at Brooklyn; went 5-for-5 and collected a single-game-record 4 triples and a then single-game-record 14 total bases in a 21–14 loss to Brooklyn's Jack Harkins

George Strief joined the semipro Ludlow, KY, club in 1875 but jumped to nearby Covington, KY, when the Ludlows failed to pay him the $12 a week he had been promised. The following season he was earning $75 a month in Covington when he learned the team's park was about to be torn down and fled to the independent Columbus Buckeyes. Strief stayed with the Buckeyes in 1877 when the club affiliated with the International Association. Years later he described his state of mind at that moment to *TSN*: "I had just been married to a Cincinnati girl and 100 big cart wheels a month looked like a fortune then." But when Columbus left the IA prior to the 1878 season, putting Strief again on the move, he joined the IA Allegheny club long enough to hit .208 and then finished the season with the newly formed Cleveland Forest Citys.

Still a member of Cleveland when it joined the NL in 1879, he began the year at 2B and then went to CF to open a spot for Jack Glasscock. But a .174 BA relegated him to playing independent and minor league ball again in 1880–81. Strief's next ML opportunity came when the rebel AA formed in 1882. He played all but one game at 2B that season for Pittsburgh but again hit below .200 (.195). His .185 career BA at that point was the lowest yet of anyone with as many as 500 ML at-bats. Nevertheless, the St. Louis Browns hired him to play 2B in 1883 and then retained him when he hiked his BA to .225. But the Browns thought better of their choice midway through the 1884 season. Before the campaign ended, Strief played for four different franchises, setting a record for wearing the most different AA uniforms in a season.

He donned yet another set of threads in 1885 when he signed with the Philadelphia A's. Despite a record-setting day on June 25 and a .274 season overall that lifted his final career BA 10 points from .197 to .207, he was released in early September. Strief played several more seasons in the minors, finishing with Canton of the Tri-State League in 1890, and then made his off-season job with the Cleveland Fire Department a career. Meanwhile, he had been umpiring amateur and semipro games in Cleveland and doing well enough at it to earn an invitation from NL president Nick Young to finish the 1890 season as a regular NL umpire. Strief's first 12 games as a full-time official all came in Cleveland, but once he began calling balls and strikes in other NL cities he no longer found the job to his liking. Returning to Cleveland, he joined the local police force and later was a bailiff in the U.S. Federal Court in Cleveland for twenty years before retiring in 1943. Prior to his death at his Cleveland home at 89 from natural causes, he was the oldest living former member of a Forest City ML team. (DN)

Sweasy, Charles James (b. Swasey) / "Charlie"

B	T	HGT	WGT	G	AB	H	R	2B
R	R	5'9"	172	166	670	130	67	11

3B	HR	RBI	BB	SO	SB	BA	SA	OBP
2	0	39	17	30	3	.194	.216	.214

G	W	L	PCT	PENNANTS
19	4	15	.211	0

B. 11/2/1847 Newark, NJ **D.** 3/30/1908
TEAMS: 71OlyNA 72CleNA 73BosNA 74BalNA 74AtlNA (P/M)75RedsNA 76CinN 78ProN
DEBUT: 5/19/1871 at Chicago; played 2B and went 1-for-5 in a 9–7 loss to Chicago's George Zettlein
FINALE: 9/30/1878 at Providence; played 2B and went 1-for-3 in a 2–1 win over Boston's Tommy Bond

Charlie Sweasy came from the same New Jersey bastion as Andy Leonard. After playing with Irvington, NJ, for two years along with Leonard, Lip Pike and Rynie Wolters (and sharing the benefits of the club's notorious home-field advantage due to its menacing spectators and rough playing surface), he joined Leonard in 1868 on the Cincinnati Buckeyes. The following year Sweasy moved with Leonard and Dick Hurley to Harry Wright's new all-professional team, the Cincinnati Red Stockings, for a salary of $800. His initial NA appearance in 1871 enabled the Washington Olympics to field a lineup that included five members of the 1869 Red Stockings when he joined pitcher Asa Brainard, left fielder Leonard, catcher Doug Allison, and third baseman Fred Waterman. Owing to illness, Sweasy appeared in just 5 games with the Olympics despite being the team's captain, and even though he participated in each of the NA's five seasons as a major league, injuries and other mishaps allowed him to play regularly only in 1875 when he served as player-manager of the St. Louis Reds in all 19 games the club played against NA competition before dropping out of the loop.

Notwithstanding his uninspired play in the NA and the fact that he was best remembered in Cincinnati for a critical error in 1870 that helped the Brooklyn Atlantics to end the Red Stockings' record winning streak, the new Cincinnati NL franchise hired him to play 2B hoping he might still regain his early form. Instead Sweasy hit .204 and scored just 18 runs in 55 games in 1876. Worse yet, he played a poor 2B and by that point was deemed almost too heavy for the position. One scribe said this about his fielding, "In running to arrest a ball he had a curious fashion of suddenly turning and leaping in the air with a sidelong twist, such as may be seen among Arab vaulters." When Cincinnati declined Sweasy's services for 1877, he played for the New England League Rhode Islands. Upon joining the NL in 1878, Providence failed to find anyone better than Sweasy to man 2B and may have lost the pennant as a result. Captain Tom York not only stuck with the ex–Red Stocking all season at the keystone position but foolishly batted him second in the order during July, where his rally-killing at-bats cost the Grays several games. Sweasy rewarded York with a .175 BA and a .390 OPS.

After leaving the NL he played with independent teams, finishing with Attleboro, MA, in 1881 when his "rheumatism" grew too severe to continue. By 1888 he was making his living selling coffee from a handcart in Providence. Sweasy died at a city hospital in Newark in 1908; one obit listed the cause of death as consumption, another as heart disease. (DN/DB/EM)

Troy, John Joseph / "Dasher"

B	T	HGT	WGT	G	AB	H	R	2B
R	R	5'5"	154	292	1127	274	166	42

3B	HR	RBI	BB	SO	SB	BA	SA	OBP
20	4	51	41	52	—	.243	.327	.274

B. 5/8/1856 New York, NY **D.** 3/30/1938
TEAMS: 81–82DetN 82ProN 83NYN 84–85NYA
DEBUT: 8/23/1881 at Chicago; played 2B and went 2-for-5 in an 8–6 loss to Fred Goldsmith and Larry Corcoran
FINALE: 7/9/1885 at Pittsburgh; played 2B and went 1-for-4 in a 17–0 loss to Pittsburgh's Ed Morris

Dasher Troy was an irrepressible but reckless fielder with a reputation for throwing games (which was never proved). He nonetheless became the original Opening Day SS for the New York Giants franchise in 1883 and played 2B for the New York AA champions the following year. A Jersey City resident, Troy first appeared in 1876 with the semipro Staten Island Alaskas, named after a U.S. warship undergoing repairs in the Brooklyn Navy Yard. After the Alaskas disbanded in 1877 following the death of the club's founder and president, Hugh Brady, Troy played 2B with the independent Jersey City Browns for two years. In 1880 he went west and joined unaffiliated Dubuque, IA, until that team folded in August.

Troy then returned east to Billy Barnie's Eastern Championship Association Brooklyn Atlantics. Barnie's team played some dozen games for a baseball-starved New York public before he moved them to Jersey City. During this period many teams came and went in New York and players took advantage of the instability. Legend has it that pitcher Jack Lynch once used a fake name to help a small-time New York team win 1 game, only to have Troy homer off him, using a fake name for the opposition. In this mix, Troy's next pro-league experience came with the New York team of the shaky ECA, which had to compete with the popular New York Metropolitans. Around this time he earned the nickname "Dasher" for the way he covered so much ground defensively with his lithe 5'5" frame.

On August 23, 1881, Detroit manager Frank Bancroft borrowed Troy from Albany of the ECA, where he had since moved, for a NL game when Joe Gerhardt had to attend his father's funeral. Troy hung on for eleven appearances with a good BA but poor defense. He went unreserved after the season and signed with the Philadelphia Athletics of the upstart AA. But when Gerhardt held out in 1882 and Bancroft contacted Troy with a better offer than Philadelphia's, Troy signed with Detroit just as Sam Wise, who had a contract with Cincinnati, signed with Boston. The AA expelled Troy and Wise, and their appearance with NL teams became the source of bitter conflict between the rival leagues. Initially, Troy echoed Wise's excuse that he did not know the AA would require him to play ball on Sundays. Later he was quoted as saying he did it "for the money."

Troy started at 2B for Detroit and was embroiled in a tight pennant race until July 11, 1882. That day, with Detroit and Chicago tied for first, Chicago's George Gore spiked Troy. His season thought to be over, Bancroft released him, giving him a month's extra pay for his trouble. However, in September Troy joined Harry Wright's Providence Grays. The two contrasting types clashed almost immediately. On September 2, Troy, playing 3B, shoved Dan Brouthers while Brouthers was making the turn at the corner, and umpire Billy McLean called Brouthers out for missing the bag. The straitlaced Wright made a rare on-field appearance to protest a call that had gone in favor of his team until it was reversed.

Freed of the moralistic Wright, Troy signed with the newly formed New York NL franchise and enjoyed his first full ML season, although he made 5 errors in the franchise's inaugural game. Management shifted him to the New York AA team for 1884 and he helped the freewheeling Mets win the pennant. Troy appeared in the 1884 World's Series, considered the first in baseball history, but when he did not show up for the final game, Tom Forster, who lived in Brooklyn, had to fill in.

Troy was having a poor year in 1885 when the Mets released him to Jersey City of the Eastern League in June and then reclaimed him when Jersey City disbanded. Released again in August, Troy finished the year with Poughkeepsie of the New York State League. After spending 1887 with Manchester of the New England League, he signed with his namesake team, Troy of the International Association, for 1888. In late July, Troy argued balls and strikes with umpire Jerry Sullivan, followed him under the grandstand after the game, and beat him up. Team Troy summarily released player Troy.

With his weight now said to be near 200 pounds, Troy managed a bar under the RF stand at the Polo Grounds in 1892—visible from the playing field—and owned the peanut concession there after the bar was shut down. On June 15, 1894, he assaulted a park ticket-taker who refused to let two of his friends in for free, ending any hope he had of winning the heart of the club's future owner, the penurious Andrew Freedman.

In 1905, observing with distaste with the way "Little Ball" had taken over in the Deadball Era, Troy told New York sportswriter Sam Crane, "To hades with all this buntation business; hop 'em off their shins." Troy's son, John, still a schoolboy then, later played SS in the minors until 1915, by which time the "Dasher" was penning a monthly column for *Baseball Magazine.* At any rate, the column appeared under his name, and no one at that time appeared to dispute its source. But in 1892 Frank Bancroft had told *TSN* that Troy couldn't read a menu card when he had played under Bancroft at Detroit and was not only completely illiterate but "very rough" in the social graces. Troy died of cancer in 1938 at his home in Ozone Park, NY, and left behind a widow and three children. (DN/FV)

Truby, Harry Garvin / "Harry" "Bird Eye"

B	T	HGT	WGT	G	AB	H	R	2B
?	R	5'11"	185	70	260	73	31	5

3B	HR	RBI	BB	SO	SB	BA	SA	OBP
2	2	50	18	16	12	.281	.338	.342

B. 5/12/1870 Ironton, OH **D.** 3/21/1953
TEAMS: 95–96ChiN 96PitN
DEBUT: 8/21/1895 at Baltimore; played 2B and went 0-for-4 in a 4–2 loss to Baltimore's Bill Hoffer
FINALE: 7/14/1896 at Pittsburgh; played 2B and went 1-for-2 in a 7–0 win over Boston's Ted Lewis

Despite growing up in Ironton, OH, a baseball hotbed in the mid-1880s, Harry Truby garnered his first pro experience in 1888 with Rockford, IL, of the Central Interstate League. Precocious, he was already playing in the Texas League at 19, but his career hit a snag the following year when the loop president ruled that he had signed with both Austin and Fort Worth, causing a forfeit on Opening Day after he was declared ineligible even as he took the field, and Fort Worth refused to furnish a second baseman in his stead. Truby finished the season with independent Houghton, MI, where teammate Moxie Hengel, fed up with his ego trips, sent him a fake telegram, purportedly from Cap Anson, offering him $250 a month to play for Chicago. Truby wired back that he wanted $350 and bragged to everyone in town of the telegram before Hengel took the wind out of his sails by revealing the gag.

In the spring of 1891, Truby, though not formally blacklisted, was so undesirable that he was without a job until late April. He signed finally with Oconto, WI, and redeemed himself by playing without incident in the lowly Wisconsin State League. In 1892 he returned to Rockford, now in the Illinois-Indiana League. By 1894 Truby was in his second season in Southern League but was sick when the loop folded in July and was unable to play elsewhere until late that season when he ran quickly through three different teams in the Virginia League. He began 1895 in the Western League but was back in the Southern League with Nashville when Chicago acquired him in August.

Truby arrived in the NL with a reputation for being hit by pitches. He claimed his secret to avoiding injury was to tighten his muscles and make sure a ball never hit him squarely but always glanced off his hip or leg. Within days after joining Chicago, he learned that he would have to be more judicious in the majors, as pitchers like Amos Rusie and Pink Hawley threw at him purposely, knowing he would try to be hit anyway. But Truby still had not learned to harness his ego. After finishing his rookie season with a .326 BA, he boasted that he would have led Chicago in batting if the season had run two weeks longer, as he was climbing at the end and Bill Lange, the actual leader, was "going just the other way."

In 1896 Truby opened the season at 2B and was hitting with power when Chicago picked up popular ex-Windy City star Fred Pfeffer, sending him to the bench. Purchased by Pittsburgh on July 4 to fill in for disabled Lou Bierbauer, he injured his leg and was traded eleven days later to Albany of the Eastern League for Dick Padden. That November, Pittsburgh included him in a trade with Baltimore, which quickly released him, thereupon ending the playing phase of his ML career. Brief though the elite part of it was, Truby's overall pro playing experience lasted more than twenty years, concluding in the 1907 Class D Kansas State League. While with Augusta of the Sally League three years earlier, he had made headlines throughout baseballdom when he started a riot in a game with Columbia by slugging an umpire who called him a vile name during an argument.

Ironically, upon playing his last pro game, Truby became an umpire, working first in the Virginia League. Weighing close to 200 pounds by then and skilled at the manly arts, he seemed to have found a more lasting niche in the majors when he was made a regular NL arbiter for 1909. But as his ML playing career had lasted just 70 games, his umpiring career was even shorter. By the end of June 1909 Truby was gone from the NL umpiring ranks, having worked only 58 games. His shortcoming seemingly was that he was weak on balls and strikes, as he was never again assigned to work the plate after a contentious afternoon with John McGraw on May 12. Truby was a widower when he died of heart failure in Ironton. (DN/DB)

Wood, James Leon / "Jimmy"

B	T	HGT	WGT	G	AB	H	R	2B
?	R	5'8½"	150	102	488	162	162	33

3B	HR	RBI	BB	SO	SB	BA	SA	OBP
12	3	82	25	6	28	.333	.467	.365

G	W	L	PCT	PENNANTS
154	76	76	.500	0

B. 12/1/1843 Quebec, Canada **D.** 11/30/1927
TEAMS: (P/M)71ChiNA (P/M)72TroNA (P/M)72EckNA 73PhiNA (P/M)74–75ChiNA
DEBUT: 5/8/1871 at Chicago; played 2B and went 2-for-4 in a 14–12 win over Cleveland's Al Pratt
FINALE: 11/1/2873 at Brooklyn; played 2B and went 1-for-4 in a 12–1 loss to Brooklyn's Jim Britt

Jimmy Wood was one of the most important figures in baseball's fitful transition from amateurism to professionalism. But his career came to an abrupt end when his leg had to be amputated, and until very recently when and where he died remained unknown.

Wood was born to British immigrants. There is contradictory evidence about the place of his birth, but on most censuses it was listed as Canada. If these are correct, then Wood was the first Canadian-born major leaguer. In any event, the family soon moved to Brooklyn, allowing Wood to be a contemporary of such legends as Jim Creighton, Asa Brainard, Charley Smith, Joe Start, and Bob Ferguson. He soon took his place among them, playing for the junior Harlem Club in 1858–59 and then graduating to the Eckfords of Brooklyn in 1860. The Eckfords formed on July 17, 1855, and played their home matches in Greenpoint. It took them several years to emerge as a top club, but when they finally made the step in 1860, Wood quickly assumed a key role. He took over as the Eckfords' second baseman in 1861, and the club captured back-to-back national championships in 1862–63, at one point winning 20 straight matches, the longest such streak to that point. The 1863 campaign was especially glorious, as the Eckfords not only went undefeated but Wood averaged 3.5 runs scored per game—the best mark on any of the clubs that kept records. Yet he played much of the season with a heavy heart. His only brother, Rufus, had enlisted in the Union Army and was sent to Louisiana, where he was slain at the battle of Port Hudson. Rufus Wood was only 25 when he died on June 26, 1863, leaving behind a young widow named Sarah.

Wood remained with the Eckfords in 1864 but left at the season's end and disappeared from the baseball scene. His next three years are somewhat mysterious, but we know that he married and moved to Ohio, where he began a family. His new bride was named Sarah, and it seems likely that she was his brother's widow. Wood was back in Brooklyn by 1868 and rejoined the Eckfords, captaining the club for the next two seasons as baseball made a fitful change from increasingly nominal amateurism to rampant professionalism. During these years, Wood came into his prime, covering as much ground "as three ordinary players," and in 1869 the Eckfords returned to national prominence with a 47-8 record, but that mark paled beside the undefeated campaign of the Cincinnati Red Stockings.

As a result, when Chicago formed a professional club that December to dethrone the Red Stockings and offered Wood the captaincy, he accepted the challenge. Chicago was prepared to offer unprecedented sums—Wood himself signed for a princely $2,500. But even so, it was no easy task, since most of the game's stars were already signed for the 1870 season. Scrambling to form a team from players were still available, Wood scooped up prospects from Brooklyn and New York City and took chances on some players with shady reputations, such as Ed Duffy and William Craver. In addition, as he later explained, "In selecting my players it was more for their batting ability than anything else, knowing full well that my only hope to conquer the Reds was to outbat them, as their fielding was as near perfection as could be."

For a while, it looked as though his plan would fail. Other than Wood, the White Stockings did not feature a single established star. Things hit bottom when Chicago suffered a humiliating 9–0 loss to the New York Mutuals—the first time that a well-known club had ever played an entire game without scoring a run. Rumors of internal dissension at that point began to circulate, and Wood's job was said to be in danger. Instead it was Craver who was dismissed from the team, and new reinforcements were brought in. Slowly, the White

Stockings improved. The season culminated with a long winning streak and 2 dramatic wins over the Red Stockings, which Wood naturally viewed as sweet redemption. As he later said with pride, "It was our batting on those two occasions that defeated the greatest ball team of the early days and caused their disbandment that year." The 1870 campaign ended with most in agreement that the White Stockings were the strongest team at season's end, although the overall 1870 professional champion is still the subject of debate.

The impressive performance earned Wood a reputation as a captain with "no superior in the country," and his services were in demand throughout the five-year run of the National Association. In the circuit's inaugural 1871 season he again led Chicago and had the club in the thick of the pennant race until the Great Chicago Fire devastated the city and the team. Chicago did not field a pro club for the next two seasons, so Wood split 1872 between Troy and Brooklyn. In 1873 a new club in Philadelphia that had been assembled to rival the Athletics signed him. The upstarts got off to a 27-3 start and held a sizable lead in the pennant race for much of the year. But then word came that Chicago would again field a club in 1874 and had signed most of the club's players. The affected players soon began to show little interest in their work, and the remainder of the season was marred by suspiciously bad performances, several by Wood. The captain, although a likeable spark plug, had developed a tendency to fly off the handle, especially in key games. According to writer William Ryczek, erratic leaders like him too often "led teams which mirrored their own tendencies toward self-destruction and uneven play."

Wood nonetheless was signed to again serve as Chicago's player-manager, but an accidental self-inflicted knife wound that led to an abscess in his leg delayed his return. Eventually came the sad news that the leg would have to be amputated, ending Wood's playing days. He served as the club's nonplaying manager for the remainder of the season and again in 1875 but produced mediocre results. Moreover, few clubs could afford the luxuries of a nonplaying manager, so he was not rehired after 1875. Wood thus reached his 33rd birthday as a one-legged man who had left behind the profession he had followed since late adolescence. A lesser man might have given way to self-pity or at the very least led an unadventurous life thereafter. Wood did neither. He remained in Chicago for several years, running a saloon and raising his children. During the 1880s his daughter Carrie married businessman William Chase Temple—the originator of the Temple Cup—and Wood and his family moved to Florida. But Wood never stayed in one place very long, and over the next few decades, he managed briefly in the minors, ran a successful bar in Chicago with Ed Williamson, and spent time in Pittsburgh, New York, and New Orleans.

Wood outlived his wife and both of their children, but even in old age the one-legged former star remained extraordinarily active. He spent much of his time in New Orleans, but continued to occasionally surface in Chicago and New York and to also spend time in Florida with his granddaughter, who had kept the family tradition alive by marrying major league pitcher Del Mason. In 1928, Wood's eyesight was failing and he traveled to California for cataract surgery. But he fell ill while there and died in San Francisco on November 20, one day short of his 85th birthday. Sadly, by then, one of the game's early greats had been entirely forgotten by baseball, and it was not until quite recently that Peter Morris was able to determine when and where Wood died. (PM/DN/EM)

5 | THE THIRD BASEMEN

5. Denny Lyons's career was probably too uneven to merit Hall of Fame consideration, but when Lyons was on his game he may have been the best third baseman ever, prior to the appearance of Eddie Mathews.

Alberts, Augustus Peter / "Gus"

B	T	HGT	WGT	G	AB	H	R	2B
R	R	5'6½"	180	120	426	84	62	10

3B	HR	RBI	BB	SO	SB	BA	SA	OBP
6	1	50	52	5	27	.197	.256	.298

B. 9/?/1860 Reading, PA **D.** 5/7/1912
TEAMS: 84PitA 84WasU 88CleA 91MilA
DEBUT: 5/1/1884 at Pittsburgh; played SS and went 1-for-3 in a 9–2 loss to Philadelphia's Al Atkinson
FINALE: 9/22/1891 at Milwaukee; played 3B and went 1-for-2 in a 5–3 loss to Boston's Cinders O'Brien

In 1882 Gus Alberts served as independent Reading's SS and lead-off hitter. After occupying the same role with the Interstate Association Wilmington Quicksteps the following year, he was offered $1,200 by Pittsburgh AA for 1884. Alberts was injured in only his second game with the Allegheny club, however, and lost his job to fellow rookie Bill White. He joined Washington UA for a short spell and then finished the season with Allentown of the Eastern League. Alberts returned to the majors in 1888 after spending two seasons with Toronto of the International Association. He was expected to replace Ed McKean as Cleveland's SS, allowing McKean to move to CF, but was soon switched to 3B and proved inadequate at that task as well.

That off-season, Cleveland traded Alberts to Milwaukee as part of the price for outfielder Jimmy McAleer, but he refused to join the Western Association club unless he was paid better than minor league wages. It took Alberts considerable finagling—the trade rules in 1888–89 were still riddled with vagaries and loopholes—but eventually he got what he wanted and spent the next three seasons in Milwaukee, including the latter portion of 1891 when the Wisconsin city replaced Cincinnati in the AA. In October 1891, despite hitting just .098 during the club's ML sojourn, he was voted the most popular Milwaukee player in a contest held by the *Evening Wisconsin.* At the same time Alberts was receiving the *Evening Wisconsin* gold medal for the honor, the paper reported that he was up for release.

That winter Alberts worked in Milwaukee handling the lever of an electric tramcar. He remained in that city for the next few years while playing for a series of minor league teams. By 1894 he was with the Milwaukee Saints semipro nine, but he returned to pro ball the following year as player, manager, and part owner of the St. Joseph club in the Western League. His prominence in St. Joseph was short-lived. The December 14, 1895, *TSN* reported that Alberts had been reduced to handling the St. Joseph club's scorecard and cushion concession for 1896. In the first decade of the twentieth century Alberts managed for three years in the lower minor leagues, finishing in 1908 with Bartlesville of the Oklahoma-Kansas League. He died at Idaho Springs, CO, in 1912 of pneumonia while working as a blacksmith. (DN)

Alvord, William Crawford / "Billy" "Uncle Bill"

B	T	HGT	WGT	G	AB	H	R	2B
?	?	5'10"	187	265	1069	270	129	31

3B	HR	RBI	BB	SO	SB	BA	SA	OBP
30	3	109	44	83	27	.253	.346	.283

B. 8/10/1863 St. Louis, MO **D.** 4/7/1927
TEAMS: 85StLN 89KCA 90TolA 91CleN 91WasA 93CleN
DEBUT: 4/30/1885 at St. Louis; played 3B and went 0-for-2 in 3–2 win over Chicago's Larry Corcoran
FINALE: 7/8/1893 at Cleveland; replaced Ed McFarland at 3B and went 0-for-1 in a 9–7 loss to Baltimore's Bill Hawke

After coming of age on the St. Louis sandlots, Billy Alvord played for semipro Vincennes, MO, in 1883. He began 1884 with the St. Louis Browns' reserves and joined the independent Omaha Union Pacifics after the reserves disbanded. Alvord signed with Henry Lucas's St. Louis Maroons when Lucas finessed his way into the National League in 1885 but lasted just 2 games before being released to Milwaukee of the Western League.

By 1887 Alvord was with Western League powerhouse Topeka. That summer he grew his hair so long that he had to put it in a braid to secure it under his nightcap. Alvord may have been attempting to emulate Sampson, as his hitting, previously his weakness, zoomed to a height where he was courted by New York NL after Topeka's season ended in September. Alvord refused the Giants' offer, however, and spent the winter in St. Louis working out with Tom Dolan. By the following spring *TSN* reported that he had lost so much weight "his friends did not recognize him."

In 1888 and part of 1889 Alvord played for Sacramento in the California League along with Harry Dooms and Joe Quest, but the team was in disarray and all three were charged with breach of contract when they fled elsewhere. Alvord went back east to play with Toledo of the International Association until he was traded to Kansas City AA toward the end of the 1889 season for $1,000 plus Sam Barkley. When his wife died in childbirth in early October he left the team to bury her and then returned to the Cowboys in time to play in KC's final AA game at Louisville on October 14, only to learn a few days later that his new baby was also dying.

In 1890 Alvord played his initial full season in the majors when KC returned him to Toledo for $2,000. For the first time, ML observers had ample opportunity to assess his talents. The verdict was mixed. In the minors, where he had played mostly on skin diamonds, Alvord had been viewed as a good third baseman, but in ML parks, with grass infields, he had trouble with tricky hops. Years later, one of his Toledo teammates, pitcher Fred Smith, recalled him as being great if he got a hit in his first at-bat, but if he made out he was best removed from the game then and there. In late August 1890 Alvord led Toledo with a .309 BA but sagged badly in the final weeks of the season to finish at .273.

On October 13, 1890, Cleveland NL paid Toledo $500 for Alvord. That winter he settled in the Forest City with his second wife, Isabel. The couple bought a house, where they raised chickens, but his desire to get off to a good start with his new team went for naught when Cleveland signed second baseman Cupid Childs, scotching manager Bob Leadley's plan to move Pat Tebeau to 2B in order to make room for Alvord at 3B. Already the odd man out, Alvord's troubles were compounded when both he and his wife were critically ill over the winter, making it difficult for him to get into shape for the coming season. Nevertheless, Alvord performed well initially with the Spiders, hitting .288 in 17 games while Tebeau was injured, but was sold to Washington for some $500 after he put up a bad game against Philadelphia. In July, when St. Louis visited the nation's capital, Browns manager Charlie Comiskey offered to trade unruly third baseman Denny Lyons for Alvord, but Senators owner J. Earle Wagner foolishly refused. Little more than a month later, Alvord lost his 3B job to Gil Hatfield and was left behind when the team began its last extended road trip of the season.

Alvord played with Rochester of the Eastern League in 1892 and then announced that he was quitting the game to become a salesman for a Louisville tobacco firm that featured such brands as Kickapoo and Pick'n Shovel. But when Pat Tebeau, now the Cleveland manager, asked him to fill in for Tebeau himself, who had been injured in early July, he agreed. After 3 games as Tebeau's replacement, Alvord went back to selling tobacco and by the end of 1893 was a representative for Lorillard's House in Cleveland. He made another brief comeback in 1894 with Franklin, PA, of the Iron & Oil League but within a few months was living in Toledo and selling tobacco again. Alvord deemed himself a "cigar manufacturing magnate" three years later and called his top selling product "Little Willie."

In 1901 Alvord again had a yen for the diamond and became an umpire, joining Bob Caruthers on the Western League's officiating crew. By 1907 he had resumed his trade as a cigar salesman and was living in Buffalo with his second wife and daughter Florence. In 1909 his wife appeared in the Buffalo city directory as a widow, but actually Alvord had abandoned her and moved to Michigan after marrying another woman. Later he relocated to St. Petersburg, FL, where he died in 1927. (DN/PM/DB)

Battin, Joseph V. / "Joe"

B	T	HGT	WGT	G	AB	H	R	2B
R	R	5'10"	169	480	1953	439	228	51

3B	HR	RBI	BB	SO	SB	BA	SA	OBP
25	3	143	40	36	26	.225	.281	.241

G	IP	H	GS	CG	BB
3	7.2	12	0	0	2

SO	SH	W	L	PCT	ERA
1	0	0	0	—	3.52

G	W	L	PCT	PENNANTS
32	9	23	.281	0

B. 11/11/1851 Philadelphia, PA **D.** 12/10/1937
TEAMS: 71CleNA 73–74AthNA 75StLNA 76–77StLN (P/M)82PitA (P/M)83–84PitA (P/M)84PitUA 84BalU 90SyrA
DEBUT: 8/11/1871 at Fort Wayne; played RF and went 0-for-4 in a 15–3 loss to Fort Wayne's Bobby Mathews

FINALE: 5/28/1890 at Syracuse; played 3B and went 0-for-3 in a 5–0 loss to Louisville's Scott Stratton

Joe Battin was the last performer from the NA's inaugural season to see action in the American Association when he took the field for Syracuse in 1890. His .521 career OPS explains how he came to be the subject of a running joke that he acquired his surname because he never did "any battin." Along with being a notoriously inept hitter, Battin also bore an unsavory reputation, particularly early in his career. Twice suspected of dumping games—in 1874 with the Athletics and again in 1877 with St. Louis—he never again appeared in the NL after the latter episode, which centered around a 4–3 loss to Chicago on August 24 when a coterie of gamblers afterward named him and teammate Joe Blong as willing accomplices in orchestrating St. Louis's defeat. Though never officially expelled, Battin did not return to the majors until the AA formed in 1882 and he was invited to join the Pittsburgh entry.

The light-hitting third baseman learned the game in the late 1860s with the amateur Philadelphia Expert club, which also produced Chick Fulmer and Orator Shaffer, before joining Cleveland NA at age 19. After appearing in just 1 game with the Forest Citys, he played with the amateur Roth club of Philadelphia in 1872 and independent Easton, PA, the following year. A 3-for-5 day in a 1-game test with the 1873 Athletics earned him a contract with the club for 1874. Battin's stay with the A's was brief after Mike McGeary reportedly accused him of throwing a game against New York and the third baseman pulled a knife on his accuser. The two allegedly never spoke again, and Battin headed for St. Louis the following year. He remained with St. Louis in 1876 after it joined the fledgling NL and hit .300 for the only time in his career. The next season, after he dropped to .199 and fell under suspicion of rigging games, seemed almost certain to be his big-league coda, especially when he passed the age of 30 still in the minors.

From 1878–82, Battin played with a number of teams including Utica, where he stopped long enough to marry a woman from there, followed by stints with the National Association Washington Nationals and Philadelphia of the Eastern Championship Association before joining Pittsburgh. After hitting .211, .214 and .177 in successive seasons with the Alleghenys, no one in the Smoke City wept when he was released to the Pittsburgh UA club in 1884. Battin finished the season with a composite .164 BA for his work in both leagues and a .281 winning percentage for the 32 games he served as a pilot.

Returning to the minors, he continued his dreary hitting. In 1888 Battin stroked a nifty .196 for Syracuse with a .267 SA but was retained by the International Association pennant winner, which evidently felt it was strong enough in other areas to carry his anemic bat. When Battin encored with a .167 BA for Syracuse in 1889, he still was not cut, perhaps because he led the loop in fielding, and instead was rewarded with the Stars' 3B slot on their inaugural day as members of the AA in 1890.

Battin umpired in the NL for part of the following season and saw spot playing duty in the minors until 1894 before settling into a life as a bricklayer. When he died of pneumonia in Akron, OH, in 1937, his obit in the *Chicago Tribune* maintained that he had been the highest-salaried player in the game at one time, making $700 a month, which was possible but highly unlikely. The obit also attributed Connie Mack's discovery to him, claiming he had recommended Mack to Washington. It was news to Mack. (DN/DB)

Bradley, William Joseph / "Bill"

B	T	HGT	WGT	G	AB	H	R	2B
R	R	6'0"	185	157	573	165	89	27

3B	HR	RBI	BB	SO	SB	BA	SA	OBP
9	7	67	39	—	18	.288	.403	.341

B. 2/13/1878 Cleveland, OH **D.** 3/11/1954
TEAMS: 99–00ChiN 01–10CleAL (P/M)14BroF 15KCF
DEBUT: 8/26/1899 at Chicago; played SS and went 1-for-4 in a 10–6 loss to Brooklyn's Doc McJames
FINALE: 9/28/1915 at Kansas City; played 3B in a 3–2 win over Baltimore's George LeClair

Bill Bradley graduated from Cleveland's semipro Euclid Beach Park League to Zanesville of the Interstate League in 1897. He finished 1898 with Auburn and remained with the New York State League team in 1899 until summoned to Chicago. Because of his great range, he was tried at SS but made 3 errors in his first game there and was soon moved to 3B, where he swiftly established himself as the best hot-corner operative in the game from

1900–1905. Held by broken right wrist to just 82 games in 1906, Bradley, who had jumped to Cleveland in 1901, not only probably cost the Naps the pennant that year with his long absence but also was never the same player. In his final four years with Cleveland he hit just .218, the lowest BA of any AL position player (catchers excluded) during that span with a minimum of 1,000 PAs.

Dropped by the Naps after the 1910 season, Bradley played in the minors and then was a player-manager in the Federal League in 1900–05. He later scouted for Cleveland for some twenty-five years and was a lifelong resident of the Ohio metropolis until his death from pneumonia in 1954. Considered by many to have been Cleveland's best third baseman prior to Al Rosen, Bradley shares the credit with Jimmy Collins for perfecting the barehanded scoop and throw on bunts up the 3B line, and his .955 FA in 1904 stood as an AL record until 1914, when it was broken by his former Cleveland teammate, Terry Turner (.963). (DN)

Burns, Thomas Everett / "Tom" "Burnsie"

B	T	HGT	WGT	G	AB	H	R	2B
R	R	5'7"	152	1251	4920	1307	722	236

3B	HR	RBI	BB	SO	SB	BA	SA	OBP
69	39	683	270	454	162	.266	.365	.305

G	IP	H	GS	CG	BB
1	1.1	2	0	0	2

SO	SH	W	L	PCT	ERA
1	0	0	0	—	0.00

G	W	L	PCT	PENNANTS
364	187	170	.524	0

B. 3/30/1857 Honesdale, PA **D.** 3/19/1902
TEAMS: 80–91ChiN (P/M)92PitN (M)98–99ChiN
DEBUT: 5/1/1880 at Cincinnati; played SS and went 0-for-4 in a 4–3 win over Cincinnati's Will White
FINALE: 7/22/1892 at Washington; pinch hit unsuccessfully for pitcher Mark Baldwin in the bottom of the ninth inning of a 12–1 loss to Washington's Frank Killen and Jesse Duryea
CAREER HIGHLIGHT: 9/6/1883 at Chicago; collected a one-inning record 3 hits (since tied) against Detroit's Stump Wiedman and Dick Burns with a home run and 2 doubles as Chicago scored a record 18 runs in the seventh frame in cruising to a 26–6 win

Tom Burns grew up in the New Britain, CT, area and by 1872 was serving as the bat boy for the NA Mansfields when they played on their home grounds in Middletown, CT. When the Mansfields were on the road or had the day off, he performed with the amateur Arctics and Aetnas. In 1874, Burns graduated to the reorganized Middletown independent club. His first fully professional experience came two years later as a member of League Alliance Auburn, NY. By the end of the season, however, he had also played with Providence and Lynn, MA. A pitcher and catcher at the time, Burns did not discover that he could also play 3B until an injury to a Lynn teammate forced him to substitute there.

By 1879 Burns had advanced to Albany of the National Association and was making $15 a week when he received a stupendous offer from Chicago of $900 for the coming season. In the spring of 1880 he took over the White Stockings' SS post and by 1883, after second baseman Fred Pfeffer joined the club, was a member of the club's famous "stonewall infield" that played together as a unit for a record seven seasons. Capable at every infield position except 1B, Burns became exclusively a third baseman in 1885 after switching positions with Ned Williamson. The change was made to take advantage of his revolutionary skills at the hot corner. Burns was a master of the "hunch play." When a runner at 3B would take a lead toward home, Burns would signal catcher Mike Kelly and then take up a position blocking the baseline so that when the runner saw Kelly ready himself for a pick-off throw and tried to scamper back to the bag, Burns would give him the hip, spinning him to the ground where he could easily be tagged out once Burns received Kelly's throw. Burns also performed the first documented "bluff throw" to 1B with a runner on 3B to catch the runner leaning toward the plate in an 1885 game against New York when he and pitcher John Clarkson worked it on John M. Ward, who liked to edge off 3B on a pick-off throw across the diamond in case it was dropped.

But while regarded as one of the more heady players of his day, Burns was also prone to memorable gaffes. On June 7, 1886, against the New York Giants, with the score tied 7–7 in the top of the ninth with 2 out, 2 on base, and 3 runs already home, Burns rifled a pitch to deep center to score both runners but failed to run to 1B, thereupon negating the potential winning runs because he been under the mistaken impression that Chicago had last raps. After the Giants threw him out at 1B, the game ended in tie. Burns's blunder demonstrates that it was a prevailing custom as long as twenty-two years before the Merkle incident for a player not always to run to 1B or touch the next base as required by rule when a walk-off winning run scored.

Burns remained a defensive force throughout the 1880s but had begun to slip at the plate by the end of the decade. After three straight subpar years he revived in 1890 to score 86 runs and collect 86 RBI when PL raids diluted the pitching depth in the NL. In 1891, with Chicago in flag contention for the first time since 1886, Burns lost his job to Bill Dahlen, turning him against player-manager Cap Anson to the extent that he refused to play a September game at SS in place of Jimmy Cooney because he "was tired of being used" as only a sub. In the closing days of a tight pennant race, he was returned to 3B and Dahlen was sent to the outfield, an admission in his eyes that Anson thought him the better man at third under pressure.

By the fall of 1891, Burns, Fred Pfeffer, and Jimmy Ryan all despised Anson and were reported to be toast in Chicago. When Burns refused to sign with the Colts even after the 1892 season was under way, he was sold in May to Pittsburgh, where he was named player-manager. He had scarcely taken the job when *TSN* predicted he would fail because he was patterned after Anson as one "of the gruffest and most uncompromising" men in game and was way too rigid a disciplinarian to succeed with the laid-back Pittsburgh team. The prophecy was fulfilled when Burns was fired just 60 games into the season (although the following January a Chicago court awarded him $1,500 after he sued the Pirates for firing him allegedly for violating club rules and neglect of duty, which he successfully proved was untrue, entitling him to the unpaid amount on his contract with the club). He finished 1892 as an NL umpire and then managed Springfield, MA, of the Eastern League for the next five years.

When Anson was canned after the 1897 season, Burns was awarded Chicago manager's vacancy and riskily appointed Dahlen, a notorious foe of discipline and Anson, as team captain. Burns's managerial philosophy was also a sharp contrast to Anson's hands-on style; he was a disbeliever in signs, relying on a runner to know when to steal, and in general tried to keep the game simple. When Dahlen was a failure as captain, Burns lost the respect of many of his players when he allowed the front office to install Bill Everitt as the team leader over his own choice of Jimmy Ryan. Even though he guided the club to successive first-division finishes, he was fired after the 1899 season.

Burns returned to Springfield as manager in 1900 and remained in, Eastern League the following year when the Springfield franchise folded, first umpiring and then managing Buffalo for part of the season. Although he had none of the traditional player vices, he was an avid poker player. When he began to lose heavily at the tables in 1901, he sought another change of venue. With the help of Eastern League president Pat Powers, Burns lined up the Jersey City manager's job for 1902. Just a few weeks later, while visiting Powers at his home in Jersey City, he was found dead in bed from a heart attack. (DN)

Buttery, Frank / "Frank"

B	T	HGT	WGT	G	AB	H	R	2B
?	?	?	?	18	93	24	19	0

3B	HR	RBI	BB	SO	SB	BA	SA	OBP
0	0	8	0	2	0	.258	.258	.258

G	IP	H	GS	CG	BB
7	59	93	5	5	2

SO	SH	W	L	PCT	ERA
0	0	3	2	.600	4.42

B. 5/13/1851 Silvermine, CT **D.** 12/16/1902
TEAMS: 72ManNA
DEBUT: 4/26/1872 at Troy; played 3B and went 0-for-4 in a 10–0 loss to Troy's George Zettlein
FINALE: 7/27/1872 at Middletown; played RF and went 1-for-4 in a 26–9 loss to New York's Candy Cummings

While pitching on town teams in Connecticut, Frank Buttery had as batterymates future MLer and sportswriter Tim Murnane and HOFer Jim O'Rourke. In 1871 Buttery and O'Rourke played for the state champion Stratford Osceolas, and when the Mansfields of Middletown upgraded their team for entry into the NA in 1872, they hired the Osceolas pair as their change battery.

Buttery began the season at 3B and then played

RF while sharing the Mansfields pitching load with Cy Bentley. He garnered the club's first win on May 2 when he beat the Brooklyn Atlantics 8–2, but his 3-2 overall record for a team that went 5-19 is deceptive. Buttery probably only got the May 2 start because the Atlantics were a lamentably weak team, and in both his other wins the Mansfields scored over 25 runs, while he was tattooed for 78 runs in just 59 innings.

As a hitter Buttery holds an interesting ML record. He has the most career at-bats of anyone who was primarily a position player whose BA, OBP, and SA are identical. When Asa Brainard joined the team at the start of August, Buttery disappeared from the lineup. He appears never again to have played professionally. A native of Silvermine, a district straddling several Connecticut cities, he belonged to a family that owned a sawmill in operation since the seventeenth century. In the 1870s Buttery worked at the mill before later opening a general store in Silvermine. He died in Norwalk at 51 of erysipelas. (DN/DB)

Carpenter, Warren William / "Hick"

B	T	HGT	WGT	G	AB	H	R	2B
R	L	5'11"	186	1118	4637	1202	720	142

3B	HR	RBI	BB	SO	SB	BA	SA	OBP
47	18	543	112	91	158	.259	.322	.281

B. 8/16/1855 Grafton, MA **D.** 4/18/1937
TEAMS: 79SyrN 80CinN 81WorN 82–89CinA 92StLN
DEBUT: 5/1/1879 at Chicago; played RF and went 2-for-4 in a 4–3 loss to Chicago's Terry Larkin
FINALE: 7/31/1892 at Cincinnati; played 3B and went 1-for-3 in a 6–0 loss to Cincinnati's Jesse Duryea
CAREER HIGHLIGHT: 9/12/1883 at Cincinnati; went 6-for-7 and joined John Reilley as the first pair of teammates each to get 6 hits in the same game in a 27–5 win over Pittsburgh's Jack Neagle

Hick Carpenter's eleven full seasons, plus a farewell cup of coffee in 1892, represent easily the most substantial career of any left-hander who played 2B, 3B, or SS in ML history, and his 1,059 games at 3B are more than twice the combined total of all the other left-handers to have played that position. Although a steady fielder, his game was "marred somewhat by his famous hop-skip and jump-throw," as *TSN* noted, no doubt a result of having to pivot when he threw to 1B. However, his arm, always his greatest asset, was strong enough to compensate for the disadvantage. If Carpenter had difficulty during the last years of his career as a left-handed third baseman coping with the increasingly popular bunting game, contemporaries do not seem to have noticed it. Pitchers, who until 1893 were positioned closer to home plate than they are now, probably took care of many bunts that later-day third basemen had to handle. Carpenter himself told an interviewer long after his retirement, "I don't suppose I would get far in modern ball because the batters would bunt me to death."

As a hitter Carpenter oddly parallels Frank Fennelly, who played beside him in the Cincinnati infield, in that contemporaries describe both as having suffered from an 1887 rules change abolishing the batter's prerogative to call for either a high or low pitch, yet each player's record shows a prolonged decline beginning well before 1887. In Carpenter's case, the likely explanation is twofold: his stats in the early 1880s were inflated by the spotty pitching prevailing in the newly formed AA and he was especially vulnerable to curve balls, which grew more prevalent as the 1880s wore on. Additionally, Carpenter, despite his size, had little power, hitting only 17 home runs in nearly 5,000 PAs. His uninspired hitting was concealed in part by his heady .342 BA in 1882, the AA's inaugural season, which represented a jump of more than 100 points from the best mark he had posted in his previous three years in the stronger NL. As the AA grew in stature, Carpenter's BA dropped to .299 in 1883 and then never approached that level again. Since he rarely walked—his five bases on balls in 1888 are the fewest by any nineteenth-century player with 500 or more ABs—if his BA was low, his offensive production was correspondingly minimal.

Carpenter began his pro career in 1877 with the League Alliance Syracuse Stars, with whom he made his NL debut in 1879. In 1880 Carpenter went to Cincinnati, where he played 1B until the Reds' lineup was revamped and he moved to 3B, which proved to be a permanent shift. The Reds left the NL in 1881, but Carpenter returned to the Queen City the next year when a new team was organized to enter the AA. His teammates on the first AA champions included Bid McPhee, and the two became close friends as well as members of the same infield for eight seasons. John Reilly joined the club in 1883, and, with periodic changes at SS, the three remained a remarkably stable unit on a team that was always strong, although it could never recapture the pennant magic of 1882. "The seasons come and go," remarked the *Pittsburgh Dispatch* early in 1886, "but Biddy McPhee, Long John Reilly and Hick Carpenter always come a winner in the shuffle, and look as natural around the bases as sign-boards at the forks of country cross-roads."

That year, however, proved an unhappy one for the Reds and a turning point for Carpenter. He injured an ankle and missed a month. Still hobbling when he returned to action, he batted only .221 and fell out of favor with fans, becoming a prime target in a campaign of vilification conducted by the *Cincinnati Enquirer* against the Reds. Now 30 years old, Carpenter retained his position for three more years but became one of those marginal players who had to fend off a challenge to his job every spring.

At last he was released just before the 1890 season began and went to Kansas City in the Western League, where he became team captain and batted .288, in spite of which *TSN* complained he did not hit well enough. Nevertheless, he remained at KC until the team folded in the middle of 1892. After one final farewell ML game for St. Louis in Cincinnati, he retired from baseball to work as a conductor on a Pullman train running between Cincinnati and Jacksonville, FL.

The *Cincinnati Commercial Gazette* felt "he would be a most valuable man in that connection, for he is courteous, popular and honest to a high degree." Indeed, while Carpenter was sometimes a whipping boy for fans in his last years in Cincinnati, everyone who knew him seems to have felt much as the *Commercial Gazette* did, and his positive presence in the clubhouse may have helped extend his career. Reliable in his habits, Carpenter was nonetheless an extrovert who enjoyed a drink with the boys but knew when to stop. He was also the man who held the hat to collect money for a player in need and organized barnstorming teams to play winters in New Orleans.

In 1902 Carpenter accepted an appointment as a customs collector, eventually rising to the post of chief deputy collector in El Paso. He retired around 1931 and moved to San Diego. A widower since 1908 and childless, he lived in a hotel and resumed his old friendship with McPhee, a resident of nearby Ocean Beach. Late in 1936 a *TSN* correspondent interviewed the two and found that the octogenarian Carpenter drove to McPhee's house several times a week and the pair then set off on fishing trips. Their relationship described by the interviewer was probably much as it had been half a century earlier, with Carpenter doing most of the talking and McPhee, always rather quiet, although by no means inarticulate, throwing in a comment now and then. Perhaps the only difference was that the more sedate pastime of fishing had replaced the venturesome hunting trips the two men used to take after the baseball season was over in the 1880s.

McPhee and Carpenter still enjoyed watching PCL games. In addition, each had been given a lifetime pass to NL games, and they told *TSN* they hoped to visit Cincinnati during the following season to see the Reds play. But Carpenter, who seemed so lively and vigorous to their interviewer, would pass away from a heart attack only a few months later, two days before Opening Day in Cincinnati. (DB/DN)

Casey, James Patrick / "Doc"

B	T	HGT	WGT	G	AB	H	R	2B
B	R	5'6"	157	172	674	177	91	18

3B	HR	RBI	BB	SO	SB	BA	SA	OBP
8	1	61	29	—	43	.263	.318	.304

B. 3/15/1870 Lawrence, MA **D.** 12/31/1936
TEAMS: 98–99WasN 99–00BroN 01–02DetAL 03–04ChiN 05–07BroN
DEBUT: 9/14/1898 at Washington; replaced Win Mercer at SS and went 2-for-5 in an 8–5 loss to Cleveland's Nig Cuppy
FINALE: 10/5/1907 at Boston; played 3B and made 1 hit in an 11–0 loss to Boston's Sam Frock

Originally a catcher, Doc Casey switched to 3B and was a solid ML player for a number of years. He was among the many credited with convincing Nap Lajoie to try pro ball. Lajoie supposedly was dubious about his chances until he saw the 5'6" Casey, then in his second pro season, catching for Portland of the New England League in 1894. Casey moved to 3B in 1898 while with Toronto of the Eastern League and almost instantly looked at home there. Called to Washington late that season after hitting .328, he seemingly caught a break when he was included in a mammoth trade with

Brooklyn the following April. But after just one year with the pennant-winning Superbas, he was traded to Detroit of the newly renamed American League early in the 1900 season. When the AL went major in 1901, Casey was made Detroit's captain but was idled by a dog bite when he "cuffed the nose of a bull terrier." Then a local paper griped, "He is no better fitted for the position of captain of a base ball club than a placid sea is for a yacht race."

Notwithstanding the pointed criticism, Casey held his captaincy the following season and then returned to the NL in 1903 with Chicago. He left the Cubs in December 1905 when they were on the eve of becoming a dynasty as part of a trade with Brooklyn for outfielder Jimmy Sheckard. Like many infielders in the heart of the Deadball Era, Casey grew increasingly challenged offensively. After batting in the low .230s for three successive seasons, he was cut by Brooklyn and finished his career in 1911 as player-manager of Fort Wayne in the Central League. Casey then returned to Detroit, where he set up a dental practice and also had a part interest in a drug store, having married May Bristol of that city in 1901. He had fallen down on his luck and was working as a guard at the Detroit Municipal Court Building at the time of his death in 1939. (DN)

Cleveland, Elmer Ellsworth / "Elmer"

B	T	HGT	WGT	G	AB	H	R	2B
R	R	5'11"	190	80	298	78	52	11

3B	HR	RBI	BB	SO	SB	BA	SA	OBP
5	4	20	24	33	8	.255	.366	.317

B. 9/15/1862 Washington, D.C. **D.** 10/8/1913
TEAMS: 84CinU 88NYN 88PitN 91ColA
DEBUT: 8/29/1884 at Cincinnati; played 3B and went 3-for-4 in a 9–2 win over Kansas City's Barney McLaughlin
FINALE: 4/23/1891 at Columbus; played 3B and went 0-for-4 in a 6–5 loss to Boston's Clark Griffith

Elmer Cleveland was among the many young men of his day named after Elmer Ellsworth, the first Union Army man to fall in the Civil War. His father reportedly was a first cousin of Grover Cleveland, and though his son denied they were related, the president himself claimed a connection in 1891. A good hitter in the minors, Cleveland also did reasonably well in the majors at the plate and had a great arm but was an erratic fielder and an awkward base runner. He first played for pay with independent Johnstown, PA, in 1883 and was with Oil City of the Iron & Oil Association in 1884 when he was garnered by Cincinnati UA on the recommendation of Jack Glasscock and Jim McCormick, who had faced him in exhibitions. One of the many casualties when the UA folded, Cleveland played with Atlanta in the fledgling Southern Association the following year and occasionally pitched. According to the *Atlanta Constitution*, "It was almost impossible to see his balls. They were delivered like lightning."

After starring in the Western Association in 1887 and winning the *St. Paul Globe* medal for leading the local club in homers, he was favored to win the Giants' coffin-corner job in the spring of 1888 but fielded just .667 in 9 games. In his final contest with New York he hit a mammoth triple against Pittsburgh that induced Pittsburgh manager Horace Phillips to trade holdout third sacker Art Whitney for him. Cleveland's fielding woes persisted, however, and Phillips released him in September, accepting *TSN*'s judgment that he was "too beefy to play good ball."

In 1889 Cleveland batted cleanup for Frank Selee's Omaha club and led the Western Association flag winner in home runs and total bases, but despite his prodigious slugging he languished in the WA the following year even after the PL added eight teams to the majors. When Omaha stunned its followers by releasing Cleveland in March 1891 to make room for Jim Donnelly, a better fielder, Columbus AA manager Gus Schmelz grabbed him. The Senators' Opening Day third baseman, he lasted only 12 games. After an *Ohio State Journal* headline appeared on April 24, 1891, proclaiming, "Why Not Place an Indian Tobacco Sign on the Third Base Bag?" following a costly error by Cleveland, he was literally run out of the Ohio capital by local boo birds the next evening when he had another bad game that afternoon against St. Louis. He fled with his valise after telling his roommate, catcher Tom Dowse, that he could no longer tolerate the roasting fans gave him every time he showed his face on the street.

Cleveland traveled full circle in his career the following year when he served as player-manager of the Johnstown Johnnies in the Pennsylvania

State League. He later ran hotels in Johnstown and Zimmerman, PA, before dying in his hotel room in the latter city at 51. (DN)

Clingman, William Frederick / "Billy"

B	T	HGT	WGT	G	AB	H	R	2B
B	R	5'11"	150	682	2310	566	337	75

3B	HR	RBI	BB	SO	SB	BA	SA	OBP
24	6	240	250	94	86	.245	.306	.322

B. 11/21/1869 Cincinnati, OH **D.** 5/14/1958
TEAMS: 90CinN 91CinA 95PitN 96–99LouN 00ChiN 01WasAL 03CleAL
DEBUT: 9/9/1890 at Cincinnati; played SS and went 1-for-6 in an 8–4 loss to Cleveland's Ed Beatin
FINALE: 7/16/1903 at Boston; replaced Nap Lajoie at 2B and went 0-for-2 in an 11–4 loss to Boston's Tom Hughes

A wood engraver by trade, Billy Clingman was an avid fan of the Cincinnati Reds before joining them in 1890 after they absconded to the NL. He had begun the season with the amateur Cincinnati Indians and then cashed several paychecks with Mansfield, OH, of the Tri-State League prior to returning to his hometown. In his second appearance with the Reds, a DH against Pittsburgh on September 11, 1890, Clingman drew his first rave review: "The fielding of Clingman, the Reds' new short stop, was the feature of both games." But as would be true his entire career, the plaudits were solely for his defense. At the close of the pre-expansion era in 1960, Clingman's career .246 BA ranked last by a fraction of a point among all switch hitters since 1893 with a minimum of 3,000 PAs.

In December 1890, following a 7-game trial with the Reds, Clingman had several attractive offers from minor league teams but could not accept them because Cincinnati still held him under reserve solely as insurance while it waited for the uncertainty over whether there would be a rival Queen City team in the Players League to be resolved when the PL folded. At that late juncture Clingman had to scramble before finally landing a post with the Northwestern League Terre Haute Hottentots.

When the Hottentots' loop dissolved in midseason, he got a 1-game trial in 1891 with the new Cincinnati AA entry before the club decided to keep Yank Robinson. It would be his last taste of ML ball until 1895, when Pittsburgh drafted him from Milwaukee of the Western League. Traded to Louisville the following spring, Clingman led all NL third basemen in assists and then captured the hot-corner FA crown in 1897 after learning to switch hit that spring. Previously only a right-handed hitter, Clingman hoped for improvement over his .246 career BA to that point but instead regressed to .228. He broke .250 after being moved to SS the following season, however, and again in 1899 after surviving typhoid malaria to hold off a swarm of competitors for his SS post that included practically every player on the club except one named Honus Wagner.

With Louisville verging on extinction, Clingman was sold to Chicago in December 1899. The *Chicago Tribune* had a mixed reaction to his acquisition, noting, "In two seasons recently he has averaged a greater number of chances per game than any other man in his position. Yet Clingman does not have the reputation of being one of the star shortstops." He opened 1900 at SS with the Windy City club but hit just .208 and was released in August to Kansas City of the newly renamed American League. When he hit .310 for the Blues in the last six weeks of the season, manager Jim Manning added him to the crew Manning took to Washington after landing the D.C. pilot's job for the AL's inaugural season as a major league. Clingman emerged as the AL's first leader in SS assists and FA, but his bat was too light to survive another ML season. He served out the rest of his career in the minors, save for a short stint with Cleveland in 1903 that was memorable only in that he was traded to Columbus of the American Association for Terry Turner, still the all-time leader in games played in a Cleveland AL uniform.

Clingman returned to the American Association for a while, finishing with Toledo in 1906, and then opened the Clingman Engraving Company in Louisville. He died in Cincinnati at 88. (DN/DB)

Corey, Frederick Harrison / "Fred"

B	T	HGT	WGT	G	AB	H	R	2B
R	R	5'7"	160	432	1738	427	239	70

3B	HR	RBI	BB	SO	SB	BA	SA	OBP
43	7	124	60	70	—	.246	.348	.273

G	IP	H	GS	CG	BB
93	656.1	764	74	59	98

SO	SH	W	L	PCT	ERA
168	3	27	46	.370	3.32

B. ?/?/1857 S. Kingston, RI **D.** 11/27/1912
TEAMS: 78ProN 80–82WorN 83–85PhiA
DEBUT: 5/1/1878 at Providence; caught by Lew Brown and lost 1–0 to Boston's Tommy Bond
FINALE: 10/5/1885 at Philadelphia; played SS and went 4-for-4 in a 9–1 win over Brooklyn's Henry Porter

A member of the Rhode Islands in the fly-by-night 1877 New England League, Fred Corey pitched Providence's initial game in the NL the following year. In 1880 he was in CF for Worcester when the NL team's ace, Lee Richmond, threw the first perfect game in big league annals. Then in 1883 he played on the last Philadelphia team to win a ML pennant in the nineteenth century, and two years later he tied the record for the most hits by a ML player in his final game. Yet he stands as one of the most luckless players in ML history.

The winter of 1885–86 Corey took a load of buckshot in his left eye while on a hunting expedition with his brother in Westerly, RI. Cut as a result by the Philadelphia A's, he remained jobless until the following May, when he signed with Lancaster of the Pennsylvania State Association. But within a week he was out of work again when the club was forced to disband after its business manager ran off to New York on payday with all of the team's cash. By that point Corey had begun to fear that the game was behind him anyway, as the sun blinded his impaired eye whenever he attempted to catch a fly ball. Two benefit games were scheduled for Corey at the A's park with him scheduled to play 3B in one and pitch in the other. *Sporting Life* cajoled in its ad for the contests, "Give the unfortunate player a lift and if you do not care to go buy a ticket anyhow."

That fall *TSN* reported that Corey was "fast regaining the use of his left eye" and would make a comeback the following year. So he did—or at least tried. In February, with the help of his old A's crony, Charlie Mason, he was hired to manage Hastings, NE, and play 3B but then was fired in April before the season began after having failed to convince the Western League team via letter that his sight was back to normal when it was actually still badly damaged. From time to time over the remaining years of his life Corey would be the recipient of another benefit game or a handout from a former teammate. He died on a cold autumn night in 1912 in a Providence hotel room, asphyxiated while reading in bed. Alone in the world at the time, he had traveled from his home in Plainfield, NJ, to visit the city where it had all begun for him on May 1, 1878, in a 1–0 loss to what would be both the best pitcher and the best team in the game that year. (DN/DB)

Davis, James J. / "Jumbo"

B	T	HGT	WGT	G	AB	H	R	2B
L	R	5'11"	195	453	1723	468	266	69

3B	HR	RBI	BB	SO	SB	BA	SA	OBP
37	14	270	108	41	151	.272	.379	.322

B. 9/5/1861 New York, NY **D.** 2/14/1921
TEAMS: 84KCU 86–87BalA 88–89KCA 89StLA *(89BroA) 90StLA 90BroA 91WasA
DEBUT: 7/27/1884 at St. Louis; played 3B and went 0-for-4 in a 9–4 loss to St. Louis's Henry Boyle
FINALE: 5/22/1891 at Washington; played 3B and made 1 hit in a 9–6 win over Louisville's Ed Daily and Red Ehret

Jumbo Davis was a skilled trap shooter, an excellent handball player, and a fine third baseman—at times. Born in New York, he grew up in St. Louis and joined the Kansas City UA team in 1884 while they were visiting the Mound City after first playing for pay with Quincy of the 1883 Northwestern League until he was dropped for refusing to travel to the local ballpark on a streetcar. He spent 1885 and part of 1886 in the New England League before Baltimore AA acquired him in late July 1886.

After hitting just .194 as an Orioles frosh, Davis weighed retiring to work for the St. Louis fire department. Changing his mind, he returned to Baltimore in the spring of 1887 but was unhappy all season under the aegis of manager Billy Barnie. By July, Davis grew so disgusted with Barnie's mode of operation that he tried to orchestrate a deal for himself with the Browns, but Barnie lied and claimed the Browns didn't want him, which alarmed Davis into staying. He finished the year with 109 RBI and a loop-leading 19 triples but was never able to get back on track and appears to be another example of a potentially outstanding player who was more or less ruined by the place where he played. In February 1888, Baltimore, rather than grant him a pay increase, rewarded him by selling him to the new Kansas City AA expansion team for $700. Stuck on a near-certain last-place club, a demoralized Davis slipped to .267 but still led the Cowboys in BA, hits, total bases, and SA.

Remaining with the Cowboys, Davis started poorly in 1889, perhaps playing for his release, and was dropped in late August for "inefficiency" by new KC manager Bill Watkins. He finally got his wish when St. Louis signed him, but after only 2 games he was cut when the Browns started to lose and owner Chris Von der Ahe, looking for a "Jonah," made him the target. In October, Davis was picked up for injury insurance prior to the World Series by NL champion Brooklyn—there were no rules then on Series eligibility—and appeared in one game at SS in the Bridegrooms' loss to the Giants.

Davis was still without a baseball job in April 1890 when Von der Ahe, with his club riddled by PL defections, rehired him. Joining the Browns while still not in top condition, he was unable to seize the open 3B slot and was dropped after making 28 errors in his first 21 games of the season. Having no other options, Davis signed with the Brooklyn Gladiators, the AA doormat, and underwent a revival, hitting .303 before the club folded. Joining Washington the following spring, he pushed Will Smalley off 3B but again was overweight and lost the job to Billy Alvord when he "couldn't stop a ground ball with a bushel basket." At that point Davis became an AA umpire, lasting at his new post until September 11, 1891, despite a historic game on August 2, when he allowed George Van Haltren's walk to force home the winning run for Baltimore even though Columbus rightfully protested that Van Haltren went to the Baltimore bench without touching 1B as the rule required. After that, Davis remained in St. Louis working at racetracks. He died of diabetes in the Mound City at 50. (DN)

Denny, Jeremiah Dennis
(b. Eldridge) / **"Jerry"**

B	T	HGT	WGT	G	AB	H	R	2B
R	R	5'11½"	180	1237	4946	1282	714	238

3B	HR	RBI	BB	SO	SB	BA	SA	OBP
76	74	667	173	602	130	.260	.384	.287

G	IP	H	GS	CG	BB
1	4	5	0	0	4

SO	SH	W	L	PCT	ERA
1	0	0	0	—	9.00

B. 3/16/1859 New York, NY **D.** 8/16/1927
TEAMS: 81–85ProN 86StLN 87–89IndN 90–91NYN 91CleN 91PhiN 93–94LouN
DEBUT: 5/2/1881 at Providence; played 3B and went 1-for-4 in a 4–2 loss to Boston's Jim Whitney
FINALE: 7/10/1894 at Louisville; played 3B and went 2-for-4 in a 13–7 win over Brooklyn's Hank Gastright and Danny Daub

Jerry Denny was a nineteenth-century Graig Nettles, a low-average free swinger with power who provided superb defense at 3B. His contemporaries were nearly unanimous in naming him as the best fielding third baseman of his day. One of the last barehanded infielders, Denny was especially adept at spearing line drives with either hand and at making right-handed pickups of bunts and throwing to 1B in the same motion. Although practically forgotten today, for half a century after his ML career concluded he was regarded as one of the outstanding players in baseball's early history. As late as the mid-1930s Denny was the only nineteenth-century player listed on sportswriter Hugh Fullerton's all-time team and one of only two nineteenth-century third basemen originally named as candidates—John McGraw was the other—for election to the HOF. Fullerton's evaluation, though perhaps a bit extravagant, nonetheless had a firm basis. In the decade of the 1880s (1881–90), Denny stood alone among third basemen in almost every major career fielding department.

A New York native, Denny was orphaned after moving to San Francisco in childhood. From 1877–79 he attended St. Mary's College, where he played baseball. To hide the fact that he was also playing for pay on some of the best teams in San Francisco, he dropped his last name and subsequently was known simply as Denny, even after he had left St. Mary's. In the winter of 1880–81 John M. Ward spotted him playing for the San Francisco Athletics and brought him east to play for Ward's Providence team. Entering the 1884 season, Denny, after only three years, had already established himself as one of the best third basemen in the game. At that time he held the ML season record for home runs by a third sacker with 8. More important, he was regarded as an outstanding fielder and had led the league in several defensive categories. While playing for the NL-pennant-winning Grays against the AA's first-place New York Mets in the fall of 1884, Denny added to his growing laurels when he hit the first home run in World's Series history, but ever after that, even though he continued to be a stellar fielder, his batting marks were mostly negative.

Denny's gradual downhill ride started in 1885, as Providence suffered a disastrous season, plagued by injuries and dissension as well as poor attendance. When manager Frank Bancroft was asked before a September game in New York whether it was true that Denny was anxious to join the Giants, he replied, "Denny is probably anxious to leave Providence. That is, I judge so from his conduct. He is down stairs trying to consume the stock of whiskey sours." As the reporter watched Denny climb the grandstand stairs on the arm of a friend, Bancroft added, "Judging from his appearances and his unsteady gait, he has made great progress in his self-appointed task." Denny was soon suspended, and Providence folded at the end of the season. In the ensuing dispersal of players, the Giants coveted Denny but instead he was assigned to St. Louis to bolster a weak sixth-place team. To his great frustration, after five years with Providence, one of the NL's strongest teams, he was mired on a succession of poor playing, and generally poor paying, ball clubs for the rest of his years in the NL. For a while his hitting showed considerable improvement, but only because from 1887 to 1889 in Indianapolis he found himself in surroundings ideally suited to his talents. During those seasons he hit 41 home runs, the third most in the majors during that span, but 37 of them—exactly half of his career total—came at his tiny Indianapolis home park. The Giants were regularly reported to be eager to secure him, and he hoped to go to New York, but by the time the formation of the PL in 1890 reconfigured the two veteran major leagues and finally freed him from Indianapolis, his best years were behind him.

Denny was a newspaperman's dream: a quotable extrovert with a fine singing voice who also made great copy with the tales that emanated from his heavy drinking. After a well-publicized spree, such as the one in New York, he would take the pledge yet another time and then almost immediately fall off the wagon again. Denny seems to have conquered his habit after leaving the majors, however, for he demonstrated a degree of personal stability, success and longevity that his previous history would not have predicted. He married a Connecticut woman two years after the death of his first wife in 1891, and settled down in that state, playing minor league ball there until he was 43. Denny then became a hotelier, running Denny's Inn in Derby, CT, along with a local men's clothing store, and serving as player-manager of the Derby Angels. He later ran another hotel in Bridgeport and was mentioned several times as a potential owner of Connecticut League clubs. In the early 1920s he left Bridgeport with his wife, Catherine, and moved to Houston, where he died of heart failure in 1927. (DB/DN)

Donnelly, James B. / "Jim"

B	T	HGT	WGT	G	AB	H	R	2B
R	R	5'11"	160	654	2388	549	322	56

3B	HR	RBI	BB	SO	SB	BA	SA	OBP
28	2	237	169	144	173	.230	.279	.285

B. 7/19/1865 New Haven, CT **D.** 3/5/1915
TEAMS: 84IndA 85DetN 86KCN 87–89WasN 90StLA 91ColA 96BalN 97PitN 97NYN 98StLN
DEBUT: 8/11/1884 at Columbus; played 3B and went 0-for-3 in an 11–3 loss to Columbus's Dummy Dundon
FINALE: 5/12/1898 at Cincinnati; replaced Lave Cross at 3B and went 1-for-1 in an 8–5 loss to St. Louis's Ted Breitenstein

Jim Donnelly appears on no one's list of the great third basemen in his day, but there were none better at handling rejection. He left Connecticut at age 17 to play for Terre Haute and graduated from the Indiana Northwestern League team to the lone Indiana major league team the following year when he joined Indianapolis AA long enough to convince his manager, Bill Watkins, to include him among the players Watkins brought with him from the disbanded Hoosier Western league entry after he took the Detroit NL pilot's job the following spring. Donnelly made his NL debut on June 25 and held the Wolverines' 3B slot for most of the rest of the season before being sold to the new Kansas City NL entry when Watkins garnered third sacker Deacon White from the disbanding Buffalo NL franchise.

In 1886, his first full ML season, Donnelly hit .201 for KC and led all NL third basemen in errors. Undeterred, he moved to Washington the following year after KC left the loop and topped all NL third basemen in assists while losing a point off his BA. Donnelly then followed his .201 and .200 seasons by hitting .201 again in 1888, giving him a composite .201, the lowest aggregate mark in ML history by a qualifier in three consecutive seasons. Still impervious to adversity, he went to spring training with Washington again in 1889 but was released after just 4 games and rejoined Detroit, now a minor league entry in the International Association. Donnelly started 1890 with Detroit but was summoned to St. Louis in July. Handed the Browns' 3B post, he promptly strained his arm and had to be sent home.

Not one to be discouraged by a mere injury, Donnelly tried his hand with the Columbus AA team in August 1891. After collecting just 13 hits in 17 games, all singles, he was sent by manager Gus Schmelz to the Ohio Mississippi ticket office in St. Louis to buy ten tickets to Baltimore for the team. That night Schmelz informed Donnelly he was released, and he "went off to celebrate the release with the tickets in his pocket." Schmelz then had to purchase ten more tickets at his own expense.

After so many failed ML opportunities, Donnelly seemed ready to serve out his days in the minors. In 1895 he was spending his second consecutive season with Tom Burns's Springfield Eastern League club when Baltimore drafted him for 1896. Donnelly assumed he had been acquired to be used as fodder in spring practice games before being returned to Springfield, and that would no doubt have been the case if John McGraw had not been felled by a near-fatal bout with typhoid prior to the 1896 season. Stuck with Donnelly, Orioles manager Ned Hanlon cringed at his every at-bat as the interim replacement hit .114 (5-for-44) through the first 10 games of the season. Just as Hanlon was about to install rookie Bill Keister at 3B, Donnelly suddenly caught fire and hit .355 the rest of the way, a truly amazing streak by a player whose career BA, minus his stats during that skein, was .208. An ulcerated tooth kept him out of some games near the end of the year, and meanwhile McGraw had recovered enough to play every inning at the coffin corner in the postseason Temple Cup Series against Cleveland.

Still, a third baseman with a .328 season BA could only take on a new luster, and Pittsburgh demanded Donnelly as part of a November 1896 trade it swung with Baltimore. He opened 1897 at 3B for the Pirates, hit .193, jumped the team, and was released to the Giants, who needed a third baseman so that Bill Joyce could move to 1B. But Donnelly was not the solution, hitting a composite .191 for the season. That fall, the Giants traded him to St. Louis, where the Browns' new manager, Tim Hurst, thought so highly of him that he was awarded 3B in spring training. But Donnelly was released before the season started and then recalled via telegram when Lave Cross was spiked on May 11 at Cincinnati. By the time Donnelly arrived the following morning, Cross's wound was found to be only minor, but he nonetheless got to appear in 1 final ML game that afternoon when Cross was ejected for excessive bench jockeying. He then returned to the minors, finishing in 1900 shortly after his old manager, Tom Burns, released him from Springfield of the Eastern League because his arm was "gone." Donnelly died of tuberculosis at his home in New Haven at 49. (DN/DB)

Farrell, Joseph F. (aka Lavin) **/ "Joe"**

B	T	HGT	WGT	G	AB	H	R	2B
R	?	5'6"	160	353	1489	345	187	43

3B	HR	RBI	BB	SO	SB	BA	SA	OBP
15	5	132	35	115	5	.232	.291	.249

B. ?/?/1857 Brooklyn, NY **D.** 4/18/1893
TEAMS: 82–84DetN 86BalA
DEBUT: 5/1/1882 at Cleveland; played 3B and went 1-for-4 in a 5–4 win over Cleveland's Jim McCormick
FINALE: 8/29/1886 at Brooklyn; played 3B and went 1-for-5 in a 9–7 loss to Brooklyn's Jack Harkins

A product of the Brooklyn sandlots, Joe Farrell began playing with organized teams in the Brooklyn area when he was in his late teens, sometimes under an alias. After calling himself "Lavin" in 1879, Farrell spent 1880 with three different teams in the National Association and 1881 with two clubs in the Eastern Championship Association. He then signed with Detroit in 1882, making his ML debut at age 25.

Farrell began 1882 as the Wolverines' regular third baseman but shifted to 2B in July when the team acquired Bob Casey. On July 27, in a game at Detroit, Farrell was hit by a Larry Corcoran pitch in the eighth inning and had to be removed from the game. He was unable to return to action until the end of August. By then Detroit's infield was in complete disarray, with only first baseman Mart Powell remaining at the same post where he had opened the season. Farrell was installed at SS when he first returned to the lineup, but after only 9 games there, went back to 2B. In 1883 Farrell regained the Detroit 3B job and held it through 1884 before a rheumatoid condition hobbled him for the entire 1885 season and no doubt continued to handicap him after he was able to return, perhaps even contributing to his early death.

Let go when the Wolverines acquired third sacker Deacon White, Farrell won the Baltimore 2B slot in the spring of 1886. In July, Orioles manager Billy Barnie, desperate to avoid a cellar finish for the second straight season, made Farrell and third baseman Mike Muldoon switch positions. The move failed to pan out, as Muldoon hit just .199 and Farrell soon lost his job to outfielder Joe Sommer and, as a last resort, was tried for one game in the outfield to the dismay of T.T.T., Baltimore's *SL* correspondent, who wrote, "Farrell is no more a success as an outfielder than an infielder, and his clumsy and awkward movements do not add to the beauty of the game. When he makes a muff or a fumble he does it in such an awful manner that it wilts the spectators to an idiotic languor that is almost fatal."

Released on August 31, 1886, Farrell departed with a .549 career OPS, the lowest between the introduction of the fifty-foot pitching distance in 1881 and the close of the nineteenth century among all ML players with at least 1,000 career ABs whose primary position was 3B. Farrell finished his pro career two years later with Bloomington, IN, of the Central Interstate League and then worked for the Nassau Gaslight Company in Brooklyn. Upon his death in Brooklyn in 1893, his aging mother was left almost destitute. Several veteran players staged a benefit game for her at the Brooklyn NL park in late April. (DN)

Foley, William Brown / "Will"

B	T	HGT	WGT	G	AB	H	R	2B
R	R	5'9½"	150	253	982	224	112	23

3B	HR	RBI	BB	SO	SB	BA	SA	OBP
10	0	76	20	62	0	.228	.272	.244

B. 11/15/1855 Chicago, IL **D.** 11/12/1916
TEAMS: 75ChiNA 76–77CinN 78MilN 79CinN 81DetN 84Chi-PitU
DEBUT: 8/23/1875 at Chicago; played 3B and made 2 hits in a 13–11 win over Boston's Jack Manning
FINALE: 5/22/1884 at Chicago; played 3B and went 2-for-5 in a 10–6 win over Baltimore's Ed Smith and Henry Oberbeck

Chicago boy Will Foley earned this accolade from the *Chicago Tribune* after his NA debut in 1875: "The new third-baseman of the White Stockings proved to be a valuable acquisition. Although a trifle nervous at first, he subsequently rallied, and by his fine stops and throws contributed largely to the victory." Excess baggage when Chicago owner Will Hulbert snared Boston's "Big Four" and launched the NL in 1876, the 19-year-old third baseman signed with Cincinnati. Never again would he gain the acclaim that came to him after his initial ML game.

Foley spent two undistinguished years with Cincinnati. On May 11, 1876, after beginning a game against St. Louis on the bench, he replaced injured catcher Dave Pierson in the first inning and piled up 12 miscues, contributing to an 11–0 loss and one of George Bradley's record 16 shutouts. After hitting .190 in 1877, Foley was dismissed by Cincinnati. Luckily, the Milwaukee expansion team was short a third baseman when it joined the NL in 1878. In 56 games with the Cream Cities, Foley hit a decent .271 but tallied just 33 runs. Rehired by Cincinnati after Milwaukee folded, he compiled a .461 OPS, the lowest in the NL by a veteran position player, and returned to the semipro ranks.

Except for a 5-game stint with Detroit in 1881, Foley had been out of the majors for four seasons when the UA formed and Chicago landed a franchise. When he appeared at 3B on Opening Day for the UA Chicago Browns, he became the only player ever to debut with one Chicago ML team and finish with another without ever playing for Windy City entries in either the NL or the AL. An excellent start with the Browns produced a .282 BA after 22 games. At that point Foley cut his own throat. Offered "a cool 300 extra a month above his salary" by St. Paul manager Bob Hunter, the third baseman jumped the UA to play in the Northwestern League, only to learn too late, according to the *Police Gazette,* that it was three-hundred cents, not dollars, that he contracted to play for. Reportedly, Foley thus had disgraced himself permanently in baseball circles for a mere $30 a month.

When he left pro play two years later to become an amateur and semipro umpire, *SL* noted that he was "quite a young looking fellow for such an old timer." At the time he was actually still in his early thirties. By November 1916 Foley was living in a loft in his brother George's barn on Carroll Avenue in Chicago. He was found dead one morning when George broke down the loft door after he hadn't seen his brother for two days. Foley's terrier Jack was standing guard over his body. He was presumed to have died from exposure since the loft was unheated. (DN/DB)

Gilbert, Peter / "Pete"

B	T	HGT	WGT	G	AB	H	R	2B
?	R	5'8"	180	206	761	184	120	20

3B	HR	RBI	BB	SO	SB	BA	SA	OBP
9	5	105	54	87	48	.242	.311	.321

B. 9/6/1867 Baltic, CT **D.** 12/31/1911
TEAMS: 90–91BalA 92BalN 94BroN 94LouN
DEBUT: 9/6/1890 at Baltimore; played 3B and went 0-for-4 in a seven-inning tie 2–2 against Toledo's John Healy
FINALE: 9/30/1894 at Louisville; played 3B and went 0-for-1 in a 12–4 loss to Brooklyn's Ed Stein

Still officially a rookie in 1891, Pete Gilbert set an all-time frosh record with 28 HBPs. He also set season records for the most HBPs by a third baseman and the lowest OBP (.317) by a player hit by as many as 28 pitches. Gilbert then missed most of 1892 while suffering from an undisclosed illness. After spending 1893 with Springfield of the Eastern League, he earned a second ML shot when Brooklyn purchased him for $500. Soon after the 1894 season began, Brooklyn loaned Gilbert to Buffalo, but the Eastern League team swiftly returned him to Brooklyn for "poor play." Gilbert then rotted on the Brooklyn bench for several months before Louisville took on his contract late in the 1894 season. Despite being one of only two players on the team to finish with a .300 BA in as many as 100 ABs, Gilbert was let go. He then played with Springfield, MA, for rest of his pro career, finishing in 1898, and made the city his permanent home after marrying a local woman in 1897.

Gilbert's first pro paycheck came from Norwalk of the Atlantic Association in 1888, and by 1890 he was with Newark of the same league. Sold to Baltimore when Newark folded in August, Gilbert joined the Orioles several weeks after they had deserted the Atlantic loop to replace the defunct Brooklyn AA team. He did well with Baltimore in the final month of the 1890 season and then seemingly gave little hint that he belonged in ML company until he joined Louisville with a few weeks left in the 1894 campaign. But there was more to Gilbert than meets the eye. Besides his .851 FA, which is tied with Bill Joyce for the second worst among third basemen in a minimum of 200 games since his 1890 debut year, and his lowly .242 BA, is his 120 runs—the most scored by anyone prior to 1900 with a sub-.245 BA and less than 800 ABs—and his 87 RBI—the third most by anyone within the same parameters. Gilbert finished his playing career in the 1898 Eastern League and then sold cigars before dying of heart disease in Springfield. (DN)

Gladmon, James Henry (aka Gladman) / "Buck" "The Level"

B	T	HGT	WGT	G	AB	H	R	2B
?	?	?	?	101	380	56	35	10

3B	HR	RBI	BB	SO	SB	BA	SA	OBP
6	2	15	15	32	5	.147	.221	.186

B. 11/?/1863 Washington, D.C. **D.** 1/13/1890
TEAMS: 83PhiN 84WasA 86WasN
DEBUT: 7/7/1883 at Philadelphia; played 3B and went hitless, fanning three times in a 15–4 loss to Boston's Jim Whitney
FINALE: 7/17/1886 at Washington; played 3B went 0-for-4 in an 8–1 loss to Philadelphia's Charlie Ferguson

Buck Gladmon began 1883 with the independent Washington Nationals, playing in the same infield with Pop Joy (1B), Tom Evers (2B), and Bill White (SS) until he somehow drew the NL Philadelphia Quakers' attention. When Gladmon left the Quakers after just one game, he was savaged in both Philadelphia and Washington for keeping the Quakers' advance money and then quitting. But several years later it emerged that he had departed after learning he had been expected to purchase new clothes with his advance, and he resented the notion that he looked downtrodden. Gladmon's sensitivity emanated from the fact that he came from "The Level," a particularly rough section of Washington, and, to his mortification, was nicknamed "The Level" upon arriving in Philadelphia.

In 1884 Gladmon opened the season at 3B for Washington AA and went 3-for-5 in the club's first game and then 2-for-4 the following day. In his next 53 games he was just 28-for-211 (.133) but saved a bit of face by going 2-for-4 in his AA finale on August 2 to lift his overall season BA to .156, still the worst season ever by a third baseman with a minimum of 200 ABs.

The following season Gladmon returned to the Washington Nationals, which had been a UA entry in 1884 but was now a member of the Eastern League, and hit .257, inducing the new Washington NL club to sign him for 1886. When his hitting was even worse than it had been in 1884—.138 in 44 games—he was released in July and joined Syracuse of the International Association. A dud there as well, he returned to Washington and played in local semipro leagues until his death in 1890 at 26.

Gladmon was not only a wretched hitter at the ML level, but he was also ragged in the field, finishing with an .812 career FA at 3B, the third worst in history among players in a minimum of 90 games at the hot corner. Nor has there ever been a worse hitter at 3B with as many as 400 career PAs. Gladman left with a .407 OPS, challenged in all the years since only by John Vukovich's .425. (DN/DB/PM)

*Gleason, John Day / "Jack"

B	T	HGT	WGT	G	AB	H	R	2B
R	R	?	170	343	1425	384	253	59

3B	HR	RBI	BB	SO	SB	BA	SA	OBP
14	9	31	95	2	8	.269	.349	.320

B. 7/14/1854 St. Louis, MO **D.** 9/4/1944
TEAMS: 77StLN 82–83StLA 83LouA 84StLU 85StLN 86PhiA
DEBUT: 10/2/1877 at St. Louis; played CF and went 1-for-4 in a 3–0 loss to Louisville's Jim Devlin
FINALE: 8/31/1886 at Philadelphia; played 3B and went 0-for-4 in a 5–4 loss to New York's Ed Cushman

Jack Gleason was the older brother of shortstop Bill "Brudder" Gleason. The two were the first siblings to play beside one another in the same infield in an ML game, achieving that distinction on May 2, 1882, the AA's inaugural day as a major league. Gleason not only participated in St. Louis's first game in the AA but also the first St. Louis NL representative's last game as a member of the senior loop in 1877 and both the St. Louis Maroons' first and last games as members of the Union Association.

Commencing in 1874 with the semipro St. Louis Stocks, the two Gleasons played together for eight years prior to first becoming teammates on the ML level in 1882. The elder Gleason opened that campaign as the Browns' third baseman and leadoff hitter, but slipshod fielding at the hot corner sent him to RF in early August. When third sacker Arlie Latham joined the Browns in 1883, Gleason demanded his release after manager Ted Sullivan informed him his permanent spot now was in the outfield, where he despised playing. Gleason then signed with Louisville after he was promised the Colonels' 3B post.

Some sixteen years later Gleason told *TSN* that after the A's lost 3 straight games in their season-ending series at Louisville to put St. Louis back in the 1883 AA pennant race, Browns owner Chris Von der Ahe sent him a telegram promising each Louisville team member a $60 overcoat if Louisville beat the A's for a fourth straight time in the final game of the season. Gleason informed his teammates of the incentive and was stunned when pitcher Guy Hecker just lobbed the ball up to A's hitters and outfielder Pete Browning missed several easy flies, helping the A's to prevail in ten innings and clinch the AA pennant. Not until after the game did Gleason learn that several of his teammates had gone to A's manager Lon Knight during pregame practice. When they informed Knight of Von der Ahe's offer, he promised each Louisville player a gold watch if the A's won the game. Gleason averred that everyone on the Louisville team subsequently got a gold watch but him. Such a tale today, even one told sixteen years after the fact, would prompt at the very minimum either an emphatic denial from the players accused or a full investigation, but in the permissive moral climate that pervaded pro baseball prior to the Black Sox Scandal, Gleason's provocative story passed without comment.

As was true of many ML players who jumped to the UA in 1884, Gleason had his career year in the rebel loop with the St. Louis Maroons. But unlike the NL, which rescinded its pledge to blacklist UA contract jumpers before the beginning of the 1885 season, the AA did not do so until late in the campaign; as a result, Gleason played just 2 games in 1885 after Louisville, which retained the rights to him, allowed him to rejoin the Maroons, by then in the NL. The AA Athletics then signed him for 1886 when Louisville released him upon acquiring minor leaguer Joe Werrick over the winter. Gleason opened 1886 as an A's regular but sagged badly after injuring his leg in a pregame collision with Jack Milligan while chasing a pop fly.

Cut before the end of the 1886 season, Gleason went home to St. Louis and turned his off-season job as a fireman into a full-time position. In June 1893 he had a narrow escape when he leaned out a window at his firehouse and accidentally touched a live wire. After his brush with instant death, Gleason lived another half century and was the last surviving member of the UA's lone champion prior to his passing in St. Louis at 90. (DN)

Hague, William L. (b. Haug) **/ "Bill" "Limpy Bill" "Martha Washington"**

B	T	HGT	WGT	G	AB	H	R	2B
R	R	5'9"	164	301	1276	303	134	23

3B	HR	RBI	BB	SO	SB	BA	SA	OBP
2	2	114	19	90	3	.237	.264	.249

B. ?/?/1852 Philadelphia, PA **D.** 9/21/1898
TEAMS: 75StLNA 76–77LouN 78–79ProN
DEBUT: 5/4/1875 at St. Louis; played 3B and made 1 hit in a 15–0 win over the St. Louis Reds' Pidgey Morgan
FINALE: 8/15/1879 at Troy; played 3B and went 2-for-5 in a 16–7 win over Troy's George Bradley

Bill Hague's .513 career OPS is the second worst in ML history among third basemen with a minimum of 1,000 career ABs, trailing only Hunter Hill's .510. Nicknamed "Limpy Bill" because he was prone to leg injuries and "Martha Washington" for his stoic demeanor, he kept an ML job for five seasons simply because he had an absolute gun for an arm and could knock any first baseman in the game off his feet with a throw from 3B. A member of the Binghamton Crickets in the early 1870s, he later moved to St. Louis, where he became one of the original St. Louis Browns and appeared in the club's lineup in its inaugural NA game. When the NL formed in 1876, he joined Louisville and gave the Grays two solid seasons at the hot corner. In his second year Louisville seemed headed for the NL pennant until suffering a mysterious late summer collapse that was strongly suspected of having been designed by several team members to throw the pennant to Boston.

Uninvolved in the "Louisville Scandal," Hague was free to sign with the new Providence NL entry in 1878 after the Kentucky city withdrew from the league. He played every inning at 3B but produced just a .204 BA, a .436 OPS, and only 21 runs, the fewest of any NL regular. Despite being retained for 1879, Hague was on thin ice, especially when his offensive contributions continued to be negligible. Still, he would probably have finished the season with Providence and joined in the team's pennant celebration were it not for a torn tendon in his throwing arm that forced manager George Wright to replace him with Jack Farrell in the final weeks of the season.

Although Hague had an operation on his once seemingly indestructible arm that winter, he received no offers for 1880 and remained in Philadelphia, operating a cigar store and playing the next two seasons for an independent team. When no ML offers came in 1882 either, even though the rebel AA had created six new ML teams, Hague ran the newly organized Atlantics of Philadelphia. The same situation persisted until the July 12, 1884, *Police Gazette* announced, "Billy Hague has received his diploma as an Eastern League umpire, having graduated June 12, at the point of Secretary Diddlebock's toe."

Hague later umpired in the Southern League as well but was not a success. By the late 1880s he drove a horse car in Philadelphia and worked summers as a ticket taker at the AA club's Athletic Park. For years he was known at last report in the early 1890s to have a paper route. Not until recently was Hague learned to have been working in a flower market when he died in Philadelphia of euremia. (DN/DB)

Hankinson, Frank Edward / "Frank"

B	T	HGT	WGT	G	AB	H	R	2B
R	R	5'11"	168	849	3272	747	410	122

3B	HR	RBI	BB	SO	SB	BA	SA	OBP
39	13	344	170	211	31	.228	.301	.267

G	IP	H	GS	CG	BB
32	266.2	281	28	28	31

SO	SH	W	L	PCT	ERA
81	2	16	12	.571	2.50

B. 4/29/1856 New York, NY **D.** 4/5/1911

TEAMS: 78–79ChiN 80CleN 81TroN 83–84NYN 85–87NYA 88KCA

DEBUT: 5/1/1878 at Indianapolis; played 3B and went 1-for-4 in a 5–4 win over Indianapolis's "The Only" Nolan

FINALE: 10/14/1888 at Louisville; played 2B and went and 0-for-4 in a 9–1 loss to Louisville's Scott Stratton

BIZARRE RECORD: 6/2/1883 at New York; in Chicago's first ever appearance at the Polo Grounds in a NL game, batted last and went 0-for-6 but scored 4 runs—a ML record for the most runs in a game without any hits, walks, or HBPs—in a 22–7 win over Chicago's Larry Corcoran and Fred Goldsmith

The son of a brick mason who was born in Lancashire, England, Frank Hankinson was primarily a pitcher with the amateur Staten Island Alaskas at age 20. He returned to the Alaskas in 1877 but was kicked off the team in June for a time and subsequently was reinstated by the League Alliance nine in September. In 1878, his rookie ML season with the Chicago White Stockings, Hankinson was installed at 3B and hit .267, which was to be his career high. He was used only once in the box—in the season finale on September 14 when he lost 9–6 to Cincinnati. Nevertheless, Hankinson was made into a change pitcher in 1879 by Chicago player-manager Cap Anson and appeared only sparingly at other positions. Anson's reason for the switch was the arrival in Chicago of Ned Williamson from the defunct Indianapolis team. Hankinson did little to help his cause for more playing time by hitting just .181. As a pitcher, however, he was quite effective, posting a 15-10 record, and it is a puzzle that he never again served as a regular boxman. Although initially among the five players Chicago reserved for 1880, Hankinson may have been the first player sold from reserve rather than a contract when he went to Cleveland after Chicago signed pitchers Larry Corcoran and Fred Goldsmith, but after he hit .209 the Blues chose not to reserve him for 1881.

The following year Hankinson found a home with Troy that proved equally short-lived when his BA dipped to .193 and he scored the fewest runs (34) of any NL performer in 80 or more games. Reduced to semipro ball in 1882, Hankinson revived his ML career when the Troy franchise went to New York in 1883. Though he was still the same weak hitter who scored few runs, his durability at 3B made him popular in Gotham. Typically, Hankinson scored just 40 runs in 94 games in 1883, but 7 of them came, remarkably, in a 3-game series with Chicago in early June that saw him garner just 2 hits and no walks.

After two years with the New York NL club, he was more or less traded prior to the 1885 season to the AA New York Mets (*see* John Day). A weak season in 1885 was followed by his best overall campaign in the majors. In 1886 Hankinson was second on the Mets only to lead-off hitter Candy Nelson in walks, garnering a career-best 49 free passes. After another strong season with the Mets in 1887, Hankinson began to make the sham trade with the Giants that had seemed so one-sided two years earlier almost palatable to Mets followers. But Gotham's AA entry folded after that season, and in 1888 Hankinson was ticketed, much to his displeasure, for Kansas City, the Mets' replacement in the AA. Injured in preseason practice, he recovered in time to play KC's opening game in the AA on April 21 but lost his 3B post to Jumbo Davis soon afterward. While he rode the bench, Hankinson raged against conditions in Kansas City, contending that the team's park was so hot during games that it "was a regular death trap." He received an unexpected last opportunity to retrieve his ML career toward the end of the 1888 season when Sam Barkley was fired as KC's player-manager, leaving the club without a second baseman, but finished with a .174 BA in 155 ABs.

Hankinson played several more seasons of semipro ball and one final campaign in the minors, when he served primarily at 1B for Ottawa of the Illinois-Iowa League in 1891. His lone return to the public eye came in March 1890 when he sued his wife, Mamie, in New York for divorce and also sought custody of their two daughters, claiming she had committed adultery with both a local fireman and a boarder at the house on MacDougal Street where she had secretly moved with her children after he learned of her initial act of adultery from a family servant. Her infidelity allegedly began in 1888, when Hankinson played for Kansas City while she remained behind in New York. It was customary then for wives, particularly those with young children, not to accompany their husbands around the country each time their baseball careers required them to relocate.

In November 1898 *TSN* noted that Hankinson was now "a gentleman of leisure" and living in uptown Manhattan on Seventh Avenue. He later moved to New Jersey and died in Palisades Park just prior to the opening of the 1911 season. (DN/DB)

Hartman, Frederick Orrin / "Fred" "Dutch"

B	T	HGT	WGT	G	AB	H	R	2B
R	R	5'6"	170	348	1353	387	190	44

3B	HR	RBI	BB	SO	SB	BA	SA	OBP
31	7	192	79	11	43	.286	.380	.337

B. 4/25/1868 Allegheny, PA **D.** 11/11/1938
TEAMS: 94PitN 97StLN 98–99NYN 01ChiAL 02StLN
DEBUT: 7/26/1894 at Pittsburgh; played 3B and went 1-for-3 in a 9–8 win over Cleveland's Tony Mullane
FINALE: 9/8/1902 at Brooklyn; played 3B and made 1 hit in a 6–1 loss to Brooklyn's Doc Newton

After playing in the Tri-State, New York–Pennsylvania, and Pennsylvania State leagues from 1890–93, Fred Hartman was invited to train the following spring with the Phillies. He stayed long enough to appear in the team photograph before returning to the Pennsylvania State League. Although he hit .319 after he joined Pittsburgh in late July 1894, he returned to the minors until 1897 when the Browns planted him at 3B and then traded him to New York that fall after he led the club in doubles and RBI.

Hartman retained the Giants' 3B job until two months into the 1899 season, when he was cut after a slow start. He finished the year in the Connecticut State League and then moved to Chicago of the newly renamed American League in 1900. Hartman was a key part of the White Sox' pennant-winning juggernaut in both 1900 and 1901 but was dissatisfied with the money owner Charlie Comiskey paid him and also became a target of boo birds seated behind 3B at South Side Park. The stumpy third sacker opted to jump to the NL Cardinals in 1902. It was a bad mistake. Hartman's bat never came alive in 1902, and he finished with the second-lowest OPS of any NL qualifier (.505). By 1903 he was back in the minors to stay with Buffalo of the Eastern League. Hartman finished his pro career in 1907 with McKeesport of the Pennsylvania-Ohio-Maryland League and remained in that city until his death in 1933. (DN)

Hickman, Charles Taylor / "Charlie" "Piano Legs"

B	T	HGT	WGT	G	AB	H	R	2B
R	R	5'9"	215	167	597	190	85	23

3B	HR	RBI	BB	SO	SB	BA	SA	OBP
24	10	115	20	—	11	.318	.528	.361

G	IP	H	GS	CG	BB
19	107	84	12	8	53

SO	SH	W	L	PCT	ERA
23	3	7	2	.778	3.87

B. 3/4/1876 Taylortown, PA
D. 4/19/1934 Morgantown, WV
TEAMS: 97–99BosN 00–01NYN 02BosAL 03–04CleAL 04–05DetAL 05–07WasAL 07ChiAL 08CleAL
DEBUT: 9/8/1897 at Boston; relieved Fred Klobedanz in a 17–5 win over St. Louis's Bill Hart
FINALE: 7/31/1908 at Cleveland; played 1B and went hitless in a 16–3 win over New York's Jack Chesbro and Harry Billiard

Charlie Hickman's heavy legs were the inspiration for his nickname. Among the more ponderous performers of his era, he stole only 72 bases in twelve ML seasons and never scored more than the 74 runs he tallied in 1902, when he hit a career-high .361 and led the AL in hits with 193. Hickman compiled 59 home runs, the fifth highest total among players active during his 1897–1908 career span, indicating why he was moved permanently from the mound to everyday play after the 1901 season, but glaring defensive shortcomings prevented him from ever finding a position that he could be trusted to make his regular home.

Taylortown, where Hickman grew up, was near West Virginia University in Morgantown, and in

1895 he studied law there and was a classmate and teammate of Fielding "Hurry Up" Yost, the future coach of the University of Michigan's famed "Point a Minute" team. The following year he began his pro career with New Castle, PA, of the Interstate League. Hickman was in his second season with New Castle when Boston NL purchased him for $1,000 and then reneged when he hurt his arm and had to go home. Even after he was healthy enough to rejoin Boston, owner Arthur Soden refused to pay the agreed-upon price for him until New Castle threatened legal action. Hickman was 6-0 as a pitcher in his third ML season, but *TSN* cited him as a prime example of the meaninglessness of winning percentage since his poor control rendered him an undependable moundsman.

When Hickman ruptured a blood vessel in his arm in September 1899, Soden ignored his perfect pitching record and .397 BA and let him choose between being farmed to Worcester of the Eastern League in 1900 or sold to New York. Hickman elected to go to the Giants, where he was put at 3B in 1900 and made 86 errors. His corresponding .842 FA was a post-1892 record low for a third sacker, but his .313 BA and club-high 91 RBI demanded that a place be found for him somewhere. Such did not occur in 1901, when Hickman played every position for the Giants except catcher before jumping that winter to the American League. (DN)

Irwin, Charles Edwin / "Charlie"

B	T	HGT	WGT	G	AB	H	R	2B
B	R	5'10"	160	728	2725	747	447	107

3B	HR	RBI	BB	SO	SB	BA	SA	OBP
42	14	405	220	42	49	.274	.359	.337

B. 2/15/1869 Clinton, IL **D.** 9/21/1925
TEAMS: 93–95ChiN 96–01CinN 01–02BroN
DEBUT: 9/3/1893 at Baltimore; played SS and went 1-for-4 in a 9–8 win over Baltimore's Tony Mullane
FINALE: 10/3/1902 at Philadelphia; played 3B and went 2-for-4 in a 7–0 win over Philadelphia's Bill Duggleby

From ages 17 through 21, Charlie Irwin played 3B for the Rivals in the Chicago City League. In 1891 he turned pro, traveling all the way to Seattle to play in the fledgling Pacific Northwest League. Comprised for the most part of veteran minor leaguers and ex–big leaguers, the loop had only three first-year pros who played regularly, and Irwin made the best showing of the trio, surpassing catcher Lou Graff of Portland and one of his Seattle teammates, Bill Lange.

In late 1893, after two seasons with Oakland of the California League, Irwin joined Lange, then also a rookie, on the Chicago Colts. The following spring Chicago player-manager Cap Anson could not decide whether Irwin or Bill Dahlen was the better SS. Irwin opened the season there with Dahlen at 3B, but the two later switched positions. Despite a solid rookie year, Irwin lost his 3B post to rookie Bill Everitt in 1895 when he injured his arm. He then spent most of 1895 at SS with St. Paul of the Western League, hitting .358.

Irwin returned to the majors with Cincinnati in 1896, replacing the popular Arlie Latham at 3B. A below-average hitter, he held the Reds' hot-corner post for the next five and a half seasons by virtue of his strong fielding. In 1897 Irwin played every inning of every game at 3B for Cincinnati and made a case for being the Reds' MVP by leading the club in hits, runs, and RBI despite hitting just .289. That winter he and his wife, the former Stella O'Keefe of Brighton Park, IL, lived in California while he acted as the betting commissioner for jockey Charlie Thorpe. Irwin continued to winter in California during the remainder of his ML career. A right-handed hitter until age 30, he learned to bat lefty in the spring of 1899. Injuries, ranging from arm trouble to a severe case of blood poisoning, reduced Irwin's playing time in several seasons, but he rebounded to become a full-time regular again after he was released to Brooklyn on July 2, 1901. That summer he also managed his brother-in-law Jack Keefe, who fought in the 112-pound division.

Irwin's final ML season, in 1902 with Brooklyn, was in many ways his best; he exceeded his career BA, OBP, SA, and FA and played 131 games. After leaving the majors he then played for and managed San Francisco in the PCL for several years and later umpired in both the American Association and the Sally League. Irwin returned to Chicago later in life and was living on Grand Boulevard when he was run over by a Chicago city bus at 56. (DN/DB)

*Irwin, John / "John"

B	T	HGT	WGT	G	AB	H	R	2B
L	R	5'10"	168	32	1269	312	222	55

3B	HR	RBI	BB	SO	SB	BA	SA	OBP
19	3	93	102	74	56	.246	.326	.308

B. 7/21/1861 Toronto, Ontario, Canada
D. 2/28/1934
TEAMS: 82WorN 84BosU 86PhiA 87–89WasN 90BufP 91BosA 91LouA
DEBUT: 5/31/1882 at Worcester; played 1B, made 4 errors and went 0-for-4 in a 10–6 loss to Cleveland's George Bradley
FINALE: 8/9/1891 at Louisville; played 3B and went 1-for-5 in an 11–5 win over Washington's Kid Carsey and Ed Eiteljorge

John Irwin was the younger brother of ML shortstop and manager Arthur Irwin. His ML debut was among the more regrettable ones, when he played a single wretched game with Worcester as a substitute for Ed Cogswell in 1882. Irwin then split 1883 between Bay City of the Northwestern League and the amateur Aetna club of Boston and was elevated to the Hub UA entry in 1884. After going 3-for-5 on Opening Day, he held the club's coffin-corner post all season. The experience would prove to be his lone ML campaign as a regular although he later would play parts of six other seasons in the majors.

Poor fielding hampered Irwin from ever again winning a full-time job after the UA collapsed. Primarily a third baseman, he finished his ML career with a .829 FA, the third lowest among players in a minimum of 250 games at the hot corner. Irwin also had trouble with ML pitching, although he hit well in the minors. In 1886 he led Haverhill in batting and ranked fifth in the New England League at .325. Irwin enjoyed another good year with Newark of the International Association in 1887 before joining Washington. When he hit .355 for the Senators in a season-ending 8-game trial, he began 1888 as captain of the club. By June, however, he was being called "a crocus player," and the *Washington Star* sighed, "There never was a man who stopped so many balls or hit so many balls in the month of April as that same man Irwin, but when the June roses bloomed where was he?"

Released in July, Irwin finished 1888 with Wilkes-Barre of the Central League but returned to Washington in 1889 to play 58 games and bat .286. His performance duped Buffalo PL into snatching him to play 3B in 1890, but after scoring 5 runs against Cleveland on Opening Day he spent most of the season drawing a salary for not playing. Irwin began 1891 with Lincoln of the Western Association but was released in May. When his brother Arthur, who was managing the AA Boston Reds, signed him as a replacement for the injured Hardy Richardson, the rest of the Reds hollered nepotism. Irwin nonetheless remained on the Reds for several weeks. When his brother installed him at SS in a Sunday game at St. Louis, the Boston press howled until it was pointed out that *someone* had to play SS that afternoon, as Paul Radford, the regular there, refused to play on Sundays. When Irwin hit just .222 for the Reds in 19 games, his brother finally relented to public pressure and released him.

After 14 games later that season with Louisville, Irwin finished his career as a player-manager in the minors while spending his winters running a billiard and bowling establishment in Boston with former ML catcher Miah Murray. His last pro season came in 1900 when he was the bench manager of the Newark Atlantic League entry. Later Irwin coached baseball for several years at Bowdoin College and then ran a resort hotel he had built on Peddock's Island a few miles off the Boston coast. He died at 62 in a Dorchester, MA, hospital of pneumonia following surgery. (DN)

Joyce, William Michael / "Bill" "Scrappy"

B	T	HGT	WGT	G	AB	H	R	2B
L	R	5'11"	185	906	3310	971	822	153

3B	HR	RBI	BB	SO	SB	BA	SA	OBP
106	70	609	721	282	266	.293	.467	.435

G	W	L	PCT	PENNANTS
316	179	122	.595	0

B. 9/27/1867 St. Louis, MO **D.** 5/8/1941
TEAMS: 90BroP 91BosA 92BroN 94–96WasN (P/M)96–98NYN
DEBUT: 4/19/1890 at Boston; played 3B and went 0-for-1 with 3 walks in a 3–2 loss to Boston's Matt Kilroy
FINALE: 10/12/1898; played 1B and went 1-for-3 in a 6–2 win over Baltimore's Jerry Nops
CAREER HIGHLIGHT ONE: 7/2/1891 at Boston; reached base in his then ML-record sixty-ninth straight game before breaking an ankle sliding in a 12–4 win over Washington's Frank Foreman; his skein ended on 10/3/91 in his first game back in the lineup after his injury
CAREER HIGHLIGHT TWO: 8/20/1894 at Washington; went 4-for-5 with 3 home runs in an 8–7 win over Louisville southpaw Phil Knell to become the first left-handed hitter in ML history to hit 3 home runs in a game against a left-handed pitcher

CAREER HIGHLIGHT THREE: 5/18/1897 at Pittsburgh: matched George's Strief's all-time single-game record when he slammed 4 triples in an 11–5 win over Pittsburgh's Pink Hawley and Jim Gardner
CAREER HIGHLIGHT FOUR: Collected an all-time rookie record 123 walks with Brooklyn PL in 1890

Bill Joyce used a bat with a blue band painted around the end of it after homering with such a bat in a Texas League game in 1889. He stood almost on top of the plate, explaining why he received so many walks, and was an agonizingly patient hitter, an excellent bunter, a good base runner, and with all the perfect qualities for a lead-off hitter except one: he hit with such tremendous power that he was wasted there. During his final six seasons in the NL, Joyce was the best infielder at combining power, average, and an ability to get on base, and he was nearly the best in the game, period. His 60 home runs led the entire ML domain in 1893–98, outfielders included. On defense, though, Joyce had his problems. He logged the worst FA in history among third basemen in a minimum of 500 games at 3B (.851). Nor was he much better at 1B. In 1898, his only full year at the first sack, he topped the NL in errors while also leading in assists.

The son of Ireland-born parents, Joyce began his career as a pitcher in St. Louis amateur circles and in 1886 came to independent Abilene, TX, his first pro team, as a catcher. Except for a 7-game stay in the Western League in 1887, he remained in Lone Star loops through 1889 when he led the Texas League in homers with 18 but batted just .235 for first-place Houston before heading north after the TL season was truncated to finish the campaign with Toledo of the International Association.

That fall, Joyce showcased his game against a barnstorming group of St. Louis Browns, hitting so impressively that Charlie Comiskey recommended him to John M. Ward after third baseman Jerry Denny reneged on his pledge to join Ward's Brooklyn PL team. One of the few freshmen in the Brotherhood loop, Joyce played every inning for Brooklyn at 3B, scored 121 runs, and led the circuit in walks despite garnering just 123 hits. As part of the settlement when the PL collapsed, all rookies were made free agents, enabling him to join the powerhouse Boston Reds the following year. Joyce was well ahead of his frosh pace in every major batting department when he broke an ankle sliding and was idled until after the Reds clinched the final AA pennant.

When the NL and AA consolidated prior to 1892, Joyce was reunited with Ward on Brooklyn NL but got off on the wrong foot with his first big league manager when he obstinately trained on his own in Hot Springs, AR, until April 1 because his contract did not officially start until then. Again his season was marred by a leg injury that knocked him out of action for all of August and most of September. In February 1893 Brooklyn owner Charlie Byrne sent his rebellious third baseman to Washington along with $2,000 for Danny Richardson, and few were surprised when Joyce, always his own man, refused to join his projected new team and instead obstinately sat out the entire 1893 season rather than join the Senators. When Joyce's intransigence met with what may have been an early form of collusion by all the other ML owners to leave him in limbo, he grudgingly reported to Washington in the spring of 1894 and compiled a phenomenal 1.146 OPS before yet another mishap ended his season and required surgery to reattach torn ligaments to his left hip joint.

In August 1896, after some two and a half seasons with dismal Washington teams, Joyce escaped to New York in a trade for Duke Farrell, pitcher Carney Flynn, and $2,500. Named player-manager of the Giants, he held the job until 1898 when Cap Anson took his place and then was hastily restored to command when Anson could not abide New York owner Andrew Freedman. Joyce also had his share of travails with Freedman but owned a stellar .598 career winning percentage at the finish of the 1898 season even though team morale was low and attendance had fallen off badly.

That winter he tried to engineer another escape from baseball hell but seemingly had resigned himself to returning to New York in 1899 when Freedman could not work out an acceptable trade for him. Then, at the last minute, Joyce decided to stay home in St. Louis and train on his own. Stymied, Freedman pondered Cleveland's offer of Tommy Dowd for him, but the deal fell through when Joyce wanted too much money. "You'll never find Bill Joyce among the cheap men," said Joyce to a *TSN* correspondent during a morning workout with the St. Louis team. Stubborn and proud to the end, he maintained the same regimen for the entire year, morning workouts and afternoons at the racetrack, where he usually won. Meanwhile, Joyce went into the hotel and saloon business with Pat Tebeau. Joyce eventually got back into the game for a time as a minor league owner and scout for the St. Louis Browns. He then worked at a city job in St. Louis until shortly before his death in 1941 from hypertrophy of the prostate. (DN)

Knowles, James / "Jimmy" "Darby"

B	T	HGT	WGT	G	AB	H	R	2B
R	?	5'9"	160	357	1388	334	185	40

3B	HR	RBI	BB	SO	SB	BA	SA	OBP
28	9	132	89	81	83	.241	.329	.288

B. 9/5/1856 Toronto, Ontario, Canada **D.** 2/11/1912
TEAMS: 84PitA 84BroA 86WasN 87NYA 90RocA 92NYN
DEBUT: 5/2/1884 at Pittsburgh; played 1B and went 0-for-4 in an 11–2 loss to Philadelphia's Bobby Mathews
FINALE: 10/12/1892 at New York; played SS and went 0-for-1 before being removed in a 9–4 loss to Baltimore's Tom Vickery

Jimmy Knowles had an unremarkable ML career that included one solid season (with Rochester in 1890) but enjoyed a distinguished minor league career as both a player and a manager. His strongest feature was his reputation for being a team player, always putting winning ahead of his own personal records. Knowles's early years are shadowy. He played mostly with independent teams before coming to Pottsville of the Interstate Association in 1883. Signed by Pittsburgh for 1884, the 27-year-old rookie first baseman was the Allegheny club's heaviest hitter in the preseason but struggled when the games began to count and was released in favor of Jay Faatz. Knowles then went to Brooklyn but did not win a regular job with the yearling AA entry until he switched to 3B on September 27.

When the AA lopped off four teams prior to 1885, he joined the Washington Nationals and led the Eastern League club with a .303 BA while working at the government printing office. Knowles gave up that job when he made the Washington NL team in the spring of 1886. Splitting the season between 2B and 3B, he hit just .212. Dumped by Washington, Knowles played a few games with the AA Mets in 1887 but otherwise languished in the minors until 1890 when his 1889 Rochester International Association club filled an empty AA slot for one season only.

Despite hitting .281 in 1890 and pacing Rochester in RBI, Knowles's ML career was basically at an end. He played a few games with the Giants in 1892 but was already 36. Knowles had one last highlight four years later when he batted .359 while serving as Atlanta's player-manager. The following year, after passing his 40th birthday and losing out with Norfolk of the Atlantic League, he tried umpiring in the minors but was unsuited for it. Knowles died in Jersey City in 1912. (DN)

Kuehne, William J. (b. Knelme) / "Willie" "Bill" "Count" "Three Bagger"

B	T	HGT	WGT	G	AB	H	R	2B
R	R	5'8"	185	1085	4277	993	533	145

3B	HR	RBI	BB	SO	SB	BA	SA	OBP
115	25	403	136	260	150	.232	.337	.258

B. 10/24/1858 Leipzig, Germany **D.** 10/27/1921
TEAMS: 83–84ColA 85–86PitA 87–89PitN 90PitP 91ColA 91–92LouN 92StLN 92CinN 92StLN
DEBUT: 5/1/1883 at Columbus; played 2B and made 1 hit in a 6–5 loss to Louisville's Guy Hecker
FINALE: 10/15/1892 at Kansas City; played 3B and went 0-for-4 in a 1–0 loss to Chicago's Bill Hutchison
CAREER HIGHLIGHT: 5/24/1889 at Washington; set a ML record (since tied) for the most errorless chances by a third baseman in a nine-inning game with 13 (10 put-outs and 3 assists)

In June 1883 Columbus manager Horace Phillips moved Pop Smith to 2B while Willie Kuehne, a 24-year-old rookie whom Phillips had imported from Chicago semipro circles and allegedly took a kickback from initially just to keep him on the roster, was switched to 3B, where he would play nearly 800 of his 1,087 ML games. In the course of his ten seasons Kuehne would set a ML record (since tied) for the most triples in a season without hitting a home run—19 in 1885—and another record (since broken by Tommy Corcoran) for the lowest SA (.337) by a player who compiled as many as 100 career triples. In 1886, as Kuehne was assembling a record fourth consecutive season in which he collected more triples than doubles, *TSN* nicknamed the son of Germany-born parents "Three Bagger" or "Dreisocker," the German word for triple.

The following year, while he was on his way to his best season (.299), *SL* observed, "Kuehne has the sympathy of his many friends in his trouble with his wife. The good-natured player made an unfortunate choice. As yet no testimony in the case has been taken. No ball players are mixed up in the affair as reported. It is said that the woman several times invited members of the [Pittsburgh] club there during her husband's absence, but none of them accepted the invitation. The woman came from Columbus [OH]. She is very homely. It is reported that she has left the city. An officer hunted high and low for her a day or so ago to serve a subpoena, but she could not be found. He will no doubt get his divorce." Through it all, Kuehne remained at his post every day with Pittsburgh and suffered not a whit in popularity. His closest friend on the club, pitcher Ed Morris, remained his partner in a Pittsburgh billiard hall the two ran during the winter months. Meanwhile, Kuehne resumed his quest to spawn some of the weirdest and most paradoxical stat combinations in ML history. In 1889 he also became the first player from the Pittsburgh franchise to play every position in a season except pitcher and catcher.

His popularity still at a peak, Kuehne was invited to join Morris on the Smoke City PL entry the following season on the heels of a .243 BA and just 43 runs scored, but he slipped to .239 and was released to Louisville AA in the spring of 1891. A model of fidelity in that he remained with each of his teams for the full term in his first eight ML campaigns, Kuehne then switched clubs five times in his final two seasons.

Though nearly 34, he was hardly ready to leave the game. Kuehne played in the minors until the end of the century. After missing part of 1898 with blood poisoning, he worked that winter at a woven wire factory in the St. Louis. Kuehne then signed with Fort Wayne of the Interstate League but was released in June 1899 while facing steep medical bills for the treatment of a cancerous growth under his left eye that had spread to the left nostril. To pay for his surgery he raffled off a treasured double-barrel shotgun at 50¢ a chance. Kuehne was able to return to the game he loved the following spring, joining the Hargadine-McKittrick Dry Goods Company so he could play on its industrial league team with former MLer Paul McSweeney. He eventually left St. Louis for Sulphur Springs, OH, where he died of pneumonia in 1921. When Kuehne was asked his occupation on his deathbed, though he had had many in his life, he instantly replied in the thick German accent that his teammates could never quite imitate, "I am a ballplayer." (DN/DB)

Latham, Walter Arlington / "Arlie" "Jimmy Fresh" "The Freshest Man on Earth"

B	T	HGT	WGT	G	AB	H	R	2B
R	R	5'8"	150	1625	6830	1836	1480	245

3B	HR	RBI	BB	SO	SB	BA	SA	OBP
85	27	563	589	240	739	.269	.341	.334

G	W	L	PCT	PENNANTS
3	0	3	.000	0

B. 3/15/1860 West Lebanon, NH **D.** 11/29/1952
TEAMS: 80BufN 83–89StLA 90ChiP 90–95CinN (P/M)96StLN 99WasN 09NYN
DEBUT: 7/5/1880 at Buffalo; played SS, went 1-for-4, and scored the game's lone run in the tenth inning when he doubled and Bill Crowley then doubled him home in a 1–0 win over Worcester's Lee Richmond
FINALE: 9/30/1909 at Pittsburgh; pinch hit unsuccessfully for catcher Art Wilson in the ninth inning of a 9–1 loss to Pittsburgh's Sam Frock
CAREER HIGHLIGHT: Is recognized as the first man to serve as a full-time ML base coach when Cincinnati hired him strictly for that purpose in August 1900

Watching returning Civil War veterans playing the game in his small New Hampshire hometown first ignited Arlie Latham's interest in baseball. Between 1877–79 he worked in a shoe factory and played with several New England semipro clubs. In 1880 Latham made his big league bow with Buffalo NL, playing SS, catcher, and in the outfield. After a rousing debut that culminated with him scoring the winning run in a 1–0 game was followed by twenty-one lackluster outings, Latham was dropped by the Bisons. The following two years the slender infielder, who preferred to be known by a derivation of his middle name, played for Philadelphia minor league teams before he was come upon by Ted Sullivan. Looking for players for the AA St. Louis Browns, Sullivan signed Latham for $100 a month to play 3B for the struggling second division team. Latham would remain with St. Louis for seven seasons and become one of the Browns' top stars and, arguably, their biggest drawing card. By the time he finished his ML career he had scored 100-plus runs nine times, logged the third-highest single-season stolen base total (129) in ML history, and compiled 739 career steals, good for eighth on the all-time list despite playing three full seasons (1883–85) when his thefts were not tabulated. However, "Jimmy Fresh" is best remembered today as "The Freshest Man on Earth" and an unbridled and unpredictable free spirit, determined to use baseball as his personal stage.

The list of Latham antics during his career is long and varied but includes such things as doing cartwheels down the third base line after hitting a home run, making speeches, and singing to the crowd from his 3B position, pretending to faint after what he perceived to be a poor call by an umpire and heckling the opposition, and somersaulting at home plate as he scored a key run. Browns owner Chris Von der Ahe was one of the favorite targets of Latham's rapscallion wit. He enjoyed perpetrating practical jokes on the St. Louis owner and delighted even more in mimicking his thick German accent. After his playing days ended, Latham estimated that Von der Ahe had probably fined him over $1 million for his clowning, very little of which, of course, was ever paid. Latham also was a pioneer in the nineteenth-century style of base coaching characterized by obnoxious yelling that was designed to rattle opposition players and umpires. A pivotal figure, to say the least, in the Browns' rowdy march to four consecutive pennants, Latham not only used his skills as an entertainer and performer on the field but also in the off-season. For several years he toured with a theater troupe, performing comedic pieces, singing, and dancing to generally positive reviews.

But far from all of Latham's exploits and behavioral quirks were favorably received. He and his first wife were famed for their violent screaming quarrels, usually about trivial subjects. Finally, in June 1886, he was granted a divorce from her and two days later married a woman of dubious repute named Ella Garvin. The following September, Latham was one of the ringleaders on the Browns who cabled Von der Ahe to inform him the team would not play a scheduled exhibition game against the black Cuban Giants after Von der Ahe had already purchased train tickets for the entire club. In late March 1888 a woman with whom he had spent the night and had a previous relationship with that no one could ever imagine he would renew allegedly robbed him of a $150 diamond stickpin, and she accused him in turn of leveling a false charge to get even with her. Then in 1889, during the heat of the AA pennant race while the Browns were trying to hoist their fifth straight pennant, Latham was suspended just days after Von der Ahe reportedly said the Browns would not take $100,000 for him when it emerged that he was associating with the same Washington gambler who had been linked to pitcher Dupee Shaw in 1886 after suspicions arose that Shaw might be dumping games. When nothing untoward was proven against Latham, player-manager Charlie Comiskey coaxed Von der Ahe to reinstate him, only to suspend him again when he went on a bender with pitcher Elton Chamberlin. As a consequence of all the turmoil, Latham played only 118 games, slipped to .246, and Brooklyn ended the Browns' four-year reign as AA champions.

In 1890, Latham, like most of the Browns' top players, jumped to the PL, joining Comiskey in Chicago, but he was let go after he hit just .229 in 52 games. He was then allowed to join Cincinnati NL rather than return to St. Louis because Von der Ahe no longer wanted any part of him and had gotten waivers the previous winter from other AA clubs, all of whom felt similarly about him after the brush with the Washington gambler. Although Latham regained a measure of respectability as both a player and a man with Cincinnati, he probably hurt the Reds as much as he helped them during his five and a half seasons in the Queen City. In 1891 manager Tom Loftus appointed him captain and lead-off hitter, but by September the skipper was accusing his third baseman of giving the team "the double cross all season." The following month Loftus acknowledged in *TSN* that Latham had been a disaster as captain and admitted his mistake in allowing Latham too much latitude, which encouraged him to come to practices late or not at all and generally behave like a spoiled brat. On the field Latham retained much of his speed and range at 3B but began to acquire a reputation for ducking hard-hit balls and playing "for the record" (his personal stats). Yet, while he continued to score 100-plus runs a season, the only stat of his from the 1890s for which he is remembered today occurred in 1892, when he became the first player in ML history to post as many as 600 ABs in a season (626) without hitting a home run.

By the close of 1895 Cincinnati was anxious to unload Latham, and he was returned to St. Louis as part of a six-player trade. In the spring of 1896 Browns manager Harry Diddlebock named him bench captain since he was only a sub at the moment and made SS Monte Cross field captain. Latham then embarked on constantly overruling Cross and meanwhile had his way with Diddlebock. The rest of the team, led by Cross, came to loathe him as both a captain and as a player—by now Latham just waved his glove at hard-hit balls whenever he was in the field—but Von der Ahe nonetheless made him the manager on May 8 in place of Diddlebock. Latham's first act as pilot was to bench Cross and put Tom Niland, a sycophantic friend of his, at SS. The move reeked of Latham's mutual dislike for Cross and resulted in his almost immediate dismissal as manager on May 10.

Latham finished 1896 with Columbus of the Western League and then played in the minors until 1899, when Washington NL manager Arthur Irwin hired him as a combination utilityman and base coach. Latham lasted only 6 games as a player, and when Irwin had no wish to retain him just as a coach, Nick Young hired him in early July to finish the season as a regular NL umpire. The following August, after flitting most of the season between playing with a team in Atlantic City and umpiring a few NL games, he was hired by Cincinnati strictly as a base coach. The groundbreaking move was seen at first by the media as a publicity stunt to draw fans, and local scribes feared Latham would undermine Reds manager Bob Allen's authority, while Cincinnati players saw the move as a ruse for Latham to spy on their participation in the newly formed Players Protective Association. By September 1900, however, the *Cincinnati Times-Star* was praising Latham's coaching and the team's prescience in hiring him to do it. But it was not until 1909 that Latham found a permanent home for his base-coaching skills with the New York Giants. In addition, Giants manager John McGraw used him in 4 games at age 49 and reveled when he stole a base.

It was during his days with the Giants that Latham restored his image as a colorful character and a goodwill ambassador for baseball. During World War I, while in England to organize baseball for American soldiers, he was invited to Buckingham Palace and took it upon himself to show King George V how to throw a baseball. He later said of the king, "He had a middling fair arm but it was hard to break him of the habit of his stiff arm way from playing cricket."

Latham remained in England for some years as the administrator commissioner of baseball. After returning to the United States in 1923, he operated a delicatessen in uptown Manhattan and was the press box custodian for both the Yankees and the Giants, depending on which team was at home. Latham enjoyed his duties, especially because it gave him an audience for his downpour of tales about his playing days. Beat writers welcomed having him in the press box, and he held the position until his death at 92 in Garden City, NY.

Prior to his death, Latham had been one of the last remaining bridges between the old and the modern game. His passing resulted in a celebration of a man who combined a lifelong love for baseball with a unique flair for adding comedic elements to it. Until the day he died he retained a sharp mind and a sprightliness that endeared him to everyone he met, in part because it included an ability to admit that he had not always been a model player. Latham was even able to laugh at his contribution to the baseball vernacular. An "Arlie Latham" today is a hard shot that an infielder dodges because it is too hot to handle. (DN/JK)

Lauder, William / "Billy"

B	T	HGT	WGT	G	AB	H	R	2B
R	R	5'10"	160	248	944	251	116	31

3B	HR	RBI	BB	SO	SB	BA	SA	OBP
13	3	157	53	—	21	.266	.342	.306

B. 2/23/1874 New York, NY **D.** 5/20/1933
TEAMS: 98–99PhiN 01PhiAL 02–03NYN
DEBUT: 6/25/1898 at Louisville; played 3B and made 1 hit in a 7–3 win over Bert Cunningham, Bill Magee, and Red Ehret
FINALE: 9/26/1903 at Pittsburgh; played 3B and made 1 hit in a 4–1 win over Pittsburgh's Roaring Bill Kennedy

In the spring of 1898, at the rather advanced age of 24 and having already played a touch of pro ball as early as 1895, Billy Lauder was still a college student at Brown University, where he captained the baseball team that also included Dave Fultz, the team's captain the two previous years. After being selected as the third baseman on the All-American college team (with Yale's legendary Walter Camp at SS), he signed with the Phillies and with his first appearance took over the club's hot-corner post for the rest of the season. Lauder had another excellent year in 1899. Nonetheless, he announced that winter that he was quitting baseball to become a representative for a New York jewelry house. At first Lauder denied that he had quit because of any "soreness" toward the Phillies, but in April *TSN* reported that he had left the team after a "lowball" salary offer from Phils owner John I. Rodgers. In addition to his work in the jewelry business, Lauder contracted with Detroit AL owner Arthur Vanderbeck to have Arlie Latham recreate Detroit's games on a theater stage as they were being played. The experiment proved unpopular and lasted only a few weeks, but Lauder won some $325 after suing Vanderbeck when he backed out of the contract.

In the winter of 1900–1901, Lauder again refused to play for the Phillies, claiming he was happy as a jeweler. But when he came to Philadelphia in September 1901 "on a business matter," having an afternoon to himself, he visited his old college teammate, Fultz, who was by then a member of the AL Philadelphia A's. Upon learning from Fultz that Bones Ely would be out that day with a stiff neck, Lauder volunteered to jump in and take his place. After Lauder's second day with the A's, manager Connie Mack wanted to sign him but could not pay him enough to lure him away from his lucrative jewelry job. Still, his 2-game taste rekindled an old spark, inciting him to sign with the New York Giants after the Phillies agreed not to stand in his way. Lauder remained on the Giants through 1903 but then quit rather than report to the Phillies after he was sold to them prior to the 1904 season. That fall he again changed his mind, claiming that he wanted to return to active play, but ML teams apparently had endured his mercurial antics long enough.

The following summer found Lauder with Plattsburg of the Northern League. Though his career seemed at a dead end, he played for parts of two more seasons in 1907–08 and later became a successful college coach at Williams and then at Columbia and Yale. While at Columbia, he helped develop Eddie Collins. In 1925, Collins, then managing the White Sox, hired his old mentor as a coach. Lauder remained with the Sox for two years and subsequently wrote a book, *How to Play Baseball*. After his first marriage ended in divorce, he remarried in 1932, scarcely a year prior to his death from a heart attack at his home in Norwalk, CT. (DN)

Leach, Thomas William / "Tommy"

B	T	HGT	WGT	G	AB	H	R	2B
R	R	5'6½"	150	160	576	152	95	11

3B	HR	RBI	BB	SO	SB	BA	SA	OBP
8	6	734	58	—	27	.264	.342	.332

B. 11/4/1877 French Creek, NY **D.** 9/29/1969
TEAMS: 98–99LouN 00–12PitN 12–14ChiN 15CinN 18PitN
DEBUT: 9/28/1898 at Louisville; played 3B and went 1-for-3 in a 6–1 win over Chicago's Clark Griffith
FINALE: 9/2/1918 at Chicago; pinch ran for Bill Hinchman in the ninth inning of a 4–3 loss to Chicago's Speed Martin

Tommy Leach's family moved to Cleveland in the early 1880s and he grew up near the Delahantys, the family that produced a record five major league players. Inspired by the eldest brother Ed's success in baseball, Leach's father encouraged his son to forsake a career as a printer's devil to test his skills with Hanover, VA, of the Cumberland Valley League in 1896. By the end of the season Leach had moved to Hampton of the Virginia League under manager Charles Boyer. He renewed his contract with Hampton for 1897 but ultimately played for Geneva and Youngstown, OH, when the Virginia League suspended operations. That winter Boyer signed Leach for Charleston of the Southern League but was ordered to release him prior to spring training so that Charleston would not have to pay train fare for his long jump from Cleveland. Boyer then recommended him to John Farrell of the Auburn, NY, team. When Leach hit .325 and led the New York State League in runs and home runs, Farrell tried to steal the credit for his discovery from Boyer and sell him to the New York Giants. Giants owner Andrew Freedman passed on the offer when he saw how small Leach was, and Farrell then sold him to Louisville for $650.

Initially, Leach seemed overmatched both at bat and in the field against NL competition. Early in 1899 Louisville farmed him to Worcester of the Eastern League but then recalled him scarcely a week later when manager Fred Clarke needed a replacement for injured SS Bill Clingman. Leach was tried at SS for 25 games and then moved to 3B when he averaged an error a game so that Clarke could send Honus Wagner (one of the few men on the club whom he did not try at SS) back to the outfield. Installed as a regular, Leach bloomed, hitting .288 in his official rookie season. When the core of the Louisville team went to Pittsburgh after the Colonels disbanded, he was fortunate to remain on the Pirates' roster in 1900 as a sub since the club already had Jimmy Williams, the NL's top rookie in 1899, at the coffin corner. Even though Williams fell prey to the sophomore jinx in 1900, Leach's future with the Pirates looked bleak when he hit just .212 in sub roles. (DN)

Lyons, Dennis Patrick Aloysius / "Denny"

B	T	HGT	WGT	G	AB	H	R	2B
R	R	5'10"	185	1123	4300	1334	933	244

3B	HR	RBI	BB	SO	SB	BA	SA	OBP
69	62	756	623	216	224	.310	.442	.407

B. 3/12/1866 Cincinnati, OH **D.** 1/2/1929
TEAMS: 85ProN 86–90PhiA 91StLA 92NYN 93–94PitN 95StLN 96–97PitN
DEBUT: 9/18/1885 at St. Louis; played 3B and went 1-for-4 in a 7–3 loss to St. Louis's Jack Kirby
FINALE: 7/23/1897 at Pittsburgh; played 3B and went 0-for-3 in an 8–7 loss to Baltimore's Arlie Pond

Denny Lyons is best known for running up a then record 52-game hitting streak in 1887 when walks were counted as hits. After being collared on May 25 by Cincinnati's Billy Serad, he tallied at least one hit or a walk in his next 52 contests before being stopped on August 29 by Cincinnati's Tony Mullane. The irony—one of many in Lyons's vastly underrated career—is that both his last hitless game before the streak began and the game that ended it came in the city where he was born and always wanted to play but, unhappily, never did during his long career.

A harsher irony is that in 1950, when Pie Traynor was voted the best third baseman in the first half of the twentieth century (with Frank Baker second), and Jimmy Collins was rated as the top third baseman prior to 1900, none of the three ranked anywhere near Lyons as the top offensive force among ML players to that point with a minimum of 1,000 games at 3B.

	OPS	AVG	SLG	RC/G	AB	G
1. Denny Lyons	.849	.310	.442	9.29	4294	1121
2. Harlond Clift	.831	.272	.441	6.65	5730	1582
3. Bob Elliott	.823	.294	.445	6.33	6021	1629
4. Frank Baker	.805	.307	.442	6.17	5985	1575
5. Freddie Lindstrom	.800	.311	.449	5.73	5611	1438
6. Pinky Higgins	.798	.292	.427	5.75	6636	1802
7. Pie Traynor	.797	.320	.435	5.70	7559	1941
8. Stan Hack	.791	.301	.397	6.40	7278	1938
9. Buddy Lewis	.789	.297	.420	5.80	5261	1349
10. Ken Keltner	.778	.276	.441	5.19	5683	1526

Lest Lyons be regarded as a strong hitter misplaced at the hot corner where sharp fielding prior to 1950 was more valued than strong hitting, the fact is that he matched up well with even the top fielders of his era in range factor, assists, and double plays.

Why then is Lyons practically an unknown name to current followers of the game? There are all the usual reasons plus one or two more: 1) He never played on a pennant winner; 2) Most of his best seasons occurred in the rebel AA rather than in the NL; 3) Although his ML career lasted 13 years, many of those were only partial seasons; 4) He had a reputation for being egocentric, a lusher, and a disorganizer; 5) None of Lyons's major accomplishments, save for his hitting streak, have previously been noted anywhere but in this book.

Lyons first played for pay in 1883 with semipro Kenton, KY. As early as 1884, while he was serving at 3B for independent Lexington, KY, Providence manager Frank Bancroft, better at scouting players than he was at managing them, grew aware of his budding talent and carried him on the Grays' reserves for a while. Bancroft then appears to have attached a string to Lyons while he spent the 1885 season with Columbus, GA, of the fledgling Southern League, for he was recalled to Providence for a 4-game trial shortly before the Grays disappeared from the ML map. Even though Lyons hit just .227 in the SL and .125 in his short stint with Providence, Bancroft was not about to quit on him. The trail that led Lyons to the AA Philadelphia A's in 1886 after he tied Blondie Purcell for the SL home run crown and hit a solid .327 is faint at this long distance in time, but it is probably significant that Bancroft managed the A's in 1887, Lyons's first full ML season.

Again Lyons faltered against ML pitching, hitting just .211 in the final month of the 1886 season, but 3B had long been a snake pit for the A's, making him the incumbent almost by default the following spring. He responded with the best season by a third sacker in the ten-year history of the AA, finishing fourth in batting at .367, third in total bases with 298, and third in hits (209). The latter figure set a record for that position that lasted until 1899. Nevertheless the A's finished only fifth in 1887 and never better than third in any of Lyons's three remaining seasons with the club. The fault was never his. In 1888 he was leading the AA in hitting on July 10 at .404, but a string of minor injuries shaved his final mark to .325. Despite another fine year in 1889, he was seemingly left alone by PL raiders, helping to foster the view that he was too self-concerned to appeal to John M. Ward and his minions. As a result, Lyons was far and away the best player in the diluted AA in 1890—when he wanted to be—as he led the A's in just about everything and the AA in SA, OPS, and OBP. In mid-June, when both Lyons and teammate Curt Welch began playing badly, A's manager Billy Sharsig accused the New York PL club of tampering with them and encouraging them to play for their release so they could join the rebel loop. Buck Ewing denied the accusation but candidly admitted he had wanted both before the season started, belying the notion that the PL viewed Lyons as an undesirable.

When the A's went into a tailspin in August 1890 and stopped paying their players regularly, Lyons jumped the team after a game with Columbus on the 28th and signed with the St. Louis Browns, claiming his freedom because the A's were not honoring the salary clause in his contract. But he then refused to join the Browns when he wanted $800 to finish the season in St. Louis and owner Chris Von der Ahe would agree to only $375 a month. In addition, Lyons would not consent to sign for longer than the rest of the 1890 season because he and Browns outfielder Tommy McCarthy were both verbally committed to joining the Chicago PL club the following year.

After the PL collapsed, Lyons reluctantly joined the Browns in 1891 and had another excellent year. Unquestionably the best all-around third baseman in the game at that point, his only negative features were an occasional bender and a readiness to defy authority, whether it be an owner or a manager. Unable to see eye to eye with Browns player-manager Charlie Comiskey, Lyons nearly jumped the team in July to sign with Pittsburgh NL. Fearing another rebellious act, Comiskey released him in September, and the third baseman promptly signed with the embryonic Chicago club that was slated to join the AA in 1892. Instead the AA and NL combined that winter, leaving Cap Anson's Colts as the only ML club in the Windy City.

Now officially a free agent, Lyons hoped to sign with Pittsburgh for 1892 but was awarded to New York when Pittsburgh's enemies cited the Sam Barkley row in 1886, the Lou Bierbauer piracy in 1891, and the team's reprehensible reputation in general. The actual truth probably was that the NL, needing a strong franchise in New York, wanted to beef up the struggling Giants. But the Gotham club was so dissension-ridden, what with the daily friction between Buck Ewing and SS Jack Glasscock, that it sank to eighth in the new twelve-team league and Lyons had his worst season ever as a regular, hitting just .261. Belatedly granted his wish to join Pittsburgh, he rebounded in 1893 to play every inning at 3B and was a key factor to the Pirates' surprising rise to second place.

The following season started Lyons on the down slope even though he was still just 28. Several clashes with manager Al Buckenberger culminated with his suspension in July followed by his release when rookie Fred Hartman seemed up to the task at 3B. Lyons signed with St. Louis in August 1894 but spent the remainder of the summer at his home after spraining his ankle during a practice session in Cincinnati. His imprudence in returning to Von der Ahe's Browns was demonstrated even before Memorial Day in 1895. After Lyons injured his knee on May 12 in a game against Brooklyn, Von der Ahe suspended him without pay later in the month after accusing him of malingering while his teammates openly carped that their owner was just trying to avoid paying a disabled player. The following month Lyons was still at odds with Von der Ahe over the severity of his injury, as was Doggie Miller, who had dislocated his shoulder. The owner ordered the pair to report to Sportsman's Park one morning and then threatened them with a loaded revolver before they wrestled the weapon away from him. When Lyons was still crippled and suspended without pay in July, his teammates reportedly kicked in money to support him. Released finally in August when Von der Ahe withered under an almost daily barrage of criticism from the local press, Lyons sued the owner for back pay, as his contract called for him either to be paid during times of disability or else released, and Von der Ahe for weeks had done neither.

After playing only 105 games in the previous two seasons, Lyons returned to Pittsburgh in 1896 and had his last good year, hitting .318 and scoring 103 runs. Still just 30, he had incurred so many injuries by then that he had the body of a fifty-year-old. Moved to 1B in 1897, he suffered two broken fingers on May 17 when he was hit by an Amos Rusie pitch and was unable to grip a bat firmly for months afterward. By August he was home in Cincinnati, his hand too sore even to play in the minors.

Lyons got into 62 games the following year in the Western League, all of them at 1B, before being released when his injured knee grew so arthritic that he was reduced on some days to a shuffle. He then dropped down to Wheeling of the Interstate League for his final two full seasons in pro ball. In 1901 Lyons quit after playing a few games with Marion, IN, of the Western Association. After sitting out the rest of 1901 and all of 1902, he agreed to serve as player-manager of Beaumont of the South Texas League in 1903 and hit .274 as a halftimer with the last-place Oil Gushers. Lyons died of influenza in 1929 at his sister's home in Covington, KY. (DN)

Mayer, Edward H. / "Ed"

B	T	HGT	WGT	G	AB	H	R	2B
?	?	5'8½"	158	185	752	167	73	27

3B	HR	RBI	BB	SO	SB	BA	SA	OBP
9	1	101	36	65	27	.222	.286	.269

B. 8/16/1866 Marshallville, IL **D.** 5/18/1913
TEAMS: 90–91PhiN
DEBUT: 4/19/1890 at New York; played 3B and went 1-for-4 in a 4–0 win over New York's Amos Rusie
FINALE: 9/30/1891 at Brooklyn; played 3B and went 1-for-4 in a 7–6 loss to Brooklyn's Bob Caruthers

Ed Mayer was so good on pop flies that he was tried in the outfield when he demonstrated that he was weak in almost every other facet of 3B play. He seemed doomed to an undistinguished career in Midwestern minor leagues until the spring of 1890 when Joe Mulvey stunned the Phils by jumping to the PL at the last minute. Mayer was ticketed for a certain return to the minors when he scored the fewest runs of any Phils regular (49) in 1890 and hit just .242, but again Mulvey saved him when Mulvey had money issues with the team's ownership prior to the 1891 season and signed with the AA Philadelphia club instead. Mayer, who had been working out with the reserves in the hope of rejoining the varsity, celebrated his return to the club by marrying Katherine Bonner in late April 1891.

In August 1891, when Mayer was hitting below .200 and his release was imminent, he circulated a story that Pittsburgh wanted him. The ploy worked when the Phils offered him an ironclad contract for the rest of the season. The following year Mayer joined Kansas City of the Western League but was idled for most of the year when he broke his arm in the late spring. Released by KC, he finished the summer with Menominee of the Wisconsin-Michigan League. By 1893 Mayer was living in Chicago and playing in the Chicago City League. His last connection with ML baseball came on August 6, 1893, when he acted as a substitute NL umpire in Chicago's game with Louisville that afternoon. Mayer died in Chicago at 80. (DN)

McCormick, James J. / "Jerry"

B	T	HGT	WGT	G	AB	H	R	2B
?	?	5'11"	170	202	841	220	104	36

3B	HR	RBI	BB	SO	SB	BA	SA	OBP
10	0	—	7	—	—	.262	.328	.268

G	IP	H	GS	CG	BB
1	2	5	0	0	0

SO	SH	W	L	PCT	ERA
3	0	0	0	—	9.00

B. 12/31/1861 Philadelphia, PA **D.** 9/19/1905
TEAMS: 83BalA 84PhiU 84WasU
DEBUT: 5/1/1883 at Baltimore; played 3B and went 0-for-4 in a 4–3 win over New York's Tim Keefe
FINALE: 10/19/1884 at Kansas City; played 3B and went 0-for-3 in a 12–1 loss to Kansas City's Bill Hutchison

Jerry McCormick faced two of the nineteenth century's top pitchers in his debut and his final appearance. A badly bruised hand caused him to miss Baltimore's last western road trip in September 1883, but otherwise he played almost every game in his two ML seasons. McCormick's chief distinction is his extraordinary impatience as a hitter. Among position players in a minimum of

200 career games since the fifty-foot pitching distance was set in 1881, he heads the list for the fewest walks with 7.

Yet he was a decent batsman, all considered. Owing to his common surname, little more is known about the son of Ireland-born parents or his baseball career. He died of phthisis pulmonalis in the city that was his lifetime home. Since his middle initial was J, our guess would be that his middle name was Jeremiah. (DN)

McCormick, William Joseph / "Barry"

B	T	HGT	WGT	G	AB	H	R	2B
R	R	5'9"	140	498	1884	463	270	56

3B	HR	RBI	BB	SO	SB	BA	SA	OBP
28	10	256	157	30	91	.246	.320	.308

B. 12/25/1874 Maysville, KY **D.** 1/28/1956
TEAMS: 95LouN 96–01ChiN 02–03StLAL 03–04WasAL
DEBUT: 9/25/1895 at Louisville; played SS and went 1-for-2 in an 11–4 loss to Pittsburgh's Pink Hawley
FINALE: 8/30/1904 at Washington; played 2B and had his left forearm broken by a pitch in his first at bat in a 3–2 loss to St. Louis's Barney Pelty
FAMOUS GAME: 5/1/1920 at Brooklyn; served as the plate umpire in the record twenty-six-inning 1–1 tie between Brooklyn's Leon Cadore and Boston's Joe Oeschger

Barry McCormick grew up in Cincinnati and was a neighbor at one time of Buck Ewing's family. In 1895 he graduated from the semipro Cincinnati Deltas to New Orleans of the Southern League. Louisville offered him a trial after the SL season ended but paid him per diem rather than sign him to a regular contract. The Colonels' parsimony freed Chicago to draft him that fall and farm him to Indianapolis of the Western League the following spring. The Colts then recalled McCormick late in the season to play 3B in place of the erratic Bill Everitt, who was moved to the outfield. At the time, McCormick probably weighed in the neighborhood of 135, and *TSN* described his physique as "of the exclamation point build like Connie Mack." Fast, sure-handed, and versatile, he played regularly at various times at 2B, 3B, and SS in his six seasons with Chicago and contributed a surprising amount offensively for a sub-.250 hitter with little power. In 1898 McCormick collected 78 RBI, just 1 short of the club lead, despite logging a .625 OPS. When he scored only 42 runs in 102 games the following year, however, he opened 1900 on the bench. But by midsummer he was at SS in place of Bill Clingman, whose bat was even less productive.

McCormick jumped to St. Louis AL in 1902 and led all third basemen in double plays. The following summer he was traded to Washington for Joe Martin, a rookie who never developed. McCormick followed a composite .216 BA in 1903 with a .218 mark in the first year the AL schedule was increased to 154 games, but he nonetheless held down 2B on a daily basis for the Senators until a broken arm ended his 1904 season and ultimately his ML career. He remained active in the minors until 1912 and then set his sights on umpiring. McCormick's first ML officiating experience came in the 1914–15 Federal League. He later umpired in both the AL and NL and appeared in two World Series, 1922 and 1925. McCormick's officiating highlight came in 1920 when he was behind the plate in the Brooklyn-Boston record twenty-six-inning tie game. He died of a heart attack in Cincinnati in 1956 on the street outside the YMCA, where he was living at the time. (DN)

McDonald, James Augustus / "Jim"

B	T	HGT	WGT	G	AB	H	R	2B
R	?	5'9½"	180	45	167	24	11	3

3B	HR	RBI	BB	SO	SB	BA	SA	OBP
0	0	0	2	4	—	.145	.164	.156

B. 8/6/1860 San Francisco, CA
D. 9/14/1914
TEAMS: 84WasU 84PitA 85BufN
DEBUT: 6/22/1884 at Cincinnati; played 3B and went 1-for-4 in a 4–2 loss to Cincinnati's Gus Shallix
FINALE: 10/10/1885 at Elmira, NY; in Buffalo's final contest as a member of the NL played SS and went 0-for-2 in a 7–3 loss to Providence's Dupee Shaw

Part of the pack of West Coast players who descended on the East Coast in the spring of 1884 when word circulated there were now twenty-eight ML teams, Jim McDonald brought less to the table than most of his cohorts despite six years of pro experience in the California League. His main asset was versatility. Although he played in just 45 games, he saw duty at every spot except pitcher and 1B. After his abysmal introduction to ML ball in 1884, he began 1885 with Toledo of the Western League and then lingered in the East after the WL folded until Buffalo ran short of players after selling its "Big Four" to Detroit in September.

McDonald made other forays to the East in the next few years but saw most of his action in the California League. In the winter of 1889 he and his brother-in-law, ex-ML pitcher Charlie Sweeney, opened a sporting house on Market Street in San Francisco that they called the Base Ball Resort. Soon after that McDonald turned mainly to umpiring and gained considerable acclaim at his new calling. When he signed to officiate in the Western League in 1894, *TSN* said that several years earlier he had beaten up Jim Corbett in a free-for-all brawl. The following season McDonald was hired by Nick Young as a regular NL umpire and made his mark so quickly that he, Tim Hurst, and Tim Keefe were named to umpire the Temple Cup series that fall between Cleveland and Baltimore, with each receiving $25 per game.

McDonald remained on the NL staff through 1899 and also worked as a fight referee in the winter months. In 1900 he joined the umpiring staff of the newly renamed American League but was not invited back for 1901 by loop president Ban Johnson, who termed him the "weakest" official the AL had in its fledgling season inasmuch as he was the only one who tolerated excessive kicking by players. McDonald returned to California and officiated West Coast games until his death in San Francisco at 54. (DN)

McGarr, James B. / "Chippy"

B	T	HGT	WGT	G	AB	H	R	2B
R	R	5'9"	168	827	3256	875	538	116

3B	HR	RBI	BB	SO	SB	BA	SA	OBP
28	9	388	184	157	267	.269	.330	.311

B. 5/10/1863 Worcester, MA **D.** 6/6/1904
TEAMS: 84Chi-PitU 86–87PhiA 88StLA 89KCA 89BalA 90BosN 93–96CleN
DEBUT: 7/11/1884 at Boston; played 2B and went 0-for-4 in a 10–2 loss to Boston's Fred Tenney
FINALE: 9/26/1896 at Louisville; played 3B went 0-for-3 in a 3–2 win over Louisville's Art Herman
CAREER HIGHLIGHT: 9/23/1886 at Philadelphia; played SS, went 4-for-5 and became the first rookie ever to hit for the cycle in a 15–6 win over St. Louis's Nat Hudson

When Chippy McGarr joined his hometown Worcester Massachusetts State Association independent team in 1883, fellow players immediately noticed that he was a look-alike for ML pitcher Daisy Davis. That July, he was part of a contingent of Worcester players who jumped to Chicago while the UA club was visiting Boston. Released after 19 games when he hit just .157, he spent the next season and a half with Haverhill in a forerunner of the New England League before being purchased by Philadelphia AA.

In his official rookie year McGarr took over at SS and became the first ML frosh to hit for the cycle. He then had a solid follow-up season with the A's in 1887 before being part of a major trade between Philadelphia and the Browns. Regarded as a key figure in the deal, he was rendered superfluous when St. Louis acquired Bill White from Louisville to play SS. Released in July on waivers, he was claimed by Cleveland AA but went to Omaha of the Western Association instead when he and the Blues could not agree on terms.

McGarr opened 1889 in RF for Kansas City AA and seemingly did well but was still farmed out in early June to St. Joseph of the Western Association. After hitting .260 for the Clay Eaters, he returned later that year for 3 games with Baltimore and then filled in at 3B for Boston NL in 1890 while Billy Nash spent the season in the PL. McGarr subsequently returned to the minors, his career at a standstill until 1893, when his work with Savannah of the Southern League drew this *TSN* notice: "He is not a man who does brilliant work one afternoon and then disappoints everybody for a month." Cleveland NL had been in search of a steady hand at 3B ever since trading George Davis to the Giants. McGarr was that and no more in the Forest City for the next three and a half seasons. Far below the league average in almost every offensive department and barely adequate defensively, he at one time had been a fine all-around athlete, but by the mid-1890s his lone remaining asset was that he fit in perfectly with the Spiders' image as the NL's most foulmouthed and roughneck team.

After McGarr had yet another subpar season in 1896, fans assumed the Spiders had cut him when his name no longer appeared in the club's 1897 box scores, but such was not the case. McGarr had arm trouble in the spring and, by the time he could throw normally again, converted pitcher Bobby Wallace had grabbed 3B. For a while McGarr sat on the bench and drew his salary but finally had his fill of not playing and demanded his release. He was let go to Columbus of the Western League, where he rebounded to hit .321. But when his arm faltered again the following year, he applied to work as an NL umpire, and while he did not get a job at that time, Nick Young remembered him in May 1899 when Jack Brennan took sick. Given an indicator, McGarr finished the NL season but was not rehired in 1900. He officiated some college games in the spring and then was committed to an asylum and diagnosed with severe melancholia over losing his job. Within months the diagnosis changed to something much grimmer. McGarr died of paresis in 1904 while still institutionalized in the Worcester Insane Hospital. (DN)

Meyerle, Levi Samuel / "Levi" "Long Levi"

B	T	HGT	WGT	G	AB	H	R	2B
R	R	6'1"	177	307	1443	513	306	86

3B	HR	RBI	BB	SO	SB	BA	SA	OBP
31	10	277	10	14	19	.356	.479	.360

G	IP	H	GS	CG	BB
3	19	29	2	2	3

SO	SH	W	L	PCT	ERA
0	0	0	2	.000	5.21

B. 7/?/1845 Philadelphia, PA **D.** 11/4/1921
TEAMS: 71–72AthNA 73PhiNA 74ChiNA 75PhiNA 76PhiN 77CinN 84PhiU
DEBUT: 5/20/1871 at Boston; played 3B, batted eighth, and went 3-for-5 in an 11–8 loss to Boston's Al Spalding
FINALE: 4/26/1884 at Philadelphia; played 1B and went 0-for-4 in a 7–4 loss to Baltimore's Bill Sweeney
CAREER HIGHLIGHT: In 1871 hit .492, the highest BA in ML history by a qualifier

A Philadelphia paper once wrote, "If it be true that handsome babes grow into ill-favored adults, then [Levi] Meyerle . . . must have been an infant remarkable for his heavenly beauty," and writer William Ryczek described "Long Levi" as "a queer, quaint-looking fellow—long, lank and lazy-looking . . . with a little, round, expressionless and bearded face." In the Athletics' 4–1 victory over Chicago on October 30, 1871, that ultimately decided the initial ML championship, Meyerle played his typical game that year at 3B: 3 hits and 1 error. It was actually a better-than-average game for him in the field—he made 45 errors in 26 games for a .646 FA—but his 1.200 OPS more than atoned for his numerous defensive lapses, and his loop-leading .492 BA almost certainly will always stand as the highest season mark ever by a qualifier. There was nothing fluky about Meyerle's performance, no rule quirks, park effects, or whatever to account for those astronomical figures. Meyerle simply could hit a baseball better, farther, and more often than any other player of his day. When the National Association disbanded after the 1875 season, his .365 career BA ranked second only to Ross Barnes's .391.

Meyerle appears to have first turned to baseball in 1867, when he served as a pitcher at times on the Henry Clay club of Philadelphia and also was a regular position player for the Geary nine. He returned mainly to pitching in 1868. The following spring Meyerle made his debut with the Philadelphia Athletics on April 24, and before the season was out had appeared at several positions as well as one of the seven pitchers the A's tried in Dick McBride's absence. By the end of the season his reputation as a batsman had spread far beyond the Northeast. Offered $1,500 to leave his native city, he accompanied teammate Ned Cuthbert in 1870 to Chicago, where he hurled 217 innings. Meyerle returned to Philadelphia in 1871 to live with his parents and help carry the Athletics to the inaugural NA pennant. He remained in Philadelphia through 1873 and then was enticed back to Chicago, where he captured his second NA batting crown in 1874 with a more earthly .394 BA.

Two years later Meyerle appeared at 2B for Philadelphia in the first game in NL history on April 22, 1876, and played errorless ball. Oddly, 2B was probably his best position, although he was also competent at 1B. In his last full ML season Meyerle hit .340 for the A's before they quit rather than make their last western road trip. He remained with the A's after they were expelled from the NL and played as an independent team until July 20, 1877, when he accepted an offer to join the reorganized Cincinnati NL club. Less than two weeks after arriving in the Queen City, he sprained his ankle in a game against Chicago. The popular assumption that he left the majors after the 1877 season because he was never the same player after the ankle injury is not supported by the facts. Actually Meyerle played through the injury and led the team in batting (.327) in the second half of the season. In what proved to be his final NL game on September 29, 1877, at Cincinnati, he went 1-for-3 and played errorless ball at SS in an 11–10 win over Chicago's George Bradley. Splitting his time between 2B and SS, he played capably at both positions, and his composite .854 FA was a career high. Hence the explanation for his abrupt departure from the majors appears to lie elsewhere.

Meyerle played in lesser leagues and for independent teams off and on through 1880 while continuing to live with his parents and work in construction as a skilled laborer. In the spring of 1884 his former teammate on the 1871 Athletics, Fergy Malone, cajoled him into attempting a comeback with Malone's Philadelphia entry in the rebel Union Association. It took Meyerle only 3 games to realize that after his long layoff from the game he was embarrassing himself. Shortly thereafter he married and moved out on his own. By the end of the century he was a prosperous lather in Philadelphia.

Meyerle's wife died in 1905. The marriage produced no children, and he seems to have lived alone in near obscurity until his death from heart disease. His passing in 1921 went unnoted by all of the Philadelphia papers and led historian Lee Allen later to observe that he had "simply been swallowed up by the city." (DN/EM)

Mulvey, Joseph H. / "Joe" "Katie"

B	T	HGT	WGT	G	AB	H	R	2B
R	R	5'11½"	178	987	4063	1059	598	157

3B	HR	RBI	BB	SO	SB	BA	SA	OBP
71	28	532	134	257	147	.261	.355	.287

B. 10/27/1858 Providence, RI **D.** 8/21/1928
TEAMS: 83ProN 83–89PhiN 90PhiP 91PhiA 92PhiN 93WasN 95BroN
DEBUT: 5/31/1883 at Providence; played SS after replacing injured Jack Farrell and went 0-for-3 in a 5–3 loss to Cleveland's Jim McCormick
FINALE: 5/14/1895 at Brooklyn; played 3B and went 1-for-3 in a 6–1 loss to St. Louis's Dad Clarkson

Joe Mulvey played for amateur and semipro teams in the Providence area while working as a jeweler until the NL Grays added him to their reserve squad in the spring of 1883. His career nearly ended that June when he was shot in the shoulder while leaving the Providence park with several teammates after a practice session. According to the *Police Gazette*, the shooter, one James Murphy, was aiming for Grays outfielder Cliff Carroll. Prior to the workout, Carroll had taken a hose and drenched Murphy, a fan who was there to watch his favorite team practice. Murphy then went home, got his gun, and returned to the park. The rookie infielder might almost have been grateful when Providence loaned him shortly thereafter to the peaceable Philadelphia NL cellar dwellers and never reclaimed him.

In 1884 Mulvey seized control of the Quakers' 3B post and held it until he jumped to the PL. During his six years under manager Harry Wright, he was a poster boy for the kind of club that Wright seemed to like: good afield and weak at the plate. Throughout his tenure under Wright, Mulvey was second among NL third basemen only to Jerry Denny in put-outs and assists but compiled a .262 BA and a .632 OPS, figures that were well below those of the better-hitting hot-corner men of his era.

In December 1889 Mulvey joined teammates Al Myers and Sam Thompson in reneging on an agreement with the Philadelphia PL club for the following season but then changed his mind in time to avoid being labeled a traitor to the Brotherhood. Nevertheless he kept the $1,250 advance Wright had given him on his 1891 contract and refused to return it after the PL folded. Even though he signed with the Philadelphia AA club to avoid repayment, *TSN* indicated that he would have to return the $1,250 to Wright, but it is not clear whether he ever did.

The 1891 season marked Mulvey as having worn the uniform of three different Philadelphia teams in three different major leagues in the space of only three seasons. It also marked his last season as a regular. Returning to Wright's club in 1892 after the NL and AA merged, he was seldom used, appearing in only 25 games before he was cut in July reportedly suffering from Bright's disease. But teammate Kid Carsey insisted that Mulvey was merely malingering and playing for his release so he could join Washington, where he would play regularly. Mulvey spent the rest of July "making book" at racetracks in New Jersey and then did indeed join Washington prior to its game on August 1, 1892, at Brooklyn. He practiced with the Senators before the game and sat on the bench ready to play if needed but then went missing the next day. *TSN* said the reason was that Mulvey had received a better offer from St. Louis but could not sign there as Washington had put in a prior claim, but Mulvey denied he had ever agreed to sign with the D.C. club, and *TSN* then acknowledged, "For reasons best known to himself [Mulvey] refused to finish out the season with [Washington]."

Over the winter, when no better offers appeared, Mulvey again changed his mind and reported to Washington. After opening 1893 at 3B, he was suspended in August and jumped to the Reading of the Pennsylvania State League. Finding minor league life not to his palate, a subdued Mulvey returned to Washington in the spring of 1894 and played hard in training camp, hoping to connect as a sub since Bill Joyce was now ensconced at 3B. Failing in his bid, he signed with Mike Kelly's Allentown minor league club, which began the season with stronger personnel than many ML nines. Mulvey looked so good with Allentown that Brooklyn owner Charlie Byrne signed him for 1895. He began the Bridegrooms' season at the coffin corner, only to discover he was merely holding the job until Billy Shindle was fit for duty.

Mulvey then spent several seasons with Rochester in the Eastern League. His 1896 campaign ended when Scranton's Joe Corbett beaned him on June 27, but he recovered to play one more partial season in the Eastern League. Some years after leaving the game Mulvey renewed ties with Philadelphia NL and was working as a night watchman at the club's Baker Bowl facility in 1928 when he was found dead of a heart attack in the Phillies' locker room after attending a boxing match at the park the previous night before going on duty. (DN)

Myers, James Albert / "Bert"

B	T	HGT	WGT	G	AB	H	R	2B
R	R	5'10"	?	160	592	150	66	14

3B	HR	RBI	BB	SO	SB	BA	SA	OBP
12	0	52	56	32	11	.253	.318	.321

B. 4/8/1874 Frederick, MD **D.** 10/12/1915
TEAMS: 96StLN 98WasN 00PhiN
DEBUT: 4/25/1896 at St. Louis; played 3B and went 1-for-4 in an 8–3 win over Louisville's Gus Weyhing
FINALE: 4/27/1900 at Philadelphia; played 3B and went 0-for-4 in a 9–4 loss to Brooklyn's Joe McGinnity

Bert Myers grew up in the Washington area and hoped to play for the local NL team eventually after he turned pro in 1893 with Petersburg in the Virginia League. He was ready to settle for neighboring Baltimore instead when the Orioles signed him in January 1895, but he was farmed to Nashville of the Southern League. Over the summer Baltimore lost interest in the third baseman whom *TSN* described as being "a large man, and rather clumsy in his movements," and he was drafted that fall by St. Louis. Loath to play for the pathetic Browns, Myers wanted $1,500 for 1896 before he would sign. It is uncertain whether he got it prior to joining St. Louis.

After a lifeless rookie year in which he stole only 8 bases and made a loop-leading 62 errors, Myers was traded to Milwaukee of the Western League for Fred Hartman. Claiming he was glad because he would not only escape St. Louis but also would make the same money in the WL for a season that was some six weeks shorter, Myers grew disenchanted with the Brewers by the spring of 1898 and staged a holdout. An accommodation was made enabling him to fulfill his lifelong ambition and play for Washington after the Senators' Harry Reitz likewise was a holdout, leaving the club short of infielders on the eve of the 1898 season. In his second crack at a regular ML job, Myers again bungled it. Although he hit reasonably well (.264), manager Arthur Irwin found him weak on bunts and slow-hit balls and also accused him of not keeping in the best of shape.

After a .276 season in the 1899 Eastern League, yet a third opportunity to play in the majors fell into Myers's lap in 1900 when Billy Lauder quit the Phils, forcing them to open the season without a qualified third baseman, but he was released to Hartford of the Eastern League in late April when Philadelphia purchased Harry Wolverton from Chicago. Myers finished his pro career the following season in the Southern Association and eventually returned to the Washington area, where he died in 1915 of tetanus that developed after he stepped on a rusty nail.

Although Myers's career stats reflect that he never hit a home run in the majors, that is only technically true. On May 14, 1896, at St. Louis he ripped a drive over the LF fence off Washington's Les German but was awarded just a single as per the rule at the time because Joe Quinn was on 3B and scored the lone run needed to win the game 9–8. There are numerous instances in the nineteenth century, however, where players were credited with home runs in similar circumstances (*see* Fred Dunlap). (DN)

Nash, William Mitchell / "Billy"

B	T	HGT	WGT	G	AB	H	R	2B
R	R	5'8½"	167	1550	5854	1608	1072	267

3B	HR	RBI	BB	SO	SB	BA	SA	OBP
87	60	979	803	384	265	.275	.381	.366

G	IP	H	GS	CG	BB
2	1.1	1	0	0	1

SO	SH	W	L	PCT	ERA
0	0	0	0	—	0.00

G	W	L	PCT	PENNANTS
130	62	68	.477	0

B. 6/24/1865 Richmond, VA **D.** 11/15/1929
TEAMS: 84VirA 85–95BosN 96–98PhiN (P/M)96PhiN
DEBUT: 8/5/1884 at Richmond; played 3B and went 0-for-4 in a 14–0 loss to Philadelphia's Bobby Mathews
FINALE: 5/28/1898 at Chicago; played 3B and went 0-for-4 in a 10–4 win over Chicago's Walt Woods

Billy Nash owns the highest career BA (.275) among HOF-eligible position players who never had a .300 season or partial season. Although officially credited with managing only one year—in 1896 with the Phillies—he also was the field leader of the 1890 PL champion Boston Reds and later was given free rein by Frank Selee to run the Boston NL club on the field for several seasons in the early 1890s. Nash made his reputation on his fielding—he had a strong arm and was dynamite on bunts—but he was a much better hitter than most third basemen of his era. In his fifteen-year career span (1884–98), he ranks third in OPS and RC/G among players at his position with 3,000 or more PAs, trailing only Bill Joyce and Denny Lyons.

Born in Richmond, Nash played for the local club from 1882 through its final game as an AA replacement team in 1884 and on into August 1885 after it dropped back down to the minor Eastern League before he and outfielder Dick Johnston were sold as a package to Boston NL for $1,250. After taking over 3B, Nash anchored the right side of the Boston infield until he jumped to the PL in 1890 and played on his first pennant winner. Prior to returning to the NL Hub entry in 1891, he married Rose Currier of San Francisco. Nash was then a key component on three straight Boston flag winners but began to rile manager Frank Selee in 1895. By the end of that season Selee had won a long battle to gain full control over the Boston club and also came to view rookie Jimmy Collins as his third baseman of the future. In November 1895 Nash was traded to Philadelphia for Billy Hamilton and named the Phillies' player-manager. On May 15, 1896, his career nearly ended when Louisville pitcher Tom Smith beaned him. Some sources hold Nash partly responsible for the mishap, claiming that Louisville catcher Charlie Dexter realized the Phils were relaying his signals to batters and changed them. Nash, who had been tipped that a fastball was coming, stepped into a pitch that proved to be an "inshoot." If true, the episode indicates that the Phillies, culprits in several notorious signal-tipping episodes later in the decade, were doing it as early as Nash's brief stay at their helm.

Reduced to a player only in 1897, Nash was never the same after the beaning. After holding out the following spring when he was faced with a pay cut to $1,800 and asked to sign an abstinence clause, he played just 20 games before drawing his release. Nash worked as a player-manager in the minors in 1899 and then opened a hotel in Buffalo, NY, with former Boston teammate Sam Wise. In 1901 he tried his hand at umpiring in the NL but quit after one season in reaction to Giants owner Andrew Freedman's successful endeavor to ban him from ever officiating in New York again following a volcanic contest at the Polo Grounds on May 17, 1901, in which he ejected three Giants players. After leaving the game, Nash worked in the medical field and was inspecting the board of health building in East Orange, NJ, with his brother-in-law and an associate when he dropped dead of a heart attack in 1929. (DN)

O'Rourke, Timothy Patrick / "Tim" "Red" "Voiceless Tim"

B	T	HGT	WGT	G	AB	H	R	2B
L	R	5'10"	170	387	1510	440	272	43

3B	HR	RBI	BB	SO	SB	BA	SA	OBP
23	1	204	197	58	81	.291	.352	.380

B. 5/18/1864 Chicago, IL **D.** 4/20/1938
TEAMS: 90SyrA 91ColA 92–93BalN 93–94LouN 94StLN 94WasN
DEBUT: 6/14/1890 at Rochester; played 3B and went 0-for-4 in a 4–3 win over Rochester's Bob Barr
FINALE: 8/7/1894 at Washington; played 2B and went 3-for-5 in a 16–8 loss to New York's Amos Rusie

Nicknamed "Voiceless Tim" (partly a play on the more famous Jim O'Rourke's nickname of "Orator Jim") either because his voice was inordinately husky as a consequence of being hit in the Adam's apple in the early 1890s by a bad-hop grounder and having cartilage crushed back into his throat (according to Hughie Jennings, in 1925) or else when he was hit in the throat by a foul tip while catching for Lima of the Tri-State League in 1888 (according to *TSN* in 1897), Tim O'Rourke was more often called "Red" because of his hair color. After making his pro entry in 1886 with Minneapolis of the Northwestern League, he remained a catcher as late as 1889 with Galveston in the Texas League. The following season he began the transition to 3B and played that position when he debuted with Syracuse AA after coming to the Stars from Houston of the TL.

A good hitter throughout his five-year stay in the majors, O'Rourke had his troubles in the field and probably should have been stationed permanently at 1B, which he played respectably. But in the early 1890s that position was still a bastion for players who possessed a fair amount of power, and O'Rourke had almost none. Not until the mid-1890s, after he was gone from the majors, did such a dearth of first basemen develop that the position eagerly embraced anyone who could hit, period. However, 1B also demanded skill at handling bunts, and Harry Pulliam once said O'Rourke "was about as shifty of foot as a diver with his business shoes on."

His struggle to find a regular ML job began in earnest in 1891. Despite hitting .283 as a rookie, he was forced to return to the minors when the majors contracted from three leagues to two. Already a multiple minor league batting-title winner, he was leading the Western Association in hitting in late July 1891 shortly before Columbus AA acquired him from St. Paul to replace Jim Donnelly at 3B. When the AA abandoned Columbus after merging with the NL, O'Rourke again found himself back in the minors as contraction reduced the number of ML teams from sixteen to twelve. He spent most of 1892 with Columbus of the Western League before joining Baltimore on July 20.

In 1893, for the first time in his career, O'Rourke was in the majors on Opening Day. Stationed at 3B with Baltimore, he was hitting .363 on June 7 when he was traded to Louisville for first baseman Harry Taylor and SS Hughie Jennings. Although unfathomable in retrospect from a Louisville perspective, the deal made sense at the time, as Jennings had been something of a disappointment with the Colonels, and by 1893 Taylor was more interested in becoming a lawyer than in furthering his baseball career. O'Rourke's BA predictably began to drop as soon as he arrived in Louisville, but his was still one of the more productive bats on the weakest-hitting team in the majors until he suffered a severe leg injury late in the season. The following year he seemed to lose motivation and on June 14 gave "the worst exhibition of listless playing at short ever seen in Boston . . . quitting no less than four times on ground balls when there were men in base." Soon after that O'Rourke was released to St. Louis and within a few weeks the Browns also cut him. Washington then tried him at 2B but swiftly became the third team in little over a month to bounce him when he proved "a rank failure," although it is hard to see why given his 3-for-5 coda.

O'Rourke finished 1894 in the Western League and then played in the minors until 1900. He died in Seattle in 1938. None of his obits shed any light as to the true version of how he came by his famous baseball nickname. (DN/DB)

---

*Parrott, Walter Edward / "Jiggs"

B	T	HGT	WGT	G	AB	H	R	2B
R	?	5'11"	160	317	1317	309	174	35

3B	HR	RBI	BB	SO	SB	BA	SA	OBP
23	6	.152	37	90	62	.235	.310	.258

B. 7/14/1871 Portland, OR **D.** 4/16/1898
TEAMS: 92–95ChiN
DEBUT: 7/11/1892 at Boston; played 3B and went 0-for-3 in a 3–2 loss to Boston's Kid Nichols
FINALE: 6/6/1895 at Baltimore; finished the game in LF, and went 0-for-1 in a 13–10 win over Baltimore's Duke Esper and George Hemming

Jiggs Parrott was the brother of MLer Tom Parrott. The source of his nickname is unknown. One of five ball-playing brothers, he starred for several years with top amateur teams like the Willamettes in the Portland, OR, vicinity before becoming the first native of his state to play ML ball. Parrott had moved from the Pacific Northwest League to Minneapolis of the Western League in 1892 when he was summoned to Chicago NL in July. After hitting .201 as a rookie third baseman, he had a .267 OBP in 1893, the first season at the new hitter-friendly pitching distance, and then, in 1894, was switched to 2B and had his career year, such as it was, when he hiked his OBP to .274. That season, Parrott and his brother also became the only sibling batter-pitcher combination in ML history to compile 500 ABs and 300 innings pitched, respectively, in the same season. Meanwhile, Chicago observers grew progressively annoyed that player-manager Cap Anson continued to grant Parrott regular duty despite glaring evidence that he was the most ineffectual position player in the majors in his first three seasons (1892–94), averaging only 3.59 runs created per game, with Charlie Comiskey's 3.70 the lone figure nearly as bad.

In the spring of 1895 doubts about Anson's sanity were allayed when rookie Ace Stewart won the 2B post. After being farmed that June to Jacksonville, IL, of the Western Association, where he did poorly and was often guilty of sulking, Parrott moved to Rockford of the same circuit, hit .351, and returned to Chicago the following spring. On the eve of the 1896 season Anson finally bowed to the local press, which had been clamoring for years that Parrott had no business being in the majors, and released him permanently. In August 1896 Bill Everitt offered the *Chicago Tribune* an explanation for Anson's strange fondness for Parrott, claiming that the Oregonian was a constant target of cruel hazing, particularly in his first few months with Chicago. Chided for being too slow, Parrott was counseled to put on seven heavy sweaters and run around the field in the hot sun to improve his speed. After he did as advised he was worthless for several weeks. According to Everitt, teammates also frequently stole Parrott's clothes after practice while he was in shower. Conceivably all of this bullying made Anson take pity on him and become his guardian angel of sorts.

Parrott played in the Western League in 1896, but when he reported to spring training with Columbus the following year, he seemed sluggish and lethargic. Sent back to the Western Association, he played 15 games with Dubuque and then returned to his Portland home. In the fall of 1897 Parrott went to Phoenix to escape the damp West Coast winter climate. He died there in April 1898 of consumption. (DN)

Pinkney, George Burton / "George"

B	T	HGT	WGT	G	AB	H	R	2B
L	R	5'7"	160	1163	4610	1212	874	170

3B	HR	RBI	BB	SO	SB	BA	SA	OBP
56	21	539	526	135	296	.263	.338	.345

G	IP	H	GS	CG	BB
1	2	2	0	0	0

SO	SH	W	L	PCT	ERA
0	0	0	0	—	4.50

B. 1/11/1859 Orange Prairie, IL **D.** 11/10/1926
TEAMS: 84CleN 85–89BroA 90–91BroN 92StLN 93LouN
DEBUT: 8/16/1884 at Boston; played SS and went 1-for-3 in a 4–3 loss to Boston's Jim Whitney
FINALE: 9/29/1893 at Louisville; played 3B and went 0-for-2 in a 6–5 win over Baltimore's Bill Hawke
CAREER HIGHLIGHT: Played a nineteenth-century record 577 consecutive games, the last on April 30, 1890; the following day Pinkney's streak ended when he was spiked by Boston's Chippy McGarr as McGarr slid into 3B in a game that was later rained out

George Pinkney was Brooklyn owner Charlie Byrne's best-kept secret. An excellent lead-off hitter who walked a lot and ran well, he was the ideal player in almost every respect. Pinkney not only was ready, willing, and able to play every day, but he also never asked Byrne "for a cent of advance money." If he could be said to have had a weakness, it was that he was a "chess fiend." Pinkney's closest friend from his first day in the majors was first baseman Bill Phillips. The pair met when Pinkney joined Cleveland in 1884, and they were part of the contingent that was sold to Brooklyn when the Forest City club folded after that season. In the City of Churches they were so inseparable that they became known as "Pink and his dad."

Pinkney came late to pro ball and was already 24 (though he claimed to be only 21) in 1883 when he first donned the threads of his hometown Peoria club in the Northwestern League. He remained with Peoria until August 1884 when Cleveland acquired him to replace SS Jack Glasscock, who had jumped to the Union Association. Pinkney lacked the range for SS and was soon switched to 2B, where he remained when he first joined Brooklyn in 1885. Midway through the season he swapped locales with third baseman Bill McClellan, and for the rest of the decade Brooklyn never had to worry about who would man the hot corner.

Pinkney's high point came in 1888 when he played every inning of every game as per usual and led the AA in runs. He hit a career-high .309 and tallied 100 or more runs two years later, for the fifth straight year. After slipping to just 80 runs in 1891, Pinkney lost his job when Byrne garnered Bill Joyce from defunct Boston AA. Byrne then rewarded his most trustworthy employee for the past seven years by releasing him summarily to the St. Louis Browns. Despondent at finding himself suddenly with an eleventh-place team, Pinkney hit .172 and finished 1892 on the bench. When his bat showed no life again in 1893, Louisville released him in August and then rehired him almost immediately after realizing it had no one to replace him.

Upon leaving pro ball in 1894 after playing briefly in the Western League, Pinkney worked in the ticket office of the Peoria and Pekin Union Railroad and eventually advanced to the auditing department. He scouted for Brooklyn after Ned Hanlon took over the club but was not notably successful at it. In the summer of 1900 Pinkney was sent on a scouting mission to evaluate pitcher Tom Hughes, infielder Sammy Strang, and catcher Johnny Kling, and he told Hanlon that none of the three significant future ML contributors would do. Pinkney died in Peoria in 1926, a year after retiring from railroad work. (DN)

*Reccius, Philip / "Phil"

B	T	HGT	WGT	G	AB	H	R	2B
?	?	5'9"	163	261	975	225	117	28

3B	HR	RBI	BB	SO	SB	BA	SA	OBP
16	4	99	54	—	12	.231	.305	.280

G	IP	H	GS	CG	BB
27	179.1	179	17	15	38

SO	SH	W	L	PCT	ERA
56	0	6	12	.333	3.26

B. 6/7/1862 Louisville, KY **D.** 2/15/1903
TEAMS: 82–87LouA 87CleA 88LouA 90RocA
DEBUT: 9/25/1882 at Louisville; played CF and went 0-for-4 in an 8–4 loss to Cincinnati's Will White
FINALE: 7/5/1890 at Louisville; played RF and went 0-for-4 in an 8–3 loss to Louisville's Scott Stratton

A member of Louisville's "first family of baseball" and the first Louisville AA team in 1882, Phil Reccius was thought for a long while to also be a part of the first set of twins to play ML ball. However, cemetery records revealed that his brother, John, was born on October 29, 1859, not June 7, 1862, as once thought.

The family included four brothers and ran a sporting goods store in Louisville in the 1880s and 1890s. The Recciuses were also well-known in Louisville baseball circles for their celebrated namesake semipro baseball club and ballpark (Reccius Park). Of the four brothers, Phil had the most extensive pro career, most of it spent in the minors, where he continued to be active until 1901 as player-manager of Evansville in the Three-I League. Principally a third baseman, he also played some outfield and SS and was 6-12 as a pitcher. Reccius's *Louisville Courier Journal* obit of February 16, 1903, reckoned his "crowning test as a ballplayer" in 1887 when he defeated coming world champion Detroit 3–0 in a spring exhibition at Louisville.

In 1892, according to several sources, Reccius was pitching for Spokane of the Pacific Northwest League against Seattle when he was unable to avoid a scorching line drive through the box. The ball struck him above the left temple (suggesting that he might have been a left-hander, assuming the ball hit him as he was following through on his delivery) and dropped him to the ground. His basic instinct enabled him to throw the runner out before collapsing, but the head injury (a loose bone fragment) later caused his insanity and led to his death. Bizarrely, Reccius was the third player from the 1885–87 Louisvilles to be institutionalized and die at an early age, joining Jimmy Wolf and Pete Browning. (PVB/DN)

Reilly, Charles Thomas (b. O'Reilly) **/ "Charlie" "Princeton Charlie" "Rowdy Reilly"**

B	T	HGT	WGT	G	AB	H	R	2B
B	R	5'11"	190	642	2381	595	342	80

3B	HR	RBI	BB	SO	SB	BA	SA	OBP
24	17	311	180	161	132	.250	.325	.314

B. 2/15/1867 Princeton, NJ **D.** 12/16/1937
TEAMS: 89–90ColA 91PitN 92–95PhiN 97WasN
DEBUT, CAREER HIGHLIGHT, AND FAMOUS FIRST: 10/9/1889 at Columbus; played 3B, went 3-for-3 in a 10–4 win over Philadelphia's Gus Weyhing, and became the first ML player to hit 2 home runs in his debut
FINALE: 9/27/1897 at New York; played 3B and went 1-for-3 in a 6–3 win over New York's Jouett Meekin before being replaced by Tom Leahy

Charlie Reilly had no connection with Princeton apart from having been born in the town where the university resides. Throughout his career he was usually called either "Charlie" or else "Rowdy Reilly." After making his pro debut in 1887 in the Southern and Northwestern leagues, Reilly moved to St. Paul the following season and in 1889 spurred the Apostles to second place in the Western Association when he hit .341 and hammered a loop-leading 27 home runs. Sold to Columbus AA for $1,500, after the WA campaign ended he appeared to be the bargain of the century when he clubbed 2 dingers in his debut and hit .478 in 6 games before going home for the winter.

In 1890 Reilly had a disappointing rookie year with Columbus, finishing at .266 and leading all AA third baseman in errors, but it proved to be the best full season of his career. A switch hitter, he had convinced even mediocre pitchers by his second trip around the league that he could not hit a decent curve ball from either side of the plate. That winter, Reilly signed to return to Columbus but jumped his contract to join Pittsburgh NL after a war developed the two leagues. The dispute raged into the 1892 season when a Cincinnati judge refused to enjoin Reilly from playing for the Pirates. In April, Reilly and Mark Baldwin, another Columbus jumper to Pittsburgh, reportedly passed through the Cincinnati Grand Central Passenger Station without being recognized because they disguised themselves as farmers to evade Columbus police detectives who had been alerted they were on the train. Gleeful at his escape, Reilly was unhappy in Pittsburgh almost as soon as the NL season started, and he wrote Columbus manager Schmelz begging to return to the Ohio capital. Pirates fans meanwhile recoiled all year at his poor play and rejoiced when he was given his 10-day release notice.

Reilly signed with Philadelphia for 1892 and hit an anemic .196 but miraculously held his job. Although he remained with the Phillies through 1895, he was only a scrub by the end of his stay. When Reilly married Lizzy Severs in Trenton that September, he sought a raise despite his indifferent play, but the following spring the Phils gave him his release instead to take a job as Syracuse's player-manager. The dual role did not agree with his temperament, and owner George Kuntzsch was piloting the club by summer. Reilly returned to the NL in 1897 with Washington and expected to be no more than the interim third baseman until Harvey Smith finished his medical school year, but he did surprisingly well and stole Smith's job out from under him. In late July a ground ball broke the index finger on his throwing hand. He slumped after that and Tom Leahy finished the season at the coffin corner.

Reilly concluded his pro playing career on the West Coast in 1904 as player-manager of Spokane in the Pacific Northwest League. The previous year he had handled the first Los Angeles entry in the fledgling Pacific Coast League. In the summer of 1900 Reilly had bought a cattle ranch in Arapahoe County, CO, and intended to spend the rest of his life there after he left baseball but changed his mind when his wife died of heart failure in 1902. He settled in Los Angeles instead and opened a laundry business. In 1914 the *Los Angeles Times* said Reilly "today finds himself literally bloated with wealth." He remained in the City of Angels until his death in 1937. (DN/DB)

***Say, James I. / "Jimmy"**

B	T	HGT	WGT	G	AB	H	R	2B
?	?	?	?	57	217	57	25	8

3B	HR	RBI	BB	SO	SB	BA	SA	OBP
5	1	12	3	—	0	.263	.359	.273

B. ?/?/1862 Baltimore, MD **D.** 6/23/1894
TEAMS: 82LouA 82PhiA 84WilU 84KCU 87CleA

DEBUT: 7/22/1882 at Baltimore; played 3B and went 1-for-4 in an 8–3 loss to Baltimore's Doc Landis
FINALE: 9/6/1887 at Philadelphia; played 3B and went 2-for-4 in a 9–6 win over Philadelphia's Ed Seward

Jimmy Say was the younger brother of ML shortstop Lou Say. In 1882 he was playing for the amateur Peabody club in Baltimore when Louisville came to town with three of its men unable to play. Say replaced player-manager Denny Mack at SS for 1 game but evidently impressed Mack sufficiently either to be recommended to the Philadelphia A's or else to accompany the Kentucky team back to Louisville, where he was loaned to the A's when they arrived in town on August 8. On that date Say replaced his brother in the A's lineup. He then remained with the AA club for the balance of 1882.

In 1884 Say was with the Eastern League Wilmington Quicksteps when the Delaware team was invited to join the UA as a replacement club. He played 10 UA games with the Quicksteps and later saw action in 2 games with Kansas City UA after the Quicksteps folded. Say began the following year at 3B with Omaha of the Western League alongside his brother Lou at SS. He moved to Utica of the International League after the WL collapsed. In mid-August 1887 the *Washington Post* mistakenly reported that Say had signed with Baltimore AA, but he instead joined Cleveland after the Forest City AA club made him a better offer. Despite hitting .369, he was released after just 16 games. Cleveland's reason for cutting him was no mystery. In his sixteen contests at 3B, Say averaged over an error a game. At that, his .714 FA was an improvement over his previous glovework at 3B in the majors. Among men who played a minimum of 30 ML games at 3B since the NL was formed in 1876, Say ranks last in career FA, with a .690 mark.

Say returned to the minors in 1888 with Scranton of the Central League. In August 1889 he was suspended for three days and fined $200 after he slugged John Henry, his manager at Hartford. Hartford still invited Say to return in 1890, but by June he was back in Baltimore, where he resided until his death four years later from consumption. (DN)

Schafer, Harry C. / "Harry" "Dexter" "Silk Stocking"

B	T	HGT	WGT	G	AB	H	R	2B
R	R	5'9½"	143	367	1655	449	339	64

3B	HR	RBI	BB	SO	SB	BA	SA	OBP
15	4	215	12	45	23	.271	.335	.277

B. 8/14/1846 Philadelphia, PA **D.** 2/28/1935
TEAMS: 71–75BosNA 76–78BosN
DEBUT: 5/5/1871 at Washington; played 3B and made 2 hits in a 20–18 win over Washington's Asa Brainard
FINALE: 8/31/1878 at Chicago; played RF and went 0-for-4 in a 5–2 win over Chicago's Terry Larkin

Harry Schafer was the first ML player to spend a career of eight or more seasons all with the same franchise. Before coming to Boston, he developed his game on Philadelphia's Parade Grounds along with Bill Hague and Tom Miller and first appeared with the local Arctic club in 1867. A strong hitter early in his career—he led the 1870 Athletics club in batting—by the inception of the NA he was rated only a mediocre hitter but a very accurate thrower, though a trifle slow at getting rid of the ball.

Schafer had several nicknames but was known best to fellow players as "Dexter," the name of a famous racehorse in the 1870s. After serving as a regular in each of his five NA seasons with Boston, he played every inning at 3B in 1876 but was demoted the following year to scrub status. When all of Boston's regulars played almost every inning of every game in 1878, Schafer frequently appeared in exhibitions but saw action in only two official contests even though he was on the team all season. Seeing no more future for himself in the Hub, he joined several other ex-Boston players on the National Association Albany club in the spring of 1879, had a brief stay there, and then had an equally brief one with the Rochester Hop Bitters.

As late as 1886 Schafer considered making a comeback but wisely refrained in view of his age. He was among the many ex-Boston players the *Chicago Tribune* cited three years later for being owed back pay from 1877, when Boston taxed the entire team 50¢ a day while on the road and $30 for uniforms and held the assessed amount out of their last paychecks. Although the players agreed to it at the time because owner Arthur Soden cried poor and claimed the club was losing money, they squawked when Soden began making money hand over fist a few years later and did nothing to cover his old debts. Not surprisingly, nothing came of the Chicago paper's plea for belated retribution. Over the next thirty years Schafer often appeared at old-timers' events. In May 1921, on the anniversary of Boston's first ML game fifty years earlier, he was among the four players from the team still alive. Schafer was residing then in Philadelphia, having moved there from Boston several years earlier. He died in the city of his birth at 88 after being in failing health for some time. (DN/EM/DB)

Schenck, William G. / "Bill"

B	T	HGT	WGT	G	AB	H	R	2B
?	?	5'7"	171	103	386	91	51	15

3B	HR	RBI	BB	SO	SB	BA	SA	OBP
3	3	0	9	—	—	.236	.313	.255

G	IP	H	GS	CG	BB
2	10	6	1	1	1

SO	SH	W	L	PCT	ERA
4	0	1	0	1.000	0.90

B. 7/?/1854 Brooklyn, NY **D.** 1/29/1934
TEAMS: 82LouA 84VirA 85BroA
DEBUT: 5/29/1882 at Pittsburgh; played 3B and went 1-or-5 in a 15–7 win over Pittsburgh's Harry Arundel
FINALE: 9/7/1885 at NY; played 3B and went 0-for-4 in a 2–0 loss to New York's Jack Lynch

Bill Schenck had a rather baffling career. In his lone ML pitching start, he beat Baltimore 5–1 on August 24, 1882, in a game shortened by rain to six innings, and he also pitched so effectively in a relief assignment that he finished his career with only 6.30 base runners allowed per nine innings, the best of any pitcher in the nineteenth century who either made at least one start or hurled a minimum of ten innings. We surmise that he did not pitch more only because the team had Tony Mullane and Guy Hecker, destined to become two of the premier pitchers in the AA's ten-year history.

Equally puzzling is that he spent his lone ML season of substance in Louisville despite having played exclusively for eastern teams prior to then, commencing in 1877 with the League Alliance Brooklyn Chelseas. Even a decent year with Louisville in 1882 could not save him from returning to Brooklyn's Interstate Association entry in 1883. Yet when Brooklyn joined the AA in 1884, Schenck did not accompany the club but instead joined Trenton of the Eastern League, where he lasted only until late July when he was released, according to the *Police Gazette,* because his movements resembled those of "a snail" and he was hitting a mere .248. Soon after that Schenck was summoned to Richmond to play for the AA Virginias, a replacement team, and installed at SS. Whatever the Virginias expected from a SS that had been compared to a snail, it must have been more than the .205 BA and 14 runs that Schenck produced in 42 games.

Back in the minors in 1885, he was finally granted an opportunity to play a ML game for his hometown team and put in the lead-off spot to boot. The gift proved to be for one day only, however, and he finished his career playing for teams like Little Falls in New York's Mohawk Valley League. By the end of the decade Schenck was driving an ice wagon in Brooklyn but still held illusions that his return to the pro baseball arena was imminent. How long that fantasy lasted we do not know, but it may just have been until he died in Brooklyn a few months short of his 80th birthday. (DN)

Shindle, William D. / "Billy"

B	T	HGT	WGT	G	AB	H	R	2B
R	R	5'8½"	155	1424	5815	1564	993	226

3B	HR	RBI	BB	SO	SB	BA	SA	OBP
97	31	759	388	241	318	.269	.357	.323

B. 9/5/1860 Gloucester, NJ **D.** 6/3/1936
TEAMS: 86–87DetN 88–89BalA 90PhiP 91PhiN 92–93BalN 94–98BroN
DEBUT: 10/1886 at Washington; played SS and went 3-for-4 in a 10–7 win over Washington's John Henry
FINALE: 9/17/1898 at Brooklyn; played 3B and collected 3 hits in an 8–8 tie with Pittsburgh's Bill Hart
CAREER HIGHLIGHT: In 1890 led PL shortstops in total chances but also committed a PL-record 119 errors

Billy Shindle began his career with great promise and fulfilled it as a fielder, ranking second all-time among third basemen in chances per game, but his offense at times was atrocious; he finished as the only MLer to be a regular in each of the first six seasons after the pitching distance increased in 1893 without ever batting .300.

Little is known about his personal life or what finally drew him to a diamond career. Shindle played semipro ball in his native Gloucester in the early 1880s before turning pro in the 1885 Eastern League at the late age of 25. Aware of his disadvantage, he shaved three years off his birth date, making it appear that he was still only 23 when he debuted with Washington NL the following year after spending most of the summer with International Association champion Utica. Shindle went to spring training with Detroit in 1887 heralded as the game's next great third baseman. That March the New York Giants reportedly offered $5,000 for him, but the Wolverines demurred even though Shindle was not about to replace incumbent third baseman Deacon White. Instead he spent most of the season on the bench yearning to go to the Kansas City Western League club to gain more experience. But several ML teams blocked his sale to the minors, wanting him for themselves. Finally, in late October after the season ended, Detroit sold him to Baltimore AA for somewhere around $2,000.

In 1888 Shindle lived up to his reputation as a stellar third baseman, leading the AA in almost every major fielding department, but hit only .208 for the Orioles. A 106-point BA improvement the following year brought the Brotherhood to his doorstep. Shindle spent 1890 with the Philadelphia PL club and would undoubtedly have received a wealth of MVP votes had there been such an award when he was stationed for that one season only at SS. In hot demand after the PL collapsed, Shindle joined the NL Phillies in March 1891 but suffered from pleurisy that summer and sagged to .210. The Phillies understandably put up little fuss when he returned to Baltimore after the NL and AA consolidated. Shindle served two seasons with the Orioles continuing in his good-field, no-hit mode and then was traded to Brooklyn with outfielder George Treadway for Willie Keeler and Dan Brouthers—in retrospect an appallingly one-sided deal. Moreover, he had the ill luck to leave Baltimore just before the Orioles launched their three-year reign at the head of the NL.

Five years later Shindle suffered a similar fate with Brooklyn. Tired of losing and being harangued by the City of Churches fans during a season that yielded him just 124 total bases in 120 games, he quit after finishing on a high note with 3 hits. His departure on the eve of syndicate ownership taking over the Brooklyn club and stocking it with most of Baltimore's best players again denied him a place on a championship team, as Brooklyn swept to the last two NL pennants in the nineteenth century. Meanwhile, Shindle finished his pro career in the 1902 Eastern League, hitting .269 for Jersey City, still short of his 40th birthday according to his baseball age but in reality he was verging on age 42. He worked for a Camden, NJ, firm until retiring and died of nephritis at his home in Lakeland, NJ, in 1936. (DN)

Smith, Charles J. / "Charley"

B	T	HGT	WGT	G	AB	H	R	2B
?	?	5'10½"	150	14	72	19	15	2

3B	HR	RBI	BB	SO	SB	BA	SA	OBP
1	0	5	1	1	6	.264	.319	.274

B. 12/11/1840 Brooklyn, NY **D.** 11/15/1897
TEAMS: 71MutNA
DEBUT: 5/18/1871 at Troy; played 3B and went 2-for-7 in a 14–3 win over Troy's John McMullin
FINALE: 7/31/1871 at Rockford; played 3B and went hitless in a 18–5 loss to Rockford's Cherokee Fisher

Called the greatest third baseman of his day by Harry Wright, Charley Smith's day was nearly over by 1871. In his 14 games with the Mutuals he fielded just .688, although he could still hit reasonably well.

Three of Smith's brothers would also make names for themselves on the diamond. He was the unquestioned star of the family, however, and while still a teenager he began to earn accolades with junior clubs. On October 18, 1858, although still only 17, he joined the Atlantics and remained with that club until 1870, captaining it during a period when the Atlantics were recognized five times as national champions (seven times according to some sources). While the Atlantics had many stars, including players like Dickey Pearce and Joe Start whose names are now much better known as the result of careers that extended deep into the professional era, those who saw the club play during the 1860s considered Smith to be the Atlantics' "shining light."

It was an era when pitcher still actually pitched the sphere like a horseshoe, which placed a premium on having fielders who could handle the sharply hit balls that resulted. Smith often held down the key position of 2B, and was sometimes described as the best player at that position in the country. But most observers believed that he was even better at 3B. In 1869 open professionalism came to baseball and many of the greats of the amateur era headed for the sidelines. Smith had good reason to do so, as the concurrent liberalization of pitching restrictions had begun to make the pitcher and catcher of prime importance at the expense of the other fielders. Instead he remained in the game and had his last hurrah in 1870 when he manned 3B as his Atlantics ended the two-year undefeated streak of the Red Stockings of Cincinnati.

The lack of a meaningful statistical records from the 1860s makes it difficult to assess the claims that have been made about Smith, but those who saw him had no doubt. In 1897 a contemporary of his said, "Anyone who knew Charley Smith when he belonged to the Enterprise and Atlantic clubs would recognize him now. Of course, he looks older, but he has that same slight, muscular, athletic build that made him one of the great ball players of his day. . . . Charley is still the unassuming gentleman he was on the ball field . . . if I was called upon to name 'the noblest Roman of them all,' it would be that gentlemanly, unassuming one who occasionally drops into my office, one who will not thank me for bringing him into prominence again, the great third baseman of the old Atlantic Club of Brooklyn—Charley Smith."

Within a few months of this panegyric, Smith was gone. In his obit the *Brooklyn Eagle* said he was conceded to be one of the greatest players of his day "who never struck out or missed a ball hit his way." Smith lived in a small neat cottage in Great Neck, NY, at the time of his death. (PM/DN)

Steinfeldt, Harry M. / "Harry"

B	T	HGT	WGT	G	AB	H	R	2B
R	R	5'9½"	180	330	1208	312	167	63

3B	HR	RBI	BB	SO	SB	BA	SA	OBP
21	2	152	94	—	42	.258	.351	.320

B. 9/29/1877 St. Louis, MO **D.** 8/17/1914
TEAMS: 98–05CinN 06–10ChiN 11BosN
DEBUT: 4/22/1898 at Cincinnati; played 3B and went 2-for-5 in Ted Breitenstein's 11–0 no-hit win over Pittsburgh's Charlie Hastings
FINALE: 7/1/1911 at New York; played 3B and was hitless in a 9–1 loss to New York's Rube Marquard
FAMOUS FIRSTS: Is among the candidates for the first player to wear shin guards in a ML game

Little promise was seen in Harry Steinfeldt when he went to spring training with Cincinnati in 1898. Observers disliked his swing, grousing, "He just snaps at the ball." Too, he rarely fielded a ball cleanly but rather "shinned" it, blocking grounders with the rudimentary shin guards he wore and then scooping them up. Steinfeldt argued that he wore the shin guards only for protection—they were made of whale bone and similar to those worn by cricket players at the time—and had started using them when a player spiked him at 3B, although he acknowledged they were useful as well on grounders since the ball would never bounce more than a couple of feet away. Midway through spring training, though, he was no longer stopping everything with his shins, and his arm was the sensation of the Reds' camp. By the end of his rookie season, Steinfeldt, secure that he had made the club to stay, dispensed with shin guards, claiming that they interfered with his running. He then closed the century two years later as one of the better defensive infielders in the game, although it was still unclear whether he belonged at 2B or 3B.

Born in St. Louis, Steinfeldt moved with his family to Fort Worth in 1882. His father went into the brewery business there, and Steinfeldt played for the company team and also for Al Field's touring Minstrels until 1895, when he signed with Houston of the Texas-Southern League. The following season Steinfeldt came home to Fort Worth to play before heading north in the spring of 1897 to hit .319 at age 19 after he was drafted by Detroit of the Western League. That fall, the Cincinnati Reds drafted both Steinfeldt and pitcher Noodles Hahn off the Wolverines' roster to the dismay of many observers who felt that neither would ever make the grade.

At the close of the century Hahn was the Reds' top hurler, but the jury was still out on Steinfeldt. After batting .295 as a rookie, in 1900, for the second season in a row, he hit in the mid-.240s, seldom walked, and scored the fewest runs (57) of any NL player with 500 or more ABs. On the plus side were his frugality and his devotion to his family. By 1900 Steinfeldt owned two houses in Fort Worth, one occupied by his parents and himself and one for the rental income. He was also paying the tuition for his sister to go to college in St. Louis. (DN)

Sullivan, Suter Grant / "Suter" "Uncle"

B	T	HGT	WGT	G	AB	H	R	2B
?	?	6'0"	170	169	617	148	47	19

3B	HR	RBI	BB	SO	SB	BA	SA	OBP
3	0	67	38	—	17	.240	.280	.298

G	IP	H	GS	CG	BB
1	6	10	0	0	4

SO	SH	W	L	PCT	ERA
3	0	0	0	—	1.50

B. 10/14/1872 Baltimore, MD **D.** 4/19/1925
TEAMS: 98StLN 99CleN
DEBUT: 7/4/1898 at Louisville; played SS and went 1-for-4 in a 2–1 loss to Louisville's Bill Magee
FINALE: 10/15/1899 at Cincinnati; played 3B and went 2-for-4 in a 19–3 loss to Cincinnati's Noodles Hahn

Suter Sullivan was a capable minor leaguer for most of his fifteen-year career, commencing in the 1896 Interstate League, but only a perfect chain of circumstances made him a major leaguer for a season and a half. In July 1898 the St. Louis Browns, in search of any able bodies they could acquire on the cheap, purchased Sullivan from Wilkes-Barre of the Eastern League for $750—probably sight unseen, for at the time he had a hand injury and had just made 5 errors in a game. Used in a utility role the rest of the season, he hit poorly and almost surely would have returned to the minors if syndicate ownership had not combined the Browns and the Cleveland Spiders the following spring and awarded Cleveland most of the Browns' dregs. Sullivan was nearly the worst of the worst. The Spiders' regular third baseman for the entire 1899 season, he scored the fewest runs of any ML player in the nineteenth century who accumulated a minimum of 500 PAs in a season (37), breaking Billy O'Brien's previous record of 42, set in 1888.

The following spring, when the NL jettisoned the Spiders, St. Louis, which still retained ownership of Cleveland's personnel, sold Sullivan to Detroit of the newly renamed American League. After 22 games with the Tigers, he was then peddled to the Cleveland AL entry but was not retained when the AL went major the following season. Sullivan found his niche during the next decade in the then Double A Eastern League and the American Association. In the spring of 1905 he received an unexpected final ML opportunity at age 32 when the Tigers invited him to training camp. When he again "could not make the grade," he was consigned to Louisville of the American Association, where owner George Tebeau made him team captain. Sullivan returned to Louisville as captain in 1906 and remained with the Kentucky club for the rest of the decade, popular with management for his steadying influence on younger players. He died in Baltimore at 52. (DN)

Sweeney, Peter Jay / "Pete"

B	T	HGT	WGT	G	AB	H	R	2B
R	R	5'9"	178	134	521	109	53	14

3B	HR	RBI	BB	SO	SB	BA	SA	OBP
7	1	47	37	35	19	.209	.269	.280

B. 12/31/1863 ?, California **D.** 8/22/1901
TEAMS: 88–89WasN 89–90StLA 90LouA 90PhiA
DEBUT: 9/28/1888 at Washington; played LF and went 1-for-4 in a 4–2 loss to Indianapolis's Bill Burdick
FINALE: 10/2/1890 at Columbus; played 3B and went 1-for-4 in a 10–2 loss to Columbus's Hank Gastright

Pete Sweeney began playing for pay in earnest in the 1884 California League and then waited four years before coming east in the spring of 1888 to join the Troy club. When the International Association season ended with him having hit .251, Washington NL invited him to remain in the East a few weeks longer. Sweeney batted just .182 in a late-season trial, but the Senators nonetheless designated him their regular third baseman the following spring. When he continued to struggle against ML pitching, Washington dropped him in midseason. The Senators were also unhappy with Sweeney's work at 3B—he fielded just .802—as were the St. Louis Browns, his next port of call in 1889. Although Sweeney hit a stellar .368 in 9 games as an emergency fill-in, Browns manager Charlie Comiskey shuttled him back to the Cal League when he fielded a horrible .780.

Over the winter, however, the Browns rehired Sweeney after losing third baseman Arlie Latham to the Players League. Given a second opportunity to earn a regular ML job, Sweeney again threw it away, hitting just .179 for the Browns. Temp jobs with Louisville and Philadelphia only sank his BA even lower. Sweeney finished 1890 at .175, shaving his ML career BA to .209 and tying him with

Will Smalley for the worst career BA among nineteenth-century third baseman with a minimum of 500 PAs.

For several more years Sweeney swung back and forth between the Cal League and eastern minor leagues. His last significant eastern engagement was in 1895 with Rochester, where he played SS and 3B and also served as the team's manager for a spell. Sweeney continued to be active in California baseball circles until his death in San Francisco at 37. He was survived by his widow Mamie (nee Regan) whom he had married in Sacramento in 1892. (DN)

Warner, Frederick John Rodney / "Fred"

B	T	HGT	WGT	G	AB	H	R	2B
?	?	5'7"	155	257	1034	242	115	29

3B	HR	RBI	BB	SO	SB	BA	SA	OBP
5	1	47	27	58	0	.234	.275	.254

B. ?/?/1855 Philadelphia, PA **D.** 2/13/1886
TEAMS: 75CenNA 76PhiN 78IndN 79CleN 83PhiN 84BroA
DEBUT: 4/30/1875 at New York; played CF and went 0-for-4 in a 4–3 loss to New York's Bobby Mathews
FINALE: 9/11/1884 at Columbus; played 3B and went 0-for-3 in a 13–10 loss to Columbus's Ed Morris and Dummy Dundon

A weak bat condemned Fred Warner to a spotty ML career. In 1879 with Cleveland, one of the era's poorest-hitting teams, he had his best year at the plate with a .244 BA but collected just 22 RBI and scored only 32 runs in 76 games. A lengthy sojourn in the minors ensued, ending in 1883 when he played for the Camden Merritts before they disbanded while leading the Interstate Association and before ML teams quickly snapped up many of their members. Warner returned to his home city of Philadelphia, joining the last-place Quakers but was not reserved after he hit .227 in 39 late-season games. In 1884, his final ML season, his BA fell to .222. Warner spent part of 1885 with Trenton of the Eastern League before failing health forced him to quit play. He died the following February at his Philadelphia home. (DN)

Waterman, Frederick A. / "Fred"

B	T	HGT	WGT	G	AB	H	R	2B
?	?	5'7½"	148	61	303	101	81	9

3B	HR	RBI	BB	SO	SB	BA	SA	OBP
7	0	38	11	3	11	.333	.409	.357

G	W	L	PCT	PENNANTS
9	2	7	.222	0

B. 12/?/1845 New York, NY **D.** 12/16/1899
TEAMS: 71–72OlyNA (P/M)72OlyNA 73WasNA 75ChiNA
DEBUT: 5/5/1871 at Washington; played 3B and went hitless in a 20–18 loss to Boston's Al Spalding
FINALE: 9/23/1875 at Chicago; played 3B and went hitless in a 5–0 loss to Philadelphia's George Zettlein

Prior to joining the legendary Cincinnati Red Stockings in 1868 and serving at 3B on their undefeated juggernaut in 1869, Fred Waterman apprenticed at a ball ground located at the corner of Third Avenue and 63rd Street in Manhattan and played two seasons with the New York Mutuals. Even in his youth he had a drinking problem and was eventually driven out of the game before his time when beer made him too corpulent. Waterman's alcoholism was also instrumental in the Red Stockings' demise in 1870 when he was taken on a tour of the Windy City's nightspots by Chicago kranks the night before a game with the local nine and reported to the park the following afternoon in wretched shape but had to play because Cincinnati had no subs on hand.

Waterman's drinking problem after he left baseball only grew more debilitating. In the fall of 1899 he returned to Cincinnati, the site of his greatest moments, but *TSN* reported that by then he was "a wreck and friendless." Waterman succumbed to pneumonia in a Cincinnati hospital just before winter arrived. He was about to be interred in potter's field when funds arrived at the last minute to provide him with a decent burial. (DN/EM/DB)

Werrick, Joseph Abraham / "Joe"

B	T	HGT	WGT	G	AB	H	R	2B
R	R	5'9"	161	392	1534	383	217	53

3B	HR	RBI	BB	SO	SB	BA	SA	OBP
34	10	212	102	—	83	.250	.348	.300

B. 10/25/1861 St. Paul, MN **D.** 5/10/1943

TEAMS: 84StPU 86–88LouA
DEBUT: 9/27/1884 at Cincinnati; played SS and went 0-for-3 in a 6–1 loss to Cincinnati's Dick Burns
FINALE: 10/14/1888 at Louisville; played 3B and went 1-for-4 in a 9–1 win over Kansas City's Henry Porter

A paperhanger by trade, Joe Werrick played for little more than pocket change throughout most of his pro career. A SS in 1884 when he made his ML debut with the late-season St. Paul UA replacement entry, he moved to 3B in 1886 after coming to Louisville from Nashville of the Southern League. Colonels manager Jim Hart slotted Werrick eighth in the batting order when the season began, but he eventually worked up to the third spot and led the team in ABs, games played, and triples. A low-ball hitter and weak on curve balls, Werrick was able to disguise his batting flaws in 1887, the initial season the majors abolished the high-low rule, but the following year he began to see a steady diet of chest-high curves. The corresponding 70-point drop in his BA, from .285 to .215, contributed heavily to Louisville's seventh-place finish and led to his release.

Werrick probably expected that he would climb back to the majors, but he never even came close to it. He played in the high minors for a time and then moved out to the Montana State League with Butte, where he worked as a policeman in the off-season. In December 1894 Werrick resurfaced in St. Paul after having been "out of sight" for several years, played with Minneapolis of the Western League in 1895, and then headed to Springfield of the Eastern League. In 1897 Werrick began a three-year run with Mansfield, OH, of the Interstate League that ended in June 1899 when he was released to Dayton in the same loop. He then played semipro ball for a time in the Chicago area before returning to Minnesota. When Werrick died in 1943 of cardiovascular disease in St. Peter, MN, he was the last surviving member of the only ML team to represent the state of Minnesota prior to 1961. (DN)

White, William Warren
(aka William Warren) / **"Warren"**

B	T	HGT	WGT	G	AB	H	R	2B
?	?	5'10½"	170	168	723	184	96	13

3B	HR	RBI	BB	SO	SB	BA	SA	OBP
4	0	64	2	6	8	.254	.284	.257

G	W	L	PCT	PENNANTS
58	9	49	.155	0

B. ?/?/1844 Milton, NY **D.** 6/12/1890
TEAMS: 71OlyNA (P/M)72NatNA 73WasNA (P/M)74BalNA 75ChiNA 84WasU
DEBUT: 6/17/1871 at Washington; played 2B and went 0-for-4 in an 11–4 loss to the Philadelphia Athletics' Dick McBride
FINALE: 6/27/1884 at Washington; played 3B and went 0-for-3 in an 8–7 loss to Kansas City's Alec Voss

Warren White had a long but sporadic involvement with baseball as a player and organizer, culminating in 1884 with his filling the role of secretary of the Union Association. Nevertheless, when he died six years later, there was no mention of his death, and only recently has it become possible to determine some of the most basic facts about his life. White was born in New York state around 1844. Around 1850 his family moved from the small town of Milton to Rochester, where White was living when he enlisted in the 14th New York Heavy Artillery on July 8, 1863. He served until the Civil War's end, receiving his discharge on May 15, 1865, and appeared in the Washington city directory that year as a clerk for the paymaster general. He remained in Washington for the rest of his life, always working in the Treasury Department.

Several other Rochester ballplayers, including Seymour Studley and Dennis Coughlin, served in the war and then moved to Washington to play for the Nationals and work in the Treasury Department. The dual roles were no coincidence, as Arthur Poe Gorman had a high position in the Treasury Department and was an officer of the Nationals. It would seem logical to assume that White had likewise established a record as a talented ballplayer in Rochester and that Gorman also orchestrated his move to Washington. There is, however, no evidence that that was the case, as White does not seem to have ever played for the Nationals or any other D.C.-area club between 1865–70. Stranger still, with no known prior playing record, White played a few NA games in 1871 and 1872, then became a regular for the next three years. In another puzzling twist, he usually played under the name "Warren," although his identity was no secret. The long gap in his career is still unexplained. Perhaps he played in the 1860s under some name other than White or Warren, but why?

White left pro baseball when the NL was founded in 1876, but he remained involved in the Washington baseball scene. In the late 1870s he was player-manager for a club called the Eagles, and then in 1881 he signed to play with a professional club organized by Mike Scanlon. In 1883 he organized another club and gave it the hallowed name of Nationals, and then in 1884 he became involved in the UA. White served as the circuit's secretary, and was renowned for letters that matched the defiant tone of the upstart league. "You will please go to the devil, with my compliments," read one of his missives in its entirety. Though now 40, he also played on the Washington UA reserves and even served with the regular team in several games.

When the UA folded after a single season, White's association with organized baseball ended. Even so, his days on the diamond were not over—in 1889 he was involved in yet another incarnation of the National Club. A year later White died in Little Rock, AR, where he was attending to Treasury Department business. An obituary listed his survivors as his wife, Susie, and two young sons, and they must have been quite young, as the Whites had no children when the 1880 census was taken. Yet three years later, when Susie died, a Civil War pension application was filed on behalf of White's grandson, Charles J. Bell. As of yet no plausible explanation for this last mystery has been advanced. (PM/DN)

---

*Whitney, Arthur Wilson / "Art"

B	T	HGT	WGT	G	AB	H	R	2B
R	R	5'8"	155	978	3681	820	475	89

3B	HR	RBI	BB	SO	SB	BA	SA	OBP
32	6	349	302	173	67	.223	.269	.285

G	IP	H	GS	CG	BB
5	28.1	39	2	1	15

SO	SH	W	L	PCT	ERA
16	0	0	1	.000	4.76

B. 1/16/1858 Brockton, MA **D.** 8/15/1943

TEAMS: 80WorN 81DetN 82ProN 82Det N 84–86PitA 87PitN 88–89NYN 90NYP 91CinA 91StLA
DEBUT: 5/1/1880 at Worcester; played 3B and went 2-for-5 in a 13–1 win over Troy's Mickey Welch
FINALE: 8/22/1891 at St. Louis; played 3B and went 0-for-3 in a 5–3 loss to Columbus's Phil Knell

Art Whitney was the younger brother of ML outfielder Frank Whitney. Their father owned three hotels in Brockton, MA, and Art worked winters in the family lodging places and also as a piano maker. In the late 1890s he and a third brother, C. B., launched the Victor Sporting Goods Company.

In 1875, at age 17, Whitney teamed with his brother Frank on the semipro Lynn Live Oaks. He then joined Lowell and remained with the New England minor league entry until 1879 when he moved to Worcester of the National Association in time to accompany the club when it enlisted in the NL the following year. As a rookie in 1880, Whitney had one of his best seasons at the plate even though pitching dominated in the last year before the distance was lengthened to fifty feet. But a good season for Whitney was one in which he hit over .220—his career BA of .223 is the second lowest in ML history among third basemen with a minimum of 3,000 ABs, surpassed only by Lee Tannehill's .220.

When Whitney dipped to .182 with Detroit in 1881, he spent parts of the next three seasons in the minors before establishing a firm ML base with Pittsburgh in 1885. He stayed with the Allegheny club through 1887 before being sold to Detroit when he demanded a raise to $2,500 and Pittsburgh would go no higher than $2,000. Whitney refused to acknowledge the sale and later refused a proposed trade to Detroit for pitcher Henry Gruber, threatening to sit out the entire 1888 season instead. Finally, he was traded to the New York Giants in June 1888 for third baseman Elmer Cleveland.

Initially, Whitney had trouble adjusting in New York, as the Giants were divided into rabid cliques and the "[Buck] Ewing gang" in particular gave him grief. By the end of the season, however, he had established himself as the regular third baseman on the best team in baseball and held the position again the following year when the Giants repeated as World's Series champions. Entrenched by then with the dominant clique on the Giants,

Whitney accompanied Ewing and several other teammates in their jump to the Players League in 1890. But even in the most hitter-friendly loop prior to 1893, when the pitching distance was again changed, he finished with the poorest offensive stats of any PL qualifier—a .219 BA and only a .582 OPS.

Having acquired third baseman Jerry Denny in the interim, the Giants slammed the door on Whitney when the PL folded, and he was forced to sign with the weak Cincinnati AA entry. After collecting just 86 total bases in 93 games before the Queen City club folded, he filled in at 3B for 3 games with St. Louis but was dropped after he went 0-for-11. In November 1891 Whitney signed with Pittsburgh for the following season because he was "the best man today not already under contract," but the team had reservations about bringing him back to a city that had booed him unmercifully in 1888.

The following spring Whitney was cut on the eve of the 1892 season. At first he refused to accept his release and threatened to take Pittsburgh to court, but eventually he hired on as player-manager with Lowell of the New England League. Whitney remained in the NEL for the next two seasons, finishing his pro career in the city where it began, and then went into the sporting goods business. After his own firm was failed, he was a traveling representative for the A. G. Spalding Company for many years. Upon his death in Lowell in 1943, he was survived by his brother Frank and a niece. (DN)

Williams, James Thomas / "Jimmy" "Buttons"

B	T	HGT	WGT	G	AB	H	R	2B
R	R	5'9"	175	259	1037	330	199	43

3B	HR	RBI	BB	SO	SB	BA	SA	OBP
38	14	184	92	—	44	.318	.473	.362

B. 12/20/1876 St. Louis, MO **D.** 1/16/1865
TEAMS: 99–00PitN 01–02BalAL 03–07NYAL 08–09StLAL
DEBUT: 4/15/1899 at Cincinnati; played 3B and went 0-for-3 in a 5–2 win over Cincinnati's Pink Hawley
FINALE: 10/3/1909 at St. Louis; played 2B and went 0-for-2 in a 3–1 loss to Cleveland's Willie Mitchell
CAREER HIGHLIGHT ONE: Produced an all-time rookie record 28 triples in 1899
CAREER HIGHLIGHT TWO: Hit in a then rookie-record 26 straight games (ended on 6/10/99 by Louisville's Deacon Phillippe) and broke his own record later that season with a 27-game streak that was again ended by Phillippe on 8/8/1899

Of Welsh heritage, Jimmy Williams was born in St. Louis, but in the late 1870s his family moved to Denver. In 1892, although still just 15, he took a train 110 miles south to play for the Rovers, a semipro team in Pueblo, and was still with the club when it joined the Colorado State League in 1895. The loop disbanded the following season, compelling Williams to relocate to Leadville, CO, until the fall, when he signed on with the Albuquerque Browns, the emergent champions of an independent team tournament in Albuquerque that October.

Still short of his 21st birthday, Williams found himself among the more experienced players on his St. Joseph club in the spring of 1897 and reacted accordingly, leading the Western Association in homers with 31 and at one point hammering a four-bagger in 7 consecutive games. The performance earned him the nickname "Home Run" Williams, but it was forgotten the following season, when he joined Kansas City, where dingers were considerably harder to achieve. Playing SS for the second year in a row, Williams hit .343 against Western League pitching, inducing Pittsburgh to purchase him for 1899 delivery.

Charles Power of the *Pittsburgh Leader* warned the Pirates not to expect much, as Williams's .343 mark was 8 points lower than Bill Gray (whom he was expected to replace at 3B) had batted in the WL in 1897. But whereas Gray hit a dismal .229 for the Pirates in 1898, 122 points below his 1897 WL mark, Williams actually *exceeded* his WL stats in fashioning the best season of any of the unparalleled rich crop of rookies in 1899. After drawing the collar in his ML debut, he collected his first hit the following day; significantly it was a triple off Cincinnati's Bill Dammann, one of a rookie-record 28 he would hit (though most sources curiously continue to omit his blow against Dammann and credit him with only 27). In addition, Williams led the Pirates in almost every major offensive department, topped all NL third basemen in chances, and set not just one but two rookie hitting-streak records in the course of his frosh season.

For an encore, Williams was expected to carry

Pittsburgh to its first NL pennant in 1900, especially after the Pirates scooped up the core of the disbanding Louisville team. Instead he was held to just 106 games by an ankle injury and "inflammation of the bowels," plummeting his BA 91 points to a mediocre .264. Still, Williams was so confident he would return to form that he married Nannie Mae Smith of Pittsburgh on December 5. The couple then wintered in Denver and parted temporarily in late March 1901 when Williams boarded a Denver train bound for Hot Springs, AR, where the Pirates were slated to train. The train arrived without him after cohorts of John McGraw, the manager of the Baltimore AL entry, shanghaied him en route and persuaded him to jump his Pittsburgh contract and cast his fate with the NL's newest rival for big league status. (DN)

Williamson, Edward Nagle / "Ned"

B	T	HGT	WGT	G	AB	H	R	2B
R	R	5'11"	210	1201	4553	1159	809	228

3B	HR	RBI	BB	SO	SB	BA	SA	OBP
85	64	667	506	532	88	.255	.384	.332

G	IP	H	GS	CG	BB
12	35	38	1	1	5

SO	SH	W	L	PCT	ERA
7	0	1	1	.500	3.34

B. 10/24/1857 Philadelphia, PA **D.** 3/3/1894
TEAMS: 78IndN 79–89ChiN 90ChiP
DEBUT: 5/1/1878 at Indianapolis; played 3B and went 0-for-3 in a 5–4 loss to Chicago's Terry Larkin
FINALE: 9/29/1890 at Chicago; played 1B and went 1-for-4 in a 6–1 win over Brooklyn's Gus Weyhing
CAREER HIGHLIGHT: hit a pre-1919 ML record 27 home runs in 1884 after hitting a pre-1887 record 49 doubles in 1883, many of which were counted as homers in 1884 when the Chicago park ground rules changed

Ned Williamson is remembered today as one of the great nineteenth-century sluggers, but in his time it was his fielding that drew the most plaudits. Equally capable at both 3B and SS, he posted season-loop-leading defensive stats at each position and was also a decent catcher, pitcher, first baseman, and second baseman. Cap Anson, his manager for most of his thirteen-year ML career, called him "In my opinion, the best all-around ballplayer the country ever saw."

Williamson learned the game at the Parade Grounds near Philadelphia's Moyamensing Prison and was said by Ned Cuthbert, who saw him play in the early 1870s, to be the greatest third baseman in the game even then. Tall and rangy at the time, probably weighing around 160, Williamson was also exceptionally fast and a slashing batsmen who stood at the plate with both feet together facing the pitcher before the hurler began his delivery. It was an unusual stance even for its day, but one he would never modify to any appreciable extent.

After beginning his semipro career with the New Castle, PA, Neshannocks in 1876, Williamson moved to the Allegheny club of the International Association the following year. In 1878 he made his first ML foray at age 21. Now up to 170 pounds, he played every inning at 3B for Indianapolis but was overwhelmed as a hitter, batting a weak .232 with just a .300 SA. Nevertheless, Chicago saw enough raw talent to quickly snatch him when the Indiana entry fled the NL after just one season. Overnight, Williamson developed into a formidable hitter, leading the Chicagos in SA, total bases, and runs, all by a wide-margin, meanwhile playing such a wide-ranging 3B that he took many balls that should normally have belonged to SS John Peters. The following year Chicago emerged as an NL powerhouse, taking the first of what would be five pennants in a seven-year span, even though Williamson slipped back to his 1878 form as a hitter. As a fielder, however, he seemed actually to improve on skills that had already been the best in the game.

Williamson continued to fall short of his 1879 performance at the plate until 1883, when Chicago moved to a new park adjacent to railroad tracks with fences so short that it must have felt like playing in someone's backyard. Along with their new park the White Stockings acquired a new second baseman, Fred Pfeffer, giving them the last component of their famous "Stonewall Infield," which also numbered Anson and Tom Burns. Ironically, in its first season in a new park, the club watched its three-year pennant run come to a halt and then lost again the following year, finishing no better than tied for fourth despite hitting a nineteenth-century team record 142 home runs. A pitching breakdown contributed heavily to the decline, but the larger problem may have been the new park. In an effort to take full advantage of its exceptionally short porch in RF, right-handed hitters Anson,

Pfeffer, and Williamson began coming out early for batting practice prior to home games and grooving their swings to hit everything to RF, which seriously hamstrung them when the club went on the road. Of Williamson's 27 homers in 1884, 25 came at home. All of Pfeffer's 25 dingers were at home, and Anson, who hit 21 homers that season at age 32, had tabulated only 5 career four-baggers prior to then.

The following season, when Chicago moved to another new grounds, it immediately resumed its winning ways, and Williamson was on two more championship teams before reaching his 30th year. But insidiously after his jackpot home run season he began putting on weight. By his 30th birthday he was over 200 pounds and yet he was still a solid fielder, even leading NL shortstops in assists in 1888.

That fall, Williamson accompanied the Chicago team on its winter-long world tour and hurt his knee the following March in a game at Paris. A temporary brace was put on the leg, and following a rough English Channel crossing, he saw a doctor in London whom he claimed "nearly butchered" him. In June, with his leg still heavily bandaged, Williamson headed for Hot Springs, AR, after admitting to the local press that he was not being paid by the Chicago team while he recovered and that he had borne almost all of his medical expenses himself since his injury. Although club president Al Spalding was vilified, especially after he had the additional audacity to charge Williamson $500 for his wife's "accrued world tour expenses" when she came to his aid in England after his injury, he continued to refuse to open his coffers, and Williamson's fellow players had to take up a collection to help keep him afloat.

By mid-July 1889, Williamson was able to return to the team and sit on the bench in uniform, but it was another full month before he was in shape to play his first game on August 14. He finished the season having taken part in just 47 contests and was invited to play for the Chicago PL entry in 1890 more as a tribute to his past performance than in any real expectation that he would be of help. Used sparingly, he hit poorly and left the team in June to be at the bedside of his dying sister, who requested he remain with her until the end. Upon returning to action, he was grossly out of shape. Williamson blamed his enormous weight gain on his bad knee, which rendered him barely able to run, but his patent disregard for conditioning probably bore equal responsibility. Williamson had always been profligate, a devotee of billiards and faro, and often owed the Chicago club money by the end of the season because he drew his salary early to pay off gambling debts.

The following March, Williamson announced his official retirement from the game and invited all his baseball friends to a saloon on Dearborn Street that he and Jimmy Wood had purchased and renamed the "Base Ball Wigwam." By the winter of 1893–94 he was back in Hot Springs suffering from a liver complaint and confined to his room. Some five weeks after his arrival he died of cirrhosis of the liver, which he was said not to have taken seriously until it was too late. It was even speculated that if he had gone to Hot Springs sooner he might have been cured, although ex-teammate Billy Sunday later reported that when the coroner took out Williamson's liver it "was as big as a tobacco bucket." Williamson was survived by his wife, Nellie, whom he had met while the Chicago team trained in New Orleans in 1881 and wooed successfully in spite of her mother's objections to ballplayers after she became friendly with teammate Silver Flint's wife, who put in a good word for him. (DN/EM)

Wolverton, Harry Sterling / "Harry" "Fighting Harry"

B	T	HGT	WGT	G	AB	H	R	2B
B	R	5'11"	205	216	832	237	98	25

3B	HR	RBI	BB	SO	SB	BA	SA	OBP
19	4	109	53	—	20	.285	.375	.337

B. 12/7/1873 Mount Vernon, OH **D.** 2/4/1937
TEAMS: 98–00ChiN 00–01PhiN 02WasAL 03–04PhiN 05BosN (P/M)12NYAL
DEBUT: 9/25/1898 at Chicago; played 3B and went 2-for-4 in a 7–4 win over Pittsburgh's Bill Hart
FINALE: 9/25/1912 at Boston; in the ninth inning pinch hit for pitcher Al Schulz and singled in a 6–0 loss to Boston's Joe Wood.

Harry Wolverton attended Kenyon College while learning the game on the Columbus, OH, sandlots and was primarily a pitcher when he joined the local Western League team for a brief whirl in 1896. By August 1897 *TSN* regarded him as the best infielder in the Western Association after he converted to 3B when he came to Dubuque that spring and hit .298. Wolverton experimented continually with batting styles as well as positions in his early years, sometimes switch hitting, sometimes hitting only from the left side. He was said to have "a quick nervous movement with the bat and [to hit] in a short choppy style."

After spending 1898 back in the Western League with Columbus and compiling a .315 BA, Wolverton arrived in Chicago in late September and immediately claimed the club's 3B job. He opened at the hot corner the following year and gained instant popularity on May 8 when he belted a walk-off 3-run homer over the RF scoreboard in the bottom of the ninth inning to beat St. Louis 8–7.

Little more than a month later Wolverton collided with catcher Art Nichols on June 11, 1900, while both were chasing a pop foul and suffered a "fractured skull and severe internal injuries." The incident drew the wrath of the local media when no Chicago players came to the aid of the injured pair and manager Tom Burns remained on the bench "as if unconcerned" while St. Louis players rushed to help both men. Held to just 99 games by the injury, Wolverton helplessly watched Bill Bradley appear on the scene while he was out of action and all but steal his job. The following spring he was sold to the Phillies. On August 14, 1900, St. Louis first baseman Dan McGann hit Wolverton in the back of the head with a ball, sparking a fight that put the third sacker on the DL. He had scarcely returned to the lineup when he became the subject of this story in Philadelphia papers:

"A serious, and what may prove a fatal accident happened to Third Baseman Harry S. Wolverton last night [September 5] as he was riding on a trolley car. . . . Owing to the crowded condition of the car, [Wolverton] stood on the steps and was struck by one of the poles that stood between the tracks. Policeman McElhatton was on the car and hurried to Wolverton's assistance. He found him unconscious, he having, it is thought, been struck on the head. . . . At the Samaritan Hospital he was found to have concussion of the brain, and it is feared his skull is fractured. Wolverton has been particularly unfortunate since he has been a member of the Philadelphia Club, having a fractured finger early in the season, and on the Phillies' last trip West, being so badly hurt by a ball thrown at him by First Baseman [Dan] McGann of the St. Louis Club, that he was unable to play for a week."

Wolverton mended in time to answer the bell the following season but by the end of August was again out for the year after breaking his collarbone in a collision with Boston first baseman Fred Tenney. While he was disabled, Phils owner Colonel John I. Rogers accused him of signing with Washington AL for 1902 and conspiring to get teammates to jump to the junior loop and then suspended him without pay. Phillies players debated whether to go on strike in protest, but first baseman Hughie Jennings counseled against it because the club was on the road and a strike would save Rogers not only salary expenses but also travel money. Meanwhile, it emerged that even though Rogers had it on good authority that Ed Delahanty also had signed for 1902 with Washington, he took no action against his star. Eventually, Wolverton and Delahanty both fled to Washington the following season, but by July Wolverton had caved to legal threats and returned to the Phillies. In 1903 he enjoyed his first ML season in comparatively good health, missing time but not a lot, and hit .303 while leading all NL third sackers in FA. After another injury plagued year in 1904, he was traded to Boston NL that December along with pitcher Chick Fraser for pitcher Togie Pittinger. A weak year with a weak team under a manager (Fred Tenney) whom he could not abide drove Wolverton to invest in the Williamsport, PA, club in the Tri-State League and serve as his own player-manager. Enormously successful in Williamsport, he moved up to Newark in the Eastern League in the same capacity and later took over the Oakland Oaks in the PCL.

By the close of 1911 Wolverton was one of the most highly regarded young managers in the minors. He was then offered a chance to replace Hal Chase as manager of the Yankees. Dissension-ridden under Chase's devious guidance, the club was no better off when the first baseman returned solely to the playing ranks in 1912. Wolverton gave it his best. He ran through a then AL-record 46 players and served so successfully as his own pinch hitter that he paced the AL in pinch blows. But his reward was the Yankees' only last-place finish prior to 1966. Fired at the end of the season, he subsequently returned to the West Coast and served as a player-manager in the PEL until 1917. He then settled in Oakland and took a job as a special officer with the Oakland Police Department. On February 4, 1937, Wolverton was killed by a hit-and-run driver while walking his beat on a downtown Oakland Street. (DN)

6 | THE SHORTSTOPS

6. Bones Ely played only 64 games at shortstop prior to his 30th birthday, but he left the majors at age 39, ranking sixth at the time in career games played at shorts.

Allen, Robert Gilman / "Bob"

B	T	HGT	WGT	G	AB	H	R	2B
R	R	5'11"	175	607	2216	534	338	77

3B	HR	RBI	BB	SO	SB	BA	SA	OBP
45	14	306	297	209	53	.241	.335	.334

G	W	L	PCT	PENNANTS
179	87	87	.500	0

B. 7/10/1867 Marion, OH **D.** 5/14/1943
TEAMS: 90–94PhiN (P/M)90PhiN 97BosN (P/M)00CinN
DEBUT: 4/19/1890 at New York; played SS and went 0-for-2 in a 4–0 win over New York's Amos Rusie
FINALE: 6/1/1900 at Boston; played SS and went 1-for-2 in a 9–2 loss to Boston's Nig Cuppy

The son of a prominent Ohio banker, Bob Allen helped revolutionize the SS position with his daring one-hand pickups. His total chances (906) as a rookie in 1890 set a new ML season record for shortstops but lasted only until 1892 when, with the schedule lengthened to 154 games for that one season only, he, Germany Smith, and Hughie Jennings all surpassed his old mark.

Allen debuted with independent Shamokin, PA, in 1886 and then joined Mansfield of the Ohio State League in 1887. Since he clerked winters in his father's banks, the 18-year-old was made manager of ill-organized Mansfield in late May. But apart from his financial acumen, he "never displayed any particular genius for leadership" and gave up the position on June 10. In 1888 Horace Phillips signed Allen for Pittsburgh NL, but he had "weak ankles and a weak bat" and was cut after opening day without making an appearance. Allen caught on with Mansfield again but suffered a broken leg on July 14, ending his season. In 1889, playing for Davenport of the Central Inter-State League, "the wizard shortstop took the town by storm" and once again was promoted to manager in midyear. Davenport was in first place on September 11 when the team dropped out of the league.

A free agent, Allen signed with Philadelphia NL, which, like most NL clubs, was thin on talent after PL desertions, and put on a dazzling display with his glove, regarded then as just a protective piece of equipment. Playing every inning of every game and snagging hot balls with one hand, he became the "coming king-pin of shortstops." On May 22 manager Harry Wright, battling what seemed to be the flu, woke up blind, and the Phillies played into the summer with a succession of managers. Fifteen days shy of his 23rd birthday, Allen became the club's fourth pilot of the season, again chosen for his financial expertise, while catcher Jack Clements ran the team on the field. Under Allen's watch the Phils won 16 straight games, and took over first place in the NL on July 17 before fading.

With his big cap pulled down over his eyes, Allen quietly captained the Phils in 1891. He missed some weeks after suffering a sprained ankle on August 13 and upon returning too soon was criticized for having a hitch in his throw and being slow on the double play pivot. When the rival AA Athletics were dissolved during the AA-NL merger in December, Wright—per a geographical claim—had first crack at their roster but passed on Tommy Corcoran believing Allen his superior. Philadelphia newspapers lambasted Wright for choosing Allen, but in 1892 he had a busy year, finishing second in total chances to Hughie Jennings despite being idled for three weeks after a bad-hop grounder on Labor Day weekend chipped his right cheekbone.

The defining injury of Allen's career came eight weeks into the 1894 season. Made captain again that spring, he was beaned under the right eye in the ninth inning of the June 15 game by Cincinnati's Elton Chamberlin. The blow shattered his cheekbone and lower orbital. Allen's career was thought to be over. He underwent a month of surgeries to remove pieces of bone from his face and slipped back into his family's banking business. On Christmas 1896 Western League Detroit began negotiations with Allen to return to baseball as SS-manager, and he finally signed in early February. Allen squabbled with Detroit's ownership, hit just .237, and was sold to Boston NL on July 12, 1897. At the time he had a standing offer to manage Indianapolis and only signed with Boston after the Beaneaters agreed not to reserve him.

Allen gave superb service as Herman Long's backup in 1897 but took the Indianapolis job in 1898 for $2,500. He lost the Western League pennant in the final days and accused last-place St. Joseph of working in cahoots with first-place Kansas City when St. Joseph claimed the field conditions were too poor to play an end-of-season make-up game after a rainstorm. Other sources insinuated that Kansas City had paid St. Joseph to intentionally flood the field. Allen won the WL pennant the next year when pitcher Ed Scott won 12 in a row in

August and left-hander Doc Newton threw a pennant-clinching DH victory over Milwaukee on the next-to-last day of the season. Allen then signed to pilot Cincinnati for 1900 but the team finished 7th. Scott and Newton, whom he brought along with him from Indy, were two of the top rookies in the NL, but the rest of the club played poorly after the grandstand burned down on May 28.

Allen returned to banking that fall but later entered the lumber business in eastern Arkansas and remained out of the game (except for 1908 when he managed Mansfield, OH) until he purchased the Montgomery Southern Association club in 1914 and moved it to Little Rock. In 1930 he sold Little Rock to purchase Nashville and then sold that franchise in 1931 to acquire Knoxville, TN. Allen still owned Knoxville at the time of his death in 1943 and was revered by then as the "dean of Southern Association club owners." (DN/FV)

Bastian, Charles A. / "Charlie"

B	T	HGT	WGT	G	AB	H	R	2B
R	R	5'6½"	145	504	1806	342	241	49

3B	HR	RBI	BB	SO	SB	BA	SA	OBP
26	11	144	179	308	57	.189	.264	.268

G	IP	H	GS	CG	BB
1	6	6	0	0	0

SO	SH	W	L	PCT	ERA
2	0	0	0	—	3.00

B. 3/?/1858 Philadelphia, PA **D.** ?/?/?
TEAMS: 84WilU 84KCU 85–88PhiN 89ChiN 90ChiP 91CinA 91PhiN
DEBUT: 8/18/1884 at Washington; played 2B and was 0-for-3 in a 4–3 win over Washington's Charlie Geggus
FINALE: 8/22/1891 at Philadelphia; played SS but was replaced after he was hit by a pitch in his first AB of a 9–5 win over New York's Amos Rusie

In his prime years Charlie Bastian was rated as good at 2B as Fred Dunlap—if only he could have hit like Dunlap. In 1883 he served with Trenton of the Interstate Association before joining Wilmington the following season. In the Quicksteps' brief stopover as a member of the Union Association, Bastian hit just .200 but led the team in SA and collected the only 2 four-baggers the team hit. When the Quicksteps folded after their game on September 12, 1884, Bastian went to Kansas City UA. Unlike the vast majority of players the UA introduced, Bastian found a home in one of the established major leagues when Harry Wright bagged him to play SS for Philadelphia NL in 1885. He scored 67 runs but hit just .167, reducing him to utility duty for most of his three remaining years with the Phils.

Prior to the 1889 season Bastian was classified as a $2,000 player even though he was regarded as "the best fielding infielder in the league." Viewed as insubordinate by Wright when he refused to sign for less than $2,500, he was sold to Chicago for a "paltry $1,000" according to *TSN* but continued his holdout until he finally got the amount he wanted. Bastian left Philadelphia on particularly bad terms, especially after Philadelphia owner John I. Rogers said in the April 6, 1889, *TSN*, "The trouble with Bastian is that he is a coward. . . . He is too much afraid of injury to play the base well." Bastian in truth was brittle and worked winters in his brother-in-law's saloon to boot but nonetheless became a welcome addition to the Chicago team when SS Ned Williamson's off-season knee injury was slow to respond. The salutary feeling was short-lived, however, after he hit just .135 and compiled only 19 total bases in 46 games. Both are season record lows among nineteenth-century position players with a minimum of 175 ABs.

Remarkably, despite his abject showing in 1889, Bastian was hired by the Chicago PL entry the following year and began the season as the club's SS. But another sub-.200 performance left him homeless when the major leagues contracted to just sixteen teams in 1891. In July he signed with Cincinnati AA to replace Yank Robinson at 2B but could not report immediately because he was out of shape. There were also rumors of domestic trouble. Cincinnati saw enough after just one game to know that Bastian was no improvement on Robinson. Perhaps Harry Wright felt sorry for Bastian. In any event, he was hired to play short for the Phils on August 22 in Tim Keefe's first Philadelphia outing against his old New York Giants teammates. In his first at-bat in the second inning Bastian was hit on the hand by an Amos Rusie fastball and had to leave the game. The Phils released him rather than wait for him to mend.

Bastian played with the Philadelphia Eastern League club in 1892 before illness forced him to quit temporarily. After a year away from pro ball, he returned in 1894 and spent the next four seasons in the minors before joining the army. In 1898 Bastian was with the 1st Calvary, stationed in Tampa, FL. Ted Sullivan reported three years later that he was in the Philippines "trying to kill [Aguinaldo's] followers." After mustering out of the army, Bastian worked as a furniture polisher in the Philadelphia area and was alive as late as 1930 before disappearing. (DN/DB)

Beard, Oliver Perry / "Ollie"

B	T	HGT	WGT	G	AB	H	R	2B
R	R	5'11"	180	331	1307	353	195	34

3B	HR	RBI	BB	SO	SB	BA	SA	OBP
34	4	173	112	61	73	.270	.357	.330

B. 5/2/1862 Lexington, KY **D.** 5/28/1929
TEAMS: 89CinA 90CinN 91LouA
DEBUT: 4/17/1889 at Cincinnati; played SS and went 1-for-4 in a 5–1 loss to St. Louis's Silver King
FINALE: 6/28/1891 at Louisville; played 3B and went 0-for-4 in a 7–1 win over Cincinnati's Frank Dwyer

At age 14 Ollie Beard was already playing SS for the independent Lexington, KY, team. His father, also named O. P. Beard, was a Mexican War hero and a well-known racetrack steward and city official in Lexington. The elder Beard was also famed for having invented "Burgoo" soup while serving in Mexico. After his father's death Beard moved with his mother and siblings to Cincinnati, where he played ball in the West End flats and in 1884 signed to play professionally with Evansville of the Northwestern League along with Lefty Marr, another Cincinnatian with whom he would often be associated throughout his career.

The following spring the two were among several future ML players who were given tryouts by Chicago NL, but neither could win a spot on Cap Anson's star-laden roster. Beard and Marr went to Nashville, where they played two years and ran a saloon that was a popular hangout for Southern League players and then spent two more seasons together at Syracuse. In the first Beard led a clique of former Southern League players who would play well behind pitcher Dummy Dundon, an ex–Southern Leaguer, but poorly behind the team's other pitchers. When Joe Simmons became the Syracuse manager and hired African American Bob Higgins, the clique exploded and caused tremendous dissension on the club.

The following year Beard finished third in the International Association batting race with a .350 mark and led the league's shortstops in FA. He was purchased after the season by Cincinnati. According to newspaper reports, Beard's price was $2,500, and he then wangled a salary of $2,200. If correct, these figures represent considerable sums at a time when the nominal ML salary limit was $2,000; clubs frequently evaded the limit, but to do so for an unproven rookie was an extreme rarity. Bob Gilks, a fellow Cincinnati native who had observed Beard for several years, called him "a splendid player" without a weak point. However, Ban Johnson of the *Cincinnati Commercial Gazette* wrote that many disagreed, saying that what Beard might add in the way of improved hitting he would more than give back in the field.

During his two years as a Red, Beard gave the Cincinnati management some trouble with his drinking and at the end of the 1889 season was fined $100. Yet he seems to have made a good impression generally, since he twice served as team captain. In the end, however, Johnson's warnings proved well founded. At the start of the 1890 season Beard was moved to 3B, an indication that his range was poor for a SS, and although he soon switched back to short, with his friend Marr inserted at 3B, his days with Cincinnati were numbered. After the 1890 season, the dissolution of the Players League produced a concentration of ML talent, with players bouncing each other out of jobs like pool balls caroming around a table. John M. Ward, head of the vanquished Brotherhood and formerly with the Giants, went to Brooklyn, while the Brooklyn incumbent Germany Smith, a light hitter but superb fielder, was picked up by Cincinnati. Reduced to a scrub, Beard was released and signed with Louisville, where he in turn replaced Phil Tomney at SS and was named team captain. However, he quickly resigned the captaincy and within a few games was moved to 3B again. At the end of June he was released and joined Denver of the Western Association. Beard subsequently enjoyed a long minor league career as a player and player-manager, best remembered for his tenure in the latter capacity at Detroit in 1898, his final active season, and his trademark green-tipped bat.

Beard's post-baseball career is difficult to follow. In 1900 he was reportedly arrested in Louisville and charged with sending obscene material through the mail. Four years later he was said to be selling slot machines in the same city. Beard later returned to Cincinnati, and in 1926 he lost the use of his legs and went into retirement. According to a son, he possessed a valuable collection of books on baseball and wrote occasional articles on the game, but it has proven difficult to ascertain where—or even if—they were ever published. Beard died in his sleep at 67 of a heart attack at his Cincinnati home, leaving behind a widow and four adult children. (DB/DN)

Berger, John Henry / "Tun"

B	T	HGT	WGT	G	AB	H	R	2B
?	R	?	204	173	622	150	88	22

3B	HR	RBI	BB	SO	SB	BA	SA	OBP
6	1	57	54	42	18	.241	.301	.313

B. 12/6/1867 Pittsburgh, PA **D.** 6/10/1907
TEAMS: 90–91PitN 92WasN
DEBUT: 5/9/90 at Cincinnati; caught Pete Daniels and went 2-for-4 in a 10–5 loss to Cincinnati's Jesse Duryea
FINALE: 8/28/92 at St. Louis; caught Frank Killen and went 0-for-3 in a 4–3 win over St. Louis's Bill Hawke

Tun Berger was oddly built for a shortstop. He seems to have been around 5'8" and weighed over 200. Too, he was not overly talented, but conscientious, a hard worker, and above all, a Pittsburgh boy who was a natural fit with the poor Pirates teams in the early 1890s.

After making his pro debut in 1887 with Johnstown of the Pennsylvania State Association, Berger spent part of 1889 with independent McKeesport along with Henry Youngman. Both men faced Pittsburgh in an exhibition game on October 19, 1889, and were remembered by the NL club when it was riddled by Players League defections later that fall. While Youngman was in over his head in 1890, Berger proved to be Pittsburgh's top rookie and one of its few players worth retaining. That winter he worked at a glass house in Lawrence, PA, and got married, only to learn, when he and his wife were packing to go to spring training in St. Augustine, FL, that the team's new manager, Ned Hanlon, had imposed a rule requiring all players to leave their spouses home. Soon after arriving in Florida, Berger professed to be homesick, but Hanlon had little time for mooncalves, especially when his club proceeded to lose every exhibition game it played in the south. Pittsburgh started off badly in the regular season as well, and the June 20, 1891, *TSN* proclaimed that Berger was just about the only player on the team who was exceeding expectations.

Barely five days later, on June 25, Hanlon yanked Berger from a game at Cleveland after he made a critical error at SS. After that Berger seldom played. Pittsburgh released him in October and then waffled all winter about whether to rehire him. Berger eventually signed for 1892 with Indianapolis of the Western League. He joined Washington in July after the Hoosier club went defunct.

Following his first practice with the Senators, the *Washington Post* said, "Berger has more life than both the other catchers combined." But less than a month later, with his BA below .150, he played his last ML innings. Berger spent the next two seasons with Erie of the Eastern League, returned to the Western League with St. Paul for a while, and next played briefly with Wheeling along with his brother Ben, a third baseman. By 1897 Berger was down to advertising for a baseball job in *TSN* and finally landing one as team captain with Cortland in the lowly New York State League. He finished his pro career in the 1898 Atlantic League and later tried umpiring in that loop but had to quit when he was called home by his brother's death.

Berger worked at his pre-baseball trade as a glass blower until he died at his Allegheny, PA, home of kidney disease in 1907. The source of his nickname is unknown, but it may actually have been "Ton" or else a contraction of the word rotund. (DN/EM)

Burke, Michael E. / "Mike"

B	T	HGT	WGT	G	AB	H	R	2B
R	R	6'0"	190	28	117	26	13	3

3B	HR	RBI	BB	SO	SB	BA	SA	OBP
0	0	8	2	5	—	.222	.248	.235

B. ?/?/1854 New York, NY **D.** 6/9/1889
TEAMS: 79CinN
DEBUT: 5/1/1879 at Cincinnati; played SS and went 0-for-5 in a 7–5 win over Troy's George Bradley
FINALE: 7/19/1879 at Cincinnati; played 3B and RF and went 1-for-6 in a 7–6 loss to Troy's George Bradley

Mike Burke grew up in Cincinnati and starred at SS for the Cumminsville Blue Stockings, a popular local team, from their formation in 1873 through 1875. After two years with the independent Columbus Buckeyes, he had an outstanding season in 1878 for London of the International Association and was brought home in 1879 to play for Cincinnati NL.

Much was expected of Burke, but he went hitless and committed an error in his debut on May 1 and never righted himself all season, hitting poorly and fielding worse, with a tendency to overthrow first baseman Cal McVey. In early June the Reds' infield was shuffled, with Will Foley taking 3B and Burke sitting. He received another trial as a replacement in RF for Mike Kelly, as yet simply another rookie going through a bad stretch, but the Cincinnati management wisely chose to stay with Kelly. Burke got a last chance when Foley was injured in July, but although he finally began to hit, his fielding deteriorated even further. On July 19 he made two wild throws and fumbled a grounder at 3B, then switched positions with Kelly and committed another error in RF.

When Burke reported for Cincinnati's next game two days later, Reds assistant secretary Con Howe handed him a notice of release. The distraught Burke tried to attack Howe, threatened a police officer that intervened, and then went out on the field and challenged player-manager McVey. Led to the clubhouse, he finally collapsed in tears. Not surprisingly, he was reported to have been drunk when he made this scene, but the Cincinnati papers gave no such color to this story and stated explicitly that he was released for poor playing, not misbehavior.

The fullest account of Burke's exodus, by Opie Caylor in the *Cincinnati Enquirer*, is quite sympathetic. Several times during the season the *Enquirer* had publishing encouraging notes calling Burke a fine player who would live up to his potential once he started to relax. Now, Caylor described him as an earnest and conscientious player, perhaps too highly strung, whose natural zeal to succeed had been heightened by the knowledge that he must provide not only for a wife but also for a daughter born just a few days before his initial benching. As a result, once he began in bad luck Burke pressed and played even worse. (Years later Caylor would reveal that Foley, Burke's competitor for playing time, had kept him all the more on edge with artful needling.)

After the unfortunate incident, Caylor wrote that Burke, having apologized manfully for "doing what no sane man would have done" when he received the bad news, could be expected to go elsewhere and play as brilliantly as he had with London. Burke did join Albany of the National Association, but after playing 3B for that team in 1880 he retired from baseball and settled down in Albany. Caylor could report some while later that he had become a successful businessman. Sadly, however, life's happy turns of events are rarely conclusive. In 1889, still only in his mid thirties, Burke died in Albany. (DB)

Carey, Thomas Joseph / "Tom"

B	T	HGT	WGT	G	AB	H	R	2B
R	R	5'8"	145	536	2394	645	405	77

3B	HR	RBI	BB	SO	SB	BA	SA	OBP
14	5	270	16	61	27	.270	.320	.275

G	W	L	PCT	PENNANTS
49	27	21	.563	0

B. 3/?/1846 New York, NY **D.** 8/16/1906
TEAMS: 71KekNA 72–73BalNA (P/M)73BalNA (P/M)74MutNA 75HarNA 76–77HarN 78ProN 79CleN
DEBUT: 5/1/1871 at Fort Wayne; played SS in the first game in ML history, batted sixth, and went 0-for-3 in a 2–0 win over Cleveland's Al Pratt
FINALE: 9/29/1879 at Cleveland; played SS and went 2-for-4 in a 13–1 loss to Cincinnati's Will White

Tom Carey served with the 17th New York Infantry in the Civil War. On October 11, 1905, he was discharged from a veteran's home in Napa, CA, after being under care there for some time, and disappeared. It was recently learned that he died in San Francisco the following August.

While with Fort Wayne in 1871, Carey appears to have attached himself to the team's star pitcher, Bobby Mathews. The two moved as a unit to Baltimore in 1872 after the Kekiongas disbanded and then switched to the New York Mutuals in 1874 once the Baltimore club dissolved. Carey began 1874 as the Mutes captain but was replaced by Dick Higham on June 27. He then played in Hartford in 1875 and remained with Hartford through 1877 while it played its home games in Brooklyn. His final two ML campaigns, with Providence and Cleveland, were colored by a marked decline in hitting but otherwise might appear to be as nondescript as the rest of his career. However, a closer examination reveals that Carey had one extraordinary distinction: he was almost impossible to walk. In 2,426 plate appearances Carey drew only 16 bases on balls. Even allowing for the infrequency with which hitters walked in the 1870s, Carey stands as the all-time anti-walk king. Upon departing Cleveland, Carey played in the California League through 1880. Later he umpired 29 games in the AA in 1882, its fledgling season. (DN)

Caskin, Edward James / "Ed"

B	T	HGT	WGT	G	AB	H	R	2B
R	R	5'9½"	165	482	1871	427	229	50

3B	HR	RBI	BB	SO	SB	BA	SA	OBP
10	2	163	82	170	0	.228	.269	.261

B. 12/30/1851 Danvers, MA **D.** 10/9/1924
TEAMS: 79–81TroN 83–84NYN 85StLN 86NYN
DEBUT: 5/1/1879 at Cincinnati; played SS and went 2-for-5 in a 7–5 loss to Cincinnati's Will White.
FINALE: 9/24/1886 at Boston; played SS and went 2-for-4 in a 16–8 loss to Boston's Bill Stemmeyer

In the early 1870s Ed Caskin enlisted in the army, learned to play ball there, and then decided baseball would be more rewarding than fighting Indians and got an early discharge by convincing his superiors that he had heart disease. A catcher-outfielder at that point, he joined independent Lynn, MA, in 1876. After two seasons with Rochester of the International Association, Caskin signed for 1879 with the new Troy NL entry and led the club in total bases and was second in hits and runs while serving as both a SS and a catcher. The following season he missed only one game at SS but hit just .225 and was released by Troy on September 25, 1881, when he was able to raise his BA only a single point to .226 in his sophomore year.

Subsequently blacklisted over contractual issues, Caskin returned to the majors in 1883 after the Troy franchise was abandoned and replaced by the New York Giants (nee Gothams). Despite an occasional good day, Caskin seemed little improved as a hitter, finishing at .238 with just a .285 SA. Another weak season in 1884 brought his release when Jim Mutrie took over as manager and opted to move John M. Ward from 2B to SS and hire Joe Gerhardt to man 2B.

Caskin signed for 1885 with the St. Louis Maroons, a NL replacement franchise for Cleveland, and began the season on the bench but took over at 3B on May 8. Some 70 games later he was given his pink slip after batting just .171. In 1886 Caskin was playing with Lynn, MA, of the New England League when the Giants arrived in Boston and John M. Ward was unavailable. Given a day's pay, he made his final ML game something he could remember fondly when he tallied 2 hits and played errorless ball. Throughout the 1880s Caskin continued to be noted for his quiet demeanor and conscientious effort as the game around him turned increasingly rowdy. Toward the end of the century he ran a shoe store in Lynn with his brother. Caskin died in Danvers, MA, of cancer in 1924. (DN/DB)

Connaughton, Frank Henry / "Frank"

B	T	HGT	WGT	G	AB	H	R	2B
R	R	5'9"	165	134	486	141	95	12

3B	HR	RBI	BB	SO	SB	BA	SA	OBP
4	4	77	44	15	26	.290	.356	.344

B. 1/1/1869 Clinton, MA **D.** 12/1/1942
TEAMS: 94BosN 96NYN 06BosN
DEBUT: 5/28/1894 at Boston; caught Harry Staley and went 1-for-4 in an 18–12 win over Washington's Charlie Petty
FINALE: 10/5/1906 at New York; played SS and went 0-for-4 in a 7–1 win over New York's Henry Mathewson

Frank Connaughton debuted with Woonsocket in the New England League in 1891 and remained in that loop until 1893 when he finished the season with Savannah of the Southern League. The following year he joined Boston as a replacement for catcher Charlie Bennett, who had lost both legs over the winter. Although Connaughton hit well—.345 in 46 games—he was not retained. The reason may have been that Boston did not have a spot for him. Not a particularly good catcher, when he was called on to fill in at SS after Herman Long was hurt he could only play the position as long as he wore his catcher's mitt, which was legal at the time. Connaughton went to spring training with Boston in 1895 but was farmed to Kansas City of the Western League, where he learned to play a better SS. Acquired by the Giants, he opened 1896 at short but lost his job when Bill Joyce joined New York and took over at 3B, freeing George Davis finally to assume his best position at SS.

Toward the end of the century Connaughton seemed more interested in playing roller polo than baseball. Blacklisted by Kansas City late in the 1898 season, he sat out all of 1899 on the ineligible list. Returning to the game with Worcester of the Eastern League in 1900, he played poorly and blamed the condition of the team's infield for his frequent errors. Connaughton decided to leave the game again and go into the wholesale liquor business but changed his mind before the 1901 season was out. It led to a return to Boston NL in 1906 for 12 games after the New England League season ended. Connaughton remained an active player in the minors until he was 44, finishing in 1913 with New Bedford, MA, where he served as SS Rabbit Maranville's player-manager and later was praised for having taught the future HOFer the tricks of the trade. He died in a Boston hospital in 1942 after being hit by a car. (DN)

#Cooney, James Joseph / "Jimmy"

B	T	HGT	WGT	G	AB	H	R	2B
B	R	5'9"	155	324	1302	315	221	35

3B	HR	RBI	BB	SO	SB	BA	SA	OBP
14	4	118	148	48	77	.242	.300	.324

B. 7/9/1865 Cranston, RI **D.** 7/1/1903
TEAMS: 90–92ChiN 92WasN
DEBUT: 4/19/1890 at Cincinnati; played SS and went 2-for-4 in a 5–4 win over Cincinnati's Jim Duryea
FINALE: 7/29/1892 at Washington; played SS and went hitless in a 7–5 loss to Baltimore's Sadie McMahon

The father of twentieth-century MLers Jimmy and Johnny Cooney made his pro debut with Bridgeport of the Eastern League in 1885 as a catcher and began the conversion to SS over the next several seasons, but he continued to catch as late as 1889 while with Omaha of the Western Association under manager Frank Selee. In November 1889 a question arose as to whether the contracts James Cooney and catcher Tom Nagle had signed with Chicago were valid after Selee contended he had gotten a retainer from Chicago owner Al Spalding to purchase them. But, as happened so often in similar controversies involving Chicago in those years, the Colts got their way by somehow persuading Omaha not to put the two players on the auction block.

In 1890 Cooney was one of the top rookies in the NL, scoring 114 runs and leading the loop with a .936 FA. The following year he seemingly succumbed to the sophomore jinx when he compiled just 135 total bases, though he again led the NL in fielding. But when the slump continued in 1892, Chicago released him after 65 games with a .172 BA. The tailspin continued when he arrived in Washington and made 4 errors and just 4 hits in his first 6 contests in Washington. Given his ten days notice, Cooney finished the season in Providence and soon became a fixture in that Eastern League bastion through the 1899 season. Since he was considered the top fielding SS in the EL during most of that period, it would seem only his lack of offensive punch obstructed him from ever receiving another chance in the NL. Cooney finished his playing career in 1900 as the SS and manager of Bristol in the Connecticut State League. He died in Cranston of pneumonia three years later, when his sons Jimmy and Johnny were 9 and 2 years old, respectively. (DN)

Corcoran, Thomas William / "Tommy" "Corky"

B	T	HGT	WGT	G	AB	H	R	2B
R	R	5'9"	164	1438	5861	1551	884	190

3B	HR	RBI	BB	SO	SB	BA	SA	OBP
118	27	716	281	205	285	.265	.352	.302

B. 1/4/1869 New Haven, CT **D.** 6/25/1960
TEAMS: 90PitP 91PhiA 92–96BroN 97–06CinN 07NYN
DEBUT: 4/19/1890 at Pittsburgh; played SS and went 1-for-4 in a 10–2 loss to Chicago's Silver King
FINALE: 7/10/1907 at New York; played 2B and made 1 hit in a 7–1 win over St. Louis's Art Fromme and Stoney McGlynn
CAREER HIGHLIGHT: 8/7/1903 at St. Louis; made a record 14 assists in a nine-inning game at SS in a 4–2 win over St. Louis's Chappie McFarland

When Tommy Corcoran played his last ML game in 1907, he held the record for the most career games at SS (2,073) as well as the most assists and most double plays. He was remembered for some years as tough, one of the last to play SS in the majors barehanded (he began using a glove in the early 1890s), a roll-your-own cigarette smoker, an ace sign stealer, and a tournament-caliber trap shooter in "shoot from the hip" competition.

Yet by the middle of the twentieth century, when the list of men who compiled 2,000 or more career hits had reached 90, Corcoran was probably its most forgotten member even though he ranked fifty-seventh with 2,252. There were a number of reasons that he had lapsed into obscurity by then, one being that he had never played on a pennant winner. But the most prominent was that despite his high career hit total, he had simply not been a very good hitter. Among all retired players with 2,000 hits, Corcoran has the worst career ratio of runs created versus league (-1.69), with Larry Bowa a very distant second at -1.08.

After pitching for an independent team in New Haven for most of 1886, Corcoran sought a position with Little Rock of the Southern League in 1887 but instead landed in Lynn, MA, of the New England League as a change pitcher and infielder. He moved to SS the following season with Wilkes-Barre of the Central League and remained with the Pennsylvania club until he was suspended in May 1889, at which point he joined his hometown team in the Atlantic Association and hit .232. Former ML catcher Bill Holbert, who appreciated fielding, recommended Corcoran to Pittsburgh PL manager Ned Hanlon in 1890. Although wary of his weak bat, Hanlon gambled on the 21-year-old and was rewarded when he and Bill Joyce were the two most enduring rookie position players to cut their teeth in the Brotherhood loop.

Corcoran was returned to New Haven when the PL folded, as per a National Agreement stipulation, and then auctioned off to Philadelphia AA. A's owner J. Earle Wagner promptly stiffed New Haven, claiming his club owed nothing because the Association had withdrawn from the National Agreement. When the AA and NL merged in December 1891, Corcoran was awarded to Brooklyn. He held the Bridegrooms' SS post until a November 1896 trade with Cincinnati for SS Germany Smith, pitcher Chauncey Fisher, and $1,000. A poor trade from Brooklyn's standpoint, it was largely made because of Corcoran's "erratic conduct" and to break up cliques on the Bridegrooms, set off by the acquisition of outfielder Tommy McCarthy, a notorious manufacturer of discord.

After batting .288 in his first season with his new club, Corcoran only twice hit over .250 in his eight remaining seasons in Cincinnati. At the close of the 1906 campaign he was reportedly sold to the Giants for $4,500, but that price seems steep given his .207 BA and 27 runs in his Reds finale. Corcoran finished his active career as a player-manager with New Bedford of the New England League in 1908. His last-known connection with the game was as an umpire in the Federal League in 1915. Corcoran lived quietly in his remaining years and died in a Plainfield, CT, nursing home at 91, leaving four sons and a daughter. (DN)

Cross, Montford Montgomery / "Monte"

B	T	HGT	WGT	G	AB	H	R	2B
R	R	5'8½"	148	828	2930	737	424	103

3B	HR	RBI	BB	SO	SB	BA	SA	OBP
49	22	353	329	100	190	.252	.343	.335

B. 8/31/1869 Philadelphia, PA **D.** 6/21/1934
TEAMS: 92BalN 94–95PitN 96–97StLN 98–01PhiN 02–07PhiAL
DEBUT: 9/27/1892 at Baltimore; played SS and went 0-for-4 in a 4–3 loss to New York's Silver King
FINALE: 10/4/1907 at Washington; played SS and got 1 hit in an 8–0 win over Washington's Tom Hughes

One of the last ML players to sport facial hair prior to the 1970s, Monte Cross on occasion wore a small black mustache similar to Charlie Chaplin's while with the AL Philadelphia A's. A graduate of Philadelphia's Central High School, he played with the local amateur Solar Tips before joining Milford, a member of the shaky 1889 Delaware League. Despite a four-year apprenticeship in the minors, Cross was still nowhere near ready for the bigs when he finished the 1892 season with Baltimore. Earning a .160 BA in 15 games rocketed him back to the sticks in 1893 with Savannah of the Southern League. Late in the season, despite being very popular with Georgia ladies, he jumped the team when "he was goaded to desperation by the attitude and actions of certain men prominent in Savannah baseball circles," namely manager Jim Manning. Back north the following year with Syracuse, Cross was happier, especially when Pittsburgh acquired him late in the season. His .442 BA in the Pirates' final 13 games was even more aberrant than his introduction to the majors two years earlier. In Cross's thirteen remaining ML seasons he never again would top .286—his mark with St. Louis in 1897—and twice would hit below .200 as a qualifier, with a nadir of .189 as a member of the 1904 A's, the lowest season BA in ML history by a player with as many as 500 ABs.

After 1895, his official rookie year, Cross was traded along with pitcher Bill Hart and $750 to St. Louis for Fred Ely. It was an odd exchange inasmuch as the two clubs did little more than swap weak-hitting shortstops who were about equal as fielders. Cross did have the good fortune, however, to suffer only two seasons with the "Done" Browns before he was part of a seven-player deal with the Phillies in November 1897. By 1901 Cross was spending his fourth season with the Phils and leading NL shortstops in put-outs for the fourth straight year. After jumping to the AL Philadelphia A's in 1902, he also led the junior circuit in that department for the next two seasons before his range began to slip as he approached his middle thirties.

Cross ultimately played on two AL pennant winners in Philadelphia before leaving the majors in 1907. He then played, managed, and umpired in the minors until 1914, when he was hired to officiate in the rebel Federal League. Leaving that position after just one season, he later coached Maine University and umpired in the Blue Ridge and Virginia leagues before taking a position as a clothing salesman at Gimbel's Department Store in Philadelphia. An outstanding amateur bowler, he seemingly was still in excellent shape when he attended the wedding of Connie Mack's son in Washington in 1934, but he died of a heart attack shortly after returning to his apartment in Philadelphia. (DN)

Easterday, Henry P. / "Henry" "Harry"

B	T	HGT	WGT	G	AB	H	R	2B
R	R	5'6"	145	322	1129	203	141	23

3B	HR	RBI	BB	SO	SB	BA	SA	OBP
15	9	92	112	57	43	.180	.251	.259

B. 9/16/1864 Philadelphia, PA **D.** 3/30/1895
TEAMS: 84PhiU 88KCA 89–90ColA 90PhiA 90LouA
DEBUT: 6/23/1884 at Philadelphia; played SS and went 2-for-4 in a 6–5 loss to Washington's Bill Wise
FINALE: 9/21/1890 at Louisville; replaced Harry Raymond at 3B and went 1-for-2 in a 16–3 win over Philadelphia's Bill Stecher

Henry Easterday played for amateur and independent Philadelphia-area nines before joining the UA Keystones in June 1884 to fill a longstanding SS hole. After the Keystones folded, he spent the next three seasons in the minors, usually struggling to break .200, before returning to the show in 1888 with Louisville AA. Before he even got into a game with the Colonels he was sold in May to the Kansas City AA replacement team for $1,200. Easterday demonstrated almost immediately that he was among the best fielding shortstops in the game and an even worse hitter than most pitchers. In 1888 he topped AA shortstops in FA but batted just .190.

Released when Kansas City acquired rookie SS Herman Long, Easterday signed for 1889 with Columbus AA. On Opening Day he went 3-for-5 against Baltimore's Matt Kilroy but hit just .166 after that. The following season Columbus released him when he was batting .157 after 58 games. On one of his last days with the Ohio club, the *Ohio State Journal* wrote, "Harry Easterday stands without a peer for his inability to make a hit or even a sacrifice in a pinch." The ink was scarcely dry when Bobby Wheelock was hired to replace him. Easterday then caught on with Philadelphia AA but lasted only long enough to hit .147 in 19 games. He finished the ML portion of his career with Louisville as an injury replacement for Phil Tomney. Cut once Tomney was healthy again, Easterday played in the minors until 1894, finishing with Lynchburg of the Virginia League just a few months prior to his death from typhoid fever at his Philadelphia home. (DN/DB)

Ely, William Frederick / "Bones"

B	T	HGT	WGT	G	AB	H	R	2B
R	R	6'1"	155	1128	4375	1146	588	126

3B	HR	RBI	BB	SO	SB	BA	SA	OBP
61	23	551	227	109	151	.262	.335.	309

G	IP	H	GS	CG	BB
9	52	77	5	4	34

SO	SH	W	L	PCT	ERA
32	0	0	5	.000	5.75

B. 6/7/1863 N. Girard, PA **D.** 1/10/1952
TEAMS: 84BufN 86LouA 90SyrA 91BroN 93–95StLN 96–00PitN 01PhiAL 02WasAL
DEBUT: 6/19/1884 at Buffalo; caught by George Myers and finished the game in RF in his 18–2 loss to Detroit's Frank Meinke
FINALE: 9/24/1902 at Washington; played SS and went 2-for-4 in an 8–2 win over Boston's Tully Sparks

If one word could characterize Bones Ely's ML career, it would be perseverance. As early as 1886, in addition to being called "Bones" for his pencil-thin physique, he was also nicknamed "Tourist" because he did so much traveling and so little playing. Yet some twenty years later, when most of his 1886 teammates had long since left the diamond and ceased all forms of violent physical activity, Ely would still be putting on a uniform each summer and working winters as a circus acrobat.

On the strength of an early-season exhibition game against Buffalo, Ely was invited by the Bisons to leave his Meadville, PA, semipro team in 1884 to test his mettle against NL competition. He was headed back to Meadville within hours after he allowed 17 hits, 15 runs, and 5 walks in just five innings of work against last-place Detroit. A good year with Birmingham of the fledgling Southern League in 1885 earned him a second trial in 1886 with Louisville AA. Found wanting both in the box and as an outfielder, he nonetheless remained on the team until manager Jim Hart finally cut him in September. After seeing him appear in only 11 games, a Louisville paper claimed that he had had "the easiest time this summer of any man in the profession."

The following season, recognizing that even though he had terrific speed, poor control would always hamper him in the box, Ely began the transition to another position. When he returned to the majors with Syracuse in 1890, it was as a left fielder, but in the closing weeks of the season he moved to SS. Ely began 1891 back in the minors with St. Paul of the Western League after Syracuse abandoned the AA. When St. Paul moved to Duluth and the franchise then disbanded, John M. Ward sent Ely train fare in August to join Brooklyn. But Ward left after the season to take over the reins in New York, and Brooklyn's new manager, Dave Foutz, saw no point in retaining a 29-year-old utilityman.

Ely headed south in 1893 for his second stint in the Southern League and stunned the entire baseball community when he led the loop in homers with 19. Hurriedly summoned to St. Louis, Ely replaced ailing Frank Shugart and then seemed to demonstrate that his SL season had been no fluke when he topped the Browns in both homers and RBI in 1894, his first season as a full-time ML shortfielder at the advanced age of 31. But if Ely had lost a step, no one noticed. *TSN* actually remarked that he played so deep at SS "that he could easily shake hands with the left fielder" and implied that it was to show off his great arm. Other Browns observers contended that he could not only play deep but also position himself close to 3B because he had "tremendous range to his left," or glove, side.

By 1895 the thrill had worn off the novelty of being a big league regular, especially with a team as poor as the Browns, and Ely tried to escape St. Louis by claiming the hardware business he and his brother ran in Giard, PA, demanded his twenty-four-hour presence, but owner Chris Von der Ahe saw the ploy for what it was and refused to release the discontented SS so that he could sign elsewhere. After the season, however, he was traded to Pittsburgh for Monte Cross, pitcher Bill Hart, and $750. In 1896 Ely had a good year with the Pirates by his standards, batting .286. But by 1898 he had dropped to .212 and collected just 140 total bases in 148 games. Ely continued to hold the Pirates' SS post as late as the summer of 1901 even though the team by then had acquired none other than Honus Wagner. Not until a rumor circulated that Ban Johnson was itching to install an AL franchise in Pittsburgh in 1902 and Ely meanwhile had been enlisted to recruit his Pirates teammates to jump to the junior loop did manager Fred Clarke agree to release his 38-year-old SS on July 25 and test Wagner as his replacement.

Ely finished 1901 with the Philadelphia A's and then was cast adrift again. Signing with Washington, he played 105 games in 1902 and hit .262, but the September 29 *Washington Post* noted that both he and pitcher Bill Carrick took their last paychecks and "fled the city as soon as season ended" when they were not offered contracts for 1903. Ely subsequently played and managed for a string of West Coast teams and then settled there permanently. He died of Alzheimer's in 1952 at California's Napa State Hospital. (DN)

Fennelly, Francis John / "Frank"

B	T	HGT	WGT	G	AB	H	R	2B
R	R	5'8"	168	786	3042	781	609	102

3B	HR	RBI	BB	SO	SB	BA	SA	OBP
82	34	408	378	78	175	.257	.378	.345

B. 2/18/1860 Fall River, MA **D.** 8/4/1920
TEAMS: 84WasA 84–88CinA 88–89PhiA 90BroA

DEBUT: 5/1/1884 at Brooklyn; played SS and went 0-for-5 in a 12–0 win over Brooklyn's Sam Kimber
FINALE: 6/18/1890 at Philadelphia; played 3B and went 2-for-4 in a 6–4 loss to Philadelphia's Eddie Green

In the middle of Frank Fennelly's career his offensive production was hindered by an important rule change. Prior to 1887 the strike zone was divided horizontally, with batters allowed to call for either a high or low strike and a pitch in the wrong zone deemed a ball. Fennelly was decidedly a low-ball hitter, and once batters could no longer call for their pitch, the selectivity that had been the mark of a disciplined batter now turned the SS into a hitter with holes in his strike zone. So runs the testimony of his contemporaries, yet Fennelly's record shows he started his ML career in 1884 as an exceptional hitter, especially for a SS, and then began a gradual erosion that bottomed out only in 1888. Yet he remained a far-ranging if error-prone SS and an excellent base runner but one averse to sliding.

Although a New Englander, Fennelly began his career with the Philadelphia League Alliance club in 1882 before going to Camden of the Interstate Association in 1883 and finishing the season with champion Brooklyn after Camden folded. In 1884 he joined Washington's new AA team, becoming the lone bright light in a dismal aggregation. The beginning of the end for the Washingtons was signaled at the start of August, when they sold their star SS to Cincinnati for $1,000. When the team disintegrated soon thereafter, the cash from the Fennelly sale was supposed to pay up the team's salary arrears, but the following January one of Washington's old players wrote *Sporting Life* wondering where the money had gone.

In Cincinnati, Fennelly filled a huge gap at SS and joined an otherwise exceptionally gifted infield consisting of John Reilly, Bid McPhee, and Hick Carpenter. Fennelly debuted for the Reds on August 13, winning the spectators' hearts with a home run, and went on from this propitious beginning to establish himself as arguably the hottest hitter in the AA until a sprained ankle ended his season prematurely in late September. After marrying in early 1885, he had another fine year, finishing among the AA's best in home runs and leading in RBI (according to retrospective calculations). Matters began to curdle for him the following year, however. He suffered an offensive decline, with his BA falling to .249, but made up for it by finishing among the leaders again in runs and home runs. However, his gigantic total of 117 errors, a huge amount even for the era, made him a target for the *Cincinnati Enquirer,* which was conducting a vicious campaign against the local club. The *Enquirer's* feud ended after the season in the wake of a change in the Reds' ownership and management, but Fennelly seems to have been left sensitive to criticism by the 1886 experience. There were periodic reports that he was drinking and wanted to get away from Cincinnati. In spite of his dissatisfaction, he was made team captain in the spring of 1887 and kept the position until he was sold to Philadelphia AA on September 24, 1888. He cost the Athletics $1,000, the same price Cincinnati had paid for him, but during that period baseball was in a furious bull market for player sales, so that in relative terms his value had diminished significantly in four years.

In Philadelphia, Fennelly replaced ponderous Bill Gleason at SS and played every inning of the 1889 season at the position. Around February 1890 the Brooklyn Gladiators, a new AA team, purchased him. The sale was probably in part a goodwill gesture by the Athletics, made to set a new franchise on its feet, and partially a response to Fennelly's demand for a raise and a multiyear contract. The 30-year-old Fennelly now found himself back where he had started in more ways than one, returning to Brooklyn, where he had played in 1883, and joining a competitively weak, financially unstable first-year ML team as he had in 1884. Although he was not the hitter he had been, his .247 BA was 26 points above the team average, and he had his usual strong extra-base numbers. In June he tore ligaments in his legs running the bases, however, and was released on July 5.

Fennelly went home to his native Fall River and ran his string of barbershops and also a grocery store there. He continued to play pro ball, manage, and umpire sporadically during the 1890s but did so primarily in and about Fall River, where he could tend to his business interest. From 1905–08 Fennelly served in the Massachusetts state legislature. Some twelve years later he died in Fall River of a probable heart attack. (DT/DB/DN)

Flowers, Charles Richard / "Dickie"

B	T	HGT	WGT	G	AB	H	R	2B
?	?	?	?	24	120	37	40	5

3B	HR	RBI	BB	SO	SB	BA	SA	OBP
4	0	22	6	2	8	.308	.417	.341

G	IP	H	GS	CG	BB
1	1	1	0	0	0

SO	SH	W	L	PCT	ERA
0	0	0	0	—	0.00

B. ?/?/1850 Philadelphia, PA **D.** 10/6/1892
TEAMS: 71TroNA 72AthNA
DEBUT: 6/3/1871 at Philadelphia; played SS and went 2-for-5 in a 15–5 loss to the Athletics' Dick McBride
FINALE: 6/12/1872 at Boston; played SS and went 1-for-3 in a 13–4 loss to Boston's Al Spalding

Dickie Flowers could do everything well but play SS. He made two wild throws in his ML debut, 3 errors in his finale, and 30 errors in 21 games at SS in between. Four days after his coda with the Athletics, the *New York Times* announced that the A's were "reconstructing their nine" and Flowers and Denny Mack would go their own way, which is indeed what happened. Flowers died in Philadelphia of dropsy of the liver when he was around 42. (DN)

Force, David W. / "Davy" "Wee Davy"

B	T	HGT	WGT	G	AB	H	R	2B
R	R	5'4"	130	1029	4250	1059	653	141

3B	HR	RBI	BB	SO	SB	BA	SA	OBP
27	1	373	156	268	35	.249	.296	.276

G	IP	H	GS	CG	BB
4	25	45	1	1	0

SO	SH	W	L	PCT	ERA
0	0	1	1	.500	6.84

B. 7/27/1849 New York, NY **D.** 6/21/1918
TEAMS: 71OlyNA 72TroNA 72–73BalNA 74ChiNA 75AtlNA 76PhiN 76NYN 77StLN 79–85BufN 86WasN
DEBUT: 5/5/1871 at Washington; played SS and made 1 hit in a 20–18 loss to Boston's Al Spalding
FINALE: 8/20/1886 at Washington; played SS and went 0-for-3 in an 11–1 loss to Philadelphia's Charlie Buffinton

When detectives came east from California searching for Davy Force, suspected of murdering one Joe Manning in what turned out to be a case of mistaken identity, the description they got from NL president Nick Young must have been out of the ordinary for a murder suspect. Young told the detectives that Force was short, bowlegged, and "a good fielder and a fair hitter." The physical description may have been helpful, but the characterization of Force's baseball talents would have been less useful. If the detectives were fans, they would have recognized "fair hitter" as a euphemism of the period meaning, "I hate to put it bluntly, but the man really can't hit at all."

Yet Young, who had known Force since both were active in Washington baseball circles thirty years earlier, would have remembered a time when Force was a very fine hitter. He began his career in 1862 with the Unknowns in Harlem, then a New York suburb. According to his commonly listed birth date, he would only have been 12 or 13 at the time, but the 1870 census lists him as 22, and if that information is correct, then, like many players, he was actually older than his baseball age.

Force moved to Washington in 1867 to catch Olympics pitcher A. G. Mills and work as a clerk in the Treasury Department. But unlike many other players of that time, his was not a patronage appointment as he actually did work at his clerical job, according to Mills's later recounting. Force soon moved to the infield and remained with the Olympics for five seasons until they cut back their salaries drastically, and he then began a peripatetic career typical of the pro player of the day, playing for six clubs in as many years.

During the winter of 1874–75, Force triggered a major controversy when he signed contracts first with his current Chicago team and then the Philadelphia A's. The A's exploited minor irregularities in Force's Chicago contract and the influence of Charles Spering, president of both their own club and the NA, to have the resulting dispute resolved in their favor. The Force affair has sometimes been described as the key incident in the replacement of the NA by the NL. Although this is an exaggeration, a considerable hullabaloo truly was aroused along with much dissatisfaction, especially among the club officials of Chicago and the A's longtime rivals in Boston.

Force had a day to remember on June 27, 1876, when he rapped 6 hits, but he hit just .214 in his other 60 games that season and in other respects, too, things were not going his way. While the Chicago team he had spurned was trotting to the NL's inaugural championship, Force's A's were playing poorly and having a difficult time meeting their payroll. In 1877 Force left Philadelphia to play for a St. Louis Brown Stockings team widely suspected of game throwing. Some of the suspicion adhered to Force, perhaps in part because of ill repute arising from the Chicago-Philadelphia matter. With the exception of these controversies, Force was generally regarded as a sober, hardworking, and responsible player, and there is no sound evidence that he ever engaged in game selling.

When St. Louis disbanded after the 1877 season, Force went to Buffalo as the highest-paid player on a strong International Association championship team. He reentered the ML in 1879 when Buffalo joined the NL and remained a Bison for seven more seasons, playing both SS and 2B. The smallest man in ML history to play 1,000 games at SS, Force was an unprepossessing athlete, but he got the most out of his 5'4" body. During his early pro seasons he was a very good hitter, although his best BA, a .418 mark good for second in the NA in 1872, was achieved with the help of a lively ball used by his Troy club. An excellent fielder as well, he was generally considered the best SS in the game with the exception of George Wright. From the middle 1870s onward, however, he suffered an offensive decline, resulting from the development of faster pitching, the widespread use of the curve ball, and the abolition of the fair-foul rule. A hitter substantially above league average until 1875, he became Young's "fair hitter" thereafter, only once reaching an AOPS as high as 95, and otherwise ranking from 80 down into the mid-30s. He did not walk much, was too small to hit for power, and batted above .217 just once in his last six seasons as a regular infielder. Such an unproductive a hitter could not hold a full-time job today, but Force remained an outstanding defensive player when fielding was a critically important skill. Over his career he was far above the average SS in range factor and nearly 50 points above league average in FA.

By 1885 Force was in his midthirties and was in and out of the regular lineup. Buffalo, along with Providence, folded at season's end, and Force was put on a list of players to be distributed between the replacement franchises. Washington, one of the new clubs, rejected him, and he was then offered to other teams with no takers although the NL reportedly priced him as low as $200. Eventually, the Washington officials changed their mind, and picked up Force on the advice of Paul Hines. He was given the SS job, but his light hitting was a luxury a club with a team BA of .210 could not afford. He played his last game on August 20 and was released less than two weeks later.

After playing and managing for two seasons in the minors and umpiring briefly in the Western Association, Force went to work for the Otis Elevator Company, whose vice president was A. G. Mills, the former NL president who had signed Force for his first engagement in ML ball with the Washington Olympics long ago. When Force was mistakenly suspected of the California murder in 1897, Mills released a public statement endorsing Force as an employee of his company for seven years and "a steady, hard-working man." Force continued working for Otis in New York until he retired. He died in 1922 in Englewood, NJ, from a cerebral thrombosis. (DB/DN)

Fuller, William Benjamin / "Shorty"

B	T	HGT	WGT	G	AB	H	R	2B
R	R	5'6"	157	964	3678	863	651	96

3B	HR	RBI	BB	SO	SB	BA	SA	OBP
43	6	349	444	198	.260	.235	.289	.322

B. 10/10/1867 Cincinnati, OH **D.** 4/11/1904
TEAMS: 88WasN 89–91StLA 92–96NYN
DEBUT: 7/19/1888 at Washington; played SS and went 0-for-4 in a 2–0 win over Boston's John Clarkson
FINALE: 6/2/1896 at New York; played SS and made 1 hit in an 8–5 win over Chicago's Clark Griffith

The brother of one-game MLer Harry Fuller was aptly nicknamed Shorty. Fuller had large hands for a man his size, an asset in the field, but nothing seemed to go his way when those hands held a bat. During his last four ML seasons (1893–96), which were exceptional hitters' years, his .632 OPS was the lowest among NL positions players with a minimum of 1,000 ABs.

Fuller graduated from the semipro Cincinnati Clippers to New Orleans in 1887, led all Southern League shortstops in fielding, and stroked .325. Midway through his second season in Louisiana, he was purchased by Washington. It was a bad omen when he did not get his first ML hit until his fourth game, on August 3. Exactly two weeks after that Fuller made a record 4 errors in the second inning in an 11–7 loss to Indianapolis and soon afterward went on the DL after he was beaned. Eager to get rid of him, Washington put him up for sale after the season but could find no takers until St. Louis owner Chris Von der Ahe, disenchanted with Bill White, his own SS, offered $800.

The St. Louis press had wanted the club to land either minor league star Jack Pickett or an established big leaguer and received Fuller's acquisition poorly. Aware that he was already unwelcome in St. Louis, the little SS refused to sign when he was offered a salary of $1,900, until Von der Ahe pointed out to him that the AA had not adopted John T. Brush's classification system and, unless he signed with St. Louis, he risked being returned to the NL, where he would probably be saddled with the lowest classification, entitling him to only $1,500.

Fuller proved a pleasant surprise in 1889, when he missed just 1 game and was enjoying an even better year in 1890 until late August when he was fined $100 when a private detective hired by Von der Ahe caught the SS in the "fearful offense" of drinking a glass of beer. No sooner had the fine been rescinded and Fuller restored to Von der Ahe's good graces than he twisted his ankle on October 7 in a game with Columbus, shelving him for the remainder of the year. Nevertheless, he led the Browns in walks and was second in numerous other batting departments.

Fuller continued to be productive in 1891, scoring 105 runs for the Browns despite hitting just .212, but the 1892 campaign signaled the beginning of the end for him as an offensive force. In 141 games with his new team, the Giants, the SS tabulated just 137 total bases. The 1893 season was no better, as Fuller was one of the few hitters who seemed not to benefit from the change in the pitching distance.

Despite losing his job prior to the season to rookie Tot Murphy, Fuller rebounded in 1894 to have his best year at the plate since 1890. Given a reprieve when Murphy injured a foot, Fuller rapped 4 hits, including a home run on his first day back in the lineup, a June 15 DH with the Phillies. Some 20 days later he had a 4-for-4 day against Louisville, strengthening Giants manager John M. Ward's conviction to leave Murphy on the bench. Ward's decision proved correct when Fuller helped spark New York to a second-place finish and the right to battle for the first-ever Temple Cup. In 1895, however, the SS resumed his offensive woes. He began the year hitting leadoff, helping him to tally 84 runs, but by midseason was often batting last, as he finished with just 120 total bases.

The trapdoor opened beneath Fuller the following year. Over the winter his brother Harry and two sisters all died of consumption just six weeks apart. Then, after an even softer beginning at the plate than usual—.167 BA in his first 18 games—Fuller lost his job to journeyman Frank Connaughton and was released. Tom Burns, the former Chicago third baseman who was now managing Springfield, MA, took him aboard his Eastern League club for the next season and a half, but when Burns moved up in 1898 to pilot Chicago, Springfield let Fuller go once the club's new manager, Billy Lush, took his job at SS.

Fuller played briefly that season in the Western League, hitting .148 for Detroit in 17 games, and then returned to Cincinnati. As late as 1903 he talked of making a comeback and joined a local semipro team. But soon after the season started, his health began to decline rapidly. Fuller died the following April of consumption at his Cincinnati home. (DN/DB)

*Fulmer, Charles John / "Chick"

B	T	HGT	WGT	G	AB	H	R	2B
R	R	6'0"	158	583	2439	635	361	70

3B	HR	RBI	BB	SO	SB	BA	SA	OBP
30	8	262	43	67	14	.260	.323	.273

G	IP	H	GS	CG	BB
2	5	7	0	0	1

SO	SH	W	L	PCT	ERA
0	0	0	0	—	3.60

B. 2/12/1851 Philadelphia, PA **D.** 2/15/1940
TEAMS: 71RokNA 72MutNA 73–75PhiNA 76LouN 79–80BufN 82–84CinA 84StLA
DEBUT: 6/5/1871 at Philadelphia; played SS and went 0-for-2 in an 11–10 loss to Philadelphia's Dick McBride
FINALE: 8/16/1884 at Cincinnati; played 2B and went 0-for-5 in a 14–8 loss to Cincinnati's Gus Shallix

Chick Fulmer was the brother of MLer Wash Fulmer. Years after he was released by Cincinnati, his former Reds teammate John Reilly—himself no mean storyteller—told reporters he intended to write a book of anecdotes from Fulmer's "interesting life." Reilly's book never appeared, but we know a fair amount about this enterprising and quick-witted man nonetheless. Fulmer's father was a butcher who served as a major in the Union Army during the Civil War. In 1895 Fulmer told *SL* he himself had been a drummer boy in the war, but much later he admitted he had tried to join up, only to be sent home from Baltimore when the officers realized he was just 14. Back in Philadelphia, Fulmer followed his older brother Wash as a baseball player for local teams. In 1869 he failed a trial when the Philadelphia Athletics needed a replacement during the illness of star pitcher Dick McBride. Fulmer later recalled having quit the A's because he wanted to buy a ticket to a show in which his sister was singing and treat her afterward, and he thought the $2 offered by the Athletics was inadequate. By his own account, however, the score of the game he had pitched was 51–49, so perhaps $2 was really all his pitching was worth.

He was more successful as an infielder, playing SS and 3B professionally with Cleveland, Rockford, IL, and the New York Mutuals before spending three years with his hometown Philadelphia club, for whom he boasted (bogusly) having turned the first unassisted triple play in history in 1873. He moved to Louisville in 1876, the NL's first season, but left after one year because he had trouble getting his pay, thereby avoiding the game-throwing scandal that tainted the 1877 Kentucky team. Fulmer subsequently played primarily for Eastern teams, most notably for 1878 International Association champion Buffalo.

Fulmer was a witty extrovert and the sort that would entertain the crowd with impressions of famous pitchers' deliveries. An energetic spirit (who was once timed to be the fastest player in the game at getting into his uniform) and a man with an eye on various ways to make a dollar, he ran a cigar stand in the clubhouse while playing for Buffalo and during off-seasons in the early 1880s managed touring theatrical companies playing the ubiquitous Gilded Age chestnut *Uncle Tom's Cabin*. Fulmer campaigned for the state legislature in 1880 and later won election as a Philadelphia city magistrate, an office with constabulary rather than judicial, responsibilities, but the spring of 1881 found his career at a low ebb following his release the previous August by Buffalo. He caught on as captain of an independent team being organized on a shoestring in his home city of Philadelphia, where pro baseball had been in the doldrums for several years. Called the new Athletics, the club was said to have started with $9 and a set of uniforms, renting a ballpark for $3 a day and paying its players a share of the gate in lieu of fixed salaries. But the three owners profited from a return of enthusiasm for baseball and made money in large quantities. After co-owner Horace Phillips was pushed out, Billy Sharsig and Charlie Mason took in Fulmer to replace Phillips in their partnership. When the Athletics received a franchise in the newly organized AA in the fall, no longer merely a player, Fulmer served on the committee to draft a constitution for the new league and gained a seat on its board of directors. At the 1882 loop spring meeting, however, he was released by the A's and quickly signed with Cincinnati. Accounts differ as to why he made the switch: the *Cincinnati Enquirer* attributed it vaguely to "some political trouble;" and co-owner Lew Simmons said later that Fulmer had merely preferred to take the more reliable course of accepting a salary as a player. The move, in any case, was made so suddenly that until the paperwork could be finalized in June, Fulmer remained nominally an owner of the A's while playing SS for Cincinnati. His new team, as it turned out, easily swept to the first AA championship. Fulmer batted a solid .281 and was singled out by the *Enquirer* as the best defensive SS in the AA, especially good at backpedaling on pop flies.

Fulmer at one time was credited incorrectly with having managed the 1882 Reds as well but truly did play a crucial quasi-managerial role in a landmark event at the end of the season. Teams normally played postseason exhibitions in those days, but the Cincinnati management apparently decided postseason games would not pay unless NL opponents could be scheduled. However, as a result of several contract disputes the AA forbid games against NL opponents. Accordingly, the Reds announced that their players would be released on September 30 and "turned over to a gentleman" who would subsequently pay their salaries, meet other postseason expenses, and collect any profits. The team would be "the Cincinnati Club only in name" and thus could play NL opponents. The other AA clubs did not agree with this interpretation and the Reds subsequently narrowly escaped league discipline, but in the meantime, they had played two series with NL teams. Historians have understandably been skeptical that the never identified gentleman was anyone other than the Cincinnati owners themselves, but the surviving account book of club secretary Opie Caylor shows that the club neither paid salaries nor received revenue during October. An obscure *Sporting Life* note suggests that the mysterious gentleman was in fact Fulmer, or rather, that at Fulmer's suggestion the Reds avoided a money-losing postseason by allowing the players to play their NL opponents under their own auspices, collecting a share of the gate receipts rather than receiving their usual salary. In this way, Fulmer is responsible for what has sometimes been called the first World's Series—a debatable characterization, but the two contests with NL winner Chicago were at any rate the first in baseball history to match the champions of two major leagues, and by splitting a pair of well-played games with the great White Stockings the Reds did much to establish the credibility of the AA.

At the start of the 1883 season Fulmer actually was named manager of a sort in a capacity that made him solely responsible for maintaining order and team discipline off the field. But he was on bad terms with Caylor, whose position was roughly that of a modern GM. Early in the season Fulmer resigned as manager, and with the Reds struggling to stay in the pennant race, Caylor benched the SS in July after a tough loss at St. Louis. The result was a remarkable furor in Cincinnati. Fulmer was swiftly reinserted in the lineup, and Caylor, evidently fearing for his job, became lavish in his praise of the SS in the columns he wrote for the *Cincinnati Commercial Gazette.* At the time, no one in Cincinnati would say aloud what many insiders secretly knew—that Caylor had benched Fulmer because he believed St. Louis owner Chris Von der Ahe had paid the Reds' SS to play badly against his Browns. Even after publicly burying the hatchet with Fulmer, Caylor continued to hint in the *Commercial* that he did not trust him.

The Reds reserved Fulmer for 1884, but he was disgusted with his treatment and wanted to get away from Cincinnati. He was in a stronger position than most players, since his magistracy in Philadelphia gave him a good independent source of income, but he eventually signed to play in 1884 for a healthy 25 percent raise, telling the *Philadelphia Item* he had gone to Cincinnati intending to get his release from the Reds, but had signed a contract after being carried away with enthusiasm when he saw the players at practice. "Charlie is too old a bird to be caught on such chaffs," the *Philadelphia Sunday Dispatch* rejoined, "and the only enthusiasm he feels is for the almighty dollar." It turned out the Reds would have done better to have let Fulmer go, for over that winter he seems to have aged very quickly. He never hit and lost his job after a 6-error game in New York on June 4. When the team returned to Cincinnati, a reporter found Fulmer watching the game from the grandstand, unhappy at not playing and saying he felt he wasn't earning his money. In early August he was released and caught on with St. Louis but was dropped again after a single 2-error game at 2B.

Fulmer managed minor league teams for a time and then quit baseball and went home to Philadelphia. In the late 1930s, when the Cincinnati Reds were again in World Series contention, he appeared in the news as one of the last surviving veterans of their first championship team and still a source of good copy for newspaper reporters. He was said to attend every game the Reds played in Philadelphia, and in August 1939 he was photographed with Cincinnati manager Bill McKechnie. By this time, however, he was in decline, having been left a semi-invalid as the result of two debilitating strokes the previous year. Fulmer died in 1940 at 89, survived by his wife of more than sixty-five years and a son. The *New York Times* described him as "one of the greatest shortstops in baseball 60 years ago," which he certainly had not been, but as John Reilly could have testified long before, there was much more to his life than that. (DB/DN)

---

*Hackett, Walter Henry / "Walter"

B	T	HGT	WGT	G	AB	H	R	2B
?	?	?	?	138	540	124	79	22

3B	HR	RBI	BB	SO	SB	BA	SA	OBP
0	1	9	10	22	—	.230	.276	.244

B. 8/15/1857 Cambridge, MA **D.** 10/2/1920
TEAMS: 84BosU 85BosN
DEBUT: 4/17/1884 at Philadelphia; went 0-for-5 and remarkably had no chances at SS in a 14–2 win over Philadelphia's Sam Weaver
FINALE: 8/22/1885 at Boston; played 2B and went 1-for-4 in a 7–0 win over Providence's Dupee Shaw

Walter Hackett was the older brother of ML catcher Mert Hackett. The two were teammates for a time on the 1885 Boston NL club and were also cousins of the Clarkson brothers. The elder Hackett had been a semipro and minor leaguer for nearly a decade before the UA formed in 1884 and installed a franchise in Boston. A competent fielder, he foundered even against suspect UA pitching but nonetheless was given a second ML opportunity in 1885 while Boston's regular second baseman, Jack Burdock, was injured. Hackett later played until 1889 with eastern minor league teams and worked winters as a printer in Cambridge. He was employed in the proof room of the *Boston Globe* until shortly before his death in 1920 at his Cambridge home. (DN)

Hallinan, James H. / "Jimmy"

B	T	HGT	WGT	G	AB	H	R	2B
L	L	5'9"	172	170	760	218	142	25

3B	HR	RBI	BB	SO	SB	BA	SA	OBP
12	5	83	15	18	5	.287	.371	.301

B. 5/27/1849 ?, Ireland **D.** 10/28/1879
TEAMS: 71KekNA 75WesNA 75MutNA 76NYN 77CinN 77–78ChiN 78IndN
DEBUT: 7/26/1871 at Fort Wayne; played SS and made 2 hits in an 11–9 loss to New York's Rynie Wolters
FINALE: 8/22/1878 at Providence; played LF and went 0-for-4 in a 5–1 win over Providence's John M. Ward

Jimmy Hallinan was fast and hit with power but was not a solution at SS, his main position, because he was both left-handed and erratic. In the late 1860s and early 1870s he played with a series of semipro teams in the Chicago area including the Aetnas, the Chicago Fire Department nine, and the Franklins, whose members nearly all worked in the press room of the *Chicago Times.* Having flunked a trial with Fort Wayne NA in 1871 when he made 21 errors in 5 games and fielded .475, Hallinan was regarded as something of a risk by the *Keokuk Daily City Gate* when the local Westerns hired him to play SS and bat leadoff after joining the NA in 1875. He showed enough improvement, however, that the New York Mutuals hired him after the Iowa club disbanded.

Despite leading NA shortstops in errors in 1875, Hallinan was retained when the Mutes joined the newly formed National League the following year. He again led in errors even though the Mutes withdrew from the loop before completing their schedule. For the remaining two years of his ML career, Hallinan was only a part-time player due to chronic bouts of illness, which may have been exacerbated by excessive drinking. When the Cincinnati team disbanded temporarily in 1877, there was considerable debate over whether Hallinan was drunk when he signed with Chicago. But he was eventually allowed to remain in his home city even after the Reds were restored to the NL in good standing. Hallinan retreated to his job with the Chicago Fire Department in 1878 after playing his last ML game with Indianapolis and died the following fall of inflammation of the bowels. (DN/DB)

*Hatfield, Gilbert / "Gil" "Colonel"

B	T	HGT	WGT	G	AB	H	R	2B
?	R	5'9½"	168	317	1190	295	173	31

3B	HR	RBI	BB	SO	SB	BA	SA	OBP
18	6	129	96	109	81	.248	.319	.315

G	IP	H	GS	CG	BB
13	77.2	90	5	5	43

SO	SH	W	L	PCT	ERA
34	0	3	5	.375	5.56

B. 1/27/1855 Hoboken, NJ **D.** 5/26/1921
TEAMS: 85BufN 87–89NYN 90NYP 91WasA 93BroN 95LouN
DEBUT: 9/24/1885 at New York; played 2B and went 2-for-3 in an 11–3 loss to New York's Mickey Welch
FINALE: 5/8/1895 at Louisville; played 3B and went 2-for-4 in a 9–6 loss to Philadelphia's Willie McGill

Gil Hatfield was the younger brother of MLer John Hatfield. The two were related to the feuding Hatfields of West Virginia. In 1889 one of the enemy McCoys came to the Polo Grounds bent on making his bones by killing a major league ballplayer but was whisked out of the park before he could get within range of the Giants' utilityman. Despite not making the majors until he was 30, Hatfield lasted until he was 40 because he was versatile, kept in good shape, and was an excellent base runner even if he never slid for fear of soiling his uniform. A native of Hoboken, he played for amateur teams at the legendary Elysian Fields as well as at Prospect Park in Brooklyn and Central Park in New York. His first ML experience came in 1883, when he was a member in the spring of the AA Mets' reserve team before joining independent Newark in July after the Mets released him.

Hatfield spent 1884 in the Eastern League and was back with Newark in 1885 when Buffalo, in need of replacements after it sold its "Big Four" to Detroit, acquired him in late September after the EL campaign finished. A flop with the Bisons, he did not appear in an ML uniform again until 1887 when he finished the season at 3B with the Giants. Hatfield then made the club the following year out of the chute as a scrub. Popular with the team's central clique, he shared in the Giants' two World's Series triumphs in 1888–89 even though he played in just 60 games over that span and hit .183. Hatfield's main contribution actually came as a pitcher. His delivery was said to be similar to Elton Chamberlin's and Gus Weyhing's in that he "brings his arm far back behind him and after a kind of hang lets the ball fly." Yet even with the best team in the game behind him, Hatfield was just 2-4 in the box.

Utilizing his Giants connections, Hatfield landed a spot on the New York PL team in 1890. Miraculously, he opened the season at SS, but abysmal fielding soon put him back on the bench until he was loaned illegally to Boston PL for 3 games that were later thrown out. Upon returning to New York, he hit so well in spot duty at 3B that pundits were puzzled why team captain Buck Ewing kept him on the sidelines and played Dan Shannon (.216) at 2B. It may have been that Hatfield and Ewing had a failing out, for he was not invited to return to the Giants after the PL folded. He served as the Washington AA club's regular SS in 1891, fielding a wretched .869, and then returned to a sub role in his last two ML ventures. Hatfield finished his playing career in 1899 at age 44 as the second baseman–manager of the New London Whalers in the Connecticut League. He was working as a teller at the Hudson Trust Company in Hoboken at 66 when he died of a heart attack in the office of his brother-in-law, who was a physician. (DN)

Herr, Joseph / "Joe"

B	T	HGT	WGT	G	AB	H	R	2B
R	R	5'9½"	179	66	257	67	32	11

3B	HR	RBI	BB	SO	SB	BA	SA	OBP
2	3	50	22	—	13	.261	.354	.333

B. 3/4/1865 St. Louis, MO **D.** 7/12/1933
TEAMS: 87CleA 88StL A 90StLA
DEBUT: 4/16/1887 at Cincinnati; played 3B and went 2-for-4 in a 16–6 loss to Cincinnati's Tony Mullane
FINALE: 6/25/1890 at St. Louis; played 2B and went 0-for-5 in a 10–7 win over Louisville's Scott Stratton

A carpenter by trade, Joe Herr grew up near where the St. Louis Maroons' Palace Park was built in 1884 and by 1885 was a member of the famed semipro Peach Pies. He began 1886 with independent Bellville, IL, and then moved to St. Joseph of the Western League. Signed for 1887 by the new Cleveland AA entry, Herr was released to Lincoln of the Western League in May of that season at his own request after deciding that he could not play his best with such a weak team.

The following spring Herr was named captain of the Western Association St. Louis Whites, which were backed by Browns owner Chris Von der Ahe and shared Sportsman's Park with the Mound City AA club. In a WA game on May 1, 1888, he became only the fourth man to hammer a ball over the LF fence in Sportsman's Park, joining Harry Stovey, Dave Orr, and Tip O'Neill. Herr later also became the fifth and sixth man to perform this feat. The latter blast came in an AA game on June 27 after he had joined the Browns once the Whites folded. Having established that he had extraordinary power, Herr soon also demonstrated that he lacked the necessary range to play SS. He was tried for eight games in the outfield, but manager Charlie Comiskey already had Tip O'Neill and Tommy McCarthy at the corner positions and felt that Harry Lyons, despite hitting just .194, covered substantially more ground in CF than the former Peach Pie. Although Herr remained on the Browns for the remainder of 1888 and participated in the World's Series against the New York Giants, he collected just 172 ABs. Since RBI were not an official stat then, no one could have realized that his retrospective 43 RBI would be 12 more than any other player in AA history compiled in a season with less than 200 ABs.

Something appears to have happened to Herr that winter, or perhaps he simply lost motivation after the Browns dropped him the following spring. Herr began 1889 in the Western Association but was released by Milwaukee after 26 games when he was hitting just .174. He then played in the Central Interstate League with Evansville but again without much élan. Riddled by Players League defections, the Browns rehired him in June 1890 and then released him less than two weeks later to Waco of the Texas League, where he hit .186. That July, Herr took an offer from Jamestown of the New York State League but regretted it almost as soon as he arrived in that tiny town and was back in St. Louis by August. Over the next eighteen months or so he married and began a family, seemingly having wasted a large quantity of baseball potential. He was an unemployed carpenter living apart from his wife, Marie, in a men's shelter when he drowned in 1933. (DN/PM)

Houck, Sargent Perry / "Sadie"

B	T	HGT	WGT	G	AB	H	R	2B
R	R	5'7"	151	641	2659	666	406	106

3B	HR	RBI	BB	SO	SB	BA	SA	OBP
58	4	234	48	75	31	.250	.338	.269

B. 3/?/1856 Washington, D.C. **D.** 5/26/1919
TEAMS: 79–80BosN 80ProN 81DetN 83DetN 84–85PhiA 86BalA 86WasN 87NYA
DEBUT: 5/1/1879 at Buffalo; played SS and went 2-for-4 in a 5–0 win over Buffalo's Jim Galvin
FINALE: 9/23/1887 at Baltimore; played SS and 2B and went hitless in a 15–7 loss to Baltimore's Matt Kilroy

Sadie Houck's strong performance with the independent Washington Nationals in 1878 misled Boston manager Harry Wright into thinking that he had made a real find when the rookie SS was signed to replace Wright's brother George, who had skipped to Providence. One of three frosh in defending NL champion Boston's lineup on Opening Day in 1879, Houck got off to a rocky start at SS and spent more time in the outfield. Wright in time would view the heralded rookie's disappointing year as a major reason Boston lost what would have been its third consecutive pennant to his brother's club. When Houck again started badly in 1880, he was released to Providence, where he did no better, finishing the season with a combined .190 BA. Set adrift, he signed with the new Detroit NL entry for 1881. Returning to his original position at SS, he led the NL in double plays and had a good year in general but exasperated manager Frank Bancroft to such a degree with his drinking that he was blacklisted by the NL for the 1882 season.

Houck returned from limbo to have another good year with Detroit in 1883, but the Wolverines' new manager, Jack Chapman, liked his habits no better than Bancroft had. It has never been established whether Houck was released outright that November to Philadelphia AA or whether the A's paid Detroit for his contract. A's manager Charlie Mason installed his new acquisition in the cleanup spot on Opening Day and later moved him to the third slot. Houck displayed little power but had a decent BA and led all AA shortstops in FA. It was his best overall season to date and also his last of consequence.

Carousing caused Houck to miss significant time in 1885 and helped increase his errors at SS from 60 to 77. The following February, after the A's considered suspending him for the 1886 season, he was sold to Baltimore instead, as *SL* observed that "sympathy for [Billy] Barnie got the better of their desire for punishment." Houck lasted only 61 games under Barnie before drawing his release. He caught a southbound train to Washington and was at SS for the NL Senators on July 28, a week after playing his last game with Baltimore. Houck broke the Mendoza Line in 1886, finishing with a combined .202 BA, but his .450 OPS was the second worst in the majors, trailing only Jim Lillie. It was to be his ML coda except for a few games with the Mets the following year after he had spent the season in the New England League.

Houck played in the Southern League awhile in 1888 and subsequently opened a roadhouse in Rockville, MD. His establishment was constantly in trouble with the law. After a raid in the early 1900s he was found guilty of operating without a liquor license and running a gaming house and then fined $200 when he failed to appear for sentencing. Meanwhile his young wife, Ella, disappeared after dressing to go shopping and admitted when she was later found that she had simply been overwhelmed by the downward turn of events in her life. Houck subsequently relocated to Chicago for a time and tended bar. Toward the end of his life he returned to Washington and died there in 1919. Several explanations have been ventured for his nickname, "Sadie," but none is particularly convincing. (DN)

Hulen, William Franklin / "Billy" "Billy the Kid"

B	T	HGT	WGT	G	AB	H	R	2B
L	L	5'8"	148	107	407	100	97	19

3B	HR	RBI	BB	SO	SB	BA	SA	OBP
7	0	41	65	20	28	.246	.327	.350

B. 3/12/1870 Dixon, CA **D.** 10/2/1947
TEAMS: 96PhiN 99WasN
DEBUT: 5/2/1896 at Philadelphia; went 0-for-2 after replacing Bill Hallman at 2B in a 15–10 loss to New York's Ed Doheny
FINALE: 5/12/1899 at Brooklyn; played SS and went 0-for-2 in a 3–0 loss to Brooklyn's Roaring Bill Kennedy

When Billy Hulen made his initial appearance at SS with the Phillies on May 5, 1896, it was his first of 73 games there that season and marked the last time in ML history that a left-hander would play more than half his team's games at an infield position other than 1B. Shaky in the field (although apparently not because he was left-handed), he scored 87 runs in 88 games and drew 55 walks, excellent numbers for a lead-off hitter. Yet he played only 19 more games in the majors.

Hulen made his pro bow with Sacramento of the California League in 1891. Released in August when he was part of a large crew of players manager John McCloskey believed was working to undermine him, he joined Los Angeles and remained with the Angels until he went east in the spring of 1894 to play for Minneapolis of the Western League. Drafted by the Phillies in the fall of 1895 after he hit .359 for the Millers, he was cut the following autumn when George Stallings took over the Philadelphia reins. Hulen spent the next two years back in the Western League with Columbus, where he was commended regularly for his fielding. Rather than being handicapped at SS because he was a southpaw, he was viewed by at least one observer as having an edge, if anything, in that being a lefty "enables him to make wonderful plays on hard hit balls over second base," which suggests that he may still have been playing barehanded. After hitting .271 with a .891 FA for Columbus in 1898, Hulen was drafted by Washington. He opened 1899 as the D.C. club's SS and lead-off hitter but lasted less than a month when he hit .147 in 19 games and was released to Kansas City of the Western League.

The following year Hulen became part owner and manager of Pueblo in the new version of the Western League in addition to serving as his own SS. A snag developed when it emerged that he had never gotten his official release from Kansas City. Eventually, Pueblo fans took up a collection to raise the $500 he needed to buy his way out of his old contract. Hulen remained a player-manager and entrepreneurial force in the minors for several more years, finishing the playing portion of his career as a first baseman with Spokane of the Northwestern League in 1908. Despite having coached part-time at several colleges while still a player, including Ohio State and Santa Clara, he was never offered a full-time college coaching position. Hulen reverted to his off-season occupation as a house painter for the remainder of his working life. He died from a heart attack at 77 while visiting relatives in Petaluma, CA. (DN)

***Irwin, Arthur Albert / "Arthur" "Sandy"**

B	T	HGT	WGT	G	AB	H	R	2B
L	R	5'8½"	158	1010	3871	934	552	141

3B	HR	RBI	BB	SO	SB	BA	SA	OBP
45	5	396	309	378	93	.241	.305	.299

G	IP	H	GS	CG	BB
2	4	6	0	0	1

SO	SH	W	L	PCT	ERA
0	0	0	0	.000	2.25

G	W	L	PCT	PENNANTS
863	416	427	.493	1

B. 2/14/1858 Toronto, Ontario, Canada
D. 7/16/1921
TEAMS: 80–82WorN 83–85ProN 86–89PhiN (P/M)89WasN 90BosP (P/M)91BosA (P/M)92WasN (P/M)94PhiN (M)95PhiN (M)96NYN (M)98–99WasN
DEBUT: 5/1/1880 at Worcester; played SS and went 0-for-5 in a 13–1 win over Troy's Mickey Welch
FINALE: 6/22/1894 at Baltimore; replaced Lave Cross at SS for an inning and then hauled 1-gamer Charlie Yingling out of the stands to finish the game in his stead
FAMOUS FIRST ONE: Claimed he was the first infielder to wear a glove in 1885 after a pitch injured the little finger on his left hand so painfully that he had a glove specially made, "the finger for the little and the one next to it being in one"

FAMOUS FIRST TWO: Invented the first football score and bulletin board, first used in a Thanksgiving Day game on 11/30/1893 between Harvard and Penn, and created a stir on 1/1/1920, when a refined version of his scoreboard reproduced the Harvard-Oregon Rose Bowl game play-by-play at the Harvard Club in New York
FAMOUS FIRST THREE: In 1895 coached the Philadelphia entry in the first professional soccer league, mistakenly thought by many modern historians to have been the first pro football league because it was called the American League of Professional Football

Arthur Irwin was the brother of ML infielder John Irwin. If not for an injury early in his ML career he might have been the most outstanding defensive SS in the nineteenth century. He also might have been one of the top early-day managers with a different temperament. The complaint against Irwin was that he was not strict enough with his stars and "too pugnacious, too abrupt, and too harsh to make a hit" with his lesser lights, but he kept himself continually employed owing to his superior organizational skills and reputation for being a shrewd judge of talent in spite of his uneven treatment of his players and at times frighteningly brutal honesty.

In 1891, Irwin managed the Boston Reds to the AA pennant but felt his team was cheated out of a chance to play in what would have been the final AA and NL World's Series when Cap Anson's Chicago Colts, which had pledged to play Irwin's Reds if they won, lost an NL pennant to Boston that Anson swore had been fixed for Chicago to lose. Here is what the Irwin bluntly had to say about the episode in the October 17, 1891, *TSN*: "These charges of crookedness will kill the game unless they are explained away, and they can't be explained away. Simply because they are true, and there is plenty of proof. While the New Yorks were in Boston, Buck Ewing and Mike Kelly made no secret of the fact that the Bostons were to win all the games. They talked it over in the dressing room, and Ewing fixed up his team in Kelly's presence and talked and laughed over it in the presence of others." When asked if he could substantiate this, Irwin said, "Yes, every word of it can be proven by reputable witnesses who were in the dressing room. It was common talk in Boston, and further than that, there is no secret that Buck Ewing gave the signs of the New York pitchers to Mike Kelly." In 1912 Phillies owner Horace Fogel was banned for asserting that the umpires favored the New York Giants to assure the Gotham club of winning the NL pennant. Not only was Irwin never even mildly chastised for his analysis, but not a single member of either the New York or Boston team ever dared to step forward and publicly deny so much as one word of what he said.

After playing with the Aetna Juniors of South Boston in 1873–74, Irwin joined a Hub nine called the Amateurs for the next four seasons. He then signed with the National Association team in Worcester that graduated to the NL the following year. In his rookie season Irwin stunned senior loop observers with his extraordinary range at SS as he compiled a then record 339 assists. The following year, however, he missed a number of games in the spring while out sick and then broke his leg sliding on August 18 at Providence. Upon returning to action in 1883 his range was noticeably reduced, and while he was a steady and competent SS for the remainder of his career, he was a sub-.240 hitter once overhand pitching was legalized in 1884.

Although Irwin continued to be an active player through the 1890 season, he grew more interested in managing after receiving his first taste of having full authority over a team in 1889 as a midseason replacement in Washington for pilot John Morrill. Two years later, in his next managerial experience with the AA Boston Reds, he won a pennant in his first full season at the helm but never won another even though he managed in both the majors and the minors for some twenty more seasons.

In 1921 Irwin was managing the Hartford Eastern League entry but left the club in July claiming that he was ill and was taken to a hospital for abdominal trouble. Upon his release, he traveled to New York with a party of friends and left them around midnight in a state of obvious depression to board the steamer Calvin Austin. Irwin then told several fellow passengers on the ship that he was "going home to die." When the ship docked in Boston the next morning, he was not longer aboard.

Presumably Irwin had committed suicide by jumping into the Atlantic, but two questions haunted his wife and his son, Arthur Herbert. What became of the $5,000 Irwin withdrew from a bank before leaving New York and why did he, an impeccable dresser, wear a baggy, ill-fitting suit aboard the Calvin Austin that was the only thing left behind in his stateroom? Several days later Arthur Herbert made an unpleasant discovery. His father had led a double life and had another wife and son in New York. Irwin's Boston family still believed that he had committed suicide after learning that he had an incurable disease while in New York, but the police were obliged to investigate the possibility that he was murdered for the $5,000 and his body thrown overboard.

Of course there was another conceivable explanation for Irwin's abrupt disappearance and the fact that his body was never found. The Baseball Hall of Fame has a letter on file written in 1922 by a pitcher who knew Irwin. In it he queried, "How can Arthur Irwin be dead? I just saw him in Oklahoma." (DN)

---

*Kappel, Henry / "Heinie"

B	T	HGT	WGT	G	AB	H	R	2B
R	R	5'8"	160	105	394	106	54	14

3B	HR	RBI	BB	SO	SB	BA	SA	OBP
11	4	51	25	28	33	.269	.391	.318

B. 9/?/1863 Philadelphia, PA **D.** 8/27/1905
TEAMS: 87–88CinA 89ColA
DEBUT: 5/22/1887 at Cincinnati; played LF and went 1-for-3 in a 17–7 win over Baltimore's Matt Kilroy and Tommy Burns
FINALE: 8/1/1889 at Columbus; played 3B and went 1-for-4 in a 16–5 loss to Cincinnati's Lee Viau

The brother of MLer Joe Kappel, Heinie Kappel's story illustrates the proposition that the careers of all but the very best players are too often at the mercy of chance and circumstance. A Philadelphian who made a considerable reputation in the Southern League in 1885–86 after debuting in the 1884 Iron & Oil Association, he was signed by Cincinnati's newly appointed manager, Gus Schmelz, in the fall of 1886 as a replacement for the Reds' veteran third baseman Hick Carpenter, who had played very poorly in the season just ended. Before Kappel had ever played an inning of ML ball, Schmelz, a former Southern League manager, privately assured Cincinnati club president Aaron Stern that "we have the finest third baseman in the [American] Association."

Kappel hit very well in the 1887 preseason, but superior fielding, greater experience, and, most of all, the strong support of his veteran teammates kept Carpenter in the lineup. The Reds tried to farm Kappel to Memphis, but loans—optional assignments, as we would call them—were contrary to the rules of the day. Other Southern League teams objected to Memphis using a farmed player, and when Cleveland complained that a player it coveted had been passed to a minor league without undergoing AA waivers, Cincinnati was compelled to recall Kappel. For the next two years he remained in deep freeze, never quite able to win a regular job in the strong Cincinnati infield, while the Reds regarded him as too promising to accept one of the many offers to buy him. At a stage of his career when he should have been developing his talents, Kappel played only 59 games in two years, often at positions other than his natural 3B. When he did get in the lineup, he was rusty and insecure from lack of use, with the result that he committed errors out of nervousness and led to jeers from the spectators, which only caused him to press all the more. Eventually, he would settle down and start playing better, but by then the player he was temporarily replacing would be healthy enough to play again.

Kappel received one protracted shot at 3B in August 1887 after Carpenter's batting fell off drastically. For a week Kappel played very badly, until at last he steadied, enjoying several errorless games and continuing to hit. On August 21, just as he seemed to have made the job his own, he hit a fourth inning triple and scored a moment later on an infield grounder but injured a hand sliding. Carpenter replaced him and, given a new lease on his position, put up a much-improved brand of ball. By the time Kappel was healthy again his moment had passed.

The next May he had another extended spell of duty replacing the injured Bid McPhee, but playing out of position in place of the finest second baseman in the game, he was again nervous and error-prone. A final chance at a regular job came in the fall, when Cincinnati sold SS Frank Fennelly to the Athletics and gave Kappel a trial at the position in the last days of the season. When he again failed to impress, Cincinnati acquired minor leaguer Ollie Beard, and packaged Kappel with three other benchwarmers to Columbus's new AA team for a modest $1,500. Repeated failure to take advantage of his opportunities had apparently driven down his value. Before the 1888 season, if newspaper reports are accurate, Kappel alone had drawn offers as high as $2,000.

Nevertheless, he was only 25 and was beginning anew on a team that had a regular position for him. He could reasonably expect his future to be much brighter in Columbus. Instead it turned out to be in some respects much worse. First, Kappel suffered a severely torn muscle playing in an indoor baseball game in February. As late as April it was questionable whether he would play at all in 1889, and Columbus signed Henry Easterday as a backup. Kappel first saw action on April 24, nearly a week into the season, playing well generally but committing 2 errors at SS, the second of which cost Columbus the game. By mid-May he was hitting hard but still committing errors and was benched in favor of Easterday. From then on he was in and out of the lineup. The source of Kappel's problems was in part a mistake by the Columbus management in acquiring him in the first place to play SS. He played some stretches at 3B as well, but that position was assigned to hard-hitting rookie Ralph Johnson. Columbus really needed Kappel at short, where Easterday was not strong enough in the field to justify carrying his weak bat. Unfortunately, as his experience in Cincinnati had shown, SS was simply not a position Kappel could handle.

On August 1 the Columbus players lost a "running, roaring farce" of a game to Cincinnati, 16–5, and then gathered for their bimonthly payday. Soon reports began to emanate that the players were on the brink of revolt over large fines held out of their pay envelopes, with Kappel reportedly assessed so heavily that teammates had to chip in to help him pay his board bill. The Columbus management denied the charges, and within a day it had released Kappel, blaming him for spreading lies. He paid his own way into a game the next day, only to be ejected from the park, and eventually he turned up in Cincinnati, swearing vengeance against the Columbus club and saying he had gone hungry for four days before leaving Columbus for fear the club's officials would have him arrested. The Columbus team, having traveled to Cincinnati, made up a purse to allow him to get home to Philadelphia. Meanwhile, the newspapers in Columbus, hitherto critical of team management for not giving Kappel a fairer chance to show what he could do, turned on him as a complainer and disturbing influence. Whether he had been blackballed for his trouble in Columbus or simply failed one too many chances, Kappel never got back to the majors, although he played for several more years in the minors before finishing in 1895, playing with his brother for Bridgeton in the outlaw Southern New Jersey League. By 1904 Kappel was in a mental hospital in Philadelphia, probably a victim of syphilis, which took the sanity and then the lives of so many former ballplayers of the day. He died the next year of myocarditis.

Might Kappel's career have played out differently than it did? Perhaps not. Yet we will never know whether he might have gone on to do had he not hurt his hand sliding home in 1887, just when he seemed to have won Hick Carpenter's job. (DB/DN)

Kessler, Henry / "Henry" "Lucky"

B	T	HGT	WGT	G	AB	H	R	2B
R	R	5'10"	144	105	434	110	51	8

3B	HR	RBI	BB	SO	SB	BA	SA	OBP
0	0	23	10	15	0	.253	.272	.270

B. ?/?/1847 Brooklyn, NY **D.** 1/9/1900
TEAMS: 73–75AtlNA 76–77CinN
DEBUT: 8/4/1873 at Brooklyn; played 1B and went 1-for-5 in a 16–8 win over Elizabeth's Len Lovett
FINALE: 6/16/1877 at Cincinnati; caught Bobby Mathews and went 0-for-4 in an 8–4 loss to Louisville's Jim Devlin

Brooklyn-born Henry Kessler evidently had connections on the Atlantics that enabled him to play occasional games with the team over three seasons despite being a heavy drinker and a lackadaisical player. But his experience with Cincinnati is even more mysterious. He left the Atlantics in July 1875 for Cincinnati when the old Red Stockings club reorganized and began raiding the weaker NA teams for players. Installed at SS, Kessler led off the Queen City club's maiden NL game by fanning but banged 2 hits later in the contest, helping Cherokee Fisher to a 2–1 win over St. Louis. He finished the 1876 season with a .278 OPS and a .788 FA but was nonetheless rehired for the following season as a tenth man, thereby living up to his nickname of "Lucky."

Kessler's only 2 hits in 1877 came in an 11–2 loss at St. Louis on June 11. He was let go a few days afterward when Cincinnati temporarily disbanded, finished the season with Rhode Island of the

New England League, and then spent the next seven years in similar federations. In 1883 when his Leadville, CO, team folded while it was visiting independent Franklin, PA, he lingered and played for Franklin in the Iron & Oil Association and Hamilton in the Ohio State League, until he was sentenced to Western Penitentiary for arson after burning down a Franklin hotel. Kessler never made it back to Brooklyn. He went to a county poor farm near Franklin shortly after he got out of prison and remained there until he died a pauper of heart failure in 1900. (DN/DB)

Leary, John J. / "Jack"

B	T	HGT	WGT	G	AB	H	R	2B
?	L	5'11"	186	129	538	125	56	11

3B	HR	RBI	BB	SO	SB	BA	SA	OBP
9	4	4	10	1	—	.232	.309	.246

G	IP	H	GS	CG	BB
14	94.2	123	12	8	20

SO	SH	W	L	PCT	ERA
23	0	3	9	.250	4.56

B. 7/?/1857 New Haven, CT **D.** 12/6/1905
TEAMS: 80BosN 81DetN 82PitA 82BalA 83LouA 83BalA 84AltU 84ChiU
DEBUT: 8/21/1880 at Chicago; caught by Phil Powers, finished the game in RF, and lost 11–2 to Larry Corcoran and Tom Poorman
FINALE: 7/5/1884 at Philadelphia; in a 3–0 loss to Philadelphia's Enoch Bakely

Jack Leary's career stats offer little hint of how good a player he might have been had he taken better care of himself and made even a modest effort to feign subservience to the management of the multitude of teams for which he played. A lefty with good range at almost every position who could also handle himself in the box, he was probably ready for the majors as early as 1878, when he pitched and played the outfield for Manchester of the International Association in his second pro season and posted a .316 BA, second on the team only to John O'Rourke's .393. Instead he headed for the far West the following summer and by 1880 was playing for Bay City in the California League. After being expelled and reinstated several times for drunkenness, Leary finally skipped the club in late May and began working his way back East. He stopped off for several weeks to pitch for the independent Topeka Westerns before appearing in Chicago to start a game in the box for Harry Wright's Hub entry. Ripped for 6 runs in three innings, Leary exchanged places in RF with Curry Foley for the rest of the game and then took his act to the road again.

The following spring he became perhaps the first player brought to court for contract jumping. The *Brooklyn Eagle* wrote of his flight to the New York Mets when he grew disgusted with the poor discipline on the co-op New York team he had first joined in 1881. Later the *New York Clipper* reported an injunction had been served on Leary by the co-op club, with a trial forthcoming, and described the suit as "a novel expedient to retain the services of a player." But before the court date arrived, Leary rendered it moot, according to the *Clipper*, when he "left the Metropolitans in the lurch and joined the Detroits." Though the Mets were members of the Eastern Championship Association, they had neglected to notify Nick Young of Leary's signing, so technically he was a free agent. Leary lasted just 3 games with Detroit.

The 1882 campaign found him with Pittsburgh in the newly formed AA. He pitched and won the Alleghenys' inaugural game, beating Cincinnati 10–9, but spent most of the rest of the season shuttling between 3B and the outfield. Though Leary hit .292, he missed numerous games when he reported to the park too inebriated to play and eventually was reckoned hopeless even on manager Al Pratts' notoriously bibulous unit. Leary split 1883 between Reading of the Interstate Association and Louisville AA, where he helped lead young outfielder Pete Browning, a prodigious drinker in his own right, even further astray. The following season caught Leary in his third different major league after he signed with Altoona UA. Regarded as the team's prize catch, he batted leadoff and played CF in its opening game but went 0-for-4 in a loss to Cincinnati. A day later Leary occupied the box, absorbing a 9–2 shellacking. After just 8 games with the Pennsylvania club, he was released when he was mauled in all three of his pitching starts and hit just .088. Leary's final chance to reform came with Chicago UA, but he was cut after 10 games when he hit .175 and fielded haphazardly no matter where he was stationed.

Dreadful as Leary's UA stats were, he was still attractive to minor league teams. He signed for 1885 with Augusta of the newly organized Southern

League, where he played the infield behind dazzling young southpaw, Matt Kilroy. But as usual Leary soon got into trouble. In September he was fined $50 for incorrigibility by manager J. H. O'Brien and suspended for the season. The following day he met up with O'Brien outside the Augusta park and slashed him in the face with a cane, whereupon O'Brien drew a knife, and the pair had to be separated by bystanders. Both were arrested, but Leary could thank his teammates and the Atlanta players, who were in town at the time when they chipped in to pay his fine and raise a $20 purse so that he had money to get home to New Haven.

Leary remained in Connecticut the following season, signing with Bridgeport of the Eastern League under player-manager Jim Donnelly. But Donnelly was no pushover and was forced to suspend and reinstate his most recalcitrant player several times even before the summer began. In 1887 Leary tried to stick even closer to home signing with his local New Haven team, but that too ended abortively and he soon chose a career path that perhaps was better suited to his nature: he joined a circus. Leary died in the town where he was born in 1905. (DN)

Lochhead, Robert Henry
(aka Lockhead) / **"Harry"**

B	T	HGT	WGT	G	AB	H	R	2B
R	R	5'11"	172	148	541	129	52	7

3B	HR	RBI	BB	SO	SB	BA	SA	OBP
1	1	45	24	—	23	.238	.261	.275

G	IP	H	GS	CG	BB
1	3.2	4	0	0	2

SO	SH	W	L	PCT	ERA
0	0	0	0	—	0.00

B. 3/29/1876 Stockton, CA **D.** 8/22/1909
TEAMS: 99CleN 01DetAL 01PhiAL
DEBUT: 4/16/1899 at St. Louis; played SS and went 2-for-4 in a 6–5 loss to St. Louis's Jack Powell
FINALE: 5/15/1901 at Baltimore; played SS and made 1 hit in an 8–5 loss to Baltimore's Harry Howell

Harry Lochhead came of age with independent teams in California before joining the Sacramento Gilt Edge of the California League in 1898. Late that season former Sacramento teammate, pitcher Jay Hughes, recommended him to St. Louis NL. Lochhead went to Cleveland the following spring when the Spiders and Browns consolidated under syndicate ownership and the latter's supposedly weaker chattels were ticketed for the Lake Erie city. In Lochhead's case, no mistake in judgment was made. The rookie, though durable, collected by far the fewest total bases in 1899 among regulars with a minimum of 500 ABs with just 141.

His .909 FA was not bad, however, earning him a contract for 1900 with Detroit of the newly renamed American League after the NL dropped Cleveland. Before reporting to the Tigers, Lochhead reputedly broke his left ankle in a collision with a teammate while chasing a pop fly. Expected to shelve him for the season, the injury turned out to be only a bad sprain. Detroit manager George Stallings, while still keeping a string on Lochhead, allowed him to round into shape by spending the summer playing in the California and Montana State leagues.

Part of the original AL cast after the circuit went major in 1901, Lochhead played just 1 game with Detroit before going to the Philadelphia A's, which began the season with Dave Fultz, normally an outfielder, at SS. Handed the position, Lochhead muffed his chance when he could only manage 3 hits and an .088 BA in his first 9 games under Connie Mack. After several more failed opportunities, Lochhead called it quits in 1904 with Fort Worth of the Class C Texas League. He returned to Stockton, where he died in 1909 at 33. (DN)

Long, Herman C. / "Herman" Dutch" "Germany"

B	T	HGT	WGT	G	AB	H	R	2B
L	R	5'8½"	160	1525	6399	1846	1334	302

3B	HR	RBI	BB	SO	SB	BA	SA	OBP
91	86	912	559	262	479	.289	.406	.351

B. 4/13/1866 Chicago, IL **D.** 9/7/1909
TEAMS: 89KCA 90–02BosN 03NYAL 03DetAL 04PhiN
DEBUT: 4/17/1889 at Louisville; played SS and went 2-for-4 and scored 3 runs in a 7–4 win over Louisville's John Ewing
FINALE: 7/13/1904 at Pittsburgh; played 2B and went 1-for-4 in an 11–0 loss to Pittsburgh's Patsy Flaherty
CAREER HIGHLIGHT ONE: Was the first SS to win a loop home run crown when he led the NL in 1900

CAREER HIGHLIGHT TWO: His 91 career home runs were the most by a SS prior to 1930 when Travis Jackson surpassed him

CAREER HIGHLIGHT THREE: Holds the record for the most career errors in ML play with 1,096.

Herman Long had four brothers, all of whom grew up on the West Side of Chicago and tried to play pro ball. In July 1896 his brother Henry, a pitcher with Hagerstown in the Cumberland Valley League, slipped while trying to board a freight train and slid to his death beneath the wheels. Trained in his youth to be a shoemaker, Long had straw-colored hair and was "bow-legged . . . ungainly . . . [with a] face tanned as yellow as hide." Known as "The Dutchman" when he first arrived in the majors because he spoke German fluently, he immediately created a stir for his daring to the point of reckless play at SS and his ruthless sliding that left in its wake numerous players with severe spike wounds. Long's most epic slide came in 1893 when he blasted into Pittsburgh catcher Connie Mack at the plate, shattering a bone in Mack's lower leg and putting him out of action for several weeks. Often spiked or injured himself in sliding and baserunning collisions, Long missed a significant amount of time in several seasons but always rebounded until the early 1900s, when fellow players noted that his eyesight had begun to weaken and recalled to mind a bizarre mishap in 1894 when Long burned one of his eyes in a Washington hotel lobby while flipping lit cigars and catching them in his mouth. Two days later he returned to action with a temporary patch over the eye, but the injury may have returned to haunt him later in his career.

Long first played for pay in 1887 with Arkansas City of the Kansas League. By the end of the season he had moved up to Emporia, where he stood out not only for his flashy play in CF but also for the bright yellow uniforms the Western League Canaries wore. He began 1888 in RF with the Chicago Maroons but was sold to Western Association rival Kansas City in July and moved to SS when Blues manager Jim Manning was dissatisfied with the incumbent. Even though he finished the season with a composite .260 BA, Manning was sufficiently impressed with his work to recommend him to Kansas City AA manager Bill Watkins. In 1889, Long had such an outstanding rookie year at the plate, scoring 137 runs, that his record 122 errors were forgiven.

After withdrawing from the AA that November to rejoin the minor league Western Association, the Cowboys accommodated Long's desire to remain in the majors by selling him to Boston NL for a princely sum in the neighborhood of $6,000. In 1890, his very first year with the Beaneaters, Long compiled his signature season, leading the club in homers and steals, hitting below .300, spending a lengthy stint on the DL, scoring plenty of runs, and fielding around .900. Over the course of his thirteen years in Boston (1890–1902) he would play on five pennant winners, score over 100 runs six times, log 431 steals, and average 7 home runs a year, easily the highest figure by a SS during that span. Casual historians may attribute his high home run totals for the period to the relatively short left-field fence in Boston's South End Grounds—except that he batted left-handed. A truer explanation is that Long swung hard and often, seldom walked, and maintained steady contact until 1901, when he plummeted to .216 scarcely a year after winning the NL home run crown. Long probably needed glasses by that point, although his vision was not yet so poor that it affected his fielding. Actually his two best defensive years came back-to-back in 1901–02, when he won his only two NL fielding crowns.

Released to New York AL after collecting a mere 118 total bases in 1902, Long was traded to Detroit the following June and then cut again when he could hit only .213 in Tigers garb. He served as a player-manager in the minors until 1906, when he hit just .213 for Omaha of the Western League and then dropped out of sight for some while. When Long resurfaced in Denver in 1909, he was nearly destitute and dying of tuberculosis. (DN)

Mack, Dennis Joseph (b. McGee) **/ "Denny"**

B	T	HGT	WGT	G	AB	H	R	2B
R	R	5'7"	164	373	1505	343	309	42

3B	HR	RBI	BB	SO	SB	BA	SA	OBP
10	1	103	93	40	31	.228	.271	.273

G	IP	H	GS	CG	BB
3	13	20	1	1	3

SO	SH	W	L	PCT	ERA
1	0	0	1	.000	3.46

G	W	L	PCT	PENNANTS
79	42	38	.525	0

B. ?/?/1851 Easton, PA **D.** 4/10/1888

TEAMS: 71RokNA 72AthNA 73–74PhiNA 76StLN 80BufN (P/M)82LouA 83PitA
DEBUT: 5/6/1871 at Rockford; played 1B and went 1-for-3 in a 12–4 loss to Cleveland's Al Pratt
FINALE: 9/27/1883 at Pittsburgh; played 2B and went hitless in a 6–2 loss to St. Louis's Tony Mullane

The son of Civil War captain Dennis McGee of Carbon County, PA, "Bucktails" Denny Mack was sent to Villanova to study for the priesthood and was elected president of the university's first baseball team but quit in his last year of school after an argument with one of his professors and joined Rockford NA under the name of Mack to conceal his identity from his father. Although he played as Mack for his entire career, he continued to sign all contracts, letters, and telegrams as Dennis McGee.

After playing 1B in the NA for a season and a half, Mack set a precedent that only Nap Lajoie and Jackie Robinson have since matched at the ML level when he moved from the initial sack to a middle infield position in 1872, replacing Mike McGeary at SS for the Philadelphia Athletics so that McGeary could focus on catching. Mack led the NA in walks in 1872 but otherwise posed little offensive threat and seemed unlikely ever to return to the majors after he hit .217 with St. Louis NL in 1876. After performing with Indianapolis of the League Alliance in 1877, he played with minor league teams in the East until the winter of 1879–80, when he joined the Robert E. Lee club of New Orleans. Mack returned to the Lees as captain after flubbing a trial with Buffalo NL in 1880 and then in the spring of 1882 somehow gained the captaincy of the Louisville entry in the fledgling AA. After he hit just .188 and was said to be "very lame" by the season's end, he was not asked to return. Mack was languishing at his home in Lehigh County, PA, in the spring of 1883 when Pittsburgh, desperate for a SS, beckoned him. Even though he hit just .196, he remained in the Smoke City until the end of the season.

Mack then returned to his original position at 1B and served as player-manager with several eastern minor league teams through the 1887 season. After finishing that campaign piloting Wilkes-Barre, he planned to return in 1888. He was working as a handyman at a Wilkes-Barre hotel in early April 1888 when he fell down a flight of stairs at his lodging place and died of a cerebral hemorrhage. (DN/DB)

Macullar, James F. / "Jimmy" "Little Mac"

B	T	HGT	WGT	G	AB	H	R	2B
R	L	5'6"	155	449	1541	319	246	47

3B	HR	RBI	BB	SO	SB	BA	SA	OBP
19	7	91	155	27	23	.207	.276	.285

G	IP	H	GS	CG	BB
2	3	4	0	0	0

SO	SH	W	L	PCT	ERA
1	0	0	0	—	6.00

G	W	L	PCT	PENNANTS
27	5	21	.192	0

B. 1/16/1855 Boston, MA **D.** 4/8/1924
TEAMS: (P/M)79SyrN 82–83CinA 84–86BalA
DEBUT: 5/5/1879 at Chicago; played SS and went 1-for-4 in a 7–3 loss to Chicago's Terry Larkin
FINALE: 10/14/1886 at Philadelphia; played SS and went 2-for-4 in a 5–1 loss to Philadelphia's Cyclone Miller

Jimmy Macullar was in some respects a paradox: a right-handed hitter who threw lefty and yet played most of his ML games at SS. Indeed, he holds the record for most games played by a left-handed SS. He was also an outstanding outfielder, and Will White, a teammate in the early 1880s, said he was one of the very few gardeners of the day who perfected the art of running to the spot a fly ball would land without watching the ball. While playing winter ball in Cuba, Macullar pitched, and one obit called him the first left-hander to throw the curve. Many players of Macullar's day were credited with having invented the curve ball, so too much should not be made of this claim, but it does suggest he had some talent as a pitcher as well. He was stable, sober, and levelheaded, but for all his positive qualities his offensive skills were too limited to make him more than a journeyman player. His career AOPS is only 83 and the *Cincinnati Enquirer* said with more clarity than charity that "he is a perfect mutton-head while on the bases."

Macullar first made a name in 1874 with the semipro Boston Stars. He went on to play for a variety of minor teams around New England and upstate New York, most notably the 1878 Syracuse Stars, a strong International Association team that entered the NL in 1879, giving Macullar his first taste of ML play. During the following winter Macullar and Syracuse infielder Hick Carpenter became the first North American professionals to play in Cuba. Their names were given as George McCullar and Urban Carpenter, odd spellings that may reflect the vagaries of nineteenth-century newspaper writing refracted through a language barrier, but it also may indicate that their Colon club wanted to hide the fact that it was using imported professionals. If that was the case, the effort failed, for Carpenter and Macullar so dominated the Cuban league that other teams refused to play against them.

In 1882 Macullar went to Cincinnati, where he was reunited with Carpenter on the AA's first championship team. However, the Reds and other AA clubs used their large profits from the 1882 season to strengthen their rosters, and the light-hitting Macullar was bumped into a scrub role in 1883. Left unreserved at the end of the season, he signed with the AA's cellar dweller, Baltimore, for whom he held down the regular SS position for three years. By 1886 he was past 30 and had lost his post to Sadie Houck. He reclaimed the job when Houck failed to hit but drew his release at season's end.

Macullar then dropped to the Western League in 1887 and later played and managed in the Western Association until 1890. In 1887, while with Topeka, he led the WL in BA with a .464 mark, a figure grossly inflated by an 1887 scoring rule that counted walks as hits, as illustrated in 1888 when he hit just .238 for Des Moines. After the 1890 season Lincoln released Macullar. The following campaign he was one of a number of players from the Cincinnati teams of the early 1880s who received appointments as AA umpires from Louis Kramer, the new AA president who had been a part owner of that club. Macullar did not last long in the job and afterward seems to have stepped away from baseball altogether, returning to Baltimore, where he ran a dry goods store and then worked for many years as deputy warden in the city jail. He died there at 69. (DB/DN)

Magoon, George Henry / "George" "Maggie" "Topsy"

B	T	HGT	WGT	G	AB	H	R	2B
R	R	5'10"	160	213	739	173	85	20

3B	HR	RBI	BB	SO	SB	BA	SA	OBP
4	1	91	80	—	19	.234	.276	.285

B. 3/27/1875 St. Alban's, ME **D.** 12/6/1943

TEAMS: 98BroN 99BalN 99ChiN 01–03CinN 03ChiAL

DEBUT: 6/29/1898 at Pittsburgh; played SS and went 1-for-5 in a 4–3 loss to Pittsburgh's Jim Gardner

FINALE: 9/28/1903 at Washington; played 2B and went 2-for-5 in a 10–3 win over Washington's Abe Wilson

George Magoon spent two seasons with semipro teams in East Rochester, NH, and Camden, ME, and then served in the New England League from 1895 until he was summoned to Brooklyn in June 1898 to replace Candy LaChance, normally a first baseman, at SS. When Brooklyn and Baltimore came under syndicate ownership the following season, Magoon went to the latter team and then was traded to Chicago in August for Gene DeMont. His career highlight came in his Chicago debut the day after the trade, when "his magnificent fielding saved his team from defeat" in Ned Garvin's 1–0 win over St. Louis. But Magoon hit poorly with Chicago (.228). Released when the NL reduced to just eight teams in 1900, he signed with Indianapolis of the newly renamed AL and hit an impressive .310 while playing the deepest of any second baseman in the circuit to take full advantage of his "iron arm." In September 1900 Cincinnati purchased him, but illness kept him from reporting until the following spring.

Magoon returned to his natural position at SS in 1901 and played 127 games but was largely a defensive sub thereafter until he was traded to the White Sox in June 1903 in a quasi-legal interleague deal. He finished the season as the Sox' regular second baseman and wore a ML uniform for the last time in the Chicago City Series that fall. The following February he was traded to Indianapolis of the American Association for catcher Mike Heydon. Magoon finished his playing career in the 1911 Sally League and later coached baseball at the University of Maine and at the University of New Hampshire. He served for some four years as the city marshal in his adopted hometown of Rochester, NH, and eventually garnered a position as special officer at the local racetrack. Magoon died at his home of a heart attack in 1943, leaving behind his wife, Helen, and two sons. (DN)

*McLaughlin, Bernard / "Barney"

B	T	HGT	WGT	G	AB	H	R	2B
R	R	5'8"	163	178	696	169	84	23

3B	HR	RBI	BB	SO	SB	BA	SA	OBP
7	3	66	67	27	15	.243	.309	.312

G	IP	H	GS	CG	BB
7	48.2	62	4	4	15

SO	SH	W	L	PCT	ERA
14	0	1	3	.250	5.36

B. ?/?/1862 Lowell, MA **D.** 2/13/1921
TEAMS: 84KCU 87PhiN 90SyrA
DEBUT: 8/2/1884 at St. Louis; caught by Kid Baldwin in a 10–0 loss to St. Louis's Perry Werden
FINALE: 8/12/1890 at Louisville; played SS and went 0-for-4 in an 18–4 loss to Louisville's Mike Jones

Barney McLaughlin was the brother of MLer Frank McLaughlin, his teammate on the Kansas City Unions and the center fielder behind him in his ML pitching debut. Like his brother, McLaughlin was a handful. In 1883, while a member of the Interstate Association Pottsville Anthracite, he was suspended for ten days in August for "breach of discipline." It would be one of his lighter punishments. McLaughlin was with Reading of the Eastern League in 1884 when Kansas City UA manager Ted Sullivan sent for him. Scheduled to arrive on August 31, McLaughlin did not report until three days later, but there is no record of whether Sullivan did anything more than admonish him before sending him to the box that afternoon. Blasted 10–0 in his first outing, McLaughlin was only slightly more effective in his next three starts and spent most of his time in the outfield, where he logged a sparkling .762 FA.

He then spent the next two seasons in eastern minor leagues and was slated to play 2B with Charleston of the Southern League in 1887 when Philadelphia NL manager Harry Wright purchased him in late May after deciding his Quakers needed someone better than Charlie Bastian at 2B. Despite stroking just .220, McLaughlin had the job to himself until he went on a three-week bender in August, forcing Wright to replace him with pitcher Charlie Ferguson. McLaughlin returned to the minors with Lowell in 1888 and then went to Syracuse the following year and hit .259, just high enough for the Stars to retain him when they left the International Association the following season to join the AA as a replacement team. McLaughlin opened 1890 at SS, hiked his BA to .264, and was leading AA shortstops in FA when the Stars booted him off the team in August after he was arrested for theft. That November he was sentenced to forty days in jail for stealing a suit and other articles belonging to a Stars teammate with whom he had been rooming at a Syracuse hotel.

After doing his time, McLaughlin played several more years in the minors but not without further incident. In 1892 the Rock Island–Moline club blacklisted him in June when he never reported after being sent an advance. McLaughlin eventually sent back the money so that he could be reinstated and return to the New England League with Lowell, where he was living at the time. But then in July he was put away for "five months in the House of Correction as a result of his last spree," effectively ending his career. McLaughlin died of unknown causes in Lowell at around 64. (DN)

*McLaughlin, Francis Edward / "Frank"

B	T	HGT	WGT	G	AB	H	R	2B
R	R	5'9"	160	107	426	97	60	21

3B	HR	RBI	BB	SO	SB	BA	SA	OBP
4	5	4	18	11	—	.228	.331	.259

G	IP	H	GS	CG	BB
4	19	29	1	0	5

SO	SH	W	L	PCT	ERA
4	0	0	0	—	9.00

B. 6/19/1857 ?, Ireland **D.** 4/5/1917
TEAMS: 82WorN 83PitA 84CinU 84ChiU 84KCU
DEBUT: 8/9/1882 at Worcester; played SS and went 0-for-4 in a 4–1 loss to Buffalo's Jim Galvin
FINALE: 8/19/1884 at St. Louis; played SS and went 1-for-4 in a 12–3 loss to St. Louis's Perry Werden

Frank McLaughlin was the older brother of MLer Barney McLaughlin. Regarded as an overgrown kid by most of his managers for his drunken escapades, fittingly, on "Children's Day" in Buffalo on September 8 in his rookie year, with several hundred juveniles in attendance, he went 0-for-3 and made 3 errors in a 13–2 loss to Jim Galvin. Never able to hold a regular job because of his drinking, McLaughlin ran through five different ML teams in three seasons while playing just 107 ML games.

In 1882 McLaughlin came to Worcester from the independent Brooklyn Atlantics. Unclaimed by any other NL team when the Massachusetts franchise disbanded, he went to the worst place he could conceivably have gone given his proclivity—Pittsburgh AA, an asylum for boozers. Although McLaughlin did nothing positive in the Smoke City, he was considered one of the UA's prize acquisitions when he jumped to the Cincinnati Outlaw Reds the following year. McLaughlin began the season in the Queen City batting cleanup and went 3-for-5 on Opening Day but made 2 errors. On April 26 he hit the club's first home run of the season off Chicago's Hugh Daily but again undermined his stick work with four miscues. In mid-May McLaughlin went on a mad rampage while drunk and then had a frightening attack of the D.T.s in the Cincinnati clubhouse. He was released after going 0-for-4 and making 2 errors in May 15 in a 3–2 loss to Boston. In early June, McLaughlin joined Chicago UA but lasted just 16 games. Kansas City was his next and last stop in the majors, but after 1884 he apparently reformed to a degree, for he played several more seasons in the minors, finishing at age 35 with Lynn in the 1891 New England League. McLaughlin died in 1917 at his brother Barney's home in Lowell. He was arguably the worst defender of anyone that played as many as 50 career ML games at SS, posting a record low .769 FA and just a 3.72 range factor. (DN)

McLaughlin, Thomas / "Tom"

B	T	HGT	WGT	G	AB	H	R	2B
R	R	5'7"	?	340	1183	227	142	28

3B	HR	RBI	BB	SO	SB	BA	SA	OBP
19	2	81	75	6	16	.192	.253	.247

B. 3/28/1860 Louisville, KY **D.** 7/21/1921
TEAMS: 83–85LouA 86NYA 91WasA
DEBUT: 7/17/1883 at Louisville; played 1B and went 1-for-4 in a 5–4 win over Columbus's Dummy Dundon
FINALE: 10/3/1891 at Boston; played SS and went 0-for-3 in an 8–2 loss to Boston's George Haddock

Tom McLaughlin was a member of the amateur Louisville Red Stockings until he joined the Louisville AA reserves in 1883. A SS by trade, he played 1B and CF in the majors before debuting at his natural position on August 8, 1883. Despite a .192 BA and a .844 FA in his rookie season, McLaughlin opened 1884 at SS for Louisville and held the job most of the season before moving to 2B the following year. Unable to carry his weak bat any longer, Louisville let him go to the New York Mets in 1886. McLaughlin celebrated the change by hitting .136, the lowest season BA ever by a position player in a minimum of 250 ABs.

He then spent five seasons in the minors before coming to Washington from Syracuse of the Eastern Association at the tag end of the 1891 AA season and batting .268 in 14 games to lift his career BA from .189 to .192. McLaughlin returned to Louisville after finishing that season with Syracuse of the Eastern Association and was a fireman for a number of years before working for a local manufacturing company until his death in 1921. (DN)

#Meinke, Frank Louis / "Frank"

B	T	HGT	WGT	G	IP	H	GS
R	?	5'10½"	172	36	294	354	32

CG	BB	SO	SH	W	L	PCT	ERA
31	67	124	1	8	24	.250	3.18

G	AB	H	R	2B	3B	HR
93	344	56	28	5	7	6

RBI	BB	SO	SB	BA	SA	OBP
24	6	90	—	.163	.270	.177

B. 10/18/1863 Chicago, IL **D.** 11/8/1931
TEAMS: 84–85DetN
DEBUT: 5/1/1884 at Philadelphia; played SS and went 0-for-4 in a 13–2 loss to Charlie Ferguson
FINALE: 5/22/1885 at Boston; started the game in the box and switched places with left fielder George Wood in the sixth inning with Boston ahead 12–0 in what would be a 14–1 Boston win

Frank Meinke played 3B and pitched for Grand Rapids of the Northwestern League in 1883. After signing with the Baltimore UA entry for 1884 and instantly reneging, he came to Detroit with the expectation of continuing to play regularly on days when he did not pitch. He started his rookie season 0-for-10 and never succeeded in getting his BA above the Mendoza line, finishing at .164, the lowest BA until 1947 by a player who collected more than 5 home runs in a season. Meinke fared better as a pitcher in 1884, posting a 3.18 ERA, but still managed to win only 1 out of every 4 decisions for the last-place Wolverines.

When Detroit upgraded the following year,

Meinke was let go after making a single pitching start in Boston three weeks into the season. He went to Chattanooga of the Southern League for the remainder of 1885. Playing for Denver in the Western League in 1886, Meinke hit the longest home run ever seen to that point in Denver's park on September 10 against Topeka. Meinke's final pro season came with La Crosse of the Northwestern League in 1887. He led all third basemen in fielding but hit just .276 even with his walks being counted as hits.

Meinke returned to his Chicago home in 1888 and played in the City League while working as a railroad brakeman. He later managed minor league teams in Mattoon, IL, and helped discover Dummy Taylor, Roy Brashear, and Andy Lotshaw, among other players. In 1910 Meinke became one of the first former ML players to have his offspring also make the majors when his son Bob played 2 games with Cincinnati. Subsequently he worked as a street department foreman in Chicago's Fortieth Ward. A widower at the time of his death in 1931, Meinke spent his declining years in the Illinois Pythian home in Decatur before returning to Chicago to the house he shared with his daughter Grace. (DN/DB)

Miller, Joseph A. / "Joe" "Sidewheel"

B	T	HGT	WGT	G	AB	H	R	2B
R	?	5'9½"	165	203	762	163	90	21

3B	HR	RBI	BB	SO	SB	BA	SA	OBP
13	1	24	54	—	—	.214	.280	.269

B. 2/17/1861 Baltimore, MD **D.** 4/23/1928
TEAMS: 84TolA 85LouA
DEBUT: 5/1/1884 at Louisville; played SS and went 0-for-3 in a 5–1 loss to Louisville's Guy Hecker
FINALE: 9/15/1885 at Brooklyn; played 2B and went 0-for-3 in a 3–1 loss to Henry Porter

Joe Miller was another of the many middle infielders in the 1880s who had all the requisite major league skills but one. His manager in 1885 when he was with Louisville, Jim Hart, described the weak-hitting SS as "a funny little fellow with a wrinkled, antiquated face." A great kidder and prankster everywhere he went, Miller first surfaced in 1882 with the independent Wheeling, WV, Standards. The following year Miller moved to Toledo along with Wheeling teammates Sam Barkley and Curt Welch, and the trio accompanied the 1883 Northwestern League champion when it joined the AA for 1884. Despite hitting just .239, he finished third on the club that year in BA, SA, and OBP, a strong enough performance to earn him a contract with Louisville for 1885 after the Ohio team dropped out of the AA.

A ghastly start—his .155 BA was the lowest of any AA regular after the first month of the season—fated Miller to log the poorest OPS (.488) among all AA players with a minimum of 300 ABs in 1885 and cost him his job by mid-September. After wintering in Wheeling, his adopted home, Miller launched a nomadic tour through the minors that lasted until 1892 by joining Savannah of the Southern League in 1886. The following January he and Jack Glasscock made headlines in West Virginia papers when they were arrested on charges of being drunk and disorderly at the Wheeling Opera House. The experience may have made Miller feel unwelcome in Wheeling, for he began wintering in whichever minor league city he had played the previous season. In the spring of 1892, after four years in the Western Association, Miller retired from pro play to work on the Wheeling police force but recanted within a month and joined Bozeman of the Montana State League for one last fling with the game. When next seen, Miller was in Indianapolis driving a streetcar. He later became a boiler tender and returned to Wheeling, where he died of diabetes. (DN)

Moynahan, Michael / "Mike"

B	T	HGT	WGT	G	AB	H	R	2B
L	R	5'9"	165	169	688	202	104	30

3B	HR	RBI	BB	SO	SB	BA	SA	OBP
13	1	95	47	24	—	.294	.379	.339

B. ?/?/1856 Chicago, IL **D.** 4/9/1899
TEAMS: 80BufN 81CleN 81DetN 83–84PhiA 84CleN
DEBUT: 8/20/1880 at Buffalo; played SS and went 0-for-4 in a 1–0 win over Worcester's Fred Corey
FINALE: 6/21/1884 at Cleveland; played LF and went 2-for-5 in a 14–12 win over Philadelphia's Charlie Ferguson

Mike Moynahan played for Chicago semipro teams before joining Davenport of the Northwestern League in 1878. He remained with Davenport until the spring of 1880, when he opened the campaign with unaffiliated Dubuque. After moving to Buffalo NL in late August, he went 0-for-8 in his first two ML contests but then hit .359 in his remaining 25 games. Nevertheless, he was not reserved, allowing him to sign with Cleveland in 1881—a mistake since the Blues already had a crack SS in Jack Glasscock. Put in LF, Moynahan hit just .230 and was released to Detroit, where he was again given the axe after just one appearance.

The following year Moynahan lost a finger while playing for an independent team in Philadelphia. If it was on his right hand, it may have hampered him some in the field after he joined the AA Athletics in 1883, but his batting certainly suffered no ill effects. Moynahan rapped a solid .310 and drove in the run that clinched the AA flag for the A's when he dropped a single over SS to bring home Harry Stovey from 3B in the bottom of the tenth inning at Louisville on September 29.

That winter the A's swept Moynahan's job out from under him by signing Sadie Houck. The best-hitting SS in the game in 1883 got into only one contest with Philadelphia in 1884 before being released to Cleveland NL. The Blues tried him at four different positions, disliked him at all of them, and cut him even though he was hitting .289. Moynahan was reportedly ready to sign with Washington AA at that point, but negotiations fell through. Later in the season he joined Milwaukee of the Northwestern League and again was mysteriously allowed to slip away before the Cream Cities joined the UA in September.

Moynahan's last pro engagement of significance was with Utica of the International Association in 1886. When he was released in June while hitting .301, again without explanation, a local writer sighed, "The Uticas will miss Moynahan's batting. He was a good hitter." Moynahan returned to Chicago and went to work in the stockyards but remained active in the local city league. In March 1888 *TSN* announced, "He is still red-headed and hopeful [of a pro engagement)." Moynahan died in Chicago eleven years later, taking to his grave the reason his ML career ended almost as soon as it seemed to bloom. (DN)

Murphy, William Henry / "Tot" "Yale" "Midget"

B	T	HGT	WGT	G	AB	H	R	2B
B	R	5'3"	125	131	475	115	101	12

3B	HR	RBI	BB	SO	SB	BA	SA	OBP
4	0	45	81	36	35	.240	.282	.351

B. 11/11/1869 Southborough, MA **D.** 2/4/1906
TEAMS: 94–95NYN 97NYN
DEBUT: 4/19/1894 at Baltimore; played SS and went 3-for-4 in an 8–3 loss to Baltimore's Sadie McMahon
FINALE: 7/26/1897 at Cleveland; replaced Kid Gleason at 2B and went hitless in a 6–5 win over Cleveland's Jack Powell

Called "Tot" and "Midget" because of his size, William Murphy entered Yale University in 1889 and captained the team in 1892, his senior year. Invited to return in 1893 after he started Yale law school, he refused at first because he "was opposed to the undergraduate rule" but eventually was induced to rejoin the varsity squad by Walter Camp and his own brother, Mike, who was the Yale team trainer.

When the Giants signed Murphy in January 1894, team observers were skeptical of his size and feared he would be another Shorty Fuller, whom he was targeted to replace at SS. Initially, the tiny rookie was a surprise sensation, starting 1894 by scoring 18 runs on 20 hits in his first 14 games. But he then went into a slump both at bat and in the field, forcing player-manager John M. Ward to restore Fuller to the lineup. Toward the end of the season Murphy revived somewhat when he was used in RF and finished at .271 with a .384 OBP, but Fuller, responding to the competition, had his best season in years, hitting .283 to lock up the job for 1895.

The following spring, Murphy, previously a right-handed batter, started switch hitting. It was an ill-fated experiment—he sagged to .201 and talked of quitting the game when he entered Bellevue Medical School that fall. Murphy subsequently changed his mind, joining Bangor, ME, of the New England League in 1896, and took the New Haven, CT, club's player-manager's post the following year. In July 1897 he was recalled to the majors when the Giants ran short of subs and filled in on five occasions for SS George Davis and second sacker Kid Gleason.

Even though Murphy eventually received a

medical degree, he opted to stay in the game as a college coach and served at the University of Pennsylvania and Columbia before returning to his alma mater. On May 13, 1904, he stunned his Bulldogs players when he broke his ankle demonstrating the sliding technique and then calmly reset the bone himself before allowing team members to carry him to his room near the campus. Murphy had just been appointed athletic director at the U.S. Naval Academy when he learned he had tuberculosis. He went to Saranac Lake, NY, in the late fall of 1905, but it was too late. He was dead less than two months later. (DN)

Nelson, John W. / "Candy"

B	T	HGT	WGT	G	AB	H	R	2B
L	R	5'6"	145	817	3294	833	648	93

3B	HR	RBI	BB	SO	SB	BA	SA	OBP
27	3	207	352	33	68	.253	.300	.330

B. 3/14/1849 Portland, ME **D.** 9/4/1910
TEAMS: 72TroNA 72EckNA 73–75MutNA 78IndN 79TroN 81WorN 83–87NYA 87NYN 90BroA
DEBUT: 6/11/1872 at New York; played SS and went 1-for-4 in a 12–4 loss to New York's Candy Cummings
FINALE: 8/25/1890 at Syracuse; played SS and went 1-for-4 in a 5–4 loss to Syracuse's Charlie McCullough

Candy Nelson was the lone man to play for the NA New York Mutuals, the AA New York Mets, and the NL New York Giants, let alone the AA Brooklyn Gladiators. In addition, he played for Troy in both the NA and the NL and in 1890 was the first 40-year-old to serve as his team's regular SS. Earlier in his career Nelson forced a rule change when he "would foul the ball off with his head," by letting a pitch deliberately skull him so that it would then become a wild pitch on which runners could advance a base. Then in 1884 he set the all-time record for the most runs created per game by a player with 400 or more ABs and fewer than 150 total bases (8.64) and the following year came the closest of anyone before or since to equaling his own mark (7.56).

The Maine native was the original "Candy" in baseball circles, preceding the younger Candy Cummings, but the precise source of Nelson's nickname is unknown. After remaining out of the NA in its inaugural season, he joined Troy in 1872, expecting to replace Steve Bellan at 3B, but illness prevented him from playing until June, and even then in his first game "it was evident he had not yet recovered sufficiently to play in his old form." After just four games with Troy, Nelson moved to the Brooklyn Eckfords and then spent the next three seasons with the New York Mutuals. After hitting just .199 in 1875, he not only insured that the Mutes would dismiss him before joining the fledgling NL in 1876 but that no other ML team would gamble on him until 1878 when he opened the season at SS with the new Indianapolis NL team after serving with the Allegheny International Association club the previous year. But a .131 BA in his first 19 games brought a quick exit. Nelson finished 1878 with Albany, NY, and then moved to the independent Brooklyn Hudsons in 1879. On August 11, 1879, he joined Troy for the rest of the NL season, and though he hit reasonably well, he made 25 errors in 25 games at SS and was not reserved for 1880.

Nelson spent his next two seasons with teams in the National Association and the Eastern Championship Association before returning to the show with Worcester on August 23, 1881, as a replacement for injured SS Arthur Irwin. Despite hitting .292, he was again not reserved. Now 33, an age when even an established ML SS would be thinking of retirement, Nelson joined the League Alliance New York Mets in 1882 and at long last found his proper milieu. Serving as the club's lead-off hitter for the next five seasons, he excelled in drawing walks and twice led the AA in that department after the Mets joined that loop in 1883. No longer the fastest SS in the game, he was nonetheless a steadying force in the team's infield until 1886, when the club opted to go with a younger Tom McLaughlin and move its incumbent SS to CF. The experiment lasted less than two months; after McLaughlin hit below .150, Nelson was back at his old post. In 1887, however, Nelson's time expired when Opie Caylor took over as manager of the Mets and preferred a much younger Paul Radford at SS. In August, Nelson was forced to leave the team for a time when his wife was taken seriously ill. Soon after his return all seven other AA clubs waived on him. Nelson signed with the Giants, hoping to play 3B in the NL but was cut after just one game.

Still not ready to accept that his active days were over, he returned to the minors. In 1889, at age

40, he hit .275 in the International Association and hoped for a ML bid from one of the teams that had been victimized by PL raiders. Instead he drew an offer only from Wilmington of the Atlantic Association. In early June the AA's dreariest franchise, the Brooklyn Gladiators, hired him on the chance that memories of his Mets days could sell a few tickets. Nelson had an embarrassing moment when he was forced to reveal his true age after he and the rest of the Gladiators were arrested for trying to play a game on Sunday but otherwise did himself proud, topping the team BA by 30 points and remaining in the regular lineup until the Gladiators breathed their last. The following year he batted leadoff for a revived independent New York Mets team that numbered Dasher Troy, Chief Roseman, and Jack Lynch among others. After an unsuccessful effort to induce NL president Nick Young to hire him as an umpire, he finally left the game in the mid-1890s and worked as a milkman in his Brooklyn neighborhood. Nelson died of heart disease in Brooklyn at 61. (DN)

Pearce, Richard J. / "Dickey" "Bad Dickey"

B	T	HGT	WGT	G	AB	H	R	2B
R	R	5'3½"	161	291	1328	333	217	21

3B	HR	RBI	BB	SO	SB	BA	SA	OBP
4	2	140	33	21	13	.251	.277	.269

G	IP	H	GS	CG	BB
2	5.1	10	0	0	0

SO	SH	W	L	PCT	ERA
0	0	0	0	—	3.38

G	W	L	PCT	PENNANTS
88	49	35	.583	0

B. 2/29/1836 Brooklyn, NY **D.** 10/12/1908
TEAMS: 71–72MutNA (P/M)72MutNA 73–74AtlNA (P/M)75StLNA 76–77StLN
DEBUT: 5/18/1871 at Troy; played SS, batted leadoff, and went 2-for-6 in a 14–3 win over Troy's John McMullin
FINALE: 10/6/1877 at St. Louis; played SS and went 0-for-4 in a 7–3 win over Cincinnati's Amos Booth

One of the game's most innovative pioneers, Dickey Pearce's career began long before the birth of professionalism, outlasted the NA, and continued into the NL era. Pearce launched his career with the Brooklyn Atlantics in 1855 and is credited with inventing modern SS play and turning SS into a key defensive position. He was also one of the first to excel at place hitting and is believed to have perfected the fair-foul hit as well as the bunt.

According to author James Terry, "Short, stout and slow of foot, Pearce did not look like a star athlete. But he made up for his physical limitations with what Henry Chadwick called 'head work.'" Earlier, Al Spink had written in *The National Game* that the "position of short field was not considered important by early professional teams, until Dickey Pearce of the Atlantics commenced playing that position in the sixties . . . Pearce was the first to study the opposing batsmen, fielding very close in for the weak hitters and backing deep when the hard hitters came up. It was Pearce who turned the first double play by dropping a fly ball and then forcing the runner out."

Also one of the first to employ "scientific batting," Pearce was a lead-off hitter with little power who became adept at getting on base in front of his teammates and scoring runs. In addition to being skilled at the fair-foul hit, according to baseball historian Harold Seymour, he also "learned to baffle the defense by artfully tapping or 'bunting' the ball gently in front of home plate and scampering to first base before bewildered opponents recovered from their surprise." So gently did Pearce hit the ball in his usual at-bat that he finished with just a .274 SA, only 22 points above his career BA, and in 1874 he went the entire season with just one extra-base hit.

Although his ML career ended in 1877 at age 41, Pearce continued to play on occasion for minor league clubs until injury finally forced his retirement in 1884 at 48. Meanwhile he umpired periodically with a notable lack of success in the NL and was even unofficially banned in 1882. Pearce later opened a wine bar in Brooklyn with money raised during a benefit game held for him by the New York Metropolitans in 1881 and, in 1890 he helped design the third Polo Grounds, where he served that year as groundskeeper.

A pioneer on the field, in his later years Pearce nearly became one off it as well. On December 10, 1898, *TSN* wrote of Pearce's novel pension-plan proposal that he intended to take to the upcoming to NL meeting, where he planned to plead his case for assistance of the same kind the league had previously given Harry Wright and Chadwick in their hours of need. Undergoing hard times now himself, Pearce was of the mind that he was entitled to a pension since he had given the game twenty-seven years active service. Pearce's innovative idea in the end went nowhere and was long forgotten by the time he died of Bright's disease ten years later in Wareham, MA. (JK/DN)

Peters, John Philip / "John"

B	T	HGT	WGT	G	AB	H	R	2B
R	R	5'7"	180	615	2695	748	372	92

3B	HR	RBI	BB	SO	SB	BA	SA	OBP
12	3	249	24	77	14	.278	.324	.284

G	IP	H	GS	CG	BB
1	1	1	0	0	1

SO	SH	W	L	PCT	ERA
0	0	0	0	—	0.00

B. 4/8/1850 Louisiana, MO **D.** 1/4/1924
TEAMS: 74–75ChiNA 76–77ChiN 78MilN 79ChiN 80ProN 81BufN 82–84PitA
DEBUT: 5/23/1874 at Chicago; played 2B and went 0-for-4 in a 7–4 loss to New York's Bobby Mathews
FINALE: 6/11/1884 at Pittsburgh; played SS and went 0-for-4 in a 3–0 loss to St. Louis's George McGinnis

Born of German parents, John Peters may have been orphaned, for he spent at least part of his childhood in the home of Chris Oberbeck (*see* Henry Oberbeck). He would probably have been playing in the NA several years sooner had he not been living in St. Louis, which was beyond the westernmost boundary of the league in its early years. After performing with the St. Louis Empires in the early 1870s, he joined the original St. Louis Reds in 1873 and signed with Chicago the following season when St. Louis was still a year away from placing an entry in the NA. Though his natural position was SS, he played 2B initially for Chicago, which already had one of the game's best short fielders in Davy Force. Peters soon supplanted Force at the position, however, and by 1876 had also temporarily supplanted George Wright as the best SS in the game. That season Peters had his career year, batting .351 for pennant-winning Chicago and topping the newly formed NL with a .932 FA.

Peters remained with Chicago in 1877 and again hit well but then chose to sign with the fledging Milwaukee NL entry for 1878. One surmise is that he fled the Windy City because he did not want to play under the irascible Bob Ferguson, who was hired over the winter as Chicago's new player-manager. Supporting that is Peters's return to Chicago in 1879 when Ferguson left the team. That season, Peters played every inning at SS despite suffering a precipitous drop in both his batting and fielding as he hit just .245 and posted a weak .837 FA, the lowest by far among NL regulars at SS. The suspicion is that he had already begun to suffer a propensity to put on weight. Over the next two seasons Peters's work continued to plummet and only the arrival of the AA saved his ML career from ending at age 31. He hit .288 with the Pittsburgh club in the yearling rebel loop in 1882 but was released in June of the following year to Springfield of the Northwestern League when he got off to a .107 start.

After playing for Stillwater of the Northwestern League in 1884, Peters joined Pittsburgh for one final ML game before returning to St. Louis, where he continued to play semipro ball on weekends for several more years while working for the water department. In the late summer of 1891 *TSN* reported that he had been fired from his cushy job, which was simply to carry around a water key to turn off the water of delinquent customers. Peters apparently was connected, however, for he soon got another job as a city hall clerk. By then in his early forties, he still played on the local "Fat Men's" team. Peters was working for the St. Louis parks department at the time of his death from uremic poisoning in 1924 and was survived by his wife, Barbara, and a son. His .278 career BA, seemingly very good for a SS in his era, is deceptive in that it is accompanied by a .284 OBP and a record—certain to endure forever—of the fewest walks of any ML player (pitchers included) with a minimum of 2,500 PAs: a mere 24. (DN/DB)

Phillips, Marr B. / "Marr"

B	T	HGT	WGT	G	AB	H	R	2B
R	?	5'6½"	164	198	824	197	73	31

3B	HR	RBI	BB	SO	SB	BA	SA	OBP
8	0	53	23	13	10	.239	.296	.263

B. 6/16/1857 Pittsburgh, PA **D.** 4/1/1928
TEAMS: 84IndA 85DetN 85PitA 90RocA
DEBUT: 5/1/1884 at St. Louis; played SS and went 1-for-3 in a 4–2 loss to St. Louis's Tip O'Neill
FINALE: 7/25/1890 at Rochester; played SS and went 0-for-4 in a 7–6 loss to Toledo's Fred Smith

Marr Phillips began his career in the 1877 League Alliance and seems to have left the pro game after 1878 until resurfacing with Fort Wayne of the Northwestern League in 1883. That winter, Fort Wayne sold several players to ML clubs, including Phillips for $500 to Indianapolis. He was with Indianapolis only a short while before *SL* warned that he is "said to be ruining himself by overindulgence in the ardent. He should put a stopper on himself at once, as no player can stand up long before 'Slugger Alcohol.'" Despite this admonition, Detroit NL manager Charlie Morton grabbed Phillips for 1885 when Indianapolis was dropped from the AA and installed him as the Wolverines' Opening Day SS. Released in early July after hitting below .200 during most of his stay with Detroit, Phillips joined his hometown Pittsburgh AA team for 4 games and then returned to the minors.

Hapless against ML pitching, he hit well in lower leagues. In 1886 he batted .321 in the pitcher-dominated Southern League. Phillips spent the next two seasons with Hamilton, Ontario, of the International Association and then joined Rochester of that same loop in 1889. A .290 BA assured that he would accompany the team when it enlisted in the struggling AA the following year. Phillips opened the season for the Rochesters at SS but hit poorly and in early July was suspended by manager Pat Powers for drunkenness. He went home to Pittsburgh and received notice of his release near the end of the month. Despite being 33 in 1890 and a confirmed lusher, Phillips continued to play in the minors until the end of the century and even served a spell as a player-manager with Hamilton before finishing his pro career in that city. Phillips returned to Pittsburgh after leaving the game and worked in the Sanitary Division of the City Department of Public Health. He died in 1928 after a brief illness. (DN)

Ray, Irving Burton / "Irv" "Stubby"

B	T	HGT	WGT	G	AB	H	R	2B
L	R	5'6"	165	226	902	263	154	30

3B	HR	RBI	BB	SO	SB	BA	SA	OBP
11	3	123	86	35	59	.292	.359	.360

B. 1/22/1864 Harrington, ME **D.** 2/21/1948
TEAMS: 88–89BosN 89–91BalA
DEBUT: 7/7/1888 at Chicago; played SS and went 2-for-5 in a 9–4 win over Chicago's Gus Krock
FINALE: 9/2/1891 at Baltimore; played RF and went 4-for-5 in a 4–2 win over Milwaukee's Frank Dwyer

Irv Ray was built on the order of Cupid Childs but had less speed. In addition, he had a habit of leaving his feet to dive for grounders in an attempt to make up for his inadequate range and then was unable to rise in time to throw the runner out. But like Childs, Ray was an outstanding hitter, especially for a middle infielder. His first pro experience resulted in a .402 BA in the 1887 New England League, and he returned to that circuit the following year with Salem, MA, after graduating from Maine State College. When Boston purchased him in early July 1888, he was leading the New England League with a .410 BA. Ray failed to hit with nearly the same panache in his frosh season with Boston and began 1889 on the bench as a result. Sometime toward the end of August he was sold to Baltimore AA for $1,500. Orioles manager Billy Barnie immediately installed Ray in the cleanup spot, and he responded by hitting .340 in the final month of the AA season. Ray remained with the Orioles in 1890 when they entered the Atlantic Association. When Baltimore returned to the AA late in the 1890 campaign to replace the defunct Brooklyn franchise, his .360 BA led all AA players with a minimum of 100 ABs that season.

Ray's hitting fell off substantially in 1891, owing in part to a sore arm that caused him to miss a number of games. His 4-hit coda tied the record for the most hits by a player in his final ML appearance. When his arm failed to mend over the winter, in April 1892 Ray announced his retirement from baseball to run a grocery store in Boston. He died in the Maine town where he was born at 84. (DN)

Richmond, John H. / "John"

B	T	HGT	WGT	G	AB	H	R	2B
?	R	5'9"	170	440	1725	410	239	45

3B	HR	RBI	BB	SO	SB	BA	SA	OBP
28	5	83	103	80	1	.238	.305	.283

B. 3/4/1854 Philadelphia, PA **D.** 10/5/1898
TEAMS: 75AthNA 79SyrN 80–81BosN 82CleN 82PhiA 83–84ColA 85PitA
DEBUT: 4/22/1875 at Philadelphia; played 2B and went 1-for-4 in a 6–3 win over the Philadelphia Whites' Cherokee Fisher
FINALE: 7/10/1885 at Pittsburgh; played SS and went 1-for-4 in a 7–5 loss to New York's Jack Lynch

John Richmond played with Philadelphia amateur teams before joining the NA Athletics in the spring of 1875. Hired to replace Joe Battin at 2B, he failed to hit and was reduced to a scrub after Bill Craver joined the A's. Richmond caught for Ithaca in 1876 and alternated between catcher and SS with Binghamton of the International Association in 1877 before settling on the latter position when he joined Utica of the same loop the following season. He made his NL debut with Syracuse on Opening Day in 1879 but went back to the minors when he hit just .213.

The following year Richmond jumped Rochester of the National Association to join Boston in July. He opened the next two seasons in CF for Boston and Cleveland, respectively, but was released in midstream on both occasions. Upon leaving Cleveland, he signed with the Philadelphia A's of the fledgling AA in August 1882 to fill a hole in CF, where the A's had been using batterymen much of the season. Left homeless after hitting a composite .176, Richmond unaccountably was named captain of the new Columbus AA entry that winter. A good season at SS accompanied by a career-high .283 BA gained him future recognition from *The ESPN Baseball Encyclopedia* as the AA's top-rated position player in 1883, although his credentials for the honor seem skimpy, especially in light of the fact that he was replaced as captain in May and later was among the party of Columbus players who were suspected of bribing manager Horace Phillips to keep them on the team.

The following spring Richmond was installed as cleanup hitter by Columbus's new skipper, Gus Schmelz, and stayed in that spot for most of the season despite slipping to .251 and scoring just 57 runs in 105 games. That October, when the Ohio team prepared to disband, he was not among the cadre of its players sold to Pittsburgh AA for $8,000. Richmond spent the winter of 1884–85 advertising in sporting publications for a job without success until Pittsburgh finally agreed to hire him at the last moment. He may have either been ill or out of shape when he reported to the Alleghenys the following spring, for he seemed to have lost ground in the field and was hitting just .206 when he was axed after 34 games. Richmond played in the Southern League and the International Association in 1886 but was out of the game by that fall. Until recently his last-known sighting was in 1893 when he apparently abandoned his second wife and their two children, but it has since been learned that he died in Philadelphia of heart disease. (DN/DB)

*Rowe, John Charles / "Jack"

B	T	HGT	WGT	G	AB	H	R	2B
L	R	5'8"	170	1044	4386	1256	764	202

3B	HR	RBI	BB	SO	SB	BA	SA	OBP
88	28	644	224	177	59	.286	.323	.392

G	W	L	PCT	PENNANTS
100	27	72	.273	0

B. 12/8/1856 Hamburg, PA **D.** 4/25/1911
TEAMS: 79–85BufN 86–88DetN 89PitN (P/M)90BufP
DEBUT: 9/6/1879 at Boston; played RF and went 1-for-3 in a 10–1 loss to Boston's Tommy Bond
FINALE: 10/4/1890 at Brooklyn; played SS and went 0-for-3 in a 5–0 loss to Brooklyn's John Sowders

Jack Rowe was the brother of ML player and manager Dave Rowe. Primarily a catcher early in his career, he moved to SS in 1885 with mixed results. While the switch assured that his hands would no longer be too sore to prevent his valuable bat from being in the lineup every day, in his last six ML seasons (1885–90) he had the least range of any SS in 500 or more games (4.21), with the sole exception of Bill Gleason (4.01).

After playing for the amateur Jacksonville, IL, Blue Sox in 1876, Rowe spent 1877 with Milwaukee and Janesville, WI, of the League Alliance. In 1878 he joined the famous Peoria Reds and played the following year with Rockford, IL, until the Northwestern League disbanded after he hit .324 in 22 games, freeing him to go to Buffalo NL. The following spring Rowe took over as the Bisons' regular catcher after handling Bill McGunnigle in a win over Cleveland on Opening Day. He batted second, went 3-for-5, and remained in the heart of the order for the rest of his seven-year stay in Buffalo.

In August 1885 Rowe was among the "Big Four" that led Detroit to purchase the foundering Buffalo franchise for $7,000, and he joined Deacon White, Dan Brouthers, and Hardy Richardson on the Wolverines the following spring. He was a key component in Detroit's march to its lone NL pennant two years later, when his career-best 135 runs and .318 BA made him arguably the best SS in the game that season. But his reign was short-lived.

After a mediocre 1888 campaign, Rowe partnered with Deacon White in buying the Buffalo International Association franchise once they realized Detroit was about to disband. Their plan was to co-manage and play for their minor league club, but Detroit sold their contracts to Pittsburgh and Smoke City owner William Nimick threatened to blacklist them if they tried to play anywhere in 1889 but with his club. Rowe and White sat out the first half of the 1889 season before relenting. Neither reported to Pittsburgh highly motivated. Rowe hit just .259 in 75 games and then, with White's aid, arranged to put a Buffalo franchise in the PL the following year. Their venture met with disastrous results. Buffalo finished a hopeless last, the PL collapsed, and neither played in the majors again.

Rowe moved to the minors in 1891, joining his brother Dave at Lincoln, NE, of the Western Association. He then returned to Buffalo to play two seasons in the Eastern League, umpired in the EL briefly, and then quit baseball to run his cigar store in Buffalo. In 1896, Jim Franklin, owner of the Buffalo EL club, persuaded Rowe to return to the game solely as a manager. Rowe piloted the Bisons for three seasons before leaving when the franchise was moved to the Western League in 1899. He returned to the tobacco business until ill health forced him to sell out his interests and live with his daughter in St. Louis. He died at her home in 1911 of "leakage of the heart." (DN)

*Say, Louis I. / "Lou"

B	T	HGT	WGT	G	AB	H	R	2B
R	R	5'7"	145	298	1239	287	181	44

3B	HR	RBI	BB	SO	SB	BA	SA	OBP
8	5	52	35	39	0	.232	.292	.253

B. 2/4/1854 Baltimore, MD **D.** 6/5/1930
TEAMS: 73MarNA 74BalNA 75WasNA 80CinN 82PhiA 83BalA 84KCU 84BalU 84KCU
DEBUT: 4/14/1873 at Baltimore; played SS and went 0-for-4 in a 24–3 loss to Washington's Bill Stearns
FINALE: 10/19/1884 at Kansas City; played SS and went 1-for-4 in a 12–1 win over Washington's Abner Powell

Lou Say was the brother of ML infielder Jimmy Say; on September 23, 1884, at Baltimore, the two became the second pair of siblings to play side by side in the same infield in a ML game. The elder Say played for various amateur clubs in the Baltimore area in early 1870s before joining the ill-begotten Marylands in 1873. He participated in parts of the next two NA seasons but dropped to semipro ball with the Harrisburg Experts after the NL formed in 1876 and then spent several seasons in the minor league International Association and League Alliance. An excellent fielder according to all reports, he was plagued by weak hitting and an even more debilitating problem. Say, in historian Lee Allen's estimation, was one of the most irredeemable alcoholics ever to don a pro baseball uniform.

In 1880 he was in his second season with Albany of the minor league National Association when Cincinnati hired him. Upon joining the Reds in Buffalo, he scored a run in his initial NL game and went 4-for-4 in his next appearance but tailed off rapidly after his super start and finished at .199. After taking part in over 100 games at SS with the 1881 Eastern Championship Association New York Mets, Say was expected to occupy SS for the Philadelphia A's in the inaugural AA season but squandered his chance in a flurry of drunken escapades. He returned home to play for Baltimore the following year and then jumped to the Lobstertown UA entry in 1884. By then dissipation had taken its toll. Say committed a then record 102 errors in the field and hit just .232 against ragged UA pitching, the lowest BA by a regular (400 ABs) who had more than a modicum of previous ML experience.

Say spent part of the following year with his brother on Omaha of the Western League and then played SS for Charleston of the Southern League briefly in 1886 behind future ML star Gus Weyhing. After leaving pro ball in 1887, he apparently lost his grip completely. In February 1895 Tom Dolan got a letter from one of Say's former teammates, Jimmy Macullar, reporting that Say, who had been unemployed for several years, had his ears badly frostbitten while shoveling snow off the pavement outside the Richmond Market in Baltimore. Less than a month later the 41-year-old drifter sank to a new personal low when he was fined $1 and costs by a Baltimore court for begging.

With each passing year the punishments meted out to Say stiffened. In February 1898 he was sentenced to six months in the house of corrections for being habitually drunk and disorderly after the residents of the Western District of Baltimore had lodged repeated complaints against his presence on their streets. The charges then began to grow serious. In the final year of the century Say drew a ten-month sentence for larceny after pleading to a lesser charge for waylaying a Baltimore businessman. It may at last have been the wakeup call he needed. Say somehow managed to put together a semblance of a life for another thirty years before succumbing in Fallon, MD, at 76. (DN)

Scheibeck, Frank S. / "Frank"

B	T	HGT	WGT	G	AB	H	R	2B
R	R	5'7"	145	294	1062	258	181	26

3B	HR	RBI	BB	SO	SB	BA	SA	OBP
15	2	110	162	56	85	.243	.302	.349

G	IP	H	GS	CG	BB
1	9	17	1	1	4

SO	SH	W	L	PCT	ERA
3	0	0	1	.000	12.00

B. 6/28/1865 Detroit, MI **D.** 10/22/1856
TEAMS: 87CleA 88DetN 90TolA 94PitN 94–95WasN 99WasN 01CleAL 06DetAL
DEBUT: 5/9/1887 at Cincinnati; caught by Charlie Reipschlager and lost 18–2 to Cincinnati's George McGinnis
FINALE: 9/13/1906 at Detroit; played 2B and went 0-for-2 in an 8–0 loss to Cleveland's Otto Hess

Frank Scheibeck is the only man to play for Cleveland ML teams in both the AA and the AL, the only man to serve as a regular (90 or more games in a season) in the AA and the AL but never in the NL, and one of the only three men (Sam Thompson and Deacon McGuire are the others) to play for Detroit in both the NL and the AL. Since his career spanned twenty ML seasons (1887–1906), none of these achievements seem remarkable until the eye notes that he was in the majors in only eight of those twenty seasons and played as many as 100 games just once (134 with Toledo AA in 1890).

Scheibeck was 18 when he pitched his first game for the local Detroit Cass Club in 1884. After hurling for independent Sandusky, OH, in 1885, he joined the Maple Leafs of Guelph, Ontario, in 1886 along with two other Detroit products who would later become prominent in the game, Al Buckenberger and Count Campau. Acquired by the expansion Cleveland AA club in 1887 as a pitcher, he was allowed to hurl just 1 disastrous game and then released to Duluth of the Northwestern League after having also been found wanting in single-game appearances at both SS and 3B. Scheibeck did not receive his first sustained ML opportunity until 1890 with Toledo, when the Ohio club boarded the foundering AA. Playing every inning at SS for the Black Pirates, he swiped 57 bases and drew 76 walks but hit just .241, ensuring his return to the minors when the majors reduced from twenty-four to sixteen teams in 1891.

Scheibeck put in the next three seasons in the Western Association, the Western League, and the Eastern League, and his only distinction was that he used the lightest bat in each loop. Drafted in the fall of 1893 by Pittsburgh, he was released the following summer after playing in just 28 games because manager Buckenberger, his ex-teammate in 1886, could find no place for him even though he hit .353. Scheibeck went to Washington, where he was the regular SS at times during the next season and a half but failed to hit enough to secure the job. He then finished the century in the Western and Eastern leagues except for a 27-game return to Washington in 1899 during the D.C. club's final days as a member of the NL. Although nearing his middle thirties, he was still regarded as a solid player whose hitting alone rendered him a cut below ML standards.

In 1901 Scheibeck was the beneficiary of one final opportunity to win a regular ML job when rookie Danny Shay flopped with Cleveland in the AL's first season as a major league. Joining the Blues in Washington on May 22, he started a game-ending double play with the bases loaded and 1 out in the ninth to preserve a 6–5 win for Ed Scott, but his positive contributions after that were few, as he hit just .213 and fielded below .900 (.897). Scheibeck again returned to the minors in 1902 and finished his pro career in 1906 where it began—in Detroit, when the Tigers welcomed him and Sam Thompson, both members in 1888 of the last NL team in the Motor City, for a few token final bows in big league garb. Scheibeck remained a resident of the Motor City until his death at 91. (DN/PM)

Shugart, Frank Harry
(b. Shugarts) / **"Frank"**

B	T	HGT	WGT	G	AB	H	R	2B
B	R	5'8"	170	638	2599	700	421	102

3B	HR	RBI	BB	SO	SB	BA	SA	OBP
77	20	337	180	174	119	.269	.383	.321

B. 12/10/1866 Luthersburg, PA **D.** 9/9/1944
TEAMS: 90ChiP 91–93Pit 93–94StLN 95LouN 97PhiN 01ChiAL
DEBUT: 8/23/1890 at Philadelphia; played SS, went 0-for-1, and was replaced by Jack Boyle in a 12–10 loss to Philadelphia's Ben Sanders
FINALE: 9/27/1901 at Washington; played SS and made 1 hit in a 6–4 win over Washington's Bill Carrick
CAREER HIGHLIGHT: 5/10/1894 at Cincinnati; hit 3 home runs in an 18–9 loss to Cincinnati's Tom Parrott

Of Pennsylvania Dutch ancestry, Frank Shugart had exceptional power for a SS and was a switch hitter off and on during most of his career with pop from both sides. In all, a much better player than many middle infielders in the 1890s who had more substantial ML careers, he had one grave weakness: he made the hard plays but muffed too many easy ones.

Raised by his mother in a meager cabin outside of Dubois, PA, Shugart viewed baseball as a way out of poverty. He spent two years with Elmira of the New York State League before joining Burlington, IA, of the Central Interstate League late in the 1889 season. The following May, St. Louis AA offered $250 for him, but the Burlington owner replied that "would not buy even a lock of his hair." After Burlington folded he signed with Chicago PL and was blacklisted for playing with a club outside the National Agreement. Toward the end of the 1890 season *TSN* preached that if he had been at SS all year things might have gone differently for Chicago, but he nonetheless began 1891 back in the minors with Minneapolis of the Western Association. That July, the Millers sold him to Pittsburgh for $5,000, the highest sum ever paid to that point for a minor league infielder. Shugart seemed worth it initially but led the NL in errors in 1892 with 99. The following June the Pirates sent him to St. Louis along with $500 for Jack Glasscock, and the Browns seemed the winner of the bargain when Glasscock began to slip fast in 1894 while Shugart tallied 103 runs and successfully made the transition to CF.

That December, Shugart's career took a wrong turn when he was traded to Louisville for Tom Brown. Happy in CF, he was returned to SS and clashed repeatedly with manager John McCloskey until he was finally fined $100 for insubordination and told the last-place Colonels would not retain him. Except for a stint with the Phillies in the last six weeks of the 1897 season, Shugart spent the rest of the century in the minors with St. Paul of the Western League; after adjusting to the SS position, he continued to hit with surprising power.

Shugart accompanied St. Paul when Charlie Comiskey moved the franchise to Chicago in 1900 after the WL renamed itself the American League. Despite missing almost a third of that season, Shugart led the AL pennant winners in home runs and was back in the show the following year, when the AL declared itself a major league. On August 21, 1901, he slugged umpire Jack Haskell during at game at Washington, and the following morning AL president Ban Johnson banned him "for all time." One paper lectured, "It was a case of a player with a big weight of meanness in him, whose only control was a worn thread of decency that easily broke." But other members of the press noted reproachfully that equally heinous incidents of rowdyism that season involving players such as Hugh Duffy and Joe McGinnity had not been nearly so severely punished, and, after weeks under similar fire, Johnson was persuaded to reinstate Shugart in time to join in the first pennant celebration by an AL major league club.

Chicago reserved Shugart for 1902 but did not send him a contract. At 35 he had little prospect of another ML job and signed as captain of the San Francisco California League entry. Shugart remained in the minors until 1908, finishing with Rockford, IL. He died of cancer in Clearfield, PA, at 77. (DN)

Smith, George J. / "Germany"

B	T	HGT	WGT	G	AB	H	R	2B
R	R	6'0"	175	1712	6562	1597	907	252

3B	HR	RBI	BB	SO	SB	BA	SA	OBP
95	47	800	408	288	235	.243	.332	.289

G	IP	H	GS	CG	BB
1	1	3	0	0	0

SO	SH	W	L	PCT	ERA
1	0	0	0	—	9.00

B. 4/21/1863 Pittsburgh, PA **D.** 12/1/1927
TEAMS: 84AltU 84CleN 85–89BroA 90BroN 91–96CinN 97BroN 98StLN
DEBUT: 4/17/1884 at Cincinnati; played SS and went 1-for-4 in a 7–2 loss to Cincinnati's George Bradley
FINALE: 10/9/1898 at St. Louis; played SS and was hitless in a 2–0 loss to Chicago's Bill Phyle

Germany Smith was the prototypical good-field, no-hit SS. He led all nineteenth-century short fielders in assists by a wide margin, with 6,154 to runner-up Jack Glasscock's 5,630. Meanwhile, he also posted the lowest OPS of any nineteenth-century position player in 1,500 or more games (.620)—this despite being active in the 1893–1900 era for the last six years of his career. But while Smith was a first-rate fielder from the outset, he did not become a poor hitter until 1888. In his first four ML seasons (1884–87) Smith averaged .270. Over his eleven remaining seasons he hit .235 and had a lower OPS (.603) than even Shorty Fuller (.635), considered the weakest-hitting SS in the 1890s.

Smith left his Pittsburgh home in 1881 to play for Altoona's independent team and remained with various reincarnations of the club until it joined the rebel UA in 1884. The smallest city in ML history, Altoona lasted only 25 games, but its crack SS was still active when the American League became the NL's newest rebel challenger in 1901. After Altoona folded, Smith joined Cleveland NL in late June 1884, and in his debut he replaced second baseman Joe Ardner as Jack Glasscock's new keystone partner. That afternoon he went 3-for-4 in a 6–4 win over New York and received this accolade from *SL*: "The Clevelands won the game through the marvelous batting of their new man Smith." He finished the season with a composite .271 BA and was among the Cleveland team members Brooklyn AA coveted when it paid the disbanding Forest City club $4,000 in January 1885 for the pick of its players. Smith remained Brooklyn's SS until 1891, when John M. Ward took the reins of the club and wanted the job for himself, but despite his exceptional fielding, he was in danger every year of being replaced because he was too injury prone. In 1887 Smith missed the rest of the season after breaking his right hand on August 30 in a tag play at 2B; the following year he again missed September when Tommy Burns joined Brooklyn and took away his job; and in 1889 an early-season ankle injury so exasperated manager Bill McGunnigle that he nearly sold Smith to Louisville for a "nominal consideration." Ironically, in 1890, the first season that Smith was healthy all year and played every inning of every game for Brooklyn, he batted just .191, a new record low for a SS in a minimum of 120 games.

Handed his release that winter when Ward usurped his job, Smith signed with Cincinnati, where he teamed for the next six seasons with second baseman Bid McPhee, giving the Reds the strongest defensive keystone pairing in the league. When he managed to hike his BA only 10 points in 1891 to .201, he attributed his hitting falloff of late to the death of his child that season and the fact that he had broken a bone in his arm twice in recent years. Smith then seemed to gain credibility by improving his hitting incrementally every year until he peaked at .300, his career high, in 1895. At the end of the following season, however, Cincinnati writers began to complain that he covered 2B on steals less often than any other SS in the league, implying that he was gun-shy of base runners and would sometimes miss throws purposely to avoid collisions. The Reds' management in this case listened and traded Smith, pitcher Chauncey Fisher, and cash to Brooklyn for SS Tommy Corcoran. Smith immediately made the deal look bad in the City of Churches by batting .201 and was released at the end of the season. He hung on awhile longer in 1898 with the last-place Browns but was cut when he hit just .159 in 51 games.

Smith then spent his final three pro seasons in the minors, including 1900 with Minneapolis of the newly renamed AL, before returning to Altoona to run the local independent club. In his later years he worked as a crossing watchman for Pennsylvania Railroad. Smith was killed in 1927 when he was run over by a car as he was hurrying to catch a trolley. (DN)

Sullivan, Joseph Daniel / "Joe"

B	T	HGT	WGT	G	AB	H	R	2B
?	?	5'10"	178	415	1656	495	289	45

3B	HR	RBI	BB	SO	SB	BA	SA	OBP
29	11	227	117	80	51	.299	.381	.362

B. 1/6/1870 Charlestown, MA **D.** 11/2/1897
TEAMS: 93–94WasN 94–96PhiN 96StLN
DEBUT: 4/27/1893 at Washington; played SS and went 0-for-4 in a 7–5 win over Baltimore's Sadie McMahon
FINALE: 9/26/1896 at St. Louis; played LF and went 2-for-3 in a 7–3 win over Pittsburgh's Elmer Horton

Joe Sullivan came of age with the Cambridge Reds, the same semipro team that produced Joe Kelley. Ever popular in the Boston area, when he first visited the Hub with the Washington club on May 25, 1893, well-wishers from his hometown presented him with a gold watch and other trinkets before the game. Sullivan then nearly undermined Jouett Meekin's 7–5 win over the locals by making 2 of his staggering rookie total of 102 errors.

Seemingly the antithesis of the good-field, no-hit shortstops that prevailed even in the mid-1890s when batting marks leaped dramatically after the 1893 pitching rule changes, Sullivan was simply playing the wrong position. The possessor of one of the strongest arms in the game and a good judge of fly balls, he was ideally suited to CF, but in 1893, his rookie season, Washington already had one of the best at that position in Dummy Hoy, and when Sullivan moved to Philadelphia the following season, there in CF for the Phillies was Billy Hamilton. As a consequence, his only option was to take the job for which he had been purchased from Washington: as a replacement for the Phils' recently beaned SS, Bob Allen.

Sullivan hit .352 for Philadelphia in 1894, but it was scarcely noticed, for the whole team hit over .340. What did come under manager Arthur Irwin's scrutiny was his new acquisition's .887 FA. When Sullivan reported the following spring at below his normal weight and his power numbers dropped while his fielding remained ragged, Irwin publicly called him a "dub" and unsuccessfully tried to trade him for such flyweight hitting shortstops as Shorty Fuller and Fred Ely. Held to just 94 games by what appeared to be no more than a series of minor nagging health problems, Sullivan also dropped several points in his FA, finishing at .879.

That winter Sullivan seemingly got the break he needed when the Phils traded Billy Hamilton, putting him in competition with Tuck Turner to replace Hamilton in CF. Sullivan won the job in the spring, overcoming a spell of "fever and ague," and opened the season as the Phils' center gardener and lead-off hitter but fell out of favor with the club's new manager, Billy Nash, when his play seemed listless. On June 28, 1896, Sullivan and Turner went to St. Louis in return for outfielder Dick Cooley. For the remainder of the season Sullivan alternated between playing for a week or two and then having to recuperate when he suffered a recurrence of his spring illness. At one point he was thought to have malaria, but he finally was able to finish the season, and on a roll besides, collecting 2 hits on the closing day of the campaign in one of the Browns' rare wins.

In the spring of 1897 Sullivan reported to the Browns' training camp in "poor health" after suffering apparent bronchial trouble all winter. Obviously not ready for the opening gong, he was left behind in Hot Springs, AR, when the team headed north. The May 15, 1897, *TSN* was optimistic that he "will get into a game next week," but a week later the same paper reported he had returned to Philadelphia in search of medical treatment ("No comment is necessary, and comparison is impossible") and admitted that his playing days seemed over after players from the Baltimore, St. Louis, and Philadelphia teams had made up a purse for him of some $300. In early August 1897 Sullivan journeyed from his home in Boston to Baltimore to attend games against the Phillies and was permitted to sit on the Baltimore bench, where his former fellow players could not help but notice that he looked "very ill." Still, it was said that he was "slowly recovering from an illness that was thought to be consumption."

But, alas, it was consumption. Sullivan died at his home in Charlestown that fall. Bizarrely, a negligent member of St. Louis's front office continued to reserve him annually for several years after his death. Sullivan is currently the last remaining MLer to have played as many as 400 games and collected as many as 1,500 ABs as late as the mid-1890s without leaving any record of which way he batted or threw. (DN/DB)

Tomney, Philip Howard / "Phil" "Buster"

B	T	HGT	WGT	G	AB	H	R	2B
R	R	5'7"	155	254	882	205	148	32

3B	HR	RBI	BB	SO	SB	BA	SA	OBP
12	5	100	96	47	64	.232	.313	.313

B. 7/7/1863 Reading, PA **D.** 3/18/1892
TEAMS: 88–90LouA
DEBUT: 9/7/1888 at Louisville; played SS and went 0-for-3 in an 8–5 loss to Brooklyn's Dave Foutz
FINALE: 10/14/1890 at Louisville; played SS and went 1-for-5 in a 13–7 win over St. Louis's Bob Hart

Phil Tomney was a quick, wide-ranging SS who made a lot of errors—114 in 1889—largely because he got to more balls than the average SS. His range factor in each of his two seasons as a regular SS ranks among the top five in the AA's ten-year history.

Upon his arrival in Louisville in 1888 a local writer remarked, "Tomney, the Colonels' new short stop, is a good fielder and a fast base runner, but he is not a giant with the willow." That evaluation held true for his entire short, sad career. After making his pro debut in the 1883 Interstate Association, Tomney put in two seasons with independent Lancaster, PA, before joining Syracuse in 1886 and quickly establishing himself as the top fielding SS in the International Association. When news of the raves he was drawing reached New York, the Giants gave him a $500 advance to report the following spring, but he returned the money after realizing that he had no realistic hope of making the big league club. He remained in the minors until September 1888, when Louisville purchased him from Allentown of the Central League for $600. By the end of the season Tomney was bringing up the rear of the Colonels' batting order. After he began 1889 still batting last, Louisville talked of releasing him in early May because "he was so badly rattled that he could not do himself justice." But he was retained when the Colonels were unable to acquire Germany Smith from Brooklyn to replace him.

Despite a .213 BA the previous year, Tomney held his job in 1890 when manager Jack Chapman lacked anyone better after PL raiders stripped both major leagues of most of the better shortstops. By midseason he had emerged as the top fielding SS in the AA and one of the driving forces on a first-place club. On Saturday August 23, Tomney injured his shoulder in a base-path collision at St. Louis. It remained tender for the rest of the year, and he was rested after Louisville clinched the pennant. Then in Game 3 of the World's Series against NL champion Brooklyn, a bad-hop grounder hit "his lame shoulder," knocking him out of the action for the rest of the postseason affair.

When Tomney returned to his home in Reading after the Series, he was greeted with a brass band reception and a dinner on his behalf at the South-End Club, where he was presented with a diamond-studded badge. Just weeks later he learned that Louisville had signed Ollie Beard to man SS in 1891 and he was to be released. Tomney joined Lincoln of the Western Association but was cut in July 1891, reportedly for weak hitting even though he was batting .276. *TSN* revealed the truth several weeks later: he was dying of consumption. Tomney left behind a wife and child when he passed away at his home in Reading at 28. (DN/DB)

Wheelock, Warren H. / "Bobby"

B	T	HGT	WGT	G	AB	H	R	2B
R	R	5'8"	160	236	854	201	138	25

3B	HR	RBI	BB	SO	SB	BA	SA	OBP
4	3	70	118	70	106	.235	.285	.330

B. 8/6/1864 Charlestown, MA **D.** 3/13/1928
TEAMS: 87BosN 90–91ColA
DEBUT: 5/19/1887 at Boston; played LF and went 1-for-5 in a 5–4 loss to Pittsburgh's Jim Galvin
FINALE: 9/27/1891 at Milwaukee; played SS and went 0-for-1 in a 12–1 loss to Milwaukee's Frank Killen

Bobby Wheelock was an excellent base runner and competent enough as a hitter to have compiled a substantial ML career at SS if he had just been a better fielder. His name first turned heads in 1884 while he was a member of the amateur Boston Tremonts. A catcher at the time, he did not convert to SS until he came under manager Harry Spence in 1886 while with Portland, ME, the New England League champions. Wheelock led the NEL in runs with 93 and also ranked high in steals, inducing Boston NL to keep him on salary the entire 1887 season as an extra man. Even though Wheelock had a decent year at the plate, he failed to prove himself ready for regular duty and was not retained.

Wheelock spent 1888 with Worcester of the New

England League and then went to Detroit, where he hit .281 for the 1889 International Association champions. Early in 1890 Columbus of the AA tried to buy Wheelock, but Detroit manager Bob Leadley held on to him in the hope that he would soon be hired to manage the St. Louis Browns and could take his SS with him. Only after the Browns job failed to materialize did Columbus succeed in prying Wheelock away from Leadley. In his debut with the Ohio club on July 13, he made 3 errors in a 3–2 loss to the lowly Brooklyn Gladiators and earned this tribute in local papers the following day: "Wheelock celebrated his first game with the Columbus team by presenting the game to Brooklyn." But he settled down after that and played well enough to be kept by Columbus in 1891.

Early in his final ML campaign, Wheelock batted leadoff but was dropped in the order when he failed to hit. In addition to collecting just 131 total bases in 136 games, he also had problems in the field. Nevertheless, he topped AA shortstops in several defensive departments and played every inning of every game until the last two contests of the season, when Charlie Duffee took his place after he was abruptly released for excessive drinking. Wheelock denied the charge, claiming that the Columbus club was just looking for an excuse to get rid of him, and even though he admitted having a glass of beer in Milwaukee after what turned out to be his final ML game, he swore that manager Gus Schmelz had surreptitiously followed him for several hours fervently hoping to catch him inside a saloon.

Following his departure from Columbus, Wheelock played in top minor leagues until he broke a leg late in the 1896 Western League season. He finished his playing career in May 1900 while captaining New London of the Connecticut State League for the second consecutive year. For some time after that, Wheelock continued to participate in oldtimers' games in Boston, his lifelong home, when not working as a chef at eastern resort hotels. He died in Boston at 63 of pneumonia. (DN/DB)

White, William Dighton / "Bill" "Will"

B	T	HGT	WGT	G	AB	H	R	2B
?	R	?	?	467	1834	441	272	39

3B	HR	RBI	BB	SO	SB	BA	SA	OBP
37	6	205	125	—	76	.240	.312	.291

G	IP	H	GS	CG	BB
1	1	2	0	0	2

SO	SH	W	L	PCT	ERA
1	0	0	0	—	9.00

B. 5/1/1860 Bridgeport, OH **D.** 12/29/1924
TEAMS: 83PhiN 84PitA 86–88LouA 88StLA
DEBUT: 6/1/1883 at Philadelphia; in a 10–1 loss to Chicago's Larry Corcoran went 0-for-1 after replacing injured Blondie Purcell at 3B in the fifth inning and later moved to SS
FINALE: 10/14/1888 at Cincinnati; played SS and went 0-for-4 in a 10–1 loss to Cincinnati's Lee Viau

At the close of the 1887 season Bill White was regarded among the better shortstops in the game; a year later his reputation and career were both in tatters. A machinist by trade, White turned pro in 1881 with an independent Akron team that was loaded with future major leaguers. He joined unaffiliated Pottsville, PA, in 1882 and then signed in 1883 with the Charles S. Brown nine of Pittsburgh, where he came to the attention of the AA club in town and was signed for 1884. After battling Gus Alberts for the Alleghenys' SS post the following spring, White won out when Alberts was injured in the second game of the season. He was pushed back to the Eastern League Washington Nationals in 1885, however, after Pittsburgh bought out the Columbus AA franchise and corralled the core of its team.

In 1886 White joined Louisville along with two other infield newcomers, second baseman Reddy Mack and third baseman Joe Werrick. The trio helped spur the Falls City team into contention for most of the summer before a horrendous late-season collapse sank the club below .500. White, for his part, was second on the team in runs. He remained one of the better shortstops in 1887 but began to acquire a reputation for being fractious. His problems came to the fore in 1888 after manager "Honest" John Kelly labeled him "unmanageable" and accused him of "always holding some grievance, real or imaginary." The final straw for Kelly was White's wild throw in the tenth inning of a game at Cincinnati on June 22 that handed the Reds the 2 deciding runs.

Two weeks later White was playing SS for the St. Louis Browns, which had lost patience with Joe Herr's erratic defense. In his three months with the AA pennant winners, White tallied just 31 runs in 76 games and compiled an abysmal .458 OPS. His poor hitting continued in the World's Series that fall against the New York Giants and was compounded by numerous defensive lapses. In the 10-game affair he hit just .143 and made 10 errors, the most critical coming in Game 5 when he dropped a throw while trying to turn a double play that allowed New York to win 6–4. For the remainder of the Series, White bore the brunt of Browns owner Chris Von der Ahe's indignation over his team's loss, and, accordingly, he is viewed in many histories of the game as the first full-blown postseason "goat."

After foiling an attempt by the Browns to trade him to the Columbus AA replacement club, White joined Denver of the Western Association in 1889 and played in the minors and outlaw leagues for another decade for teams ranging geographically from Montana to Maine, and for managers as diverse as Dave Rowe, Billy Earle, and even himself. For a time in 1895 White piloted the Wheeling Interstate League team that was owned by Al Buckenberger and functioned, ironically, as a sort of farm team for the St. Louis Browns and White's nemesis, Von der Ahe. The following season he played 2B for Earle, also a renowned globetrotter, with Dallas of the Texas League. Later in life White worked as a security guard for Riverside Tube Mill in Bellaire and died in the town where he was born of pneumonia at 64. (DN/DB)

Wise, Samuel Washington / "Sam" "Modoc"

B	T	HGT	WGT	G	AB	H	R	2B
L	R	5'10½"	170	1175	4715	1281	834	221

3B	HR	RBI	BB	SO	SB	BA	SA	OBP
112	49	672	389	643	203	.272	.397	.332

B. 8/18/1857 Akron, OH **D.** 1/22/1910
TEAMS: 81DetN 82–88BosN 89WasN 90BufP 91BalA 93WasN
DEBUT: 7/30/1881 at Detroit; played 3B and went 2-for-4 in a 7–6 win over Buffalo's Jim Galvin
FINALE: 9/29/1893 at Cincinnati; played 2B and went 3-for-5 in a 10–4 loss to Chicago's Tom Parrott

Even after marrying Lizzie O'Neill of Utica, NY, in December 1887, Sam Wise continued to be an incorrigible womanizer. Far too often the Boston management had to fork over tidy sums to bail him out of "scrapes." Wise also was said to have a "wicked" arm. He had good range at SS and made many "marvelous" stops, but he was a first baseman's nightmare in that his throws naturally curved and frequently ended up in the bleachers. Nevertheless, Wise remained a middle infielder for almost his entire career and as such was far above the average as a hitter. But even with a bat in his hand he could be all over the place. In 1884 Wise was the first documented ML performer to strike out as many as 100 times in a season. During his career he batted everywhere in the order from first to last, and he also batted every which way. Even though he was primarily a left-handed hitter, he would turn up in the right side batter's box whenever the mood struck him.

Wise played with amateur and semipro teams in his hometown area until joining the Akron independent team in 1880. He remained with Akron until July 1881 when Detroit gave him a one-day test at 3B and he nearly threw the game away with late-inning errors that gave Buffalo 4 unearned runs. That winter, Wise signed with Cincinnati of the upstart AA and then reneged and signed with Boston NL, claiming that he hadn't known the AA would play Sunday games. Cincinnati fought unsuccessfully to enjoin him from playing in the Hub and gloated at first when he hit just .221 in his official rookie year. Wise followed, however, with a solid .271 for Boston's surprise NL-pennant-winning entry in 1883 and soon was generally considered the best all-around SS in the senior loop. But after a sore arm forced him to spend most of 1886 at 1B, he was plagued intermittently with recurrences of arm trouble for the rest of his career.

Wise reached his pinnacle in 1887 when he won the silver bat awarded by the *Boston Globe* for leading all Hub performers in hitting at .334. The following autumn he publicly broadcast that he had been promised a $500 bonus by Boston's triumvirate of owners if he stayed sober and in condition all season, but when Arthur Soden refused to pay his third of the agreed amount, he had been forced to settle for only $333. The revelation so embarrassed Soden that he sold both Wise and first baseman John Morrill to Washington in April 1889 for around $6,000.

Wise fled the Senators for the Players League after they finished last in 1889 but ended up with Buffalo, the PL tailender. In 1891, once the PL folded, he signed with Baltimore AA but was released in late August when he injured his leg while sporting only a .247 BA at the time. Wise spent 1892 in the Eastern League. At age 35 his ML days were presumably over, but once Jim O'Rourke took over as Washington manager in 1893, he invited his old NL adversary to compete for the club's 2B slot. Wise not only won the battle but led all Senators qualifiers in batting and slugging.

That winter, Washington sent him a contract for 1894, but he refused to sign it, snarling that he would stay with his hotel business in Akron, OH, because he felt he had not received his due recognition or pay from the club the previous season. Eventually Wise signed the contract but then played a "listless game" in spring training, prompting Washington to release him—which is probably what he had wanted all along since he raced to join Mike Kelly's "Wild Bunch," the 1894 Allentown Kelly's Killers. Wise continued to play in the minors until he was past 40, finishing in 1899 with Newark of the Atlantic League, and then umpired for a while before retiring to his winter job as a fireman in Akron. Later he worked as a foreman at a rubber company in Akron until January 1910, when he died at his Akron home of a ruptured appendix after refusing medical attention for his "discomfort" until it was too late. (DN)

*Wright, Samuel / "Sam"

B	T	HGT	WGT	G	AB	H	R	2B
R	R	5'7½"	146	45	173	29	10	4

3B	HR	RBI	BB	SO	SB	BA	SA	OBP
0	0	5	1	6	0	.168	.191	.168

B. 11/25/1848 New York, NY **D.** 5/6/1928
TEAMS: 75NHNA 76BosN 80CinN 81BosN
DEBUT: 4/19/1875 at Boston; played SS and made 1 hit in a 6–0 loss to Boston's Al Spalding
FINALE: 9/23/1881 at Boston; played SS and went 1-for-4 in a 4–3 win over Buffalo's Jim Galvin

The youngest of the three Wright brothers might never have appeared in a ML game if he had been a member of any other family in America. Sam Wright trained with his brother Harry's Boston NA club in the early 1870s but was never regarded as strong enough to use in an actual game. His oldest brother actually tried to keep him away from pro ball, believing he would fall prey to bad company. An outstanding fielder—Harry Wright once said, "When boys, Sam's fielding always pleased me better than [brother] George's"—Wright spent 1875 with the New Haven Elm Citys and then played 2 games with Harry's Boston NL club the following year before disappearing into the minors for three seasons. In 1878 he batted .184 for Lowell of the International Association and did little better in 1879 with National Association New Bedford.

Nevertheless, Wright opened the 1880 season at SS for Cincinnati NL but was cut less than three weeks later after he hit .088 for a team representing the same city that his brothers had put indelibly on the baseball map eleven years earlier. Harry gave him one last token appearance with Boston in 1881 and then probably encouraged him to quit while he was ahead after he got a hit off one of the game's toughest pitchers at the time. Wright worked for his brother George in the Wright & Ditson Company for a time and then opened his own sporting goods shop. He never married and died in Dorchester, MA, at the Wrights' old family home, of a cerebral hemorrhage. (DN/DB)

Wrigley, George Watson / "Sailor" "Zeke"

B	T	HGT	WGT	G	AB	H	R	2B
?	?	5'8½"	150	239	861	222	121	25

3B	HR	RBI	BB	SO	SB	BA	SA	OBP
20	5	117	46	1	18	.258	.351	.296

B. 1/18/1874 Philadelphia, PA **D.** 9/28/1952
TEAMS: 96–98WasN 99NYN 99BroN
DEBUT: 8/31/1896 at Washington; replaced Jack O'Brien at 2B and went 0-for-1 in a 1–0 win over Chicago's Danny Friend
FINALE: 10/14/1899 at Brooklyn; played SS and went 2-for-2 in a 6–3 win over Baltimore's Harry Howell

Teammates knew George Wrigley as "Sailor" because he worked winters as a boat skipper, but writers preferred to call him "Zeke." In 1896 he and pitcher Togie Pittinger, his 1895 compatriot with Carlisle of the Cumberland Valley League, graduated to Roanoke. Wrigley joined Washington when Roanoke disbanded but not before hitting .310, topping the Virginia League in extra-base hits, and tying for the lead in home runs with 16. After a 5-game trial at the end of the 1896 season, Wrigley spent the next two years with Washington without ever finding a regular position. His quick release made SS seem his best spot, but he lacked range. Too, he displayed little of the power that had commemorated his 1896 Virginia League performance.

After Washington quit on Wrigley, he spent 1899 with Syracuse and joined the New York Giants at the close of the Eastern League season. He had already played 4 games with the Giants when Syracuse sold him to Brooklyn, triggering an eligibility furor. At first it appeared that Brooklyn manager Ned Hanlon had used Wrigley knowing that he might lose possession of his new infielder, and there was some debate whether Brooklyn should forfeit all the games in which he played. Hanlon meanwhile contended that New York had used him illegally because he was still Syracuse property even though the EL season had ended. In the end NL president Nick Young took another of his conciliatory stances, siding with New York but ruling that Wrigley's games with Brooklyn would count as long as Brooklyn paid a $500 fine.

The whole matter became moot when Wrigley returned to Syracuse in 1900, played poorly, and was sold to Worcester for $300. After serving as Worcester's captain in 1901, he married a local woman, Margaret Torpey, and shortly afterward underwent surgery that "reduced him to a shadow of his former self." Wrigley healed by the following spring, however, and played in the high minors for another decade, compiling 1,714 career hits, before finishing in 1914 as player-manager of Trenton in the Class B Tri-State League. He died in Philadelphia in 1952. (DN)

7 | THE OUTFIELDERS

7. The 1884 Columbus Buckeyes. Jim Field and Frank Mountain stand; Field has his hand on manager Gus Schmelz's shoulder, and Mountain leans on Pop Smith. Seated are Ed Morris, Tom Brown, Fred Carroll, Rudy Kemmler, Dummy Dundon, Willie Kuehne, and Fred Mann. Shortstop John Richmond stands between Kuehne and Mann. Brown, the last member of the team to be active in the majors, was then in his third season. He eventually scored 1,521 runs in 1,786 games despite finishing with just a .265 batting average.

Abbey, Charles S. / "Charlie"

B	T	HGT	WGT	G	AB	H	R	2B
L	L	5'8"	169	452	1756	493	307	67

3B	HR	RBI	BB	SO	SB	BA	SA	OBP
46	19	280	167	107	93	.281	.404	.351

G	IP	H	GS	CG	BB
1	2	6	0	0	0

SO	SH	W	L	PCT	ERA
0	0	0	0	—	4.50

B. 10/1/1866 Falls City, NE **D.** 4/27/1926
TEAMS: 93–97WasN
DEBUT: 8/16/1893 at Washington; played LF and was 0-for-3 in a 5–0 loss to Baltimore's Bill Hawke
FINALE: 8/19/1897 at Washington; played RF and was 0-for-4 in a 10–4 loss to Chicago's Clark Griffith

Blessed with a gorgeous crop of strawberry-blond hair, Charlie Abbey was also reputedly one of the best-dressed and most highly educated players in the game, an opera buff, and during his minor league days returned each winter to Nebraska to work as a reporter for the *Lincoln State Journal.* After spending 1888 with an independent team in Beatrice, NE, Abbey joined Des Moines of the Western Association the following year and moved to St. Paul of the same loop later in the season. He remained with St. Paul in 1890, surviving a line drive by Denver's George Treadway in a game in early August that "hit that red-headed cigar sign in the head" and ricocheted over the fence to give Treadway a freak 3-run homer. The following spring, however, Abbey incurred an injury in early May while hitting just .205 and was released by St. Paul. He caught a train for the West Coast and signed with Portland, OR, of the Pacific Northwest League.

Already nearing the age of 27, Abbey must have felt his career had stalled when he had risen no higher than the Southern League by August 1893, but he caught a break when Gus Schmelz, his manager at Chattanooga, anticipated that he would be hired to pilot Washington NL in 1894 and arranged for his star outfielder to join the D.C. club after the SL folded. Abbey's ML career seemed that it would be very brief when he went hitless in his first 3 games, but after that he hit a respectable .286 to earn a contract for the following year. In 1894 Washington's new manager, Schmelz, installed Abbey in LF and looked like a genius when the redhead led the team in hits and total bases. That fall, Abbey played on Washington's Professional Association football team before returning to his customary off-season job in Lincoln. He may have sustained a gridiron injury, for he got off to a dismal start the following spring and as late as July 5 was hitting only .189. A 4-for-4 day against Cleveland's Cy Young on August 20 finally lifted him over .230 and ignited a hot streak that enabled him to finish at .276.

By that time Abbey had become a year-round Washington resident in order take full advantage of its cultural pursuits. Rather than play football again, he worked that winter managing a produce stand. But he got off to another miserable start in 1896 and was hitting just .203 in early June. Soon thereafter he found himself competing periodically with Billy Lush for his job but remained the Senators' right fielder until Jake Gettman was purchased in August 1897. On August 28 *TSN* announced Abbey's release, and he subsequently finished the campaign with Providence of the Eastern League. That winter Abbey's playing career came to a sad end when he lost an arm after being run over by a carriage. He remained in Washington operating a newsstand and often took part in old-timers' events. Abbey died from an aortic aneurysm in San Francisco in 1926. (DN/DB)

Addy, Robert Edward / "Bob" "Magnet" "Honorable Bob"

B	T	HGT	WGT	G	AB	H	R	2B
L	L	5'8"	160	274	1231	341	227	36

3B	HR	RBI	BB	SO	SB	BA	SA	OBP
13	1	171	20	9	35	.277	.330	.289

G	W	L	PCT	PENNANTS
31	8	23	.258	0

B. 2/?/1845 Rochester, NY **D.** 4/9/1910
TEAMS: 71RokNA 73PhiNA 73BosNA 74HarNA (P/M)75PhiNA 76ChiN (P/M)77CinN
DEBUT: 5/6/1871 at Rockford; played 2B and went 1-for-3 in a 13–4 loss to Cleveland's Al Pratt
FINALE: 10/6/1877 at St. Louis; played RF and went 0-for-4 in a 7–3 loss to St. Louis's Tricky Nichols

Known for his dry and often profanity-laced wit, Bob Addy is credited by some with introducing sliding into bases, and in the 1890s both *TSN* and the *Chicago Tribune* attributed the first headfirst slide to him. His nickname "Magnet" stemmed from his sure-handed fielding, but his career stats raise doubts that it was entirely deserved. In 1871, Addy, then in his seventh season with Rockford, led NA second basemen in errors with 42 in 22 games. He remained outside the fabric of the NA in 1872 after Rockford left the loop and triggered a furor in 1873 when he joined the NA champion, Boston, to man RF in midseason while allegedly still a member of an independent team in Rockford.

Addy played 2B again in 1874 and then occupied RF in almost all of his remaining ML appearances. In 1876 he was a member of his second ML pennant winner when he shared RF on the Chicago club with Oscar Bielaski. The following year he finished the ML portion of his career with Cincinnati and captained the club for 24 games. Reportedly he and Will Foley were both released after the 1877 season for drunkenness even though each had another year to go in his two-year contract. (Considerable research remains to be done on nineteenth-century players with multiyear contracts who were released before their pacts expired.)

After leaving baseball Addy ran an ice skating rink for a while and then moved to the Washington Territory and worked as a tinner. In March 1889 *TSN* reported (perhaps jokingly) that he was a Mormon and had seven wives, all of whom he would leave for a chance to play 1B again. Addy later was among the first settlers in Pocatello, ID, operating a hardware store there until he died of a stroke. In his memoirs Cap Anson wrote that Addy "was an odd sort of a genius and quit the game because he thought he could do better at something else," a decision that Anson found unimaginable. (DN/DB)

Allen, Myron Smith / "Myron" "Zeke"

B	T	HGT	WGT	G	AB	H	R	2B
R	R	5'8"	150	156	606	157	89	28

3B	HR	RBI	BB	SO	SB	BA	SA	OBP
14	4	88	45	3	30	.259	.371	.317

G	IP	H	GS	CG	BB
5	35.2	34	3	3	7

SO	SH	W	L	PCT	ERA
3	0	1	3	.250	1.77

B. 3/22/1854 Kingston, NY **D.** 3/8/1924

TEAMS: 83NYN 86BosN 87CleA 88KCA

DEBUT: 7/19/1883 at Cleveland; caught by Jack Humphries and lost 5–4 to Cleveland's Jim McCormick

FINALE: 7/1/1888 at Cleveland; played LF and went 1-for-4 in a 6–5 loss to Cleveland's Cinders O'Brien

After years of playing in obscurity, Myron Allen came into the limelight in 1883 as a pitcher-outfielder with the independent Leader club of Kingston, NY, which won 21 straight games at one point before Allen lost 9–2 to Brooklyn of the Interstate Association in July. Allen made his ML debut a few days later as a pitcher with New York NL and also played the outfield on occasion but only in exhibitions. He returned to Kingston and appeared in just one ML game during the next three years.

In 1887 Allen joined the Cleveland AA replacement entry. The club's Opening Day right fielder, Allen batted in the middle of the order all season and was second on the team in RBI but scored just 66 runs. Parting with Cleveland after the season, Allen did not sign again until the 1888 campaign was under way, joining the new Kansas City AA club on May 1. He was released in July and said to be "in poor health" at the time. Allen later played in the New York State League into his early forties while working as a caretaker at the main post office in Kingston. He died in a Kingston hospital at 69 after becoming ill at work. (DN)

*Allison, Arthur Algernon / "Art"

B	T	HGT	WGT	G	AB	H	R	2B
?	?	5'8"	150	168	741	188	106	19

3B	HR	RBI	BB	SO	SB	BA	SA	OBP
8	1	70	5	18	10	.254	.305	.259

B. 1/29/1849 Philadelphia, PA **D.** 2/25/1916

TEAMS: 71–72CleNA 73ResNA 75WasNA 75HarNA 76LouN

DEBUT: 5/4/1871 at Fort Wayne; played RF and went 1-for-4 in a 2–0 loss to Fort Wayne's Bobby Mathews

FINALE: 10/5/1876 at Louisville; played RF and went 0-for-4 in an 11–2 loss to Hartford's Candy Cummings

The brother of Doug Allison of 1869 Cincinnati Red Stockings fame, Art Allison played in the first ML game and was the first to whiff when he struck out in the second inning but reached base when catcher Bill Lennon missed his third strike. A decent hitter early in his career, he grew overmatched as the pitching grew stiffer. By his final season he was able to hit just .208 for Louisville but would not have been wanted back in any case, according to the *Chicago Tribune,* because of his fondness for drinking "cheap whisky." Allison played with two teams in the 1877 League Alliance and then occupied 1B for the independent Cleveland Forest Citys in 1878. He was working for the monotype section of the government printing office in 1916 when he was run over by a truck while crossing G Street in Washington in a blinding snowstorm. Allison was survived by his wife and a son, John, who was a professor at the University of Pennsylvania. (DN)

Anderson, John Joseph / "John" "Honest John"

B	T	HGT	WGT	G	AB	H	R	2B
B	R	6'1"	190	597	2367	707	401	114

3B	HR	RBI	BB	SO	SB	BA	SA	OBP
72	25	421	106	55	142	.298	.440	.337

B. 12/14/1873 Sarpsborg, Norway
D. 7/23/1949 Worcester, MA
TEAMS: 94–98BroN 98WasN 98–99BroN 01MilAL 02–03StLAL 04–05NYAL 05–07WasAL 08ChiAL
DEBUT: 9/8/1894 at St. Louis; played CF and went 2-for-3 in a 6–1 win over St. Louis's Pink Hawley and Ted Breitenstein
FINALE: 10/2/1908 at Cleveland; pinch hit for pitcher Ed Walsh and grounded out to Bill Bradley after almost breaking up Addie Joss's 1–0 perfect game with 2 out in the ninth when he lined a ball down the left-field line that was just foul by inches

Called "Honest John" because he so seldom protested umpires' decisions that he made them doubt their calls when he did, John Anderson had a strong arm, hit with power, and was among the few early-day players to be a loop leader during his career in both stolen bases and SA. As an added bonus, he batted equally well from both sides of the plate. Yet only a year after he won the 1898 NL slugging crown, he was among the ML regulars consigned to spend 1900 in the minors when the NL lopped off four teams, and he was never looked upon as one of the better players of his day. Anderson's most obvious deficiency was his impatience—he compiled only 310 walks in 6,341 ABs—but he had an even more glaring fault, although one had to see him play a few times to be aware of it. Even though Anderson on an infamous occasion tried to steal 2B with the bases loaded, his obits adamantly said that he was not viewed as a dumb player. His contemporaries said otherwise. As early as his second ML season *TSN* already had perceived him as, "a fine sticker [who] lacks a balance wheel in his think tank."

Born in Norway, Anderson was brought to Worcester, MA, by his parents at age 5. In 1893 he joined the Worcester Athletic Club as a pitcher and was among the team members invited to try out for the Worcester New England League entry the following spring. Anderson pitched poorly but persuaded Haverhill player-manager John Irwin to test him as an outfielder. Late that summer Brooklyn owner Charlie Byrne came to an NEL game to watch Buck Freeman, then with Fall River, but he was more impressed by Anderson and acquired him to replace injured gardener Mike Griffin. In the spring of 1895 Anderson wrested the Brooklyn LF post from Tommy Burns and led the Bridegrooms in homers but garnered only 12 walks. He continued to produce wildly uneven stats until the spring of 1898, when Brooklyn loaned him to Washington to clear a lineup opening for rookie Jimmy Sheckard and then regretted it when Sheckard was unready. Meanwhile, Anderson had made Brooklyn's new president, Charlie Ebbets, squirm by ranking among the early NL slugging leaders. Shortly after the Scandinavian outfielder married in July, Ebbets began working to retrieve him. Anderson finally left Washington on September 21 (ironically, to be replaced by Buck Freeman) and five days later reappeared in a Brooklyn uniform at Boston. In October he finished the season as the first slugging leader in ML history with a sub-.300 BA (.294).

When he dropped to a .686 OPS the following year as Brooklyn romped to the pennant, he was sold to Milwaukee of the then Western League. Anderson at first refused to report to Brewers manager Connie Mack when he was offered only $250 a month, insisting that he should receive $325, the same amount he had gotten in Brooklyn, but he eventually relented. That winter, he worked as a wrestling referee in Worcester, preparing for his first season in the newly renamed American League. (DN)

Andrews, George Edward / "Ed"

B	T	HGT	WGT	G	AB	H	R	2B
R	R	5'8"	160	774	3233	830	602	117

3B	HR	RBI	BB	SO	SB	BA	SA	OBP
26	12	278	194	245	205	.257	.320	.301

B. 4/5/1859 Painesville, OH **D.** 8/12/1934
TEAMS: 84–89PhiN 89IndN 90BroP 91CinA
DEBUT: 5/1/1884 at Philadelphia; played 2B and went 2-for-4 in a 13–2 win over Detroit's Stump Wiedman
FINALE: 7/26/1891 at Cincinnati; played LF and went 2-for-3 in a 9–5 loss to Louisville's Jouett Meekin.

Ed Andrews was a rarity in his time: a model player who later became a model citizen and a highly respected spokesman for the game. In the spring of 1883 he was still attending Western Reserve University and playing amateur ball in Cleveland when he passed his 24th birthday. After the college term ended, Andrews played with independent Akron awhile and then traveled to Toledo, where he had friends on the Northwestern League team, to help out when it played an exhibition game with Providence NL. Andrews did so well that afternoon at 3B that he was not only asked to stay with Toledo by manager Charlie Morton, but after the game he was also invited by Providence skipper Harry Wright to have a talk. Over dinner that night Wright revealed that he planned to manage the Philadelphia NL team in 1884 and proposed signing Andrews to a Philadelphia contract. Andrews said that he had no intention of playing ball full-time but after mulling it over for a few months, he decided to accept Wright's offer. When he arrived at the Philadelphia park in 1884 for preseason training, he found some thirty players milling about, no two in the same uniforms. "Some in rags, some in tags, and some in velvet gowns," Andrews later said, but no sooner did Wright arrive than he quickly organized the motley group into an orderly workout.

Wright and Andrews remained close until Wright's death in 1895. Years later Andrews confided that early in his career in a game against Detroit he had cut 3B when he saw umpire John Gaffney's back was to him. As Andrews took a seat on the Philadelphia bench after scoring, Wright reproachfully said, "Ed, I don't want any games won that way," and Andrews claimed he never did anything like that again while playing for Wright. Andrews also revealed that in the early weeks of 1890 he had been delegated to approach Wright and convince him to manage the Philadelphia PL team. But when he went to Wright's home, he left empty-handed after Wright wished him and the Brotherhood every success but said he was committed irrevocably to the NL.

Andrews spent his first five and a half seasons in the majors under Wright and was a regular from day one until he lost his job in 1889 after the Quakers acquired Sam Thompson from the defunct Detroit club. Used exclusively at 2B his rookie year, Andrews shifted to the outfield on May 8, 1885, to make room for Al Myers. The move appeared to agree with Andrews; when the NL averages were published after the games of May 27 he led the loop with a .431 mark. Over the remainder of 1885 Andrews's average cooled down to .266. The following year Wright batted him leadoff to take advantage of his speed, but while he led the league in steals, he neither hit nor walked enough to justify the move on almost any other team but Philadelphia. By 1886 Wright's club was built around players like Andrews: good at everything but hitting. After working out that winter in Jacksonville, FL, however, Andrews led all Quakers regulars in both BA and SA in 1887 (with what would have been only average marks on most other teams). His defense and fine baserunning likewise made him a player in great demand. After the season, Andrews told a Philadelphia reporter that he had not been reserved by Philadelphia in 1887 and had agreed to play for $1,800, $200 less than he had received as a rookie in 1884, only after Wright promised to take care of him if he had a good year.

Andrews then revealed that he wanted $5,000 and held out until March of 1888. With a college education and a good off-season job as a salesman, he was in a stronger position than most players to demand the limit, and other teams were eager to purchase him. However, the Quakers, suspecting tampering and probably regarding his holdout as a form of blackmail, were in no hurry to sell him. They would discuss only extravagant terms, offering him to Boston for third baseman Billy Nash plus several thousand dollars in cash and suggesting a trade for Hardy Richardson, arguably the best player on Detroit's pennant-winning team. In late March the Quakers finally concluded that Andrews meant it when he said he would sit out rather than play in Philadelphia again and agreed to sell him to Boston if Boston could come to terms with him. The complicated three-sided negotiations finally broke down, with Andrews rejoining Philadelphia and the Boston club angry at what it regarded as a breach of faith. Andrews signed for much less than his asking price but still got $2,400, a substantial sum for the day.

In 1888, despite the ill will between Andrews and the Quakers' front office, he led the team in both hits and runs, but it was no great feat as the Quakers posted just a .566 team OPS. Indeed, Andrews's individual OPS was only .569, a mere 3 points above the team average and the lowest mark ever by a team leader in both hits and runs. His stolen bases fell off sharply, and withal his season gave comfort to those who believed marriage was bad for a ballplayer; in July 1888 Andrews had wed Mary Kirby, the daughter of Dr. Edmund Kirby, a noted Philadelphia prohibitionist, and begun to lose some of his passion for baseball. His disenchantment grew when Sam Thompson's arrival relegated him to the bench in the spring of 1889. Andrews's services even as a substitute were so little needed that after he refused to be sold to Washington he was allowed to go home to Ohio and continue to draw his salary. Finally, a sale more agreeable to Andrews was arranged with Indianapolis on August 16, and he supplanted Marty Sullivan in CF. In his first game back at full duty, even though Indianapolis lost 10–3 to Chicago, Andrews had personal reason to celebrate, as he went 3-for-3 and followed by keeping his average around the .300 mark for the next two months before finishing at .306.

His return to form not only reinvigorated his interest in the game but also made him attractive to PL organizers and especially its prime mover, John M. Ward. Andrews put his education to use by writing much of the publicity material at the time of the PL's inception and signed with Ward's Brooklyn club, joining the two outfielders who had flanked him with Indianapolis, Em Seery and Jack McGeachy. But the trio doomed Brooklyn to be an also-ran in the 1890 Players League race when they logged the worst offensive numbers of all the regular outfielders in the league, with the lone exception of Buffalo's Larry Twitchell. Andrews's offensive decline continued in 1891 after he joined Mike Kelly's AA Kelly's Killers. He tried to attribute both his poor start and the team's to a flu epidemic that had felled several key members of the club in April, but the excuse failed to fly when the club showed no improvement after the epidemic subsided. Andrews's departure from Cincinnati was greased by a peculiar falling out with Kelly, who had deputed Andrews to run the team whenever Kelly was out of the game. During a July road trip Kelly left the team, and with business manager Frank Bancroft also away, Andrews was fully in charge. Upon taking command, on July 17 he told reporters that Kelly two days before had confided to him that he was going to take a vacation. Andrews at first thought Kelly was joking, but Kelly really did leave and Andrews said he had no idea where the manager had gone. Kelly's sudden departure fueled rumors that he might want to take advantage of the ongoing trade war between the AA and NL to jump to the NL. A few days later Kelly surfaced at a game in Boston, saying he had only taken a few days off to rest an injury and was furious at Andrews for stirring up trouble. Before the month was out, Andrews was released to make way for Lefty Marr in RF.

He went home to Painesville, OH, and claimed that he was entertaining offers from several ML teams. Whether or not there was any truth to it, the winter of 1891–92 found him ensconced on his new plantation in Eden, FL, adjacent to the Indian River. His baseball career was over. The buyer's market for talent that emerged from the combination of the NL and AA into one twelve-club organization was particularly unpropitious for an aging player like Andrews, and the diminished salaries teams were paying would not have tempted a man who had much better career prospects than the average ballplayer. Consequently, although he took time on occasion to umpire in the majors, he was one of the relatively few players who retired and never attempted to come back. Andrews remained a resident of Florida's east coast for the rest of his life, eventually settling in Palm Beach, where he became a wealthy real estate developer. A skilled stenographer and typist, he carved a subsidiary career as a yachting writer and was known to both his readers and Palm Beach neighbors as "Capt. George Andrews." He died of a heart attack at Palm Beach Hospital in West Palm Beach. (DN/DB)

*Bannon, James Henry / "Jimmy" "Foxy Grandpa"

B	T	HGT	WGT	G	AB	H	R	2B
R	R	5'5"	160	367	1438	460	293	76

3B	HR	RBI	BB	SO	SB	BA	SA	OBP
24	19	253	152	101	99	.320	.446	.389

G	IP	H	GS	CG	BB
3	9	18	1	0	8

SO	SH	W	L	PCT	ERA
2	0	0	1	.000	12.00

B. 5/5/1871 Amesbury, MA **D.** 3/24/1948
TEAMS: 93StLN 94–96BosN
DEBUT: 6/15/1893 at Boston; played RF and went 3-for-3 in a 5–1 loss to Boston's Harry Staley
FINALE: 8/12/1896 at Boston; played LF and went 0-for-4 in a 6–4 loss to New York's Mike Sullivan
CAREER HIGHLIGHT: 8/7/1894 at Boston; hit a grand slam homer off Philadelphia's Jack Fanning to become the first player in ML history to bang a jackpot dinger in 2 consecutive games

Jimmy Bannon was the brother of ML outfielder Tom Bannon. He received his nickname for tirelessly humming "Foxy Grandpa," a popular vaudeville song of the 1890s. Reports differ on how many brothers he had as well as on how many of them played ball. At most there were ten, at least six of whom played professionally. In any case, Tom was the last to survive. In the early 1890s, after fizzling in the 1891 New England League, Bannon pitched and Tom caught for a third brother John's amateur Thompson Houston & Company Electrics team of Lynn, MA. "Foxy" Bannon came to Boston NL in 1893 after spending the spring with the Holy Cross baseball team and was loaned to St. Louis. When he got 3 hits in his debut with the Browns, he suddenly had the look of a valuable commodity. Yet Bannon played only 26 games with St. Louis despite hitting .336. The Browns may simply have preferred using players they knew were theirs to keep, and when he hurt his ankle they swiftly released him rather than continue to pay him since they knew they were going to lose him anyway.

Bannon finished the summer pitching for a semipro team in Maryland and then re-signed with Boston in November 1893. He opened 1894, his official rookie year, in RF, but by late May, *TSN* was already warning, "Jimmy Bannon is in daily expectation of his release from Boston. He has played poorly all season. . . . As a fielder he is as rank as can be." Bannon continued to skate on thin ice in Boston until August 6, when he belted a grand slam off Washington's Al Maul and then victimized Philadelphia's Jack Fanning with a four-wheeler the following day and later in the same game added another jack against Kid Carsey. Bannon's homer barrage helped him to lead all NL rookies in almost every major batting department in 1894. He followed with another good year as a sophomore. Nevertheless, by August 1895 the local press had begun urging manager Frank Selee to get rid of him for his repeated failures to hit in the clutch, poor fielding, and erratic baserunning. The latter in particular was traceable to Bannon being trapped all year between a Billy Nash clique on the team, to which he belonged, and a Hugh Duffy clique, which made him often try to steal contrary to signs from Duffy on the suspicion that Duffy was trying to deprive him of a good stolen base record. Demoralized, Bannon started poorly in 1896, lost his RF job to Fred Tenney and was cut on August 18.

While Bannon undeniably was an uneven fielder—his career outfield FA was a wretched .877—he was not incompetent. In his official rookie season he led NL outfielders in assists and double plays in addition to errors. Bannon seems as if he might have been a victim of a Boston team that was riddled with dissension during the transition period between its three pennants in the early 1890s and its 1897–98 mini dynasty. During the next few years he starred in the Eastern League, got married, learned to switch hit, and watched as his hair turned "prematurely almost as white as snow." Bannon remained a productive minor league player and sometimes manager through the 1910 season and later coached baseball at Lehigh and the University of New Hampshire before going into the hotel business and serving for a time in the New Hampshire legislature. He died in Paterson, NJ, at 76 after a brief illness. (DN)

Barrett, James Erigena / "Jimmy"

B	T	HGT	WGT	G	AB	H	R	2B
L	R	5'7"	170	163	637	206	144	13

3B	HR	RBI	BB	SO	SB	BA	SA	OBP
11	5	52	90	—	48	.323	.402	.412

B. 3/28/1875 Athol, MA **D.** 10/24/1921 Detroit, MI
TEAMS: 99–00CinN 01–05DetAL 06CinN 07–08BosAL

DEBUT: 9/13/1899 at Washington; played CF and went 2-for-4 in a 14–4 win over Washington's Bill Magee
FINALE: 5/13/1908 at Boston; played CF and went 0-for-5 in a 10–3 loss to Detroit's George Mullin

Raised by uncles after both of his parents died when he was barely of school age, Jimmy Barrett played for an independent team in Brattleboro, VT, in 1897 before making his pro debut with Oswego of the New York State League the following year at SS. Sold to Detroit of the Western League that winter for $200, he came under manager George Stallings, who turned him into an excellent bunter and thought his speed was better suited to CF. Stallings sold Barrett to Cincinnati as the WL season was winding down, and he joined the mass influx of super rookies in 1899 when he hit .370 in the Reds' 26 remaining games and scored 30 runs. The following April, Cincinnati's new manager, Bob Allen, stationed Barrett in RF on Opening Day but soon moved him to CF to take full advantage of his exceptional throwing accuracy. Barrett's forte as a fielder was that he was always in position to throw when he caught a ball and rarely threw to the wrong base. He continued to be just as valuable with a bat in his hand, pacing the Reds in runs, walks, and steals while hitting leadoff. Expected to be Cincinnati's center fielder for years to come, Barrett crushed the hopes of Queen City fans that winter when the AL proclaimed itself a major league and George Stallings was made manager of the Detroit entry in the rebel loop. (DN)

Barrows, Franklin Lee / "Frank"

B	T	HGT	WGT	G	AB	H	R	2B
?	?	?	?	18	86	13	13	2

3B	HR	RBI	BB	SO	SB	BA	SA	OBP
1	0	11	0	0	1	.151	.198	.151

B. 10/22/1846 Hudson, OH **D.** 2/6/1922
TEAMS: 71BosNA
DEBUT: 5/20/1871 at Boston; played 2B and went 1-for-5 in an 11–8 win over the Athletics' Dick McBride
FINALE: 10/7/1871 at Boston; played LF and went 1-for-4 in a 12–3 win over Troy's John McMullin

The son of a clergyman and a teacher, Frank Barrows was born in Ohio and educated at Phillips Academy in Exeter, MA, where his father was on the faculty. In the late 1860s he was living in Boston and playing 2B for the Trimountains, a club that had introduced the codified modern rules of baseball from New York to New England about a decade earlier. When Boston's first professional team was organized in 1871, Barrows was signed, perhaps to add a native touch to a roster otherwise composed of mercenary professionals who had never lived or played in Boston. However, Barrows proved to be unready for a pro league. He occupied LF for much of the initial NA season and was an important factor in the Hub team's failure to capture the pennant. His BA was around 160 points below the team average and he scored the fewest runs of any of the eleven club members.

Barrows was not invited to return in 1872 after Boston signed Andy Leonard to play LF. He is not known to have played professionally again, yet he remained a familiar enough figure on the Boston baseball scene that in 1897 he was included on an old-timers' team that featured such famous names as Al Spalding, John Morrill, Tommy Bond, George Wright, and Leonard. He married late in life and died in Fitchburg, MA, in 1922. (DB/DN)

Barry, John C. / "Shad"

B	T	HGT	WGT	G	AB	H	R	2B
R	R	?	?	159	501	137	71	17

3B	HR	RBI	BB	SO	SB	BA	SA	OBP
12	2	70	25	—	20	.273	.367	.315

B. 10/27/1878 Newburgh, NY **D.** 11/27/1936
TEAMS: 99WasN 00–01BosN 01–04PhiN 04–05ChiN 05–06CinN 06–08StLN 08NYN
DEBUT: 05/30/1899 at Washington; played LF and went 1-for-3 in a 4–3 loss to Pittsburgh's Jesse Tannehill
FINALE: 10/7/1908 at New York; replaced Mike Donlin in RF in a 7–2 win over Boston's Al Mattern and Bill Chappelle

Even though Shad Barry played ten years in the majors, he remained so nearly a cipher that none of the media ever mentioned his height or weight, let alone anything of much interest about his personal life. Barry grew up in upstate New York and at 19 was already about to graduate from Niagara College when he led Montreal of the Eastern League in batting in 1898 after being "goldbricked away from Buffalo" in a trade for infielder Frank Shannon. Needing extra money to start law school, he refused to report the following spring when he disliked Montreal's offer. In late May 1899 Barry was sold to Washington and hit .287 for the Senators as a rookie, playing six different positions. Barry had a similar kind of year with Boston in 1900. Only twice during his career was he a full-time regular at a set position. In 1902 he played 130 games in RF for the Phillies, and three years later he was in 150 games at 1B while splitting the season between Chicago and Cincinnati.

After ending his pro career in the 1913 New York State League, during World War I Barry ran baseball programs for the American Expeditionary Forces. He then worked as a bank security officer in Los Angeles, where he died at 58 of prostate cancer. The source of Barry's nickname is unknown. (DN)

Bass, John Elias / "John"

B	T	HGT	WGT	G	AB	H	R	2B
?	?	5'6"	150	25	100	29	19	2

3B	HR	RBI	BB	SO	SB	BA	SA	OBP
10	3	19	3	4	0	.290	.600	.311

B. ?/?/1848 Charleston, MD **D.** 9/25/1888
TEAMS: 71CleNA 72AtlNA 77HarN
DEBUT: 5/4/1871 at Fort Wayne; played SS and went 0-for-3 in a 2–0 loss to Fort Wayne's Bobby Mathews
FINALE: 8/20/1877 at Brooklyn; played LF and went 1-for-4 in a 5–1 win over Louisville's Jim Devlin

A Civil War veteran, John Bass played in the first ML game, led the NA in triples in its initial season, and fell just one four-bagger short of tying for the home run crown. Moreover, his .640 SA was third in the loop. Prior to joining the 1871 Forest Citys, Bass had played SS for the Unions of Morrisania. We do not know why he played just 2 more games in the NA or how he came to play 1 NL game for Hartford in 1877. At that time, he appears to have been living in Brooklyn and playing semipro ball there. In 1883 Bass served as a substitute umpire in the AA until he resigned in early May. Five years later he became the first former MLer to die in the state of Colorado. Until recently his grave in Denver's Riverside Cemetery was unmarked. (DN/EM)

Beals, Thomas Lamb
(aka W. Thomas 1871–73) **/ "Tommy"**

B	T	HGT	WGT	G	AB	H	R	2B
R	?	5'5"	144	123	539	131	109	15

3B	HR	RBI	BB	SO	SB	BA	SA	OBP
16	0	66	8	11	4	.243	.330	.254

B. 8/?/1850 New York, NY **D.** 10/2/1915
TEAMS: 71–72OlyNA 73WasNA 74–75BosNA 80ChiN
DEBUT: 7/27/1871 at Troy; played LF and went 0-for-3 in a 3–3 tie against Troy's John McMullin
FINALE: 9/29/1880 at Chicago; played RF and went 1-for-4 in a 19–10 loss to Buffalo's Jim Galvin and Stump Wiedman

Judging by the sketchy surviving evidence, a lively story must have gone untold when Tommy Beals and his adventurous family passed from the scene without leaving an account of their lives. Connecticut native Albert J. Beals began operating a daguerreotyping business in New York City in 1846 and was a prizewinner in competitions with the likes of the famous Matthew Brady. Yet by the middle of the decade Albert had packed his family off to the rugged and remote frontier, settling in the mining boomtown of Silver City, where he operated the New York Photographic Gallery and did dental work on the side.

Around 1870 Albert's son Tommy returned to New York. What impelled him to travel back to his native city is unknown; at that early date, he is not likely to have come just to play pro baseball, but he nonetheless became perhaps the first of what would become a stream of players to leave the far west to play in the east. After playing in the New York area, Beals joined the Washington Olympics in July 1871. For reasons now unknown he appeared in box scores under the assumed name of "Thomas," but his teammates appeared to be in on his secret, as did other teams when he umpired NA games on occasion.

Beals continued to play as Thomas as late as October 1873. One of the better players on a series of dreary Washington teams, he was a little-noted substitute on a Boston club in the midst of a four-year championship run. Beals still seems to have made an impact on his teammates, for in 1879 George Wright, Boston's star SS, named his first son Beals in honor of his former teammate. Wright retained his regard for Beals in spite of the fact that in 1876 Beals had jumped the last year of a long-term contract with Boston to play for independent Cambridge, MA.

He then returned to Silver City and worked as a store clerk while continuing to play ball in the California League. We do not know how he came to join Chicago NL in 1880, but Albert Spalding, one of his Boston teammates, was a leading figure in the White Stockings organization. Nothing came of early-season talk that Boston might protest his playing for Chicago after failing to honor his contract in 1876. Disputing his services would have been pointless, for at that point in his career they were worth little. He sat on the Chicago bench until August and then began to play more often but performed poorly. At season's end he returned to Silver City, married Emma MacGregor, and fathered a son the following July. In 1894 Emma died, and by 1900 Beals was in San Francisco, living with a son and his widowed mother and following his father's trade as a photographer, probably unsuccessfully, for he later worked as a train conductor. He died in San Francisco at 65. (DB/DN)

Beaumont, Clarence Howeth / "Ginger" "Butch"

B	T	HGT	WGT	G	AB	H	R	2B
L	R	5'8"	190	249	1004	312	195	29

3B	HR	RBI	BB	SO	SB	BA	SA	OBP
17	8	88	81	—	58	.311	.397	.369

B. 7/23/1876 Rochester, WI
D. 4/10/1956 Burlington, WI
TEAMS: 99–06PitN 07–09BosN 10ChiN
DEBUT: 4/21/1899 at St. Louis; played 1B and went 1-for-4 in a 6–5 loss to St. Louis's Jack Powell
FINALE: 10/5/1910 at Cincinnati; played CF and went 0-for-2 in a 3–2 win over Cincinnati's Jack Rowan
CAREER HIGHLIGHT: 7/22/1899 at Pittsburgh; went 6-for-6 and scored 6 runs in an 18–4 win over Philadelphia's Wiley Piatt

In his rookie year with the 1899 Pirates, the 5'8" Ginger Beaumont debuted at 1B, used a fifty-five-ounce bat, usually batted down in the order, and was nicknamed "Butch," a carryover from his days at Beloit College. He would soon take over Pittsburgh's CF post, adopt a lighter bat, be called "Ginger," and become one the best lead-off hitters in the game, but he would never again equal the .860 OPS he achieved as a freshman. Beaumont was primarily a catcher until he joined Connie Mack's Milwaukee club in 1898 when the Western League season was nearly over. Moved to the outfield, he hit .354 in Milwaukee's 24 remaining games and in October was sold to Louisville along with teammate Irv Waldron. *TSN* cynically noted that it was a phony deal Mack had staged so as to keep both outfielders in 1899, but the paper was only partially right. The following month, at the urging of manager Bill Watkins, who had spotted Beaumont while on a late-season scouting trip to the Midwest, Pittsburgh acquired the novice outfielder for third baseman Bill Gray, pitcher Bill Hart, and cash. Beaumont began 1899 on the bench, as Watkins preferred to bring him along slowly, but when Patsy Donovan replaced Watkins at the helm in May, he installed the rookie in CF ahead of incumbent Tom McCreery. Only McCreery was angered by the change, as Beaumont finished the season second on the team in BA and SA only to fellow rookie Jimmy Williams.

The following season Fred Clarke took the Pittsburgh reins after the Pirates were the beneficiaries of most of the folding Louisville franchise's top players. Too smart to tamper with one of the few areas on the Pirates that had been successful in 1899, he left Beaumont in CF and moved him permanently into the lead-off spot. But the sophomore jinx claimed Beloit College's first major leaguer with a vengeance, shaving 73 points off his BA. Beaumont's precipitous decline had a large hand in Pittsburgh's failure to claim the 1900 NL pennant, but he would rebound the following year to help lead the Pirates to their first of three straight flags. (DN)

Beecher, Edward Harry / "Ed" "Harry"

B	T	HGT	WGT	G	AB	H	R	2B
L	L	5'10"	185	283	1190	325	148	52

3B	HR	RBI	BB	SO	SB	BA	SA	OBP
17	7	177	71	48	19	.273	.363	.322

G	IP	H	GS	CG	BB
1	6	10	0	0	3

SO	SH	W	L	PCT	ERA
0	0	0	0	—	12.00

B. 7/2/1860 Guilford, CT **D.** 9/12/1935

TEAMS: 87PitN 89WasN 90BufP 91WasA 91PhiA
DEBUT: 6/28/1887 at Pittsburgh; played CF and went 1-for-4 in a 8–0 win over Washington's Hank O'Day
FINALE: 7/16/1891 at Philadelphia; played RF and went 0-for-4 in a 7–6 win over Columbus's John Dolan

Ed Beecher was an avid bicycle rider who kept in fantastic shape, owned a strong arm, hit well almost everywhere he went, and does not appear to have been a discipline problem—in fact he worked as a police officer in the off-season. Yet he failed to excel in any of his five ML stops. By 1887, Beecher, then in his fifth pro season, was with Hartford and leading the Eastern League in hitting when he was sold to Pittsburgh NL. But after scoring just 15 runs in 41 games, he was cut and went to Wilkes-Barre, where he stayed until he was peddled to Washington along with third baseman John Irwin in July 1889. Beecher performed well enough with the Senators to be part of the Washington contingent that joined the Buffalo PL entry in 1890. In his only full season in the majors, the lefty-swinging redhead led the Bisons in hits and total bases but scored just 69 runs despite batting in the middle of the order. After the PL disbanded, Beecher and several other Bisons were awarded to Pittsburgh, but *TSN* reported on December 17, 1890, "Pittsburg [*sic*] doesn't want the sunset-haired ex-senator who pawed the ground as a Bison last season." Beecher then opened 1891 in LF with Washington AA and was regarded as a decent hitter but a trifle slow in the field. On June 27 he was released when he became the odd man out after Paul Hines was moved from 1B to the outfield but found a new home in RF with the Philadelphia A's. A month later Beecher was cut after being confined to his hotel room for some 10 days with "inflammatory rheumatism." Beecher went home to Hartford, his residence at the time, and played only one more full pro season, in the 1892 Eastern League, before retiring to become a full-time police officer in Hartford. In 1897 he was given a leave of absence from the force to umpire in the Atlantic League, but he soon gave up officiating and returned to police work. Beecher died at 75 after a long illness. (DN/DB)

Birchall, Adoniram Judson / "Jud"

B	T	HGT	WGT	G	AB	H	R	2B
?	?	?	?	225	1007	254	196	24

3B	HR	RBI	BB	SO	SB	BA	SA	OBP
4	1	51	32	—	—	.252	.287	.279

B. 9/12/1855 Philadelphia, PA **D.** 12/22/1887
TEAMS: 82–84PhiA
DEBUT: 5/2/1882 at Philadelphia; played LF and went 2-for-5 in a 10–7 win over Baltimore's Tricky Nichols
FINALE: 10/10/1884 at Philadelphia; played 3B and went 2-for-5 in a 9–1 win over Baltimore's Bob Emslie

The tenth of fifteen children spawned by an English father and a German mother, Jud Birchall was a fine fielder and an excellent base runner. His batting left much to be desired but might have passed muster if he had learned to be more patient at the plate. Birchall owns one of the lowest OPS figures in ML history (.566) among outfielders with a minimum of 1,000 career ABs. A longtime fixture on the Philadelphia semipro scene, chiefly as a second baseman with clubs in suburban Germantown, Birchall might never have made the majors if he had not been on the Eastern Championship Association 1881 Athletics club that was among the original entrants when the AA formed over that winter. He showed his extraordinary baserunning dexterity in a 4-game series against St. Louis in August 1882, when he tallied a phenomenal 9 runs despite going hitless. After batting .263 as a rookie, Birchall dropped to .241 the following year but nonetheless scored 95 runs after reaching base via hits and walks only 128 times. When the A's won the 1883 AA pennant, Birchall's lowly BA was forgiven and he even opened the 1884 campaign batting leadoff. But by midseason he had dropped to seventh in the order and later in the year batted last in several games.

When the A's let Birchall go following the 1884 season, he married over the winter and spent 1885 with Newark of the Eastern League but was cut once the schedule ended. His final competitive game may have been on September 23, when he played CF for the Orange Athletic Club of New Jersey behind Amos Alonzo Stagg in a 12–3 loss to the Young America team of Philadelphia. Birchall was probably already suffering from consumption by then. Upon his death two years later, only Charlie Mason and Cub Stricker from his former ML team attended his funeral. (DN)

Birdsall, David Solomon / "Dave"

B	T	HGT	WGT	G	AB	H	R	2B
R	R	5'9"	126	48	239	63	66	6

3B	HR	RBI	BB	SO	SB	BA	SA	OBP
3	0	39	7	4	7	.264	.314	.285

B. 7/16/1838 New York, NY **D.** 12/30/1896
TEAMS: 71–73BosNA
DEBUT: 5/5/1871 at Washington; played RF and went 2-for-6 in a 20–18 win over the Olympics' Asa Brainard
FINALE: 5/17/1873 at Boston; played LF and RF and went 0-for-3 in an 11–10 loss to the Brooklyn Atlantics' Jim Britt

Snappish and tough as nails, Dave Birdsall played with several New York area clubs in the 1860s, including the Morrisanias. Already nearing 33 when the NA was formed, he joined Boston and served as the Hub entry's right fielder in 1871. Too light a hitter to remain a regular gardener, he was too frail to catch faster pitching. After spending 1872 as both a substitute catcher and outfielder, Birdsall returned in 1873 only long enough to play 3 games in RF. In his later years he worked in Boston billiard rooms and was a member of the Elks club. He died in 1896 of complications from a surgery performed earlier in the year at the Boston boarding house where he had resided the last twenty years of his life. Birdsall's obit in the *Washington Post* said, "He retired after 1872 [*sic*], not being strong enough to face the more speedy pitching that came into vogue." The only former Boston teammates at his funeral were Harry Shafer and Jack Manning. (DN)

Blake, Harry Cooper / "Harry"

B	T	HGT	WGT	G	AB	H	R	2B
R	R	5'7"	165	527	1880	474	299	67

3B	HR	RBI	BB	SO	SB	BA	SA	OBP
22	8	253	231	85	55	.252	.324	.336

B. 6/16/1874 Portsmouth, OH **D.** 10/14/1919
TEAMS: 94–98CleN 99StLN
DEBUT: 7/7/1894 at Cleveland; played CF and went 2-for-5 in a 16–10 loss to Boston's Kid Nichols
FINALE: 10/9/1899 at St. Louis; replaced Mike Donlin in CF late in a 6–4 win over Cincinnati's Ted Breitenstein

Harry Blake had an exceptional arm; in August 1896 *TSN* said his throws went straight as a bullet with no elevation. He worked winters as a cashier at his father's Portsmouth butcher shop and was popular with teammates, good-natured, unassuming, and not only an excellent fielder but also smart—if only he could have hit. In 1898, Blake gave up cigarettes when Tommy McCarthy told him they impaired his vision. He then tied for the Cleveland team lead in walks but otherwise remained an unbearable liability at the plate. Among all outfielders with a minimum of 2,000 PAs in the 1893–1900 era, Blake's .660 OPS is the lowest, save for his teammate Jimmy McAleer's .638, explaining why Cleveland had so much trouble winning a pennant in that period.

Blake left Portsmouth in 1892 to play for an independent team in nearby Ironton. Two years later he began the season with Atlanta, and when the Southern League did its annual swoon he was summoned to Cleveland as an injury replacement for center fielder McAleer. When McAleer returned to the lineup, Blake moved to RF and made it his province until 1899, if only by default. Each spring he began the season on the bench while the Spiders sought a better hitter, but after a few weeks he was invariably back in the lineup. Blake also had the ignominious experience of being farmed twice, in 1896 and again in 1897, after he felt he was an established veteran. The 1898 campaign was the only one in which he collected as many as 400 ABs, but any hope that cigarettes were his bane evaporated when he hit .245.

Blake opened 1899 in CF for St. Louis after syndicate ownership relocated most of Cleveland's better players there but permanently lost his spot when Mike Donlin joined the team. On August 30 he caught a game in an emergency and did such a fine job for someone who had never before caught in the majors that it is a puzzle why he was never tried there again. St. Louis reserved him for 1900, but he was released in spring training and spent the season in the Eastern League. Blake finished his career in 1910 as player-manager of Portsmouth in the Ohio State League. He died in Chicago in 1919 when flames cut off his stairway escape route in a rooming-house fire. (DN)

Blakiston, Robert J. / "Bob"

B	T	HGT	WGT	G	AB	H	R	2B
?	?	5'8½"	180	154	594	142	87	14

3B	HR	RBI	BB	SO	SB	BA	SA	OBP
4	0	46	30	—	—	.239	.276	.280

B. 10/2/1855 San Francisco, CA **D.** 12/25/1918
TEAMS: 82–84PhiA 84IndA
DEBUT: 5/2/1882 at Philadelphia; played 3B and went 1-for-4 in a 10–7 win over Baltimore's Tricky Nichols
FINALE: 10/15/1884 at New York; played 1B and went 0-for-2 in an 18–2 loss to New York's Buck Becannon

Before coming east Bob Blakiston played for a variety of clubs in the San Francisco Bay Area beginning in 1878. Equally at home in the infield or the outfield, he survived for three full ML seasons despite never hitting enough to land a regular job. In 1884, Blakiston's final campaign, he rode the A's bench for most of the season until Indianapolis first sacker Jack Kerins was hurt on a visit to Philadelphia in early October and the A's gave the Hoosiers Blakiston as an injury replacement.

After being released by Newark in July 1885, purportedly because his salary was too high for the Eastern League club's limited budget, Blakiston announced he "was sick of the East" and would return to California. Instead he finished the season with Chattanooga of the Southern League. He then began 1886 in the California League, but he again was visited by a yearning to give eastern ball one more whirl with Rochester of the International Association. Past 30 by then, Blakiston finally reconciled himself to remaining in his native California. In 1887, with the Greenhood & Morans of Oakland, he was part of an outfield for a time that also numbered Dan Long and, on days when he didn't pitch, George Van Haltren. Blakiston later worked as a janitor prior to his death in San Francisco from tuberculosis. (DN)

Booth, Edward H. / "Eddie"

B	T	HGT	WGT	G	AB	H	R	2B
?	?	?	?	242	1016	244	129	23

3B	HR	RBI	BB	SO	SB	BA	SA	OBP
13	1	76	7	11	4	.239	.293	.244

G	IP	H	GS	CG	BB
1	5	16	0	0	0

SO	SH	W	L	PCT	ERA
0	0	0	0	—	10.80

B. ?/?/? Brooklyn, NY **D.** Unknown
TEAMS: 72ManNA 72AtlNA 73ResNA 73–74AtlNA 75MutNA 76NYN
DEBUT: 4/26/1872 at Troy; played 2B and went 2-for-4 in a 10–0 loss to Troy's George Zettlein
FINALE: 10/17/1876 at New York; played RF and went 0-for-3 in a 3–0 loss to Hartford's Candy Cummings

Eddie Booth was a multipurpose fielder but a weak hitter. He continued to play after the Mutuals were ousted from the NL in the aftermath of the 1876 season; his last confirmed sighting was in 1877 with Columbus of the International Association. Surprisingly little is known about Booth considering the length of his career and his connection for most of it with well-known teams in the New York area. There is speculation that he died in New York on December 21, 1928, but no definite proof exists as yet. (DN)

Boyd, William J. / "Bill"

B	T	HGT	WGT	G	AB	H	R	2B
?	?	?	?	147	666	192	94	30

3B	HR	RBI	BB	SO	SB	BA	SA	OBP
9	3	91	11	14	7	.288	.374	.299

G	IP	H	GS	CG	BB
1	1.2	4	0	0	0

SO	SH	W	L	PCT	ERA
0	0	0	0	—	0.00

G	W	L	PCT	PENNANTS
2	0	2	.000	0

B. 12/22/1852 New York, NY **D.** 9/30/1912
TEAMS: 72MutNA 73AtlNA 74HarNA (P/M)75AtlNA
DEBUT: 4/22/1872 at Baltimore; played 3B and went 0-for-4 in a 14–8 loss to Baltimore's Cherokee Fisher

FINALE: 10/9/1875 at Brooklyn; played 3B and made 2 hits in a 20–7 loss to Hartford's Tommy Bond

Bill Boyd had a strong arm and was a capable hitter but emerged from his four ML seasons as a near nonentity in part because he played for poor teams after his initial season. He also does not appear to have been committed wholeheartedly to playing ball. In 1874 Boyd was hitting .350 for Hartford after its game in Brooklyn against New York on July 25 when he decided to remain in Brooklyn and work for the fire department rather than return to Connecticut. His .350 BA that year was somewhat undermined by his .664 FA at 3B. By the following season Boyd was torn between umpiring and playing, officiating in 20 NA contests while participating in 36 with the Brooklyn Atlantics.

Boyd's weight is unknown, but by August 1884 the *New York Times* reported, "The portly 'Billy' Boyd, who tips the scales at 250 pounds, played with his old time vigor" in a benefit game. He died in Jamaica, NY, at 59. (DN)

Brady, Stephen A. / "Steve"

B	T	HGT	WGT	G	AB	H	R	2B
?	?	5'9½"	165	490	2030	529	313	50

3B	HR	RBI	BB	SO	SB	BA	SA	OBP
20	4	114	94	15	22	.261	.311	.296

B. 7/14/1851 Worcester, MA **D.** 11/1/1917
TEAMS: 74–75HarNA 75WasNA 83–86NYA
DEBUT: 7/23/1874 at Brooklyn; played RF and went 1-for-4 in a 13–5 loss to New York's Bobby Mathews
FINALE: 10/5/1886 at Cincinnati; played RF and went hitless in a 4–3 loss to Cincinnati's Tony Mullane

Steve Brady moved from Worcester to Hartford when very young. He was fast, had a big chin and narrow eyes, and led by example, but he did not really begin to make his mark until he was in his midtwenties. Brady's local reputation earned him a walk-on role for Hartford NA in an exhibition game hosting independent Bristol, RI, on July 22, 1874. An all-around athlete, he played at four positions for the rest of the year and hit well. Slated for a backup role again with Hartford in 1875, he was recommended to the visiting Washington Nationals on May 10 as "a heavy batter, good runner, and a pretty sure catch."

After a dismal .137 season with Washington in 1875 followed his fine .314 rookie showing the previous year, Brady descended to the minors. In 1876 he led the wobbly New England League with a .373 average, batting leadoff for Billy Arnold's Providence club. Brady then led off for and captained the International Association Rochester Hop Bitters in 1877 and played for Arnold again with Springfield IA in 1878. Worcester became his next port of call in 1879 when he led off for Jim Mutrie's National Association club.

Brady captained the Hop Bitters again in 1880. Around Labor Day, Rochester left Washington for points north when its train was apparently detained at Jersey City by Mutrie, who was looking for players for a new independent team in New York called the Metropolitans. Five Rochesters got off the train, including Brady and one-armed pitcher Hugh Daily. On September 29, when the Polo Grounds opened for baseball, Brady was the first batter to step up to the plate. He captained Mutrie's Mets until they joined the AA in 1883. On June 17 of that year, in keeping with the new vogue for team captains to be loud and boisterous, catcher Bill Holbert replaced Brady as captain. But he remained the de facto sergeant at arms of the Mets, backing up the regular captains from his RF post while appearing in at least 400 consecutive games, including the first AA versus NL World's Series in 1884. In the spring of 1886, Brady, now in his midthirties, made the mistake of reporting to training camp overweight and never really got untracked. He begged out of the lineup during the Mets' last road trip of the season. At 34, he was the third oldest regular in the AA. Brady captained the Eastern League Hartfords in 1887 until they disbanded and then filled in at 1B for the Jersey City team. When the Mets reformed as an independent team in 1889, he captained them once again. He also was part owner of an ice skating rink in Brooklyn, where he promoted the infant sport of ice hockey.

Brady later returned to Connecticut and married May Begley in New Britain in 1892. After leaving the sporting arena, he opened Brady Brothers, a soda and mineral water producer in Hartford with his brothers, Ed and Thomas. Brady died in Hartford in 1917 in the same house on Ward Street where he was raised as a boy. Despite being a high-profile player and enjoying a lengthy career in the game, Brady is the only remaining multiple-ML loop leader in games played whose choices of batting and throwing sides are still unknown. (DN/FV)

Brodie, Walter Scott / "Steve"

B	T	HGT	WGT	G	AB	H	R	2B
L	R	5'11"	180	1245	4977	1515	808	177

3B	HR	RBI	BB	SO	SB	BA	SA	OBP
81	20	817	373	148	269	.304	.384	.353

B. 9/11/1868 Warrenton, VA **D.** 10/30/1935
TEAMS: 90–91BosN 92–93StLN 93–96BalN 97–98PitN 98–99BalN 01BalAL 02NYN
DEBUT: 4/21/1890 at Boston; played RF and went 2-for-3 in a 7–6 loss to Brooklyn's Mickey Hughes
FINALE: 10/4/1902 at New York; played CF and went 1-for-2 in a 5–1 win over Boston's Vic Willis
CAREER HIGHLIGHT ONE: 6/26/1897 at Pittsburgh played in his 574th consecutive game in a 5–3 win over Philadelphia's Kid Carsey; in Pittsburgh's next game two days later a sore arm kept him out of the lineup, ending his streak just 3 games short of George Pinkney's then record 577
CAREER HIGHLIGHT TWO: Brodie's .956 FA ranks first among all nineteenth-century outfielders in a minimum of 1,000 games

Named after Sir Walter Scott and nicknamed after Steve Brodie, the bookmaker who allegedly jumped off the Brooklyn Bridge in 1886, Walter Brodie was something of a showman in his own right. He liked to treat the crowd in pregame warmups to sensational long throws—some fans even came out early just to watch him—until he began experiencing arm trouble in 1897. Born in the Shenandoah Valley as the son of a Scottish immigrant, Brodie played with the local Warrenton, VA, nine in 1884 and then moved with his family to Roanoke and performed in area industrial leagues until he joined Altoona of the Pennsylvania Association in 1887. A catcher until then, he gravitated to the outfield so that both his bat and his rifle arm could be utilized on a daily basis.

Two years later Brodie nabbed the Boston NL club's eye by hitting .302 for Hamilton of the International Association. Manager Frank Selee held him out of the Beaneaters' opening game in 1890 to assuage his nervousness, but after that the rookie appeared in every game but one and topped NL outfielders with a .953 FA. Moved to CF the following year, Brodie began earning a rep as an eccentric and something of a bonehead. Hugh Duffy's arrival in 1892 made him expendable, and he was reassigned to St. Louis in the NL-AA consolidation that winter. Unlike most of the unhappy refugees with weak teams, Brodie hustled and played well, and it did not go unnoticed. The following season, when the Browns' new manager, Bill Watkins, complained that his center fielder was a stupid base runner and not a "winning" player, Baltimore raced to the nearest telegraph office with an offer to purchase him for somewhere between $800 and $2,000. Brodie's acquisition allowed Orioles manager Ned Hanlon to move Joe Kelley to LF, his stronger position, and gave the club the final outfield component it needed to snare three straight pennants in 1894–96. The move also elevated Brodie to near star status. In three plus seasons with the Orioles, he hit a composite .340; for the rest of his career he batted just .287. Perhaps more so than any other member of the Orioles dynasty, Brodie exemplified how much a hitter's performance could be impacted when he was surrounded in the batting order by such as Kelley, Hughie Jennings, John McGraw, and Willie Keeler. At the same time, it must be said that Brodie's bat impacted positively on all of them as well.

On November 11, 1896, Hanlon seized a chance to trade Brodie at a good price, sending him to Pittsburgh in a six-player deal that brought the Orioles center fielder Jake Stenzel. After his consecutive games streak ended on June 26 at 564, he missed considerable time and finished with just 47 runs. Piqued over how badly they were stung in the trade for Brodie, the Pirates listened to their new manager, Bill Watkins (who hadn't liked Brodie in St. Louis and liked him even less now with a bad arm) and tried to farm him to the minors in June 1898. Then, when Baltimore protested that he had not cleared waivers, Watkins released him on June 11 and the Orioles reacquired him.

Brodie revived in Baltimore but not enough to survive the squeeze when the NL shrank to just eight teams after the 1899 season. He served a year in the minors in 1900 with Chicago of the newly renamed AL, hitting just .262 in 64 games, and then was turned over for free to the fledgling Baltimore AL franchise in 1901. Still mending from a broken leg, Brodie was unable to join the Orioles until late June and by the end of the year was said by Baltimore writer Frank Patterson to have "fallen by the wayside" again after losing his job as manager of the bowling alleys owned by John McGraw and Wilbert Robinson. Brodie returned to the NL with the Giants in 1902 and reunited with McGraw after the latter jumped Baltimore to manage the New York club. When he was not invited by McGraw to return, he played and managed in the minors until 1910. Two years later Brodie was named head baseball coach at Rutgers. He moved to the U.S. Naval Academy in the same capacity in 1914 and remained until 1922. Brodie was then a city parks department supervisor in Baltimore until his death from heart disease in 1935. (DN)

Brown, Thomas Tarlton / "Tom"

B	T	HGT	WGT	G	AB	H	R	2B
L	R	5'10"	168	1788	7373	1954	1523	239

3B	HR	RBI	BB	SO	SB	BA	SA	OBP
138	64	736	748	709	657	.265	.361	.336

G	IP	H	GS	CG	BB
12	49.1	56	1	1	31

SO	SH	W	L	PCT	ERA
16	0	2	2	.500	5.29

G	W	L	PCT	PENNANTS
137	64	72	.471	0

B. 9/21/1860 Liverpool, England **D.** 10/25/1927
TEAMS: 82BalA 83–84ColA 85–86PitA 87PitN 87IndN 88–89BosN 90BosP 91BosA 92–94LouN 95StLN (P/M)97–98WasN
DEBUT: 7/6/1882 at Pittsburgh; played RF and went 4-for-5 in a 9–8 win over Pittsburgh's Harry Arundel
FINALE: 5/17/1898 at New York; played CF and went 0-for-4 in a 9–3 loss to New York's Amos Rusie
CAREER HIGHLIGHT: 6/25/1891 at Boston; in Boston's 13–5 win over Baltimore's Sadie McMahon and Enoch Bakely, Brown and Bill Joyce became the first teammate duo in history to hit back-to-back home runs leading off a game, and Curt Welch also led off for Baltimore with a home run, marking only the second time in ML history that players on both teams led off with four-baggers

Tom Brown was equivalent to nineteenth-century baseball's little girl with a curl in the middle of her forehead. When he was on his game he was terrific, with an AOPS of 138 prior to 1887. When he was not, which was all too often after that, he could be just awful. Among all players in ML history who made less than 2,000 hits, Brown ranks first in runs (1,521) despite carrying a mere .265 career BA. He also topped nineteenth-century ML outfielders in assists and double plays and was second only to Mike Griffin in put-outs. Unhappily, Brown also ranks first among nineteenth-century players in documented career strikeouts with 708, and in back-to-back seasons he posted two of the worst three BAs (.227 and .240) in the twelve-team NL (1892–99) among outfielders with a minimum of 500 ABs.

In 1901 Buck Ewing said the reason Brown failed to develop into the offensive player he ought to have been was because he never learned how to bunt, but there were other reasons as well. In 1887, the first season the high-low rule was no longer in effect, Brown slipped to .217 when he was put at the mercy of pitchers who knew he could not hit low pitches. He remained a weak hitter for the rest of the decade but was still a valued commodity for his fielding and baserunning. In 1889 he set an all-time record for the most thefts in less than 400 ABs when he swiped 63 bases for Boston and, even more astonishingly, scored 93 runs in just 90 games despite hitting a paltry .232.

Brown emigrated from England to California as a boy and learned the game on the San Francisco sandlots and later in Reno, NV, while working as a gold beater. In the winter of 1881–82 he played RF for the barnstorming Providence NL team in several postseason exhibitions and followed John M. Ward east from California the following spring, hoping to make the Grays. Despite being cut, he remained in the East playing semipro ball until the fledgling Baltimore AA team hired him in July 1882. By the end of the AA's inaugural campaign, Brown was the Orioles' best player but wisely escaped to the Columbus expansion entry that winter. He moved to Pittsburgh in 1885 when the Allegheny club acquired the core players of disbanding Columbus and remained among the top outfielders in the game until Pittsburgh released him in August 1887, when he no longer wanted to play there and the feeling was mutual. Brown then joined Indianapolis NL but only long enough to hit .179 in 36 games before being left unreserved. He signed with Boston NL in 1888 and jumped to the Hub PL entry in 1890. Playing on his first pennant winner, he scored 146 runs despite hitting .274, some 8 points below the team average, and that fall owned just a .260 career BA. But then, in 1891, Brown enjoyed a season that enabled him to feast off it for the rest of his career. Remaining with the Boston PL champs when they moved almost intact to the AA, he tallied a then ML-season-record 177 runs and also led the loop in triples, hits, and steals.

When the NL and AA consolidated that winter, Brown was assigned to Louisville and remained on poor teams for the rest of his career, no doubt accounting for some of his decline. During the 1897 season he was appointed Washington's player-manager and continued in that role until he left the club the following June. That July 4, he was named temporarily to the NL umpiring staff, marking him one of the rare performers to play, manage, and officiate in the majors in the same season. Brown returned as an NL arbiter during the 1901 campaign and remained in blue through 1902 before retiring to the cigar store he owned in Washington. A magnificent storyteller with a more trustworthy memory than most players of his era, he was frequently sought by the local press for his views and reminiscences on the game. Brown died at the Washington Tuberculosis Hospital at 67. (DN/DB)

Burch, Earnest A. / "Ernie"

B	T	HGT	WGT	G	AB	H	R	2B
L	?	5'10"	190	194	768	200	134	30

3B	HR	RBI	BB	SO	SB	BA	SA	OBP
10	4	105	73	24	31	.260	.341	.328

B. 9/9/1856 Dekalb County, IL **D.** 10/12/1892
TEAMS: 84CleN 86–87BroA
DEBUT: 8/15/1884 at Providence; played LF and went 0-for-4 in a 3–2 loss to Providence's Charley Radbourn
FINALE: 7/10/1887 at Louisville; played LF and went 0-for-4 in a 14–7 loss to Louisville's Elton Chamberlin

Ernie Burch joined independent Omaha in 1883 and moved soon afterward to Peoria of the Northwestern League. He reputedly collected 5 doubles in his first 5 at-bats with his new team and remained with Peoria in 1884 until Cleveland NL acquired him. In 1885 Burch spent most of the season with Washington of the Eastern League and was reportedly ticketed for Denver in 1886 before Brooklyn won an angry squabble with the New York Mets for the rights to him. Burch was Brooklyn's left fielder in 1886, and he held the job until July 1887 when Ed Greer replaced him even though he was among the team's top hitters at the time. Brooklyn owner Charlie Byrne later explained that Burch had been released because he had invested all his money in farmland in the Dakota Territory and his mind was on his property rather than on baseball. Other team observers took a different view, accusing Burch of being "utterly without ambition, energy or pride in his work . . . a good player who went to seed through sheer laziness. It was a question half of the time if he was not asleep standing in the field." The unforgiving critique was all the more peculiar in that Burch was not a drinker.

After playing for the Western Association St. Louis Whites in 1888 and hitting .196 in 36 games, Burch did indeed quit the game to work his ranch. Apparently the enterprise failed, however, for he was back in baseball with Peoria of the Illinois-Iowa League by 1890. Burch played briefly again with Peoria in 1891 but by the end of the season was living in Red Rock, OK, without an engagement. The following October he died at 36 in Guthrie, OK. (DN/DB)

Burke, Edward D. / "Eddie"

B	T	HGT	WGT	G	AB	H	R	2B
L	R	5'6"	161	855	3516	983	747	142

3B	HR	RBI	BB	SO	SB	BA	SA	OBP
57	30	410	319	228	293	.280	.378	.352

B. 10/6/1866 Northumberland, PA **D.** 11/26/1907
TEAMS: 90PhiN 90PitN 91MilA 92CinN 92–95NYN 95–97CinN
DEBUT: 4/19/1890 at New York; played CF and went 1-for-4 in a 4–0 win over New York's Amos Rusie
FINALE: 9/19/1897 at Cincinnati; played RF and went 0-for-4 in a 5–4 win over St. Louis's Willie Sudhoff

Eddie Burke made his pro debut as a catcher in 1886 with Scranton of the Pennsylvania State Association. By 1888 he had switched to the outfield and advanced to Toronto of the International Association. Despite hitting just .237, he led the loop in steals with 107. The following year Burke hiked his BA to .315 and was acquired by Philadelphia NL. He was on his way to a solid rookie year in

1890 when Phillies manager Harry Wright traded him, pitcher Bill Day, and $1,100 to Pittsburgh for Billy Sunday in late August. It was a bad deal for both teams. Sunday was about to quit the game to become an evangelist, and Burke washed out to sea after reporting to last-place Pittsburgh and hit just .210 in the final month of the season.

Cut after Pittsburgh regained the players it had lost to the PL, Burke returned to the minors with Milwaukee of the Western Association but was soon back in the majors when the Brewers replaced the Cincinnati AA team in August 1891. When the AA and NL merged that winter, he was assigned to the Cincinnati Reds. In June 1892 Burke was targeted for release as part of a reduction so that the Reds could get down to the legal roster limit of 13, and the New York Giants gleefully snatched him, certain that Cincinnati had made a grievous mistake. Later, however, *TSN* confided that Burke was viewed in Cincinnati as a troublemaker. His reputation soon worsened in New York after he clashed with Jack Doyle and then hired a hoodlum to beat up Doyle. When Doyle was getting the better of fight, Burke pretended to try to separate the combatants. Doyle then caught on that he was fighting two opponents and "scored a knockdown at Burke's expense."

Two years later Burke went a long way toward redeeming himself in his teammates' eyes. When the Giants had a day off on August 29, 1894, most of the team went to Atlantic City. While they were at the beach, a drunk swam beyond the breakers. Burke grabbed a lifesaver ring and threw it "straight as an arrow" to the drowning inebriate, and George Davis then hauled him ashore safely. The pair were heroes, and Burke added to his new image by topping .300 for the first time and scoring 121 runs, further pleasing the regulars in the left-field bleachers at the Polo Grounds, who had dubbed their habitat "Burkeville." Still, in the 1894 offensive deluge Burke's .304 mark was below the NL average, and when he started poorly the following season, the Giants offered him for sale. Burke eventually returned to Cincinnati, although there is no record that the Reds paid anything for him. He finished 1895 with a composite .263 BA but burst forth the following year to hit .340, lead the Reds in hits, and tie for the club lead in runs. His bombshell season was considered a prime reason Cincinnati emerged as a pennant contender in 1896. The following summer, though Burke was still just 30, the Reds suddenly axed him. *TSN* said that he suffered from catarrh, but the true reason probably was that he took such poor care of himself his body was far older than its years.

By 1900 Burke was still on the fringes of the top minor leagues, and he began the year in the newly renamed AL. But after playing a handful of games with three different teams, he drifted out to the Montana State League, played awhile with Butte, and then instigated a riot while umpiring a game in which he purportedly gave Great Falls every close decision until he was snowed under by Helena players. Burke took up a bat and swung it at his assailants and then ran for it, declaring the game forfeited to Great Falls as he exited the park. Meanwhile, the Helena police swore out a warrant against him for "assault with a deadly weapon" when it was "alleged that he flourished a knife as big as a machete" as the enraged crowd pursued him down the streets outside the park. Burke escaped Montana in one piece, but little more than seven years later he was a charity patient at Utica City Hospital. His last job was as a cook on a section gang for the New York Central Railroad. Too dissipated and beaten down by then to hold on to any job for long, he died within a month after cooking his last meal. (DN)

Burns, James Milton / "Jim"

B	T	HGT	WGT	G	AB	H	R	2B
B	R	5'7"	168	169	727	222	131	29

3B	HR	RBI	BB	SO	SB	BA	SA	OBP
11	5	111	27	78	64	.305	.396	.341

B. ?/?/1861 St. Louis, MO **D.** 2/17/1909
TEAMS: 88–89KCA 91WasA
DEBUT: 9/25/1888 at Kansas City; played LF and went 1-for-5 in a 7–4 loss to Brooklyn's Al Mays
FINALE: 5/22/1891 at Washington; played RF and made 2 hits in a 9–6 win over Louisville's Ed Daily and Red Ehret

There is documentation that Jim Burns threw right-handed and batted both ways, but he was probably never a switch hitter on a consistent basis. All of his other vital stats except his death date and middle name are speculative. The March 3, 1889, *TSN* said he was 27, meaning he was probably born in either 1861 or 1862, and the September 20, 1890, *Chicago Inter-Ocean* said, "Jimmy Burns, the

Kansas City fielder of the knotted fingers [from his early days as a catcher], parts his name in the middle with 'Milton.'" Burns's failure to carve a longer ML career is a puzzle. He obviously could hit and was good on fly balls, and his only known major flaw was that he had a weak arm.

Burns first appeared fleetingly as a catcher with Quincy of the Northwestern League in 1884. At the close of the 1887 season, his second with Oshkosh of the Northwestern League, he was reportedly headed for Washington NL but instead joined Omaha of the Western Association in 1888 before being acquired by the Kansas City AA replacement team. In his rookie year Burns led the Cowboys in BA and SA and scored 103 runs. That winter, after KC left the AA to become a minor league entry he was courted by several PL teams but was dissuaded from jumping his contract by the legal action the Cowboys took against Jack Pickett for his defection to the Brotherhood loop. After spending the winter in Quincy with his parents, Burns was rewarded in the spring of 1890 by being named KC captain. But he resigned the position in late April, and after the season he lost his CF job when the Cowboys signed George Hogriever. One local scribe reported that Burns's downfall was fanning too often with the bases full.

After joining Washington AA on April 28, 1891, Burns hit well but made a key error in his last game and was released for "indifferent play" even though the Senators won. He returned to the minors and continued to hit well wherever he went. Burns finished his active career early in 1896 with St. Paul of the Western League after hitting .356 the previous year, and then he disappeared. He was discovered only recently to have died in Chicago in 1909. (DN)

Burns, Richard Simon / "Dick"

B	T	HGT	WGT	G	AB	H	R	2B
L	L	5'7"	140	130	544	145	97	26

3B	HR	RBI	BB	SO	SB	BA	SA	OBP
14	4	9	10	30	—	.267	.388	.280

G	IP	H	GS	CG	BB
58	460.1	473	53	47	80

SO	SH	W	L	PCT	ERA
199	1	25	27	.481	3.07

B. 12/26/1863 Holyoke, MA **D.** 11/16/1937
TEAMS: 83DetN 84CinU 85StLN
DEBUT: 5/3/1883 at Detroit; caught by Sam Trott and lost 10–1 to Chicago's Fred Goldsmith
FINALE: 7/23/1885 at New York; played CF and went 0-for-4 in a 15–3 loss to New York's Mickey Welch
CAREER HIGHLIGHT: 8/26/1884 at Kansas City; caught by Joe Crotty and no-hit Kansas City, winning 3–1 over Bob Black

Dick Burns began his career in the late 1870s with Massachusetts clubs, including his hometown Holyoke team of the International Association. The son of Irish immigrants, he and several brothers worked in Holyoke cotton mills until he took up pro ball. In 1884 the Detroit *Free Press* noted in passing that now that Burns was playing in the new UA, "the whilom secretary of the YMCA at Holyoke" would be required to play on Sundays. Given Burns's youth, working class background and probable Catholicism, this should probably not be taken literally but may indicate that he was a churchgoer and perhaps generally regarded as a straight arrow.

In 1883 Burns joined Detroit NL. As a pitcher, he won 2 of 14 decisions with an ERA more than a run above the NL average. After the release of outfielder Tom Mansell, he was also used sometimes in RF but hit a weak .186 and committed 8 errors in 24 garden games, a poor defensive performance even for the period. Burns was still only 19, however, and the fact that Detroit kept him for nearly the entire season suggests he must have shown potential. That fall, he was reserved, but Detroit soon released him, perhaps because it belatedly decided he was not worth the $1,000 minimum salary for reserved players.

In 1884 Burns played in the upstart UA with Cincinnati, for whom he again split his time between the outfield and pitching. He alternated in the box with veteran George Bradley until the acquisition of NL star Jim McCormick in midseason and improved his record to 23-15, making him part of the first team in ML history with a trio of 20-game winners. Against the much weaker competition of the UA, Burns's batting also improved radically. He hit .306, led the league in triples, and finished among the leaders in home runs and slugging percentage. His defensive stats, which are less responsive to the caliber of competition, also improved considerably.

During the subsequent off-season the UA collapsed, but unlike many other players who had gone into the outlaw circuit, Burns had violated neither a current contract nor the reserve clause and so needed no special dispensation to make him eligible. No ML team wanted him, however, and instead, at the young age of 21, he became player-manager of Milwaukee in the new Western League. When the loop disbanded Burns played 2 games for Waterbury of the Eastern League before skipping to join St. Louis's NL team, so desperate to shore up its outfield that it offered him $1,000 to finish the year, more than Detroit had been willing to pay him for an entire season. In Burns's second NL stint, his hitting improved marginally on his 1883 performance, but he fielded even more poorly, committing 7 errors in 14 games. A 2-error day in a 15–3 loss to New York on July 23 convinced St. Louis to release him.

No doubt discouraged, Burns never returned to the majors but continued to play in the lower echelons of the minors until he was 26. In 1894 he entered politics and was elected an alderman in his native Holyoke, MA. He later operated a cigar store there that was an affiliate of the Kaffir Cigar Co before retiring in 1930. Burns died in Holyoke 7 years later. The enormous disparity between his UA performance and his two NL stints is one of the primary proofs analysts cite in making a case that the UA was well below major league caliber. (DB/DN)

Burns, Thomas P. / "Tommy" "Tom" "Oyster" "Good Eye"

B	T	HGT	WGT	G	AB	H	R	2B
L	R	5'8"	183	1188	4645	1392	870	224

3B	HR	RBI	BB	SO	SB	BA	SA	OBP
129	65	834	464	182	263	.300	.445	.368

G	IP	H	GS	CG	BB
25	138.2	152	11	10	30

SO	SH	W	L	PCT	ERA
40	1	8	5	.615	4.09

B. 9/6/1864 Philadelphia, PA **D.** 11/11/1928
TEAMS: 84WilU 84–85BalA 87–88BalA 88–89BroA 90–95BroN 95NYN
DEBUT: 8/18/1884 at Washington; played SS and went 0-for-3 in a 4–3 win over Washington's Charlie Geggus
FINALE: 9/16/1895 at New York; played 1B and went 3-for-4 in a 9–5 loss to Philadelphia's Kid Carsey

Tommy Burns was called "Oyster" because he hailed from Maryland and also "Good Eye," the words he constantly shouted at batters while coaching the bases, but teammates generally called him either "Tommy" or "Tom." A multitalented player early in his career, capable at two of the most difficult positions, pitcher and SS, after the 1888 season he was lodged permanently in RF although he continued to play other positions occasionally.

At age 17 Burns played for the Shibe club, the 1881 Philadelphia amateur champions. He moved to semipro Atlantic City the following year and at the close of the season pitched several exhibitions for Baltimore, the AA tailender. Orioles player-manager Henry Myers took Burns with him in 1883 when he ran the Harrisburg entry in the International Association. After hitting just .220, Burns remained in that loop with the Wilmington Quicksteps after it became the Eastern League in 1884 and was hitting .361 when the Delaware club replaced Philadelphia in the UA. Burns played just two UA games with the Quicksteps before jumping to Baltimore AA along with outfielder Dennis Casey. He remained with the Orioles until September 1885 when he was knocked cold by a pitched ball and requested his release so he could join Newark. After his .366 BA helped carry the New Jersey club to the Eastern League pennant in 1886, he signed with New York NL and was nearly blacklisted for not having waited until his minor league season was over. When the uproar abated, Burns decided to return to Baltimore after Billy Barnie promised to make him team captain.

In his first year back in Lobstertown, Burns led the AA in triples and hit .341. He was relieved of his captaincy late in the season but had it restored the following spring and then was permanently dismissed when Barnie decided he was a "disturber" of team harmony and an excessive coacher who "disgusted everyone within the sound of his voice by his senseless screaming and absurd pretensions to objecting to the pitcher's delivery." On August 10, 1888, Burns was sold to Brooklyn for $4,000, triggering accusations from St. Louis that Barnie was trying to hand Brooklyn the pennant. St. Louis won anyway, but the Bridegrooms then copped two successive flags with Burns, harmonious now that he was with a good team, playing RF and usually batting cleanup. He remained one of the game's most productive hitters until 1893, when he slipped to .270, well below the NL average in the first year at the 60'6" distance. Realizing his job was in peril, Burns went on a severe training regimen over the winter. The following spring he reported twenty-five pounds lighter and in his best condition in years. His effort paid a rich dividend, as he hit .354 and led Brooklyn in RBI.

Burns then relapsed to his old training methods, spending the winter of 1894–95 managing McGroarty's Billiard Parlor in Brooklyn. A .184 start in 1895 prompted his release to New York after just 20 games. Burns hit better with the Giants in a sub role but opted to serve as player-manager with Newark of the Atlantic League in 1896 rather than ride the bench again in New York. He acted in the same capacity with Hartford the following year and then returned to Newark in 1898 after buying a piece of the team. Burns was forced to resign as manager after a player strike on July 5 over unpaid salaries and then had to surrender complete control of the club to the owner of the team's ballpark when his players began pocketing the gate receipts in order to get their due. He applied successfully to be a NL umpire in 1899 but resigned in late June after working an anxious string of games in Cincinnati. Burns was a corporate inspector for the borough of Brooklyn when he died at 64 following a stroke. (DN)

Cahill, John Patrick Parnell / "Patsy"

B	T	HGT	WGT	G	AB	H	R	2B
R	R	5'7½"	168	252	936	192	93	24

3B	HR	RBI	BB	SO	SB	BA	SA	OBP
12	1	58	24	84	50	.205	.260	.227

G	IP	H	GS	CG	BB
10	50	66	2	2	26

SO	SH	W	L	PCT	ERA
8	0	2	2	.500	8.64

B. 4/30/1865 San Francisco, CA **D.** 10/31/1901
TEAMS: 84ColA 86StLN 87IndN
DEBUT: 5/31/1884 at Baltimore; caught by Rudy Kemmler, went 2-for-5 and scored 2 runs in a 15–12 win over Baltimore's Hardie Henderson and Jim McLaughlin
FINALE: 8/9/1887 at Indianapolis; played RF and went 0-for-4 in a 10–5 loss to New York's Mickey Welch

A quick-witted, lively little black Irishman, Patsy Cahill was so popular with fans that he became one of the candidates for Ernest Thayer's prototype in his poem "Casey at the Bat." In truth, he was an unlikely choice for the role, for, in spite of excellent baserunning skills and a lively arm, the high hopes for his ML career were blighted by hitting that started impressively but swiftly got worse and worse. After spending 1883 with the semipro Redingtons of San Francisco, Cahill entrained to Baltimore that October hoping to impress Orioles manager Billy Barnie sufficiently to be offered a contract for 1884. When Barnie demurred Cahill then went to Texas and spent the winter playing for the K.O.M. team. After his aggressive play drew comparisons to Arlie Latham, Philadelphia NL manager Harry Wright, who had his finger on pulses everywhere, invited him to training in the spring of 1884. Cahill failed to make the Quakers but was steered to Columbus manager Gus Schmelz, who needed both a left fielder and a change pitcher in late May. Promptly upon joining the Ohio team in Baltimore, Cahill was put into the box and staggered to what proved to be his only CG win in the majors. In all, he made an excellent initial impression on the Columbus press, but by the time he had been with the team for a month, doubts were expressed about his hitting. When the overachieving Columbus team went into a late August slump, Cahill became one of the scapegoats. The *Columbus Times* observed that, for lack of cash, Columbus had failed to acquire a qualified outfielder. "However," the *Times* added sarcastically, "we have Cahill." A few days later Columbus no longer did after he broke a leg sliding on August 30 and was out for the season. There was talk he would be kept in 1885 to play SS, but Columbus sold out to Pittsburgh, which had no interest in retaining Cahill.

However, the San Franciscan had a godfather in Schmelz, who was an advocate of little ball and always liked speed-and-defense players like Cahill, Hugh Nicol, and Paul Radford. When Schmelz was hired to manage Atlanta in the fledgling 1885 Southern League, Cahill was one of several Columbus players he took along. The San Franciscan served as team captain and SS on the first SL champions. His popularity in the new loop was so great in 1885 that cigars, a cocktail, and babies were named after him, and some twenty-five years later the *Atlanta Constitution* claimed that he was so revered in the Georgia metropolis that his likeness was put into a cornerstone along with other Georgia notables when the new state capital was built. On the strength of his success in Atlanta, Schmelz took over the NL's St. Louis Maroons in 1886 and brought Cahill in to play RF, but the little Californian was abused by the Mound City crowd from outset of the season for his weak play, and he hit just .199, scored a mere 43 runs, and produced 124 total bases, one of the worst seasons ever by an outfielder. That winter he resurrected his image enough while playing in California that he was among the packet of players Indianapolis, the NL's newest entry, agreed to inherit from the disbanded Maroons. But the results in 1887 were even more disastrous; Cahill's AOPS dropped from 49 to 35, and he was fired after just 68 games. He played in the Southern League again for a while, this time without distinction, as the loop was much stronger than it had been in 1885, and then returned to California, where he again retrieved his reputation as one of the top players in the San Francisco Bay area.

A classic example of a player of star quality in a middle-range minor league and doomed to fail when he tried to rise above that level, Cahill remained a player and an umpire in Northern California until shortly before he died of pneumonia in Pleasanton, CA, at 36. His .487 OPS is the lowest in ML history among outfielders with a minimum of 900 career PAs. (DN/DB)

Campau, Charles Columbus / "Count" "The Smoked Italian"

B	T	HGT	WGT	G	AB	H	R	2B
L	R	5'11"	160	147	572	153	97	14

3B	HR	RBI	BB	SO	SB	BA	SA	OBP
15	10	93	46	40	63	.267	.397	.322

G	W	L	PCT	PENNANTS
42	27	14	.659	0

B. 10/17/1863 Detroit, MI **D.** 4/3/1938
TEAMS: 88DetN (P/M)90StLA 94WasN
DEBUT: 7/7/1888 at Detroit; played RF and went 0-for-4 in a 3–2 loss to Washington's Hank O'Day
FINALE: 7/17/1894 at New York; played RF and went hitless in a 7–2 loss to New York's Amos Rusie

Called "Count" because of his "olive-tinted skin," Charles Campau survived prejudice early in his career because he was mistakenly thought to be Italian and played only 147 ML games but had a long and illustrious pro career full of championships and highlights. A member of one of Detroit's pioneer families, Campau was born in 1863 of French ancestry and was related to D. J. Campau, the father of horse racing in the Motor City. He began playing baseball while attending Notre Dame (then a boarding school) in 1875. Campau subsequently played for number of independent teams, including Kokomo, where he was a teammate of the writer Booth Tarkington's brother, before joining Detroit's independent Cass Club in 1883. The following year he began his pro career with a team in Vincennes, IN. So began a long odyssey that included pennants with Erie (Interstate League, 1884), London (Canadian League, 1886), New Orleans (Southern League, 1887), Detroit (International Association, 1889), Columbus (Western League, 1892), Kansas City (Western League, 1898), and Rochester (Eastern League, 1899). It is unlikely that any other nineteenth-century player played for pennant winners in so many different leagues or cities. At least two of Campau's other clubs were in first place when their leagues disbanded, while the Binghamton club of which he was player-manager missed out on the 1902 New York State League flag by a mere half game.

Of all the pennants, the most dramatic came with Kansas City in 1898. The season ended with a 3-game series between the Blues and Indianapolis, with the winner claiming the pennant. Kansas City won the first game, but Indianapolis took the second. So the pennant came down to a single game, and as Campau told it, "The strain was something I never want to go through again. I retired at 10 p.m., but could not sleep, dressed myself and sat in a chair and smoked till 6 a.m. If I say it myself, never did I go on a field feeling so cool and collected. . . . The game was a corker from start to finish and was not won until the last man was out. With two men on the bases, Kansas City one run to the good, [Herm] McFarland . . . came to the plate and hit a corker to right. I lost it in the sun for a second, then found it and I thought it would never come down. Not a sound could be heard except from behind me I heard someone say, 'My God, will he get it?' Thanks to the Maker of all I did, and the flag of 1899 will wave over Kansas City grounds."

By the time he finally quit in 1905, Campau had played in over 2,000 pro games and amassed somewhere in the neighborhood of 2,500 hits. Perhaps his most famous feat was leading both a minor and a major league in home runs in the same season, 1890, when he was tied for the lead when the International Association disbanded, then joined the AA and despite missing its first three months also led that loop in homers.

In an 1887 game in New Orleans, Campau hit 3 four-wheelers, and gleeful fans rewarded him by throwing some $90 on the field for him to collect. It began a long love affair with the city. Eventually he married a Louisiana woman and moved to New Orleans for good, working at such jobs as ticket taker at local racetracks and gate tender at the Crescent City Jockey's Club until his death at 74. (DN/PM)

Canavan, James Edward / "Jim"

B	T	HGT	WGT	G	AB	H	R	2B
R	R	5'8"	160	541	2072	464	326	63

3B	HR	RBI	BB	SO	SB	BA	SA	OBP
49	30	291	232	147	114	.224	.345	.305

B. 11/26/1866 New Bedford, MA **D.** 5/27/1949
TEAMS: 91CinA 91MilA 92ChiN 93–94CinN 97BroN
DEBUT: 4/8/1891 at Cincinnati; played SS and went 2-for-5 in a 7–7 tie with St. Louis's Jack Stivetts
FINALE: 7/13/1897 at Chicago; played 2B and went 0-for-4 in an 11–4 loss to Chicago's Jimmy Callahan

After joining the new Cincinnati AA entry in 1891, Jim Canavan hit with power, on the bases was "on par with Hamilton and Stovey," had decent plate discipline, and was versatile, but he had such enormous holes in his swing that good pitchers were elated to face him with the game on the line. In 1891, his rookie ML season, he had a .380 SA and 10 home runs, excellent for a middle infielder, but made 103 errors and hit just .238. The errors were tolerable because Cincinnati played in Pendleton Park, which had been hastily constructed, was poorly maintained, and had terrible drainage, but Canavan's hitting swiftly got worse. When the NL and AA merged, he was assigned to lowly Louisville but went to Chicago with $1,000 on April 5 for second baseman Fred Pfeffer, Cap Anson's latest teammate friend-turned-enemy. Canavan then produced the worst season BA in ML history by a player in a minimum of 400 ABs by hitting a putrid .166.

Remarkably, rather than being sent to the sticks for further bat training, he landed with Cincinnati in 1893 and proved that his previous season had been the Real McCoy when he came in again with the lowest BA of any qualifier in the league (.226), save for over-the-hill Cliff Carroll (.224). Had Cincinnati seen enough? Hardly. Canavan held the Reds' RF post for most of 1894 and ranked among the home run leaders in early July with 10. But minor injuries and several prolonged slumps soon reduced him to his former level, and he never hit another homer after July.

Canavan played with the Reds' Indianapolis Western League farm team in 1895 and then broadcast that he would only play with his hometown New England League club thereafter because he was now "one of the custodians of the secret of the mixing" in the local copper factory, New Bedford Copper Company, that was possessed only by his father, who was growing old and would place the secret in his care. It may only have been a ploy to escape Cincinnati, for he played with Pawtucket of the New England League in 1896 and then was the surprise choice of Brooklyn's new manager, Billy Barnie, to open the 1897 campaign at 2B for Barnie's Bridegrooms. Asked prior to the season by *TSN* for his thoughts on Charlie Comiskey and Cap Anson after having played for both, Canavan, in a rare moment of candor, said that Comiskey was a great manager and Anson was highly overrated, never asking for help on points of the game from his players, and "you may be sure that they never ask his judgment."

Canavan never submitted his views on Barnie for publication after Barnie released him in July 1897 when he strained a tendon in his throwing arm. He returned to the minors the following year with Providence of the Eastern League. Then, in January 1899, *TSN* announced he had taken a job as the assistant superintendent of a copper mine in Arizona, where his uncle was superintendent, and on this occasion the report may have been accurate, for he disappeared from the game until 1900, when he resurfaced as manager of New Haven in the Connecticut State League. Canavan finished a career that had begun in the 1887 New England League back in the NEL in 1906, but he continued to play roller polo for several more years and later scouted for the Tigers. He died in New Bedford at 72. (DN/DB)

Carroll, Samuel Clifford / "Cliff"

B	T	HGT	WGT	G	AB	H	R	2B
B	R	5'8"	163	991	3972	995	729	125

3B	HR	RBI	BB	SO	SB	BA	SA	OBP
47	31	423	361	290	197	.251	.329	.320

B. 10/18/1859 Clay Grove, IA **D.** 6/12/1923
TEAMS: 82–85ProN 86–87WasN 88PitN 90–91ChiN 92StLN 93BosN
DEBUT: 8/3/1882 at Providence; played RF and went 1-for-4 in a 6–3 win over Cleveland's Jim McCormick
FINALE: 9/27/1893 at Louisville; played RF and went 0-for-5 in a 7–6 win over Louisville's Bill Whitrock

Cliff Carroll played 1B on the independent 1878 Peoria Reds, which also numbered the Rowe brothers, Charley Radbourn, and Bid McPhee, among other future MLers, along with center fielder Floyd Lauman, who later earned circus fame under the name of Alvaretta. Carroll then joined the Gleason brothers in 1879 on Ted Sullivan's Northwestern League Dubuque Rabbits before journeying west the following year to play for Oakland, CA. Well-traveled by the time he joined Providence in 1882, he finished his first ML season as a scrub, playing in just 10 games. Carroll remained a part-timer the following year but won Providence's LF slot in 1884. The lone switch hitter on that season's NL pennant winner, he finished second on the club in runs despite logging a weak .640 OPS.

Carroll slipped to a .232 BA in 1885 and was transferred to the new Washington NL franchise when Providence folded at the end of the season. With a feeble D.C. entry he appeared to lose interest. The following spring he bought a restaurant in Washington called The Bouquet and spent all his time there when an injury prevented him from playing until June. But club officials found his association with "the liquor business . . . a source of much embarrassment to the team management," and when he finished 1887 far below the league norm in every major batting department, Washington cut all ties with him. Though just 28, Carroll worried that his ML career might be at an end when Pittsburgh also jettisoned him after he began the 1888 campaign 0-for-20. Upon signing with Buffalo of the International Association, his concern deepened when manager Jack Chapman sent him home to his farm in Bloomington, IL, in September with a bad ankle and told him not to come back.

Carroll sat out the 1889 season, seemingly washed up, but then got a reprieve when the PL stripped the NL and AA of many of their top players. Signed for 1890 after Cap Anson's Chicago NL club lost its entire starting outfield to the PL, Carroll led the Colts in runs with 134. Given new life, he played three more full seasons as a regular gardener, although his 1892 sojourn in St. Louis was cut short when he left the team in late August after owner Chris Von der Ahe fined him $50 for being unable to dig a ball out of his blouse pocket in time to stop Brooklyn outfielder Darby O'Brien from taking an extra base. The following January, Carroll was traded to Boston for second baseman Joe Quinn, enabling him to finish his career with a pennant winner. Carroll left with a whimper, however, hitting just .224 for the Beaneaters, the lowest BA of any qualifier in 1893. He later played in the Western and Texas leagues before retiring to his farm. Prior to his death from heart disease in 1923, he moved to Portland, OR. (DN)

Cassidy, John P. / "John"

B	T	HGT	WGT	G	AB	H	R	2B
R	L	5'8"	168	634	2642	650	353	87

3B	HR	RBI	BB	SO	SB	BA	SA	OBP
33	5	191	84	132	0	.246	.310	.271

G	IP	H	GS	CG	BB
32	231.2	308	24	20	12

SO	SH	W	L	PCT	ERA
11	0	2	22	.083	3.19

B. ?/?/1857 Brooklyn, NY **D.** 7/2/1891
TEAMS: 75AtLNA 75NHNA 76–77HarN 78ChiN 79–82TroN 83ProN 84–85BroA
DEBUT: 4/24/1875 at Hartford; caught by Jake Knowdell in a 6–5 loss to Hartford's Candy Cummings
FINALE: 8/12/1885 at New York; played RF and went 1-for-4 in a 5–4 win over New York's Jack Lynch

John Cassidy's rookie winning percentage of .045 is the lowest among pitchers with twenty or more decisions in a season. Nevertheless, he enjoyed a ten-year ML career. His pitching record was largely the product of the dismal teams that played behind him during his seasons in the box. As a hitter and outfielder, Cassidy's performance was extremely spotty, although his strong arm was especially useful in RF, enabling him to throw out runners at 1B on potential hits. After batting .378 with Hartford in 1877, Cassidy was mortified when his mark dropped 112 points the following year. By the time he left the majors following a .213 finale with Brooklyn in 1885, his career BA had fallen to .252. If his aberrant 1877 season is deducted from his career stats, his mark drops an additional 15 points to .237. Cassidy's nadir came in 1882 with Troy, which had fired him after he hit .222 the previous year. He began the season as a first baseman with the independent Brooklyn Atlantics and first joined the upstate New York NL team on June 3 for an exhibition game with the New York Mets at the Polo Grounds. Cassidy promptly collided with fellow outfielder Pat Gillespie on a fly ball, knocking Gillespie out. After some two months with Troy, on August 13 he married a Chicago belle at his Brooklyn home; thirteen days later the Trojans released him when he collected only 21 hits in 29 games with the club for a .174 BA. Yet Cassidy inveigled Providence to sign him in 1883 and then moved to the AA when the Grays gave him his freedom for 1884.

If his birth year is correct, Cassidy was just 28 when he left the majors and debuted in his eighteenth year after coming to prominence in 1874 with the semipro Nassaus, where he was caught by Billy Barnie. He opened a billiard room in Brooklyn after he left baseball and died in Brooklyn at 34 of dropsy after ailing for over a year. (DN)

Clack, Robert S. (b. Clark) / "Bobby"

B	T	HGT	WGT	G	AB	H	R	2B
R	R	5'9"	153	82	312	38	33	1

3B	HR	RBI	BB	SO	SB	BA	SA	OBP
1	0	19	9	17	0	.154	.163	.178

G	IP	H	GS	CG	BB
2	2	0	0	0	0

SO	SH	W	L	PCT	ERA
0	0	0	0	—	4.50

B. 6/13/1850 ?, England **D.** 10/22/1933
TEAMS: 74–75AtlNA 76CinN
DEBUT: 5/13/1874 at Brooklyn; played CF and went 0-for-4 in an 8–3 win over Baltimore's Asa Brainard
FINALE: 10/9/1876 at Hartford; played RF and was hitless in an 11–0 loss to Hartford's Candy Cummings

Bobby Clack must have been one incredible fielder. His .341 OPS is the lowest among outfielders with 300 or more career ABs. Clack came to the Atlantics from the amateur Flyaways after the Flyaways beat the NA club 12–10 on May 7, 1874. It is impossible now to comprehend why Cincinnati retained Clack from its 1875 independent entry when it joined the NL in 1876. His career BA at that point was .149. After opening the season in RF and batting cleanup of all places, Clack soon moved to the bench when he failed once again to hit. He remained on the team all year, however, and appeared in Cincinnati's season finale.

Clack began 1877 with Binghamton of the newly organized League Alliance and finished the year with Utica. After he hit just .083 in 9 games in 1878, Utica severed connections with him. Though Clack was only a marginal player in the NL's maiden season, he was among its longest-lived participants. We do not know whether he attended the NL's fiftieth reunion celebration in New York in January 1926 prior to his death nearly eight years later in Danvers, MA. (DN/DB)

Cline, John P. / "Monk"

B	T	HGT	WGT	G	AB	H	R	2B
L	L	5'4"	150	232	940	245	165	39

3B	HR	RBI	BB	SO	SB	BA	SA	OBP
12	2	71	66	2	31	.261	.334	.313

B. 3/3/1858 Louisville, KY **D.** 9/23/1916
TEAMS: 82BalA 84–85LouA 88KCA 91LouA
DEBUT: 7/4/1882 at Louisville; played 3B and went 1-for-4 in a 7–1 loss to Louisville's John Reccius
FINALE: 10/4/1891 at St. Louis; played LF and went 1-for-3 in a 4–3 win over St. Louis's Willie McGill

Monk Cline's father founded the amateur Louisville Red Stockings, which graduated not only his son but also Hub Collins and Red Ehret. The younger Cline was with the Red Stockings in 1882 when Baltimore AA arrived in Louisville short of players. Despite being left-handed, Cline debuted for Baltimore at 3B, thereupon becoming one of the smallest men ever to play the position in the majors. Later that season he also played SS and 2B before claiming the Orioles' CF post. The following year Cline lost his mother in July while with Harrisburg of the Interstate Association but showed enough talent in his first full season of pro ball to induce Louisville to sign him for 1884.

The 1884 campaign proved to be Cline's only full year in the majors and also his best, as he hit a solid .290 and scored 91 runs in just 94 games. It addition, he was a favorite of manager Joe Gerhardt and popular with the team for his spunky base coaching that featured an incessant chant of "A dollar for a hit!" But late in the season Gerhardt was replaced as manager. When Jim Hart took over as Louisville pilot in 1885, he moved Pete Browning from 3B to CF. Cline vied for one of the other outfield jobs in the spring of 1885 until he suffered a broken leg in an exhibition game. He was then released in July and finished the season in the Southern League. Cline opened 1886 at SS with Atlanta and hit .320. His fine season enabled him to move up in 1887 to Rochester of the International Association, but he was soon back in the SL. He remained in the SL until it disbanded on August 21, 1888, at which point he joined Kansas City AA.

Now 30 years old, Cline was about to receive his final sustained opportunity to establish himself as a major leaguer, and he failed the test, compiling a meager .582 OPS. Fired by Kansas City, Cline signed with Sioux City for 1889 and had his finest season as a professional, leading the Western Association with a .364 BA and slugging 15 home runs to go with his 93 stolen bases. Cline continued to dominate WA pitching for the next two seasons, leading to his last stint in a big league uniform. Returning to his Louisville home in September of 1891 after the WA season ended, he was asked to join the AA Colonels after manager Jack Chapman and Colonels left fielder Patsy Donovan clashed, prompting Donovan's release. In his first appearance on September 12 he "was warmly received by the home crowd" and helped the Colonels defeat Baltimore 7–1. Even though he finished his 19-game tour as Donovan's replacement with a .300 BA and a .802 OPS, Chapman released him the following February.

Although Cline continued to flirt with pro ball for several more years, by 1893 he had turned his off-season job as a pipeman at the No. 6 Engine House of the Louisville Fire Department into a full-time position. When a falling wall seriously injured him while fighting a fire in early December 1894, his baseball career seemed at an end. But Cline later umpired in the minors and as late as the spring of 1899 claimed to be in great shape and on the verge of making a comeback with Birmingham of the Southern League. By then, though, he was nearly 41, and his size, always against him, had become an even greater handicap now that he was aging. Cline returned to the fire department and died at his Louisville home in 1916 of tuberculosis.

Cline was never able to turn his sensational minor league dossier into a steady job in the majors largely because he failed to utilize the natural advantage his small stature ought to have gained him. Despite usually serving as his club's lead-off hitter, he collected only 66 career walks, the fewest ever by a ML player under 5'5" with a minimum of 1,000 PAs. (DN)

Clinton, James Lawrence / "Jim" "Big Jim"

B	T	HGT	WGT	G	AB	H	R	2B
R	R	5'8½"	154	426	1719	438	246	45

3B	HR	RBI	BB	SO	SB	BA	SA	OBP
20	4	55	82	20	3	.255	.311	.297

G	IP	H	GS	CG	BB
19	141	178	16	11	6

SO	SH	W	L	PCT	ERA
8	0	1	15	.063	2.94

B. 8/10/1850 New York, NY **D.** 9/3/1921
TEAMS: 72EckNA 73ResNA 74–75AtlNA 76LouN 82WorN 83–84BalA 85CinA 86BalA
DEBUT: 5/18/1872 at Brooklyn; replaced David Lenz after Lenz was injured, caught Joe McDermott, and went 1-for-3 in a 24–6 loss to New York's Candy Cummings and John McMullin
FINALE: 7/15/1886 at Louisville; played RF and went 0-for-3 in a 5–3 win over Louisville's Tom Ramsey

Jim Clinton had a truly weird career. Despite being popular wherever he went, he was out of the majors for five full seasons when he seemingly should have been at the peak of his playing skills. Equally intriguing is that he is the only MLer who took his first at bat against Candy Cummings, purportedly the first great master of pitches that bend, and his last against Tom Ramsey, whose pitches, according to some batters, did tricks never seen before or since. Too, despite standing only a tad over 5'8", Clinton played every position on the diamond at least twice during his career, including 1B. What's more, he was 33 before he had his first season in the majors in which he played more than 26 games. Yet he played all or parts of 10 ML seasons and logged over 1,800 PAs along with hurling 132 innings.

Clinton's strangest season perhaps was 1876, when he played for the independent Memphis Reds in the Tennessee team's classic 1–0 win over the Allegheny club from the Pittsburgh area and then joined Louisville in time to hit .338 in 16 games, have his career day on October 4 when he went 4-for-4 against Cummings, then with Hartford, and then pitched the season finale against none other than Cummings again. For all that, Clinton was not invited back to the Falls City in 1877 and did not appear in the majors again until June 1882, after the Worcester NL club purged itself of several of its disappointing veterans. Clinton was no improvement, hitting .163 in 26 games, but the following season, out of nowhere, he produced his ML career year with a .313 BA for Baltimore that ranked third in the AA. He slipped to .270 the next year and then tumbled all the way to .238 in 1885 after being sold to Cincinnati but was excused to a degree because his 4-year-old son, Frankie, the putative Reds mascot, died suddenly in August.

After the season Clinton left Cincinnati when his wife refused to live there any longer and the Reds tired of his lame arm. He then hired on as a regular AA umpire in 1886. His new career ambition ended for the moment when an angry crowd besieged him in Brooklyn on May 19, 1886, after the locals had lost 7–4 to St. Louis. Resigning his officiating post, the following month he returned briefly to the AA playing ranks with last-place Baltimore and then put in two more seasons in the minors, finishing in the 1888 New England League. Clinton returned to umpiring in the minors for a time in the 1890s before relocating to Brooklyn, where he had been born and first played ML ball. He died there in 1921 at 71. (DN/DB)

Cone, Joseph Frederick / "Fred"

B	T	HGT	WGT	G	AB	H	R	2B
?	?	5'9½"	171	19	77	20	17	3

3B	HR	RBI	BB	SO	SB	BA	SA	OBP
1	0	16	8	2	12	.260	.325	.329

B. 5/?/1848 Rockford, IL **D.** 4/13/1909
TEAMS: 71BosNA
DEBUT: 5/5/1871 at Washington; played LF and made 1 hit in a 20–18 win over Washington's Asa Brainard
FINALE: 9/9/1871 at Boston; played LF in a 17–14 win over the Athletics' George Bechtel

Fred Cone joined the Rockfords in 1868 as a first baseman but moved to the outfield in 1870. He accompanied Al Spalding and Ross Barnes from Rockford to Boston after the NA formed. It is not clear why he spent only one season in the loop, but he continued to play for independent teams and also umpired several ML games in Chicago between 1873 and 1877. Reportedly, he considered returning to the majors with Chicago in 1876 when the NL was formed but decided there would be no future in it once he perceived how strong the Windy City lineup was likely to be.

Cone later worked as a clerk at Chicago hotels. In August 1896, after earlier in the season playing in a benefit game for Harry Wright at Rockford, he attended his first ML game in years at Chicago and marveled at the size of the pillows worn on hands by all fielders and the "mattress big enough to sleep six" worn on the catcher's chest while "around his head he wore enough steel to keep all the firm of the Long, Short & Company in confinement for years to come." Some three years later Cone's reminiscences about his experiences playing for Rockford appeared in the July 15, 1899, *Lima News*. He died of a stroke at his Chicago home at 60. (DN/DB)

Cooley, Duff Gordon / "Dick" "Sir Richard"

B	T	HGT	WGT	G	AB	H	R	2B
L	R	5'11"	158	696	3183	975	607	86

3B	HR	RBI	BB	SO	SB	BA	SA	OBP
65	19	300	228	73	144	.306	.392	.355

G	W	L	PCT	PENNANTS
2	1	1	.500	0

B. 3/29/1873 Leavenworth, KS **D.** 8/9/1937
TEAMS: 93–96StLN 96–99PhiN (P/M)00PitN 01–04BosN 05DetAL
DEBUT: 7/27/1893 at St. Louis; played RF and went 1-for-3 in a 6–3 loss to Cleveland's John Clarkson
FINALE: 8/26/1905 at Detroit; played CF, made 1 hit,

and was then replaced by Ty Cobb after he took ill in a 5–4 win over Philadelphia's Weldon Henley and Chief Bender

Despite his lord-of-the-manor baptismal name and nickname of "Sir Richard" (given him for his aristocratic appearance when he was dressed to the nines), Dick Cooley grew up on the streets of Topeka working as a bootblack and newsboy and had never been east of Kansas City until he joined the Browns in 1893. Awed by the sights on his first trips to Chicago and New York, he immediately envisioned every major crowd gathering area as a potential spot for a bootblack stand.

After serving as captain–second baseman of a team he had organized in Topeka in 1892, the following spring Cooley used his skills as a "boss newsboy" to help reorganize the Western Association as a four-team league including his own Topeka club. After 20 games, the 20-year-old player-manager was hitting .410 when the loop disbanded. The following month he joined Bill Watkins's St. Louis club and vied with fellow rookie Jimmy Bannon for playing time. Several years later Watkins, then managing Pittsburgh, revealed why he had kept Cooley and released Bannon in 1893: "Because Dick has him beaten a block in every way, particularly from the neck up." By then Watkins had been proven right after seeming dead wrong at the time.

In the 1893–94 off-season Doggie Miller replaced Watkins at the St. Louis helm and Cooley's brother died. After beginning his first full ML campaign as Miller's tenth man, he jumped the team in July to catch for St. Joseph. Then, after Browns owner Chris Von der Ahe barred him from continuing to do so, he went home to Topeka. Reinstated the following season, he led St. Louis in hits, runs, BA, RBI, and beer consumption after hooking up with the Browns' German duo of Ted Breitenstein and Heinie Peitz to form "The Five Cent Gang," so dubbed after they found a bar in Washington that sold beer at 5¢ a bottle. The gang spent around $50 in the place each night in town. The trio all wanted to escape St. Louis, but Cooley was the first to get his wish when he was traded to Philadelphia in June 1896 after staging a bitter holdout that spring and then being suspended without pay while recovering from malaria. Unable to resist leaving St. Louis without a parting shot, Cooley told a local writer that Von der Ahe "is the meanest man in the business, and there is not a man in his pay who does not thoroughly despise him."

He was not in Philadelphia long before Cooley had a rival in Dan Mills, a writer on the *Philadelphia Times*, who seemed to bear the outfielder a virulent animosity almost from the moment he donned a Phillies uniform. Cooley still played well in the City of Brotherly Love until 1899, when rookie Roy Thomas stole his CF job. Irked when he was moved to 1B, Cooley got on the bad side of owner John I. Rogers, who punished him by not playing him toward the end of the season and then offering him only $1,200 in 1900, half the NL maximum limit of $2,400.

Again an angry holdout, Cooley was finally sold to Pittsburgh in April 1900 for $1,000, "the lowest price ever exacted for a first-class player," according to *SL*. Kept at 1B, a position he detested, by his new manager, Fred Clarke, Cooley debuted with the Pirates on May 2, 1900, and collected 22 hits and 16 runs in his first 23 games with the club and even acted as interim manager for 2 games while Clarke was idled by kidney trouble. But after his next 38 games as a Pirate he was riding a .201 BA when Pittsburgh released him in early August.

Cooley went home to Topeka to await another ML offer that never came. Meanwhile he ran a local saloon that Carrie Nation and her followers invaded one night "and left nothing but a bottle of Seltzer for Dick to recover on." His spirits at low ebb, Cooley was left with little choice the following spring but to play 1B for Syracuse of the Eastern League. Late that July, Boston NL acquired him as a scrub, but by the end of the season he had claimed the Beaneaters' LF job. Cooley held that post through 1904 and then was waived to Detroit when he seemed more interested in his off-season work in vaudeville than he did in baseball. Tigers manager Bill Armour moved Cooley to CF because Jimmy Barrett's "pins" were ailing, but by late August he had "returned to his indifferent form" and lost his job to a hungry 18-year-old rookie named Ty Cobb.

For the next several years Cooley was "a monologue artist on the vaudeville stage during the winters when he cares to be," and he served as player-manager and part owner of the Topeka club in the Western League. He later owned and managed Salt Lake City in the Union Association before returning to Kansas. His last field position in baseball was as manager of Topeka in the Southwestern League in 1922. Cooley died in Dallas from the effects of heat prostration in August 1937. (DN)

Coon, William K. / "William"

B	T	HGT	WGT	G	AB	H	R	2B
?	?	?	?	57	232	52	31	5

3B	HR	RBI	BB	SO	SB	BA	SA	OBP
1	0	23	2	4	1	.224	.254	.231

G	IP	H	GS	CG	BB
2	7	9	0	0	0

SO	SH	W	L	PCT	ERA
0	0	0	0	—	5.14

B. 3/21/1855 Philadelphia, PA **D.** 8/30/1915
TEAMS: 75AthNA 76PhiN
DEBUT: 9/4/1875 at Philadelphia; caught Lon Knight and went 0-for-5 in a 6–3 win over Boston's Jack Manning
FINALE: 9/16/1876 at Philadelphia; caught George Zettlein and went 2-for-5 in a 7–6 loss to Louisville's Jim Devlin

William Coon and Lon Knight first came to the NA Athletics in September 1875 as a unit after serving as the battery for the amateur champion Shibe club of Philadelphia. After 1876 he remained with the Athletics for several more seasons while they functioned mostly as an independent team. He later worked for the U.S. mail service in Philadelphia and died in his home city of liver cancer. (DN)

Corkhill, John Stewart / "Pop" "John"

B	T	HGT	WGT	G	AB	H	R	2B
L	R	5'10"	180	1086	4404	1120	650	110

3B	HR	RBI	BB	SO	SB	BA	SA	OBP
80	31	631	174	<u>80</u>	<u>137</u>	.254	.337	.288

G	IP	H	GS	CG	BB
17	62.1	68	1	0	17

SO	SH	W	L	PCT	ERA
21	0	3	4	.429	4.62

B. 4/11/1858 Parkesburg, PA **D.** 4/3/1921
TEAMS: 83–88CinA 88–89BroA 90BroN 91PhiA 91CinN 91–92PitN
DEBUT: 5/1/1883 at Cincinnati; played CF and made 1 hit in a 6–5 win over St. Louis's George McGinnis
FINALE: 7/12/1892 at Pittsburgh; played CF and went 2-for-5 in an 11–1 win over Boston's Tom Lovett

In November 1882 Cincinnati club president Aaron Stern came to Philadelphia to sign John Corkhill, a player spending the off-season pounding a beat as a police officer. When Stern finally tracked down Corkhill after much searching, his quarry reportedly asked him, "Don't you know you can never find a policeman when you want one?"

Corkhill began his pro career as a second baseman in 1879 with the independent Philadelphia Pearls. His premature baldness led to him being nicknamed "Pop" by future Cincinnati teammate Kid Baldwin; additionally, it made him so self-conscious that he was loath to tip his cap when the crowd applauded him. By 1882 Corkhill was playing for the League Alliance Philadelphias under Billy Barnie. After the season he signed a contract to play for Barnie's AA team in Baltimore and then another for Stern's Cincinnati club, explaining that he preferred the Reds because a sister and brother lived near Cincinnati, and Barnie had agreed beforehand to release him if he so requested. Barnie saw it otherwise, but a cash offer persuaded him to sell his claim to Corkhill. The cost to the Reds was probably $400, half of which the club charged to Corkhill as a salary advance.

Previously, Corkhill had often played the infield, but the Reds placed him in the outfield, alternating between center and right. He reportedly got the cold shoulder from several Reds players who wanted Jimmy Macullar to retain his position but in short order proved himself one of the finest defensive outfielders of the 1880s. When newly acquired Hugh Nicol proved unable to handle CF in 1887, Corkhill gladly switched positions with Nicol, preferring CF because he saw more action there. Gifted with a strong throwing arm and exceptional sure-handedness, Corkhill generally recorded an outfield FA about 50 points above the league norm and reportedly once went three years without dropping a fly ball, an incredible feat in a time when many gardeners still disdained wearing gloves. Corkhill's record and attendant reputation demonstrate the importance of fielding skill for nineteenth-century players.

Corkhill also continued to play the infield capably in emergencies and beginning in 1884 was sometimes used as a relief pitcher since he could throw very hard for short stints. Even in his prime, he was no more than a fair hitter, but he was known as an excellent base runner. In addition, he carried the proud distinction all during his career of never having been fined or censured by an umpire.

Commencing in the fall of 1885, Corkhill began to push Cincinnati for a sale to an eastern team to the extent of engaging in a protracted holdout in 1887 when he claimed he could not afford to leave a grocery he now owned in Camden, NJ, and finally signed in April. According to reports, Corkhill actually wanted to leave the Reds because Cincinnati's muggy climate was bad for his health and his wife disliked the city, but there were also suspicions that he was being tempted by higher salary offers from Brooklyn and the Philadelphia A's. In 1888 the Cincinnati management began to seem dissatisfied with Corkhill's performance, and suspicions grew that he was deliberately playing poorly to force a sale. Having reached the age of 30, however, he may simply have been slowing down. On September 10 he was fined for sending word only at the last minute that he was too ill to play in a game and some two weeks later was sold to Brooklyn for $3,500. The talk about his allegedly poor attitude took a toll on his relations with Cincinnati fans. Previously a very popular player in the Queen City, Corkhill subsequently received a hostile reception whenever he returned with his Brooklyn teammates.

Corkhill was one of a number of late-season major acquisitions Brooklyn made in 1888 aiming to overtake the AA-leading Browns, but even his .380 BA over the last 19 games of the season could not do the trick. The next season however, Brooklyn won a torrid race to break St. Louis's string of four consecutive championships, but the 1889 AA pennant proved a climax to Corkhill's career, which soon took a downturn. He injured his arm in an 1890 spring exhibition making a throw home from CF and then was shelved by a lame shoulder in July. Playing in only 51 games, Corkhill suffered his worst offensive season since his rookie year. In midsummer he went home to Camden to run his grocery and did not pick up a ball again until spring when he signed with the Athletics. Although his arm recovered, his hitting dropped off still more to .209 and he was again cut. After a single game with Cincinnati, Corkhill joined Pittsburgh but had his season abruptly ended on September 29 when a stray inshoot from Cincinnati's Ed Crane broke his jaw. Corkhill returned in 1892 to claim the Pittsburgh CF post but was released for a final time in July at the close of the first half of the split-season schedule that was in effect that year.

Unlike many aging MLers of his generation, Corkhill did not go back to the minors. He appears to have made a success of his business career, running two furniture stores in Philadelphia in addition to his Camden grocery and also working at times as a machinist in a furniture factory. In 1896 he was appointed chief of police in Stockton, NJ. Corkhill was living in Pensauken, NJ, when he died following surgery for kidney cancer in 1921. Among all ML outfielders in 500 or more games prior to the increased pitching distance in 1893, Corkhill ranks second only to Mike Griffin in career FA and leads in assists. (DB/DN)

Croft, Arthur F. / "Art"

B	T	HGT	WGT	G	AB	H	R	2B
?	?	?	?	133	517	101	50	14

3B	HR	RBI	BB	SO	SB	BA	SA	OBP
2	0	45	6	40	5	.195	.230	.205

B. 1/23/1855 St. Louis, MO **D.** 3/16/1884
TEAMS: 75RedsNA 77StLN 78IndN
DEBUT: 5/4/1875 at St. Louis; played CF and made 1 hit in a 15–9 loss to the St. Louis Browns' George Bradley
FINALE: 9/13/1878 at Indianapolis; played LF and went 0-for-3 in a 3–0 loss to Boston's Tommy Bond

Art Croft occupied CF for the St. Louis Reds during their brief sojourn in the NA in 1875. Despite a .200 BA and just 5 runs in 19 games, he remained with the Reds the following year, when they were an independent team, and then was signed by the NL Browns for 1877. Croft split that campaign between 1B and the outfield and again produced horrendous offensive numbers. He nonetheless hooked on with Indianapolis when the Hoosier club joined the NL in 1878. A .361 OPS and 41 total bases in 60 games left him homeless after Indianapolis folded. Croft spent a portion of 1879 with Davenport, IA, of the Northwestern League and then returned to St. Louis to play for the independent Browns and work for a wholesale dry goods house. He quit playing ball in 1881 prior to his death from typhoid pneumonia at 29. (DN/DB)

Crowley, William Michael / "Bill"

B	T	HGT	WGT	G	AB	H	R	2B
R	R	5'7½"	159	521	2057	540	263	83

3B	HR	RBI	BB	SO	SB	BA	SA	OBP
22	8	225	102	178	0	.263	.336	.297

B. 4/8/1857 Philadelphia, PA **D.** 7/14/1891
TEAMS: 75PhiNA 77LouN 79–80BufN 81BosN 83PhiA 83CleN 84BosN 85BufN
DEBUT: 4/26/1875 at Philadelphia; played 1B and went 1-for-4 in a 10–7 win over the Philadelphia Centennials' George Bechtel
FINALE: 10/10/1885 at Elmira, NY; played LF and went 1-for-3 in a 7–3 loss to Providence's Dupee Shaw

Bill Crowley lived in Gloucester, NJ, for most of his life and died there of Bright's disease in 1891 at 34. After playing with Gloucester's top amateur team in 1874, he signed with the NA Philadelphia Pearls the following year. Still just 18, he was overpowered, hitting .081 in 9 games, but remained on the club's reserve squad all season and returned in 1876 when the Pearls became an independent team. That July, he joined independent Harrisburg, PA, after the Pearls disbanded and did well enough to earn a spot with Louisville NL for 1877. Crowley hit .282 in his lone year with the Grays and played in every one of the team's games but received no ML offers after the Grays disbanded pursuant to a scandal-ridden ending to their season. Even though Crowley was never mentioned in connection with the scandal, some historians associate him with it, if only tangentially, because he was later blacklisted by the NL, but the two events were completely disparate.

Crowley spent 1878 with Buffalo of the International Association and hit .304 for the loop champs, assuring him a job when the club joined the NL in 1879. He served two seasons with the Bisons, performing well above the league average in both, and in the second led the club in hitting but nonetheless was not reserved for 1881. At that point Crowley signed with Boston, probably a mistake, for after he reportedly went "lame" toward the end of the season, he was blacklisted. The club cited his dissipation, but how bad it was is debatable; Boston owner Arthur Soden and pilot Harry Wright were both known to be intolerant of even mild misbehavior and no doubt were also disturbed by the club's first sub-.500 finish ever in 1881.

Crowley returned to the majors in 1883 with the new NL franchise in Philadelphia as the club's center fielder, but he was released in early September after appearing in just 23 games. He finished the season with Cleveland and then was allowed to return to Boston in 1884 now that Wright had left. Crowley's outfield spot vanished that winter when the Beaneaters signed two young gardeners, Jim Manning and Tommy McCarthy, and he hooked on again with Buffalo. The foundering Bisons were on the verge of extinction, and Crowley was no help in extending their life, scoring just 29 runs in 92 games. Not surprisingly there were no buyers among the other NL teams when the NL put him in an allotment pool after Buffalo disbanded. Crowley played in the Southern League in 1886 but hit just .236 and then returned to Gloucester after fumbling another minor league chance two years later. Upon his death in 1891, *SL* reported that he was unmarried and referred to him as "the latest knight of the diamond to succumb to Father Death's curves." (DN/DB)

Cuthbert, Edgar Edward / "Ned"

B	T	HGT	WGT	G	AB	H	R	2B
R	R	5'6"	140	452	2114	537	453	74

3B	HR	RBI	BB	SO	SB	BA	SA	OBP
17	8	181	65	35	69	.254	.316	.276

G	W	L	PCT	PENNANTS
80	37	43	.463	0

B. 6/20/1845 Philadelphia, PA **D.** 2/6/1905
TEAMS: 71–72AthNA 73PhiNA 74ChiNA 75StLNA 76StLN 77CinN (P/M)82StLA 83StLA 84BalU
DEBUT: 5/20/1871 at Boston; caught Dick McBride and went 0-for-5 in an 11–8 loss to Boston's Al Spalding
FINALE: 9/4/1884 at Baltimore; played CF, batted eighth, and went 2-for-4 in a 15–5 loss to St. Louis's Charlie Sweeney

Ned Cuthbert was married to pitcher Sam "Buck" Weaver's sister until her death in 1889. Some historians consider him the first player to employ a headfirst slide to steal a base and regard him as one of the best early-day outfielders and a particularly good judge of hard-hit balls. But the November 17, 1900, issue of *TSN* took exception, claiming that he "played to the grandstand," making every fielding chance look hard so as to please the crowd.

Cuthbert was also accused of playing inordinately deep and purposely waiting until the last second as if he had misjudged a ball when it was hit in front of him and then, in a burst of speed, racing in and grabbing it off his shoe tops. Hot dog or not, he played past his time and in his last few seasons was almost a caricature of his former self.

Just before his 20th birthday in 1865, Cuthbert joined the original Philadelphia Keystones and remained with them until the spring of 1867 when he agreed to catch for the West Philadelphias. Some four months later, on August 17, he made his debut with the Philadelphia Athletics as a left fielder and change catcher. Cuthbert turned pro in 1869 and bolted the A's the following year when Chicago made him a better offer but then returned to Philadelphia after the NA formed. In his five NA seasons he ranked as one of the better defensive left fielders but was slightly below par offensively. After spending 1875 with the St. Louis Browns, a new NA entry, he returned to the club in 1876 after it transferred to the newly formed National League, and he began to call the Mound City his home. Cuthbert left the Browns after his second straight sub-.250 season and ventured to Cincinnati for the 1877 season but was dropped after he hit just .169 in 12 games while batting in the lead-off spot and finished the season with Indianapolis of the League Alliance. For the next several years he ran a saloon in St. Louis and played with the Browns, which had reorganized as an independent team. In the fall of 1881, after successfully applying for a franchise in the fledgling AA on Cuthbert's recommendation, Chris Von der Ahe rewarded the outfielder by naming him field captain of his new St. Louis entry, which took the Browns nickname, and also appointed him superintendent of the club's Sportsman's Park grounds. Promised a $1,000 bonus by Von der Ahe if the Browns won the pennant, Cuthbert never had a prayer of getting even a dime and evaded the loop cellar only because the Baltimore won scarcely more than a quarter of its games.

Cuthbert returned to the Browns as a player only for part of 1883 and then foolishly tried to prolong his career one more season with Baltimore of the rebel UA. A .202 BA and a .750 FA seemingly consigned him to saloon keeping, but in the fall of 1886, on something of a whim, he applied for a post as an AA umpire. Appointed to the regular Association staff in 1887, Cuthbert lasted only 27 games before he was bounced for inefficiency. He returned once again to the St. Louis saloon business. In 1891 he ran a place in the Grand Opera House. The following year Cuthbert expanded his sphere of operations when he bought out his partner's share in a Market Street saloon called The Drum. Apparently, at some point he overextended himself financially, for by 1895 he was working as a "uniformed driver for City Hospital" ambulance service.

In August 1904 Cuthbert suffered a major stroke and was paralyzed. His second wife, Maggie, whom he had married after Weaver's sister died and then later divorced, nursed him during his darkest hours and remarried him in a bedside ceremony just four days before his death in 1905. (DN)

Dalrymple, Abner Frank / "Abner"

B	T	HGT	WGT	G	AB	H	R	2B
L	R	5'10½"	175	951	4172	1202	813	217

3B	HR	RBI	BB	SO	SB	BA	SA	OBP
81	43	407	204	359	58	.288	.410	.323

B. 9/9/1857 Warren, IL **D.** 1/25/1939
TEAMS: 78MilN 79–86ChiN 87–88PitN 91MilA
DEBUT: 5/1/1878 at Cincinnati; played LF and went 1-for-5 in a 6–4 loss to Cincinnati's Will White
FINALE: 10/2/1891 at Minneapolis; played LF and went 0-for-3 in a 5–0 win over Columbus's Jack Easton

Abner Dalrymple is known best for leading the NL in batting as a rookie with a BA that was second to Paul Hines by today's rules, which count hits played in tied games, something not done in 1878. He should be equally well-known for leading the NL in the most bases advanced in 1880, the lone year that stat was kept. In addition, on July 3, 1883, Dalrymple was the first to crack 4 doubles in a nine-inning game; three weeks later, on July 24, 1883, he and Chicago teammate Mike Kelly shared the distinction of being the first to collect eight plate appearances in a nine-inning game; and on June 29, 1885, he became the first MLer to lead off two consecutive games with a home run. That same year Dalrymple also earned the distinction of being the first lead-off batter to top his loop in home runs.

For all of that, his career was something of a disappointment, especially in light of how sensationally it began. The son of a New-York-born auctioneer, Dalrymple left school at 14 against his father's wishes to work for the Illinois Central Railroad, ostensibly as a substitute brakeman but in reality to beef up the railroad's baseball team. When it became apparent that his abilities eclipsed the competition he was facing, he joined a stronger independent team in Freeport, IL. After playing with the independent Janesville, WI, Mutuals in 1876, Dalrymple came to Milwaukee in 1877 as "a big gawky youth" and accompanied the League Alliance club when it joined the NL in 1878. When Milwaukee folded after just one season, Chicago won a spirited bidding war for the rookie bat titlist, paying him a reported $300 a month, second on the club only to player-manager Cap Anson. Dalrymple more than earned his keep, giving the White Stockings seven straight solid seasons and playing on five pennant winners, peaking in 1885 when he won the NL home run crown and helped Chicago to tie St. Louis in that year's World Series. Up to that point he had suffered only one career glitch, that in 1883 when he had missed several games with an unspecified eye injury he suffered against Providence on May 24. But in 1886 his hitting skills suddenly deserted him.

Several theories were proffered to account for his abrupt decline that season. One was that Dalrymple, who thrived on high deliveries, was ruined by the elimination of the rule allowing a batter to call for either high or low pitches, but it is false. That rule did not come into effect until 1887. A more passable explanation was that pitchers began exploiting Dalrymple's superstition that he would not make a hit all game if he swung at the first pitch he saw that day by dropping an easy strike on the first pitch they served him. Dalrymple himself proposed yet a third possibility, that his eyes were failing him, perhaps due to the injury he had sustained to one of them three years earlier. His manager, Anson, provided the theory that gained the most credence: by 1886 the majors were loaded with good left-handed pitchers and Dalrymple, a left-handed hitter, was simply not capable of hitting a ball curving away from him. Acting on his own notion of his lead-off hitter's problem, Anson began alternating him in LF with rookie Jimmy Ryan, a right-handed hitter, one of the first instances of platooning. The results initially seemed to bear out Anson's thinking when Chicago won the pennant and faced St. Louis in the World Series for the second straight time, but the final game must have raised a sliver of doubt when Dalrymple muffed an easy fly ball that was instrumental in Chicago's losing the game and resulted in his being made the scapegoat for the demoralizing Series defeat. Decried all season for using his faulty eyesight as an excuse for his poor play, he later judiciously maintained that he had simply misjudged the ball, but as he walked off the field after St. Louis scored the winning run, he heard Anson tell him, "You can't play ball for me any more, Dal." Anson, it need be said, was never an ardent fan of Dalrymple's, even in his salad days. In his book *A Ball Player's Career*, Anson said, "[Dalrymple] was only an ordinary fielder, and a fair base runner, but excelled as a batsman. I have said that he was a fair fielder, and in that respect perhaps I am rating him too high, as his poor fielding cost us several games. . . . Dalrymple was a queer proposition, and for years a very steady [and temperate] player. He was never known to spend a cent in those days, and was so close that he would wait for somebody else to buy a newspaper and then borrow it in order to see what was going on. Later on he broke loose, however, and when he did he became one of the sportiest of sports, blowing his money as if he had found it and setting a hot pace for his followers."

Little more than a month after the 1886 season ended Dalrymple was sold to Pittsburgh, where his deterioration accelerated. In 1887 he hit just .212 in 92 games. That winter, Dalrymple played in California hoping to revive his batting stroke, and when he reported to Pittsburgh's training camp the following spring, he was wearing a glove in the field for the first time. When his hitting only worsened—.525 OPS in 57 games—students of the nineteenth-century game were provided with further ammunition for their theory that what Dalrymple really needed to wear on the field were glasses. Whether because of his earlier eye injury, a marked increase in the speed and spin with which pitches by the mid-1880s were being delivered, or a gradual deterioration of his vision due to natural causes that eventually stabilized, Dalrymple almost certainly was among the numerous ML players in the late nineteenth and early twentieth century who would have profited from wearing glasses but had to refrain so long as "cheaters" were condemned by their peers as a sign of weakness and aging. Moreover, optometry in the nineteenth century was still so rudimentary that conceivably Dalrymple might have tried glasses at some point, perhaps during his winter in California where no one really knew him, but found none that improved his vision enough to sharpen his hitting and certainly none sturdy enough to survive the vigorous demands put on him as an outfielder or a base runner.

Released by Pittsburgh at his request in September 1888, Dalrymple served out the remainder of his career in the minors with the exception of a few weeks at the tail end of 1891 when his Milwaukee Western Association club replaced the disbanded Cincinnati franchise in the AA. His performance in that juncture—he led the team in BA and SA—seemingly demonstrated that he might still have fuel left in his tank, but pundits were aware that the pitching in the AA in 1891 was no better than what he could still handle with fair success in the minor leagues. Not only did Dalrymple draw no interest from a ML team for the following season, but he could not even find a taker in the high minors and finally signed with Spokane of the Pacific Northwest League. Some three years later he was given a financial cushion that might have enabled him to quit the game when his father, after years of refusing to accept his being a ballplayer, reconciled with him shortly before his death and left him a third of a $300,000 estate. Instead, Dalrymple stubbornly continued to descend the baseball ladder, draining every last drop of his talent. His final day on the field, at 50, was with a Grand Forks, ND, semipro team in 1907.

In 1926, Dalrymple, a widower (his first marriage had been to Winifred Green, a wealthy ship owner's niece, in 1885), returned to Warren, IL, his place of birth, to marry Margaret Glasgow, a widow. His second wife had a home where he lived out his remaining years after retiring from the Northern Pacific Railroad in 1928. In 1939 Dalrymple died at his Warren home. Later that year a monument works in Galena, IL, created a granite stone for his grave, featuring the image of a left-handed batter and an inscription that ended, "Chicago White Stockings, 1879–1886." (DN/DB/PM)

Deane, John Henry / "Harry"

B	T	HGT	WGT	G	AB	H	R	2B
?	?	5'7"	150	53	225	54	32	8

3B	HR	RBI	BB	SO	SB	BA	SA	OBP
2	0	15	6	3	2	.240	.293	.260

G	W	L	PCT	PENNANTS
5	2	3	.400	0

B. 5/6/1846 Trenton, NJ **D.** 5/31/1925
TEAMS: (P/M)71KekNA 74BalNA
DEBUT: 7/20/1871 at Fort Wayne; played LF and made 1 hit in a 24–9 loss to the Athletics' Dick McBride
FINALE: 10/14/1874 at Baltimore; played CF and went 1-for-4 in a 15–2 loss to Boston's Al Spalding

Hired in July 1871, Harry Deane captained the Kekies during most of his brief 6-game stay with the Fort Wayne club. He served as Baltimore's center fielder in 1874 and later in the decade umpired 4 NL games in the Midwest, where he was living at the time. Deane began his career in the late 1860s and served as the Cincinnati Red Stockings' tenth man in 1870, replacing Dick Hurley. He died in Indianapolis at 71. (DN)

Decker, George A. / "George"

B	T	HGT	WGT	G	AB	H	R	2B
L	L	6'1"	180	704	2739	756	423	98

3B	HR	RBI	BB	SO	SB	BA	SA	OBP
51	25	416	173	127	112	.276	.376	.324

B. 6/1/1866 York, PA **D.** 6/7/1909
TEAMS: 92–97ChiN 98StLN 98–99LouN 99WasN
DEBUT: 7/11/1892 at Chicago; played RF and went 0-for-3 in a 3–2 loss to Boston's Kid Nichols
FINALE: 7/12/1899 at Washington; played 1B and went 0-for-3 in a 10–5 win over Cincinnati's Jack Taylor

George Decker was the son of a prosperous lumber merchant who moved from Pennsylvania to Illinois shortly after his son's birth and later took the family to the Los Angeles area. Decker then survived the Great Chatsworth Train Disaster on August 10, 1887, but had to be rescued after being trapped beneath the dead body of a fellow passenger for several hours after the train bound for Niagara Falls plunged into a ravine when it crossed over a trestle weakened earlier in the day by a fire, causing it to collapse and resulting in the deaths of some 85 people.

By 1887 Decker had already launched his baseball career with semipro teams in Los Angeles, playing on weekends while he attended school to become an accountant. Over the next few years he came east from time to time to play pro ball but always returned to Los Angeles. Shortly after his

26th birthday in 1892, Decker signed with Chicago but soon realized his mistake. His best position was 1B, but he was hardly about to dislodge player-manager Cap Anson. In his very first game with the Colts, the *Chicago Tribune* noted that he was playing "out of position" in RF, and that remained the case for almost his entire career. After a weak rookie season (.227 in 78 games), Decker married Louisa Stafford of Fairbury, IL, and reported to camp in the spring determined to win a regular job. He quickly demonstrated to his teammates that he was the best first baseman on the club, but that meant nothing to Anson, who used him almost everywhere else in his sophomore year. The same pattern continued in his remaining four years with the Colts. Though Decker played over 100 games on two occasions with the club, he never saw action in more than 71 games in a season at any one position.

On September 1, 1896, one of the rare days when he played 1B, his left wrist was broken in a baserunning collision. The fracture mended poorly, and when a second bone in his forearm was also found to be cracked, there was talk of releasing him to Detroit and making him player-manager of the Western League club. Decker overcame these obstacles and was off to a strong start in 1897 when Anson took 1B away from him on June 2 and he was moved to LF. Some four weeks later Louisville's Jim Jones beaned him, and he was still reeling when his wife died in July. Despite all these setbacks, in 1898, when Anson was fired, Decker seemingly was in line to finally land the Chicago 1B job, but general manager Jim Hart instead tried to get waivers on him so he could go to Chicago's Omaha farm team as a player-manager. When St. Louis thwarted the plan by claiming him, in March 1898 Decker wrote to Hart, "Whatever you do, I beg you not to sentence me to St. Louis." Hart, supposedly assured him that would not happen but then loaned him to the Browns with the proviso that he could be recalled if Chicago needed him. At that juncture the *Chicago Tribune* entered the fray: "Handsome, popular George Decker was turned over to Tim Hurst this afternoon. . . . President Hart says he is satisfied with the arrangement by which Decker is to go to St. Louis, inasmuch as Decker is satisfied."

The reader thus must judge whether Decker got off to a wretched start in St. Louis because he was disheartened to be there or for some other reason. He was soon released in any event and signed with Louisville as a free agent, overriding Chicago's protest that it still owned the rights to him. At an NL meeting in November 1898, Louisville was allowed to keep Decker and St. Louis was fined $1,000 and ordered to pay Chicago $500 for the insult, but there is some doubt that either the League or Chicago ever collected from the nearly bankrupt Browns. Decker opened 1899 at 1B with Louisville but was cut in June after having been sick for some weeks with "acute dyspepsia." After railing against Louisville for having been "thrown away like an old shoe," he joined Washington, where he lasted only 4 games.

In 1900, Decker remained at his parents' California home until early July, when he was taken to a Los Angeles hospital "in demented condition" following the deaths in recent years of his wife (1897) and son (1894). He recovered long enough to remarry and play in the California League for a time in 1901 but was forced to stop when he was afflicted by uncorrectable astigmatism and an inflammation of the optic nerve, all of which and more were perhaps triggered by his 1897 beaning. Decker then deteriorated rapidly. His mind permanently affected, he was institutionalized again and later released to live out his remaining years at his parents' home in Compton, CA. Decker died there of consumption in 1909. (DN/DB/PM)

Donovan, Patrick Joseph / "Patsy"

B	T	HGT	WGT	G	AB	H	R	2B
L	L	5'11½"	175	1330	5604	1698	1065	162

3B	HR	RBI	BB	SO	SB	BA	SA	OBP
63	15	572	353	131	424	.303	.361	.352

G	W	L	PCT	PENNANTS
266	129	129	.500	0

B. 3/16/1863 Queenstown, Ireland

D. 12/25/1953 Lawrence, MA

TEAMS: 90BosN 90BroN 91LouA 91WasA 92WasN 92–99PitN (P/M)97PitN (P/M)99PitN 00StLN (P/M)01–03StLN 04WasAL (P/M)06–07BroN (M)08BroN (M)10–11BosA

DEBUT: 4/19/1890 at Brooklyn; played CF and made 3 hits in a 15–9 win over Brooklyn's Bill Terry

FINALE: 10/5/1907 at Boston; finished the game in RF and went 0-for-1 in a 6–5 loss to Boston's Irv Young and Jake Boultes

Patsy Donovan was an excellent base runner who scored over 1,300 runs and a right fielder who led at times in outfield assists and double plays and logged a .301 career BA and 2,253 hits. But he finished with just a .702 OPS, the lowest of any career .300 hitter in ML history with a minimum of 3,000 ABs.

Born in Ireland, Donovan shaved two years off his birth year at some point after coming to the States with his family in 1866. Hence he was 23 rather than 21, as he claimed, when he left the cotton mills of Lawrence, MA, in 1886 to play for the local New England League team. Donovan then spent the following year with Salem and the next two seasons with London, Ontario, leading the International Association in batting with a .359 mark in the second of them. Injured part of 1889, he hit just .268 in 53 games but nonetheless was signed by Boston NL in 1890 when PL raids stripped the Hub entry of its entire starting outfield. When he hit very sporadically, he was cut in July and then picked up by Brooklyn as an injury replacement for Darby O'Brien. Donovan finished his rookie season with a composite .241 BA and a weak .269 SA, but Louisville manager Jack Chapman saw promise in him.

Opening the 1891 campaign in LF with the Colonels, Donovan hit well but was released to Washington when Chapman felt his new outfielder was trying to rally the team against him. Washington then foolishly released Donovan when he started poorly the following year and tried glasses without success to correct his vision problems. Pittsburgh snatched him, and his eyesight improved enough to lead the Pirates in hits and runs the second half of the season. In the spring of 1893 manager Al Buckenberger named Donovan captain and lead-off hitter. It was a role he would occupy until 1897, when he replaced Connie Mack as Pittsburgh's manager in addition to his playing duties. Unlike most performers who slip in their play after assuming added supervisory responsibilities, Donovan thrived, hitting .322, his best mark to date. But when he brought the Pirates home eighth in the 12-team league, his pilot's cap went to Bill Watkins in 1898. The following May, with the club in tenth place under Watkins, Donovan was again asked to do double duty. He lifted the team to seventh, seeming to make a case to rehire him as skipper in 1900. Instead he was sold to St. Louis that December for $1,000 when Pittsburgh inherited the cream of the about-to-disband Louisville team, including player-manager Fred Clarke. Unfazed, Donovan won his only NL stolen base crown in 1900 and hit .316, putting himself in line to be named the Cardinals' new player-manager in 1901. (DN)

*Dorgan, Jeremiah F. / "Jerry"

B	T	HGT	WGT	G	AB	H	R	2B
L	R	?	165	131	531	150	74	22

3B	HR	RBI	BB	SO	SB	BA	SA	OBP
4	0	49	14	11	—	.282	.339	.303

B. ?/?/1856 Meriden, CT **D.** 6/10/1891
TEAMS: 80WorN 82PhiA 84IndA 84BroA 85DetN
DEBUT: 7/8/1880 at Buffalo; played RF and went 0-for-4 in a 10–2 loss to Buffalo's Jim Galvin
FINALE: 6/25/1885 at Detroit; played CF and went 2-for-4 in a 7–0 loss to Providence's Dupee Shaw

The younger brother of ML outfielder Mike Dorgan, Jerry Dorgan might have been an outstanding player but for a hopeless addiction to alcohol. An excellent fielder and a strong base runner, he began as a catcher with the amateur Stowe club in his hometown of Meriden, CT. By 1879 he was catching Mickey Welch at Holyoke, MA, but by the time he made his ML debut the following year he was appearing more often in the outfield. Cut after he hit just .200 in 7 games, Dorgan split 1881 between the minor league New York Mets and independent Newark.

The Opening Day of the AA's inaugural season as a major league found him in RF and batting leadoff for the Philadelphia Athletics. In early August his irredeemable alcoholism finally became more than the A's owners could bear. Released in the middle of the month, he finished the season with independent Harrisburg. After spending 1883 with Dan O'Leary's independent Indianapolis club, Dorgan accompanied the Hoosiers when they joined the AA the following year. As in his initial AA season in 1882, Dorgan opened 1884 in RF and batting leadoff. Though he was the Hoosiers' best hitter, manager Jim Gifford came to the same unhappy conclusion that all of Dorgan's previous employers had reached: he was drunk too often to be dependable. Upon leaving Indianapolis, Dorgan caught four AA contests for Brooklyn. They were the last games he served behind the plate in the majors, as dissipation and the increased speed with which pitchers were hurling made him too prone to passed balls—he committed 29 in the 9 AA games he caught in 1884.

Dorgan received one final chance to pull his career out of the flames in 1885 and seemed ready to make the most of it when he went 4-for-4 for Detroit NL on Opening Day and was 10-for-14 in the Wolverines' 3-game sweep of Buffalo to start the season. But Dorgan then began drinking heavily. A common belief is that he lost his RF job when Sam Thompson joined the team, but actually he had been removed from the lineup a week earlier even though he ranked third at the time on the club in hitting at .286. In bidding him farewell the *Detroit Free Press* said, "Dorgan has been mastered by his arch enemy."

Dorgan's few remaining years on earth were a blur. On the night of June 9, 1891, he was found unconscious in the livery stable behind the Kilbourn House hotel in Middletown, CT. Taken to lockup, he died the following morning in his cell of acute alcohol poisoning. (DN)

---

*Dorgan, Michael Cornelius / "Mike"

B	T	HGT	WGT	G	AB	H	R	2B
R	R	5'9"	180	715	2924	802	443	112

3B	HR	RBI	BB	SO	SB	BA	SA	OBP
34	4	346	118	179	39	.274	.340	.303

G	IP	H	GS	CG	BB
18	140	123	15	13	59

SO	SH	W	L	PCT	ERA
103	0	8	7	.533	3.28

G	W	L	PCT	PENNANTS
138	67	70	.489	0

B. 10/2/1853 Middletown, CT **D.** 4/26/1909
TEAMS: 77StLN (P/M)79SyrN (P/M)80ProN (P/M)81WorN 81DetN 83–87NYN 90SyrA
DEBUT: 5/8/1877 at St. Louis; played RF and went hitless in a 3–2 win over Boston's Tommy Bond
FINALE: 6/9/1890 at New York; played RF and went 1-for-5 in a 13–7 loss to Brooklyn's Mike Mattimore

Mike Dorgan was the older brother of ML outfielder Jerry Dorgan. After serving at SS for the independent Syracuse Stars in 1876, the elder Dorgan signed with St. Louis NL in 1877 and not only played in every game as a rookie but led the club in total bases. Despite sharing retrospective Rookie of the Year honors with Chicago pitcher Terry Larkin, he left the NL in 1878 when St. Louis ceded its NL franchise. That season, Dorgan led International Association Syracuse in BA (.319) and was rated the Stars' top position player when they joined the NL in 1879.

In his second NL season Dorgan slipped a bit at the plate but demonstrated that he was arguably the most versatile player in the game, serving at every position but LF and CF. He joined Providence in 1880 after the Stars folded. The following year he was named Worcester's captain after moving to that NL club. But that August, Worcester released him owing to his "lame shoulder" and a "lack of harmony in the nine" caused by his "incompetence as captain of the team." Dorgan quickly signed with Detroit but was blacklisted after the season when it developed that Worcester had sugarcoated its reasons for cutting him. Like his brother, Dorgan had a huge drinking problem.

Forced to sit out 1882, Dorgan returned to the NL in 1883 with New York and suffered through a bad reentry year, hitting just .234. The following season he not only revived as a hitter but spent time in New York's pitching rotation, going 8-7 after a broken left thumb temporarily limited his use as an outfielder. Yet Dorgan never pitched again in the majors, perhaps because he was already experiencing the first symptoms of an arthritic shoulder that would soon impair his play.

By 1887 Dorgan had a share in a Syracuse saloon and claimed he no longer needed baseball unless the Giants met his salary demands. Eventually, he signed in time to open the season in RF but was subpar physically and soon lost his job temporarily to Danny Richardson. By the following spring Dorgan was in Hot Springs, AR, getting treatment for his shoulder. He toyed with the notion of playing for the Syracuse International Association club but then announced his retirement, only to change his mind that August and demand $900 to finish the season with the Stars. Manager Charlie Hackett opted to keep Fred Ely in LF instead, forcing Dorgan to wait until 1889 to mount a comeback.

Although 36 and the second oldest player on the Stars, he was retained for his name attraction when Syracuse joined the AA in 1890 and opened the season in RF. After being suspended for intoxication in May, he was cut the following month when his salary, the highest on the team, coupled with his .216 BA, forced the financially strapped Stars to dump their top drawing card.

Less than a year later Dorgan was incarcerated in Syracuse after beating a man "to a pulp" in a drunken brawl. Shortly thereafter he underwent the Keeley treatment (for chronic alcoholism) and asked his former Giants teammate John M. Ward to recommend him to Nick Young for post as an NL umpire, but Ward declined. The resilient Dorgan eventually found other ways to sustain himself. His son later tried out for the local Eastern League club but lacked his father's talent. Dorgan was still in reasonably good health when he opted to repair an old knee injury in 1909 at a Hartford hospital. He died of blood poisoning after undergoing surgery. (DN/PM)

Dowd, Thomas Jefferson / "Tommy" "Pink Coat" "Buttermilk Tommy"

B	T	HGT	WGT	G	AB	H	R	2B
R	R	5'8"	173	1183	4920	1334	799	145

3B	HR	RBI	BB	SO	SB	BA	SA	OBP
81	21	449	332	200	335	.271	.346	.320

G	W	L	PCT	PENNANTS
92	31	60	.341	0

B. 4/20/1869 Holyoke, MA **D.** 7/2/1933
TEAMS: 91BosA 91WasA 92WasN 93–95StLN (P/M)96–97StLN 97PhiN 98StLN 99CleN 01BosAL
DEBUT: 4/8/1891 at Boston; played RF and went 1-for-4 in an 11–7 loss to Baltimore's Sadie McMahon
FINALE: 9/28/1901 at Boston; played LF and went 2-for-3 in a 10–9 win over Milwaukee's Bill Reidy

Rather a dandy ("he of the suave smile and Italian sunset neckties"), Tommy Dowd was called "Pink Coat," a seemingly pejorative nickname, but it appears to have originated when he wore a pink coat while fox hunting or playing roller polo, two of his favorite pastimes. What can be said of Dowd that is indubitably pejorative, however, is that he played for just about all of the most execrable ML teams in the decade of the 1890s in between his short sojourn with the AA-flag-winning Boston Reds in 1891 and his final season with second-place Boston AL in 1901.

After graduating from a Holyoke high school in 1888, Dowd enrolled at Brown University, where he played 2B and was the college team's leading hitter in 1890 before signing with Boston AA. In the spring of 1891 he appeared to have won the Reds' 2B job in spring training, but when the opening bell rang, manager Arthur Irwin went with veteran Cub Stricker instead. After 4 games with Boston, Dowd was loaned without his consent to Washington, which needed a replacement for injured second baseman Fred Dunlap. He remained in Washington for two years, attended Georgetown for "special classes" (probably so that he could play football for the Hoyas), and liked everything about the city but its baseball team. Dowd nearly escaped it in May 1892 when New York wanted to swap Denny Lyons for him, but the trade that might have changed his career ran aground after Washington manager Billie Barnie vetoed the intractable Lyons. When Dowd hit just .243, he was released in December 1892.

Allowed to pass through waivers, Dowd signed with St. Louis and thrived at first, leading the Browns in runs, hits, total bases, and steals in 1893. It proved to be his best overall season in the majors as he also fielded .944 and logged 27 outfield assists. But the 1893 campaign was also the Browns' best during his stay. In 1895 the club lost 92 of 131 decisions and the following year it nose-dived into the NL cellar for the first of three successive seasons. Dowd managed the Browns for a time in both 1896 and 1897 and got the club to play at a .341 clip, better than anyone else who handled its reins during that span. Then in June 1897 he seemingly won his freedom from the NL dungeon when he was traded to the Phillies for outfielder Dick Harley and second baseman Bill Hallman. Unhappily, the Phils plummeted that season to tenth place and then added to Dowd's torment by dealing him back to the Browns in 1898.

Not having breathed anything higher than eighth-place air since 1894, Dowd had a moment to dream that he could actually be in a pennant race in 1899 when news came that Cleveland and St. Louis were merging under syndicate ownership and the Spiders' best players were ticketed for the Mound City. But he soon discovered that he was headed for Cleveland instead along with all the losers on the 1898 Browns. In 1899 Dowd led the Spiders in walks (48), steals (28), and runs (81) and otherwise did his best for the worst ML team in history, but it was never really very good, as he finished the season with a .669 OPS, cementing his position as the worst hitter during the 1890s with a minimum of 4,000 PAs whose primary position was in the outfield.

Among the many marginal players jettisoned when the NL pared to eight teams after the 1899 season, Dowd delivered an undistinguished performance in the newly renamed minor American League in 1900 but surprised pundits when he made the Boston AL club in the spring of 1901, was the first player to come to bat for the franchise in an official game, played regularly all year, and scored 100 runs for only the second time in his career. Released nonetheless, he spent several seasons in the minors, finishing in 1907 as Holyoke's player-manager, and then coached college baseball for a time and scouted for the Red Sox in the New England area.

In July 1933 Dowd's body was found floating in the Connecticut River near Holyoke. An autopsy established that he had drowned, but whether his death was accidental, suicide, or foul play was never determined, although his death certificate lists the cause as accidental. Dowd's nickname of "Buttermilk Tommy" is suspect and may belong to Tom Dowse. There are several references, however, to his other nickname. One such: "'Pink Coat' Tommy Dowd is seldom heard of nowadays," appeared in the February 9, 1906, issue of the *Washington Post.* (DN/DB/PM)

Duffee, Charles Edward / "Charlie" "Home Run"

B	T	HGT	WGT	G	AB	H	R	2B
R	R	5'5½"	151	508	1943	518	314	67

3B	HR	RBI	BB	SO	SB	BA	SA	OBP
33	35	281	180	150	110	.267	.389	.332

B. 1/27/1866 Mobile, AL **D.** 12/24/1894
TEAMS: 89–90StLA 91ColA 92WasN 93CinN
DEBUT: 4/17/1889 at Cincinnati; played CF and went 2-for-3 in a 5–1 win over Cincinnati's Tony Mullane
FINALE: 4/30/1893 at Cincinnati; played LF and went 2-for-3 in an 8–1 loss to Chicago's Gus McGinnis

In his rookie year Charlie Duffee blasted 16 homers to set a record for the most four-spots in a season by a player with a sub-.250 BA that lasted until 1914. Aptly nicknamed, he hit some of the longest jacks seen to that point but tailed off badly in the second half of his frosh season and was instrumental in the Browns' failure to capture their fifth straight AA pennant.

Duffee played near his home for the amateur Acid Iron Earths before joining the Mobile Southern League team in 1887. Initially a lead-off hitter because of his short stature, he was moved to the heart of the order once his power emerged. Duffee switched to Birmingham of the SL in 1888 when Mobile did not field a team. Acquired that winter by St. Louis, he supplanted weak-hitting Harry Lyons in CF. Duffee was left alone that winter by PL raiders but was unable to rejoin the Browns until June 1890 after missing the first two months of the season while sick at his Mobile home. Upon arrival, he played almost every inning but failed to display the same power. The following February, the early-day Hack Wilson prototype was sold to Columbus of the AA and rebounded to lead the team in BA, SA, total bases, home runs, and RBI. When Columbus was left out of the AA-NL merger that winter, Duffee was assigned to Washington. A poor season with the D.C. entry in 1892 led to his release in October. Cincinnati, needing a left fielder, was quick to snatch him, and he was in the Reds' Opening Day lineup the following spring. After beginning the season 0-for-9, he went 2-for-3 in his next game, but it was too late to save his job. Duffee returned to the Southern League with Atlanta in May 1893 and hit well right up until August 30, when the *Atlanta Constitution* reported, "Duffee's health . . . is not very good, and he has gone to his home in Mobile." He worked for a time at a saloon but was confined to a bed by the following fall and died in Mobile of consumption on Christmas Day 1894. (DN)

Dungan, Samuel Morrison / "Sam" "Dunny"

B	T	HGT	WGT	G	AB	H	R	2B
R	R	5'11"	180	244	984	285	144	45

3B	HR	RBI	BB	SO	SB	BA	SA	OBP
14	2	124	66	29	29	.290	.370	.337

B. 7/29/1866 Ferndale, CA **D.** 3/16/1939
TEAMS: 92–94ChiN 94LouN 00ChiN 01WasAL
DEBUT: 4/12/1892 at St. Louis; played RF and went 3-for-4 in a 14–10 win over St. Louis's Kid Gleason and Ted Breitenstein

FINALE: 9/27/1901 at Washington; played RF and went 2-for-4 in a 6–4 loss to Chicago's Wiley Piatt

References list Sam Dungan's arm of choice as unknown, but the February 24, 1894, *TSN* said that he "could not catch fly balls with his left hand," indicating that he likely threw righty. Dungan was an excellent contact hitter, particularly in the minors, but had little patience and was both a poor base runner and a mediocre fielder. Also militating against him was premature baldness. After he had torn up the Western League for several seasons in the late 1890s, *TSN* said that even though he was only 33 in 1900, he was considered too old, in part because he was prematurely gray in addition to being bald and looked ancient with his fringe of gray hair whenever he doffed his cap.

But despite his unprepossessing appearance, Dungan appears to have been a fair hand with the ladies. The scion of a wealthy Santa Ana family, he was a catcher with semipro teams around Los Angeles and San Diego in the late 1880s and billed himself as a Harvard graduate. In 1890 he came north to play for Oakland, moved to the outfield, and was leading the California League in hitting when he met Mamie Bogard, the daughter of a local banker, and married her on March 21, 1891, at the Ramona Hotel after she came to Los Angeles to visit him. The couple was still at the hotel when Dungan's father got wind of the marriage. After registering at the hotel as "Jones," he met with his son and convinced him that he would be disowned if he consummated the nuptials. Dungan tearfully left Mamie, saying he had to go to Santa Ana on business, and the old man, still posing as Jones, then told her that Dungan actually had deserted her and gone to Arizona to herd cattle. When Mamie went to Santa Ana to learn the truth, the Dungans refused to receive her, and she then wired her mother, realizing she had been deserted and needed money to return home to Oakland. Later she learned Dungan was playing ball in Milwaukee and followed him there. The couple then reunited, but Dungan's family continued to try to break them up. Some two years later the *Los Angeles Times* painted a very different picture of Mamie, calling her an "Oakland adventuress" who took up with other men while living with Dungan in Chicago, where he was playing for the Colts, and then went back to California where she continued to be supported by him while living with another man. When she sued him for divorce, charging desertion, he proved he had been in touch with her and had sent her support, and a bad light then fell on her for her alleged "orgies." Followers of the Dungan saga were then left on their own to reconcile the two very different versions of his relationship with his wife, but *TSN* offered some assistance in January 1893 by announcing that ex-ML pitcher Jack Fanning and Dungan's wife were "no longer friends" after a falling out over who had ownership of a diamond ring that Fanning apparently had given her after wooing her away from Dungan. The affair was part of what drove Dungan to go east to Milwaukee in 1891 (*see* Jack Fanning).

But anyone who saw Dungan as a lamb led to slaughter by a wanton woman and a nefarious Fanning might have had occasion to reframe when the Detroit papers began speculating why the outfielder, who had been loaned by Chicago to the Wolverines in 1894 and hit a ton, was having so much trouble getting untracked in 1895. Purportedly, the slump was caused by stress put on Dungan when a local Detroit physician named MacQuisten accused the outfielder of having "alienated his wife's affections." But once the doctor retracted the accusation as the idle gossip of his servant girl, the speculation developed into whether the good doctor had wanted to make the matter a court case because Dungan had family money and was thus a ripe target. Then in the summer of 1897, while Dungan was still with Detroit, MacQuisten accused the outfielder of resuming the affair and sued him for $1,500 "for estranging his wife's affections." The following May a Detroit jury could not reach a verdict, and the case against "the bald headed fielder" was thrown out, but a retrial was said to be a possibility. Meanwhile, Dungan was among the WL hitting leaders as usual. The following year he paced the loop with a .347 BA but was dropped by manager George Stallings as too old when the WL tried to bolster its status in 1900 by changing its name to the American League. After signing with Kansas City under Jim Manning, he was moved to 1B and repeated as the circuit batting champ with a .337 mark. Closing his eyes to Dungan's age and reputation for being "rather gumshoey on the bases," Manning hauled him to Washington when it became the new home of the KC franchise after the AL went major in 1901. Dungan proceeded to hit .320, still the record high by a post-1900 untarnished player with 400 ABs in his final ML season.

In January 1902 the *Washington Post* surmised that all of the Senators' regular outfielders in 1901 would be "lost in the shuffle" now that the club had acquired Ed Delahanty, Jimmy Ryan, and Bill Keister. Dungan nonetheless worked out at American Park with the rest of the club that March but was released to Milwaukee before the AL season started. He finished his playing career in 1905 by hitting .286 for Memphis of the Southern Association and then returned to California, where he operated a cigar store for a time and then bought an orange grove. Dungan died in 1939 of a heart attack at his Santa Ana home, where he had lived since he was 12 years old, and left behind a widow, Mary, and two children. (DN)

Eden, Charles M. / "Charlie"

B	T	HGT	WGT	G	AB	H	R	2B
L	L	?	168	226	935	244	118	56

3B	HR	RBI	BB	SO	SB	BA	SA	OBP
18	4	77	33	26	—	.261	.372	.296

G	IP	H	GS	CG	BB
6	27.2	34	2	1	6

SO	SH	W	L	PCT	ERA
8	0	1	3	.250	5.53

B. 1/18/1855 Lexington, KY **D.** 9/17/1920
TEAMS: 77ChiN 79CleN 84–85PitA
DEBUT: 8/17/1877 at Chicago; played RF and went 2-for-4 in a 12–6 win over St. Louis's Tricky Nichols
FINALE: 10/1/1885 at Philadelphia; played LF before switching places with pitcher Pete Meegan prior to the fourth inning, went 0-for-3, and took the 4–3 loss to Philadelphia's Bobby Mathews

Charlie Eden spent only two full seasons and parts of two others in the majors but was better than many outfielders of his time who enjoyed much longer careers in the show. He is also perhaps the lone MLer to debut as a position player and leadoff hitter and conclude his career with a pitching loss.

After playing with independent Indianapolis in 1876, Eden performed for two League Alliance teams the following year before joining Chicago NL in August and finishing the season in right field. But a .218 BA gave Chicago no incentive to retain him. Eden then went to the independent Cleveland Forest Citys and was part of the core of that team when it joined the NL in 1879. On Opening Day in 1879 Eden stepped to the plate against Providence's John M. Ward as the first Cleveland batter in NL history and ignominiously fanned on three pitches. He otherwise had a fine year, leading the NL in doubles and his team in home runs, total bases, BA, and SA. Yet to be found is an explanation for why Eden then disappeared into independent ball until he joined Grand Rapids in 1883. After leading the Northwestern League in hitting with a .359 BA, he remained with the Michigan team until it disbanded for financial reasons on August 2, 1884, freeing him to sign with Pittsburgh. In the remaining month and a half of the 1884 AA campaign, Eden was one of the few bright spots on the Alleghenys and a natural choice to be reserved for the following year.

Eden ranked among the early-season AA batting leaders in 1885 but tailed off sharply. Some of the reason for his dip may have been that he played hurt in the last third of the season. In 1891, Pete Browning, in one of his rambling recitations in *TSN*, said that in 1885 he had walloped a line drive—"I got a good square swipe at one of Morris [*sic*] dead-arm floaters"—that hit Eden in the leg and put him permanently "out of commission." In all likelihood the blow came in a late July series between Pittsburgh and Louisville, and while Browning exaggerated its effect on Eden in that Eden remained in the lineup, indications are that he was never the same player. When Pittsburgh made no effort to sign him for 1886, he played for an independent team in tiny Kankakee, IL. The following spring Eden begged Indianapolis NL for a tryout but flunked it owing to a chronic bad ankle, perhaps the lingering result of Browning's hard shot off his leg. Forced to retire from the game, Eden, who had worked winters as a railroader, accepted a promotion to a conductor's position on the Big Four railroad. He was still in the employ of the Big Four in March of 1895 when *TSN* reported that he was at "Death's Door" from injuries he sustained after stepping off a moving train. Eden survived the calamity, however, and continued to be a railroader until he succumbed to a stroke at 65. (DN)

Ellick, Joseph J. / "Joe"

B	T	HGT	WGT	G	AB	H	R	2B
?	?	5'10"	162	116	487	106	77	12

3B	HR	RBI	BB	SO	SB	BA	SA	OBP
0	0	2	19	4	1	.218	.242	.247

G	IP	H	GS	CG	BB
1	3	1	0	0	1

SO	SH	W	L	PCT	ERA
0	0	0	0	.000	3.00

G	W	L	PCT	PENNANTS
13	6	6	.500	0

B. 4/3/1854 Cincinnati, OH **D.** 4/21/1923
TEAMS: 75RedsNA 78MilN 80WorN 84ChiU (P/M)84PitU 84KCU 84BalU
DEBUT: 5/13/1875 at St. Louis; played 3B in a 15–2 loss to Chicago's George Zettlein
FINALE: 10/11/1884 at Milwaukee; played SS, went 0-for-3 and made 2 errors in a 5–2 loss to Milwaukee's Henry Porter in a game shortened to seven innings

Despite a short and unmemorable ML career, Joe Ellick was a well-recognized figure on the baseball scene until the end of the nineteenth century. Born in Cincinnati, he traveled all the way to New Orleans in 1872 to play for his first organized team, the Robert E. Lee club, and then returned to the Lees in 1874 after spending the previous season with the semipro St. Louis Empires. Ellick began 1875 with the Empires but deserted in April to play for the Eagle club of Louisville. In October 1886 he claimed to have been the first pro player the Louisville team ever had, but if so his stay was brief. By mid-May he was back in St. Louis to make his NA debut with the St. Louis Reds. Ellick resumed his iterant ways in 1876, playing in Memphis with the local independent Reds, and after a year in the League Alliance made his NL debut in 1878 with Milwaukee on June 1 as a catcher. Two years later Ellick returned to the NL for 5 games with Worcester but also played with at least four other pro teams that summer, finishing with the Cincinnati Buckeyes. He then left the game for two years to work in a Kansas City railroad freight office.

When Ellick returned to baseball in 1883, it was to captain the Springfield Northwestern League club. Approaching his 30th birthday, he seemed to have little chance of ever rising above minor league play again. That winter, however, the rebel UA formed, creating close to one hundred new openings on the ML level. Ellick nailed one of them with Chicago and later moved to Pittsburgh, Kansas City, and Baltimore. He returned to his railroad freight office post in 1885. It is not known how he persuaded NL president Nick Young to hire him as an umpire in July 1886. Initially, he was willing to work only games in Kansas City but by the middle of the month agreed to a schedule that would transfer him from city to city. That October, Ellick wrote an article for *Lippincott's Monthly Magazine* describing what a hard job umpiring was and how he had quit once he concluded that "defensive armour [*sic*] for protecting the umpire against bad language and beer-glasses is imperatively called for."

In the spring of 1887 Ellick resigned his railroad job to serve as player-manager of the Kansas City Western League club but was fired on the eve of the season, although he remained with the team for a time as a SS. He then worked as a bartender in Kansas City until around 1892, when he umpired briefly in the Kansas City-Missouri League while Fred Clarke played for St. Joseph. Later in the decade he worked in the auditor's office of the Swift & Company meatpackers in Kansas City and then became a cigar maker. Ellick died in Kansas City in 1923. (DN)

Evans, Uriah L. P. / "Jake" "Bloody Jake"

B	T	HGT	WGT	G	AB	H	R	2B
L	R	5'8"	154	472	1831	435	215	70

3B	HR	RBI	BB	SO	SB	BA	SA	OBP
21	1	168	63	172	—	.238	.300	.264

G	IP	H	GS	CG	BB
3	15	24	1	1	0

SO	SH	W	L	PCT	ERA
3	0	0	1	.000	6.60

B. 9/22/1856 Baltimore, MD **D.** 1/16/1907
TEAMS: 79–81TroN 82WorN 83–84CleN 85BalA
DEBUT: 5/1/1879 at Cincinnati; played RF and went 0-for-4 in a 7–5 loss to Cincinnati's Will White
FINALE: 5/19/1885 at Cincinnati; played RF and went 0-for-4 in a 13–5 loss to Will White

Among outfielders in at least 400 ML games, Jake Evans is arguably the weakest hitter in history. His .564 career OPS is lower than that of many pitchers of his era. Yet his defensive skills were so extraordinary than *The ESPN Encyclopedia of Baseball* assigns him a +2.0 TPR rating. In 1883 the *Boston Globe* claimed that Evans could tell within fifty feet where a ball would land by its sound off the bat and thus got a great jump on drives hit over his head. The first NL right fielder to field .900, in his six seasons of regular play he led in fielding percentage every year, often by as much as 30 points. In addition, Evans had sufficient range to play capably at SS and 2B as well as the arm strength to fill in on occasion at 3B and even pitch a few innings.

The son of a Chesapeake Bay pilot, in 1871, at age 14, Evans was playing for the amateur Baltimore Swans. By 1876 he had progressed to the semipro Wilmington Quicksteps and, at various junctures during the summer, had as teammates Buttercup Dickerson, Bill Smiley, and Bill Holbert. According to historian Newt Weaver, Evans received part of his colorful nickname on June 5, 1876, when the Quicksteps journeyed to West Chester, PA, to play the local Brandywines, known as a dirty team that specialized in intimidating their opposition with help from their home crowd. After the Quicksteps dismantled their hosts 12–4, a gang of drunken hooligans assaulted the open carriages carrying the victors away from the field. During the spitting, name-calling, and rock throwing, several players were struck, including Evans and Dickerson. When the two sprang from their coach, bats in hand, dripping blood and blasphemy, and began to chase their tormentors, the bloody portion of Evans's nickname was born, although we still don't know why he was called Jake.

Evans began his pro career the following summer with the Rhode Islands in the New England League. Despite hitting just .224, two years later he made his ML debut, arriving in Troy in 1879 from New Bedford of the International Association. Immediately Evans was installed in RF to take advantage of his arm. Early in his career, when most hitters were right-handed and few were able to pull fastballs thrown only forty-five feet from the plate, he was able to play such a shallow RF that he frequently robbed batters of hits by throwing a runner on 1B out at 2B on a line drive hit his way. Even after the pitching distance grew to fifty feet in 1881, Evans continued to be so valuable defensively that teams accommodated him in the lineup by often batting him last. But while the new fifty-foot rule helped most hitters by giving them an extra fraction of a second to tackle fastballs, Evans appears to have received only token assistance. Only one other regular outfielder, John Cassidy, posted a lower OPS in 1881, the first year at the new pitching distance, than Evans's .581.

Although most reference books list the side from which Evans batted as unknown, he probably was a left-handed hitter. Evidence of that is that while facing Larry Corcoran in a game at Chicago on June 30, 1881, Evans was struck in the right temple according to several sources, an unlikely occurrence if he had been hitting from the right side of the plate. Following the 1881 season Evans was not reserved by Troy and was made to find a new home with Worcester, MA. On September 25, 1882, Worcester manager Jack Chapman bestowed on Evans the dubious honor of pitching the club's final game as a member of the NL. In his lone ML start, he suffered a 10–7 loss to Troy. When the Worcester franchise disbanded prior to the 1883 season, all of its players essentially became free agents, allowed to sign where they pleased. Evans chose Cleveland, and at first it seemed a fortuitous choice. The Blues were a strong team in 1883 and afforded Evans his first and only opportunity to play for a contender. But the club had already begun to decline as a result of an injury to its star pitcher, Jim McCormick, when Evans suffered a disabling injury of his own. On September 5 at Buffalo, he dislocated his right shoulder making a headfirst slide into 2B. Since Cleveland was still in contention, he tried to return to action too soon, and his shoulder became a chronic problem that would haunt him for the rest of his career when he dislocated it again in an exhibition game on October 4, 1883, against the AA champion Philadelphia A's.

Even though Evans rebounded in 1884 to lead all NL outfielders in FA and set personal highs in most major batting departments, his arm was no longer a formidable weapon. Before the Cleveland franchise disbanded following the 1884 season, Evans either purchased his release or had it purchased by Orioles manager Billy Barnie so that he could sign with Baltimore, where he made his home, and had his career game shortly after the 1885 season began, going 4-for-5 on May 5 against the New York Mets' Ed Begley. But when Evans hit just .181 in his other 19 appearances, he was replaced in RF by rookie Pat Burns after drawing the collar against Cincinnati's Will White almost exactly six years after he had an O-for day against White in his ML debut. At some point that season

Evans apparently reinjured his shoulder, effectively ending his pro career although he continued to play semipro ball for teams in the Baltimore area. In 1907, Evans died suddenly in the backyard of his sister's home. The precipitating cause was probably a heart attack or a stroke, with the underlying causes listed as uremia and acute nephritis. (DN/FV/DB)

Fields, John Joseph / "Jocko"

B	T	HGT	WGT	G	AB	H	R	2B
R	R	5'10"	160	341	1319	358	212	65

3B	HR	RBI	BB	SO	SB	BA	SA	OBP
32	12	176	124	139	50	.271	.397	.338

G	IP	H	GS	CG	BB
1	1	0	0	0	2

SO	SH	W	L	PCT	ERA
0	0	0	0	—	0.00

B. 10/20/1864 Cork, Ireland **D.** 10/14/1950
TEAMS: 87–89PitN 90PitP 91PitN 91PhiN 92NYN
DEBUT: 5/31/1887 at Philadelphia; caught Jim McCormick and went 0-for-5 in a 6–5 loss to Philadelphia's Charlie Buffinton
FINALE: 6/11/1892 at New York; caught Silver King and went hitless in a 5–1 loss to Cleveland's Nig Cuppy

Hotheaded and easily goaded by bench jockeys, Jocko Fields probably would have profited from more time in the minors before he joined Pittsburgh in the spring of 1887 in just his third pro season. After making two wild throws in his ML debut, he didn't see action again until June 17. Fields continued to play only sporadically until late in the 1889, season when his hitting (.311 in 75 games) prompted Pittsburgh's new manager, Ned Hanlon, to give him more ABs. Nevertheless, Fields was a surprise addition to the Pittsburgh PL team in 1890 after Hanlon was named the club's player-manager. Despite skepticism that he could keep the pace in the fast PL company, Fields opened the season in LF for the Burghers and also caught and played 2B. He finished the campaign with 101 runs and tied for the club lead in home runs with 9.

Returning to Pittsburgh NL along with Hanlon in 1891 after the PL collapsed, Fields was slotted for a starting role but instead ended up in Hanlon's doghouse—literally. He was cut in July after hurting his hand in a wrestling match with pitcher Mark Baldwin, or so he claimed, but an informant told Hanlon the injury had actually occurred when Fields attended a dog fight and "got too close to one of the combatants." Released to Omaha of the Western Association, he returned to the NL in September with the Phillies and then signed with the Giants for 1892. A good spring at the Giants' camp in Richmond, VA, earned him a start in RF on Opening Day, but he was axed even though he hit a decent .273 when he was not up to the challenge of catching the club's ace flamethrower, Amos Rusie.

Discouraged, Fields went through the motions for a while with Somerville of the Central New Jersey League and then tackled the game with renewed vigor, signing for 1893 with Macon of the Southern League. Over the next few years in the SL, Fields's defense improved so dramatically that in September 1895 the *Washington Post* predicted he would be with the Senators in 1896, but when Deacon McGuire caught practically every inning in 1895 manager Gus Schmelz decided he could do without another backstop.

After leaving pro ball following the 1896 season, Fields, who had married his childhood sweetheart in 1888, worked for Railway Express until 1933. In 1936 he joined a group of old-timers who paraded and then attended an 1870s-style game at the Polo Grounds on August 13 to honor Jim Mutrie and celebrate the sixtieth anniversary of the National League. Ten years later, Fields, who had played on historic Elysian Field as a youth in New Jersey, was again among the ancient luminaries who took bows before a game at Hoboken commemorating the game's centennial. He died in Jersey City at 85. (DN)

Fogarty, James G. / "Jim"

B	T	HGT	WGT	G	AB	H	R	2B
R	R	5'10½"	180	751	2880	709	508	110

3B	HR	RBI	BB	SO	SB	BA	SA	OBP
55	20	320	351	327	325	.246	.343	.335

G	IP	H	GS	CG	BB
7	14	16	0	0	3

SO	SH	W	L	PCT	ERA
5	0	0	1	.000	4.50

G	W	L	PCT	PENNANTS
16	7	9	.438	0

B. 2/12/1864 San Francisco, CA **D.** 5/20/1891
TEAMS: 84–89PhiN (P/M)90PhiP
DEBUT: 5/1/1884 at Philadelphia; played RF and went 2-for-5 in a 13–2 win over Detroit's Stump Wiedman
FINALE: 10/4/1890 at Cleveland; played RF and went 1-for-3 in a 16–4 win over Cleveland's Henry Gruber

Jim Fogarty was probably the most valuable career .246 hitter ever. His high walk and steal totals more than outweighed his low BAs, and defensively he ranked among the top outfielders of his time and was perhaps the best of them all. Equally adept in CF and RF, he led the NL in outfield assists at both positions and also led multiple times in put-outs, double plays and FA. Moreover, Fogarty could play every infield position except 1B capably and was even used as a pitcher on occasion.

A native of San Francisco, in 1883 Fogarty played for four teams in that city before coming east in the spring of 1884 in quest of a job with the NL Philadelphia Quakers. By Opening Day he had captured the RF berth and was a fixture in the City of Brotherly Love for the next seven years. In 1886 Fogarty was on his way to what might have become his finest season when he hurt his knee. Limited to just 77 games, he nonetheless led the Quakers in walks despite collecting only 280 ABs. The following season Fogarty took advantage of two rule changes in effect for only that one year (4 strikes rather than 3 needed for a strikeout and walks counting as hits) to top the NL in walks, swipe 102 bases, and hit .366 (105 points over his actual BA when walks were deducted). With the four-strike rule extinct in 1888, to avoid walking Fogarty pitchers laid their deliveries right over the plate, but he still led the Quakers in free passes and steals and was second in runs despite hitting only .238. As a reward, he was invited to play for the All-Star combine that toured the world that winter, playing games against the Chicagos in every part of the globe. Something of a gagster, Fogarty wreaked mayhem on the trip after the ship's crew fed the players a pack of pirate tales one evening on the Indian Ocean. Awakening before dawn the next morning, he went up on deck and fired a rifle three times and then raced downstairs in his nightclothes and shouted that pirates were attacking the ship. Panicked, several players were about to jump overboard before Fogarty burst out laughing.

Returning to the Quakers in 1889, he led the NL in stolen bases and his team in walks and runs, again on a lowly BA (.259). Courted vigorously by the Brotherhood, he signed with Philadelphia PL for 1890 but contracted typhoid after he came east in February. No sooner had the PL season started than his knee injury from several years earlier acted up, sidelining him periodically. Compounding an already difficult season for Fogarty was a bitter money dispute in late May with the club's management followed by a fire in his Philadelphia hotel room in late August in which he burned his hands beating out flames. Finally, with Mike Griffin on the team, Fogarty was made to cede him the CF spot, though years later Dan Shannon, who played with both men in 1890, insisted that Fogarty was the better fielder.

Still, Fogarty's .239 BA in the hitter-friendly PL made him less desirable to his old team when the PL collapsed, and there were rumors that Philadelphia NL was offering him to Cleveland for Pat Tebeau since it now had an outfield consisting of Sam Thompson, Ed Delahanty, and Billy Hamilton. When Fogarty came east in the spring of 1891, he was still unsigned. In early March *TSN* reported that he was confined to his hotel room in Philadelphia with a "severe attack of the grippe" but was recovering rapidly. A week later the same paper announced that he was on the mend and had accepted an offer to play for Pittsburgh in 1891. But the updates after that grew increasingly grim until Fogarty finally died in Philadelphia at St. Joseph's Hospital, where he was cared for toward the end by the Sisters of Charity.

His body was sent by train to San Francisco but could not be buried for several days after it arrived because the parties who conveyed his remains failed to obtain a certificate in Philadelphia that his death was due to natural causes. Finally the fear of contagion was assuaged by a report that he had died from a very rapid case of consumption that had consumed all of his lung tissue in just three months. A heavy cigarette smoker since his teens, Fogarty was said to have hastened his death with the habit. In its final word on the matter, *TSN* sermonized, "His system was impregnated with nicotine and drugs used in the manufacture of the paper pipes." (DN)

Foley, Charles Joseph / "Curry"

B	T	HGT	WGT	G	AB	H	R	2B
?	L	5'10"	160	305	1305	373	192	57

3B	HR	RBI	BB	SO	SB	BA	SA	OBP
12	6	128	34	83	—	.286	.362	.304

G	IP	H	GS	CG	BB
69	442.2	511	50	39	64

SO	SH	W	L	PCT	ERA
127	2	27	27	.500	3.54

B. 1/14/1856 Milltown, Ireland **D.** 10/20/1898
TEAMS: 79–80BosN 81–83BufN
DEBUT: 5/13/1879 at Cincinnati; played RF and went 1-for-3 in a 3–2 win over Cincinnati's Will White
FINALE: 9/5/1883 at Buffalo; played LF and went 0-for-4 in a 6–1 loss to Cleveland's Hugh Daily
CAREER HIGHLIGHT: 5/25/1882 at Buffalo; played RF and became the first MLer to hit for the cycle in a 20–1 win over Cleveland's George Bradley

Curry Foley immigrated to the United States from Ireland with his family in 1863 and by 1874 was playing with Chub Sullivan on the Stars, Boston's champion junior club. He then spent four seasons with Lowell, MA, an eventual member of both the League Alliance and the International Association. In Foley's first two seasons with Lowell, Michael Doyle captained the team, and so many club members boarded with Doyle that some had to sleep on the floor. Foley first signed with Boston after the 1876 season but then had a change of heart when he saw the demoralizing effect it would have on Doyle's close-knit Lowell team if he left. He later recalled that at that point in the game's history camaraderie and fellowship were more important to many players than playing in the National League.

After Foley led Lowell in batting in 1878 with a .309 mark and also bagged 18 pitching wins, Boston made him an offer he could no longer refuse. In his rookie season he spelled Tommy Bond in the box and served as a substitute outfielder–first baseman. On July 19, 1879, at Cleveland, Foley squared off against the Blues' Bobby Mitchell in the first all-lefty duel in ML history and came out on the short end, 8–2 (*see* Bobby Mitchell). The following season he served in the same role with Boston but appeared in more than twice as many games, making him essentially a regular without a position. As a result, even though he was second on the team in batting only to Charley Jones, he was not reserved for 1881. Foley signed with Buffalo and took on the same role with the Bisons, the difference being that his time in the box was cut to just forty-one innings once it grew apparent that he was not as effective at the new fifty-foot distance. Returning to Buffalo in 1882, he at last won a full-time slot, playing all of the Bisons' 84 games in RF. Always a good hitter, he compiled career bests that season in most batting departments and ranked high among right fielders in both assists and double plays.

But by the spring of 1883 Foley was no longer the same player. Although his sudden physical deterioration was not as pronounced as Lou Gehrig's would be some fifty-six years later, it was no less evident that he was in the grip of a dreadfully debilitating disease. By Opening Day, Foley was already in such constant pain that he could play only 23 games even though he remained on the team almost the entire season. Doctors came up with a variety of diagnoses, but today it seems likely that he had a particularly virulent form of rheumatoid arthritis. But the Buffalo club believed he was faking his disability to obtain his release and refused to pay him or release him as long as he maintained he was too ill to play. Nevertheless, it reserved him for 1884, although it was now obvious his health was beyond repair.

Throughout the 1880s Foley's former teammates held periodic benefit games for him, and in November 1892 *TSN* reported that he had been a "helpless cripple for over seven years" and yet still remained good company and full of stories about the game. Actually, until almost the end of his life, Foley was a frequent contributor to the pages of both *TSN* and *SL*, and his 1898 obit in the *Boston Globe* praised his "happy faculty of extracting humor out of almost every situation" and a memory that "was trustworthy, and stored with a fund of material apparently inexhaustible." But other obits painted a darker picture of his final days, noting that he had been unable to walk a step since the late 1880s or "earn money from his pen" in nearly as long, causing him to lament that, since all he wanted was for his family to be cared for, there was no "organization of the ball players, the deserving of which would be looked out for and not be compelled to want." In commenting on Foley's pension plan recommendation, the *Boston Post* railed against the shabby way he was treated in his last years by his fellow players, none of whom contributed to his financial needs or visited him or held a benefit for him though he was cheerful and well liked. The explanation given for their callous treatment was Foley had sided with the NL against the players in the Brotherhood War. Yet at the end much was forgiven. An enormous funeral was held for Foley at his Boston home with many present from the baseball community. We still do not know the source of his nickname. (DN)

Freeman, John Frank / "Buck"

B	T	HGT	WGT	G	AB	H	R	2B
L	L	5'9"	169	306	1131	356	185	41

3B	HR	RBI	BB	SO	SB	BA	SA	OBP
41	34	209	57	2	33	.315	.514	.365

G	IP	H	GS	CG	BB
7	51	50	4	4	36

SO	SH	W	L	PCT	ERA
28	0	3	2	.600	4.41

B. 10/30/1871 Catasauqua, PA **D.** 6/25/1949
TEAMS: 91WasA 98–99WasN 00BosN 01–07BosAL
DEBUT: 7/1/1891 at Boston; caught by Deacon McGuire and lost 9–3 to Boston's Cinders O'Brien
FINALE: 4/20/1907 at New York; pinch hit unsuccessfully for Lou Criger in the ninth inning of an 8–1 loss to New York's Al Orth
CAREER HIGHLIGHT: Hit 25 home runs in 1899, a post-1892 ML season record until 1919, when it was broken by Babe Ruth

The origin of Buck Freeman's nickname is unknown. The son of a coal miner, he was working in the mines himself near Wilkes-Barre, PA, as a slate picker by the time he was 9. In his late teens Freeman began pitching for local semipro teams on his rare off days. Somehow he captured the attention of Washington AA and was sent train fare to join the team in Boston. Freeman did poorly in his first outing but showed enough to accompany the club back to Washington, where he beat Louisville in his next appearance three days later. After 44 innings against AA hitters, he owned 28 strikeouts, a 3.89 ERA, and a 3-2 log for a last-place team but was very wild, the explanation given for his release. Still, the local *Star* was only one of several voices to say in dismay that "he managed to win, and that is what he pitched for"—but Freeman's next eight pro seasons are even more of a puzzle.

After struggling for two more years in the minors to master his control, Freeman finally heeded the advice he had been given several years earlier by African American second baseman Bud Fowler that his future was brighter as a hitter than as a pitcher. In 1894, upon switching to the outfield, he smashed .386 for Haverhill to win the New England League batting crown and added 34 home runs. After failing to stick with Detroit of the Western League the following spring, Freeman joined Toronto of the Eastern League and was still stuck on the Canucks in 1898 despite having demonstrated year after year that he was one of the best hitters in the minors. But that season Freeman's fortunes finally began to change when he heeded Canucks manager Arthur Irwin's advice to stop trying to pull every pitch and use the whole field.

At the close of the 1898 EL campaign, Irwin was hired to take over Washington NL immediately and brought Freeman with him. After hitting .364 in the final 29 games of Washington's season, he became Irwin's most prized discovery in 1899, when he banged a loop-leading 25 home runs and added a .563 SA. Freeman's first full season performance so impressed *TSN* that he was asked to share his secrets in its October 29, 1899, issue. His discourse on hitting was one of the most insightful of its time but may have backfired in that it revealed that Freeman felt he ranked with Dave Orr and Nap Lajoie among the great bad-ball hitters in the game's history to that point. Assigned to Boston NL in 1900 after Washington fell victim in the loop's reduction to eight teams, Freeman suddenly began to see fewer good pitches. When he slipped to just 6 home runs, scored 49 fewer runs, and lost 117 points off his OPS, there was now a distinct possibility that rather than ranking with Orr and Lajoie he would become a one-year wonder. (DN/DB)

Gedney, Alfred W. / "Count" "Al"

B	T	HGT	WGT	G	AB	H	R	2B
?	?	5'9"	140	202	832	209	139	25

3B	HR	RBI	BB	SO	SB	BA	SA	OBP
8	5	99	13	26	8	.251	.319	.263

G	IP	H	GS	CG	BB
2	11	7	1	1	1

SO	SH	W	L	PCT	ERA
2	0	1	0	1.000	0.82

B. 5/10/1849 Brooklyn, NY **D.** 3/26/1922
TEAMS: 72TroNA 72EckNA 73MutNA 74AthNA 75MutNA

DEBUT: 4/27/1872 at Troy; played CF and went 4-for-7 in a 27–10 win over Middletown's Cy Bentley
FINALE: 10/29/1875 at New York; played LF, batted last, and went 1-for-3 in a 5–5 tie with St. Louis Browns' rookie Jim Galvin

Count Gedney's 9 games as a rookie with Troy in 1872 before the team disbanded made him seem a phenom. He hit .426, hammered 3 home runs, and compiled a 1.107 OPS, but pundits were aware that the Troy team used a very live ball in its home games. In the remaining 193 games of his career, Gedney hit .241 and was not invited to accompany the New York Mutuals to the newly formed National League after he batted .206 in 1875.

Just about Gedney's only positive feat after he left Troy came in 1875, when he won the only Mutuals game all season that was not pitched by Bobby Mathews, beating the Brooklyn Atlantics 9–2 on July 9. Gedney continued to play with New Jersey semipro teams after the Mutes dropped him, and he worked for a time as a post office clerk in the New York state senate. He died in Hackensack, NJ, in 1922. We do not know why he was called "Count." (DN/DB)

Geier, Philip Louis / "Phil" "Shorty" "Ophelia"

B	T	HGT	WGT	G	AB	H	R	2B
L	R	5'7"	145	139	485	130	81	7

3B	HR	RBI	BB	SO	SB	BA	SA	OBP
7	1	51	69	7	25	.268	.318	.365

B. 11/3/1876 Washington, D.C. **D.** 9/25/1967
TEAMS: 96–97PhiN 00CinN 01PhiAL 01MilAL 04BosN
DEBUT: 8/17/1896 at Philadelphia; replaced Sam Thompson in RF and went 0-for-1 in a 16–15 loss to Baltimore's George Hemming and Arlie Pond
FINALE: 10/8/1904 at Philadelphia; played CF and went 0-for-3 in a 4–0 loss to Philadelphia's Chick Fraser

Phil Geier began his pro career in 1895 with Norfolk of the Virginia League as an 18-year-old catcher and perhaps would have stayed at that position if he had been bigger. In 1896 he accompanied Nap Lajoie to the Phils from the loop-leading Fall River New England League team. Strictly a scrub in his rookie season, Geier struggled without success to find a regular spot in the lineup again in 1897 and then returned to the minors with St. Paul of the Western League. His second ML opportunity came in 1900 when he was drafted by Cincinnati, but he came to spring training out of shape. In his first 2 games with the Reds he played 3B while Harry Steinfeldt was being tried at 2B, but that experiment ended when he made a double error on his only chance in the first contest and two more bobbles the following day.

A flop with Cincinnati, Geier spent that winter working at his father's butcher shop in Washington, D.C., and awaiting his third ML shot, this in the AL in its fledgling season as a major circuit. But Geier again faltered in 1901, hitting just .224. After spending the following two years back in St. Paul, he won the Boston NL club's CF post in the spring of 1904 and enjoyed his only full season in the majors. But again a weak bat—he hit just .248 with a .284 SA—doomed him. Geier continued to play pro ball until he was in his midthirties, finishing in the 1911 Central League. He was among the last surviving nineteenth-century players when he died in Spokane, WA, at 90. (DN)

Genins, C. Frank / "Frank" "Frenchy"

B	T	HGT	WGT	G	AB	H	R	2B
?	R	?	?	123	413	93	60	13

3B	HR	RBI	BB	SO	SB	BA	SA	OBP
0	2	35	35	27	29	.225	.266	.289

B. 11/6/1866 St. Louis, MO **D.** 9/30/1922
TEAMS: 92CinN 92StLN 95PitN 01CleAL
DEBUT: 7/5/1892 at Cincinnati; played SS and went 0-for-3 in a 7–3 loss to Philadelphia's Gus Weyhing
FINALE: 5/23/1901 at Cleveland; played CF and was 1-for-4 as Cleveland rallied from a 13–5 deficit against Case Patten and Watty Lee of Washington by scoring 9 runs in the bottom of the ninth

Many players have claimed they prefer playing in the minors to sitting on the bench in the majors, but Frank Genins was one that meant it. He was a fine all-around athlete, an excellent ice skater, and extraordinarily versatile, perhaps the first MLer to play a full game at SS in his ML debut and a full game in CF in his finale as many as nine years later.

Genins launched his pro career with Omaha in 1886. He then spent five years in the minors while working winters for the Butler Tobacco Company in St. Louis before being acquired by St. Louis in November of 1891 from Sioux City of the Western Association. But over the winter Genins contracted a severe case of pneumonia, and the Browns put him on waivers when he was still not in shape to play in the spring of 1892. Genins then apparently signed illegally with Indianapolis of the Western League before the ten-day waiver period was up, perhaps with St. Louis's complicity. Meanwhile, Pittsburgh claimed him, as did Chicago, forcing NL president Nick Young to intervene in May 1892. Young returned Genins to St. Louis, and the Browns promptly traded him and Cub Stricker to Pittsburgh for Jim Galvin. In early July, Young further complicated matters by awarding Genins to Cincinnati. Whether Pittsburgh received compensation from St. Louis for the loss of Genins is not known, but the Pirates may have dropped the matter when Genins batted below .200 for Cincinnati and was unconditionally released. Genins's troubles were partly due to a fresh bout of pneumonia, and though he was able to return to St. Louis later in the season after recuperating at French Lick, IN, he was no more successful with the Browns than he had been with the Reds, finishing the season with a composite .186 BA in 50 games.

His health still fragile, Genins spent all of 1893 in St. Louis under a doctor's care. Not permitted to travel, he was able only to play home games for The Sporting News semipro team. Upon his recovery, he joined Sioux City in 1894 and was the Derby Medal winner at the end of the season for being voted the most popular player on the Western League pennant winners. As a further reward, Genins signed with Pittsburgh for 1895—this time for real—and spent the entire season as the Pirates' fourth outfielder, a role he had no desire to repeat. With his eager consent, he was farmed to Grand Rapids of the Western League in 1896. Over the next five seasons Genins became a fixture in the WL, culminating in 1900 when the loop changed its name to the American League. A member by then of Cleveland, he hit a solid .293, bidding the Forest City team to retain him when the AL went major the following year.

Genins opened 1901 as the Blues' center fielder but lost his job to Jack O'Brien on May 24 after hitting just .228 in 26 games. The following month he went to Omaha of the reorganized Western League. Genins later played in numerous minor leagues before completing his active playing career in 1909. He returned to his native St. Louis, where he died in 1922. (DN)

Gettinger, Lewis Thomas Leyton
(b. Gittinger) **/ "Tom" "Tired Tommy"**

B	T	HGT	WGT	G	AB	H	R	2B
L	L	5'10"	180	125	503	131	61	18

3B	HR	RBI	BB	SO	SB	BA	SA	OBP
10	6	64	30	16	14	.260	.372	.306

G	IP	H	GS	CG	BB
2	6.1	13	0	0	1

SO	SH	W	L	PCT	ERA
0	0	0	0	—	7.11

B. 12/11/1868 Frederick, MD **D.** 7/26/1943
TEAMS: 89–90StLA 95LouN
DEBUT: 9/21/1889 at St. Louis; played LF and went 2-for-4 in a 5–4 loss to Cincinnati's Tony Mullane
FINALE: 9/25/1895 at Louisville; played RF late in the game and went 1-for-1 in an 11–4 loss to Pittsburgh's Pink Hawley

Tom Gettinger first played for pay with Shamokin in the Pennsylvania Central League in 1888 under his birth name of "Gittinger." It is unknown whether he adopted the name Gettinger or simply accepted that spelling after it began appearing in box scores. Gettinger began 1889 as a teammate of Jack Stivetts's on York, PA, and, like Stivetts, was acquired by the Browns before the season was out. A sizzling .438 BA in a late-September trial earned him the Browns' LF post on Opening Day in 1890 after the club lost Tip O'Neill to the PL. Gettinger failed to hold the job because he had trouble going back on fly balls and, to escape embarrassment, played so deep that he was continually being waved in by frustrated teammates. Released in July 1890, he then embarked on a long minor league junket before returning to the show in 1895 with Louisville. The previous year had been an especially eventful one for him, inasmuch as he accidentally shot himself in the leg in January while engaging in target practice and then in August married Katie Dwyer, whom he had met in 1893 while with Mobile of the Southern League. Although Gettinger appears to have been on the Louisville club for the entire 1895 season, at no point was he a regular, and he never did anything out of the ordinary, either good or bad. Back in the minors with Grand Rapids of the Western League in 1896, he suffered a severe setback in late July, dislocating his kneecap while running for a fly ball in a game against Kansas City. Despite a second, more serious, setback in 1901, when he spent most of the Southern League season hospitalized with typhoid, Gettinger last played for pay in the 1908 Cotton States League when he was nearly 40. He died in Pensacola Hospital in 1943 just twenty-six days after retiring from a job with the city of Pensacola and reportedly being the first to draw a pension from the Florida Panhandle city. (DN)

Gettman, Jacob John / "Jake"

B	T	HGT	WGT	G	AB	H	R	2B
B	L	5'11"	185	197	772	215	108	24

3B	HR	RBI	BB	SO	SB	BA	SA	OBP
8	8	78	40	—	44	.278	.361	.322

B. 10/25/1875 Frank, Russia **D.** 10/4/1956
TEAMS: 97–99WasN
DEBUT: 8/20/1897 at Washington; played CF and went 2-for-4 in a 6–2 loss to Chicago's Danny Friend
FINALE: 5/19/1899 at Washington; pinch hit for pitcher Dan McFarlan in the second inning, singled off Harley Payne, and scored a run in a 10–3 win over Pittsburgh's Payne and Bill Hoffer

Jake Gettman was not only a switch hitter but could also throw with both arms, although he was naturally left-handed. Born in Russia, he came to Nebraska when he was around 10 years old and was already an expert cigar maker, a trade he had learned in the old country. Although fluent in English by the time he turned pro, Gettman would sometimes pretend he could speak only Russian as a way of disguising that he was cursing out an umpire.

At age 19 the switch hitter was playing 1B for Topeka of the Kansas State League. After joining Fort Worth of the Texas League the following year, Gettman became an outfielder. Upon being acquired by Washington in late August 1897, he took command of the Nationals' RF slot and held it until the close of the 1898 season. The following spring Gettman lost his job to Buck Freeman and then also lost a battle for the CF berth to rookie Jimmy Slagle. Sent to Kansas City when he was only batting .210 by the middle of May, Gettman predicted he would return to majors once he acquired a better command of the strike zone. He complained that in the Texas League, where the pitchers were wild and the umpires loath to give walks, he had just whaled away and landed tons of hits but in the majors had been ordered to wait for strikes. This strategy had worked for a time, but when he went into protracted slump and was hitting a lot of fly balls, he began swinging haphazardly again.

Only 23 when he left Washington, Gettman did not seem unrealistic in his expectations, especially when he had a string of fine years in the Eastern League in the early part of the twentieth century. But even though he continued to play in top minor league company until he was in his late thirties, he never got a second ML opportunity. Gettman finished his pro career in 1914 with Hastings, NE, where he had first learned the game and then was a rancher for nearly forty years. He died in Denver. (DN)

Gilks, Robert James / "Bob"

B	T	HGT	WGT	G	AB	H	R	2B
R	R	5'8"	178	339	1385	320	163	33

3B	HR	RBI	BB	SO	SB	BA	SA	OBP
9	1	142	49	61	47	.231	.270	.265

G	IP	H	GS	CG	BB
21	160.2	164	18	17	59

SO	SH	W	L	PCT	ERA
36	1	9	9	.500	3.98

B. 7/2/1864 Cincinnati, OH **D.** 8/21/1944
TEAMS: 87–88CleA 89–90CleN 93BalN
DEBUT: 8/25/1887 at Cleveland; played 1B and went 0-for-5 in an 8–6 loss to Philadelphia's Gus Weyhing
FINALE: 9/18/1893 at Cincinnati; played RF and went 2-for-4 in a 7–6 loss to Cincinnati's Silver King and Tom Parrott

As a player Bob Gilks never was able to equal the sum of his parts. Early in his ML career it was observed: "Gilks is the only twirler of the Clevelands who is worthy of notice, and what effectiveness he has is attained by speed." Yet he pitched only 21 games in the majors before arm problems made him an outfielder, where he became a master of the trap ball play, a gritty base runner, and a batsman of rare courage who nonetheless was a failure against ML pitching because he was a sucker for wide curves that spun out of the strike zone.

In 1889 the batting style Gilks adopted to compensate for his weakness helped initiate a rule change. On April 9, Gilks, a Cincinnati native, was staying at home with his family when Cleveland came to the Queen City for a preseason exhibition. After receiving permission to dress in the Cincinnati clubhouse, he brought his uniform to the Reds' park. In the eighth inning of the game, he reacted to brush-back pitches from Tony Mullane by complaining they were intentional, but the reality was that he had hung his head far out over plate so he could reach Mullane's wide-sweeping curves. While changing in the clubhouse after the game, Gilks had more words with Mullane and came at him with a bat. The row dissolved into a fistfight between the two and resulted in abolishing the custom whereby players who happened to live in a town their team was visiting were allowed to dress in the home team's clubhouse, a courtesy that most ML clubs had routinely extended to each other prior to the Gilks incident.

In 1884 Gilks made his pro debut with Hamilton of the Ohio State League. He then spent 1885 in the Southern League and most of the next two seasons with Binghamton of the International Association. Upon joining the Cleveland AA in late August 1887 for his ML initiation, he immediately became the eye of a tornado when he announced he expected it would be harder to play in the AA than the NL because NL teams played slow and scientific ball while AA teams, led by the St. Louis Browns, scrapped for every run and would tear a leg off to score one. He then demonstrated that even the AA might be little challenge for him by hitting .313 and finishing as the lone hurler on the Cleveland staff with a winning record (7-5) and the third-best ERA (3.08) among AA pitchers in a minimum of 100 innings. But he would never again approach any of his rookie achievements. In 1888, as Cleveland's left fielder, he collected only 136 total bases in 119 games. After being reduced to a part-time role in 1889, the following year Gilks logged just 132 total bases, an all-time season low for an outfielder with 500 or more ABs.

Released by Cleveland after the 1890 season, Gilks then embarked on a long career as a minor league player and manager, interrupted only in 1893 when he returned briefly to the NL with Baltimore. Toward the end of the 1890s Gilks was made playing captain of the Toledo Mud Hens, at the time an Interstate League powerhouse. Rumored to be returning to Cleveland as a player in 1898, instead he ended up costing Toledo a third straight pennant when he choked an umpire in a game at Toledo's Casino Park on August 7, resulting in the contest being forfeited. Then in November his wife died suddenly of heart failure while he was away on a hunting trip. His life at its nadir, Gilks refused to abandon the only occupation he knew. He eventually matured into a respected minor league manager in the Southern Association and then served as the New York Yankees' chief scout in the South until 1923. Among the players Gilks brought to pinstripes was pitcher George Pipgras. The Cincinnati native remained in the South after leaving the Yankees and died at his Brunswick, GA, home at 80. (DN)

Gillespie, Peter Patrick / "Pat" "Padney" "Paddy" "Pete" "Twist" "Gill"

B	T	HGT	WGT	G	AB	H	R	2B
L	R	6'1½"	178	714	2927	809	450	108

3B	HR	RBI	BB	SO	SB	BA	SA	OBP
45	10	351	106	216	54	.276	.354	.303

B. 11/30/1851 Carbondale, PA **D.** 5/4/1910
TEAMS: 80–82TroN 83–87NYN
DEBUT: 5/1/1880 at Worcester; played LF and went 1-for-5 in a 13–1 loss to Worcester's Lee Richmond
FINALE: 10/6/1887 at New York; played LF and went 1-for-4 in a 6–3 loss to Philadelphia's Charlie Ferguson

The son of a coal miner, Pat Gillespie worked in the mines himself, first as a breaker boy and then as a laborer, before recognizing he could make a lot more money playing baseball. He was known as "Twist" when he played for the amateur Pottsville Fern Leafs in the early 1870s, became "Padney" after joining Carbondale in 1874, and was "Pat" by the time he reached the majors in 1880 at the advanced age of 28 after hitting .411 for Holyoke the previous year to lead the National Association in batting. Gillespie's strengths were his height (which contributed to the New York NL team being dubbed the Giants in 1885), being a left-handed hitter, a gritty player, and a hard negotiator at contract time. Gillespie's obits report that he was the first player to be paid as much as $2,800, and while that is questionable, he was definitely paid handsomely considering that in most seasons he was little more than a journeyman outfielder.

Gillespie's career nearly ended tragically. Playing LF for Troy on June 3, 1882, in an exhibition game against the independent New York Mets, he collided with centerfielder John Cassidy while both were chasing a deep fly ball and was knocked senseless. Miraculously, he returned to action just nine days later after a protective silver plate the size of a half dollar piece was planted in his skull. The following season Gillespie hit a career-high .314 but scored only 64 runs. It was a perennial weakness. During the eight seasons Gillespie's career spanned (1880–87), only Bill Phillips scored fewer runs (447) than his 450 among players with a minimum of 3,000 PAs.

Gillespie began his final ML season as the Giants' Opening Day left fielder but usually gave way to Mike Dorgan against lefty pitchers and played only 76 games. Notified that he would not be rehired, he stubbornly sat at his Carbondale home awaiting another ML offer until the spring of 1888 when he returned to Troy, which was now a member of the International Association. Scarcely two weeks into the season manager Ted Sullivan released him for drinking. Gillespie then joined last-place Albany and was hitting .320 in July when he and teammate Chief Roseman "insulted a lady shamefully" while both were drunk. Released toward the end of the month, he finished the season with a Carbondale amateur team. By 1891 he was back in the mines with his father making $1 a day. At the time of his death from pneumonia in 1910, Gillespie was a widower and living at the family home in Carbondale with his mother, who was close to 100. (DN)

Glenn, Edward C. / "Ed" "Mouse"

B	T	HGT	WGT	G	AB	H	R	2B
R	R	5'10"	160	137	525	106	66	8

3B	HR	RBI	BB	SO	SB	BA	SA	OBP
11	1	29	24	8	20	.202	.265	.245

B. 9/19/1860 Richmond, VA **D.** 2/10/1892
TEAMS: 84VirA 86PitA 88KCA 88BosN
DEBUT: 8/5/1884 at Richmond; played LF and went 1-for-4 in a 14–0 loss to Philadelphia's Bobby Mathews
FINALE: 10/5/1888 at Boston; played LF and went 1-for-2 in a 5–3 win over Detroit's Charlie Getzein

Ed Glenn was playing with the top semipro team in Richmond, VA, as early as 1878 and remained with the basic fabric of the club until it joined the AA in August 1884 as a replacement for Washington. Earlier in the season the *Police Gazette* reported that Virginia had rejected an offer of $1,000 apiece for Glenn and third baseman Billy Nash from St. Louis manager Jimmy Williams, and while Williams's judgment was certainly right with respect to Nash, evidence of Glenn's value never emerged. Actually, it is unfathomable that he was given the opportunity with four different teams to establish that he was of ML caliber. Among all outfielders with a minimum of 400 career ABs, Glenn's .510 OPS is the lowest of any active in the majors as late as 1888. Nor was he a great outfielder. In 137 games he compiled only 17 assists and a mediocre .867 FA.

Yet Glenn was able to find a playing job for thirteen consecutive seasons until the spring of 1891, when the *Boston Globe* reported he was "at his home with consumption." The following February, Glenn died at his Richmond home. The cause was listed as consumption, but in March 1892 *TSN* lamented that he had died from "a blow he received in a championship game," and as a result some sources still contend that his death was attributable to a lung injury he sustained while still an active player. (DN/DB)

Glenn, John W. / "John"

B	T	HGT	WGT	G	AB	H	R	2B
R	R	5'8½"	169	315	1372	366	235	43

3B	HR	RBI	BB	SO	SB	BA	SA	OBP
7	1	157	35	33	16	.267	.311	.285

B. 1/?/1850 Rochester, NY **D.** 11/10/1888
TEAMS: 71–72OlyNA 72NatNA 73WasNA 74–75ChiNA 76–77ChiN
DEBUT: 5/13/1871 at Cleveland; played RF and went 2-for-5 in a 12–8 win over Cleveland's Al Pratt
FINALE: 9/28/1877 at Cincinnati; played LF and went 0-for-4 in a 5–5 tie against Cincinnati's Bobby Mitchell

John Glenn served with his hometown amateur Rochester Alerts before journeying south to Washington to play for both the Nationals and the

Olympics in 1870. He then spent the first three NA seasons in D.C. before heading west in 1874 to join the reorganized Chicago entry. Two years later Glenn was probably the least-known regular on the Windy City juggernaut that captured the initial NL pennant when he occupied LF. After his BA slipped to .222 the following year, Chicago flushed him away.

Glenn returned to Rochester in 1878 to play with the local International Association entry and remained in Rochester for the most part until July 1880, when he left town for a week to officiate 5 NL games in Buffalo and Boston. Glenn, who had previously umpired NA games, then returned to Rochester and continued to play and umpire locally for several more years. Reportedly, in November 1888 he was accidentally shot to death by a policeman who was trying to protect him from an angry mob seeking to lynch him for allegedly assaulting a little girl in the Sandy Hills section of Glens Falls, NY. (DN)

Gore, George F. / "George" "Piano Legs"

B	T	HGT	WGT	G	AB	H	R	2B
B	R	5'11"	195	1310	5357	1612	1327	262

3B	HR	RBI	BB	SO	SB	BA	SA	OBP
94	46	618	717	331	170	.301	.411	.386

G	W	L	PCT	PENNANTS
16	6	9	.400	0

B. 5/3/1854 Saccarappa, ME **D.** 9/16/1933
TEAMS: 79–86ChiN 87–89NYN 90NYP 91–92NYN (P/M)92StLN
DEBUT: 5/1/1879 at Chicago; played CF and went 1-for-5 in a 4–3 win over Syracuse's Harry McCormick
FINALE: 8/18/1892 at St. Louis; played CF and made 2 hits in a 13–4 win over Baltimore's Ben Stephens and Tom Vickery

Until he was in his late teens, George Gore worked in a paper mill in his Maine hometown, which was also the home of Clara Louise Kellogg, a noted opera singer. Initially a "real country boy," he wised up quickly after he joined the independent Portland, ME, team in 1877. Gore moved to New Bedford of the International Association the following year under Frank Bancroft and hit.324. Upon learning that Chicago craved his young outfielder, Bancroft counseled him to turn down the White Stockings' initial offer of $1,200 and ask for $2,500. Eventually, Gore signed for $1,900 and all too soon became worldly in other areas as well. Almost from the moment of his arrival in Chicago he clashed with player-manager Cap Anson over his extracurricular activities, and Anson later had this to say about the game's best center fielder in the early 1880s: "Women and wine brought about his downfall . . . and the last time that I saw him in New York he was broken down, both in heart and pocket, and willing to work at anything that would yield him the bare necessities of life."

But Anson was sometimes wont to exaggerate the negative qualities of a player who was never a great admirer of him, and Gore's life story is far from that of someone whose athletic skills or physical being expired prematurely. In fourteen ML seasons the outfielder with lower limbs that resembled the legs of a piano was the first player in ML history to score 1,000 or more runs and retire with an average of better than 1 run scored for every game he played. While it is true that his career year came in only his second season when he hit .360 to win the NL batting title, on several future occasions he topped the senior loop in runs and walks. Then in 1890, ten years after snagging his lone batting crown, Gore set an all-but-unbreakable season record for the most runs while playing less than 100 games when he crossed the plate for the New York PL entry 132 times in just 93 contests.

Apart from dissipation, an undeniable shortcoming, Gore also suffered a string of physical setbacks in the late 1880s. Commencing in 1887, after Chicago owner Al Spalding had sold Gore to the New York Giants the previous November for around $3,500, the outfielder had an early-season bout with malaria; the following year a hand injury limited him to just 64 games in the regular season and 3 in the World's Series against the St. Louis Browns; and after a healthy 1889, various ailments sidelined him for nearly 40 games in 1890. Gore rebounded to play 130 games in 1891 at age 37, but his legs were nearly gone and the former speed king was held to just 19 stolen bases, the same number as 41-year-old Jim O'Rourke. After a slow start the following year, Gore was released to St. Louis and briefly piloted the eleventh-place Browns in addition to hitting .205 in the final 20 contests of his career.

In the spring of 1893 the *Washington Post* noted that Gore was running a New York saloon near the

Polo Grounds on 124th Street right across from Grant's Tomb. A year later, after struggling for a time with Binghamton to hold his own against Eastern League pitching, he was socked with a messy divorce suit and by 1895 had lost his saloon and was working as a "street cleaning inspector." Gradually then, Gore began to pull his life back together. He hired on as a New York City policeman and by the 1910s was one of baseball's elder statesmen, frequently solicited for his opinions on the modern game. He died at 77 while living at a Masonic Home in Utica, NY.

Reference works list Gore as solely a left-handed batter, but there is ample evidence that he batted right against select lefties, beginning in 1880 when both he and Abner Dalrymple took the opposite batter's box whenever they faced Lee Richmond. Also in question is Gore's birth date; some sources have him born in 1852, which would have made him 40 when he finished his ML career and even less a victim of dissipation. (DN)

Green, Edward / "Danny"

B	T	HGT	WGT	G	AB	H	R	2B
L	R	?	?	267	1052	315	179	37

3B	HR	RBI	BB	SO	SB	BA	SA	OBP
19	15	132	59	—	58	.299	.413	.345

B. 11/6/1876 Burlington, NJ **D.** 11/9/1914
TEAMS: 98–01ChiN 02–05ChiAL
DEBUT: 8/17/1898 at Boston; played CF and went 2-for-4 in a 6–2 loss to Boston's Kid Nichols
FINALE: 10/8/1905 at St Louis; played RF and went hitless in a 5–3 win over St. Louis's Barney Pelty

Danny Green played for less than $40 a month for Carlisle of the Cumberland Valley League in 1896 and then leaped directly to Springfield of the fast-paced Eastern League the following year and hit .323. He came from Springfield to Chicago NL in August 1898 and in his debut played CF in Bill Lange's absence. For the rest of the season Green occupied RF. He was there again the following year but switched to CF midway through the 1900 season and in 1901 led NL outfielders in put-outs.

That winter, the AL champion White Sox procured Green from their NL Windy City counterparts with an offer of more money and a chance to play on a better team. With Fielder Jones ensconced in CF, Green resumed his former RF post. Although he hit over .300 in each of his first two seasons with the White Sox, his arm swiftly eroded. By 1904 teams were routinely taking an extra base on almost every ball hit Green's way. Jones, now the Sox' player-manager, nonetheless was not yet ready to remove Green's potent bat from the lineup. In 1905, however, Green's BA dropped below .250 (.243) and his behavior, always eccentric, now bordered on the bizarre. On road trips he refused to ride in the upper berth, preferring to sleep on the floor if he drew an upper by lot because he "no longer could tolerate heights."

The following spring, when the White Sox reported to their training camp at Wichita, KS, Jones put the veteran Green in charge of conditioning but quickly thought better of it when Green had the "yanigans" roller-skating rather than running to get their legs in shape. Near the end of April the *Washington Post* announced that Green had been ticketed for the minors. ("His arm is gone and his batting eye has dimmed.") Green played three seasons with Milwaukee of the American Association, two more in lower leagues, and then joined Jimmy Callahan's Logan Squares for a time before leaving Chicago to return to his home in New Jersey. When Green died in a Camden institution, his *New York Times* obit said it was the result of an old beaning. But earlier the *Chicago Tribune* had said he was dying of consumption, and other reports attribute his death to "locomotor atoxia and paralysis due to advanced syphilis." Green's true cause of death is still as much of a mystery as the reason he was called "Danny." (DN)

Greer, Edward C. / "Ed"

B	T	HGT	WGT	G	AB	H	R	2B
?	R	5'9"	155	232	851	183	117	26

3B	HR	RBI	BB	SO	SB	BA	SA	OBP
5	3	93	43	—	51	.215	.268	.261

B. ?/?/1865 Philadelphia, PA **D.** 2/4/1890
TEAMS: 85–86BalA 86–87PhiA 87BroA
DEBUT: 6/24/1885 at Baltimore; caught Bob Emslie and went 0-for-4 in a 10–4 loss to Philadelphia's Tom Lovett
FINALE: 10/10/1887 at Philadelphia; caught Steve Toole and went 1-for-2 in a 7–5 win over Bobby Mathews

Ed Greer was such a sensational ball hawk that when he came to Baltimore in 1885 from the amateur Westminster club of Philadelphia, *SL* soon noted, "His judgment on fly balls amounts to an instinct, and it is a very long or a very short hit indeed that he cannot get under." But Orioles manager Billy Barnie fancied him more as a catcher than an outfielder, perhaps because of his lame bat. In the spring of 1886, even though Greer shone in exhibition games as both a hitter and an outfielder, Barnie continued to view him as a catcher, and only a scrub at that. Greer got into just 11 games with Baltimore that season before being released in late July despite protestations from Baltimore sportswriters that he was more than good enough to be playing regularly for a last-place team.

Moving to Philadelphia AA, Greer caught in his A's debut on July 19. Toward the end of August *SL* observed, "Greer was hit by a pitched ball and now has a lay off. There is some wonder as to whether the feminine attraction at Westminster does not cause him to magnify such accidents." He returned to action before the end of the month, however, and in a game against Baltimore on August 29 saved pitcher Bill Hart when he snared a deep drive against the fence with 2 on and 2 out in the top of the ninth and the A's then scored a run in the bottom of the frame to win 7–6. But he finished with a miserable .185 BA, and was released early in 1887 when he again started poorly.

Picked up by Brooklyn, Greer hiked his BA to a semirespectable .254 but was suspended for intoxication in September. After signing with Toronto of the International Association, Greer was released in June 1889, when he was hitting .157 after 14 games. Though just 23, his career may have been truncated in any event, because he was an erratic catcher, unable to carry his weight offensively as an outfielder, and "lacked ambition," according to the *Philadelphia Public Ledger*. But it more likely was shortened by illness, for he died at his Philadelphia home the following February of unknown causes. (DN)

Griffin, Tobias Charles
(aka Griffith) / **"Sandy"**

B	T	HGT	WGT	G	AB	H	R	2B
R	R	5'10"	160	166	630	173	116	35

3B	HR	RBI	BB	SO	SB	BA	SA	OBP
7	5	78	77	24	25	.275	.376	.361

G	W	L	PCT	PENNANTS
6	2	4	.333	0

B. 10/24/1858 Fayetteville, NY **D.** 6/4/1926
TEAMS: 84NYN 90RocA (P/M)91WasA 93StLN
DEBUT: 5/26/1884 at NY; played RF after replacing injured Mike Dorgan and went 0-for-3 in a 10–4 loss to Providence's Charley Radbourn
FINALE: 5/27/1893 at Cleveland; played LF and went 0-for-4 in a 3–2 win over Cleveland's John Clarkson

Sandy Griffin was approaching his 25th birthday when he joined New York NL in 1884. He remained on the team for almost the entire season but missed much of it with a dislocated shoulder and appeared in only 16 games. Griffin's .177 BA made him eminently dispensable when the majors reduced from 28 to 16 teams in 1885, and he seemed destined to spend the rest of his career in the minors. But a .310 season with Rochester of the International Association in 1888, followed by a .294 campaign in 1889, tempted manager Pat Powers to retain Griffin when Rochester joined the AA as a last-minute replacement club in 1890. The 31-year-old gardener opened the season in CF and closed it as the club leader in BA and SA while hitting .307 in 107 games.

But Griffin's age weighed heavily against him when the PL folded, reducing ML jobs for the following season by a third. He began 1891 with Omaha of the Western Association but jumped the team in July along with several other players in the belief that it was about to fold. Griffin and several teammates ended up with Washington AA by the end of July. He was hitting well and appeared to have the CF job secured for the rest of the season until Cincinnati's Ed Crane beaned him on August 4. Griffin tried to return to action too soon, was in and out of the lineup the rest of the way, finished the season managing the club, and then was one of many casualties when the NL and AA merged, reducing ML jobs by a quarter. Always somewhat brittle throughout his long career, over the next several seasons Griffin suffered one major injury after another, culminating in an 1895 collision during an Eastern League game with Springfield teammate Frank Bonner, in which he was knocked unconscious and suffered a broken hand when Bonner, who was deaf in his left ear, failed to hear him call for a pop fly.

The next few seasons went smoothly for Griffin as his bat continued to cut a swathe in the eastern minor leagues, but by 1898, now that he was nearing 40, his arm failed. He could still hit, however, and had just finished the 1899 season with Syracuse of the Eastern League when he struck his head on a beam in his barn in Fayetteville, NY, severely damaging nerves in his neck. Griffin recuperated for a lengthy spell and then worked out a deal to be player-manager for Cortland in the New York State League. Finding that he was still unable to play, he turned to umpiring in the Eastern League but had to go home in July 1900 when his damaged neck was unable to tolerate the hot sun.

Griffin made one final comeback bid with Syracuse in 1902 and then managed in the New York State League until 1909, when he retired to his farm in Fayetteville. He died in a Syracuse hospital in 1925 of complications from a throat infection. (DN)

Hall, Archibald W. / "Al"

B	T	HGT	WGT	G	AB	H	R	2B
?	?	?	?	70	314	80	31	7

3B	HR	RBI	BB	SO	SB	BA	SA	OBP
3	0	14	3	13	—	.255	.296	.262

B. Unknown Worcester, MA **D.** 2/10/1885
TEAMS: 79TroN 80CleN
DEBUT: 5/1/1879 at Cincinnati; played CF, led off and went 2-for-5 in a 7–5 loss to Cincinnati's Will White
FINALE: 5/13/1880 at Cincinnati; played CF in a 1–0 loss to Cincinnati's Will White and was replaced by Doc Kennedy in the top of the first inning

In 1876 Al Hall was living in Oil City, PA, and playing for independent Syracuse. The following year he returned to the Stars and customarily played CF beside Pete Hotaling, who three years later would be beside him again on the most fateful day of his life. In 1878 Hall left the Stars to join London, Ontario, of the International Association and subsequently was signed by Troy in 1879 after it was granted a NL franchise. Hall's ML career came full circle in little more than twelve months as both his first and last games were losses to pitcher Will White in Cincinnati's home opener in back-to-back years. Apart from Ray Chapman, few ML players have had their careers end on a more tragic note.

On May 13, 1880, Cincinnati's Jack Manning led off the game by skying a lazy fly ball to left center. Hotaling, in LF for Cleveland, called for the ball, but Hall, in CF, failed to hear him and the two collided. The *New York Clipper* wrote "both bones in Hall's right ankle were broken clean off halfway between the knee and ankle." After his leg was crudely splinted, Hall was carried off the field in a makeshift litter and taken by ambulance to Cincinnati Hospital at his own expense. As was the custom in 1880, Cleveland owner John Ford Evans cut off Hall's salary once he was disabled and obliged him to pay his own hospital bill. Cleveland and Cincinnati players proposed playing a benefit game for Hall but postponed their plan when Evans refused to attend it, purportedly protesting, "I have to go to a champagne breakfast." Nevertheless, a benefit game eventually took place on May 17 and netted Hall some $500 toward his medical expenses. In late May the *Clipper* said, "Hall, who recently broke his leg in a Cleveland-Cincinnati game, is getting along finely, and his doctor thinks he will be out on crutches in a short time." But such was not the case. In mid-September a note in the *Clipper* continued to be encouraging: "Al Hall . . . is rapidly recovering the use of his limb, and thinks he will be all right again in a very few weeks."

But that also was way too optimistic. Hall never played again and died less than five years after his career-ending injury in a Warren, PA, insane asylum to which he was committed for being delusional and an acute alcoholic. (DN)

Ham, Ralph A. / "Ralph"

B	T	HGT	WGT	G	AB	H	R	2B
?	?	5'8"	158	25	113	28	25	4

3B	HR	RBI	BB	SO	SB	BA	SA	OBP
0	0	12	1	7	6	.248	.283	.254

B. 3/?/1849 Troy, NY **D.** 2/13/1905
TEAMS: 71RokNA
DEBUT: 5/6/71 at Rockford; played LF and went hitless in a 12–4 loss to Cleveland's Al Pratt

FINALE: 9/15/71 at Cleveland; played LF in a 16–8 loss to Cleveland's Al Pratt

The son of Irish immigrants, Ralph Ham was an adequate outfielder but a hideous third baseman—13 errors in 25 chances. Although he was born and died in Troy, NY, he seems to have spent a portion of his life in the Midwest. In the early 1890s he reportedly worked as a night clerk at the Grand Pacific Hotel in Chicago, but throughout most of his adulthood he was a stove molder. (DN/DB)

Harbidge, William Arthur (aka Harbridge) **/ "Bill" "Parrot Toes" "Yeller Bill"**

B	T	HGT	WGT	G	AB	H	R	2B
L	L	?	162	378	1510	373	200	47

3B	HR	RBI	BB	SO	SB	BA	SA	OBP
16	2	114	80	69	2	.247	.303	.285

B. 3/29/1855 Philadelphia, PA **D.** 3/17/1924
TEAMS: 75HarNA 76–77HarN 78–79ChiN 80TroN 82TroN 83PhiN 84CinU
DEBUT: 5/18/1875 at Brooklyn; caught Candy Cummings and went 1-for-4 in 5–0 win over the Atlantics' Jim Clinton
FINALE: 10/3/1884 at Cincinnati; played RF and went 0-for-4 in a 6–1 win over Washington's Charlie Geggus

Bill Harbidge never seemed to care how his name was spelled, making it nearly impossible now to determine whether his true surname was Harbidge or Harbridge. He appeared in box scores as both and sometimes would be carried by one name in the box score and the other in the game account. The nickname by which he was best known is also a source of dispute. The press sometimes referred to him as "Yeller Bill," but teammates called him "Parrot Toes" because of his mincing gait. By the late 1880s he was out of the game and soon was almost completely forgotten. In July 1892 *TSN* recalled: "Harbridge was always known for his gaseous qualities. His wonderful know-it-all letters to *Sporting Life* stamped him as a thorough windbag." Already 90 percent of the paper's readership had no notion whom the subject under discussion was.

Harbidge fares no better even among today's nineteenth-century historians. The debut date (May 15, 1875) listed for him in most reference works is incorrect, and many casual researchers continue to identify him as the first left-handed catcher in ML history when there had actually been several before him, most prominently Fergy Malone. In 1873 Malone became the first southpaw to catch as many as 50 games in a season. Harbidge was the first to match Malone's achievement in the NL, catching 53 games for Chicago in 1878 and leading all receivers in errors and passed balls. All that season the *New York Clipper* reported rumors of his imminent release, but he was still on the team in September. A few weeks later the *Chicago Tribune* announced that Harbidge had signed to play for Chicago in 1879, but he appeared in only 4 games with the club the following spring before being released to Holyoke of the National Association. Later that year he joined Springfield, MA, for a time before returning briefly to the NL in 1880 with Troy. Harbidge hit.370 in 9 games with the Trojans but spent most of the summer with the semipro Troy Tibbitts. After a year with five teams in the Eastern Championship Association he reconnected with the Trojans in 1882. Despite hitting just .187 in 32 games, he was hired in 1883 by the Philadelphia replacement franchise for Troy. His flexibility enabled him to play every position except RF and pitcher for the cellar-dwelling Quakers, and his .221 BA assured that he would not be mourned when he jumped to the UA in 1884.

Harbidge opened the UA season in CF for the Cincinnati Outlaw Reds. He batted leadoff on Opening Day, suggesting that manager Dan O'Leary had watched where his previous clubs had slotted him. But O'Leary, like the others, seemingly was clueless that Harbidge, a slow runner who walked infrequently and had never scored more than 32 runs in any of his previous ML seasons, was a poor choice to head a batting order. O'Leary nonetheless kept Harbidge in the lead-off spot until he was fired. His replacement, Sam Crane, then used the NL reject in the second, third, and fourth slots for the rest of the season. Crane was rewarded with a season total of 59 runs, tied for the third fewest among UA players with a minimum of 350 PAs.

Notwithstanding Harbidge's scant contributions, Cincinnati finished a strong second among full-season UA entries. When the loop folded and the Queen City franchise, after failing to gain Detroit's spot in the NL, was forced to disband, Harbidge was one of the club's leading casualties. The southpaw played with Augusta in the fledgling Southern League in 1885 and renewed his contract for the following season but was released to Syracuse after hitting .243 in 47 games. By 1888 he was reduced to advertising in sporting papers for a baseball job. Later in life he worked in construction, but his duties were limited after his foot was severely crushed in a work-related accident in 1896. Harbidge died at his home in Philadelphia at 67. As in life, his tombstone contains one surname and his death certificate another. (DN)

Harley, Richard Joseph / "Dick"

B	T	HGT	WGT	G	AB	H	R	2B
L	R	5'10½"	165	379	1470	382	189	28

3B	HR	RBI	BB	SO	SB	BA	SA	OBP
16	4	132	111	—	55	.260	.309	.331

B. 9/25/1872 Philadelphia, PA **D.** 4/3/1952
TEAMS: 97–98StLN 99CleN 00–01CinN 02DetAL 03ChiN
DEBUT: 6/2/1897 at Brooklyn; played CF and went 1-for-4 in a 10–1 loss to Brooklyn's Chauncey Fisher
FINALE: 8/1/8/1903 at Brooklyn; played RF and made 2 hits in a 6–5 win over Brooklyn's Ned Garvin

After playing for the amateur Norristown Alerts, Dick Harley attended Georgetown University in 1891 and was the team captain in 1895, his final collegiate season, and also played on the Hoyas' football squad. In the summer of 1895 he was a member of Harry Mackey's Atlantic City all-collegian amateur team and then went pro in the South New Jersey League. After hitting .357 for Springfield in the 1896 Eastern League, Harley was drafted by the Phillies, farmed to the Philadelphia Athletics in the Atlantic League, and then traded to St. Louis in June 1897 along with second baseman Bill Hallman and $300 for outfielder Tommy Dowd. Installed as the Browns' lead-off hitter, the ex-Hoya had a solid rookie year, hitting .291 with a .740 OPS, but would never again approach either of those figures while serving a full ML season.

Playing for the 1897–98 Browns no doubt quickly (and perhaps permanently) drained Harley's enthusiasm for the game. After suffering through two consecutive dreary cellar finishes, he desperately wanted out of St. Louis and got his wish but in a "Monkey's Paw" kind of way when he went to Cleveland after the Browns and Spiders consolidated under syndicate ownership in 1899. Cleveland in 1899 lost a ML record 134 games, encumbering Harley with the unenviable distinction of having played with clubs in his first three ML seasons that lost 347 games and had an aggregate .202 winning percentage.

Dropped from the NL when the loop reduced to eight teams, he spent most of 1900 with Detroit of the newly renamed American League and regained a measure of his reputation as a good contact hitter by batting .325. Returning to the majors with Cincinnati after the AL season ended, Harley was the Reds' regular left fielder in 1901 but fielded just .898 and led the loop in outfield errors. He then jumped to the AL in 1902, returning to Detroit but for just one season. After he hit .231 in his 1903 ML finale, the Cubs traded him to Toronto of the Eastern League with two other players and $700 for pitcher Bert Briggs. Harley remained in the minors until 1908 and later coached baseball at the University of Pittsburgh, Penn State, and Villanova before he and his brother opened a restaurant. He died in Philadelphia at 79. (DN)

Hassamaer, William Louis / "Bill" "Roaring Bill" "Gentle Willie"

B	T	HGT	WGT	G	AB	H	R	2B
?	?	6'0"	180	257	1059	306	163	58

3B	HR	RBI	BB	SO	SB	BA	SA	OBP
23	7	178	84	44	25	.289	.407	.342

B. 7/26/1864 St. Louis, MO **D.** 5/29/1910
TEAMS: 94–95WasN 95–96LouN
DEBUT: 4/19/1894 at Washington; played SS and went 1-for-4 in a 4–2 win over Philadelphia's Gus Weyhing
FINALE: 7/6/1896 at Louisville; played 1B and went 1-for-4 in a 5–2 win over Boston's Ted Lewis

Bill Hassamaer drove a team of horses for his father, a North St. Louis coal dealer, before investigating pro ball and continued in his father's employ winters until the finish of his baseball career. After playing for the semipro St. Louis Advance in 1886, he signed with the AA Browns the following spring but was cut in training camp. Hassamaer then spent two seasons with Kansas City minor league teams but failed to develop, hitting just .237 in 1888, and descended to Waco of the

Texas League in 1889. Released when he was at .228 in 48 games, he finished the season with Tyler, TX, and improved enough that Waco rehired him in 1890. On May 15, 1890, Hassamaer won a cash prize when he hit the first home run of the season by a Waco player, but within a few months he was made to take his game west to Portland of the Pacific Northwest League after the TL folded. That winter he drove a streetcar in Portland to support his family and then headed south in February to San Francisco, where he was hired to play SS under controversial manager Henry Harris.

Hassamaer's first encounter with Harris brought this observation from *TSN*: "A tall, heavily built man with a Peek-a-Boo Veach look . . . wandered around in a nervous sort of manner, and after some hesitation announced his name was Hassamer [*sic*]." In July 1891 Hassamaer's wife died and he asked permission to accompany her body from San Francisco to Fort Scott, KS, where it could be buried among her kinfolk. Harris threatened to blacklist his SS if he left the team, but Hassamaer was determined to go. Harris then refused to delay that day's game with Sacramento even for the hour it would take the San Francisco team to accompany Hassamaer to Oakland on the ferry while acting as pallbearers. Events then turned even more heartless when Harris refused to allow his players to collect travel money for Hassamaer, who had little of his own. At that point Sacramento manager John McCloskey got together a $50 purse among his own players and had them wear black armbands during the game while the San Francisco players wore none.

Having had his fill of Harris, Hassamaer signed a contract with Los Angeles when he returned to the West Coast that included an incentive clause. After LA manager Bob Glenalvin released him in August, Hassamaer claimed it was because he was nearing the stats that would have made the club pay him more and vowed never to play in the West again. He made good on his oath in 1893, moving to Montgomery in the Southern League. Nearly 30, that season Hassamaer caught the interest of an ML team for the first time since he had gone to training camp with St. Louis six years earlier. Joining Washington in 1894, he split his days between the infield and the outfield and led the club in runs with 106. Still, at the close of the season, in summing up Hassamaer's rookie performance, *TSN* whispered that he was "not a total abstainer."

Over the winter Washington tried to arrange a deal with St. Louis that would send Hassamaer west and bring the Senators Tommy Dowd, which would have been perfect for both men since Hassamaer still made his home in St. Louis and Dowd lived in Washington, but negotiations stalled. In Hassamaer's first exhibition appearance in the spring of 1895 he caught, a position he had played with some success in the minors but one, unfortunately for him, that was Washington's strongest, as Deacon McGuire would catch every game that year. Consequently, Hassamaer opened the season in RF even though he was awkward there. In late June he was voted "the most popular Senator." Nevertheless, scarcely eight weeks later he was sold to Louisville for a mere $200. Under the wing of John McCloskey, his benefactor when his wife had died, Hassamaer started slowly and finished poorly. The following spring he was ticketed for release by Louisville in March, but McCloskey gave him a reprieve. Soon afterward his chief supporter was fired and Bill McGunnigle took over the Colonels, launching a personnel shakeup that provoked Hassamaer to tell *SL* he was "of the opinion that it is not a string which a club has on a player. 'It's a rope and it's around a fellow's neck' is his explanation." Oddly, he later worked as a rope maker.

Back in the minors, Hassamaer seemed to lose heart for a time but revived to play until 1899, finishing with Bridgeport of the Connecticut State League under former MLer Jerry Denny. Hassamaer died in St. Louis of locomotor ataxia and is immortalized for the "Hassamaer bounce," a sharp ground ball that jumps neatly into a fielder's glove on the first hop, his typical luck at the plate. He is also among the few multiyear ML regulars in the 1890s whose batting and throwing sides are both still unknown. (DN/DB)

---

*Hatfield, John Van Buskirk / "John"

B	T	HGT	WGT	G	AB	H	R	2B
?	?	5'10"	165	206	1011	283	219	36

3B	HR	RBI	BB	SO	SB	BA	SA	OBP
11	3	146	23	20	28	.280	.346	.296

G	IP	H	GS	CG	BB
3	8	11	0	0	0

SO	SH	W	L	PCT	ERA
0	0	0	1	.000	2.25

G	W	L	PCT	PENNANTS
68	35	31	.530	0

B. 7/20/1847 ?, New Jersey **D.** 2/20/1909
TEAMS: 71–75MutNA (P/M)72–73MutNA 76NYN
DEBUT: 5/18/1871 at Troy; played LF and went 1-for-5 in a 14–3 win over Troy's John McMullin
FINALE: 5/5/1876 at Brooklyn; played 2B and made 1 hit in a 4–3 loss to Hartford's Tommy Bond

John Hatfield was the older brother of ML infielder Gil Hatfield and related to the feuding West Virginia Hatfields. He reputedly had the greatest arm in the game in his heyday, but unhappily it is still not known with which arm he set a new throwing record in 1868 at Cincinnati and later used to break his own mark on October 15, 1872, at Brooklyn's Union Grounds. Hatfield played with the Queen City Red Stockings in 1868 but was suspected of being in cahoots with gamblers and was no longer with the club in 1869 when it became the first all-professional unit. In his six ML campaigns—all spent with the New York Mutuals—he served as a regular at three different positions: 3B, 2B, and LF. In 1874, his final full season, Hatfield led all NA gardeners with an .874 FA but hit just .222, suggesting that the pitching by then had left him behind.

Field captain of the Mutes for parts of both the 1872 and 1873 seasons, Hatfield remained connected with the team until it disbanded in 1876. Afterward he relocated to St. Louis, where for some years he ran a prosperous betting parlor with fellow bookmaker Dick Roche. Hatfield made a good living at the racetracks until the mid-1890s, when he hit a long losing streak and went broke. He subsequently regrouped and remained a bookmaker and member of the Turf Benevolent Association until his death from heart failure in 1909 at his Long Island City, NY, home. (DN/DB)

Hawes, William Hildreth / "Bill"

B	T	HGT	WGT	G	AB	H	R	2B
R	R	5'10"	155	117	504	129	99	10

3B	HR	RBI	BB	SO	SB	BA	SA	OBP
7	4	9	7	13	—	.254	.325	.264

B. 11/17/1853 Nashua, NH **D.** 6/16/1940
TEAMS: 79BosN 84CinU
DEBUT: 5/1/1879 at Buffalo; played RF and went hitless in a 5–0 win over Buffalo's Jim Galvin
FINALE: 10/15/1884 at Cincinnati; played LF and went 0-for-4 in a 5–4 win over Baltimore's Al Atkinson

Bill Hawes enjoyed a long and fertile career in baseball even though little of it was spent at the big league level. He began with the amateur Bartlett club of Lowell, MA, in 1873 and soon joined the more prestigious Lowell nine. Hawes remained with Lowell through the 1878 International Association season with a year out in 1876, when he played in the Midwest. Boston signed him for 1879 on the strength of his .296 BA with the 1878 Lowells. Hawes's ML career nearly ended before it had barely begun when he went hitless in the first 5 games of the 1879 season. He finally broke the ice on May 10, going 2-for-4 and scoring 2 runs in a 7–3 win over Cleveland's Jim McCormick. But it was one of his rare good days with Boston, and he was hitting at the bottom of the order when he was dropped after a 0-for-4 effort at Chicago on July 8.

Hawes remained in the game one more year, playing for several minor league teams in 1880, and then quit to go into business in Lowell. When he broke a leg in an 1881 benefit game, it perhaps solidified his thoughts of abandoning baseball. But after umpiring a number of games in the Boston area in 1882, including a July 4 DH between Boston and Detroit, Hawes joined Saginaw of the Northwestern League in 1883. When the Union Association was launched the following year, he was among the original cast of the Cincinnati club. But against even the dubious quality of pitching in the UA Hawes struggled. After beginning the 1884 campaign as a regular, he became only a part-timer as the season wore on and finished with the second lowest OPS (.643) among UA outfielders with a minimum of 350 PAs.

The collapse of the UA plunged Hawes permanently back into the minors. His career reached its zenith when he joined Minneapolis of the strong Western Association in 1887 and remained in that loop for four seasons. Hawes then returned to Lowell to finish out his career in the New England League. In 1892, at age 38, he experienced rejuvenation and had 36 stolen bases for Lowell by the end of June, causing *TSN* to inquire, "What's the matter with the New England League catchers?" Hawes was working in Lowell as a pawnbroker and was seemingly out of the game for good, but two years later *TSN* warned, "The old passion is still strong and he has hung three base balls over his door." Soon Hawes was back in the harness with Lowell under manager Bill McGunnigle. The following winter he was tending bar at Hood's Sarsparilla in Lowell when he again succumbed to the urge. Hawes continued to be part of the baseball scene in the Lowell-Boston area deep into the twentieth century. Later in life he served on the Lowell Board of Cemetery Commissioners while serving as the sole proprietor of the James Green & Company pawn shop. Hawes died at his Lowell home in 1940 at 86 and was among the last alive to have made their ML debuts when pitchers still delivered the ball only forty-five feet from home plate. (DN)

Heidrick, R. Emmet / "Emmet" "Snags"

B	T	HGT	WGT	G	AB	H	R	2B
L	R	6'0"	185	250	1006	319	170	29

3B	HR	RBI	BB	SO	SB	BA	SA	OBP
24	4	135	55	—	80	.317	.406	.350

B. 7/9/1876 Queenstown, PA **D.** 1/20/1916
TEAMS: 98CleN 99–01StLN 02–04StLAL 08StLAL
DEBUT: 9/14/1898 at Washington; played CF and went 4-for-5 in a 6–5 win over Washington's Pop Williams
FINALE: 10/6/1908 at Cleveland; played RF and went 3-for-4 in a 5–1 loss to Cleveland's Jack Ryan

Emmet Heidrick first learned the workings of the pro game under Ed Barrow in 1896 as a member of the Paterson, NJ, Atlantic Association club, where he often appeared in the same lineup with Honus Wagner. By September 1898 he was ready to graduate to the majors with Cleveland, and in a 19-game trial hit a neat .303. Heidrick won St. Louis's RF post the following season after syndicate ownership reassigned most of the Spiders to the Mound City entry and led the team in hits and steals and all NL outfielders in assists, but his fine rookie year was eclipsed by the welter of other great frosh performances in 1899.

Paid $1,500 that season, Heidrick sought a raise to $3,200 in 1900 after teammates assured him he was worth it but was laughed out of owner Frank Robison's office when he presented his demand. Over the winter he worked for his father's lumber company in Wisconsin and refused to sign for 1900 until spring training was under way. That June, Heidrick tore a hamstring and then reinjured it in early July on his first afternoon back in the lineup. When he was held to just 85 games, Robison's claim that he was a shirker forced him to get a doctor's letter proving his leg had been in a cast during his time on the DL before Robison would give him his last paycheck of the season.

In the winter of 1900–1901, Heidrick reached an agreement with his father that he would play baseball one more year and then join the family business. When Robison again tried to lowball him on salary, he jumped to the rebel AL, signing an option with Chicago, but then reneged and returned to St. Louis for what was slated to be his final season. In July 1901, Heidrick was leading the NL in batting when his father suddenly died. After returning from the funeral, he reinjured his leg, missed several games, and watched teammate Jesse Burkett overtake him in the batting race when his leg injury made it so "he could not shift his position to meet the ball."

His agreement to retire rescinded by his father's death, Heidrick opted to play again in 1902. He remained blacklisted by the AL for having backed out of his 1901 deal with Chicago until AL president Ban Johnson hired Jimmy McAleer to run the new St. Louis Browns' AL entry, and McAleer discovered that Bobby Wallace, Burkett, Dick Padden, Jack Powell, and Jack Harper would agree to jump from the Cardinals to the Browns only if Heidrick came along. McAleer persuaded Johnson to get Chicago owner Charlie Comiskey to agree to lift the ban on Heidrick but was disappointed when his prized acquisition slipped to .289, his lowest mark to date.

Heidrick played two more seasons and then, still unable to regain the speed that had been his forte before his rash of hamstring injuries, quit in the fall of 1904 to go into the lumber business with his brother in Clarion, PA. He remained on the retired list until the closing weeks of the 1908 season, when the Browns were among the four closely packed contenders in the AL race. McAleer at that point induced the 32-year-old outfielder to rejoin his old club in return for a $3,000 windfall just to finish the season. Heidrick looked as if he might be worth all that money initially, but the rust soon began to show. Only a 3-for-4 performance in his ML finale pulled his 1908 BA above .200 (.215). Heidrick returned to Clarion and his lumber business until his death from influenza at 39. (DN)

Hines, Paul Aloysius / "Paul"

B	T	HGT	WGT	G	AB	H	R	2B
R	R	5'9½"	173	1658	7062	2133	1217	399

3B	HR	RBI	BB	SO	SB	BA	SA	OBP
93	57	855	372	310	163	.302	.409	.340

G	IP	H	GS	CG	BB
1	1	3	0	0	0

SO	SH	W	L	PCT	ERA
0	0	0	0	—	0.00

B. 3/1/1852 Washington, D.C. **D.** 7/10/1935
TEAMS: 72NatNA 73WasNA 74–75ChiNA 76–77ChiN 78–85ProN 86–87WasN 88–89IndN 90PitN 90BosN 91WasA
DEBUT: 4/20/1872 at Washington; played 1B and went 1-for-5 in a 21–1 loss to Baltimore's Cherokee Fisher
FINALE: 7/3/1891 at Washington; played CF and made 1 hit in a 2–2 fourteen-inning tie with Cincinnati's Will Mains
CAREER HIGHLIGHT: In the view of most historians won the first ML Triple Crown in 1878

Washington native Paul Hines graduated from the amateur Rosedales to the NA Nationals in 1872. From the outset of his career he played without a glove—in 1900 he told *TSN*, "I never wore a mitt in my life" and scoffed that any player ever should—and by the 1880s had begun to lose his hearing, a handicap that did not prevent him from continuing to be a fertile source of copy for reporters.

When the National League was founded in 1876, Hines starred in CF for the champion Chicago team. He became an original member of the Providence Grays in 1878 and was the only player to survive the small city's entire eight-year run as a ML entity. On May 8, 1878, Hines made what some historians believe was the first unassisted triple play in ML history and still the only one by an outfielder. According to Tim Murnane—a witness to the play as a member of the Boston club—after making a spectacular running catch in short left-center of Boston second baseman Jack Burdock's low line drive, Hines sprinted to 3B and touched the bag, thereupon retiring two runners who had passed it by then and would have been required to come back and tag it before returning to their original bases. Murnane's account, if correct, would have made Hines's play indeed unassisted according to the rule in 1878, but in the July 6, 1889, *TSN* other witnesses challenged Murnane's recollection, noting that the trailing runner, Jack Manning, had not yet reached 3B, forcing Hines to throw to second baseman Charlie Sweasy for the third out.

Also in dispute are Hines's Triple Crown season in 1878, in that his margin of victory in the batting race came from hits made in tie games whose stats the NL did not then count, and yet a third famous first, that he introduced sunglasses while playing the outfield. In 1879, Hines, without argument, set a ML record with 146 hits that lasted until 1883, won the batting title, and led the Grays to their first pennant. Five years later Hines was still in CF for the Grays when they won a second pennant. He led off in every game at a time when lineups were customarily constructed to get the best hitters the most at-bats, but his batting stats, although still good, were no longer exceptional. The Grays' success was built on pitching and defense, and Hines by reputation was an excellent outfielder, known for spectacular one-hand barehanded catches. But in 1885, when Providence plummeted from being a runaway pennant winner to a sub-.500 team, Hines contributed heavily to the demise, slumping to .270 and scoring just 63 runs. The Grays still finished in the NL's first division, but in his remaining six years in the majors he would never play on a team that finished so high again. Actually, he would find himself on many of the worst teams in the 1880s. In 1886, while Hines's last-place Washington NL club was hitting .210 as a unit, he batted .312, 83 points higher than any other regular on the club, and was all that stood between the wretched D.C. entry and an aggregate .196 team BA.

There is some question about Hines's birth year, whether it was 1852 or 1855, but in any case he was nearly out of gas when he played his last ML game. The following day the *Washington Post* observed that he had been guilty of such bad fielding, missing balls in the sun and failing to charge a reachable pop fly, and such bad baserunning as well that he was "paving the way to be replaced by [Mike] Slattery" in CF, as indeed transpired. Hines sat out the 1892 season and then returned as a player-manager in the minors, finishing with Mobile of the Southern League in 1896. His home remained in Washington, where he had made many influential contacts during his playing days. Among them was William McKinley, a former congressman, who rewarded Hines with a position as postmaster for the Department of Agriculture after he was elected president. In Hines's later years, however, things did not go well for him. In 1922 he was arrested in Washington as a pickpocket and a decade later was deaf and blind, living in the Sacred Heart Home for seniors, where he died at 83. (DN/DB)

Hodes, Charles / "Charlie"

B	T	HGT	WGT	G	AB	H	R	2B
?	R	5'11½"	175	62	273	63	57	10

3B	HR	RBI	BB	SO	SB	BA	SA	OBP
1	2	44	8	2	3	.231	.297	.253

B. ?/?/1848 New York, NY **D.** 2/14/1875
TEAMS: 71ChiNA 72TroNA 74AtlNA
DEBUT: 5/8/1871 at Chicago; caught George Zettlein and made 2 hits in a 14–12 win over Cleveland's Al Pratt
FINALE: 7/16/1874 at Hartford; played 2B and went 0-for-5 in a 6–2 win over Hartford's Cherokee Fisher

Although best as a catcher, Charlie Hodes played every position in the majors except LF and pitcher. He spent two seasons with the Brooklyn Eckfords before coming to Chicago in 1870 and working nights as a printer. In 1898 *TSN* said that after an 1871 game against Troy, Hodes put his fist through a glass window that night when the saloon where he and the Chicago team were imbibing closed too early for his taste, and he was able to play no more that year. Like so many stories told years after the fact, there may not have been much truth to it since Hodes participated in every official Chicago contest in 1871. Yet it wasn't completely a distortion, for Hodes definitely had a serious alcohol problem. After he joined Jimmy Wood in the mass exodus of Chicago players to Troy in the wake of the Great Fire that forced the Windy City team to disband, the *Chicago Tribune* noted the following April, "It would be premature to say that Hodes has entirely abandoned his enemy of last year; yet his appearance now is all that any athlete could ask for." But when Troy started badly in 1872 despite its influx of Chicago talent, Hodes was made the "Jonah." By June he was back in Chicago playing for the semipro Aetnas and working mainly as a printer.

Hodes remained out of the NA in 1873 before returning to play for the Brooklyn Atlantics. When he scored just 8 runs in his first 22 games in 1874 and hit .148, he was informed he had played his last innings in the majors. Hodes is believed to have died the following February in Brooklyn, but there were reports that he worked as a letter carrier in Chicago after he left baseball. Moreover, the January 30, 1892, *TSN* stated, "Ten years ago . . . they buried him in Chicago." (DN)

Hogan, Robert Edward / "Eddie"

B	T	HGT	WGT	G	AB	H	R	2B
R	?	5'7"	153	121	426	88	88	23

3B	HR	RBI	BB	SO	SB	BA	SA	OBP
7	0	24	87	—	42	.207	.293	.357

B. ?/?/1862 ?, Illinois **D.** 3/17/1923
TEAMS: 84MilU 87NYA 88CleA
DEBUT: 9/27/1884 at Milwaukee; played RF and went 0-for-3 in a 2–0 win over Washington's Charlie Geggus
FINALE: 10/17/1888 at Philadelphia; played RF and went 2-for-4 in a 14–4 loss to Philadelphia's Gus Weyhing

Eddie Hogan could do it all on the diamond except catch and pitch, but the only areas where he excelled were in coaxing walks—87 in 429 career ABs as opposed to just 88 hits—and stealing bases. A Chicago native, he played for the local semipro Green Stockings in 1882 and joined Peoria of the Northwestern League the following spring. He was with Milwaukee of the same loop when it enlisted in the UA late in 1884.

Hogan then played in the Western and in Southern leagues before coming to New York AA in August 1887 from Nashville. His career highlight was actually a gaffe. In a game at New York's Staten Island ballpark on August 12, 1887, after he fumbled a ball hit by Philadelphia's Gus Weyhing, it rattled around on the park's resplendent "Babylon" platform in deep RF. The park rule stated that a ball landing on the platform was an automatic double, so Weyhing, who had made 3B, was ordered back to 2B, and the A's protested in vain to umpire Jerry Sullivan that the rule didn't apply since Hogan had touched the ball. The game was ultimately forfeited to the Mets, who were ahead 9–7 at the time.

In 1888 Hogan was leading Cleveland in runs scored per game when he was hobbled in September by a chronic rheumatoid condition that ended his career. He later umpired in the minors and officiated a NL twin bill at Chicago on August 2,

1897. Hogan died in Chicago in 1923. His .357 career OBP (all of it achieved before the number of balls needed to walk were shaved to four) tops all ML players with a minimum of 400 career ABs and a sub-.210 BA. (DN)

Holdsworth, James / "Jim"

B	T	HGT	WGT	G	AB	H	R	2B
R	R	?	?	319	1484	432	221	38

3B	HR	RBI	BB	SO	SB	BA	SA	OBP
22	0	138	8	20	8	.291	.346	.295

B. 7/14/1850 New York, NY **D.** 3/22/1918
TEAMS: 72CleNA 72EckNA 73MutNA 74PhiNA 75MutNA 76NYN 77HarN 82TroN 84IndA
DEBUT: 5/4/1872 at Washington; played SS and went 2-for-5 in a 13–10 win over Washington's Bill Stearns
FINALE: 6/9/1884 at Baltimore; played CF and went 1-for-3 in an 11–10 loss to Baltimore's Bob Emslie

After playing for the independent Brooklyn Eckfords in 1871, Jim Holdsworth signed with Cleveland for 1872 but returned to the Eckfords after the Forest City team disbanded. Despite being tarred from time to time with accusations of dishonest play along with most of the New York Mutuals, he remained a solid player throughout the NA's tenure but began to falter as a hitter in 1876 when the NL formed and the pitching sharpened. By 1878, with New Bedford–New Haven and Allegheny in the International Association, he saw his BA drop to .208. Holdsworth remained in the game nonetheless. As late as 1883 he still had illusions, advertising in *SL* for a baseball position in early August and claiming to be in "fine trim." The following spring he evidently developed a connection with someone affiliated with the Indianapolis AA club but was given his walking papers after hitting .111 in 5 games. Holdsworth continued to play in benefit games and old-timers' events for several more years in New York. When he died at 67, funeral services were held at his apartment in Manhattan. (DN/PM)

*Holliday, James Wear / "Bug" "Hall"

B	T	HGT	WGT	G	AB	H	R	2B
R	R	5'11"	151	930	3658	1141	735	162

3B	HR	RBI	BB	SO	SB	BA	SA	OBP
72	65	621	360	211	252	.312	.449	.377

G	IP	H	GS	CG	BB
2	5	17	0	0	3

SO	SH	W	L	PCT	ERA
0	0	0	0	—	9.00

B. 2/8/1867 St. Louis, MO **D.** 2/15/1910
TEAMS: *(85ChiN) 89CinA 90–98CinN
DEBUT: 10/17/1885 at St. Louis; played RF in Game 4 of the World's Series and went 0-for-4 in a 3–2 loss to St. Louis's Dave Foutz
FINALE: 6/30/1898 at Cincinnati; played LF and went 1-for-4 in a 17–3 loss to Philadelphia's Red Donahue

For half a dozen seasons James Holliday was one of the game's better outfielders, an outstanding hitter, and a base runner so fast that it earned him the nickname of "Bug." His illustrious career ended prematurely and sadly as a result of a debilitating illness, but he still has the distinction of having been the only player to make his ML debut in a World Series game. That such a thing could happen indicates the relative informality of the affair between the two league champs that was known as the World's Series in the 1880s. Not until 2006 would another player, Mark Kiger, make his ML debut in a postseason game—the ALCS—and Kiger had a substantial pro career behind him at the time. In contrast, Holliday was an 18-year-old semipro in his native St. Louis in 1885 when Chicago manager Cap Anson needed an outfielder for a Series game against the St. Louis Browns. Holliday did nothing to turn heads, batting ninth and going hitless. Nevertheless, he moved into more serious competition with St. Joseph of the Western Association the next season.

For reasons known only to himself, Holliday played under the name of "Hall" for much of 1886 but was quick to adopt his own name when he established himself as a top prospect in 1887 with Walt Goldsby's Topeka Western League champion. That fall, Holliday was nearly acquired by the St. Louis Browns, but Des Moines of the Western Association was eventually awarded his rights in a contract dispute. A year later Holliday was the center of another controversy, as Des Moines agreed to sell him to Philadelphia for a reported $1,500 and then reneged so as to take a much larger offer from Cincinnati, prompting Philadelphia mogul John I. Rogers to sponsor a new rule making the acceptance of a purchase offer binding on the selling club. In Cincinnati, Holliday stepped into the CF position left vacant after Pop Corkhill's sale. Holliday was not Corkhill's equal on defense—few outfielders were—but he was far superior at bat. A fastball hitter who stood on his right foot with his left toe barely touching the ground, he met the ball with tremendous topspin, swinging so hard that he spun around three or four times on occasion. Not overly analytical about his craft, Holliday once said, "All I know is that I smack out at any thing that I think is in reach." His ML career got off to a quick start, as he was hitting .387 in early June 1889 and still led the AA in batting in July before finally finishing at .321. He also tied for the AA home run crown with 19 despite batting leadoff most of the season. After a sophomore slump in 1890, Holliday posted four more fine seasons. He was a league leader in homers again in 1892 and over his first six seasons compiled 63 dingers, only 2 behind Roger Connor, the ML leader during that span. In an era when inside-the-park homers predominated, this was a tribute to Holliday's speed as well as his big swing and the strength that allowed the slender outfielder to use a bat that most players could not even lift, according to teammate Ollie Beard.

Early in the 1895 season a ruptured appendix felled Holliday. For a while his life was in danger, and as late as July he remained too weak to play more than a few innings. Although Holliday would remain a Red for another four years, he never regained his full physical strength and former skills, let alone his regular position. Judged by normalized OPS, Holliday's best post-illness season barely equals his worst before his illness.

Handsome, good-natured, and quick-witted, Holliday nonetheless remained exceptionally popular in Cincinnati and used his contacts to secure lucrative employment. After hitting a weak .236 as a part-timer in 1898, he put away his spikes at the age of 31 when he was offered a job as a cashier in "a race pool room" in Covington, KY, across the river from Cincinnati. By the following year he was working for Eddie Austin, one of the top bookmakers in the country. In the fall of 1902, however, Holliday was drawn to apply for a position as an NL umpire. Hired only as a sub, he nonetheless worked 53 games in 1903 and then officiated briefly in the minor league American Association the next season before resigning near the end of July.

In the fall of 1894, just before the downward turn in his career, Holliday had made a remarkable marriage. Mary Thurman was the black-sheep daughter of the Ohio senator and Democratic presidential candidate Allen Thurman and sister of the elder Thurman's namesake, who had briefly been the controversial president of the AA. She met Holliday when he was playing winter ball on the West Coast, and he became her third husband. Mary Holliday would stand by him in his last years even as he faced a health crisis far more serious than the one he suffered in 1895. Like many players of the day, Holliday had contracted syphilis, and he suffered symptoms that eventually developed into locomotor ataxia, a cruelly debilitating and ultimately fatal disease. By the fall of 1907 he was so ill that a benefit game was played in his behalf. The affair netted Holliday $800, a substantial sum for the day, but the expenses of his illness soon consumed the money. Ultimately, a leg was amputated, after which he went into a steady decline. Long before he died at his Cincinnati home in 1910, he was reported to be penniless. (DB/DN)

Holmes, James William / "Ducky"

B	T	HGT	WGT	G	AB	H	R	2B
L	R	5'6"	170	443	1712	507	241	73

3B	HR	RBI	BB	SO	SB	BA	SA	OBP
27	9	233	109	14	116	.296	.380	.373

G	IP	H	GS	CG	BB
4	26	42	2	1	12

SO	SH	W	L	PCT	ERA
3	0	1	1	.500	6.58

B. 1/28/1869 Des Moines, IA **D.** 8/6/1932
TEAMS: 95–97LouN 97NYN 98StLN 98–99BalN 01–02DetAL 03WasAL 03–05ChiAL
DEBUT: 8/8/1895 at Pittsburgh; played SS and went 2-for-4 in a 9–6 loss to Pittsburgh's Jim Gardner
FINALE: 9/5/1905 at Philadelphia; pinch hit for Nick Altrock in the fifth inning and fanned in an 11–1 loss to Philadelphia's Chief Bender

The stocky Ducky Holmes and his trademark waddle first came to prominence in 1892 with Beatrice, NE. Living in Carroll, IA, at the time, he caught and played LF and was the best hitter on the Nebraska State League team. Later that season he also did some pitching with St. Joseph and remained with the Missouri club in 1893 long enough to top the Western Association in hitting with a .519 BA before the loop disbanded. By 1895 Holmes was playing SS with Omaha of the WA when he was summoned to Louisville. He hit a snazzy .373 in 43 games and seemed to be the only keeper among the many rookies the Colonels auditioned that season.

The following March, Holmes broke his collarbone when he fell while chasing a fly ball in an exhibition game and was never completely healthy all season. He then rode the Louisville bench in 1897 until he was traded to New York in May for General Stafford. Unhappy with the Giants, that November he was sent to St. Louis in a four-player swap but was on the move again the following June when he joined Baltimore along with $2,500 for Jake Stenzel and Joe Quinn. Some six weeks later, on July 25, 1897, at the Polo Grounds, Holmes fanned in the top of fourth inning, and as he slunk back to the Baltimore bench, a Giants fan hollered, "Holmes, you're a lobster. That's what you left here for." Holmes retorted, "It's a good thing I'm not working for a f*** Sheeny now." Between innings, Giants owner Andrew Freedman stormed onto the field and ordered umpire Tom Lynch to remove Holmes from the game for besmirching his ethnicity. Lynch said he hadn't heard Holmes say anything insulting, and Freedman then secured the police and refused to let the game continue until Holmes was removed from the park. Lynch, after attempting to mollify Freedman, threw up his hands and forfeited the game to Baltimore, whereupon the crowd demanded its money back and threatened violence until Freedman grudgingly assented. Meanwhile, Holmes was given a protective escort from the grounds.

In explaining his version of the incident in *TSN*, Holmes observed, "Freedman treated me like a dog when I was a member of his team, and I can not say that I'm sorry he has made a monkey of himself." NL president Nick Young later prodded the board of directors to endorse what he thought was a reasonable compromise: suspending Holmes and fining Freedman for causing the forfeit. But when that decision failed to pacify either Freedman's or Holmes's supporters, Young eventually rescinded both the suspension and the fine. Still, despite rapping .320 with Baltimore in 1899 and swiping 50 bases, Holmes was frozen out of the NL when the loop reduced to eight teams.

He served with Detroit in the newly renamed AL in 1900 and hit .291. When the rebel loop went major the following year, Holmes was the Tigers' first right fielder and scored 90 runs on a .294 BA. His only achievement of note in the remaining years of his ML career was leading AL gardeners in assists in 1903 despite playing in just 96 outfield games. Holmes finished his playing days as player-manager of the Lincoln Western League entry in 1907 but later returned to manage one final minor league season in 1922. He died in Truro, IA, of diabetes at 63. (DN)

Hoover, William James / "Buster"

B	T	HGT	WGT	G	AB	H	R	2B
R	R	6'1"	178	127	525	151	114	23

3B	HR	RBI	BB	SO	SB	BA	SA	OBP
14	1	16	37	13	16	.288	.390	.337

B. 4/12/1863 Philadelphia, PA **D.** 4/16/1924
TEAMS: 84PhiU 84PhiN 86BalA 92CinN
DEBUT: 4/17/1884 at Philadelphia; played LF and went 1-for-5 in a 14–2 loss to Boston's Tommy Bond
FINALE: 10/15/1892 at Cincinnati; played LF and went 0-for-4 in Bumpus Jones's 7–1 no-hit win over Pittsburgh's Mark Baldwin on the final day of the season

Buster Hoover used a heavy bat, hit the ball hard, and was fast for his size. Off the field he was glib, educated, and a conqueror with the ladies, his tall, blond figure a constant recipient of the distaff element's gifts and nosegays prior to games. Compared to Pete Browning as a dangerous right-handed batsman, he also drew comparison to Browning in that his "trouble with the flowing bowl" continually harmed his ML prospects. After playing in the 1883 Interstate Association, Hoover joined Philadelphia UA in 1884 and was among the circuit's top hitters at .364 and the second player in the loop to reach 100 hits (Fred Dunlap was the first) when the Keystones folded. He joined the NL Quakers almost immediately and hit his only career home run on August 21 off Cleveland's John Henry but otherwise was such a disappointment that he got into only 10 games before being dropped.

Hoover picked up where he had left off with the Keystones after signing with the Washington

Nationals of the Eastern League in 1885. His .299 performance in D.C. won him the Opening Day CF post with the AA Orioles in 1886, but again he demonstrated that he could not hit topflight pitching. Hoover then led one minor league team after another in both batting and fines for misbehavior, highlighted by his 1890 sojourn with Kansas City when he topped the Western Association with a .336 BA. Resentful that local fans nonetheless adored his teammate Elmer Smith more, Hoover sulked and went on repeated benders the following season until KC manager Jim Manning was forced to suspend him indefinitely.

In 1892 Hoover led the Eastern League in homers. Summoned to Cincinnati when the EL season ended, he hit just .176 in 14 games but was reserved by the Reds for 1893. Hoover failed to make the team even though Cincinnati had a glaring lack of quality outfielders and returned to the EL. When Syracuse released him the following year for his usual transgressions, he began 1895 without an engagement. Recognizing that his playing days were over, Hoover wrote to Jim Manning, begging his former nemesis to recommend him for job as a Western League umpire. Hoover died in Jersey City in 1924. Apart from his partial .364 season in the suspect UA, his ML career BA was .204. (DN)

Hornung, Michael Joseph / "Joe" "Ubbo Ubbo"

B	T	HGT	WGT	G	AB	H	R	2B
R	R	5'8½"	164	1123	4784	1230	788	172

3B	HR	RBI	BB	SO	SB	BA	SA	OBP
90	31	564	120	498	159	.257	.350	.277

G	IP	H	GS	CG	BB
1	3	2	0	0	1

SO	SH	W	L	PCT	ERA
0	0	0	0	—	6.00

B. 6/12/1857 Carthage, NY **D.** 10/30/1931
TEAMS: 79–80BufN 81–88BosN 89BalA 90NYN
DEBUT: 5/1/1879 at Buffalo; played LF and went 0-for-3 in a 5–0 loss to Boston's Tommy Bond
FINALE: 10/3/1890 at Chicago; played LF and was replaced in the first inning by Pat Murphy when he took sick

Joe Hornung's strange nickname was given to him by teammates for his shouting something that sounded like "ubbo ubbo" whenever he made a great catch. He grew up near Utica and was taken north to London, Ontario, in 1876 by Utica resident Juice Latham. Hornung remained with the Tecumsehs until they folded in 1878 and then joined Buffalo in time to share in its International Association championship run. Although Hornung hit just .236 with the Bisons, he was retained when the franchise moved to the NL in 1879. He ended his rookie year batting cleanup but would never again occupy that prime spot in the order on a regular basis.

Hornung made his reputation as a fielder, collecting a ML-record eleven chances in LF on September 23, 1881. In 1884 he reportedly went the entire season without muffing a fly ball despite playing his whole career barehanded, and the *Washington Post* contended that he "was in a class by himself" with his strong arm and quick release. At that point Hornung was at his apex; the previous season he had topped the NL in runs with the pennant-winning Bostons. In 1885, however, he began the season mysteriously incapacitated and did not appear in the lineup until May 25. The following day the *Boston Globe* remarked, "Joe is not a well man yet, and until he can play as only he can, his presence in the team is no improvement." Hornung continued to appear on occasion until July 21. A few days later the *Globe* noted, "Joe Hornung, at his own request, will leave for his home today. He isn't a well man, and until fully recovered will not play ball again." Hornung then finished the season umpiring in the New York State League.

The following year he returned to his customary role in LF and batting leadoff, an odd spot for someone who walked only 10 times and scored just 67 runs in well over 400 PAs. Still, he remained a fixture in Boston until July 1888, when his release was rumored to be eminent because he "was a disagreeable factor to the club." Shortly after *TSN* wrote, "Hornung's tongue is an unruly member and often gets its owner into trouble," his long stay with Boston terminated. Baltimore AA then signed him for 1889 largely on his former reputation. Devastated in the spring when his child died, he had a dismal year with the Orioles.

When Players League raids stripped the Giants of most of their regulars, manager Jim Mutrie signed Hornung in the spring of 1890 as a last resort. Hornung left the Giants that October having batted just .244 in the last half of his twelve-year career (1885–90). He played in the minors until

Providence of the Eastern League dropped him in July 1893. Hornung then umpired in the NL for the rest of the season, returned to the playing ranks in the minors for a time, and then became an umpire in the minors after breaking his ankle sliding in a New England League game.

Hornung's last job in baseball was as a special policeman at the Polo Grounds, a position to which his combative nature was well suited. He died in Howard Beach, NY, in 1931. Hornung's 120 career walks are the fewest among ML outfielders with a minimum of 3,000 ABs. (DN)

Hotaling, Peter James / "Pete" "Monkey"

B	T	HGT	WGT	G	AB	H	R	2B
L	R	5'8"	166	840	3492	931	590	148

3B	HR	RBI	BB	SO	SB	BA	SA	OBP
63	9	371	224	161	78	.267	.353	.314

B. 12/16/1856 Mohawk, NY **D.** 7/2/1928
TEAMS: 79CinN 80CleN 81WorN 82BosN 83–84CleN 85BroA 87–88CleA
DEBUT: 5/1/1879 at Cincinnati; played CF and went 1-for-5 in a 7–5 win over Troy's George Bradley
FINALE: 9/15/1888 at Cleveland; played CF and went 1-for-3 in a 6–5 win over Baltimore's Matt Kilroy

Pete Hotaling grew up in Ilion, NY, and by 1876 was catching for the local semipro Clippers. He signed his first pro contract in 1877 with Syracuse of the International Association. Still a catcher, he was hit in the eye by a foul tip early in the season. When Hotaling returned to the lineup, he wore a protective device similar to the wire mask invented earlier that year by Fred Thayer of Harvard. Some historians credit Hotaling as the first to wear a mask in a pro game, but that acknowledgment is highly disputable. In any case, his appearance in the "cage" led to him being nicknamed "Monkey." In 1878, his encore year with Syracuse, then in the International Association, Hotaling hit .278 and played mostly in the outfield.

When Hotaling arrived in Cincinnati the following spring, the *Cincinnati Enquirer* wrote after his debut, "Hotaling . . . will prove a taking card. He is a broad-shouldered, heavily-built, handsome young fellow, who does everything with a manner that bespeaks confidence." Nevertheless, Cincinnati did not retain him the following season. Hotaling moved to Cleveland, launching a pattern. Until 1884 he never spent two consecutive seasons with the same ML team. That year marked the finish of his second tour with Cleveland, when the Forest City club surrendered its franchise and sold most of its top players to Brooklyn AA.

Hotaling resumed the pattern in 1885, lasting only one season with Brooklyn before losing his job to Jim McTamany. He served the following year as player-manager of Savannah of the Southern League and then seized an invitation to return to the majors in 1887 as captain of the Cleveland AA replacement team.

In 1883 Hotaling had married Forest City native Buena Vista Perry. Since then the couple had maintained a residence in Cleveland even while he was playing elsewhere, and he had come to regard the Forest City as his home. After the Blues turned his CF job over to Bob Gilks in September 1888, Hotaling split the following season between two minor league teams and then settled permanently in Cleveland. For several years he ran a grocery business with his uncle. Restive, Hotaling eventually hired on as a machinist with the White Motor Company. He died in Cleveland of pneumonia at 71. (DN)

Hoy, William Ellsworth / "Dummy"

B	T	HGT	WGT	G	AB	H	R	2B
L	R	5'6"	160	1593	6309	1811	1269	206

3B	HR	RBI	BB	SO	SB	BA	SA	OBP
108	36	647	880	211	558	.287	.371	.385

B. 5/23/1862 Houcktown, OH **D.** 12/15/1961
TEAMS: 88–89Wasn 90BufP 91StLSA 92–93WasN 94–97CinN 98–99LouN 01ChiAL 02CinN
DEBUT: 4/20/1888 at Washington; played CF and went 1-for-4 in a 6–0 loss to New York's Cannonball Titcomb
FINALE: 7/17/1902 at Cincinnati; played CF and made 2 hits in a 6–3 loss to New York's Christy Mathewson

Like the numerous players called "Dummy" in the cruelly frank atmosphere that pervaded the nineteenth-century game, William Hoy was deaf but not a mute. Late in the 1900 season *TSN* noted that he spoke in high, squeaky voice. Years earlier the same paper had reported that he avoided outfield collisions by yelling, "I'll take it." While these reports are credible, other current portrayals of Hoy's role in the game's evolution are somewhat suspect. In 1900 *TSN* discussed how he had coached on other teams or else infielders on his own team signal umpires' pitch calls to him by raising their right hands for strikes and left hands for balls so he could keep count. Hoy recommended, as did others, that it become a rule for umpires to signal calls in this same way, belying the popular notion that his presence in the majors had already led to this innovation.

As for Hoy the man, all sources are in agreement that he was bright, extroverted, worked hard at making connections with the hearing people around him, and was an extremely popular teammate everywhere he went. Born on a small Ohio farm, Hoy contracted meningitis when he was 3, rendering him deaf and vocally challenged. After graduating from the Ohio School for the Deaf, where he had been class valedictorian and a teammate of future ML pitcher Dummy Dundon, he opened a shoe shop and played ball only as a sideline, accounting for his late start professionally. Reportedly, a good day while playing for semipro Kenton, OH, against Urbana and its future ML pitcher Bill Hart convinced Hoy that he too could play for pay, and he eventually persuaded Billy Harrington, manager of Oshkosh in the Northwestern League, that his skill would supersede his handicap. A second season with Oshkosh in 1887 under future ML pilot Frank Selee brought Washington scout Ted Sullivan west to sign him.

In his rookie season Hoy led the dreadful 1888 Senators in almost every offensive department despite hitting just .274. He escaped Washington in 1890 for a team that was even worse, landing with Buffalo, the PL's cellar dweller in its lone year extant. A free agent when the PL collapsed, Hoy signed with St. Louis AA. Despite producing 136 runs and a loop-leading 119 walks, he was released in October 1891 when Browns owner Chris Von der Ahe declined to raise his salary.

After the NL and AA merged that December, Hoy found himself back in Washington with a different franchise but one just as bad—so bad actually that it foolishly traded him to Cincinnati in November 1893 for journeyman pitcher Mike Sullivan. Hoy's four seasons with the Ohio team were almost certainly his happiest in the game, which is probably why he returned to the Reds in 1902 when his career was nearing its end. Competitive throughout his tenure, Cincinnati nonetheless failed to win a pennant, and the same gap in his resume persisted after he was traded to Louisville with two other players for pitcher Bill Hill following the 1897 season. That same fall, Hoy announced his engagement to Anna Lowry, a teacher of the deaf, who was also deaf. The couple married the following October and later raised three children to adulthood, two of whom became schoolteachers and the third a judge.

Hoy had an excellent 1898 season with Louisville and an even better one in 1899, tallying 116 runs and leading the club in walks. The Colonels were considering making him team captain in 1900 before they were dropped when the NL downsized to eight teams. When no other NL team claimed him over the winter, owing perhaps to his age, Hoy signed with Chicago of the newly renamed American League. Now 38, he hit just .254 in 1900 but led AL center fielders in fielding marks as Chicago marched to the pennant. When the White Sox repeated the following year after the AL went major, Hoy was finally on his first ML pennant winner in what turned out to be his last full ML season.

Leaving the game after a .257 season in the 1903 Pacific Coast League, Hoy bought a dairy farm in Mount Healthy, OH. He also worked briefly as a personnel director for the Goodyear Tire Company. After his children had left the nest, he worked for a book firm until retiring at 75. In 1961 Hoy threw out the ceremonial first pitch before Game 3 of the World Series between the Reds and the Yankees in Cincinnati. At the time, he was the oldest living former MLer and the last bridge between a game that had still required five balls for a walk in his rookie season and the postexpansion era. Hoy died that December in Cincinnati at 99 and was cremated as per his wishes. (DN/DB)

Johnson, William F. / "Bill" "Sleepy Bill" "Lefty"

B	T	HGT	WGT	G	AB	H	R	2B
L	L	?	167	169	636	168	121	15

3B	HR	RBI	BB	SO	SB	BA	SA	OBP
17	2	90	98	61	45	.264	.351	.368

B. 9/?/1862 ?, New Jersey **D.** 7/17/1942
TEAMS: 84PhiU 87IndN 90–91BalA 92BalN
DEBUT: 6/27/1884 at Philadelphia; played LF and went 0-for-4 in a 6–4 loss to St. Louis's Billy Taylor

FINALE: 4/27/1892 at Brooklyn; played LF and went 0-for-4 in a 4–1 loss to Brooklyn's Dave Foutz

Bill Johnson was nicknamed "Sleepy Bill" because he was unflappable to the point of appearing almost comatose. *SL* said that when he coached the bases, "The silence is so dense you can't cut it with the butt of an axe. No sound but the gentle zephyr sighing through the dreary expanse of a bald eyebrow."

After a brief stint with Philadelphia UA in 1884, Johnson labored in the minors until Indianapolis acquired him in August 1887 to replace Mark Polhemus in RF. In his first game with the Hoosiers, on August 12, he went 3-for-5 but was only 5-for-37 after that. Johnson next found a home with Newark of the Atlantic Association until he and Pete Gilbert were sold as a package to Baltimore in early September 1890. In the remaining weeks of the AA season, he hit well but not with men on base, driving home just 6 runners in 24 games.

Johnson then had an excellent year in the AA's final campaign, compiling a .758 OPS. Among the few Orioles manager Ned Hanlon retained when the team moved to the consolidated NL-AA in 1892, Johnson opened the season batting cleanup and playing RF. He was cut after 4 games, however, when he had just 2 hits and a .667 FA. Johnson played several more years in the minors, finishing his playing career with Titusville of the Iron & Oil League. He died in Chester, PA, at 79. (DN/DB)

Johnston, Richard Frederick / "Dick"

B	T	HGT	WGT	G	AB	H	R	2B
R	R	5'8"	155	746	2992	751	453	109

3B	HR	RBI	BB	SO	SB	BA	SA	OBP
68	33	386	133	233	151	.251	.366	.285

B. 4/6/1863 Kingston, NY **D.** 4/4/1934
TEAMS: 84VirA 85–89BosN 90BosP 90NYP 91CinA
DEBUT: 8/12/1884 at New York; played CF and went 0-for-4 in a 13–5 loss to New York's Jack Lynch
FINALE: 8/16/1891 at St. Louis; played CF and went 0-for-2 in an 8–0 loss to St. Louis's George Rettger

Said to have an uncanny ability to take off at the crack of the bat and race to exactly where the globe would descend, Dick Johnston is considered by some historians to have been the best defensive outfielder in the nineteenth century. Only a sudden mysterious decline as a hitter has made him a scarcely remembered figure today rather than one of the game's top early-day stars.

In 1883 Johnston was working as a typesetter in his Kingston, NY, hometown and earning $2.50 a game playing on weekends and holidays with the local team. The following year he joined the Virginias of Richmond and accompanied the team's new manager, Felix Moses, when Moses took the club from the Eastern League to the AA as a replacement for the disbanded Washington franchise. The rookie outfielder went 0-for-17 against AA pitching before singling on August 21 for his first ML hit. After a 1-for-20 start, he hit .317 for the remainder of the season to finish at .281.

Returning to the Virginias the following year when they rejoined the Eastern League, Johnston was leading the team with a .365 BA at the end of July, 82 points better than teammate Billy Nash. A month later Boston NL acquired the pair as a package. Both made their Hub debuts on September 1, 1885, in a 2–0 win over Providence and by the end of the season had established themselves as regulars. In 1886, his first full ML season, Johnston led all NL outfielders in putouts but scored just 48 runs, in part because he was able to collect only 3 walks in 413 ABs. The following year he again excelled in the field and collected 339 outfield put-outs, a record that stood until 1891. He also improved markedly as a hitter, lifting his OPS 95 points. In 1888 Johnston reached his apex, leading Boston in runs, total bases, and hits. Seemingly on the verge of stardom at age 25, he then plummeted the following year to .228, the lowest BA by all outfield qualifiers in the NL. His unaccountable slump cost his team dearly, as Boston finished just game out of first place. Still, despite intimations that the root of Johnston's sudden decline might be a mushrooming drinking problem, it was seen as an aberration, and he was quickly grabbed that winter to play CF for the Boston PL entry. But just 2 games into the 1890 season he was abruptly benched. A month later Johnston was sold to the New York PL club, which had outfield injury problems, but finished the season with a .238 BA, 36 points below the league average.

Unlike most PL players who returned perforce to their former teams when the rebel loop folded, Johnston was no longer wanted in Boston. He sat at home without an engagement for 1891 before finally signing with Cincinnati, a late entry that

Mike Kelly had been persuaded to run in order to give the AA a necessary eighth team. Johnston's old Boston teammate stuck with him even though he hit just .221, but once Kelly's Killers disbanded in mid-August there were no other takers for an outfielder whose drinking had descended so far out of control that he had an aggregate sub-.230 BA for the past three seasons.

After drawing a string of releases from minor league teams over the next years, Johnston returned to Kingston and ran the local team for a short spell without much success. He then resumed the printing trade until the early 1920s when he relocated to Detroit and worked at the local house of corrections until he was stricken with throat cancer around Christmastime in 1933 and died the following April. (DN)

Jones, Fielder Allison / "Fielder"

B	T	HGT	WGT	G	AB	H	R	2B
L	R	5'11"	180	623	2456	768	486	74

3B	HR	RBI	BB	SO	SB	BA	SA	OBP
33	11	256	266	15	153	.313	.383	.388

B. 8/13/1871 Shinglehouse, PA
D. 3/13/1934 Portland, OR
TEAMS: 96–00BroN 01–03ChiA (P/M)04–08ChiAL (P/M)14–15StLF (M)16–18StLAL
DEBUT: 4/18/1896 at Brooklyn; played RF and went 1-for-4 in a 6–2 loss to Baltimore's Arlie Pond
FINALE: 9/1/1915 at Pittsburgh; served as a pinch runner in a 7–2 win over Pittsburgh's Clint Rogge

In the early 1890s Fielder Jones and his brother Willard formed a battery for the amateur Shinglehouse team, with Willard doing the pitching. Jones then followed his older brother into the engineering and surveying business, and the pair eventually wove their way west to Portland, OR. While there, Jones played for the local team in the Oregon State League as a side venture in 1893 and then decided to make the game his livelihood. He played in New York State League until July 1895 when the loop folded and then moved to Springfield of the Eastern League under manager Tom Burns. During the off-season Burns was offered the New York NL pilot job in 1896 but turned it down when Giants owner Andrew Freedman refused to let him bring Jones and two other Springfield players with him because Freedman didn't "think them fast enough."

Jones went to Brooklyn NL in the spring of 1896 instead but was farmed to Hartford of the Atlantic League after he got off to a slow start. Recalled by Brooklyn when John Anderson was injured, he went on a roll that produced a final BA of .354 to lead his club as well as all NL rookies. The mark proved to be Jones's career high by a wide margin, but he remained a steady offensive force in the Brooklyn lineup for the remainder of the century. A right fielder exclusively in his first two ML seasons, Jones opened the 1898 campaign at SS in the hope he could fill a hole there but was swiftly returned to the outfield after making 6 errors in the first 2 games of the season. The following year he was moved to CF, replacing holdout Mike Griffin but lost his job temporarily to Anderson when an injury caused him to miss over a third of the season. Healthy again in 1900, Jones reclaimed CF and played an integral role as Brooklyn repeated as the NL pennant winner.

Having married Mabel Schaney, a woman from his hometown, in 1898, Jones was ripe for the taking when American League raiders began dangling fat contracts in front of NL luminaries toward the end of the 1900 season. He eventually signed with the Chicago AL entry, joining Boston NL catcher Billy Sullivan and veteran Chicago NL hurler Clark Griffith, who was named manager of the fledgling ML club in 1901. Jones and Sullivan thought of themselves only as players at that point in their careers, but in time both of them would also manage Chicago and Jones would spearhead the club to its first world championship. (DN)

Kennedy, Edward / "Ed"

B	T	HGT	WGT	G	AB	H	R	2B
?	?	5'6"	150	299	1105	225	142	20

3B	HR	RBI	BB	SO	SB	BA	SA	OBP
13	5	23	47	—	1	.204	.259	.239

B. 4/1/1856 Carbondale, PA **D.** 5/20/1905
TEAMS: 83–85NYA 86BroA
DEBUT: 5/1/1883 at Baltimore; played LF and went 2-for-5 in a 4–3 loss to Baltimore's John Fox
FINALE: 8/25/1886 at Brooklyn; played LF and went 0-for-4 in a 2–1 win over New York's Ed Cushman

Ed Kennedy was a four-star fielder who excelled at tracking down deep drives, often snagging them with his back to the plate. On June 21, 1881, while playing in an exhibition contest for the New York Mets against the Olympics at Paterson, NJ, he saved the game by capturing a blast that looked like a cinch home run and then turning a complete somersault after making the catch without dropping the ball. For years afterward witnesses to the play deemed it the greatest catch they had ever seen, made all the more amazing by the fact that its architect played his entire career without a glove.

Kennedy's offensive prowess was another matter. The best that was ever said of that phase of his game was, "Kennedy occasionally gets in a telling hit at the bat, and is a very clever base-runner." But the sad truth was that Kennedy was not just an especially weak hitter for an outfielder; he was arguably the worst-hitting outfielder ever. Among flychasers with a minimum of 1,000 career ABs Kennedy ranks dead last in batting average (.204) and slugging average (.259).

Kennedy began his career in the mid-1870s as a catcher with teams in the Carbondale, PA, area. In 1876 he graduated to independent Binghamton, where he served as a SS in addition to catching. Over the next several years he played with numerous eastern teams including New Bedford, where he first met Jim Mutrie, before finally coming under Mutrie's supervision again in August 1880 as a member of the fledgling New York Metropolitans. A left fielder by now, the following season Kennedy played in 149 games, a record at the time. Once the Mets joined the AA in 1883, their left fielder since their inception was among the first players Mutrie signed for the coming season. But after going 2-for-5 in his debut and homering in the Mets' home opener on May 11, Kennedy barely managed to keep his BA above the Mendoza line, finishing at .219. His .884 FA led all left fielders, however, and he scored 57 runs despite reaching base only 95 times via a hit or a walk. In his sophomore season, with the pitching swifter as more hurlers edged toward overhand deliveries, Kennedy fell to .190, the lowest BA ever by a qualifier on a pennant winner.

When he continued his dreary hitting in 1885, with Mutrie gone by then to the NL New York entry, the original Met had no one to champion his fielding as a reason to keep him, and he was released the following spring. In April 1886 Kennedy signed with Dan O'Leary's independent Elmira club, which became the Scranton entry in the Pennsylvania State Association by July. That August, he returned to the majors for 6 games with Brooklyn AA as a fill-in for injured Ernie Burch under a rule then that allowed teams to use unsigned players for a few games in emergencies. Kennedy then finished his minor league career in 1890 and also played for the Mets, which reorganized as a cooperative nine on several occasions in the late 1880s and early 1890s.

Kennedy spent his last years as a laborer living in a cramped Manhattan flat with his wife, Mary, and four children. He died in New York City at 49 of heart disease. Despite all the glowing reports of his fielding and the converse stories about his hitting, the sides with which he batted and threw are still unknown. (DN)

*King, Stephen F. / "Steve"

B	T	HGT	WGT	G	AB	H	R	2B
?	?	5'9"	175	54	272	96	78	18

3B	HR	RBI	BB	SO	SB	BA	SA	OBP
6	0	55	2	3	4	.353	.463	.358

B. ?/?/1844 Lansingburgh, NY **D.** 7/8/1895
TEAMS: 71–72TroNA
DEBUT: 5/9/1871 at Troy; played LF in a 9–5 loss to Boston's Al Spalding
FINALE: 7/23/1872 at Middletown; played LF and went 3-for-4 in a 7–0 win over Middletown's Cy Bentley

The brother of MLer Mart King, Steve King was a member of the original Troy Haymakers in 1866, when they were still known as the Unions of Lansingburgh. One story is that the team received its new nickname during a game against the Brooklyn Atlantics on August 9, 1866. The field was muddy and both clubs were slipping and sliding until the Unions removed their cleated baseball shoes and played barefoot to cries of "Just look at the haymakers!"

Among the local team's top batsmen from the outset of his career, King was 30 when the Haymakers left the NA and evidently had no desire at the time to play elsewhere, because his hitting must have made him desirable to other NA clubs. He died at his home in the Lansingburgh section of Troy in 1895. (DN)

Lange, William Alexander / "Bill" "Little Eva"

B	T	HGT	WGT	G	AB	H	R	2B
R	R	6'1½"	190	813	3202	1056	691	134

3B	HR	RBI	BB	SO	SB	BA	SA	OBP
80	39	579	350	86	399	.330	.458	.400

B. 6/6/1871 San Francisco, CA **D.** 7/23/1950
TEAMS: 93–99ChiN
DEBUT: 4/27/1893 at Cincinnati; played LF and went 0-for-4 in an 11–1 loss to Tony Mullane and Bumpus Jones
FINALE AND FAMOUS FIRST: 10/15/1899 at Chicago; in the 1st game of a three-team DH went 1-for-3 and scored 1 run in a 7–0 win over St. Louis's Tom Thomas, and in the second game went 1-for-4 and scored 1 run in a 9–5 loss to Louisville's Deacon Phillippe, thereupon becoming the first and only player to score runs against two different teams on the final day of his ML career

Bill Lange was the uncle of HOFer George Kelly. There are several stories as to how he acquired the fetching nickname of "Little Eva." One is that it came to him for being the youngest player in the Pacific Northwest League in 1888, when he made his pro debut with Port Townsend at age 17. Lange's own version was that one year an attractive young woman began appearing at Chicago's games in the East and the Colts kept winning with her in the audience until in Boston a "hoodoo" was hired to counteract her magical effect. To ensure that she would continue to attend all their road games, Lange and several other Colts went to her home and discovered that she was playing Little Eva in a current production of *Uncle Tom's Cabin* and her husband was none other than the hoodoo. Because Lange was the most smitten by her, he was dubbed Little Eva. The reader is left to judge which tale is more credible.

The reader also must judge whether Lange was a great player who missed out on his historical due because he quit while still in his prime or else simply a very good player whose press clippings exceeded his actual achievements. Al Spink, founding editor of *TSN*, contended some twenty years after Lange retired that he was "Ty Cobb enlarged, fully as great in speed, batting skill and baserunning." Yet Mike Grady, who caught for the Giants, claimed that Lange was mortally terrified of the Giants' twin speedballers, Amos Rusie and Jouett Meekin. Grady would thus call for the first pitch of the game to Lange from either of them to be up and in, and Lange would then be pudding for the rest of the day upon rising from the ground "all atremble."

Lange spent four years in early versions of the Pacific Northwest League, a long time in any case for a budding star to play in such a lowly circuit, before joining Oakland of the California winter loop in the fall of 1892. He convinced any lingering local skeptics that he was the genuine article in a game against San Francisco when he belted the longest home run ever seen at that point on the Haight Street grounds, rattling the tin clubhouse roof in distant CF on the fly. Upon joining Chicago in 1893, Lange immediately presented manager Cap Anson with a dilemma: where to play him. After the rookie made 42 errors in 57 games at 2B and also looked shaky at 3B and SS, he finished 1893 in CF, replacing the injured Jimmy Ryan, and took over Ryan's spot permanently the following year.

In time Lange would be viewed by some as the top center fielder in the NL, but fielding stats from his seven ML seasons (1893–99) suggest that there may have been several better. None, however, was ever credited with a catch anywhere near as stunning as the two that Lange made against Washington on August 31, 1896, and July 4, 1897, respectively. The former occurred at Washington on a day when Lange arrived late at the park. Told by Anson as he took the field that he would be fined, he earned a reprieve when he smashed into the fence in hauling down a drive that was "headed for the Potomac" to preserve a scoreless tie (although Chicago eventually lost 1–0 to Win Mercer).

Some of Lange's batting stats are likewise suspect. In 1895 he produced his career year, leading the Colts in every major batting department. While there is no question of his club leadership, the final averages in *TSN* at the season's end credit him with having hit .402, 14 points above the figure that researchers now deem correct (.388). Scorekeepers in almost every NL city were notorious in those years for padding the BAs of local stars, but none so much as those in Chicago, where batting titles on more than one previous occasion had been rigged for a certain favorite son to win. Even if the same favor were never done for Lange, the claim that he would be a cinch HOFer had he not terminated his career before it reached the necessary ten-year minimum meets with firm opposition when it is taken into account that no less than twelve players who had a minimum of 2,000 PAs during his 7-year tenure had higher runs created per game ratios than his 9.42, and three of them—Bill Joyce, Jake Stenzel, and Elmer Smith—have never had a soul touting them for enshrinement.

Still, Lange's many champions might be forgiven their fervor if he could be shown to have sparked Chicago to heights the club would never have reached without him. Actually, his impact on the team seems to have grown progressively less positive. With each passing year Lange played fewer and fewer games until by 1899, his final season, he missed nearly a third of the action. In 1899 he also began to draw fire from the Chicago press for "malingering" and from his own teammates for squawking to the press about dissension on the club.

As early as February of his last season, Lange began talking of quitting to marry the daughter of a prominent Bay Area attorney. He reiterated his intent in October 1899 but then seemed to vacillate. In January 1900 he informed Chicago that he might be willing to sign for $600 a month, but when April came and his marriage occurred, club officials began to take his retirement seriously. Reportedly, he turned down colossal offers from AL raiders later in 1900 when both his wife and father-in-law, who had set him up in business, continued to disdain baseball. Lange eventually did some scouting on the West Coast for Cincinnati and also coached baseball for a time at Stanford, but his main interest remained his real estate and insurance business even after he and his wife divorced. He died from a heart attack at his San Francisco home at 79. (DN/PM)

Leonard, Andrew Jackson / "Andy"

B	T	HGT	WGT	G	AB	H	R	2B
R	R	5'7"	168	501	2394	715	481	86

3B	HR	RBI	BB	SO	SB	BA	SA	OBP
27	4	343	29	52	74	.299	.362	.307

B. 6/1/1846 County Cavan, Ireland **D.** 8/21/1903
TEAMS: 71OlyNA 72–75BosNA 76–78BosN 80CinN
DEBUT: 5/5/1871 at Washington; played 2B and made 1 hit in a 20–15 loss to Boston's Al Spalding
FINALE: 7/6/1880 at Cincinnati; played SS and went 0-for-4 in a 5–2 win over Boston's Tommy Bond and John Morrill

A member of the legendary 1869 Cincinnati Red Stockings, Andy Leonard made the same mistake that several of his teammates who were accustomed to playing for pay did when the NA formed. They went where they were offered the most money without regard to the quality of the team around them. Leonard thus found himself on a .500 club that lacked a second baseman after Charlie Sweasy took ill, forcing him to serve in the infield rather than LF, where his exceptional flychasing made him more useful.

Not eager to repeat the experience, he joined Boston the following year and served on four straight NA pennant winners, spending most of his afternoons at his customary LF spot. Leonard remained a valued if never treasured member of Boston for another three seasons after it moved to the NL when the NA disbanded and played on two more pennant winners, hiking his total to six in his eight ML seasons to date. He then spent the following year with Albany and Rochester of the minor league National Association before returning to Cincinnati for his ML finale.

By 1880 Leonard was 34 and probably needed to be hidden in RF, the least demanding outfield position at the time, but Cincinnati captain John Clapp put him at 3B instead and then tried him at SS. The ex–Red Stockings legend hit just .211 in 33 games before exiting from the Queen City in early July.

Leonard moved back to Newark, NJ, the town where he had come of age, but a political upheaval cost him his city job. In 1895 he returned to Boston, where his three sons resided, and ran a family dry goods firm until his old teammate, George Wright, gave him a job at the Wright-Ditson sporting goods concern. Leonard remained in Boston until his death in 1903. (DN/DB)

Lillie, James J. (b. Lilly) **/ "Jim" "Grasshopper"**

B	T	HGT	WGT	G	AB	H	R	2B
R	?	?	?	390	1518	332	179	41

3B	HR	RBI	BB	SO	SB	BA	SA	OBP
11	6	134	23	221	13	.219	.272	.230

G	IP	H	GS	CG	BB
6	31	46	1	0	8

SO	SH	W	L	PCT	ERA
8	0	0	2	.000	4.65

B. 7/27/1861 New Haven, CT **D.** 11/9/1890
TEAMS: 83–85BufN 86KCN
DEBUT: 5/17/1883 at Buffalo; started the game in LF and replaced George Derby in the box in the third inning and went 0-for-5 in Derby's 13–9 loss to Providence's Charley Radbourn
FINALE: 10/11/1886 at Washington; played LF and went 1-for-4 in a 7–5 win over Washington's John Henry

Jim Lillie's career hitting stats are so dismal that the casual fan today is baffled that he could have lasted four seasons as a ML regular. The explanation is simply that he was the best fielder of his time at the most important outfield position in the early game: LF. Lillie was among the first to master the one-handed catch, often with his bare hand. Furthermore, he had a fine arm, as evidenced by his having been called in from the outfield to pitch in his very first ML game. Following his final appearance some three and a half years later, *SL* remarked, "Lillie's fielding was the feature of the game," and such was often the case all during his career.

In the fall of 1882 Lillie was discovered on a New Haven sandlot by Buffalo player-manager Jim O'Rourke and brought to the Bisons' training camp in the spring of 1883. His small "Grasshopper" size was initially regarded as too much of a handicap, and he began the season on the bench, with O'Rourke himself manning LF. Lillie's first opportunity to play did not come until the third week of the season, when O'Rourke went behind the bat in a game against Providence. Despite a rocky start in which he went hitless and made 2 errors, Lillie was again on the lineup card in Buffalo's next game and made his first two ML hits in a 7–4 win over New York's Mickey Welch. He then served for the rest of the season as a jack-of-all-trades, playing every position except 1B.

Lillie still was denied his true calling the following year, as O'Rourke stubbornly positioned himself, the weaker fielder, in LF and sent Lillie to RF. After missing just 1 game in 1884, Lillie played every inning of Buffalo's 112 contests in 1885, usually in LF after Jack Chapman replaced O'Rourke as manager. When the Bisons disbanded and their players were dispersed, Lillie went to the Kansas City NL replacement entry. In KC, Lillie experienced his finest moment. The Cowboys played in Independence Park, which was set in a ravine about fifty feet below street level and had a steep hill running up to the fence in LF. Lillie was expert at playing the hill. The December 31, 1898, *TSN* recalled a game-saving catch he made in 1886. With two out in ninth inning, Boston's Sam Wise sent a shot to deep left. Lillie scrambled up the hill but halted when center fielder Paul Radford shouted that he had overrun the ball. Turning back to the field, Lillie lunged and caught the ball in his left hand before slipping on one of the stones that littered the hill and falling and hitting his head against a rock. Despite being knocked senseless, he held on to the ball. Unfortunately, the more sensational Lillie's fielding grew, the worse his hitting got. His stats in 1886 are the poorest season marks ever by an ML outfielder with a minimum of 400 ABs, ranking last in BA (.175), SA (.197), OBP (.197), and OPS (.394). When the Cowboys dropped out of the NL following the 1886 season, Lillie remained in Kansas City, playing for its Western League entry in 1887 when no ML team, after scanning his 1886 batting marks, knocked on his door. But his fielding continued to impel observations such as, "This 'pyrotechnic' fielder makes phenomenal catches."

On December 29, 1887, Lillie married Nellie O'Shea, the daughter of a wealthy Kansas City contractor. He began 1888 with Fort Worth of the Texas League but quit when his wife became pregnant and asked him to come home. On September 4, 1888, Nellie gave birth to a stillborn daughter. Two days later, while trying to ignite a cooking stove, she accidentally set herself on fire and was enveloped instantly in flames. Hearing her screams, Lillie rushed into the kitchen and tried to subdue the inferno, severely burning his hands. But his efforts to save his wife were in vain, and his hands were so badly damaged that he was expected to lose fingers on both. The following spring, on April 9, Lillie's misfortunes deepened when his vindictive father-in-law convinced a Kansas City court to remove him as executor of his wife's estate because he had "improperly handled it." Through it all, Lillie held out hope of returning to baseball and joined an amateur team in Kansas City that summer, somehow playing with his maimed hands.

In late October 1890 Lillie came down with typhoid after attending a funeral. Alone now in the world, he stayed at the Kansas City home of a friend, Charley Morrissey, to recover. But within ten days of his taking ill peritonitis set in, and Lillie recognized death was imminent. According to one of his obits, his last words were, "I'm afraid, Charley, it's three strikes and out." (DN)

Long, James M. / "Jim"

B	T	HGT	WGT	G	AB	H	R	2B
?	?	5'10"	160	61	251	54	36	8

3B	HR	RBI	BB	SO	SB	BA	SA	OBP
1	2	29	19	33	24	.215	.279	.286

B. 11/15/1862 Louisville, KY **D.** 12/12/1932
TEAMS: 91LouA 93BalN
DEBUT: 8/9/1891 at Louisville; played LF and went 2-for-5 in an 11–5 win over Washington's Kid Carsey and Buck Freeman
FINALE: 8/30/1893 at Baltimore; played LF and went 0-for-4 in a 12–7 loss to Cleveland's Cy Young

Red hair and freckles made Jim Long look younger than his years. In 1891, after two unsuccessful minor league ventures, he was playing with the Deppens semipro team in Louisville when Patsy Donovan hurt his arm in early August. "His work was first-class," said *SL* after Long's debut as Donovan's replacement, but Louisville manager Jack Chapman disagreed and released him. Chapman also let *TSN* know, "He is not a very young man as has generally been supposed, and has been playing for over fifteen years."

That was probably somewhat of an exaggeration, for Long was still considered promising enough that Denny Long (no relation), who owned Atlanta of the Southern League, signed him for 1892. Outfielder Long followed owner Long to Charleston of the Southern League in 1893 and faced Baltimore in several spring exhibitions. After watching the redheaded outfielder, Orioles manager Ned Hanlon began negotiating with Denny Long and his manager, Jack Carney, and eventually landed his catch for $1,800.

Long took over in LF for Baltimore on June 26 in St. Louis, replacing Harry Stovey. After compiling only a .560 OPS in over 50 games, he was jettisoned after the Orioles acquired Steve Brodie from St. Louis in late August. It appears that Long received more of an opportunity to make good with the Orioles than his talent warranted (probably because of the price paid for him), but upon leaving the team he blasted Hanlon and vowed that he would never play for Baltimore again.

He returned to Atlanta in 1894, but in June *TSN* noted, "Jim Long has proven to be a great failure." Shortly thereafter he was released. Nevertheless, Long later returned to the Southern League and finished his pro career there with New Orleans in 1899. He then worked as a city meat inspector in Louisville prior to his death at his Louisville home at 70. (DN/DB)

Lush, William Lucas / "Billy"

B	T	HGT	WGT	G	AB	H	R	2B
B	R	5'8"	165	105	382	93	77	9

3B	HR	RBI	BB	SO	SB	BA	SA	OBP
11	4	47	68	50	28	.243	.356	.361

B. 11/10/1873 Bridgeport, CT **D.** 8/28/1951
TEAMS: 95–97WasN 01–02BosN 03DetAL 04CleAL
DEBUT: 9/3/1895 at Washington; played RF and went 1-for-4 in a 17–9 loss to Louisville's Mike McDermott and Gus Weyhing
FINALE: 10/8/1904 at Detroit; played CF and went 0-for-1 in a 3–0 loss to Cleveland's Otto Hess

Billy Lush was the older brother of MLer Ernie Lush. The younger Lush was scarcely 9 years old when his elder began making his name with the St. Joseph Temperance Society team in Bridgeport, CT, in 1893. After playing for Worcester of the New England League in 1894, Lush took a job in the Bridgeport post office and seemed ready to quit baseball until Jim O'Rourke encouraged him to give it one more try and recommended him to Rochester manager Jack Chapman. By the time Washington purchased him for $1,000 from Rochester in July 1895, he was rated the most sensational center fielder in the Eastern League. Lush's forte was his arm. He frequently boasted that he could throw as far as John Hatfield, but when pressed to prove it he would always say, "I'm not going to take the chance of throwing out my arm."

In a 5-game trial with Washington late in the 1895 season, Lush did well but was hampered by an injury to the middle finger of his left hand. For a while it was feared the finger might have to be amputated, but by the time Lush enrolled in Yale law school that fall the danger had passed. The following spring he wrestled Charlie Abbey for the Washington RF job but hit just .247. Before the year was out he had married Mary Heenan of New Haven, increasing his motivation when he reported for spring training in 1897. At the suggestion of teammate Tom Brown, Lush learned to bat left-handed, and though he eventually became a switch hitter, initially the experiment fizzled. After Lush went hitless in his first 3 games of the season, manager Gus Schmelz routed him to Toronto of the Eastern League.

That winter, Lush agreed to take the player-manager post with the Springfield EL club in 1898 but resigned the manager's portion of the job in late May when the team got off to a poor start and his youth was blamed as the reason some veteran players were playing indifferently. The club remained dissension-ridden even after Billy Barnie took over the reins, and Lush was eventually released for taking part in a strike when he and his teammates were not paid in a timely fashion.

He finished 1898 with Syracuse of the Eastern League and then tried the player-manager role again the following year with Derby of the Connecticut League. In late May 1899 Lush was embarrassed in front of his players when Derby's gate receipts were attached while the team was in Bridgeport so that a local tailor could collect an outstanding bill their manager owed. He finished the season with Rochester, the scene of his greatest triumphs in pro ball thus far, and remained with the Eastern League club until Boston NL acquired him late in 1901. Before leaving the game in 1904, Lush spent three unspectacular offensive seasons as a regular ML outfielder but finished his career with 74 outfield assists in 461 games, a total exceeded only by Ray Demmitt (79) among gardeners in less than 500 games since the strong-armed Bridgeport native first appeared on the scene in 1895. Lush died at 77 in Hawthorne, NY. (DN)

Lyons, Harry Pratt / "Harry"

B	T	HGT	WGT	G	AB	H	R	2B
R	R	5'10½"	157	407	1713	401	236	31

3B	HR	RBI	BB	SO	SB	BA	SA	OBP
21	7	198	97	35	120	.234	.289	.277

G	IP	H	GS	CG	BB
1	3.2	8	0	0	1

SO	SH	W	L	PCT	ERA
2	0	0	0	—	12.27

B. 3/25/1866 Chester, PA **D.** 6/29/1912
TEAMS: 87PhiN 87–88StLA 89NYN 90RocA 92–93NYN
DEBUT: 8/29/1887 at Philadelphia; played LF and went 1-for-5 in a 7–6 loss to Pittsburgh's Ed Morris
FINALE: 7/4/1893 at New York; played CF and went 1-for-2 in a 2–1 loss to St. Louis's Ted Breitenstein

The son of a Philadelphia police lieutenant, Harry Lyons played with Kingston, NY, in 1886–87, along with a 1-game stint with the NL Quakers, followed by a trip back to the minors and then two appearances with the AA Browns at the tail end of that season. Lyons's natural position was SS, and when he appeared there for St. Louis in 2 World's Series games against NL champion Detroit, it was expected to spell the end of the Browns' longtime SS, Bill Gleason.

Such came to pass when Gleason was traded in the off-season to the Philadelphia A's, but Browns manager Charlie Comiskey had to install Lyons in CF in place of Curt Welch (who was traded with Gleason) after everyone else Comiskey tried in center during spring training failed. Lyons began 1888 batting leadoff and finished it batting sixth despite hitting only .194. A badly sprained wrist suffered in a late-season game threatened to keep him out of the World's Series when the Browns swept to their fourth straight pennant. Lyons was back at his post, however, when the fall affair began, only to sustain a severe injury in a Game 5 collision with a teammate that seemed as if it might end his career. His questionable physical condition in conjunction with a .118 BA in the limited Series action he saw against New York NL induced the Browns to release him.

Lyons was with Worcester of the Atlantic Association in 1889 when a rash of outfield injuries forced the pennant-bound New York Giants to acquire him in August, but he was quickly returned to Worcester when he hit just .100 as a fill-in. Lyons then had a busy off-season, successfully suing Browns owner Chris Von der Ahe in October for $71.40, his share from the 1888 World's Series that Von der Ahe had withheld from him after he was injured. In early February he wed a Camden, NJ, woman after the PL formed, providing extra incentive for him to return to the majors with the Rochester AA replacement team.

Playing every inning of every game, Lyons led the AA in ABs in 1890 but logged just a .626 OPS, rendering him unwanted again when the PL collapse shaved ML jobs by a third. After spending 1891 with Buffalo of the Eastern Association, Lyons started 1892 with a minor league team in Philadelphia. In late June he was summoned to New York to replace aging George Gore in CF. Opie Caylor, by then a Gotham sportswriter, warned Giants fans to expect a good-field, no-hit player, and Lyons lived up to his billing, compiling just 105 total bases in 411 ABs. He was nonetheless retained for 1893 and opened the season in CF but soon lost his job to young Willie Keeler, only to regain it when Keeler was hurt and then lose it once and for all to General Stafford. But if Stafford was an improvement on offense, the *New York Times* wrote, "When it comes to fielding he cannot cover half as much ground as the released player."

Meanwhile Lyons joined Providence of the Eastern League, where for the next five years he carved his niche as an excellent fielder and base runner but a barely marginal hitter before being cut in August 1898 while hitting just .246. Upon leaving the game, Lyons ran a newspaper and cigar store in Philadelphia for a time and then was a clerk for the city water department until his death at 46 of paralysis. (DN)

Mann, Fred J / "Fred"

B	T	HGT	WGT	G	AB	H	R	2B
L	R	5'10½"	178	577	2277	597	388	104

3B	HR	RBI	BB	SO	SB	BA	SA	OBP
68	12	181	163	15	67	.262	.383	.323

B. 4/1/1858 Sutton, VT **D.** 4/6/1916
TEAMS: 82WorN 82PhiA 83–84ColA 85–86PitA 87CleA 87PhiA
DEBUT: 5/1/1883 at Boston; played 3B and went 3-for-5 in a 6–5 loss to Boston's Jim Whitney
FINALE: 10/10/1887 at Philadelphia; played CF and went 0-for-3 in a 7–5 loss to Brooklyn's Steve Toole

Despite a strong debut with Worcester and a good start in general, Fred Mann was benched prior to the June 3, 1882, contest with Chicago. He was tried again at 3B in mid-June and then let go to Philadelphia AA, as was pitcher Frank Mountain around the same time. The peculiarity of these two early-day transactions between clubs in rival major leagues has never been adequately explained. Mann did poorly with the A's, enabling the expansion Columbus AA club to sign him for 1883. Converted to CF, he continued to struggle in his first season in Ohio but blossomed in 1884 to lead the second-place Senators in home runs and SA.

In 1885, after Mann was among the core of the disbanding Columbus team that was sold to Pittsburgh, his home run total dropped to zero even though he broke a 3–3 tie against Guy Hecker at Louisville on April 21 in the bottom of the thirteenth inning with a drive over the RF fence. Since Willie Kuehne, who was on 2B at the time, scored the winning run ahead of Mann, he was not credited with a home run as per the rule at that time. After slipping to .250 in 1886, Mann again was made part of a package to furnish an Ohio AA expansion team with a startup roster. He opened 1887 batting cleanup for the fledging Cleveland Blues and was leading the club in both batting and slugging when he was mysteriously dropped in favor of Scrappy Carroll, who had blown two previous ML trials and would soon botch a third by hitting .199 in 57 games. Observers assumed that Mann had somehow annoyed Cleveland manager Jimmy Williams. The mystery deepened when Mann returned to his original AA team, the Athletics, finished the season with a composite .293 BA, and then joined two other A's in being traded that winter to St. Louis for Bill Gleason and Curt Welch.

Expected to replace Welch in the Browns' outfield, Mann instead was cut in April 1888 without ever playing an official game in St. Louis garb. He then had his first taste of the minors in the 1888 Southern League and moved to Hartford in the Atlantic Association in 1889 but hit just .239. Mann's sudden decline as soon as he left the majors made it appear that Williams, Billy Sharsig, and Charlie Comiskey, his final three ML managers, all correctly sensed he was losing it as a productive player. Additionally, there is some evidence that his arm was dead. He operated a hotel in Springfield, MA, until just before his death of prostate cancer in 1916. (DN/DB)

Manning, James H. / "Jim"

B	T	HGT	WGT	G	AB	H	R	2B
B	R	5'7"	157	364	1384	298	188	39

3B	HR	RBI	BB	SO	SB	BA	SA	OBP
25	8	149	107	168	68	.215	.297	.278

B. 1/31/1862 Fall River, MA **D.** 10/22/1929
TEAMS: 84–85BosN 85–87DetN 89KCA (M)01WasAL

DEBUT: 5/16/1884 at Boston; played CF and went 0-for-3 in a 4–2 loss to Detroit's Dupee Shaw
FINALE: 10/13/1889 at Louisville; played LF and made 1 hit in a 6–5 win over Louisville's Mike McDermott

Jim Manning was an intense, cagey player capable of playing every position except 1B and catcher, a team leader wherever he went, and a man with only good habits but one large flaw that kept him from stardom. Manning's .215 career BA is the lowest of any ML switch-hitting position player with a minimum of 1,000 ABs prior to expansion in 1961. A graduate of the Massachusetts College of Pharmacy and a druggist both before and after he played pro ball, Manning was drawn to the game by the success of his Fall River friend Frank Fennelly and wrote letters in the winter of 1882–83 to teams in the Midwest, fearing to appear in the East in front of people who knew him until he had proven himself. Hired by Springfield, IL, of the Northwestern League, he played 3B in his 1883 pro introduction. Manning advanced to Boston NL in 1884 and had his best full season in the majors as a rookie, belying the assumption that he was rushed into top company before he was ready. Toward the end of the following year Boston let Manning go after he slipped to .206, and he finished the season as Detroit's SS. In 1886 he opened the year in LF for the Wolverines but broke his left forearm in the first game of a Memorial Day DH at New York when he collided with SS Jack Rowe on a pop fly and missed most of the rest of the year.

The following spring Manning went to camp with Detroit but was unable to crack the lineup of what would be the best team in the majors in 1887 and was in effect farmed to Kansas City of the Western League, although he was recalled later in the season after second baseman Fred Dunlap was injured. Soon afterward he embarked on a relationship with the town of Kansas City that would last until early in the twentieth century. After captaining a football team that fall comprised of players wintering in KC, he acted as player-manager of the Western Association champion KC Blues in 1888 and then moved up to the AA KC Cowboys in 1889, where he was reunited with Bill Watkins, his manager at Detroit. The 1889 season was Manning's last in the majors, and for good reason. Alternating between 2B and LF, he hit .204, the ML season record until 1933 for the lowest BA by a switch hitter with a minimum of 500 ABs.

Manning remained with KC when it left the AA in 1890. Once again serving as player-manager, he steered the team to the Western Association pennant. The following year the Blues slipped to second, but Manning topped the WA with 138 runs. In 1892 he shepherded KC into the newly formed Western League and then assumed the player-manager's post with Southern League champion Birmingham after the WL collapsed. Manning subsequently returned to Kansas City when the Western League reorganized, and he remained at the club's helm until the fall of 1900. On January 3, 1895, he married Mary Dennis, whom he had first met in KC in 1891. The November following his marriage he made history, according to *TSN*, when he had his KC club draft pitcher Jack Barnett (20-19) from Syracuse and catcher Fred Lake (.343) from Toronto. The St. Louis paper observed that the 1895 transaction was "the first time on record one minor league team had drafted players from another."

After the 1900 season, when the AL voted to deem itself a major circuit, Manning was offered a new franchise in Washington. Backed by the millionaire owner of the *Cincinnati Enquirer* and the *Washington Post*, John McLean, who also owned the Washington Gas Light Company, Manning took advantage of the loose restrictions in that era by initially retaining his interest in his KC minor league club after helping to launch the new AL entry in Washington. One of his first actions upon assuming the Senators' reins was to entice three NL players to jump to the AL: pitcher Bill Carrick, catcher Boileryard Clarke and outfielder Jimmy Slagle. Slagle later recanted and remained in the NL, but Clarke, and Carrick emerged as Manning's top battery in 1901.

When Washington finished sixth that year and failed to make money, Manning worried that adding new players to improve his Senators would prove too costly. He chose instead to sell his interest in the club to Fred Postal, owner of the Griswold House hotel in Detroit. Postal then replaced him as manager with Tom Loftus, who had just been canned by the Chicago NL club, claiming that Manning "was liked but too conservative for the progressive element in the league." Squeezed out of the majors by a man whom *TSN* would ironically call "the main squeeze" on the Washington team, Manning never managed again. He moved to Houston and worked as a land appraiser for the

Missouri Pacific Railroad for a number of years. Manning died of diabetes at 67 in Edinburg, TX. (DN/DB)

Manning, John E. / "Jack"

B	T	HGT	WGT	G	AB	H	R	2B
R	R	5'8½"	158	833	3505	922	562	170

3B	HR	RBI	BB	SO	SB	BA	SA	OBP
37	14	360	181	198	34	.263	.345	.300

G	IP	H	GS	CG	BB
96	573.1	694	63	41	70

SO	SH	W	L	PCT	ERA
78	1	39	27	.591	2.79

G	W	L	PCT	PENNANTS
20	7	12	.368	0

B. 12/20/1853 Braintree, MA **D.** 8/15/1929
TEAMS: 73BosNA 74BalNA 74HarNA 75BosNA 76BosN (P/M)77CinN 78BosN 80CinN 81BufN 83–85PhiN 86BalA
DEBUT: 4/23/1873 at Boston; played 1B and went 1-for-4 in an 8–5 loss to Philadelphia's George Zettlein
FINALE: 10/14/1886 at Philadelphia; played RF and went 0-for-4 in a 5–1 loss to Philadelphia's Cyclone Miller
CAREER HIGHLIGHT: 10/9/1884 at Chicago; became the first visiting team player to hit 3 home runs in a ML game in a 19–7 loss to Chicago's John Clarkson

After beginning his career as a versatile utilityman with a claim to being one of the first notable relief pitchers, in the 1880s Jack Manning developed into an outfielder whose primary asset was his arm. In his final four ML seasons (1883–86) he totaled 100 assists, ranking him forth among the leaders during that span. The son of an Irish-born stonemason, Manning left school in his native Boston to clerk in a store. After Boston NA manager Harry Wright discovered him playing 2B for the Boston Juniors in 1872, Manning spent the next half dozen years bouncing back and forth between the Red Stockings and other teams without ever quite finding a place in the talented lineup of the strongest club in the NA and later the NL. Although he played a fair amount of infield, he did not really have the necessary skills there, and in Boston he was primarily used in RF. Manning also used his arm strength to pitch. The rules of the day allowed substitutions only in case of injury, so a relief pitcher had to be brought in from another position. Wright, an outfielder-pitcher himself, was very aggressive in using change pitchers and frequently brought Manning in from RF to pitch in midgame. Saves were not a stat in those days, but retrospective calculations credit Manning with 12 saves in 20 relief appearances in 1875–76, an exceptional number for the era.

Following the 1876 season, however, Manning was loaned by Boston to Cincinnati and seldom appeared in the box. He had been known for violating the rules requiring underhand pitching, and it may be that the rest of the league simply caught up with him once other pitchers acquired the knack of throwing undetected from a higher elevation. Manning spent most of the late 1870s and early 1880s in the minor league National Association and League Alliance but returned in 1883 with the new Philadelphia NL entry. There he was reunited with Wright, who became the Quakers' manager in 1884. It was not a happy reunion, however, as the two engaged in acrimonious off-season battles over salary, with Wright publicly denigrating Manning's fielding and baserunning. Manning's defenders replied by suggesting that if Wright valued Manning so lightly, he should release him, but Manning remained the Philadelphia right fielder through 1885. Just before the 1886 season he escaped Wright at last when he was waived out of the NL and acquired by Baltimore AA. Manning batted only .223 for the Orioles, but with an abysmal club playing in a park favoring pitchers, he led the team in hits, total bases, BA, SA, and OBP. Nevertheless, he was cut after the season, probably because of his diminished speed and weak fielding; his 1.32 range factor was the lowest that year among AA gardeners in 100 or more games.

Manning claimed, with tongue in cheek, that "early piety" had turned his hair prematurely gray, leading managers to think he was older than he was. ML clubs then refused to buy his story that he actually was the age he claimed to be (33), and he finished his career at age 34 playing for New England minor league teams. After retiring, Manning worked as a groundskeeper for the Boston PL club and then as a theater stagehand and a janitor. A lifelong bachelor, he died in Boston at 75. (DB/DN)

*Mansell, John / "John"

B	T	HGT	WGT	G	AB	H	R	2B
L	?	5'10"	168	31	126	30	17	3

3B	HR	RBI	BB	SO	SB	BA	SA	OBP
1	0	17	4	—	—	.238	.278	.262

B. ?/?/1861 Auburn, NY **D.** 2/20/1925
TEAMS: 82PhiA
DEBUT: 5/9/1882 at Baltimore; played CF and went 1-for-4 in a 4–2 win over Baltimore's Bill Wise
FINALE: 7/22/1882 at Philadelphia; played CF and went 3-for-4 in a 9–8 win over St. Louis's George McGinnis

John Mansell made his pro debut with the independent Akrons in 1880. The following year he joined his brothers Tom and Mike on the Albany National Association club to form pro ball's first sibling trio to play together in the same outfield. Mansell may have been injured in the 1882 preseason, for Philadelphia opened the AA's inaugural campaign using someone different in CF almost every day until the strongest arm on the team made his first appearance. His departure from the A's is baffling in that he played brilliantly in his finale, but there is some evidence that he met with a season-ending accident at that point. Mansell was with Saginaw of the Northwestern League in 1883 and later played in the Southern and Western leagues. He appears to have left pro ball in 1886 after 2 games with Chattanooga of the Southern League and died in Willard, NY, thirty-nine years later. (DN)

*Mansell, Michael R. / "Mike"

B	T	HGT	WGT	G	AB	H	R	2B
L	?	5'11"	175	371	1471	352	237	43

3B	HR	RBI	BB	SO	SB	BA	SA	OBP
43	9	25	61	82	—	.239	.344	.271

B. 1/15/1858 Auburn, NY **D.** 12/4/1902
TEAMS: 79SyrN 80CinN 82–84PitA 84PhiA 84VirA
DEBUT: 5/1/1879 at Chicago; played LF and went 0-for-4 in a 4–3 loss to Chicago's Terry Larkin
FINALE: 10/15/1884 at Richmond; played RF and went 1-for-4 in a 9–7 win over Toledo's Hank O'Day

Mike Mansell was the best of the trio of brothers who all played ML ball and in 1881 was part of the first-ever all-sibling pro outfield with Albany until he hurt his knee and left the team. He was regarded as a sure catch, a sharp base runner and a hard hitter, and at his peak he was rated one of the fastest sprinters in the country, good enough to hold open a standing offer for several years to race any other pro ballplayer at a distance of one hundred yards. Yet his career almost ended before it had scarcely begun when he suffered a near-fatal bout with typhoid while with the semipro Columbus Buckeyes in 1876.

Just 18 at the time, Mansell put in the next two seasons with the minor league Syracuse Stars before they joined the NL in 1879. Pundits questioned whether he was ready when he hit just .215 in his rookie year, but Cincinnati saw enough promise to sign him for 1880. After his BA dropped to .193 in the Queen City, the Reds released him in midsummer and he joined his brother John on the Akron, OH, independent team.

After playing with both of his brothers on the Albany club in 1881, the following year Mansell had the good fortune to be among the first crop of players to participate in the American Association's inaugural season as a major league but the dubious luck to land in Pittsburgh, a mismanaged team that included some of the worst lushers in the game's history. In 1882 Mansell had a solid year, pacing the AA in both doubles and triples. His encore season in Pittsburgh was less auspicious, culminating when he was suspended in August and fined $100 for "dissipation."

Come 1884 by mid-June, just before the Allegheny club released him, Mansell had been dropped to eighth in the batting order after hitting a robust .140 in the first 27 games of the season. He then joined Philadelphia AA for 20 games and managed to lift his mark to .200 with the A's before being released again. The Virginia replacement club in the AA picked Mansell up in the final month of its short ML sojourn and was rewarded with a team-best .301 BA and .770 OPS. Notwithstanding Mansell's seeming revival, he never wore a ML uniform again even though he played professionally until he was in his midthirties. The explanation probably lies in his personal conduct. Never the most popular teammate, Mansell often could be downright bellicose. On March 22, 1889, he got into a savage fight with fellow Auburn resident Tug Arundel, himself no pantywaist, in a bar near their Auburn homes. Arundel, usually the decisive victor in such brawls, got by far the worst of it.

By 1896 Mansell had been out of pro ball four years after a .216 season in the 1892 Eastern League and was a guard at Auburn state prison, in charge of the outer gate. When Cincinnati played an exhibition game that summer against Mark Baldwin's Auburn independent team, the Reds players visited the prison afterward, and Bid McPhee expressed a curiosity to feel what it was like to be electrocuted. Seating himself in the death chair, he was strapped in by Mansell and told to expect a very slight jolt of electricity just to get a mild taste of the experience, but the operator miscalculated and McPhee was nearly fried. Mansell had left prison work and was running a saloon when he died of pneumonia in 1902. He was the first of his brothers to be laid to rest in the family plot at St. Joseph Cemetery in Auburn. (DN)

*Mansell, Thomas Edward / "Tom" "Brick"

B	T	HGT	WGT	G	AB	H	R	2B
L	R	5'8"	160	191	767	199	132	23

3B	HR	RBI	BB	SO	SB	BA	SA	OBP
11	0	74	39	22	—	.259	.318	.300

G	IP	H	GS	CG	BB
1	6.2	21	0	0	5

SO	SH	W	L	PCT	ERA
3	0	0	0	—	18.90

B. 1/1/1855 Auburn, NY **D.** 10/6/1934
TEAMS: 79TroN 79SyrN 83DetN 83StLA 84CinA 84ColA
DEBUT: 5/1/1879 at Cincinnati; played LF and went 1-for-4 in a 7–5 loss to Cincinnati's Will White
FINALE: 10/15/1884 at Philadelphia; played LF and went 1-for-3 in a 17–7 loss to Philadelphia's Billy Taylor

The oldest of three brothers who formed the first all-sibling professional outfield with Albany, NY, in 1881, Tom Mansell enjoyed one remarkable ML season—or rather, partial season. He played two seasons in the minors, beginning as a right fielder with the 1877 Auburn, NY, Alliance club before making his NL debut for Troy in 1879. Mansell subsequently played with Washington of the National Association until that team moved to Albany, where he was reunited with brothers Mike and John.

In 1883 Mansell returned to the NL with Detroit but hit only .221 while fielding very poorly in RF. Released in early July, he caught on with St. Louis AA. In his July 4 debut with the Browns, Mansell recorded 3 hits and went on to bat .402 in 28 games. The AA's *Reach Guide* named him the league's batting champ, although he had only 112 ABs. No official criteria for eligibility existed at the time, and the choice of Mansell was believed in some quarters to have been motivated by the desire to give the Association a leader with a higher BA than NL titlist Dan Brouthers. In reality, the AA, in its second year of operation, though improving its caliber of ball, still lagged behind the NL, and the fact that a player could be released by a bad NL team, move to the AA, and improve his BA by nearly 200 points was hardly a mark in the junior loop's favor.

Mansell would have played more often for the Browns had he not returned to his Cincinnati hotel after a night on the town in early August and walked into an open elevator shaft, breaking a leg. He had a reputation as a drinker, but St. Louis manager Ted Sullivan insisted he had not been intoxicated and had been sitting innocently in the hotel lobby for an hour before the accident. Mansell was in action again by the time the 1883 season ended, and his gaudy average persuaded St. Louis to try to sign him that winter, but Cincinnati owner Aaron Stern got his name on a contract first. He began 1884 playing LF for the Reds but never got his bat untracked. A fielder of limited range and so lacking in confidence that he made catches by trapping the ball against his chest, Mansell was of little value to a team unless he hit. Released on August 26, he signed with Columbus to replace Patsy Cahill, who had just suffered a season-ending broken leg, but his offensive production dropped off even more sharply, as he batted below .200.

Columbus exited the AA at season's end, and another ML team did not pick up Mansell. He finished his pro career in the 1887 Western League with Kansas City and became a fixture in that city for several years after retiring from baseball. After working as a cable-car grip man, Mansell joined the police force and eventually rose to be the police chief of Kansas City, KS. He retired in 1931 and returned home to Auburn, where he died three years later in the home of his sister, Minnie. (DB/DN)

Marr, Charles W. / "Lefty"

B	T	HGT	WGT	G	AB	H	R	2B
L	L	5'9"	180	363	1445	417	244	54

3B	HR	RBI	BB	SO	SB	BA	SA	OBP
35	2	186	166	80	92	.289	.379	.368

B. 9/19/1862 Cincinnati, OH **D.** 1/11/1912
TEAMS: 86CinA 89ColA 90–91CinN 91CinA
DEBUT: 4/16/1889 at Baltimore; played LF and went 2-for-6 in a 13–3 win over Baltimore's Matt Kilroy
FINALE: 8/16/1891 at St. Louis; played RF and went 0-for-5 in an 8–0 loss to St. Louis's George Rettger

Although he was left-handed, Charles Marr could play any position except pitcher. He was a fine headfirst slider and a good hitter, but for all his versatility he was not a strong fielder, passable only in RF, and he carried a reputation as a lusher. Only by the time his talents were on the wane did Marr realize he had been misguided to believe a drink before a game helped him relax and begin to take the field sober.

Marr worked as a carpet stretcher in Shillito's department store in his native Cincinnati until 1884, when he turned pro with Evansville of the Northwestern League. He did well enough to earn a trial with Chicago NL in the spring of 1885 but could not crack the White Stockings' star-studded roster and spent 1885–86 with Nashville of the Southern League. In 1885 Marr was involved in one of the most famous on-field tragedies in baseball history when his knee speared Atlanta's Louis Henke in a collision at 1B. Henke, a fellow Cincinnatian whom Marr had previously played with in Queen City semipro circles, was taken to his hotel room and died the next afternoon of a ruptured liver.

Marr joined Syracuse of the International Association toward the end of the 1886 season and received a trial with Cincinnati in CF during fall exhibition games but returned to Syracuse the next spring. The move may have been voluntary, for at the time the minor leagues did not have reserve rights to players, and Marr may have preferred to remain in the minors, where he could make his own deal every season rather than move up to the majors and subjugate himself to the reserve clause. In 1888 he batted .338 for Syracuse, but with reserve rights restored to the minors, he had little reason not to acquiesce when Syracuse sold him after the season to Columbus's new AA team.

Marr's rookie year was easily his best, as he led Columbus in SA and OBP. He started the season in RF but spent much of the summer at 3B and SS, covering weaknesses in the Senators' lineup and generally putting up a good game. However, in a crucial contest at the end of the season that clinched the AA championship for Brooklyn, Marr committed 4 errors at SS. Rumors that he had taken money to throw the game were so rampant that the Columbus club finally was forced to hold a formal inquiry prior to exonerating him.

The bad taste the incident left, and perhaps some tampering by Cincinnati club officials, led Marr to demand a sale to his hometown Reds. He claimed he had offers to jump to the newly formed PL but preferred to give Columbus a chance to recoup its investment in his purchase by selling him to Cincinnati. On January 20, 1890, Columbus reluctantly sold him to the Reds for a reported $2,000. With his new team Marr enjoyed a solid season, first playing 3B and then moving to RF after Arlie Latham was acquired. In 1891, however, his hitting fell off and an egregious baserunning blunder in a game against Chicago on June 26 may have sealed his fate. Released soon afterward, he moved across town to Cincinnati's AA team, only to find his new club folding within weeks of his signing. Marr ended the season barnstorming with other unemployed pro players.

In subsequent seasons Marr moved through the minors from Butte to Macon to Allentown. In 1896, in his lone experience as a manager, he piloted the Richmond Virginia League club and hit .341 but was fired as a poor handler of men. As late as 1898, at age 36, he was playing for New Britain of the Connecticut State League. He then settled in that city and ran a bowling alley with pitcher Tom Vickery for a time. Marr was later employed briefly by the Stanley Works, a tool-making concern, and played ball in a local factory league. In his final months he worked as a bartender and took on odd jobs like chopping wood and cleaning saloons. Nearly destitute, Marr was found dead in a room at New Britain's Central Hotel in 1912. (DB/DN)

*Maskrey, Samuel Leech / "Leech"

B	T	HGT	WGT	G	AB	H	R	2B
R	R	5'8"	150	418	1601	360	190	52

3B	HR	RBI	BB	SO	SB	BA	SA	OBP
26	2	94	61	—	4	.225	.294	.256

B. 2/11/1854 Mercer, PA **D.** 4/1/1922
TEAMS: 82–86LouA 86CinA
DEBUT: 5/2/1882 at St. Louis; played LF and went 1-for-5 in a 9–7 loss to St. Louis's George McGinnis
FINALE: 7/7/1886 at Cincinnati; finished the game in CF and went 0-for-1 in a 6–4 win over New York's Jack Lynch

Leech Maskrey was a sometimes business partner of his 1-game ML brother, Harry. When Harry played CF for Louisville on September 21, 1882, and Leech played LF, the two became only the second pair of siblings in ML history to play beside one another in the same outfield. Baseball never seemed as if it should be more than a sideline for Maskrey. Highly educated, he was a water colorist, a musician, and a voracious reader of the classics. What kept him in the game for two decades despite his limited success will probably never be ascertained. Maskrey's primary contribution to baseball may have occurred in 1881 as a member of the strong, independent Akron, OH, team, which also featured Ed Swartwood, Tony Mullane, team captain Charlie Morton (Maskrey's cousin), Sam Wise, and Bid McPhee. When McPhee, after a year's absence from the game, got off to such a dismal start that Morton talked of releasing him, Maskrey, who had played with the struggling second baseman at Davenport, IA, in 1878, coaxed his cousin to give the future HOFer one more chance.

Hired by the fledgling Louisville AA team in 1882 to join hometown products Pete Browning and Jimmy Wolf in the outfield, Maskrey scored just 30 runs as a rookie, the fewest of any regular gardener in the majors. The following year he batted just .202 yet contrived to hold his job through the 1885 season. In the spring of 1886 Maskrey was cut by Louisville's directors against the wishes of manager Jim Hart. He was picked up by Cincinnati but soon was cleaning out his locker in the Reds' clubhouse after hitting .194 in 27 games. Then 32, given his many other talents and dim prospects of ever returning to the majors, Maskrey seemingly would have moved on to a new pursuit. Instead he returned to the minors, where he remained a weak-hitting player and manager until the late 1890s.

In 1890 Maskrey was dispatched to England by the Spalding Brothers Sporting Goods Company to "represent the firm there" by introducing pro baseball to the British. He organized a four-team league with nines representing the cities of Derby, Stoke, Preston, and Birmingham and took the reins of the Preston club himself. Players in the loop received a pound a week (worth about $5 then), although some got as much as a pound and twelve shillings ($7.50). The enterprise miscarried when the Derby manager broke a covenant to use only Englishmen as pitchers by presenting a battery of ex-ML catcher Sim Bullas and southpaw Jack Reidenbach, who had pitched for a Cleveland semipro team with Bullas as his catcher. Maskrey responded by putting himself in the box for Preston. Derby then agreed to bench its American battery but began re-employing it after suffering a string of losses, and the club subsequently detonated the league by quitting when a dispute flared up again.

Maskrey married Ollie Goff in his hometown of Mercer two years later and opened a hotel there along with his brother. He nonetheless returned to the game that spring as a nonplaying manager with Atlanta of the Southern League but wore his uniform so he could appear on the field and coach 3B. Eventually, the desire to play again overtook him, and he put himself in CF. Soon after that he was fired. By 1897 Maskrey was running the Revere Hotel in Kent, OH, along with his brother and captaining a local team that included future ML pitcher Bob Spade. At 43 he was near the end as a player, but he continued to be a hotelier until his death in Mercer, PA, from a heart attack. (DN/DB)

McAleer, James Robert / "Jimmy" "Loafer"

B	T	HGT	WGT	G	AB	H	R	2B
R	R	6'0"	175	1114	3971	1004	620	114

3B	HR	RBI	BB	SO	SB	BA	SA	OBP
40	11	469	365	290	262	.253	.311	.322

B. 7/10/1864 Youngstown, OH
D. 4/29/1931 Youngstown, OH
TEAMS: 89CleN 90CleP 91–98CleN (P/M)01CleAL (P/M)02StLAL (M)03–06StLAL (P/M)07StLAL (M)08–09StLAL (M)10–11WasAL
DEBUT: 4/24/1889 at Indianapolis; played CF and went 1-for-5 in a 10–3 loss to Indianapolis's Charlie Getzein
FINALE: 7/8/1907 at St. Louis; pinch ran in a 3–2 win over Washington's Charlie Smith and Oscar Graham

Jimmy McAleer was peerless in his time at going back on fly balls, but he was injury prone and such a poor hitter that only a team with no other weak spots in its batting order could afford to carry him. Unhappily, Cleveland in the 1890s was not such a team, and McAleer's daily presence almost undoubtedly helped cost the Spiders a pennant or two. Among outfielders with a minimum of 2,000 PAs between 1889 (the first year of the four-ball rule) and 1900, McAleer owned the lowest OPS (.632), and teammate Harry Blake was right behind him (.660).

McAleer played with his Youngstown, OH, hometown team in 1883–85 in three different small minor leagues. He then served over two years in the Southern League before advancing to Milwaukee of the Western Association in June 1888 and hitting .284. But it was his defensive prowess that enticed Cleveland to trade Ed Keas and Gus Alberts for him, and he remained in the Forest City through 1898. In his rookie year McAleer tallied just 126 total bases in 110 games before tearing a leg muscle in a rundown play at Philadelphia on September 7, 1889. The following year another serious leg injury held him to only 86 games with Cleveland PL. McAleer then survived the next two seasons injury-free and led the NL in games played in 1891 and all loop outfielders in put-outs the following year. The 1893 campaign again found him sidelined for a lengthy period and resulted in a .237 BA in a season when most other outfielders were hitting 100 points higher. McAleer's most positive contribution that season was innovating a play where, instead of throwing the ball to 2B when a batter singled, he would fire it to 1B, hoping to nail an unwary runner who had rounded the bag as a matter of course.

After spending the bulk of 1894 on the trainer's table with a pulled hamstring, McAleer put together his best two-year stretch, hitting .289 and .271 in back-to-back seasons while missing very little time, as Cleveland, not coincidentally, made back-to-back Temple Cup appearances in 1895–96. He then opened 1897 in CF but played only 23 more games and in July claimed to be "out of the game for good." Tired of his anemic offense, the local press rejoiced in February 1898 when he reiterated that he would rather retire than play again in a city where he was unappreciated. But before the spring was out McAleer was back in uniform to amass 90 total bases, the fewest of any player in the 1893–1900 era with a minimum of 350 ABs.

That October, McAleer swore he would retire rather than go to St. Louis when rumors began to surface that the Cleveland team might move there in 1899. Other Spiders echoed his sentiments, but he was the only one who lived up to his word. In 1899 McAleer served as player-manager with Youngstown of the Interstate League after syndicate ownerships transferred most of his former teammates to St. Louis. The following March he initially turned down an offer to manage the fledgling Cleveland entry in the newly renamed American League but then reconsidered after Cleveland secured his official release from St. Louis NL. McAleer guided the Lake Shores home sixth and was rehired when the team nickname was changed to the Blues after the AL announced it would operate as a major league in 1901. (DN)

McAllister, Lewis William / "Sport" "Texas Jack"

B	T	HGT	WGT	G	AB	H	R	2B
B	R	5'11"	180	181	639	148	62	16

3B	HR	RBI	BB	SO	SB	BA	SA	OBP
10	1	52	36	2	9	.232	.293	.277

G	IP	H	GS	CG	BB
17	113.1	140	11	10	44

SO	SH	W	L	PCT	ERA
21	0	4	7	.364	5.32

B. 7/23/1874 Austin, MS **D.** 7/17/1962
TEAMS: 96–99CleN 01DetAL 02BalAL 02–03DetAL
DEBUT: 8/7/1896 at Cleveland; played RF and went 2-for-4 in a 3–3 tie against Pittsburgh's Frank Killen
FINALE: 9/29/1903 at New York; played SS and was hitless in a 10–4 loss to New York's Ambrose Atkins and Merle Puttnam

Sport McAllister was a Mississippi boy who played a bit in Vicksburg in 1892 but otherwise remained a Texas League stalwart from age 17 in 1892 until Cleveland acquired him in 1896. Known as "Texas Jack" during his days in the Lone Star state, he acquired the nickname "Sport" after making the majors. At the time Cleveland purchased him from the Fort Worth club, he was billed as "the best all-around ball player in Texas," and for good reason. McAllister could play every position on the diamond and did so in the majors, although pitching was a challenge for him. He had short, stubby fingers that made it difficult for him to grip the ball but that still could give it some "puzzling twists."

McAllister had the distinction of being the only player to be a member of the NL Cleveland Spiders in the last five years of their existence, which is not a plus. When the Spiders merged with St. Louis prior to the 1899 season and Cleveland's best players headed for the Mound City, McAllister was left behind, although he technically became St. Louis property. Once Cleveland disbanded at the close of the 1899 season, St. Louis sold him to Detroit of the newly renamed American League. McAllister remained in the Motor City for the next four years except for a 3-game stint in 1902 when he was more or less loaned to the foundering Baltimore AL team.

Versatility kept McAllister in the majors for some seven seasons and weak hitting prevented him from staying longer. After leaving the AL at the close of the 1903 campaign, he found his appropriate playing level in the Eastern League, where he became a fixture at Buffalo until he was in his midthirties and then played three more seasons before terminating his 23-year pro career with Lincoln of the Western League at age 40. After coaching baseball for a time at the University of Michigan, the crusty McAllister was replaced by Branch Rickey and eventually returned to Detroit and became a stage actor. His death in 1962 at 88 removed the last living member of the 1899 Spiders. McAllister holds two other significant distinctions. In 1899 he became the first ML player to serve at every position on the diamond since 1893, when the pitching distance was set at 60'6". That same season his 29 runs were the fewest in the nineteenth century of anyone with a minimum of 400 PAs. (DN/DB)

McBride, Algernon Griggs / "Algie" "Teddy"

B	T	HGT	WGT	G	AB	H	R	2B
L	L	5'9"	162	305	1202	361	212	42

3B	HR	RBI	BB	SO	SB	BA	SA	OBP
26	8	122	113	3	33	.300	.399	.373

B. 5/23/1869 Washington, D.C. **D.** 1/10/1956
TEAMS: 96ChiN 98–01CinN
DEBUT: 5/12/1896 at Chicago; played LF and went 0-for-3 in a 5–2 win over Boston's Jim Sullivan
FINALE: 9/16/1901 at New York; pinch hit unsuccessfully for Jim Miller in a 3–2 loss to Boston's Bill Dinneen

Algie McBride was a small left-handed slap hitter who got off to a late start in pro ball and was at his prime or perhaps even past it by the time he reached the NL. His ML career was further abbreviated by limitations in his game as well as injuries. Born in Washington, McBride was the son of a Government Printing Office employee. After flunking several earlier minor league trials, he attracted considerable attention in 1895, playing for Austin and recording enough ABs before that team disbanded in August to lead the Texas-Southern League with a BA of .444, outstanding even in an era of astronomical averages. A Galveston reporter wrote, "There never was a surer or more timely batter in the Texas League circuit." Upon leaving Austin, McBride signed with Chicago and, after appearing in 1 exhibition game, was loaned to Rockford in the Western Association, where he again topped the.400 mark (.407).

McBride was promoted the next season to Chicago and showed an unusual ability to handle the difficult sun in LF at West Side Park, but playing in the NL proved a tougher proposition than the weak competition he had seen in 1895. He batted only .241 in 9 games and in June was loaned to Grand Rapids of the Western League. After a strong 1897 season in which he topped the WL in batting at .381, he was acquired by Cincinnati from St. Paul in exchange for two outfielders and $2,000 in cash.

Throughout his stay with the Reds, McBride competed for playing time in a somewhat crowded outfield. In 1899 he hit .347, easily his best ML mark, but suffered a severe knee injury and missed considerable time and then was benched again late in the year with a dislocated finger. McBride had already damaged his other knee in 1898, his rookie season. In the fall of 1899 the Reds disposed of Kip Selbach and handed McBride a full-time outfield job. However, his hitting fell off to .275 and he lost favor with manager Buck Ewing, who considered him a poor bunter and tentative on the bases, perhaps as a result of his knee injuries. McBride then played only semiregularly in 1900 until he moved to New York late in June when his BA plummeted to .236. After a final ML appearance as an unsuccessful pinch hitter, McBride played a year in the then outlaw American Association and later worked as a railroad express messenger. At 86 years old he was still in good health, but he then suffered a severe fall and died in Georgetown, OH, six weeks after it occurred. (DB/DN)

McCreery, Thomas Livingston / "Tom"

B	T	HGT	WGT	G	AB	H	R	2B
B	R	5'11"	180	536	1973	600	381	73

3B	HR	RBI	BB	SO	SB	BA	SA	OBP
55	19	257	220	73	66	.304	.426	.376

G	IP	H	GS	CG	BB
10	52.2	58	5	3	44

SO	SH	W	L	PCT	ERA
14	1	3	2	.600	6.32

B. 10/19/1874 Beaver, PA **D.** 7/3/1941

TEAMS: 95–97LouN 97–98NYN 98–00PitN 01–03BroN 03BosN

DEBUT: 6/8/1895 at Boston; relieved Mike McDermott in a 17–3 loss to Kid Nichols that was charged to McDermott

FINALE: 9/27/1903; played CF and went 2-for-5 in a 10–3 loss to Chicago's Bob Wicker

Tom McCreery was a second baseman–pitcher for a Washington YMCA team in 1892–93. After enrolling at Georgetown University in the fall of 1893, he turned pro in the 1894 Virginia League and also began to play the outfield. The following spring he fanned 33 hitters over a 4-game stretch while pitching for Georgetown, fetching a telegram from Louisville manager John McCloskey offering him $150 a month. McCreery nearly didn't respond, thinking it was a joke, and later wished he hadn't. Expected to step into the Louisville rotation, he rode the bench instead for most of his rookie season after McCloskey decried his poor control: 38 walks in 48⅔ innings.

In the spring of 1896, McCloskey, desperate to add punch to a team that had only one bona fide hitter (Fred Clarke), tried McCreery in RF and struck gold when the sophomore switch hitter posted a .956 OPS, by far the club's best since it had joined the NL in 1892. At that juncture, however, McCreery's career took an unfortunate turn. Anxious to escape the last-place Colonels, he waited with bated breath that winter as first Boston and then Pittsburgh tried to acquire him. Negotiations ended when Boston's Hugh Duffy refused to go to Louisville and the Colonels demanded that promising southpaw Jesse Tannehill be included in any Pirates deal. Had McCreery gone to Pittsburgh he would have replaced fading Lou Bierbauer at 2B, his original position and still his best—he excelled particularly in handling throws and making the tag on steal attempts. Instead he languished in Louisville, losing much of his spark, and was traded to New York in August 1897 for pitcher Dad Clarke and cash. Playing on the largest stage in the league, McCreery found himself under sharp scrutiny and responded poorly, alienating player-manager Bill Joyce, fellow teammates, the New York fans, and, finally, volatile owner Andrew Freedman. Although he led the league in games played (138) and sacrifice hits (30), against that he also led in outfield errors with 31 and fell 229 points short of his 1896 OPS figure.

Given a chance to redeem himself, McCreery opened 1898 in RF but was benched after he hit .198 and then belatedly was granted his earlier wish when he signed with Pittsburgh after the Giants released him in June. McCreery recovered to hit a composite .267 for the season and had a comeback year in 1899, hitting .323. His career then suffered another derailment. Ironically, in 1900 his old Louisville team furnished Pittsburgh with so much talent before it went defunct that there was no room for him in the Pirates' lineup. Appearing in only 43 games, he was further hampered when he was hospitalized for a month with an illness. After Pittsburgh released him, McCreery announced he was quitting to go into the insurance business with his father but then changed his mind and signed with Brooklyn. In the fall of 1901 he again threatened to quit, but his new bride sensed that his heart was still in baseball. McCreery played two more seasons in the majors, hitting below .250 in each, and then spent three years in the Double A American Association before launching a new career with the American Sheet and Tinplate Company, an affiliate of U.S. Steel. He retired in 1938 because of failing health and died three years later at his home in Beaver, PA. (DN/DB)

McGeachy, John Charles
(b. McGeachey) **/ "Jack"**

B	T	HGT	WGT	G	AB	H	R	2B
R	R	5'8"	165	608	2464	604	345	106

3B	HR	RBI	BB	SO	SB	BA	SA	OBP
18	9	276	57	148	164	.245	.314	.265

G	IP	H	GS	CG	BB
5	16	25	0	0	13

SO	SH	W	L	PCT	ERA
6	0	0	1	.000	10.13

B. 5/23/1864 Clinton, MA **D.** 4/5/1930
TEAMS: 86DetN 86StLN 87–89IndN 90BroP 91PhiA 91BosA 91PhiA
DEBUT: 6/17/1886 at Detroit; played LF and made 2 hits in an 11–4 win over Kansas City's Pete Conway
FINALE: 8/24/1891 at Boston; played LF and went 0-for-4 in a 5–3 loss to Boston's George Haddock

Although he spoke with a heavy Irish brogue, Jack McGeachy was a native of Clinton, MA. In his third pro season he was playing with Long Island of the Eastern League when it disbanded on May 22, 1886. In great demand, he was signed by Detroit, a free-spending team eager to find a left fielder to fill the lone weak spot in its powerful lineup. After a 6-game trial McGeachy was benched and then reportedly offered in sale to the St. Louis Maroons of the NL. The Maroons wisely passed, enabling them to sign him for free a few weeks later when Detroit released him. In the final weeks of the 1886 season, he served as St. Louis's center fielder.

Signing with the Maroons was a decision that cost McGeachy dearly. At that time, only ML teams had the right to reserve players, and McGeachy had minor league salary offers that would have paid him about as well as the Maroons' offer while leaving him free to make another deal for himself when the season ended. McGeachy signed with St. Louis, however, on the strength of manager Gus Schmelz's promise not to reserve him in October. But by then the financially strapped Maroons had changed ownership, and after Schmelz resigned as manager in the waning days of the season, the new owner refused to honor Schmelz's commitment to McGeachy. Since the promise had no weight under baseball law, McGeachy remained under the Maroons' control and subsequently was compelled to play for Indianapolis after the Maroons disbanded and its players were reassigned. "It seems to be good base ball for club officials to break a promise made by their authorized agent," observed *SL*, "but if a ball player violates a promise he has made, there is a great hullabaloo raised and efforts are immediately made to blacklist him."

McGeachy remained a regular throughout Indianapolis's NL tenure but found himself in the baseball Siberia of his day, playing on losing teams and working for a penurious small-market outfit under six different managers in 3 years. McGeachy no doubt resented being stuck in Indianapolis even more keenly for having been thrust there by a broken promise. He jumped the club in August 1887 to go home to join his new wife in Clinton but reluctantly returned late in the season, only to hold out into early May of 1888 before signing.

McGeachy's long-awaited chance to leave Indianapolis occurred when the PL organized in 1890. The grievances of the Hoosiers players had played a large part in sparking the Brotherhood revolt, but when it occurred owner John T. Brush acted aggressively to retain many of his malcontents by offering large salary increases and exploiting internal tensions in the Brotherhood ranks. McGeachy could not be persuaded by Brush's enticements and was one of only four Hoosiers to jump to the PL. He joined John M. Ward's Brooklyn Ward's Wonders and told the *Brooklyn Eagle* that he had been "with the Indianapolis team for three years and says he is sorry for it." But when the PL collapsed after the 1890 season and Ward moved over to Brooklyn's NL club as manager of that team, he chose not to take McGeachy with him after the outfielder compiled the lowest OPS (.601) of any regular on Ward's squad.

McGeachy eventually signed with Philadelphia AA in 1891. Released in mid-June, he was picked up by pennant-bound Boston AA to replace the injured Hardy Richardson in LF and then, after Richardson healed, allowed to return to the A's. McGeachy played his last game with Philadelphia on August 24 and was then released. Unlike many players, he did not descend to the minors when his major league days were over, although in 1893 he was reported to have written Ward saying that "his leg was all right" and that he wanted to play again, and then in 1895 he played a few games in the New England League.

Although McGeachy was considered an outstanding prospect as a rookie, it is difficult to understand how he lasted more than five years as an ML regular given that his career .579 OPS was the lowest among all post-NA nineteenth-century outfielders with a minimum of 2,000 ABs. When the Athletics released McGeachy in 1891, he was reportedly living in East Orange, NJ, near New York City, and the following year he was said to be running a saloon in New York. In the mid-1890s, however, he returned to Massachusetts, where he worked as a drugstore clerk and later ran his own drugstores in Clinton and other towns. He died in Cambridge, MA, in 1930. (DB/DN)

McKelvy, Russell Errett / "Russ"

B	T	HGT	WGT	G	AB	H	R	2B
R	R	?	?	64	257	57	3	4

3B	HR	RBI	BB	SO	SB	BA	SA	OBP
3	2	36	5	38	—	.222	.284	.237

G	IP	H	GS	CG	BB
4	25	38	1	1	3

SO	SH	W	L	PCT	ERA
3	0	0	2	.000	2.16

B. 9/8/1854 Swissvale, PA **D.** 10/19/1915
TEAMS: 78IndN 82PitA
DEBUT: 5/1/1878 at Indianapolis; played CF and went 0-for-5 in a 5–4 loss to Chicago's Terry Larkin
FINALE: 8/24/1882 at St. Louis; played RF and went 0-for-4 in a 7–2 win over St. Louis's Bert Dorr

In 1876 Russ McKelvy was a pitcher-outfielder for the semipro Braddock, PA, team. The following year he joined the International Association Allegheny club. On June 2, 1877, he hurled a nineteen-inning 3–2 exhibition game loss to the Memphis Reds that was rumored to have been rigged for Memphis to win so it would gain credibility as a strong independent team. Then on September 1 he beat the NL St. Louis Browns 1–0 in fifteen innings.

As a ML rookie pitcher-outfielder with Indianapolis in 1878, however, McKelvy was considerably less auspicious, losing his only start 8–5 on August 9 to Providence's John M. Ward, and being equally challenged as a hitter. Even though he had some power, none of the incumbent NL teams cared to take him aboard when Indianapolis left the NL following the 1878 season. He spent the next several years with independent teams before joining Pittsburgh AA in 1882 for his last ML bow. By 1886 McKelvy had become the player-manager of the Omaha Union Pacifics independent team. The following year he was elected secretary of the Western League in July but turned down the job because he wanted to remain an active player. McKelvy spent the next several years moving back and forth between Omaha and Denver before settling in Omaha in the early 1890s and working as a scout and occasional Western League umpire in addition to his regular job with the Pacific Express Company. He continued to play on an Omaha YMCA team until he was past 40 years old, and he died in Omaha in 1915 of kidney disease. (DN/DB)

McMullin, John F. / "John" "Lefty"

B	T	HGT	WGT	G	AB	H	R	2B
R	L	5'10"	160	244	1081	307	233	32

3B	HR	RBI	BB	SO	SB	BA	SA	OBP
13	4	135	40	41	38	.284	.349	.310

G	IP	H	GS	CG	BB
37	283.1	490	31	30	79

SO	SH	W	L	PCT	ERA
15	0	14	15	.483	5.43

B. 4/1/1849 Philadelphia, PA **D.** 4/11/1881
TEAMS: 71TroNA 72MutNA 73–74AthNA 75PhiNA
DEBUT: 5/9/1871 at Troy; caught by Mike McGeary, went 1-for-4 and lost 9–5 to Boston's Al Spalding
FINALE: 10/25/1875 at Philadelphia; played CF and went 1-for-4 in a 17–2 win over St. Louis's George Bradley

John McMullin was the first documented left-handed pitcher in ML history and also the first to win a game, when he beat Boston 29–14 on May 16, 1871. An outfielder when he was not pitching, McMullin was a competent hitter and skillful bunter and was seldom used as a pitcher after his initial season. His last known connection with the ML game came in 1876 when he umpired three NL contests, but he later played with the 1877 Philadelphia League Alliance entry. McMullin died in Philadelphia of pneumonia ten days after his 32nd birthday. (DN)

McTamany, James Edward / "Jim"

B	T	HGT	WGT	G	AB	H	R	2B
R	R	5'8"	190	813	3102	794	693	135

3B	HR	RBI	BB	SO	SB	BA	SA	OBP
58	19	334	535	158	255	.256	.355	.373

B. 7/1/1863 Philadelphia, PA **D.** 4/6/1916
TEAMS: 85–87BroA 88KCA 89–91ColA 91PhiA
DEBUT: 8/15/1885 at Philadelphia; played LF and went 1-for-4 in a 4–1 win over the A's Bobby Mathews
FINALE: 10/15/1891 at Philadelphia; played CF and went 0-for-3 in a 6–0 loss to Boston's George Haddock

Jim McTamany was among the more superstitious players of his day, rivaling even Pete Browning. Clean shaven in some pictures, in others he sported the largest and most garish handlebar mustache in baseball history. Yet, for all that, McTamany was quiet, educated, temperate, gentlemanly, and a speedy and sure-handed outfielder who brought a rare confidence to his teams that fly balls hit his way would be caught. He seemed to backpedal effortlessly and consistently ranked in the top three in the majors in range and fielding percentage. Right fielders and left fielders who played alongside him were able to play near the lines, sometimes to ridiculous extremes. Descriptions of his catches were never of a sensational order. Often he "ran to get under" a "corker," indicating that he liked to get set for his catches and make hard plays look routine. The *Brooklyn Eagle* summed it up, saying that he offered "solid, downright, get everything that's getable fielding."

Bat in hand, McTamany seemed a different sort of player at first glance. He swung hard, missed often, and was a fly-ball hitter. Nevertheless, McTamany is the only player in ML history to log both 100 walks and 100 runs in his final season. That achievement was in keeping with his overall career and is part of what makes it seem that he was one of the most underappreciated players ever. His contemporaries probably noted only that he never hit above .280, struck out too much, and compiled stolen-base totals that were on the low end for a lead-off-type hitter. Too, he seems to have had spells when he only went through the motions. Toward the end of Brooklyn's disappointing 1887 season, *SL* lamented that McTamany "seemed bereft of life and energy, and if a ball hit to the outfield happened to touch ground . . . seemed lost." But while all that was held against him, no one in his time could have foreseen that he would compile the highest OBP (.373) of any outfielder in ML history with a minimum of 3,000 career ABs and a sub-.260 BA, and this for the most part before the rule was established that only four balls were needed for a walk; second to McTamany on this intriguing list is Jim Wynn at .366.

McTamany had four years of Philadelphia sandlot and amateur experience prior to his pro debut in 1884 with Lancaster of the Eastern League. He played CF and showed such a good arm that he was used as a change pitcher. In August of the following year, McTamany and Dave Oldfield were borrowed from Lancaster by Brooklyn AA for an exhibition game in Atlantic City against the Philadelphia A's. Both were impressive enough that they stuck with Brooklyn. McTamany played regularly for the next six years, missing substantial time only in 1890 after a bad ankle sprain suffered in a home-plate collision in a game against Louisville.

Initially, when Brooklyn, a team on the rise, signed Bob Caruthers and Dave Foutz for 1888, McTamany was considered to be a key part of the club's future. However, in January 1888, to his immense disappointment, he was sold to the Kansas City AA replacement team after Brooklyn acquired the core of the disbanded New York Mets, including outfielder Paul Radford. Judging Radford the more valuable of the two, the Bridegrooms let McTamany go, a move that may have cost Brooklyn the pennant when he outhit Radford by 30 points and scored 46 more runs.

He again was a victim of expansion machinations the following season, when Kansas City sold him to Columbus, the newest AA stepchild. Off to a hot start, McTamany was leading the Ohio club in hitting when he had his most regrettable display of temper on a ball diamond on June 24, 1889. The normally mild-mannered outfielder threatened substitute umpire Bill Paasch with his bat after being called out on strikes. The following season McTamany was named Columbus captain on May 18 but relinquished the post in 1891 shortly before his release when the club claimed he had lost his batting eye, while he attributed his decline to being unable to get along with a certain member of the front office. On July 24, 1891, McTamany signed with Philadelphia AA and made an inspirational homecoming to his native city three days later, when he batted cleanup and collected 2 of the A's 5 hits in a 3–0 loss to Washington's Kid Carsey. The following month he and Ted Larkin became only the second pair of teammates in ML history to lead off a game with back-to-back homers when they picked on Cinders O'Brien on August 21 in a contest at Boston. Although McTamany played every inning of every game after joining the A's, he left the majors the following winter when the Philadelphia team was discarded in the NL-AA merger. He captained the Rochester Eastern Association entry in 1892 but hit only .221 and after that played just parts of two more seasons in the minors before retiring to pursue his trade as a wigmaker until his death in Lenni, PA, at 52. McTamany holds a further distinction that will never be surpassed: the all-time record for the most ML games (813) by a performer who never played in the NL or the AL. (DN/FV)

Mertes, Samuel Blair / "Sam" "Sandow"

B	T	HGT	WGT	G	AB	H	R	2B
R	R	5'10"	185	364	1319	383	220	46

3B	HR	RBI	BB	SO	SB	BA	SA	OBP
32	17	202	117	10	129	.290	.412	.363

B. 8/6/1872 San Francisco, CA **D.** 3/11/1945
TEAMS: 96PhiN 98–00ChiN 01–02ChiAL 03–06NYN 06StLN
DEBUT: 6/30/1896 at Brooklyn; played CF and went 1-for-3 in a 5–4 loss to Brooklyn's Dan Daub and Ed Stein
FINALE: 9/15/1906 at St. Louis; played CF and made 1 hit in a 6–2 loss to Chicago's Jack Taylor

Sam Mertes's nickname stemmed from his resemblance to Eugene Sandow, a contemporary strongman. Multitalented, a strong hitter, and an excellent base thief, he was among the best players of his era but lost several years early in his career when he was held back in the minors and subsequently never stayed with any team long enough to achieve the recognition he merited. In 1902 Mertes played every position except LF, won the only ML game he ever pitched, fielded a perfect 1.000 in 5 games at SS, and led all AL outfielders in assists. He followed by leading the NL in RBI in 1903 after jumping from the White Sox to the Giants. Two years later Mertes enjoyed his best RBI season with 108 and played on John McGraw's first Giants' World Series entrant but was released before the following season was out when his hitting dropped off sharply at age 34.

Born in San Francisco, Mertes spent 1891 in the Central California League and 1892 with a semipro nine in Santa Rosa, CA, before joining his hometown California League Pioneers in 1893. The following spring he came east to play for Lincoln of the Western Association under player-manager Buck Ebright but was released after he and Ebright quarreled, and he finished the season with Quincy. A .345 season with Quincy in 1895 propelled Mertes to the Western League with St. Paul before he was traded to the Phillies for pitcher Willie McGill. Installed as Philadelphia's new lead-off hitter, Mertes started slowly but might have survived his failure to live up to his minor league press clippings if he had held his ego in check. In September the *Washington Post* chortled, "Sandow Mertes, he of the swelled chest and ditto caput, who was swellheaded into popularity by the Philadelphia papers when he joined the Phillies last June, has been sent to Billy Sharsig's farm [the Philadelphia Athletics of the Atlantic League]." Released by the Phils that fall, Mertes hit .337 with Columbus in 1897 but remained frozen in the WL until July 1898 when he was traded to Chicago for pitchers Bert Briggs and Danny Friend. The deal marked him the first minor leaguer to be swapped twice to ML teams for established ML players.

Mertes stayed with Chicago NL through 1900 and then jumped to the AL Second City entry. Switched to 2B, in 1901 he played on the junior loop's first flag winner. He then returned to the outfield in 1902 to make room at 2B for new acquisition Tom Daly and remained in LF for the balance of his career.

After arriving in the majors to stay in 1898, Mertes ranked second in stolen bases and forth in RBI among players active during the remaining nine years of his career (1898–1906). Little is known of his life after he played his last pro innings in the 1909 California League. Mertes died in Guerneville, CA, of a heart attack in 1945. (DN)

Miller, Charles Bradley / "Dusty"

B	T	HGT	WGT	G	AB	H	R	2B
L	R	5'11½"	170	656	2561	771	445	139

3B	HR	RBI	BB	SO	SB	BA	SA	OBP
51	22	421	174	75	206	.301	.421	.353

B. 9/10/1868 Oil City, PA **D.** 9/3/1945
TEAMS: 89BalA 90StLA 95–99CinN 99StLN
DEBUT: 9/23/1889 at Baltimore; played LF and went 0-for-4 in a 10–9 loss to Philadelphia's Sadie McMahon
FINALE: 8/20/1899 at Cincinnati; played CF and went 1-for-5 in a 10–1 win over Cincinnati's Ted Breitenstein

Dusty Miller played briefly for Niagara University and went into minor league ball at 18. A heady player from the start, while playing the outfield in 1888 for Lima, OH, which had a swampy downhill dip before the fence in which high grass grew, Miller hid balls that he would scoop up instead of the batted ball to throw out runners trying to stretch hits. There is no evidence that he was the first to employ this trick, only testimony from Bug Holliday that he had it in his arsenal some years before the NL Orioles gained fame for "inventing" it.

Columbus AA acquired Miller late in the 1889 season from Canton after he had topped the Tri-State League in batting, fielding, and baserunning. But he did poorly in an 11-game trial, making 16 errors in his 8 contests at SS alone, and was swiftly released. Sensing his potential, Indianapolis signed him in December 1889. Miller was tentatively assigned to Pittsburgh when Indianapolis sold its franchise to the NL prior to the 1890 season but could not work out an arrangement with the Smoke City NL club. Instead, he went to Evansville, did well, and received another trial with St. Louis late in 1890 but again failed to hit and also displayed the first signs of the chronic arm trouble that would hound him throughout his career.

In 1891 Miller disappeared back into small-town ball and did not seek ML company again for more than four years. His first step back into top competition came with Toledo in the Western League. After a good 1894 season, Miller was purchased by Cincinnati from Toledo. In his early pro years Miller had often played SS, but by the time he reached Cincinnati he was used almost exclusively in RF. His overall NL fielding stats were only slightly above average, but in Cincinnati he bore the disadvantage of contending with a notoriously difficult sunny field during the 1890s. Years later Miller was remembered as "the only Red to successfully negotiate the sun garden until Mike Mitchell" joined the team, but even then his status remained intact as the Reds were playing in a different park by the time Mitchell arrived.

Miller was able to overcome his early habit of stepping in the bucket against lefties by using a long bat. In his first two years in Cincinnati he hit well, leading the team in many offensive categories. In 1897 Miller's play slipped and he fell into a hostile relationship with the bleacherites. Manager Buck Ewing began efforts to trade him, but the Reds set his price high, and he remained on the 1898 roster to play all but a small handful of games in RF. In 1899, however, Ewing made an expensive acquisition in Kip Selbach. Miller began the season on the bench and then replaced Algie McBride in RF but hit just .251 and was released toward the end of July. A batting average 50 points below his career mark might seem sufficient reason to jettison a player, but according to one report, Miller had also fallen out of favor because he liked to mimic the facial tics of club owner John T. Brush, who was afflicted with a nervous disease. Miller was picked up by St. Louis and played 10 games in CF as a replacement for Harry Blake, who was home with his sick wife, but when his BA barely topped .200, he was released shortly after his last game on August 20. Miller then played minor league ball until he was 40 before retiring.

During the early 1890s Miller had played in Cygnet, a little town in Wood County in northwestern Ohio. Small as many of Wood County's towns were, they were enjoying an oil boom, and they began to import professionals to bolster their semipro teams. Findlay boasted such fine black players as Grant Johnson and Bud Fowler while its archrival Cygnet hired Miller as well as pitcher Jerry Nops. Miller settled down for a time in Cygnet, opening a store and acquiring a farm on which oil was discovered in 1895. That October, it was reported that when nine wells had been opened on his land, he was living "on easy street" and his new pseudonym would be "Greasy" rather than "Dusty." Eventually, however, Miller moved south, probably liking what he found when he played in the Southern League. In 1945 he died of a heart attack at his home in Memphis. He had earlier been in the real estate business, but he had apparently run through most of whatever money he had accumulated from his oil wells and real estate investments, for at the age of 77 he was working as a clerk in a liquor store. He left no relatives.

According to one story, Miller's nickname came

early in his career when he adopted the habit of deliberately raising clouds of dust to impair the umpire's vision every time he stole a base. Another version notes that "Dusty Miller" was the name of a "little roan mare" that was a famous trotting horse circa 1891. (DB/DN)

Nicol, George Edward / "George" "Kid"

B	T	HGT	WGT	G	AB	H	R	2B
R	L	5'7"	155	43	147	51	24	8

3B	HR	RBI	BB	SO	SB	BA	SA	OBP
5	0	26	6	6	4	.347	.469	.381

G	IP	H	GS	CG	BB
15	91.1	118	12	7	84

SO	SH	W	L	PCT	ERA
45	0	5	7	.417	7.19

B. 10/17/1870 Barry, IL **D.** 8/10/1924
TEAMS: 90StLA 91ChiN 94PitN 94LouN
DEBUT AND CAREER HIGHLIGHT: 9/23/1890 at St. Louis; caught by Jack Munyan and pitched a seven-inning no-hitter against Philadelphia's Eddie Green, winning 21–2
FINALE: 9/29/1894 at Louisville; played RF and went 0-for-4 in an 11–4 loss to Brooklyn's Ed Stein

George Nicol pitched a no-hitter in his ML debut while still a teenager and followed it with a one-hitter in his next start. He went on to compile a career batting average of .362. Yet rather than being a first-ballot HOFer, he spent most of his career in the minor leagues and there is no reason to believe he was the victim of any injustice. Nicol spent the summer of 1890 with a Mount Sterling, IL, independent team and went 21-4 before joining St. Louis in September. He was immediately nicknamed "Kid" by local writers who mistakenly thought his name was Nichols, the same as Boston's star rookie hurler that year. Given a start against a wretched Philadelphia team in utter disarray on September 23, 1890, Nicol became the first pitcher in ML history to throw a no-hitter in his debut, although it has never been counted as such by MLB because the game went only seven innings. In Nicol's next start he beat Philadelphia again, 7–3 in a five-inning game, but he was unmasked in his third and final appearance of the 1890 season on October 6, when he lost 10–3, and *TSN* noted, "Young Nichols [*sic*], the sixteen-year-old [*sic*] phenomenon from the wilds of Illinois, proved an easy mark for the Toledo team."

Still, his overall performance in his initial taste of ML competition appears to have made Nicol cocky almost beyond endurance—at least until the following January, when he was forced to advertise for a pitching job in *TSN*. He eventually signed with Davenport of the Illinois-Iowa League and was 16-5 in July when Nick Young forced him to join Chicago to appease Cap Anson, who had missed out on another Davenport pitcher he wanted. A dud with the Colts, Nicol continued to do so well in the minors that his cockiness soon resurfaced. Although unpopular with teammates everywhere he went, he was a favorite of managers because he was a winner and a workhorse. In 1893 Nicol pitched Los Angeles to the forefront of the California League before the loop folded and then joined Erie, PA, in July and launched Charlie Morton's club on a drive to the Eastern League pennant by beating Springfield, MA, in his first start. But after hurling some 60 games that season, he was damaged goods when Pittsburgh drafted him in the fall. The Pirates loaned his lame arm to Franklin, PA, of the Iron & Oil League in July 1894 and then traded him to Louisville the following month for pitcher Jock Menefee.

Having noted that Nicol could hit perhaps even better than he could pitch, Colonels manager Billy Barnie sent him to RF and soon incurred the ire of center fielder Tom Brown when Nicol's excellent range enabled him to snare many of the fly balls that Brown was accustomed to handling. Moreover, Nicol led the Colonels in hitting during his month and a half in Kentucky. Near the end of the season his arm went south again, however, and he was released despite his .352 BA. One suspects team chemistry may have been the real issue, as Nicol was a fine pinch hitter and could still have served in that role despite an ailing wing.

Nicol finished the century as an outfielder in the Western League. In 1896, with Milwaukee, he led the loop in steals, but by 1899 he had lost his job on the Brewers to Bunk Congalton. He stayed in Milwaukee running billiard halls and saloons after temporarily leaving the game following the 1900 season and then returned to pro ball for several seasons in the Three-I League. In 1908 he finally retired.

Nicol died under mysterious circumstances. On the evening of August 3, 1924, he returned to his Milwaukee home about 10:30 and went to bed without indicating that anything was out of the ordinary. He died in his sleep, and an autopsy revealed he had four broken ribs. There was speculation that he had suffered a fall or been the victim of an assault, but police turned up no leads and the mystery of his death was never solved. (PM/DN)

Nicol, Hugh N. / "Hugh" "Wee Hugh"

B	T	HGT	WGT	G	AB	H	R	2B
R	R	5'4"	145	888	3465	813	631	91

3B	HR	RBI	BB	SO	SB	BA	SA	OBP
29	5	272	337	88	383	.235	282	.307

G	W	L	PCT	PENNANTS
40	8	32	.200	0

B. 1/1/1858 Campsie, Scotland **D.** 6/27/1921
TEAMS: 81–82ChiN 83–86StLA 87–89CinA 90CinN (M)97StLN
DEBUT: 5/3/1881 at Chicago; played LF and went 0-for-5 in a 6–0 win over Cleveland's Jim McCormick
FINALE: 8/2/1890 at Cincinnati; played LF and went 1-for-4 in an 11–3 win over Philadelphia's Tom Vickery and Kid Gleason

Born outside Glasgow, Hugh Nicol was the seventh of eight children in a family that immigrated to Rockford, IL, an early baseball stronghold, where he learned the marble-cutting trade while playing ball on local teams. He was at SS for the Rockford Northwestern League club in 1879 when Ross Barnes, the finest player Rockford ever produced, recommended him to Cincinnati NL. When the Reds passed on him, Nicol was signed the following year by another old Rockfordite, Al Spalding, president of the Chicago club.

Nicol received an excellent grounding in the fundamentals of baserunning from manager Cap Anson and the aggressive, well-schooled Chicago players, but he could not break into the White Stockings' powerful lineup. After the 1882 season, eager to play regularly, he signed with St. Louis AA and became that team's right fielder, remaining with the Browns through 1886. He imported the lessons he had learned in Chicago and played an integral part in developing the potent running game that fueled the Browns' drive to AA championships in 1885 and 1886. But when Nicol fell ill in 1886 he lost his RF berth and that November 12 was traded to Cincinnati for catcher Jack Boyle and $350 in the first player trade (as distinct from a sale) between two major league clubs. St. Louis owner Chris Von der Ahe explained that Nicol's health issues and a drop-off in his batting had fostered the trade. Nicol had hit below .210 in each of the two previous years, and Von der Ahe expected that new rule changes would further hamper his limited hitting skills.

Gus Schmelz, Cincinnati's new manager, was a particular devotee of the little ball tactics used so effectively by the Browns and made the trade in order to provide the Reds with a player who could "infuse life and ginger into the team." He briefly placed Nicol in CF, but after the wee outfielder had trouble adjusting to that position, he was moved back to his accustomed RF post and retained it through 1889. By that point he was in his thirties and experiencing a natural decline in talent, but it may not be coincidence that after his patron Schmelz left the club in the fall of 1889, Nicol went to the bench very early in the next season when his hitting fell off again. He drew his release in August 1890.

Nicol could look back on a distinguished if not truly outstanding career of ten ML seasons, yet if we view him through the prism of modern baseball it would be difficult to understand how he survived at all. A skillful outfielder, speedy on the bases and an excellent headfirst slider, disciplined, intelligent, and always well conditioned, he was nonetheless a hitter so weak that he could never have held his own as an outfielder today, no matter what other qualities he might possess. Too small to drive the ball for power, he recorded a career BA of a mere .235 and hit .215 or below more seasons than not. In all of baseball history no other outfielder with so lengthy a career has been as weak a hitter as Nicol. In the 1880s, however, a player with his combination of skills could make a contribution to his team out of all proportion to his batting abilities. By simply putting the ball in play, any hitter could expect to reach base on errors about once every 3 games in the 1880s, adding the equivalent of about 70 or 80 points of OBP to whatever he earned through hits and walks. Once on base, a runner of Nicol's mettle would then manufacture runs the hitters behind him could not otherwise produce. Rules changes during the 1880s made bases on balls increasingly common and enabled the little outfielder to reach base even more often.

As Chris Von der Ahe predicted, the new rules introduced in 1887 had a negative effect on his BA, but his walks rose sufficiently to compensate for it. As a result, Nicol led the AA in steals in 1887 and finished second in 1888 and fourth in 1889. His throwing arm was likewise far more valuable than it would be today, as is shown by his string of outfield assists in 8 consecutive games—a remarkable record when he made it in 1884, but one that would be unimaginable now.

After the Reds released him, Nicol signed with Kansas City, where he had made his home since marrying May Little of that city in 1886. In 1891 he returned to Rockford as a player-manager and, after bouncing around awhile, came back to Rockford as owner of its Western Association franchise, which he ran for a time as an informal farm club for his former Chicago team. In 1897 he went back to another of his old clubs, the Browns, as manager, but the once-proud St. Louis team was now in disarray and Nicol left after losing 32 of 40 games.

In 1905 Nicol sold his interest in the Peoria club and the next year became baseball coach and the first athletic director at Purdue University, where he proved an innovative and effective administrator until he retired in 1915 due to failing heath while continuing to scout for several ML teams. He died in 1921 after diabetes required the removal of several toes. A 16-year-old son, Lyle, had died in 1906 as the result of a football injury, but Nicol was survived by two other children and his wife. (DB/DN)

O'Brien, John Joseph / "Jack"

B	T	HGT	WGT	G	AB	H	R	2B
L	R	6'1"	165	127	468	132	68	11

3B	HR	RBI	BB	SO	SB	BA	SA	OBP
5	6	51	31	—	17	.282	.365	.331

B. 2/5/1873 Watervliet, NY **D.** 6/10/1933
TEAMS: 99WasN 01WasA 01CleAL 03BosAL
DEBUT: 4/14/1899 at Philadelphia; played LF and was 0-for-4 in a 6–5 loss to Philadelphia's Wiley Piatt
FINALE: 9/28/1903 at Boston; played CF and was 2-for-4 in a 5–0 win over St. Louis's Willie Sudhoff

In 1897, his third pro season, Jack O'Brien replaced the popular Tom Bannon in the Syracuse outfield. He remained with the Eastern League team in 1898 before joining Washington. O'Brien survived a horrific 0-for-22 start to reward manager Arthur Irwin's patience by hitting a solid .282 as part of the Senators' all-NL freshman outfield, with Buck Freeman and Jimmy Slagle. Unlike his two counterparts, O'Brien was left homeless when the NL reduced to eight teams after the 1899 season and went to Kansas City in the newly renamed American League. Finishing second in the loop in hits and rapping .298 earned him an invitation to return to Washington when it became part of the AL in 1901 after it assumed major league status. A poor start caused him to be waived to Cleveland, where he hit .283 but was not retained.

O'Brien spent 1902 with Milwaukee of the Western League under Hugh Duffy and led the loop in runs. Acquired by the Boston AL club to play CF, he hit a disappointing .210. O'Brien's last ML action came in the 1903 World Series in two unsuccessful pinch-hitting appearances. In 1904 he returned to Milwaukee, which by then had become a member of the Double A American Association and finished his career there the following year with a .228 BA in 123 games. O'Brien returned to his hometown after leaving the game and joined the local police force. He served for a time as its chief before dying from kidney disease at 60. (DN)

O'Neill, James Edward / "Tip"

B	T	HGT	WGT	G	AB	H	R	2B
R	R	6'1½"	189	1052	4248	1385	879	222

3B	HR	RBI	BB	SO	SB	BA	SA	OBP
92	52	757	420	146	161	.326	.458	.392

G	IP	H	GS	CG	BB
35	289	307	33	29	115

SO	SH	W	L	PCT	ERA
91	0	16	16	.500	3.39

B. 5/25/1858 Woodstock, Ontario, Canada
D. 12/31/1915
TEAMS: 83NYN 84–89StLA 90ChiP 91StLA 92CinP
DEBUT: 5/5/1883 at New York; caught by John Clapp in a 3–1 loss to Providence's Charley Radbourn
FINALE: 8/30/1892 at Cincinnati; played LF, went 0-for-4 and was replaced by Frank Genins after he "was taken sick" in a 6–1 win over Boston's Jack Stivetts
CAREER DAY: 5/7/1887 at St. Louis; hit for the cycle for the second time in an eight-day period when he followed a 6-for-7 day with 2 home runs on 4/30

with a perfect 5-for-5 performance in which he scored 4 runs in a 12–7 win over Louisville's Guy Hecker

The scion of a hotel-keeping family in Woodstock in southwestern Ontario, Tip O'Neill began his career as a hot pitching prospect after learning the game in the late 1870s from American pro players who vacationed at his father's luxury O'Neill House hotel. In 1879 O'Neill was the featured performer on the Woodstock Actives. The independent club was extremely successful that summer, touring the United States and claiming the Canadian baseball championship, but it would be another two years before O'Neill crossed the waters to the States to play for pay. Near the close of the 1881 NL season, he traveled to Detroit, hoping to pitch for the NL Wolverines, but they let him slip away. The following spring the lean right-hander first began to make his mark south of the border with the League Alliance New York Metropolitans.

By 1883 club president John Day and his partners owned not only the AA Mets but also New York NL, and O'Neill was working for the latter club. That fall, Day and manager Jim Mutrie conspired to convey him back to the Mets after he went just 5-12 as a 25-year-old freshman. Under the rules then prevailing, they could not simply transfer O'Neill between the clubs; instead he had to be released from his current contract and then undergo a ten-day waiting period before signing with his new team. Nevertheless, Day and his partners released him from their NL club and, in their impatience, got his name on the second contract without waiting the ten days and transmitted an official notification to league officials. Then they handed O'Neill a nice bonus and sent him home to Canada.

But Jimmy Williams spotted New York's notice of the new contract and recognized it was illegal. As it happened, Williams was serving his last days as the American Association's secretary before taking over as manager of the AA St. Louis Browns. Williams went to Woodstock and, as soon as the ten days had passed, got O'Neill's signature on a contract with his new club. The Mets protested, but the National Board of Arbitration found that their contract was not valid. Day and his partners had their bonus money returned, but the Browns got O'Neill, who in the fullness of time would become the offensive lynchpin of St. Louis's four American Association champion teams and would log one of the greatest hitting seasons in ML history when he won the Triple Crown in 1887.

It seemed at first that O'Neill might not be worth all the fuss, for while he won 11 of 15 decisions for St. Louis, he continued to struggle with a chronic arm injury. Between his ailing arm and the Browns' acquisition of Dave Foutz and Bob Caruthers, O'Neill was unlikely to see much more duty as a pitcher. With a bat in his hand he was clearly more than competent, however, and since the Browns were badly in need of offense, they used him increasingly in LF, where he blossomed into the only really heavy hitter on a team that showcased strong pitching and hard, heady baserunning to win four consecutive pennants. So enormous, in fact, were O'Neill's offensive contributions that Browns manager Charlie Comiskey was willing to overlook what were arguably the most glaring shortcomings of any ML outfielder in the nineteenth century. In addition to a reputation for being lazy at times on the bases and often removed for a courtesy runner in an era when the rules still allowed one, O'Neill covered little ground in the field and, owing perhaps to the weakened condition of his once strong arm, presented little challenge to runners seeking to take an extra base. Among all gardeners in a minimum of 750 AA games, his 59 career assists are a whopping 92 short of the next-lowest man on the list, Jim McTamany (151).

In 1887 a thoroughgoing revision of the rules created excellent offensive conditions, but as compensation to pitchers, the privilege of calling either for a high or a low pitch was removed from hitters. Batsmen who had been particularly good at hitting one type of delivery or the other were disadvantaged, and among them was O'Neill, a notorious low-ball hitter whom the *Cincinnati Enquirer* predicted would be unable to hit high pitches. Once the season started, however, O'Neill rocketed to perhaps the most dominant offensive season in history. Thanks to a scoring rules change that counted walks as hits, he was credited at the close of the 1887 campaign with a BA of .492. Modern statisticians, using the current definition of the base hit, have deflated that figure to an only marginally less remarkable .435. Although no one was counting RBI as yet, O'Neill is now credited retroactively with the Triple Crown, and he also led the AA in a host of other offensive categories.

Yet the Canadian clouter is not remembered altogether fondly for his contributions to the game in 1887. On September 11 of that year, O'Neill went to Browns owner Chris Von der Ahe and handed him a letter, signed by eight team members, stating that the players would "not agree to play against Negroes." While Browns manager Charlie Comiskey was willing to believe the revolt, which led to the cancellation of a potentially lucrative exhibition game, was due to the fact that O'Neill and the other players merely wanted a day off in the middle of a long eastern road trip, some historians see this event as a milestone on the road to the establishment of baseball's color line.

In 1888, following a spate of new rule changes that favored pitchers, O'Neill's hitting fell off dramatically, yet he managed the extraordinary feat of winning a second batting championship in a season in which his BA dropped a full 100 points. Nevertheless, in July when he claimed that he was too ill to play, the mercurial Von der Ahe accused him of malingering. A controversy arose when Charlie Byrne, president of St. Louis's archrival, Brooklyn, enlisted Doc Bushong, a former Brown now playing for Byrne, to write O'Neill letting him know Brooklyn would like to have him and Von der Ahe formally accused Byrne of tampering with his star hitter (*see* Charlie Byrne).

O'Neill remained with St. Louis, but when an opportunity arose to escape in 1890, he followed Browns player-manager Charlie Comiskey in jumping to the rebel Chicago PL team. At 32, O'Neill was starting to decline, and two years later, playing for Comiskey again at Cincinnati, his decay was so palpable that he had only a .327 SA after 109 games. In early September he left the Reds in a dispute over whether he would get paid while he convalesced from a rib injury. When Comiskey reportedly reneged on a promise to keep him on the payroll at half his salary until he recovered, O'Neill refused to return to Cincinnati in 1893 and became a bookmaker and later a gambling-house operator in Montreal. Meanwhile, he kept a hand in his love for sports by managing prizefighters and, toward the end of the century, umpired in the Eastern League, which at that time included two Canadian teams, Montreal and Toronto.

O'Neill's extraordinary 1887 season, two batting titles, and .326 career BA have never earned him even token HOF consideration largely because in his time baseball was foremost a fielding and base running game, and he was decidedly weak at both of these critical departments. In 1888, playing for a pennant winner, he became the first man in ML history to play 120 or more games, win a batting title, and score fewer than 100 runs (96). Yet he was nonetheless a very valuable player at his peak and a member of the first class inducted into the Canadian Baseball HOF in 1983. Indeed, the Tip O'Neill Award is given annually to the best Canadian player in the major. According to Von der Ahe, O'Neill was nicknamed "Tip" because "he merely seemed to 'tip' the ball when batting. He stood at the plate straight as an arrow, a giant in physique, and it seemed that he would just push out his bat and the ball would shoot off it like lightning." But according to *SL*, as a schoolboy in Woodstock O'Neill joined a company of amateur tragedians and "never being possessed of a serious disposition suggested that an old farce, 'Tip and Slasher,' be put on." O'Neill played Tip, and even though his performance was poorly received, the nickname stuck. On the final day of 1915 O'Neill suffered a fatal heart attack while aboard a Montreal street car. (DN/DB/JK)

*O'Rourke, John W. / "John"

B	T	HGT	WGT	G	AB	H	R	2B
L	L	6'0"	190	230	945	279	148	58

3B	HR	RBI	BB	SO	SB	BA	SA	OBP
24	11	98	47	64	—	.295	.442	.329

B. 8/23/1849 Bridgeport, CT **D.** 6/23/1911
TEAMS: 79–80BosN 83NYA
DEBUT: 5/1/1879 at Buffalo; played CF and went 2-for-5 in a 5–0 win over Buffalo's Jim Galvin
FINALE: 9/10/1883 at Louisville; played CF and went 3-for-5 in a 13–4 win over Louisville's Sam Weaver

John O'Rourke was the older brother of HOF outfielder Jim O'Rourke and might be nearly as well remembered today as his famous sibling if baseball had been paramount in his life. Record of his early involvement in the game is sketchy. In 1875 at age 26 he was a member of the nefarious T.B.F.U.S. team that represented his home city (*see* Terry Larkin). O'Rourke continued to play in and around Connecticut through the 1878 season when he led the International Association with a .393 BA and .483 SA while playing in his second season with Manchester. The following year he became the first

30-year-old impact rookie in ML history when he hit .341 with Boston, topped the NL with a .521 SA, and tied Charley Jones for the loop RBI lead with 62.

On September 19, 1879, O'Rourke incurred the first of several major injuries that helped shorten his career, when he was hurt sliding against Cleveland and missed the last 7 games of the season. Healthy at the start of his second ML campaign, he led all Boston hitters in spring training with a .383 mark and opened the 1880 season in CF. On May 8 his brother Jim played beside him in RF for the first time, but some two weeks later the pair were temporarily separated when the elder O'Rourke crashed into the CF fence in Troy on May 24 while chasing Roger Connor's long drive. He sustained a five-inch gash in his throat and had to be carried off the field. Scarcely had he returned to the lineup when he collided with Sadie Houck on June 1 as the pair pursued a long fly ball. Hampered by the rapid succession of injuries, O'Rourke was further discouraged when Boston dropped out of contention, but what finally turned him against the game was team owner Arthur Soden's refusal to pay his players in a timely fashion, especially when they were on the road. At the finish of the 1880 season O'Rourke took a steady-paying railroad job, played occasionally in 1881 for Philadelphia of the Eastern Championship Association, and shunned all offers to return to the majors for the next two years. Finally, in 1883, Chief Roseman, a former teammate on the 1875 T.B.F.U.S. team, induced O'Rourke to join the New York AA expansion club. He showed his rust after a two-year absence from top competition but was beginning to hit his stride when he abruptly quit for the season while the Mets were in Louisville. O'Rourke then returned to his railroad job. By 1898 he was baggage master on the New York Central Railroad, working out of Grand Central Station. He later rose to be a national official in the rail-workers' union prior to his death in Boston of heart disease. (DN/DB)

Pabor, Charles Henry / "Charlie"
"The Old Woman in the Red Cap"

B	T	HGT	WGT	G	AB	H	R	2B
L	L	5'8"	155	170	715	204	101	13

3B	HR	RBI	BB	SO	SB	BA	SA	OBP
12	0	80	8	8	3	.285	.337	.293

G	IP	H	GS	CG	BB
10	51.1	81	4	3	10

SO	SH	W	L	PCT	ERA
0	0	1	4	.200	5.96

G	W	L	PCT	PENNANTS
77	13	64	.169	0

B. 9/24/1846 New York, NY **D.** 4/22/1913
TEAMS: (P/M)71–72CleNA 73AtlNA 74PhiNA (P/M)75AtlNA (P/M)75NHNA
DEBUT: 5/4/1871 at Fort Wayne; in the first game in ML history played CF and went 0-for-4 in a 2–0 loss to Fort Wayne's Bobby Mathews
FINALE: 10/28/1875 at New Haven; played LF and made 3 hits in a 10–7 loss to Boston's Cal McVey

Charlie Pabor may have been the first left-handed pitcher of note in 1867 when he was a member of the Morrisanias with Dave Birdsall as his catcher. The origin of his intriguing nickname is unknown, but there are references to it in the *Chicago Tribune* as late as 1878. In the course of his five-year career in the NA, Pabor did it all—manage, pitch, and umpire in addition to playing the outfield. Apart from his appearance in the first game in ML history, his most interesting achievement came on July 6, 1872, when he was forced into the box after both Al Pratt and Rynie Wolters deserted the Cleveland team, leaving it understaffed, and beat the Brooklyn Eckfords with only two outfielders behind him. The headline in the *New York Times* the following day was, "The Eckfords Beaten by Eight Men."

In 1876, when New Haven's bid to join the newly formed NL was unsuccessful, Pabor remained the captain of the Elm Citys and their highest paid player at $1,600. The following year he signed with the League Alliance Columbus Buckeyes and became Mike "King" Kelly's first pro manager. By 1880 Pabor was out of the game and working as a New Haven policeman. He later was that city's police chief before becoming a policeman in New York and running a flower shop there with his son. Said to have made and lost a fortune in investments early in life, just prior to his death Pabor claimed he hadn't seen a baseball game in twenty-five years and ridiculed the notion that any modern SS could be as good as George Wright. Pabor died of pneumonia at 66 in New Haven. (DN)

Parks, William Robert / "Bill"

B	T	HGT	WGT	G	AB	H	R	2B
R	R	5'8"	150	29	121	21	13	0

3B	HR	RBI	BB	SO	SB	BA	SA	OBP
0	0	6	1	2	1	.174	.174	.180

G	IP	H	GS	CG	BB
16	112	157	11	9	6

SO	SH	W	L	PCT	ERA
3	0	4	8	.333	3.54

G	W	L	PCT	PENNANTS
8	1	7	.125	0

B. 6/4/1849 Easton, PA **D.** 10/10/1911
TEAMS: (P/M)75WasNA 75PhiNA 76BosN
DEBUT: 4/26/1875 at Washington; played LF and made 1 hit in an 8–2 loss to Boston's Al Spalding
FINALE: 4/22/1876 at Boston; played LF and went 0-for-4 in a 6–5 win over Philadelphia's Lon Knight

A Civil War veteran, Bill Parks ran away from home several times to enlist until his father finally tired of retrieving him from recruiting stations and permitted him to join the Union Army despite being underage. His baseball high point came on July 4, 1875, when he took the box and won Washington's final game as a member of the NA, topping the St. Louis Reds 12–5. His low point came in the very first NL game ever played, when he made a key error, dropping a line drive hit by Dave Eggler. The following day John Morrill replaced Parks in the Boston lineup, but he remained on the team for several more weeks and played in a number of exhibition games. Writer George Tuohey in 1897 recounted that Boston got rid of Parks by having a fake letter sent to him purportedly from someone on the St. Louis club offering him $100 more than Boston was paying, provided he could get his release. When Parks did as asked, he discovered he had been bamboozled. By the close of the 1870s he was pitching for the local team in Easton and working as a barber. Self-employed all of his life, Parks died in 1911 while sitting in his barbershop waiting for his first customer of the day.

More time has elapsed since Park's last NL appearance on April 22, 1876, than any other player's in the league's long history. Lou Gehrig's record has been broken and Nolan Ryan's may some day fall, but Park's mark is unassailable. (DN/DB)

***Parrott, Thomas William / "Tom" "Tacks" "Tacky Tom"**

B	T	HGT	WGT	G	AB	H	R	2B
R	R	5'10½"	170	281	999	301	157	40

3B	HR	RBI	BB	SO	SB	BA	SA	OBP
26	15	163	41	53	26	.301	.438	.329

G	IP	H	GS	CG	BB
115	795	1055	89	69	307

SO	SH	W	L	PCT	ERA
166	2	39	48	.448	5.33

B. 4/10/1868 Portland, OR **D.** 1/1/1932
TEAMS: 93ChiN 93–95CinN 96StLN
DEBUT: 6/18/1893 at Chicago; caught by Mal Kittridge, relieved in the fifth inning by Al Mauck and later Willie McGill, with Mauck taking the 16–12 loss to St. Louis's Kid Gleason and John Dolan
FINALE: 9/26/1896 at St. Louis; played 1B and went 2-for-4 in a 7–3 win over Brooklyn's Elmer Horton

Tom Parrott was the older brother of ML infielder Jiggs Parrott and followed him by a year as the second native Oregonian to play in the majors. In 1894 the pair became the only sibling pitcher–position player combo in ML history to collect 500 PAs and 300 innings pitched, respectively, in the same season. The elder Parrott was a man of many talents who played the cornet well enough to have been a racetrack bugler and was a frequent winner in the minors of both sprint and throwing contests in baseball Field Day events. He was also an unstoppable hot dog with "the famous $10,000 arm and 50-cent head" and, early in his career, had been a hapless greenhorn, the butt of many practical jokes and so cowed by his father that he sent all his money home and kept only enough for his board and tobacco. Yet Parrott without question had the ability to play in the majors as both a pitcher and a hitter. When on the mound he went through elaborate gyrations before each pitch, making him very hard to hit until a batter had faced him a few times, and owned a "delusive slow ball" that may actually have been an early form of the blooper. In 1896 Joe Sugden described the pitch in *TSN*: "He hoops the ball in the air high above the batter's head. Few batsmen will go after it. The pitch looks ridiculous, and everybody laughs when Tommy uses it." But that observation came in Parrott's final ML season. Earlier in his career he had been so effective that he had been named Cincinnati's Opening Day starter in 1894. Overall, Parrott compiled the highest OPS (including only his PAs while serving as a pitcher) of any hurler with a minimum of 500 PAs since the four-ball rule was adopted in 1889, as his .810 mark tops Wes Ferrell by 13 points and Jack Stivetts by 19.

In 1890 Parrott and his brother graduated from the Willamettes, a Portland amateur team, to the Portland entry in the newly formed Pacific Northwest League. He remained in the loop until it disbanded after the 1892 season and then joined Birmingham of the Southern League. In June 1893 Parrott signed illegally with Chicago NL even as Birmingham was in the process of selling his contract to Cincinnati NL. He pitched 4 games for Chicago before the Board of Arbitration properly awarded him to Cincinnati. After joining the Reds in July, he logged the best winning percentage on the staff. But when he followed his rookie year with a composite 5.54 ERA in 1894–95, he was traded to St. Louis as part of a six-player deal. After two hapless April starts with the Browns, Parrott was made into a full-time outfielder. He hit a team-high .291 in 1896 and was paid $4 nightly to play three cornet solos with owner Chris Von der Ahe's brass band, which served as a side attraction during night horse races under electric lights at Sportsman's Park. His overall performance seemed worthy of an encore in the Mound City, but instead he was forced to return to the minors when the Browns chose not to reserve him for 1897. Parrott spent two seasons in the Western League, sat out a year after his father died, and then was active in the game until 1907, when he played his last innings with Houston of the Texas League and hit .234. He remained in the Lone Star state for a number of years, making his living as a musician. Parrott eventually returned to Oregon after his second wife died and was living with a cousin in Dundee at the time of his death in 1932. His nickname "Tacky" was period slang for a weirdo. (DN)

Peltz, John / "Jack"

B	T	HGT	WGT	G	AB	H	R	2B
R	R	5'8"	175	230	871	195	106	25

3B	HR	RBI	BB	SO	SB	BA	SA	OBP
26	4	48	45	—	18	.224	.326	.266

B. 4/23/1861 New Orleans, LA **D.** 2/27/1906
TEAMS: 84IndA 88BalA 90BroA 90SyrA 90TolA
DEBUT: 5/1/1884 at St. Louis; played LF and went 0-for-3 in a 4–2 loss to St. Louis's Tip O'Neill
FINALE: 10/13/1890 at Columbus; played CF and went 0-for-2 in a 6–0 loss to Columbus's Elton Chamberlin

Jack Peltz was a lifelong resident of New Orleans and first commanded attention in that city while playing almost every position for the amateur J. S. Wright club in 1880. Three years later he had worked his way north to independent Indianapolis. Peltz remained on the Hoosier club in 1884 after it joined the AA, serving as its left fielder at a time when LF was still where many managers stationed their best flycatcher. Though he finished with an anemic .219 BA, he led the club in extra-base hits with 33 and topped the AA in games played in LF with 106.

Surplus baggage when the majors reduced to sixteen teams in 1885, the New Orleans native spent the next three seasons in the Southern League with four different teams and briefly served as a player-manager with two of them—Macon in 1886 and Memphis late the following season. Following two seasons with Rochester of the International Association in 1888–89, Peltz was ticketed to return to the majors when the upstate New York club joined the AA prior to the 1890 campaign. Before the season opened, however, Rochester parted with Peltz to help stock the AA's weak sister, the Brooklyn Gladiators. On the surface, he was readily expendable. Peltz hit just .227 in 98 games with Brooklyn and did no better in short stints with both Syracuse and Toledo after the Gladiators folded. But despite logging the lowest OPS (.587) of any AA outfielder in 1890 with a minimum of 400 ABs, he played CF during his tour of duty with each club, suggesting that he was strong defensively. The evidence supports this, as he finished third among AA gardeners in total chances, trailing only noted ball hawks Curt Welch and Harry Lyons.

Peltz returned to the minors in 1891, finishing his pro playing career in the Southern League 3 years later. Throughout the 1890s he umpired periodically in that circuit while continuing to play for semipro teams in New Orleans. Peltz died of consumption at his New Orleans home at 44. (DN)

Pickering, Oliver Daniel / "Ollie" "Pig"

B	T	HGT	WGT	G	AB	H	R	2B
L	R	5'11"	170	155	596	176	95	16

3B	HR	RBI	BB	SO	SB	BA	SA	OBP
8	3	65	49	11	51	.295	.364	351

B. 4/9/1870 Olney, IL **D.** 1/20/1952
TEAMS: 96–97LouN 97CleN 01–02CleAL 03–04PhiAL 07StLAL 08WasAL
DEBUT: 8/11/1896 at Louisville; played CF and went 3-for-5 in a 6–6 tie against Cleveland's Cy Young
FINALE: 10/8/1908 at Washington; played RF and made 1 hit in a 1–0 win over New York's Jack Warhop

Ollie Pickering may be the only player to face Cy Young in an NL uniform in his debut and play behind Walter Johnson in his finale. Despite a pro career spanning over twenty years—nearly half of it spent in the majors—he remains among the more obscure players of his time even though there is ample testimony that he was quite fascinating in his own way and willing to go to almost any lengths to pursue his dream of playing ball for a living. In 1902, after he had at long last earned steady ML employment, Pickering revealed to *TSN* that he "went bankrupt in the spring of 1892 buying postage stamps" so he could write for a baseball job. When no teams answered his pleas, he hopped a freight from his Olney, IL, home to San Antonio, and there, with his last stamp, the reply wrote to John McCloskey in Houston and lived "under a high sidewalk" while awaiting the manager's reply. When it was encouraging he grabbed a "pig train" to Houston. Arriving disheveled and malodorous, he was asked how he had traveled, and he replied, "Pigged it." Pickering admitted that as a result of his years of hopping freights to get from one place to another in his early days in the game it was years "before I could ride in a Pullman without holding on with both hands."

After spending most of 1896 with Lynchburg of the Virginia League and logging a .345 BA, Pickering joined Louisville in August. His bumpkin ways immediately made him a target of veteran Colonels players, led by Jim Rogers, who called him "Rube" and "Hayseed" and worked to undermine his confidence and force him off the team. The brutal hazing resumed in 1897 until Pickering stopped hitting and was released to Cleveland. With the Spiders, he rained hits in the final weeks of the season, finishing at .352 in 46 games. Nevertheless, Pickering went to spring training the following year having to battle for a job and lost out when veteran Jimmy McAleer ended a bitter holdout on the eve of the season.

Pickering subsequently began 1898 on the Giants' roster but was farmed out before he ever played a game for New York. Still undeterred, he dropped down to the Western League and remained in that loop with Cleveland in 1900 after it became the American League. That season, Pickering finished third in the AL in batting, second in total bases and steals and first in runs and hits, assuring him of Cleveland's CF post when the AL went major in 1901. He then alternated good and bad years in his six AL seasons, with a two-year hiatus in 1905–06 when he served with Columbus of the American Association. Pickering later returned to the AA after his final ML season in 1908 and last appeared in pro garb as the player-manager of Redfield in the South Dakota League at age 50.

How good was Pickering? Not bad for a man over 30 before he found regular work in the majors. In his six seasons in the AL, Pickering averaged 4.56 runs created per game, ranking him just below Willie Keeler and a notch ahead of Danny Hoffman among AL outfielders in a minimum of 500 games during that period. Pickering died at his home in Vincennes, IN, at 81. (DN)

Poorman, Thomas Iverson / "Tom"

B	T	HGT	WGT	G	AB	H	R	2B
L	R	5'7"	135	496	2043	498	396	65

3B	HR	RBI	BB	SO	SB	BA	SA	OBP
43	12	172	102	99	165	.244	.335	.285

G	IP	H	GS	CG	BB
15	109.2	147	11	10	30

SO	SH	W	L	PCT	ERA
14	0	3	9	.250	4.02

B. 10/14/1857 Lock Haven, PA **D.** 2/18/1905
TEAMS: 80BufN 80ChiN 84TolA 85–86BosN 87–88PhiA
DEBUT: 5/5/1880 at Cleveland; caught by Jack Rowe

and Bill Crowley and lost 22–3 to Cleveland's Jim McCormick

FINALE: 9/18/1888 at Cincinnati; played RF and went 0-for-3 in a 7–6 win over Cincinnati's Elmer Smith

An outstanding base runner with a streaky bat, Tom Poorman lost five years trying to succeed as a pitcher with little more than a "slow ball" and was "considered the quietest and most remote player" of his time. In the mid-1880s a window of opportunity opened for fleet players like Poorman who ran aggressively and masterfully assessed the risks of advancing a base during a time of barehanded fielders and increasing pitch velocities. Poorman specialized in manufacturing runs after reaching on an error or a passed ball. He continues to hold the ML record for the most career runs scored (396) by a player with fewer than 500 hits.

After starring for semipro Sunbury, PA, at age 19, the 135-pound Poorman came east in 1878 and replaced Frank Hankinson as pitcher on the Staten Island Alaskas. He signed with the Jersey City Browns in July and pitched against other independent teams with John Farrow as his catcher. Although the NL had a rule forbidding midseason exhibitions in 1879, Jersey City became a regular stop for League teams passing through New York. Poorman went 14-21 against them, and when Jim Galvin held out in 1880 and threatened to spend the season on the West Coast, Buffalo signed Poorman as a fallback replacement. His high blooper pitches, which even "deceived the umpire," failed to impress his Buffalo teammates and they reportedly intentionally lost games behind him to get him released after his first start ended in an execrable 22–3 loss. On June 10 Poorman became the first pitcher to give up 2 home runs to the same batter in one inning when Boston's Charley Jones took him deep twice in the eighth frame of a 19–3 loss. Soon after that he was released with a 1-8 record. Chicago signed Poorman on July 22 to fill in for ailing pitcher Fred Goldsmith, but he rode the bench almost the entire time until a September departure.

In 1881 Poorman served as Hugh Daily's backup pitcher on the minor league New York Mets and learned to play the outfield when he was not in the box. The following season he stayed close to his Renovo home and played for unaffiliated Shenandoah, PA. That fall the Northwestern League was created, and Poorman signed as an outfielder with Toledo. He batted .276 in 1883 as Toledo won the pennant. When Charlie Morton moved the club to the enlarged twelve-team American Association in 1884, Poorman played regularly again, making his last pitching start on May 10 in an 11–1 loss to Cincinnati before returning to the outfield.

With Toledo one of the four teams slated to be pared from the AA after the season, when their contracts expired on October 23, Poorman and four other Toledo players made a secret pact to sign with St. Louis once their ten-day waiting period expired. Browns owner Chris Von der Ahe sequestered the five players at a hotel, but only two—Sam Barkley and Curt Welch—ultimately signed with the Browns. Poorman was released from his obligation when Von der Ahe exercised his option not to take aboard certain of the five players, and he signed instead with Bill Watkins's Western League Indianapolis club. When Indianapolis disbanded after 31 games, underachieving Boston NL grabbed Poorman. He debuted for the Hub entry on July 17 and immediately became the finest base runner on the team. Poorman often batted third or cleanup for Boston, the wrong spot given a twenty-first-century evaluation of his batting stats. However, Poorman, whose "reached on errors" total, possibly as high as 40–50 per year, might have seen his OBP figure soar to over .350. In 1886 Poorman introduced "blue goggles" to keep the sun out of his eyes, scored a run in 13 consecutive games, and was leading the team in runs scored on September 2 when his season was cut short by a bad case of the flu.

After Boston acquired Mike Kelly in the 1886–87 off-season, the following April, Poorman was sold to the AA Philadelphia Athletics for $750. A's skipper Frank Bancroft moved him to the lead-off spot, and he had a career year in all departments, tallying a club-leading 140 runs on just 155 hits and a .265 BA. In 1888, however, Poorman slumped badly and was benched in Cincinnati on September 19, mired in a 1-for-33 skid. The next day he showed up at the park drunk, embarrassed the team with his antics, and had to be dragged off the grounds. Banished by the A's, Poorman played two seasons with Milwaukee in the Western Association and was hitting .309 in 1891 with Sioux City of the WA when he was inexplicably cut on June 23. By the following year he was playing for Demarest, a semipro team in Williamsport, PA. Poorman subsequently worked for railroad companies and then helped out in a Cortland, NY, dry goods business before succumbing to consumption in 1905 at his sister's home in Lock Haven. (FV/DN/DB)

Radford, Paul Revere / "Paul" "Shorty"

B	T	HGT	WGT	G	AB	H	R	2B
R	R	5'6"	148	1361	4979	1206	945	176

3B	HR	RBI	BB	SO	SB	BA	SA	OBP
57	13	462	790	373	346	.242	.308	.351

G	IP	H	GS	CG	BB
10	43.1	85	4	3	17

SO	SH	W	L	PCT	ERA
13	0	0	4	.000	8.52

B. 10/14/1861 Roxbury, MA **D.** 2/21/1945
TEAMS: 83BosN 84–85ProN 86KCN 87NYA 88BroA 89CleN 90CleP 91BosA 92–94WasN
DEBUT: 5/1/1883 at New York; played RF and went hitless in a 7–5 loss to New York's Mickey Welch
FINALE: 9/22/1893 at Cleveland; played LF and went 0-for-3 in a 6–5 loss to Cleveland's Mike Sullivan

Flare-hitting Paul Radford was endowed with limited baseball skills and an ineradicable passion for the game. Eight times in eight successive years subsequent to 1884 his ML career seemed over, but on each occasion yet another team or a league transfer kept him afloat and enabled him eventually to set a record by playing regularly for eight different teams in eight seasons.

From a wealthy family, Radford was a mischievous clubhouse presence with a reputation for being nimble with the ladies. He led his teams in circus catches, finding good-luck charms and identifying bad omens. Because of his great range and arm, Radford could serve at almost any position. The 1891 Boston AA team won the pennant with him at SS. Radford also pitched in 10 ML games, although his deliveries had so little command that he was used mostly in mop-up roles. Meanwhile, he kept to his pledge never to play baseball on Sunday. After his first two ML teams, Boston in 1883 and Providence in 1884, won pennants, Radford was seen as a providential mascot. His lone drawback was that it seemed his main goal when he batted was to coax a walk. When Radford retired in 1894 he ranked third all-time in free passes, behind only Cap Anson and Roger Connor, despite having just a .648 OPS.

A resident of Hyde Park, MA, Radford started his own independent club in 1879 along with two brothers. By 1882 the team had grown in stature and Radford, then a pitcher, claimed a 22-6 record. Boston signed him to play RF and bat ninth in 1883. The pet of captain John Morrill, he debuted in the New York NL franchise's opening game in front of 15,000 baseball-starved fans at the Polo Grounds, and General Grant but was hitless and made 2 errors. From then on Radford saw limited duty as a rookie until he started on May 27 with Boston riding a 9-game losing streak. He went 0-for-4 but the team won. Radford started again in both games of a Memorial Day DH and went 0-for-7, but the team won a pair as he made four impressive catches in his home park debut and became a fan favorite on a struggling team. "Sure death on a fly," the *Boston Globe* wrote, "quick as a cat and lithe as an eel." Radford's hitless streak grew to 0-for-25, but he superseded it with his fielding. When Boston won the NL championship, the rookie became a rabbit's foot even though he was not reserved for 1884. Signing with Providence, Radford fit in well with the Grays' bunt-and-run offense. For an entire month, starting on August 7, he batted .132, but Providence won 20 straight games and broke open the 1884 NL race.

After his first two seasons, Radford owned a .200 career BA but had pocketed first-place bonus checks of $100 and $75, respectively. In 1885 his father began adding to his coffers by paying him $5 every time he scored a run. Providence disbanded that year and the NL awarded Radford to a new Kansas City franchise, which lasted only one season. When the league auctioned off KC players, the AA New York Mets picked him up. Radford moved to SS, where he showed surprising range, but the Mets played poorly. Once the Mets disbanded, Radford was purchased by Brooklyn, rebuilding to end the St. Louis dynasty. Radford was soon ensconced in center field, and Brooklyn held first place as late as July 19, 1888. However, when St. Louis pulled ahead, Radford's weak bat was seen as a liability, and Tommy Burns was purchased from Baltimore. Radford was sent home in August while Brooklyn fell 11 games back. After he rejoined the club in September, Brooklyn went 29-9, but it was too late.

Sold to Cleveland for 1889, Radford led off for

most of the year, topping the team in runs and walks. In 1890 he defected to the Cleveland PL entry, but while he hit a career-high .292, his club tanked. On February 10, 1891, Arthur Irwin, player-manager of the star-studded new AA franchise in Boston, recognized Radford for the team player he was and signed him to play SS, freeing Irwin to quit active play. Radford again fielded well, and Boston claimed the last flag awarded in the ten-year history of the AA. He signed again with the Reds for 1892 but on Christmas Day was assigned to the NL for placement after the NL and AA merged. Radford headed reluctantly to lowly Washington, where, after three uneven years, he rounded out his ML career before his 32nd birthday. After three seasons in the minors, Radford went into business in Hyde Park as the "head of a mechanical industry," according to the *Atlanta Constitution*. He died at his Hyde Park home in 1945. (FV/DN)

*Reccius, John / "John"

B	T	HGT	WGT	G	IP	H	GS
?	?	5'6½"	168	14	99	116	10

CG	BB	SO	SH	W	L	PCT	ERA
9	22	31	1	4	6	.400	3.00

G	AB	H	R	2B	3B	HR
92	329	72	56	14	3	1

RBI	BB	SO	SB	BA	SA	OBP
3	30	—	—	.219	.289	.284

B. 10/29/1859 Louisville, KY **D.** 9/1/1930
TEAMS: 82–83LouA
DEBUT: 5/2/1882 at St. Louis; played CF and went 2-for-5 in a 9–7 loss to St. Louis's George McGinnis
FINALE: 7/11/1883 at Louisville; played CF and made 1 hit in a 7–3 loss to Cincinnati's Will White

John Reccius and his younger brother Phil at one time were believed to have been the first set of twins to play in the majors. His older brother Bill was also prominent in Louisville baseball circles, and the three siblings at one juncture were partners in a sporting goods firm that acted as the sole agent for Louisville Bats and was a favorite local hangout for current and former Louisville players. Reccius began pitching with the amateur Eclipse, a forerunner of the 1882 AA entry in 1878 and achieved his career high point on May 15, 1881, when he no-hit the Cincinnati Gymnasium Club 11–0. The following year he was expected to be the fledgling AA club's top hurler and occupy CF on days when he was not in the box, but he neither pitched nor hit up to AA standards. When Reccius continued to struggle the following year, he was released to Harrisburg of the Interstate Association and quit pro ball in 1886 to return home to the family sporting goods business.

Reccius remained an active part of the Louisville baseball scene until the end of the nineteenth century and meanwhile became an illustrious doll maker. He operated a combination doll store and doll "hospital" until not long before his death in Louisville from a stroke at 70. (DN)

Riley, William James / "Billy" "Pigtail Billy"

B	T	HGT	WGT	G	AB	H	R	2B
R	R	5'10"	160	57	194	28	18	3

3B	HR	RBI	BB	SO	SB	BA	SA	OBP
0	0	10	3	27	0	.144	.160	.157

B. ?/?/1855 Cincinnati, OH **D.** 11/9/1887
TEAMS: 75WesNA 79CleN
DEBUT: 5/4/1875 at Keokuk; played RF and made 1 hit in a 15–1 loss to Chicago's George Zettlein
FINALE: 9/30/1879 at Cleveland; played LF and went 1-for-5 in a 9–5 win over Cincinnati's Will White

Billy Riley's .317 career OPS is the lowest in ML history among outfielders with a minimum of 175 ABs. It is unclear how the Cincinnati native landed in Keokuk, IA, in 1875 and secured the Westerns' RF post despite fielding just .667. Except for 1877, when he was with Indianapolis of the League Alliance for part of the season, Riley's next few years are sketchy until he occupied LF for Cleveland in its inaugural game in the NL in 1879 and was hitting .212 at the end of May but batted only .101 in his remaining 109 ABs. Riley missed a number of games in midsummer, perhaps due to an injury, before returning to the lineup in September. He later umpired a handful of games in the AA prior to his death in Cincinnati at age 32 or thereabouts from a ruptured appendix. Riley's nickname of "Pigtail Billy" was pinned on him by fellow players who thought he looked part Chinese. (DN)

Roseman, James John / "Chief" "Jim"

B	T	HGT	WGT	G	AB	H	R	2B
R	R	5'7"	167	681	2761	726	443	120

3B	HR	RBI	BB	SO	SB	BA	SA	OBP
49	17	222	133	41	19	.263	.360	.312

G	IP	H	GS	CG	BB
4	16	20	1	0	7

SO	SH	W	L	PCT	ERA
1	0	0	1	.000	7.88

G	W	L	PCT	PENNANTS
15	7	8	.467	0

B. 7/4/1856 New York, NY **D.** 7/4/1938
TEAMS: 82TroN 83–86NYA 87PhiA 87NYA 87BroA (P/M)90StLA 90LouA
DEBUT: 5/1/1882 at Troy; played RF and went 0-for-4 in a 9–3 loss to Providence's John Ward
FINALE: 8/25/1890 at St. Louis; played 1B and went 0-for-4 in a 13–2 loss to St. Louis's Tom Ramsey

James Roseman was nicknamed "Chief" for the blood-curdling war whoops he unleashed in the heat of battle while a member of the New York Mets. When teammates began imitating him, the Mets for a time became more commonly known in the New York press as the "Indians." Roseman graduated from the semipro ranks in 1877 to the League Alliance, where he divided the season among three different teams. He remained in the minors through 1881, when he spent most of his time with the Eastern Championship Association New York Mets.

In his ML debut with Troy in 1882, Roseman hit a weak .236 and compiled just 41 runs in 82 games. After Troy disbanded he returned to the Mets, now a member of the AA. Despite hitting just .251 in 1883 with little power, Roseman was installed as the Mets' cleanup hitter the following season by manager Jim Mutrie. Mutrie's seemingly absurd move paid huge dividends when Roseman had his best overall ML season, logging career highs in runs, hits, and total bases, and the Mets won the AA flag.

It would be Roseman's lone full season on a championship club. In 1885, despite another good year from him, the Mets slipped to seventh and finished in the same spot the following season as he hit a meager .227 and notched just 6 stolen bases, making him arguably the slowest runner on a notoriously slow team. The rumor in the Mets' clubhouse was that Roseman and Dave Orr were both playing for their releases so they could join Brooklyn, which had tried to snatch them in December 1885 when it looked as though the AA might expel the Mets. If this was the case, Roseman was thwarted when the Mets sold him to Philadelphia AA for $750 in March 1887. Roseman opened that season in RF for the A's but was suspended for a month in late April and fined $100 for going on a bender. In June, after he went 0-for-3 in a loss to last-place Cleveland, the exasperated A's released him. Two days later, on June 16, 1887, Roseman was back with the Mets playing CF, a sign of the New Yorker's desperation as he had little range by then and a weak arm. Roseman lasted just 60 games with the Mets before manager Opie Caylor booted him for leaving the team shorthanded one afternoon after wiring that he couldn't play because his bartender had been arrested and he had to appear in court as a character witness.

Subsequently, Roseman finally got his wish to play for Brooklyn, albeit for just 1 game. That appearance seemed as if it would be his ML finale, especially after he worked over ex-ML outfielder Tom York, his manager the following season with Albany of the International Association, after York suspended him and teammate Pat Gillespie for assaulting a female patron one evening at their bar of choice. But after being exiled from pro ball for a year and a half, Roseman got a reprieve when PL raiders decimated ML rosters in the winter of 1889–90, forcing teams to scramble for replacements. Better yet, for the first time since 1884, Roseman found himself on a winner when the St. Louis Browns, second in the AA in 1889, hired him.

In the spring of 1890 player-manager Tommy McCarthy rashly bought Roseman's boast that his best spot was CF. When McCarthy was fired as manager shortly after the season started, team owner Chris Von der Ahe compounded the foolishness by letting Roseman persuade him that he was the ideal candidate to replace McCarthy. Jack Stivetts later revealed that after every game under Roseman's command the Browns attended "a glass convention" (drinking festival) and recalled that the Chief's arm muscles "stood out like ripcords" from lifting beer steins.

Roseman quickly exhausted Von der Ahe's patience as a manager and by the middle of August also was finished in St. Louis as a player despite leading the Browns at the time in batting and the majors in hit by pitches with 29. (Curt Welch later overtook him, finishing with 34) He was granted a brief stay of execution when Louisville manager Jack Chapman needed a first baseman so that Harry Taylor could fill in for ailing SS Phil Tomney.

In 1891 Roseman snubbed an offer to play in the New England League in order to join several former teammates in reviving the old Mets as a semipro nine. Among the opponents the Mets scheduled were several "colored" teams, including the Cuban Giants. After noting how well these games drew in the New York area, Roseman toyed with the notion of forming a colored team of his own but soon abandoned the plan to devote himself to his saloon in Brooklyn. When the Raines Bill forced him to close the establishment in 1896, he announced that he was down to 200 pounds, his lowest weight in years, and primed to make a comeback. This plan also came to naught. Roseman eventually left the saloon business to work as a fireman and then for the New York City Bureau of Sewers until retiring in 1934. He died in Brooklyn four years later at 82. The cause of death, however improbable it may seem given his advanced years, was listed as paresis. (DN/DB)

***Rowe, David Elwood / "Dave"**

B	T	HGT	WGT	G	AB	H	R	2B
R	R	5'9"	180	347	1458	383	223	77

3B	HR	RBI	BB	SO	SB	BA	SA	OBP
32	8	90	42	63	4	.263	.376	.284

G	IP	H	GS	CG	BB
4	23	54	3	2	11

SO	SH	W	L	PCT	ERA
3	0	1	2	.333	9.78

G	W	L	PCT	PENNANTS
176	44	127	.257	0

B. 10/9/1854 Harrisburg, PA **D.** 12/9/1930
TEAMS: 77ChiN 82CleN 83BalA 84StLU 85StLN (P/M)86KCN (P/M)88KCA
DEBUT: 5/30/1877 at Chicago; played RF and went 2-for-3 in a 5–1 loss to Cincinnati's Bobby Mathews
FINALE: 6/17/1888 at Kansas City; played CF and went 0-for-4 in a 7–6 loss to Louisville's Scott Stratton

Dave Rowe was the older brother of MLer Jack Rowe. He played and managed professionally for some fifteen years, including all or parts of seven seasons in the majors, and seems to have gotten by on smoke and mirrors—for the ML portion of his career anyway.

After debuting in RF with Chicago in 1877, Rowe pitched the following day and lost 3–1 to Louisville's Jim Devlin. His inaugural ML game in the box was his only one that approached respectability. When Rowe hurled his first ML game at the fifty-foot distance five years later for Cleveland on July 24, 1882, Chicago slaughtered him 35–4. In all, the pitching portion of Rowe's ML career is best left unexhumed. Among all ML hurlers who appeared in 25 innings or less, he heads the list in runs allowed with 51, ten more than the second-place Sid Schacht.

With the exception of his sojourn with Chicago in 1877, Rowe was a teammate of his brother's everywhere he played early in his career. The two were with semipro Jacksonville, IL, in 1876, Peoria in 1878, and Rockford in 1879 until Jack joined Buffalo and remained in the majors for the next decade. His older sibling meanwhile languished in independent ball until Cleveland beckoned in 1882 after he had failed a trial that spring with the fledgling Cincinnati AA entry. Unreserved for 1883, the elder Rowe began the season back in the minors and finished it with last-place Baltimore of the AA at SS, going 4-for-5 in the season finale against Columbus to lift his BA to .313. Jumping to the UA St. Louis Maroons in 1884, he again showed his versatility, finishing the season at SS. Blacklisted for 1885 along with many other UA jumpers, Rowe did not have the ban on him lifted until late in the season. His ML career seemed at an end when he hit just .161 with the Maroons.

But Rowe had connections in Kansas City, where he had played in 1880, and led efforts to bring a team from that city into the NL in 1886. Rewarded with the dual role of manager and center fielder, he showed his gratitude by hitting .243, fielding .851, and piloting KC to a .248 winning percentage. His second-place finish as player-manager of Western League Lincoln in 1887 seduced another KC group into enlisting him to lead the expansion AA entry from that city in 1888. Slowed by malaria in the spring of that season, Rowe nonetheless opened the campaign exactly as he had with the 1886 Kansas City NL entry, managing and playing CF. Although he wisely benched himself after hitting .161 in 32 games, it could not save his job. Fired when KC won only 14 of its first 50 decisions, he continued to serve as a player-manager for Midwestern minor league teams until the mid-1890s and even was named president of the Western Association for a time while operating the Denver club in that circuit.

While Rowe was of only marginal ML caliber as a player, he was a successful enough manager in the minors to argue that his dismal .257 career winning percentage as a ML pilot was largely the result of being at the controls of poor teams. Rowe died in 1930 in Glendale, CA. (DN/DB)

Seery, John Emmett / "Em" "Emmett"

B	T	HGT	WGT	G	AB	H	R	2B
L	R	5'7"	145	916	3547	893	695	152

3B	HR	RBI	BB	SO	SB	BA	SA	OBP
68	27	300	471	426	240	.252	.356	.345

G	IP	H	GS	CG	BB
2	7	8	0	0	3

SO	SH	W	L	PCT	ERA
2	0	0	0	—	7.71

B. 2/13/1861 Princeville, IL **D.** 8/7/1930
TEAMS: 84BalU 84KCU 85–86StLN 87–89IndN 90BroP 91CinA 92LouN
DEBUT: 4/17/1884 at Baltimore; played LF and went 0-for-4 in a 7–3 win over Washington's Milo Lockwood
FINALE: 6/10/1892 at Washington; played RF and went 1-for-4 in a 7–3 win over Washington's Frank Killen

Em Seery entered top competition in 1884 with Baltimore UA after playing with a string of amateur and semipro teams as far back as 1877, when he was a member of the Natick, MA, club. Spending his rookie season in LF, his position for most of his career, Seery batted .311 and led his team in nearly every major offensive category. On the final day of the campaign, after Baltimore had released its entire club rather than provide train fare to their homes from Cincinnati, he played a single game with the Kansas City UA entry, and when the entire rebel loop folded that winter he moved with the KC club to the newly formed Western League. By June 1885 the WL had also collapsed and Seery signed with the St. Louis Maroons, making his NL debut on June 29. Over the rest of the season he batted a meager .162, holding his job only through capable fielding, good baserunning and, most important, the fact that the Maroons were extremely weak in the outfield. Seery then improved dramatically in 1886, raising his average more than 70 points to a still modest .238 but also ranking among the NL leaders in walks.

Seery's years in St. Louis were eventful if not always pleasant. In a well-publicized incident, he was sucker punched by hard-drinking, short-tempered teammate Charlie Sweeney, and a few days before July 4, 1886, he was the only Maroon in the clubhouse when a premature explosion of some stored fireworks hurled him across the room. The durable Seery played that day in spite of a sprained wrist. In the spring of 1887 the Maroons franchise was transferred to Indianapolis. Modifications to the playing rules in 1887 made walks easier to obtain, advantageous for a player of Seery's skills, while the scoring rules were amended to count walks as hits. Seery finished fourth in the NL in walks, and his average, when calculated according to the revised rule, leaped to .325. By the traditional rule, he hit only .224 but made up for his low mark in part by shining as a base thief. In 1887 he was tenth in the NL in steals, and in 1888 he was just nipped by Dummy Hoy for the NL lead in that category. His last season in Indianapolis, 1889, was also his finest, when he hit .314, nearly 30 points better than he batted in any other ML season except his rookie year in the weak UA.

In five NL seasons to date, Seery had only once played on a team that finished as high as sixth place. His chance to escape the doldrums came in 1890 when the PL formed and four Hoosiers, including the team's entire outfield, were signed by John M. Ward's Brooklyn club. Seery's new team finished third, but snaring the entire Indianapolis outfield proved to Ward's detriment. Light hitting had been a weak point of the Indianapolis trio, and while Seery had made up for his lack of punch in other ways, during his year in Brooklyn he suffered from malaria, missing 30 games and hampering his effectiveness when he did play. While his statistics to the casual observer appear similar to those he had registered prior to 1889, the PL was a high-octane league, averaging 1.3 more runs per game than the NL, and Seery's 5.86 runs created per game put him forty-fourth among the fifty-seven players with enough at-bats to qualify for the list.

When the PL disbanded, Seery was expected to return to St. Louis and play for the Browns. But once the AA put a team in Cincinnati shortly before the 1891 season, St. Louis president Chris Von der Ahe, who provided much of the financing for the new entry, met Seery in the Queen City on March 20 and signed him to a Cincinnati contract, probably as the Browns' contribution to the new club. Back in the second division but playing RF regularly for the first time in his ML career, Seery returned to his 1889 form offensively. However, when Cincinnati folded in August he was surprisingly left without a berth and sat out the rest of the season. He began 1892 as Louisville's right fielder but failed to hit and was released in June. Seery had one more shot at the ML, failing in a tryout with Cincinnati before the 1893 season. He subsequently played in the minors but was out of the game before the 1895 campaign was completed.

A chess player, musician, and sometimes actor in an amateur light opera company in Indianapolis during the winter months, Seery seems to have been a man of better education than most players. After leaving baseball he owned a pineapple plantation in Florida, where his neighbor and close companion for a time was Ed Andrews, his teammate on three different teams between 1889 and 1891. Seery died in Saranac Lake, NY, the famous tuberculosis sanitarium, in 1930. (DB/DN)

Selbach, Albert Karl / "Kip"

B	T	HGT	WGT	G	AB	H	R	2B
R	R	5'7"	190	892	3427	1070	689	170

3B	HR	RBI	BB	SO	SB	BA	SA	OBP
102	33	500	484	76	246	.312	.451	.402

B. 3/24/1872 Columbus, OH **D.** 2/17/1956

TEAMS: 94–98WasN 99CinN 00–01NYN 02BalAL 03–04WasAL 04–06BosAL

DEBUT: 4/19/1894 at Washington; played RF and went 1-for-2 in a 4–2 win over Philadelphia's Gus Weyhing

FINALE: 6/29/1906 at New York; pinch hit for pitcher Bill Dinneen in the ninth inning and walked in an 8–4 loss to New York's Jack Chesbro

Kip Selbach got his nickname as a youngster in Columbus because he liked to pretend he was a policeman and the officer on the local beat was named Kip. An excellent bowler and all-around athlete, he began his career as a catcher and did not move to the outfield until he joined independent Findlay, OH, in 1893 before finishing the season in the Southern League. Owing to his late start as a gardener, he was still weak on balls hit over his head when he arrived in Washington and was made to switch places with right fielder Bill Hassamaer, who was nearly as inept. The rookie pair kept center fielder Charlie Abbey busy chasing balls they misjudged and contributed heavily to Washington's eleventh-place finish.

Selbach also brought with him an annoying ritual that was rarely seen before the postexpansion era. Between pitches, for countless seconds he would knock the dirt off his spikes, pull up his trousers, tug down his cap and run his hands up and down his bat before getting back in the batter's box.

Still, he was having a fine rookie year until a leg injury sidelined him after just 97 games. Selbach rehabbed over the winter running YMCA gym classes in Columbus and returned to produce an even better sophomore campaign, leading the NL in triples. The following spring he coached The Ohio State University's baseball team before going to camp with Washington and proceeded to lead the club in runs, RBI, walks, and steals. That December, Selbach severely burned his left hand trying to save his house from a devastating fire over the holidays but rebounded to again top Washington in several batting departments. After he had another solid year in 1897, Cincinnati reportedly offered Eddie Burke, Claude Ritchey, Dusty Miller, Dummy Hoy, and Red Ehret for him but was rebuffed. But toward the end of the 1898 season Selbach tore a tendon in his ankle, causing his batting to sag in the late going, and when Cincinnati proposed another offer on Christmas day—a straight $5,000 in cash—Washington grabbed it. Asked after the deal what he thought of the Cincinnati team, Selbach made the welcome mat the Queen City was preparing for him shrivel to the size of a pea when he told the *Cincinnati Tribune*, "There's the best team of ball players in the circuit, but some of the boys have a yellow streak. They ought to be dropped and let aggressive be the watchword this year."

The following July, *TSN* reported that Selbach was unhappy in Cincinnati where the papers, not surprisingly, were a tad harsh on him. Even though he improved after manager Buck Ewing finally figured out he was not a center fielder and returned him to his normal station in left, in March 1900 the Reds sold both him and recalcitrant pitcher Pink

Hawley to the New York Giants for an undisclosed sum but probably not as much as the Reds had paid for Selbach alone fifteen months earlier. In his next four seasons Selbach had the unpleasant distinction of playing on cellar dwellers in three different ML cities before landing with Boston AL on July 4, 1904 (Selbach had a way of getting himself dealt on holidays), after a trade with Washington. He helped secure Boston's second straight AL pennant with a dazzling catch of Kid Elberfeld's sinking line drive in the flag-clinching game but was denied a World Series appearance when the Giants snubbed a postseason invitation. Selbach dropped below .250 the following year and then sank to .211 in 1906, when he finished his thirteen-year ML career on yet another basement finisher, Boston's first as a member of the AL, then hung on in the minors until 1910.

Selbach, who had been captain of the All America bowling team in 1902 and won the American Bowling Congress doubles tournament in Indianapolis the next fall, ran a bowling alley in Columbus until 1943, thirteen years before his death following a lengthy illness. (DN)

Sensenderfer, John Phillips Jenkins / "Count" "Sensy"

B	T	HGT	WGT	G	AB	H	R	2B
?	?	5'9"	170	51	234	79	55	6

3B	HR	RBI	BB	SO	SB	BA	SA	OBP
2	0	34	0	3	5	.299	.342	.299

B. 12/28/1847 Philadelphia, PA **D.** 5/3/1903
TEAMS: 71–74AthNA
DEBUT: 5/20/1871 at Boston; played CF and went 1-for-5 in an 11–8 loss to Boston's Al Spalding
FINALE: 10/21/1874 at Philadelphia; played RF and went 1-for-4 in an 11–3 loss to the Philadelphia Pearls' Candy Cummings

Nicknamed "Count" for being deft with both women and a piano keyboard, John Sensenderfer played with Philadelphia junior clubs in the early 1860s before joining the Olympics in 1867 and remained with them until August 9, 1867, when he played his first game in CF with the Athletics. By the early 1870s, however, the game was more of a sideline for him. In his last three ML seasons he played infrequently while pursuing his political ambitions but continued to make an appearance every now and then with local teams throughout the 1870s. After teammate West Fisler also retired from the game, Sensenderfer and he opened a men's clothing store next to Al Reach's sporting goods house. The partnership dissolved when Sensenderfer became prominent enough in Democratic circles to focus on politicking. He was later a city commissioner for a number of years before his death in Philadelphia from a ruptured stomach. (DN)

***Shaffer, George W.** (b. Shafer) **/ "Orator"**

B	T	HGT	WGT	G	AB	H	R	2B
L	R	5'9"	165	871	3552	1000	601	162

3B	HR	RBI	BB	SO	SB	BA	SA	OBP
52	10	308	227	218	32	.282	.367	.326

B. 10/?/1851 Philadelphia, PA **D.** 1/21/1922
TEAMS: 74HarNA 74MutNA 75PhiNA 77LouN 78IndN 79ChiN 80–82CleN 83BufN 84StLU 85StLN 85–86PhiA 90PhiA
DEBUT: 5/23/1874 at Philadelphia; played RF and went hitless in a 12–4 loss to the Athletics' Dick McBride
FINALE: 9/16/1890 at Philadelphia; played RF and went 0-for-3 in a 5–1 loss to Baltimore's Les German

Unlike Jim O'Rourke, who was nicknamed "Orator" for his eloquence, George Shaffer received the handle because he was garrulous almost to the point of being insufferable. He rattled on even when there was no one around to listen and was notorious long before Pete Browning arrived for referring to himself in the third person. Shaffer and his younger brother, ML second baseman Taylor Shaffer, were born "Shafer." Since that was unknown until their death certificates were recently found, we are carrying them under the surname they used while playing. The elder Shaffer was with the amateur Philadelphia Eurekas prior to his ML debut. After spending part of 1875 with the Philadelphia Pearls, he remained with that club in 1876 when it functioned as an independent team. Invited to join Louisville the following year, he led the NL in both outfield assists and errors and gained acclaim for nailing runners at 1B on apparent singles to RF, with many of his miscues coming on errant throws. When Louisville folded, Shaffer went to Indianapolis and in 1878 led the new NL entry in almost every major batting department. In hot demand after Indianapolis also disbanded, he signed with Chicago for 1879 and again led the NL in outfield assists but left the Second City after getting into a brawl with Ned Williamson that shamed him when he took a savage beating.

Shaffer was never again the same player. Although he continued to be a strong fielder, his hitting increasingly became a liability. Initially, the decline was attributed to his patent inability to hit left-handed pitching, but by 1886 there were also questions about his eyesight. Throughout, Shaffer tried to blame rheumatism, claiming it "tied up" his shoulder muscles. However, in 1884 facing an assortment of marginal pitchers in the UA, he hit a career-high .360 for the champion St. Louis Maroons, with the added edge of not having to bat against his own team's pitchers, which were the best in the league. After slipping below .200 the following year and starting poorly in 1886, Shaffer was cut by Philadelphia AA. Although he talked of going into the saloon business, eventually he stooped to playing in the minors. Against weaker pitching his hitting improved to the point that he was among the leading hitters in the Western League in 1887 prior to his season-ending suspension in September for slugging umpire Ben Young.

Shaffer remained in the high minors until 1890, when the A's rehired him as a replacement for Harry Stovey, who had been lost to PL raiders. He hit a solid .282—but, again, against thinned pitching staffs—before quitting in September when the A's could no longer meet their payroll. Shaffer, his brother and outfielder Blondie Purcell all played their final ML innings with the 1890 A's. By the mid-1890s the threesome was haunting racetracks along the Eastern seaboard, writing sheets for bookmakers and wagering on horseflesh for a living. Not long afterward all of them disappeared, and Purcell remains missing to this day. (DN)

Sheckard, Samuel James Tilden / "Jimmy"

B	T	HGT	WGT	G	AB	H	R	2B
L	R	5'9"	175	350	1266	367	241	57

3B	HR	RBI	BB	SO	SB	BA	SA	OBP
31	11	192	141	—	120	.290	.381	.378

B. 11/23/1878 Upper Chanceford, PA
D. 1/15/1947 Lancaster, PA
TEAMS: 97–98BroN 99BalN 00–01BroN 02BalAL 02–05BroN 06–12ChiN 13StLN 13CinN
DEBUT: 9/14/1897 at Brooklyn; played SS and went 1-for-4 in a 7–5 win over New York's Cy Seymour
FINALE: 9/28/1913 at Cincinnati; pinch hit unsuccessfully for pitcher Jack Rowan in the seventh inning of a 5–3 loss to Brooklyn's Eddie Stack

Jimmy Sheckard owed his birth name to his father's admiration for New York governor Samuel Tilden, the loser of the controversial 1876 presidential election. After moving to Pennsylvania's Lancaster County, where he learned the game, he made his pro debut in 1896 at age 17 as a pitcher-utilityman with a whirlwind tour of four minor league clubs. In 1897 Sheckard joined Brockton of the New England League as a pitcher-infielder. After he led the loop with a .377 BA and went 3-2 on the hill, he came to Brooklyn and finished the year at SS, replacing veteran Germany Smith, but a .753 FA relegated him to LF the following spring. Sheckard started the 1898 campaign 17-for-34 and was leading the NL with a .500 BA in early May but finished at .277 and scored just 51 runs in 105 games.

His lackluster performance in his first full ML season led Brooklyn's new manager, Ned Hanlon, to ship him to Baltimore when syndicate ownership brought the two clubs under the same umbrella in 1899. Under John McGraw, who took over the Orioles reins from Hanlon, Sheckard led the loop in steals with 77. The performance sparked Hanlon to bring him back to Brooklyn in 1900, but even though he hit .300 he was unable to secure a regular outfield berth, usually playing only when Hanlon used Joe Kelley at 1B. That winter, Sheckard studied dentistry at the Baltimore Medical College and played handball on the school team, confident that he would do full-time duty with Brooklyn the following season when he learned that left fielder Fielder Jones had jumped to Chicago of the rebel AL. (DN)

Shoch, George Quintus / "George"

B	T	HGT	WGT	G	AB	H	R	2B
R	R	5'6"	158	707	2540	671	414	89

3B	HR	RBI	BB	SO	SB	BA	SA	OBP
28	10	323	298	115	138	.264	.333	.354

G	IP	H	GS	CG	BB
1	3	2	0	0	1

SO	SH	W	L	PCT	ERA
0	0	0	0	—	0.00

B. 1/6/1859 Philadelphia, PA **D.** 9/30/1937
TEAMS: 86–89WasN 91MilA 92BalN 93–97BroN
DEBUT: 9/10/1886 at Washington; played RF and went 1-for-3 in a 4–1 loss to Philadelphia's Charlie Ferguson
FINALE: 10/2/1897 at Brooklyn; played 2B and went 1-for-3 runs in a 15–6 win over Boston's Ted Lewis

George Shoch was a shrewd one. He schemed so that his name, for effect, was spelled "Shock" in box scores until writers caught on to his trick. Shoch also shaved four years off his birth date and beefed up his height and weight. Probably no one had any idea that he was really 38 and not 34 when he played his last ML game. He undoubtedly did not want it broadcast either that he was the first position player in history other than a catcher to play ten ML seasons without ever being a full-time regular.

Shoch's best all-around season was 1891, when he posted an .844 OPS after returning to the show late in the summer with the Milwaukee AA replacement team following a year and a half in the minors. His most active campaign came with Brooklyn in 1893, when he played 94 games and notched 327 ABs. His most regrettable season was 1892, when he was Baltimore's SS until he broke his right arm in a July practice session stepping on a ball and falling hard. His most improbable season was his 1897 finale, which saw him finish the year with Brooklyn at 2B and then be traded in November to St. Louis, which sold him to Milwaukee of the Western League not only without his consent but also, it appears, without going through the required waiver process.

Given no choice, Shoch reported to Milwaukee and served at 3B in 1898 and SS in 1899 before succeeding Dick Cooley as player-manager of the Philadelphia Athletics of the Atlantic League in 1900. Since he was only "34" when he left the majors in 1897, he completed his twenty-one-year pro career in the minors in 1905, when he was really 47 years old. Shoch died at 78 in Philadelphia, where he was born and raised and never, to his disappointment, got to play with any of the local four ML teams extant during his lengthy career. (DN)

Simmons, Joseph S. (b. Chabriel) **/ "Joe"**

B	T	HGT	WGT	G	AB	H	R	2B
?	?	5'9"	166	58	272	60	45	12

3B	HR	RBI	BB	SO	SB	BA	SA	OBP
2	0	30	2	4	6	.221	.279	.226

G	W	L	PCT	PENNANTS
31	3	28	.097	0

B. 6/13/1845 New York, NY **D.** 7/24/1901
TEAMS: 71ChiNA 72CleNA 75KekNA (P/M)75WesNA (M)84WilU
DEBUT: 5/8/1871 at Chicago; played RF and went 1-for-3 in a 14–12 win over Cleveland's Al Pratt
FINALE: 6/14/1875 at Keokuk; played CF and went hitless in a 1–0 loss to New York's Bobby Mathews

Joe Simmons was a ML player, manager, and umpire but was conspicuously unsuccessful at each. His only full season of ML activity was his first when he played 27 games with Chicago and hit .217. In 1875 Simmons finished below .200 and had piloted Keokuk to a 1-12 record when the team folded after his final ML game. Nine years later, now solely a bench manager, he ushered Wilmington into the UA as a late-season replacement and guided the Quicksteps to a 2-18 mark before they also folded.

In 1882 Simmons signed in early July to umpire in the newly formed American Association. Some six weeks later, on August 25, he would have been drawn and quartered by an enraged Cincinnati crowd "had not the Cincinnati managers pulled him away under the escort of a posse of police" after he helped Philadelphia to a key 2–1 win by signaling a game-ending double play a on bases-loaded, one-out grounder that he said forced Cincinnati outfielder Joe Sommer at 2B even though the throw seemed to pull Cub Stricker off the bag. He also ruled Hick Carpenter out at 1B after Juice Latham appeared to block Carpenter's path to the base and then failed to touch it when Carpenter bowled him over. The following day Simmons bravely returned to Cincinnati's grounds and umpired without incident when Cincinnati won.

Subsequent to 1884 Simmons managed for a number of years in the minors before disappearing. His date and place of death in Jersey City were not found until recently. (DN)

Simon, Henry Joseph / "Hank"

B	T	HGT	WGT	G	AB	H	R	2B
R	R	5'6"	155	130	539	144	100	22

3B	HR	RBI	BB	SO	SB	BA	SA	OBP
14	2	61	51	—	35	.267	.371	.333

B. 8/25/1862 Hawkinsville, NY **D.** 1/1/1925
TEAMS: 87CleA 90BroA 90SyrA
DEBUT: 10/7/1887 at St. Louis; played LF and went 1-for-3 in a 12–2 loss to St. Louis's Bob Caruthers
FINALE: 10/12/1890 at Pittsburgh; went 4-for-4 and scored 3 runs in a 12–5 win over. Philadelphia's John Sterling

Hank Simon made his pro debut with Utica of the New York State League in 1885 and finished with Albany of the same loop in 1904. He was probably the best minor league player in the nineteenth century who never played for a team south of Albany, NY, or west of Rochester, NY, except for 1890 and 3 AA games at the close of the 1887 season that were all played in St. Louis. Were it not for the aberrant 1890 campaign he would also probably be the best minor league player in the nineteenth century who never played at least one full season in the majors. Simon's 4-hit coda tied the still extant record, first set by Ed Rowen in 1884, for the most hits by a player in his final ML game. He worked as a cigar maker in Utica after leaving the pro amphitheater and died in Albany of a heart attack in 1925 while changing trains there so that he could visit his sister in Connecticut. (DN)

Slagle, James Franklin / "Jimmy" "Rabbit" "Shorty" "The Human Mosquito"

B	T	HGT	WGT	G	AB	H	R	2B
L	R	5'7"	144	288	1173	328	207	31

3B	HR	RBI	BB	SO	SB	BA	SA	OBP
17	0	86	115	—	56	.280	.335	.348

B. 7/11/1873 Worthville, PA **D.** 5/10/1956
TEAMS: 99WasN 00–01PhiN 01BosN 02–08ChiN
DEBUT: 4/17/1899 at Philadelphia; pinch hit unsuccessfully for pitcher Kirtley Baker in the ninth inning of an 11–4 loss to Philadelphia's Wiley Piatt
FINALE: 10/3/1908 at Cincinnati; replaced Del Howard in CF and went 0-for-1 in a 16–2 win over Cincinnati's Billy Campbell and Marty O'Toole
CAREER HIGHLIGHT: In the 1907 World Series stole 6 bases against Detroit, a record that stood until Lou Brock broke it in 1967

Jimmy Slagle's game relied on speed and snagging balls that few other outfielders could reach. His outstanding range hurt him in fielding ratings in an era when scorekeepers were unforgiving of balls a fielder touched but failed to secure. As a result, among outfielders active during his ten-year sojourn (1899–1908) he ranked third in career errors. After spending two seasons in Pennsylvania independent leagues, Slagle served most of 1895 in the Western Association and then moved to Houston of the Texas League in 1896. That September, Baltimore manager Ned Hanlon wired him an advance and travel money after the TL season ended but lost him to Boston when Frank Selee offered him more plus the assurance that he would be with the Beaneaters in 1897. In the fall of 1896 Slagle played LF for Boston in several exhibition games, but the following spring Selee reneged on his promise and loaned his acquisition to Grand Rapids of the Western League. In midseason Grand Rapids manager Bob Leadley bought Slagle outright from Boston for $425, but Grand Rapids went bankrupt before the check could be cashed, and Boston owner Arthur Soden further muddied matters by claiming that Selee had not been authorized to sell Slagle and Boston wanted him back forthwith. Meanwhile, St. Paul manager Charlie Comiskey paid Slagle the $325 Grand Rapids owed him in back salary and cut Boston a new check for $425. Eventually Western League president Ban Johnson intervened; Comiskey got his money back and Slagle went to Kansas City, where he led the WL with a .378 BA in 1898 and was acquired by Washington NL.

Upon arriving in the majors two years later than he had been promised, Slagle got malaria in the spring of 1899 but recovered in time to take the Senators' CF job away from veteran Jake Gettman. In his rookie season he set a new ML record for outfield putouts with 407 but saw his BA drop as the season progressed when catchers caught on to his propensity to bunt and began playing up close behind the plate for him. After Washington was among the four teams dropped from the NL prior to the 1900 campaign, the NL took ownership of Slagle and sold him to the Phillies. Having no chance to wrest the Phils' CF post away from Roy Thomas, one of the NL's many 1899 rookie sensations, Slagle switched to LF and played every inning of every game in 1900. But when he got off to a .202 start the following season, the Phils released him, and before September was out Boston NL had also cut him. Viewed as a light hitter of little use once his bunting game was taken away from him, Slagle seemed headed for the minors again until the manager who had once betrayed him, Frank Selee, claimed him for the Cubs, the team Selee had just signed to manage for 1902.

All was forgiven Selee when Slagle was awarded a regular spot in his first season as a Cub and remained a fixture in either LF or CF through the 1908 season. Handicapped his entire career by a lack of power, he finished with a .268 BA but just a .317 SA. Slagle was a regular cast member on the Cubs' 1906–08 NL dynasty but participated only in the 1907 World Series. In both of the club's other postseason appearances, manager Frank Chance replaced him in CF with Solly Hofman, a stronger hitter. Axed by the Cubs after the 1908 Fall Classic, Slagle spent two full seasons with Jack Dunn's Baltimore Eastern League club and subsequently owned a laundry in Chicago. He retired in 1946 and died at his Chicago home ten years later. (DN)

Slattery, Michael J. / "Mike" Kangaroo"

B	T	HGT	WGT	G	AB	H	R	2B
L	L	6'2"	210	374	1481	372	229	44

3B	HR	RBI	BB	SO	SB	BA	SA	OBP
21	8	135	62	71	53	.251	.325	.284

B. 11/26/1866 Boston, MA **D.** 10/16/1904
TEAMS: 84BosU 88–89NYN 90NYP 91CinN 91WasA
DEBUT: 4/17/1884 at Philadelphia; played CF and went 1-for-5 in a 14–2 win over Philadelphia's Sam Weaver
FINALE: 7/23/1891 at Washington; played LF and went hitless in a 6–1 loss to Boston's Charlie Buffinton

Mike Slattery is the youngest regular position player in ML history if his birth date is accurate, and there is reason to believe it is not. The April 30, 1889, *TSN* said he was 24; if true, that would mean he was born in 1864. In 1892 the same paper gave his birth date as October 28, 1865. Slattery was nicknamed "Kangaroo" when he won the amateur high jumping championship of Massachusetts as a youth and was also a competitive sprinter early in his baseball career. One of the fastest men in the game, paradoxically he was reported as being big, awkward, and a poor fielder. Both portraits may be correct. In 1888 Slattery was capable of doing an adequate job in CF for the New York Giants' first pennant winner despite an increasing propensity to put on suet; earlier in his career he had weighed around 175. Three years later Washington released him just hours after he made his final ML appearance when it grew apparent that he could no longer play the outfield. The following month *TSN* suggested that Slattery's career was shortened by arthritic knees. He continued to try to make a go of it in the minors for a time but desisted in 1895 soon after *TSN* callously noted, "Mike Slattery is making the summer rounds among Eastern League clubs. He averages a release and a new engagement every week."

Discovered by Tim Murnane while playing for an amateur team in South Boston, Slattery remained Murnane's darling throughout his rookie ML season despite an abysmal .448 OPS. The following year he and several Boston Unions teammates joined Biddeford of the Eastern New England League. Although Slattery never hit especially well even in the minors, Jim Mutrie acquired him from Toronto for the Giants after he topped the International League in runs and stolen bases in 1887. The newcomer was an instant smash with New York fans. On May 3, 1888, when George Gore was listed as the starter in LF, the crowd "howled for Slattery and was so persistent that captain Ewing retired [Gore] and put in Slattery." After appearing in 103 games in 1888, Slattery was held by physical problems and a corresponding weight gain to just 12 games the following year but returned for four World's Series contests against Brooklyn. He then jumped with several other Giants to the New York PL entry and again was reduced by ailments to a part-timer. The following summer, when he played his last ML game, he was still just 26 at the very oldest.

Slattery went into the clothing business after leaving baseball following the 1895 New England League seasons. By then he was a salesman at McManus & Company in Boston. The following year he was stabbed when he tried to detain a shoplifter but survived to become head salesman of the clothing firm. Slattery died in Boston of stomach trouble in 1904. The clues, though sketchy, point to the possibility that he suffered from a severe rheumatoid arthritic condition that compromised his immune system and caused internal organ damage. (DN)

Smith, Elmer Ellsworth / "Elmer" "Mike"

B	T	HGT	WGT	G	AB	H	R	2B
L	L	5'11"	178	1217	4632	1446	908	195

3B	HR	RBI	BB	SO	SB	BA	SA	OBP
135	37	662	631	139	231	.312	.437	.399

G	IP	H	GS	CG	BB
149	1210.1	1167	136	122	422

SO	SH	W	L	PCT	ERA
525	9	75	57	.568	3.35

B. 3/23/1868 Pittsburgh, PA **D.** 11/3/1945
TEAMS: 86–89CinA 92–97PitN 98–00CinN 00NYN 01PitN 01BosN
DEBUT: 9/10/1886 at Brooklyn; started, was relieved by Abner Powell, and finished the game in LF in his 8–4 loss to Brooklyn's Henry Porter
FINALE: 6/15/1901 at Pittsburgh; pinch hit unsuccessfully for George Grossart in the ninth inning of a 1–0 loss to Pittsburgh's Jack Chesbro

Elmer Smith was an outstanding left-handed pitcher who converted to the outfield after showing even more ability as a hitter. By no means the nineteenth century's answer to Babe Ruth and practically unremembered today, Smith was nonetheless one of the better outfielders of the 1890s. Unlike Ruth, Smith probably could not have had a significant career as a pitcher, for his early pro experience gave ample evidence of a fragile arm. He grew up in Allegheny, the home of the Pittsburgh ML club's park. In the spring of 1886, barely 18, he ventured to Nashville, where was hailed as "the boy phenomenon" of the Southern League whose "speed is something marvelous." But after making just eight starts he was resting a sore arm back in Allegheny, temporarily unable to pitch. One day in early September, Smith showed up at Pittsburgh's Recreation Park to ask manager Opie Caylor of visiting Cincinnati for a tryout. Caylor thought he had the look of a pitcher, and then as now everyone liked a left-hander. Signed to a trial contract, Smith was given a start some days later in Brooklyn. Rusty after his long layoff and working with a catcher unfamiliar with his style, he lost 8–4. Nevertheless, Smith pitched regularly for the rest of the season and showed considerable potential, dominating those games in which his sometimes uncertain control did not betray him.

Owing to his uneven performances, Smith was considered a work in progress and his role on a rebuilding pitching staff in 1887 was unclear. While the Reds' management tried other candidates, Smith did not get his first start until May 18, but when the Reds' volatile pitching ace, Tony Mullane, jumped the club around that time, he took full opportunity of the opening. By the time Mullane returned to the team some six weeks later, Smith had established himself as the AA's premier pitching newcomer and eventually rang up a 34-17 record in spite of his paucity of early-season opportunities. As fast as things had coalesced for Smith, just as quickly they began to crumble. He developed a sore shoulder in the spring of 1888 and, in spite of periodic optimistic reports, did not improve. Only 19 when he had his breakout season, Smith was a finished product as a pitcher but unfinished as a man. Already married, he also supported his widowed mother and two younger brothers. When his pitching arm failed he must have felt under enormous pressure, and his personal immaturities only exacerbated matters. He failed to work diligently in the gymnasium, gained weight, and drank too much. His love of animals was a more endearing quality, but when he finally left Cincinnati after his release in the fall of 1889, a full day was needed to clean his rented home of the empty growlers (beer kegs) and his dogs' leavings.

Smith went to Kansas City, which dropped to the minor Western Association in 1890, and was put to work in the outfield. A solid hitter for a pitcher, he carried a reputation as a terrible fielder, lax about covering 1B on grounders and unwilling even to catch a pop fly if he could avoid it. Given regular outfield duty, however, he became excellent defensively and batted over .300 and topping the Western Association in runs. His arm recovered—or so he said—with the aid of salve made by "an old man in Sioux City," and he continued to do some pitching for several more years. Given his past history, it is likely Smith's arm would have gone bad again with regular work in the box, and, if he had not proven too valuable an outfielder to use for more than spot duty as a pitcher, his story might have ended much like that of many of his contemporary pitchers who made a big splash as youngsters and then quickly vanished.

After another fine season in 1891, Smith was snared in the minor league draft by his hometown Pittsburgh team. His metamorphosis from an incompetent fielding pitcher to a capable outfielder seems to have reflected a general personal maturation, and former Reds teammates were surprised to see Smith trim and fit rather than the "fat, flabby" pitcher they remembered. During his half-dozen years with the Pirates, Smith was one of the best hitters on a team that featured such potent batsmen as Jake Beckley, George Van Haltren, and Jake Stenzel. In 1893 and 1896, his best seasons, he was the team leader in most offensive categories. It was in Pittsburgh, too, that he acquired the nickname "Mike," the source of which is unknown.

Smith's tenure with the Pirates ended on November 10, 1897, when he was traded to Cincinnati with pitcher Pink Hawley for five players, most of them surplus from the Reds' strong Indianapolis farm club, which had been managed by Pittsburgh's new manager Bill Watkins. Along with another seven-man deal made on the same day between St. Louis and Philadelphia, it was the largest trade of the nineteenth century in terms of numbers of players exchanged. Smith batted .342 for Cincinnati in 1898, but by the time he returned to the Reds he was 30 and on the downgrade. Too, he persisted in using one of the heaviest bats in the game, around fifty ounces, and with his advancing age, his power numbers declined accordingly. After his wife died in 1899 of consumption, Smith appeared in only 87 games and logged just 24 RBI in 339 ABs. By the turn of the century Smith was a scrub. In 1902 he was released to minor league KC, where he had enjoyed his renaissance over a decade before. He traveled around the minors for a few years more, ending on a high note with a .313 season for Binghamton in 1906 and then left baseball and went home to Pittsburgh and Allegheny Kennels, the bird and dog store he had opened in July 1900. More devoted to his dogs than ever after his wife's death, Smith bred bull terriers and eventually expanded his love for animals to include an Angora cat farm. He died in Pittsburgh at 78. (DB/DN)

Sneed, John Law / "Jack"

B	T	HGT	WGT	G	AB	H	R	2B
L	?	5'8"	160	263	982	253	197	26

3B	HR	RBI	BB	SO	SB	BA	SA	OBP
21	4	130	132	29	68	.268	.349	.364

B. ?/?/1861 Shelby County, TN **D.** 12/27/1898
TEAMS: 84IndA 90TolA 90–91ColA
DEBUT: 5/1/1884 at St. Louis; played CF and went 1-for-4 in a 4–2 loss to St. Louis's Tip O'Neill
FINALE: 9/22/1891 at Columbus; played RF and went 1-for-5 in a 10–8 win over Baltimore's John Healy

Little is known about Jack Sneed's early life, probably because he wanted it that way. A man with many dark corners, he moved from job to job and woman to woman, but wherever he went there were two constants: he loved dogs and always kept himself in top playing condition. Sneed began as a pitcher with the unaffiliated Knoxville Reds in the late 1870s and later played for the independent Memphis Riversides and the Omaha Union Pacifics before joining the Indianapolis AA expansion club in 1884. Released when he hit just .216 in 27 games, he moved to Nashville in the fledgling Southern League in 1885 and then took a hand in forming the Memphis SL entry the following year and hit .292. In June 1887 Sneed was in his second season as Memphis's player-manager when he was accused of scheming to break up the SL. To avoid being blacklisted he bought his own release, temporarily leaving behind his share in the tool and cutlery store in Memphis that he owned jointly with his brother, and went to Topeka to play for the 1887 Western League champions. After Sneed hit .273 with Toledo of the International Association two years later, he accompanied the Black Pirates when they joined the AA as an interim replacement team in 1890.

Sneed lasted only 9 games with Toledo before friction exploded between him and captain Perry Werden. Realizing Sneed and Werden would not get along, manager Charlie Morton said he would release Sneed if he could find a new home. But when Columbus manager Al Buckenberger wanted him, Morton refused to let him go to Toledo's AA archrival. So Sneed faked a telegram saying minor league Omaha had agreed to sign him, and Toledo released him. Sneed went forthwith to his home in Toldeo and showed up the next day at Toledo's park in a Columbus uniform, much to Morton's consternation. Sneed then spent the next two seasons in Ohio's capital nursing his ailing wife, Amelia, and dealing with conflicting opinions as to whether he had a good attitude or was a divisive element. In late September 1891 Buckenberger's replacement, Gus Schmelz, finally decided he was the latter. Sneed quit the game at that point but remained in Columbus working as a scalper at the Chittenden Hotel. In January 1892 his Columbus home burned to the ground, destroying everything he owned, but he took it in stride, "quietly running a ticket office in Columbus and laughing at the troubles of the boys in his profession." The following February, Sneed deserted his wife and absconded with $9,000 worth of her jewelry and Alice Shipley, his stenographer. The two fugitives laid a false trail and appear to have lived for a time in Louisville. In March 1894 Sneed was run to earth in Cincinnati after twenty or so "1,000 mile" tickets went missing from a local Pennsylvania Railway office that he frequented. He denied all of his crimes initially but finally agreed to return to Columbus and face the music. Not only did he somehow beat the charges against him but he even got another job in a ticket brokerage office. By then Sneed's wife had divorced him and gained custody of their 8-year-old daughter after charging him with mental cruelty, neglect, desertion, "and the intimacy of the defendant with one of the fair sex." Meanwhile, Sneed was in St. Louis with little interest in baseball anymore although he was confident he could still suit up. His last known connection with the game came when he mailed a bat to Cincinnati outfielder Bug Holliday that he had swiped from Holliday in 1887 when the two were minor league teammates with Topeka. Sneed died in Jackson, TN, of typhoid fever in 1898. (DN/DB)

Sommer, Joseph John / "Joe"

B	T	HGT	WGT	G	AB	H	R	2B
R	R	5'11"	185	920	3675	911	617	109

3B	HR	RBI	BB	SO	SB	BA	SA	OBP
42	11	342	238	53	101	.248	.309	.297

G	IP	H	GS	CG	BB
6	14	33	0	0	7

SO	SH	W	L	PCT	ERA
3	0	0	0	—	9.64

B. 11/20/1858 Covington, KY **D.** 1/16/1938

TEAMS: 80CinN 82–83CinA 84–89BalA 90CleN 90BalA

DEBUT: 7/18/1880 at Cincinnati; played SS and went 0-for-4 in a 19–5 loss to Boston's Tommy Bond

FINALE: 10/15/1890 at Baltimore; played LF and went 1-for-2 in a 9–5 win over Rochester's Bob Miller and Jack Grim

As a youth, Joe Sommer played both the infield and outfield on teams in his hometown of Covington, KY, sometimes teaming with his brother Ben, who was a good amateur catcher and umpired in the AA prior to his premature death in 1883. In 1880 Cincinnati's struggling NL team picked up Sommer as a surrogate for Harry Wheeler, another local player. Sommer provided little offense but impressed observers with his self-discipline and work habits as well as his strong fielding in LF, which made him a distinct improvement on Wheeler, who hit even less and was a defensive liability.

In 1881 Cincinnati left the NL and Sommer went to Louisville to play for the semipro Eclipse. He came back home the following year, signing with the Cincinnati entry in the newly organized AA. After some experimentation with its new cast of players, Cincinnati played Sommer every inning of the season in LF and received a solid .288 BA as the club rolled to the first AA pennant. The following season was a disappointment; the Reds finished third, and Sommer was criticized for failing to slide into bases and briefly benched in early July. That fall, Sommer signed with Baltimore after the Cincinnati management misinterpreted the rules of the National Agreement, thinking they could omit the outfielder from their reserve list after inking him prematurely to a contract. For the next six years Sommer was a Baltimore mainstay. His hitting gradually declined, but he fielded well. Nevertheless, Sommer came to regret his decision to leave Cincinnati after years of constant losing with the weakest team in the AA. By the end of the 1886 season there was talk that he would be traded for Reds outfielder Charley Jones. "You just bet your sweet life I would like to go back to Cincinnati and play ball," Sommer said, but he spent another three years in Baltimore despite coming off a year in which he logged the lowest OPS (.506) of any nineteenth-century player with 500 or more ABs.

But other attributes overshadowed his weak bat in the view of *SL*'s Baltimore correspondent: "Joe is a model in habits and a strong player even under disheartening circumstances." Throughout his career, Sommer neither drank nor smoked, and *TSN* called him "one of the quietest, most unassuming and gentlemanly ball players of the country," while *SL* commented that "his intelligent training and earnest, patient ambition to do his best for himself and his employers will, if he chooses, make him sought after as a ball player, when some of his comrades have been laid on the shelf for years."

In 1889 Sommer's batwork slipped beyond the pale when he clocked in at .220 in a hitter's year, resulting in his release late in the season. He signed with Cleveland NL for 1890 but after just 9 games lost the LF job to Bob Gilks, who ironically went on to fashion an OPS that year that is second worst only to Sommer's 1886 season. Upon his release from Cleveland, Sommer then returned to Baltimore, which rejoined the AA late in the 1890 season and played every inning of the team's 38 games at his traditional LF post. Now past 30, he was released after hitting just .256. Sommer played two final seasons in the minors and then went on to confirm the forecast that he would long outlast most of his contemporaries. On the occasion of *Sporting Life's* twenty-fifth anniversary in 1908, Cincinnati writer Ren Mulford looked back at all the personnel of the two major leagues in 1883 and found that only Sommer "still dons a uniform and knocks around the minors and semi-pros."

In Sommer's youth, his family had operated Covington's Central Hotel, for which he himself had clerked. Subsequently, in 1883, his last year with the Reds, he opened a Cincinnati saloon with Charlie Reising, another local player, and later he ran a combination hotel and saloon in his native Covington. From about 1920 on Sommer was "in charge of various amusement devices at the Cincinnati zoo," according to his obit. When he died from heart disease in Cincinnati at 79, he had receded sufficiently from public consciousness that none of the local newspapers realized he had been a big league ballplayer. (DB/DN)

*Stafford, James Joseph / "General" "Jamsey"

B	T	HGT	WGT	G	AB	H	R	2B
R	R	5'8"	165	570	2137	585	341	60

3B	HR	RBI	BB	SO	SB	BA	SA	OBP
19	21	291	164	96	118	.274	.349	.330

G	IP	H	GS	CG	BB
12	98	123	12	11	43

SO	SH	W	L	PCT	ERA
21	0	3	9	.250	5.14

B. 7/9/1868 Webster, MA **D.** 9/18/1923
TEAMS: 90BufP 93–97NYN 97–98LouN 98–99BosN 99WasN
DEBUT: 8/27/1890 at Brooklyn; caught by Connie Mack and beat Brooklyn's John Sowders 10–9
FINALE: 10/12/1899 at Washington; played 2B and went 0-for-4 in a 5–4 loss to New York's Ed Doheny

The brother of ML pitcher John Stafford, the elder Stafford had an arm that could fire a ball on a line from deep CF to nail a runner at the plate. During his lengthy career, General Stafford played every position in the majors except catcher and for the most part was with teams that received extensive press coverage. Yet as late as the 1980s most of his ML achievements were still being credited to Bob Stafford, a career minor leaguer, and not one of his vital statistics was known. Stafford is perhaps the prime example of how rudimentary baseball research still was as recently as twenty-five years ago, and the reason he was called "General" is still a mystery, though one theory is that he was nicknamed after Confederate brigadier gen. L. A. Stafford, who was killed at the battle of Wilderness.

After pitching semipro ball in Hartford in 1886, Stafford made his pro debut with independent Springfield, MA, in 1887 as a pitcher-outfielder and by 1890 had moved up to Worcester of the Atlantic Association until the club disbanded, permitting him to join the abysmal Buffalo PL team. He showed poorly and returned to the minors for the next two and a half seasons before the Giants acquired him in 1893 from Augusta of the Southern League to replace lame-hitting Harry Lyons in CF. An adequate performance went for naught when New York traded for George Van Haltren that offseason. Stafford began 1894 on the bench, briefly replaced Mike Tiernan in LF when Tiernan experienced a slump, and then was farmed to Nashville of the Southern League. Recalled in 1895, Stafford replaced the newly retired John M. Ward at 2B and again did adequate work, only to lose his spot the following spring to Kid Gleason. Stafford opened and closed the 1896 campaign as the Giants' regular left fielder—his third different position as a regular on the club—but sat out a large chunk of the campaign after he suffered a broken right wrist when a pitch hit him in a July game against Louisville. Accused of playing poorly upon his return to the lineup, Stafford alluded to his injury, but writer Opie Caylor blamed Stafford's corrosion on his being smitten with one Mattie Hughes, whom he planned to marry after the season.

The following May the newlywed was traded to Louisville for outfielder Ducky Holmes. He ended the season as the Colonels' regular SS and ranked as the third-best hitter on the team, trailing only Fred Clarke and Perry Werden. Although Stafford began the 1898 campaign hitting .298, he was let go to Boston, where he served as a substitute outfielder. He remained a scrub with Boston in 1899 until he was released in August and signed 10 days later with Washington. After hitting .302 with Boston, Stafford slipped to .248 with the Senators and was not retained when the NL contracted to eight teams prior to the 1900 season.

Stafford spent the next two years with Providence of the Eastern League and then appeared to get a reprieve in January 1902 when the Giants signed him to replace Kip Selbach, who had jumped to the AL. New York released him soon after spring training ended, however. By then Stafford already had a hearing problem that would eventually leave him totally deaf. He remained in the Eastern League until 1904, when he concluded an eighteen-year pro career that included eight seasons in the majors and yet left him totally unrecognized for his service by historians until the mid-1980s. After leaving baseball Stafford operated a farm near Dudley, MA, until his death in 1923 following surgery at a Worcester hospital. (DN)

Stenzel, Jacob Charles (b. Stelzle) / **"Jake"**

B	T	HGT	WGT	G	AB	H	R	2B
R	R	5'10"	168	768	3031	1024	664	190

3B	HR	RBI	BB	SO	SB	BA	SA	OBP
71	32	533	300	71	292	.338	.479	.408

B. 6/24/1867 Cincinnati, OH **D.** 1/6/1919

TEAMS: 90ChiN 92–96PitN 97–98BalN 98–99StLN 99CinN

DEBUT: 6/16/1890 at Chicago; caught Jack Luby and went 0-for-4 in a 5–4 win over Pittsburgh's Guy Hecker

FINALE: 7/23/1899 at Cincinnati; pinch hit unsuccessfully in the ninth inning for Ted Breitenstein in an 8–5 loss to Washington's Gus Weyhing

Jake Stenzel was the Lefty O'Doul of his time in that he spent the early portion of his career at a position he was unsuited for, performed meteorically in the majors once he converted to the outfield, and then saw his star swiftly descend after only a handful of outstanding seasons in an era that was particularly charitable to hitters. But while it is true that Stenzel's peak years coincided with the first few seasons after the pitching distance was lengthened, so did those of his numerous contemporaries, and only one with a minimum of 2,000 career ABs (Willie Keeler) had a higher career BA than his .357 at the close of the 1897 season after he had reached 2,000 ABs.

Born Stelzle, Stenzel apparently changed his name before launching his pro career with Wheeling of the Tri-State League in 1887. A catcher at the time, he progressed slowly through the minors even though it was clear that he could hit. In 1889, after two years with Wheeling, Stenzel still had risen no higher than Springfield, OH, of the Tri-State League, and despite scoring 121 runs that season and finishing second in the loop in steals with 81, the best offer for the following year came from Galveston of the wobbly Texas League. When that loop disbanded in June 1890 with Stenzel hitting .307, he accompanied batterymate Jack Luby to Chicago NL. But while Luby stuck with the team and set a rookie winning-streak record, Stenzel was unable to overcome a 0-for-12 start and was released in August.

In 1892, as Stenzel was about to spend his second straight season in the Pacific Northwest League, he finally conceded that he was a much better hitter than a catcher. Now with Portland, OR, in July he became a full-time outfielder and two months later was purchased by Pittsburgh. Going 0-for-9 in a 3-game trial at the end of the 1892 season condemned him to begin 1893 on the bench and might even have earned his release if the Pirates had not been loath to sacrifice the money they had paid for him. As it was, Stenzel spent most of the season as an injury replacement both at catcher and in the outfield even though he hit .362. The moment that finally elevated Stenzel in manager Al Buckenberger's judgment came on July 15 when he hit a grand slam home run and a bases-loaded triple against Washington, but just as Buckenberger decided to make him a regular, Cleveland's Jesse Burkett spiked him in the left foot in early August.

Stenzel's sudden emergence nonetheless convinced Buckenberger to sell center fielder George Van Haltren to the Giants that winter. For the next three seasons Stenzel reigned supreme among Pirates hitters but ranked in the lower half defensively among the loop's center fielders. In November 1896, Pittsburgh grew enamored of Baltimore's three straight pennant triumphs with Steve Brodie in CF and consented to a multiplayer swap that featured the exchange of Stenzel for Brodie. The deal was a bad one for Pittsburgh but a disappointment for Baltimore as well. Stenzel was far superior to Brodie as a hitter but not his equal in the field. His days under Baltimore manager Ned Hanlon were numbered after a misplay in a pivotal game against Boston on September 27, 1897. With an overflow Baltimore crowd ringing the field behind him, Stenzel tracked a long fly ball, but then, as the crowd made way for him to catch it, he played the ball diffidently and dropped it, leading to a huge Boston inning that helped cost Baltimore the pennant.

When Stenzel started slowly in 1898, hitting just .254 in 35 games, Hanlon shipped him to last-place St. Louis. He decayed rapidly in the Mound City but still was one of the few members of the 1898 Browns who were retained when syndicate ownership transferred most of Cleveland's better players to St. Louis in the spring of 1899 in exchange for St. Louis's dregs. He opened his final ML season on the bench and then replaced weak-hitting Harry Blake in CF for a time before being waived to his Cincinnati hometown, where he finished his career. Soon after leaving the Reds, Stenzel bought out Jim Keenan's share in a saloon Keenan partly owned. The following spring he officially announced his retirement, blaming his demise on Hanlon, whom he claimed wrecked his career by forcing him to play with an injured leg in 1897. Stenzel sold his portion of his saloon in 1917 and worked as a night watchman until he died at his Cincinnati home in 1919 from a stroke while suffering from influenza. (DN)

Stires, Garrett / "Gat" "The Terrible Hayseed"

B	T	HGT	WGT	G	AB	H	R	2B
L	R	5'8"	180	25	110	30	23	4

3B	HR	RBI	BB	SO	SB	BA	SA	OBP
6	2	24	7	5	3	.273	.473	.316

B. 10/13/1849 Hunterdon County, NJ **D.** 6/13/1933
TEAMS: 71RokNA
DEBUT: 5/6/1871 at Rockford; played RF and went 1-for-3 in a 12–4 loss to Cleveland's Al Pratt
FINALE: 9/15/1871 at Cleveland; played RF and went 1-for-5 in a 16–8 loss to Cleveland's Al Pratt

Gat Stires was born in New Jersey but grew up on a stock farm and ranch near Byron, IL. He joined the Rockford Forest Citys in 1868 and was expected to be one of the mainstays of the club when it enlisted in the NA in 1871 after leading the team in total bases in 1870. A swing-from-the-heels hitter (the type that Henry Chadwick loathed), Stires hit one of the longest home runs ever seen in an 1870 victory over the vaunted Cincinnati Red Stockings. Stationed in RF for most of his career, Stires was a sure fielder but prone to making wild throws. An old-time player reminiscing in 1897 for *TSN* described him as "old Gat Stires," always lame and needing someone to run for him. Stires retired to the family ranch after only one year of ML play and made it into one of the most prosperous in the Byron area. He was later the postmaster in Byron, IL, and was put in a rest home there when his health began to decline in the 1920s. Stires never married and died in Oregon, IL, at 83. (DN/DB)

Sullivan, Martin C. / "Marty"

B	T	HGT	WGT	G	AB	H	R	2B
B	R	?	?	398	1618	441	280	56

3B	HR	RBI	BB	SO	SB	BA	SA	OBP
32	26	220	162	168	99	.273	.395	.341

G	IP	H	GS	CG	BB
1	2.1	6	0	0	1

SO	SH	W	L	PCT	ERA
1	0	0	0	—	7.71

B. 10/20/1862 Lowell, MA **D.** 1/6/1894
TEAMS: 87–88ChiN 89IndN 90–91BosN 91CleN
DEBUT: 4/30/1887 at Pittsburgh; played LF and went 1-for-4 in a 6–2 loss to Pittsburgh's Jim Galvin
FINALE: 8/17/1891 at Cincinnati; played RF and

went 1-for-4 in a 3–2 loss to Cincinnati's Tony Mullane

Arriving in Chicago in the spring of 1887 after spending the previous year with the New England League Boston Blues, Sullivan slipped so fast after a solid rookie campaign that he clearly was beset by serious physical or personal problems—actually both. Given to despondency that triggered bouts of drinking, Sullivan reached the depths of his natural tendency toward depression in late June 1889, when he was forced to leave the Indianapolis team to be with his wife in her final moments before she died. The previous year his eighteen-month-old son had died, the second child he had lost in a twelve-month period, and in the fall of 1887, after going west with the Chicago team on a postseason barnstorming tour, his mother's illness had bade him to cut the trip short and return home.

But personal misfortunes were only part of what dogged Sullivan. Though he hit well as a frosh with Chicago, he was erratic both on the bases and in the field and also swiftly began to see his batting marks decline once pitchers realized he was a chance hitter, the 1880s term for a free swinger. Moreover, Sullivan was involved in two incidents in 1888 that diminished his popularity in Chicago. On Opening Day of his sophomore year he got into an altercation on the field with Indianapolis first baseman Tom Esterbrook that Esterbrook instigated by punching him after the two collided in a play at 1B. When Sullivan failed to retaliate, Cap Anson, who was coaching at 3B, bolted across to diamond to rebuke him. Viewed as cowardly for his passive role in the exchange, Sullivan belatedly attempted to atone the following day by racing in from LF when Esterbrook knocked down Fred Pfeffer in a play at 2B and forcing his teammates to restrain him from tackling Esterbrook.

Despite the disdain Sullivan's teammates rained on him following the Esterbrook incidents, coupled with his having to learn to bat left-handed during the 1888 season so he could remain in the lineup against right-handers and nonetheless losing his regular outfield post in August, when both Hugh Duffy and George Van Haltren began to emerge as coming stars, he was invited to accompany the team that winter on its famous postseason world tour. In Italy, however, Sullivan incurred not only the ire of his teammates but also Al Spalding's displeasure when he swiped a conductor's horn, resulting in the tour train being detained and the whole team placed under arrest for some two hours before the matter was resolved. Soon after the tour group returned to the States, Spalding released Sullivan along with three other club members in what he claimed was a cost cutting measure made necessary after the world tour was a financial fiasco for players and management alike, costing most players between $400 and $1,000 in expenses rather than making money for them as promised. But in Sullivan's case, the true reason for his release more likely was that there was no longer room for him in the Chicago outfield.

Sullivan signed for 1889 with Indianapolis, a team in dire need of outfielders with offensive punch, and was hitting well until he lost his wife and had to leave the club for a spell in midseason. Soon after his return, the Hoosiers acquired Ed Andrews, not his equal as a hitter but sufficiently better as both a fielder and a base runner that Sullivan was relegated to the bench and then released. Left to fend for himself, he signed a conditional contract with Boston NL that stipulated he could be released at any time if he was caught drinking, a problem that had begun to magnify in 1888 when his otherwise unbearable string of personal losses began.

Under first-year manager Frank Selee, Sullivan experienced a resurgence in 1890, leading Boston in SA. That winter, to further demonstrate his sincerity in reforming his ways, he joined the Mathew Temperance Institute in Lowell, MA, his hometown. Selee rewarded Sullivan by keeping him at his post in the spring of 1891. But after just 17 games Sullivan was cut and his LF spot given to Link Lowe. He offered himself to the Philadelphia A's, but they declined, leaving him idle until Cleveland sought an outfielder to replace slumping Ralph Johnson. In his first game with the Spiders, Sullivan injured his foot, and though he finished the contest, he never played pro ball again. Upon his departure from the only thing that had held his psyche together after the loss of his wife in addition to his two children, Sullivan watched his life swiftly disintegrate. He began drinking heavily again and during a scuffle with a bartender in February 1893 stabbed him after his adversary hit him over the head with a bottle. Within a year the 33-year-old former ML outfielder was dead, expiring at his home in Lowell after a long illness (probably tuberculosis). (DN)

Swartwood, Cyrus Edward / "Ed" "Ned" "Swarty"

B	T	HGT	WGT	G	AB	H	R	2B
L	R	5'11"	198	724	2876	861	607	120

3B	HR	RBI	BB	SO	SB	BA	SA	OBP
63	14	229	325	11	120	.299	.400	.379

G	IP	H	GS	CG	BB
2	5.1	8	0	0	1

SO	SH	W	L	PCT	ERA
1	0	0	0	—	6.75

B. 1/12/1859 Amherst, OH **D.** 5/15/1924
TEAMS: 81BufN 82–84PitA 85–87BroA 90TolA 92PitN
DEBUT: 8/11/1881 at Cleveland; played RF and went 1-for-4 in an 8–7 win over Cleveland's "The Only" Nolan
FINALE: 5/21/1892 at Chicago; played RF and went 0-for-2 in a 1–0 loss to Chicago's Bill Hutchison

Ed Swartwood was a brainy athlete who nearly always captained his teams and readily confronted owners during contract negotiations. Yet he mixed some of the best AA batting numbers with stretches of uninspired play, fueling suspicions that he was aloof and disinterested. In hindsight, it may simply have been that Swartwood never was able to combine his brilliant potential with the pressures of captaining his teammates. Born in nearby Amherst, Swartwood moved to Cleveland as a youth and debuted with the local amateur Red Stockings in 1878. The following year he gained national attention by batting .319 for an independent Detroit team. When Detroit captain Charlie Morton was offered a manager's job in Akron he took Swartwood with him. For two years Akron was a top independent club and Swartwood played alongside such future stars as Bid McPhee and Tony Mullane. On August 11, 1881, after playing in an exhibition game against Buffalo the day before, Swartwood was asked by the Bisons to take part in a NL contest at Cleveland when Buffalo pitcher Jim Galvin was called away to attend to a sick child. Occupying RF when Curry Foley moved from the outfield to pitch, Swartwood made his ML debut with a single and a walk in a Buffalo win. When the AA was formed that November, the Akron team was raided of its top players. Swartwood, Billy Taylor, and Jack Neagle all signed with the Pittsburgh Alleghenys, Swartwood reportedly for $100 a month.

The hard-hitting, solidly built Swartwood served surprisingly as a lead-off batter and led Pittsburgh by substantial margins in nearly every offensive category. His 1883 season was even better. Swartwood batted .357 with power, speed, and walks and became the only lefty hitter prior to 1891 to win an AA batting crown. On August 22 manager Ormond Butler picked him to captain the club. Swartwood couldn't reverse the team's seventh-place pace but quickly showed he was no toady to his manager. On September 5, as Cincinnati's Charlie Snyder was about to take his place in the batter's box, Butler yelled that he was batting out of order. Pittsburgh having thus lost the chance for an out, Swartwood ripped into the manager, roaring, "You have no business interfering with the men while on the field!"

When 1884 opened and the veteran Bob Ferguson was signed to manage, Swartwood had a lackluster year after losing the captain's bonus money and began to put on weight, a problem that would haunt him for the rest of his career. On July 20 Ferguson was released and Joe Battin was picked as his successor. The next day Swartwood made 4 glaring errors at 1B in a loss to weak Washington. In a later game against Louisville he was embarrassingly picked off 2B by center fielder Monk Cline, who crept up behind him while he was tying his shoe. Swartwood's painful season resulted in his sale to Brooklyn. In July of 1885 he replaced veteran John Cassidy as Brooklyn's captain. Swartwood was sensitive to his players' needs, switching his catchers to give them rest in the middle of a game and benching himself against strong left-handed pitchers such as Ed Morris and Matt Kilroy. He remained captain through 1886, the first winning season of his career. On June 12 Brooklyn awakened in first place, the latest in the season any team except St. Louis was able to occupy the top spot in the first three years of the Browns' four-year AA dynasty.

In 1887 Brooklyn rolled to a 13-6 start but by the end of the season had fallen to 15 wins below .500. Swartwood had a leading role in the slump, producing his worst offensive season and leaving the team near the end of the year under the guise of illness in order to tend bar in his hometown Pittsburgh. Released by Brooklyn, in 1888 he signed with Hamilton, Ontario, of the International Association. The following year he was made captain and manager, but Hamilton played poorly, sunk to last place, and nearly disbanded. After Abner Powell replaced him as manager, he finished out the year living apart from his teammates in a boarding house. Toward the end of 1888 Swartwood had also been separated from the team by a long bout with pneumonia but recouped to hit .297 and then resume his off-season job in Pittsburgh as a cigar salesman.

Charlie Morton, Swartwood's Akron manager in 1881, obtained his release from Hamilton when Morton became pilot of the 1890 Toledo AA team. Swartwood had a strong season, but despite a stellar .327 BA he did not survive ML contraction that winter, instead following three Toledo teammates to Sioux City of the Western Association and captaining the club to the pennant under manager Al Buckenberger. Buckenberger took Swartwood and catcher Billy Earle along when Pittsburgh NL appointed him its general manager in 1892. In just the eighth game of the season, however, Swartwood injured his throwing elbow in a collision with St. Louis's George Pinkney at 3B. A comeback bid in the Eastern League brought a .307 BA but no NL offers, and by 1893 he had become a regular umpire in the EL. Swartwood did so well that he was eventually recommended to NL president Nick Young. Though said to be firm, not one to rattle, and able to discuss controversial decisions calmly with players, he had difficulties in 1894, his first year as an NL arbiter, and returned to the Eastern League for further seasoning. Swartwood resurfaced in the NL in 1898 weighing close to 250 pounds and wearing a new type of chest protector that covered a much wider area when he worked the plate. He umpired in the senior loop through 1900 and later officiated again in the Eastern League. Winters he worked in law enforcement in Pittsburgh and ran a saloon in Allegheny.

Swartwood was serving as the hangman for Allegheny County and a chief deputy sheriff under former ML pitcher Ad Gumbert when the two were involved in the infamous McKees Rock strike riots in 1909 (*see* Ad Gumbert). One of his last connections with baseball occurred in 1915 at a Federal League game in Pittsburgh. In his role as a deputy sheriff, he served papers on the Baltimore club, which were initiated by future HOF pitcher Chief Bender to collect $1,085 in back salary owed him by the Terrapins. Swartwood died nine years later in Pittsburgh after a long illness. (DN/FV/BM/DB)

Sylvester, Louis J. / "Lou"

B	T	HGT	WGT	G	AB	H	R	2B
R	R	5'6"	165	173	654	159	138	22

3B	HR	RBI	BB	SO	SB	BA	SA	OBP
14	66	43	67	—	18	.243	.347	.315

G	IP	H	GS	CG	BB
6	32.2	32	1	1	6

SO	SH	W	L	PCT	ERA
7	0	0	1	.000	3.58

B. 2/14/1855 Springfield, IL **D.** 5/5/1936
TEAMS: 84CinU 86LouA 86CinA 87StLA
DEBUT: 4/18/1884 at Cincinnati; played LF and went 0-for-4 in a 9–2 win over Altoona's Jack Leary
FINALE: 8/14/1887 at St. Louis; played RF and went 0-for-3 in an 8–1 win over Cleveland's Jack Kirby

Lou Sylvester's parents were from the Madeira Islands but married in 1851 in Springfield, IL, where their son was born four years later. The elder Sylvester was a watchmaker who moved to Elgin, IL, and by the early 1880s his son was working for the large Elgin's Watch Company and playing on the Watch Factory Nine, a well-known industrial team that also featured Charlie Comiskey and Rudy Kemmler. His career before he broke into the majors is difficult to track, in large measure because he played professionally only once, in 1877 with a Springfield independent team. In 1879 Sylvester married Jennie Figueira, who may have been a relative since his mother's maiden name was also Figueira. For the next few years he seems to have followed his trade as a watchmaker while playing ball on the side, as a semipro in Brooklyn and then in 1883 in Waltham, MA. Since another important watch manufacturer was located then in the latter city, it is likely Sylvester's trade had drawn him there.

In 1884 Sylvester joined Cincinnati UA. He pitched for the club's reserves initially but spent most of the season playing the corner outfield positions on the regular squad. When the UA collapsed, Sylvester went to Memphis and then Augusta of the Southern League. In July 1886 Augusta disbanded, and despite lugging just a .204 BA, Sylvester signed with Louisville AA but was cut in early September after Louisville obtained Hub Collins to take his outfield spot. Sylvester landed on his feet, returning to Cincinnati, where the Reds needed outfield help. After the season, Cincinnati added two new gardeners, George Tebeau and Hugh Nicol, and Sylvester began 1887 with AA champion St. Louis, for whom he played occasionally as a sub until he was released in August and went back to the minors with Milwaukee of the Northwestern League. He continued to play for Midwestern minor league teams until 1889 and then went west, working winters as a store clerk and playing in Texas and California while earning a growing reputation as an umpire. By 1899 Sylvester was reported to be serving as president of the San Diego Baseball Association. To be closer to his daughter he eventually returned to the East and remained a watchmaker before dying in Brooklyn at 81. Although Sylvester hit reasonably well in the weak UA, in two years of AA competition his composite BA was just .218. (DB/DN)

*Tebeau, George E. / "George" "White Wings"

B	T	HGT	WGT	G	AB	H	R	2B
R	R	5'9"	175	628	2319	623	441	96

3B	HR	RBI	BB	SO	SB	BA	SA	OBP
54	15	311	324	129	228	.269	.376	.364

G	IP	H	GS	CG	BB
2	13	30	1	1	8

SO	SH	W	L	PCT	ERA
1	0	0	1	.000	11.77

B. 12/26/1861 St. Louis, MO **D.** 2/4/1923
TEAMS: 87–89CinA 90TolA 94WasN 94–95CleN
DEBUT AND FAMOUS FIRST: 4/16/1887 at Cincinnati; played CF, went 2-for-5 in a 16–6 win over Cleveland's George Pechiney, and homered in his first ML at-bat to share with Mike Griffin (who also did it on 4/16/1887) the distinction of being the first MLers to perform this feat
FINALE: 9/29/1895 at Louisville; played RF and went 1-for-4 in a 13–8 loss to Louisville's Tom McCreery

George Tebeau was the older brother of ML player-manager Pat Tebeau and cousin of minor leaguer Al Tebeau. He may well have been nicknamed "White Wings" because he was brash and abrasive, the antithesis of the white-winged dove of peace. Tebeau was regarded as an excellent fielder, a team leader, and a valuable base coach who always kept his head in the game. Seemingly, he was a cut below ML standards as a hitter, especially for an outfielder, but actually his .740 OPS is the highest among nineteenth-century players with a minimum of 2,000 PAs and a sub-.275 BA

Before turning pro, Tebeau played on the amateur St. Louis Shamrocks with his brother Pat. A member of Western League champion Denver in 1886, he joined several other highly touted hitters from the "Mile High" Mountain Lions in moving to the AA the following year. Tebeau opened the 1887 campaign in CF for Cincinnati, replacing the injured Hugh Nicol, and homered in his first ML at-bat but then had to wait until June before he could wrest the regular LF post away from aging Charley Jones.

After a promising start Tebeau remained the Reds' left fielder for the next two seasons and hit for low averages but was nonetheless a potent offensive force. In 1889 he led Cincinnati in both runs and walks despite batting just .252. Upon being cut unexpectedly by the Reds the following April, he signed with Toledo AA but cooked himself when he "spoke words to [manager] Morton that you cannot find in the Bible," was fined $100, and then refused to play next day and was suspended.

Tebeau spent the next three seasons in the minors before resurfacing as Washington's right fielder on Opening Day in 1894. When he hit just .225 in the first half of the season, he was released to his brother's Cleveland team. Over the next season and a half, Tebeau was the Spiders' most productive outfielder save for Jesse Burkett but could never win a regular job. Since the elder Tebeau's competition consisted only of two lame hitters, Jimmy McAleer and Harry Blake, the reason may simply have been that his brother feared being accused of nepotism.

Tebeau finished 1895 in RF but missed the Temple Cup series against Baltimore that fall and was asked by the Cleveland ownership to become player-manager of the Spiders' Fort Wayne farm team the following spring. Tebeau continued to play minor league ball through 1901 and then changed to managing from the bench and coaching lines. He later owned a piece of several midwestern minor league teams before leaving the game and settling in Denver. Tebeau died there of diabetes in 1923. (DN/DB)

*Thomas, Roy Allen / "Roy"

B	T	HGT	WGT	G	AB	H	R	2B
L	L	5'11"	150	290	1078	346	269	16

3B	HR	RBI	BB	SO	SB	BA	SA	OBP
7	0	80	230	—	79	.321	.349	.454

G	IP	H	GS	CG	BB
1	2.2	4	0	0	0

SO	SH	W	L	PCT	ERA
0	0	0	0	—	3.38

B. 3/24/1874 Norristown, PA
D. 11/20/1959 Norristown, PA
TEAMS: 99–07PhiN 08PitN 09BosN 10–11PhiN
DEBUT: 4/14/1890 at Philadelphia; played 1B and went 1-for-2 in a 6–5 win over Washington's Frank Killen
FINALE: 9/4/1911 at Brooklyn; pinch hit unsuccessfully for Bunny Madden in a 6–2 loss to Brooklyn's Elmer Knetzer

Roy Thomas was the brother of twentieth-century MLer Bill Thomas. He played 14 games at 1B in his first ML season and was a center fielder almost exclusively for the rest of his career. Among the top defensive outfielders of his day, Thomas had the misfortune to begin his career as the 1893–1900 hitters' era was ending and by the early 1900s, just when he was reaching was prime, was thrust into the downward draft of the Deadball Era. A comparable player to Willie Keeler but with even less power, Thomas, like Keeler, needed to be able to slap pitches deliberately foul to wait for one that he could pop into an infield gap, and he was arguably the primary target of the NL's imposition of a foul-strike rule in 1901 and subsequently shared with Keeler the unhappy distinction of being its primary victim.

Perhaps the most unique feature of Thomas's career is that he did not play in his first pro game until he was 25 years old, and then it was at the big league level. From 1892–95 he played summers for the Cape May "college boy" team while attending the University of Pennsylvania and from the outset was obviously the best player in the summer amateur league. In 1892, his first season, Thomas hit .525, and each spring thereafter he was also among the elite members of a strong Penn team. After earning his bachelor's degree from the Ivy League school in 1894, he debated playing college ball one more year but then resigned his team captaincy that winter and spent the next four seasons with the Orange, NJ, Athletic Club as an outfielder in the summer and the quarterback on the club's football team in the fall. In December 1898 *TSN* reported that Thomas hadn't dropped a fly ball in three years, intensifying the Phillies' conviction that he would be a prize gardener if they could induce him to sign.

It is unclear what finally convinced Thomas to test his mettle against the best players of his day, but from the moment of his arrival in the majors it was obvious that he belonged among them. In 1899 he scored an NL rookie-record 137 runs and also collected 115 walks. The following season he topped the loop in both departments and also ranked high in several fielding categories. But Thomas had one irremediable drawback: zero power. He finished in 1911 with just 160 extra-base hits, the fewest ever by a ML player with as many as 1,500 hits, but he also accumulated more than 1,000 runs and even more walks. (DN/PM)

Tiernan, Michael Joseph / "Mike" "Silent Mike"

B	T	HGT	WGT	G	AB	H	R	2B
L	L	5'11"	165	1478	5915	1838	1316	257

3B	HR	RBI	BB	SO	SB	BA	SA	OBP
162	106	853	748	318	428	.311	.463	.392

G	IP	H	GS	CG	BB
5	19.2	33	0	0	7

SO	SH	W	L	PCT	ERA
3	0	1	2	.333	8.69

B. 1/21/1867 Trenton, NJ **D.** 11/9/1918
TEAMS: 87–99NYN
DEBUT: 4/30/1887 at Philadelphia; played CF and went 1-for-4 in a 15–9 loss to Philadelphia's Charlie Ferguson
FINALE: 7/31/1899 at Louisville; played LF and went 1-for-3 in an 8–3 loss to Louisville's Deacon Phillippe

Mike Tiernan was lightning fast, both on his feet and on ice skates, and he frequently won sprint races against other players on field days. As a hitter, he was unique for his time in that he used a comparatively light bat and did not swing hard. Nevertheless, his quick wrist snap produced exceptional power and was envied but rarely imitated successfully by other hitters. As Tiernan was nearing retirement, Kid Nichols confessed that the Giant was the batter he had most feared when he was in his prime. Tiernan was also a manager's and owner's dream in every other respect: never one to grumble or complain (in keeping with his nickname), always at the park on time and ready to play, reportedly never fined or ejected by an umpire, and loyal almost to a fault. Tiernan is the only nineteenth-century player with an ML career of ten years or longer who played for only one team.

Born almost in the shadow of Trenton state prison, Tiernan played for the local Athletic Juniors before traveling west in 1884 at age 17 to pitch, play the outfield, and bat cleanup for Chambersburg of the patchy Keystone Association. At least twice during the season Tiernan beat ML clubs in exhibition games and in addition fanned 15 in a loss to Providence. The following year he shared the box for his hometown Trenton Eastern League club with Mike Mattimore. In 1886, his last season of minor league apprenticeship, Tiernan became more comfortable in the outfield, batting .332 for Jersey City. Then, still short of his 20th birthday, he pledged himself to the New York Giants for 1887 and remained a Giant for thirteen seasons and 1,478 games.

Tiernan's career stats deliver a somewhat inaccurate picture of the kind of player he was. He scored 100 or more runs on seven occasions but only once had over 89 RBI in a season, the profile of a table setter geared to bat first or second in the order. Yet he topped all performers with a minimum of 2,000 ABs prior to the 1893 change in pitching distance in home runs per plate appearance with 2.18. And despite his exceptional speed and the fact that he served either in CF or RF for almost his entire career, only one player in ML history who played a minimum of 1,000 games in the garden (Greg Gross, 1.39) owns a poorer range rating than his 1.48. Further complicating efforts to assess Tiernan is the relative brevity of his career considering that he was already a ten-year man at age 29. As early as February 25, 1899, *TSN* implied that Tiernan might be finished in New York. When he returned north from training camp that March, it was feared that he might be in the early stages of consumption. Happily, he was only suffering from a severe upper respiratory infection and was able to return to the lineup by June. After just 35 games, however, he was released when the snap in his swing was gone and he seemed lethargic on the bases.

Tiernan agreed to play for ex-teammate Jerry Denny's Derby, CT, team in 1900 but quit after 18 games and a .243 BA. He then retired to run a café in Manhattan. In August 1902 Tiernan was in the news for one of the rare times after he left the game when his 9-year-old son Joseph accidentally shot himself in the hand with a blank cartridge and developed tetanus. Drs. William Bevings and John Slevin broke new ground in medicine when they cured Joseph's lockjaw by injecting antitoxin into his spinal cord rather than into his brain, "as heretofore" had been done. Tiernan continued to be plagued by upper-respiratory ailments until his death in New York from tuberculosis. (DN)

Tipper, James / "Jim"

B	T	HGT	WGT	G	AB	H	R	2B
?	?	5'5½"	148	110	466	114	70	13

3B	HR	RBI	BB	SO	SB	BA	SA	OBP
1	0	39	2	14	1	.245	.277	.248

B. 6/18/1849 Middletown, CT **D.** 4/21/1895
TEAMS: 72ManNA 74HarNA 75NHNA
DEBUT: 4/26/1872 at Troy; played LF and went 1-for-3 in a 10–0 loss to Troy's George Zettlein
FINALE: 10/28/1875 at New Haven; played CF and made 1 hit in a 10–7 loss to Boston's Cal McVey

A member of the Mansfields since their inception in the late 1860s, Jim Tipper debuted in their initial NA appearance in 1872 and left the majors three years later as the only man to play for all three ML franchises to date that have been based in Connecticut. Quick, a good fielder, and a weak hitter, he had his career shortened by a felon on his throwing hand, though which hand that was is still unknown. After the NA dissolved, he played for the Lynn Live Oaks in 1876 and later was part of the Rochester contingent that manager Jack Chapman took to Cuba in the fall of 1877 before finishing his career in 1879 with Manchester of the National Association. In 1895 he was found dead of consumption in a New Haven lodging house. (DN)

Treadway, George B. / "George"

B	T	HGT	WGT	G	AB	H	R	2B
L	L	6'0"	185	328	1290	368	259	58

3B	HR	RBI	BB	SO	SB	BA	SA	OBP
46	13	227	165	115	60	.285	.432	.370

B. 11/11/1866 Greenup County, KY **D.** 11/5/1928
TEAMS: 93BalN 94–95BroN 96LouN
DEBUT: 4/27/1893 at Washington; played RF and went 2-for-5 in a 7–5 loss to Washington's Jouett Meekin
FINALE: 6/21/1896 at Louisville; played 1B and went 0-for-3 in a 10–5 loss to St. Louis's Ted Breitenstein

George Treadway's ML career got off to such a promising start that he was a key figure in a trade that helped launch the mid-1890s Baltimore NL dynasty. But his career and life were soon derailed and he died in obscurity. Born in Kentucky, Treadway and his five younger siblings all grew up in Ironton, OH. He was of a dark complexion, and rumors arose early in his career that he was African American, but all indications are that they were untrue. After five minor league seasons, four of them in the Western Association, Treadway reached the majors with Baltimore in 1893, and shortly thereafter the *Louisville Courier-Journal* ran the headline: "Is the Orioles Right Fielder an Ethiopian?" Treadway vehemently denied the allegation and traced its history to an incident while he was with Denver when Dave Rowe called him a "n***" in a heated argument. He then added that the foul name was later given life by an ex-member of the Orioles who tried to run him off the team, but Baltimore manager Ned Hanlon would have none of it and kept him.

While Treadway's rookie year in Baltimore was not spectacular, he showed enough promise to be coveted in a major trade at the season's end. The deal was originally designed to send Treadway to Brooklyn for first baseman Dan Brouthers, but then Brooklyn asked for Billy Shindle as well, so Hanlon requested Willie Keeler in return and the trade became a two-for-two deal. At first, Treadway looked as though he might make it a mutually helpful swap, as he batted a robust .326 in 1894 and swatted 26 triples while displaying a stellar throwing arm in the outfield. But when his career collapsed after that and Shindle was a disappointment in Brooklyn, it developed that Baltimore had gotten two future HOFers at very little cost.

After substandard seasons in 1895 and 1896, Treadway left the majors and his life went into a tailspin. By 1899 his wife of six years sued him for divorce, claiming that he had gone broke before the honeymoon ended and hadn't had any money since. Whenever her husband couldn't get a baseball engagement, she alleged that he "seemed content to lie around her parents' house." She believed him to be living in New York and working for a machine shop, but maintained that he had sent her no money, forcing her to support herself by taking in boarders.

By 1901 Treadway was living in Chicago and playing semipro ball. The following year he returned to the pro ranks in the Pacific Northwest League. In 1905, his playing career over, Treadway was hired to umpire in the minors but was fired for excessive drinking. After that, he disappeared from sight entirely. Then in 1928 two teenage boys were hiking near Perris, CA, and happened on a shack whose elderly occupant was in obvious distress. The location was so remote that it took several hours to get an ambulance to the shack, and by the time the prospector could be rushed to the closest hospital he was on the verge of death from nephritis. The man's age was estimated at 85, but when authorities were sent to his shack to identify him, a different picture emerged. Among the papers of the man, who had apparently been living alone there for several years, was a Professional Ball Players of America membership card that identified him as George Treadway. Despite his ancient appearance, the man who had once been traded for Dan Brouthers and Wee Willie Keeler was only a year or two over 60 years old. (PM/DN)

Turner, George A. / "Tuck"

B	T	HGT	WGT	G	AB	H	R	2B
B	L	5'6½"	165	379	1504	482	298	67

3B	HR	RBI	BB	SO	SB	BA	SA	OBP
38	7	215	129	69	53	.320	.430	.378

G	IP	H	GS	CG	BB
1	6	9	0	0	0

SO	SH	W	L	PCT	ERA
3	0	0	0	—	7.50

B. 2/13/1867 W. New Brighton, NY **D.** 7/16/1945
TEAMS: 93–96PhiN 96–98StLN
DEBUT: 8/18/1893 at Philadelphia; played CF and went 0-for-4 in a 3–2 loss to St. Louis's Ted Breitenstein
FINALE: 6/10/1898 at Philadelphia; played RF and went 2-for-4 in a 3–1 win over Philadelphia's Al Orth

Tuck Turner went 1-for-4 in his second ML game to raise his career BA at that point to .125. From that day forward through the close of the 1895 season he hit .390 (271-for-695) and yet had still never played regularly for more than a few days at a time. The reason: he was the fourth outfielder behind Ed Delahanty, Sam Thompson, and Billy Hamilton, who all hit .388 or better during the same span.

In 1891 Turner had Willie Keeler as his teammate on the amateur Plainfield, NJ, club. Turner remained an amateur until 1893 when the Phils lured him away from the Corinthian Athletic Club on Staten Island to serve as an injury replacement for Hamilton. The following year Turner usually played only when Thompson or Hamilton was hurt or when Delahanty was used in the infield. He scored 91 runs in 80 games, hit .416, and collected 82 RBI in just 339 ABs. That winter, he fell on a patch of ice and hurt his right hand. The hand still troubled him in the spring of 1895, but once again there would have been no room for him in the Phils' outfield even if he had been the complete picture of health.

Prior to the next season Hamilton was traded to Boston for third baseman Billy Nash, who was made the Phils' manager. Turner chose that winter to stage a holdout, leaving Nash without a center fielder and forcing the club to open the season with Joe Sullivan, normally a SS, at the position. Upon joining the team, Turner hit .219 in his first 13 games back in harness, triggering the Phils first to farm him out to St. Paul as punishment and then to swap both him and Sullivan to St. Louis for Dick Cooley. St. Paul manager Charlie Comiskey initially refused to surrender Turner, claiming the Phils had promised to leave him in the Western League for the entire season, and in truth, Turner would have preferred remaining in the minors to going to the dreary Browns. Sullivan also did not want to go, but neither had a choice now that player permission was no longer needed for a trade to be effected. Demoralized, Turner hit just .243 for the year but rebounded in 1897 to bat .291 in 109 games and survive a potentially serious beaning on August 13 when he had to be carried off on a stretcher after being nailed by Cleveland's Zeke Wilson.

Turner opened 1898 as the Browns' RF incumbent but faded to .199 and was sold to Kansas City of the Western League when Jake Stenzel was acquired. He went home during the ten-day waiver period in the hope someone would claim him before he had to report to KC and then opted to stay home when no other NL team did. At some point Turner's sale appears to have been voided, for he was allowed to join Hartford of the Eastern League in 1899 for 56 games. Turner played two more seasons in the EL and finished his pro career in 1905. He then returned to Staten Island, where he died in 1945 of heart trouble. His story is a puzzle that may never be solved. Was he a potential star who got trapped on the wrong team early in his career and lost his spirit when he was traded to a tailender? Or was he swept up in the tsunami attack the Phils possessed in his first three seasons to heights that he never would have scaled with a weaker-hitting team? In any event, at the close of the nineteenth-century Turner owned the highest BA (.320) of any universally recognized switch hitter with a minimum of 1,000 career ABs. (DN)

Twitchell, Lawrence Grant / "Larry"

B	T	HGT	WGT	G	AB	H	R	2B
R	R	6'0"	185	639	2571	676	362	103

3B	HR	RBI	BB	SO	SB	BA	SA	OBP
40	19	384	168	231	84	.263	.356	.313

G	IP	H	GS	CG	BB
42	280.2	307	29	26	135

SO	SH	W	L	PCT	ERA
70	0	17	11	.607	4.62

B. 2/18/1864 Cleveland, OH **D.** 8/23/1930
TEAMS: 86–88DetN 89CleN 90CleP 90BufP 91ColA 92WasN 93–94LouN
DEBUT: 4/30/1886 at St. Louis; caught by Charlie Bennett in an 8–6 loss to St. Louis's Henry Boyle
FINALE: 7/7/1894 at Louisville; relieved Phil Knell in Knell's 14–6 loss to New York's Jouett Meekin
CAREER HIGHLIGHT: 8/18/1889 at Cleveland; batted cleanup, went 6-for-6, scored 5 runs, and hit for the cycle while appearing in relief of Enoch Bakely before returning to his outfield post in a 19–8 win over Boston's Kid Madden; his box appearance enabled him to join Jimmy Ryan as the only two players in ML history to hit for the cycle and pitch in the same game

Larry Twitchell was tall, blond, and a distaff favorite until he married in the winter of 1887–88. A carpenter by trade, he took up baseball because he had a great arm, was fast, and could hit the globe hard. But although he had his share of memorable moments, he was never able to build on the tremendous potential he exhibited in 1887, his official rookie season, and played his last ML game before he was 30. Twitchell began as a pitcher with independent Columbus, OH, in 1885 and moved to Zanesville of the Ohio State League after Columbus disbanded. After tossing a four-hitter against Detroit in an October 1885 exhibition, he was acquired by Wolverines manager Bill Watkins and was paid by the NL club for the entire 1886 season even though he made just four box appearances after straining a tendon in his arm. The following year Twitchell alternated between the box and the outfield, hit .333, and made Detroit the first team in ML history to have four pitchers with double-figure win totals when he went 11-1, thanks to the torrential run support his pennant-winning Detroit teammates gave him in almost every outing. Ironically, in his best-pitched game of the year, Twitchell drew his only loss, when Boston edged him 4–3 on May 30.

Unimpressed by Twitchell's glittering won-lost record, Watkins made him a full-time outfielder the following year, and it may have ruined his career. The Forest City native produced only one noteworthy season as a gardener—in 1889 when he came home to Cleveland after Detroit disbanded and hit .275 with 95 RBI. It was not that his arm had gone bad; he continued to pitch on occasion and in 1893, while in the Southern League, made a couple of throws that nearly broke the then world record.

After Twitchell finished 1893 with Louisville NL by hitting .310 in 45 games, he opened 1894 in LF for the Colonels but was gone in July when he hit only 4 points above his career mark of .263. Twitchell finished pro play with St. Paul of the Western League in 1896 and then returned to Cleveland. He sold insurance for a while and later worked as an inspector. In 1910 his son captained the Case Institute team, and some eleven years later, on July 29, 1921, Twitchell helped Cleveland celebrate its 125th anniversary by playing with the old-timers against a team of Cleveland sandlot players prior to an Indians game. He was a construction inspector when he died in Cleveland from heart disease, leaving behind his wife, Rebecca. (DN)

Van Dyke, William Jennings / "Bill" "The School Master"

B	T	HGT	WGT	G	AB	H	R	2B
R	R	5'8"	170	136	530	134	78	15

3B	HR	RBI	BB	SO	SB	BA	SA	OBP
11	2	56	25	2	74	.253	.334	.290

B. 12/15/1863 Paris, IL **D.** 5/17/1933
TEAMS: 90TolA 92StLN 93BosN
DEBUT: 4/17/1890 at Columbus; played LF and went 0-for-5 in a 14–9 loss to Columbus's Hank Gastright
FINALE: 9/30/1893 at St. Louis; played LF and went 1-for-4 in a 17–6 loss to St. Louis's Ted Breitenstein

Known as "The Schoolmaster" because he was educated and cultured, Bill Van Dyke played a good outfield and was an exceptional base runner, a hard slider, and usually the fastest player on his team. Were he active today he would have been platooned, as he could hit left-handers fairly well but was pie for any right-hander with a decent curve ball. His ML career BA, though a mediocre .253, was in all probability higher than his minor league career BA. Van Dyke's first pro season was 1884 with Terre Haute of the Northwestern League. In his debut with Terre Haute on May 2, he went 0-for-4 against Grand Rapids's Will Sawyer, a harbinger of what lay ahead. By 1887 Van Dyke was in a new version of the Northwestern League, where his weak hitting came fully to the fore with Des Moines. Even with walks counting as hits, he stood dead last among all loop regulars in late August 1887, with a .237 BA. A strong September lifted his final mark to .271 and brought him an invitation to return to Des Moines in 1888. Van Dyke stayed in the Iowa city that winter, working as a boot and shoe salesman, a job he would dare to pursue again the next winter after hitting all of .195 and then begging for work with Toledo of the International Association. Despite hitting just .254 in 1889, Van Dyke was retained by Toledo manager Charlie Morton when the Black Pirates ascended to the American Association in 1890.

After drawing the collar in his ML debut, Van Dyke collected his first hit the following day off Columbus's Jack Easton and then went on a tear over the next month that produced a .365 BA after the games on May 19, 1890, and ranked him third in the AA. But he hit less than .250 for the remainder of the season, finishing his rookie year at .257. When Toledo left the AA that winter, *TSN* reported that Van Dyke had been released so that he could remain in the AA with the revamped Philadelphia A's. But the A's never sent Van Dyke advance money, and he signed instead with Sioux City. When Sioux City won the Western Association flag, its manager, Al Buckenberger, earned a return ticket to the majors, as did Van Dyke despite hitting just .213. In November 1891 he signed with St. Louis and then moved his family to the Mound City, where he resumed his usual winter employment as a boot and shoe salesman in the expectation of winning a job the following spring as a substitute outfielder. Instead Van Dyke found himself in CF on Opening Day in 1892 after the Browns' entire outfield cast ditched the AA and signed with NL teams before the two loops struck a peace settlement. But he was released just 4 games into the season when he reached base only twice in his first 16 ABs.

Van Dyke nonetheless continued to make his home in St. Louis. His presence there after his 1893 minor league season ended enabled him to play his last 3 games in the majors when Boston came to the Mound City for its final series of the 1893 campaign needing a LF replacement for Cliff Carroll, who had gone home early. Van Dyke subsequently played in the minors until 1897. Despite his educational background and an early life of culture and refinement, his final days were spent as a widower at the County Poor Farm in El Paso, TX, living in destitute circumstances and probably suffering from Alzheimer's along with hardening of the arteries and malnutrition. (DN)

Waitt, Charles C. / "Charlie" "Charlie Fresh"

B	T	HGT	WGT	G	AB	H	R	2B
?	R	5'11"	165	113	407	67	35	14

3B	HR	RBI	BB	SO	SB	BA	SA	OBP
0	0	14	15	11	3	.165	.199	.194

B. 10/14/1853 Hallowell, ME **D.** 10/21/1912
TEAMS: 75StLNA 77ChiN 82BalA 83PhiN
DEBUT: 5/25/1875 at St. Louis; played 3B and made 1 hit in a 3–2 win over Keokuk's Mike Golden
FINALE: 9/18/1883 at Philadelphia; played CF and went 1-for-3 in a 4–0 loss to Buffalo's Jim Galvin

Al Spalding recalled that he once saw Charlie Waitt wearing a novel flesh-colored glove to play 1B in a game at Boston. Frank Bancroft also chipped in a recollection in 1900 of a game in 1878 when he was managing New Bedford and Waitt came to the bench after an inning in the field in which he had muffed a fly. Bancroft said he released his gardener when he saw he was wearing a glove. Whatever the truth regarding Waitt's early adventures with gloves, his misfortune was that while gloves in his day were optional, bats were not. With a bat in his hand Waitt was an atrocity. His .393 OPS is last among position players with a minimum of 400 career ABs, and his .370 OPS with Baltimore in 1882 is the season low in the AA's ten-year's history among players with a minimum of 250 ABs and was achieved despite the fact that he led the club in walks with 13.

Waitt spent 1871–72 with the amateur G. M. Roth club of Philadelphia before joining independent Easton, PA, for the next two seasons and then heading west to play for the St. Louis Brown Stockings in the final NA campaign. Although he never hit well even in the minors, he seems to have had little trouble finding teams to hire him, indicating that he was a better outfielder than his .843 career FA suggests. Even after his wretched year with Baltimore in 1882, Waitt was named player-manager of Wilmington for 1883 but "soon became unpopular with both players and public, caused by his overbearing manner" and was fired as manager in July, although he remained captain of the Interstate Association team until he left in September to join Philadelphia NL for his final ML innings and followed by playing one last season in the minors. By 1912 Waitt was working as a window washer in San Francisco when he died from blood poisoning that developed after he hurt his arm in a fall on the job. (DN)

Walker, Oscar / "Oscar"

B	T	HGT	WGT	G	AB	H	R	2B
L	L	5'10"	166	282	1128	287	155	46

3B	HR	RBI	BB	SO	SB	BA	SA	OBP
23	11	51	34	56	0	.254	.365	.278

B. 3/18/1854 Brooklyn, NY **D.** 5/20/1889
TEAMS: 75AtlNA 79–80BufN 82StLA 84BroA 85BalA
DEBUT: 9/17/1875 at Brooklyn; played RF and went 0-for-2 in a 12–3 loss to the Athletics' George Bechtel

FINALE: 9/4/1885 at Philadelphia; played RF and went 0-for-3 in a 2–1 win over Philadelphia's Bobby Mathews
CAREER LOWLIGHT: 6/20/1879 at Troy; became the first player to fan 5 times in a ML game in an 8–3 win over Providence's George Bradley, who logged only 6 whiffs in the entire game

Oscar Walker had excellent power but gaping holes in his swing. His chief distinctions are: in 1882 he won the rebel AA's initial home run crown, and the following year he became the only reigning ML home run king save for Count Campau to be consigned to the minors. Walker first gained prominence as the first sacker of the independent Memphis Reds in 1877 but jumped to the St. Paul Red Caps, pennant winners that year in the very informal thirteen-club League Alliance. Walker joined St. Paul in midseason 1877 but was subsequently expelled after a home game with Manchester for leaving town with the New Hampshire club while still under contract to St. Paul. An anonymous reporter known as "RED CAP" wrote in the *Chicago Tribune* on August 5 that Walker's actions were "as aggravated a case of 'revolving' as ever cursed the season of 1876, and it is to be hoped that the machinery of the Alliance will effectually impair the culprit's usefulness for 1877." The League Alliance ban stuck, and Walker played no more the rest of that year or the next with sanctioned teams. The Walker case is of particular interest because he had a family and we can only wonder where they lived and what they lived on while he was engaged in his unprofitable globe hopping.

Walker returned to the majors in 1879 for the first time since a token appearance with the 1875 Brooklyn Atlantics and hit .275 as a rookie. After a slow start the following year, he was released shortly after batting cleanup for Buffalo in John M. Ward's perfect game against the Bisons on June 17. Walker spent 1881 with two Eastern Championship Association teams in New York followed by a spell with the new version of the Brooklyn Atlantics. The formation of the AA brought him another ML chance in 1882, and he responded by winning the upstart loop's first dinger crown and finishing seventh in SA despite batting just .239. The arrival of rookie first baseman Charlie Comiskey in St. Louis the next spring rendered Walker superfluous.

He returned to his Brooklyn hometown to play for the Interstate Association champion Grays and then accompanied the team when it was added to the AA in 1884. Although Walker seemingly hit fairly well in his second crack at AA pitching, he again lost out to a better man when Brooklyn acquired Bill Phillips from the disbanded Cleveland NL team prior to the 1885 season. Walker spent that year with Newark of the Eastern League until summoned to Baltimore AA in September for his final ML at bats. By 1887 his health had declined to a point where a benefit game was played for him at Arctic Park in New York on October 17. Walker died less than two years later of consumption at his Brooklyn home with his wife and two sons at his bedside. (DN/DB)

Ward, Frank Gray / "Piggy"

B	T	HGT	WGT	G	AB	H	R	2B
B	R	5'9½"	196	221	780	223	172	23

3B	HR	RBI	BB	SO	SB	BA	SA	OBP
16	1	90	156	73	86	.286	.360	.419

B. 4/16/1867 Chambersburg, PA **D.** 10/24/1912
TEAMS: 83PhiN 89PhiN 91PitN 92–93BalN 93CinN 94WasN
DEBUT: 6/12/1883 at Philadelphia; played 3B and went hitless in a 5–4 win over Cleveland's Jim McCormick in twelve innings
FINALE: 9/30/1894 at St. Louis; played SS and went 1-for-3 in a 10–4 loss to St. Louis's Pink Hawley

Some say Frank Ward received his unflattering nickname because of his tendency to arrive at training camp each spring grossly overweight, but in 1897 *TSN* wrote, "Piggy Ward . . . with the countenance that suggests a scene at the Chicago stock yards when the tragedies of the porkers are being enacted," making it seem that he had more than a weight handicap. Despite his bulk, Ward was considered an excellent base runner and a very good slider, but his primary forte was his extraordinary patience as a hitter. Among all players in ML history who have appeared in more than 200 games but collected fewer than 1,000 PAs, Ward's .419 OBP heads the list by a significant margin of 27 points over Olaf Henriksen's .392.

Yet there is little question why his ML career was so spotty. Ward never found a position that he could play particularly well even though he was tested at all of them except pitcher. His best site was probably 1B, but his lack of height militated against him. A more serious fault, however, was his unfortunate penchant for following the same pattern with almost every new team he joined, starting off so poorly that he was nearly dumped and then catching fire only after his cause had begun to seem hopeless. There were times, too, when he would not be retained long enough to reverse course. The most prominent came in 1889 when he was given his first genuine opportunity to win a ML job. Sold to Philadelphia NL in early June by New Orleans of the Southern League, he hit .160 and lasted only 7 games as a replacement for injured Ed Delahanty before *TSN* adjudged he "has been given a thorough chance to distinguish himself and has thoroughly failed." It would be another three years before Ward received a lengthy trial in the majors and only in his last season did he succeed in playing enough to be a qualifier for the batting title.

Although Ward is credited with having played a game at 3B with the 1883 NL Quakers at age 16, it is undoubtedly an error. The man who appeared at 3B that day was said to be a Philadelphia amateur, and, in addition, there was no mention that Ward had previously played for the Quakers when he came to the team in 1889. The likelihood is that Ward made his pro debut with Allentown of the Eastern League in 1884 and remained with Pennsylvania minor league teams until he joined New Orleans in 1889 prior to coming to Philadelphia. After leaving the Quakers he probably played in nearly ten different minor league or independent ball cities before returning to the majors for a 6-game whirl with Pittsburgh NL in 1891.

Ward began the following season with Milwaukee of the Western League and did so well that he was dispatched to Baltimore on Brewers manager Billy Barnie's recommendation when the Western League folded in July. In early August 1892 Ward took over at 2B for Orioles captain Cub Stricker after Stricker's jaw was broken in an altercation with teammate Jocko Halligan. Even though he hit .290 in 56 games, he was released to New Orleans until June 1893 when Baltimore manager Ned Hanlon begged him to return. Hanlon's motive may simply have been to make Ward a pawn in a trade on June 16 for aging Cincinnati pitcher Tony Mullane, but the Reds immediately put Ward to work in RF. By mid-August he had compiled 44 runs, 37 walks, and 27 stolen bases in just 41 games with the Reds and yet went from being a strong favorite of the fickle crowd that occupied the RF bleachers to "a dirty deuce in a clean deck" after his "yellow fielding" in several games. Given his ten-days notice, Ward finished the season in the humble Pennsylvania State League.

That winter, he drove a delivery truck for an oyster and fish house in Altoona, his adopted home. In the spring of 1894 Ward won the Washington 2B job by default when Gus Schmelz, the Senators' new manager, could find no one better. He struggled in Pittsburgh, where fans "roused the ire of Senator Frank Ward by calling him 'Old Razor Back'" and also suffered a broken thumb that restricted him to the coaching lines for several weeks but still hit .303, led Washington in steals, and was second only to Bill Joyce in walks despite playing just 98 games. None of those good deeds outweighed his vile tongue and wobbly fielding in Schmelz's estimation, and he was released.

Ward won the Eastern League batting championship the following year, when he hit .372 for Scranton but was unable to excite any of the twelve NL teams enough to rehire him. He played another decade in the minors, finishing in the 1906 Hudson River League, and then returned to doing teamster and construction work in Altoona. In 1911 Ward attended Charlie Comiskey's 52nd birthday party in Chicago, belying an earlier report that he had been killed in the South grasping a live wire. He died the following October, however, of paresis, reportedly exacerbated by falling off a telephone pole three years earlier. (DN)

Weaver, William B. / "Buck" "Farmer"

B	T	HGT	WGT	G	AB	H	R	2B
13	?	5'10"	170	751	3073	853	421	114

3B	HR	RBI	BB	SO	SB	BA	SA	OBP
38	9	342	185	86	162	.278	.348	.330

B. 3/23/1865 Parkersburg, WV **D.** 1/23/1943
TEAMS: 88–91LouA 92–94LouN 94PitN
DEBUT: 9/16/1888 at Kansas City; played CF and went 2-for-4 in a 6–4 win over Kansas City's Frank Hoffman
FINALE: 9/29/1894 at Pittsburgh; caught Jock Menefee and went 3-for-4 in a 6–5 loss to Philadelphia's George Hodson

William Weaver was the second man in ML history with his surname to be nicknamed "Buck." Ironically, he was also called "Farmer" at times early in his career, largely because he had buckteeth, although he truly did have a half interest in a farm in Kansas. In 1896 *TSN* noted, "Buck Weaver's prominent teeth have given him the title of 'The Teddy Roosevelt of Base Ball.'"

Weaver came to Louisville in August 1888 from San Antonio of the Texas League. The following season, in his official rookie year, he won the Colonels' CF job and logged excellent numbers, but they went unnoticed because they came with a bad team in a campaign that was rich with outstanding frosh performances. Weaver continued to build his portfolio in 1890 when Louisville went from worst to first by hitting .289 and scoring 101 runs despite missing time in late June to be with his wife, Dora, after she accidentally shot herself with a revolver she kept under her pillow while he was away when she thought she heard a burglar and sprang up to investigate. After that, however, he plateaued in his development and may even have regressed.

Weaver's lone noteworthy achievement over the remainder of his career came in 1892 when he topped the NL in sacrifice hits with 68. Louisville fired him two years later after he hit just .221 in 64 games. Even though Weaver rebounded to hit .348 in the latter part of the season after joining Pittsburgh, the Pirates cut him the following March. He played in the minors until 1905 and later returned for two partial seasons as a player-manager in the Kansas State League in 1909–10. In 1911 his life unraveled when his wife divorced him for cruelty and his underage adopted daughter was discovered to be carrying his child. Convicted of rape, Weaver entered the Kansas state penitentiary in 1912 but received a controversial parole two years later from Gov. George Hodges, an amateur teammate of his in the mid-1880s. Weaver later worked for the Goodyear Tire and Rubber Company in Akron. He died at his Akron home of cardiac and renal disease in 1943. (DN)

Welch, Curtis Benton / "Curt"

B	T	HGT	WGT	G	AB	H	R	2B
R	R	5'10"	175	1107	4385	1152	915	215

3B	HR	RBI	BB	SO	SB	BA	SA	OBP
66	16	503	381	93	453	.263	.353	.345

G	IP	H	GS	CG	BB
1	1	6	0	0	0

SO	SH	W	L	PCT	ERA
1	0	0	0	—	54.00

B. 2/11/1862 E. Liverpool, OH **D.** 8/29/1896
TEAMS: 84TolA 85–87StLA 88–90PhiA 90–91BalA 92BalN 92CinN 93LouN
DEBUT: 5/1/1884 at Louisville; played CF and went 0-for-3 in a 5–1 loss to Louisville's Guy Hecker
FINALE: 5/23/1893 at Louisville; played LF and went 0-for-4 in an 8–4 loss to Cincinnati's Tony Mullane

Described by the *Boston Globe* as "a brilliant . . . (and) peerless outfielder," Curt Welch gained fame for one of the legendary plays of nineteenth-century baseball—his walk-off "$15,000 Slide" to end the 1886 World's Series—although most eyewitness reports indicate that he crossed the plate standing up with the winning run in the deciding game of the only postseason affair ever won by the AA (*see* Mike Kelly). Less than seven years later the uncouth and uneducated Welch had drunk himself out of the majors just weeks after passing his 31st birthday.

In his heyday, however, Welch was generally regarded as the premier center fielder in the majors. Stationing himself extraordinarily shallow in order to snare what would otherwise be line singles, he was believed by many who saw him play to have been the best outfielder prior to Tris Speaker at backpedaling on deep fly balls. Welch was also known as a smart, aggressive player who "would take any chance when running the bases and would buck a stone wall if that sort of thing was necessary." The *Boston Globe* wrote that he "had no fear of personal injury and would plunge headlong after the ball. At the bat he would brave the fastest pitching. He frequently permitted the ball to hit him in order to secure a base." So deft in fact was Welch at allowing pitches to nick him while pretending to dodge them that the NL adopted a revision to the hit-by-pitch rule in 1892, known unofficially as the Welch Amendment, stipulating that a batter would no longer be given his base if he were struck by a pitch on the hand or forearm. The revision survived until an incident in 1896 demonstrated its absurdity (*see* Thomas Daly).

Remembered as a shy and insecure youth, Welch joined his hometown Crockery City Club in 1877 by happenstance at the age of 15. The club was about to leave for a match in Steubenville, OH, when it learned that its catcher had injured his hand. According to the *East Liverpool Review*, "Someone noticed (Welch) in the crowd of admirers present, and suggested they give (him) a chance to prove his ability." Playing well, Welch earned a permanent spot on the club. The following year he helped to organize the Stars of East Liverpool and excelled as the team's pitcher. Rejoining the Crockery City Club in 1879, Welch was regarded as the best player on the team.

In June 1883 Welch left the Crockery Club to join Toledo of the Northwestern League on the recommendation of Sam Barkley. He and Barkley remained with the club the following season after it moved up to the AA. While with Toledo, Welch developed a trick play whereby, with a runner on second, the SS and second baseman would leave 2B uncovered, tempting the runner to take a long lead. After the pitcher deliberately threw wide to the plate, the catcher would fire the ball to 2B, where Welch, streaking in from CF, would snatch the throw and tag out the runner. In 1884 the rookie center fielder became even more renowned, however, for another ploy. While playing at home in Toledo's wooden park, Welch would conceal a mug of beer behind a loose slat in the center field fence and sneak a swig whenever there was a break in the action while his team was in the field.

When Toledo was unable to retain its AA franchise, it sold Welch and several teammates to St. Louis AA in October 1884. The price tag for Welch alone was believed to be around $500, but he would have been a bargain at ten times that figure. In his first season in the Mound City, he topped the Browns in batting and tied for the club lead in runs. More important, he paced all AA outfielders in put-outs and FA. Welch continued to rank annually among the club's offensive leaders and the AA's defensive chieftains, but by his third season with the Browns his unsavory off-field conduct had begun to madden player-manager Charlie Comiskey. After the 1887 campaign Welch and teammate Bill Gleason were traded to Philadelphia for Fred Mann, Chippy McGarr, Jack Milligan, and $3,000. The trade culminated a gigantic Browns winter fire sale and was in itself a historic transaction, as it involved the most players ever traded in one fell swoop to that point and would remain the largest deal of its kind for almost eight years. From the Browns' standpoint, the trade of Welch and several other stars of their three-time AA championship squad strengthened the team's financial situation by bringing in cash and cheaper players at a time when money was tight. It also beefed up several other clubs in the AA, creating a more balanced and competitive league. But most of all it appeased some of Comiskey's worries by ridding the club of malcontents and replacing them with eager new faces.

While the Browns streaked to their fourth straight pennant in 1888 without him, Welch did well in Philadelphia. Continuing to be productive both on offense and defense, he signed a contract that made him one of the highest-paid outfielders in the game, and additionally, in 1890, he received a bonus of $450 for acting as the A's captain. When Philadelphia flirted with bankruptcy late that season and discontinued paying its players, Welch, after a fight for his services, joined Baltimore. In 1891 he enjoyed one last illustrious year, scoring 122 runs and leading the AA for the third time in HBPs, but the following summer he tested the Orioles' new manager, Ned Hanlon, once too often and was bounced when he appeared on the field at Pittsburgh intoxicated after having been caught just a few days earlier drinking between innings under the grandstand. Welch signed with Cincinnati and expected to finish out the season there, but in mid-August a fall off the wagon cost him his job with the Reds, as it had in Baltimore.

He then worked at the McNichol Pottery in East Liverpool for $1.50 a day until an offer came to join Louisville NL in the spring of 1893. Welch opened the season in LF but looked lost at the plate, hitting just .170 in 14 games before he was dropped. The following year he tried to prolong his career with Syracuse of the Eastern League but already exhibited the early symptoms of consumption, according to writer Harry Merrill, who noted that the once raucous outfielder could now speak only in a "coarse whisper." Welch nonetheless remained with Syracuse until July 1895, when he was released after he resumed drinking heavily despite a doctor's orders to stop. He finished the season in the Pennsylvania State League and then tried to resume his job at the pottery but soon found the work too taxing.

Welch's last public appearance was at a benefit game for him in July 1896. He sat in the grandstand at the East Liverpool park, part of a crowd of about 200, and watched a game between the local Eclipse club and his old Crockery City team. The benefit brought his family around $500 and paid his funeral expenses when he died the following month. (DN/JK)

Wheeler, Harry Eugene / "Harry"

B	T	HGT	WGT	G	AB	H	R	2B
R	R	5'11"	165	257	1122	256	152	29

3B	HR	RBI	BB	SO	SB	BA	SA	OBP
21	2	32	23	32	—	.228	.297	.244

G	IP	H	GS	CG	BB
14	97.2	117	10	8	43

SO	SH	W	L	PCT	ERA
41	0	7	6	.538	4.70

G	W	L	PCT	PENNANTS
4	0	4	.000	0

B. 3/3/1858 Versailles, IN **D.** 10/9/1900
TEAMS: 78ProN 79–80CinN 80CleN 82CinA 83ColA 84StLA (P/M)84KCU 84Chi-PitU 84BalU
DEBUT: 6/19/1878 at Providence; caught by Lew Brown in a 9–3 win over Indianapolis's "The Only" Nolan
FINALE: 10/15/1884 at Cincinnati; played RF and went 2-for-4 in a 5–3 loss to Cincinnati's George Bradley

In 1878 Harry Wheeler was working as a Cincinnati bartender and playing semipro ball when his effective work in preseason exhibitions against Cincinnati NL earned him a June trial as Providence's regular pitcher. Although Wheeler won six of seven games, his ERA was more than a run above the NL average and he lost his job to rookie John M. Ward. Wheeler began 1879 as Cincinnati's change pitcher, but the durable Will White needed little help, and he pitched only 1 game, in which he was battered 17–1. A decent hitter, Wheeler subsequently turned to outfielding. After a game as an injury sub for Cleveland NL early in 1880, he got a trial in LF with Cincinnati NL in August, which he failed in decisive fashion. By the time Joe Sommer replaced him, Wheeler was fielding .750, batting barely above .100, and had more than twice as many errors as hits.

Wheeler finally established himself in pro ball in 1882 when the rebel AA formed. The Cincinnati entry in the new loop released first baseman–pitcher Dave Rowe just before the season began and added Harry McCormick as a change pitcher and Bill Tierney to play 1B. But the rules then forbade bringing in a new player except in case of injury, so it was more strategic to have an additional pitcher who could also play in the field than strictly a position player. Tierney was released in favor of Wheeler. As matters turned out, Wheeler seldom worked as the third pitcher. Meanwhile, he proved unable to handle 1B, reaching his nadir with a four-error day on May 20. Soon afterward, the Reds signed Henry Luff to man 1B, but by then Wheeler had contributed enough at bat that he was kept in the lineup in RF, a job he held the rest of the season.

The pennant-winning Reds had no intention of standing pat in 1883 and particularly intended to improve their outfield. Although not the liability in RF that he had been at 1B, Wheeler's habit of playing too deep suggested a lack of confidence, understandable since in an incomplete season as the RF regular he committed nearly as many errors as the other two Reds regular outfielders combined. In the spring he was released and signed with Columbus. Axed again after a poor season, he caught on briefly with St. Louis in 1884 but played little. In early June, Wheeler signed with Kansas City in the upstart UA and was named manager, but he was fired from that position after losing his first 4 games and then released as a player a short while later. He finished 1884 bouncing around with two more UA teams.

By the middle 1880s, with the UA disbanded and the AA having taken giant steps toward upgrading its rosters, ML jobs were scarcer. Wheeler reached his appropriate level as a minor leaguer, most notably at Waterbury, CT, where he captained a team that included future HOFer Billy Hamilton and reportedly taught Hamilton the art of baserunning and "sliding out of harm's way." After 1888 he left baseball and returned to Cincinnati, where he had continued to tend bar winters, and opened his own saloon. Like so many players of his day, Wheeler had contracted syphilis. Before long he was an invalid, unable to support his wife and two children. Extroverted and musically talented, Wheeler had always been popular wherever he had played, and when word of his condition spread, contributions poured into a benefit fund for the support of his family from well-wishers in Cincinnati and elsewhere. By the fall of 1898 more than $1,500 had been amassed. The money was put in the hands of Aaron Stern, formerly president of Cincinnati's 1882 champion team, who doled out $35 a month to Wheeler's family over a period that lasted until after Wheeler passed away in October 1900. (DB/DN)

Wilmot, Walter Robert / "Walt"

B	T	HGT	WGT	G	AB	H	R	2B
B	R	5'9"	165	962	3988	1100	727	152

3B	HR	RBI	BB	SO	SB	BA	SA	OBP
92	58	594	350	226	383	.276	.404	.337

B. 10/18/1863 Plover, WI **D.** 2/1/1929
TEAMS: 88–89WasN 90–95ChiN 97–98NYN
DEBUT: 4/20/1888; played LF and went 0-for-4 in a 6–0 loss to New York's Cannonball Titcomb
FINALE: 6/14/1898 at New York; in the ninth inning pinch hit unsuccessfully for pitcher Ed Doheny in a 3–2 loss to Brooklyn's Roaring Bill Kennedy
CAREER HIGHLIGHT: 8/22/1891 at Chicago; collected a record 6 walks in 6 plate appearances in a 10–4 win over Cleveland's Cy Young and Lee Viau

Walt Wilmot came to St. Paul of the Northwestern League in 1886 as a pitcher but fared poorly, looked weak in the outfield, and was also up for release until the sports editor of the local *Pioneer Press* prevailed upon manager Jack Barnes to stick with him a bit longer. By 1887 Wilmot was Barnes's best hitter and tied for the loop lead in triples with Oshkosh's Dummy Hoy. Washington NL acquired both men that off-season, and while Hoy thrived immediately in the majors, Wilmot struggled. Not yet a switch hitter, he was benched whenever the Senators faced a lefty.

He improved the following season, leading the NL in triples, and then purportedly signed a three-year contract for $4,000 per annum with Chicago when the Colts bought him from Washington after the Senators feared he would otherwise jump to the PL. He rewarded the Second City by leading the NL in homers in 1890, but that winter, while working at his off-season job in a Minneapolis bank, he learned the PL was about to disband and asked Chicago president Al Spalding for his release, fearing that otherwise Hugh Duffy would return to the club and take his job. Wilmot's fears were alleviated when Duffy signed with Boston AA instead. Then in March, he suffered a more serious setback when he was compelled to sue his wife, Frankie, for divorce, charging desertion and adultery; they had married in 1886 and she had since "run away to Spokane Falls with a traveling man."

The divorce was granted in late June 1891, freeing Wilmot to concentrate on baseball again. He had another solid year, nearly matching his 1890 stats, but then fell off drastically in 1892 and lost his job to George Decker for long stretches. After winning the Foley Emblem (awarded to the amateur billiards champion of St. Paul) in November for the third straight year, Wilmot refused to accept the huge pay reduction Chicago wanted to levy for his poor year and held out deep into the spring of 1893. Upon returning, he put up decent numbers that year and followed with his last strong season in 1894 before drawing his release in November 1895 so that he could take the player-manager's job with Minneapolis, which had unofficially become a Chicago farm club. Wilmot remained at that post until July 1897, when Doggie Miller replaced him. He joined the NL Giants toward the end of the season and upon his release in June 1898 returned to his former station in Minneapolis when the Millers fired manager Gus Schmelz. Wilmot remained with Minneapolis through 1900. That fall, he remarried, wedding Clare McDonald, the daughter of a Kansas City judge. Now in his late thirties, he spent 1901 with Grand Rapids of the Western Association and then returned to Minneapolis for two more years before finishing his pro career in 1905 as the player-manager of Butte in the Pacific National League. In his remaining years Wilmot promoted automobile shows in the Midwest. He died in Chicago of cancer at 65. (DN/DB)

Wolf, William Van Winkle / "Jimmy" "Chicken"

B	T	HGT	WGT	G	AB	H	R	2B
R	R	5'9"	190	1196	4959	1439	779	212

3B	HR	RBI	BB	SO	SB	BA	SA	OBP
109	18	592	229	71	186	.290	.388	.327

G	IP	H	GS	CG	BB
3	10	19	0	0	3

SO	SH	W	L	PCT	ERA
2	0	0	0	—	10.80

G	W	L	PCT	PENNANTS
65	14	51	.215	0

B. 5/12/1862 Louisville, KY **D.** 5/16/1903
TEAMS: 82–88LouA (P/M)89LouA 90–91LouA 92StLN
DEBUT: 5/2/1882 at St. Louis; played RF and went 2-for-5 in a 9–7 loss to St. Louis's George McGinnis
FINALE: 8/21/1892 at St. Louis; played RF and went 0-for-4 in an 8–2 loss to Baltimore's George Cobb
FAMOUS INCIDENT: 8/22/1886 at Louisville; hit 2 home runs in a 5–3 win over Cincinnati's George Pechiney in eleven innings, with the second bounding over the CF fence as a small dog raced on the field and held Reds center fielder Abner Powell by the leg for several seconds, preventing him from retrieving the ball (as the rules then permitted) while Wolf circled the bases
FAMOUS FIRST: Was the first player in ML history to spend his first ten seasons in the majors with the same franchise

William Wolf was reputedly nicknamed "Chicken" after stuffing himself on stewed chicken prior to a game and then playing poorly, but the source of "Jimmy," his primary nickname, is still a mystery. The only player to be a member of the AA from the day it began in 1882 until its last hurrah in 1891, Wolf had the additional distinction of being the first performer in ML history to reach the ten-year mark in career longevity while spending his entire term with the same team. Pete Browning and Guy Hecker may have been the face of Louisville baseball before the club joined the NL, but Wolf was the soul of it.

A product of the Louisville sandlots, Wolf first graduated to the Eclipse in 1880 and remained with the club when it formed the core of the franchise that represented Louisville in 1882, the AA's initial season as a major league. Some fourteen years later, after he was no longer an active part of the game, Wolf revealed that he was only receiving $35 a month at the time he made his ML debut, and newspaper notes indicate that he was added to the original Eclipse roster only when the club could not land an experienced outfielder. Pestered each winter by a weight problem, he finally resorted to going to Hot Springs in the late 1880s to "sweat it off" in the baths, but not until 1889 did he finally begin to come into his own. Performing for the worst team in AA history, Wolf paced the last-place Colonels in batting, played wherever he was needed, and, after Tom Esterbrook was relieved of the captaincy, "received every vote" to replace him. Nevertheless, in August a Louisville *TSN* correspondent labeled him the worst right fielder in the AA and predicted he was playing his last season in the Falls City.

Instead Wolf returned in 1890 after Browning had jumped to the PL and Hecker to manage the Pittsburgh NL club and enjoyed a banner year, leading Louisville in almost every major offensive department and topping the AA in batting, overriding his purported admission to the *Ohio State Journal*, which was partial to Columbus's Ralph Johnson, that, "I'll lead the association all right. I may not be entitled to the honor, but the official scorers of the Louisville club will swell my average enough to beat out Johnson." When the rest of the team fell into step with Wolf, Louisville marched from worst to first and he became the only member of the original Louisville AA team to play in an AA vs. NL World's Series. As was Wolf's custom, he did not work that winter—baseball was his only employment during his active career—and spent most of his time caring for and seasoning two new bats he had made for him by the Hillerich Company. But the bats were unable to stem a brutal slide the following season. By July 1891 the Louisville public was already clamoring for his release. Overweight and no longer able to cover his position, Wolf dropped 110 points off his 1890 BA and was cut the following January just days before his father died. He began 1892 with Syracuse in the Eastern League but was called to St. Louis in August in the vain hope that he could revive his game. After just three outings with the Browns, Wolf went to owner Chris Von der Ahe to request his release because he felt he "was out of luck" and could no longer play good ball.

Wolf finished strongly, hitting .348 in the 1893

Eastern League after starting an off-season job with the Louisville Fire Department that he now decided to make his full-time profession. Periodically, he was called on to serve as a substitute umpire in a local NL game, but any thoughts of making that a career were quashed when he was almost torn limb from limb by the entire New York Giants team after squeezing pitcher Amos Rusie unmercifully in the second game of a DH on July 16, 1897, causing a flood of protested walks. Two years later, as Wolf was responding to a fire call near his Louisville home, his fire engine collided with a pushcart, causing the horse team to separate from the wagon. Wolf was dragged across the cobblestones for several hundred yards and suffered a serious head injury that left him "mentally unbalanced" and forced his commitment to the Central Asylum for the Insane outside Louisville in 1901. Although he was eventually released, his final months were a misery. Late in 1901 one of his sons died and his own health continued to fail. Wolf died of multiple causes in Louisville's city hospital in 1903. (DN/PVB)

Wood, George Albert / "George" "Dandy"

B	T	HGT	WGT	G	AB	H	R	2B
L	R	5'10½"	175	1280	5371	1467	965	228

3B	HR	RBI	BB	SO	SB	BA	SA	OBP
132	68	601	418	547	113	.273	.403	.329

G	IP	H	GS	CG	BB
5	12	18	0	0	5

SO	SH	W	L	PCT	ERA
3	0	0	0	—	5.25

G	W	L	PCT	PENNANTS
125	67	55	.549	0

B. 11/9/1858 Prince Edward Island, Canada
D. 4/4/1924
TEAMS: 80WorN 81–85DetN 86–89PhiN 89BalA 90PhiP (P/M)91PhiA 92BalN 92CinN
DEBUT: 5/1/1880 at Worcester; played LF and went 3-for-5 in a 13–1 win over Troy's Mickey Welch
FINALE: 9/29/1892 at Cincinnati; played RF and went 0-for-3 in a 10–4 loss to Chicago's Ad Gumbert
CAREER HIGHLIGHT: 5/29/1884 at Chicago; Wood and Chicago's Abner Dalrymple became the first batters in ML history to hit lead-off homers for their respective teams in the same game in Larry Corcoran's 15–5 win over Detroit's Stump Wiedman

George Wood had a live bat and a strong arm that was used to pitch on occasion. In 1882 he was the first lead-off hitter to lead a ML loop in homers when he topped the NL with 7 dingers.

Why was he batting leadoff? Good question. Even though Wood seldom walked, was not particularly fast and was never much of a threat to steal, he remained a lead-off hitter for most of his career. The result was some of the most bizarre and contradictory season stats in history. In 1882 the NL home run king was credited with just 29 RBI. Two years later he hiked his total to eight but again collected only 29 RBI. Knowledgeable historians know that RBI figures during Wood's time are guesstimates, but still there is no sane explanation for why he continued to bat leadoff until the tail end of his career. Actually, Harry Wright's persistence in using Wood there after he came to Philadelphia in 1886 reeks of masochism. All during the outfielder's four-year tenure with the Quakers the team suffered mortally from the lack of a decent run producer in the middle of the order.

Wood spent parts of his first two pro seasons with Worcester minor league entries before the city joined the NL in 1880. Despite a passable rookie season, in 1881 he was allowed to go to Detroit, a new franchise replacing the expelled Cincinnati team. Wood had the misfortune to be sold by Detroit to Philadelphia in November 1885 just as the Wolverines were about to flower into one of the NL's premier teams. In his first year with the Quakers he led the club in BA, SA, and total bases while batting at several different spots in the order. Wright bafflingly took that performance to mean that Wood was ideal for the lead-off slot the following year, and there he stayed until he was released in the waning days of the 1889 season, allegedly for his role in recruiting teammates to jump to the PL that fall. In 1890, batting in the middle of the order, he had his first 100-RBI season for Philadelphia PL. Rather than returned to Wright's NL club in 1891, he joined the reorganized Philadelphia AA entry. Playing for his third different Philadelphia team in three different leagues in a three-year span, Wood had his career year at 33 and also garnered his only ML managerial experience. Expected to pilot the A's only on an interim basis after Billy Sharsig stepped down, he ended up managing them the rest of the season. Amid charges that he was incompetent to do anything more than make out a lineup card, Wood guided the A's to a surprise first division finish in the AA's final campaign as a major league.

After the AA and NL merged, Wood began 1892 without a team after he was assigned to Washington in the consolidation and the Senators released him in the belief that Patsy Donovan would work cheaper and do as well. Their judgment proved accurate when Wood hit just .208 in stints with Baltimore and Cincinnati. Released by the Reds when he was deemed "too fat" to play the outfield anymore, he lingered in the minors until 1896 despite his mushrooming weight problem—"George is a hitter when he hits. He is not a runner when he runs"—and then tried umpiring.

In 1898 Nick Young hired Wood for the NL's regular officiating staff, but he encountered an embarrassing situation his very first day on the job. On April 15, Opening Day at Cincinnati, Reds outfielder Dusty Miller tried to steal 3B and the throw from Cleveland catcher Jack O'Connor appeared to beat him. Wood, working the bases, said nothing, figuring that Ed Swartwood behind the plate had a better view and would make the call. From Swartwood's angle Miller looked out, but many felt he had eluded the tag. When Miller remained on 3B, Swartwood ordered him to vacate it, thinking Wood had called him out. After the game it developed that neither umpire had made the call, but since Cincinnati won no protest was lodged. The incident nonetheless demonstrated a serious flaw in the double-umpire system as well as Wood's lack of officiating wherewithal. He lasted in his blue coat and cap only until the end of July. Former ML pitcher John Tener, then governor of Pennsylvania, later appointed Wood the marshal of the Pennsylvania state public service commission. He served at that post until shortly before his death from a heart attack in Harrisburg. (DN)

York, Thomas Jefferson / "Tom"

B	T	HGT	WGT	G	AB	H	R	2B
L	?	5'9"	165	963	4005	1095	743	217

3B	HR	RBI	BB	SO	SB	BA	SA	OBP
89	15	502	198	202	20	.273	.383	.309

G	W	L	PCT	PENNANTS
96	56	37	.602	0

B. 7/13/1851 Brooklyn, NY **D.** 2/17/1936
TEAMS: 71TroNA 72–73BalNA 74PhiNA 75HarNA 76–77HarN (P/M)78ProN (P/M)81ProN 78–82ProN 83CleN 84–85BalN
DEBUT: 5/9/1871 at Troy; played CF in a 9–5 loss to Boston's Al Spalding
FINALE: 10/1/1885 at Baltimore; played RF and went 2-for-4 in a 13–9 win over 3 Louisville pitchers

Tom York performed with the amateur Brooklyn Crystals in 1867 and the Brooklyn Powhatans in 1868–69 before turning pro with Troy in 1870. Leaving Troy after just one NA season, he then spent two years with the Lord Baltimores and is the only man to play regularly with Baltimore clubs in the NA and the AA. Even though he participated in fifteen consecutive ML seasons and was a regular in all but the last of them, he is among the least-remembered nineteenth-century performers. Adding to York's unwarranted obscurity, he managed and umpired in the majors, was a key member of Providence's first NL pennant winner in 1878, and was among the Grays' best players over the course of the four seasons he was with them.

York had his last distinguished ML season in 1881, when he led the Grays in slugging and OBP while playing every game in LF. He left Providence for Cleveland after the 1882 campaign when he was promised the Blues' captaincy. During the 1883 season, although Frank Bancroft is officially listed as the manager, it was York who really ran Cleveland on the field. After just one season in the Forest City, York wanted out, ostensibly because his wife was ailing and hated the climate in Cleveland, and she purchased his release. Baltimore reimbursed him for the amount in the form of a salary increase and also granted him the scorecard concession at its park. York opened the 1884 AA campaign as Baltimore's captain and cleanup hitter but batted just .223. He remained on the Orioles one final season as a scrub and then tried umpiring. In May 1886, York replaced Jim Clinton as a regular AA official but resigned after just 16 games to take a similar job in the NL. He quit as a senior loop umpire after a game in New York on July 22, 1886, in which the crowd hissed him. York later served as part owner and manager of the Albany, NY, minor league team and was ruined financially by the venture. By the mid-1890s he was an inspector on Al Johnson's Nassau electric streetcar line in Brooklyn. In the winter of 1897–98, York suffered a stroke but was back at work by the summer and appointed to a superintendent's position soon afterward. He died in New York at 84. (DN)

BIBLIOGRAPHY

BOOKS

Adelman, Melvin. *A Sporting Time*. Chicago: University of Illinois Press, 1986.

Alexander, Charles. *John McGraw*. New York: Viking, 1988.

———. *Our Game*. New York: Henry Holt, 1991.

Allen, Lee. *The Cincinnati Reds*. New York: G. P. Putnam's Sons, 1948.

———. *The Hot Stove League*. New York: A. S. Barnes, 1955.

———. *The World Series: The Story of Baseball's Annual Championship*. New York: G. P. Putnam's Sons, 1969.

Anson, Adrian C. *A Ball Player's Career*. Chicago: Era, 1900.

Appel, Martin, and Burt, Goldblatt. *Baseball's Best*. New York: McGraw-Hill, 1980.

Axelson, G. W. *"Commy": The Life Story of Charles A. Comiskey*. Chicago: Reilly & Lee, 1919.

Ball, David. *Nineteenth Century Transactions Register*. Cincinnati: David Ball, 2009.

The Baseball Encyclopedia. New York: Macmillan, 1968, 1976, 1982, 1993, and 1996.

Benson, Michael. *Ballparks of North America*. Jefferson NC: McFarland, 1989.

Bowman, Larry G. *Before the World Series*. Dekalb: Northern Illinois University Press, 2003.

Bready, James. *Baseball in Baltimore*. Baltimore: The Johns Hopkins University Press, 1998.

Brown, Warren. *The Chicago Cubs*. New York: Putnam's, 1952.

Caillault, Jean-Pierre. *A Tale of Four Cities*. Jefferson NC: McFarland, 2003.

Casway, Jerrold L. *Ed Delahanty in the Emerald Age of Baseball*. Notre Dame IN: University of Notre Dame Press, 2004.

Coombs, Samm, and Bob West, eds. *Baseball: America's National Game 1839–1915 by Albert G. Spalding*. San Francisco: Halo, 1991.

Dewey, Donald, and Nicholas Acocella. *Encyclopedia of Major League Baseball Teams*. New York: Harper Collins, 1993.

Freyer, John, and Mark Rucker. *Nineteenth-Century Baseball in Chicago*. Charleston SC: Arcadia, 2003.

Goldstein, Warren. *Playing for Keeps: A History of Early Baseball.* Ithaca NY: Cornell University Press, 1989.
Graham, Frank. *The Brooklyn Dodgers.* New York: Putnam's, 1945.
———. *The New York Giants.* New York: Putnam's, 1952.
Hetrick, J. Thomas. *Chris Von der Ahe and the St. Louis Browns.* Lanham MD: Scarecrow, 1999.
Hetrick, J. Thomas. *Misfits! Baseball's Worst Ever Team.* Clifton VA: Pocol, 2001.
Ivor-Campbell, Frederick, Mark Rucker, and Robert L. Tiemann, eds. *Baseball's First Stars.* Cleveland OH: Society for American Baseball Research, 1989.
James, Bill. *The Bill James Historical Baseball Abstract.* New York: Villard, 1988.
Johnson, Lloyd, and Miles Wolff, eds. *The Encyclopedia of Minor League Baseball,* 2nd edition. Durham NC: Baseball America, 1997.
Kaese, Harold. *The Boston Braves.* New York: G. P. Putnam's Sons, 1948.
Kirsch, George. *The Creation of American Team Sports: Baseball and Cricket, 1838–72.* Urbana IL: University of Illinois Press, 1989.
Koppett, Leonard. *Koppett's Concise History of Major League Baseball.* Philadelphia: Temple University Press, 1998.
Lange, Fred W. *History of Baseball in California and Pacific Coast Leagues, 1847–1938.* Oakland CA: privately published, 1938.
Lanigan, Ernest J., ed. *The Baseball Cyclopedia.* New York: The Baseball Magazine, 1922.
Lansche, Jerry. *Glory Fades Away.* Dallas TX: Taylor, 1991.
Lee, Bill. *The Baseball Necrology.* Jefferson NC: McFarland, 2003.
Levine, Peter. *A. G. Spalding and the Rise of Baseball: The Promise of an American Sport.* New York: Oxford University Press, 1985.
Lewis, Franklin. *The Cleveland Indians.* New York: Putnam's, 1949.
Lieb, Frederick G. *The Baseball Story.* New York: Putnam's, 1950.
———. *The St. Louis Cardinals: The Story of a Great Baseball Club.* New York: Putnam's, 1947.
Lowry, Phillip J. *Green Cathedrals.* Cooperstown NY: Society for American Baseball Research, 1986.
Mack, Connie. *My Sixty-Six Years in Baseball.* Philadelphia: Winston, 1950.
Macht, Norman L. *Connie Mack and the Early Years of Baseball.* Lincoln NE: University of Nebraska Press, 2009.
Miklich, Eric. *Rules of the Game.* North Babylon NY: privately published, 2002.
Morris, Peter. *Baseball Fever.* Ann Arbor MI: University of Michigan Press, 2003.
———. *But Didn't We Have Fun.* Chicago: Ivan R. Dee, 2008.
———. *A Game of Inches, The Game on the Field: The Stories Behind the Innovations that Shaped Baseball.* Chicago: Ivan R. Dee, 2006.
———. *Level Playing Fields: How the Groundskeeping Murphy Brothers Shaped Baseball.* Lincoln NE: University of Nebraska Press, 2007.
Nemec, David. *The Baseball Rookies Encyclopedia.* Dulles VA: Brassey's, 2004.
———. *The Beer and Whisky League.* New York: Lyons & Burford, 1995.
———. *The Great American Baseball Team Book.* New York: New American Library, 1992.
———. *Great Baseball Feats, Facts, and Firsts.* New York: New American Library, 1987.
———. *The Great Encyclopedia of Nineteenth-Century Major League Baseball.* Tuscaloosa AL: University of Alabama Press, 2006.
———. "Last Call for the Beer Ball League." *Hot Stove Baseball* (Winter 1991).
———. *The Official Rules of Baseball Illustrated.* New York: Lyons, 2006.
———. *The Ultimate Baseball Book.* With Daniel Okrent and Harris Lewine. Boston: Houghton Mifflin, 2000.
Palmer, Harry. *Stories of the Base Ball Field.* Chicago: Rand McNally, 1890.

Palmer, Pete, and Gary Gillette, eds. *The ESPN Baseball Encyclopedia*, 5th edition. New York: Sterling, 2008.
Peverelly, Charles A. *A Book of American Pastimes*. Self-published.
Povich, Shirley. *The Washington Senators*. New York: Putnam's, 1954.
Rankin, June. The *New York and Brooklyn Base Ball Clubs*. New York: Richard Fox, 1888.
Reichler, Joseph L. *The Great All-Time Baseball Record Book*. New York: Macmillan, 1993.
Richter, Francis. *A Brief History of Base Ball*. Philadelphia: Sporting Life, 1909.
Ritter, Lawrence. *The Glory of Their Times*. New York: Random House, 1985.
Ryczek, William J. *Blackguards and Red Stockings: A History of Baseball's National Association, 1871–75*. Jefferson NC: McFarland, 1992.
———. *When Johnny Came Sliding Home*. Jefferson NC: McFarland, 1998.
Seymour, Harold, and Dorothy Seymour Mills. *Baseball: The Early Years*. New York: Oxford University Press, 1960.
Shannon, Bill, and George Kalinsky. *The Ballparks*. New York: Hawthorne, 1975.
Shatzkin, Mike, ed. *The Ballplayers*. New York: William Morrow, 1990.
Spalding, John. *Always on Sunday: The California Baseball League, 1886–1915*. Manhattan KS: Ag Press, 1992.
Spatz, Lyle. *Bad Bill Dahlen: The Rollicking Life and Times of an Early Baseball Star*. Jefferson NC: McFarland, 2004.
The Sporting News Official Baseball Record Book. St. Louis: The Sporting News, 1984.
Stevens, David. *Baseball's Radical for All Seasons: A Biography of John Montgomery Ward*. Lanham MD: Scarecrow, 1998.
Sullivan, Dean A. *Early Innings: A Documentary History of Baseball, 1825–1908*. Lincoln NE: University of Nebraska Press, 1995.
Sullivan, Ted. *Humorous Stories of the Ball Field*. Chicago: M. A. Donohue, 1903.
Thompson, S. C. *All-Time Rosters of Major League Baseball Clubs*. New York: A. S. Barnes, 1973.
Thorn, John, and Pete Palmer, eds., with Michael Gershman. *Total Baseball*, 5th edition. Viking, 1997.
Terry, James L. *Long before the Dodgers: Baseball in Brooklyn, 1855–1884*. Jefferson NC: McFarland, 2002.
Tiemann, Robert L. *Dodger Classics*. St. Louis: Baseball Histories, 1983.
Tiemann, Robert L., and Mark Rucker, eds. *Nineteenth-Century Stars*. Cleveland OH: Society for American Baseball Research, 1989.
Turkin, Hy, and S. C. Thompson. *The Official Encyclopedia of Baseball*. New York: A. S. Barnes, 1951.
Vincent, Ted. *Mudville's Revenge*. New York: Seaview, 1981.
———. *The Rise and Fall of American Sport*. Lincoln NE: University of Nebraska Press, 1994.
Voigt, David Quentin. *American Baseball, Volume One*. University Park PA: Pennsylvania State University Press, 1983.
———. *The League that Failed*. Lanham MD: Scarecrow, 1998.
Von Borries, Phillip. *American Gladiator: The Life and Times of Pete Browning*. Bangor ME: Booklocker.com.
———. *Legends of Louisville*. West Bloomfield MI: Altwerger and Mandel, 1993.
Westlake, Charles. *Columbus Baseball History*. Columbus OH: Pfeiffer, 1981.
Wright, Marshall. *The National Association of Base Ball Players*. Jefferson SC: McFarland, 2000.
Zang, David. *Fleet Walker's Divided Heart*. Lincoln NE: University of Nebraska Press. 2007.

NEWSPAPERS

Atlanta Constitution
Boston Globe
Boston Herald
Boston Post
Brooklyn Daily Eagle
Chicago Inter-Ocean
Chicago Tribune
Cincinnati Commercial
Cincinnati Commercial Gazette
Cincinnati Enquirer
Cincinnati Gazette
Cincinnati Times-Star
Cleveland Leader
Cleveland Plain Dealer
Cleveland Press
Covington Daily Commonwealth
Detroit Free Press
Hartford Courant
Indianapolis Journal
Los Angeles Times
Louisville Courier Journal
Missouri Republican
New York Clipper
New York Herald
New York Times
Philadelphia Inquirer
Pittsburgh Dispatch
Pittsburgh Leader
Pittsburgh Post
Pittsburgh Telegraph
Police Gazette
Providence Journal
St. Louis Post-Dispatch
St. Louis Republican
Toledo Bee
Washington Post
Washington Star

BASEBALL GUIDES

Beadle's Dime Base-Ball, 1865
Players League Guide, 1890
Reach's Official Base Ball Guide. Philadelphia: A. J. Reach & Bros., 1884–1901
Spalding's Official Base Ball Guide. Chicago: A. G. Spalding and Bros., 1876–1901

MAGAZINES, JOURNALS, AND OTHER PUBLICATIONS

Lippincott's Monthly Magazine
Sporting Life, 1883–1910
Sporting News, 1886–1975
Thorn, John, and Mark Rucker. *The National Pastime: A Review of Baseball History*. Special Pictorial Issue: The Nineteenth Century. A publication of the Society for American Baseball Research, 1984.

MANUSCRIPTS AND ARCHIVES

Chadwick, Henry. Personal scrapbooks. On microfilm. New York Public Library, Albert G. Spalding Collection.

CONTRIBUTORS

David Ball is employed by the Classics Library at the University of Cincinnati, from which he graduated with a degree in ancient history. He has studied nineteenth-century baseball for many years and is the author of several biographical sketches of players and book reviews for publications and websites of the Society of American Baseball Research (SABR), as well as two articles for *Base Ball Magazine* dealing with organizational issues in early professional baseball. Ball has also created a register of major league sales and trades of the nineteenth century.

Jeffrey Kittel is the curator of This Game of Games website (http://thisgameofgames.blogspot.com/), which is dedicated to the history of nineteenth-century baseball in St. Louis. He studied history at the University of Illinois and Southern Illinois University at Carbondale, where he learned to master a microfilm scanner, read old newspapers, and scour obscure texts for any references to baseball. His current obsessions include researching the 1875–1877 Brown Stockings team of St. Louis, and investigating the spread of premodern baseball in southern Illinois. Kittel's favorite nineteenth-century baseball player is Packy Dillon; he also strenuously holds to the belief that Chris Von der Ahe and Fred Dunlap are two of the most underrated figures in the history of the nineteenth-century game. He was born, raised, and currently resides in Granite City, Illinois.

Brian McKenna was born and raised in Baltimore, coming of age to joyfully witness the last few years of Brooks Robinson's career. He is the author of *Early Exits: The Premature Endings of Baseball Careers* (2006) and is writing a forthcoming biography of Clark Griffith. He also has contributed over fifty entries for the Society for American Baseball Research's Biography Project, as well as "Professional Baseball and Football: A Close Relationship," an article jointly published by SABR and the Professional Football Researcher's Association. McKenna is currently working on a documentary film of Eddie Plank, titled *Gettysburg Eddie*, and a novel based on a mixture of the careers of pre–Negro leaguers Bud Fowler, Frank Grant, and Charlie Grant.

In 1998 **Eric Miklich** began playing nineteenth-century style baseball where the "rebirth" of the sport began in 1980, at Old Bethpage Village Restoration (OBVR) in Old Bethpage, New York. He became a volunteer nineteenth-century baseball coordinator at Old Bethpage in 2000. Miklich has competed in close to six hundred matches under varying nineteenth-century baseball rules, mainly as a pitcher, at OBVR, with the Mutual Club of New York, and for the Dark Blue Club of Hartford. Elected in 2005 as a trustee for the Vintage Base Ball Association, he became its historian in 2009. Miklich owns *19th Century Base Ball Inc.*, which sells authentic baseballs and other period items, and he has written and complied a six-hundred-page website dedicated to nineteenth-century baseball (www.19cbaseball.com). In 2008 he was hired by Da-Cor Pictures to advise, design, direct, and pitch in the reshooting of the professional baseball scenes for the independent film "Dummy Hoy." Miklich has spoken about nineteenth-century baseball three times at the Baseball Hall of Fame, most recently in September of 2009, and appeared in a live Internet classroom program with Ozzie Smith in 2005.

Currently Miklich lives in North Babylon, New York. He has a daughter, Christina, 7½ and a black lab, Smokey, 12. He is honored to be included in this latest project and would like to thank David Nemec for his contributions, friendship, and support.

Peter Morris is the author of six books, including the award-winning *A Game of Inches.*

David Nemec is a baseball historian, novelist, and playwright. He has published six novels and authored or coauthored over thirty books on baseball. His most important works have dealt with the game's embryonic years. In 1994 Lyons & Burford published *The Rules of Baseball,* an anecdotal look at the evolution of the rules of our national pastime. The following year the same publisher brought out *The Beer and Whisky League*, a history of the American Association during its tenure as a rebel major league. In 1997 Donald I. Fine Books introduced Nemec's *The Great Encyclopedia of Nineteenth Century Major League Baseball.* Nemec has received *The Sporting News* Research Award, playwrighting grants from the Impossible Ragtime Theater and the Huntington Playhouse, fellowships in creative writing, and numerous residency fellowships at the Corporation of Yaddo, the MacDowell Colony, the Virginia Center for the Creative Arts, and the Edward Albee Foundation. Nemec has taught writing at the College of Marin, at St. Mark's Church in the Bowery, and at prisons in the San Francisco Bay Area.

Lyle Spatz is the author of five books on baseball history and the editor of two baseball record books. He and coauthor Steve Steinberg recently completed *1921: The Yankees, the Giants and the Battle for Baseball Supremacy in New York* (Nebraska 2010). Spatz has also contributed chapters to several collections of baseball works, and his articles have appeared in various newspapers and magazines. He has presented papers at the Babe Ruth Conference and at the Jackie Robinson Conference. Since moving to Florida in 2002 he has lectured on baseball history to Elderhostel groups and various civic organizations around the state. A member of SABR since 1973, Lyle has served as the chairman of SABR's Baseball Records Committee since 1991. In 2000 SABR presented Spatz with the L. Robert Davids Award, its most prestigious honor.

John Thorn is a historian, writer, and producer of sports encyclopedias, anthologies, and pictorial biographies. He conceived and continues to edit *Base Ball: A Journal of the Early Game,* a semiannual publication (McFarland). Apart from his creation, with Pete Palmer, of *Total Baseball,* Thorn is often visible on ESPN, the History Channel, MLB Network, and other television outlets as a sports authority and commentator. He was also a major on-screen presence in and chief consultant to Ken Burns's PBS series *Baseball*. Thorn coauthored *The Hidden Game of Baseball*, which established alternative statistics that were later recognized and adopted as official by Major League Baseball. He has written many other baseball books over the past three decades. Thorn also helped create *Total Football* as the official encyclopedia of the NFL. He serves as publishing consultant to the Pro Football Hall of Fame and the Museum of the City of New York, which published his *New York 400* (2009).

Dick Thompson began writing baseball historical pieces in his early twenties and quickly gained renown for his generosity in aiding fellow researchers. A longtime friend and colleague of the late Tom Shea, Thompson shared Shea's deep passion for delving into the lives of little-known major league players and was dedicated to bringing to light their overlooked greatness. Thompson was the author of *The Ferrell Brothers of Baseball*, which made a persuasive case that Wes Ferrell, and not Lefty Grove, was the best pitcher of his era. At the time of his death, Thompson was working on a biography of Bill Jackman, the most prominent African American pitcher in the New England era between the two world wars. An extraordinarily scrupulous researcher and a magnificent storyteller, in 2004 Thompson received the L. Robert Davids Award, SABR's highest honor, and earlier he compiled the Society for American Baseball history book, for which he also wrote the "History of SABR" section.

Frank Vaccaro was born in Rome, Italy, and graduated from Stony Brook University. He is a Local Union 812 teamster and shop steward with Pepsi-Cola, representing eighty workers at the College Point facility. With notes on all major league games played prior to 1963, he self-published the game data in, *All Games Baseball* and the pennant race graphs *Game Dots*. He has contributed to *Total Baseball*, *The National Pastime*, the SABR BioProject, SABR's Casey Stengel chapter newsletter, *Retrosheet*'s nineteenth-century game scores, the SABR-L electronic bulletin board, and many other projects. Vaccaro lives in Long Island City, New York, with his wife, Maria.

Philip Von Borries, a leading authority on Louisville baseball, has written on the subject for some twenty-five years. At his suggestion, Hillerich & Bradsby—along with the city of Louisville—erected a new honorary marker over Pete Browning's grave in 1984. Von Borries co-designed the marker, which was dedicated during the celebration of the centennial of the Louisville Slugger. The author of *Louisville Diamonds* and *American Gladiator* (the latter the first biography of Pete Browning), Von Borries has written historical articles for the Chicago Cubs and the Oakland Athletics. He is also one of the few turfwriters to have won both of this country's top horse race–writing prizes: the Eclipse (thoroughbred racing) and the John Hervey (standardbred racing). His racing books include *Racelines*.

INDEX

Page numbers in bold indicate a main biographical entry. †† preceding a name indicates that this figure's biography appears in volume 2. Page numbers in italic indicate photographs.

PREVIOUS WORKS BY DAVID NEMEC

NOVELS AND SHORT FICTION

Bright Lights, Dark Rooms (Doubleday, 1980)
Early Dreams (Baseball Press, 1999)
Mad Blood (Dial, 1983)
Remember Me to My Father (Robert D. Reed, 2001)
Stonesifer (Robert D. Reed, 1999)
Survival Prose (Bobbs-Merrill, 1971)
The Systems of M. R. Shurnas (Riverrun Press/John Calder, 1985)

NONFICTION

This Day in Baseball History (Taylor, 2008)
The Ultimate St. Louis Cardinals Baseball Quiz Book (Taylor, 2008)
The Ultimate Boston Red Sox Baseball Quiz Book (Taylor, 2008)
The Ultimate Chicago Cubs Baseball Quiz Book (Taylor, 2007)
The Ultimate New York Yankees Baseball Quiz Book (Taylor, 2007)
The Great Encyclopedia of Nineteenth-Century Major League Baseball (Donald I. Fine, 1997; updated and reissued by the University of Alabama Press in 2006)
The Rules of Baseball Illustrated (Lyons & Burford, 1994; updated and reissued in 1999 and 2006)
The Great American Baseball Box (Shout, 2005)
"The History of Baseball" (CD)
The Encyclopedia of Major League Rookies (Brassey's, 2004)
The Ultimate Baseball Book (Houghton Mifflin, 1979; updated and reissued by Hilltown in 2000)
The Great Book of Baseball Knowledge (Contemporary Books/Masters, 1999)
150 Years of Baseball (Publications International, 1996)
The Beer and Whisky League (Lyons & Burford, 1995)
1001 Fascinating Baseball Facts (Publications International, 1993)
The Great American Baseball Team Book (New American Library, 1992)
Players of Cooperstown (Publications International, 1992)
The Baseball Challenge Quiz Book (New American Library, 1991)
20th-Century Baseball Chronicles (Publications International, 1991)
The Most Extraordinary Baseball Quiz Book Ever (New American Library, 1990)
Great Baseball Feats, Facts, and Firsts (New American Library, 1987; updated and reissued annually)
A History of Baseball in the San Francisco Bay Area (Woodford, 1985)
The Even More Challenging Baseball Quiz Book (Macmillan, 1978)
The Absolutely Most Challenging Baseball Quiz Book, Ever (Macmillan, 1977)